PEARSON
mysoclab™

Save Time.

....

Improve
Results.

MySocLab is an online learning system for
Sociology: A Down-to-Earth Approach, Fifth Canadian
Edition. This fun and easy-to-navigate site enhances
Sociology: A Down-to-Earth Approach,
with a variety of learning resources.

To take advantage of all that MySocLab has to offer,
you will need an Access Code. If you do not already
have an access code, you can buy one
online at www.mysoclab.com.

PEARSON

Personalized Learning!

In MySocLab you are treated as an individual with specific learning needs.

The study and assessment resources that complement your textbook allow you to review content and develop your skills and knowledge online, on your own time, and at your own pace.

MySocLab provides

- pre-tests
- post-tests
- learning and assessment activities with immediate scoring and feedback
- online writing assessment with peerScholar—a powerful tool for writing open-ended assignments in class. Improve your writing and communication skills with peerScholar.

- a gradebook where you can store your grades and view reports showing your progress as the term unfolds
- instructors can view the gradebook, too. Some instructors assign homework, monitor class results, and adapt their lectures based on students' progress.

Sociology

A Down-to-Earth Approach

Fifth Canadian Edition

James M. Henslin • Dan Glenday • Norene Pupo • Ann Duffy

Southern Illinois University · Brock University · York University · Brock University

Pearson Canada

Toronto

To a new and hopeful generation of sociology students

Library and Archives Canada Cataloguing in Publication

Sociology : a down-to-earth approach / James M. Henslin ... [et al.].—5th Canadian ed.

First Canadian ed. written by James M. Henslin, Adie Nelson.
Includes bibliographical references and index.
ISBN 978-0-205-60149-3

1. Sociology—Textbooks. I. Henslin, James M

HM586.S63 2010   301   C2008-904272-7

ISBN-13: 978-0-205-60149-3
ISBN-10: 0-205-60149-9

Vice President, Editorial Director: Gary Bennett
Editor-in-Chief: Ky Pruesse
Senior Acquisitions Editor: Laura Paterson Forbes
Marketing Manager: Arthur Gee
Senior Developmental Editor: Joel Gladstone
Production Editors: Leanne Rancourt, Söğüt Y. Güleç
Copy Editor: Sally Glover
Proofreaders: Leanne Rancourt, Julia Hubble
Production Coordinator: Janis Raisen
Composition: Macmillan Publishing Solutions
Permissions and Photo Research: Sandy Cooke
Art Director: Julia Hall
Cover and Interior Design: Anthony Leung
Cover Image: Veer Inc.

1 2 3 4 5   13 12 11 10 09

Printed and bound in USA.

BRIEF CONTENTS

CONTENTS

PART 3

SOCIAL INEQUALITY 111

CHAPTER 6

Social Inequality: The Canadian Experience in a Global Context 111

CHAPTER 11
The Economy: Money and Work   239

CHAPTER 12
Politics: Power and Authority   259

CHAPTER 13

The Family: Initiation into Society   279

CHAPTER 14

Education and Religion   308

PART 5
SOCIAL CHANGE   361

CHAPTER 16
Crime and Social Deviance   361

LIST OF FEATURES

TO THE STUDENT

Welcome to sociology! I've loved sociology since I was in my teens, and I hope you enjoy it, too. Sociology is fascinating because it holds the key to so much understanding of social life.

If you like to watch people and try to figure out why they do what they do, you will like sociology. Sociology pries open the doors of society so you can see what goes on behind them. *Sociology: A Down-to-Earth Approach* stresses how profoundly our society and the groups to which we belong influence us. Social class, for example, sets us on a path in life. For some, the path leads to better health, more education, and higher income, but for others it leads to poverty, dropping out of school, and even a higher risk of illness and disease. These paths are so significant that they affect our chances of making it to our first birthday, as well as of getting in trouble with the police. They even influence how our marriage will work out, the number of children we will have—and whether or not we will read this book in the first place.

When I took my first course in sociology, I was "hooked." Seeing how marvelously my life had been affected by these larger social influences opened my eyes to a new world, one that has been fascinating to explore. I hope that this will be your experience also.

From how people become homeless to how they become presidents, from why people commit suicide to why women are discriminated against in every society around the world—all are part of sociology. This breadth, in fact, is what makes sociology so intriguing. We can place the sociological lens on broad features of society, such as social class, gender, and race-ethnicity, and then immediately turn our focus to the small-scale level. If we look at two people interacting—whether quarreling or kissing—we see how these broad features of society are being played out in their lives.

We aren't born with instincts. We don't come into this world with preconceived notions of what life should be like. At birth, we have no ideas of race-ethnicity, gender, age, or social class. We have no idea, for example, that people "ought" to act in certain ways because they are male or female. Yet we all learn such things as we grow up in our society. Uncovering the "hows" and "whys" of this process is also part of sociology's fascination.

One of sociology's many pleasures is that as we study life in groups (which can be taken as a definition of sociology), whether those groups be in some far-off part of the world or in some nearby corner of our own society, we constantly gain insights into our own selves. As we see how *their* customs affect *them*, effects of our own society on us become more visible.

This book, then, can be part of an intellectual adventure, for it can lead you to a new way of looking at your social world—and in the process, help you better understand both society and yourself.

I wish you the very best in college—and in your career afterward. It is my sincere hope that *Sociology: A Down-to-Earth Approach* contributes to that success.

James M. Henslin
Department of Sociology,
Southern Illinois University,
Edwardsville

PREFACE

To study sociology is to embark on a fascinating journey into a new world of perception and understanding. It is an exploration of other worlds and ideas far from your own—as well as a quest to understand your own world and ideas. Since this book is designed to help you on this journey, we'd like to show you how it is organized and review its themes and features.

THE ORGANIZATION OF THIS TEXT

The text is organized into five parts. Each has a broad focus and is designed to help you acquire the sociological perspective. This will enable you to better analyze social relations—and the particular corner of life in which you find yourself.

Part I focuses on the sociological perspective, which we introduce in the first chapter; in Chapter 2 ("What Do Sociologists Do?"), we present the methods used by sociologists.

Part II builds on this foundation as we continue our sociological exploration of the significant influence that social groups have on our lives. We present an overview of culture, introduce socialization, and conclude with a new chapter entitled "Globalization."

Part III focuses on social inequality, which has such a tremendous impact on our lives. Because social stratification is so significant—and to understand social life we need to know that it penetrates every crevice of our existence—we start with the Canadian experience and place it in the global context, which presents an overview of the principles of stratification, then turn the sociological spotlight on social class. After establishing the broader context, we focus on gender, the most global of the social inequalities. Following this, we examine the inequalities of race, ethnicity, and age.

In Part IV, we turn to those engulfing social arrangements called social institutions. Social institutions are so significant that without understanding them we cannot understand life in society. First, we examine the impact of bureaucracy and the corporation turn to an analysis of the overarching institutions of economy and politics, which exert an incredible amount of control over our lives. Following this, we look at four other social institutions that also play significant roles in the world—family, education, religion, and medicine.

In Part V, you will gain insight into why your world is changing so rapidly, as well as a glimpse of what is yet to come. This concluding part opens with crime and social deviance, which students often find to be among their favourite topics in sociology. The next chapter examines population, urbanization, and the environment, issues that impact us all. Lastly, we look at the fascinating areas of collective behaviour and social movements.

THEMES AND FEATURES

Perhaps the single greatest goal of the introductory sociology course is to show the connection between the individual and society—to understand how social forces shape our behaviour. To help students reach this goal, this text has five central themes: down-to-earth sociology, cultural diversity and globalization, technology and society, critical thinking, and the growing influence of mass media on our lives.

Let's look at these themes in more detail.

Down-to-Earth Sociology

Why shouldn't sociology be presented in a manner that conveys its inherent excitement? Without any doubt, sociology is the most enticing of all the social sciences. Yet textbooks often make sociology seem dull, and thereby fail to reach students.

The choice of subtitle for this book, *A Down-to-Earth Approach*, is deliberate, for our goal is to share sociology's excitement as we embark on this fascinating journey. To note how the basic substance of sociology penetrates our everyday lives is to make visible the influence of the social on who we are. We know that you already have an awareness of the influence of the social on your life, and we hope to build on this awareness.

This down-to-earth approach is present in the vignettes that open each chapter. Many of these lively vignettes are based on the personal sociological experiences of the authors. To stimulate your sociological imagination, we use examples that you can relate to. Threaded through the examples are the central insights provided by sociology's major perspectives. As we apply symbolic interactionism, for example, you will see how symbols create social life. As we examine functionalism, you will see how people's actions have both manifest and latent consequences. And you will have no difficulty seeing the far-reaching implications for your own life of the conflict perspective's view that groups compete for scarce resources. The inclusion of feminist theories complements the three major theoretical perspectives of the discipline, while postmodernism brings a fresh, new perspective to some of the issues raised.

Down-to-Earth Sociology boxes underscore this approach. They focus on such topics as Sociological Findings versus Common Sense (Chapter 1), Careers in Sociology (Chapter 1), Expressing Yourself Online (Chapter 3), The Big Win: Life After the Lottery (Chapter 6), The Inuit Expulsion (Chapter 8), Polygamous Canada (Chapter 13), and Youth Unemployment and Crime in Canada (Chapter 16).

We have attempted to reinforce the down-to-earth theme with a writing style that is also "down-to-earth"—that is, one that is accessible and inviting. We have tried, then, to avoid unnecessary jargon so you won't have to endure linguistic torture in order to grasp basic ideas. These ideas are of utmost importance in your sociological journey, and in introducing them we try to use concise explanations, clear (but not reductive) language, and relevant examples.

DOWN-TO-EARTH SOCIOLOGY
The New Shorthand: Expressing Yourself Online

Talking online has become a favourite activity of millions of people, young and old. Teenagers rehash the day's events with friends, grandmothers keep in touch with grandchildren in different provinces, hobbyists correspond about special interests, and businesspeople seal deals with the click of the Send button. All of them appreciate the speed of online communications.

Online communication doesn't allow its users to convey nuances that are transmitted during face-to-face talk. To make up for this, users have developed symbols to convey humour, disappointment, sarcasm, and other indications of mood or attitude. Some are listed below. If you tilt your head to the left as you read, the symbols will be clearer.

- :-) Smile
- :-)) Laugh
- :-(Sad
- :-((Very sad
- :-X My lips are sealed
- >:-) Feeling in a devilish mood
- :-O WOW! (What a surprise!)

Some correspondents also use the following abbreviations, which add a touch of whimsy and make their communications even more succinct:

- ILY I Love You
- LOL Laughing Out Loud
- IMHO In My Humble Opinion
- TTFN Ta-Ta for Now
- WB Welcome Back
- BTW By the Way
- GMTA Great Minds Think Alike
- WTG Way to Go!
- J/K Just Kidding
- D/L Downloading
- IAB I Am Bored
- LBR Later
- TTYL Talk to You Later

Cultural Diversity and Globalization

Any attempt to explain Canadian society must pay keen attention to its diverse populations, for ours is truly a multicultural society. It must also explore the many implications of the globalization of the world's societies.

Discussions of diversity, such as the *Perspectives* box in Chapter 8 (Over Half a Century of Citizenship), help you apply your growing sociological imagination to fundamental changes occurring in our society. They will also help you see connections among key sociological concepts, such as culture, socialization, norms, race, gender, and social class. As your sociological imagination grows, you will better understand the social structure of our society—and your own place in it.

PERSPECTIVES
Over Half a Century of Citizenship

Most Canadians do not realize that our citizenship is a relatively new achievement. As late as 1946, Canadians were considered British subjects residing in Canada, not Canadian citizens.

It was not until 1947, with the passage of the first *Citizenship Act*, that the idea of a distinctly Canadian citizenship was introduced. The year 1997 saw the fiftieth anniversary of this step toward true nationhood for Canada.

The *Citizenship Act* came into being largely due to the efforts of Paul Martin, Sr., father of the former prime minister of Canada. It has been said that while visiting a military cemetery in France just after World War II, Paul Martin, Sr. was visibly shaken by the rows and rows of wooden crosses marking the graves of Canadians who had given their lives in the service of their country and for the peace and freedom that everyone now enjoys.

Martin was impressed by the various ethnic and religious backgrounds of the names on the graves. Despite their differences, these soldiers had come together in a struggle against the Nazi dictatorship and fascism and had died for what they believed in. When Martin returned to Canada, he set wheels in motion that led to the establishment of the *Citizenship Act* as a tribute to their memory. On January 1, 1947, Canada took a bold step toward independence when the *Citizenship Act* came into being, and in so doing established a separate Canadian identity, new rights for Canadian women, and our own Canadian passport.

Source: Adapted from Citizenship and Immigration Canada website.

Global interconnections profoundly affect our lives. With this in mind, the latest edition of the text provides a separate chapter on globalization and its implications. For example, the dawn of a global economy—new to world history—influences the kinds of skills and knowledge you need to make a living, the types of work that will be available to you, and the variety and costs of the goods and services you consume. This new global economy, which has married our fate with that of other nations, also determines other essential aspects of your life, such as whether you will experience war or peace. Of course, global changes are not simply or primarily economic. As McDonald's and KFC open up shop in Cairo and Beijing, there are profound cultural changes at hand.

Sociology and the New Technology

One of the most profound social forces is the accelerated rate of technological change. In just a single generation, computers have been integrated into our daily lives; alternative, or niched, media outlets have proliferated, including online services and the internet; "sci-fi"–like technologies are being used to aid reproduction; distance learning is becoming common. *Sociology and the New Technology* boxes address these issues. Topics selected both for their relevance and timeliness include Global Village or Big Brother? (Chapter 3), Gender and Reproductive Technology (Chapter 7), and Technology and the Dilemma of Medical Rationing (Chapter 15).

French sociologist Jacques Ellul feared that technology was destroying civilization, while Canadian Marshall McLuhan celebrated the "global village." The emerging sociological theory of technology, rather than regarding technology as an out-of-control force that drives culture and upon which all social change depends, emphasizes that individuals and groups—with all their values and special interests—shape technology. In addition to the impact of technology on our daily lives, this edition introduces the student to the growing influence of environmental sociology in Canada (Chapter 17).

Critical Thinking

Thinking Critically about Social Controversy is another important feature of this text. These sections, which address pressing and often controversial social issues, underscore the significance of sociology for understanding the events that are challenging our ideas and changing our lives. They consider interesting issues, ranging from Are Sex Offenders Sick? (Chapter 2) to Why Canadian Mothers Work for Pay (Chapter 13). The Thinking Critically sections make excellent points of departure for class discussions, since they contrast several points of view or theoretical interpretations about areas of social controversy. Critical thinking questions at the end of each chapter ask you to further apply such insights. Each of these boxes also appears in MySocLab as a peerScholar assignment.

Mass Media and Social Life

These sections stress how the mass media affect our behaviour and permeate our thinking. We consider how they penetrate our consciousness to such a degree that they influence how we perceive our own bodies. As you consider this theme, you should begin to see mass media in a different light, which should further stimulate your sociological imagination.

We have included a series of boxed features called *Mass Media in Social Life* to make such issues more prominent. Among these are analyses of the worship of thinness and how it affects our own body images (Chapter 1), how gender is portrayed on television in the popular cartoon *The Simpsons* (Chapter 7), and how the popular media avoid representing seniors as sexual beings (Chapter 9).

THE FIFTH CANADIAN EDITION

The fifth Canadian edition is a substantial revision aimed at making content current, relevant, and of increased interest to Canadian students, particularly in the areas of globalization, feminism, postmodernism, social issues, social inequalities, and the mass media. By enhancing topic coverage in these areas while retaining the best features of the previous edition and drawing on the latest research and statistical reports, it appeals to instructors who teach social action-oriented mainstream courses to university and college students. In addition, new *Talking About Theory* tables are included in selected and relevant chapters.

Features

- A timeline covering Canadian and sociological events
- A thorough but concise text of 18 chapters
- Current perspectives: an emphasis on "inclusivity," including the diversity of the Canadian experience, integrating feminist, postmodernist, queer, and critical race perspectives to address the needs of many users
- An enhanced focus on globalization and its implications
- Challenging and informative content that draws on issues that are "in the news," such as employed mothers, violence against women, problems of poverty, and homelessness
- The latest Canadian data, examples, studies, issues, and photos
- Enhanced pedagogy to make content more accessible and engaging

Highlights in the Fifth Canadian Edition

CHAPTER 1   WHAT IS SOCIOLOGY?

- Careers in Sociology
- Recent trends in feminism, such as postmodern feminism and emergent queer and critical race theories
- **Expanded Coverage**—English Canadian and Quebec sociology, including coverage of early Canadian feminist sociologists
- Inclusion of macro and micro dimensions of postmodernism

CHAPTER 2   WHAT DO SOCIOLOGISTS DO?

- Updated table on the number of spousal homicides in Canada, the provinces, and territories by sex of victim
- **Expanded Coverage**—Rapport, the researcher's personal characteristics, and qualitative interviews
- **New**—Down-to-Earth Sociology box: "Three Ways to Measure Average"
- Feminist methodology
- **Expanded Coverage**—How to read a table
- Diagrammatic representation of quantitative and qualitative research strategies
- **Expanded Coverage**—Desroches's replication in Canada of Humphreys's research into the tearoom trade

CHAPTER 3   CULTURE

- **Revised coverage**—Overview of values in Canada, including a comparison of value clusters in Quebec and the rest of Canada
- **New**—Introduction to Pierre Bourdieu and cultural capital

- Highlights from the history of the *Indian Act*
- Up-to-date survey results of Canadian responses to the Americanization of Canadian values

CHAPTER 4   SOCIALIZATION

- Socialization as an important key to exploring social and gender inequalities and serious issues, such as violence against women
- Life course analysis of the Canadian socialization experience from birth to old age
- **New**—Discussion of social structure and social interaction

CHAPTER 5   GLOBALIZATION

- **New**—Globalization distinguished from earlier historical periods of expansion, such as colonialism and imperialism
- **New**—Globalization's role in international migration and in making tourism the world's largest industry
- **New**—Introduction to the major international institutions, such as the International Monetary Fund, the World Bank, and the World Trade Organization
- **New**—The pros and cons of globalization, including the anti-globalization movement and the World Social Forum
- **New**—Globalization and women's work
- **New**—Canada's position in the world economy
- **New**—Globalization and world poverty

CHAPTER 6   SOCIAL INEQUALITY

- Global stratification and the status of women
- Complexities of inequality
- **New**—Down-to-Earth Sociology: "The Big Win: Life After the Lottery"
- **New**—Feminist and anti-racist approaches

CHAPTER 7   INEQUALITIES OF GENDER

- **New**—Michelle Dumaresq and the challenge of gender
- **Revised**—Data and analysis on Canadian women's educational achievements and changes in the occupational structure
- **New**—Theoretical perspectives on gender
- Women in sports

CHAPTER 8   INEQUALITIES OF RACE AND ETHNICITY

- **New**—The changing ethnic composition of Canada, 2001–2006
- **New**—Top ethnic origins reported for Montreal, Toronto, and Vancouver
- **New**—Learning from association

- The three major classifications in Canada: native peoples, the "Two Charter Groups," and immigrants
- Multiracial feminism and inequality

CHAPTER 9 INEQUALITIES OF AGE

- Locates aging in the life course—the latest trend in research literature—while integrating critical social gerontology; notably, aging from a feminist perspective
- **New**—Proportion of the Canadian population aged 65 and over, 1956 to 2006
- Latest trends in social analysis, combining aging as a social problem (social isolation and physical impairment), along with seniors' empowerment and a positive perspective on the aging process
- Generational conflict, the future role of seniors in paid employment, and efforts to address elder abuse

CHAPTER 10 BUREAUCRACY AND THE CORPORATION

- **New**—Feminist and critical approaches to the study of organizations
- Virtual organizations and hotelling
- Community service: coercion or volunteerism?
- The Canadian establishment
- Scientific management

CHAPTER 11 THE ECONOMY: MONEY AND WORK

- **New**—Changes in the top, middle, and bottom 20 percent of Canadian income earners based on 2006 Census data
- **New**—Young Canadians, especially young men, are poorer than their parents
- **New**—Five largest federal Crown corporations
- Neo-liberalism and social conservatism
- Corporate concentration in Canada
- Federal and provincial Crown corporations and their profitability
- Work in Canadian society; for example, the highest- and lowest-paying jobs in Canada

CHAPTER 12 POLITICS: POWER AND AUTHORITY

- The Canadian parliamentary system, including the evolution of the political party system
- **New**—Back-to-back minority governments
- Updated employment equity at the "executive" level in the federal civil service
- Updated top-eight arms sellers and buyers in the world
- **New**—Post-traumatic stress disorder and Canada's military

CHAPTER 13 THE FAMILY: INITIATION INTO SOCIETY

- Critical feminist perspectives on family studies
- **Expanded Coverage**—The power struggle over housework
- **New**—*Sociology and the New Technology* box: "Finding a 'Significant E-other': Looking for Romance in All the New Places"
- Diversity in Canadian families—including racial and ethnic differences, one-parent families, childless families, blended families, gay and lesbian families
- **New**—Common-law unions among older Canadians
- Up-to-date information on the changing Canadian family, including the sandwich generation, boomerang kids, delayed marriage, and gay marriage

CHAPTER 14 EDUCATION AND RELIGION

- **New**—The feminist perspective on education
- School leavers and inequality of access to education
- Characteristics of religion in Canada
- Differences between Canada and the U.S. on the role of religion in society
- Female spirituality and feminist themes in Christianity and Judaism
- **New**—Themes in feminism and Islam

CHAPTER 15 MEDICINE: HEALTH AND ILLNESS IN CANADA

- **Updated**—Selected leading causes of death, by sex
- **Updated**—Federal expenditures on health
- **New**—Latest results for Canada from the *Health Behaviour in School-Aged Children* study led by the World Health Organization
- The development of the sociology of health in Canada
- Feminist perspectives on sexism and the gendered experience of health and illness

CHAPTER 16 CRIME AND SOCIAL DEVIANCE

- Youth unemployment and crime
- **Updated**—Violence in hockey, the Roy incident, and proposals to curb violence
- Youth crime and the risk society
- Canadian criminal justice system
- Postmodern theories of crime and social deviance
- Feminist theories and male violence against women
- Diagrammatic representation of crime and social deviance as a continuum

CHAPTER 17 POPULATION, URBANIZATION, AND THE ENVIRONMENT

- **Updated**—Demographic profile of Canada
- **New**—Global growth in cities with over 1 million residents
- **New**—Settlement patterns in the least developed countries
- Feminism and the population debate
- Canadian immigration policy

- The environmental paradigm
- **New**—Environmental injustice
- Discussion of ecofeminism and the environment

CHAPTER 18 SOCIAL MOVEMENTS AND SOCIAL CHANGE

- The pros and cons of trade unions in Canada
- **New**—Transnational and metaformative social movements
- Feminist and postmodern theories of social change

In-Text Learning Aids

Sociology: A Down-to-Earth Approach includes a number of other pedagogical aids to help your learning. These include:

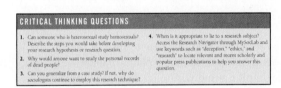

New! *Talking About Theory* tables are provided in selected and relevant chapters to provide students with a quick overview of how the various theoretical perspectives consider the subject at hand.

Critical Thinking Questions encourage students to use the Research Navigator tool (provided through MySocLab). This helps students develop their research skills and will bring them into contact with a wide scope of materials and resources.

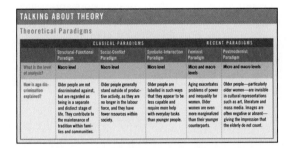

CRITICAL THINKING QUESTIONS

1. Can someone who is heterosexual study homosexuals? Describe the steps you would take before developing your research hypothesis or research question.
2. Why would anyone want to study the personal records of dead people?
3. Can you generalize from a case study? If not, why do sociologists continue to employ this research technique?
4. When is it appropriate to lie to a research subject? Access the Research Navigator through MySocLab and use keywords such as "deception," "ethics," and "research" to locate relevant and recent scholarly and popular press publications to help you answer this question.

Learning Outcomes summarize what students will learn in each chapter.

LEARNING OUTCOMES

After you have studied this chapter, you will be able to answer the following questions:

1. What is a valid sociological topic?
2. Why isn't common sense adequate?
3. How do sociologists gather data?
4. How do sociologists choose a particular research method?
5. What are the eight basic steps of scientific research?
6. How important are ethics in sociological research?
7. What is the relationship between theory and research?
8. What happens when the ideal meets the real?

Inequalities of Gender

In Tunis, the capital of Tunisia, on Africa's northern coast, I met some postsecondary students, with whom I spent a couple of days. When they said they wanted to see Tunis's red-light district, I wondered if it would be worth the trip. I had already seen other such districts, including the unusual one in Amsterdam where the state licenses prostitutes, requires medical checkups (certificates are available for customers to inspect), sets the prices, and pays social security at retirement. The women sit behind lighted picture windows while customers, interspersed with tourists and neighbourhood residents, stroll along attractive canal side streets, browsing from the outside.

Opening Vignettes pique interest and alert students to key topics. Many are based on the authors' own experiences.

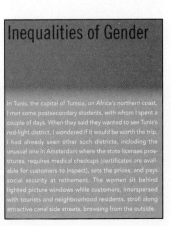

Focus Questions draw attention to important aspects of topics and issues being discussed.

In Sum boxes appear at various spots in the chapters to help review important points before going on to new materials.

Summary and Review reinforces the important concepts and issues discussed in the chapters. A question-and-answer format enhances learning.

Key Terms: Learning new terms can be difficult. Key terms are highlighted and introduced within a context that explains or illustrates them. They are listed together at the end of each chapter along with page numbers identifying where the concept is first defined in the chapter. To learn sociology, it is necessary to learn the sociologist's basic vocabulary. These terms provide working definitions of the most important sociological concepts.

Weblinks: At the end of each chapter a set of useful Weblinks helps you use the internet to explore ideas.

Comprehensive Glossary: Complete and with clear definitions, the glossary is designed to bring together the important concepts and terms introduced in the text, organizing them into a single, accessible format at the end of the text.

Supplements

MYSOCLAB WITH PEERSCHOLAR A personal access code card is provided with every copy of the fifth Canadian edition.

What Is MySocLab? MySocLab combines a complete electronic version of the fifth Canadian edition of *Sociology: A Down-to-Earth Approach* with video, audio, animations, research sup-port, practice tests, exams, peerScholar topics, and more. MySocLab gives students the opportunities and tools they need to extend their learning experience, practise, and enhance their performance.

MySocLab is a state-of-the-art interactive solution for introductory sociology.

Features and Benefits for Students

- **Practise** and study with pre-tests, post-tests, and personalized study plans

- **Explore** important sociological concepts through animations of important data, maps, graphs, and concept diagrams.

- **Watch** video clips that illustrate key sociological concepts.

- **Listen** to interviews with prominent researchers and social scientists.

- **Read** current newspaper articles.

- **Use** *Research Navigator*™ anytime. It is the easiest way for students to start a research assignment. Complete with extensive help on the research process and four exclusive databases of credible and reliable source material—including the EBSCO Academic Journal and Abstract Database, *New York Times* Search by Subject Archive, and the "Best of the Web" Link Library.

Features and Benefits for Instructors

- **MySocLab** gives instructors quick and easy access to a vast array of resources for teaching and administering a sociology course.

- **A wealth of instructor support material** simplifies and enriches the teaching experience. **MySocLab** saves time, giving you one-stop access to electronic, text-specific materials and course management materials such as a Class Gradebook and discussion centre.

- Access to peerScholar, a unique peer-to-peer online assignment program. Ready-made assignments are available, including one controversy text box per chapter. Use these assignments as they are, adapt them, or add your own. Students complete assignments online and then grade one another. It's an excellent way to integrate critical thinking and writing assignments into a large class. Students discover what makes a great writing assignment great, and they learn from their peers.

The following instructor supplements are available through MySocLab, located in one place for easy retrieval and organization.

INSTRUCTOR'S MANUAL This useful teaching aid provides chapter summaries, learning objectives, detailed lecture outlines, suggestions for introducing each chapter, discussion questions, class activities, student projects, and internet activities.

POWERPOINT PRESENTATION This PowerPoint presentation provides graphic and text images for complete multimedia presentations in the classroom.

IMAGE LIBRARY The image library provides electronic versions of the figures and tables that appear in the text.

TEST ITEM FILE The test item file contains more than 2000 questions in multiple-choice, true-false, short-answer, and essay formats, and is available in both Word and MyTest formats.

MyTest for *Sociology: A Down-to-Earth Approach* from Pearson Education Canada is a powerful assessment generation program that helps instructors easily create and print quizzes, tests, exams, and homework or practice handouts. Questions and tests can all be authored online, allowing instructors ultimate flexibility and the ability to efficiently manage assessments at anytime, from anywhere.

These supplements are also available on an Instructor's Resource CD-ROM (ISBN 0-205-67583-2) or by accessing the password-protected section of Pearson Education Canada's online catalogue (**http://vig.pearsoned.ca**). Navigate to your book's catalogue page to view a list of available supplements. See your local sales representative for details and access.

Ask your Pearson representative for an instructor access code for MySocLab.

TECHNOLOGY SPECIALISTS Pearson's Technology Specialists work with faculty and campus course designers to ensure that Pearson technology products, assessment tools, and online course materials are tailored to meet your specific needs. This highly qualified team is dedicated to helping schools take full advantage of a wide range of educational resources by assisting in the integration of a variety of instructional materials and media formats. Your local Pearson Education sales representative can provide you with more details on this service program.

COURSESMART CourseSmart is a new way for instructors and students to access textbooks online anytime from anywhere. With thousands of titles across hundreds of courses, CourseSmart helps instructors choose the best textbook for their class and give their students a new option for buying the assigned textbook as a lower cost eTextbook. For more information, visit **www.coursesmart.com**.

Additional Supplements

TRANSPARENCIES The Allyn & Bacon Transparencies for Sociology 2008, 5/E (ISBN 0-205-52103-7) package includes more than 125 colour acetates featuring illustrations both from the seventh U.S. edition of the text and other sources.

ALLYN & BACON DIGITAL MEDIA ARCHIVE CD-ROM FOR SOCIOLOGY, 2006 EDITION, 1/E Want more electronic presentations in your classroom? This CD-ROM (ISBN 0-205-46727-X) contains hundreds of graphs, charts, and maps to supplement your lectures and illustrate key sociological concepts. If you have full multimedia capability, you can use the DMA's video segments and links to sociology websites.

Some of these instructor supplements are also available for download from a password-protected section of Pearson Education Canada's online catalogue, **http://vig.pearsoned.ca**. Navigate to your book's catalogue page to view a list of available supplements. See your local sales representative for details and access.

ACKNOWLEDGMENTS

The gratifying response to earlier editions of the text indicates that our efforts at making sociology down to earth have succeeded. The years that have gone into writing this book are a culmination of the many more years that preceded its writing—from graduate school to the equally demanding endeavour of classroom teaching. No text, of course, comes solely from its authors. Although we are responsible for the final words on the printed page, we have received excellent feedback from instructors and students who have used this book.

Numerous individuals at Pearson have provided invaluable support and assistance in the development of the Canadian edition. Thanks are due to Arlene Mahood (whose early intervention at Prentice Hall provided the basis for this project). The most recent edition owes much to the efforts of Joel Gladstone and Laura Forbes, who guided the authors through the complex process of revisions. It is difficult to heap too much praise on such fine and capable people. Their efforts, often going "beyond the call of duty" as we faced pressing deadlines, coalesced with ours in producing this text. Students, whom we constantly kept in mind as we prepared this edition, are the beneficiaries of this intricate teamwork.

Since this text is based on the contributions of many, we would count it a privilege if you would share your teaching experiences with this book, including any suggestions for improving the text. Both positive and negative comments are welcome. It is in this way that we learn.

We wish you the very best in your teaching. It is our sincere desire that *Sociology: A Down-to-Earth Approach* contributes to that success.

—JMH, DG, NP, AD.

It is often the case that an author acknowledges the "invaluable contribution" made by his/her spouse or partner. In this case, no such salutary statement will be made. Instead, the revisions to the original text were written during long periods of solitary confinement in my basement office. On numerous occasions, I was "liberated" from my work by Rick, my spousal partner. These interruptions may have caused some at Pearson Education to fret, but they prevented me from becoming a morose recluse.

—DG

To my family members, John, Jennifer, and Gregory Barkans—thank you for your ongoing support and patience during the long hours I spent at my desk.

—NP

I wish to thank Dusky, Mayra, and Hermana for their loving support through the years.

—AD

The Canadian authors would like to thank the following reviewers for their help in developing the fifth Canadian edition of *Sociology*:

Francis Adu-Febiri, Camosun College

Joan Harkness, Camosun College

Chris MacKenzie, University of British Columbia

Tara Milbrandt, Trent University

Dan Popowich, Mohawk College

Sian Reid, Carleton University

ABOUT THE AUTHORS

James M. Henslin was born in Minnesota and graduated from high school and junior college in California and from college in Indiana. Awarded scholarships, he earned his Master's and doctorate in sociology at Washington University in St. Louis, Missouri. He was awarded a postdoctoral fellowship from the National Institute of Mental Health and spent a year studying how people adjust to the suicide of a family member. His primary interests in sociology are the sociology of everyday life, deviance, and international relations. Among his more than a dozen books is *Down to Earth Sociology: Introductory Readings* (Free Press), now in its eleventh edition. This book of readings reflects some of his sociological interests. He also has published widely in sociology journals, including *Social Problems* and *American Journal of Sociology*.

While a graduate student, Jim Henslin taught at the University of Missouri at St. Louis. After completing his doctorate, he joined the faculty at Southern Illinois University, Edwardsville, where he is Professor Emeritus of Sociology. He says, "I've always found the introductory course enjoyable to teach. I love to see students' faces light up when they first glimpse the sociological perspective and begin to see how society has become an essential part of how they view the world."

Henslin enjoys spending time with his wife, reading, and fishing. His two favourite activities are writing and travelling. He especially enjoys living in other cultures, which brings him face to face with behaviours that he cannot take for granted, experiences that "make sociological principles come alive."

Dan Glenday was educated in Quebec, where he earned a BA with Distinction from Sir George Williams University—now Concordia University—and an MA from McGill University, and was awarded a PhD from Carleton University in Ontario. He has taught at the University of Toronto, Queen's University, and Eastern Michigan University, and is now at Brock University, where he is a full professor of Sociology and founder and director of the Centre for Labour Studies. His present research has led him into the work world of professional wrestlers. His most recent books include *The Shifting Landscape of Work: Surviving and Prospering in the New Economy* (with Ann Duffy and Norene Pupo), *Canadian Society: Meeting the Challenges of the Twenty-first Century* (with Ann Duffy), and *Good Jobs, Bad Jobs, No Jobs: The Transformation of Work in the 21st Century* (with Ann Duffy and Norene Pupo).

Norene Pupo (PhD at McMaster University, 1985) is an associate professor in the Department of Sociology at York University and the director of the Centre for Research on Work and Society of the same university. Professor Pupo has researched and published in the areas of women and work, part-time employment, women and social policy, and unions and economic restructuring. She has co-authored *The Part-time Paradox* and *Few Choices: Women, Work and Family,* and has co-edited *Good Jobs, Bad Jobs, No Jobs: The Transformation of Work in the 21st Century*. She is currently co-editing two books on work issues: *Interrogating the New Economy,* with Professor Mark Thomas, and *The Shifting Landscape of Work,* with Professors Duffy and Glenday. Norene Pupo has been principal investigator of a project entitled *Restructuring Work and Labour in the New Economy,* a SSHRCC-funded Initiative on the New Economy Research Alliance. Under this grant, she has studied changes in work time and labour processes within a globalized economy.

Ann Doris Duffy was educated in Ontario (BA, MA, and PhD at McMaster University). She is currently a full professor in the Department of Sociology at Brock University, where she is cross-appointed to the Labour Studies program and is active in the Women's Studies and Master's Program in Social Justice and Equity Studies programs. She is currently active in the development of an MA program in critical sociology at Brock. In 1995, she received the Ontario College and University Faculty Associations' Teaching Award. Her research interests include women's employment, family violence, and aging. She has co-authored and co-edited a number of books, including *Few Choices: Women, Work and Family; The Part-Time Paradox; Good Jobs, Bad Jobs, No Jobs: The Transformation of Work in the 21st Century; Family Violence: A Canadian Introduction;* and *Canadian Families: Diversity, Conflict and Change.* In 2008, she co-authored *Connection, Compromise, and Control: Canadian Women Discuss Midlife.*

1

The Sociological Perspective

Even from the dim glow of the faded red-and-white exit sign, its light barely reaching the upper bunk, I could see that the sheet was filthy. Resigned to another night of fitful sleep, I reluctantly crawled into bed—tucking my clothes firmly around my body like a protective cocoon.

The next morning, I joined the long line of dishevelled men leaning against the chain-link fence. Their faces were as downcast as their clothes were dirty. Not a glimmer of hope among them.

No one spoke as the line slowly inched forward. When my turn came, I was handed a Styrofoam cup of coffee, some utensils, and a bowl of semi-liquid that I couldn't identify. It didn't look like any food I had seen before. Nor did it taste like anything I had ever eaten.

My stomach fought the foul taste, every spoonful a battle. But I was determined. "I will experience what they experience," I kept telling myself. My stomach reluctantly gave in and accepted its morning nourishment.

The room was strangely silent. Hundreds of men were eating, but each was sunk deeply into his own private hell, his head aswim with disappointment, remorse, bitterness.

As I stared at the Styrofoam cup holding my solitary post-breakfast pleasure, I noticed what looked like teeth marks. I shrugged off the thought, telling myself that my long weeks as a sociological observer of the homeless were finally getting to me. "That must be some sort of crease from handling," I concluded.

I joined the silent ranks of men turning in their bowls and cups. When I saw the man behind the counter swishing out Styrofoam cups in a washtub of water, I began to feel sick at my stomach. I knew then that the jagged marks on my cup really had come from a previous mouth.

How much longer did this research have to last? I felt a deep longing to return to my family—to a welcome world of clean sheets, healthy food, and "normal" conversations.

Source: Based on the personal experiences of James Henslin.

LEARNING OUTCOMES

After you have studied this chapter, you will be able to answer the following questions:

1. What is the sociological perspective?

2. What is science, and where does sociology fit in?

3. When did sociology first appear as a separate discipline, and what factors contributed to its emergence?

4. Is the only purpose of social research to advance human understanding, or should it also be used to reform society?

5. How do sociologists use *Verstehen* and social facts to investigate human behaviour?

6. What was the position of women in early sociology?

7. What universities in Canada were considered the historical centres of sociology in English-speaking Canada? How were they different?

8. What is a theory and what are the major theoretical perspectives?

9. What is the difference between pure (or basic) and applied sociology?

THE SOCIOLOGICAL PERSPECTIVE

Why were these men silent while waiting in line for their food? Christopher Hauch's important study of skid row in Winnipeg in 1984 dealt with the experience of homelessness. Hauch listed silence as a method of surviving on the street. Why do you think not speaking to someone in line is better or safer than talking? How would you feel living with homeless men and women if you knew you could leave at any time and return to the comforts of your home and family?

In this text you will find yourself looking at your own world in a different light. As you observe other groups or your own family and friends, the sociological perspective (or imagination) opens a window into unfamiliar worlds and offers a fresh look at well-known surroundings. In fact, this is what many find appealing about sociology.

The sociological perspective has been a motivating force in the lives of the authors of this text. Since we embarked on our first introductory courses in sociology, we have thoroughly enjoyed both observing other groups and questioning our own assumptions about life. We sincerely hope that the same happens to you.

Seeing the Broader Social Context

The **sociological perspective** stresses the social contexts in which people live and how these contexts influence their lives. At the core of this perspective is the sociological imagination, a term coined by C. Wright Mills (1959). The **sociological imagination** is a sociological vision—a way of looking at the world that allows links between the apparently private problems of the individual and important social issues. At the centre of the sociological perspective is the question of how people are influenced by their **society**—the group of people with whom they share a culture and territory.

To find out why people do what they do, sociologists look at **social location**, or where people are located in a particular society. Sociologists consider occupation, income, education, gender, age, and ethnicity. Consider, for example, how growing up identified with a group called females or a group called males affects our ideas of what we should attain in life. Growing up as a male or a female influences not only our aspirations, but also how we feel about ourselves and how we relate to others in dating and establishing households and at work.

LEVELS OF SOCIOLOGICAL ANALYSIS

Sociologists Elijah Anderson (1978, 1990, 1997) and Elliot Liebow (*Street Corner Society*, 1997) have written fascinating accounts of homeless men. Although homeless ("street-corner") men may appear to be disorganized—simply coming and going as they please and doing whatever feels good in the moment—Anderson and Liebow have concluded that these men are influenced by the norms and beliefs of our society in the same way other men are. This will become more apparent as we examine the two levels of analysis used by sociologists.

Macrosociology and Microsociology

Macrosociology focuses on the broad features of society. Sociologists who use this approach analyze such things as social class and patriarchy. If macrosociologists were to analyze street-corner men, for example, they would stress that they are at the bottom of the social class system. Their low status, according to men's feminism, means that they will be denigrated by other men because they possess few skills and little education. As "able-bodied" men, however, they are not eligible for welfare, so they hustle to survive and, as a consequence, spend their lives on the street. These men are viewed as being of little social value and potentially dangerous to other men and women.

Conflict theory, functionalism, and feminism focus on the broader picture and are examples of the macrosociological approach. The goal of these theories is to examine and interpret the large-scale social forces that influence people.

A second approach used by sociologists is **microsociology**. Here, the emphasis is placed on **social interaction**, or what people do when they come together. Microsociologists are likely to focus on homeless men's survival strategies ("hustles"); their rules for dividing money, wine, or whatever other resources they have; their relationships with girlfriends, same-sex partners, family, and friends; where they spend their time and what they do there; their language; pecking order; and so on. With their focus on face-to-face interaction and discourse analysis, symbolic interactionism, queer theory, postmodernism, and feminism that emphasizes the social construction of gender are examples of microsociology.

While the macrosociological approach stresses the broad features of society, the microsociological approach has a narrower focus, placing its emphasis on *face-to-face social interaction*, language and discourse, or what people do when they are in each other's presence.

Sociologist C. Wright Mills (1959: p. 2) said of sociology: "The sociological imagination or perspective enables us to grasp the connection between history and biography." As a result of history, each society has certain broad characteristics—such as its ideas of the proper roles of men and women. In using the term biography, Mills is referring to the individual's specific experiences in society. In short, people don't do what they do because of inherited characteristics such as instinct. Rather, *external* influences—our experiences—become part of our thinking and motivations. A sociology student must develop a sociological imagination if she or he is to grasp the extent to which her or his "personal troubles" are linked to broader "public issues" arising

An ad for Kellogg's Special K cereal shows an 18-month-old girl wearing nothing but a diaper. She has a worried look on her face. A bubble caption over her head has her asking, "Do I look fat?" (Krane et al., 2001).

When you stand before a mirror, do you like what you see? To make your body more attractive, do you watch your weight or work out? You have ideas about what you should look like. Where did you get them?

Television and magazine ads keep pounding home the message that our bodies aren't good enough, that we've got to improve them. The way to improve them, of course, is to buy the advertised products: wigs, hairpieces, hair trans-

plants, padded brassieres, diet pills, and exercise equipment. Female movie stars effortlessly go through tough workouts without breaking a sweat. Muscular hunks show off machines that magically produce steel abs and incredible biceps—in just a few minutes a day! Women and men are led to believe that attractive members of the opposite sex will flock to them if they purchase that wonderworking exercise machine.

Although we try to shrug off such messages, knowing they are designed to sell products, they still get our attention. They penetrate our thinking and feeling, helping shape ideal images of how we "ought" to look. Could those models so attractively clothed and coiffed sashaying down the runway be any thinner? For women, the message is clear: you can't be thin enough. The message for men is also apparent: you can't be strong enough.

Woman or man, your body isn't good enough. It sags where it should be firm. It bulges where it should be smooth. It sticks out where it shouldn't and doesn't stick out enough where it should. And—no matter what your weight—it's too much. You've got to be thinner.

Exercise takes time and getting in shape can be painful. Once you get

there, if you slack off it seems to take only a few days for your body to return to its former drab, slothful appearance. You can't let up, you can't exercise enough, and you can't diet enough.

But who can continue at such a torrid pace, striving for these unrealistic cultural ideals? A few people, of course, but not many. Liposuction becomes appealing: just lie there, put up with a little discomfort, and the doctor will suck the fat right out of you. Surgeons can transform flat chests into super breasts overnight. They can lower receding hairlines and smooth furrowed brows. They remove lumps with magical tummy tucks and reverse a decade with rejuvenating skin peels and face lifts.

With the bosomy girls on *Baywatch* the envy of all, and impossibly shaped Victoria's Secret models the standard to which women hold themselves, even teens call on plastic surgeons. Anxious lest their child violate peer ideals and trail behind in the race for popularity, parents foot the bill. Some parents pay up to $25,000 to give their daughter a flatter tummy (Gross, 1998).

With peer pressure to alter the body already intense, surgeons stoke the fire. A sample ad reads: "No Ifs, Ands or Butts. You Can Change Your Bottom Line in Hours!" Some surgeons even offer gift

All of us contrast the reality we see when we look in the mirror with our culture's ideal body types. Mischa Barton represents an ideal body type that has developed in some parts of Western culture. Cultural ideals can make it difficult for larger people to maintain positive images of their bodies. These women in Florida have struggled against cultural stereotypes.

certificates, so you can give your loved ones liposuction or Botox injections along with a greeting card (Dowd, 2002).

The thinness craze has moved to the east, too. Glossy magazines in Japan and China are filled with skinny models and ads touting diet pills and diet teas. In China, where famine used to abound, a bit of extra padding was valued as a sign of good health. Today, the obsession is thinness (Rosenthal, 1999). Not-so-subtle ads scream that fat is bad. Some teas come with a package of diet pills. Weight-loss machines, with electrodes attached to acupuncture pressure points, not only reduce fat but also build breasts—or so the advertisers claim.

Not limited by our rules, advertisers in Japan and China push soap that supposedly "sucks up fat through the skin's pores" (Marshall, 1995: p. B1). What a dream product! After all, even though the television models smile as they go through their paces, those exercise machines look like a lot of hard work.

Then there is the other bottom line: attractiveness pays off. Economists have studied physical attractiveness and earnings and found that "good-looking" men and women earn the most, "average-looking" men and women earn more than "plain" people, and the "ugly" are paid a "pittance" (Hamermesh & Biddle, 1994). Consider obese women: their net worth is less than half that of their slimmer sisters ("Fat is a Financial Issue," 2000). "Attractive" women have another cash advantage—they attract and marry higher earning men.

More popularity *and* more money? Maybe you really can't be too thin, after all. Maybe those exercise machines are a good investment. If only we could catch up with the Japanese and develop a soap that would suck the fat right out of our pores. You can practically hear the jingle now.

For Your Consideration
What image do you have of your body? How do cultural expectations of "ideal" bodies underlie your image? Can you recall any advertisement or television program that has affected your body image?

Most advertising and television programs that focus on weight are directed at women. Women are more concerned than men about weight, more likely to have eating disorders, and more likely to express dissatisfaction with their bodies (Honeycutt, 1995; Stinson, 2001). Do you think that the targeting of women in advertising creates these attitudes and behaviours? Or do you think that these attitudes and behaviours would exist without the ads? Why?

from changing views of social inequalities from generation to generation. When and where we grow up, then, influences our sociological understanding of behaviour.

People around the globe take their particular worlds for granted. Something inside Canadians tells us that hamburgers are delicious, small families are attractive, and designer clothing is desirable. Yet something inside some Sinai Desert Arab tribes used to tell them that warm, fresh camel's blood made a fine drink and that everyone should have a large family and wear flowing robes (Murray, 1935; McCabe, Terrence, & Ellis, 1990). That "something" certainly isn't an instinct: as sociologist Peter Berger (1963: p. 93) put it, that "something" is "society within us."

This brings us to *you*—to how your social groups have shaped *your* ideas and desires. Over and over in this text, you will see that the way you look at the world is the result of your exposure to specific social groups and your ignorance of others. We think you'll enjoy the process of self-discovery offered by sociology.

The Growing Global Context

As is evident to all of us—from the labels on our clothing to the components in our cars—our world is becoming a global marketplace. Communications used to be so slow that in the War of 1812 the Battle of New Orleans was fought two weeks after the United States and Great Britain had signed a peace treaty. The armed forces had not yet heard that the war was over (Volti, 1995).

Today, most of us use the internet to communicate with our friends, neighbours, and people all over the planet. New economic agreements such as the North American Free Trade Agreement (NAFTA) and the World Trade Organization (WTO) connect Canada not only with the United States and Mexico, but also with France, Japan, Korea, and China. However, we continue to occupy small corners of life, marked by a particular space and differences in family background, religion, occupation, gender, ethnicity, and social class. In these corners, we learn distinctive ways of viewing the world.

One of the beautiful—and fascinating—aspects of sociology is that it is able to analyze the two parts of our current reality: the changes that incorporate us into a global network and our unique experiences in our smaller corners of life. In this text, we shall examine both of these vital aspects of the contemporary experience.

SOCIOLOGY AND THE OTHER SCIENCES

To satisfy our basic curiosity about the world, humans gradually developed **science**—systematic methods of studying the social and natural worlds and the knowledge obtained by those methods. **Sociology**, the scientific study of society and human behaviour, is one of the sciences developed by modern civilization.

A useful way of comparing the sciences—and of gaining a better understanding of sociology's place—is to first divide them into the natural and the social sciences.

Sociologists have a particular interest in the social consequences of material goods, group structure, and belief systems, as well as how people communicate with one another.

The Natural Sciences

The **natural sciences** are the intellectual and academic disciplines designed to comprehend, explain, and predict events in our natural environment. The natural sciences are divided into specialized fields of research according to subject matter, such as biology, geology, chemistry, and physics. These are further subdivided into even more highly specialized areas, with a further narrowing of content. Biology is divided into botany and zoology, geology into mineralogy and geomorphology, chemistry into its inorganic and organic branches, and physics into biophysics and quantum mechanics. Each area of investigation examines a particular "slice" of nature (Henslin, 1997b).

The Social Sciences

In the pursuit of a more adequate understanding of life, people have also developed fields of science known as the social sciences, which examine human relationships. Just as the natural sciences attempt to understand the world of nature, the **social sciences** attempt to understand the social world, and just as the world of nature contains ordered (or lawful) relationships that are not obvious but must be discovered through theoretical advances and controlled observation, the ordered relationships of the human or social world are not obvious. However, unlike nature, humans create and re-create their second nature—their particular society. Fortunately—or unfortunately for some—there are several theoretical perspectives that help us understand ourselves, our society, and the countries and nations around us. Each

theory is based on observations derived from specific methods. (See Chapter 2 for detailed descriptions of these methods.)

Like the natural sciences, the social sciences are divided into specialized fields on the basis of their subject matter. These divisions are political science, economics, anthropology, psychology, and sociology.

POLITICAL SCIENCE *Political science* focuses on how people govern themselves: the various forms of government, their structures, and their relationships to other institutions in society. In studying a constitutional democracy such as Canada's, political scientists also analyze voting behaviour.

ECONOMICS *Economics* is the social science that deals with the theory and management of the production, distribution, and consumption of goods.

ANTHROPOLOGY *Anthropology*, with the exception of physical anthropology, which studies anatomy and biology, examines the origins of human migration and the development of tools, techniques, kinships, value systems, and social relationships. Anthropological fieldwork or ethnography is a specific form of inquiry involving long-term exposure to the daily life of the people being studied. Well-known anthropologists include Margaret Mead, famous for her work in Samoan and New Guinea cultures, and Jane Goodall, who has made significant discoveries about primate societies, especially those of chimpanzees. (See the website of the Department of Anthropology at the University of Winnipeg, available at www.uwinnipeg.ca/index/anthropology-index.)

It is said that in the recent past, five wise men and women, all blindfolded, were led to an elephant and asked to explain what they "saw." The first, a psychologist, feeling the top of the head, said, "This is the only thing that counts. All feeling and thinking take place inside here. To understand this beast, we need study only this."

The second, a political scientist, feeling the gigantic ears, said, "This is the power centre. What goes in here controls the entire beast. Concentrate your studies here."

The third, an economist, feeling the mouth, said, "This is what counts. What goes in here is distributed throughout the body. Concentrate your studies on this."

The fourth, an anthropologist, tenderly touching the top of the head, the ears, mouth, trunk, and tusks, said, "I am interested in understanding the meaning behind these different attributes. I will concentrate on these and possibly other aspects of the animal by spending more time with it."

Then came the sociologist (of course!), who, after feeling the entire body, said, "You can't understand the beast by concentrating on only one part. Each is but part of the whole. The head, the trunk and tusks, the ears, the mouth—all are important. But so are the parts of the beast that you haven't even mentioned. We must remove our blindfolds so we can see the larger picture. We have to see how everything works together to form the entire animal."

Pausing for emphasis, the sociologist added, "And we also need to understand how this creature interacts with similar creatures. How does their life in groups influence their behaviours?"

We wish we could conclude this fable by saying that the psychologist, anthropologist, political scientist, and economist threw away their blindfolds and, joining together, began to examine the larger picture. But, on hearing this sage advice, all stubbornly bound their blindfolds even tighter to concentrate all the more on the single parts. And if you listened very carefully you could even hear them mutter, "The top of the head is mine—stay away from it." "Don't touch the tusks." "Take your hand off the ears." "Stay away from the mouth—that's my area."

PSYCHOLOGY The focus of *psychology* is processes that occur within the individual. Psychologists are primarily concerned with mental processes: intelligence, emotion, perception, and memory.

SOCIOLOGY Simply put, sociology is the disciplined study of human social behaviour, especially the investigation of the origins, classifications, institutions, and development of human society on a global level. Sociology ranges from understanding passing encounters between individuals on the street to understanding global social processes.

Unlike political scientists and economists, sociologists do not concentrate on a single social institution. And unlike psychologists, sociologists stress factors *external* to the individual to determine what influences people. The Down-to-Earth Sociology box above revisits an old fable about how members of different disciplines perceive the same subject matter.

Focus Question

Why is sociology different from the other social sciences?

The Goals of Science

The first goal of each science is to *describe* and *explain* why something happens. The second goal is to make generalizations—that is, to go beyond the individual case and make statements that apply to a broader group or situation. For example, a sociologist wants to explain not only why Mary went to university or became a renowned astrophysicist, but also why people with her characteristics are more likely than others to go to university or become astrophysicists. To achieve generalizations, sociologists look for patterns, recurring characteristics, or events. The third scientific goal is to *predict*—to specify what will happen in the future in light of current knowledge.

To attain these goals, scientists need to examine evidence with an open mind so that their work can be checked in future by other trained scientists. Secrecy, prejudice, and other biases go against the grain of science.

Sociologists and other scientists move beyond common sense, or beyond those ideas that prevail in a society that "everyone knows" are true. "Everyone" can be mistaken today just as easily as when common sense dictated that the

Some findings of sociology support common-sense understandings of social life, while others contradict them. Can you tell the difference? To fully enjoy this quiz, complete *all* the questions before looking at the next Down-to-Earth Sociology box to check your answers.

1. **True/False** The earnings of Canadian women have just about caught up with those of Canadian men.

2. **True/False** When faced with natural disasters such as floods and earthquakes, people panic and social organization disintegrates.

3. **True/False** Revolutions are more likely to occur when conditions remain poor than when they are improving.

4. **True/False** Most people on welfare are lazy and looking for a handout. They could work if they wanted to.

5. **True/False** Compared with men, women touch each other more often when talking.

6. **True/False** Compared with women, men maintain more eye contact when conversing.

7. **True/False** How long people live depends on their genetic or biological makeup and therefore is not strongly influenced by any social differences.

8. **True/False** Not long ago the family was a stable unit, but today we face an explosion of broken and dysfunctional families.

9. **True/False** Today, because women face more stress and anxiety at work and in the home, more women than men commit suicide.

10. **True/False** Wars have been fought throughout history because humans have aggressive instincts.

world was flat or that no human would ever walk on the moon. As sociologists examine people's assumptions about the world, their findings may contradict common-sense notions about social life. Sometimes the explorations of sociologists lead them to study things that people would prefer remain unexplored. For example, a sociologist might study how some people decide to commit a crime, engage in switching (wife/spouse swapping), or work for Greenpeace. Because above all sociologists want to understand social life, they cannot cease their studies because some people feel uncomfortable. With all realms of human life considered legitimate avenues of exploration by sociologists, their findings sometimes challenge cherished ideas. To test your own "common sense," read the Down-to-Earth Sociology box above.

It seems that every organization or group nourishes a pet image that it presents to the public. Sociologists are interested in knowing what is really going on behind the scenes, however, so they peer beneath the surface to get past such sugar-coated imagery (Berger, 1963). This approach sometimes brings sociologists into conflict with people who feel threatened by that information—which is all part of the adventure—and risk—of being a sociologist.

Focus Question
What makes sociology a science?

THE ORIGINS OF SOCIOLOGY

How did sociology begin? In some ways this is a difficult question to answer. However, all science requires the development of theories that can be tested by research.

This standard simplifies the question of the origin of sociology. Sociology is clearly a recent discipline. It emerged at about the middle of the nineteenth century, when European social observers began to use scientific methods to test their ideas. Three factors combined to lead to its development.

The first was the Industrial Revolution. By the middle of the nineteenth century, Europe was evolving from an agriculture-based society to one dependent on factory production. Masses of people were forced from their land. They moved to cities, where they were greeted by horrible working conditions: low pay; long, exhausting hours; dangerous work; foul smoke; and much noise. To survive, families were forced to send their children to work in these conditions, some of whom were even chained to factory machines to make certain they did not run away.

Such negative changes in people's lives sparked transformations in what they believed to be true and false, good and evil. In the realm of ideas, Enlightenment philosophers such as Jean Jacques Rousseau (1712–1778, French) and John Locke (1632–1704, English) pointed out that human growth and development of society occurs when tradition gives way to reason. Reason and science, in turn, contribute to the ability of people to comprehend, change, and perhaps control not only their society but also the world as a whole. Enlightenment philosophers foresaw a world free from religious dogma, within human control, and leading ultimately to emancipation for all humankind (Sydie, 1987; Zeitlin, 1990). The Enlightenment's scientific ideas for the application of reason and rationality to the physical and social world and human progress swept through Europe and North America. In the realm of politics and the economy, these philosophers encouraged the

1. **False.** Over the years, the income gap has narrowed, but only slightly. On average, full-time working women earn only about 65 percent of what full-time working men earn. This low figure is actually an improvement; in the 1970s, women's incomes averaged about 60 percent of men's.

2. **False.** Following such disasters, people develop *greater* cohesion, cooperation, and social organization to deal with catastrophe.

3. **False.** Just the opposite is true. When conditions are consistently bad, people are more likely to be resigned to their fate. Rapid improvement causes their aspirations to outpace their circumstances, which can increase frustration and incite revolution.

4. **False.** Most people on welfare are children, elderly, sick, mentally or physically handicapped, or young mothers with few skills. Less than 2 percent meet the common stereotype of an able-bodied male. See also "Exploring Myths about the Poor" in Chapter 6.

5. **False.** Men touch each other more during conversations (Whyte, 1989).

6. **False.** Female speakers maintain considerably more eye contact (Henley, Hamilton, & Thorne, 1985).

7. **False.** The poor are less healthy on average than the rich because their diets are worse and their work lives are more physically demanding.

8. **False.** The proportion of children living with single parents was probably as high 200 years ago as it is today because many more people died at a young age. This was the result of the premature death of one parent (usually the mother) due to inadequate health care. Today, it is the result of separation and divorce.

9. **False.** In Canada, suicide rates for males have been at least three times higher than for females since the 1950s, with the difference increasing to four times higher in the 1990s and decreasing to three and a half times by 2003 (Centre for Suicide Prevention, June 1998, 2003, http://www.suicideinfo.ca/csp/assets/alert30.pdf).

10. **False.** Humans do not have instincts—that is, fixed and inherited patterns of behaviour (Berger, 1963).

idea that individuals could possess land, property, and inalienable rights.

Tradition, in the form of religious beliefs, imbued the opposite: "We do this because it has always been done this way." Since the answers are already provided, why search for explanations? Sweeping change sparked by the Industrial Revolution, however, achieved the opposite: by upsetting the existing order, it encouraged questioning and demanded answers.

The second factor that stimulated the development of sociology was imperialism. The new European colonial empires, stretching from Asia through Africa to North America, exposed them to radically different cultures. Startled by these contrasting ways of life, Europeans began to ask why cultures differed. Anthropology concentrated on providing insight into the colonies of the Western European empires, while sociology slowly took on the task of understanding the social changes happening in the burgeoning cities of England, Europe, and later, North America.

The third impetus for the development of sociology was the success of the natural sciences. At the time that the Industrial Revolution and imperialism moved people to question fundamental aspects of their social worlds, the **scientific method**—objective, systematic procedures used to acquire knowledge based on empirical evidence—practised in chemistry and physics uncovered truths about the physical world that had been concealed in nature. Given these successes, it seemed logical to apply this method to questions being raised about the social world.

Auguste Comte

Auguste Comte (1798–1857) was the founder of French **positivism**. Positivism was a theory of knowledge based on experience alone and not on metaphysical speculation or ungrounded philosophical concepts. Knowledge, to be positive, must also be situated in its proper historical context.

Auguste Comte (1798–1857), considered the founder of sociology, began to analyze the bases of social order. Although he stressed that the scientific method should be applied to the study of society, he did not apply it himself.

Comte argued that human understanding of the world was initially religious, defined by the significance of supernatural forces. It then advanced to a metaphysical stage of abstract principles, and finally proceeded to positive or scientific knowledge based on an empirical grasp of the relations between observable phenomena.

With the French Revolution fresh in his mind, Comte left the small, conservative town of Montpellier, where he had grown up, and moved to Paris. The changes he experienced led to his interest in the twin problems of social order and social change (which he called "social statics" and "social dynamics"). What holds society together? he wondered. Why is there social order instead of anarchy or chaos? And once society becomes set on a particular course, what causes it to change? Why doesn't it always continue in the direction it began?

Comte concluded that the right way to answer his questions about social order and social change was to apply positivism to social life. This new approach would not only uncover society's fundamental laws, but would also apply them to social reform. Comte is often credited as the founder of the discipline because he called this new science *sociology*— "the study of society" (from the Greek *logos*, "study of," and the Latin *socius*, companion, "being with others").

Karl Marx

Karl Marx (1818–1883) not only influenced sociology but also left his mark on world history. Marx's influence has been so great that the *Wall Street Journal* called him one of the three greatest modern thinkers (the other two being Sigmund Freud and Albert Einstein).

Marx believed that the engine of human history is **class conflict** and that capitalism is the highest stage of human development. He said that the *bourgeoisie* (the controlling class of *capitalists*, or those who own the means to produce wealth—capital, land, factories, and machines) are locked in conflict with the *proletariat* (the exploited class—the mass of workers who do not own the means of production).

According to Marx, this bitter struggle can end only when members of the working class unite in revolution and throw off their chains of bondage, resulting in a classless society, one free of exploitation (Marx & Engels, 1848/1967).

Marxism is not the same as communism. Although Marx stood firmly behind revolution as the only way for workers to gain control of society, he did not develop the political system called *communism*. Indeed, Marx himself felt disgusted when he heard debates about his insights into social life. After listening to some of the positions attributed to him, he even declared, "I am not a Marxist" (Dobriner, 1969b, p. 222; Gitlin, 1997, p. 89).

Unlike Comte, Marx did not think of himself as a sociologist. He spent years studying in the library of the British Museum in London, where he wrote widely on history, philosophy, and, of course, economics and political science. Because of his insights into the relationship between the social classes, especially the class struggle between the "haves" and the "have-nots," many sociologists today claim Marx as a significant early sociologist. He also introduced one of the major perspectives in sociology: conflict theory, which is discussed later in this chapter.

Emile Durkheim

Emile Durkheim (1858–1917) grew up in eastern France and was educated there and in Germany. At the beginning of his academic career, sociology within the university was viewed as an offshoot of history and economics (Coser, 1977). Durkheim sought recognition for sociology as a separate academic discipline and achieved his goal when he received the first academic appointment in sociology in France at the University of Bordeaux in 1887.

Durkheim also had two other major goals (Giddens, 1978). One was to study how individual behaviour is shaped by social forces. In one of his most enduring studies, he compared the suicide rates of several European countries. Durkheim (1897/1966) found that each country's suicide rate was different and that it remained remarkably stable year after year. He also found that different groups within a

Karl Marx (1818–1883) believed that the roots of human misery lay in the exploitation of the proletariat, or propertyless working classes, by the capitalist class—those who own the means of production. Social change, in the form of the overthrow of the capitalists by the proletariat, was inevitable from Marx's perspective. Although Marx did not consider himself a sociologist, his ideas have profoundly influenced many in the discipline, particularly conflict theorists.

French sociologist Emile Durkheim (1858–1917) contributed many important concepts to sociology. When he compared the suicide rates of several countries, he discovered an underlying social factor: people are more likely to commit suicide if their ties to others in their communities are weak. Durkheim's identification of the key role of social integration in social life remains central to sociology today

Durkheim believed that modern societies produce feelings of isolation, much of which come from the division of labour. In contrast, members of traditional societies who work alongside family and neighbours and participate in similar activities experience a high degree of *social integration*. The Sudanese women in the photo on the right are building a house.

country had different suicide rates. For example, unmarried Protestant males killed themselves at a higher rate than Catholics, Jews, females, and married people. From his research findings, Durkheim drew the highly insightful conclusion that suicide is not simply a matter of individuals here and there deciding to take their lives for personal reasons; instead, social factors underlie the act.

Durkheim identified social integration, or the degree to which people are tied to their social group, as a key factor in suicide. He concluded that people with weaker social ties are more likely to commit suicide. This factor, he said, explained why unmarried Protestant males have higher suicide rates. Durkheim argued that Protestantism encourages greater freedom of thought and action, males are more independent than females, and unmarried people lack the ties and responsibilities of marriage. However, this freedom comes at a cost—the loss of social anchors inhibiting the individual from taking his life. In other words, because their social integration is weaker, people with these characteristics have fewer social ties that keep them from committing suicide. Durkheim called this egoistic suicide. It is prevalent in industrial societies dominated by large cities and ideas such as reason, science, and individualism.

Although strong social bonds help protect people from suicide, Durkheim noted that in some instances they actually encourage suicide. This type of suicide, which Durkheim termed altruistic suicide, can occur when some people kill themselves following the death of a dearly loved spouse. Their own feelings are so integrated with those of their mate that they prefer death rather than life without that person.

Durkheim singled out a third type of suicide—anomic suicide—also characteristic of industrial capitalist societies. For Durkheim, capitalism was an economic system based on greed and the unattainable goal of material wealth for almost everyone. When aspirations of wealth become unfulfilled, such as during a severe economic depression, some individuals may feel so passionately about their "loss" that they contemplate suicide.

Because of its scientific rigor and excellent theoretical interpretations, Durkheim's study is still quoted over a hundred years later. His research was so thorough that the principle he uncovered still applies: people who are less socially integrated have higher rates of suicide.

Durkheim's third concern was that social research be practical. He concluded, for example, that the new individualism or selfishness emerging during the nineteenth century was a characteristic of capitalism and not pathological; it was an expected outcome of a changing society. When individualism goes too far, however, it then poses the danger of what Durkheim called anomie—a breaking down of the controlling influences of society. Under such conditions, individuals become detached from society and are left with too little moral guidance. This is dangerous, as their desires are no longer regulated by social norms (Coser, 1977). Durkheim suggested that sociologists intervene: to prevent anomie, they should promote the creation of new social groups to stand between family and the state. These groups, such as professional associations and even trade unions, would help meet the need for a sense of belonging that was being eroded by the new, impersonal industrial society.

In sum, Durkheim achieved his three goals. First, he made sociology an accepted academic discipline in France and then elsewhere in the world. Second, he showed how social forces shape individual behaviours. Suicide, for example, appears to be such an intensely individual act that we might expect psychologists, rather than sociologists, to examine it. Yet, as Durkheim illustrated, if we look at suicide only in individualistic or psychological terms, we miss its *social* basis. Finally, he showed how to make social research practical.

Max Weber (1864–1920) was another early sociologist who left a profound impression on the discipline. He used cross-cultural and historical materials to help us understand modern bureaucracies, charismatic leaders, and theories of domination.

Max Weber

Max Weber (1864–1920), a German sociologist and a contemporary of Durkheim, also held professorships in the new academic discipline of sociology. Weber is one of the most influential sociologists; you will encounter his writings and theories numerous times in the coming chapters.

One of Weber's most important contributions to sociology was his study of the rise of capitalism. How, he asked, did capitalism come about—and why did some countries adopt it with enthusiasm while others lagged behind? Weber suspected that religion might be the key. As background, we need to understand that the typical approach to life before the development of capitalism was not to strive "to get ahead," but to work only enough to maintain one's usual way of life. Weber (1904/1958) theorized that all religions except Protestantism encouraged their followers to cling to this traditional way of life, while the Protestant belief system, and especially Calvinism, encouraged people to embrace change. Protestantism pushed people to work hard, to save money, and to invest it. Weber called this religious doctrine the **Protestant Ethic**. He termed the readiness to invest capital to make more money the **spirit of capitalism**. Thus, Weber theorized, Protestantism included the set of ideas that were sufficient to push-start capitalism.

To test his theory, Weber compared Roman Catholic and Protestant countries and found that Protestant countries were much more likely to embrace the new economic system called capitalism. This theory was controversial when Weber developed it, and it continues to be debated today (Dickson & McLachlan, 1989; Zou, 1994).

THE ROLE OF VALUES IN SOCIAL RESEARCH

Weber raised another issue that remains controversial among sociologists when he declared that sociology should be **value-free**. By this he meant that a sociologist's values—personal beliefs about what is good or worthwhile in life and about the way the world ought to be—should not affect his or her research. Weber wanted **objectivity** to be the hallmark of sociological work.

All sociologists agree that objectivity is an important goal in the sense that sociologists should not distort data to make it fit preconceived ideas or personal values, and that research reports must accurately reflect actual, not desired, findings. On the other hand, sociologists are members of a particular society at a given point in history and their values inevitably play a role in their research. For example, values may be in part responsible for why one sociologist chooses to research the Mafia while another turns a sociological eye on kindergarten students. As a way of uncovering any unintended distortions in original research, sociologists stress the need for **replication**—that is, repeating a study to compare secondary results with initial findings. If values have unwittingly influenced research findings, replication by other sociologists should uncover this problem and correct it.

Another related problem faced by sociologists centres on the proper purpose and use of sociological research (Seubert, 1991; Hewa, 1993). Some sociologists believe that the proper role of sociology is to advance understanding. Others are convinced that sociologists have a responsibility to explore harmful social arrangements in society—to investigate what causes poverty, crime, war, and other forms of human exploitation (see Figure 1.1).

Regarding the *uses* of sociology, those who assert that understanding is sociology's s proper goal take the position that the knowledge gained by social research belongs to the scientific community and the world. Accordingly, sociologists should not be concerned with how their research is funded because it can be used by anyone for any purpose. In contrast, those who say that the goal of sociology should be to explore harmful social arrangements believe that sociologists should use their studies to alleviate human suffering and make society a better place to live.

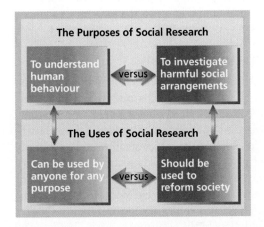

FIGURE 1.1   The Debate Over Values in Sociological Research

Sociologist John Galliher (1991) perhaps best expresses today's majority position when he says:

> Some argue that social scientists, unlike politicians and religious leaders, should merely attempt to describe and explain the events of the world but should never make value judgments based on those observations. Yet a value-free and nonjudgmental social science has no place in a world that has experienced the *Holocaust*, in a world having had *slavery*, in a world with the ever-present threat of *rape* and other *sexual assault*, in a world with frequent, *unpunished crimes in high places*, including the production of products known by their manufacturers to cause death and injury as has been true of asbestos products and continues to be true of the cigarette industry, and in a world dying from *environmental pollution* by these same large multinational corporations.

VERSTEHEN AND SOCIAL FACTS

Weber and *Verstehen*

Weber stressed that one cannot understand human behaviour simply by looking at statistics, because numbers must be interpreted. To understand people, he said, we should use *Verstehen*—a German word meaning "to understand." By emphasizing *Verstehen*, Weber meant that we must pay attention to what are called **subjective meanings**—the ways in which people interpret their own behaviour. We can't understand what people do, Weber insisted, unless we look at how people view and explain their own behaviour.

To better understand this term, let's return to the homeless example in the opening vignette. Why were the men silent?

When Henslin interviewed men in homeless shelters (and, in other settings, homeless women), he observed their feelings of despair. We know that people in despair feel a sense of hopelessness; the future looks bleak, hardly worth plodding toward. Consequently, what is there worth talking about anyway? Who wants to hear another hard-luck story?

By applying *Verstehen*—your own understanding of what it means to face various situations in life—you gain a better understanding of people's behaviour—in this case, the silence and lack of communication Henslin observed among the homeless.

Durkheim and Social Facts

In contrast, Durkheim stressed what he called **social facts**—the patterns of behaviour that characterize a social group, community, or nation. (Note, however, that Weber did not disagree about the significance of social facts, for they are the basis of his conclusions about Protestantism and capitalism.) Examples of social facts in Canada include June to August being the most popular months for weddings, July 1 being the most popular date for moving in Montreal, suicide being higher among Native peoples and, more recently, Quebec teenagers, and more births occurring between Tuesdays and Thursdays than any other days of the week.

People all over the country don't just coincidentally decide to do similar things, be it getting married or committing suicide. If that were the case, in some years middle-aged people would be most likely to kill themselves; in other years, young people, and so on. Patterns that hold true year after year, however, indicate that as thousands and even millions of people make individual decisions, they are responding to conditions in their society. These are social facts.

How Social Facts and *Verstehen* Fit Together

Social facts and *Verstehen* go hand in hand. As a member of Canadian society, you know that summer weddings are related to the end of the school year and how these months, now locked in tradition, common sentiment, and advertising, carry their own momentum. As for suicide among Canada's Native peoples or the recent burst in the suicide rate among Quebec's teenagers, you probably already have a sense of the greater isolation or anomie that many Native peoples and some teenagers feel about living in their communities.

SEXISM IN EARLY SOCIOLOGY

Attitudes of the Time

As you may have noticed, all the sociologists we have discussed so far are male. In the 1800s, sex roles were rigidly defined, with women assigned the roles of wife and mother. In the classic German phrase, women were expected to devote themselves to the four Ks: "*Kirche, Küchen, Kinder, und Kleider*" (church, cooking, children, and clothes). To dare to break out of this mould was to risk severe social disapproval.

Most women received no education beyond basic reading and writing, and many not even that. A few women from wealthy families, however, insisted on pursuing higher education, which at the time was reserved almost exclusively for men. A few managed to study sociology, although deeply entrenched sexism in universities stopped them from obtaining advanced degrees or becoming professors. In line with the times, their research was almost entirely ignored.

Harriet Martineau

When Harriet Martineau (1802–1876), who had been born into a wealthy English family, first began to analyze social life, she hid her writing beneath her sewing when visitors arrived, for "writing was 'masculine' and sewing 'feminine'" (Gilman, 1911/1971, p. 88).

An active advocate for the abolition of slavery, she toured the United States in 1834 and wrote two volumes based on her travels, entitled *Society in America* and *Retrospect of Western Travel,* and a methodological treatise called *How to Observe Manners and Morals* (Hoecker-Drysdale, 1992). *Society in America* was published in 1837, two or three

Interested in social reform, Harriet Martineau (1802–1876) studied sociology and discovered the writings of Comte. She became an advocate for the abolition of slavery, travelled widely, and wrote extensive analyses of social life.

decades before Durkheim and Weber were born, and criticized America's failure to live up to its democratic principles. Among her suggestions in the book, Martineau argued for improvement in women's education so that "marriage need not be their only object in life." (John Simkin, www.spartacus.schoolnet.co.uk/Wmartineau.htm). At the end of her life, she defended the right to unionize and strike. Martineau is primarily known for her 1853 translation into English of Auguste Comte's *Cours de philosophie positive* rather than her pioneering work on culture and methodology. Her translation allowed Comte's ideas of positivism to be circulated in the English-speaking world.

SOCIOLOGY IN QUEBEC, CANADA, AND THE UNITED STATES

Sociology in Quebec

The establishment of sociology as an academic discipline in Canada followed a different course than the history of sociology in the United States. Sociology in Canada is the story of the "Two Solitudes" (MacLennan, 1946), or Quebec sociology and sociology in the rest of Canada.

Quebec sociology owes its early development in the late nineteenth and early twentieth centuries to conservative European (mainly French) developments. Gaudrée Boilleau, a student of the conservative French sociologist Frédéric LePlay, conducted the first known study of a Quebec family in 1886. The sociology of Leon Gérin, the pre-eminent Quebec sociologist of the early twentieth century, was deeply influenced by LePlay's sociology of the family. Gérin spent his "career" as a sociologist studying rural family life in Quebec (Glenday & McMullan, 1970). Until the arrival of Everett Hughes at McGill University in the early 1940s, sociology in the province concentrated on the microcosm of the individual and family in rural Quebec society.

FROM THE QUIET REVOLUTION TO THE PRESENT Until his untimely death in 2002, the contributions of Hubert Guindon (1964, 1968, 1978, 1988) made it easier for English-speaking sociologists, political scientists, and policy makers in Canada to better understand the social roots of not only the Quiet Revolution but the seemingly inexplicable rise of the nationalist and separatist movement in Quebec. Guindon was the first social scientist to identify the Quiet Revolution as state modernization; that is, the expansion of the province's health, education, and welfare bureaucracies. The burgeoning public sector during the 1960s meant well-paying careers for the growing number of well-educated, French-speaking Quebecois professionals. The private sector, however, remained firmly in English-speaking hands. For Guindon, a good part of the explanation for the rise of nationalist, and even separatist, sentiment during the 1960s and beyond rested with the struggle over "opening up" the linguistic barrier in the private sector in Quebec to qualified French-speaking Quebecois. Certainly, there were other sources of discontent expressed by Quebec nationalists, both then and now.

However, Hubert Guindon was a rare Canadian sociologist. His genius was his ability to communicate to *both* sides in this deeply divisive debate in Canada. This was achieved through a combination of his engaging prose and his personal charm and convivial wit. All who read and met him agreed that his work helped bridge the gap of misunderstanding separating Quebecois from Anglophone sociologists, political scientists, and public policy makers. Today, unfortunately, there are few willing or able to communicate across the linguistic and cultural duality that is at the core of Canadian society. A case in point is the year-long commission into "reasonable accommodation" in Quebec. Headed by Charles Taylor (political scientist and philosopher) and Gerard Bouchard (sociologist) and entitled "Building the Future: A Time for Reconciliation," the report deals with major issues such as freedom of religion and gender equality and the hierarchical ordering of rights facing not only Quebec society but Canadian society at large.

What little is known about this contentious issue in English-speaking Canada is the hyperbole reported in the media. Instead of addressing, for example, the lack of debate and discussion over similar issues facing the rest of Canada, Montreal's English-language newspaper would accentuate the "we versus them" distinction in Quebec with headlines such as, "Language debate creeps into Quebec hearings on cultural accommodation" (September 27, 2007) and "leaked portions" of the report allegedly stating "Quebec francophones [must] open their minds, get informed and learn more English" (May 20, 2008), as if to suggest that the anglophone minority stands above ethnic and racial conflict.

Sociology in Quebec carries on its connection to state-building in the province. Granted, there remain sociologists committed to some form of political independence, but many are now tackling issues as diverse as teenage suicide, immigration and multiculturalism, workplace health and safety, and criminology.

Sociology in English-Speaking Canada

British and American traditions influenced the development of sociology in English-speaking Canada. The British tradition was centred at the University of Toronto, while the U.S. influence was positioned at McGill University. To most historians of sociology, University of Chicago–trained sociologist Carl Dawson is credited with introducing the discipline to an English-speaking audience in Canada. Even though sociology courses had been offered at the University of Manitoba and in the Maritimes, Canada's first major program in sociology began in 1922 at McGill University under Dawson's leadership. During the period known as the "Chicago connection" (1920s to the mid-1950s), Dawson brought many Chicago sociologists and anthropologists to McGill, with Everett Hughes considered the most notable in terms of the development of sociology in Quebec and Canada. Until the early 1960s, Dawson's work on rural settlements in western Canada helped to establish the prevalence of community studies in early Canadian sociology.

Unlike French or American influences, the British tradition outside Quebec did not involve a separate department of sociology among the social sciences. On the contrary, until the 1960s, when an independent department of sociology was established at the University of Toronto, any sociology done was through the auspices of the Department of Political Economy.

For several years, Harold A. Innis headed the Department of Political Economy at the University of Toronto. Innis was an economic historian who had created the model of economic development known as the staples theory of international trade. Historically, Canada's usefulness, first to the French and later to Great Britain and the United States, was its abundance of natural resources. Staples such as furs, fish, timber, mineral ores, oil, and so on were, for the most part, exploited by "foreign" rather than Canadian capitalists.

According to Innis, these staple exports created the conditions for a particular pattern of Canadian economic development. For example, companies involved in the building of Canada's railways and canals were needed in order to cheaply ship exports out of the country. In other words, the conditions for the development of a more complex Canadian society were dependent on the number and kind of staple exports. Today, for example, the oil rich province of Alberta has the lowest unemployment rate in the country (in 2006, Alberta's unemployment rate was 3.4 percent compared to 6.3 percent in Canada as a whole).

Samuel D. Clark, an M.A. graduate of the Department of Sociology at McGill University who worked alongside Harold Innis, became the lead sociologist among a group of social scientists working at the University of Toronto during the late 1930s and 1940s. Clark built on the work of Innis by showing how the staples approach helped shape our society over the past 250 years—from the French Regime to the mid-twentieth century. It is especially interesting to note the parallel development of distinctive sociologies in English and French Canada during this period, a phenomenon exemplified by S.D. Clark's important study entitled *The Social Development of Canada* (1942), which was published at about the same time as Everett Hughes's *French Canada in Transition* (1943).

The 1960s, however, witnessed a large influx of American-trained sociologists into universities across Canada. Their interest in the discipline did not rest either in the development of a distinctive sociology in Canada or in community studies or historical sociology; instead, their interest lay in social problems and in rigorous research methods, especially statistical research methods. As a result of their training in the United States, these sociologists did very little research on the changing dynamics of Canadian society. There were few courses taught in which either the content or course descriptions dealt with Canadian topics.

THE CANADIANIZATION MOVEMENT While Quebec sociologists were enmeshed in the province's political struggles in the 1960s and 1970s, Canadian English-speaking sociologists were faced with their own dilemma. The expanding university system in Canada meant an increase in undergraduate and graduate student enrollments. However, many feared there would be few career openings to Canadian-trained PhD graduates. In 1975, the Commission on Canadian Studies of the Association of Universities and Colleges issued a report entitled *To Know Ourselves*—otherwise known as the Symons Report. Among its recommendations, the report called on the Canadian government and policy makers to increase knowledge of Canadian society through research, publications, and the hiring of Canadian-trained faculty.

SOCIOLOGY IN PRESENT-DAY ENGLISH-SPEAKING CANADA Unlike sociology in Quebec, sociology in English-speaking Canada is not concerned with nation building. According to Robert Brym and Céline St. Pierre (1997), one of the defining features of English-speaking sociology is its Leftist nature.

Wallace Clement (b. 1952) is considered by many to be Canada's pre-eminent sociologist. His books include *The Canadian Corporate Elite, Continental Corporate Power,* and *Relations of Ruling: Class and Gender in Postindustrial Societies* (with John Myles). Wallace Clement is discussed in Chapters 8 and 12.

Aileen Ross (1902–1995)

In addition to her pioneering work on philanthropy, Aileen Ross pursued field work in India and published two very different books in one year (1961): *The Hindu Family in its Urban Setting* and *Becoming a Nurse*. Several years later she followed her first book on India with her second, entitled *Student Unrest in India: A Comparative Approach*.

Kathleen "Kay" Herman (b. 1920)

First appointed assistant professor of Sociology in the Department of Political Science at Queen's University in 1966, "Kay" Herman became one of the founding members of the new Department of Sociology in 1969, where she taught until her retirement in 1989.

Annie Marion MacLean (1870–1934)

Chicago-trained sociologist Annie Marion MacLean (pictured) was born on Prince Edward Island. She taught for almost 30 years at Adelphi College, where she championed women's rights in the workplace. She is considered one of the pioneers, if not the "mother," of modern ethnographic research.

Building on the 1960s connection with political economy, sociologists such as Wallace Clement and William Carroll have written about Canada's corporate structure and role in globalization. In addition to political economy, the impact of feminist scholarship—and, to a lesser extent, postmodernism—has contributed to the perception of sociology's activist nature in English-speaking Canada. Among feminist scholars, Margrit Eichler and Dorothy Smith stand out as excep-tional contributors to their field. Margrit Eichler (1988b) is widely recognized for her work in nonsexist research methods, while Dorothy Smith (1987, 1999) is best known for her studies of feminist theory, especially her work on the everyday world of women and men. We will have more to say about feminist theories in the next section of this chapter (see the Down-to-Earth Sociology box: Early Women Sociologists in Canada).

Dorothy Smith, born in England in 1926, has taught at O.I.S.E. in Toronto since 1977. In 1999, she was awarded the Distinguished Scholarship Award by the American Sociological Association (ASA). Among her more notable publications is *The Everyday World as Problematic: A Feminist Sociology* (1987)

John Porter (1921–1979) was one of the leading sociologists in Canada during the post–World War II period. His book *The Vertical Mosaic* is considered a benchmark in scholarship and practical public policies. John Porter is discussed in Chapters 8 and 12.

Sociology in the United States

THE BEGINNINGS At first, sociology in the United States was dominated by the department at the University of Chicago, founded by Albion Small (1854–1926), who started the *American Journal of Sociology* and was its editor from 1895 to 1925. George Herbert Mead (1863–1931), who developed the symbolic interactionist perspective examined later, was an early member of the same department.

EARLY WOMEN SOCIOLOGISTS The position of women in North America was similar to that of European women, and their contributions to sociology met a similar fate. Denied faculty appointments in the discipline, many turned to working with the poor and became social activists (Young, 1995). Among the early women sociologists in the United States were Jane Addams, Alice Hamilton, Florence Kelley, Elsie Clews Parsons, and Alice Paul.

JANE ADDAMS Jane Addams (1860–1935), like Harriet Martineau, came from a background of wealth and privilege.

Addams worked tirelessly for social justice (Addams, 1910/1981). She founded Hull-House in Chicago's notorious slums, which was open to any person needing refuge—immigrants, the sick, the elderly, the poor. At her invitation, sociologists from the nearby University of Chicago were frequent visitors at Hull-House. Her efforts at social reform were so outstanding and so effective that in 1931 she was a co-winner of the Nobel Peace Prize, the only sociologist ever to win this coveted award.

W.E.B. DU BOIS With the racism of this period, African-American professionals also found life difficult. The most notable example is provided by W.E.B. Du Bois (1868–1963) (Lemert, 1994).

Du Bois's writings, numbering almost 2000, preserve a picture of race relations of that period. Frustrated at the lack of improvement in the issue, he turned to social action. Along with Jane Addams, Florence Kelley, and others from Hull-House, he founded the National Association for the Advancement of Colored People (NAACP) (Deegan, 1988). Combating racism both as a sociologist and a journalist, Du Bois eventually embraced revolutionary Marxism. Dismayed that so little improvement had been made in race

Jane Addams (1860–1935), a recipient of the Nobel Peace Prize, tirelessly worked on behalf of poor immigrants. With Ellen G. Starr, she founded Hull-House, a centre to help immigrants in Chicago. She was also a leader in women's rights (women's suffrage) and in the peace movement.

relations, at the age of 93 he moved to Ghana, where he was eventually buried (R. Stark, 1989).

SOCIAL REFORM VERSUS SOCIAL THEORY Like Du Bois, many early American sociologists combined the role of sociologist with that of social reformer. During the 1920s and 1930s, for example, Robert Park and Ernest Burgess not only studied prostitution, crime, drug addiction, and juvenile delinquency, but also offered suggestions for how to alleviate these social problems.

During the post–World War II period, sociology in the United States took a different direction. Its rise as the dominant force in the capitalist world did not go unchallenged. The Soviet Union was viewed as the communist threat to its influence in the developed European nations and less-developed world. In this milieu of U.S. supremacy, great emphasis was given to earning academic respect for sociology, and the focus shifted from social reform to serving the interests of U.S. global capitalism. Talcott Parsons (1902–1979), for example, developed abstract models of society known as structural functionalism that exerted great influence on sociology and political science. These models of how parts of society work harmoniously together did little to stimulate social activism among its adherents either at home or abroad. Consequently, Parsons had critics, among whom was C. Wright Mills.

C. Wright Mills (1916–1962) deplored the theoretical abstractions of the period, which he said were accompanied by empty research methods. Mills (1956) urged sociologists to return to social reform, seeing imminent danger to freedom from the coalescing of interests of the powerful elite—the wealthy, politicians, and the military. After his death, turbulence in U.S. and Canadian universities during the 1960s and 1970s fuelled by the Vietnam War also shook the dominance of structural functionalism. As U.S. supremacy in the world weakened, interest in social activism was revived, and Mills's ideas became popular among a new generation of sociologists.

Robert Merton (1910–2003) stressed the need for sociologists to develop **middle-range theories**—explanations

George Herbert Mead (1863–1931) is one of the founders of symbolic interactionism, an important theoretical perspective in sociology. His lectures at the University of Chicago were very popular. Though he wrote very little, after his death his students compiled his lectures into an influential book, *Mind, Self, and Society.*

C. Wright Mills was a controversial figure in sociology because of his analysis of the role of the elite in U.S. society. Today, his work is taken for granted by many sociologists and members of the public.

that tie together many research findings but avoid sweeping generalizations that attempt to account for everything. Such ideas, he claimed, are preferable because they can be tested. Merton's theories (1949/1968) contend that U.S. society's emphasis on attaining material wealth encourages crime and delinquency.

THE PRESENT Since the 1970s, U.S. sociology has not been dominated by any one theoretical orientation. Some sociologists are content to study various aspects of social life, interpret their findings, and publish them in sociology journals (for example, the *American Journal of Sociology*). Others direct their research toward social change and actively participate in community affairs to help bring about a vision of a more just society (see *Social Problems*, the journal of the Society for the Study of Social Problems).

What Do Sociologists in Canada and the United States Do Now?

Over the past two decades, the activities of sociologists have broadened. Early PhD graduates in sociology had difficulty finding work beyond university teaching. Although many in the field still teach, the government has become the second-largest employer of sociologists. Many others work for private firms in management and planning positions. Still others work in criminology and demography, in social work, and as counsellors. Sociologists put their training to use in such diverse efforts as tracking the spread of AIDS and helping teenage prostitutes pursue other lifestyles. Later we will look more closely at some of the careers open to sociology graduates.

At this point, however, let's concentrate on a better understanding of sociological theory.

THEORETICAL PERSPECTIVES IN SOCIOLOGY

Facts never interpret themselves. A number is just a number, a statistic is simply a statistic. In everyday life, we interpret what we observe by using common sense. That is, to understand our experiences (our "facts"), we situate them in a framework of more-or-less-related ideas. Sociologists place their observations into a conceptual framework called a theory. A **theory** is a general statement about how some parts of the world fit together and how they work. It is an explanation of how two or more facts are related to one another. By providing a framework for observations, a theory interprets social reality in a distinct way.

Sociologists in Canada use six major theories: symbolic interactionism, functional analysis, conflict theory, feminist theories, postmodernism, and queer theory. Let's examine the main elements of each of these theories (see Table 1.1).

Symbolic Interactionism

Unlike functionalism or conflict theory, which focus on organizations, institutions, or national societies, symbolic interactionism studies specific behaviours of interacting individuals caught in identifiable face-to-face social settings or encounters. We can trace the origins of symbolic interactionism to the Scottish moral philosophers of the eighteenth century, who noted that people evaluate their own conduct by comparing themselves with others (Stryker, 1990). This micro-theoretical perspective was developed by sociologists Charles Horton Cooley (1864–1929), William I. Thomas (1863–1947), and George Herbert Mead (1863–1931). We will discuss in more detail how symbols form the basis of our individual self-concept in Chapter 4.

Symbolic interactionists view *symbols*—things to which we attach meaning—as the basis of social life. Without symbols, we would have no mechanism for perceiving others in terms of relationships (aunts and uncles, employers and teachers, and so on). Symbols define what such family relationships mean to us. For example, if you think of someone as an aunt or uncle, you behave in certain ways, but if you think of that person as a boyfriend or girlfriend, you behave quite differently. And without symbols, we could not coordinate our actions with others. If we lacked the ability to specify time, materials, sizes, or goals, we could not build bridges and highways. Without symbols, there would be no books, movies, or musical instruments. We would not have schools or hospitals, government, or religion. In short, symbols make social life possible.

IN SUM

Symbolic interactionists explain order and personal stability using the symbols we share with others in our community and define change in terms of the changing symbols (or meanings) associated with particular institutions, such as family, the economy, or universities.

TABLE 1.1 Major Theoretical Perspectives in Sociology

Perspective	Usual Level of Analysis	Focus of Analysis	Key Terms
Symbolic interactionism	Microsociological—examines small-scale patterns of social interaction	Face-to-face interaction; how people use symbols to create social life	Social act Dramaturgy Social object Generalized other
Functional analysis (also called functionalism and structural functionalism)	Macrosociological—examines large-scale patterns of society	Relationships among the parts of society; how these parts are functional (have beneficial consequences) or dysfunctional (have negative consequences)	Objective social factors Scientific research Functions (manifest and latent) Equilibrium
Conflict theory	Macrosociological—examines large-scale patterns of society	The struggle for scarce resources by groups in a society; how dominant elites use power to control the less powerful	Rational self-interest Progress Conflict Control Domination Exploitation
Feminist theories	Microsociological—individual and small groups Macrosociological—patterns of patriarchy	Individuals in face-to-face interaction, predominately women	Patriarchy Sexism Coercive structures Gender division of labour
Postmodernism	Macrosociological—language and culture Microsociological—describing the socially constructed postmodern individual	Texts—documents, film, photos, video, collages, and so on	Spectacle Free-floating signifiers Simulation Sign/image
Queer theory (emergent: from the 1990s onward)	Microsociological—individual sexual identities	Texts, films, photography	Heterosexual identity Subversions Bodies LGBT (lesbian, gay, bisexual, transgendered) Drag queens Homophobia
Critical race theory (emergent: from the 1970s onward)	Macrosociological—discrimination and the law	Texts, fieldwork	Racism Critical legal studies Discrimination

Sources: Various, including Kenneth Allan, *Contemporary Social and Sociological Theory,* London: Pine Forge Press, 2006, and *The Condition of Postmodernity* (p. 43), by David Harvey, 1989, Oxford, England; New York: Blackwell.

Functional Analysis

Functional analysis, also known as *functionalism* and *structural functionalism*, is a macrosociological theory that views society as a unit made up of interrelated parts that work together (J. H. Turner, 1978). When all the parts of a society fulfill their functions, that society is in a "normal" state. If they do not fulfill their functions, the society is in an "abnormal" or "pathological" state. To understand society, then, func-tionalists contend that we must look at both *structure* (how the parts of a society fit together to make a whole) and *function* (what each part does and how it contributes to society).

Continuing the work of Durkheim, Robert K. Merton used the term *functions* to refer to the beneficial consequences of people's actions that help keep a group (society or social system) in equilibrium. In contrast, *dysfunctions* are consequences that undermine a system's equilibrium.

Functions can often be both manifest and latent. If an action is intended to help some part of a system, it is a *manifest function*. For example, suppose the tuition at your university is doubled. The intention, or manifest function, of such an increase may be to raise faculty salaries and thus recruit better staff. Merton pointed out that actions can also have *latent positive functions*, or unintended consequences that help a system adapt. Suppose the tuition increase worked and the quality of the faculty improved and significantly increased the university's position in the *Maclean's* ranking of universities across Canada. As a result, the school was flooded with new student applicants and was able to expand its programs and its campus. The expansion contributed to the growth and stability of your university, but it was an unintended positive consequence of the tuition increase.

Sometimes actions have the opposite effect, of course, and hurt or weaken the social system. Because such consequences are usually unintended, Merton called them *latent dysfunctions*. Let's assume that doubling the tuition backfired, and that half the student body couldn't afford the increase and dropped out. With this loss of income, the university had to reduce salaries and lost ranking in the *Maclean's* annual poll. Because these results were not intended and resulted in harm, they represent a *latent dysfunction* of the tuition increase.

Finally, structural functionalism contends that individuals living in a normally functioning social system will share a number of values—beliefs about what is right and wrong—that help hold a society together. Values help maintain a state of social equilibrium. The process of socialization, to be discussed in Chapter 4, contributes to the social integration of individuals in society.

IN SUM

From the perspective of functional analysis, society is a functioning unit, with each part related to the whole. Whenever we examine a smaller part, we need to look for its functions and dysfunctions to see how it is related to the larger unit. This basic approach can be applied to any social group—an entire society, a university or college, or even a group as small as a family.

Conflict Theory

Conflict theory provides a third perspective on social life. Karl Marx witnessed the Industrial Revolution that transformed Europe. He saw that peasants who left the land to seek work in urbanizing areas were forced to work for wages that barely provided enough to eat. The average worker died at age 30, and the wealthy lived to 50 (Edgerton, 1992, p. 87). Shocked by this suffering and exploitation, Marx developed **conflict theory**, concluding that class struggle is the key to all human history. In each society, one small group controls the means of production and exploits those who do not. In industrialized societies, the struggle is between the **bourgeoisie**, the small group of capitalists who own the means to produce wealth, and the **proletariat**, the mass of workers they exploit. The capitalists also control politics, so that when workers rebel, they are able to call on the power of the state for control (R.C. Angell, 1965).

When Marx made his observations, capitalism was in its infancy and workers were at the mercy of their employers. Workers had none of what we take for granted today—the right to strike (for unionized workers), minimum wages, eight-hour days, coffee breaks, five-day workweeks, paid vacations and holidays, medical benefits, sick leave, unemployment compensation, and government pension plans. His analysis reminds us that these benefits came not from generous hearts, but from workers who forced such concessions from their employers.

Some current conflict sociologists use conflict theory in a much broader sense. Ralf Dahrendorf (b. 1929) sees conflict as inherent in all relations that have authority. He points out that **authority**, or power that people consider legitimate, runs through all layers of society—in small groups, a community, or an entire society. People in positions of authority try to enforce conformity, which in turn creates resentment and resistance. The result is a "contested terrain" over who has authority over what within business organizations, political bureaucracies, and even families (J.H. Turner, 1978).

Another sociologist, Lewis Coser (b. 1913), asserts that conflict is especially likely to develop among people who are in close relationships. Such people are connected by a network of responsibilities, power, and rewards, and to change something can easily upset carefully worked out arrangements. Consequently, we can think of even close relationships as a balancing act—of maintaining and reworking a particular distribution of responsibilities, power, and rewards.

IN SUM

Unlike functionalists, who view society as a harmonious whole with parts working together, conflict theorists see society as composed of groups competing for scarce resources. Although alliances or co-operation may prevail on the surface, a struggle for power lies beneath. Marx focused on struggles between the bourgeoisie and proletariat, but today's conflict theorists have expanded this perspective to include smaller groups and even basic relationships such as the family and its kinship networks (see Chapter 13, The Family).

Feminist Theories

There are, at present, at least three variants of **feminist theories**: Marxist feminist theories, liberal feminist theories, and non-Marxist radical feminist theories. While they differ in important ways from one another, especially when it comes to their programs for changing society, they share a few common characteristics, which we will outline after briefly describing each approach.

MARXIST FEMINIST THEORIES Marxist feminists share the view of Marxists that social class is more fundamental than gender in explaining inequality. Like Marxists, they assert that women's position in society is a consequence of the property relations of capitalism. Women and men are viewed as property, but the exploitation of women includes their objectification in roles that serve men's interests. Marxist feminists argue that revolutionary changes in the world economy are the only way to change both men's and women's exploitation by capitalism. Modern-day Marxist feminists see one of their goals as combating the "false consciousness" of women's groups such as Real Women, who dignify women's traditional role of subservience and exploitation in the traditional family.

LIBERAL FEMINIST THEORIES Liberal feminists claim that legal restraints and customs are at the root of women's subservient role in society. While they recognize the importance of class, ethnicity, and race as valid criteria in understanding women's inequality, our society's laws and customs stand out as the principal factors. Liberal feminism has been criticized for being exclusionary—preserving middle-class women's position in universities and society at the expense of women of colour or women from poor backgrounds. Moreover, liberal feminists have attracted controversy over their opposition to prostitution and soft pornography as exploitative. On the other hand, liberal feminists have been at the forefront of changes that have tackled sexist privileges in the existing structure—changes such as pay equity, provision of day care for working mothers, better education for women, and opening nontraditional career options to women.

RADICAL FEMINIST THEORIES Radical feminists believe patriarchy oppresses women. Patriarchy is characterized by power, dominance, hierarchy, and competition. Not only must patriarchy's legal structures and gender socialization be changed, but society's cultural and social institutions that keep women "in their place" must be transformed. Institutions such as the traditional family, the church, and academia are often singled out for restructuring. While many radical feminists point to women's biology (e.g., childbearing) as a critical factor in their relegation to second-class status, they endeavour to support those initiatives that can overcome whatever socially constructed negative effects biology may have on both men and women.

Recent developments in feminist theory include lesbian feminism, men's feminism, and postmodern feminism. Lesbian feminism argues that if heterosexual relationships are exploitative by nature, then women should build a separate culture for themselves. Men's feminism applies feminist theories to the study of men and masculinity. Postmodern feminism undermines previous theories based on an optimistic belief in progress (Lorber, 1998, p. 174).

WHAT IS COMMON TO FEMINIST THEORIES? These three feminist theories share a number of commonalities:

1. Biological sex differences account for differing genitalia between the sexes (although this is not a perfect relationship, as transgendered individuals will attest) and physical strength, but gender differences are not simply derived from biology; they are a product of complex social, historical, and cultural factors.

2. The gender division of labour is hierarchical, with men's roles dominant and better rewarded and women's roles subordinate and less valued.

3. Relations between the genders are so intertwined that changes in one area affect many other aspects of social life. Social issues such as abortion or homosexuality are related to the "liberation of women" from the structures of subservience in society. Gains or losses in the struggle for women's rights influence the direction of change in other areas such as gay and lesbian rights.

4. The knowledge of science, ourselves, and society has been largely derived from an androcentric bias—that is, men's experiences—because men have held positions of authority in academia. The contributions made by women and other "invisible" minorities must be uncovered and communicated for the benefit of all.

IN SUM

The three variants of feminist theory are Marxist, liberal, and non-Marxist radical. All feminist theories share at least four characteristics.

Postmodernism

Postmodernism in present-day society could be viewed as the logical rejection of modernity. Modernity, as a sociological concept, was first employed by Max Weber to describe the society or civilization that had emerged from feudalism, otherwise known as industrial capitalism. It was a society based on the Enlightenment ideas of reason, science, and freedom. Modernity meant that change was possible because humans could act collectively. In addition, science could make society materially better while reason promised to unmask prejudices based on religious or other irrational ideas and lead all humanity toward personal freedom.

C. Wright Mills was the first sociologist to argue that we are living in a "postmodern period," by which he meant a society where "the ideas of freedom and of reason have become moot; that increased rationality may not be assumed to make for increased freedom" (1959, p. 167). The advent of two world wars, nuclear weapons, the Cold War, and so on meant that personal freedom was not automatically linked to progress, reason, science, capitalism, or communism—quite the contrary. Many horrors against humanity were and continue to be visited in the name of these ideas.

Postmodernism as a theory of present-day society recognizes diversity where modernity pushes sameness. Postmodernism recognizes cultural and sexual differences while modernity looks for uniformity of tastes and habit. In other words, the culturally homogenized world promised by modernity with the spread of capitalism is being replaced with a view of present-day society as a cultural collage where people can live in their own cultural and social space as free individuals. For some analysts, such as David Harvey (1989), postmodernity as a theory of diversity in an otherwise culturally homogeneous capitalist world is made possible as a result of the computer revolution. Computers and other information technologies contribute to the economic viability of small businesses based in culturally distinct communities. Instead of assimilation or marginalization, information technologies make cultural diversity a reality. In an age of conglomerates, it is increasingly possible to make a comfortable living working from home or starting a small business, in part because the internet links us to a world market.

The computer is a place where image is dominant and the symbol supreme. Jean Baudrillard (1983, 1993, 1995), a French theorist of postmodernity, is noted for his developmental theory of the symbol. In preindustrial societies, signs or symbols are passed on in festivals, rites of passage, and rituals, and are often expressed in the exchange of gifts. In industrial capitalist societies—which Baudrillard labels productionist—signs and symbols and the real world are the same. Statements such as "The clothes make the man/woman" capture the essence of a link between signs and the real world; that is, the clothes someone wears confer his or her status in society. The rise of postmodernity breaks the link between symbols and the real world. Signs and symbols become autonomous. In cyberspace, for example, image is more important than the real world. Young people today play video games in realms of their own choosing. For postmodern theorists, image, symbols, and signs are steadily encroaching on modernity.

Postmodernism can also be viewed as both macrosociology and microsociology. The link between macro- and microsociology begins with language as the primary social bond in contemporary society. Postmodernists call their emphasis on language *discourse analysis*. Language and culture form the structures within which individuals become social beings. Lyotard (1984) defines the postmodern condition as skepticism toward all universal or absolute truths that have been used to legitimize political and scientific projects such as communism (Marx) or the dominance of the unconscious mind (Freud). Modern information and communications technologies (ICTs) have brought about the postmodern condition. To some postmodernists, homeless men and women embody the tragic fallout of modernism. Today's world has no need for past or future; it is made up of two "presents"—one that is based in the virtual reality of new ICT technologies and media, and the other "real" present that appears to many as elusive or even borderline. To escape the angst of the "real-world" present, a postmodern person might enjoy cybersex with Lulu, the first porn star of virtual reality, for example. Or, with the advent of the "teledildonic" suit, made up of a head piece with video and audio inputs connected to a suit that stimulates the erogenous zones, a player can take on any idealized persona and enjoy distant, uncommitted, and safe sex (Appignanesi & Garratt, 2000).

The major criticisms of postmodernism centre on its preoccupation with surface reality. In addition, postmodern theorists often view society as a closed system in which events happen but seemingly under no one's control. Why some images, symbols, or signs are more important than others are questions of power that are usually left unasked by postmodern theorists.

IN SUM

Postmodernism emphasizes cultural diversity in opposition to the cultural homogeneity promised by modernism. Information and communications technologies help make cultural diversity a reality. The concept of power, however, is absent from most postmodern theories.

Queer Theory (from the 1990s onward)

Queer theory is an emerging theory that has become associated with gay and lesbian studies—a recent academic achievement spanning the social sciences and humanities. However, queer theory owes its origins to the pioneering work of several researchers and theorists. Only two will be discussed here. In her 1990 book *Gender Troubles*, Judith Butler, a professor of comparative literature and rhetoric at the University of California, Berkeley, rejects the feminist argument that "women" are a group with common characteristics and interests. In place of a binary view of gender and sexuality, Butler points to the significance of the human body in defining the parameters of a person and his or her personality in her later book, *Bodies That Matter* (1993). Today, the fluidity of gender identities is understood in Freudian terms, and especially Oedipal law.

Gayle Rubin, in her widely cited essay "Thinking Sex" (1984), discusses the oppressions that fall upon groups of lesbians and gay men in the context of a more general intolerance of sexual difference and a fear of (or at least a distaste for) sex itself. She sees intolerance of gays and lesbians as part of a broader "moral panic" (Chapter 18) that targets pornography, sadomasochism, leather, prostitution, birth control, divorce, and even masturbation, especially among the young. Morality crusaders attack obscene literature, nude paintings, abortion, birth control information, and "sexual" public dancing. On the other hand, Rubin claims that sexual norms are constantly being challenged and contested. As a result, social dynamics constitute the substance of queer theory.

Queer theory deliberately challenges all notions of fixed identity. Therefore, instead of viewing sex, gender, and desire as a continuum, queer theory smashes any link between them. Gender and desire/pleasure become more free-floating and based on individual attraction—regardless of the sex of the other person.

Critical Race Theory (from the 1970s onward)

Critical race theory—another emerging theory—is linked to the development of African-American legal thought in the post–civil rights era (Tate, 1996). For some civil rights scholars, the pace of legal reform during the 1960s and 1970s slowed appreciably. Derrick Bell, a lawyer who served as the executive director of the NAACP in the 1970s, is considered to be the first activist scholar to fashion arguments that were designed to expand the reformation of existing laws in the United States (Bell, 1993).

Today, **critical race theory** encompasses the disciplines of anthropology, sociology, history, philosophy, and politics. Notions of the social construction of race and race identity and the reality of discrimination are ever-present in the writings of contemporary critical race theorists.

Focus Question
What are the major sociological theories and the two emerging ones?

Levels of Analysis: Macro and Micro

A major difference between the theoretical orientations described above is their level of analysis. Functionalists, conflict theorists, and critical race theorists focus on **macro-level analysis**; that is, they examine large-scale patterns of society. In contrast, symbolic interactionists, postmodernists, and queer theorists usually focus on **micro-level analysis**—they analyze social interaction, or what people do when they are in one another's presence. Feminist theories engage in both levels of analysis (see Table 1.1).

Let's return to the example of homelessness to make the distinction between micro and macro analysis levels clearer. In studying the homeless, symbolic interactionists would focus on what is said and done, analyzing what homeless people do when they are in shelters and on the streets, focusing especially on their communications—both speech and **nonverbal interaction** (how they communicate by gestures, silence, use of space, and so on). The observations made earlier about the despair and silence of the homeless, for example, would be areas of interest to symbolic interactionists, as well as to critical race theorists and queer theorists. Unfortunately, postmodern theories have difficulty grasping the reality of homelessness.

Analysis at the micro level would be of no interest to functionalists and conflict theorists. They would focus instead on the macro level. Functionalists would examine how changes in society are related to homelessness. They might look at how changing relationships in the family unit (size, divorce rate) and economic conditions (higher rents, inflation, fewer skilled jobs, loss of jobs overseas) cause homelessness among people who are unable to find jobs and do not have a family to fall back on. Conflict theorists would stress the struggle between social classes, attributing the disproportionate numbers of homeless Native Canadians to the policies of the wealthy that push certain groups into unemployment and homelessness. Feminists would be capable of understanding the plight of homeless women and would attribute the disproportionate number of homeless women with children to patriarchy.

Putting the Theoretical Perspectives Together

Which theoretical perspective should we use to study human behaviour? Which level of analysis is correct? As you have seen, each theoretical perspective provides a different and often sharply contrasting picture of the world. No theory or level of analysis encompasses all reality. Rather, by focusing on different aspects of social life, each provides a distinctive interpretation. Consequently, it is necessary to use all six theoretical lenses to analyze human behaviour. By putting the contributions of each perspective and level of analysis together, we gain a more comprehensive picture of social life.

APPLIED AND CLINICAL SOCIOLOGY

Sociologists Paul Lazarsfeld and Jeffrey Reitz (1989) divide sociology into three phases. As we have already learned, sociology was initially indistinguishable from attempts to reform society. The primary concern of early sociologists was making the world a better place—analyzing social conditions to improve social life.

During the discipline's second phase of development, the goal of sociologists was to establish sociology as a respected field of knowledge. To this end, sociologists sought to develop **pure** or **basic sociology**—that is, research and theory aimed at making discoveries about life in human groups.

During sociology's third phase, there has been an attempt to merge sociological knowledge and practical work. Dissatisfied with "knowledge for the sake of knowledge," many sociologists use their sociological skills to bring about social change—to make a difference in social life.

Efforts to blend sociological knowledge with practical applications are known as **applied sociology**. Today's applied sociologists work in a variety of settings, recommending practical changes that can be implemented. A business firm may hire a sociologist to solve a problem in the workplace; sociologists may do research for government commissions or agencies investigating social problems such as pornography, crime, violence, or environmental pollution. The Down-to-Earth Sociology box on the next page describes several careers in sociology.

Clinical sociologists deal with specific problems for particular organizations. Examples include those who work with drug addicts and ex-convicts, or others who work with families to change basic relationships between husbands and wives or children and parents. Figure 1.2 contrasts basic and applied sociology.

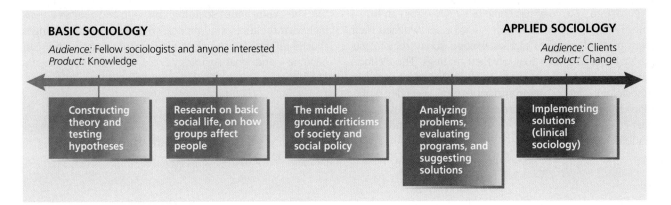

FIGURE 1.2 Comparing Basic and Applied Sociology

Source: Based on "Basic and Applied Sociological Work: Divergence, Convergence, or Peaceful Co-existence?" by J.R. DeMartini, 1982, *The Journal of Applied Behavioral Science, 18*, 2, pp. 203–215.

Contrary to popular belief, sociologists use their skills in a variety of settings, not just in universities. They can be found counselling children, consulting with businesses and/or governments, and improving relationships in the workplace.

Pat Eklund graduated with an undergraduate degree in sociology and several hundred hours of "time" spent as an intern in a local correctional facility. According to Pat, "that time and those experiences in prison [as an intern] have been the springboard for my career in criminal justice." Underlying these experiences was his sociological perspective: "I am always looking for why things happen, what is underneath someone's behaviour. This is where my degree in sociology has proved invaluable."

Mary's interest in sociology included writing a departmental honours thesis. While practical applications intrigued her, Mary was passionate about abstract modelling. Because of extenuating circumstances, Mary was unable to pursue her studies in graduate school. Instead, she worked at a variety of jobs, one of which involved conducting training seminars on abuse for police officers. She used her sociological training to develop models for identifying abusive situations. Without the models, the police officers might not have recognized the potential for abuse in certain situations. According to Mary, "The problem is that people experience so much of their lives as a kind of chaos. They don't really see how the things that happen are interconnected. . . . If you are going to have a real effect on people's lives, then making them aware of the larger picture—the model—is a real gift."

Dave Blume and Bob Chase both earned undergraduate degrees in business. Each also earned a second degree in sociology. According to Dave, "The competition in the business world can be very intense. You have to give potential employers a reason to select you over other candidates who have the same business degree that you do. Sociology, with its focus on groups, organizations, and human interaction, is a natural complement to business. And, it is a degree which is increasingly well received in the business world." Bob adds, "Sociology prepares you for understanding change and anticipating it. The degree is a real asset."

Donna decided to pursue sociology because in many ways it defined her own life. "It seemed that my whole life has been spent working with people in groups—my work, my children, and their groups like Girl Scouts and other organizations. I have had to learn how to get along with many different people in many different settings." Donna focused her course work on the sociology of politics and power and started a career as an independent consultant and trainer. Donna's consultations and training sessions often take the form of workshops that cover a wide variety of topics, including cultural diversity, women, organizational creativity, and power and organization.

For some, this kind of work can be difficult to grasp. Donna suggests that "workshops like I do are an ongoing part of the business and government worlds. Simply because you haven't heard about them doesn't mean that they do not exist. You could begin by contacting convention bureaus and getting a list of industry conventions or annual meetings which have come to your city. Then ask for convention schedules. You will see for yourself the array of workshops offered. But this is only a start."

THE FUTURE Sociology has come full circle. From an initial concern with improving society, sociologists switched their focus to developing abstract knowledge. Today, sociologists are again seeking ways to apply their findings. These efforts have gained momentum in recent years. Many departments of sociology offer courses in specialties such as gender, workplace issues, criminology, and family violence, and some offer co-op programs and internships at graduate and undergraduate levels.

The evolution of sociology has allowed renewed contact with the discipline's roots, with invigorating changes that challenge us to grasp a vision of what society can become—and what sociology's role will be in that process of change.

Focus Question
What can you do with a degree in sociology?

SUMMARY AND REVIEW

The Sociological Perspective

WHAT IS THE SOCIOLOGICAL PERSPECTIVE?
The **sociological perspective** stresses that people's social experiences—the groups to which they belong and their particular experiences within these groups—underlie their behaviour. C. Wright Mills referred to this as the intersection of biography (the individual) and history (social factors acting on the individual). pp. 2–4.

Sociology and the Other Sciences

WHAT IS SCIENCE, AND WHERE DOES SOCIOLOGY FIT IN?
Science is the application of systematic methods to obtain knowledge and the knowledge obtained by those methods. Science is divided into the **natural sciences**, which seek to comprehend, explain, and predict events in the natural environment, and the **social sciences**, which seek to understand the social world objectively by means of controlled and repeated observations. **Sociology** is the scientific study of society and human behaviour. pp. 4–7.

The Origins of Sociology

WHEN DID SOCIOLOGY FIRST APPEAR AS A SEPARATE DISCIPLINE, AND WHAT FACTORS CONTRIBUTED TO ITS EMERGENCE?
Sociology emerged as a separate discipline in the mid-1800s in Western Europe during the onset of the Industrial Revolution. Industrialization brought social changes so sweeping that they affected all aspects of human existence—where people lived, the nature of their work, and interpersonal relationships. Early sociologists who focused on these social changes include Auguste Comte, Karl Marx, Harriet Martineau, Emile Durkheim, and Max Weber. pp. 7–11.

The Role of Values in Social Research

IS THE ONLY PURPOSE OF SOCIAL RESEARCH TO ADVANCE HUMAN UNDERSTANDING, OR SHOULD IT ALSO BE USED TO REFORM SOCIETY?
All sociologists concur that social research should be **value-free**: the researcher's personal beliefs should be set aside to permit objective findings. But sociologists do not agree on the uses and purposes of social research. Some believe its purpose should only be to advance understanding of human behaviour; others contend that its goal should be to reform harmful social arrangements. pp. 11–12.

Verstehen and Social Facts

HOW DO SOCIOLOGISTS USE VERSTEHEN AND SOCIAL FACTS TO INVESTIGATE HUMAN BEHAVIOUR?
According to Weber, to understand why people act as they do, sociologists must try to put themselves in their shoes. He used the German term **Verstehen**, "to grasp by insight," to describe this essentially subjective approach. Emile Durkheim, although not denying the importance of *Verstehen*, emphasized the importance of uncovering "social facts" that influence human actions. **Social facts** are objective social conditions that influence how people behave. Contemporary sociology uses both approaches to understand human behaviour. p. 12.

Sexism in Early Sociology

WHAT WAS THE POSITION OF WOMEN IN EARLY SOCIOLOGY?
Only a few wealthy women received advanced education, and their writings were largely ignored. Harriet Martineau is an example. pp. 12–13.

Sociology in Quebec, Canada, and the United States

WHAT UNIVERSITIES WERE CONSIDERED THE HISTORICAL CENTRES OF SOCIOLOGY IN ENGLISH-SPEAKING CANADA? HOW WERE THEY DIFFERENT?
McGill University and the University of Toronto. Sociology in English-speaking Canada was influenced by two traditions, the British and the U.S. The British influence was centred at the University of Toronto, while the U.S. influence emerged at McGill University.

Canada's first major program in sociology began in 1922 at McGill University under the leadership of Carl Dawson. Dawson used the program at the University of Chicago, the leading centre of U.S. sociology in this period, as a model for establishing sociology at McGill University. He was instrumental in bringing several Chicago-trained sociologists to McGill.

The British tradition treated sociology as a branch of political economy. Unlike at McGill, an independent department of sociology was not established at the University of Toronto until the 1960s. There was a healthy disdain for the U.S. brand of sociology among the sociologists, political economists, and historians that dominated the Department of Political Economy. Their main criticisms were that U.S. sociology was practised as little more than the study of social problems such as poverty and delinquency and that it lacked research and theoretical rigour. pp. 13–17.

Theoretical Perspectives in Sociology

WHAT IS A THEORY AND WHAT ARE THE MAJOR THEORETICAL PERSPECTIVES?

A **theory** is a general statement about how sets of facts are related to one another. A theory provides a conceptual framework within which facts are interpreted.

Sociologists make use of five primary theoretical frameworks to interpret social life. **Symbolic interactionism** examines how people use symbols to develop and share their views of the world. Symbolic interactionists usually focus on the micro level—on small-scale patterns of human interaction. **Functional analysis**, in contrast, focuses on the macro level—on large-scale patterns of society. Functional theorists stress that a social system is made up of various parts. When working properly, each part contributes to the stability of the whole, fulfilling a function that contributes to a system's equilibrium. **Conflict theory** also focuses on large-scale patterns of society. Conflict theorists stress that society is composed of competing groups struggling for scarce resources.

Feminist theories focus on both microsociological and macrosociological analysis. All three variants of feminist theory stress the importance of biology and patriarchy in determining the position of both women and men in society.

Postmodernism also concentrates on macrosociological and microsociological levels of analysis. Postmodern theorists are concerned with analyzing the importance of symbols, signs, and images in present-day society.

Queer theory and **critical race theory** are two emerging theories. The former owes much to developments in feminist and postmodern scholarship, while the latter is a more distinctly U.S.-based multidisciplinary theory.

Because no single theory encompasses all of reality, at different times sociologists may use any or all of the seven theoretical lenses. With each perspective focusing on certain features of social life and each providing its own interpretation, their combined insights yield a more comprehensive picture of social life. pp. 17–22.

Applied and Clinical Sociology

WHAT IS THE DIFFERENCE BETWEEN PURE (OR BASIC) AND APPLIED SOCIOLOGY?

Pure (or basic) sociology is sociological research whose only purpose is to make discoveries. In contrast, **applied sociology** is the use of sociology to solve problems. pp. 22–24.

KEY TERMS

WEBLINKS

All URLs listed are current as of the printing of this book.

Sociologists for a New Millennium
www.arts.ualberta.ca/cjscopy/newmill/
A special issue of the *Canadian Journal of Sociology Online* asking graduate students, recent graduates, and junior faculty to write about the people and works that influenced their development as sociologists and where they think those influences will take both them and the discipline in Canada in the twenty-first century.

Pearson Education Canada's Sociology Resource Site
www.pearsoned.ca/sociology
Information about the study of sociology. Material concerning the history of sociology and its theoretical underpinnings, as well as its diverse areas of interest.

World Wide Sociology WebRing
http://a.webring.com/hub?ring=sociology
The World Wide Sociology WebRing (WWSW) is being developed for the purpose of bringing together sociologists and students from colleges around the world to establish a community where the free exchange of ideas may take place. This web ring will also be a place where published and unpublished papers can be made available to all conducting research in the social sciences.

Dead Sociologists' Society
http://media.pfeiffer.edu/lridener/DSS/DEADSOC.HTML
A list of various theorists, some biographical information, and a summary of their work can be found in the Dead Sociologists' Index. Students can check out the Dead Sociologists Gallery or the original chart from which the site was developed.

Social Science Departments in Canada
http://www.sociosite.net/socdeps/canada.php
A complete listing of sociology departments in Canada.

CRITICAL THINKING QUESTIONS

1. Do all sociological theories espouse progress—that is, the view that all societies advance from one stage of civilization to the next?

2. Why are symbolic interactionism and queer theory regarded as microsociology?

3. Why are functionalism, conflict theory, and critical race theory considered to be macrosociology?

4. Why are feminist theories and postmodernism both microsociological and macrosociological?

5. Considering the macro and micro approaches in sociology, which one do you think best explains social life? Access the Research Navigator through MySocLab and use keywords such as "micro," "macro," and "social life" to locate relevant and recent scholarly and popular press publications to help you answer this question.

 **PEARSON mysoclab** Explore the topics covered in this chapter on MySocLab using the access information provided with this text. Interactive resources for studying include multimedia tutorials, video clips, practice tests, quizzes, and animated maps and figures.

What Do Sociologists Do?

Carol Meredith and Barclay McKie were 19 years old when they met in Wetaskiwin, Alberta. On July 28, 1997, barely a month after Meredith had decided to leave McKie, her husband, he sexually assaulted her and dropped her off at a shopping mall near Calgary, Alberta. A warrant was issued for McKie's arrest and Meredith fled to her sister's home in Cold Lake, Alberta, 600 kilometres north-east of Calgary. According to RCMP officials, on July 31, 1997, less than nine hours after she had arrived at her sister's home, a man beat her sleeping brother to near death, attacked her, and dragged her by the hair for half a block down one of Cold Lake's busiest streets and shoved her into a brown van. Six days later, Meredith was found dead from a blow to the head in a van some 30 kilometres from town. The day before she was discovered, Barclay McKie was arrested while buying a bus ticket to Edmonton, Alberta.

At about the same time as the murder, Statistics Canada released crime figures showing that incidents of wife assault had *declined* by 18 percent since 1993, from 14 420 to 11 829 cases per year. Feminists and public-shelter advocates across Canada dismissed the figures; women and children seeking shelter in Alberta alone had risen 10 percent between 1996 and 1997 to 20 139 individuals. The Centre for Justice Statistics reported that between 1998 and 2000, there had been a 4 percent decline in the number of women and children residing in shelters. However, the Alberta Council of Women's Shelters reported that in the same time period, 3835 women and 3006 children *could not* be accommodated due to overcrowding. The *average* number of spousal (wife only) homicides per year between 1975 and 2004 (see Table 2.1) had slightly declined, to 72.6 deaths as compared to 74.1 for the previous period (1975–2000). What accounted for these disparities in research findings?

First, Statistics Canada relied on *reported* cases to police, while workers in the field based their statistics on who came through their doors asking for help.

Second, the decline in reported cases may have been due to a much-applauded public policy of zero tolerance for domestic violence. Under zero tolerance, many women who might previously have called the police to defuse a domestic incident may not have called for fear of losing their men to prison, thereby leaving them in a potentially dangerous environment.

This discrepancy illustrates the importance of understanding the nature of social problems and how they are researched. It also helps us understand the relationship between what Robert K. Merton called the *manifest function* of a good public policy (in this case, zero tolerance of family violence) and its unintended consequences, which often make matters more difficult to understand.

LEARNING OUTCOMES

After you have studied this chapter, you will be able to answer the following questions:

1. What is a valid sociological topic?

2. Why isn't common sense adequate?

3. How do sociologists gather data?

4. How do sociologists choose a particular research method?

5. What are the eight basic steps of scientific research?

6. How important are ethics in sociological research?

7. What is the relationship between theory and research?

8. What happens when the ideal meets the real?

TABLE 2.1 Number of Spousal Homicides[1] in Canada, by Province and Sex of Victim, 1975–2004

	Total Number of Victims		Average Number of Victims Per Year (1975–2004)	
	Female	Male	Female	Male
Newfoundland and Labrador	15	7	0.5	0.2
Prince Edward Island	6	1	0.2	0.0
Nova Scotia	62	24	2.1	0.8
New Brunswick	52	7	1.7	0.2
Quebec	497	87	16.6	2.9
Ontario	753	186	25.1	6.2
Manitoba	123	48	4.1	1.6
Saskatchewan	98	59	3.3	2.0
Alberta	244	97	8.1	3.2
British Columbia	293	104	9.7	3.5
Yukon	9	5	0.3	0.2
Northwest Territories[2]	22	11	0.7	0.4
Nunavut[3]	4	2	0	0
Canada	2178	638	72.6	21.3

1. Includes married, common-law, separated, divorced, and (ex) same-sex spouses.
2. Data prior to 1999 include the territory of Nunavut.
3. Reflects the number of spousal victims reported by police since 1999.

Data source: Statistics Canada, Canadian Centre for Justice Statistics, Homicide Survey.
Table source: Statistics Canada, 2006, *Measuring Violence Against Women: Statistical Trends*, catalogue number 85-570-XWE2006001.

WHAT IS A VALID SOCIOLOGICAL TOPIC?

Sociologists conduct research on nearly every area of human behaviour. At the macro level, we study such broad matters as the military (Moscos & Butler, 1997), race relations (W.J. Wilson, 1996), and multinational corporations (Kanter, Wiersema, & Kao, 1997). At the micro level, we study individualistic matters, such as pelvic examinations (Henslin & Biggs, 1997), how people interact on street corners (W.H. Whyte, 1989, 1997), and how people decorate their homes at Christmas (Caplow, 1991). In fact, no human behaviour is ineligible for sociological scrutiny, whether routine or unusual, respectable or reprehensible.

The case of Meredith and McKie discussed in the opening vignette is not only an incident of family violence, it is also a valid topic of sociological research.

COMMON SENSE AND THE NEED FOR SOCIOLOGICAL RESEARCH

Why do we need sociological research? Why can't we depend on common sense—on what "everyone knows"? As discussed in Chapter 1, common-sense ideas may or may not be true. For example, common sense would lead us to believe that strangers are responsible for most violence against women and children. Nothing could be further from the truth (see Chapter 13). Common sense also tells us that if a woman or man is abused, she or he should leave their abusive husband or same-sex partner. Research shows, however, that the reality of abuse is much more complicated. Some women and gay men leave right away, but for a variety of reasons—primarily because they feel trapped and can't see viable alternatives—many put up with abuse for years.

Because all human behaviour is open to be researched by sociologists, studies range from the unusual to the routines of everyday life. Sociologists might look at broad-scale social change, such as the globalization of capitalism, or the practices and rituals around tattooing, piercing, and body painting. Shown here is a tattooed and pierced woman at an international tattoo exposition in London, England.

also suppose that your university's enrollment is large, making it impractical to **survey**, or question, every student. You must select a **sample** of individuals from among your target **population**. The population of your study is the total number of students at the university. How you choose a sample is critical, for the choice will affect the results of your study.

A survey of only first-year students, only seniors, only those enrolled in introductory sociology courses, or only those in advanced physics classes will produce unrepresentative results in each case. To be able to generalize your findings to the entire campus, you must select a sample that is representative of the campus (called a "representative sample").

The best representative sample is a **random sample**. *In a random sample, everyone in the population has the same chance of being included in the study.* In this case, since the population is every student enrolled in your university, every student, whether first-year, male or female, full time, part time, or graduate, must have the same chance of being included in the sample.

How would you get a random sample in this case? You'd need a list of all the students enrolled in your university. You could assign a number to each name on the list and, using a table of random numbers, determine which students would become part of your sample. (Random numbers are available on tables in statistics books or can be generated by a computer.)

Because a random sample represents the population—in this case, all students enrolled at your university—you can generalize your findings to all the students on your campus, whether they were included in the sample or not.

Sociological research helps explain why some put up with abuse and others don't. We may also want to know something entirely different, such as why men are more likely to inflict abuse or why some people abuse persons they say they love.

Regardless of the research question, we must look beyond guesswork and common sense to find out what is really going on. For accurate answers, we need sociological research.

SIX RESEARCH METHODS

Sociologists use six **research methods** (or **research designs**) for gathering data: surveys, participant observation, qualitative interviews, secondary analysis, documents, and unobtrusive measures. To understand these strategies better, note how the choice of method depends on the questions we want to answer.

Surveys

Let's assume that your resources allow you to investigate alcohol and marijuana consumption at your university. Let's

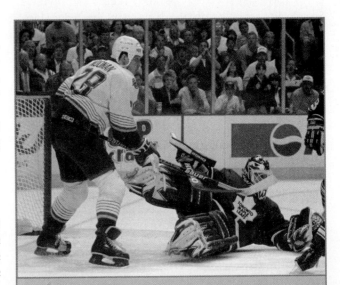

Because sociologists usually cannot interview or observe every member of the group they wish to study, such as the spectators at this hockey game, they must select a sample that will let them generalize the entire group. The text explains how samples are selected.

The term *average* seems clear enough. However, sociologists use three statistics to summarize data by describing the average score in a distribution of outcomes. This is called the three measures of central tendency. Consider the following results from seven sociology exams:

35 52 65 78 78 82 95

1. Mean: The *mean* is the average of a group and is most often used as the starting point in the calculation of more advanced statistics. Add together the results from each exam, then divide by the number of exam results. The mean in this case is 69 (485/7).

2. Median: The *median* is the middle score in a distribution. List the exam results from lowest to highest (as shown above) and find the middle one. The median is 78. This measure divides the exams into two categories: "highs" and "lows."

3. Mode: The *mode* is the most frequently occurring result in a distribution. The mode above is 78. It is the only score that appears more than once. This measure can be used to find the most common score and is the only measure that can be used with nominal level data, such as sex (male or female) and ethnicity/race.

ASKING NEUTRAL QUESTIONS After you have determined a population and sample, your next task is to make certain that your questions are not biased to one point of view or another. Your questions must allow **respondents**, people who respond to a survey, to select appropriate responses to standardized questions. If your questions are biased, your answers will be, too—and biased findings are worthless. For example, if you were to ask, "Don't you agree that men who beat their wives deserve a prison sentence?" you would be tilting the answers toward agreement with the position stated. For other examples of flawed research, see the following Down-to-Earth Sociology box.

QUESTIONNAIRES AND STRUCTURED INTERVIEWS Sociologists not only strive to ask questions that reduce bias, they are also concerned with how **questionnaires**, the list of questions to be asked, are administered (carried out). The technique most often used is to ask respondents to fill in their answers. Such **self-administered questionnaires** allow a large number of people to be sampled at a relatively low cost.

In other cases, **structured interviews** work best. Both self-administered questionnaires and structured **interviews** use **closed-ended questions**. Each question is followed by a list of possible answers. The advantages of structured interviews are that they are fast to administer and make it easy for the answers to be *coded* (categorized) so that they can be fed into a computer for analysis. The primary disadvantage is that the answers listed on the questionnaire may not include all the respondents' opinions.

ESTABLISHING RAPPORT The example of research on spousal abuse also brings up another significant issue.

It is vital for researchers to establish **rapport**, or a feeling of trust, with their respondents, especially when it comes to sensitive topics, areas about which people feel embarrassment, shame, or other deep emotions. Feminist researchers and queer theorists in Canada have been in the forefront of not only including women in research but also of recognizing the importance of validating the experiences of women and gay men. Although researchers must take care not to influence their informants in ways that might distort their behaviour or statements, the necessity of establishing a rapport in order to gain access to what might be sensitive or closely guarded information means that the degree of detachment associated with quantitative research may not be viable or desirable. Getting too close, or "going native" is a significant research issue, but so is adopting an approach that is too superficial and that merely provides a veneer of plausibility. These are important issues when researching sensitive topics and ones that all good researchers understand and grapple with, especially in the study of violence against women, gay men, and other minorities.

Once a rapport has been established (e.g., by asking non-sensitive questions first), participants will generally talk to researchers about personal, sensitive issues.

Participant Observation (Fieldwork)

In **participant observation**, or **fieldwork**, the researcher participates in a research setting and *observes and records* what is happening in that setting. Simply put, the researcher spends a great deal of time with the people he or she is studying. The research with the homeless mentioned in Chapter 1 is an example of participant observation. Participant observation was a well-established research technique in the early history of sociology in Canada. Sociologists and anthropologists often spent at least a year in a small town or village in rural Quebec, Ontario, the Maritimes, or the Prairies to understand the social, religious, political, and economic life of its inhabitants. Examples include Everett Hughes's study of the effects of industrialization on traditional institutions in Drummondville, Quebec, otherwise known as *French Canada in Transition* (1943), or John

Can the methods of social science lend themselves to distortion, misrepresentation, and fraud?

Some consumer researchers "load the dice." Hired by firms that have a vested interest in the outcome of the research, they deliver the results their clients are looking for. There are four basic ways of loading the dice:

1. *Choosing a biased sample.* If you want to "prove" that Canadians prefer Chryslers to Toyotas, for example, you might interview unemployed union workers who can trace their job loss to Japanese imports. The answer is fairly predictable. You'll get what you're looking for.

2. *Asking biased questions.* Even if you select an unbiased sample, you can phrase questions in such a way that most people see only one logical choice. How would you answer this question (asked in an actual survey)? "It is estimated that disposable diapers account for less than 2 percent of the trash in today's landfills. In contrast, beverage containers, third-class mail, and yard waste are estimated to account for about

21 percent. Given this, in your opinion, would it be fair to ban disposable diapers?" It isn't surprising that 84 percent of the survey's respondents said that disposable diapers are better for the environment than cloth diapers.

3. *Listing biased choices.* Another way to load the dice is to use closed-ended questions that push people into the answers you want. Consider this finding: "Canadian university students overwhelmingly prefer Levi's 501 to the jeans of any competitor." Sound good? Before you rush out to buy Levi's, what if you discovered that the researchers had asked a sample of Canadian university students which jeans would be the most popular in the coming year, and their list of choices included no other jeans but Levi's 501?

4. *Discarding undesirable results.* Researchers might choose to keep silent about results they find embarrassing, or could continue to survey samples until they find one that matches what they are looking for.

As stressed in this chapter, research must be objective if it is to be scientific. Obviously, none of the preceding results qualify. The underlying problem with the research cited here—and with many surveys bandied about in the media as fact—is that survey research has become big business. Simply put, the vast sums of money offered by corporations have gone unquestioned by many university administrators and academics in Canada. In an era of "tight money," with the proportion of government financing of higher education shrinking, the potential exists for the commercial corruption of social research.

The beginning of such corruption is subtle. Paul Light, dean at the University of Minnesota, put it this way: "A funder will never come to an academic and say, 'I want you to produce finding X, and here's a million dollars to do it.' Rather, the subtext is that if the researchers produce the right finding, more work—and funding—will come their way." He adds, "Once you're on that treadmill, it's hard to get off."

Sources: Crossen (1991); Goleman (1993); F. Barnes (1995).

Jackson's study of high schools and language conflicts in Tecumseh, Ontario (1975).

Participant observation can be used in research as diverse as the study of the subculture of motorcycle gangs, jazz or blues musicians, or professional wrestlers. Suppose you are interested in the world of professional wrestling. You may want to know if the time spent becoming a professional wrestler has changed the hopes, dreams, or self-concepts of men or women in the profession, or how it has affected their relationships with their partners. Participant observation can provide detailed insight into such questions.

To some sociologists, participant observers face the problem of **generalizability**, the ability to apply findings to larger populations. However, generalizability is rarely a concern in modern-day science. Participant observations are rich in description and often provide significant theoretical insight.

Focus Question

What is the difference between survey research and participant observation?

Qualitative Interviews

A **qualitative** or **field interview**, commonly referred to as a **structured conversation**, is the third research method. A researcher might begin by creating an interview schedule or list of questions about the topic he or she wants to study. For example, when interviewing gay and lesbian couples about their lifestyles, both parties—the researcher and the interviewee—should view themselves as participants in a conversation, even if the interviewer is asking most of the questions and the conversation is being tape-recorded. The interviewer should not be afraid to stop and listen when his or her participant strays from the guided tour of questions.

THE FAR SIDE® BY GARY LARSON

"Anthropologists! Anthropologists!"

A major concern of sociologists and other social scientists is that their research methods must not influence their findings. Respondents often change their behaviour when they know they are being studied.

A qualitative or field interview is like a journey into a new territory, where we seek help from those who know what to see and do, what to look for, and what not to expect along the route.

A researcher's personal characteristics are extremely important in fieldwork. Their sex, age, race, personality, and even height and weight can affect their findings (Henslin, 1990a). For example, should a male researcher conduct participant observation of women who have been beaten by their husbands? Given the sensitivity of the topic, a female

sociologist would be better suited to conduct this study, and thus more likely to achieve valid results.

In recent years, a number of feminist writers have argued for a distinctive feminist methodology (Eichler, 1988b; Stanley & Wise, 1993). The traditional claim made by most social scientists is that knowledge about our social world can be objective. However, for many feminist sociologists and queer theorists, sexist value judgments and homophobia explicitly or implicitly inform researchers' choice of study, how to investigate a particular social phenomena, and even the interpretation of findings.

Many feminist methodologists reject the emphasis on control and the impersonal nature of scientific research. Instead, they are drawn to qualitative techniques, principally interviewing. (However, this does not mean that it is not possible to do quantitative research in a feminist way.) The interview, from a feminist point of view, is like a conversation between equals and allows women to "tell their own stories" in a manner that is non-exploitative and descriptive. Increasingly, sociologists in Canada, both men and women, acknowledge the contributions made by feminist sociologists in qualitative research interviewing.

Secondary Analysis

In **secondary analysis**, a fourth research method, researchers analyze data that have already been collected by others. If you were to examine original data from a previously completed study of women who have been abused by their husbands, for example, you would be doing secondary analysis. Ordinarily, researchers prefer to gather their own data, but lack of resources, especially money and time, may make that impossible.

DATA LIBERATION INITIATIVE (DLI) To avoid many of the methodological pitfalls of secondary analysis, such as the reliability and validity of collected data, many researchers in Canada use Statistics Canada databases to conduct secondary analyses. The recent creation of the Data Liberation Initiative (DLI) has proved invaluable to students and faculty across the country. The DLI, begun in 1996 as a five-year pilot project, is a co-operative effort of the Social Sciences and Humanities Research Council of Canada, the Canadian Association of Research Libraries (CARL), the Canadian Association of Public Data Users (CAPDU), the

Improperly worded questions can steer respondents toward answers that are not their own, thus producing invalid results.

Canadian Association of Small University Libraries (CASUL), Statistics Canada, and other government departments. It provides low-cost access to Statistics Canada data files and databases for Canadian university faculty, staff, and students for teaching and research purposes. Each university pays an annual fee to download files and make them available for use.

DLI databases include the Canadian Socio-economic Information Management System (CANSIM), the National Population Health Survey (NPHS), the Labour Force Historical Review, the General Social Survey (GSS), Canada's Alcohol and Other Drugs Survey (CADS), Family Expenditure and Food Expenditure surveys (FAMEX and FOODEX), and others. These are large files of anonymous survey responses that can be analyzed using statistical packages.

A complete list of available files is given on the DLI website, along with a list of DLI contacts at each Canadian university and other background information on the program (see the Weblinks section at the end of the chapter).

Documents

The use of **documents** (written sources) is a fifth research method used by sociologists. To investigate social life, they examine such diverse sources as film, videos, photographs, books, newspapers, diaries, bank records, police reports, household accounts, immigration files, and records kept by various organizations.

To study spousal abuse, you might examine police reports and court records. These could reveal what proportion of complaints result in arrest and what proportion of the men arrested are charged, convicted, or even put on probation. If these were your questions, police statistics would be valuable (see recent Statistics Canada *Juristat* data).

A crisis intervention centre might have records that provide other key information. Diaries kept by abuse victims would yield important insights into their reactions, especially how their attitudes and relationships with others change over time.

We are presenting an ideal situation, however, in which the crisis intervention centre would welcome your inquiries. In reality, the centre might not co-operate at all, neither asking victims to keep diaries nor allowing you access to its records. Access is another problem faced regularly by researchers. Simply put, you can't study a topic unless you can get access to it.

Queer theorists and postmodern researchers have minimized the problem of access by using available sources such as videos, pictures, texts, and other published materials.

Unobtrusive Measures

The sixth method is **unobtrusive measures**: observing the behaviour of people who do not know they are being studied. For example, social researchers studied the level of whisky consumption in a town that was officially "dry" by counting empty bottles in trash cans, and the degree of fear induced by ghost stories by measuring the shrinking diameter of a circle of seated children (Webb, Campbell, Schwartz, & Sechrest, 1966). A sociology student studied gender differences by recording all the graffiti in every public restroom in two towns (Darnell, 1971). An example of commercially applied social research is the outfitting of shopping carts with infrared surveillance equipment. After tracing customers' paths through a store and measuring their stops, retailers use their findings to change the presentation of their products (M.J. McCarthy, 1993). Another technique for studying the social makeup of small towns or villages is

Sociologists use different methods of research to answer different questions. Among the methods that could be used to study spouse abuse might be the examination of the documents kept by shelters for battered women, which log the number of calls and visits made by victims. This woman is answering calls at a sexual assault hotline.

Research from the 1920s known as the Hawthorne experiments became a classic case in the study of sociology.

The managers of the Hawthorne plant of Western Electric Company near Chicago wanted to know how different levels of lighting would affect productivity. Several groups of women participated in what were known as the Relay Room Experiments. In a control room, the level of lighting was held constant, while in the experimental room the lighting was varied. To everyone's surprise, output increased in *both* locations. In the experimental room, productivity remained high even when the lights were dimmed to about the level of moonlight, so low that workers could barely see what they were doing.

To solve this mystery, management called in a team of researchers headed by Elton Mayo of the University of Chicago. The team tested 13 different work conditions. When they changed the workers' pay from hourly wages to piecework, productivity increased. When they served refreshments, output again went up. When they added two five-minute rest periods, productivity jumped. When they changed the rest periods to two 10-minute periods, again output increased. When they let the workers go home early, they found the same result. Confused, the researchers restored the original conditions, offering none of these added benefits. The result? Even higher productivity.

The situation grew even more confusing when men were observed in what was known as the Bank Wiring Room Study. Here, the researchers did not change work conditions at all. They simply observed the men while they worked and interviewed them afterward. Instead of there being no change in productivity, as might have been expected, productivity *dropped*.

None of this made sense. Finally, Mayo concluded that the results were the result of the research itself. The women, aware that they were being studied and pleased at the attention paid to them, responded by increasing their efforts. The men, in contrast, were suspicious about why the researchers were observing them. They feared that if they had higher productivity, they would be expected to produce more each day or that higher productivity might even cost some of them their jobs. Consequently, they decreased their output.

The Hawthorne experiment is important for what it revealed about the research process itself. Today, researchers carefully monitor the *Hawthorne effect*— the change in behaviour that occurs when people know they are being studied.

Sources: Based on Roethlisberger & Dickson (1939), Mayo (1966), Baron & Greenberg (1990).

---

to visit and spend some time examining the community's graveyards. Important insights into the town's history, infant mortality rate, ethnic makeup, and so on can come from using this technique.

Focus Question

What is the difference between using documents and unobtrusive measures as research strategies?

Focus Question

What are the six major research techniques used by sociologists?

Deciding Which Method to Use

How do sociologists choose from among these methods? Four primary factors affect their choice. First and foremost concerns the purpose of the research—the questions that the sociologist wishes to answer. Some methods are better for answering some questions and not others. Participant observation, for example, is good for uncovering the meanings people give to their behaviour, while surveys work better at revealing attitudes toward public issues such as abortion, gay adoption, the *Youth Criminal Justice Act*, or Quebec independence. Second, resources or sources of funding are crucial. Sociologists must match methods to available resources. Although they may want to conduct a survey, researchers might find that finances will not permit it, and instead might turn to the study of secondary sources. The third significant factor is access to subjects. If people in a sample live in remote parts of the country, researchers may have to mail questionnaires or conduct a telephone survey even if they would prefer face-to-face interviews. Fourth, the researcher's background or training comes into play. After graduate school, sociologists generally use the methods in which they have had the most training.

Thus, sociologists who have been trained in **quantitative research methods**, which emphasize measurement, numbers, and statistics, are likely to use structured questionnaires or surveys. Sociologists with training in **qualitative research methods**, which emphasize observing, describing, and interpreting people's behaviour, lean toward participant observation or qualitative interviews. Figure 2.1 illustrates the two common paradigms for social research. In the Down-to-Earth Sociology box on the next page, you can see how a combination of quantitative and qualitative methods is used in applied sociology. The Thinking Critically about Social

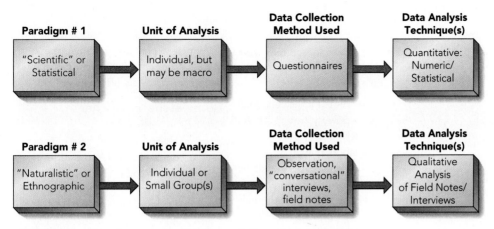

FIGURE 2.1 Two Common Social Research Strategies or Paradigms

To increase sales, manufacturers try to improve the "position" of their products. "Position" is marketing jargon for how customers think about a product.

This is where marketing researchers come into play. They find out what customers think they want, how they select and use products, and what images they hold of a product or service.

To do this, marketing researchers use a combination of qualitative and quantitative techniques. One example is "focus groups," groups of about 10 people who are invited to discuss a product. A moderator leads a discussion in front of a one-way mirror, where team members observe or videotape the session. To control for regional variations, other focus groups may be held at the same time in other cities. Sociologist Roger Straus points out that his training in symbolic interactionism is especially useful in interpreting these results.

Marketing researchers also use quantitative techniques. For example, they may conduct surveys to determine what the public thinks of a new product. They also gather sales data from the bar codes found on almost all products. They use statistics to analyze data and prepare tables and graphics that summarize their findings for clients.

Sources: Based on R.A. Straus (1991) and communication with R.A. Straus, 1993.

Controversy box illustrates the significance of the choice of research method and how sociologists can find themselves in the midst of controversy for applying rigorous research methods.

Focus Question
What is the difference between qualitative and quantitative research?

THINKING CRITICALLY ABOUT SOCIAL CONTROVERSY
Doing Controversial Research: Counting the Homeless in Toronto

What could be simpler, or more inoffensive, than counting the homeless? Even basic research can be difficult to conduct and politically controversial.

In 1997, the United Way of Greater Toronto called for the creation of a task force on homelessness. As such, Mel Lastman, the newly elected mayor of Toronto at the time, created the Homelessness Action Task Force in January 1998.

Which method or methods do you think would be most suitable for counting the homeless in Toronto and suggesting remedies? Surveys? Interviews? Secondary analysis? Focus groups? To survey a population, you need to know the size of the population or the geographical space it occupies. Since no one knew the exact number of homeless persons in Toronto, nor what constituted their geographical space, the survey method was ruled out.

Who Are The Homeless?

The initial research task was to establish an operational definition of "homeless." The task force settled on the following:

- those who are "visible" on the streets or staying in hostels
- the "hidden" homeless, who live in illegal or temporary accommodation
- those at risk of soon becoming homeless

Research Methods

The researchers chose a multi-method approach that included:

- an extensive review of the existing literature on the homeless in North America and Europe
- close to 200 hours spent by each member visiting local sites and listening to presentations made by professionals and community stakeholders
- consultation with homeless people through individual interviews and focus groups
- interviews with 17 homeless Aboriginal people to develop a distinct strategy for Toronto's Aboriginal population
- working with municipal staff familiar with the homeless

What Causes Homelessness?

The principal causes for the new wave of homelessness in Toronto isolated by the task force were:

- an increase in both the incidence and the depth of poverty brought about, in large part, by changes in the structure of the labour market
- restrictions and cutbacks in income security programs, such as employment insurance and social assistance (the shelter component of welfare is too low to cover typical rental payments in Toronto)
- the removal of support for social housing development by the provincial and federal governments
- spousal abuse, reported to be the main cause of homelessness for more than one in four women using the hostel system
- physical or sexual abuse, which accounts for almost three out of four young people who are homeless
- severe mental illness or addictions, which are the significant cause(s) of homelessness among single adults
- distinct problems of the one in seven street homeless who are Aboriginal

The "typical" homeless person is no longer a single, alcoholic adult male. Youth under the age of 18 and families with children are the fastest-growing groups of homeless persons. Together, these groups accounted for almost half the people using hostels in Toronto in 1996.

Homelessness in Other Canadian Cities

While members of the task force did not have a comprehensive knowledge of homelessness in other Canadian cities, they did analyze the causes of and responses to homelessness in the larger metropolitan areas and discovered that Toronto is not unique. In Calgary, the homeless population includes employed and unemployed people. In Montreal and Vancouver, homeless youth are a major problem. The root causes of homelessness in all big Canadian cities are the same: poverty, a lack of affordable housing, abuse, mental illness, and addictions. Experts in major Canadian cities reported that the federal government's withdrawal of funding from social housing was a primary cause of the rise in homelessness five years preceding the study.

There was widespread consensus on what is needed to combat the problem. First and foremost, there must be programs to preserve the existing stock of low-cost housing while increasing the supply in all major Canadian cities.

Research sometimes lands sociologists in the midst of a dispute. Most people would agree with the figures released by the Toronto task force on the homeless, but the solutions offered generated controversy. Recognizing the need for publicly funded social housing is one such controversial remedy for homelessness.

A RESEARCH MODEL

As shown in Figure 2.2, there are eight basic steps in sociological research.

1. **Selecting a Topic** What do you want to know more about? Always look for a topic in which you have a personal interest. Many sociologists simply follow their curiosity: studying the homeless, women, and part-time work (Duffy & Pupo, 1996); examining how new technologies are changing the workplace (Glenday, 1997, 1995); or understanding the makeup of the Canadian economic and political elites (Porter, 1965; Clement, 1978; Olsen, 1980). Some sociologists choose a topic because funding is available; others because social problems such as domestic violence, young offenders, or corporate crime have become pressing social issues and the sociologist wants to gather data that will help people better understand and perhaps contribute to public policy solutions.

2. **Defining the Problem** The second step involves specifying exactly what you want to learn about your chosen topic. For example, you might start with a general interest in how or why the homeless grew in number over the 1980s and 1990s in the major cities of Canada and the United States. Or you may want to compare the job ghettos of nursing and hairdressing for women and gay men. You might want to know what can be done to reduce spousal abuse. Sociologists conduct research on any aspect of social life that interests them.

3. **Reviewing the Literature** The third step is to review existing literature to see what has been written on the problem. This is the *most* important step in the research process if sociologists are to distinguish themselves from nonscientists (such as newspaper or television reporters). Reading research reported by others helps narrow down the problem, pinpointing particular areas to examine. Reviewing the research may also provide ideas about what other questions to ask.

4. **Formulating a Hypothesis or Research Question** The fourth step is to formulate a **hypothesis** or research question: a statement of what you expect to find

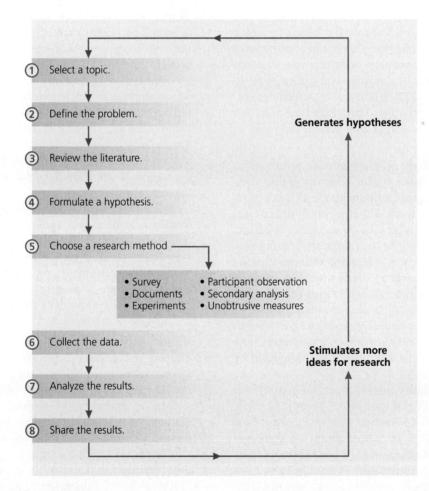

FIGURE 2.2 The Research Model

Source: Modification of Figure 2.2 of Schaeffer, 1989.

according to predictions from a sociological theory and what other researchers have found. A hypothesis predicts a relationship between or among **variables**, factors that change or vary from one person or situation to another. Generally, there are two variables: independent and dependent. An independent variable is the hypothesized cause or influence on a dependent variable, while the dependent variable is the effect or outcome variable. For example, the statement "The more strongly religious people are, the more racist their attitudes will be toward visible minorities in Canada" is a hypothesis in which religiosity (how religious a person is) is the independent variable and racist attitudes are the dependent variable. Hypotheses need **operational definitions**—precise ways to measure their variables. In this example, we would need operational definitions for three variables: religiosity, racist attitudes, and visible minorities.

Unlike a research hypothesis, a research question generally seeks theoretically informed, in-depth descriptions of sociological events, issues, or places. More often than not, sociologists use qualitative research methods such as semi-structured or conversational interviews.

5. **Choosing a Research Method** The means by which sociologists collect data are called research methods (or research designs), which can be further classified into two broad categories—quantitative and qualitative methods. Sociologists use six basic research methods, as outlined earlier in the chapter. They select the one(s) that will best answer the particular questions they want to address.

6. **Collecting the Data** Sociologists take great care to assure both the validity and the reliability of their data. If you are using a quantitative method, such as a questionnaire, **validity** is the extent to which operational definitions measure what they are intended to measure. Our operational definition must make sense and be precise enough that there is little question about what we are measuring. For example, how should we measure religiosity? Is the number of times a year a person goes to a place of religious worship an accurate reflection of how religious that person is? Wouldn't we also want to know what religion means to him or her—a much more difficult question that is probably best answered by qualitative methods?

The term **reliability** refers to the extent to which different studies result in similar results. If one study finds that 1 percent of the women in a certain city have been the victims of spouse or partner abuse, while another study finds that the fraction is 10 percent, sociologists might use the term "unreliable" to describe these studies. However, many sociologists today employ a technique known as triangulation to compensate for the weaknesses of various methods. **Triangulation** is a research strategy that includes not only the comparison of different data sources, but also the use of different data-gathering techniques and methods to investigate a single phenomenon. By gathering and comparing multiple datasets, triangulation helps to counteract threats to validity. This approach has been applied in diverse subfields of sociology to strengthen conclusions about observations and to reduce the risk of false interpretations by drawing upon multiple independent sources of information

---

Focus Question

What is the difference between reliability and validity in sociological research? Why is triangulation a useful strategy in compensating for the weaknesses characteristic of quantitative and qualitative methods?

7. **Analyzing the Results** To analyze collected data, sociologists use qualitative and quantitative techniques. *Qualitative* analysis is especially useful for data gathered by participant observation and in-depth interviews. That is, sociologists classify statements people have made in qualitative interviews to identify the main themes. This process can also be used by queer theorists and postmodernists to uncover themes in movies, music videos, television programs, newspapers, or any visual or written document. The goal is to faithfully reproduce the world of the people being studied. In Henslin's research on cab drivers (1967, 1993), for example, he tried to picture the world as cabbies see it, so that anyone reading the analysis would understand not just what cabbies do, but also why they do it.

Quantitative analysis involves statistically analyzing relationships between variables, sometimes known as number-crunching (see Table 2.2). Quantitative analysis is especially useful in testing hypotheses. The computer has become an especially powerful tool for quantitative analysis because statistical packages such as MicroCase and the Statistical Package for the Social Sciences (SPSS) can analyze huge amounts of information and identify basic patterns in an instant.

8. **Sharing the Results** In this step, researchers write a report to share their findings with the scientific community. The report includes a review of the preceding steps to help others evaluate the research. It also shows how the findings are related to the literature, the published results of other research on the topic. When research is published, usually in a scientific journal or a book, it then "belongs" to the scientific community. Table 2.2 illustrates how published research is often displayed.

TABLE 2.2 How to Read a Table

Survey Question	National Average (%)	18–34 Years Old (%)	35–54 Years Old (%)	55+ Years Old (%)	Female (%)	Male (%)	18–35 + Weekly** (%)	18–34 <Weekly*** (%)
Disapproval and Non-Acceptance of Children's Sexual Behaviour by Age, Gender, and Religious Service Attendance								
How do you feel—or did you feel/would you feel—about your children...								
1. Engaging in premarital sex prior to age 18	29*	19	28	40	18	20	57	11
2. Engaging in premarital sex when 18 or older	11	9	9	18	8	10	37	3
3. Engaging in homosexual acts	45	27	45	63	24	31	71	18
4. Informing you that they are gay or lesbian	22	12	23	32	12	13	29	9
5. Having children without being married	17	8	16	30	8	7	28	3
6. Living with a partner without being married	12	9	10	17	8	10	37	3
7. Having sexual relations other than with their spouse	74	69	74	79	74	63	90	65

* % indicating the respondents "Disapprove and Do Not Accept"
** Respondents indicated they attended religious services weekly
*** Respondents indicated they attended religious services less than weekly
Data collection was carried out by mail over about a five-month period spanning March 15 to August 15, 2003. A total of 2093 adults aged 18 and over participated in the survey: 830 had participated in previous Project Canada surveys for Professor Bibby and 1263 were new respondents.

Source: Vanier Institute of the Family (with Reginald Bibby), *The Future Families Project: A Survey of Canadian Hopes and Dreams*, 2004 (www.vifamily.ca/library/future/future_toc.html).

A table is a concise way of presenting information. Because sociological findings are often presented in tabular form, it is important to understand how to read a table. Tables contain five elements: a title, headings, columns, rows, and a source. When you understand how these elements work together, you know how to read a table.

1. The title states the topic of a table, and is usually located at the top. What is the title of this table? Please determine your response before looking at the correct answer below.
2. The headings tell what kind of information is contained in the table. Are there any headings in this table?
3. The columns present information vertically arranged. What does the first column tell you?
4. The rows present information arranged horizontally. Read questions 1 and 3. Are there any differences between the young people who are religious and those who are not?
5. The "source" of a table, usually given at the bottom, provides information on where the data shown in the table originated. Often, as in this instance, the information is specific enough for you to consult the original source. What is the source for this table?
6. Tables sometimes include notes. This table indicates the number of survey participants. How many people participated in the survey?
Some tables are much more complicated than this, but all follow the same basic pattern.

Answers
1. The title reads "Disapproval and Non-Acceptance of Children's Sexual Behaviour by Age, Gender, and Religious Service Attendance."
2. Yes. The headings are "Survey Question," "National Average," "18–34 years old," "35–54 years old," etc., beginning at column 1.
3. The first column tells you the survey questions.
4. Yes, religious young people are much less accepting of their children engaging in premarital and homosexual sex.
5. *The Future Families Project: A Survey of Canadian Hopes and Dreams*, Vanier Institute of the Family (with Reginald Bibby), 2004 (www.vifamily.ca/library/future/future_toc.html).
6. A total of 2093 adults aged 18 and over participated in the survey.

These findings are available for **replication**; that is, others can repeat the study to see if they come up with similar results.

ETHICS IN SOCIOLOGICAL RESEARCH

In addition to choosing an appropriate research method, sociologists must also consider ethics. Their research must meet the profession's ethical criteria, which centre on basic assumptions of science and morality (Canadian Sociology and Anthropology Association, 1995). Research ethics require openness (sharing findings with the scientific community), honesty, and truth. Ethics clearly forbid the falsification of results, as well as *plagiarism*—stealing someone else's work. Another basic ethical guideline is that research subjects should not be harmed by the research. Sociologists are required to protect the identity of people who provide information, which can sometimes be intimate, potentially embarrassing, or otherwise harmful to them. Finally, although not all sociologists are in agreement about this, it generally is considered unethical for researchers to misrepresent themselves.

Conducting sociological research also involves the issue of funding: Where will the money come from and are there any "strings attached"? Virtually all research foundations in Canada, such as the Donner Foundation or "think tanks" like The Fraser Institute, have a political agenda. What ethical questions are raised when spokespersons for these organizations stipulate the general orientation a research initiative should take? Unfortunately, this question is being asked less frequently. Instead, the majority of questions on ethics in sociological research deal with the responsibility of individual sociologists. The examples that follow represent some of the ethical considerations individual sociologists can be confronted with when doing their research. To illustrate the extent to which researchers will go to protect their respondents, consider the following research conducted by two U.S. sociologists, Mario Brajuha and Rik Scarce.

The Brajuha Research

Mario Brajuha, a graduate student at the State University of New York at Stony Brook, conducted participant observation of restaurant work (Brajuha & Hallowell, 1986). He had lost his job as a waiter when the restaurant where he was working burned down. The fire turned out to be of "suspicious origin," and during their investigation detectives learned that Brajuha had taken field notes. They asked to see them. When Brajuha refused, the district attorney subpoenaed the notes. Brajuha still refused to hand them over. The district attorney then threatened to send Brajuha to jail. By this time, Brajuha's notes had become rather famous, and unsavoury characters, perhaps those who had set the fire, also began to wonder what was in them. They, too, demanded to see them—accompanying their demands with threats of a different nature. Brajuha unexpectedly found himself in a very disturbing double bind.

Brajuha refused to hand over his notes for two years, even though he had to appear at numerous court hearings and became filled with anxiety. Finally, the district attorney dropped the subpoena. When the two men under investigation for setting the fire died, so did the threats to Brajuha, his wife, and his children.

Ethics in social research are of vital concern to all sociologists. As discussed in the text, sociologists may disagree on some of the issue's finer points, but none would approve of slipping LSD to unsuspecting subjects "just to see what would happen," as was done to U.S. servicemen in the 1960s under the guise of legitimate testing.

The Scarce Research

In 1991, a group calling itself the Animal Liberation Front broke into a research facility at Washington State University, released animals, and damaged computers and files. Rik Scarce, a doctoral student in sociology at the university who was doing research on radical environmental groups, was summoned before a federal grand jury investigating the break-in. Scarce was not a suspect, but law enforcement officers thought that during his research, Scarce might have come across information that would help lead them to the guilty parties.

Scarce answered scores of questions about himself and topics related to the raid, but refused to answer questions that would violate his agreements of confidentiality with research subjects.

A federal judge did not agree with Scarce's ethics and put him in the Spokane County Jail for contempt of court. Although he could have obtained his freedom at any time simply by testifying, he maintained his laudable ethical stance and continued to refuse, in his words, "to be bludgeoned into becoming an agent of the state." Scarce served 159 days in jail. The longest any previous U.S. scholar had been held in contempt was one week (Scarce, 1993a, 1993b, 1994).

The Humphreys Research

Sociologists agree on the necessity of protecting respondents, and applaud the professional manner in which Brajuha and Scarce handled themselves. Let's look at the Humphreys case,

which forced sociologists to rethink and refine their ethical stance.

Laud Humphreys, a classmate of Henslin's at Washington University in St. Louis, was an Episcopal priest who was training to become a sociologist. For his PhD dissertation, Humphreys (1970, 1971, 1975) decided to study social interaction in "tearooms," public restrooms where some men go for quick, anonymous oral sex with other men.

Humphreys found that some restrooms in Forest Park, across from the campus, were "tearooms." He first conducted participant observation by hanging around the restrooms. He found that in addition to two men having sex, a third person—called a "watchqueen"—served as a lookout for police and other unwelcome strangers. Humphreys took the role of watchqueen, watching not only for strangers but also observing what the men did. He systematically recorded these encounters, and they became part of his dissertation.

Humphreys became curious about the regular lives of these men. Impersonal sex in "tearooms" was a fleeting encounter, and the men clearly spent most of their time doing other things. What things? With whom? And what was the significance of the wedding rings worn by many of the men? Humphreys hit on an ingenious technique: after observing an encounter, he would leave the restroom and record the licence plate number of the subject's car. With the help of a friend in the St. Louis police department, Humphreys then obtained each man's address. About a year later, he arranged for these men to be included in a medical survey conducted by some of the sociologists on the Washington University faculty. Disguising himself with a different hairstyle and clothing, and driving a different car, he

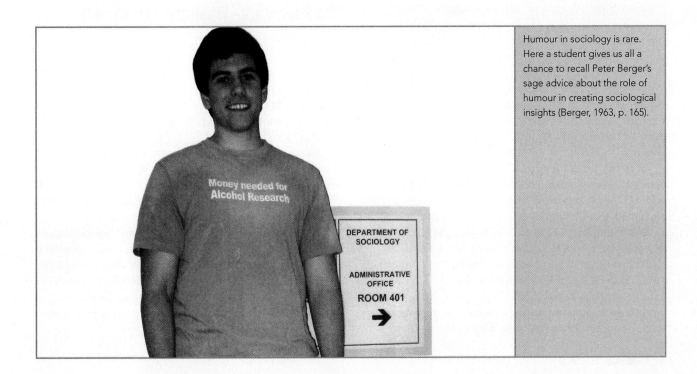

Humour in sociology is rare. Here a student gives us all a chance to recall Peter Berger's sage advice about the role of humour in creating sociological insights (Berger, 1963, p. 165).

visited these men at their homes. He conducted interviews, supposedly for the medical study.

Humphreys said that no one recognized him—and he obtained the information he was looking for: family background, education, income, health, religion, and even details about the men's relationships with wives and children. He found that most of the men were in their mid-thirties and had at least some college education. Surprisingly, the majority were married, and a higher proportion than in the general population turned out to be Roman Catholic. Moreover, these men led very conventional lives. They voted, mowed their lawns, and took their kids to Little League games.

Humphreys also found that although most of the men were committed to their wives and families, their sex lives were far from satisfactory. Many reported that their wives were not aroused sexually or were afraid of getting pregnant because their religion did not allow them to use birth control. Humphreys concluded that these were heterosexual men who were using the "tearooms" for an alternative form of sex, which, unlike affairs, was quick (taking no time away from their families), inexpensive (zero cost), and nonthreatening (the encounter required no emotional involvement to compete with their wives). If a wife had discovered her husband's secret sex life, she would have been devastated. However, Humphrey's research findings have done much to dispel the myth that only gay men engage in such behaviours in public washrooms.

This study stirred controversy among both sociologists and non-sociologists (Goodwin, Horowitz, & Nardi, 1991). Humphreys was severely criticized by many sociologists, and a national columnist wrote a scathing denunciation of "sociological snoopers" (Von Hoffman, 1970). Concerned about protecting the identity of his respondents, Humphreys placed his master list in a safety deposit box. As the controversy grew more heated, however, he feared that the names might be subpoenaed (a court case was threatened), and had the list destroyed. Humphreys had a contract to remain at Washington University as an assistant professor but was fired before he could begin teaching. (Although other reasons were involved, his research was a central issue. There was even an attempt by one professor to have his doctorate revoked.)

Was this research ethical? That question is not easily decided. Although many sociologists sided with Humphreys, and his book reporting the research won the highly acclaimed ASA C. Wright Mills Award, criticisms mounted. At first, Humphreys vigorously defended his position but, five years later, in a second edition of his book (1975), he stated that he should have identified himself as a researcher.

Several years later, Frederick Desroches (1990) replicated Laud Humphrey's study in Canada. Desroches, however, worked with the police in five cities across the country. In total, Desroches found 190 men who had been arrested by police. Consistent with Humphrey's observations, the majority of the men were married and primarily heterosexual. Like their U.S. counterparts, most Canadian "tearoom" participants (a) communicated through nonverbal gestures and seldom spoke, (b) did not attempt to learn one another's identity or exchange biographical information, and (c) did not use force or coercion or attempt to involve youths or children. There were two exceptions: there were no watchqueens or lookouts in Canada, and these acts were more likely to take place in a shopping mall than in public parks. However, the men's behaviour in both studies showed significant consistency across time and place.

HOW RESEARCH AND THEORY WORK TOGETHER

As previously discussed, sociological research is based on a sociologist's personal interests, access to subjects, appropriate methods, and ethical considerations. But the value of research is related to sociological theory. On one hand, as sociologist C. Wright Mills (1959) forcefully argued, research without theory is of little value and is simply a collection of unrelated "facts." On the other hand, theory unconnected to research is abstract and empty, unlikely to represent the way life really is.

Research and theory are both essential for sociology. As such, theory stimulates research. And as sociologists conduct research, they often come up with surprising findings—findings that, in turn, stimulate the development of theory to explain them.

The Real World: When the Ideal Meets the Real

Although one can list the ideals of research, real-life situations often force sociologists to settle for something that falls short of the ideal. Consider the research presented in the Thinking Critically about Social Controversy box on the following page for a look at how two sociologists confronted the ideal and the real.

Sociology needs more imaginative and sometimes daring research conducted in an imperfect world under less than ideal conditions. This is really what the discipline is all about. Sociologists study what people do, whether those behaviours are conforming or nonconforming, whether they are pleasing to others or disgust them and arouse intense anger. No matter what the behaviour studied, systematic research methods, together with the application of social theory, take us beyond common sense. They allow us to penetrate surface realities to allow a better understanding of human behaviour and, in the ideal case, to make changes to help improve social life.

Two sociologists, Diana Scully and Joseph Marolla, were not satisfied with the typical explanation that rapists are "sick," psychologically disturbed, or different from other men. They developed the hypothesis that rape, like most behaviour, is learned through interaction with others. That is, some men learn to think of rape as appropriate behaviour.

When presented with the opportunity to interview convicted rapists in prison, Scully and Marolla jumped at it. They sent 3500 letters to men serving time in seven prisons in Virginia, the state where they were teaching. About 25 percent of the prisoners agreed to be interviewed. They matched these men on the basis of age, education, race, severity of offence, and previous criminal record, resulting in a sample of 98 prisoners who had been convicted of rape.

Scully and Marolla discovered something that goes against common sense: most rapists are not sick and are not overwhelmed by uncontrollable urges. They found that the psychological histories of rapists and nonrapists were similar. Rapists, they concluded, are emotionally average men who have learned to view rape as appropriate in various situations. Some rape spontaneously, while others plan their attacks. Others use rape as a form of revenge, to get even with someone, not necessarily the victim.

The researchers also found support for what feminists had been pointing out for years—that power is a major element in rape. According to one subject:

Rape gave me the power to do what I wanted to do without feeling I had to please a partner or respond to a partner. I felt in control, dominant.

Rape was the ability to have sex without caring about the woman's response. I was totally dominant.

The discovery that most rape is calculated behaviour, that rapists are not "sick," that the motivating force is power rather than passion—the criminal pursuit of pleasure rather than mental illness—is extremely significant.

Connecting Research and Theory

Such findings go far beyond simply adding to our storehouse of "facts." As indicated in Figure 2.2, research stimulates both the development of theory and the need for more research.

Sources: Scully & Marolla (1984, 1985); Marolla & Scully (1986); Scully (1990); Foley, Evancic, Karnik, King, & Parks (1995).

SUMMARY AND REVIEW

What Is a Valid Sociological Topic?

WHAT IS A VALID SOCIOLOGICAL TOPIC?
Any human behaviour is a valid sociological topic, even disreputable behaviour. Spousal abuse is an example. Sociological research is based on a sociologist's interests, access to subjects, appropriate methods, and ethical considerations. p. 28.

Common Sense and the Need for Sociological Research

WHY ISN'T COMMON SENSE ADEQUATE?
Common sense does not provide reliable knowledge. When subjected to scientific research methods, common-sense ideas are often found to be very limited or false. pp. 28–29.

Six Research Methods

HOW DO SOCIOLOGISTS GATHER DATA?
Sociologists use six **research methods** (or research designs) for gathering data: **surveys**, **participant observation**, qualitative interviews, **secondary analysis**, **documents**, and **unobtrusive measures**. pp. 29–34.

HOW DO SOCIOLOGISTS CHOOSE A PARTICULAR RESEARCH METHOD?
Sociologists choose their research method on the basis of the research questions to be answered, their access to potential subjects, the resources available, their training, and ethical considerations. pp. 34–36.

A Research Model

WHAT ARE THE EIGHT BASIC STEPS OF SCIENTIFIC RESEARCH?

1. Selecting a topic
2. Defining the problem
3. Reviewing the literature
4. Formulating a hypothesis or research question

5. Choosing a research method
6. Collecting the data
7. Analyzing the results
8. Sharing the results
   pp. 37–40.

Ethics in Sociological Research

HOW IMPORTANT ARE ETHICS IN SOCIOLOGICAL RESEARCH?

Ethics are of fundamental concern to sociologists, who are committed to openness, honesty, truth, and protecting their subjects from harm. In addition, most research foundations and think tanks in Canada have political agendas that can seriously undermine the ethical neutrality of sociological research. The Brajuha research on restaurants, the Scarce research on the environmental movement, and the Humphreys research on "tearooms" were cited to illustrate ethical issues and the personal responsibility expected of sociologists. pp. 40–42.

How Research and Theory Work Together

WHAT IS THE RELATIONSHIP BETWEEN THEORY AND RESEARCH?

Theory and research are interdependent. Sociologists *must* use theory to interpret the data they gather. Theory without research is not likely to represent real life, while research without theory is merely a collection of unconnected facts. p. 42.

WHAT HAPPENS WHEN THE IDEAL MEETS THE REAL?

As illustrated by the Scully-Marolla research on rapists in prison, real-life situations often force sociologists to conduct research under real-life conditions. Although conducted in the *natural social world*, social research stimulates sociological theory, more research, and the potential of improving human life. p. 42.

KEY TERMS

closed-ended
   questions   30
documents   33
field interview   31
fieldwork   30
generalizability   31
hypothesis   37
interview   30
operational
   definitions   38

participant
   observation   30
population   29
qualitative interview   31
qualitative research
   methods   34
quantitative research
   methods   34
questionnaires   30
random sample   29

rapport   30
reliability   38
replication   40
research designs   29
research methods   29
respondents   30
sample   29
secondary analysis   32
self-administered
   questionnaires   30

structured
   conversation   31
structured interviews   30
survey   29
triangulation   38
unobtrusive
   measures   33
validity   38
variables   38

WEBLINKS

All URLs listed are current as of the printing of this book.

Data Liberation Initiative (DLI)
www.statcan.ca/english/Dli/dli.htm
Visit the DLI website and locate your university's DLI contact person(s).

The Canadian Sociological Association
www.csaa.ca
Visit the CSAA website and locate the Professional Code of Ethics. What does the code say about an organization's ethical responsibilities to its researchers and research participants?

Statistics Canada
www.statcan.ca/start.html
Canada's national statistical agency profiling Canada's business, economics, and society.

CASS Home Page: An ESRC Resource Centre
www.s3ri.soton.ac.uk/cass
CASS is an ESRC (Economic and Social Research Council) resource centre run jointly by the National Centre for Social Research, the University of Southampton, and the University of Surrey. It provides short courses in survey methods and is developing a survey question bank for use by social scientists and social researchers in the academic world, governments, market researchers, and the independent and voluntary sectors.

Canadian Journal of Sociology Resources Online
www.ualberta.ca/~cjscopy/resource.html
Online resources for Canadian students doing research on Canadian sociology topics.

CRITICAL THINKING QUESTIONS

1. Can someone who is heterosexual study homosexuals? Describe the steps you would take before developing your research hypothesis or research question.

2. Why would anyone want to study the personal records of dead people?

3. Can you generalize from a case study? If not, why do sociologists continue to employ this research technique?

4. When is it appropriate to lie to a research subject? Access the Research Navigator through MySocLab and use keywords such as "deception," "ethics," and "research" to locate relevant and recent scholarly and popular press publications to help you answer this question.

Explore the topics covered in this chapter on MySocLab using the access information provided with this text. Interactive resources for studying include multimedia tutorials, video clips, practice tests, quizzes, and animated maps and figures.

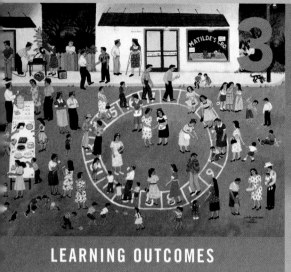

Culture

LEARNING OUTCOMES

After you have studied this chapter, you will be able to answer the following questions:

1. What is culture?

2. What are the components of nonmaterial culture?

3. Why is language so significant to culture?

4. How do values, norms, folkways, mores, and sanctions reflect culture?

5. How do subcultures and countercultures differ?

6. What are cultural relativism and ethnocentrism?

7. What are the values of Canadian and Quebec societies?

8. Do cultural universals exist?

9. Do animals have culture?

10. How is technology changing culture?

I stood in the oppressive heat of the Moroccan-Algerian border. I had never felt heat like this before. The sweat poured off me as the temperature soared past 110 degrees Fahrenheit.

As we were herded into a building—without air conditioning—hundreds of people lunged toward the counter at the rear. With body crushed against body, we waited as uniformed officials behind windows leisurely examined each passport.

When I arrived in Morocco, I found the sights that greeted me exotic—not far removed from my memories of *Casablanca*, *Raiders of the Lost Ark*, and other movies that had become part of my collective memory. Men, women, and children really did wear white robes that reached down to their feet. In spite of the heat, every woman wore not only a full-length gown, but also a head covering that reached over her forehead and a veil that covered her face from the nose down. All that was left showing were their eyes—and every eye the same shade of brown.

And how short everyone was! The Arab women looked to be about five feet tall, on average, and the men only about three or four inches taller. As the only blue-eyed, blond, six-foot-plus person around, wearing jeans and a pullover shirt in a world of white-robed short people, I stuck out like a sore thumb. Everyone stared. No matter where I went, they stared. It was different from home, where, if you caught someone staring at you, the person would immediately look embarrassed and glance away.

The concept of orderly lines apparently didn't exist. Buying a ticket for a bus or train meant pushing and shoving toward the ticket man (always a man—no women were visible in any public position), who took money from whichever outstretched hand he decided on.

The notion of germs didn't seem to exist here, either. Flies swarmed over the food in restaurants and unwrapped loaves of bread in the stores. Shopkeepers considerately shooed away flies before handing me a loaf. They also had home delivery of bread. I still remember a bread vendor delivering an unwrapped loaf to a woman standing on a second-floor balcony. She threw her money to the vendor, who threw the unwrapped bread up in return. His throw missed, and the bread bounced off the wrought-iron balcony railing and landed in the street filled with people, wandering dogs, and the ever-present burros. The vendor simply picked up the loaf and threw it again. This certainly wasn't his day—he missed again. The man made it on his third attempt, and the woman smiled, satisfied, as she turned back into her apartment.

Pressed body to body, the man behind me decided that this was a good time to take a nap. Determining that I made a good support, he placed his arm against my back and leaned his head against his arm. Sweat streamed from my back at the point that his arm and head touched me.

Source: Based on the personal experience of James Henslin.

WHAT IS CULTURE?

What is culture? The concept is sometimes easier to grasp by description than by definition. Suppose you meet a young woman who has just arrived in Canada from India. That her culture is different from yours is immediately evident: you can see it in her clothing, jewelry, makeup, and hairstyle. You can also hear it in her language and see it in her gestures. Later, you may hear her express unfamiliar beliefs about the world and different opinions about what is valuable in life. All these characteristics are indicative of **culture**, the language, beliefs, values, norms, behaviours, and even material objects that are passed from one generation to the next.

Technology is central to social life. From this photo, we can see how technology limits or expands human activities and, ultimately, how it plays a significant role in the types of societies we develop.

In North Africa, a Canadian would be surrounded by a culture quite alien to her or his own. Evidence would be everywhere. The **material culture** Henslin witnessed in Morocco—jewelry, art, buildings, weapons, machines, and even eating utensils, hairstyles, and clothing—provided a sharp contrast to what he was used to. There is nothing inherently "natural" about material culture. That is, it is no more natural (or unnatural) to wear gowns on the street than it is to wear jeans.

Henslin also found himself immersed in a contrasting **nonmaterial culture**—ways of thinking (beliefs, values, and other assumptions about the world) and doing (common patterns of behaviour, including language, gestures, and other forms of interaction). Here again, no particular custom is "right." People simply become comfortable with the customs they learn during childhood, and uncomfortable when their basic assumptions about life are challenged.

IN SUM

To avoid losing track of the ideas under discussion, let's pause for a moment to summarize, and in some instances clarify, the principles covered so far.

1. There is nothing "natural" about material culture. Arabs wear gowns on the street and feel that it is natural to do so; Canadians do the same with jeans.
2. There is nothing "natural" about nonmaterial culture; it is just as arbitrary to stand in line as it is to push and shove.

COMPONENTS OF SYMBOLIC CULTURE

Sociologists sometimes refer to nonmaterial culture as **symbolic culture**, because one of its central components is the symbols that people use to communicate. A **symbol** is something to which people attach meaning and which they then use to communicate. They include gestures, language, values, norms, sanctions, folkways, and mores.

Gestures

Gestures, the use of one's body to communicate with others, are useful shorthand ways of giving messages without using words. While people in every culture use gestures, their meaning may change completely from one culture to another. Canadians and Americans, for example, communicate a succinct message by raising the middle finger in a short, upward stabbing motion. We wish to stress *Canadians and Americans,* for that gesture does not convey the same message in South America or most other parts of the world.

For Mexicans, for example, the rudest gesture—placing the hand under the armpit and moving the upper arm up and down—means "Your mother is a whore," absolutely the worst possible insult in that culture.

Gestures thus not only facilitate communication but can also lead to misunderstandings, embarrassment, or worse. In Mexico, raising your hand to a certain height to indicate how tall a child is may result in laughter. Mexicans use several hand gestures to indicate height, and there are separate ones for people, animals, and plants (see Figure 3.1).

To get along in another culture, it is important to learn that culture's gestures. In many cultures, for example, you would provoke deep offence if you were to offer food or a gift with your left hand, because the left hand is reserved for dirty tasks such as wiping after going to the bathroom. Left-handed Canadians visiting Arabs, please note!

FIGURE 3.1   Gestures to Indicate Height, Southern Mexico

Is it really true that there are no universal gestures? There is some disagreement on this point. Some anthropologists claim that no gestures are universal (Ekman et al., 1984). However, ethologists—researchers who study biological bases of behaviour—claim that expressions of anger, pouting, fear, and sadness are built into our biology and are universal (Eibl-Eibesfeldt, 1970, p. 404). They point out that even infants who are born blind and deaf, who have had no chance to learn these gestures, express themselves in the same way. Although this matter is not yet settled, we can note that the meanings attached to the same or similar gestures vary remarkably around the world.

IN SUM

1. Culture penetrates deep into the recesses of our thinking and affects the way we see the world and obtain our perception of reality.
2. Culture provides implicit instructions that tell us what we ought to do in various situations. It provides a fundamental basis for decision-making.
3. Culture also provides a "moral imperative"; that is, by internalizing a culture, people learn ideas of right and wrong. (Canadians, for example, believe it is unacceptable to push and shove to get ahead of others in a line.)

Language

The primary means of communication for people is **language**—a system of symbols that can be strung together in an infinite number of ways for the purpose of communicating abstract thought. The significance of language for human life is difficult to overstate. Language itself is universal in the sense that all human groups possess it, but there is nothing universal about the meanings given to particular

sounds. Thus, as with gestures, in different cultures the same sound may mean something entirely different or may have no meaning at all. As the first Down-to-Earth Sociology box illustrates, symbols can take on unique meanings within a unique culture—in this case, the culture of online communication. The second Down-to-Earth Sociology box (see page 50) points out differences between French-speaking Quebecois and English-speaking Canadians that exist in many areas of social life, including mores around teenagers and sex at home.

LANGUAGE ALLOWS HUMAN EXPERIENCE TO BE CUMULATIVE Through language, we pass ideas, knowledge, and even attitudes on to the next generation. This allows young people to build on experiences they may not undergo themselves. Hence the central sociological significance of language: *language allows culture to develop by freeing people to move beyond their immediate experiences.*

Without language, human culture would be little more advanced than that of the lower primates. You could grunt and gesture that you want a drink of water, but in the absence of language, how would you share ideas and *feelings* concerning past or future events?

LANGUAGE PROVIDES A SOCIAL OR SHARED PAST AND FUTURE Using language, events can be codified—that is, attached to words and then recalled so they can be discussed in the present. Talking allows people to arrive at the shared understandings that form the essence of social life.

Language also extends our time horizons forward. When people talk about past events, they share meanings that allow them to decide how they will or should act in similar circumstances in the future. Because language enables people to agree with one another concerning times, dates, and places, it also allows them to plan activities together.

Think of the difficulty—perhaps impossibility—of conveying even a slight change in the sentiment: "I can't make it tomorrow."

The New Shorthand: Expressing Yourself Online

Talking online has become a favourite activity of millions of people, young and old. Teenagers rehash the day's events with friends, grandmothers keep in touch with grandchildren in different provinces, hobbyists correspond about special interests, and businesspeople seal deals with the click of the Send button. All of them appreciate the speed of online communications.

Online communication doesn't allow its users to convey nuances that are transmitted during face-to-face talk. To make up for this, users have developed symbols to convey humour, disappointment, sarcasm, and other indications of mood or attitude. Some are listed below. If you tilt your head to the left as you read, the symbols will be clearer.

:-)	Smile
:-))	Laugh
:-(	Sad
:-((	Very sad
:-X	My lips are sealed
>:-)	Feeling in a devilish mood
:-0	WOW! (What a surprise!)

Some correspondents also use the following abbreviations, which add a touch of whimsy and make their communications even more succinct:

ILY	I Love You
LOL	Laughing Out Loud
IMHO	In My Humble Opinion
TTFN	Ta-Ta for Now
WB	Welcome Back
BTW	By the Way
GMTA	Great Minds Think Alike
WTG	Way to Go!
J/K	Just Kidding
D/L	Downloading
YGG	You Go, Girl!
IAB	I Am Bored
L8R	Later
TTYL	Talk to You Later

LANGUAGE ALLOWS COMPLEX, SHARED, GOAL-DIRECTED BEHAVIOUR Common understandings enable people to establish a *purpose* for getting together. Suppose you want to go on a picnic. You use speech not only to plan the picnic (who will drive; who will bring the hamburgers, potato chips, and drinks; where you will meet; and so on), but also to decide on reasons for the picnic, which may range from "because it's a nice day that shouldn't be wasted studying" to "because it's my birthday." Only with language can you participate in such a common yet complex event.

LANGUAGE AND PERCEPTION: THE SAPIR-WHORF HYPOTHESIS In the 1930s, anthropologists Edward Sapir and Benjamin Whorf became intrigued when they noted that the Hopi Indians of the southwestern United States had no words to distinguish between the past, the present, and the future. In contrast, English, German, French, Spanish, and so on can carefully specify when something takes place. From their observation, Sapir and Whorf concluded that language is embedded with ways of looking at the world. The French have a unique phrase to convey this meaning: "*prise de conscience.*" The Germans say "*weltanschauung.*" There is nothing similar in English. Therefore, when we learn a language, we learn not only words, but also a certain way of thinking and perceiving (Sapir, 1949a, 1949b; Whorf, 1956).

The implications of the **Sapir-Whorf hypothesis** alert us as to how extensively we are affected by language. *The hypothesis reverses common sense*: It suggests that rather than objects and events forcing themselves into our consciousness, our language *determines* our consciousness, and hence our perceptions of objects and events. Inuit, for example, have many words for snow. As Inuit children learn their language, they learn distinctions between types of snowfalls that are imperceptible to non-Inuit speakers. Other Canadians might learn to see heavy and light snowfalls, wet and dry snowfalls, and so on, but not having words for "fine powdery," "thicker powdery," and "more granular" snowfalls actually prevents us from perceiving snow in the same way as Inuit do.

Although Sapir and Whorf's observation that the Hopi do not have tenses was incorrect (Edgerton, 1992, p. 27), we must still take their conclusion seriously. Sociologist Eviatar Zerubavel (1991) presents a different example. Hebrew, his native language, does not differentiate between jam and jelly. Only when Zerubavel learned English could he "see" this difference, which is "obvious" to native English speakers. Similarly, if you learn to classify students as "Jocks," "Emos," "baby bats" (Young Goths), and "indies," you will perceive them in an entirely different way than someone who does not know these classifications.

Language also allows us to expand our connections far beyond our immediate, face-to-face groups, so that our *individual* biological and social needs are met by extended networks of people. This development, in turn, leads to far-flung connections with fellow humans extending outward from our family and local communities to worldwide networks of production and distribution. Although language by no means *guarantees* co-operation among people, it is an *essential* precondition of collaboration. Without language, the extended co-operative human endeavours on which society is based simply could not exist (Malinowski, 1945; Hertzler, 1965; Blumer, 1966).

For more than 20 years, *Maclean's* polls have shown that Canadians are generally tolerant and liberal.

But what about parents, teens, and sex? Would Canadian parents permit their 18-year-old son with a steady girlfriend to have sex in their home? Two out of three Canadians say no. One province stood out as an exception, however. In Quebec, 57 percent—almost three times the result of any other province—say they would allow their 18-year-old to have sex at home. Additionally, 42 percent of Quebecers would allow their 18-year-old *gay* son with a steady boyfriend to have sex at home—a rate between three and six times higher than that any other province in the nation (B.C.=7 percent yes; Ontario=13 percent yes).

Consider explanations from two sets of parents.

Pierre (fictitious name) and his wife Céline (fictitious name) have raised two children: a daughter, 21, and son, 18. The family talks openly about sex. Both kids have been allowed to have sex at home with their steady partners since they were 17.

Their children say most of their friends enjoy the same policy at home. The son doesn't have a girlfriend now—but when he did, she would stay the night.

> During the day we're around the house with my parents, but at night, we go into my bedroom and close the door.

For Pierre and his wife, the freedom they allow their teenagers sends a strong message: the house belongs to all of them . . . and it's a safe haven from the chaotic world of teenage life. Céline says:

> School, work, and friends demand so much from my kids. They are faced with all kinds of rules and limitations. When they're at home, I want them to feel safe, secure, and natural.

It's a different story for a family in southwestern Ontario, where the teenage daughters are younger: 13 and 15. Their father, John (fictitious name)—a teacher—was surveyed and answered no when asked: if his girls were 18, would he allow them to have sex in the house?

His wife, Ann (fictitious name), agrees, because, she says, the older sister has to set an example. The older sibling says many of her friends are having sex, but she's not ready. And when the time does come, she agrees with the house rules.

> I wouldn't feel comfortable having sex in my parents' house, especially when they are home. It has to do with the whole respect thing my parents talk about.

On other matters of sex and teenagers, the mother says:

> I would encourage my daughters to talk to me if they ever decide to have sex with someone. I would want to talk to them about birth control.

On the issue of teenagers and sex in the home, many French-speaking Quebecers are more tolerant than most Canadians (see Figure 3.2). Why? In Quebec, the family is seen as a refuge against a hostile world, while in Ontario, the family offers other compensations. (For a discussion of the nature of the family in Quebec, see Gerin, 1928. For a broader view of the role of the family in the social and political life of society, see Todd, 1995, 1998.)

Source: Adapted from The National Magazine/ Maclean's Poll, 1998. Retrieved September 25, 2002 from www.tv.cbc.ca/national/pgminfo/ poll/index.html.

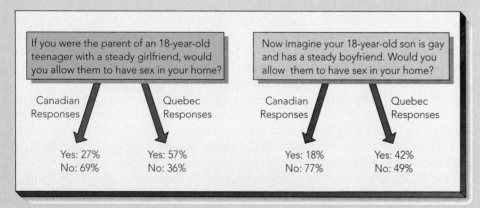

If you were the parent of an 18-year-old teenager with a steady girlfriend, would you allow them to have sex in your home?

Canadian Responses
Yes: 27%
No: 69%

Quebec Responses
Yes: 57%
No: 36%

Now imagine your 18-year-old son is gay and has a steady boyfriend. Would you allow them to have sex in your home?

Canadian Responses
Yes: 18%
No: 77%

Quebec Responses
Yes: 42%
No: 49%

FIGURE 3.2 Differences between Quebec and the Rest of Canada on Matters of Parenting, Sex, and Teens

Language is the basis of human culture. The past decade has seen a major development in communication—the ease and speed with which we can "speak" to people across the globe. This development is destined to have vital effects on culture.

IN SUM

The sociological significance of language is that it takes us beyond the world of apes and allows culture to develop. Language frees us from the present by giving us the capacity to share understandings about the past and to develop common perceptions about the future. Consequently, as in the case of the picnic, each individual is able to perform a small part of a larger activity, aware that others are carrying out related parts. In this way, a series of separate activities becomes united into a larger whole.

Focus Question

Why is language so important to human culture?

Values, Norms, and Sanctions

To learn a culture is to learn people's **values**, their ideas of what is desirable in life. When we uncover people's values, we learn a great deal about them, for values are the standards by which people define good and bad, beautiful and ugly.

Sociologists use the term **norms** to describe the expectations, or rules of behaviour, that develop out of a group's values. They use the term **sanctions** to refer to positive or negative reactions to the ways people follow norms. **Positive sanction** refers to an expression of approval given for following a norm, while **negative sanction** denotes disapproval for breaking a norm. Positive sanctions can be material, such as a money reward, prize, or trophy, but in everyday life, they usually consist of hugs, smiles, a pat on the back, soothing words, or even handshakes. Negative sanctions can also be material—a fine, for example—but they, too, are more likely to consist of gestures, such as frowns, stares, harsh words, or raised fists. The North American finger gesture described earlier is a negative sanction.

Folkways and Mores

Norms that are not strictly enforced are called **folkways**. We expect people to comply with folkways, but we are likely to shrug our shoulders and not make a big deal about it if they don't. If someone insists on passing you on the left side of the sidewalk, for example, you are unlikely to take corrective action. However, if the sidewalk is crowded and you must move out of the way, you might give the person a dirty look.

Other norms, however, are taken much more seriously. We think of them as essential to our core values, and we insist on conformity. These are called **mores** (MORE-rays). A person who steals, rapes, or kills has violated some of society's most important mores, which results in formal sanctions otherwise identified as the criminal justice system (see Chapter 16). As sociologist Ian Robertson (1987, p. 62) explained,

> A man who walks down a street wearing nothing on the upper half of his body is violating a folkway; a man who walks down the street wearing nothing on the lower half of his body is violating [a] mores, the requirement that people cover their genitals and buttocks in public.

It should also be noted that one group's folkways may be another group's mores. For example, to walk down a sidewalk in a nudist camp with the entire body uncovered would be conforming to that subculture's folkways.

A **taboo** refers to a norm so strongly engrained that even the thought of its violation is greeted with revulsion. Eating human flesh and having sex with one's parents are examples of such behaviours (Benales, 1973; Read, 1974; Henslin, 1997c).

Pierre Bourdieu and Cultural Capital

French sociologist Pierre Bourdieu developed the concept of *cultural capital* in the early 1960s to help address the fact that "economic obstacles are not sufficient to explain" disparities in the educational attainment of children from different social classes (Bourdieu & Passeron 1979: p. 8). He noted that certain "cultural habits and... dispositions" inherited from family are fundamentally important to school success (Bourdieu & Passeron 1979: p. 14). According to Bourdieu, children from the middle and upper classes possess cultural capital or a set of "habits and dispositions" that give them advantages over children from the working class.

In proposing his theory, Bourdieu broke sharply with traditional sociological conceptions of culture, which tended to view it primarily as a source of *shared* norms and values. Instead, Bourdieu maintained that culture shares many of the properties that are characteristic of economic capital. In particular, he maintained that certain cultural "habits and dispositions" comprise a *resource* capable of generating "profits." They are cultural competencies or skills that become part of an individual's identity and can be continuously "cashed-in" when called upon or needed. Those without cultural capital are left behind. Moreover, under appropriate conditions,

these skills can be *transmitted* from one generation to the next (Lareau & Weininger, 2003).

Bourdieu's concept of cultural capital contributes to our understanding of how wealth, privilege, and poverty can be transmitted (see Chapter 14, Education).

Subcultures and Countercultures

A **subculture** consists of people whose experiences have led them to a distinctive way of looking at life. Canadian society contains thousands of subcultures. Some are as broad as the way of life we associate with teenagers, others as narrow as those we associate with bodybuilders or philosophers. Ethnic groups also form subcultures: their values, norms, and foods set them apart. So might their religion, language, and clothing. Occupational groups also form subcultures, as anyone who has hung out with cab drivers (F. Davis, 1959; Henslin, 1993), the police (Pepinsky, 1980), factory workers (Halle, 1984), artists (McCall, 1980), or construction workers (Haas, 1972) can attest. Even sociologists form a subculture, and, as you are learning, use a unique language for carving up the world.

The values and norms of most subcultures are compatible with the larger society to which they belong. In some cases, however, a group's values and norms place it in opposition to the dominant culture. Sociologists use the term **counterculture** to refer to these groups. Heavy-metal adherents who glorify Satanism, hatred, cruelty, sexism, violence, and death are an example of a counterculture. Note that motorcycle enthusiasts who emphasize personal

The violation of mores is usually a very serious matter. In this case, it was serious enough that police at this rugby match in Dublin, Ireland, swung into action to protect the public from seeing a "disgraceful" sight, at least as designated by this group. Yet unlike reactions to most violations of mores, this scene also shows barely suppressed laughter.

freedom and speed and affirm cultural values of success are members of a subculture. In contrast, the members of an outlaw motorcycle gang who also stress freedom and speed but add the values of despising women and selling drugs and prostitution form part of a counterculture (Watson, 1988).

Countercultures do not have to express negative values but can encourage over-conformity to some of society's mainstream values. Fundamentalist Christian groups in the U.S. and Canada who seek to politically impress their view of the world on all of us are another example of a counterculture. Skinheads who are members of SHARP (Skinheads Against Racial Prejudice), ARA (Anti Racist Action/Alliance), or Queer Skinhead Brotherhood (QSB) counter the negative image presented by neo-Nazi skinhead groups in Canada, such as the Western Guard and Heritage Front, but are more correctly seen as a subculture. Each of the three groups above is international, with chapters in North America and Europe. Unfortunately, neo-Nazi groups are given more press and media coverage than SHARP.

Culture and Taken-for-Granted Orientations to Life

To develop a sociological imagination, it is essential to understand how culture affects people's lives. While meeting someone from a different culture may make us aware of culture's pervasive influence, attaining the same level of awareness regarding our own culture is quite another matter. *Our* speech, *our* gestures, *our* beliefs, and *our* customs are usually taken for granted. We assume that they are "normal" or "natural," and we almost always follow them without question. As anthropologist Ralph Linton (1936) said, "The last thing a fish would ever notice would be water." Except in unusual circumstances, the effects of our own culture generally remain imperceptible to us.

Yet culture's significance is profound; it touches on almost every aspect of who and what we are. We came into this life without language, values, or morality, and with no ideas about religion, war, money, love, use of space, and so on. Yet at this point in our lives, we all have them. Sociologists call this "culture *within* us." *Culture becomes the lens through which we perceive and evaluate what is going on around us.* The rare instances in which these assumptions are challenged, however, can be upsetting. Our Canadian values and norms, or our nonmaterial culture, can fail us and leave us feeling embarrassed or out of place. For example, if you are travelling and participating in the cultural life of Southeast Asia—living and experiencing their culture—there will be many occasions when you will be introduced to new ways of handling your experiences with food, dress, polite conversation, and (if you are male) relationships with women. You will feel uneasy when, for example, someone is talking to you no more than five centimetres from your face. Not only that, you can smell his breath and it's

not pleasant! But you feel you can't move away; you are somehow locked in this social encounter. When this happens—when your nonmaterial culture fails to make sense of your surroundings—the disconnection you experience is known as culture shock. Additionally, the relationships between men and women, men and men—otherwise known as "male bonding"—and women and women vary greatly from culture to culture.

An important consequence of culture within us is **ethnocentrism**, a tendency to use our own group's ways of doing things as a yardstick for judging others. All of us learn that the ways of our own group are good, right, proper, and even superior to other ways of life. As sociologist William Sumner (1906), who developed this concept, said, "One's own group is the center of everything, and all others are scaled and rated with reference to it." Ethnocentrism has both positive and negative consequences. On the positive side, it creates in-group loyalties. On the negative side, ethnocentrism can lead to harmful discrimination against people whose ways differ from ours, such as those of Muslim, Caribbean, and other non-white immigrants.

The effects of culture on our lives fascinate sociologists. By examining more explicitly just how profoundly culture affects everything we are, this chapter will serve as a basis from which you can start to analyze your previously unquestioned assumptions of reality and thus gain a different perspective on social life and your role in it.

Practising Cultural Relativism

To counter our tendency to use our own culture as a standard to judge other cultures, we can practise **cultural relativism** by trying to understand a culture on its own terms.

For example, many Canadians may appear to have strong feelings against raising bulls for the sole purpose of stabbing them to death in front of shouting crowds. According to cultural relativism, however, bullfighting must be viewed strictly within the context of the culture in which it takes place—*its* history, *its* folklore, *its* ideas of bravery, and *its* ideas of gender roles.

As a Canadian, you may still regard bullfighting as wrong because our culture has no history of the activity. We all possess culturally specific ideas about cruelty to animals, ideas that have evolved slowly and match other elements of our culture. Consequently, practices that once were common in some areas—cock-fighting, dog-fighting, and so on—have been gradually weeded out (Bryant, 1993). Cultural relativism, however, is an attempt to refocus our cultural lens and thereby appreciate other ways of life rather than simply asserting that "our way is the right way."

Although cultural relativism is a worthwhile goal and helps us avoid cultural smugness, this view has come under attack. In a provocative book, *Sick Societies* (1992), anthropologist Robert Edgerton points out that some cultures endanger their people's health, happiness, or survival. He

Many Canadians perceive bullfighting as a cruel activity that should be abolished. To Spaniards and those who have inherited Spanish culture, however, bullfighting is a beautiful, artistic sport in which matador and bull blend into a unifying image of power, courage, and glory. *Cultural relativism* requires that we suspend our own perspectives in order to grasp the perspectives of others, something that is much easier described than attained.

suggests that we should develop a scale to evaluate cultures on their "quality of life." He also asks why we should consider cultures that practise female genital mutilation, gang rape, or wife beating, or sell daughters into prostitution, as morally equivalent to those that do not. Cultural values that result in exploitation, he says, are inferior to those that enhance people's lives.

IN SUM

1. Although the particulars of culture differ from one group of people to another, all people have culture. There are no exceptions. A society cannot exist without developing shared, learned ways of dealing with the demands of life.
2. Coming into contact with a radically different culture challenges our basic assumptions of life.
3. All people are ethnocentric, which has both functional and dysfunctional consequences.

Edgerton's sharp questions and incisive examples bring us to a point that will come up repeatedly in this text—disagreements that arise between scholars as they confront changing views of reality. It is such questioning of assumptions that keeps sociology interesting.

VALUES IN CANADIAN SOCIETY
An Overview of Canadian Values

As you know, Canada is a **pluralistic society**, made up of many different religious, racial, and ethnic groups, as well as countless interest groups centering on such divergent activities as collecting Barbie dolls and hunting deer. However, the study of national cultural values is of interest to many sociologists, not just in Canada, but in the United States, Europe, and many other countries (see Hofstede, 1980, 2001 for an interesting examination of masculine and feminine characteristics of many national cultures).

Some recent Canadian analysts, such as Hiller (1996) and literary icon Margaret Atwood (1972, cited in Lipset, 1986: p. 124), point palpably to our vast geography to account for the existence of a national set of values based on "survival" in an inhospitable environment. However, John Porter (1965), English Canada's pre-eminent sociologist, was the first to point to Canada's geography as a unifying principle in our national political culture. That is why the call for more provincial autonomy, whether it comes from Alberta or Newfoundland, or the occasional stirrings of Quebec nationalism otherwise known as "separatism," evokes such strong emotions over national unity in the rest of the country. We need look no further than the paintings of the Group of Seven or to note that Canada's national motto—*A mari usque ad mare*—from sea to sea—is stamped on all our paper currency to reinforce the importance of geography in Canada's history. That said, is that all there is to Canadian culture?

A more serious analysis goes deeper. Seymour Martin Lipset (1986, 1990), for example, contrasts the "revolutionary" national values of the United States with the "counterrevolutionary" main beliefs of the dominant anglophone culture throughout the nineteenth and well into the twentieth century. He locates this contrasting set of values in the historical experiences of both countries. The United States "broke away" from Great Britain in the "successful" revolution of 1776 and established a unique constitution that promoted individual rights, personal freedoms, and the pursuit of happiness through profit or capitalism. Canada, however, maintained its colonial status within the British Empire. For Lipset, this means Canadian identity is caught up in our

Many Canadians outside Quebec perceive "la fête nationale du Quebec" with suspicion. To most French-speaking Quebecois and those who have inherited Quebec culture, "la fête nationale du Quebec" is a colourful and joyous time for family and friends. Cultural relativism requires the suspension of our own perspectives in order to grasp the perspectives of others, which is sometimes much easier said than done.

Britain and enshrined in law Canada's *Charter of Rights and Freedoms*, that we matured as a nation. Therefore, as Canadians, we have often defined ourselves by what we *are not*; namely, Americans. Table 3.4 (see page 60) provides evidence of our perceptions of cultural distance from American culture throughout recent history. What is startling about this data is the dramatic break in 2006, when the responses for "Essentially Different" from American culture was *halved* from 31 percent in 2004 to only 17 percent in just two years. Note that for Quebec, this is not as significant an issue as for the rest of Canada. Let's examine Quebec culture and what makes it different from the rest of Canada.

Throughout the nineteenth century, until the beginning of the Quiet Revolution in 1959/60, Quebec was viewed by social scientists as a rural peasant society controlled by the Roman Catholic Church (Glenday & McMullan, 1970; Miner, 1964) (for dissenting views, see Garigue, 1964). A set of collective values that upheld clericalism, agriculturalism, and anti-industrialism was said to dominate French-speaking Quebec society (Taylor, 1964). The Quiet Revolution dramatically changed all that. Hubert Guindon called this societal transformation and its accompanying secularization of Quebec society "state modernization" (see Chapter 10 for a discussion of bureaucracy). That is, the modernization of Quebec society witnessed not only the creation of a new middle class of professionals with well-established careers in the provincial government bureaucracies of health, education, and welfare (Guindon, 1964, 1978, 1988), it also meant the dramatic decline of the role of the Catholic Church in the lives of most French-speaking Quebecois.

Having said that, what has replaced the societal values of clericalism, agriculturalism, and anti-industrialism? Hubert Guindon suggests an important societal and political value for most Quebecers was the belief that the establishment of Canada as a nation in 1867 was constituted by "two founding peoples"—the French and the English—or what John Porter referred to as the "two charter groups," much like the image suggested by Hugh MacLennan's novel entitled *Two Solitudes,* first published in 1945 (see Chapter 12 for a discussion of this political value and its significance for Canadian society).When it comes to personal value clusters, the secularization of Quebec society has meant the almost complete disappearance of Catholic morals. We will examine this concept further after we discuss some of the similarities among Canadians on matters of sexual mores.

For over 20 years (since 1983), *Maclean's* magazine has polled Canadians on a wide variety of topics, from taxes to sex, politics, and morality. One of the latest polls, in 2003, was conducted by Toronto-based *The Strategic Counsel*, and involved a national telephone survey of 1200 adult Canadians aged 18 years or older.

What are Canadians telling pollsters about what is important and what is not? Table 3.1 provides evidence of a move to more liberal moral values for most Canadians. The

"successful" counterrevolution. As such, Lipset concluded that anglophone Canadians are more elitist; that is, we are more deferential to authority than Americans. In addition, Canadian political and economic culture is more collectivist than that in the U.S. This fact, Lipset argues, helps explain the existence in Canada of a social democratic party on the traditional left (the NDP), much like the Labour Party in Great Britain or the Socialist Party in France. The collectivist tradition leads Canadians to accept more than Americans government intervention in the economy. We are also more likely to accept the social status we were born into. In a word, there is no equivalent in Canadian economic cultural history to the Horatio Alger myth—the notion that anyone could achieve material success with enough hard work.

It was not until 1982, when Pierre E. Trudeau, then prime minister, repatriated the constitution from Great

The study of national cultural values has become much more interesting for sociologists as Canadian society has grown in complexity and created a mosaic that envelopes its two-founding-nations status.

data compare Canadian attitudes, over a 25-year period, toward premarital and homosexual relations. The most dramatic shift comes with Canadians' acceptance of homosexual relations, regardless of age group, although young people (those aged 18–34 years) exhibit the largest percentage change from 1975 to 2000. Support for premarital relations has always scored high among young people, but in 2000 all age categories were overwhelming in their support for premarital relations.

In terms of sexual mores, Quebec differs from other Canadians on the following issue. Figure 3.2 (page 50) shows the differences between Quebec and the rest of the country on matters of parenting, sex, and teens. Quebec is much more accepting of teenagers, whether gay or straight, having sex at home with a steady partner than any other province or region.

Why? In the Down-to-Earth Sociology box earlier in the chapter, two different explanations were provided, representing marked differences in the perception about the character of the home in Quebec and the rest of Canada.

When it comes to other differences in values and beliefs, Quebec is a paradox. There are values that Quebecers share with the rest of Canada and there are those they do not. This should not be surprising. Quebec's history is bound-up with French language and culture and, until recently, with agriculturalism and Catholicism. Quebecers live within a language frontier that generates a sense of collective belonging. Moreover, Quebec has its own media and star system. An examination of Table 3.2 reveals an interesting paradox. On one hand, Quebecers report greater concern over social problems than do individuals in the rest of Canada. However, when

TABLE 3.1 Sexual Mores in Canada by Age, 1975–2000

Attitudes Toward Premarital Relations	1975 (%)	2000 (%)
Nationally	68	84
18–34	90	93
35–54	65	89
55+	42	74
Attitudes Toward Homosexual Relations		
Nationally	28	73
18–34	42	75
35–54	25	64
55+	12	42

Sources: Vanier Institute of the Family (with Reginald Bibby), *The Future Families Project: A Survey of Canadian Hopes and Dreams*, 2004 (www.vifamily.ca/library/future/2.html#2_4).

it comes to the personal values of compassion and social conscience, Quebecers score *lower* than other Canadians.

Allan Gregg, a well-known Canadian pollster, once stated that when he asked Canadians whether they agreed or disagreed with the statement: "eat, drink, and be merry, for tomorrow you may die," 77 percent of Quebec teenagers agreed, compared with only 17 percent of teens in British Columbia (Aubin, 2001–2002). He coined the term "hedonist-individualist" to characterize the response of Quebec teenagers. For Gregg, this dramatic shift in values represented more than a simple break with Catholic morals. It represented a break from the traditional values of agriculturalism and clericalism to a new postmodern value for this generation of Quebecers. The results reported in Table 3.2 speak to this dramatic shift in values. Leslie Laczko, a sociology professor at the University of Ottawa, may have a more salient answer, which is that Quebec has a much higher proportion of people who are single and who live in common-law relationships than the rest of Canada. "That itself is a significant part of this big puzzle that social scientists are trying to solve," he says, because single people are more likely to feel bored and isolated than married couples.

Just as interesting is the fact that when Quebecers look outside their province, they tend to "skip" Canada and adopt a continental or global view. According to Table 3.2, Quebecers are more guarded of their personal liberties than the average Canadian since they are less likely to give up personal freedom to combat terrorism.

TABLE 3.2 Social Problems versus Personal Values (2006); International Issues (2002); Quebec and the Rest of Canada

Social Problem*	Quebec	Rest of Canada
Poverty	48%	28%
Child Abuse	53%	32%
Suicide	42%	14%
Violence	39%	28%
Racism	21%	11%
Terrorism	35%	24%
Personal Values**		
Friendliness	53%	78%
Courtesy	64%	83%
Forgiveness	60%	80%
Generosity	45%	58%
Politeness	66%	77%
Honesty	87%	94%
International Issues (2002)		
More Likely to Support		
Canada re-evaluating its Israeli-Palestinian policies	63%	49%
Less Likely to Support		
Canadian involvement in Afghanistan	65%	83%
More funding for the Canadian military	48%	74%
Giving up some freedoms to combat terrorism	47%	63%

* Percentage of respondents who were "Very Serious" when asked how concerned they were about the issues above

** Percentage of respondents who indicated that the personal values above were "Very Important" to them

Sources: For 2006 data, see Cameron Ainsworth-Vincze, "Values lost in translation," *Maclean's* Vol 119, July 3, 2006, Issue 27/28. For 2002, data see "Where Solitudes Meet," by Benoit Aubin, *Maclean's*, Vol 114, p 32.

TABLE 3.3 Highlights from the History of the *Indian Act*

1.	1876	The first *Indian Act* was passed by Parliament. a. The concept of enfranchisement was a key provision of the act. This meant and still means the total assimilation of the First Nations population in Canada. b. The *Indian Act* gave substantial powers to the federal government to control First Nations people living on reserves. It explicitly forbade the selling or leasing of any reserve land unless it was first surrendered or leased to the federal government. c. It also distinguished between Status and non-Status Indians. (Status Indians are those who are registered with the federal government as Indians according to the terms of the *Indian Act*. Non-Status Indians are those who are not registered.) d. The *Indian Act* of 1876 also made provision for the election of First Nations chiefs. Essentially, chiefs functioned as agents of the federal government, exercising limited power within federal supervision. The act was so limiting that First Nations band members could not leave reserves without a special pass, and their children were taken away to residential schools to be assimilated. After returning from fighting for Canada in World War II, Aboriginal men fought against the injustices of the *Indian Act*. In the 1940s, Aboriginal leaders began to emerge as champions of Native rights.
2.	1951	The *Indian Act* was revised, but Indian status and enfranchisement clauses were retained. The law banning Indian ceremonies was repealed and First Nations members were given the right to enter public bars.
3.	1960	First Nations were allowed to vote in federal elections.
4.	1973	Native leaders reclaimed their right to educate their children through their culture, and church-operated or residential schools soon disappeared.
5.	1975/78	The first modern land claims settlement was signed by the Cree and the Quebec government in 1975 and the Naskapi and Quebec in 1978. A total of $225 million was awarded as compensation to the James Bay Cree and the Inuit of Northern Quebec.
6.	1988	The federal government amended the *Indian Act,* enabling First Nations to pass bylaws to levy property taxes on reserve lands that they would lease.
7.	1996	The 13 First Nations and the Department of Indian Affairs signed the Framework Agreement on First Nations Land Management in February 1996, which allows First Nations to pass their own laws to develop, conserve, protect, manage, and use their lands. The 13 First Nations are Westbank, Musqueam, Lheit-Lit'en, N'Quatqua, Squamish, Siksika, Muskoday, Cowessess, Opaskwayak Cree, Nipissing, Mississaugas of Scugog Island, Chippewas of Georgina Island, and Chippewas of Mnjikaning.
8.	1999	The creation of Nunavut ("our land") as the largest and newest territory in Canada with a population of approximately 29 500. The federal government agreed to pay Nunavut $1.2 billion over a period ending in 2007.

Source: Adapted from The First Nations Governance Act, by Linda Ward, June 14, 2002, CBC News Online. Accessed at www.cbc.ca/news/features/indian_act.html and www.ainc-inac.gc.ca/pr/info/info14_e.html.

Focus Question
In what ways do Canadians outside of Quebec differ from Quebecers, and in what ways are they similar?

Native Peoples in Canada

The multicultural aspect of recent Canadian history is often viewed as positive. Many ethnic groups celebrate their differences and similarities as Canadians at numerous festivals, carnivals, and celebrations every year in Canada. Native Canadians, however, have very little reason to rejoice and make merry. Their present status as Canadians was enshrined in the *Indian Act* of 1876. Today, the Minister of Indian Affairs and Northern Development administers the *Indian Act* at the federal level. As shown in Table 3.3, the *Indian Act* has served to isolate Natives from mainstream Canadian society by keeping them on reserves. More importantly, and in many ways because the federal government controls their social life, Native peoples in Canada are afforded few opportunities for meaningful employment or for starting business ventures that respect their diverse cultures.

Neither are the living conditions on many reserves healthy. Nor are there opportunities for young people to explore their place in the Native way of life. The combination of adverse social, psychological, and economic conditions serves to heighten susceptibility to illness and poor health. It is little wonder, then, that Native peoples report the highest incidences of death due to respiratory disease, accidents, violence, and poisoning (Jarvis & Boldt, 1983; Department of Indian Affairs and Northern Development, 2001).

Value Contradictions and Social Change

Not all values fall into neat, integrated packages. Some may even contradict one another. The **value contradiction** of group superiority violates freedom, democracy, and equality. There simply cannot be full expressions of freedom, democracy, and equality alongside racism and sexism. Something has to give. One way Canadians sidestepped this contradiction in the past was to say that the values of freedom, democracy, and equality applied only to certain groups. The contradiction was bound to surface, however, and did, as is evident from the internment of the Japanese during World War II and the women's liberation movement during the 1960s and 1970s. However, most Canadians who live and work with many different subcultural groups continue to extend the values of freedom and equality and, as we saw earlier when discussing values in Canadian society, tolerance to more and more groups. As a result, we are reducing the emphasis on a single national group superiority.

As society changes, some values are challenged and undergo modification. Change may be gradual, with people slowly adjusting their behaviours and ideas, or it may come suddenly and be extremely disruptive. It is precisely at the point of value contradictions that we are able see a major force for social change in a society.

Value Clusters

Values are not independent units. Instead, some come together to form a larger whole, or **value cluster**. As previously discussed, "hedonistic individualism" represents a recent Quebec value cluster, while Seymour Martin Lipset distinguished "counterrevolution" as a value cluster for the anglophones that have dominated Canadian history.

EMERGING VALUE CLUSTERS A value cluster of four interrelated core values—leisure, self-fulfillment, physical fitness, and youth—appears to be emerging in Canada and the United States. A fifth—concern for the environment—has established itself on a global scale.

1. *Leisure.* The emergence of leisure as a value is reflected in the rapid growth of a huge recreation industry—from computer games, boats, and motor homes to sports arenas, vacation homes, and a gigantic travel and vacation industry.

2. *Self-fulfillment.* This value is reflected in the "human potential" movement, a concern with becoming "all one can be," "self-help," "relating," and "personal development."

3. *Physical fitness.* There is much greater emphasis being placed on both men and women today to appear attractive. For men, the standard is the Calvin Klein poster boy look of "Marky Mark" Wahlberg, or, for the sophisticated urban man, what Mark Simpson (1994) called the "Metrosexual Male." This trend can be seen in the mushrooming of health clubs and physical fitness centres, the "natural" foods craze, and brew bars, and in the obsessive concerns about weight and diet.

4. *Youth.* While valuing youth and disparaging old age is not new, some sociologists note a new sense of urgency. Aging baby boomers are targeted by advertisers to buy products that are said to fight the normal physical changes that happen with growing older. Advertising, to be sure, fuels cosmetic makeovers, but so do so-called experts, one of whom recently claimed that "aging is not a normal life event, but a disease" (G. Cowley, 1996). It is not surprising that techniques of youth enhancement—from cosmetics to surgery—have become popular.

   These first four items in the cluster are a response to needs and interests resulting from fundamental changes in Canadian and American society. Not long ago, Canadians were preoccupied with forging a nation and fighting for economic survival. Today, advertisers push an increasing variety of wares and services, not only to mass markets but especially to emerging, age-specific "niche" markets such as kids, teenage boys and girls, and young adults.

5. *Concern for the environment.* Throughout most of Canadian history, the environment was seen as a challenge—a wilderness to be settled, forests to be chopped down, rivers and lakes to be fished, and animals to be hunted for their furs. Today, most Canadians have developed a genuine and long-term concern for the environment because we now recognize our dependence on natural resources. In fact, the environment is increasingly linked to health and is associated with judgments about our quality of life and economic success (K. Reil, 2001).

When Values Clash

Core values do not change without meeting strong resistance from traditionalists—those who hold them dear. Consequently, many people are upset at the changes swirling around them, seeing their way of life challenged and their future growing insecure. Efforts to change gender roles, for example, arouse intense controversy, as do support of alternative family forms and changes in sexual behaviour. Alarmed at such onslaughts to their values, traditionalists fiercely defend idealized family relationships and gender roles. The majority of Canadians, unlike many of their American neighbours, are embracing the changing moral values of tolerance and respect for other cultures and ways of life, including gay and lesbian lifestyles.

The Americanization of Canadian Values?

As John Porter (1965) remarked over three decades ago, Canadians, unlike Americans, lack a unifying ideology. Canadians are not brought up with a set of beliefs and values that tell us who we are and what we should strive for in order to make our lives meaningful and fulfilling. At the same time, we have been preoccupied with who we are as a nation. Many of us have been known, on frequent occasion, to ask the proverbial question, "What is the Canadian identity?" Many social scientists, Canadian and non-Canadian, have sought answers to this perplexing national question.

Could it be that we are losing what distinctiveness we possess as Canadians as we become more closely tied economically with the United States—that is, as our trade, capital, and people move north and south? As shown in Table 3.4, it seems we want to see ourselves as essentially different from Americans even though the latest data suggests a shift in perception. However, what constitutes truly Canadian values remains elusive to us. American filmmaker Michael Moore underlined some similarities between Canadian and American societies in his film *Bowling for Columbine*, in which he asked the question, "What is responsible for the exceptionally high level of killing in America?" Not a large number of guns, Moore answered, because other countries, including Canada, have proportionally as many guns. Neither is it a love of violent movies, video games, poverty, unemployment, and ethnic diversity, because

Canada has as much ethnic diversity and more unemployment. Two things, according to Moore, are primary causes: the U.S. media, which, as he shows, constantly encourages fear among the American populace; and the government in Washington, which solves problems by bombing people somewhere in the world. According to Moore's argument, perhaps the Canadian media differs in some respects from that in the United States—and certainly the Canadian government exercises much less military power than the U.S. government does. What do you think? Are there unique Canadian values worth preserving?

CULTURAL UNIVERSALS

With the amazing variety of human cultures around the world, are there any **cultural universals**—values, norms, or other cultural traits that are found everywhere?

Anthropologist George Murdock (1945) sought to answer this question and drew up a list of customs concerning courtship, cooking, marriage, funerals, games, laws, music, myths, incest taboos, and even toilet training. He found that although activities such as these are present in all cultures, *the specific customs differ from one group to another.* There is no universal form of family, of disposing of the dead, or of toilet training.

Even incest is defined differently from group to group. For example, some groups allow some men to marry their own daughters (La Barre, 1954). In certain circumstances, some groups require that brothers and sisters marry one another (Beals & Hoijer, 1965). The Burundi of Africa even insist that, to remove a certain curse, a son have sexual relations with his mother (Albert, 1963). Such sexual relations are allowed only for special people (royalty) or in a special situation (such as that of a lion hunter before a dangerous hunt), and no society permits generalized incest for its members.

In short, although there are universal human activities (speech, music, storytelling, marrying, disposing of the dead, preparing food, and so on), there is no universally accepted way of *doing* any of them. Humans have no biological

TABLE 3.4 Canada-United States: Are We Getting Closer Culturally?*

Response	1999 (%)	2002 (%)	2004 (%)	2006 (%)	2006 Quebec (%)
Essentially the same	8	7	12	6	3
Mainly the same	44	34	32	44	27
Mainly different	23	29	23	32	47
Essentially different	24	28	31	17	22

*Survey question asked of Canadians, "Would you describe Canadians and Americans as essentially the same, mainly the same but with small differences, mainly different but with small similarities, or essentially different?"

Source: "The Nation's Mood," *Maclean's*, December 27, 2004. www.macleans.ca/topstories/polls/article.jsp?content=20041220_145019_3484.

imperative that results in one particular form of behaviour throughout the world.

Focus Question
Is there a universally accepted way of conducting basic human activities such as cooking, marriage, and so on?

ANIMALS AND CULTURE

Let us digress for a moment to follow a fascinating and related issue: do animals have culture? Do they have language?

Do Animals Have Culture?

According to our definition of culture as a learned way of life passed on to others, it would seem that animals could not have culture. The basic sociological question is this: are there any behaviours that animals learn and then pass on to others?

We begin with Jane Goodall, who extensively studied chimpanzees in Tanzania, Africa (Van Lawick-Goodall, 1971).

When the chimps became accustomed to Goodall and allowed her to join them, she slowly figured out how they communicate. Eventually she was even able to participate in their gestures, hoots, and facial expressions. For 30 years, Goodall lived in the remote jungle (J. Walters, 1990). She observed that wild chimps make and use **tools**; that is, they modified objects and use them for specific purposes. Until her observation, it was assumed that only humans used tools. The chimps would pick a blade of grass, then strip off its leaves and lick one end. Next they would poke the sticky end into a nest of termites. After waiting a bit, they would pull it out covered with termites, then savour the taste as they licked off the stick. In 1977, Goodall founded the Jane Goodall Institute for Wildlife Research, Education and Conservation to provide ongoing support for field research on wild chimpanzees. Today, she is on a globe-spanning crusade to promote conservation and improve conditions for captive chimps (J.J. Miller, 1995). In 2003, Queen Elizabeth II named Dr. Goodall a Dame of the British Empire.

A related question that has intrigued both scientists and nonscientists is whether animals have language. Social scientists think of language as more complex than mere sounds. They view it as symbols that can be infinitely strung together to communicate abstract thought. Animal sounds, however, appear to be closer to a baby's cries. A cry of distress, even though it brings a parent running, is not language. The cry is merely a biological response to pain, similar to reflexes.

Stimulated by Goodall's discovery, scientists began trying to determine the extent of **animal culture**—learned, shared behaviour among animals (Eibl-Eibesfeldt, 1970).

Focus Question
What makes humans different from all other animals?

TECHNOLOGY IN THE GLOBAL VILLAGE
New Technologies

In addition to symbolic or nonmaterial culture, there is also a material aspect, a group's things, ranging from houses to toys. Central to a group's material culture is its **technology**; that is, the skills or procedures necessary to make and use tools.

We can use the term **new technology** to refer to emerging technologies, such as computers, satellites, and various forms of microelectronics-based media.

The sociological significance of technology is that *the type of technology a group has sets the framework for its nonmaterial culture.* Technology influences the way people think and how they relate to one another, a focus of the box on

"COOL! A KEYBOARD THAT WRITES WITHOUT A PRINTER."

Technological advances have become so rapid that the technology of one generation is practically unrecognizable by the next.

Sociology and the New Technology. Consider gender relations. Through the centuries and throughout the world, it has been the custom (a group's nonmaterial culture) for men to dominate women. Today, with instantaneous communications (the material culture), this custom has become much more difficult to maintain. For example, when women from many nations gathered in Beijing for a U.N. conference in 1995, satellites instantly transmitted their grievances around the globe. Such communications may create discontent, or sometimes a feeling of sisterhood, and taken together women will agitate for social change (see Chapters 7 and 18). In addition, the internet has facilitated an explosion in small businesses in Canada and the U.S. owned by entrepreneurial women. It is much easier to offer online payments to customers for products through companies such as PayPal or CCNow, for example, than it is for a woman to get a merchant's account from one of Canada's chartered banks.

Cultural Lag and Cultural Change

A couple of generations ago, sociologist William Ogburn (1922) coined the term **cultural lag**. By this, Ogburn meant that not all parts of a culture change at the same pace. Ogburn pointed out that *a group's material culture usually changes first, with the nonmaterial culture lagging behind*, playing a game of catch-up. For example, when we get sick, we could type our symptoms into a computer and get an immediate printout of our diagnosis and best course of treatment. In fact, in some tests, computers outperform physicians (Waldholz, 1991). Yet our customs have not caught up with technology, and we continue to visit doctors' offices.

Technology and Cultural Levelling

Except in rare instances, humans have always had some contact with other groups. In this process, called **cultural diffusion**, groups are eager, for example, to adopt superior

---

SOCIOLOGY AND THE NEW TECHNOLOGY
Information and Communications Technologies (ICTs): Global Village or Big Brother?

A sign over a photocopy machine:

WARNING! This machine is subject to break downs during periods of critical need ... Threatening the machine with violence only aggravates the situation. Keep cool and say nice things to the machine. Nothing else seems to work. Never let the machine know you are in a hurry.

All over the country, users of copiers have laughed at some version of this attempt to turn frustration into humour. This sign comes close to a point of view called **technological determinism**, the idea that technology is the single greatest force shaping our lives (D. Chandler, 1995).

Two Canadian analysts from the University of Toronto, Harold Innis and Marshall McLuhan, examined the effects of technological revolutions on our culture. For Innis, oral cultures were limited to the size of small communities. However, the ability to write made human geographical expansion possible because a literate group could keep in touch through writing. In Innis's mind, bureaucratic empires became possible when people could check records and develop standards of judgment.

Marshall McLuhan built on Innis by portraying communications technologies as extensions of the human body. Just as a pole increases the reach of your arm, the new and varied ways we communicate with one another today extend the power of our senses. But not all senses share equally in their extension. Literacy may amplify one's eyes, McLuhan observed figuratively, but shrink one's ears. A computer, for example, extends the power of our brain and ears with the use of computer games and access to new music over the Web, but not our sense of touch or smell. The more we use a cell phone, computer, or MP3 player, the smaller our world becomes. We are living in what McLuhan coined "The Global Village."

Sherry Turkle (1984, 2005; 1995) takes McLuhan several steps further by arguing that information and communications technologies, when incorporated into toys, video and internet games, helps create separate virtual realities that play on our fantasies, both sexual and nonsexual.

For Your Consideration

Technological determinists highlight a significant issue: are we in control of

Marshall McLuhan.

technology, or is technology in control of us?

In today's world, the long-accepted idea that it is proper to withhold rights because a person is a women or gay no longer holds. What is usually invisible in such a revolutionary change is the role of technology in joining the world's nations into a global communication network. Can you explain how it is possible for global information technologies to bring about the expansion of human rights?

This Barbie doll, sold in Japan, is dressed in the stage costume of a Japanese singer. As objects diffuse from one culture to another, they are modified to meet the tastes of the adoptive culture. In this instance, the modification has been done intentionally as part of the *globalization of capitalism*.

cooking pots, steel axes, and even bits of clothing spun in mills in North America. Although the direction of cultural diffusion today is primarily from the West to other parts of the world, cultural diffusion is not a one-way street, which can be seen in architectural designs, food (bagels, falafel, Thai, and so on), and leisure items such as the hammock.

Not long ago, a trip from Canada to Africa was so unusual that only a few hardy people made it, and newspapers would herald their feat. With today's technology in travel and communications, cultural diffusion is occurring rapidly. Air travel has made it possible to journey around the globe in a matter of hours. Hundreds of thousands now make the trip every year.

The changes in communication are no less vast. Today's electronic communications transmit messages across the globe in a matter of seconds. In fact, travel and communication unite us. One result is **cultural levelling**, a process in which cultures become similar to one another as expanding industrialization brings not only technology, but also Western culture to the rest of the world.

Cultural levelling, occurring rapidly around the world, is apparent to any traveller. The golden arches of McDonald's welcome today's visitors in Tokyo, Paris, London, Madrid, and even Moscow, Beijing, and Hong Kong. In Mexico, the most popular piñatas are no longer of donkeys but of Mickey Mouse and Fred Flintstone (Beckett, 1996). "Thanks to MTV," says an Indian girl in Calcutta, "I can wear a miniskirt to a disco" (Brauchli, 1993b).

Some would argue globalization facilitated the spread of U.S. popular culture around the world. In addition to the pervasive influence of U.S. television, movies, and magazines, sports such as basketball, football, and baseball are played in many countries. A much maligned but fascinating form of sports entertainment, the World Wrestling Entertainment franchise, has followers in almost every corner

weapons and tools. During these contacts, people learned from one another, adapting some part of the other's way of life. In remote areas of South America, one can find metal

PERSPECTIVES
Pro Wrestling 101 at Brock University

Professional wrestling draws millions of men, women, and children from diverse backgrounds and ages. It is not just a North American trend; professional wrestling is a worldwide cultural phenomenon.

Recently, professional wrestling has been on the receiving end of academic criticism for its misogyny, homophobia, and violence. Is this an accurate representation of what happens in the "squared circle"? Or is there more to professional wrestling

than what some academics have argued?

Until now, there has been little sociological research on professional wrestling as a worldwide cultural phenomenon. Starting in September 2006, students at Brock University in St. Catherines, Ontario, are able to study professional wrestling in a course offered through the Department of Sociology cross-listed with Sports Management. One important topic in the course is the critical examination of recent psycho-

logical research that places the blame for such social problems as bullying, domestic violence toward women, and increasing homophobia on the antics of professional wrestlers. Another topic explores why sociologists in Canada and the U.S. neglected the study of professional wrestling as a worldwide cultural spectacle.

Students attend a local professional wrestling card to witness firsthand the athletes/performers and their audience.

of the world. Professional wrestling, with its soap opera antics, staged violence, and comedic rituals, fascinates an increasingly large number of young men and women (see the Perspectives box on Pro Wrestling on page 63).

The bridging of geography and culture by electronic signals does not in itself mark the end of traditional cultures. Japan, for example, has adapted not only Western economic production but also Western forms of dress and music. These changes, superimposed on Japanese culture, have turned Japan into a blend of Western and Eastern cultures.

Globalization, a topic to be discussed in Chapter 5, is a process of transnational economic activity that has contributed to the resurgence of religious and ethnic nationalism in various parts of the world.

SUMMARY AND REVIEW

What Is Culture?

WHAT IS CULTURE?

All human groups possess **culture**—language, beliefs, values, norms, and material objects passed from one generation to the next. **Material culture** consists of objects (art, buildings, clothing, and tools). **Nonmaterial** (or **symbolic**) **culture** is a group's way of thinking and patterns of behaviour. p. 47.

Components of Symbolic Culture

WHAT ARE THE COMPONENTS OF NONMATERIAL CULTURE?

The central component is **symbols**, anything to which people attach meaning and use to communicate with others. Universally, the symbols of nonmaterial culture are **gestures**, **language**, **values**, **norms**, **sanctions**, **folkways**, and **mores**. p. 47.

WHY IS LANGUAGE SO SIGNIFICANT TO CULTURE?

Language allows human experience to be goal-directed, co-operative, and cumulative. It also lets humans move beyond the present to share a past, future, and other common perspectives. According to the **Sapir-Whorf hypothesis**, language even shapes our thoughts and perceptions. pp. 48–49.

HOW DO VALUES, NORMS, FOLKWAYS, MORES, AND SANCTIONS REFLECT CULTURE?

All groups have **values**, standards by which they define what is desirable or undesirable, and **norms**, rules or expectations about behaviour. Groups use **positive sanctions** to show approval of those who follow their norms, and **negative sanctions** to show disapproval of those who do not. Norms that are not strictly enforced are called **folkways**, while **mores** are norms to which groups demand conformity because they reflect core values. pp. 51–52.

HOW DO SUBCULTURES AND COUNTERCULTURES DIFFER?

A **subculture** is a group whose values and related behaviours distinguish its members from the general culture. A **counterculture** holds values that in some way stand in opposition to those of the dominant culture. pp. 52–53.

WHAT ARE CULTURAL RELATIVISM AND ETHNOCENTRISM?

People are naturally ethnocentric; that is, they use their own culture as a yardstick for judging the ways of others. In contrast, those who embrace **cultural relativism** try to understand other cultures on those cultures' own terms. pp. 53–54.

Values in Canadian Society

WHAT ARE THE VALUES OF CANADIAN AND QUEBEC SOCIETIES?

Although Canada is a **pluralistic society** made up of many groups—each with its own set of values—tolerance and liberal moral values dominate. For Canadians, sex and morality means acceptance and tolerance. There are differences in values between Quebecers and the rest of Canada.

Some values come together (**value clusters**) to form a larger whole. **Value contradictions** (such as equality and racism) indicate areas of social tension, which are likely points of social change. Changes in a society's fundamental values are opposed by people who hold strongly to traditional values. Leisure, physical fitness, self-fulfillment, and concern for the environment are emerging core values. **Ideal culture** is a group's ideal values and norms and their goals. **Real culture**, people's actual behaviour, often falls short of their cultural ideals. pp. 54–60.

Cultural Universals

DO CULTURAL UNIVERSALS EXIST?

Cultural universals are values, norms, or other cultural traits found in all cultures. Although all human groups have customs concerning cooking, funerals, weddings, and so on, because the specific forms of these customs vary from one culture to another, there are no cultural universals. pp. 60–61.

Animals and Culture

DO ANIMALS HAVE CULTURE?

To the extent that some animals teach their young certain behaviours, such as using tools, animals also have a rudimentary culture. No animals have language in the sociological sense of the term. p. 61.

Technology in the Global Village

HOW IS TECHNOLOGY CHANGING CULTURE?

Ogburn coined the term **cultural lag** to refer to a group's nonmaterial culture lagging behind its changing technology. With today's technological advances in travel and communications, **cultural diffusion** is occurring rapidly. This leads to **cultural levelling**, whereby many groups are adopting Western culture in place of their own customs. Much of the richness of the world's diverse cultures is being lost in the process. pp. 61–64.

KEY TERMS

animal culture   61
counterculture   52
cultural diffusion   62
cultural lag   62
cultural levelling   63
cultural relativism   53
cultural universals   60
culture   47
ethnocentrism   53

folkways   51
gestures   47
language   48
material culture   47
mores   51
negative sanction   51
new technology   61
nonmaterial culture   47
norms   51

pluralistic society   54
positive sanction   51
sanctions   51
Sapir-Whorf hypothesis   49
subculture   52
symbol   47
symbolic culture   47
taboo   52

technological
    determinism   62
technology   61
tools   61
value cluster   59
value contradiction   59
values   51

WEBLINKS

Maclean's Poll
www.macleans.ca/article.
jsp?content=20060701_130104_130104
Since 1983, *Maclean's* magazine has polled Canadians on topics from taxes to sex, politics, and morality. Here, you can see the results from the 2006 poll.

Culture and Tradition: The Canadian Graduate Student Journal of Folklore and Ethnology
www.ucs.mun.ca/~culture
Canada's longest-running bilingual folklore journal, published for nearly 20 years in French and English. It is currently run by graduate students in Folklore at Memorial University of Newfoundland. Topics covered include the traditional arts, music, cuisine, architecture, beliefs, cultural psychology, and sociological structure of regional ethnic, religious, and industrial groups in Canada.

Multicultural Canada Home Page
www.pch.gc.ca/progs/multi/evidence/contents_e.cfm/
In 1971, Canada became the first country in the world to adopt multiculturalism as an official policy. The 1971 Multiculturalism Policy of Canada also confirmed the rights of Aboriginal peoples and the status of Canada's two official languages.

Tables of Contents for All Issues of *Postmodern Culture*
http://jefferson.village.virginia.edu/pmc/
Postmodern Culture, an electronic journal of interdisciplinary criticism, is published by Johns Hopkins University Press with support from the University of Virginia's Institute for Advanced Technology in the Humanities.

CRITICAL THINKING QUESTIONS

1. Are all cultures equally valid? Can you think of a culture (e.g., Nazism) that you would find unacceptable? Why do you feel the way you do?

2. Do the media influence our culture, or does the expanding cultural diversity in our society influence the changes we find expressed in the media?

3. Is sexual orientation simply the product of a person's cultural upbringing? What role does biology play in our sexual preferences?

4. Why do many teenagers rebel against authority? Access the Research Navigator through MySocLab and use keywords such as "teenage" and "authority" to locate relevant and recent scholarly and popular press publications to help you answer this question.

PEARSON
mysoclab

Explore the topics covered in this chapter on MySocLab using the access information provided with this text. Interactive resources for studying include multimedia tutorials, video clips, practice tests, quizzes, and animated maps and figures.

Socialization

LEARNING OUTCOMES

After you have studied this chapter, you will be able to answer the following questions:

1. What is the "nature versus nurture" debate, why is it important, and what is the latest thinking on the contributions of biology to human behaviour?

2. In what ways does social experience create and structure our human existence, including our beliefs, values, goals, and even our perceptions?

3. How is gender identity created through gender socialization?

4. Why might the changing of socialization messages through resocialization be a powerful instrument of control?

5. What are the stages of human socialization and what kinds of transitions do we experience as we live through the life course?

6. What are the limitations of socialization as an explanation of human behaviour?

Anyone exposed to crime news, television programs, and popular movies in contemporary North America might seriously question the line between humans and animals. In an actual event, a Toronto father sexually abused his infant daughter and recorded the event for the internet. A string of popular movies (for example, *Saw, Saw II, III,* and *IV*) portray the horrific torture and murders of innocent victims. At a loss for more satisfying explanations, television crime series openly speculate whether certain people are simply "born bad." Seeking to understand human behaviour, including behaviour that deviates so profoundly from what is considered "'normal," is at the foundation of the sociological enterprise.

In 2007, a 48-year-old big-rig truck driver confronted three cars street-racing down the highway toward him. He veered his truck off the highway rather than slam into oncoming traffic. His bravery is posthumously recognized (Westell, 2008). In the same year, three young men in British Columbia risked their lives to rescue a woman from her burning vehicle (Peters, 2007). In March 2008, three Alberta teenagers, in the course of vandalizing a neighbour's home, microwaved the family's cat. They left a message for their victims, "Nice cat. Look in microwave" (Montgomery, 2008). How can we explain such disparate displays of human behaviour? Clearly, simply saying, "It's human nature" is not a satisfactory or helpful explanation.

What does it mean to be a human being? What is our "nature" and why and how do we differ from other animals? Many people assume that human beings will show empathy for those who are smaller and weaker and not mindlessly inflict pain and death. According to this popular viewpoint, while non-human animals are amoral and may kill their own young, human beings are different. For years, scientists pointed to the "fact" that animals do not use tools, do not employ symbols, and do not communicate with spoken language as evidence of our distinctly human category. Recent scientific research indicating that animals do use tools, are capable of using symbols, and, in fact, can be taught limited spoken language has dramatically blurred the lines between humans and other animals, and the question of what it means to be human and where "human nature" is located remains more troubling than ever.

BIOLOGY, SOCIOBIOLOGY, OR SOCIALIZATION

For generations, one of the major issues every sociology student has been introduced to is an exploration of the "nature versus nurture" debate. Two competing perspectives have long struggled against one another. Are people's fates, likes and dislikes, and behaviours dictated by biologically inborn characteristics—in other words, genetic material—or are our lives the product of our exposure to the culture, historical period, family, and friendship groups we happen to belong to? The "human nature" explanations are basically biological or genetic; people act in specific ways because of their in-born nature. If human behaviour is the result of "human nature," then this conclusion has profound implications. After all, if your "bad" acts are the result of genetics, how can we blame you and how can we hope to change your behaviour? Similarly, if certain races or genders are "genetically inferior," then their social subordination is simply "natural."

In the nineteenth and early twentieth centuries, many researchers embraced the idea of **biological determinism**—the belief that the way we act reflects in-built biological traits such as the need to reproduce, the need to survive, and so on. Strongly influenced by the then-emerging field of modern biology and its new theory of evolution, many analysts pointed to aspects of human biology—such as "instincts" (the mothering instinct, for example) and biological differences (especially "racial" differences)—as the root causes of human actions. These beliefs later informed Nazi ideology. After all, if some people and some races are "naturally" inferior, they should be weeded out so that the superior races can flourish. Sociology, which was also emerging as a discipline at the turn of the century, was influenced by this debate, and North American sociologists vigorously challenged this kind of "born in the bone" thinking. They argued that human behaviour is in large measure a reflection of societal and cultural forces. In other words, through the process of **socialization**, our beliefs, values, attitudes, and even our emotions are sculpted throughout our lives by our contact with parents, siblings, peers, schools, religion, media, and a wide variety of major societal institutions (Gerth & Mills, 1953).

Today, the debate over whether human behaviour is at root social or biological is far from resolved. In general conversation, people often explain human actions in terms of "human nature," and popular culture still provides support for biological determinism. We all have heard the phrases "That's just like a man" or "just like a woman" to explain specific behaviours. These are implicitly explanations based on biological differences by gender. Even more troubling are commonplace "racial" explanations, such as "Group X members are all bad drivers" or "Group X is always good at math or good at sports." Such biological explanations suggest that differences in biology "by race" can account for our behav-iour. What "racial" justification ignores is that among scientists, "race" is considered a meaningless concept—it is inaccurate, lacks consistency, and has no scientific reality (Sorenson, 2003: p. 37).

In our society, where biology affects our everyday understandings of the world, it is not surprising that the mass media continues to popularize this perspective. A recent Canadian newspaper article maintains that "biological differences between the sexes" are hard-wired. The explicit implication is that we should simply accept "ancient stereotypes about the sexes" and just try to live with the patterns "that nature and evolution laid down long, long ago" (Brooks, 2006). Another columnist advances the theory that men will keep winning most of the Nobel prizes because they are "genetically wired to win at all costs" (Wente, 2007). In a recent magazine article, an author explores the argument that even our political viewpoints—conservative or liberal—are "pre-programmed into our genes and brain activity" (Giles, 2008).

Further, this enthusiasm for biology remains respectable in some scientific spheres, including among some sociologists who term themselves *sociobiologists* and argue that much human social behaviour can and should be explained in terms of our evolutionary heritage and resultant biological makeup. Not long ago, a psychologist at the University of Western Ontario ignited a media fire storm by asserting that his research demonstrated there are racial differences in the intelligence of whites, Asians, and blacks—with the conclusion that blacks are inferior and Asians superior. While numerous scientists around the globe pointed out the flaws in the research and analysis, this work reflects the ongoing preoccupation with explaining people in terms of their biological make-up. Consider, however, the implications of explaining who you are in terms of, as suggested by a leading primatologist, your "inner ape." Are you in a significant way simply a reflection of humans' evolutionary past and our primate genes (De Waal, 2005)? Similarly, what are the implications of accepting a "sociobiological" explanation of male violence? Should we simply acknowledge, as suggested by a leading Canadian criminologist, that men are "'hard wired' to respond with violence (Boyd, 2000)?

Today, many social scientists continue to vigorously oppose biologically based explanations. In her humorously titled book *Shopping is Not a Gene,* Canadian researcher Anne Innis Dagg (2004) vigorously challenges genetic explanations of male violence, homosexuality, and intelligence. One of the most important things you will learn in sociology is a healthy skepticism about narrowly formulated biological explanations of human behaviour. "Human nature" remarks will never sound quite the same. You will inevitably wonder what role inequality, socialization, and culture play in creating the so-called "biological" reality. And, once you know that social factors play a role, it becomes possible to change social reality. After all, unlike most biology, society is subject to change and reform.

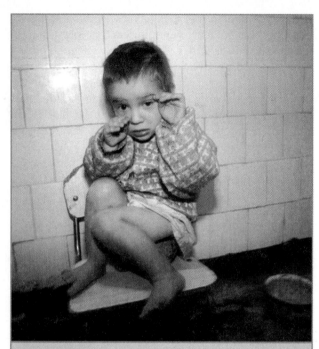

Under Communist rule, orphans in Romania received horrible treatment. These children will carry emotional scars into adulthood. In severe cases, their treatment is likely to affect their ability to reason and function as adults.

Blurring Boundaries Between Biology and Sociology

It is neither fair nor accurate to suggest that biological and sociological explanations confront one another as mutually exclusive and competing viewpoints. The most recent research suggests that neither social nor biological determinism is entirely satisfactory in explaining human behaviour. Leading sociologists and biologists are moving increasingly to a more nuanced and complex analysis. On one hand, it is now recognized that the "genetic" mandate may not be as fixed and clear as once assumed. For example, biologists contend that human evolution is ongoing and that humans are evolving "away from each other" as a result of new diseases and more anonymous societies (McIlroy, 2007). Culture and biology may, in fact, interpenetrate, so that living in a specific cultural context (a contemporary complex society, for example) may favour some genetic traits over others. Further, genetic materials may alter in response to our social environment. Montreal researchers reported in 2008 that there were genetic changes in the brains of adult suicide victims who, as children, had suffered abuse (sexual, physical, and emotional abuse or neglect). It appears that an abusive early social environment literally changes the epigenetic markings in the brains of abused people (Fidelman, 2008). Consistent with the critiques of "race," scientific research continues to disclose much more variability among human populations (and among human biologies) than has been previously accepted (Wente, 2008).

As a result of this work, recent cutting-edge discussions of the nature versus nurture debate are articulating a subtler vision of human behaviour: humans are both free-willed and driven by biology and culture. Human genes both "set" the paths of human behaviour and also absorb and respond to human experiences (Ridley, 2003). Within this highly complex and interactive vision of the relationship between nature and nurture, it seems most accurate to conclude that human biology does establish some general parameters for human development, but that social experiences are pivotal to understanding human behaviour. For example, the numerous studies that, over the centuries, have examined "feral children"—that is, children who were brought up deprived of most human contact—suggest that our biological makeup sets time limits on our abilities to acquire language and make connections to others. In recent years, there continue to be reports of children who have been severely deprived of normal socialization—confined to basements, dog kennels, or cribs throughout their formative years. For example, for seven years, three Austrian girls were imprisoned in their home by their mentally ill mother. They were kept in complete darkness and never allowed to leave the home. Rescued by police in 2005, the girls have been in specialized therapy ever since. However, reflecting research in other cases, it is believed that they will never fully recover (www.feralchildren.com). Their language abilities are impaired and they are extremely fearful of human contact. The oldest girl (13 when the imprisonment began and now 21) is reported to spend long periods of time standing on one foot staring at the floor. In this instance and others, it seems that the absence of social interaction during the early years of human development results in impairments that cannot ever be fully eliminated (Pancevski, 2007).

In case of "feral" or "isolated" children, the loss of language appears key. In order to interact with other human beings, we need some form of shared symbols. Some severely isolated children have created their own language to use among themselves. This language system may take various forms—spoken, spoken and written, or, as with American Sign Language, signed. Without such a shared symbol system, we are cut off from communicating with others. Helen Keller, who became deaf, blind, and mute as a result of early childhood illness, was trapped in her own world until one day she realized that the hand symbols created by her teacher in fact stood for elements in her environment. Once she understood the notion of **symbols**—that something can stand for something else—the world of communication and social relationships opened up. Without language, we not only cannot connect with others, we have no means of developing self-awareness—without a symbol (name) for "me," it isn't possible to think about "me." Without language, there can be no culture—no shared way of life—and shared culture is essential to what people become. Research with isolated and deprived children suggests our human biology allows us to acquire extensive language skills only for a specific period of time during childhood. If this opportunity is denied or undermined, it appears it can never be fully made up. There is a developmental timetable that is biologically limited. For most human beings, this biological matrix establishes the framework within which complex and diverse social learning occurs.

Focus Question

What questions could you use to challenge a friend who is continuously explaining human behaviour (women's driving abilities, men's approach to dating) by saying, "It's just human nature"?

IN SUM

There is considerable scientific evidence that society and social experience intersect with biological potential to make us human. It seems likely that if babies could be raised in isolation from human contact, they would mature into full-size adults but would not develop into "human beings" as we understand them. In particular, without the use of language or other symbol systems, humans reared in isolation would not experience or grasp relationships between people, would not be able to share the knowledge of others, and would be unable to chronicle their own history. However, for most human beings, biology provides only the basic framework upon which social experience superimposes who we become and how we act.

THE SOCIAL DEVELOPMENT OF THE SELF, MIND, AND EMOTIONS

At birth, we have no idea that we are separate beings. Babies will cry in anguish when they bite their own feet. How do we develop a **self**, the picture we have of how others see us, our view of who we are? The overall process by which we learn the ways of society (or of particular groups) is called socialization. This is what sociologists have in mind when they say, "Society makes us human."

Cooley and the Looking-Glass Self

In the 1800s, Charles Horton Cooley (1864–1929), pioneering sociologist at the University of Michigan, theorized about the emergence of human identity. In contrast to the biological explanations of his day, he argued that the unique aspect of "humanness" called the "self" is *socially created*; that is, our sense of self develops from interaction with others. In other words, he was suggesting that to become human beings we must *interact* with one another, and this interaction is premised on a shared set of *symbols* (typically, language). Only in this context do we develop a sense of our

"self" as a separate and manageable entity. For example, parents teach their children symbols—certain sounds ("Mama") that stand for certain objects. Once the child makes this profound discovery, it is possible to learn the next fundamental lesson: that the child herself is an object that can also be referred to by a sound (her name). The door opens to complex interaction with others and with our "selves." Cooley coined the term **looking-glass self** (1902) to describe the process by which a sense of self develops, which he summarized in the following couplet:

Each to each a looking-glass

Reflects the other that doth pass.

The looking-glass self entails three ingredients. First, we imagine how we appear to others around us. Second, we interpret their reactions, and, third, based on our interpretations of the reactions of others, we develop feelings and ideas about ourselves. As infants, we might register that our mother is speaking loudly in our direction, for example. We then interpret this action as a sign of anger directed toward us. In response to this interpretation, we might feel sad and angry with ourselves.

Mead and Role-Taking

Another influential symbolic interactionist, George Herbert Mead (1863–1931), who taught at the University of Chicago, suggested that play is also a critical element in the development of a self. In play, children learn **taking the role of the other**—that is, putting themselves in someone else's shoes to understand how someone else feels and thinks and anticipating how that person will act.

Young children attain this ability only gradually. Mead suggests that *taking the role of the other* is an essential part of learning to be a full-fledged member of a group and of society. At first, we are able to take the role only of *significant others*—individuals who significantly influence our lives, such as parents or siblings. Later, we develop the capacity to take the role of the *generalized other*—we can imagine how people in general might react to our behaviour. This second step is essential not only for extended co-operation but also for the control of antisocial desires (Mead, 1934; Coser, 1977).

Young children are only able to act out the roles of **significant others**: mother, father, sister, or brother. By assuming these roles during play, such as dressing up in their parents' clothing, children cultivate the ability to put themselves in their place.

As the self gradually develops, children internalize the expectations of larger numbers of people. The ability to take on roles eventually extends to being able to take the role of an abstract entity, "the group as a whole." When we consider doing something (especially something unusual), we may actively consider the abstract proposition—"What will 'people' think?" Mead gave the term **generalized other** to this perception of how people in general think of us. This

To help his students understand what the term *generalized other* means, Mead used baseball as an illustration. The text explains why team sports and organized games are excellent examples of this concept.

understanding allows us to modify our behaviour before acting by anticipating the reactions of others. As discussed earlier, severely isolated children often lack this ability and as a result have difficulties interacting.

Prominent Canadian sociologist Marlene Mackie uses Mead's game analogy of the three stages of "learning to take the role of the other" in order to explain how we learn our **gender roles**—the behaviour that is socially defined as appropriate to boys or girls (1987, pp. 124–127).

1. *Imitation/preparatory stage.* Children under three can only mimic others. They do not yet have a sense of self as separate from others. This stage is not actually role-taking but prepares the child for it. Gradually, the child learns that there are symbols and that they are often distinguished by gender. Boys and girls usually have different kinds of names. The gender difference is socially defined as very important (unlike, for example, eye colour) since the child also witnesses that boys and girls are treated differently by caregivers, wear different clothes, play with different toys, and so on.

2. *Play stage.* During the second stage, from the age of about three to five or six, children tend to take the roles of specific people. Girls will play at being mother or teacher while boys pretend to be hockey players or firefighters. They still often have an imperfect understanding of gender roles—thinking that hair length or urination posture determines gender. Caregivers, parents, and peers directly and indirectly convey the message that boys and girls are profoundly different.

3. *Game stage.* This third stage, organized play or team games, begins roughly at age seven and lasts through to puberty. The significance for the development of the self is that to play games, an individual must be able to take on multiple roles. Mead used the analogy of a baseball game. In order to play baseball, it is important to know not only what to do when you go up to bat but also what to expect from the other players in the game: what will the catcher, first base, umpire, and so on be doing in the game? Without knowledge of the entire game and these diverse roles, it is impossible to really participate. Similarly, boys and girls learn that gender roles are complexly related to one another. The role of "being a girl" hinges on some other who will be "acting the role of boy and who understands the overall 'game.'"

Needless to say, the actual processes of gender socialization at each stage of development are very subtle and complex. In recent years, some feminist sociologists have increasingly explored these complexities through the work of Philippe Bourdieu (1930–2002), who became one of the most eminent French sociologists in the later part of the twentieth century. Bourdieu argues for a complex vision of socialization, including gender socialization, in which learning is often unconscious and/or symbolic. Gender socialization extends into adulthood, and women, for example, may learn to function in an institutional context (a university or corporation) that is implicitly premised on masculine dominance. In being socialized into this institutional arrangement, the dominant power arrangements are culturally reproduced and the dominated (in this instance, women) come to accept as legitimate their own condition of domination (a process termed "symbolic violence" by Bourdieu).

So, for example, the established gender arrangements in a university—that women predominate as administrative

Gender Socialization and Time Pressures

Recent Canadian research into the time use patterns of Canadian adolescents provides a useful example of Bourdieu's perspective. Researchers examined the amount of time that boys and girls aged 12 to 19 spent doing school work (including homework), domestic work, personal care, and leisure activities. Interestingly, older girls spent significantly more time on domestic work on school days than boys. On Sundays, among both younger and older adolescents, girls had a larger total workload (one third larger) than boys, and continued to spend more time on domestic work. There was also a significant difference in the amount of free time for boys and girls. On schools days, boys aged 12 to 14 had 42 minutes more free time than girls, and older boys (aged 15 to 19) had 25 more minutes per day. On Sundays, younger boys had 87 minutes more free time and older boys 54 more minutes. Even though a portion of the gender difference was due to girls spending more time on "personal care" and on school homework, the results indicate that even as adolescents, girls learn to assume more of the domestic burden, to juggle diverse responsibilities, and to get by with less free time (Hibrecht, Zuzanek, & Mannell 2008; Marshall, 2007).

Following Bourdieu, girls learn the prevailing gendered "rules of the game"—that as women, they will assume more domestic responsibilities, they will have more time-pressured lives, and their male counterparts will have more free time. This "habitus" (an acquired pattern of thinking, acting, and viewing social reality) they construct as adolescents and carry into adulthood is premised on not only gender differences but also on gender inequalities.

---

assistants, that very few senior administrators are female, that female academics tend to be found in the social sciences, and so on—come to be experienced as simply natural—this is the way the world is. In this complex and ongoing process, men and women come to embody **habitus**—that is, they embrace a set of skills and a way of looking at the world that reflects (rather than questions or challenges) the hierarchical social structures they inhabit. Often we do what we are "supposed" to do, without needing to refer to explicit rules or even pondering alternatives. Through socialization, our identity is permeated by "a set of relatively permanent and largely unconscious ideas and dispositions about how society works" (Reimer, 2008: p. 38).

Focus Question

What have Mead, Bourdieu, and contemporary feminists provided that helps us understand gender socialization as a complex and subtle process?

Freud, the Development of Personality, and Civilizing the "Id"

Along with the development of the mind and the self comes the development of personality. Let's look at a theory that has profoundly influenced the Western world.

Physician Sigmund Freud (1856–1939) founded *psychoanalysis*, a technique for treating emotional problems through long-term, intensive exploration of the subconscious mind.

Freud proposed that personality consists of three elements. Every child is born with an **id**, Freud's term for inborn drives for self-gratification. The id of the newborn is evident in cries of hunger or pain. The pleasure-seeking id operates throughout life, demanding the immediate fulfillment of basic needs: attention, safety, food, sex, aggression, and so on.

The id's drive for immediate and complete satisfaction runs directly against the needs of other people. As a child comes up against norms and other constraints (usually represented by parents), he or she must adapt to survive. To adapt to constraints that block his or her desires, a second component of the personality emerges, which Freud called the **ego**. The ego is the balancing force between the id and the demands of society that suppress it.

The ego also serves to balance the id and the **superego**, the third component of the personality, more commonly called the conscience. The superego represents *culture within us*, the norms and values we internalize from our social groups. As the *moral* component of the personality, the superego gives us feelings of guilt or shame when we break social rules, or pride and self-satisfaction when we follow them.

Freud's theorizing continues to have a profound and far-reaching impact on Western thought about human and social development (Thurer, 2005). Freud (1930) went on to argue that civilization must, by necessity, repress our impulses. If we were freed from the repressions of society, life would become so chaotic that culture would be impossible. Freud's ideas were adopted by Talcott Parsons as he built his theory of socialization.

Freud's theories have been rejected by many analysts, including feminist theorists, who vehemently challenge a number of his central assertions. His suggestion that women have a deep-seated desire for a penis (a longing that, according to Freud, is only resolved by the birth of a child) and his

Smoking cigarettes provides a useful example of the power and complexity of the socialization process. There is no evidence that people have any inborn drive to inhale tobacco smoke. Nonetheless, we live on a planet where growing numbers of people engage in smoking while a growing body of scientific evidence documents that it may harm your health and shorten your life. The World Health Organization estimates that, globally, 1 billion deaths will be attributable to tobacco use during the twenty-first century, and 100 million people died as a result of this behaviour in the past century (Picard, 2008).

Enormous effort and expense have been put toward educating the public about these risks. Yet around the world, numerous young men and women (typically, under 19 years of age) become "smokers." In Canada in 2005, slightly more than one in five men (aged 15 and older) and one in six women smoked daily or occasionally. Among Canadian teens aged 15 to 19, slightly fewer than one in five were smokers. The highest rates persist among men and women aged 20 to 24; more than a quarter of these men (29 percent) and slightly less than a quarter of same-age females (23 percent) identified themselves as smokers in 2005 (Statistics Canada, 2006). Why?

To understand this behaviour, it is important to recognize the powerful societal and cultural pressures that create smoking as a socially desirable activity.

Smoking is a habit that, while biologically reinforced through physical addiction, must first be learned. As it is learned, specific meanings and even identities are associated with the activity (Hughes, 2003). Historically, smoking was a male-dominated behaviour—a sign of masculinity—and women who smoked were likely to be seen as lower-class or deviant. Only in the early twentieth century, as the tobacco industry dramatically expanded its efforts to promote the product, did women take up smoking.

Popular magazines played an important role at that point in socializing young women to smoke by translating smoking into a glamorous, "modern," and rebellious behaviour (Tinkler, 2001). Product placement in popular movies along with advertisements that portray woman celebrities and social leaders as smokers have a long history of legitimating smoking as "classy" and desirable behaviour (Sargent et al, 2007).

Today, smoking socialization persists worldwide. Researchers in Britain report that smoking imagery (not advertising) in films and youth style magazines is experienced as a positive by first-year university students. Simply seeing a lead actor in a film smoking a cigarette sends a powerful message. Smoking behaviour is seen as "risky, sociable, indulgent, and acceptable." Young people reported that smoking signalled adulthood and independence (MacFayden, Amos, Hastings, & Parkes, 2003).

Such implicit messages in movies are reinforced by direct cigarette advertisements that associate smoking with youthful, attractive, slender young men and women who are having fun. Indicative of the impact of such advertisements, recent research indicates that Joe Camel (a cartoon character used in Camel cigarette advertising) is as recognizable to U.S. five-year-olds as Mickey Mouse (www.kidshealth.org/teen/drugalcohol/tobacco/smoking.html2007).

Socialization into cigarette consumption intertwines with powerful gender socialization messages. Picking up on the fact that 30 percent of their customers are women, Camel cigarettes (R.J. Reynolds Tobacco) is marketing cigarettes in pink foil, with pink logos and in rose-bedecked boxes highly reminiscent of Chanel perfume boxes (Kobayashi, 2007). Gendered advertising ploys also draw on women's body-image concerns. Not surprisingly, female teens aspiring to live up to the media ideal of "thinness" for women often embrace the popular belief that smoking helps consumers lose weight and ignore food cravings. In this context, it is revealing that cigarette advertisements frequently employ "thin" models and even promote "thin" cigarettes specifically to women.

The ways that meaning is constructed around smoking vary considerably depending upon historical and cultural context. In contemporary China, a country of avid smokers where a third of the world's cigarettes are consumed, young people look up to teenage smokers as "cool" and fashionable. Further, the smoking of specifically American cigarettes, a very costly commodity in China, is an important mechanism for conveying to others that one is not only "hip," but also affluent (Cheng, 1999).

In India, a staggering 120 million people regularly smoke local cigarettes called "bidis," but smoking is taken up later in life. Further, the overwhelming majority are men; 37 percent of men and only 5 percent of women smoke. In this social context, smoking is "seen" primarily as a male activity. It is estimated that in India, smoking accounts for one in five deaths among men and one in twenty among women. Needless to say, increases in smoking rates coupled with a growing population promise a boom in smoking-related deaths (Picard, 2008: p. A15).

Smoking behaviour also provides an intriguing example of efforts to both alter socialization patterns and to **resocialize** (provide different socialization messages to) established smokers. Although this is a global concern, Canada has adopted one of the strictest anti-smoking positions in the world. In recent years, the numbers of public areas that are designated by law to be smoke-free has proliferated. Today, most universities, restaurants, movie theatres, and so on ban on-site smoking completely, and there is proposed legislation banning smoking in all personal cars when children are present. By 2006, only 12 percent of employed smokers worked where there were no smoking restrictions, down from 24 percent in 1998 (Statistics Canada, 2007). In addition, more than half (55 percent) of private households with children younger than 15 ban smoking in the home. These efforts have been coupled with graphic warnings on cigarette packages and extensive restrictions on cigarette advertising.

There is evidence that these resocialization efforts are having an impact. When smoking was banned in the workplace, 27 percent of smokers quit over the course of two years; when there was no ban on smoking, only 13 percent of smokers stopped. In private households that banned smoking, 42 percent of smokers either quit recently or maintained their "quit smoking" status. In homes with no bans, the figure was 15 percent. Even when smokers continue to smoke, they reduce their daily cigarette consumption when living in homes or working in environments that are smoke-free. Even in the face of powerful physical addiction, changes in the social environment (both private and public) produce significant changes in human behaviour. Between 2000 and 2006, the percentage of Canadians who smoked daily or occasionally dropped from 24 percent to 18 percent (Statistics Canada, 2007).

Focus Question

What social forces socialize young people to become cigarette smokers and how can they be resocialized?

Cigarette advertisers (along with other advertisers) have long recognized that appealing to gender roles and gender stereotypes may provide a powerful purchasing inducement. "Manly" cigarettes have been commonplace in the mass media. Today, there is a more concerted effort to construct a "feminine" tobacco product.

refusal to publicly acknowledge that many of his female patients were actually the victims of child sexual abuse have been criticized as evidence of his patriarchal biases. Nonetheless, Freud's ideas have contributed profoundly to an acknowledgement of the complexities of human social experience, including the "unconscious aspects" that were utilized in Bourdieu's work.

Goffman and the Presentation of the Self

No review of the theoretical influences of socialization is complete without mention of eminent Canadian sociologist Erving Goffman (1922–1982), whose work provided a provocative new approach to understanding the emergence and presentation of the self (Smith 2006; Scheff, 2006). Goffman developed **dramaturgical analysis** of human interactions; that is, he used the image of a drama on stage as a way to analyze everyday life. Through socialization, we not only learn "scripts" (gender scripts, employee scripts, and so on), we also learn to navigate a **backstage** (where we rehearse our performances) and a **frontstage** (where we perform our roles). Before a job interview, for example, you might practice how you will perform at home, even using your parents as an audience. Your actual performance on stage then occurs in the interview situation.

Goffman's emphasis on symbolic meanings—even in terms of how we dress, stand, and gesture—was crucial to fleshing out not only how we "play" our particular scripts but also how we learn specific ways to embody them. As discussed later in the chapter, Goffman's analysis of **total institutions** was important to exploring the limits on social control and resocialization.

What kinds of direct and indirect socialization did you experience when you first came to college or university and learned to "act" the role of a student?

IN SUM

Prominent social theorists have attempted to explain how we develop a sense of self, a mind, the capacity to reason, and a set of emotions. Through this ongoing work, we have developed an appreciation for the complex process of socialization that occurs in every culture and at every historical moment. Viewed from this theoretical perspective, our fundamental sense of self—what we desire, who we love, how we experience sadness—is rooted in our socialization experiences (Settersten & Owens, 2002).

SOCIALIZATION INTO GENDER

One of the key ways in which Canadian society channels behaviour is through gender socialization. By reinforcing and then expecting different attitudes and behaviours from us *because* we are male or female, the social group nudges boys and girls in separate directions in life. This foundation of contrasting attitudes and behaviours is so thorough that, as adults, most of us simply take gendered behaviour for granted. Since gender socialization is a universal experience, let's briefly consider the gender messages we receive from family and the mass media.

Gender Messages in the Family

Our parents are usually the first significant others in our lives and typically first teach us our part in the gender division of society. Often they do so implicitly, perhaps by painting a girl's room pink rather than blue or by encouraging her to wear frilly dresses rather than pants. Gender messages from parents may also be explicit. For example, in many cultures, boys are specifically allowed more freedom and independence than girls and at an earlier age—"because they are boys." Most significantly, they are often expressly discouraged from "acting like girls" (Blakemore & Craig, 2008; Nelson, 2006).

As we mature, gender lessons from parents become more complex and have greater lifelong implications. For example, research suggests that mothers and fathers often hold gender-stereotypic views about their sons' and daughters' abilities—their prevailing assumption is that boys are better than girls at science and computers. Not surprisingly, their interactions with their children unwittingly reflect and reinforce these gendered views (Tenenbaum & Leaper, 2003).

In this context, parents, consciously and unconsciously, set many young men and women on a narrow gendered path. Whether young people accept or reject this path, they cannot help but struggle with its subtle and not so subtle pressures. By the time a child enters the formal education system, the family (along with the media, toys, sports, and so on) have firmly established gender roles—boys and girls both understand the behaviour and attitudes considered

The family is one of the primary ways that we learn gender. Shown here is a woman of the Chin tribe in Myanmar as she farms her field. What gender messages do you think her daughter is learning?

appropriate for each sex and, importantly, know where they personally are situated in this gender schema.

However, the process of parental gender socialization is often not straightforward and predictable. Understandably, experiences are varied and contradictory. For example, parents themselves are far from uniform; after all, there are numerous parents who are lesbians, gays, and/or feminists (Arnup, 2005). When parents explicitly reject traditional gender roles and when their own lives are in contradiction to those roles, what is the impact on daughters and sons? Initial research indicates that feminist mothers and fathers are more likely to treat their sons and daughters similarly and feminist fathers are more involved with their children's upbringing than traditional ones.

The complex relationship between parenting and gender roles is underscored in research with lesbian parents. Lesbian parents tend to be more liberal with regard to children's gendered behaviours and are more likely to share an egalitarian spousal relationship (care work and paid work are divided more equally). However, preliminary research suggests that it is not parents' stated beliefs and values or the fact of having lesbian parents that impact gender development. Rather, it is the way parents act out their roles as parents—whether they share parenting and paid labour responsibilities—that most powerfully influences children's acceptance or rejection of gender stereotypic beliefs (Fulcher, Sutfin, & Patterson, 2008). In other words, if feminist and/or lesbian parents actually live an egalitarian lifestyle, this appears to most directly impact their children's gender beliefs and attitudes (Blakemore & Hill, 2008).

Gender Messages in the Mass Media

Parents, no matter how much they may try to insulate their children from the surrounding social context, will find that the social environment mediates any messages they instill in their children (Sutfin, Fulcher, Bowles, & Patterson, 2008). The **mass media**—forms of communication directed to large audiences—are a particularly prominent element in contemporary gender socialization and play a pivotal role in both creating and reinforcing cultural expectations of gender. Of the many ways they do this, we will more closely examine television and video games.

TELEVISION Fifty years ago, televisions entered Canadian homes and in a relatively short time transformed our private and public lives. Today, nearly 30 percent of Canadian adults watch television 15 or more hours a week, and it plays an important role in the early socialization of most North Americans (Statistics Canada, 2008).

A recent U.S. study found that half of all infants, toddlers, and preschoolers live in homes with three or more televisions. A 2003 study of media habits of U.S. children reported that almost 70 percent of all children *under two years of* age spend two hours a day watching television shows or videos. These very young children are spending the equiv-

alent of about a month a year consuming television (Moscovitch, 2007).

As children continue to mature, television remains a continuous and constant source of social information. A recent study of time use among Ontario adolescents found that boys aged 12 to 14 spend approximately 2½ hours on Sundays and 1 1/3 hours on school days watching television (and videos), while girls of the same age watch an average of slightly less than 11/4 hours each day (Hillbrecht, Zuzanek, & Mannell 2008: pp. 349–350). Various studies, including international research, indicate that boys watch more television than girls.

What are we learning from all these hours of "entertainment"? Of particular concern to feminists is the tendency of television programming to reinforce traditional gender stereotypes and social patterns in which women play subordinate or supportive roles. Things have changed from the early days of I Love Lucy and Bewitched, where women were restricted to family roles. And today, in television series, women are often portrayed leading independent lives, pursuing successful careers and working side-by-side with male colleagues. Nonetheless, gendered themes have not been eradicated. Much popular prime time television still tends to prioritize male characters and establish men as "leaders" (in CSI and its offshoots, for example). Similarly, "serious" television (concerning politics and recent events) typically involves a male host, and evening news programs have hardly been enthusiastic in their employment of female news anchors.

Gendered messages on television are not lost on children. In a revealing study, children in Grades 1 and 2 were exposed to one of three videotaped television commercials. In one instance, only boys were portrayed playing with two toys; in another, only girls were portrayed playing with the toys. In the control condition, the children were exposed to non-toy commercials. When then asked to sort six toys (including the toys in the commercials) into one of three categories—for boys, for girls, or for both—children exposed to "all boy" commercials were more likely to report that the toys were for boys, and children exposed to "all girl" commercials were more likely to report that the toys were for both girls and boys (Pike & Jennings, 2005). Children absorb what they see, even in television commercials, accept its accuracy, and then use that information in real life (Kilbourne, 2004).

Television directed toward adults as consumers perpetuates this overall pattern of gender inequity. A recent survey of prime-time commercials on major American networks found that in the 1990s, just as in the 1980s, women were under-represented as primary characters. Further, the roles men and women played in commercials followed a traditional gender script—men were the consumers in automobile, electronics/appliance, and financial commercials, while women were consumers in health and beauty products. Predictably, the women in these commercials were typically younger than their male counterparts and were cast in supportive roles vis-à-vis the male characters (Baker, 2005).

Implied here is one of the key gendered messages in the media. Only certain types of women are "visible" in television—young, slender, and "physically attractive." Older, heavier, and/or less attractive women are typically obliterated. Recent research reveals that 13 percent of male characters on television are above average weight compared with only 7 percent of female characters (Fouts & Vaughan 2002: p. 440). When older and heavier women do appear, it is typically in comedies, and in this context, stereotypes about their age and weight are an important source of humour. As a result, women are not likely to see themselves reflected in the media reality of *Sex in the City* and *Friends*. The television female ideal is far from average—the 36-24-36-inch figure translates into a size 4 hip measurement, size 2 waist, and size 10 bust.

A recent study of college students found that the greater their exposure to ideal-body images on television, the more likely the approval from males and even more from females for women's use of breast augmentation surgery and lipoplasty to improve their bodies (Harrison, 2003). It appears that many women are digesting the media message that they are not "good enough" and that only through the consumption of goods and services can they transform their unsatisfactory bodies into acceptable products. Further, the embedded media message is that women's primary value is in relation to men: youthful, attractive (slender) women have a place in the idealized media reality, while older, heavier, and/or unattractive (to men) women are rendered invisible (Cruikshank, 2003).

It is not only women that have a media-generated gender script to live up to. While women may be confronted by media representations of unrealistic beauty and youthfulness standards, men have long faced demands to be strong, emotionally controlled, successful, and fiercely competent. From *Gunsmoke* to *Mission: Impossible* to *Survivor*, "real" men (and increasingly women) have confronted a strict, even rigid, gender script on television. As extensively discussed in the sociology of gender, to the degree that men embrace this model of masculinity and fail, for example, to emotionally express themselves, particularly with intimate partners, their successful gender performance may place them at risk for depression, substance abuse, violence, and non–help-seeking behaviours. However, there is some evidence that male gender stereotypes are changing, and this is reflected in new television images of masculinity. Research into popular situation comedies on television found that male characters are expressing themselves emotionally and more frequently than females. Further, when men disclosed their feelings to other men or women, the average audience response was somewhat favourable (Good, Porter, & Dillon, 2002). Male characters on sitcoms such as *Will and Grace*, *Friends*, and *Frasier* suggest a new model of masculinity—one that supports the new "consumer" image of males—the heterosexual males appearing on television whose lifestyle includes excessive grooming and interest in fashion (for example, the male protagonists on *Nip and Tuck*). However, this "new" model of masculinity may offer little in the way of liberation and may be cynically seen as television characters extending the traditional male gender role in order to benefit the dominant consumer culture (Conseur, Hathcote, & Kim, 2008).

VIDEO GAMES AND GENDER MESSAGES While television viewing remains a ubiquitous experience and an important contributor to gender socialization, it is also clear that our media consumption habits are changing. In 1998, the average daily television consumption was almost a whole hour *more* per day than in 2005; we are watching less television or we are combining this activity with other media such as listening to MP3 players and talking on the internet. Almost all families now own DVDs, more and more children have their own television sets, and television viewing is less commonly a family group activity and more often a solitary pastime. Recent U.S. research found that a quarter of toddlers under age two had a television set in their bedroom. The majority of Canadian homes have computers and internet access, and half of 16-year-old Canadian students have their own internet-connected computer (Vanier Institute of the Family, 2007). Prominent in these new patterns of media consumption is the popularization of video games.

Video games are clearly a booming segment of the media industry. In 2004, sales in the United States reached $10 billion (Miller & Summers, 2007: p. 733). In 2006, Canadians spent $933 million on video gaming (games and equipment), a 22 percent increase from 2005. Research indicates that 60 percent of Canadian boys in Grades 3 to 6 play video/computer games almost daily, often for up to two hours. The majority of children, even children aged 8 and 9, indicated that their parents were not involved in supervising what games they could play and how long they could play (Vanier Institute of the Family, 2007). U.S. research in 2005 indicated that 83 percent of 8- to 18-year-olds have at least one game console in their homes and 92 percent of boys and 80 percent of girls play video games. The consumption of video games is not just the domain of children and teens—more than two thirds of gamers are over age 18 and almost a third of women over 18 play video games (Ogletree & Drake, 2007: p. 537; Burgess, Stermer, & Burgess, 2007: pp. 419–20). In these many hours of activity, extending through childhood and into adulthood, what kinds of messages about gender are being communicated?

Ironically, evidence suggests that video games have taken up where television left off in the perpetuation of sexist depictions of male and female roles—portrayals in which women are not only different to men but inferior to them. Content analyses of video games, video game covers, and video game magazines suggest that female characters are consistently less common than male characters, that their roles are often supplemental to male roles, and that they are

Young people who spend a lot of time playing video games are subjected to many disturbing and skewed gender messages from the games' characters.

much more likely to be portrayed in terms of an exaggerated and objectified sexiness. Males are more likely to be heroes or main characters and use "more weapons," "have more abilities," and are "more muscular and powerful" (Miller & Summers, 2007). For example, on game covers, male characters are represented almost four times more frequently than female characters, and males have significantly more game relevant action (Burgess, Stermer, & Burgess, 2007). Consistent with traditional gender roles, female characters are much more likely than their male counterparts (60 percent to 1 percent) to be "sexualized." For example, 39 percent of female characters and only 8 percent of males are presented as scantily clad (Dill & Thill, 2007). They are not only wearing more revealing clothing, they are more stereotypically attractive and typically "curvaceously slim."

Concerns about the impact of video games are myriad. A number of analysts suggest video games may be a key source of increased youth aggression and violence in society (Sternheimer, 2007). Relatively little public attention has been paid to the more subtle impact on gender stereotypes—an impact that may be at least as significant. Researchers suggest that video games may provide a media that legitimates male dominance and aggression and reaffirms traditional gender arrangements in which women are not only subordinate to men, but primarily function as decorative/sexual objects.

Boys and men are much more likely than females to routinely play video games, and young women more frequently complain that their "significant other" plays video games too much and that it interferes with "couple time" (Ogletree & Drake, 2007). Further, hopes that the popularization of powerful female characters in video games, such as Lara Croft, may minimize the negative gender impact are problematic. Despite an increased number of female characters in video games, the prevailing tendency is to provide an abundance

of "hypermuscular" men and "hypersexualized" women. Virtual women serve as "eye candy" for men—both as video game characters and video game players they are objects for male consumption. Importantly, women who play video games will likely be confronted with female characters who are disproportionately thin, embody exaggerated female characteristics, and represent stereotypic ideals of beauty and femininity (Jansz & Martis, 2007). In a societal context in which women confront extreme and unhealthy body images in much of the media, video games function as one more site of oppression.

Focus Question
What gender messages would a five-year-old boy and five-year-old girl learn from watching the most popular current television show and from playing the leading video game?

THE CONTRADICTIONS OF SOCIALIZATION: MALES IN CRISIS

Many analysts now argue that the traditional male role in many Western countries is unclear and "in crisis." Specifically, many boys are often brought up to fit into a rather rigid and strict gender role—one that emphasizes strength, aggression, autonomy, competitiveness, success, and emotional control. To the degree to which this is true (it is less the case in more "feminine" countries. such as Spain and Italy), boys confront a very demanding and unforgiving gender agenda (Calvo-Salguero, Garcia-Martinez, &Monteoliva, 2008). For example, a recent report from the Canadian Vanier Institute of the Family suggests that traditional male socialization creates many boys and young men who are sad, lost, confused, and/or angry (Mathews, 2003; Baxter, 2003). After all, boys are much more likely to be charged with juvenile crime, less

Perhaps one thing we typically confront as a biological entity is our body. Our facial characteristics, eye colour, height, and so on all seem to be fixed biological realities. However, as has become increasingly apparent in recent years, societal beliefs and values about the ideal shape have resulted in an amazing variety of products and services that change our bodies. The market for cosmetic surgery, non-surgical procedures, and cosmetics has become a billion-dollar international industry. Purchases of these products and interventions have become an important signifier of social class.

Through most of human history, for the overwhelming majority of human beings, simply having access to enough nutritious food was a daily and lifelong struggle. Obesity or being overweight was a problem for only a miniscule portion of the human population. Beginning primarily in the second half of the twentieth century, the weight of our bodies and the distribution of our fat became increasingly problematized, especially for women. As discussed in more detail below, parents, peers, and the media were soon consistently perpetuating the socialization message that being overweight was bad, especially for girls and women.

The result has now been several generations of women, of whom many—if not most—are preoccupied with monitoring and managing their weight. Their strategies may be socially legitimate, such as purchasing diet pills, participating in a gym, joining a weight loss organization, or "being on a diet"; but a significant minority engage in socially deviant behaviour such as anorexia and bulimia. While "Ana" and "Mia" may be commonplace in youth cultures such as high schools, they are understood by the general society to be activities that jeopardize physical well-being and even life.

In Canada, almost 50 percent of girls aged 12 to 18 report that they are unhappy with their weight. A recent Ontario study reported that among young adolescents aged 10 to 14, almost a third (29.3 percent) are currently trying to lose weight. Today, about one in five Canadian female teenagers is on a diet and as many as two thirds have attempted to lose weight at some point in their lives. In many instances, teenage girls seeking weight loss may not be engaging in eating disorders, but their eating may be considered "disordered" since it involves fasting, skipping meals, excessive exercise, or extreme dieting (Canadian Paediatric Society, 2004; McVey, Tweed, & Blackmore, 2004).

Alarmingly, there is every indication that this is increasingly a global phenomenon that is intensifying. Recent U.S. research reported that between 1995 and 2005, the numbers of teenage boys and girls engaged in weight control activities increased every year. The end result was 54 percent of teen girls dieting and 24 percent of teen boys (CBC News, 2007). Research in mainland China and Hong Kong also indicates that a thin body is central to current female appearance ideals (Jackson & Chen, 2008). Further, multi-ethnic and lifespan research in the U.S. suggests that ethnic and age differences among women produce only small differences in body dissatisfaction. Young and middle aged, Asian American, and Black American women in the U.S. and China are surprisingly likely to indicate dislike for some aspect of their bodies, especially their weight (Frederick, Forbes, Grigorian, & Jarcho, 2007; Forbes & Frederick, 2008; Bessenoff & De Priore, 2007).

Although dissatisfaction with one's body is a complex issue and may include psychoanalytic and psychological dimensions, the historical shifts and documented global dimensions suggest a significant role for cultural factors. A growing body of research suggests that contemporary Western mass media—especially appearance-related advertisements in magazines, on television, and elsewhere—play a key role in generating body dissatisfaction. Several recent studies report that when female U.S. undergraduates were exposed to appearance-related magazine advertisements (ads featuring a thin woman), their body dissatisfaction scores worsened and/or their weight-related appearance anxiety intensified. Women who were not exposed to such advertisements evidenced no change (Hamilton, Mintz, & Kashubeck-West, 2007; Harper & Tiggemann, 2008). Other research indicates that when teenage girls frequently read magazine articles about dieting and weight loss, they become at increased risk of eating disorders; that is, they are more likely to lose weight by fasting or smoking cigarettes (CBC, 2007).

The media does not act alone as a socializing agent. Researchers have also found that girls, much more than boys, are vulnerable to pressure from their mothers to attain a thin ideal. Interestingly, the experience of this maternal pressure is more likely to result in girls being dissatisfied with their bodies than actually engaging in weight control behaviours. Boys seem to be less susceptible to pressures from mothers and from the media. It seems likely that while dissatisfaction with one's body crosses gender lines, it is still a gendered phenomenon. Boys experience pressures to be muscular and fit, while women confront demands for extreme thinness (Peterson, Paulson, & Williams, 2007).

This exploration of the impact of socialization on our bodies and how we treat them is important in a variety of ways. First, it underscores once again that biology is subject to social pressures. Second, it is clear that history has an important place in understanding socialization. In a specific historical context, body weight became socially relevant for the majority of people. Third,

likely to graduate from high school, less likely to be university students, and four times as likely to commit suicide (Frenette & Zeman, 2007). Researchers argue that standard masculine socialization—as conveyed by the media, sports, religion, peers, and teachers—places boys at a disadvantage in education, employment, and social life in general (McCloskey, 2003; Mathews, 2003; Baxter, 2003; Levitt, Swanger & Butler, 2008).

The popular culture's construction of young masculinity contributes its share to the problem. Emulating the high-risk behaviour of male role-model celebrities—drugs, alcohol abuse, fast cars, guns, smoking—may put young men at increased risk for personal injury, addiction, and other health problems (Nelson & Robinson, 2006). Similarly, embracing the masculine norm that boys/men should stand on their own and not seek assistance means that many men do not seek help from physical and mental health agencies even when they are in need (Addis & Hahalik, 2003). In short, following the lead of prominent gender role models may have negative and destructive consequences. These gendered difficulties are compounded if a young man is a Native Canadian, a visible minority, gay, disabled, a recent immigrant, poor or working-class, and so on (Roper & Halloran, 2007).

Focus Question

What happens to the gender socialization of a star high-school football quarterback who becomes a quadriplegic as a result of a car accident?

IN SUM

Biological sex is one of the most important "sorting" principles in Canadian society. We learn to divide the world into male and female and to locate ourselves within this gendered reality. Although we may differ in our specific notions of masculinity and femininity and may select different gender orientations—from Miley Cyrus or Britney Spears to John Mayer or Justin Timberlake—we are socialized to organize our lives around notions of gender.

SOCIALIZATION INTO GROUPS

Sociologists often make a direct connection between social groups and the socialization process. In most instances, socialization teaches us to fit into **social groups**; that is, people who regularly and consciously interact with one another over an extended period of time.

Groups in Society

Some social groups are involuntary, such as the family or gender group into which we are born, and some are voluntary, including the clubs and sports teams we join. The family is a key example of what Charles Horton Cooley termed a **primary group**—a group characterized by intimate face-to-face association and cooperation. In these kinds of groups, such as close friends, we develop a sense of belonging and feelings of self-esteem. However, much of our life is spent in **secondary groups**—ones that are larger, more anonymous and temporary, and more formal and impersonal, such as a workplace or university class.

Sometimes groups are organized into **in-groups** (groups we feel loyal to) and **out-groups** (groups we feel antagonistic toward). These group allegiances may play an important role in group relations. In-groups are somewhat similar to **cliques**—close-knit clusters of individuals or factions within groups that tend to set themselves off from the rest of the group.

In-groups built around ethnic/racial distinctions may be important in encouraging **ethnocentrism**—the belief that our group is superior to another. In certain historical and social situations, in-group/out-group conflicts may turn into **xenophobia**—a fear of strangers. For example, if we encounter an economic recession and employment is difficult to find, in-group perspectives will encourage attacks on immigrants and pressures to keep immigrants out.

Groups may also take the form of **reference groups**—groups we use as standards to evaluate ourselves. For example, if you want to become a politician, you might start dressing like Stephen Harper, reading *The Economist,* and watching parliamentary debates. Reference groups may then serve as a form of social control—you might use them to measure and improve your own performance.

Groups are not necessarily positive social forces. Sometimes, our groups can encourage us to conform to behaviours we are not personally comfortable with. Famous experiments by Stanley Milgram (1963, 1965) and Solomon Asch (1952) reveal the tremendous influence of *groupthink*. Groups may cultivate tunnel vision about social reality and members may become blind to the nature and consequences of their actions. Using Goffman's approach, a group may come to define a situation and by doing so create social

SOON WE'LL GIVE UP DOLLS AND HOPSCOTCH---BUT THEY'LL BE INTO FOOTBALL FOREVER.

The gender roles we learn during childhood become part of our basic orientations to life. Although we refine these roles as we grow older, they remain built around the framework established during childhood.

reality. Consider, for example, some contemporary reactions to the "terrorist threat": certain groups defined anyone who was "different" (a Sikh wearing a turban) as a potential threat and acted upon this reality by assaulting or imprisoning innocent Canadian citizens. These acts reflect sociologist W.I. Thomas's classic theorem (Thomas Theorem), "If people define situations as real, they are real in their consequences." Even in the absence of any threat, a volatile and violent social reality is constructed.

Groups may coalesce to provide a sense of *community*. Such groups are ones we feel we belong to and identify with. In recent years, the internet has provided an entirely new medium for the creation and maintenance of community. Electronic communities (e-communities) allow people worldwide to connect, and in some instances, their interaction online leads to a sense of belonging together. The impact of these new communities on society provides a rich source for social research.

Groups as Agents of Socialization

Socialization is a pervasive and lifelong series of processes. Every time we enter a new social environment—get a new job, go to a new school, move to a new neighbourhood, take retirement, are diagnosed as cancer patients, become a mother or father—we go through a socialization process. Directly or indirectly, formally or informally, we learn what to say, what to do, who has power and who doesn't, what to wear, and where and when to talk, along with all the other complex information that is needed to function in the new social context. The social institutions, organizations, groups, and individual people who socialize us are called **agents of socialization**, and through their intervention, our self-concept, emotions, attitudes, and behaviours may be profoundly changed. Of the numerous agents of socialization active in contemporary Canadian society, we will briefly examine the following groups and institutions: family, religion, day care, school, peers, sports, and the workplace.

The Family

Around the world, the first group to have a major impact on almost all humans is the family. Unlike some animals, we cannot survive by ourselves, and as babies we are utterly dependent on our caregivers, typically our family. Our experiences in the family are so intense that, as Freud and others have pointed out, they have a lifelong impact on us (Putney & Bengston, 2002). They lay down our basic sense of self, establishing our initial motivations, values, and beliefs. The family gives us ideas about who we are and what we deserve out of life. In the family, we begin to think of ourselves as strong or weak, smart or dumb, good-looking or ugly, or somewhere in between.

As Goffman puts it, the family is a "socialization depot" (1977, p. 314). This is where our journey begins and where we pick up most of our baggage. Around the globe and in contemporary Canadian society, we generally assume that a person's family is key to the development of "productive and responsible" adults (Heath, 2004). For example, supportive and responsive parenting is more likely to produce adolescents who are willing to speak up or take action in the interest of fairness and justice and, conversely, harsh and restrictive parenting tends to result in adolescents who are hesitant in situations demanding moral courage (Bronstein, Fox, Kamon, & Knolls, 2007). While our families are only part of the picture, as a culture, we recognize that they are a crucial early socializing agent. Conversely, we recognize that "dysfunctional" families may contribute to social problems.

Structural functionalist Talcott Parsons identified socialization in the family unit as a key social process in ensuring that children fit neatly into the social order. However, as Parsons would no doubt acknowledge, real family life is much messier and more diverse than implied by the structural-functional model. Parson's ideal-typical family—with a loving dad who "earned" the bacon and a dutiful mother who cooked it, and a flock of happy, obedient children—was more a creation of 1950s television than a reflection of actual life. And, in subsequent generations, family life has moved further away from this Parsonian model—most mothers, even of young children, are now working for pay outside the home, children are more likely to grow up in formal or informal day care, more families are divided by divorce, and peer groups along with e-communities appear to be increasingly important in young people's lives. Discussing family socialization today means addressing a much more complex and diverse process—one that acknowledges these major historical changes and structural shifts.

How are Canadian families changing and what do these changes mean in terms of childhood socialization?

Religion: A Declining Influence?

Some social commentators suggest that Canada is increasingly becoming a secularized society. In the past several decades, religious attendance has declined. Nearly half of Canadians (43 percent) in 2004 reported that they had no religious affiliation and/or hadn't attended religious services in the previous 12 months (Clark & Schellenberg, 2006).

Based on these trends, it seems reasonable to argue that the impact of formal religion on the socialization of Canadians has diminished over the past several decades. However, it must also be pointed out that religious activities continue to play a significant role in the lives of many Canadians. Despite increasing time pressures, almost a third of Canadians attend religious services at least monthly. Further, more than half (53 percent) indicated they engage in religious activities (prayer, meditation, worship, and/or reading sacred texts) on their own at least monthly. Reflecting these patterns, 44 percent of Canadians in 2004 "placed a high degree of importance on religion in their life." The aging Canadian population, along with the continuing inflow of immigrants (who tend to have a higher degree of religiosity than native-born Canadians), will likely mean that religion will remain prominent on the social landscape (Clark & Schellenberg, 2006).

As long as religion remains a significant social institution and religious beliefs and values are seen to be reflected in major social issues, religion will be an important ingredient in the socialization of many Canadian children. Organized religions and specific religious beliefs continue to be central to personal positions on gay rights, capital punishment, gay marriage, abortion, and the status of women. Religion has been at the centre of a variety of recent public debates, including the rights of girls to wear religious head coverings while attending Quebec schools and the rights of non-Catholic religious schools to receive state funding. Whether children are attending after-school religious programs, attend private religious schools, or are simply sharing religious discussions with adults, they are engaged in a process of religious socialization that may help establish their most fundamental beliefs and values. In 2001, over a third of Canadian children (under 12 years of age) attended religious services at least once a month. More than half of Canadian children attended at least occasionally. Canada and its influential neighbour, the United States, are far from secular at this point in history and religion must be understood as an important contributor to childhood socialization (Ecklund, 2008; Wilcox, 2006).

Day Care: The New Normal?

According a recent government report on child care in Canada, in 2002/2003, 54 percent of Canadian children (aged six months to five years) were in some form of non-parental child care, a marked increase from the 42 percent of children in child care in 1994/95. Certain types of families had particularly high rates of child-care usage—64 percent of children in single-parent households and 71 percent of children in dual-income households received child care (Bushnik, 2006: p. 10 in 2002/2003). The growing participation in child care reflects the dramatic increase in the number of employed mothers. In 2004, 67 percent of mothers of children under age six were employed—a sharp increase from the 37 percent of mothers of young children who held paid employment in 1976 (Statistics Canada, 2006: p. 105). Not only have the numbers of children in child care increased, the format of that care has shifted. There has been a decline in the use of care provided by a non-relative and an increase in the use of both care by a relative and day-care centres. Particularly when children's parents were born outside Canada, they are more likely to be cared for inside the home by a relative. In contrast, in Quebec (where childcare is heavily subsidized by the province) and in lower-income households, there has been a shift to a greater use of day-care centres. Even outside day-care centres, care providers are much more likely to be licensed and trained today than in the past.

Taken together, these new statistics reveal intriguing shifts in childhood socialization. More and more children are spending some portion of their childhood in the care of others. However, the nature of that care may be dramatically different. On one hand, the children of immigrants may be cared for in the home by their grandmother, while children of lower-income families may be in a day-care centre staffed by a diversity of licensed individuals. Regardless of the quality of the experience, it is likely that these socialization experiences will be profoundly different.

Given this dramatic shift in child-rearing patterns, it is not surprising that day care remains a contentious issue. Some condemn the trend to day care as a reflection of our growing materialism and a loss of family values (Shaw, 2003). Others counter that parents have little choice but to take paid work and that day care in fact benefits many children. But while day care may be a necessity, what effects does it have on our children?

Recent examinations of the impact of non-parental child care on children continue to point to the same conclusion: it depends. It depends on the child (and his or her temperament), on the parents (and their strengths or weaknesses as parents), and on the quality of the child-care arrangements themselves. Some children who are coming from overburdened, deprived, or abusive backgrounds may benefit enormously from a safe, well-staffed day-care centre (Wrigley & Dreby, 2006). Similarly, children who attend a day-care centre that allows them to explore their specific cultural background (for example, Aboriginal day-care centres) may experience important growth in self-esteem. Furthermore, if parents provide high-quality parenting in the hours that they do spend with their children, any problems may be minimized.

Generally, if child care is well-funded and facilitated by qualified and dedicated staff, it is more likely to have a positive impact on the child and also on the parents (Gagne, 2003; Canadian Council on Learning, 2006; University of Waterloo, 2006, & Albanese, 2006). There is little evidence to suggest that the shift to non-parental child care has profoundly altered or jeopardized the process of child socialization. The strongest evidence, perhaps, is the fact that the children of prior generations who personally experienced non-parental child care are now placing their children in day-care centres and other child-care arrangements.

Child-care arrangements are embedded in history. This is evidenced, for example, by the introduction of the $7-a-day day-care policy in Quebec that resulted in a significant increase in the numbers of children cared for at licensed day-care centres. Today, corporations play an increasing role in the global provision of child care—so-called "big box" day care. Major corporations are emerging that seek to provide standardized day-care services in a variety of Western countries. For example, Australian corporation Groves has created a $2.2-billion "kiddie care kingdom," operating 2400 ABC Learning Centres on three continents. This type of development may spell significant changes in the typical day-care experience for children (Cribb & Brazao, 2007). In the continued absence of a national government-funded child-care program for Canadian children, some analysts fear the expansion of a "for-profit" corporate-based approach may reduce the quality of day-care experiences.

Focus Question

Viewed from the perspective of a four-year-old, what might be the costs and benefits of being placed in a day-care centre?

The School: More Years of Socialization

One of the most important sites of socialization is school. Not only do we learn to "do student," but we acquire the specific knowledge and skills needed to function in the social order (Prus, 2007). If asked how schools socialize students, you might stress the formal knowledge and skills they transmit, such as reading, writing, and arithmetic. From a structural-functionalist perspective, the **manifest functions**, or intended purpose, of formal education, transmitting such skills is certainly part of socialization. Our schools' **latent functions**, the unintended or hidden consequences that help the social system, are also significant. Let's look at this less visible aspect of education.

Sociologists have identified a *hidden curriculum* in our schools. This term refers to the latent function of education—namely, the inculcation of values that, though not explicitly taught, form an inherent part of a school's "message." One of the unspoken but prominent tasks of

schools is to produce graduates that are "polite, well-dressed and on time" (Raby, 2007). In addition, there are indirect lessons in the stories and examples used to teach math, English grammar, or Canadian history—messages that may bring with them lessons in gender or racial inequality and help to create, for example, a "chilly climate" for girls and Native Canadians (Nelson, 2007; Restoule, 2005).

If women and Native Canadians are essentially absent from history texts, an important message is conveyed. These indirect educational messages may then be reinforced as female students find, for example, that they receive less mentoring than their male colleagues at the undergraduate, graduate, and post-doctoral levels of education (Nolan, Buckner, Marzabai, & Kuck, 2008).

Conversely, some groups will find that the educational process helps to secure their position of power and privilege. Elite private schools are typically structured to provide the personal friendships, manners, and social values that are key to establishing the upper-class credentials of students and providing access to more prestigious post-secondary institutions (Maxwell & Maxwell, 1971; Gabler & Kaufman, 2006).

For members of subordinate social groups (out-groups), educational qualifications have been important in challenging social hierarchies. Aboriginals in Saskatchewan have used their growing post-secondary educational attainments to create a new, more positive public identity—a new intellectual class—that is engaging in political advocacy for their communities (Kumar, 2007).

The process of educational socialization in contemporary Canadian universities and community colleges also indirectly communicates a strong corporate agenda. Today, the daily experiences of most post-secondary students are embedded in a corporate landscape where everything from buildings and classrooms to elevators and stadiums hold plaques thanking corporate sponsors and campuses are inundated with brand-name product placement (Turk, 2000). In short, as we participate in education, we not only learn facts and figures, we assimilate important messages about acceptable behaviour, gender arrangements, social status, and corporate branding.

The impact of education on socialization complexly intersects with the other socializing influences. A recent report based on Canada's National Longitudinal Survey of Children and Youth, which tracked 20 000 children from birth to adulthood from 1994 to 2006, reported that our primary group—notably, our parents—are an important ingredient in determining school success (Statistics Canada and Human Resource Development Canada, 2005). Researchers report that "children perform better in school when parents monitor their behaviour, are responsive to their needs, and encourage independence" (Sokoloff, 2004: p. A8). As children are assigned increasingly large amounts of homework throughout grade school and high school, the role of parents in providing assistance and/or securing tutoring is clearly very significant in influencing children's educational outcomes.

Similarly, family and schooling intersect for university students. Research indicates that coming from a family where parents or older siblings have already attended university allows for greater **anticipatory socialization** (learning to play a role before we enter it) of university life. First-generation students may be at a disadvantage, since they report that they have to work harder to manage the university experience, to learn about the new university student role, and to navigate into a career (Shields, 2002; Reimer & Mueller, 2007).

Peer Groups: Bullying and Popularity

Almost every social behaviour, from success at school to drug use and reading pornography, has been associated with the influence of **peer groups**. Considerable research has focused on the ways in which peers reinforce gender norms. It is thanks to the social pressures mobilized by peers in "teenage tribes," for example, that certain girls are labelled "sluts" and become the object of derision and avoidance (White, 2002). Often, appearance—socially constructed by clothing as well as biological factors such as weight, height, and figure—is used by peer groups to establish social hierarchies among girls (Pomerantz, 2006).

A study of female adolescents in southern Alberta found that, just as Goffman predicted, appearance played a powerful role among high school girls—ranging from the elite to the wannabes to those "in the middle" and ending with those on the fringe. While not all girls subscribe to the importance of physical appearance or accept the rank order established by peer groups, they are aware it exists (Matthews, 2005). Through this pattern, peers may play an important role in contributing to eating disorders among young women.

Peer groups can also form around and support "deviant" sets of values. The trend toward increasing female youth violence and "girl gangs" may be seen as one example of such group influence. There is evidence suggesting that girls are now more likely to engage in violent attacks on other girls and that this behaviour is reinforced by peer group values. However, it is also important to keep in mind that minority racial status, poverty, inner-city residence, and residence on a rural reserve are all related to the likelihood that a girl will be charged with a criminal offence, engage in violence, or be the victim of violence (A. Duffy, 1996; Hussain, 2006; Jiwani, 2006).

The role of peers in bullying must be balanced by recognizing their role in providing the social support that allows for individual survival and even the courage to challenge societal constraints (Daniels & Leaper, 2006). Among Aboriginal girls engaged in prostitution—usually victims of sexual abuse, racism, family breakdown, or economic marginalization—peers provide the sense of community and self-worth that allows for not only survival but the possibility of personal transcendence (Downe, 2006). A recent study of Alberta homeless youth (12 to 17 years of age) underscores that for this particular population, peers may be an especially invaluable resource. Homeless boys and girls relied heavily on their peers as a source of community and spent most of their days "hanging out" with friends. As the researchers note, "they often described friends as family." More than the adult homeless, these young people appeared to rely on the support and companionship of their peers (Miller, Donahue, Este, & Hofer, 2004).

Sports: Hidden Lessons

Sports participation has long been considered a powerful socializing process. Sports teach not only physical skills but also values and self-esteem (Daniels & Leaper, 2006). About half (49.5 percent) of Canadian children aged 5 to 14 regularly took part in some organized sport activity in 2005—55 percent of boys and 44 percent of girls. Soccer was most popular, followed by ice hockey, swimming, and baseball (Statistics Canada, 2008). If we include watching sports events and supporting sports teams, there are a tremendous number of Canadians engaged in sports. What are they learning?

Canadians may be learning that sports participation is primarily a facet of youth: sports involvement is highest among young people (59 percent of teenagers aged 15 to 18 were active in 2005). These individuals are not only more likely to be physically fit, but occupy institutional contexts (high schools) that explicitly encourage organized sports activities. As Canadians age, they often are under pressure to focus their attention on other pursuits. Among Canadians aged 25 to 34, 45 percent indicated in 2005 that they lacked the time (and are presumably busy establishing careers and new families) to be regularly involved in a sport.

Sports involvement tends to reaffirm class differences among Canadian adults and children. Only 43 percent of children from lower income families (less than $40 000 annual income) were active in sports in 2005, in contrast to 65 percent of children from higher income families ($80 000 or more annual income). It seems that low-income families cannot afford to create a climate in which sports activities are encouraged. Families with household incomes of $80 000 a year or over were twice as likely to participate in sports in 2005, in contrast with families with annual incomes of less than $30 000 (Statistics Canada, 2008).

Extensive research has documented the role of sports in gender socialization. Until the second half of the twentieth century, most Canadian sports were generally constructed as male activities. Even in 1998, 43 percent of men, compared with only 26 percent of women, were regularly active in a sport. While the difference narrowed in 2005 to 36 percent for men and 21 percent for women and there were more female coaches (up 400 percent since 1992), referees, officials, and umpires, it is clear that a gender discrepancy persists (Statistics Canada, 2008; Cunningham, 2008).

The actual gender socialization mechanisms at work may be a complex mix of lack of role models, parental and peer pressure to conform to more stereotypic models of femininity, and a general social context that does not revere or reward the accomplishments of female athletes (Ross & Shinew, 2008). The role of sports as a forum to perpetuate the restraints of the female gender role may be only part of the picture. Some analysts suggest that sports help maintain gender inequities by supporting aggressive forms of masculinity that may contribute to male violence and sexual aggression against women (Murnen & Kohlman, 2007).

Sports may play a crucial role in fitting Canadians into an increasingly organized, urbanized, and corporatized society. Earlier in Canadian history, sports activities were often unorganized and spontaneous. Neighbourhood boys played baseball in empty fields; a frozen pond was an invitation to

The workplace—quite often the fast-food or call centre industry—is a major socializing agent for teenagers.

a hockey game. As our culture changed—as communities became more intensely urbanized and suburbanized, families became increasingly time-pressured, and organized sports became more like business enterprises—the experience of sports has been transformed. Boys and girls enrolled in soccer leagues are learning very different lessons about life than their counterparts who played soccer spontaneously and without adult supervision.

While the shift in sports socialization may have diverse implications, it is interesting to realize that today, we are being socialized to be less physically active. Across all age groups, education levels, income brackets, both sexes, and almost all provinces, the rates of participation in one or more sports dropped from 45 percent of adult Canadians in 1992 to 28 percent in 2005 (Statistics Canada, 2008).

The Workplace: Adult Socialization

Socialization—learning how to think and behave according to the norms and values of a specific social location—is a lifelong process. In the course of life, most Canadians will learn how to fit into a workplace and function as an employee.

Focus Question

What important socialization lessons are learned through part-time work at a fast food restaurant?

After trying out various jobs, most of us eventually become committed to some particular line of work. Although we may not find our "dream job," we will likely start to engage in anticipatory socialization, or learning to play a role before entering it—a sort of mental rehearsal for some future activity. We may read books or watch movies about people who work in a career, talk to them, or take a summer internship. This allows us to gradually identify with the role, to become aware of some of its expectations and rewards, and, perhaps, reject it as a career choice.

An interesting aspect of work as a socializing agent is that the more you participate in a line of work, the more the work becomes a part of your self-concept, such as saying, "I am a teacher, personal chef, or lawyer," for example.

Acquiring certain professional identities—such as becoming a doctor—entails particularly powerful socialization processes. Several classic American and Canadian sociological studies focus on the training of medical students (Merton et al, 1957; Becker et al., 1961; Haas & Shaffir, 1987; Lingard, Garwood, Schryer, & Spafford, 2003). A recent Canadian examination of the process of becoming a doctor reports that the socialization process is remarkably unchanged (Beagan, 2007).

Medical students must focus on constructing a professional appearance; adopting appropriate ("doctorly") patterns of language, thinking, and communicating; learning (and deferring to) the complex hierarchy within medicine; and negotiating the patient–doctor relationship. Despite changes in the medical profession—in particular, the dramatic increase in the number of women doctors and medical students—many of the problematic aspects of medical socialization persist—notably, the messages to pretend competence and confidence, to establish emotional distance with patients, to work oppressively long hours, and to sacrifice family, friends, and outside interests in order to pursue a medical career (Beagan, 2007). As this example reveals, the workplace as an agent of socialization may have a contradictory or even negative impact on an individual's identity.

The negative consequences of workplace socialization are not randomly scattered throughout the population. A considerable body of research suggests that learning to fit in to a workplace often brings with it a sense of exclusion and structured inequality for specific segments of society. Women, racialized groups, the disabled, gays and lesbians, seniors, and others may find that learning to "fit in" at work means accepting a restricted or negative sense of self (see, for example, Galabuzi, 2006).

IN SUM

Many agents of socialization guide us throughout our lives. From the moment of birth until our death, we are encouraged to act, think, and feel in a socially specified fashion. The most intimate components of our identity—how we feel love and joy, how we experience grief and despair—are moulded by our interactions with family members, with religion, with day care and education, with peers and sports, with the mass media, and within our workplaces. Some agents of socialization are particularly powerful in demanding conformity and punishing deviance. The socialization process and its agents are powerful determinants of who we are and who we wish to become.

RESOCIALIZATION

As discussed with regard to smoking, socializing agents may seek to change or redirect socialization messages. The process of **resocialization**—which may take many different forms—involves learning new norms, values, attitudes, and behaviours. In its most common form, resocialization occurs

Resocialization often is a gentle process, as we are gradually exposed to different ways of thinking and doing. Sometimes, however, resocialization can be swift and brutal, as it is for those incarcerated in Canada's federal prison system.

every time we learn something contrary to our previous experiences. Most resocialization is mild, with only a slight modification of things already learned. Resocialization can be intense, however. Drug rehabilitation programs or psychotherapy, for example, may not only change an individual's behaviour, but she or he may learn a fundamentally different way of looking at life.

The Case of Total Institutions

Relatively few of us experience the most powerful expressions of socialization that Goffman (1961) called the total institution. He coined this term to refer to a place where people are cut off from the rest of society and come under almost total control of those who run the place. Boot camps, prisons, concentration camps, group homes for juvenile offenders, convents, some religious cults, along with some elite boarding schools, are all examples of total institutions.

Sociologists continue to study total institutions, since they provide insight into the complexities and contradictions of social control and underscore the enormous impact of socialization. The powerful experience not only leaves an indelible mark on an individual, but also on overall society. Although the application of total institutions is typically disproportionately directed toward the poor, visible minorities, and Aboriginals, every Canadian knows that imprisonment faces those who deviate from societal norms (Western, 2006; Hallett, 2006; Kivett & Warren, 2002).

A person entering a total institution is typically greeted with a **degradation ceremony** (Garfinkel, 1956; Santos, 2006), or an attempt to remake the self by stripping away the individual's current identity and stamping a new one in its place. This unwelcome greeting may involve fingerprinting, photographing, shaving the head, and banning the person's **personal identity kit** (items such as jewelry, hairstyles, clothing, and other body decorations used to express individuality). Newcomers may be ordered to strip, be examined (often in humiliating, semipublic settings), and then be given a uniform to designate their new status. (For prisoners, the public reading of a verdict and being led away in handcuffs by armed police also form part of the degradation ceremony.) As evidenced in recent pictures of inmates at Abu Ghraib and practises at the detention centre in Guantanamo Bay, total institutions continue to follow this kind of regimen.

Total institutions are extremely effective in stripping away people's personal freedom. They are isolated from the public (walls, bars, or other barriers not only keep inmates in, but also keep outsiders from interfering). They suppress preexisting statuses (prison inmates, for example, learn that their previous roles—such as spouse, parent, worker, or student—mean nothing, and that the only thing that counts is their current role). Total institutions suppress the norms of "the outside world," replacing them with their own rules, values, and interpretation of life. They also closely supervise the entire lives of the residents—eating, sleeping, showering, and recreation are all standardized. Information flow is also

Sociologists point out that children look up to and emulate role models. However, who is seen as a suitable role model may change dramatically through the course of historical events.

controlled, which helps the institution shape the individuals' ideas and "picture" of the world. Finally, they control rewards and punishments. (Under conditions of deprivation, simple rewards for compliance, such as sleep, a television program, a letter from home, extra food, or even a cigarette, are powerful incentives in controlling behaviour.) The institution also holds the power to punish rule-breaking—often severely: for example, in prisons by solitary confinement or acceptance of inmate violence and assaults (Kupers, 1999).

IN SUM

Resocialization is an important aspect of the socialization process. When individuals are identified by others or identify themselves as being improperly socialized, various agencies may step in to replace earlier socialization messages with more appropriate ones. In some instances, resocialization efforts are voluntary (as in drug rehabilitation programs); in others, a state or other social agent may deploy their own resources (as in prisons and jails) not only to punish inappropriate behaviour but to inculcate more socially acceptable actions.

SOCIALIZATION THROUGH THE LIFE COURSE

In recent decades, sociologists have increasingly employed a life course approach to socialization processes. Although there are tremendous diversities in our experiences and the sequences of our lives, there often appears to be a series of socially constructed stages—childhood, adolescence, relationship formation, parenting, middle-age, retirement, early

and late old age—that comprise our lives and our understanding of our lives (Giele & Elder, 1998; Hunt, 2005; Hostetler, Sweet, & Moen, 2007). A life course approach does not assume that events and roles inevitably proceed in a particular sequence or that all stages occur in all lives. In terms of current general trends, there is evidence of increased **individuation**—a growing diversity of individual paths through the life course.

The life course approach accepts that historical events and ongoing social interaction interplay with established patterns of biological and psychological development to produce diverse and changing outcomes from childhood to death. For example, when children grow up, their views on gender roles are not simply a reflection of gender messages in their parents' home. After all, many women lawyers, corporate executives, and political leaders grew up in traditional male breadwinner/female homemaker families. Furthermore, as we go through our life span, our gender beliefs and attitudes often change; for example, in old age, men are much more likely to identify with both masculine and feminine personality traits than younger and adolescent males (Strough, Leszczynski, Neely, Finn, & Margrett, 2007). Below, we examine some of the major stages in the life course, discuss their current means, and consider how their social construction has shifted through the course of history.

Childhood (Birth to About Age 12)

What a child "is" differs from one culture to another and from one historical period to the next (Goelman, Marshall, and Ross, eds., 2004). To understand this point, consider

Historically and cross-culturally, ideas of childhood vary. For instance, from paintings such as this 1642 British painting by the Le Nain brothers, *A Woman and Five Children*, some historians conclude that Europeans once viewed children as miniature adults who assumed adult roles at the earliest opportunity.

how different your childhood would have been if you had grown up during the Middle Ages or in contemporary Myanmar.

When historian Philippe Ariès (1962) examined European paintings from the Middle Ages, he noticed that children were always dressed up in adult clothing. If they were not stiffly posed for a family portrait, children were depicted as engaging in adult activities. Ariès concluded that at that time and in that place, childhood was not regarded as a special time of life. Rather, Europeans considered children miniature adults.

Childhood was harsh at different times in history. Lloyd DeMause (1975) documented the nightmare of childhood in ages past. Beating children used to be the norm. Parents who did not beat their children were considered neglectful of their social duty to keep them off the road to hell. Even teachers were expected to beat their students, and one nineteenth-century German schoolteacher methodically recorded every beating he administered.

The physically harsher realities of childhood persist in both poor and rich nations. Visitors to emerging nations are often struck by the fact that children are expected to work side-by-side with adults in helping to support the family, but this reality also persists in impoverished and marginalized neighbourhoods in the most affluent countries (Heesterman, 2005). Nonetheless, in more well-to-do regions around the globe, economic development has meant that most children have been afforded the leisure to go to school. Reflecting this shift, children came to be thought of as tender and innocent, as needing more adult care, comfort, and protection. Today, children, especially the very young, are often represented in our culture as needing gentle guidance if they are to develop emotionally, intellectually, morally, socially, and even physically.

Society continues to change, so does our conception of childhood. Contemporary social analysts have repeatedly questioned whether modern childhood is being eroded.

Children today are not only spending more of their lives connected to televisions, computers, and video games, but the dramatic increase in the use of psychiatric drugs on young children, including Ritalin and anti-depressants, and the numerous examples of young celebrities whose sexualized appearance, illicit drug use, and/or sexual behaviour is role-modelled by young people, have all raised concerns. Some analysts suggest that the increased generalized pressures on young people in our society are creating an experience of childhood that "sucks the joy" out of being a kid (Honore, 2008). Others argue that the new post-industrial experience of childhood is in crisis and demand new forms of selfhood and socialization (Block, 2005). As parents juggle double and triple days and children confront unclear but demanding educational and personal agendas, together they rush from one activity to the next with little if any chance to "enjoy the moment" (McDonnell, 2002). Viewed from this perspective, the golden era of childhood may have come and gone.

Adolescence/Youth (About Age 13 to 17)

In earlier centuries, societies did not mark out adolescence as a distinct time of life. People simply moved from childhood into young adulthood, with no stopover in between. The Industrial Revolution, over time, reduced the need for child labour while increasing the need for skilled labour and, thus, the demand for education. The convergence of these two forces in industrialized societies created a gap between childhood and adulthood—hence the "discovery" of "adolescence" in the early twentieth century (Hall, 1904).

DOWN-TO-EARTH SOCIOLOGY
Creating Little Consumers

One of the most dramatic historic shifts in childhood has been related to the creation and expansion of consumerism. Since World War II, most Western societies have been transformed into consumer societies—societies in which there has been an explosion in the number of goods and services being marketed to meet every possible human need and a dramatic expansion in the time devoted to consumer activities. As a result, very young children are learning to approach their lives in terms of consumer products and consumption.

Fifty years ago, malls were uncommon on the Canadian landscape and shopping was not viewed as a significant "leisure activity" by most young people. Today, malls are often the social and economic centres of our communities, and children spend considerable time in these spaces. Equally important, the mass media are continuously inculcating consumer values and consumer knowledge. Young children learn quickly that the consumer market provides key social objects and that acquisition of these objects is directly relevant to

self-worth, popularity, and even identity. Advertisers recognize that efforts to market to children are extremely worthwhile in terms of accessing parents' resources. By adolescence, children, particularly girls, have typically been well-socialized into the meanings of corporate brand names and the significance of consumption as a social activity (Bauman, 2007; Zukin, 2005; Schor, 2004; Quart, 2003; Kenway & Bullen, 2001).

The experience of adolescence has changed dramatically in the past 100 years. Youth culture is now much more likely to be reflected in music, television, movies, and computer technology. A significant segment of the consumer market is devoted to this demographic and often makes explicit connections between youth identity and resistance to the larger social order. A recent study of raves in southern Ontario suggests that rave culture provides youth with "an escape from and a reaction against a mainstream culture where people are intolerant of one another and are poor communicators, and where day-to-day life is so intense that 'letting go' is almost impossible" (Wilson & Jette, 2005, p. 79).

The framing of adolescence as "rebellious" is apparent in the emerging stereotype of youth as the "whatever" generation. Although individual adolescents—depending on gender, sexual orientation, disability, race, and so on—have varying experiences, sociologists are concerned that pressures on adolescents are so intense that they are destructive. In his aptly titled book *The Road to Whatever,* Elliott Currie argues that the harsh "winner/loser" world of middle-class adolescence—where there is little in the way of compassionate help to deal with educational, social, and economic pressures and where there is an increasingly punitive approach to adolescent misbehaviours—is producing a life stage that is experienced by many as desperate and painful (2004).

Young Adulthood (About Age 18 to 29)

Historian Kenneth Keniston suggests that industrialized societies seem to be adding a period of prolonged youth to the life course; a period in which young adults are no long adolescents but not yet sociological adults (1971). As education, particularly for middle and higher classes, extends increasingly into college, university, and graduate or professional school, the attributes of adulthood—marriage, home ownership, parenthood—are often delayed. In 1971, three quarters of 22-year-old Canadians had finished school, almost half were married, and a quarter had children. In contrast, 30 years later, 50 percent of 22-years-olds were still in school, only 20 percent were in a conjugal union (mostly common-law), and only one in eleven had children (Clark, 2007: p. 21; Mitchell, 2007). The shift in patterns of young adulthood is also striking in terms of the once-momentous step of "moving out." Today, increasing numbers of young Canadians are continuing to live with their parents or to move out and then back in (**boomerang kids**) as they go through periods of schooling, employment, and family-building. In 1981, only 12 percent of Canadians aged 25 to 29 lived with their parents. In 2006, this figure had grown to 26 percent (Beaupre, Turcotte, & Milan, 2006: p. 8; Statistics Canada, 2007).

The Middle Years (About Ages 30 to 65)

During the early middle years (ages 30 to 49), most people enter more firmly into adult status. Many men and women enter into conjugal unions and become parents during this stage of life. In 2003, the average age at first marriage for men was 30.2 years and for women 28.2 years—in sharp contrast to the 1960s and 70s, when women were marrying for the first time at around age 22 and men at around age 25. The average age of first birth for mothers was 29.2 years in 2005, and almost half (48.9 percent) of mothers giving birth that year were over 30 years of age. At the same time, the numbers of births to teens has been in decline for the past 31 years. The net result is that for many Canadians, the thirties and forties is a period for formalizing long-term relationships and entering into parenthood.

Both of these new identities—spouse and parent—typically involve intense socialization and may also entail problematic outcomes, such as divorce. In 2003, slightly more than a third (35.3 percent) of marriages ended in divorce (before the twenty-fifth year of marriage), and most of the men and women divorcing were in their early forties. The average age at divorce was 43.4 for men and 40.8 for women (Human Resources and Social Development Canada, 2008).

Resocialization of the self to accommodate such ruptures in expectations and self-conceptualization may be a years-long process. Even stable relationships may entail painful adjustments in an economy where there is tremendous pressure to consume, coupled with sometimes inadequate support systems. Single parents and adults who must juggle care for their children and extensive paid employment may feel trapped by conflicting pressures and lack of time. Even though they are now fully-fledged adults, men and women during these years may be constantly adjusting their sense of self to accommodate personal and societal demands.

During their later middle years (ages 50–65), people attempt to resolve past issues and come to terms with what lies ahead. They may take time to compare what they have accomplished with how far they had hoped to get. Although many do not like the gap they see between where they now are and where they had planned to be, most adjust fairly well (Carr et al., 1995). During this time of life, many people find themselves caring not only for their own children but also for their aging parents. Because of this often crushing set of twin burdens, people in the later middle years are sometimes referred to as the **sandwich generation**. Health and mortality concerns may also begin to loom large and some people may experience a "mid-life crisis" as they address the frustrations associated with their personal relationships and/or public accomplishments.

The Older Years (About Age 66 Onward)

In industrialized societies, the older years begin around the mid sixties. This, too, is recent; in preindustrial societies, when most people died early, old age was thought to begin at around age 40. For those in good health, being over 65 today is often experienced not as old age, but as an extension of the middle years. People who continue to work or are active in rewarding social activities are especially unlikely to see themselves as old. However, the ability to stay healthy and socially active while growing old varies depending on social class, gender, and other significant social markers (Mandell, Wilson, & Duffy 2008).

As with the preceding periods of life, except the first, there is no precise beginning point to the last stage—later older years. For some, the seventy-fifth birthday may mark entry into this period. For others, that marker may be the eightieth or even the eighty-fifth birthday. For many, this stage is marked by growing frailty and illness; for all who reach this stage, by impending death. Physical decline may be slow, and increasing numbers of people now manage to see their hundredth birthdays (although for many centarians, quality of life is compromised by cognitive and/or physical disabilities). Increasing numbers of Canadians will experience old age and very old age. In 2005, life expectancy at birth was 78 years for men and 82.7 years for women; further, men could expect to spend 68.3 years of their life in good health and women 70.8 years. With the growing aging of the Canadian population, we can expect that efforts to enhance the socialization of seniors into healthy, productive old age will intensify.

Focus Question
What specific steps might be taken by Canadian society to socialize seniors to be healthier and more socially productive in their old age?

Focus Question
In what ways are your own experiences of the "life course" different from those of your parents and your grandparents?

IN SUM

According to life course analysis, our lives often involve a series of stages: childhood, adolescence, young adulthood, the middle years, and the older years. However, how we experience these stages depends on a complex interplay of factors—in particular, historical location and culture. In all stages of life, social location, such as social class, gender, and race, is typically highly significant. However, within these complexities, patterns of human life tend to establish the general boundaries for us at each stage. As a result, we can speak of "boomerang kids," "the sandwich generation," or "mid-life crisis" and strike a chord with many Canadians at those particular stages. For instance, as we enter the later older years, almost all of us will be coming to terms with common issues such as increasing frailty and the prospect of death.

THE LIMITATIONS OF SOCIALIZATION

Socialization is an extremely appealing explanation for human behaviour. It makes a great deal of sense to look to the influence of father, mother, friends, media, and schooling in order to understand who we are, what we value, and how we act. However, even the framers of socialization theory understood its limitations. George Herbert Mead emphasized the powerful impact of social forces on our lives; he even argued that *the human mind is a social product*. According to Mead, we need symbols to be able to think, and these symbols come from society when we learn our language. If society did not provide the symbols, we would not be able to think and would not possess what we call the mind.

Despite Mead's strong endorsement of a socialization perspective, he also wanted to allow for human freedom in his framework. He was not prepared to argue that we are simply the sum total of societal inputs. He introduced the concepts of the "I" and the "me." The "I" is *the self as subject*, the active, spontaneous, creative part of the self, as in "*I* throw the ball." In contrast, the "me" is the *self as object*, made up of attitudes internalized from our interactions with others, as in "They made *me* do it." Mead stressed that the individual is not only a "me," like a computerized robot passively absorbing the responses of others. Rather, the "I" actively makes sense of those responses and then acts. With this inclusion in his theory, Mead made provision not only for **human agency** (the ability to individually or collectively resist social pressures and provide for social change) but also for human responsibility. We are the products of socialization, but we also make choices.

SUMMARY AND REVIEW

Biology, Sociobiology, or Socialization

WHAT IS THE "NATURE VERSUS NURTURE" DEBATE, WHY IS IT IMPORTANT, AND WHAT IS THE LATEST THINKING ON THE CONTRIBUTIONS OF BIOLOGY TO HUMAN BEHAVIOUR?

The "nature versus nurture" debate refers to the ongoing controversy regarding the sources of human behaviour. Some argue that how we act is basically determined by our biology and our evolutionary past. In popular conversation, this perspective is reflected in comments about "human nature" and "mother instinct." In contrast, advocates of the "nurture" perspective maintain that human behaviour is not genetically determined but rather an outcome of our experiences growing up in a particular society at a particular point in history. Our attitudes toward "mothering," for example, reflect the cultural beliefs and values we learned in childhood. The debate between nature and nurture has been going on for a long time and continues to be reflected in our mass media. Each viewpoint has important implications. If men are, by nature, violent, or if some races are, by nature, inferior, then how can we hope to reduce domestic violence against women or improve human productivity through education? Currently, the biological and sociological viewpoints appear to be acknowledging a complex interplay between biology and social input. In this latest thinking, biology is not set in stone and may be influenced by social factors. Conversely, social influences are understood to be restricted by certain biological elements, such as the development timetable that establishes restrictions on our ability to learn language. pp. 67–69.

The Social Development of the Self, Mind, and Emotions

IN WHAT WAYS DOES SOCIAL EXPERIENCE CREATE AND STRUCTURE OUR HUMAN EXISTENCE, INCLUDING OUR BELIEFS, VALUES, GOALS, AND EVEN OUR PERCEPTIONS?

In every way, how we feel, what we value, what we want to achieve, what we believe, and even what we see is influenced by our social environment. If you imagine a typical day in your life, virtually every act, from brushing your teeth with your favourite brand to worrying about gaining weight over breakfast to going off to school, is a socially constructed activity. We act in particular ways and value or enjoy those actions because we have been directly and/or indirectly taught that these are things we should do and should value.

Through our experience in social relationships, our basic identity is constructed. In the absence of such human contact, it is likely that not only our beliefs, values, and goals would be absent, but our basic perceptions would be altered. The process of social interaction, starting at birth, constructs who we are, what we want, and even what we perceive. pp. 69–74.

Socialization into Gender

HOW IS GENDER IDENTITY CREATED THROUGH GENDER SOCIALIZATION?

Gender socialization commences before birth, since it is rooted in the gender socialization of our parents. As soon as we are born, our parents are likely to provide direct and indirect messages about gender (pink and frilly clothes for baby girls, for example). These gender messages then permeate our childhood and adolescence and are reflected in almost every aspect of our social existence. The mass media and education play an important role in affirming the importance of gender differences. Even seemingly unrelated activities such as smoking become gendered when women are targeted with "feminine" cigarette advertising campaigns. Some gender socialization is profoundly indirect and we are often unaware of it. For example, young men and women have different levels of responsibilities in terms of household work and paid work and males tend to have more "free" time. Both men and women are likely to be unaware that the temporal structures of their lives are gendered. Gender

socialization may have profoundly negative or profoundly different outcomes for males and females. Young women are much more likely to engage in self-destructive behaviours, such as eating disorders, while young men are more likely to be risk-takers (such as with alcohol use, for example). pp. 74–77.

Resocialization

WHY MIGHT THE CHANGING OF SOCIALIZATION MESSAGES THROUGH RESOCIALIZATION BE A POWERFUL INSTRUMENT OF CONTROL?

Socialization messages may become powerful determinants of who we are throughout our lives. In particular, specific instruments of resocialization—prisons, rehabilitation centres—may strive intentionally to alter our socialization. Specifically, different sets of beliefs, values, and attendant behaviours may be rewarded while prior patterns are challenged. Many societies employ resocialization organizations to maintain social control and eradicate what they define as inappropriate patterns of behaviour or attitudes. pp. 85–87.

Socialization through the Life Course

WHAT ARE THE STAGES OF HUMAN SOCIALIZATION AND WHAT KINDS OF TRANSITIONS DO WE EXPERIENCE AS WE LIVE THROUGH THE LIFE COURSE?

Life course analysis suggests that most contemporary Canadians will go through the following life stages: childhood, adolescence, young adulthood, middle years, and senior years. Research suggests a variety of changes in childhood—more and more children are spending some portion of the weekday in non-parental child care as their mothers and fathers both engage in paid employment. Further, there is concern that children are subject to much greater adult supervision and educational pressures. Old age has also changed significantly, as increasing numbers of Canadians can anticipate growing old and remaining healthy. Further, senior Canadians are becoming a significant component of the Canadian population and soon will outnumber children. As a result, a growing number of goods and services are now being directed toward older Canadians. pp. 87–90.

The Limitations of Socialization

WHAT ARE THE LIMITATIONS OF SOCIALIZATION AS AN EXPLANATION OF HUMAN BEHAVIOUR?

Socialization may become a kind of blanket explanation. Why do we drive on the right/left hand side of the road? Because we are socialized to do so. While it is important to recognize that we are tremendously influenced by the beliefs, values, and norms we are taught in a particular social context and that we often unconsciously follow societal rules, we are not simply the end result of various socialization inputs. Rather, leading socialization theorists allow for the possibility that individuals will reject or resist socialization messages. Even in total institutions, inmates may find ways to express their individuality or "get around" the rules. Sometimes, members of society take contradictory socialization messages and arrive at their own paths for navigating life. Socialization reveals the pressures to act in a particular manner but it does not imply that we necessarily succumb to those pressures. p. 90.

TALKING ABOUT THEORY

Theoretical Paradigms

CLASSICAL PARADIGMS		
Structural-Functional Paradigm	**Social-Conflict Paradigm**	**Symbolic-Interaction Paradigm**
What is the level of analysis? Macro level	Macro level	Micro level
What is the importance of socialization for society? Socialization is key to fitting the individual into society and its various institutions.	Socialization is key to understanding conformity in society and the role of specific institutions in providing social control. However, there must be an allowance for human agency.	Socialization provides us with the roles, techniques, and strategies that allow us to perform in specific social interactions.
Has socialization changed over time? How? Somewhat. The primary function remains the same, but the specifics have changed. For example, the internet and mass media have provided new socializing agents.	Somewhat. The process of socialization has intensified in some instances (for example, prolonged education) and there are more extensive uses of socialization in social control. However, the overall process of socialization remains intact.	Somewhat. The process of socialization and the construction of social meanings remain intact, but the specific roles we acquire and learn to perform (for example, adolescence) have changed.

KEY TERMS

agents of
    socialization   80
anticipatory
    socialization   83
backstage   73
biological
    determinism   67
boomerang kids   89
cliques   79
degradation
    ceremony   86

dramaturgical analysis   73
ego   71
ethnocentrism   79
frontstage   73
gender roles   70
generalized other   69
habitus   71
human agency   90
id   71
individuation   87
in-groups   79

latent functions   82
looking-glass self   69
manifest functions   82
mass media   75
out-groups   79
peer groups   83
personal identity kit   86
primary group   79
reference groups   79
resocialization   85
sandwich generation   89

secondary groups   79
self   69
significant others   69
social groups   79
socialization   67
superego   71
symbols   68
taking the role of the
    other   69
total institution   73
xenophobia   79

WEBLINKS

All URLs listed are current as of the printing of this book.

National Longitudinal Study of Children and Youth
www.statcan.ca/english/survey/household/child/
child.htm
A long-term study of Canadian children that follows their development from birth to early adulthood.

Media Awareness Network
www.media-awareness.ca
This website provides information and links for those interested in media literacy programs for youth.

CRITICAL THINKING QUESTIONS

1. Socialization in terms of formal education, for example, is intended to turn us into conforming members of society. As a result, we are under considerable pressure to "do the right thing." Explain some of the more powerful social forces that push us to act appropriately and then consider how socialization would also be useful in explaining the behaviour of the numerous individuals, from white-collar criminals to wife abusers, who deviate from social norms.

2. Postmodern feminists emphasize that a dualistic (male/female) understanding of gender socialization ignores the complexities and diversities of gender in our society. Using the gender messages in the mass media, consider the complex and sometimes contradictory ways gender is portrayed.

3. Socialization is presented as such a powerful social process that students sometimes have the impression that people are empty vessels filled with social messages—"this is what you should eat, wear, say, and so on." However, socialization theorists usually accept that each of us is *actively* involved in the social construction of the self. Thinking of your own upbringing, consider the ways in which you are not simply a reflection of your family and early childhood experiences and outline some reasons for these differences.

4. Do traditional gender socialization and its resulting gender roles make it more difficult for North American men than women to connect emotionally to others? Access the Research Navigator through MySocLab and use keywords such as "masculinities," "homophobia," "sports," and "militarism" to locate relevant and recent scholarly and popular press publications to help you answer this question.

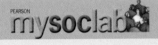

PEARSON **mysoclab** Explore the topics covered in this chapter on MySocLab using the access information provided with this text. Interactive resources for studying include multimedia tutorials, video clips, practice tests, quizzes, and animated maps and figures.

5 Globalization

LEARNING OUTCOMES

After you have studied this chapter, you will be able to answer the following questions:

1. What is globalization?

2. How does globalization impact the movement of people?

3. How does globalization impact the paid and unpaid work of women?

4. What are the main arguments for and against globalization?

5. How are the world's nations stratified?

6. What are the main sociological theories of economic and social development?

7. What makes Canada a semi-peripheral country and why is this important to know?

8. How is the system of global stratification maintained?

Let's consider three "average" families from different parts of the world:

For Getu Mulleta, 33, and his wife, Zenebu, 28, of rural Ethiopia, life is a constant struggle to keep themselves and their seven children from starving. They live in a 320-square-foot (30 m²) manure-plastered hut with no electricity, gas, or running water. They have a radio, but the battery is dead. Surviving on $130 a year, the family farms teff, a cereal grain.

The Mulletas' poverty is not the result of a lack of hard work. Getu works about 80 hours a week, while Zenebu works even more. "Housework" for Zenebu includes fetching water, making fuel pellets out of cow dung for the open fire over which she cooks the family's food, and cleaning animal stables. Like other Ethiopian women, she eats after the men.

In Ethiopia, the average male can expect to live to 48, and the average female to 50.

The Mulletas' most valuable possession is their oxen. Their wishes for the future? More animals, better seed, and a second set of clothing.

In Guadalajara, Mexico, Ambrosio and Carmen Castillo Balderas and their five children, ages two to ten, live in a four-room house. They also have a walled courtyard, where the family spends a good deal of time. They even have a washing machine, which is hooked up to a garden hose that runs to a public water main hundreds of metres away. Like most Mexicans, they do not have a telephone, nor do they own a car. Unlike many, however, they own a refrigerator, a stereo, and a recent purchase that makes them the envy of their neighbours—a television.

Ambrosio, 29, works full-time as a produce wholesale distributor. He also does welding on the side. The family's total annual income is $3600. They spend 57 percent of their income on food. Carmen works about 60 hours a week taking care of their children and keeping their home spotless. The neatness of their home stands in stark contrast to the neighbourhood, which is lined with littered dirt roads. As in many other Mexican neighbourhoods, public utilities and road work do not keep pace with people's needs.

The average life expectancy for males in Mexico is 70. For females, it is 76.

The Castillo Balderas' most valued possessions are their refrigerator and television. Their wish for the future? A truck.

Sources: Menzel (1994); Population Reference Bureau (1995); *Statistical Abstract* (1997), Tables 713, 723; Statistics Canada (2001a); Statistics Canada (2005c) Average income after tax by economic family types (2001–2005) www40.statcan.ca/l01/cst01/famil21a.htm.

"Worlds Apart" would be an appropriate title for these photos, which illustrate how life chances depend on global stratification. On the left is the Mulleta family of Ethiopia, featured in the opening vignette, standing in front of their home with all their material belongings. On the right is the Skeen family of Texas, also surrounded by their possessions.

Kitchener, Ontario, is home to the Kellys—Rick, 36, Patti, 34, Julie, 14, and Michael, 10. The Kellys live in a four-bedroom, 2100-square-foot (195 m²), carpeted, ranch-style house, with central heating and air conditioning, a basement, and a two-car garage. Their home is equipped with a refrigerator, washing machine, clothes dryer, dishwasher, garbage disposal, vacuum cleaner, food processor, microwave, and toaster. They own three radios, two CD players, four telephones (three cellular), two televisions, a camcorder, a DVD player, an Xbox with dozens of games, two iPods, two computers with printers, and a laptop. They also have numerous other small appliances, including blow dryers, an answering machine, a coffee maker, and electric toothbrushes. There are stereo-radio-CD and DVD players in their van and car.

Rick works 40 hours a week as an electrical power line and cable worker for the provincial power company. Patti is an elementary school teacher. Together they make $73 000* a year, plus benefits. The Kellys can choose from among dozens of

*This figure represents the median income for a Canadian family in 2006.

super-stocked supermarkets. They spend $7046 on food for their home, and another $3520 eating at restaurants—a total of nearly 15 percent of their annual income.

In Canada, the average life expectancy is 78 for males, 82 for females.

On the Kellys' wish list are a new Jeep, a Nintendo Wii, a MacBook Air laptop, a boat, a camping trailer, and—one day—a vacation cabin.

WHAT IS GLOBALIZATION?

Globalization is the latest stage in a process characterized by the spread and intensification of capitalism across the globe (see Figure 5.1). Today, globalization involves the interaction and integration of increasing numbers of people through international trade and investment, travel and tourism, and information technology and the mass media. Let's look at

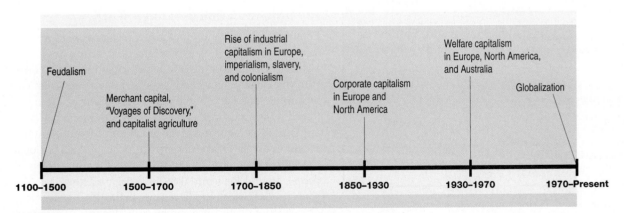

FIGURE 5.1   Stages of Capitalism, Expansion, and Intensification

how globalization impacts the movement of people around the world.

GLOBALIZATION AND PATTERNS OF MOVEMENT OF PEOPLE

Immigration

International migration has mushroomed in recent decades. In 2005, 190 million people migrated to different countries in the world. The United States had the highest migration rate, with Canada placing sixth after Saudi Arabia and France (see Table 5.1). Together, the countries with the top ten migration rates in 2005 accounted for over 51 percent of total world migration. What accounts for this upsurge in international movement? Partly, migration can be attributed to the age-old search for a better life in the richer countries of the world. Another factor, according to Anny Hefti (1997), is the globalization of communications technology. The pervasiveness of mass communication, including television, film, video, and music, has reinforced dreams of an "easy life" abroad. Hefti contends that fax machines and cell phones have replaced snail mail communications and that relations between immigrant communities abroad and home communities have been facilitated by these new communications technologies. As a result, migration has become very attractive.

TABLE 5.1　Top 10 Countries with the Largest Number of International Migrants (in thousands, 2005)

	Number of Immigrants
United States	38 354 709
Russian Federation	12 079 626
Germany	10 143 626
France	6 471 029
Saudi Arabia	6 360 730
Canada	6 105 722
India	5 700 147
United Kingdom	5 408 118
Spain	4 790 074
Australia	4 097 204
Top 10 Total	99 510 985
World	190 633 564

Note: As countries collect statistics on immigrants in varying ways, it is often difficult to harmonize data across countries; differences in counting deeply affect rank orders.

Source: United Nations, *Trends in Total Migrant Stock: The 2005 Revision,* data in digital form, 2006. Available at http://esa.un.org/migration/index.asp?panel=1

Globalization and Tourism

The growth in tourism is one indicator of the spread of international contact between people facilitated by cheap air travel, global communications, and the internet. In 1990, 486 million international tourist arrivals were recorded worldwide. That figure jumped to 846 million in 2006—nearly doubling in size. Europe was the primary destination in terms of money spent by international tourists in 2006, claiming just over 51 percent of the $733 billion spent worldwide. Asia and the Pacific shared second place, and the United States received approximately 21 percent of tourism dollars spent globally.

Today, tourism is arguably the world's largest industry. According to predictions from the World Tourism Organization, international tourist arrivals will climb from 850 million this year to 1.6 billion in 2020. Tourism is and will remain the privilege of a few, however: only about 4 percent of the world's population travel abroad.

As new forms of tourism gain prominence—ecotourism, ethnic tourism, "roots" and heritage tourism—the industry has increasingly become integral to every nation in the world. Many developing countries, facing debt burdens and worsening trade terms, have turned to tourism in the hope that it will attract foreign exchange and investment. Simultaneously, leading international agencies such as the World Bank and the United Nations, and business organizations such as the World Travel & Tourism Council (WTTC) have been substantially involved in making tourism a run-for-profit global industry. However, critics often view tourism in developing countries as an extension of former colonial conditions. Unequal trading relationships, dependence on foreign interests, and the division of labour have relegated poor countries in the South to becoming even more involved in the uneven and often environmentally detrimental development of tourist attractions and facilities to placate the expectations of tourists from the affluent North. The flip side to globalization and tourism is legal and illegal emigration from developing countries to more affluent regions such as Canada, the United States, and the European Union.

Globalization and Women's Work

Economic globalization includes cutting costs, especially labour costs, which usually means downsizing or closing facilities in Canada or the U.S. and re-locating to other countries where labour costs and taxes are low and environmental protections lax. People in poorer countries are often forced from rural farms and either travel to where new jobs are located or leave in search of a better life in the richer countries of the world economy. The push and pull of global capitalism accounts for the unprecedented migration of people around the world (see Table 5.1), whether from the countryside to small and large cities in the developing world or in pursuit of affluence and an easier life in rich countries such as Canada, the United States, France, and Germany.

With few transferable skills, many new immigrants, especially women, find employment as domestics or alongside national workers in "soft" sectors such as the garment industry. In these and similar precarious employment options, women's paid work often means accepting lower pay, increasing workloads both at work and at home, and more stress. In the private sector, for example, a preponderant number of women work in less skilled jobs in the garment industry, while in the public and not-for-profit sectors women form the largest share of health care professionals such as nurses, home care, and personal support workers.

The textile and garment industries were among the first industries to be globalized. United Colors of Benetton, or the Benetton Group, an Italian family-run clothing multinational, began operations in the mid 1960s. Today, the company is known not only for its images of beautiful faces and youth from around the world, but also for its ability to communicate through music, theatre, photography, publishing, and the internet. Benetton is the precursor to companies such as Gap and Old Navy.

The garment industry in Canada—be it along Spadina Avenue in Toronto or in the Chabanel District of Montreal—experienced massive changes under the force of globalization. Consider the Exchange District in Winnipeg, now a designated historic site, or the rapid demise of Mr. Jax in Vancouver, and the dramatic effects of globalization are obvious. The existing industry in Montreal and Toronto faces hard times in a global economic world. Employment in the clothing sector in Quebec fell from 57 000 in 2003 to 30 000 in 2005—a massive change in a short period of time. Most of those affected were women; many were recent immigrants.

Offshore textile and garment manufacturing is certainly global in scope. In many Asian countries, young girls are lured to tax-free "factory cities," called **"export processing zones,"** by the promise of good jobs manufacturing products for export. Among the hazards they are confronted with are forced overtime, stiffling hot factories with poor ventilation, forced pregnancy tests, sexual violence, and unclean drinking water.

Job loss in Canada and hazardous offshore working conditions tell only half the story. What happens when women return home? Who does the housework? What happens if their husband or partner loses his job? During the recent Asian economic crisis, the Korean government called upon women to "get your husband energized" if he had lost his job, and help offset the impact of the economic crisis on men who, as government ads pointed out, were subject to depression and possible suicide.

Education is critical in order for women in Canada and the rest of the world to compete as equals in the professional world and earn a decent income of their own. However, in Canada, student debt has skyrocketed. On average, female graduates earn less than their male counterparts, resulting in longer debt repayment periods. Those without a university education are particularly disadvantaged. When the Canadian government eliminated the National Training Act in 1996, which included training programs geared toward women, good paying jobs for women in non-traditional sectors became even harder to get.

University education and skills development remain significant factors for achieving equity in the workplace, both in Canada and elsewhere around the world.

GLOBALIZATION: THE ISSUES

More important than the movement of people around the world has been the movement of goods, services, and capital. Since 1950, the volume of world trade has increased twentyfold, and the flow of direct investment doubled from $468 billion in 1997 to $827 billion in 1999. Subsidiaries of transnational corporations, such as Toyota's CAMI Automotive plant in Ingersoll, Ontario, or the slew of Wal-Marts in almost every province are examples of direct investment.

Globalization involves more than the building of large manufacturing and retail businesses controlled outside the community or country; it often means the disappearance of local enterprises, restaurants, and entertainment venues in favour of branch plants of foreign-based transnational corporations. It can even affect the choices of food and beverages offered at your university. Chances are that Sodexho and Pepsi-Cola have a monopoly at your school. As such, globalization impacts the world's environment, national and local cultures, national and local governments, the physical well-being of individuals, and human rights.

Globalization has both advocates and detractors. Its proponents argue that poor countries and their citizens benefit economically from increased employment opportunities and rising standards of living. In order to benefit, it is argued, nations must open their borders to international trade. Tariffs and other barriers to the "free" movement of capital, goods, and services must be eliminated. International organizations such as the World Bank, the International Monetary Fund (IMF), and the World Trade Organization (WTO) (formerly the General Agreement on Tariffs and Trade (GATT)) foster a climate of trade and investment liberalization across the globe. They maintain that globalization will generate a more level playing field on which countries can compete for capital and labour, thereby decreasing worldwide inequalities of wealth and poverty.

Opponents of globalization point to the benefits amassed by transnational corporations such as Time Warner, Exxon Mobil, AT&T, Johnson & Johnson, or Sony Corporation at the expense of local enterprises, local cultures, and ordinary people. They contend that increased inequalities of wealth, power, and privilege accrue at the expense of the less developed and poorer regions of the world. Democracy, human rights, and labour rights are said to be undermined by institutions such as the IMF and the World Bank.

In July 1944, delegates from 44 nations gathered at the United Nations Monetary and Financial Conference in

Bretton Woods, New Hampshire. They reached an agreement, known as the Bretton Woods Agreement, that created two international institutions: the International Bank for Reconstruction and Development, known today as the World Bank, and the IMF.

WORLD BANK With considerable financial power, the World Bank shapes development policies across Africa, Latin America, Asia, and Eastern Europe. Its self-proclaimed primary objective is to eradicate poverty, yet evidence suggests that World Bank programs often increase social inequalities and cause environmental destruction.

IMF The IMF was founded in 1944 as a result of the financial turmoil of the Great Depression of the 1930s and the devastation caused by World War II. The organization provided financial stability in the decades following the Second World War in order to increase world trade. Today, the IMF has a membership of 184 countries and has intervened in such financial crises as the 1995 crash of the Mexican peso and the 1997/98 East Asian financial crisis. IMF policies have been criticized for increasing poverty and suffering among ordinary citizens while shielding multinational corporations and their backers in wealthy countries.

WTO Growing out of the Uruguay Round of GATT trade talks (1986 to 1994), the WTO was founded in January 1995 as an international body of 146 member countries whose purpose, like the GATT, is to promote free trade. Unlike the GATT, WTO decisions are absolute and every member must abide by its rulings. As such, it has become closely associated with globalization.

GATT The GATT was first signed in 1947 as a United Nations treaty, rather than an organization. The agreement was designed to provide an international forum to encourage free trade between member states.

GLOBALIZATION, INEQUALITY, AND DEVELOPMENT

Until recently, a simple model consisting of *First*, *Second*, and *Third Worlds* was used to depict global stratification. "First World" referred to industrialized capitalist nations, "Second World" to communist nations, and "Third World" to any nation that did not fit into the first two categories. After the collapse of the Soviet Union in 1989, these terms became outdated. In addition, although "first," "second," and "third" did not mean "best," "second best," and "worst," they sounded like it. An alternative classification now in use—*developed, developing*, and *undeveloped nations*—has the same drawback. By referring to ourselves as "developed," it sounds as though we are mature and the "undeveloped" nations lack our desirable trait. Consequently, we employ more neutral descriptive terms: *most industrialized, industrializing*, and *least industrialized nations*.

Such descriptions are used to depict on a global level three primary dimensions: property, power, and prestige. The most industrialized nations have greater property (wealth), power (they get their way in international relations), and prestige—rightly or wrongly, they are looked up to as world leaders with something to contribute to humanity. As illustrated in Figure 5.2, internationally, more than 1.2 billion people—or one in five—survive on less than U.S.$1 a day (United Nations, 2003, p. 5). The past few decades have seen some improvements in the least industrialized countries: life expectancy increased by eight years and literacy rates improved dramatically (United Nations, 2003, p. 2). However, during the 1990s, average per capita income growth was less than 3 percent in 125 countries, and actually declined in 54 of them (United Nations, 2003, p. 3). The poorest countries face critical, life-threatening crises: increasing poverty, food shortages, and increased rates of hunger.

To further understand the tremendous differences between the richest and poorest people in the world, consider income share. In the first years of the twentieth century, the richest 1 percent of people received income equal to 57 percent of the world's poorest people. Further, the income of the world's richest 10 percent of the population was 127.7 times that of the poorest 10 percent (Centre for Social Justice, 2001; United Nations, 2001). The three families sketched in the chapter's opening vignette provide insight into the far-reaching effects of globalization on citizens around the world, as does the Thinking Critically about Social Controversy box on Children as Prey.

Over the past two centuries, the gap between the richest and poorest countries has grown tremendously. In 1820, the richest countries were roughly three times richer than the poorest, based on Gross Domestic Product (GDP) per capita. This ratio rose to 15 times by 1950 and to 19 times by 1998 (Lee, 2002). The world's richest people's share of total GDP has skyrocketed over the past 40 years (see Table 5.2).

TABLE 5.2 Share of the Total GDP of the World's People: Richest 20 Percent versus Poorest 20 Percent

Year	Share of Top 20% Compared to Bottom 20%
1960	30x
1970	32x
1980	45x
1989	59x
1997	74x

Note: In 1997, the top 20 percent received 74 times the income of the bottom 20 percent.

Source: Based on "The Global Divide: Inequality in the World Economy" by Marc Lee, 2002, *Behind the Numbers: Economic Facts, Figures and Analysis, 4,* No. 2. Ottawa: Canadian Centre for Policy Alternatives. Reproduced from United National Development Program, *Human Development Report 1999.* New York: Oxford University Press, pp. 36–37.

In Phnom Penh, Cambodia, the city dump is home to many people, and a highly developed social organization has emerged. Pictured here, after garbage has been delivered by truck, people stream around it, struggling to be the first to discover something of value. Workers use metal picks, like the one this child is holding, to sift through the trash. Note that children work alongside adults.

Sociologist Martha Huggins (1993) reports that in Brazilian slums, poverty is so deep that children and adults swarm over garbage dumps searching for enough decaying food to keep them alive. To add insult to injury, the owners of these dumps hire armed guards to keep the poor out—so they can sell the garbage for pig food. Even more shocking, poor children are systematically killed. Every year, Brazilian police and death squads murder close to 2000 children. Some associations of shop owners go so far as to put hit men on retainers and auction victims off to the lowest bidder. The going rate is half a month's salary—figured at the low rate of a Brazilian minimum wage.

A life of slavery is bad enough—but death squads for children? To understand, we must recognize Brazil's long history of violence. Brazil has an extremely high rate of poverty, only a small middle class, and is controlled by a small group of families who, under a veneer of democracy, make the country's major decisions. Hordes of homeless children, with no schools or jobs to attend, roam the streets. To survive, they wash windshields, shine shoes, beg, and steal. These children, part of what are known as the "dangerous classes," threaten the status quo.

The "respectable" classes see them as nothing but trouble. They hurt business, for customers feel uncomfortable or intimidated when they see a group of begging children clustered in front of stores. Some shoplift; others dare to sell items in competition with local shops. With no social institutions to care for these children, some see killing them as a solution. As Huggins notes, murder sends a clear message, especially if accompanied by ritual torture—pulling out eyes, ripping open chests, cutting off genitals, raping girls, and burning victims' bodies.

The plight of these Brazilian children is replicated around the globe. Worldwide, 1.2 billion persons live on a dollar a day or less. Tens of millions of children are on the streets, locked out of schools because their parents cannot afford school fees. And more than a million children die each year from diarrhea because they do not have access to clean drinking water (Mokhiber & Weissman, 2002).

In some societies, even the law fails to provide adequate protection. In China, children younger than 16 are forbidden from working, but an estimated 10 million school-age children, usually girls and often from rural areas, are

assemblers in manufacturing plants or work illegally in any number of other activities. Some of these children have been kidnapped. "Children, some as young as four, roam China's relatively prosperous coastal cities, begging on the streets or selling roses deep into the night, apparently victims of schemes that use youngsters as bait" (Ni, 2005). In some cases, "rural schools have contracted out entire classes of students to work in urban factories, supposedly to help defray school costs" (Ni, 2005). And child labourers face appallingly dangerous, unhealthy, and dirty working conditions, including 12-hour shifts with no time off. For these children, there are no alternatives. They drop out of school because their families cannot afford tuition.

For Your Consideration
Can the most industrialized nations do anything about this situation? Or are they partially responsible? Are these problems "internal" affairs that should be left to the Brazilians or Chinese to handle as they wish? Or are they the result of globalization? Can you do anything to help?

The Most Industrialized Nations

	Nation	Income per Person
1	Luxembourg	$58,900
2	United States	$39,820
3	Norway	$38,680
4	Switzerland	$35,660
5	Ireland	$32,930
6	Iceland	$31,900
7	Austria	$31,800
8	Denmark	$31,770
9	Hong Kong (a part of China)	$31,560
10	Belgium	$31,530
11	United Kingdom	$31,430
12	Netherlands	$31,360
13	Canada	$30,760
14	Sweden	$29,880
15	Japan	$29,810
16	Finland	$29,800
17	France	$29,460
18	Australia	$29,340
19	Germany	$28,170
20	Italy	$28,020
21	Singapore	$27,370
22	Taiwan	$25,300
23	Israel	$23,770
24	New Zealand	$22,260

The Industrializing Nations

	Nation	Income per Person
25	Spain	$24,750
26	Greece	$22,230
27	Slovenia	$20,830
28	Korea, South	$20,530
29	Portugal	$19,240
30	Czech Republic	$18,420
31	Hungary	$15,800
32	Slovakia	$14,480
33	Saudi Arabia	$13,810
34	Estonia	$13,630
35	Poland	$12,730
36	Lithuania	$12,690
37	Argentina	$12,530
38	Croatia	$11,920
39	Latvia	$11,820
40	South Africa	$10,960
41	Chile	$10,610
42	Malaysia	$9,720
43	Russia	$9,680
44	Mexico	$9,640
45	Costa Rica	$9,220
46	Uruguay	$9,030
47	Romania	$8,330
48	Brazil	$7,940
49	Bulgaria	$7,940
50	Thailand	$7,930
51	Bosnia	$7,230
52	Colombia	$6,940
53	Venezuela	$5,830

The Least Industrialized Nations

	Nation	Income per Person		Nation	Income per Person
54	Botswana[3]	$9,580	70	Lebanon	$5,550
55	Turkey	$7,720	71	Peru	$5,400
56	Namibia	$7,520	72	Albania	$5,070
57	Tunisia	$7,430	73	Philippines	$4,950
58	Belarus	$6,970	74	El Salvador	$4,890
59	Kazakhstan	$6,930	75	Paraguay	$4,820
60	Dominican Republic	$6,860	76	Jordan	$4,770
61	Panama	$6,730	77	Suriname	$4,300
62	Macedonia	$6,560	78	Guatemala	$4,260
63	Belize	$6,500	79	Morocco	$4,250
64	Ukraine	$6,330	80	Sri Lanka	$4,210
65	Algeria	$6,320	81	Egypt	$4,200
66	China	$5,890	82	Armenia	$4,160
67	Gabon	$5,700	83	Jamaica	$3,950
68	Turkmenistan	$5,700	84	Azerbaijan	$3,810
69	Swaziland	$5,650	85	Guyana	$3,800
			86	Ecuador	$3,770

FIGURE 5.2 Global Stratification: Income of the World's Nations

The Oil-Rich Nations

Nation	Income per Person
149 United Arab Emirates	$24,090
150 Qatar	$23,200
151 Kuwait	$21,610
152 Bahrain	$19,200
153 Oman	$14,680
154 Iran	$7,530
155 Iraq[2]	$2,100

The Least Industrialized Nations

Nation	Income per Person	Nation	Income per Person	Nation	Income per Person	Nation	Income per Person
87 Syria	$3,500	102 Cameroon	$2,120	119 Nepal	$1,480	135 Zambia	$890
88 Indonesia	$3,480	103 Mauritania	$2,050	120 Cote d'Ivoire	$1,470	136 Madagascar	$840
89 Nicaragua	$3,480	104 Zimbabwe	$2,040	121 Uganda	$1,450	137 Yemen	$810
90 India	$3,120	105 Bangladesh	$1,970	122 Bhutan	$1,400	138 Afghanistan	$800
91 Cuba	$3,000	106 Moldova	$1,950	123 Chad	$1,340	139 Niger	$780
92 Georgia	$2,900	107 Angola	$1,930	124 Djibouti	$1,300	140 Ethiopia	$750
93 Honduras	$2,760	108 Mongolia	$1,900	125 Rwanda	$1,240	141 Congo	$740
94 Equatorial Guinea	$2,700	109 Gambia	$1,890	126 Burkina Faso	$1,170	142 Guinea-Bissau	$690
95 Vietnam	$2,700	110 Laos	$1,880	127 Mozambique	$1,170	143 Congo, Democratic Republic	$680
96 Bolivia	$2,600	111 Krygyzstan	$1,860	128 Tajikistan	$1,160	144 Tanzania	$670
97 Cambodia	$2,310	112 Uzbekistan	$1,860	129 Kenya	$1,130	145 Burundi	$660
98 Papua-New Guinea	$2,280	113 Sudan	$1,810	130 Central African Republic	$1,100	146 Malawi	$630
99 Ghana	$2,220	114 Burma	$1,700	131 Benin	$1,090	147 Somalia	$600
100 Pakistan	$2,170	115 Korea, North	$1,700	132 Nigeria	$970	148 Sierra Leone	$550
101 Guinea	$2,160	116 Senegal	$1,660	133 Eritrea	$960		
		117 Togo	$1,510	134 Mali	$950		
		118 Haiti	$1,500				

[1]Income is a country's purchasing power parity based on its per capita gross domestic product measured in U.S. dollars. Since some totals vary widely from year to year, they must be taken as approximate. [2]Iraq's oil has been disrupted by war. [3]Botswana's relative wealth is based on its diamond mines.

Sources: By the author. Based on *Statistical Abstract of the United States* 2007: Table 1324, with a few missing countries taken from the CIA's latest *World Factbook*.

GDP measures the dollar value of all final goods and services produced *within* the borders of a country such as Canada or the United States in a given year. GDP must be distinguished from GNP, or Gross National Product, which does not include goods and services produced by *foreign* producers but does include the dollar value of goods and services produced by all Canadian-owned firms operating in foreign countries. GDP is the preferred measure of whether an economy is expanding or contracting used by economists and other social scientists.

According to the U.S. Institute for Policy Studies, there were 497 billionaires worldwide in 2001, with a combined wealth of $1.54 trillion, a figure that exceeded the combined GNPs of all the nations of sub-Saharan Africa or those of the oil-rich regions of the Middle East or North Africa. Moreover, the billionaires' combined wealth was "greater than the combined incomes of the poorest half of all of humanity" (IPS, quoted in Mokhiber & Weissman, 2002).

Modifying the Model

The classification of nations into the most industrialized, industrializing, and least industrialized is helpful in that it pinpoints gross differences among them. But it also presents problems. How much industrialization does a nation require in order to be classified as "most industrialized" or "industrializing"? Several nations have become "postindustrial." Does this new stage require a separate classification? The oil-rich nations of the Middle East are not industrialized, but by providing the oil and gasoline that fuel the machinery of the most industrialized nations, they have become immensely wealthy. Consequently, to classify them simply as "least industrialized" glosses over significant distinctions, such as their modern hospitals, extensive prenatal care, pure water systems, abundant food and shelter, high literacy, and computerized banking.

Kuwait, on whose behalf the United States and other most industrialized nations fought Iraq in the First Gulf War, is an excellent example of the difficulties posed by this classification system. Kuwait is so wealthy that almost none of its citizens are employed. The government simply pays each resident a generous annual salary. Migrant workers from poor nations do most of the onerous chores of daily life, while highly skilled workers from the most industrialized nations run the specialized systems that keep Kuwait's economy going—and, on occasion, fight its wars. Table 5.3 reflects this significant distinction.

SOCIOLOGICAL THEORIES OF GLOBAL AND SOCIAL ECONOMIC DEVELOPMENT

How did the world come to be divided into such distinct worlds of development? The obvious answer is that the poorer nations have fewer resources than the richer ones. As with so many other "obvious" answers, however, this one,

TABLE 5.3   An Alternative Model of the Global Economy

Four Worlds of Development
1. Most industrialized nations
2. Industrializing nations
3. Least industrialized nations
4. Oil-rich, non-industrialized nations

too, falls short, for many of the industrializing and least industrialized nations are rich in natural resources, while one of the most industrialized nations, Japan, has few. Four competing theories explain how some countries developed faster than others and how globalization came about.

Imperialism and Colonization

The first theory suggests that the first European nations to industrialize got a jump on the rest of the world. Beginning in Great Britain about 1750, industrialization spread throughout Western Europe. Powerful new technology produced great wealth, resulting in surplus capital. According to economist John Hobson (1858–1940), the industrialized nations lacked enough consumers to make it profitable to invest all excess capital at home. Consequently, business leaders persuaded their governments to embark on **imperialism**, to take over other countries so they could expand their markets and gain access to cheap raw materials.

Backed by the powerful armaments developed by their new technology, the industrialized nations found easy prey elsewhere (Harrison, 1993). The result was **colonization**, where more powerful nations made colonies out of weaker ones. After invading and subduing a country, colonizers left a controlling force to exploit its labour and natural resources. At one point, there was virtually a free-for-all among European industrialized nations as they rushed to divide the continent of Africa. As Europe sliced it into pieces, even tiny Belgium got in the act and acquired the Congo—a country 75 times its own size. While the powerful European nations planted national flags in a colony and sent representatives to directly run the government, the United States, after it industrialized, usually chose to plant corporate flags in a colony and let corporations dominate the territory's government. Central and South America are prime examples of U.S. *economic imperialism*. No matter the form, whether benevolent or harsh, the purpose was the same—to exploit another nation's people and resources for the benefit of a "mother" country.

Western imperialism and colonization shaped the least industrialized nations (Martin, 1994). In some instances, the most industrialized nations were so powerful that to divide their spoils, they drew lines across a map, creating new states without regard for tribal or cultural considerations (Kennedy, 1993). Britain and France followed this policy in North

Africa and parts of the Middle East, which explains why the national boundaries of Libya, Saudi Arabia, Kuwait, and other nations are so straight.

World System Theory

Sociologist Immanuel Wallerstein (1974, 1979, 1984, 1990) proposed a **world system** theory. Since the 1500s, Wallerstein argued, economic, political, social, and cultural interactions have grown between nations. Today, these links are so great that they tie most of the world's countries together. At the beginning of the expansion of capitalism from its European origins, Wallerstein identified four groups of interconnected nations. The first group is comprised of the *core nations*, those that first embraced capitalism. These regions (Britain, France, Holland, and later Germany) grew rich and powerful. The second group—the nations around the Mediterranean—Wallerstein called the **semiperiphery**. Their economies stagnated as a result of their dependence on trade with the core nations. The third group, the **periphery**, or fringe, consists of the eastern European countries. Because they were primarily limited to selling cash crops to the core nations, their economies developed even less. The fourth group, the *external area*, includes most of Africa and Asia. These nations were left out of the development of capitalism and had few economic connections with the core nations.

Capitalism's relentless expansion gave birth to a **capitalist world economy**, dominated by the most industrialized nations. This economy is so all-encompassing that today, no single region is outside the reach of global capitalism. All the nations of the world can be classified as core, semiperiphery, or periphery.

CANADA AS A SEMIPERIPHERAL COUNTRY At a time when most sociologists and political economists argued that Canada was a developed core nation, one of the authors of this text, a graduate student of Immanuel Wallerstein in the mid 1970s, tackled the question of whether this was true or whether Canada displayed the characteristics of a semiperipheral country. In an article entitled "Rich but Semiperipheral: Canada's Ambiguous Position in the World Economy," Dan Glenday (1989) presented evidence for Canada as a semiperipheral nation. Canada's major economic sectors, with the exception of banking, insurance, and transportation, are heavily foreign owned and/or controlled. Canada ships its natural resources to the U.S., Japan, and China, but operates its own direct investment outlets in the Caribbean and in other peripheral countries of the world economy.

Why was this important? Semiperipheral countries, according to Wallerstein, possess unique characteristics. First, they act like core countries when trading with the periphery, but appear to behave as peripheral nations when engaged in economic relations with core regions. Semiperipheral nations also display direct and immediate interest in the control of the market at both internal and international levels (1989: p. 238). Clearly, from the point of view of global economic relations, Canada behaved and still behaves like a semiperipheral country.

Glenday argues that Canada's state policies, such as the Free Trade Agreement and, later, the North American Free Trade Agreement, were critical in defining our status in the world economy. Would these initiatives raise Canada's status in the world economy and thereby increase economic and social advantages for all Canadians? Or would they push Canada downward, distancing it from the core countries, and, as a result, negatively impact our economic and social future?

Recently, Glenday (2009) offered an assessment of these and other state policies on Canada's position in the world economy. While Canada remains defined as a rich nation, we are sliding downward in the world economy. How does Canada's descent impact on the kind of job opportunities available to young Canadians, the social choices we can make, and the life chances for this and future generations?

Developed core countries offer their citizens access to many economic, social, medical, and cultural advantages, especially when compared to poorer peripheral countries. In relation to semiperipheral countries such as Canada, core countries such as France, Germany, Great Britain, and Japan are better off economically, socially, and culturally. Canada's good fortune lies in our rich endowment of natural resources, from oil and gas to gold and diamonds. Our natural resources are exported to other countries, where they are processed and re-sold in the global marketplace, expanding employment, social choices, and life chances in those regions. Today, Canadians in Alberta and Saskatchewan benefit from the export of oil and natural gas. Tomorrow, Canadians in Newfoundland and Nova Scotia will likely benefit from the discovery and exploitation of offshore natural resources. Instead of unifying the country, the uneven distribution of natural resources is transforming Canada into a patchwork of natural resource "sheikdoms." How long will our good fortune last? On what other industries is our economy being built? What will the extent of social choices be for this and future generations of Canadians? These questions must be addressed and openly debated.

INFORMATION TECHNOLOGY AND THE NEWS As noted at the beginning of the chapter, the extensive movement of capital, technology, people, and ideas between nations that was ushered in by the expansion of capitalism is called **globalization** (Kanter, 1997b). Although globalization has been under way for several hundred years, today's new forms of communication and transportation have greatly intensified the process.

Our extensive interconnection has been made possible in part by the existence of cable news. Satellite, fibre-optic, and other technologies bring events that are happening in remote parts of the world into our living rooms. Communications technology has made the world smaller, with international outlets such as CNN, Fox News, the BBC, and Al Jazeera creating a "global news village" in which those with the means can watch stories from around the world. People can now claim certain commonalities on which to base a shared experience, even though they live in very different cultures and nations.

Conversely, much technology is owned and controlled by a small group of companies and as a result has made the world more divisive—the heavy influence of "Americanized" news underscores the disparity between the United States and the rest of the world. Instead of serving to unite the "global news village," the news often inserts a wedge between civilizations. Deep divisions about how to interpret what is happening in the world are reproduced in news presentations worldwide. All societies today, no matter where they are, are part of a global social system with built-in contradictions.

Dependency Theory

The third theory is sometimes difficult to distinguish from world system theory. **Dependency theory** stresses how the least industrialized nations became dependent on the most industrialized nations (Cardoso, 1972; Furtado, 1984). According to dependency theory, the first nations to industrialize turned other nations into plantations and mines, harvesting or extracting whatever they needed to meet their growing appetite for raw materials and exotic foods. As a result, many of the least industrialized nations began to specialize in single cash crops. Brazil became a coffee plantation for the most industrialized nations. Nicaragua and other Central American countries specialized in bananas (hence the term "banana republic"). Chile became the primary source of tin, and Zaire (then the Belgian Congo) was transformed into a rubber plantation. Nations in the Middle East were turned into gigantic oil wells. A major point of dependency theory is that the domination of the least industrialized nations rendered them unable to develop independent economies.

There is substantial evidence that as capital has moved around the world, poverty has increased and quality of life for millions of people has deteriorated. The process of globalization has accelerated economic competition among countries. To compete with one another in world markets, many nations have lowered wages, eliminated worker support programs and environmental protection, decreased social spending, and dismantled public health care and other essential services (Brecher & Costello, 1998; McNally, 2002). Sociologists such as James Petras and Henry Veltmeyer (2001) argue that globalization is a modern form of imperialism that advances the interests of the powerful and privileged and neither enhances quality of life nor extends social justice to ordinary people.

Culture of Poverty

An entirely different explanation of global poverty was proposed by economist John Kenneth Galbraith (1979), who contends that the least industrialized nations were held back by their own cultures. Building on the ideas of anthropologist Oscar Lewis (1966a, 1966b), Galbraith argued that some nations are crippled by a **culture of poverty**, a way of life that perpetuates poverty from one generation to the next. Most of the world's poor live in rural areas, where they barely eke out a living from the land. Their marginal life offers little room for error or risk, so they tend to stick closely to tried-and-true, traditional ways, according to Galbraith. Experimenting with new farming or manufacturing techniques is threatening, because if they fail, the result could be hunger or death. Their religion also reinforces traditionalism, for it teaches fatalism, the acceptance of one's lot in life as God's will.

Evaluating the Theories

Most sociologists prefer imperialism, world system theory, and dependency theory to Galbraith's culture of poverty theory, given that the latter places blame on the victim—the poor nations themselves. It faults the characteristics of poor nations rather than international arrangements that benefit the most industrialized nations at their expense. But even taken together, these theories yield only part of the picture, as becomes evident from the example of Japan. After World War II, with a religion that stressed fatalism and two major cities destroyed by atomic bombs, Japan—through stripped of its colonies—became an economic powerhouse that turned the Western world on its head. Looking at detailed socio-historical national studies examining the way in which culture, political structure, and class relations affect global economic positioning may provide us with the clearest understanding of globalization, inequality, and development.

Focus Question
Which theory or theories do you think most adequately explain globalization?

THE STRUCTURES OF GLOBALIZATION

Regardless of how globalization developed, why do the same countries remain rich year after year, while the rest stay poor? Let's look at how world inequality is maintained by some of the structures of globalization.

Neocolonialism

Sociologist Michael Harrington (1977) argued that nineteenth century colonialism was replaced by twentieth century **neocolonialism**. When World War II changed public sentiment about sending soldiers and colonists to weaker countries, the most industrialized nations turned to international markets as a way of controlling the least industrialized nations. These powerful nations determine how much they will pay for tin from Bolivia, copper from Peru, coffee from Brazil, and so forth. They also move hazardous industries into the least industrialized nations.

As many of us learn, falling behind on a debt often means that we find ourselves dangling at the end of a string pulled by our creditor. The same is true for neocolonialism. Selling weapons and other manufactured goods to the least industrialized nations on credit turns those countries into eternal debtors. The capital they need to develop their own industries goes instead to debt, ever bloated with mounting interest. As debtors, these nations are also vulnerable to trading terms dictated by the agents of globalization, such as the IMF and World Bank (Tordoff, 1992; Carrington, 1993).

Thus, although the least industrialized nations have their own governments—whether elected or dictatorships—they remain almost as dependent on the most industrialized nations as they were when those nations occupied them.

Transnational Corporations

Transnational or **multinational corporations**, companies that operate across many national boundaries, also help maintain the global dominance of the most industrialized nations. In some cases, multinational corporations directly exploit the least industrialized nations. A prime example is the United Fruit Company, which controlled national and local politics in Central America for decades, running these nations as fiefdoms for the company's own profit while the U.S. Marines waited in the wings in case the company's interests needed to be backed up. Most commonly, however, transnational corporations help maintain globalization simply by doing business. A single transnational may do mining in several countries, manufacturing in many others, and run transportation and marketing networks around the globe. No matter where profits are made or where they are reinvested, the primary beneficiaries are the most industrialized nations, and especially the one in which the multinational corporation has its world headquarters. As Michael Harrington (1977) stressed, the real profits are made in processing the products and in controlling their distribution—profits that are withheld from the least industrialized nations. For more on multinational corporations, see Chapter 11.

Transnational corporations try to work closely with the elite of the least industrialized nations (Lipton, 1979; Waldman, 1995a; Sklair, 2001). Those elite, who live a sophisticated upper-class life in the major cities of their home countries, send their children to Oxford, the Sorbonne, McGill, or Harvard to be educated. Multinational corporations funnel investments to this small circle of power, whose members favour projects such as building laboratories and computer centres in capital cities, projects that do not help the vast majority of people living in poor, remote villages eking out a meagre living on small plots of land.

The end result is an informal partnership between transnational corporations and the elite of the least industrialized nations. The elite benefit by receiving subsidies (or payoffs); the corporations gain access to the countries' raw materials, labour, and market. Both benefit through political stability, necessary to keep the partnership alive.

This is not the full story, however. Transnational corporations also play a role in changing the process of development in some countries, such as in India and China. This is an unintentional by-product of their worldwide search for cheap resources and labour. By moving manufacturing from the most industrialized nations with high labour costs to the least industrialized nations with low labour costs, they not only exploit cheap labour, but, in some cases, also bring prosperity to certain regions within those nations. Although workers in the least industrialized nations are paid a pittance, it is more than they can earn elsewhere. With new factories come opportunities to develop new skills and a capital base. This does not occur in all nations, but the Pacific Rim nations, nicknamed the "Asian tigers," are remarkable. They have developed such a strong capital base that they have begun to rival the older capitalist nations.

Technology and the Maintenance of Global Domination

The race between the most and least industrialized nations to develop and apply new information technologies can be compared to a marathon runner competing against a one-legged man. The vast profits amassed by multinational corporations allow the most industrialized nations to invest huge sums in the latest technology. Wal-Mart, along with a few restaurant chains, controls 54 percent of the direct sales market in Mexico, with 687 stores in 71 cities (Ribeiro, 2005). Multinationals often use technologies to track their customers' purchases and streamline production processes in order to shave what sometimes amounts to only a fraction of a cent off costs. Gillette spent $100 million to adjust its output "on an hourly basis" (Zachary, 1995). Many least industrialized nations would greatly benefit from a $100 million investment in their national economy, much less to fine-tune production in a single organization. In short, new technologies accrue even more advantages for the most industrialized nations.

ANTI-GLOBALIZATION

José Bové is considered by many to be an important representative of the anti-globalization movement. He is widely known for campaigning against genetically modified crops and has led protests in Brazil and France. His most publicized protest was directed at the cheese used by McDonald's restaurants, which he viewed as the most effective way to protest U.S. trade restrictions against locally made Rocquefort cheese. On August 12, 1999, Bové led a group known as the Peasant Confederation to vandalize a McDonald's restaurant in Millau, France. He was sentenced to three months in prison and, together with nine others, became known as the Millau 10. (BBC, February 15, 2001)

Targeting the negative practices of transnational corporations is one major strategy of the anti-globalization movement. Such protests usually focus on the following:

- aim for the maximization of profits
- locate where the salaries are lowest
- employ children and women in factories
- destroy the environment through production
- obliterate cultural identities
- amass greater power than many nation states

A second target of anti-globalization protestors is international organizations such as the World Bank, the International Monetary Fund, and the World Trade Organization, whose objective is to promote policies of free trade and balanced state budgets. According to the movement, such policies put an intolerable weight on the shoulders of the poor countries by increasing debt loads and pushing for reductions in social expenditures. Often, protesters request that rich countries "forgive" the debts owed to them by poorer nations.

World Social Forum

Founded in 2001 in Porto Alegre, Brazil, the World Social Forum (WSF) is not an organization or formal group; rather, it uses the internet as an "open space" to bring together social

Eight-year-old Mahashury is a *bonded laborer* who was exchanged by her parents for a 2000 rupee loan (about $14). To repay the loan, Mahashury must do construction work for a year. She will receive one meal a day and a single set of clothing for the year. Because this centuries-old practice is now illegal, the master bribes Indian officials, who inform him when they are going to inspect the construction site.

movements, organizations, NGOs, and individuals to discuss alternatives to globalization. In its own words, the WSF seeks to bring together all those who oppose "neo-liberal globalization" and "imperialism in all its forms." It meets in January of every year in order to counterbalance the discussions of the World Economic Forum, which is a Geneva-based foundation whose annual meetings in Davos, Switzerland, bring together leaders of the most powerful economic organizations (companies with annual earnings over $1 billion), national political leaders (presidents, prime ministers, and others), and selected intellectuals.

Globalization, Forced Child Labour, and Slavery

Before attending university, many young Canadians worked part-time. However, in all provinces and territories, there are several laws prohibiting employers from hiring a young person for full-time work (see Chapter 11 for a description of the Canadian labour market and labour laws). The most important restriction is compulsory school attendance. In every province, a young person must attend school until graduation from high school or until she/he reaches the age of 18 (Labour Law Analysis, International and Intergovernmental Labour Affairs, Labour Program, Human Resources and Social Development Canada, October 15, 2006; www.hrsdc.gc.ca/en/lp/spila/clli/eslc/minage(e).pdf). At least five Canadian provinces allow children under the age of 14 to work with permission from their parents and the Director of Employment Standards (www.cbc.ca/childlabour/ilo.html).

The International Labour Organization, a United Nations agency, has established conventions regarding child labour. Convention 138 deals with the minimum age of working and recommends a minimum age of 15 for employment of any kind. Convention 182 deals with dangerous work environments for children. On June 22, 2008, Canada signed on to Convention 182 but not Convention 138 (http://webfusion.ilo.org/public/db/standards/normes/appl/appl-ratif8conv.cfm?Lang=EN).

THINKING CRITICALLY ABOUT SOCIAL CONTROVERSY
Poverty: A Global Warning

Poverty and growing social inequality are not simply local problems; they have global dimensions. Current estimates suggest that one in five people in the world live on less than $1 per day and 8 million people die each year as a result of poverty (Williams, 2004; Sachs, 2005). Almost 11 million children die each year before the age of five in developing countries and almost half of their deaths are from preventable causes such as diarrhea, measles, malaria, and acute respiratory infection ("Bid to Cut Mortality Rate," 2005). While the industrial countries have long been aware of global inequalities, economic globalization—along with the increasing prominence of global organizations such as the World Trade Organization (WTO), the World Bank, and the International Monetary Fund (IMF)—have heightened Canadians' awareness of broader poverty issues. In particular, the events of September 11, 2001, resulted in many analysts pointing to the growing chasm between rich and poor nations as a trigger for international violence and terrorism and a threat to world security.

The issue of global poverty is particularly pressing since the neo-liberal course proposed by the WTO and others has become increasingly suspect. The vision that international investment in the economies of developing countries, combined with open markets and more liberalized trade, would level the playing field and trickle down to the world's poor has not been fulfilled. Developing countries, in particular in

Africa, have made relatively little headway in reducing poverty levels. Indeed, the World Bank suggests that the economic situation for most of Africa is worse today than it was 40 years ago. Although Africa is home to about 10 percent of the world population, its gross domestic product (GDP—the value of all goods and services produced annually) is only about 1 percent of the global GDP, and the continent receives less than 1 percent of foreign direct investment. Meanwhile, protectionist policies (tariffs and quotas on foreign imports) in North America and the European Union make it almost impossible for African goods to enter these markets (Rees, 2002; Khalif, 2002).

The problem is not confined to Africa. Around the globe, the rich have become richer and the poor, poorer. In 1970, the richest 10 percent of the world's population earned 19 times the income of the poorest 10 percent. By 1997, the ratio grew to 27:1. By this time, the wealthiest 1 percent of the world's population earned as much income as the poorest 57 percent, and the 25 million wealthiest Americans (0.4 percent of the global population) received an income larger than that of the poorest 2 billion people on earth (43 percent of the global population) (Rees, 2002). This economic pattern of inequality translates into a myriad of other inequalities. Currently, 90 percent of the world's medical health research dollars focus on the health problems of 20 percent of the

global population. Cancer and heart disease take pre-eminence while the infectious diseases such as malaria and tuberculosis, which cause half the deaths in developing countries, receive relatively little attention (Calamai, 2002). The AIDS pandemic brings into clear focus the life and death consequences of global inequities. There are an estimated 25 million people in sub-Saharan Africa with HIV/AIDS and, despite the development of life-saving drug regimens in Western countries, 2.3 million of those afflicted die each year. In some areas, the population of 15- to 24-year-old females has been decimated and children are left to the care of orphanages, aging relatives, or the streets (www.stephenlewisfoundation.org).

The rich nations have not rushed forward to resolve the global inequalities. The IMF is a specialized United Nations agency with 182 member countries, created in 1944 to help maintain the world monetary system. The World Bank was set up as a lender of last resort to the least industrialized nations. The WTO (which is a successor to other international trade organizations) is intended to bring countries together to improve international trade and, indirectly, encourage global standards in environmental protections, worker protections, and so on. The history of the various global governing agencies is complex, but their roles remain hotly debated and global inequality is a growing concern.

Even more direct efforts at assisting developing countries through the provision of foreign aid have had limited results and elicited only limited enthusiasm on the part of richer nations. Only Denmark, the Netherlands, Sweden, Norway, and Luxembourg have met the United Nations target of contributing 0.7 percent of their GDP to foreign aid. Canada contributes a scant 0.25 percent, behind much smaller economies such as Portugal and New Zealand. Indeed, Canadian foreign aid contributions in 2008 were at their lowest level in 30 years. Interestingly, at the bottom of the pack of 22 wealthy nations providing developmental aid to foreign countries is the United States, contributing 0.10 percent of its GDP ("Saturday Special," 2002, p. A25).

Currently, about one in three of the world's 6 billion people live in a state of "extreme poverty" and inhabitants in 21 countries are subsisting on average incomes of less than U.S.$1000 a year, while at the wealthy end of the scale, citizens of 17 wealthy nations average U.S.$20 000 a year. As widely publicized by Live Aid and other anti-poverty groups, if less than 1 percent of the income of the wealthiest countries was redirected to the poorest, almost everyone on the globe would have enough to eat as well as adequate health and education (Williams, 2004). At present, however, the future for global poverty appears bleak. The global population is expected to grow by another 2 billion people over the next 25 years, 97 percent of whom will

live in poorer countries (Rees, 2002; Crane, 2000).

Certainly, if the growing strains of global and local inequalities are not addressed, the negative consequences will likely impact on both the rich and poor (Laxer, 1998). Globalization—with its world trade and world travel in the midst of a world economy—ensures that we all share the outcomes. Ultimately, while the wealthy nations have attempted to create "gated communities," disease and environmental destruction cannot be kept out. If poor countries continue to plunder their natural resources in order to survive and in the process disregard environmental consequences, everyone on the planet will bear the results.

While the restrictions vary between provinces and Canada has yet to sign Convention 138, the exploitation of child labour in Canada is not knowingly tolerated. Child labour exists in many other parts of the globe, however. Globalization exposes the poorest people to some of the harshest working conditions. Consider chocolate, for example. Many Canadians and Americans were shocked to learn in early 2000 that some of their favourite candies might have been produced by child labourers in West Africa. In 2000, the U.S. State Department, Knight Ridder, and the BBC reported that roughly 15 000 children worked in conditions of forced labour picking beans in Ghana and Ivory Coast. Trafficked from extremely poor countries such as Mali and Burkina Faso, the children worked on some of the 1.5 million small cocoa farms in West Africa. These farms produce more than half the world's cacao, used to make candy, cookies, or cocoa butter for cosmetics. Attempts have been made to curb child labour on the cocoa plantations. One recent result is the Cocoa Protocol, a partnership of the major chocolate companies, government officials, and others. It called for a deadline of July 1, 2005, to ensure that all cocoa bean products would be grown and processed without

violating internationally accepted labour standards. Unfortunately, child labour still thrives on cocoa plantations even amid efforts by activists and others who have filed suit against Nestlé, ADM, and Cargill for their violations of international child labour laws.

All forms of slavery have not been eliminated. Child slavery in the form of the trafficking of young girls for the sex trade affects all parts of the globe, even Canada (see Chapter 6 for a more in-depth discussion of slavery).

A CONCLUDING NOTE

Consider again the three families in the opening vignette. Remember that they represent three worlds of development—that is, globalization, inequality, and development. Their life chances—from access to material possessions to their opportunities for education and even the likely age at which they will die—are profoundly affected by globalization and its consequences. The division of the globe into interconnected units of nations with more or less wealth and more or less power and prestige is much more than a matter of theoretical interest. In fact, it is *your* life we are talking about.

SUMMARY AND REVIEW

What Is Globalization

WHAT IS GLOBALIZATION?

Globalization involves the interaction and integration of increasing numbers of people in the world through international trade and investment, travel and tourism, and information technology and the mass media. pp. 95–96.

Globalization and Patterns of Movement of People

HOW DOES GLOBALIZATION IMPACT THE MOVEMENT OF PEOPLE?

The globalization of communications technology, the pervasiveness of mass communication—including television, film, videos, and music—and cheap air travel open the world to more people through increased tourism and immigration. pp. 96–97.

HOW DOES GLOBALIZATION IMPACT THE PAID AND UNPAID WORK OF WOMEN?
Globalization involves cutting costs, especially labour costs. This means factories and offices are closed in developed countries and transplanted to less developed countries, where labour—and women's labour in particular—is cheap. In the developed world, globalization means depressing wages and benefits for workers, especially vulnerable workers such as immigrant women. pp. 96–97.

Globalization: The Issues

WHAT ARE THE MAIN ARGUMENTS FOR AND AGAINST GLOBALIZATION?
Proponents of globalization argue that poor countries and their citizens benefit economically from increased employment opportunities and rising standards of living. Opponents of globalization point to the increased wealth, power, and privilege enjoyed by the developed and rich parts of the world that come at the expense of the less developed and poorer regions of the globe. Democracy, human rights, and labour rights are said to be undermined by institutions such as the IMF and the World Bank. pp. 97–98.

Globalization, Inequality, and Development

HOW ARE THE WORLD'S NATIONS STRATIFIED?
The model favoured by the authors of this text divides the world's nations into three groups: most industrialized, industrializing, and least industrialized. This layering represents relative property, power, and prestige. The oil-rich nations are an exception. pp. 98–102.

Sociological Theories of Global and Social Economic Development

WHAT ARE THE MAIN SOCIOLOGICAL THEORIES OF ECONOMIC AND SOCIAL DEVELOPMENT?
The main sociological theories that seek to account for global stratification are **imperialism** and **colonization**, **world system theory**, **dependency theory**, and the **culture of poverty**. pp. 102–105.

WHAT MAKES CANADA A SEMIPERIPHERAL COUNTRY AND WHY IS THIS IMPORTANT TO KNOW?
Canada's major economic sectors, with the exception of banking, insurance, and transportation, are heavily foreign owned and/or controlled. Canada ships its natural resources primarily to core countries but has direct investment outlets in the Caribbean and in other peripheral countries of the world economy. Canada's state policies, such as the FTA and NAFTA, which make us "open for business" to globalization, have consequences for Canadian employment and social and life choices. pp. 103–104.

The Structures of Globalization

HOW IS THE SYSTEM OF GLOBAL STRATIFICATION MAINTAINED?
There are three basic explanations for why nations remain stratified. **Neocolonialism** is the ongoing dominance of the least industrialized nations by the most industrialized nations. A second explanation attributes stratification to the influence of **multinational corporations**, which operate across national boundaries. New technologies give further advantage to the most industrialized nations. pp. 105–106.

KEY TERMS

capitalist world economy 103
colonization 102
culture of poverty 104
dependency theory 104

export processing zones 97
globalization 104
imperialism 102

multinational corporations 105
neocolonialism 105
periphery 103

semiperiphery 103
transnational corporations 105
world system 103

WEBLINKS

All URLs listed are current as of the printing of this book.

Globalization and Tourism
www.planeta.com
Planeta.com is the first website focusing on ecotourism, conservation, and tourism's effects on local communities.

The Stephen Lewis Foundation
www.stephenlewisfoundation.org
The Stephen Lewis Foundation website provides information on the AIDS pandemic in Africa and the need for greater

action from Western countries. Stephen Lewis, a prominent Canadian, is the United Nations' special envoy for HIV/AIDS in Africa.

Runaway World: A BBC 1999 Lecture Series by Anthony Giddens
http://news.bbc.co.uk/hi/english/static/events/reith_99/
The website provides access to text, audio, and video lectures given by Anthony Giddens, who plainly and succinctly dissects the links between globalization and its impact on tradition, the family, and democracy.

Globalization 101
www.globalization101.org/
Sponsored by The Levin Institute (a graduate institute of the State University of New York), this website provides useful, up-to-date information about globalization.

Anti-Globalization
www.anti-marketing.com/anti-globalization.html
An introduction to anti-globalization, including links to anti-globalization and pro-globalization organizations.

World Social Forum
www.wsf2008.net/
The main web page of WSF2008, an anti-globalization network.

CRITICAL THINKING QUESTIONS

1. Do you think that the low wage factories of multinational corporations, located in such countries as Mexico or China, represent exploitation or opportunity? Why?

2. Think of something you use every day—such as a cellphone or iPod, or Starbucks or Tim Horton's coffee— and find out where it was manufactured and/or assembled, marketed, and sold. How easy was it to find out? What did your journey of discovery teach you about globalization?

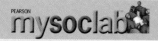

PEARSON
Explore the topics covered in this chapter on MySocLab using the access information provided with this text. Interactive resources for studying include multimedia tutorials, video clips, practice tests, quizzes, and animated maps and figures.

Social Inequality: The Canadian Experience in a Global Context

Ah, downtown Vancouver—that wonderful western gateway. Memories of past visits stirred my thoughts—lush gardens, a thriving metropolis, scenic waterways, sailboats, the yacht club, and the sights and sounds of a vibrant arts community.

Images of shelters for the homeless in the Lower Mainland startled me back into reality. The shelters were much like those I had visited in central and eastern Canada—dirty and crowded—and among the worst conditions I had encountered while conducting research on poverty.

The men looked dishevelled and haggard, with unmistakable expressions of despair—just like the homeless anywhere in the country. Poverty wears the same tired face wherever you are, I realized. The surroundings may differ, but the look remains unchanged.

I had grown used to the sights and smells of abject poverty. They no longer surprised me. But after spending a few hours in shelters with the homeless, I saw something that did.

A block or so from the shelter, I was startled by life-size, full-colour photographs mounted on the transparent Plexiglas shelter of a bus stop. Staring back at me were images of finely dressed men and women proudly modelling elegant suits, dresses, diamonds, and furs. Across the street from the bus shelter was a spa for dogs, featuring gourmet treats and home-baked goodies.

A wave of disgust swept over me. "Something is cock-eyed in this society," I thought, my mind juxtaposing these images of extravagance with the suffering I had just witnessed. Occasionally, the reality of social class hits home with brute force. This was one such moment.

The disjunction I felt that day was triggered by the ads, but it was not the first time I had experienced this sensation. Whenever my research abruptly transported me from the world of the homeless to one of another social class, I experienced a sense of disjointed unreality. Each social class has its own way of being, and because these fundamental orientations to the world contrast so sharply, the classes appear to be in different worlds altogether.

Source: Based on the personal experiences of James Henslin. Adapted for the Canadian edition.

LEARNING OUTCOMES

After you have studied this chapter, you will be able to answer the following questions:

1. **What are the four major systems of social stratification?**

2. **What is social class, and how do sociologists measure it?**

3. **What are three criteria used to measure social class?**

4. **What is meant by the term *status inconsistency*?**

5. **How do nations maintain social stratification?**

6. **What models are used to portray the social classes?**

7. **How does social class affect people?**

8. **What are the three types of social mobility?**

9. **Who becomes poor?**

10. **Why are individualistic explanations of poverty more popular than structural explanations?**

11. **How is the Horatio Alger myth functional for society?**

Startling contrasts in wealth and quality of life are found in urban areas, and Vancouver in no exception. These contrasting images of beautiful downtown Vancouver—a thriving metropolis with scenic waterways, gardens, yacht clubs, and business towers—and an impoverished area of the city were taken within walking distance of one another.

WHAT IS SOCIAL STRATIFICATION?

Some of the world's nations are wealthy, others are poor, and some are in-between. This layering of nations, or of groups of people within a nation, is called *social stratification*. Social stratification is one of the most significant topics discussed in this text, for it affects our life chances—from material possessions to the age at which we die.

Social stratification also affects our orientations to life. If you relied on a homeless shelter in Vancouver for survival, you would expect hunger to be a part of life and not be too surprised when people died around you. If you lived life as one of the models portrayed in the bus shelter ad, you would have quite different views of the world.

It is important to emphasize that social stratification does not refer to individuals. It is *a way of ranking large groups of people into a hierarchy that shows their relative privileges*. **Social stratification** is a system in which people are divided into layers according to their relative power, property, and prestige.

Let's examine how inequalities profoundly affect everyone's chances in life. But first we'll review the major systems of social stratification.

SYSTEMS OF SOCIAL STRATIFICATION

Every society stratifies its members in some form. Some, such as agricultural societies, draw firm lines that separate group from group, while others, such as hunting and gathering societies, show much greater equality. Regardless of its forms, however, the existence of social stratification is universal. There are four major systems of social stratification: slavery, caste, clan, and class.

Slavery

Slavery, with its essential characteristic of *ownership of some people by others*, has been common throughout world history. The Israelites of the Old Testament kept slaves, as did the ancient Africans. In classical Greece and Rome, slaves worked while free citizens engaged in politics and the arts. Slavery was least common among nomads, especially hunters and gatherers, and most common in agricultural societies (Landtman, 1938/1968).

Contrary to popular assumption, slavery was not always based on racism, but on one of three other factors. The first was debt. In some cultures, an individual who could not pay a debt could be enslaved by the creditor. The second was a violation of the law. Instead of being killed, a murderer or thief might be enslaved by the family of the victim as compensation for their loss. The third was war and conquest. When one group of people conquered another, it was often convenient to enslave at least some of the vanquished (Starna & Watkins, 1991). Historian Gerda Lerner (1986) notes that through this practice the first slaves were women. When premodern men raided a village or camp, they killed the men, raped the women, and then brought the women back as slaves. Women were valued for sexual purposes, reproduction, and extra labour. Slavery, then, was a sign of defeat in battle, of crime, or of debt, and not the sign of some inherently inferior status.

Indentured service represents a fuzzy line between a contract and slavery (Main, 1965; Elkins, 1968). Many people who desired to start a new life in the American colonies were unable to pay their passage. Ship captains would carry them on credit, depending on someone to "buy their paper" when they arrived. This arrangement provided passage for the penniless, payment for the ship's captain, and servants for wealthier colonists for a set number of years. During that specified period, servants had to serve their master—and could be captured and forcibly returned if they ran away. At the end of the period of indenture, servants became full citizens, able to live where they chose and free to sell their labour.

When colonists found that there were not enough indentured servants to meet their growing need for labour,

Negroes for Sale.

A Cargo of very fine stout Men and Women, in good order and fit for immediate service, just imported from the Windward Coast of Africa, in the Ship Two Brothers.——
Conditions are one half Cash or Produce, the other half payable the first of January next, giving Bond and Security if required.
The Sale to be opened at 10 o'Clock each Day, in Mr. Bourdeaux's Yard, at No, 48, on the Bay.
May 19, 1784.   JOHN MITCHELL.

Under slavery, humans are sold like a commodity. This 1784 announcement says that slaves could be bought for cash or exchanged for produce (crops).

they tried to enslave Indians. This attempt failed miserably, however. Among other reasons, when Indians escaped they knew how to survive in the wilderness and were able to make their way back to their tribes. The colonists then turned to Africans, who were being brought to North and South America by the Dutch, English, Portuguese, and Spanish.

Finding it profitable to make people slaves for life, slave owners developed an **ideology**, a system of beliefs that justifies social arrangements. Essential to an ideology that would justify lifelong slavery was the view that slaves were inferior. Some said that they were locked in a helpless, child-like state, which meant that they needed to be taken care of by superior people—white colonists, of course. Others even contended that slaves were not fully human. With such views, colonists developed elaborate justifications for slavery on the presumed superiority of their own race.

Patterns of legal discrimination did not end after the Civil War. Until 1954, for example, the United States operated two separate school systems. Even until the 1950s, to keep races from "mixing," it was illegal in Mississippi for a white and an African-American to sit together on the same seat of a car. To allow for African-American chauffeurs, there was no outright ban on both races being in the same car.

SLAVERY TODAY Slavery has surfaced in current times in Sudan, Mauritania, and Ivory Coast (Tandia, 2001; Bales, 2002; Del Castillo, 2002; Henslin, 2005). This region has a long history of slavery, and the practice was not officially abolished until 1980 in Mauritania, 1987 in Sudan (Ayittey, 1998), and 2004 in Niger (Andersson, 2005). However, although officially abolished, slavery continues to exist.

Caste

The second system of social stratification is caste. In a **caste system**, status is determined by birth and is life-long. In sociological terms the basis of a caste system is ascribed status. Achieved status cannot change an individual's place under this system. Someone born into a low-status group will always have low status, no matter how much that person may accomplish in life.

Societies with this form of stratification try to make certain that the boundaries between castes remain firm. They practise **endogamy**, marriage within their own group, and prohibit intermarriage. To prevent contact between castes, they even develop elaborate rules about *ritual pollution*, teaching that contact with inferior castes contaminates the superior caste.

INDIA India provides the best example of a caste system. Based on religion rather than race, the caste system has existed in India for almost 3000 years (Chandra, 1993a, b; Jaffrelot, 2006). India has four main castes, or *varnas*. These are subdivided into thousands of specialized subcastes, or *jati*, with each *jati* working in a specific occupation. For example, knife-sharpening is done only by members of a particular subcaste.

The *Harijan*, the lowest group, is actually so low that it is beneath the caste system altogether. *Harijans*, along with some *Shudras*, make up India's "untouchables." If someone of a higher caste is touched by an untouchable, that person becomes unclean. In some cases, even the shadow of an untouchable is contaminating. If anyone becomes contaminated, religion specifies ablution, or washing rituals, to restore purity (Lannoy, 1975).

Although the Indian government abolished the caste system in 1949, the force of centuries-old practices cannot be easily eliminated, and the caste system remains part of everyday life in India (Sharma, 1994). The ceremonies followed at births, marriages, and deaths, for example, are still dictated by caste (Chandra, 1993a). As a result of globalization, however, this system is breaking down as practices from around the globe are incorporated into everyday Indian life.

Clan

The **clan system** was once common in agricultural societies. In this system, every individual is linked to a large network of relatives called a **clan**. A clan is like a greatly extended

These photographs, taken at the end of the nineteenth century, illustrate the different worlds social classes produce within the same society. The boys on the left worked full-time when they could get work. They did not go to school, and they had no home. The children on the right, Cornelius and Gladys Vanderbilt, are shown in front of their parents' estate. They went to school and did not work. You can see how the life situations illustrated in these photos would have produced different orientations to the world—and, therefore, politics, ideas, and so on—the stuff of which life is made.

family. Just as in a family, if a clan has a high status, so do individual members. Similarly, an individual's resources—whether few or many—are the same as the clan's. And like a family, allegiance to a clan is a life-long obligation.

Clans are like castes in that membership is determined by birth and is life-long. Unlike castes, however, marriages can cross clan lines. In fact, marriages may be used to forge alliances between clans, for the obligations that a marriage establishes between in-laws can bind clans together (Erturk, 1994).

Just as globalization is eroding the lines that separate the castes of India, it also makes clans more fluid, eventually replacing them with social classes.

Class

As we have seen, stratification systems based on slavery, caste, and clan are rigid. The lines marking the divisions between people are so firm that, except for marriage between clans, there is no movement from one group to another. A **class system**, in contrast, is much more open, since it is based primarily on money or material possessions. It, too, begins at birth, when an individual is ascribed the status of his or her parents, but, unlike slavery, caste, and clan, one's social class may change as a result of what one achieves (or fails to achieve) in life, although to some extent we carry some of the subtle "marks" of class even after changes in status. In addition, there are no laws that specify occupation on the basis of birth or that prohibit marriage between classes.

A major characteristic of this fourth system, then, is its relatively fluid boundaries. A class system allows for the *possibility* of **social mobility**—that is, movement up or down the class ladder. The potential for improving one's social circumstances or class is one of the major forces that drives people to go far in school and to work hard. However, the family background inherited by an individual at birth may bestow such obstacles that a child has little chance of climbing very far—or it may provide such privileges that it is almost impossible to fall very far down the class ladder.

Global Stratification and the Status of Women

In *every* society of the world, gender is a basis for social stratification. In no society is gender the sole basis for stratifying people, but gender cuts across *all* systems of social stratification (Huber 1990). In all systems, on the basis of their gender, people are sorted into categories and given different access to the good things available in their society.

Apparently such distinctions always favour males. It is remarkable, for example, that in *every* society of the world, men's earnings are higher than women's. Men's dominance is even more evident when we consider forms of violence committed against women, including rituals such as female circumcision. That most of the world's illiterate are female also drives home women's relative position in society. Of the several hundred million adults who cannot read, about two-thirds are women (UNESCO, 2006). Because gender affects so much of what happens to us in life, it is the focus of Chapter 7.

WHAT DETERMINES SOCIAL CLASS?

In the early days of sociology, a disagreement arose about the meaning of social class in industrialized societies. Let's compare how Marx and Weber viewed the matter.

Karl Marx: The Means of Production

As discussed in Chapter 1, when the feudal system broke down, masses of peasants were displaced from their traditional lands and occupations. Fleeing to cities, they competed for few available jobs. Offered only a pittance for their labour, they dressed in rags, went hungry, and slept under bridges and in shacks. In contrast, factory owners built mansions, hired servants, and lived in the lap of luxury. Seeing this great disparity between owners and workers, Karl Marx (1818–1883) concluded that social class depends on a single factor: people's relationship to the **means of production**—the tools, factories, land, and investment capital used to produce wealth (Marx, 1844/1964; Marx & Engels, 1848/1967).

Marx argued that the distinctions people often make between themselves—such as clothing, speech, education, or relative salary—are superficial matters. They camouflage the only real significant dividing line. People either own the means of production (the **bourgeoisie**) or they work for those who do (the **proletariat**). According to Marx, this is the only distinction that counts, and these two classes make up modern society. In short, people's relationship to the means of production determines their social class.

Marx recognized that other groups were part of industrial society: farmers and peasants; a *lumpenproletariat* (marginal people such as migrant workers, beggars, vagrants, and criminals); and a middle class (self-employed professionals). Marx did not consider these groups social classes, however, for they lacked **class consciousness**—common identity based on their position in the means of production. They did not see themselves as exploited workers whose plight could be solved only by collective action. Consequently, Marx thought of these groups as insignificant in the coming workers' revolution that was destined to overthrow capitalism.

Capital becomes concentrated, Marx said, which makes capitalists and workers increasingly hostile toward one another. When workers recognize capitalists as the source of their oppression, they unite and throw off the chains of their oppressors. In a bloody revolution, they seize the means of production and usher in a classless society, where the few will no longer grow rich at the expense of the many. What holds back the workers' unity and their revolution is **false consciousness**—workers mistakenly identifying with capitalists and their interests. For example, workers with a few dollars in the bank often forget that they are workers and instead see themselves as investors or as capitalists who are about to launch a successful business.

The only distinction worth mentioning, then, is whether a person is an owner or a worker. This decides everything else, Marx stressed, since property determines people's lifestyles, shapes their ideas, and establishes their relationships with one another.

Max Weber: Property, Prestige, and Power

Max Weber (1864–1920) became an outspoken critic of Marx. He asserted that property is only part of the picture. Social class, he said, is actually made up of three components—*property*, *prestige*, and *power* (Gerth & Mills, 1958; Weber, 1922/1968). Some call these the three Ps of social class. (Although Weber used the terms "class," "status," and "power," some sociologists find "property," "prestige," and "power" to be clearer terms. To make them even clearer, some substitute *wealth* for "property.")

Property (or wealth), said Weber, is certainly significant in determining a person's standing in society: on that he agreed with Marx. But, added Weber, ownership is not the only significant aspect of property. For example, some

The text describes the many relationships among Weber's three components of social class: property, prestige, and power. What mix of the three do you think apply to John A. Macdonald and Governor General Michaëlle Jean?

powerful people, such as managers of corporations, *control* the means of production even though they do not *own* them. If managers can control property for their own benefit—awarding themselves huge bonuses and magnificent perks—it makes no practical difference that they do not own the property they so generously use for their own benefit.

Prestige, the second element in Weber's analysis, is often derived from property, since people tend to look up to the wealthy. Prestige, however, can also be based on other factors. Olympic gold medalists, for example, may not own property, yet they have very high prestige. Some are even able to exchange their prestige for property—such as being paid to say that they start their day with a particular breakfast cereal or for endorsing a brand of sportswear. In other words, property and prestige are not one-way streets: although property can bring prestige, prestige can also bring property.

Power, the third element of Weber's social class, is the ability to control others, even over their objections. Weber agreed with Marx that property is a major source of power, but added that it is not the only source. Prestige can be turned into power. For example, actor Arnold chwarzenegger became governor of California, and previously, another actor, Ronald Reagan, was president of the United States. For other interrelationships of property, prestige, and power, see Figure 6.1.

Focus Question

What are some of the differences between Marx's and Weber's approaches to social class?

IN SUM

For Marx, social class was based solely on a person's position in relation to the means of production—as a member of either the bourgeoisie or the proletariat—while Weber argued that social class is a combination of property, prestige, and power.

COMPLEXITIES OF INEQUALITY

In this chapter, we closely examine social class as a dimension of inequality. However, inequalities are highly complex, and in order to unravel that complexity we must question the interrelationships among various inequalities. We refer to this as **intersectionality**, and feminists and other sociologists who adopt a critical perspective approach studies of inequality by considering the ways in which class, gender, and race intersect (McCall, 2001). In other words, from this perspective, we are not only interested in how each of these dimensions may affect a person's life experiences, but we suggest that it is important to consider class, race, and gender simultaneously, since we may uncover inequalities in the interconnections of these dimensions.

Defining Social Class

"There are the poor and the rich—and then there are you and I, neither poor nor rich." That is about as far as most Canadians' consciousness of social class goes. Let's try to flesh this out.

Our task is made somewhat difficult because sociologists have no clear-cut, agreed-upon definition of social class. As noted above, conflict sociologists (of the Marxist orientation) see only two social classes: those who own the means of production and those who do not. A problem with this view, say most sociologists, is that it lumps too many people together. Physicians and corporate executives with incomes of $250 000 a year are lumped together with hamburger flippers working at McDonald's for $10 000 a year.

Most sociologists agree with Weber that there are more components of social class than a person's relationship to the means of production. Consequently, most sociologists use the components Weber identified and define **social class** as a large group of people who rank closely to one another in wealth, power, and prestige. These three elements separate people into different lifestyles, give them different chances in life, and provide them with distinct ways of looking at the self and the world.

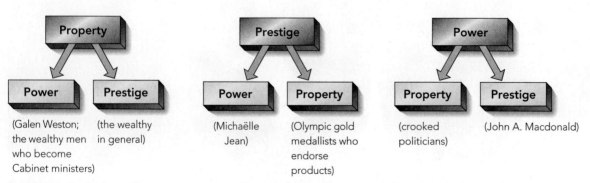

FIGURE 6.1　Weber's Three Components of Social Class and the Interrelationships between Them

Measuring Social Class

We will examine wealth, power, and prestige in the next section, but first let's look at three different ways of measuring social class.

1. *Subjective method.* The **subjective method** involves asking people what their social class is. Although simple and direct, this approach is filled with problems. First, people may deny that they belong to any class, claiming, instead, that everyone is equal. Second, people may classify themselves according to their aspirations—where they would like to be—rather than where they actually are. Third, when asked which class they belong to, most Canadians identify themselves as middle-class, as do most citizens of industrialized nations (Kelley & Evans, 1995; Forcese, 1997). This perception removes the usefulness of the subjective method for most purposes.

2. *Reputational method.* In the **reputational method**, people are asked what class others belong to on the basis of their reputations. Social anthropologist W. Lloyd Warner (Warner & Hunt, 1941; Warner, Hunt, Meeker, & Eels, 1949) pioneered this method in a study of a community he called "Yankee City." Its use is limited to smaller communities, where people are familiar with one another's reputation.

    Three of Warner's colleagues used the reputational method to study "Old City," a small southern town in the U.S. (Davis, Gardner, & Gardner, 1941). They found that just as people at each class level see life differently, so too they carry around different pictures of society's classes. People see finer divisions at their own class level, but tend to lump people together as one social class as they recede from them. Thus people at the top see several groups of people at the top, but tend to lump the bottom into a single unit ("the poor"), while people at the bottom see several distinctions among the poor but tend to see just "the rich" at the top.

3. *Objective method.* In the **objective method**, researchers rank people according to objective criteria such as wealth, power, and prestige. This method has the advantage of letting others know exactly what measurements were made, so that they can test them.

Given the three methods of determining social class, sociologists primarily use the objective method. The studies reported in this chapter are examples of the objective approach.

THE COMPONENTS OF SOCIAL CLASS

Let's look at how sociologists measure the three components of social class: wealth, power, and prestige.

Wealth

The primary dimension of social class is **wealth**. Wealth consists of property and income. Property comes in many forms, such as buildings, land, animals, machinery, cars, stocks, bonds, businesses, and bank accounts. Income is money received as wages, rents, interest, royalties, or the proceeds from a business.

PROPERTY Overall, Canadians are worth a hefty sum. Most of this wealth is in the form of real estate, corporate stocks, bonds, and business assets and is highly concentrated. If we consider wealth distribution, in 1984, families in the top 10 percent held 52 percent of aggregate household wealth, while the bottom 50 percent held only 5 percent. This concentration of wealth increased from 1984 to 1999 and again from 1999 to 2005. By 2005, the top 10 percent increased their share of Canadians' net worth to 58 percent, and, in fact, it was only those in the top 10 percent who increased their share of total wealth between 1984 and 2005 (Morissette & Zhang, 2006: p. 6). Another way to describe the pattern is that during this period the poorest fifth of Canadian families experienced a negative net worth, while the wealth of the richest fifth grew by 64 percent. This group, the wealthiest 20 percent of families, holds 75 percent of Canada's personal wealth (Morissette & Zhang, 2006; Dunphy, 2006).

When compared with other countries, and with the U.S. in particular, Canada has a small percentage of the world's wealthiest, or the super-rich. According to estimates, in 2001, 315 000 Canadians held over $1 million in investable assets, excluding real estate. But the number of Canadians who are at the top of this elite group is relatively small. Only 25 out of 1125 billionaires are Canadian. Or, in other words, Canada could claim only 2 percent of the world's billionaires in 2008 (CBC News, 2008).

Power and wealth are very concentrated within Canadian society. Table 6.1 provides a list of Canada's 10 wealthiest individuals or families and their major corporate fields. The web of ownership, wealth, power, and property weave a complex network, making it very difficult to indicate precisely the nature of this concentration, although sociologists such as Porter (1965) and Clement (1975), along with journalists Peter Newman (1979) and Diane Francis (1986), have all demonstrated it (Forcese, 1997). Earlier estimates suggest that, for example, a third of all corporate assets in Canada are controlled by only twelve families and five conglomerates, while about 80 percent of the Toronto Stock Exchange's list of 300 companies are controlled by eight conglomerates (Allahar & Coté, 1998).

Family dynasties hold a prominent place among the wealthy and powerful of Canada. Some family names, including Weston, Black, Desmarais, Irving, Thomson, and Bronfman, have appeared on lists of the richest people for years. Most Canadians are unaware of such levels of

Each year on January 2, about the time most Canadians begin a new year of work, Canada's top paid CEOs will already be having a good year. They'll pocket the equivalent of the national average wage ($38 998 in 2006) by 10:33 a.m. that day. They will continue to earn the average Canadian wage every nine hours and 33 minutes for the rest of the year. That's what happens when your average annual income is $8 528 304,

the average earnings of Canada's 100 best paid CEOs in 2006. Canada's top-paid CEOs make more than 218 times someone working full-time for a full year on the average Canadian weekly wage. For Canadians making minimum wage, the gap is even more astounding. By 1:04 p.m. on New Year's Day, the top-paid CEOs will pocket what will take a minimum-wage worker the entire year to earn. Every four hours and four min-

utes, they will keep pocketing the annual income of a full-time, full-year minimum-wage worker.

Are those at the top of the income ladder really worth that much? And are those at the bottom worth that little?

Source: Hugh Mackenzie. The Great CEO Pay Race: Over Before it Begins. Ottawa: Canadian Centre for Policy Alternatives, 2007.

TABLE 6.1   Canada's Super-Rich Top 10

	Billions of Canadian Dollars
1. Thomson family (media)	25.4
2. Ted Rogers, Jr. (media)	7.6
3. Galen Weston (groceries)	7.3
4. Paul Desmarais, Sr. (Power Corporation)	5.6
5. Irving family (diversified)	5.3
6. Jimmy Pattison (diversified)	4.52
7. Jeff Skoll (eBay)	4.48
8. Mike Lazaridis (Research in Motion)	4.36
9. Jim Balsillie (Research in Motion)	4.09
10. Barry Sherman (Apotex)	3.61

Source: *Canadian Business* (December 2007).

concentration of wealth and power, but nevertheless are touched by this concentration as they go about their daily routines and activities. As Diane Francis (1986) graphically notes, "Everything from your glass of orange juice in the morning, to the clothes you put on, to the office where you work, to the department store and mall where you shop, to that after-work beer and a night at the ball game—are likely to be produced by these families and conglomerates."

The distribution of wealth is more unequal than that of income, and the distribution of inherited wealth is much more unequal than that of wealth in general (Davies, 1999). While income has to be declared for taxation purposes, it is unclear how much wealth there is in Canada. The majority of the population will never inherit significant wealth, and a small minority receives outrageous amounts. This extreme concentration makes inheritance an important determinant of wealth inequality (Davies, 1999).

INCOME   How is income distributed in Canada? Very unequally, it turns out, as shown in Table 6.2. Income distribution in

TABLE 6.2   Family Income, 2001*

Quintile	Market Income	Shares of Market Income	After Tax/Transfer Income	After Tax/Transfer Income Shares
Bottom	$8362	2.6%	$20 721	7.1%
Second	$32 362	10.2%	$36 830	12.7%
Middle	$54 127	17.0%	$51 074	17.6%
Fourth	$78 389	24.6%	$67 878	23.4%
Top	$145 580	45.6%	$113 615	39.2%

* Data are for economic families of two or more people in constant 2001 dollars

Source: Statistics Canada, *Income in Canada* CD-ROM (Ottawa, 2001), Table T802, cited in Jackson, 2005: p. 25).

Canada can be configured into a typical pyramid shape, with a very small percentage of Canadians (1 percent) at the top with very high incomes and the majority residing near the bottom. Economist Paul Samuelson (Samuelson & Nordhaus, 1989, p. 644) put it this way: "If we made an income pyramid out of a child's blocks, with each layer portraying $500 of income, the peak would be far higher than Mount Everest, but most people would be within a few feet of the ground" (see Figure 6.2).

Evidence suggests there is a growing disparity in income, and this mirrors a growing disparity in the distribution of wealth (Valpy, 2008). As with wealth, the disparity between the highest and lowest income earners in Canada has grown over the past two decades. For example, in 1982, the top 5 percent of individual incomes equalled 322 percent of the median income that year, but by 2004, this had increased to 364 percent (Murphy, Roberts, & Wolfson, 2007: p. 7). The gain among the super-rich was even more dramatic. In 1982, the income threshold for individuals in the top 1 percent was 55 times larger than the median, but by 2004, it was over 115 times larger (Ibid.).

In 2005, the median income of all Canadian families was just over $60 600; for two-parent families with children under 18, it was about $67 600 (Statistics Canada, 2007). Yet compared with the "Mount Everest" incomes of a select few, the earnings of the typical Canadian family would bring it only three metres off the ground. The fact that some Canadians enjoy the peaks of Mount Everest while most make it only a few metres up the slope presents a striking image of income inequality in Canada.

Another way to present the contrasts in income is to visualize the following: "If the average CEO is perched atop the CN tower, Canadians making the average wage are merely two steps up a six-foot ladder. Comparatively, the minimum wage worker is standing in a three-foot deep hole" (Mackenzie, 2007: p. 5).

Another picture emerges if we consider the percentage of Canadian families distributed within high- and low-income groups. If we divide all families into 10 groups based on their income levels that we refer to as "deciles," with each group representing 10 percent of the total number of families, we uncover vast inequalities among Canadian families, as indicated in Figure 6.2. In 2004, the after-tax income of families in the top decile averaged $135 810, and the combined income of these families totalled over 29 percent of the income of all Canadian families (Yalnizyan, 2007: p. 8, 12). In contrast, families at the other end—in the bottom decile—had incomes below $23 300, and the combined total income of these families was about 1 percent of the total Canadian family income (see Figure 6.3)

Two features of the data available on incomes are outstanding. First, income inequality has remained remarkably consistent through the years. Second, the changes that do occur indicate growing inequality. Since the 1940s, the richest 20 percent of Canadian families have grown richer, while the poorest 20 percent have grown poorer. In spite of numerous social welfare programs, the poorest 20 percent of

Some Canadians: Higher than Mount Everest

If a 4-centimetre child's block equals $500 of income, the average Canadian is only 2 metres off the ground, and the average family just over 3 metres, while the income of some families propels them past the top of Mount Everest.

2 metres

Average Canadian

Just over 3 metres

Average Canadian Family

FIGURE 6.2 Inequality of Canadian Income

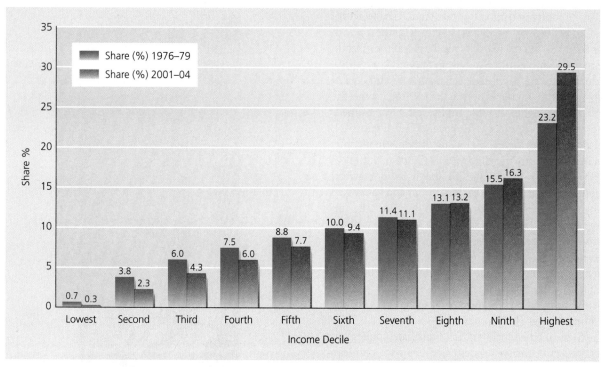

FIGURE 6.3 Share of Earnings of Families with Children by Income Percentile, 1976–79 and 2001–04

Source: Yalnizyan, *The Rich and the Rest of Us.* 2007: p 12.

Canadians receive less of the nation's income today than they did in the 1940s. The richest 20 percent, in contrast, receive more than ever. In 2004, about 3.5 million Canadians were in low-income jobs, earning less than $20 000. Nearly 1.4 million of these workers were working full-time, or, in other words, one in seven full-time workers were in low-wage jobs in 2004 (Statistics Canada, Income Statistics Division, 2006). Earning $20 000 a year for full-time work means working for $10 an hour for 50 weeks a year at a rate of 40 hours each week. Women, recent immigrants, lone parents, and young workers are overrepresented among low-wage workers.

Census data from 2006 indicates gains in wealth and income by the richest 5 percent of Canadians, with the poorest falling further behind (Valpy, 2008). Impacting heavily upon those falling behind is a labour market increasingly characterized by low-paid, insecure, entry-level jobs. Table 6.3 makes clear that the earnings grew for the top 20 percent while earnings for the bottom 20 percent fell. In 2005, over 600 000 workers (full-time, full-year) earned over $100 000, representing a 25.7 percent increase from 2000. Between 1980 and 2005, the percentage of earners receiving over $100 000 almost doubled, from 3.4 to 6.5 percent. Between

TABLE 6.3 Median Earnings[1] of Full-Time, Full-Year Earners by Quintile

Quintile	Year 1980	1990	2000	2005	% Change 1980–2005	2000–2005
Bottom	$19 367	$16 345	$15 861	$15 375	−20.6%	−3.1%
Middle	$41 348	$40 778	$40 433	$41 401	0.1%	2.4%
Top	$74 084	$76 616	$81 224	$86 253	16.4%	6.2%

[1] In constant 2005 dollars

Source: Frenette, Marc, Hou, Feng, Morissette, Rene, Wannell, Ted, & Webber, Maryanne. *Earnings and Incomes of Canadians Over the Past Quarter Century, 2006 Census.* Statistics Canada, Catalogue 97-563-X, May 2008, p. 11. Calculated from Statistics Canada, Censuses of Population, 1981, 1991, 2001, and 2006.

Toronto Blue Jays's owner and media mogul Ted Rogers's net worth makes him the richest person in Canada.

States piqued his students' curiosity when he lectured on poverty in Latin America. That weekend, one of his students borrowed his parents' corporate jet and pilot, and in Monday's class he and his friends reported on their personal observations on the problem. Others, in contrast, must choose whether to spend the little they have at the laundromat or on milk for their baby. In short, divisions of wealth represent not mere numbers, but choices that make real differences in people's lives.

Displays of prestige and social position vary over time and from one culture to another. Elizabeth I became Queen of England and Ireland in 1558 at the age of 25 and ruled for 45 years, until 1603. This painting hangs in the National Portrait Gallery.

1980 and 2005, the percentage of those earning over $150 000 more than doubled, from 1 percent in 1980 to 2.2 percent in 2005 (Frenette et al., 2008: p. 11).

Across the border in the United States, former Microsoft CEO Bill Gates is wealthier than the bottom 45 percent of American households. In 1997, his wealth surpassed the total GNP of Central America (including Guatemala, El Salvador, Costa Rica, Panama, Honduras, Nicaragua, and Belize). The following year, Gates's wealth grew to $60 billion, more than the GNPs of Central America plus Jamaica and Bolivia (Mokhiber & Weissman, 1999). He continues to rank as one of the world's top billionaires (Pitts, 2002; Ribeiro, 2005). However, Gates has met his match in the family of the late Sam Walton. Along with their mother, Sam Walton's widow, the four Walton "boys" control 38 percent of the shares of Wal-Mart, "19th among the 100 most powerful economies in the world," and each of the five family members has a net worth of over $20 billion (Robeiro, 2005). Yet while five of the ten richest people in the U.S. are Wal-Mart heirs, in 2006 the average Wal-Mart employee earned $17 530, an amount that was $1820 below the poverty line for a family of four (Jerrery, 2006).

Imagine how you could live on a seven-figure income. For most people, it is even difficult to dream about living with such wealth. Beyond the cold numbers lies a dynamic reality that profoundly affects people's lives. The difference in wealth between those at the top and the bottom of the Canadian class structure means vastly different lifestyles for each. For example, a colleague of one of the authors who was teaching at an exclusive eastern university in the United

Power

Like many people, you may have said to yourself, "Sure, I can vote, but somehow the big decisions are always made in spite of what I might think. Certainly *I* don't make the decision to raise taxes. It isn't *I* who decides to change welfare benefits."

Another part of you might say, "But I do it through my representatives in Parliament." True enough—as far as it goes. The trouble is, it just doesn't go far enough. Such views of being a participant in the nation's "big" decisions are a playback of the ideology we learn at an early age— an ideology that Marx said is put forward by the elites to both legitimize and perpetuate their power. Sociologists Daniel Hellinger and Dennis Judd (1991) call this the "democratic façade" that conceals the real source of power in society.

In the 1950s, sociologist C. Wright Mills (1956) was criticized for insisting that **power**—the ability to carry out your will in spite of resistance—was concentrated in the hands of the few, for his analysis contradicted an almost sacred ideology of equality. As discussed in Chapter 1, Mills coined the term **power elite** to refer to those who make the big decisions in society.

Mills and others have stressed how wealth and power coalesce in a group of like-minded individuals who share ideologies and values. They belong to the same private clubs, vacation at the same exclusive resorts, and even hire the same bands for their daughters' debutante balls. These shared backgrounds and vested interests all serve to reinforce their view of the world and of their special place in it (Domhoff, 1978, 1997). The elite wield extraordinary power in Canadian society. Although there are exceptions, *most* prime ministers and Cabinet ministers come from this group—rich white males from families with "old money" (Baltzell & Schneiderman, 1988).

Continuing in the tradition of Mills, sociologist William Domhoff (1990, 1996) argues that this group is so powerful that no major government decision is made without its approval. He analyzed how the group works behind the scenes with elected officials to set both the nation's foreign and domestic policies—from establishing taxes to determining trade tariffs. Although Domhoff's conclusions are controversial—and alarming—they certainly follow logically from the principle that wealth brings power, and extreme wealth brings extreme power.

Prestige

OCCUPATIONS AND PRESTIGE What would you like to do with the rest of your life? Chances are you don't have the option of relaxing under palm trees at the beach. Almost all of us have to choose an occupation and go to work.

Why do people give some jobs more **prestige**—respect or regard—than others? Generally, the most prestigious jobs share four elements:

1. They pay more.
2. They require more education.
3. They entail more abstract thought.
4. They offer greater autonomy (freedom or self-direction).

If we reverse this idea, it means that people give less prestige to jobs that are low-paying, require less preparation or education, involve more physical labour, and are closely supervised. In short, the professions and some white-collar jobs are ranked at the top with respect to prestige, while blue-collar (and pink-collar) jobs are at the bottom.

One of the more interesting aspects of ranking occupations by prestige is how consistent they are across countries and over time. For example, people in every country rank university professors higher than nurses, nurses higher than social workers, and social workers higher than janitors. Similarly, the occupations that were ranked high in the 1970s are still ranked high today.

DISPLAYING PRESTIGE In times past, only emperors and their families could wear purple in some countries. In France, only the nobility could wear lace. In England, no one could sit while the king was on his throne. Some kings and queens required subjects to walk backward as they left a room—so that no one would "turn his (or her) back" on the "royal presence."

Concern with the display of prestige has not let up—and for some, it is almost an obsession. Western kings and queens expect curtsies and bows, while their Eastern counterparts demand that their subjects touch their faces to the ground. The prime minister enters a room only after others are present—to show that *he* isn't the one waiting for *them*. Military officers surround themselves with elaborate rules about who must salute whom, while bailiffs, sometimes armed, make certain everyone stands when a judge enters a courtroom.

The display of prestige permeates society. Addresses in Toronto's Rosedale or Montreal's Westmount are well recognized as among the most prestigious places to live in Canada. Many willingly pay more for clothing that bears a "designer" label. Prestige can be a primary factor in deciding which university to attend. Everyone knows that the prestige of a degree from Oxford compares with a degree from Harvard, Princeton, Yale, or Cambridge.

Status symbols vary with social class. Clearly, only the wealthy can afford certain items, such as yachts. But beyond affordability lies a class-based preference in status symbols. For example, the "nouveau riche" are quick to flaunt labels and other material symbols to show they have "arrived," while those with old money, more secure in their status, often prefer to flaunt their own status symbols, such as the "right" addresses and Rolex watches.

Status Inconsistency

Ordinarily, a person has a similar rank in all three dimensions of social class—wealth, power, and prestige. Such people show **status consistency**. Sometimes individuals have a mixture of high and low ranks, a condition called **status inconsistency**. This leads to some interesting situations.

Sociologist Gerhard Lenski (1954, 1966) observed that each of us tries to maximize our **status**, or social ranking. Individuals who rank high on one dimension of social class but lower on others expect people to judge them on the basis of their highest status. Sometimes, however, people hoping to maximize their own position may respond on the basis of people's lowest status.

A classic study of status inconsistency was conducted by sociologist Ray Gold (1952). He found that after apartment-house janitors unionized, they made more money than some of the people whose garbage they carried out. Tenants became upset when they saw their janitors driving more expensive cars than they did. Some attempted to "put the janitor in his place" by making "snotty" remarks. Similarly, during a strike by outside workers (including garbage collectors) in July 2002 in the City of Toronto, several media commentaries questioned the rights and motives of garbage collectors to strike for higher wages and job security. Interestingly, as the stench of rotting garbage in the summer heat rose and as serious health concerns issued by public officials escalated, few acknowledged the essential contribution of these workers to our communities, our safety, and our well-being.

Instant wealth, the topic of the Down-to-Earth Sociology box below, provides an interesting case of status inconsistency.

Individuals with status inconsistency, then, are likely to confront one frustrating situation after another. They claim the higher status, but are handed the lower. The sociological significance of this condition, said Lenski, is that such people tend to be more politically radical. An example is university professors: their prestige is high, but their incomes are relatively low. Hardly anyone in Canadian society is better educated, yet university professors don't come close to the top of the income pyramid. In line with Lenski's prediction, the political beliefs of many professors are left of centre.

Focus Question
What are some of the ways we define or measure social class?

DOWN-TO-EARTH SOCIOLOGY
The Big Win: Life After the Lottery

Many Canadians dream about winning the lottery, thinking that with a win, life would be good and problems would disappear. Canadian households shell out an average of $280 a year on lotteries and games of chance (Statistics Canada, December 12, 2006), with the glimmering hope that they'll hit it big.

Most are lucky to win $10 or another scratch-off ticket, but sometimes there are big hits. What happens to these winners? Do they live worry-free in the lap of luxury?

According to sociologist H. Roy Kaplan, who surveyed hundreds of lottery winners in Canada and the U.S., winning becomes a disruption in people's lives, heightening their anxieties and changing their attitudes (Brean, 2008). Kaplan's conclusions were confirmed by Professor Richard Tunney, who studied big winners in Britain, and Professor Mark Lutter of the Max Planck Institute in Germany, whose research found that winning may even decrease one's happiness. Lutter notes that suddenly acquiring wealth changes the balance in life and that such an abrupt change in affluence may contribute to deviant behaviours, including suicide (Brean, 2006).

Why does this happen? Our connections with others provide the basis

for our orientations in life and how we feel about the world. Sudden wealth can rip these moorings apart, and the resulting status inconsistency can lead to a condition sociologists refer to as **anomie.**

Shock is generally the first emotion after a big win, and is accompanied by reporters asking about plans for the newfound wealth. Then come the calls. Some callers offer sincere congratulations, but long-forgotten friends and distant relatives often suddenly remember how close they are to you—and, strangely enough, they all have emergencies that your money can solve. You may even get calls from strangers with ailing mothers, terminally sick kids, sick dogs . . . Winners often have to unplug their phones or get unlisted numbers.

Some lottery winners are flooded with marriage proposals. These individuals surely didn't become more attractive or sexy overnight—or did they? Maybe money makes people sexy.

Winners have trouble trusting people, not knowing what their real motives are. The normal becomes the abnormal. Even picking out a wedding gift becomes a problem—if they give the usual toaster or blender, everyone will think they're cheap, but should they write a cheque for $25 000? If so, they'll be

invited to every wedding in town—and everyone will expect the same.

Winning big has resulted in numerous court battles over questions of who owns the winning ticket, how the winnings should be split, and what agreements had been made prior to the draw. And the battles are nasty, often with family members, co-workers, or longtime friends throwing accusations at one another.

Winners who avoid *anomie* seem to be people who don't make sudden changes in their lifestyle or behaviour. They maintain their old friendships, routines, and other anchors in life that give them identity and a sense of belonging. Some even keep their old jobs—not for the money, but because working affords them an identity with which they are familiar and comfortable. To a certain degree, most Canadians relate to this behaviour. In a recent poll by Ipsos Reid of over 2000 workers, the majority— 65 percent—said they would not quit their jobs or retire permanently if they won the lottery (Morrissy, 2008).

Sudden wealth, in other words, poses a threat that must be guarded against. Of course, as we check our numbers in the weekly draws, most of us say we are willing to accept any risks that winning big may bring.

WHY IS SOCIAL STRATIFICATION UNIVERSAL?

What is it about social life that makes all societies stratified? We shall first consider the explanation proposed by functionalists, which has aroused much controversy in sociology, followed by criticisms of this position. We then explore theories proposed by conflict theorists.

The Functionalist or Conservative View

Functionalists take the position that the patterns of behaviour that characterize a society exist because they are functional for that society. They contend that because social inequality is universal, inequality must help societies survive. Using this principle, sociologists Kingsley Davis and Wilbert Moore (1945, 1953) concluded that stratification is inevitable for the following reasons:

1. Society must make certain that its positions are filled.

2. Some positions are more important than others.

3. The more important positions must be filled by the more qualified people.

4. To motivate the more qualified people to fill these positions, society must offer them greater rewards.

Let's look at some examples to flesh out the functionalist argument. The position of a university president is deemed much more important for society than that of a student, because the president's decisions affect many more people. Any mistakes he or she makes carry implications for a large number of people, including many students. The decisions of university presidents affect careers, paycheques, and, in some cases, even life and death.

Positions with greater responsibility also require greater accountability. University presidents are accountable to boards of trustees for how they perform. How can society motivate highly qualified people to enter such high-pressure positions? What keeps people from avoiding them and seeking less demanding jobs?

The answer, according to functionalists, is that society offers greater rewards for its more responsible, demanding, and accountable positions. If higher salaries, benefits, and greater prestige were not offered, why would anyone strive for these positions? Thus, a salary of $2 million, a country-club membership, a private jet, and a chauffeured limousine may be necessary to motivate the most highly qualified people to compete with one another for a certain position, while a $35 000 salary without fringe benefits is enough to get hundreds of people to compete for a less demanding position. Similarly, higher rewards are necessary to recruit people to positions that require rigorous training. Why suffer through taking tests and writing papers in university or graduate school if you can get the same pay and prestige with a high-school education?

The functionalist argument is simple and clear. Society works better if its most qualified people hold its most important positions. For example, to motivate highly talented people to become surgeons—to undergo many years of rigorous training and cope with life-and-death situations on a daily basis—requires a high payoff.

The Conflict Approach: A Critical Response

The functionalist view makes many sociologists uncomfortable, for they see it as coming close to justifying the inequalities of society.

Melvin Tumin (1953) was the first sociologist to point out what he saw as major flaws in the functionalist position. He developed four major arguments.

First, how is the importance of a position measured? It can't be measured by the rewards a position carries, for that argument is circular. An independent measure of importance must exist to test whether the more important positions actually carry higher rewards. For example, is a surgeon really more important to society than a garbage collector, since the garbage collector helps prevent contagious diseases?

Second, if stratification worked according to functionalist theory, society would be a **meritocracy**; that is, all positions would be awarded on the basis of merit. Ability, then, should predict who goes to university. Instead, the best predictor of university entrance is family income—the more a family earns, the more likely their children are to go to university, as we will see in Chapter 14. Similarly, while some people get ahead through ability and hard work, others simply inherit wealth and the opportunities that go with it. Moreover, if a stratification system places most men above most women, it does not live up to the argument that talent and ability are the bases for holding important positions. In short, factors far beyond merit give people their relative positions in society.

Third, the functionalist view places too much emphasis on money and fringe benefits. These aren't the only reasons people take jobs. For example, if money were the main motivator for professors, why would they spend four years in university, plus another six or seven pursuing a PhD—only to earn wages that are far behind those of physicians, lawyers, and other highly educated professionals? Obviously, university teaching offers more than monetary rewards: high prestige, autonomy (university professors have considerable discretion about how they do their job), rewarding social interaction (much of the job consists of talking to people), security (when given tenure, professors have lifetime employment), and leisure and the opportunity to travel (many professors work short days, enjoy several weeks of vacation during the school year, and have the entire summer off).

Fourth, if social stratification is functional, it ought to benefit almost everyone. In reality, however, social stratification is *dysfunctional* to many. Think of the people who could have made invaluable contributions to society if they had not been born into poverty and forced to drop out of school, taking menial jobs to help support their families; or the many who, born female, are passed over for promotions or are paid wages unequal to those of their male colleagues, as we will discuss further in Chapter 7. In other words, the functionalist perspective of social stratification does not explain why women and members of minority groups are vastly underrepresented among those most highly paid in Canada.

The Conflict Perspective and Competition for Scarce Resources

Conflict theorists sharply disagree with the functionalist position. They stress that conflict, not function, is the basis of social stratification. Sociologists such as William Domhoff (1990, 1997), C. Wright Mills (1956), and Irving Louis Horowitz (1966) assert that in every society, groups struggle with one another to gain a larger share of their society's limited resources. Whenever a group gains power, it uses that power to extract what it can from the groups beneath it. It also uses social institutions to keep other groups weak and itself in power. Class conflict, acccording to conflict theorists, is the key to understanding social stratification, since society is far from being a harmonious system that benevolently distributes greater resources to its supposedly more qualified members.

All ruling groups—from slave masters to modern elites—develop an ideology to justify their position at the top. This ideology often seduces the oppressed into believing that their welfare depends on keeping society stable. Consequently, the oppressed may support laws against their own interests and even sacrifice their children as soldiers in wars designed to enrich the bourgeoisie.

The day will come, Marx believed, when class consciousness will overcome ideology. When the workers' eyes are opened, they will throw off their oppressors. At first, the struggle for control of the means of production may be covert, taking the form of work slowdowns or industrial sabotage, but it will ultimately break out into open resistance. The revolt, though inevitable and bloody, will be difficult, for the bourgeoisie control the police, the military, and even education (where they implant false consciousness in the minds of workers' children).

Some sociologists have refocused conflict theory. C. Wright Mills (1956), Ralf Dahrendorf (1959), and Randall Collins (1974, 1988), for example, stress that groups within the same class also compete for scarce resources—power, wealth, education, housing, and even prestige—whatever benefits society has to offer. The result is conflict not only between labour unions and corporations, but also between the young and the old, women and men, and among racial and ethnic groups. Unlike functionalists, conflict theorists hold that just beneath the surface of what may appear to be a tranquil society lies overt conflict—only uneasily held in check.

Feminist and Anti-Racist Approaches

Critical thinkers drawing from feminist and anti-racist perspectives believe that people should be valued equally and seek explanations for unequal treatment and inequalities of wealth and power within Canadian and other societies. They argue that classic analyses of inequality from functionalist and conflict perspectives do not account for the relative lack of power, resources, and wealth experienced by women and racialized minorities. In their analyses, they argue that gender and race are socially constructed and form the bases for limitations to equality of condition and opportunity. These critical approaches consider the ways in which women and racialized minorities, including some men, have been oppressed within patriarchy and the capitalist economy. They consider how people come to be exploited and dominated by others, and the characteristics of those exploited as opposed to those who dominate.

In particular, feminists argue that underlying women's oppression and inability to achieve equality with men are their roles in social reproduction; that is, in unpaid household and family labour. As we will discuss in Chapter 7, women's unpaid work at home has an effect on their wages and ability to achieve equality with men in the labour force.

In addition to the questions raised by feminists about gender inequality, anti-racist theorists also consider structural aspects of inequality and the ways in which categories of race and ethnicity affect life chances, opportunities, and social class position. In examining inequalities within the labour market, for example, they will consider the ways in which inequalities of gender, race, and class are intertwined and argue that the labour market is split along these divisions. An anti-racist theorist might contend that these multi-layered inequalities are complexly woven by unequal structures of power and are based on assumptions regarding the different characteristics people bring to the structures of opportunity.

HOW DO ELITES MAINTAIN SOCIAL INEQUALITY?

Suppose you are part of the ruling elite of your society. What can you do to maintain your privileged position? The key lies in controlling ideas and information, in social networks, and, least effectively, the use of force.

Ideology versus Force

Medieval Europe provides a good example of the power of ideology. During Medieval times, land was owned by only a small group of people called the "aristocracy" and was the primary source of wealth. With the exception of the clergy and some craftsmen, most citizens were peasants working for this small group of powerful landowners. Peasants farmed the land, took care of cattle, and built roads and bridges. Every year, they had to turn over a designated portion of their crops to their feudal lord. This system was followed for centuries. Why?

CONTROLLING IDEAS Why didn't the peasants rebel? There were many reasons, not the least of which being that the army was controlled by the aristocracy. Coercion, however, only goes so far, for it breeds hostility and nourishes rebellion. It is much more effective to convince people to *want* to do what the ruling elite desires. This is where *ideology* comes into play, and medieval aristocracies used it to great effect. They developed an ideology known as the **divine right of kings**—the idea that the king's authority came directly from God—and could be traced back several thousand years to the Old Testament. The king could delegate authority to

nobles, who, as God's representatives, also had to be obeyed. To disobey was to commit a sin against God; to rebel meant physical punishment on Earth and a sentence to suffer in eternal hell.

The control of ideas, then, can be remarkably more effective than brute force. Although this particular ideology no longer governs people's minds today, the elite in every society develop ideologies to justify their position at the top. For example, schools around the world teach that their country's form of government—*whatever form of government that may be*—is the best. Each nation's schools also stress the virtues—rather than the vices—of governments past and present. Religion also teaches that we owe obedience to an authority, and that laws are to be obeyed. To the degree that the elites' ideologies are accepted by the masses, political arrangements are stable.

CONTROLLING INFORMATION To maintain their positions of power, elites also try to control information (Carroll & Hackett, 2006). In dictatorships, this is accomplished through the threat of force. Dictators can—and do—imprison editors and journalists for publishing reports that are critical of them, and sometimes for simply publishing unflattering information (Timerman, 1981). The ruling elites of democracies accomplish the same purpose by manipulating the media through the selective release of information, withholding whatever they desire "in the interest of national security." But just as coercion has its limits, so does the control of information—especially given its new forms (satellite communications, fax machines, e-mail, and the internet) that pay no respect to international borders (Kennedy, 1993).

SOCIAL NETWORKS Also critical in maintaining stratification are *social networks*—the social ties that link people (Higley, Hoffmann-Lange, Kadushin, & Moore, 1991). These networks, expanding outward from an individual to gradually encompass more and more people, supply valuable information and tend to perpetuate social inequality. Sociologists William Domhoff (1983, 1990), John Porter (1965), Wallace Clement (1975), and Bill Carroll (2004) have documented how members of the elite move in a circle of power that multiplies their opportunities. Contacts with people of similar backgrounds, interests, and goals allow the elite to pass privileges from one generation to the next. In contrast, the social networks of the poor perpetuate poverty and powerlessness.

TECHNOLOGY The desire of elites to preserve their position is aided by recent developments in technology, especially monitoring devices. These devices—from "hot telephones" (taps that transform a telephone into a microphone even when off the hook) to machines that can read the entire contents of a computer without leaving a trace—help the elite monitor citizens' activities without their knowledge. Dictatorships have few checks on how such technology can

The *divine right of kings* was an ideology that made the king God's direct representative on Earth—to administer justice and punish evildoers. This theological-political concept was supported by the Roman Catholic Church, whose representatives crowned the king. Shown here is Pope Clement IV crowning Charles Anjou as king of Sicily in 1226.

be employed, but in democracies checks and balances, such as constitutional rights and the necessity of court orders, at least partially curb their use.

IN SUM

Underlying the maintenance of the system of social inequality is control of a society's institutions. In a dictatorship, the elite *make* the laws. In a democracy, the elite *influence* law. In both systems, laws are enforced by the legal establishment. The elite also command the police and military and can give orders to crush a rebellion—or even to run a post office or air traffic control unit if workers go on strike. As noted, force has its limits, and a nation's elite generally finds it preferable to maintain its stratification system by peaceful means, especially by influencing the thinking of its citizens.

APPLYING SOCIOLOGICAL MODELS OF SOCIAL CLASS

The question of how many social classes exist is a matter of debate. Sociologists have proposed various models, but none has gained universal support. There are two main models: one based on Marx, the other on Weber.

Applying Marx

Marx argued that there are two classes—capitalists and workers—with membership based solely on a person's relationship to the means of production. Sociologists have criticized these categories as too broad. For example, executives, managers, and supervisors are technically workers because they do not own the means of production. But what do they have in common with assembly-line workers? Similarly, the category of "capitalist" takes in too many types; the decisions of someone who employs a thousand workers directly affect a thousand families, for example. Compare this with a man the authors know in Calgary, Alberta. Working on cars in his own backyard, he gained a following, quit his regular job, and in a few years put up a building with an office and five bays. This mechanic is now a capitalist who employs five or six other mechanics and owns the tools and building (the "means of production"). But what does he have in common with a factory owner who controls the lives of a thousand workers? Not only is his work different, but so are his lifestyle and the way he looks at the world.

Sociologist Erik Wright (1985) resolved this problem by regarding some people as members of more than one class at the same time. They have what he called **contradictory class locations**. By this, Wright meant that people's position in the class structure can generate contradictory interests. For example, the automobile-mechanic–turned–business-

TABLE 6.4 Social Class and the Means of Production

Marx's Class Model (based on the means of production)
1. Capitalist (bourgeoisie)
2. Workers (proletariat)
Wright's Modification of Marx's Class Model (to account for contradictory class locations)
1. Capitalists
2. Petty bourgeoisie
3. Managers
4. Workers

owner may want his mechanics to have higher wages, since he, too, has experienced their working conditions. At the same time, his current interests—making profits and remaining competitive with other repair shops—may lead him to resist pressures to raise wages.

Because of such contradictory class locations, Wright modified Marx's model. As summarized in Table 6.4, Wright identified four classes: (1) *capitalists*, business owners who employ many workers; (2) *petty bourgeoisie*, small business owners; (3) *managers*, who sell their own labour but also exercise authority over other employees; and (4) *workers*, who simply sell their labour to others. As you can see, this model allows finer divisions than the one Marx proposed, yet maintains the primary distinction between employer and worker.

The question of how many social classes exist and how they relate to one another is highly complex. Even with Wright's modifications to Marx's model, problems persist. How do we categorize university professors who employ research assistants with their research grants, for example? As you know, there are huge differences in the power and resources of managers. An executive at General Motors, for example, may be responsible for a thousand workers, while a shift manager at the local McDonald's may oversee only a handful. They, too, have little in common.

Updating Weber

Sociologists Dennis Gilbert and Joseph Kahl (1993) developed a six-class model to portray the class structure of the United States and other capitalist countries. Think of their model, illustrated in Figure 6.4, as a ladder. Our discussion will start with the highest rung and move downward. In line with Weber, on each lower rung there is less wealth, less power, and less prestige. Note that in this model education is a primary criterion of class.

THE CAPITALIST CLASS The super-rich, who occupy the top rung of the class ladder in Canada, comprise only about

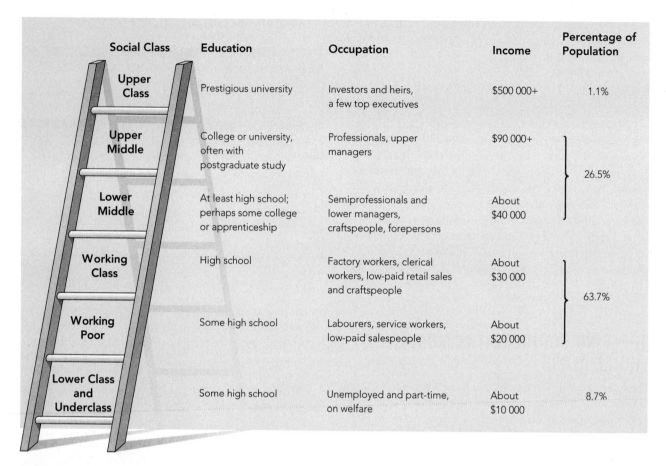

Social Class	Education	Occupation	Income	Percentage of Population
Upper Class	Prestigious university	Investors and heirs, a few top executives	$500 000+	1.1%
Upper Middle	College or university, often with postgraduate study	Professionals, upper managers	$90 000+	26.5%
Lower Middle	At least high school; perhaps some college or apprenticeship	Semiprofessionals and lower managers, craftspeople, forepersons	About $40 000	
Working Class	High school	Factory workers, clerical workers, low-paid retail sales and craftspeople	About $30 000	63.7%
Working Poor	Some high school	Labourers, service workers, low-paid salespeople	About $20 000	
Lower Class and Underclass	Some high school	Unemployed and part-time, on welfare	About $10 000	8.7%

FIGURE 6.4   The Canadian Social Class Ladder

Source: Based on Gilbert & Kahl (1993); Forcese (1997).

1.1 percent of the population. As mentioned, this 1.1 percent is so wealthy that its members are worth more than the entire bottom 90 percent of the nation. Their power is so great that their decisions open or close jobs for millions of people. Through their ownership of newspapers, magazines, and radio and television stations and their access to politicians, this elite class even helps shape public consciousness. Its members perpetuate themselves by passing on to their children their assets and influential social networks.

The capitalist class can be divided into "old" and "new" money (Aldrich, 1989). In general, the longer wealth has been in a family, the more it adds to the family's prestige. Many people entering the capitalist class have found it necessary to cut moral corners, at least occasionally. This "taint" to the money disappears with time, however, and the later generations of Kennedys, Rockefellers, Vanderbilts, Mellons, Du Ponts, Chryslers, Fords, Eatons, Molsons, Bronfmans, and so on are considered to have "clean" money simply by virtue of the passage of time. Able to be philanthropic as well as rich, they establish foundations and support charitable causes. Subsequent generations attend prestigious prep schools and universities, and male heirs

are likely to enter law. These old-money capitalists wield vast power and they use their extensive political connections to protect their huge economic empires (Sklair, 2001; Domhoff, 1990, 1997, 2006; Clement, 1975; & Newman, 1979, 2004).

Some members of the capitalist class who possess vast sums of money and power are referred to as the *nouveau riche* because their money is "new." Although such people may have made fortunes in business, the stock market, inventions, entertainment, or sports, they don't necessarily share the social networks that come with old money. Donald Trump, for example, is a member of this group. The children of new-monied families can ascend into the upper part of the capitalist class if they attend the right schools *and* marry into old money.

THE UPPER-MIDDLE CLASS Of all the classes, the upper-middle is the one most shaped by education. Almost all members of this class have at least a bachelor's degree, and many have postgraduate degrees in business, management, law, or medicine. These people manage the corporations owned by the capitalist class or operate their own business or profession. As Gilbert and Kahl (1982) say, these positions

The Bronfmans are among Canada's oldest wealthy families. Old-money capitalists wield vast power and have numerous political, social, and economic connections that they draw on in order to protect their huge economic empires.

may not grant prestige equivalent to a title of nobility in the Germany of Max Weber, but they certainly represent the sign of having "made it" in contemporary America... Their income is sufficient to purchase houses and cars and travel that become public symbols for all to see and for advertisers to portray with words and pictures that connote success, glamour, and high style.

Consequently, parents and teachers push children to prepare them for upper-middle-class jobs.

THE LOWER-MIDDLE CLASS Members of the lower-middle class follow orders given by those who have upper-middle-class credentials. Their technical and lower-level management positions earn them a decent living—albeit one constantly threatened by rising taxes and inflation—and they generally enjoy a comfortable, mainstream lifestyle. They usually feel secure in their positions and anticipate moving up the social class ladder.

The distinction between lower-middle class and working class on the next lower rung are more blurred than those between other classes, and it may be that as the economy changes and more full-time, relatively well-paid unionized and secure jobs are replaced by part-time or temporary and less-secure jobs, there will be no discernible distinction between these groups. As a result, these two classes merge somewhat. Members of the lower-middle class work at jobs that have slightly more prestige, however, and their incomes are generally higher.

THE WORKING CLASS This class includes relatively unskilled or deskilled blue-collar and white-collar workers. Compared with the lower-middle class, they have less education and

lower incomes. Their jobs are also less secure, more routine, and more closely supervised. One of their greatest fears is being laid off. The average member of the working class has little hope of climbing up the class ladder. Job changes are usually "more of the same," so most concentrate on getting ahead by achieving seniority in a job rather than by changing their type of work.

THE WORKING POOR Members of this class work at unskilled, low-paying, temporary and seasonal jobs, such as migrant farm work, housecleaning, and day labour. Most are high-school dropouts. Many are functionally illiterate, finding it difficult to read even the want ads. Recent immigrants are often members of the working poor; 40 percent earned less than $20 000 in 2000 despite their skills and previous work experience (Statistics Canada, 2003b, p. 12).

Large numbers among the working poor work full-time, trapped in low-wage, precarious work (Statistics Canada, 2003b, p. 8), and in some cases, despite working harder and longer (Yalnizyan, 2007), they must depend on help from social programs such as food banks to supplement their meager incomes. It is easy to see how it is possible to work full-time and still be poor. Suppose you are married with a three-month-old baby and a two-year–old toddler. Your spouse stays home to care for them, so you are responsible for earning a living for the family. As a high-school dropout, all you can get is a low-wage job. At $9.00 an hour, you earn $360 for 40 hours, which totals less than $19,000 a year—before deductions. Your nagging fear—and daily nightmare—is of ending up "on the streets."

THE UNDERCLASS On the lowest rung, and with next to no chance of climbing anywhere, is the **underclass** (Myrdal, 1962; Kelso, 1995). Concentrated in the inner city, this group has little or no connection with the job market. Those who are employed or on workfare perform menial, low-paying, temporary work. If they qualify, welfare and food banks are their main supports, and most members of other classes consider these people the ne'er-do-wells of society. Life is tough in this class, and it is filled with despair. Children's chances of getting out of poverty are relatively slim.

The Homeless

Homeless men, women, and children are the "fallout" of the post-industrial economy. Technically, the homeless are members of the underclass, but their poverty is so severe and their condition in life so despairing that we can think of them as occupying an unofficial rung below the underclass. How do Canadians become homeless? Recent studies have concluded that homelessness is caused by two factors: lack of income and lack of affordable housing. In other words, homelessness and poverty are interrelated.

Homelessness has been on the rise in Canada. More than 14 000 people across the country were living in homeless shelters in 2001 (Olive, 2007: p. A1). In 2005, the federal government-sponsored National Homelessness Initiative estimated that there were approximately 150 000 homeless Canadians. However, non-governmental organizations working with this population have suggested that the figure is much higher—closer to 200 000 or 300 000 people (Ethos Strategy Group, 2007: p. 7). Many Canadians wish the homeless would just "go away." Their presence on city streets bothers passersby from more privileged social classes—which includes just about everyone. "What are those dirty, foul-smelling people doing here, cluttering up my city?" appears to be a common response. A few respond with sympathy and a desire to help. But how? Almost all of us simply shrug our shoulders and look the other way, despairing of a solution and somewhat intimidated by their presence.

The largest population of homeless persons is in Toronto, Canada's largest city, but all major cities and even some small towns have homeless populations.

In another era, the homeless would have had plenty of work—tending horses, working on farms, digging ditches, shovelling coal, or running the factory looms. Some would have explored and settled the West. Others might have followed the lure of gold to the Yukon, California, Alaska, and Australia. Today, however, with no unsettled frontiers, factory jobs scarce, and even farms becoming technological marvels, we have little need for unskilled labour, and these people are left to wander aimlessly about the city streets.

Most of us feel powerless to help the homeless, especially as their numbers increase in Canada's major centres.

CONSEQUENCES OF SOCIAL CLASS

Each social class can be thought of as a broad subculture with distinct approaches to life. Of the many ways that social class affects people's lives, we will briefly review new technology, physical and mental health, family life, education, religion, politics, and crime.

Technology

The higher the rung on the social class ladder, the more technology is a benefit. For the capitalist class, technology and new forms of communication and transportation have made dreams come true: global profits through global integration. No longer are national boundaries an obstacle. Rather, a product's components are produced in several countries, assembled in another, and the product is marketed throughout the world. New technologies also benefit the upper-middle class in that their education prepares them for leading roles in the management of this global system for the capitalist class, or for using technologies to advance in their chosen professions.

Below these two classes, however, new technologies add to the uncertainty of life, with levels of insecurity increasing the farther one moves down the ladder. New technologies have transformed the workplace, eliminating jobs and out-dating skills. People in lower management can transfer their skills from one job to another, although in shifting job markets the times between periods of employment can be precarious. Those in crafts are even less secure, for their training is more specific and the changing occupational world can reduce the need for their narrower, more specialized skills.

From the middle of the ladder down, people are hit the hardest. The working class has been ill prepared for changes ushered in by new technology, and are still haunted by the spectre of unemployment. The low technical skills of the working poor make them even more vulnerable, since they have even less to offer in the new job market. As unskilled jobs dry up, more and more working poor are consigned to day labour and getting by on whatever meager bits of work they can find, however temporary and however dangerous, underpaid, and exploitative. The underclass, with no technical skills, is bypassed entirely.

The playing field is far from level. Some even fear that the current trend of exporting Canadian jobs means Canadian workers are becoming an expendable luxury, destined to be replaced by low-paid, non-unionized—and more compliant—workers on other continents. In short, new technologies open and close opportunities for people largely by virtue of their position on the social class ladder.

Physical and Mental Health

Social class even affects our chances of living and dying. The homeless, for example, experience numerous increased health risks and high levels of morbidity and mortality (Hwang, 2001). The principle is simple: the lower a person's class, the more likely that individual is to die before the expected age. Among the top 25 percent of income earners in Canada, men can expect to live 6.3 years longer and be free of disability for 14.3 years more while women in this group can expect to live 3 years longer and have about 7.6 more years without disability compared to their lower-income counterparts (Health Canada, 1999). Among status Indians, many of whom have very low incomes, life expectancy was seven years less than the average for the Canadian population in 1991 (Health Canada, 1999). Although Canada has one of the highest life expectancies in the world, there are wide variations by region. The life expectancies of Canadians living in remote regions and in the North are closer to those in less developed countries than to rates in other parts of Canada (Statistics Canada, 2005c). Infants born to the poor are more likely than other infants to die before their first birthday. A study of 140 000 births in Toronto between 1996 and 2001 found that babies born to women living in the poorest neighbourhoods were 53 percent more likely to be underweight and 25 percent more likely to be premature than those born to mothers living in more affluent areas (Lewis, 2007: p. A10). Overall, health researchers have established a link between low incomes and

higher risks of babies born prematurely or with low birth weights, even at full term (Urquia, Frank, Glazier, & Moineddin, 2007).

In old age—whether 70 or 90—the poor are more likely to die of illness and disease. In Canada, the highest life expectancies are found in large metropolitan and urban centres where education levels are high, while people in remote northern communities, where a large percentage of the population is Aboriginal and where income and education levels are low, have the lowest life expectancies (Shields & Tremblay, 2002; Statistics Canada, 2005c; Allard, Wilkins & Berthelot, 2004). A recent study of life expectancy in Inuit-inhabited areas of Canada found that the life expectancy of the Inuit population was 12 to 15 years less than the figures for Canada as a whole (Wilkins et al., 2008).

From a comparative global perspective, Canadians enjoy relatively healthy and long lives. A recent report by the World Health Organization placed Canada twelfth on a new life expectancy measure. This means that on average, Canadians will live about 72 years free of disease or disability while total life expectancy is over 78 years. In Japan, the top-ranked country, people might expect to live illness-free 74.5 years; in contrast, people living in African countries such as Zimbabwe, Botswana, and Sierra Leone can expect less than 35 years of good health. Interestingly, the United States, the most prosperous nation in the world, ranked twenty-third on the health-expectancy scale. This relatively poor ranking is explained by the tremendous gap between rich and poor in the United States, where Native Americans, rural blacks, and the inner-city poor enjoy far fewer years free of health problems than others (Philp, 2000). A recent study found that air pollution along one of the major NAFTA trucking routes at Ciudad Juarez in Mexico is contributing to increased sickness and death among children living near this border crossing. However, when data from other border crossings were compared, the increased mortality at Ciudad Juarez was clearly linked to lower incomes and poverty (Bueckert, 2003).

During both childhood and adulthood, the poor are also more likely to be killed by accidents, fires, and homicide. Underlying these different death rates is unequal access to medical care and nutrition. Despite Canada's government-funded health care system, the higher classes receive better medical treatment. A recent study in Ontario showed that the rate of myocardial infarction (heart attack) was 38 percent higher for those living in the poorest 10 percent of the province's communities, compared with those in the richest 10 percent. Yet people in poorer neighbourhoods were less likely to receive surgery or necessary medical care. Relative to the rate of heart disease present, people in wealthy areas received 60 percent more surgery than those living in poorer areas (Talaga, 1999). Poor people are also less educated about nutrition, and their meals tend to be heavy in fats and sugars, neither of which are healthy. Children living in poor neighbourhoods and low-income families are at greater risk of being overweight or obese because the foods available to them are of lower nutritional value and they have fewer opportunities to be physically active (Statistics Canada, November 4, 2005).

Social class also affects mental health. From the 1930s until now, sociologists have found that the mental health of the lower classes is worse than that of the higher classes (Faris & Dunham, 1939; Srole et al., 1978; Brown & Gary, 1988; Lundberg, 1991; Burman, 1996; Capponi, 1997). This difference reflects the greater stresses experienced by those in the lower classes, such as unpaid bills, unemployment, dirty and dangerous work, the threat of eviction, unhappy marriages, and broken homes. People higher up the social class ladder also experience stress in daily life, of course, but their stresses are generally less and their coping resources greater. Not only can they afford vacations, psychiatrists, and counsellors, but *their class position gives them greater control over their lives, a key to good mental health*.

The Reach of Social Class

Social class plays a significant role in all aspects of life. How social class affects various aspects of life, including our personal lives—such as family life or choice of marital partner—and our public lives, such as which school we will attend and for how long, are examined throughout the chapters of this book. Below are some examples of the consequences of social class.

- *Choice of Husband or Wife*. The capitalist class strongly emphasizes family tradition and continuity, stressing the importance of ancestry, history, and even a sense of purpose or destiny in life (Baltzell, 1979; Aldrich, 1989). Children of this class learn that their choice of husband or wife affects not just themselves but the whole family unit, and that their spouse will have an impact on the "family line." Consequently, their field of "eligibles" is much narrower than it is for the children of any other social class. In effect, parents in this class play a greater role in their children's mate selection. Marriage has even become a class indicator—"an important class divider" (Wente, 2007: p. A25). Women with more education are not only more likely to marry, but are more likely to stay married and raise children with their biological father. When marriage breaks down, there is a greater likelihood that the children will grow up in a household where their mothers struggle to make ends meet.

- *Divorce*. The more difficult daily life of the lower social classes, especially the many tensions that come from insecure employment and inadequate incomes, leads to more marital friction and a greater likelihood of both spouse and alcohol abuse. Consequently, the marriages of the poor are more likely to fail and their children are more likely to grow up in broken homes.

- *Child-Rearing*. Sociologist Melvin Kohn (1977) finds significant class differences in child-rearing. Lower-class parents are more concerned that their children conform to conventional norms and obey authority figures. Middle-class parents, in contrast, encourage their children to be more creative and independent and tolerate a wider range of behaviours (except in speech, where they are less tolerant of bad grammar and curse words).

- *Education*. As was shown in Figure 6.4, education increases as one goes up the social class ladder. It is not just the amount of education that changes, but also the type. Children of the capitalist class bypass public schools entirely in favour of exclusive private schools, where they are trained to take a commanding role in society. Prep schools such as Upper Canada College teach upper-class values and prepare students for prestigious universities (Beeghley, 1996).

- *Religion*. Classes tend to cluster in different denominations. Anglicans, for example, are much more likely to recruit from the middle and upper classes, Baptists draw heavily from the lower classes, and Methodists are more middle-class. Patterns of worship also follow class lines: those that attract the lower classes have more spontaneous worship services and louder music, while the middle and upper classes prefer more "subdued" worship.

- *Politics*. As has been stressed throughout this text, symbolic interactionists emphasize that people see events from their own corner in life. Political views are no exception to this principle, and the rich and poor walk different political paths. The working class, which feels much more strongly than the classes above it that government should intervene in the economy to make citizens financially secure, is more likely to vote New Democrat, while those in higher classes are more likely to vote Conservative. The Liberal Party is the party of the centre. However, voting patterns and party allegiance are mixed. There is no clear class majority supporting any one party (Forcese, 1997). Although the working class is more liberal on *economic* issues (i.e., they favour government spending), members are more conservative on *social* issues (such as opposing abortion) (Lipset, 1959; Houtman, 1995). People toward the bottom of the class structure are less likely to become politically active—to campaign for candidates or even vote (Gans, 1991a; Gilbert & Kahl, 1993; Curtis, Grabb, & Guppy, 1999).

- *Crime and the Criminal Justice System*. Justice certainly is not blind when it comes to one's chances of being arrested (Henslin, 2008). In Chapter 16, we will discuss the different styles of crime the upper and lower social classes engage in. The white-collar crimes of the more privileged classes are more likely to be dealt with outside the criminal justice system, while the street crimes of the lower classes are dealt with by the police. One consequence of this class standard is that poor people, especially non-white poor people, are far more likely to be on probation, on parole, or in jail (National Council of

Welfare, 2000; Reiman, 2001). In addition, since people tend to commit crimes in or near their own neighbourhoods, the lower classes are more likely to be robbed, burglarized, or murdered.

Focus Question
In everyday life, what are some of the ways in which social class differences may be observed?

SOCIAL MOBILITY

No aspect of life, then—from marriage to politics—goes untouched by social class. Because life seems much more satisfying for the more privileged classes, people strive for upward social mobility. What affects people's chances of climbing the class ladder?

Three Types of Social Mobility

There are three basic types of social mobility: intergenerational, structural, and exchange mobility. **Intergenerational mobility** refers to adult children ending up on a different rung of the social class ladder than their parents—a change that occurs between generations. For example, if the child of someone who sells used cars goes to university and eventually buys a Toyota dealership, that person experiences **upward social mobility**. Conversely, if the child of the dealership owner parties too much, drops out of university, and ends up selling cars, he or she experiences **downward social mobility**.

We like to think that individual efforts—or faults—are the reason people move up or down the class ladder. In these examples, we can see hard work, sacrifice, and ambition on the one hand, and indolence and alcohol abuse on the other. Although individual factors underlie social mobility, sociologists consider **structural mobility** to be the crucial factor. This second basic type of mobility refers to changes in

society that cause large numbers of people to move up or down the class ladder.

To better understand structural mobility, think of the opportunities that opened when computers were invented. New types of jobs appeared overnight. Huge numbers of people took workshops and crash courses, switching from blue-collar to white-collar work. Although individual effort was certainly involved—some seized the opportunity while others did not—the underlying cause was a change in the *structure* of work. Or consider the other side: the closing of opportunities in a depression, when millions of people are forced downward on the class ladder. In this instance, too, their changed status is due less to individual behaviour than to *structural* changes in society.

The third type, **exchange mobility**, occurs when large numbers of people move up or down the social class ladder, but on balance the proportions of the social classes remain about the same. Suppose a million or so working-class people are trained in computers and move up the social class ladder—but a vast surge in imports forces about a million skilled workers into lower-status jobs. Although millions of people change their social class, there is in effect an *exchange* among them; that is, the net result more or less balances out and the class system remains basically untouched.

Ignoring Women

Sociologists used to focus only on the social mobility of men. For example, major studies of intergenerational mobility concluded that about half of sons moved beyond their fathers, about a third stayed at the same level, and only about a sixth dropped to a lower level on the social class ladder (Blau & Duncan, 1967; Featherman & Hauser, 1978; Featherman, 1979).

Fathers and sons? What about the other half of the population? Feminists pointed out this obvious absence (Davis & Robinson, 1988). They also objected to the idea that women were assumed to have no class position of their own

The term *structural mobility* refers to changes in society that push large numbers of people either up or down the social class ladder. A remarkable example was the Great Depression, during which thousands suddenly lost their jobs and wealth. People who had once "had it made" found themselves standing on street corners selling apples or, as depicted here, selling their possessions at fire-sale prices.

and were simply assigned the class of their husbands. The defence was that too few women were in the labour force to make a difference. Today, with the majority of women working for pay, recent studies include women, tracking their movement into higher ranking professional occupations, management, and traditionally male-dominated fields such as engineering and politics.

Gender, Class, and Race

As we noted earlier, there is a complex interrelationship between gender, class, and race and how these relationships play out in the economy and other social structures such as family, school, media, and politics (McCall, 2001; Brenner, 2000). What is clear from studies of working-class lives is that life's choices are constrained by gender as well as race and there is a complex relationship between these issues and social class. Inequalities spring from the complex interaction of social class with race and gender in the course of daily life (Rubin, 1976; Johnson, 2002).

New Technology and Fears of the Future

Movement on the ladder also goes down, which strikes fear in the hearts of many workers. If Canada fails to keep pace with global change and remain highly competitive by producing low-cost, quality goods, its economic position will decline. The result will be shrinking opportunities—with Canadian workers facing fewer good jobs and lower incomes. Such a decline would result in the children of the next generation having less status than their parents.

Perhaps this decline has already begun. We have lost millions of manufacturing jobs to Mexico, South America, and Asia. These jobs have taken with them the dreams of upward mobility for millions of Canadians. For others, this loss means downward mobility (Dentzler, 1991). Consider Alphonse Brown:

> Twenty-two years ago, Alphonse's mother, Letitia, the daughter of a migrant worker, easily found work at a parts plant in St. Catharines, Ontario. There she earned good money, built seniority, and enjoyed excellent benefits. Alphonse, in contrast, has given up hope of joining the assembly line. For ten years, he has moved from one low-paying, no-benefits job to another. Letitia says, "There's nobody left with less than 14 years' seniority. We're on our way back to being migrants."

In short, with global competition nipping at the heels of Canadian industry, the richest rewards are reserved for the highly educated or for those who work in jobs sheltered from foreign competition. The result is that millions of workers in the lower half of the Canadian labour force are hitting a brick wall (Swift, 1995; Jackson, 2005).

The foundation of this brick wall is new technology, especially computers and satellites. When corporations move factories overseas, their top-level managers, through the wonders of satellite-based communications, are able to monitor the production process from the comfort of their U.S. or Canadian offices. In many instances, this makes North American workers an expendable luxury, easily replaced by low-paid, non-unionized, and more compliant workers on other continents.

Of the thousands of examples, consider the following:

> Ireland is one of the poorest of European countries. Its workers, though, receive a solid high school education, generally superior to our high schools, and are willing to work for a fraction of what Canadian and American workers make. Consequently, many health insurance claims forms and grocery store redemption coupons are flown overnight to Ireland, where Irish workers efficiently process them, and return them, again overnight, to the United States.

A MATTER OF CONTROVERSY Fears of the future are apparent, but whether or not social mobility has decreased is a matter of heated debate. Although millions of jobs have been exported, millions more have been created. The question to be decided by empirical research is whether the new jobs bring sufficient incomes and status to maintain the social mobility to which Canadians have become accustomed—or whether most of them lead to a social-class dead end (Duffy, Glenday, & Pupo, 1997a). Although the answer will not be decided for some time, it is apparent that education remains the key to qualifying for better positions and thus to maintaining or improving one's social class.

POVERTY

Many Canadians find the "limitless possibilities" of the "Canadian dream" elusive. More than one in four Canadians (29.6 percent) experienced poverty for at least one year between 1996 and 2001. More than a million were poor for all six of those years. Over 4.9 million Canadians, or about one in six, currently live in poverty. This number is greater than the total population of British Columbia (4.2 million) (National Council of Welfare, 2006). Children, of course, are not exempt. About 1.2 million (17.6 percent) of children under the age of 18 live in poverty (National Council of Welfare, 2006). The impoverishment of some Canadians is also evident in the numbers of homeless people and the proliferation of food banks and food bank users across the nation (Cheadle, 2000). Across Canada in 2007, over 720 000 people relied on food banks each month, and almost 39 percent of food bank users were children (Canadian Association of Food Banks, 2007). This impoverishment is occurring in the midst of dramatic growth in the wealth of the richest Canadian families. In recent years, the old adage "the rich get richer" has accurately described the Canadian situation. Between 1980 and 2004, the richest 20 percent (quintile) of families improved their after-tax income by 17.4 percent ($ 16 400) to an average of $110 700 per annum. The poorest quintile only marginally improved by 4.3 percent during this time and averaged an after-tax income of $12 200 in 2004. The second and third poorest quintiles lost ground, by

TABLE 6.5 Income Shares by Quintile and Income Type, 2004

Quintile	Market Income	Total Income	After-Tax Income
Poorest	2.2%	4.2%	4.8%
Second	7.5%	9.7%	10.7%
Third	14.7%	15.6%	16.4%
Fourth	24.4%	23.7%	24.0%
Richest	51.2%	46.8%	44.0%
TOTAL	100.0%	100.0%	100.0%

Source: Statistics Canada, *Income Trends in Canada 1980–2004,* Table 2020703. Cited in National Council of Welfare, Poverty Statistics 2004, October 2007.

2.9 percent and 4.4 percent respectively, resulting in average after-tax incomes of $26 900 and $41 200. Finally, the fourth wealthiest quintile improved by only 2.5 percent and averaged an after-tax income of $60 400. The net result appears to be a growing chasm between the haves and the have-nots in Canada and a marked decline in the economic well-being of the "middle classes" (National Council of Welfare, 2007). Table 6.5 indicates the differences in the income shares of Canadians by quintile, providing another way of understanding the vast differences between the rich and poor.

In considering the data in Table 6.5, we can conclude that Canada is following in the footsteps of the United States and Great Britain, where income inequality has grown markedly since the 1980s (Statistics Canada, 2005e; Yalnizyan, 2007; Jackson, 2005).

Currently, 43.7 percent of the total after-tax income in Canada goes to the richest 20 percent of families. The share of income for the poorest 20 percent was only 5.0 percent. Between 1980 and 2003, the richest 20 percent of families increased their after-tax incomes by 14.4 percent, whereas the poorest 20 percent increased their after-tax incomes by only 4.3 percent (National Council of Welfare, 2006). The poorest 20 percent of family units has absolutely no net worth and is living month to month, spending all or most of what is earned and having little or nothing to set aside for RRSPs and RESPs (Kerstetter, 2001). Young families with children, single mothers, recent immigrants, visible minorities, and disabled Canadians are all confronting increasingly uncertain economic futures (Carey, 2001). At the same time, the social welfare net, made up of employment insurance payments, welfare assistance, disability payments, and so on, has grown increasingly bare-boned. In recent years, Ontario, British Columbia, and Alberta have instituted welfare reforms that have resulted in reduced funding for welfare recipients. Poverty and inequality have taken centre stage in understanding Canadian society.

Drawing the Poverty Line

Most Canadians will be surprised to learn that Canada does not have an "official" poverty line. Indeed, determining who is and is not poor remains a contentious issue. The National Council of Welfare (2004) documents nine different poverty lines that appear in reports on urban poverty (p. 135). It is easy to see that homeless, starving children in Guatemala or nineteenth-century Montreal are poor; it is much more difficult to agree upon present-day Canadians who have so little that they cannot meaningfully participate in Canadian society. According to some analysts, if individuals are not starving, not homeless, and not in immediate physical peril due to their economic plight, they are not *really* poor. In a contentious thesis under the aegis of the conservative Fraser Institute, Christopher Sarlo (1992) argued that if you adopt a "basic needs" approach, "poverty ... has been virtually eliminated" in Canada and "is simply not a major problem" (p. 2). This physical survival argument suggests a very narrow understanding of poverty.

Currently, most discussions of poverty in Canada rely on more generous standards of impoverishment. In particular, Statistics Canada's *low-income cut-offs* (LICOs) are frequently employed as informal poverty lines. Adopted in 1973 (and reset in 1992), the before-tax LICOs seek to establish a specific income level below which individuals are considered to be living in "straitened circumstances." The assumption underlying the cut-offs is that poor families are those whose income requires them to spend more than 54.7 percent of their gross income on food, clothing, and shelter. Since the average Canadian family spends 34.7 percent of its income on these necessities, it is assumed (arbitrarily) that an additional 20 percent results in an economic burden (National Council of Welfare, 2004, p. 134). As a result of these expenditures on absolute necessities, little, if anything, is left over for transportation, health, personal care, education, household operation, recreation, insurance, savings, and so on.

The LICOs are set up so that they vary depending upon the size of the family unit (how many dependants are

WIZARD OF ID

THE KING WILL NOW OUTLINE HIS PLAN TO ELIMINATE POVERTY

IN THE FUTURE, THERE WILL BE NO MONETARY AMOUNT USED TO DEFINE POVERTY

GEE, I FEEL RICHER ALREADY!

This cartoon pinpoints the arbitrary nature of the poverty line.

supported by the family income) and the size of the community (town, city, or area)—a population of more than 500 000, 100 000 to 499 000, and so on—in which the family/individual lives. These calculations result in 35 separate LICOs for all of Canada. For example, in 2006, a family of three living in Montreal would be poor if the total income for the family was $32 450 or less; the same family living in a rural area would be poor if they received $22 338 or less (Canadian Council on Social Development, 2008).

It is important to be aware that other "poverty lines" have been proposed. Some analysts, for example, have argued for a "market basket measure." This approach, which seeks to create an absolute, long-term measure, develops a basket of necessities for families and then prices the basket in terms of local costs. The net result is a much more restrictive measure of poverty, which, if adopted, would dramatically reduce the number of people who are considered poor in Canada (CCSD, 2000, pp. 14–30).

The definitional struggle is far from resolution. Every now and then, the conflict bursts open and there is, as with Sarlo, much discussion of who is "really" poor in Canada and, implicitly, who really needs help.

This problem is by no means uniquely Canadian. Around the world, there are frequent disagreements about who is or is not poor. It is part of the magical sleight-of-hand of modern bureaucracy that a modification in the official measure of poverty instantly adds—or subtracts—millions of people from the category (Sainath, 1996). Governments use the definition not only to decide who will and will not receive help but also to represent to the world the relative health of their national economy. Using the prevailing definition of poverty in Canada—Statistics Canada's LICOs— let's see who is poor. But first, compare your ideas of the poor with the myths explored in the following Down-to-Earth Sociology box.

DOWN-TO-EARTH SOCIOLOGY
Exploring Myths About the Poor

Myth 1: **Most poor people are lazy. They are poor because they do not work.**
It's important to keep in mind that many poor people are either disabled or too old or young to work and, as a result, are limited in their ability to support themselves. In addition, a whole range of societal prejudices, including ageism, racism, and ableism, may stand in their way of finding employment (Jackson, Robinson, Baldwin, & Wiggins, 2000). Furthermore, many poor people actually do work. In 2004, more than half of poor Canadians under age 65 earned more than 50 percent of their total

incomes from paid work (National Council of Welfare, 2007). However, even when work is secured, it is no guarantee against poverty.

Although many poor people are employed, their jobs pay so poorly that one income does not lift them above the low-income cut-offs. In 2004, the poverty rate for two-parent families with one earner was 26.5 percent, and 6.6 percent of families with two earners were considered poor (National Council of Welfare, 2007). Low-wage or minimum-wage jobs, along with part-time, contract, and seasonal work, often simply

are not enough to rescue families from poverty. Finally, poverty rates tend to rise and fall with unemployment rates, which suggests that many poor people grab the chance for paid employment whenever possible.

Myth 2: **Most poor people are single mothers and their children.**
Being a single mother with children is a high-risk formula for poverty. In 2004, 43.4 percent of single-parent mothers were poor (National Council of Welfare, 2007). However, it is important to keep in mind that mother-headed families make up a minority of poor families. Only

40 percent of poor children are living in mother-headed families. The majority (54 percent) of poor kids are in two-parent families, with a fraction (4 percent) in single-father families or other living arrangements (3 percent) (National Council of Welfare, 2007).

Myth 3: Poverty is a big-city problem. Since many Canadians live in large metropolitan areas, it is not surprising that many poor individuals do as well. In 2003, 50 percent of poor unattached individuals and 56 percent of poor families lived in cities of 500 000 or more (National Council of Welfare, 2006: 61). Poverty rates are higher in larger cities and metropolitan areas and lower in rural regions and smaller cities because of the way the low-income cutoffs are calculated in relation to the cost of living. Not surprisingly, the poor in rural areas and small towns, such as Atlantic Canada, for example, may be particularly vulnerable to economic restructuring as traditional sources of employment (fishing, mining) are lost and changes in employment insurance policies remove the significant alternative of reliance on welfare payments. In short, poverty is a pressing issue across the country, from small towns and farming communities to large urban areas (Heisz, 2001).

Myth 4: The poor live on welfare. In one sense this is true. Living on welfare means living in poverty, since welfare incomes are substantially below the LICOs. However, it is not true that the majority of poor Canadians depend on welfare. In 2004, only 12 percent of poor couples with children and only 28 percent of single-parent mothers relied on welfare as their only source of income; further, only 9 percent of poor couples with children and 26 percent of single-parent mothers relied on a combination of earnings and welfare. More than three-quarters of poor families and almost half of single-parent mothers were not drawing on welfare as a primary source of income that year (National Council of Welfare, 2007). Furthermore, the idea that welfare fraud runs rampant is simply untrue. A study by law professors Janet Mosher and Joe Hermer found that in Ontario, the number of welfare fraud cases was extremely low—the equivalent of about 0.1 percent of the total social assistance load for the province. Further, they found that only 1 percent of the allegations in welfare fraud cases resulted in convictions (McCormack, 2007: p. A17).

Focus Question
What are some of the popular myths about the poor and why is this misinformation still widely believed?

Who Are the Poor?

GEOGRAPHY Poverty is not evenly distributed across Canada. Reflecting differences in local economies (and, as a result, opportunities for employment), poverty rates for all persons in Canada in 2003 ranged from a high of 20.1 percent in British Columbia to a low of 11.8 percent in Prince Edward Island (National Council of Welfare, 2006: p. 29). We know relatively little about the Yukon, the Northwest Territories, or Nunavut since Statistics Canada does not include them in their income surveys. However, high rates of Aboriginal poverty suggest that impoverishment is a very significant issue in these areas (National Council of Welfare, 2001, pp. 23–26). However, the greatest predictor of whether Canadians are poor is not geography, but rather the race/ethnicity, education, age, disability, and sex of the head of household. Let's examine these factors more closely.

RACE/ETHNICITY Despite Canada's official multiculturalism, being a visible minority, immigrant, or Aboriginal Canadian carries with it an increased risk of poverty. The national poverty rate among visible minorities is about twice that of other groups, and, in specific provinces such as Newfoundland and Nova Scotia, visible minorities are more likely than other Canadians to be poor. Between 1993 and 1998, at least 21 percent of visible-minority Canadians experienced low income for four or more years, compared with only 7 percent of other Canadians (Morissette & Zhang, 2001, p. 26). A recent study of Statistics Canada income data revealed that white Canadians earn about 25 percent more than non-whites (Campbell, 2001).

Predictably, immigrants, and especially recent immigrants, are also disadvantaged (Frenette et al., 2008). Between 1980 and 2005, the employment income of recent immigrants slipped further behind their Canadian-born counterparts. In 1980, while both male and female recent immigrants received 85 cents for each dollar earned by Canadian-born men, by 2005, the numbers fell to 63 cents for recent immigrant men and 56 cents for recent immigrant women (Ibid.: p. 6). For immigrant families in which the major income earner came to Canada after 1989, the poverty rate is 29.8 percent, while for families in which the income earner was born in Canada, the rate is 9.8 percent (National Council of Welfare, 2006, pp. 52–53). Even highly educated recent immigrants often find themselves stuck in low-education, low-income jobs (Galarneau & Morissette, 2004).

Not surprisingly, Aboriginal peoples also face increased economic risk. In several provinces in Canada, the poverty rate among Aboriginal peoples is more than twice that of non-Aboriginals, and in Saskatchewan and Manitoba in 2000 more than half of all Aboriginals were living in poverty (CCSD, 2000, pp. 75, 77). The overall Canadian picture is bleak. Almost half (44 percent) of all Canadian Aboriginals and 60 percent of Aboriginal children are reported to be living below the LICOs (Federal, Provincial, and Territorial Advisory Committee, 1999, p. 47).

EDUCATION As discussed earlier, education is also a vital factor in poverty. Unattached persons with eight years of education or less have an astounding poverty rate of 57 percent, while for those with a university bachelor's degree the rate is 21.7 percent (National Council of Welfare, 2006: p. 48). This disparity is also reflected in earnings patterns. Compared to their counterparts without a high school diploma, for example, young men between the ages of 25 and 34 who had a trade or apprenticeship in 2006 earned $8000 more per year (Frenette et al., 2008: p. 17). The median income for women aged 45 to 54 with a bachelor's or postgraduate degree is $30 000 more than the median income for women who did not graduate from high school (Ibid.: p. 18). Ironically, while education may serve as a way out of low income situations for many, rising tuition costs and mushrooming student-loan debt appear to be deterring many students from low-income families from attending postsecondary institutions (Rushowy, 2000).

Education, however, is not a guarantee against bad economic times. Many poor heads of families have education beyond high school and still end up in poverty. Between 1993 and 1998, 20 percent of Canadians who had completed some or all of a postsecondary program experienced a year or more of low income (Morissette & Zhang, 2001). Indeed, in 2003, 50 percent of all poor two-parent family major income earners had education beyond the high school level (National Council of Welfare, 2006: p. 51). Recent surveys of food bank clients also support the impression that education does not guarantee against poverty, especially for certain groups of Canadians. In 2002, 59 percent of immigrant users of food banks were "highly educated" (Quinn, 2002). This pattern suggests that poverty may be as much a result of too few or inadequate employment opportunities as too little education.

AGE As discussed in Chapter 9, the reduction of poverty among seniors is one of the great poverty success stories. Poverty among Canadians 65 and older dropped from 33.9 percent in 1980 to 16.8 percent in 2001 and further to 14 percent in 2004 (National Council of Welfare, 2004, p. 11; National Council of Welfare, 2007). This dramatic improvement is largely the result of changes in government policies. The creation of the Canada and Quebec pension plans in 1966 and the introduction of the Guaranteed Income Supplement and Old Age Security programs were crucial steps. More recent income security policies have further improved the lives of many seniors (National Council of Welfare, 1999a).

However, seniors are not entirely poverty-free. Senior women, in particular, remain at risk, with poverty rates often twice those of senior men. Unattached women are at a very high risk, with 45.6 percent living below the LICOs, resulting in the highest poverty rate of any of the most common family types in Canada (National Council of Welfare, 2004, p. 30).

Similarly, aged seniors appear to be at a disadvantage. Among older seniors (85+), 28.6 percent of women are living in poverty regardless of marital status (National Council of Welfare, 2006, p. 41). In short, a substantial number of very old seniors, especially those not sharing expenses with a partner, are struggling with poverty.

Further, senior poverty remains a significant problem in certain provinces. In British Columbia, for example, the poverty rate for all persons 65 and older is 19.6 percent, compared to Alberta at 9.6 percent (National Council of Welfare, 2006: p. 121).

WOMEN The other major predictor of poverty is gender—the so-called **feminization of poverty**. If we look at the ratio of female-to-male poverty rates—in other words, the poverty rate of women compared to the poverty rate of men—we consistently find that women are at a greater risk. This gender difference has fluctuated over the past two decades, tending to narrow somewhat in tough economic times, but has consistently favoured men (National Council of Welfare, 2004, p. 4; National Council of Welfare, 2006).

Women's greater vulnerability to poverty can primarily be explained by high poverty rates in three types of families: unattached women under 65, unattached women 65 and older, and single-parent mothers under 65 with children under 18. Women seniors, women on their own, and women who head families are at a greater risk of poverty than their male counterparts.

Single mothers are particularly vulnerable. They comprise 85 percent of single-parent families in Canada and more than 90 percent of poor single-parent families (National Council of Welfare, 2004, p. 14). However, there has been progress. In 2003, the poverty rate for single mothers was 48.9 percent. The poverty rate for single fathers, a much smaller portion of the population, was 20 percent in that year and has typically been less than half that of their female counterparts (National Council of Welfare, 2006: p. 39). The number of two-parent families living below the poverty line has, with notable ups and downs, remained fairly stable at slightly more than 9 percent.

A variety of social factors contribute to the economic vulnerability of single mothers. Women's work in traditional women's occupations tends to result in less well-paid employment with fewer benefits. Women who interrupt their work or decrease their paid hours to part-time to care for home and family find themselves disadvantaged in the labour market. In the event of divorce, persistent difficulties in obtaining child-support payments from non-custodial parents may exacerbate financial problems. Lack of adequate, accessible, and affordable child care may make it difficult for single mothers to improve their financial situation. Between 2001 and 2006, there was a steep drop in the number of new regulated child care spaces, leaving Canadians lagging far behind many other industrialized countries providing child support programs for families (Canadian Press, 2008). As one analyst concludes, the simple fact is that single mothers earn less than men, but have the primary responsibility for the custody of their children in the event of marital breakup, and never-married mothers are in an even worse situation (Finnie, 2000, p. 31). Many single mothers turn to social welfare and other government transfer payments in order to maintain their families, and the level of these income transfers guarantees that their families will be living below the low-income cut-offs (CCSD, 2000). Not surprisingly, these poor single mothers may find themselves sinking further and further into debt. A recent study reported that while one in six Canadian families fell behind two months or more on a bill, loan, rent, or mortgage payment, almost one in three single mothers were in the same situation (Pyper, 2002).

Women who are not married and who do not have children at home may also fare poorly. In 2003, the poverty rate for unattached women under age 65 was 40.9 percent, while for men of the same age and marital status it was 34.4 percent (National Council of Welfare, 2006: p. 39). Again, inequalities in the labour market along with work interruptions, divorce, and so on may create these patterns of disparity. Consider, for example, the plight of a 55-year-old recently-divorced woman with little experience in the paid labour force and not yet eligible for old age security.

As women age, the poverty imbalance persists. The poverty rate for unattached women 65 and older was 45.6 percent in 2001 while for comparable men it was 32.8 percent. Since earlier generations of women frequently dropped out of the paid labour force in order to bear and raise children, they often receive little or no pension income when they retire. Once widowed, divorced, or otherwise single, senior women frequently find themselves in financially precarious situations (Morissette & Zhang, 2001).

THE DISABLED Canadians who are born with or acquire a disability are likely to experience economic difficulties. According to the 2001 Participation and Activity Limitation Survey (PALS), excluding people living in institutions, roughly 2 million Canadians between the ages of 15 and 64 are living with a disability—that is, a long-term condition that limits daily activity at home, work, school, and in other activities (Williams, 2006: p. 10). Compared to the non-disabled population, people with disabilities experience higher rates of unemployment, are less likely to work in management, are more likely to work reduced or part-time hours, and have lower incomes (Ibid.). For example, the median employment income of persons with disabilities in 2001 was 17 percent lower than that of the non-disabled labour force (Ibid.: p. 19). The degree of difference between disabled and non-disabled workers, however, varies with the degree of severity of the disability. Yet despite the inequalities faced by persons with disabilities in the labour force, workers with disabilities have more education on average than their non-disabled counterparts (Ibid.: p. 18).

Almost 30 percent of disabled men and a third of disabled women (in contrast to 18 percent of other Canadians) are poor. Discrimination in hiring practices, limited accommodations in work environments, and inadequate disability benefits all set the stage for this pattern. (CCSD, 2000, p. 76; Morissette & Zhang, 2001, p. 28).

IN SUM

Poverty is a social issue that is not as straightforward as it might seem. Determining who "qualifies" as poor is a contentious political issue. Understanding the realities of poverty means questioning popular myths about the poor. It is important to recognize that poverty is not simply a result of poor character or bad luck. Particular categories of individuals, notably women, seniors, members of racial and ethnic minorities, the disabled, and children whose primary parents belong to these categories, are much more likely to be poor. The failure of Canadians and their governments to adequately address poverty over the past recent decades does not bode well for the future.

CHILDREN Despite government promises to end child poverty in Canada by 2000, in 2004 there were 1 196 000 children living below the LICOs in Canada (National Council of Welfare, 2007). Nationally, according to the annual Report Card on Child Poverty (2005), the child poverty rate is about 18 percent, but almost 50 percent of recent immigrant children, 40 percent of Aboriginals living in urban areas, and 33 percent of children who are visible minorities live in poverty (Brown, 2005: p. A11). The fact that this many Canadian children are reared in poverty is shocking when one considers our nation's wealth and supposed concern for the well-being of our children. The tragedy of poverty is the topic of the next Thinking Critically about Social Controversy box (page 140).

Focus Question

Which categories of Canadians are more likely to be poor at some point in their lives?

THE DYNAMICS OF POVERTY

In the 1960s, Michael Harrington (1962) and Oscar Lewis (1966a) suggested that the poor tend to become trapped in a **culture of poverty**. They assumed that the values and behaviours of the poor "make them fundamentally different . . . and that these factors are largely responsible for their continued long-term poverty" (Ruggles, 1989, p. 7). This perspective is closely linked to the notions of deserving and undeserving poor discussed in the Thinking Critically about Social Controversy box on page 141. Implied by this "culture of poverty" approach is the idea that many poor people are lazy and bring poverty on themselves. Is a self-perpetuating culture, transmitted across generations that locks poor people into poverty, the basic reason for its existence?

Until recently, we knew little about how long Canadians spend in poverty and how they move in and out of it. In the early 1990s, Statistics Canada began tracking individuals over six-year stretches to determine how their financial circumstances changed.

As a result, we now have longitudinal information on the financial lives of Canadians, and these data suggest (1) that

In 1989, the House of Commons unanimously resolved to eradicate child poverty in Canada by 2000. In 1991, Canada ratified the United Nations Convention on the Rights of the Child. Successive governments have pledged improvement in the provision of child care and, more recently, a national system of early childhood education and care (Campaign 2000, 2003, p. A26). Instead of improvements, the past decade has witnessed a series of disappointing failures. In an affluent and progressive country, about one child in six is living in poverty (National Council of Welfare, 2004, p. 111).

This is a particularly sorry record when compared to the efforts of other countries. While the United States, Britain, and Russia have an even more dismal record on child poverty, when we turn our attention to countries such as Sweden, Finland, the Netherlands, and Denmark it is apparent that much more could be accomplished in reducing poverty and income inequality (Bradshaw, 2002; Federal, Provincial, and Territorial Advisory Committee, 1999; Statistics Canada, 2005e). For example,

while the poverty rate for lone-parent mothers is 42.4 percent in Canada (2001) and 47 percent in the United States, in Sweden only 3 percent of lone-parent mothers are impoverished (National Council of Welfare, 2001, 2004).

Of course, most children are poor in Canada because they happen to be born into poor families. Their risk of impoverishment simply reflects the patterns of racism, sexism, ableism, and economic marginalization that result in patterns of growing social inequality. For example, child poverty is higher where the children's families are headed by young people (under age 25), only one parent (especially if that parent is the mother), visible minorities or Aboriginals, or a disabled adult. Clearly, for more and more poor children, having only one parent to support them is a crucial ingredient in impoverishment. However, many children are the victims of an economy that has generated large numbers of "bad jobs" (part-time and/or part-year jobs with very low rates of pay) and high rates of unemployment, along with a social assistance "net" that is increasingly inadequate (characterized not only

by decreases in social assistance payments but also increased restrictions on employment insurance benefits and scant increments to minimum wage levels) (National Council of Welfare, 2004, pp. 100–105; National Council of Welfare, 2006, pp. 112-120; Morissette & Picot, 2005; Sussman & Tabi, 2004).

The statistical profile of child poverty provides only a sanitized impression. Poverty permeates children's lives. Being born into poverty, for example, means a higher risk of dying at birth and a greater risk of being unhealthy. Growing up poor means living in inadequate and unhealthy housing in unsafe neighbourhoods. Growing up in poverty means less of a chance at a good education, which in turn reduces the opportunities for satisfying, well-paid employment. Growing up in poverty may mean poorer health and higher rates of hospitalization and heart disease (Raphael, 2001). Growing up poor may mean being viewed by social workers, police, and judges as less reputable, less trustworthy, and less worthy of lenience (National Council of Welfare, 2000). Not having adequate work leads to insufficient

The number of Canadian children living in poverty is shocking considering our country's wealth and concern for the well-being of children and families.

pensions and an old age marked by struggle rather than rest (Federal, Provincial, and Territorial Advisory Committee, 1999).

On a day-to-day basis, being poor may mean having to miss a school trip with other children, not having enough to eat, or always feeling on the outside, wanting the clothes, vacations, and experiences that others have and that the media promote (Hurtig, 1999).

For Your Consideration

Many social analysts—liberal and conservative—are alarmed at the persistence of child poverty. They emphasize that it is time to stop blaming the victim; instead, we must focus on the structural factors that underlie child poverty. To relieve the problem, they say, we must take immediate steps to establish national programs of child nutrition, child care, health care, and housing. Solutions will require at least these fundamental changes: (1) removing obstacles to employment; (2) improving education; and (3) supporting parents and strengthening families. To achieve these changes, what specific programs would you recommend?

Sources: Moynihan (1991); C. Murray (1993); Sandefur, 1995; *Statistical Abstract* (1997, Tables 22, 736, 739, 1338); National Council of Welfare (1999c, 2004).

---

poverty is much more common among Canadians than is often assumed and (2) that long-term poverty is relatively uncommon and impacts disproportionately on certain segments of the population. We know that nearly a third (30.7 percent, almost twice the annual poverty rate of 15.5 percent) of Canadians experienced at least one year of low income between 1996 and 2001. However, only 5.9 percent of Canadians were poor for all six years during this time period (National Council of Welfare, 2006: p. 71). Predictably, certain segments of the population are particularly vulnerable to long-term impoverishment, but this does not suggest a "culture of poverty." Rather, happenstance—being born into a low-income family, being old, being disabled, being divorced—is strongly related to long-term poverty.

THINKING CRITICALLY ABOUT SOCIAL CONTROVERSY
The Welfare Debate: The Deserving and Undeserving Poor

Throughout Canadian history, we have divided the poor into two types: the deserving and the undeserving. The deserving poor are people who, in the public mind, are poor through no fault of their own. Most of the working poor, such as the Lewises, are considered deserving:

> Nancy and Ted Lewis are in their late 30s and married with two children. Ted works three part-time jobs; Nancy takes care of the children and house. Their total income is $22 000 a year. To make ends meet, the Lewises rely on welfare and food bank support.

The undeserving poor, in contrast, are viewed as having brought on their own poverty. They are thought of as freeloaders who waste their lives in sloth, alcohol and drug abuse, and unwed motherhood. They don't deserve help, and, if given anything, will waste it on their dissolute lifestyles. Some people would see Joan as an example:

> Joan's grandmother and her six children were supported by welfare. Joan's parents are alcoholics—and on welfare. Joan started having sex at 13, bore her first child at 15, and, now at 23, with three children, is expecting her fourth. Her first two children have the same father, the third a different father, and Joan isn't sure who fathered her coming child. Joan parties most nights, using alcohol and whatever drugs are available. Her house is filthy and social workers have threatened to take away her children.

This division of the poor into deserving and undeserving underlies a heated debate about welfare. "Why should we use *our* hard-earned money to help *them*? They are just going to waste it. Of course, there are those who want to get on their feet, and helping them is okay."

For Your Consideration

What is the purpose of this division of the poor into deserving and undeserving? Would we let some people starve because they "brought poverty upon themselves"? Would we let children go hungry because their parents are unmarried, uneducated, or unskilled? Try to look beyond such a simplistic division and use a sociological perspective to explain poverty without blaming the victim. What *social* conditions (conditions of society) create poverty? What *social* conditions propagate this lifestyle?

Changes in the Welfare Response to Poverty

After decades of debate, welfare programs across Canada (most notably in British Columbia, Ontario, and Alberta) have been reformed. In many provinces, welfare incomes, already well below the LICOs, have been further reduced and programs have been introduced to force many recipients to accept welfare work ("workfare") or participate in training programs in order to qualify for social welfare. At the same time, other government programs that provide assistance to those in economic stress, such as employment insurance, disability payments, and legal aid, have been dramatically cut back in some provinces. Critics call this an attack on the poor, saying that the new rules and restrictions will push many people, notably single mothers, poor kids, and the disabled, deeper into poverty (Bashevkin, 2002). Supporters of welfare reforms claim that the changes rescue people from poverty—transforming them into self-supporting and hard-working citizens—and reduce welfare costs (A. Cohen, 1997). Welfare rolls have dropped but the numbers of homeless people in our urban centres have markedly increased. In 2004, for example, there were 8664 people in Ottawa who were homeless and stayed at a shelter at some point (Alliance to End Homelessness, 2005). Reducing the safety net while at the same time increasing the gap between rich and poor may have dramatic social consequences.

Deferred Gratification

One consequence of a life of deprivation punctuated by emergencies—*and seeing the future as more of the same*—is a lack of **deferred gratification**, giving up things in the present for the sake of greater gains in the future. It is difficult to practise this middle-class virtue if one does not have a middle-class surplus—or middle-class hope.

In 1967, sociologist Elliot Liebow noted this precise problem among African-American street-corner men. Their jobs were low-paying and insecure, and their lives were pitted with emergencies. With the future looking exactly like the present, and any savings gobbled up by emergencies—theirs or those of friends and relatives—saving for the future was fruitless. The only thing that made sense from their perspective was to enjoy what they could at the moment. Immediate gratification, then, was not the cause of their poverty, but its consequence. Cause and consequence loop together, however; their immediate gratification, in turn, helped perpetuate their poverty.

If both causes are at work, why do sociologists emphasize the structural explanation? Reverse the situation for a moment. Suppose the daily routine of the middle class involved an old car that ran only half the time, threats from the utility company to shut off the electricity and heat, and a choice between buying medicine, food, and diapers or paying rent. How long would they practise deferred gratification? Their orientations to life would likely make a sharp U-turn.

Sociologists, then, look at the behaviours of the poor more as driven by their poverty than as a cause of it. Poor people would love the opportunities that would allow them the chance to practise the middle-class virtue of deferred gratification. They just can't afford it.

"Pull Yourself Up by Your Own Bootstraps": The Social Functions of a Myth

Around the turn of the twentieth century, one of the United States' most talked-about fictional heroes was Horatio Alger, whose rags-to-riches exploits and startling successes in overcoming severe odds motivated thousands of boys of that period. Although he has disappeared from literature, the ideology remains alive and well in the psyche of Canadians. From abundant real-life examples of people of humble origins who climbed far up the social class ladder, Canadians know that anyone can get ahead if they really try. In fact, they believe that most Canadians, including minorities and the working poor, have an average or better-than-average chance of getting ahead—obviously a statistical impossibility (Kluegel & Smith, 1986).

Functionalists would stress that this belief is functional for society. On one hand, it encourages people to compete for higher positions, or, as the song says, "to reach for the highest star." On the other hand, it places blame for failure squarely on the individual. If you don't make it—in the face of ample opportunities to get ahead—the fault must be your own. The myth helps to stabilize society; since the fault is viewed as the individual's rather than society's, current social arrangements are satisfactory. This reduces pressures to change the system.

As Marx and Weber observed, social class penetrates our consciousness, shaping our ideas of life and our proper place in society. When the rich look around, they sense superiority and control over destiny. In contrast, the poor see defeat and a bitter buffeting by unpredictable forces. Both know the dominant ideology, that their particular niche in life is the result of their own efforts, that the reasons for success—or failure—lie solely with the self. Like fish not seeing water, people tend not to see how social class affects their own lives.

What Is Social Stratification?

The term **social stratification** refers to a hierarchy of relative privilege based on power, property, and prestige. Every society stratifies its members. p. 112.

Systems of Social Stratification

WHAT ARE THE FOUR MAJOR SYSTEMS OF SOCIAL STRATIFICATION?

The four major stratification systems are slavery, caste, clan, and class. The essential characteristic of **slavery** is ownership of some people by others. Initially, slavery was based not on race but on debt, punishment, or defeat in battle. Slavery could be temporary or permanent, and was not necessarily passed on to one's children. In North America, slaves had no legal rights, and the system was gradually buttressed by a racist ideology. In a **caste system**, status is determined by birth and is life-long. People marry within their own group and develop rules about ritual pollution. In a **clan system**, people's status depends on lineage that links them to an extended network of relatives. A **class system** is much more open than these other systems as it is based primarily on money or material possessions. Industrialization encourages the formation of class systems. Gender discrimination cuts across all forms of social stratification. pp. 112–114.

What Determines Social Class?

Karl Marx argued that a single factor determines social class: If you own the **means of production**, you belong to the **bourgeoisie**; if you do not, you are one of the **proletariat**. Max Weber argued that three elements determine social class: *property*, *prestige*, and *power*. pp. 114–116.

Complexities of Inequality

WHAT IS SOCIAL CLASS, AND HOW DO SOCIOLOGISTS MEASURE IT?

Most sociologists have adopted Weber's definition of **social class** as a large group of people who rank closely to one another in wealth, power, and prestige. There are three ways to measure social class. In the **subjective method**, people assign themselves to their own social class. In the **reputational method**, people identify the social class of others on the basis of knowledge of their circumstances. In the **objective method**, researchers assign subjects to a social class on the basis of objective criteria such as wealth, power, and prestige. pp. 116–117.

The Components of Social Class

WHAT ARE THE THREE CRITERIA USED TO MEASURE SOCIAL CLASS?

Wealth, power, and prestige are most commonly used to measure social class. **Wealth**, consisting of property and income, is concentrated in the upper classes. The distribution of wealth in Canada has changed over the past couple of generations: the richest quintile is receiving a larger share of the country's wealth and the poorest quintile a much smaller share than they did in the 1940s. **Power** is the ability to carry out one's will, even over the resistance of others. C. Wright Mills coined the term **power elite** to refer to the small group that holds the reins of power in business, government, and the military. **Prestige** is often linked to occupational status. People's rankings of occupational prestige have changed little and are similar from country to country. Globally, occupations that pay more, require more education and abstract thought, and offer greater autonomy are given greater prestige. pp. 117–122.

WHAT IS MEANT BY THE TERM *STATUS INCONSISTENCY*?

Status is social ranking. Most people are status-consistent; that is, they rank high or low on all three dimensions of social class. People who rank higher on some dimensions than on others are status-inconsistent. The frustrations of status inconsistency tend to produce political radicalism. pp. 122–123.

Why Is Social Stratification Universal?

To explain why stratification is universal, functionalists argue that to attract the most capable people to fill its important positions, society must offer higher rewards. Critics argue that if this view were correct, society would be a **meritocracy**, with all positions awarded on the basis of merit. Conflict theorists argue that stratification comes about because resources are limited, requiring groups to struggle against one another for them. pp. 124–125.

How Do Elites Maintain Social Inequality?

HOW DO NATIONS MAINTAIN SOCIAL STRATIFICATION?

To maintain social stratification within a nation, the ruling class uses an **ideology** that justifies current arrangements. It also controls information, and, when all else fails, depends on brute force. The social networks of the rich and poor also perpetuate social inequality. pp. 125–127.

Applying Sociological Models of Social Class

WHAT MODELS ARE USED TO PORTRAY THE SOCIAL CLASSES?

Two models that portray the social classes were described in this chapter. Erik Olin Wright developed a four-class model based on Marx: (1) capitalists or owners; (2) petty bourgeoisie or small business owners; (3) managers; and (4) workers. Gilbert and Kahl developed a six-class model based on Weber. At the top is the capitalist or upper class, and in descending order are the upper-middle class, the lower-middle class, the working class, the working poor, and the **underclass**. pp. 127–130.

Consequences of Social Class

HOW DOES SOCIAL CLASS AFFECT PEOPLE?
Social class leaves no aspect of life untouched. It affects people's chances of benefiting from new technology, dying early, becoming ill, receiving good health care, and getting divorced. Class membership also affects child rearing, educational attainment, religious affiliation, political participation, and contact with the criminal justice system. pp. 130–133.

Social Mobility

WHAT ARE THE THREE TYPES OF SOCIAL MOBILITY?
The term **intergenerational mobility** refers to changes in social class from one generation to the next. **Exchange mobility** is the movement of large numbers of people from one class to another, with the net result that the relative proportions of population in each class remains about the same. The term **structural mobility** refers to social changes that affect the social class membership of large numbers of people. pp. 133–134.

Poverty

WHO BECOMES POOR?
Poverty is unequally distributed in Canada. Women, seniors, members of racial and ethnic minorities, the disabled, recent immigrants, and children whose primary parents are members of these categories are much more likely to be poor. pp. 134–139.

The Dynamics of Poverty

WHY ARE INDIVIDUALISTIC EXPLANATIONS OF POVERTY MORE POPULAR THAN STRUCTURAL EXPLANATIONS?
Some popular analysts argue that characteristics of individuals, such as the lack of a "work ethic" or the desire for immediate gratification, cause poverty. While "blaming the victim" is easy, it ignores many of the complexities of poverty. Sociologists examine structural features of society, such as employment opportunities, to find the causes of poverty. Sociologists generally conclude that life orientations are a consequence, not the cause, of people's position in the social class structure. pp. 139–142.

HOW IS THE HORATIO ALGER MYTH FUNCTIONAL FOR SOCIETY?
The Horatio Alger myth—the belief that anyone can get ahead if only he or she tries hard enough—encourages people to strive to get ahead and deflects blame for failure from society to the individual. We are free to blame individuals for their failures rather than questioning fundamental social and economic arrangements p. 142.

TALKING ABOUT THEORY

Theoretical Paradigms

	CLASSICAL PARADIGMS		RECENT PARADIGMS
	Structural-Functional Paradigm	Social-Conflict Paradigm	Feminist and Anti-Racist Paradigm
What is the level of analysis?	Macro level	Macro level	Macro and micro levels
How are social stratification and inequality explained?	The most qualified people are rewarded with high-ranking positions, decision-making power, and high income.	Conflict between social classes for resources—power, wealth, status—is the basis of social stratification.	Gender and race are the basis by which people are limited from equality of condition or opportunity.
How is the gap between rich and poor explained?	People are rewarded on the basis of merit and members of the wealthy and powerful classes have proven themselves through their achievements.	Class system reproduces itself, and within the structure of capitalist society, there are many limitations—low wages, poor benefits, high cost of housing—that keep the classes separate.	The labour market and opportunities for mobility are split along race, ethnicity, gender, and class lines.

National Anti-Poverty Organization
www.napo-onap.ca
NAPO is a non-profit, non-partisan organization that represents the interests of low-income Canadians. It was founded in 1971 at Canada's first nationwide poor people's conference.

National Council of Welfare
www.ncwcnbes.net
The NCW was established in 1969 as a citizens' advisory body to the federal government on matters of concern to low-income Canadians.

Anti-Slavery International
www.antislavery.org
This site provides information on slavery in the contemporary world and efforts to eradicate all forms of enslavement.

World Bank
www.worldbank.org
Information on emerging economies and development issues.

KEY TERMS

anomie 123
bourgeoisie 115
caste system 113
clan 113
clan system 113
class consciousness 115
class system 114
contradictory class locations 127
culture of poverty 139
deferred gratification 142
divine right of kings 126

downward social mobility 133
endogamy 113
exchange mobility 133
false consciousness 115
feminization of poverty 138
ideology 113
indentured service 112
intergenerational mobility 133
intersectionality 116
means of production 115

meritocracy 124
objective method (of measuring social class) 117
power 122
power elite 122
prestige 122
proletariat 115
reputational method (of measuring social class) 117
slavery 112
social class 116

social mobility 114
social stratification 112
status 122
status consistency 122
status inconsistency 122
structural mobility 133
subjective method (of measuring social class) 117
underclass 130
upward social mobility 133
wealth 117

CRITICAL THINKING QUESTIONS

1. What are some of the differences in opportunities and obstacles encountered by the daughter of a fisherman living in Newfoundland, the son of a Saskatchewan grain farmer, the daughter of an auto worker in central Canada, and the children of Canada's most prominent families?

2. We observe many social class differences in everyday life. Besides differences in income, how does social class position affect quality of life and life circum-

stances? Access the Research Navigator through MySocLab and use keywords such as "social class differences" and "socioeconomic status" to find recent articles that establish connections between social class position and personal or family well-being.

3. Despite the existence of a relatively well-developed social welfare system in Canada, why has poverty persisted and social inequality intensified?

PEARSON
mysoclab

Explore the topics covered in this chapter on MySocLab using the access information provided with this text. Interactive resources for studying include multimedia tutorials, video clips, practice tests, quizzes, and animated maps and figures.

7 Inequalities of Gender

In Tunis, the capital of Tunisia, on Africa's northern coast, I met some postsecondary students, with whom I spent a couple of days. When they said they wanted to see Tunis's red-light district, I wondered if it would be worth the trip. I had already seen other such districts, including the unusual one in Amsterdam where the state licenses prostitutes, requires medical checkups (certificates are available for customers to inspect), sets the prices, and pays social security at retirement. The women sit behind lighted picture windows while customers, interspersed with tourists and neighbourhood residents, stroll along attractive canal side streets, browsing from the outside.

I decided to follow the students.

We ended up on a narrow street opening onto the Mediterranean. Each side was lined with a row of one-room wooden shacks, the structures touching one another, side wall to side wall. In front of each open door stood a young woman. Peering from outside into the dark interior of one shack, I could see a tiny room with a well-worn bed.

The street was crowded with men looking at the women. Many of them wore sailor uniforms from countries that I couldn't identify.

As I looked more closely, I saw runny sores on the legs of some of the women. Incredibly, with such visible evidence of their disease, customers still entered. Evidently, the low prices were too much to resist.

With a sickening feeling in my stomach, I kept a good distance from the beckoning women. One tour of the two-block area was more than sufficient.

Out of sight, I knew, was a group of men whose wealth came from exploiting these women, who were condemned to a short life punctuated by fear and prolonged by misery.

ISSUES OF SEX AND GENDER

This chapter examines **gender inequality**—males' and females' unequal access to power, property, and prestige on the basis of sex. Gender inequality is especially significant because it cuts across *all* aspects of social life. No matter what our social class, age, or racial or ethnic classification, we are labelled *male* or *female*. The images and expectations attached to these labels guide our behaviour in everyday life. They are especially significant in determining power and privilege. In this chapter's fascinating journey, we will look at inequality between the sexes in Canada, and to some extent around the world. We will explore whether biology or culture makes us the way we are, and review issues such as sexual harassment, unequal pay, and violence against women. This excursion will provide a good context for understanding the power differences between men and women that lead to such situations as the one described in our opening vignette. It should also give you insight into your own experiences with gender.

When we consider how females and males differ, the first thing that usually comes to mind is **sex**, the *biological characteristics* that distinguish males and females. *Primary sex characteristics* consist of a vagina or penis and other organs related to reproduction; *secondary sex characteristics* are the physical distinctions between males and females that are not directly connected with reproduction. Secondary sex characteristics become evident at puberty, when males develop more muscles, a lower voice, and more hair and height while females form more fatty tissue, broader hips, and larger breasts.

Gender, in contrast, is a *social* rather than biological characteristic. Gender varies from one society to another; it is what a group considers proper for its males and females. Whereas sex refers to male or female, *gender* refers to masculinity or femininity. In short, you inherit your sex, but you learn your gender as you are socialized into behaviours and attitudes thought appropriate for your sex.

The sociological significance of gender is that it is a device by which society controls its members. Gender sorts us, on the basis of sex, into different life experiences. It opens and closes access to power, property, and even prestige. Like social class, gender is a structural feature of society. Cassie Campbell, a member of the Canadian national women's ice hockey team, declares, "I hate the words *feminine* and *masculine*, because who is the person who decides? Who decides who's more feminine than someone and who's more masculine. . . . It's important to be yourself and at the same time know you can go to the gym and sweat. That's okay" (quoted in Doren & Jones, 2000, p. 97).

Before examining inequalities of gender, let's consider why men and women act differently. Are they just born that way?

Biology or Culture? The Continuing Controversy

Why are most males more aggressive than most females? Why do women enter "nurturing" occupations such as nursing in far greater numbers than men? To answer such questions, many people respond with some variation of "They're just born that way" or "They have the right characteristics for the job."

Is this the correct answer? Certainly, biology is an extremely significant part of our lives. Each of us begins as a fertilized egg. The egg, or ovum, is contributed by our mothers, the sperm that fertilizes the egg by our fathers. At the very moment the egg is fertilized, our sex is determined. Each of us receives 23 pairs of chromosomes from the ovum and 23 from the sperm. The egg has an X chromosome. If the sperm that fertilizes the egg also has an X chromosome, we become female (XX). If the sperm has a Y chromosome, we become male (XY).

That's the biology. The sociological question is: Do these biological differences control our behaviours? Do they make females more nurturing and males more aggressive and domineering, for example? Almost all sociologists take the side of "nurture" in the "nature versus nurture" controversy, but a few do not, as you will see in the Thinking Critically about Social Controversy boxes that follow.

The Dominant Position in Sociology

The dominant sociological position is represented by symbolic interactionists. They stress that the visible differences of sex do not come with meanings built into them. Rather, each human group determines what these physical differences mean to its members, and on that basis assigns males and females to separate groups. Here, people learn contrasting expectations of life and, on the basis of their sex, are given different access to their society's privileges.

Despite the great strides women have made in the workforce, there are still many "male" work roles in which they are not accepted by society.

For sociologist Cynthia Fuchs Epstein (1988, 1989, 2007), differences between males' and females' behaviours are solely the result of social factors—specifically, socialization and social control. Her argument is as follows:

1. A re-examination of the anthropological record shows greater equality between the sexes in the past than we first thought. In hunting and gathering societies, both women's and men's roles are less rigid than those created by stereotypes. For example, the Agta and Mbuti are clearly egalitarian and thus prove that hunting and gathering societies exist in which women are not subordinate to men. Anthropologists claim that in these societies, women have a separate but equal status.

2. The types of work that men and women perform in each society are determined not by biology but by social arrangements. When socially constructed barriers, including informal customs and laws, are removed, women's and men's work habits are similar to one another.

3. The human behaviours that biology "causes" are limited to those involving reproduction or differences in body structure. These differences are relevant for only a few activities, such as playing basketball or "crawling through a small space."

4. Female crime rates are rising in many parts of the world. This indicates that aggression, often considered a biologically dictated male behaviour, is related instead to social factors.

When social conditions permit, such as when women become lawyers, they exhibit "adversarial, assertive, and dominant behaviour."

In short, rather than "women's incompetence or inability to read a legal brief, perform brain surgery, [or] to predict a bull market," social factors—socialization, gender discrimination, and other forms of social control—are responsible for gender differences in behaviour. Arguments that assign "an evolutionary and genetic basis" to explain differences in sex status are simplistic. They "rest on a dubious structure of inappropriate, highly selective, and poor data, oversimplification in logic and in inappropriate inferences by use of analogy."

Most sociologists find the argument compelling that if biology were the principal factor in human behaviour, we would find women around the world to be one sort of person and men another. In fact, ideas of gender—and resulting male–female behaviours—vary greatly from one culture to another.

Opening the Door to Biology

The matter of "nature versus nurture" is not so easily settled, however, and some sociologists who take the "nurture" side still acknowledge that biological factors may be involved in some human behaviour other than reproduction and child-bearing. Alice Rossi, for example, a feminist sociologist and former president of the American Sociological Association, has suggested that women are better prepared biologically for "mothering" than men. She (1977, 1984) contends that women are more sensitive to stimuli such as an infant's soft skin and nonverbal communications. Her basic point is that the issue is not biology or society, but rather nature provides biological predispositions, which are then overlaid with culture. This argument is supported by the events surrounding a bizarre medical accident.

A MEDICAL ACCIDENT The drama began in 1963, when seven-month-old identical twins were taken to a doctor to be circumcised (Money & Ehrhardt, 1972). The inept

Throughout history, women have been denied the right to pursue various occupations on the basis of presumed biological characteristics. As society—and gender roles—have changed, women have increasingly entered occupations traditionally reserved for men.

Sociologist Steven Goldberg (1986, 1993) finds it astonishing that anyone should doubt "the presence of core-deep differences in males and females, differences of temperament and emotion we call masculinity and femininity." Goldberg's argument, that it is not environment but inborn differences that "give masculine and feminine direction to the emotions and behaviours of men and women," is as follows:

1. The anthropological record shows that all societies for which evidence exists are (or were) **patriarchies** (societies in which men dominate women). Stories about long-lost **matriarchies** (societies in which women dominate men) are myths.

2. In all societies, past and present, the highest statuses are associated with males. In every society, politics are ruled by "hierarchies overwhelmingly dominated by men."

3. The reason that men dominate societies is that they "have a greater tendency to exhibit whatever behaviour is necessary in any environment to attain dominance in hierarchies and male-female encounters and relationships." Men are more willing "to sacrifice the rewards of other motivations—the desire for affection, health, family life, safety, relaxation, vacation and the like—in order to attain dominance and status."

4. Just as a six-foot-tall woman does not prove the social basis of height, so

exceptional individuals, such as highly achieving and dominant women, do not refute "the physiological roots of behaviour."

In short, only one interpretation of why every society from that of the Pygmy to that of the Swede associates dominance and attainment with males is valid. Male dominance of society is "an inevitable resolution of the psychophysiological reality." Socialization and social institutions merely *reflect*— and sometimes exaggerate—inborn tendencies. The point is that biology leads males and females to different behaviours and attitudes—regardless of how we feel about it or wish it were different.

physician, who was using electrocautery (a heated needle), turned the electric current too high and accidentally burned off the penis of one of the boys. You can imagine the parents' reaction of disbelief—followed by horror as the truth sank in.

What can be done in a situation like this? The damage was irreversible. The parents were told that the child could never have sexual relations. After months of soul-wrenching agony and tearful consultations with experts, the parents decided that their son should have a sex change operation. When he was 17 months old, surgeons used the boy's own skin to construct a vagina. The parents then gave the child a girl's name, dressed him in frilly clothing, let his hair grow long, and began to treat him as a girl. Later, physicians gave the child female steroids to promote female pubertal growth (Colapinto, 2001).

At first the results were extremely promising. When the twins were 4½ years old, the mother described her daughter as "neat and tidy," "very proud" of her appearance, dainty, and "quite different" from her son (Money & Ehrhardt, 1972).

About a year later, the mother described how their daughter imitated her while their son copied his father:

> I found that my son, he chose very masculine things like a fireman or a policeman. . . . He wanted to do what daddy does, work where daddy does, and carry a lunch kit. . . . And [my

daughter] didn't want any of those things. She wants to be a doctor or a teacher. . . . But none of the things that she ever wanted to be were like a policeman or a fireman, and that sort of thing never appealed to her. (Money & Ehrhardt, 1972)

If the matter were this clear-cut, we could use this case to conclude that gender is entirely up to nurture. Seldom are things in life so simple, however, and a twist occurs in this story. In spite of the promising start and her parents' coaching, the twin whose sex had been reassigned did not adapt well to femininity. She rejected dolls and tried to urinate standing up. Classmates called her a "cavewoman" because she walked like a boy (Diamond, 1982). At age 14, in despair over her inner turmoil, she tried to commit suicide. In a tearful confrontation, her father told her about the accident and her sex change. She then chose to stop her hormone therapy, and later had extensive surgery to partially reconstruct a penis. At age 25 he married a woman and adopted her children (Gorman, 1997a; "Sexual Identity Is Inborn Trait," 1997; Wente, 2000). There is an unfortunate end to this story, however. In 2004, David (his new name) committed suicide.

In another high-profile case, following a successful sex-change operation, Canadian army sergeant Sylvia Durand declared, "This is a rebirth. I feel the way I should have felt at my birth. I'm at peace with myself" (quoted in Peritz, 2000).

Like any athlete, Canadian downhill mountain bike racer Michelle Dumaresq trains hard and dreams of national and world championships.

Mountain biking is her passion and she has proven herself repeatedly since her first race in 2001. But it is neither her status as an elite racer nor her speed and agility in the competitive sport of racing that makes news. Michelle Dumaresq lived the first 20 years of her life as a male, and she is Canada's first trans-gendered athlete on a national team.

Michelle's struggle to gain acceptance from teammates and other racers has been an uphill climb. From her very first race as a woman, she faced hostility and criticism from others in the sport. Some of the most vocal opponents she had considered to be her friends—those with whom she had shared her deepest thoughts about her transformation and her new identity.

Michelle Dumaresq has faced a two-pronged attack from her critics. Some questioned her right to compete. They suggested that the 20 years she spent as a boy give her an unfair advantage, given both biological differences in muscular development and testosterone levels, as well as social differences acquired from having lived in the "more competitive" masculine world. Michelle has encountered numerous roadblocks at all levels, including license suspensions from the Canadian Cycling Association and the Swiss-based Union Cycliste Internationale, which regulates the World Cup and Tour de France. Her revised birth certificate now indicates that she is female. Other critics cut to the core of the matter, challenging her identity as a woman. This was the most difficult challenge for Michelle—the struggle for acceptance as a woman. With Michelle's story, in the context of fairness in competition and sport, we are challenged to ask questions and explore the nature and definition of gender.

Canadian filmmaker Karen Duthie produced a documentary, *100% Woman* (2005), about Michelle Dumaresq, her racing, and her struggle for acceptance.

Sources: Hargrove (2002); Billman (2004); Kingston (2006); Grisdale (2007).

Focus Question

What are some of the main arguments in support of the position that differences between males' and females' behaviours are the result of biological factors?

IN SUM

We await further studies about sex and gender, but what has been published so far is intriguing: some behaviours sociologists usually assume are entirely the result of socialization are, in fact, also influenced by biology. The findings are preliminary, but extremely significant. In the years to come, this should prove to be an exciting—and controversial—area of sociological research. One stage will be to document differences that are clearly due to biology. The second stage, of much greater sociological significance, is, as sociologist Janet Chafetz (1990, p. 30) puts it, to determine "how 'different' becomes translated into 'unequal.'"

GENDER INEQUALITY IN A GLOBAL PERSPECTIVE

Around the world, gender is *the* primary division between people. Every society sets up barriers to provide unequal access to property, power, and prestige on the basis of sex. The barriers *always* favour men as a group. Some analysts have speculated that in hunting and gathering societies, women and men were social equals (Leacock, 1981; Hendrix, 1994) and that horticultural societies also had much less gender discrimination than exists in our contemporary world (Collins, Chafetz, Blumberg, Coltrane, & Turner, 1993). In these societies, women may have been equal partners with men. They may even have contributed about 60 percent of the group's total food. Yet, after reviewing the historical record, historian and feminist Gerda Lerner (1986) concluded that "there is not a single society known where women-as-a-group have decision-making power over men (as a group)." Consequently, sociologists classify females as a **minority group**. You may question this terminology since women outnumber men; however, the term *minority group* applies because it refers to people who are discriminated against on the basis of physical or cultural characteristics.

Sex Typing of Work

Anthropologist George Murdock (1937), who surveyed 324 premodern societies around the world, found that in all of them activities are **sex-typed**; in other words, every society associates certain activities with one sex or the other. He also found that activities considered "female" in one society could be considered "male" in another. In some groups, for example, taking care of cattle is women's work, while other groups assign this task to men.

Metalworking was the exception, being men's work in all the societies examined. Three other pursuits—making weapons, pursuing sea mammals, and hunting—were almost universally the domain of men. In a few societies, women participated in these activities. Although Murdock found no specific work that was universally assigned to women, he did find that making clothing, cooking, carrying water, and grinding grain were almost always female tasks. In a few societies, however, such activities were regarded as men's work.

From Murdock's cross-cultural survey, we can conclude that nothing about biology requires men and women to be assigned different work. Anatomy does not have to equal destiny when it comes to occupation; as we have seen, pursuits considered feminine in one society may be deemed masculine in another, and vice versa.

Prestige of Work

You might ask whether this division of labour really illustrates social inequality. Does it perhaps simply represent arbitrary forms of dividing labour, rather than gender discrimination?

That could be the case, except for this finding: *Universally, greater prestige is given to male activities—regardless of what those activities are* (Linton, 1936; Rosaldo, 1974; Ashford, 2001). If taking care of goats is men's work, then the care of goats is considered important and carries high prestige, but if it is women's work, it is considered less important and given less prestige. Or, to look at an example closer to home, when delivering babies was "women's work" and done by midwives, it was given low prestige. But when men took over this task, its prestige increased sharply (Ehrenreich & English, 1973). Similarly, when women began to outnumber men as bank tellers and office workers, wages, along with the prestige accorded these occupations, declined (Lowe, 1987). In short, it is not the work that provides the prestige, but the gender with which the work is associated.

Other Areas of Global Discrimination

Let's briefly consider four additional areas of global gender discrimination. Later, when we focus on Canada, we will examine these same areas in greater detail.

EDUCATION Statistics illustrate how extensively females are discriminated against in education: Approximately 1 billion adults around the world cannot read; two-thirds are women (UNESCO, 2006). In 2002, close to 100 million children of primary school age were not enrolled in school, and 55 percent of these children were girls (UNESO, 2006: p. 47.) Women constitute 64 percent of the world's illiterate today, an increase from 58 percent in 1960 (UNESCO, 2006: p. 165). The rate of women's illiteracy may not be surprising, since there is a strong relationship between illiteracy and poverty—and the majority of the world's poor are women. Overall, while the gender gap in school enrolments closed

somewhat during the 1990s, the gap widened in less developed countries where girls are more likely to quit (or be pressured to quit) school, often for family-related reasons (Ashford & Clifton, 2005).

POLITICS That women lack equal access to national decision-making can be illustrated by the global fact that in no national legislature in the world are there as many women as there are men. In 2005, in a survey of 187 countries, researchers found that women held only 16.2 percent of seats in the lower houses and 14.8 percent in upper houses of parliaments or congresses (United Nations, Inter-parliamentary Union, 2005: p. 3). Although these numbers have increased dramatically over the past 15 years, in some countries today, women cannot even vote. In most nations, as in Canada, women hold a minority of national legislative seats (Ashford & Clifton, 2005).

THE PAY GAP In every nation, women average less pay than men. Despite years of trying to close the gendered pay gap, on average, women in Canada earn between 70 and 80 cents for every dollar earned by Canadian males, although the average pay gap varies considerably across occupations and by level of education (Jackson, 2005; Brennae, 2008). Between 1993 and 2004, women in Canada were twice as likely as men to hold low wage jobs (Statistics Canada, April 2006: p.8). At a global level, women earn 16 percent less than males, on average, but the differences in the gender wage gap vary considerably. In some countries, women earn 60 percent less and overall account for an increasing proportion of the world's poor and working poor (International Trade Union Confederation, 2008). For example, a recent UNICEF report found that women's earnings were estimated to be 30 percent of men's in several countries in the Middle East and North Africa, 40 percent in Latin America and South Asia, 50 percent in sub-Saharan Africa, and 60 percent in East Asia (Teotonio, 2006: p. A10).

Women also have fewer resources than men and most often are not landowners. In Cameroon, for example, women own less than 10 percent of the land although they are responsible for 75 percent of the work. Similarly, women own 10 percent of land in Brazil and 27 percent in Paraguay (Ibid.). Generally, as women's earnings increase, they have more decision-making influence in the family, which means that they devote more of the family's resources to health and well-being, particularly of their children. Multi-country studies indicate that women usually face the stressful situation of dual responsibilities of work both outside and inside the home.

VIOLENCE AGAINST WOMEN Violence against women is a global human rights issue (Human Rights Watch). Perhaps the most infamous historical examples are foot binding in China, suttee (burning a living widow with her dead husband's body) in India, and witch burning in Europe. Rape, wife beating, forced prostitution (as was likely the case in our

Violence against women has taken many forms throughout history. Foot binding was practised in China until about 1900. A woman's tiny feet, which made it difficult for her to walk, were a status symbol, indicating that her husband was wealthy and did not need her labour. It also made her dependent on him. To make feet even smaller, sometimes a baby's feet were broken and wrapped tightly. Some baby's toes were cut off. This photo was taken in Hubei Province, China. The woman getting the pedicure is reportedly 105 years old.

opening vignette), female infanticide, and female genital mutilation are prevalent forms of extreme violence against women. In India, where daughters are considered to be a financial burden, particularly among the poor, the government has recently taken a positive step toward stopping the practice of aborting female fetuses by offering families financial incentives—nutrition and health support and a lump sum at the daughter's eighteenth birthday. To be eligible, daughters must be sent to school and unmarried (Buncombe, 2008: p. A12).

Another form of violence against women is "honour killing." In societies such as Pakistan, Jordan, India, and Kurdistan, a woman who is thought to have disgraced her family's honour is killed by a male relative, usually a brother or husband, but often by her father or uncles. In Pakistan in 2002, there were more than 450 honour killings and almost 250 women were killed and another 750 seriously disfigured and injured by acid attacks (Human Rights Watch). Women are regarded as commodities—the property of males who have the right to make decisions about their fate. What threat to a family's honour can be so severe that a woman is murdered? The usual reason is marital infidelity or premarital sex. However, women have been killed

for being raped, for flirting, for poor cooking, or even for failing to be on time (CNN World News, 2002; Mayell, 2002; Henslin, 2005). Killing a girl or woman removes the "stain" she has brought to her family, restoring the family's honour in the community. Currently, these killings are on the rise in many countries. The practice is generally ignored by the police because these killings are viewed as family matters.

GENDER INEQUALITY IN THEORETICAL PERSPECTIVE

As noted earlier, gender is *the* primary division between people and therefore helps define a minority group. For an overview of gender discrimination in a changing society, see the Perspectives box on the next page.

What is the origin of discrimination against women? Let's consider a popular theory. It assumes that patriarchy is universal and, accordingly, looks to universal conditions to explain its origin—biological factors coupled with social factors.

The Origins of Patriarchy

The major theory of the origin of patriarchy—men dominating society—points to social consequences of the biology of human reproduction (Lerner, 1986; Friedl, 1990). In early human history, life was short, and to balance the death rate and maintain the population, women bore many children. Because only females get pregnant, carry a child nine months, give birth, and nurse, women were limited in activities for a considerable part of their lives. To survive, an infant needed a nursing mother. With a child at her breast or in her uterus, or one carried on her hip or on her back, a woman was physically encumbered. Consequently, around the world women assumed tasks associated with the home and child care, while men took over the hunting of large animals and other tasks that required greater speed and absence from the base camp for longer periods of time (Huber, 1990).

As a consequence, males became dominant. It was the men who left camp to hunt animals, who made contact with other tribes, who traded with these other groups, and who quarrelled and waged war. It was also men who made and controlled the instruments of death—the weapons used for hunting and warfare. It was they who accumulated possessions in trade and gained prestige by triumphantly returning with prisoners of war or with large animals to feed the tribe. In contrast, little prestige was given to the routine, taken-for-granted activities of women—who were not seen as risking their lives for the group. Eventually, men dominated society. Their weapons, items of trade, and knowledge gained from contact with other groups became sources of power. Women were transformed into second-class citizens, subject to men's decisions.

Mao, the leader of China's 1949 Communist revolution, is often quoted as saying that women hold up half the sky. By this, he meant that women are as important as men. One of the revolution's goals was to free women from their traditional low status.

Although women have never become the social equals of men, their status under Mao did improve. Today, with China's cautious transition to capitalism, however, the situation of women is deteriorating.

For the first time, factory managers are under pressure to produce a profit. Under the old system, production without profit was the norm: managers were assigned production goals and given enough workers to meet those goals. Now, managers say that with maternity leaves and the requirement that they provide childcare centres and rooms for nursing mothers, women workers are more expensive than men. Consequently, women have become the last hired and first fired.

Women are also being encouraged to enter "traditional" women's occupations. Working as nurses, nursery school teachers, grade school teachers, and street sweepers, women are among the least skilled workers and, as such, are poorly paid. Responding to international criticism, China passed a law that guarantees equality for women in employment, education, housing, and property rights. The flaw? There is no mechanism to enforce it. It remains propaganda.

Westernized ideas have begun to pervade the culture, as is illustrated by an emphasis on appearance rather than on skills. In an adaptation of Western-style advertising, scantily clad women are shown perched on top of sports cars. A new cosmetic surgery industry has sprung up to give Chinese women Western-looking eyes, stencilled eyebrows, and bigger breasts.

While adopting new Westernized ideas of beauty, parts of China maintain a centuries-long tradition of bride-selling. In this blend of old and new worlds, women are commodities for men's consumption. The situation is fuelled by the Chinese government's strict enforcement of its one-child policy. Since sons are preferred, female infanticide is common, resulting in a shortage of women of marriageable age. Yet behind the scenes, women have formed study groups. Without slogans or drawing public attention, which could be dangerous, a women's movement is emerging. As in the West, the political struggle must begin with a changed consciousness of women's status.

Sources: Chen (1995); Rosenthal (2001); Johansson (1999).

Evaluating the Theory

Does this theory adequately explain women's second-class status? Remember that the answer lies buried in human history, and there is no way of testing it. Male dominance may be due to some entirely different cause.

Another theory, proposed by anthropologist Marvin Harris (1977), argued that universal physical differences between men and women together with universal social conditions account for patriarchy. In other words, because men are more often stronger and larger than women and because hand-to-hand combat was the key to survival for most tribal groups, men were coaxed to become warriors with the promise of rewards for their bravery or the threat of punishment for their refusal. Ultimately, to entice them to do battle, warriors were rewarded with females. For this system to work, it was essential that all women, even those who were as strong as or stronger than some men, be excluded from combat. From birth, men were prepared for their roles in combat while women were socialized into submissiveness.

Frederick Engels's explanation of women's inequality also proposed that social conditions or social structure contributed to women's inequality. He argued that patriarchy (male dominance of a society) developed with the origin of private property (Lerner, 1986). He could not explain why private property should have produced patriarchy, however. Gerda Lerner (1986) suggests that patriarchy may have had different origins in different places. Whatever its origins, support for patriarchy has been interwoven with culture, custom, ideology, and practice. A closed, circular system of thought evolved. Men developed notions of their own inherent superiority, based on the evidence of their dominant position in society. They then consolidated their power, enshrouded many of their activities with secrecy, and constructed elaborate rules and rituals to avoid "contamination" by females, whom they openly deemed inferior. Even today, patriarchy is always surrounded with cultural supports to justify male dominance, such as designating certain activities as "inappropriate" for women.

As tribal societies developed into larger groups, men, enjoying their power and privileges, maintained their dominance. Long after hunting and hand-to-hand combat ceased to be routine, and even after large numbers of children were no longer needed to reproduce the human group, men held on to their power. Male dominance in contemporary societies, then, is a continuation of a millennia-old pattern whose origin is lost in history. Let's consider perspectives on gender inequality.

Focus Question

How do theorists explain women's inequality and male dominance?

Theoretical Perspectives on Gender

In explaining the division of labour by gender, the *functionalist perspective* considers the different roles in family and society typically played by men and women as distinct and as necessary for well-being. This perspective does not place importance on the question of power and inequality, but rather derives from biological explanations, as previously discussed.

By contrast, the *conflict perspective* explains gender differences within families, workplaces, and social institutions as based on power differences between men and women and men's assumption of political, institutional, economic, and social power. Conflict theorists question men's control over women broadly at the societal level, and also interpersonally at the level of individual relationships. Frederick Engels (1942) argues that within the family, unequal power relations between men and women have their origin in the private ownership of the means of production. Men have control over property, and this power, in turn, provides them with power over women. Within this context, marriage guarantees proprietorship over women and children, and therefore enforces male dominance. Feminist analyses draw on a conflict approach to explain and elaborate on gender inequality.

Focus Question

How is patriarchy defined, and, according to Engels, how is it supported or maintained?

FEMINIST PERSPECTIVES **Feminism** is the fundamental belief in equality between women and men. Feminists argue that gender has been socially constructed and has impacted the lives of men and women differentially. All feminists are engaged in struggle against gender discrimination and argue from a human rights perspective that equality gains are essential to dignity, respect, and freedom. Feminist perspectives vary from more liberal approaches to radical ones. Below we elaborate on the particular stances taken by liberal, socialist, and radical feminists. Liberal feminism is mainly concerned with equality of opportunity or equal access to educational, economic, and political resources within society. In aiming for women to have the same chances as men, liberal feminists argue that changing attitudes regarding appropriate male and female roles and behaviours are necessary for real change to occur. The aim of liberal feminism is to work within the existing system to make things work more equitably for women through legislative reform and changes in workplaces, education, and families.

Further along the political continuum, socialist feminists zero in on women's dual roles, both paid and unpaid, and argue that in a patriarchal capitalist system, women are exploited within the economy and within the home (Hartmann, 1976). Socialist feminists are concerned with relationships of class and gender, and capitalism and patriarchy. In the economy, women's low wages and inferior, low-paid, low-status jobs relate to their unpaid work in the home. That women are responsible for the lion's share of unpaid domestic work and child/family care devalues their work in the paid labour market. These feminists call for equality rights for women, and argue that this would be possible within a socialist economic framework.

Radical feminism calls for the end of patriarchy, arguing that men's power over women is the root of women's oppression (Firestone, 1970). Because men occupy positions of power within the broader society, their decisions and the institutions they govern, including the media, maintain women's subordination. The way to change, say radical feminists, is through the development of alternative women-centred organizations and institutional arrangements that meet women's needs.

QUEER THEORY By the early 1980s, disagreements among feminists broke out around questions of sexuality. In particular, debate erupted between lesbians who identified themselves as cultural feminists who embraced more "traditional" sexual practices and lesbian feminists who embraced more radical sexual practices. Essentially, new practices of lesbianism broke down the old notions that there were two forms of women's sexuality—heterosexual and lesbian—because the disagreements gave rise to the understanding that there are multiple expressions of sexuality (Martindale, 2001). The discussion around sexual practices helped initiate the emerging disciplines of lesbian and gay studies and their theories of sexuality, known as *queer theory*. Queer theory attempts to break down the binary gay–straight categorization of people and their sexuality. Queer theorists give meaning and understanding to gay and lesbian cultures and the deep forms of oppression, including the silencing, experienced by gays and lesbians. However, recently, some argue that queer theory may ignore multiple diversities and oppressions and thereby call for greater inclusiveness in understanding sexual marginalization (Martindale, 2001).

POSTMODERNISM Interrelated to theories of feminism, the postmodern approach starts with the understanding of gender as socially constructed and interrelated with race, class, and sexual orientation, all of which are also socially constructed (Elliott & Mandell, 2001). Postmodernists ask us to question our categorizing and conceptualizations of "others," emphasizing the importance of understanding identities from the individual's viewpoint, rather than through universal assumptions about gender, oppression, and patriarchy by categorizing women as a group and assuming that they share common values, beliefs, and histories. Postmodernists caution against generalizing about others, asking researchers to avoid drawing conclusions based on "hard and fast" definitions or characterizations of people based on objective, scientific methods that may obscure individuals' experience of their own complex identities.

GENDER INEQUALITY IN CANADA

Inequality is not some accidental, hit-or-miss affair; the institutions of every society work together to maintain its particular forms. Custom, venerated by history, both justifies and maintains arrangements of gender inequality. Although men have resisted sharing their privileged positions with women, changes are occurring.

Fighting Back: The Rise of Feminism

To see how far we have come, it is useful to see where we used to be. In early Canadian society, the second-class status of women was taken for granted. A husband and wife were legally one person—him (Chafetz & Dworkin, 1986). Women who worked for wages could not even collect their own paycheques—single women were often required to hand them over to their fathers; married women, to their husbands. Women could not serve on juries; nor could they vote, make legal contracts, or hold property in their own name. These conditions were generally seen as part of the *proper* relations of the sexes. How could times have changed so much that such conditions sound like fiction?

A central lesson of conflict theory is that power yields tremendous privilege; that, like a magnet, it draws to the elite the best resources available. Because men held tenaciously on to their privileges and used social institutions to maintain their position, basic rights for women came only through prolonged and bitter struggle (Offen, 1990).

Unlike its counterparts in Britain and the United States, where suffragists adopted militant tactics, the "first wave" of the Canadian women's movement was regarded as a war of words. One of the most outspoken suffragists was Nellie McClung, whose passionate statements were strong and compelling.

Feminism, the view that biology is not destiny, and that, therefore, stratification by gender is wrong and should be resisted, met strong opposition—both by men who had privilege to lose and by many women who accepted their status as morally correct. In Great Britain and the United States, for example, women had to directly confront men, who first denied them the right to speak and then ridiculed them when they persisted in speaking in public. Leaders of the feminist movement, then known as *suffragists*, chained themselves to posts and to the iron grillwork of public buildings—and then went on protesting while police sawed them loose. When imprisoned, they continued to protest by going on hunger strikes. Threatened by such determination and confrontations, men spat on demonstrators for daring to question their place, slapped their faces, tripped them, pelted them with burning cigar stubs, and hurled obscenities at them (J. Cowley, 1969).

Although heavily influenced by developments in the United States and Britain, the Canadian women's movement may be characterized as a war of words. The militant tactics of British and American suffragists were not adopted by Canadian feminists, who instead employed a relatively peaceful approach. The Canadian movement upheld Nellie McClung's motto: "Never retract, never explain, never apologize, get the thing done and let them howl" (cited in S. J. Wilson, 1991). These words were strong and compelling, yet moderate. While they may have offended some aspects of the prevailing social etiquette prescribed for women, they were not suggestive of a radical departure from conventional social norms.

This "first wave" of the women's movement had a conservative branch that concentrated on winning the vote for women and a radical branch that wanted to reform all the institutions of society (Chafetz & Dworkin, 1986). Both groups worked toward winning the right to vote, but after the vote was won in 1917 in Canada (and in 1920 in the United States), many declared that the movement had achieved its ultimate purpose, and some argue that this victory left the movement with no unifying goal. However, women continued to struggle for change, by working to establish their voice and presence in trade unions, in the workplace, within the political process, through the courts, and in educational institutions. Every victory was hailed, but feminists realized that barriers to women's social and economic equality, including attitudes and beliefs about women's status and rights, would not be easily changed.

The "second wave" began in the 1960s. Sociologist Janet Chafetz (1990) points out that up to this time, most women thought of work as a temporary activity to fill the time between completing school and getting married. When larger numbers of women began to enter the labour force, however, they began to compare their working conditions with those of men. This shift in reference group created a different view of working conditions, launching a "second wave" of protest and struggle against gender inequalities. The goals of this second wave are broad—from changing work roles to changing policies on violence against women.

The second wave is also broken into liberal and conservative factions. Although each holds a different picture of what gender equality should look like, they share several goals, including nondiscrimination in job opportunities and pay. Through ongoing discussions, which sometimes include divergent views, the women's movement will continue to take shape and affect public policy.

Although women enjoy fundamental rights today, gender inequality continues to play a central role in social life. In some instances, it can even be a life-and-death matter, as with the medical situations discussed in the Down-to-Earth Sociology box that follows.

Let's now look at gender relations in education and everyday life, and then, in greater detail, at discrimination in the world of work.

Gender Inequality in Education

In education, too, a glimpse at the past sheds light on the present. About a century ago, leading educators claimed that women's wombs dominated their minds. This made higher education a burden on women's frail capacities. Dr. Edward Clarke, of Harvard University's medical faculty, expressed the dominant (nineteenth century) sentiment this way:

> A girl upon whom Nature, for a limited period and for a definite purpose, imposes so great a physiological task, will not have as much power left for the tasks of school, as the boy of

whom Nature requires less at the corresponding epoch (cited in Andersen, 1988).

Because women were seen as so much weaker, Clarke urged them to spend only a third of the amount of time that young men spent studying—and not to study at all during menstruation.

Over 200 years ago, in 1792, Mary Wollstonecraft, a well-known early feminist, published *A Vindication of the Rights of Woman*, in which she discussed male power as the underlying cause of society's problems (Mackie, 1991, p. 252). She believed that education was the key to liberating both men and women. Although she was heavily criticized as a man-hating crusader, her ideas on the importance of education in contributing to women's equality were not only subsequently echoed by John Stuart Mill and other historical thinkers, but also became part of the foundation of the suffrage movements.

According to Marlene Mackie (1991), the problem of access to higher education was the spark that initiated the Canadian suffrage movement. In the 1860s, schoolteacher Emily Stowe found herself supporting her disabled husband and their three children. Although she managed to save enough money to study medicine, Canadian medical schools denied her admission because of her gender. Eventually she was admitted to an American medical school, and upon her return, became Canada's first female physician. She continued to struggle with others for the acceptance of women in the professions. As a result, the University of Toronto began to admit women in 1886.

DOWN-TO-EARTH SOCIOLOGY
Making the Invisible Visible: The Deadly Effects of Sexism

Medical researchers were perplexed. In the early 1990s, reports indicated that women, who live longer than men, were twice as likely to die after coronary bypass surgery. This prompted researchers at numerous sites across the U.S., Canada, and elsewhere to consider why these differences were occurring. Researchers at Cedars-Sinai Medical Center in Los Angeles, for example, checked their own hospital's records and found that of almost 2300 coronary bypass patients, 4.6 percent of women died as a result of the surgery, compared with only 2.6 percent of men.

These findings presented a sociological puzzle. To solve it, medical researchers first turned to an answer based on biology. In coronary bypass surgery, a blood vessel is taken from one part of the body and stitched to a coronary artery on the surface of the heart. Perhaps this operation was more difficult to perform on women because of their smaller coronary arteries. To find out, researchers measured the amount of time surgeons kept patients on the heart-lung machine while they operated. They were surprised to learn that women spent less time on the machine than men, indicating that the operation was not more difficult to perform on women.

As the researchers probed, a surprising answer unfolded—unintended sexual discrimination. Referring physicians had not taken the chest pains of

their women patients as seriously as those of their men patients. Physicians, it turned out, were *10* times more likely to give men exercise stress tests and radioactive heart scans.

They also sent men to surgery on the basis of abnormal stress tests but waited until women showed clear-cut symptoms of coronary heart disease before sending them to surgery. Being referred for surgery after the disease has progressed decreases the chances of survival. In another study, researchers found that women who are hospitalized for heart attacks are less likely than men to be referred to rehabilitation programs that have the potential to decrease the risk of death by 25 percent. Women who have had a heart attack are more likely than men to have a second heart attack, are less likely to recover well, and more often die within the first year (Yelaja, 2002). Overall, the majority of Canadians with cardiac conditions are not referred for rehabilitation, and income may be a critical barrier along with gender.

Despite the similarity in the presenting condition (moderate knee osteoarthritis), researchers in Toronto recently found that women were less likely to be recommended for knee-replacement surgery than males (Pearce, 2008: p. L1). How is this difference explained? The lead researcher, Dr. Borkhoff, suggests that there may be a number of answers, but the most likely is the "subconscious bias" held by doctors, both male and female, who may not recognize women's symptoms as being equally as serious as those of their male patients. Some doctors are under the false assumption that female patients do not benefit as much as males from this type of surgery. However, the findings point out that women are more likely to be recommended for surgery when their condition is at a more advanced stage, and generally when surgery is performed at a earlier stage, it is more likely to be successful (Pearce, 2008: p. L4).

Not only may doctors be overlooking the seriousness of women's complaints, but thorough diagnosis involving medical tests may be delayed as well. With regard to overall diagnostic testing, women's wait times were considerably longer than those for men (53.1 days for women, compared to 31.4 for men) and for magnetic resonance imaging (MRI), in particular, the gap was even greater (70.3 days for women compared to 29.1 days for men) (Kazanjian, Morettin, & Cho, 2004: p. 10).

Other researchers wondered if the sex of the physician matters when it comes to ordering Pap smears and mammography. They examined the records of 98 000 patients and found that it does make a difference—women physicians are much more likely to order these screening tests. However, in her study of knee replacements and gender bias, Dr. Borkhoff suggests that the social stereotyping that affects doctors' decisions may be as widely held by female physicians as it is by males (Pearce, 2008: p. L4).

For Your Consideration

In short, gender bias is so pervasive that it operates beneath our level of awareness and so severe that it can even be a matter of life or death. It is important to note that the doctors are unaware that they are discriminating. They have no intention of doing so. In what ways does gender bias affect your own perceptions and behaviour?

Sources: Bishop (1990); Lurie, Slater, McGovern, Ekstrum, Quam, & Margolis (1993).

Over the years, the situation gradually improved, but discrimination persisted. Through the 1960s, for example, girls were not welcome in shop classes, which were reserved for boys. Instead, they were routed to home economics, considered appropriate for their station in life. (Even today, whenever I attend Toronto Raptors basketball games, I still see an organized group of women, at times scantily clad in short, brightly coloured outfits, wildly cheering from the sidelines. There is no such group of young men leading organized cheers in the WNBA.)

The situation has so changed from what it used to be, however, that some measures of education make it look as though discrimination may be directed against males. For example, more women than men are enrolled in Canadian universities, and in 2006 accounted for 58 percent of students in all bachelor degree programs. This represents a dramatic increase from the 1970s, when about one in three full-time students was female. In addition, about half of Master's students and 45 percent of Ph.D. students are women (Canadian Council on Learning, 2007: p. 77). Graduation rates for women are also higher and climbing whereas rates for men are declining (Ibid.).

Probing below the surface, however, degrees follow gender, thus reinforcing male-female distinctions. Extremes at the bachelor's level highlight gender tracking: Men earn over 75 percent of bachelor's degrees in engineering and 67 percent in mathematics and physical sciences, considered "masculine" fields, while women are awarded 73 percent of bachelor's degrees in health professions and occupations, over 71 percent in education, and 68 percent in fine and applied arts, traditionally "feminine" fields (Statistics Canada, 2004e). While business, management, marketing, and related support services were the most popular fields of study among both men and women, according to the 2006 census data, the top fields of study for men and women otherwise differ widely. Tables 7.1 and 7.2 list the top 10 fields of study for men and women in Canada in 2006.

Because gender socialization gives men and women different orientations to life, they enter postsecondary education with gender-linked aspirations. It is this socialization—rather than any presumed innate characteristics—that channels them into different educational paths.

If we trace the steps of those who earn doctoral degrees back into colleges and universities, we find gender stratification in both prestige and income. Overall, women hold about 27 percent of all earned Ph.D.s in Canada, but again they are vastly underrepresented in fields traditionally dominated by men, including science and engineering, physics, computer and physical sciences, and mathematics (McKenzie, 2007: p. 24). A recent study conducted in 2007 based on a survey and interviews with 2500 workers concluded that women leave science, technology, and engineering professions in disproportionate numbers, despite their advances in education

TABLE 7.1 Top 10 Fields of Study for Female Postsecondary Graduates in Canada, 2006

No.	Fields of Study	Number
1	Business, management, marketing, and related support services	1 357 160
2	Health professions and related clinical sciences	1 080 745
3	Education	583 560
4	Personal and culinary services	271 825
5	Visual and performing arts	182 880
6	Social sciences	182 625
7	Family and consumer sciences/human sciences	170 020
8	Computer and information sciences and support services	150 220
9	Legal professions and studies	130 190
10	Public service administration and social service professions	126 575

Source: Statistics Canada, Census of Population, 2006 www12.statcan.ca/english/census06/analysis/education/tables/table7.htm.

in these fields, because of the "hard hat," "lab coat," and "geek" cultures, all of which are unaccommodating and intimidating to women (Belkin, 2008: p. A13). Some suggest that the "hard sciences" are the most difficult environments for women because of firmly rooted beliefs that women are not as good at math and science as men are.

In universities throughout Canada, women are less likely to be full professors, the highest, most prestigious rank. It is important also to note that full professors are paid more than the lower ranks (instructor, assistant professor, and associate professor) and enjoy greater status. In 2004/05, almost a third of university professors were women, but women numbered fewer than one in five full professors (Perkel, 2007). To see the extent of the inequality, we can note that even when women are full professors, they average less pay than men who are full professors—$6000 less in 2004/05. At all ranks, the median salary of female professors is lower than that of their male colleagues. Sociologists Janice Drakich and Penni Stewart argue that although the situation for female professors has improved tremendously since the 1990s, it is still the case that "'systemic discrimination is alive and well in the academy'" (Ibid.).

TABLE 7.2 Top 10 Fields of Study for Male Postsecondary Graduates in Canada, 2006

No.	Fields of Study	Number
1	Business, management, marketing and related support services	801 605
2	Mechanic and repair technologies/technicians	542 370
3	Engineering	450 960
4	Engineering technologies/technicians	427 840
5	Construction trades	388 990
6	Precision production	290 625
7	Computer and information sciences and support services	257 385
8	Health professions and related clinical sciences	204 560
9	Education	196 165
10	Social sciences	194 795

Source: Statistics Canada, Census of Population, 2006 www12.statcan.ca/english/census06/analysis/education/tables/table7.htm.

Some encouraging changes are taking place in higher education. Although we are still a long way from equality, the proportion of professional degrees earned by women has increased sharply. In Canada today, women constitute almost half of all graduates in medical studies and research and are studying dentistry in increasing numbers. In addition, women are now the majority among graduates in two previously male-dominated professional fields—pharmacy and veterinary medicine—outnumbering their male counterparts by almost two to one.

Gender Inequality in Everyday Life

Of the many aspects of gender discrimination in everyday life that could be examined, we only have space to look at two: the general devaluation of femininity and male dominance of conversation.

GENERAL DEVALUATION OF THINGS FEMININE Leaning against the water cooler, two men—both minor executives—are nursing their cups of coffee, discussing last Sunday's game, postponing for as long as possible the moment when work must finally be faced.

A vice-president walks by and hears them talking about sports. Does he stop and send them back to their desks? Does he frown? Probably not. Being a man, he is far more likely to pause and join in the conversation, anxious to prove that he, too, is "one of the boys," feigning an interest in football that he may very well not share at all. These men—all men in the office—are his troops, his comrades-in-arms.

Now, let's assume that two women are standing by the water cooler discussing whatever you please: women's liberation, clothes, work, any subject—except football, of course. The vice-president walks by, sees them, and moves down the hall in a fury, cursing and wondering whether it is worth the trouble to complain—but to whom?—about all those bitches standing around gabbing when they should be working. "Don't they know," he will ask, in the words of a million men, "that this is an office?" (Korda, 1973, pp. 20–21).

As illustrated in this scenario, women's capacities, interests, attitudes, and contributions are not taken as seriously as those of men. Masculinity is valued more highly, representing success and strength. In contrast, femininity is devalued; it is perceived as representing weakness and lack of accomplishment (Schur, 1984).

During World War II, sociologist Samuel Stouffer noted the general devaluation of femininity. In his classic study of combat soldiers, *The American Soldier*, Stouffer reported that officers used feminine terms as insults to motivate soldiers (Stouffer et al., 1949). To show less-than-expected courage or endurance was to risk the charge of not being a man. An officer might say, "Whatsa matter, Bud—got lace on your drawers?" A generation later, to prepare soldiers to fight in Vietnam, accusations of femininity were still used as motivating insults. Drill sergeants would mock their troops by saying, "Can't hack it, little girls?" (Eisenhart, 1975). The practice continues today.

The same phenomenon occurs in sports. Sociologist Douglas Foley (1997) notes that football coaches insult boys who don't play well by saying that they are "wearing skirts," and sociologists Jean Stockard and Miriam Johnson (1980), who observed boys playing basketball, heard boys who missed a basket called a "woman." This pattern continues in professional sports, and hockey players who are not rough enough on the ice are called "girls" (Gallmeier, 1988, p. 227). So commonplace is the mocking of boys in feminine terms that it has prompted women athletes to sport T-shirts, popular in women's locker rooms, retorting: "You only wish" (front) . . . "you played like a girl" (back).

Such name-calling is sociologically significant because the insults embody a generalized devaluation of females and there is no comparable phenomenon among women (Stockard & Johnson, 1980, p. 12). Girls' coaches do not ridicule them by calling them "boys." Quite the contrary. In some athletic circles, such as in rowing, which demands rigorous strength training, pumping iron and pulling "like a man" is laudable.

GENDER INEQUALITY IN CONVERSATION As you may have noticed in your own life, gender inequality shows up in everyday talk. Because men are more likely to interrupt a conversation and to control changes in topic, sociologists have noted that talk between a man and a woman is often more like talk between an employer and an employee than between social equals (West & Garcia, 1988; Smith-Lovin & Brody, 1989; Tannen, 2007). Even in college, men interrupt their instructors more often than do women, especially if the instructor is a woman (Brooks, 1982). In short, conversations between men and women mirror their relative positions of power in society.

Derogatory terms and conversation represent only the tip of the iceberg, however. Underlying these aspects of everyday life is a structural inequality based on gender that runs throughout society. Let's examine that structural feature in the workplace.

GENDER RELATIONS IN THE WORKPLACE

To examine the work setting is to make visible basic relations between men and women. Let's consider changes in the labour force, the pay gap, and opportunities for women.

Women's Participation in the Labour Force

While women have always worked, over the past 35 years there has been a massive movement of women, including those with young children, into the paid labour force. Women's high level of involvement in paid work has prompted sociologists to examine the ways women's employment differs from that of men. This includes comparisons between men's and women's jobs, wages, patterns of employment, and opportunities for promotion, and how women's

These protestors are lobbying for pay equity at Bell Canada. In 1992, the Canadian Human Rights Commission ruled that former female Bell Canada operators had suffered from pay discrimination. The case has been in court ever since, with demands that Bell pay its male and female operators equitably, and that the company pay some 800 former female employees $400 million in pay equity money.

paid work experiences are affected by familial responsibilities and expectations.

The *labour force participation rate* is the proportion of men and women 16 years and older who are in the labour force, working full- or part-time. A century ago, almost all married women were full-time housewives. While married women often worked in the informal economy (e.g., sewing at home or taking in laundry or boarders), they did not usually participate formally in the labour force. In 1891, two-fifths of employed women were servants or were working at jobs that mirrored their domestic roles. Eventually the range of occupations open to women widened somewhat and certain jobs became regarded as "women's work." In 1901, about 25 percent of clerical workers were women, but by 1921 more than 40 percent were women (cited in Duffy & Pupo, 1992, pp. 15–17). Today, retail sales work is the most prevalent occupational category for women (Statistics Canada, 2008c: 70).

With the increased demand for workers during and immediately following the world wars, women's labour force participation grew from 17 percent in 1921 to 20 percent in 1931 and from 24.4 percent in 1939 to 33.5 percent in 1944 (cited in Duffy & Pupo, 1992, p. 17). After a decline following World War II, when millions of women left factories and offices to return home as full-time wives and mothers, women's labour force participation steadily climbed from the mid 1950s on. Today almost 60 percent of all women aged 15 and over and 77 percent of women between the ages of 25 and 54 work for pay (Statistics Canada, 2007: pp. 6,7). Differences among women, however, persist. Female recent

immigrants, for example, experience lower work-force participation rates than males who immigrated at the same time, as well as compared to Canadian-born women (Statistics Canada, 2008c: 72).

The Pay Gap

How would you like to earn an extra $800 000 at your job? If this sounds appealing, read on. All you have to do is average an extra $20 000 a year between the ages of 25 and 65.

Is this hard to do? Not if you are a man. Comparing workers who have bachelor's degrees, $800 000 is precisely how much more the average man will earn compared to the average woman. Hardly any single factor pinpoints gender discrimination better than this total. A gender gap in earnings shows up at all levels of education and exists in all industrialized nations.

The gender gap in wages is pervasive. In 2005, the average annual earnings of men working full-year, full-time was $55 700, while women working full-year, full-time averaged $39 200. In other words, women (full-time, full-year) were paid an average of 70.5 cents for every dollar their male counterparts earned. For those working full-time, full-year with a university degree, the gap was wider—women earned 67.5 percent of their male counterparts' wages (Statistics Canada, cited in Canadian Labour Congress, 2008a). While the gap today represents huge gains from the late 1960s, when Canadian women were only earning 58 cents for every dollar earned by males, it is persistent, and there is some indication it may be widening among younger workers.

What logic can underlie the gender pay gap? Earlier we saw that university degrees are gender-linked, so perhaps this gap is due to career paths. Maybe women tend to work at lower-paying jobs, such as primary school teaching, whereas men are more likely to go into better-paying fields such as business and engineering. Actually, researchers have found that less than *half* the pay gap can be attributed to such factors. The balance, however, is due to workplace characteristics, such as high performance systems, degree of foreign ownership, and the rate of part-time work, and to gender discrimination (Drolet, 2002; Iyer, 2002; Jackson, 2005; Canadian Labour Congress, 2008). A key factor contributing to the gender pay gap is the "child penalty"—women missing out on work experience and opportunities while they care for children. In other words, women are placed on the "mommy track" rather than the "career track," and it is presumed that they not as committed to their paid work as their male colleagues.

Depending on your sex, then, you are likely either to benefit from gender discrimination—or to be its victim. Because the pay gap will be so important in your own work life, let's consider women's presence is corporate Canada. According to a survey in 2005, only 12 percent of directors (508 out of 4225) of Canada's 500 largest corporations were women (Flavelle, 2006: p. A16). For the first time, over half (52.8 percent) of these companies had at least one women director. Just over 25 percent had multiple women directors and women held 25 percent or more of the directorships on 12.6 percent of the boards. These figures represent improvements since 2003. However, there are tremendous discrepancies among corporations, with women faring considerably better at Crown corporations, where they hold 28.5 percent of directorships, compared to publicly traded firms, where only 9.2 percent of directors are women (Ibid.)

Your best chance to reach the top is to be named—in this order—John, Robert, James, William, or Charles. Edward, Lawrence, and Richard are also advantageous. Amber, Candace, Leticia, and María, however, apparently draw a severe penalty.

Struggling for pay equity has paid off for many Canadian women. A settlement of female civil servants in Ontario in 2001 provided each woman about $45 000 in retroactive pay, and recently, a settlement with Bell Canada will bring female operators' pay in line with that of their male counterparts. These two recent decisions, both favourable toward mending the gap, will continue to pay off for thousands of others waiting to have their cases heard.

Focus Question
How can the pay gap between men and women be explained?

Women in Manufacturing and IT

Gaining equity in the workplace for women has been an uphill climb. Overall, women's jobs tend to be lower-paying, with fewer benefits and lower rates of unionization, often part-time and located in the service sector. What happens when we look at a work sphere traditionally associated with males? Are women's job prospects any better? In contrast to service sector jobs (the so-called McJobs), those in manufacturing usually offer a better deal—higher wages, more benefits, including pension plans, and higher rates of unionization. For example, the average hourly wage in manufacturing is almost $21, compared to just over $15 in retail (Canadian Labour Congress, 2008b). However, over the past five years, Canadians have experienced significant job loss in the manufacturing sector, largely due to plant closures, work relocation overseas, corporate downsizing, and other factors, and these changes have impacted women's access to and ability to hang on to manufacturing jobs.

According to the Canadian Labour Congress, there have been over 300 000 manufacturing jobs lost in the past five years, and women's losses in manufacturing are greater relative to those of men—9 percent of women in manufacturing faced job loss compared to 7 percent of men (Canadian Labour Congress, 2008b). When women lose their manufacturing positions in industries such as auto, auto parts, aerospace, and food and fish processing, the jobs available to them are frequently insecure McJobs.

The number of women in information technology (IT) and high-tech occupations doubled between 1991 and 2001 (Statistics Canada, 2003c). Will new developments in technology and other highly skilled fields make a difference for women? In a recent study, Krista Scott-Dixon (2004) traced women's paths in developing careers in IT. The women she studied worked in high-tech industries, applying technological, scientific, and engineering skills and knowledge in their jobs. Yet despite their knowledge and skills, women in a variety of technological occupations continue to face barriers preventing them from reaching their full potential.

The Glass Ceiling or the Glass Escalator?

THE GLASS CEILING What keeps women from breaking through the "glass ceiling," the mostly invisible barrier that keeps women from reaching the executive suite? Researchers have identified a "pipeline" that leads to the top—marketing, sales, and production—positions that directly add to the corporate bottom line (Hymowitz, 2004). Stereotyped as better at "support," women are often steered into human resources or public relations. There, successful projects are not appreciated as much as those that bring in corporate profits—and bonuses for their managers.

Another reason the glass ceiling is so powerful is that women lack mentors—successful executives who take an interest in them and show them the ropes. Some men executives fear gossip and sexual harassment charges if they get close to a woman in a subordinate position. Others don't mentor women because of stereotypes of women as less qualified or lacking the necessary commitment to the job. To lack a mentor is no trivial matter, especially since women often experience a "chilly climate" in executive boardrooms or decision-making chambers.

The glass ceiling is cracking, however slowly, and more women are reaching the executive suite (Flavelle, 2006: p. A16). Policy shifts may significantly crack the ceiling further. On the eve of International Women's Day in 2002, the Norwegian government announced a plan that would force companies to guarantee that at least 40 percent of boardroom seats are held by women (Doyle, 2002). As a result, by 2004, Statoil, a Norwegian petroleum refining company, ranked second on the *Fortune* Top 200 global corporations for female representation, at 44.4 percent (AT&T News, 2004). (The top ranked for female representation with 50 percent [5/10 directors were women] was Albertsons, a U.S. retail firm.) While the Norwegian plan specified that businesses would not have these quotas formally imposed if they undertook action voluntarily, it does provide us with an idea of a structure that might contribute to gender equity. A look at women above the glass ceiling reveals highly motivated women with a fierce competitive spirit who are highly committed to their work and career. Often they play by "men's rules," developing a style that makes men comfortable. In order to play the game successfully, these women establish a support system with their partners or through paid help for household and family work.

THE GLASS ESCALATOR Sociologist Christine Williams (1995) interviewed men and women who worked as nurses, elementary school teachers, librarians, and social workers. She found that the men in these traditionally women's occupations, instead of bumping into a glass ceiling, had climbed aboard a *glass escalator*. That is, compared with women, the men were accelerated into more desirable work assignments, higher-level positions, and larger salaries. The motor that drives the glass escalator is the stereotype that because someone is male, he is more capable.

Gender and the Control of Workers

Conflict theorists argue that capitalists exploit gender divisions among workers in order to control them—the "divide and rule" principle. Their method is not overt, but rather owners and managers divide workers in subtle ways. For example, a manufacturing firm in the Silicon Valley, California, specifies the colour of the smocks that it requires workers to wear. The colour of the men's smocks depends on the particular job they do, but all the women wear the same colour, regardless of their jobs.

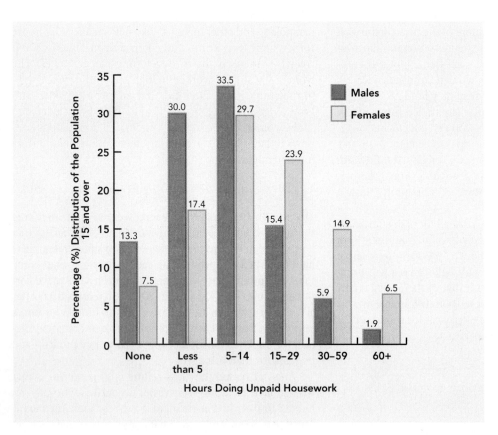

FIGURE 7.1 Percentage of Males and Females, Aged 25 to 54, by Number of Hours Doing Unpaid Housework, Canada, 2006 Census

Source: www12.statcan.ca/english/census06/data/topics/Print.cfm?PID=92108&GID=771240&D1=2&D2=0&D3=0&D4=0&D5=0&D6=0

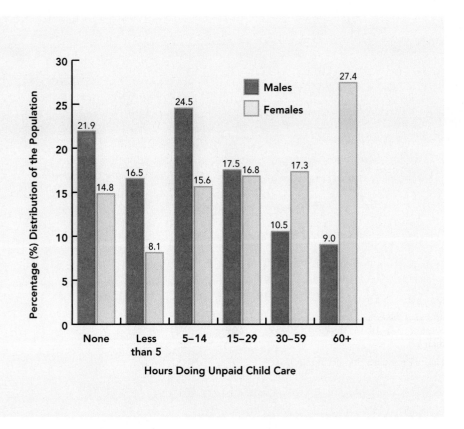

FIGURE 7.2 Percentage of Males and Females Aged 25 to 54 Doing Unpaid Child Care, Canada, 2006 Census

Source: www12.statcan.ca/english/census06/data/topics/Print.cfm?PID=92108&GID=771240&D1=2&D2=0&D3=0&D4=0&D5=0&D6=0

Why should management have such a policy? According to sociologist Karen Hossfeld (2000), who studied these workers, the underlying message is: no matter what your job is, you are primarily a woman. Encouraging the women to think of themselves not as workers, but as *women* workers, makes them easier to control. Hossfeld found that when their bosses flirted with them, the women were not inclined to file grievances.

The same company has a "Ladies' Corner" in its newsletter. The subtle message: it is a men's newsletter with a little corner devoted to women. In other words, men are the *real* workers, but women are there, too.

Women, Family, and Inequality

Women are more likely than their partners to be the caretakers of the family, to nurture it through the hard times. Women usually take greater responsibility for caring roles—with children, elders, disabled family members—for maintaining family ties (such as sending greeting cards), and spend considerably more time doing housework. Consequently, most employed women face greater role conflict than do their partners.

The greatest constraint limiting women's labour-force participation or their career advancement is the pressure they face from their family-related roles, expectations, and responsibilities. The burdens of reconciling family and work fall particularly heavily on the shoulders of mothers with small children whose personal costs (the guilt they feel, not having time for themselves, not living up to the image of the "good mother") for working outside the home are tremendously high. As Figures 7.1 and 7.2 indicate, women are far more engaged than their male partners in housework and child care. Even when both partners work full-time, there is a substantial difference between males and females in the hours they spend on housework and care-giving. A recent case study by Luxton and Corman (2001) of working-class men and women in Hamilton, Ontario, confirms this pattern. Most women in the labour force work a *double day*—that is, a shift of unpaid work at home following or before their shift in the workplace. Not surprisingly, most women at some point face the likelihood of leaving their paid jobs in order to undertake their domestic responsibilities, including care-giving to senior, young, or disabled family members, on a full-time basis (see Figure 7.3).

To help resolve this conflict, Felice Schwartz (1989) suggests that corporations offer women a choice of two parallel career paths. The "fast track" consists of high-powered, demanding positions that may require 60 or 70 hours of

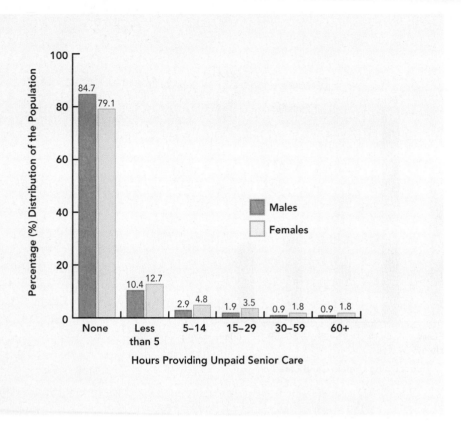

FIGURE 7.3   Percentage of Males and Females, Aged 25 to 54, by Hours Spent Providing Unpaid Care or Assistance to Seniors, Canada, 2006 Census

Sources: www12.statcan.ca/english/census06/data/topics/Print.cfm?PID=92108&GID=771240&D1=2&D2=0&D3=0&D4=0&D5=0&D6=0, and www12.statcan.ca/english/census01/Products/Reference/tech_rep/unpaid_work/table10a.cfm

work per week—regular responsibilities, emergencies, out-of-town meetings, and a briefcase jammed with work at night and on weekends. Instead, women may choose a "mommy track," which would allow for a lower commitment to the firm, freeing time for a higher commitment to family.

What is wrong with this proposal is that a "mommy track" would encourage women to be satisfied with lower aspirations and fewer promotions and confirm men's stereotypes of women executives. Because there is no "daddy track," it also assumes that child-rearing is primarily women's work (Starrels, 1992). To encourage women to slow down in the race to climb the corporate ladder would perpetuate, or even increase, the pay gap. The "mommy track," conclude critics, would keep men in executive power and relegate women to an inferior position in corporate life.

Critics suggest that a better way to confront the conflict between work and family is for partners to take greater responsibility at home and for workplaces to provide on-site day care, flexible work schedules, and parental leave without loss of benefits (Auerbach, 1990; Galinsky & Stein, 1990; Duffy & Pupo, 1996). Others maintain that the choice

between family and career is artificial, that there are ample role models of family-oriented, highly successful women, from Hilary Weston, former lieutenant-governor of Ontario, to judges Rosalie Abella and Louise Arbour and CEO Christine Magee.

Parenting and work often bring conflict, some of which we will examine in Chapter 13. The next Sociology and the New Technology box presents a controversy surrounding motherhood that has been ushered in by technology (page 166).

Sexual Harassment

Until the 1970s, women considered it a personal matter when they experienced unwanted sexual comments, touches, looks, or pressure to have sex. The term **sexual harassment**, which refers to these activities, especially in occupational or school settings, was unknown. In 1979, Catharine MacKinnon, an activist lawyer, published *Sexual Harassment of Working Women: A Case of Sex Discrimination*. MacKinnon stressed that such unwanted sexual advances are a *structural* problem; that is, they are built into the social structure. It is not a case of a man here and a man there

Boys are pilots.

Girls are stewardesses.

Boys are presidents.

Girls are First Ladies.

Boys are doctors.

Girls are nurses.

Boys build houses.

Girls keep houses.

By looking at the past we get an idea of how far we have come. This illustration from a 1970s children's book shows the mind-set of the day. You can see how children who grew up during this period were taught to view gender and work.

Source: Anthony Cortese, *Provocateur: Images of Women and Minorities in Advertising*, 2nd ed., Boulder, CO: Rowman and Little Publishers, 2003.

doing obnoxious things because they are attracted to a woman; rather, it is a case of men abusing their positions of authority to force unwanted sexual activities on women.

Although the targets of sexual harassment are usually women, the number of male victims has been increasing as women have moved into positions of power. Male victims are less likely than female victims to receive a sympathetic ear. Like women victims, however, these men report that they feel powerless and used. Social norms and symbolic perceptions, we assume, will eventually catch up to this emerging reality of women abusing power and men as victims. With most authority and power vested in men, the majority of sexual harassers are men.

As symbolic interactionists stress, labels affect our perception. Today the term *sexual harassment* sheds a different light on unwanted sexual attention as compared to the understanding of this behaviour by earlier generations. The meaning of sexual harassment continues to be redefined as court cases change what the term does and does not include. Sexual harassment laws apply to homosexuals who are harassed by heterosexuals, and by extension, to heterosexuals who are harassed by homosexuals.

Central to sexual harassment is the abuse of power. Like other dynamic terms in our language, this one, too, continues to undergo shifts.

Focus Question

What are some of the ways in which women are disadvantaged in the labour force?

GENDER AND VIOLENCE

While most Canadian communities are usually regarded as relatively safe, many residents are increasingly fearful of robberies, home invasions, kidnappings, and sexual assault. Only a couple of generations ago, Canadians left their homes and cars unlocked. Today, a growing number are having security systems installed in their homes and cars, escorting their children to and from schools, and organizing neighbourhood watch networks. Lurking behind these fears is gender inequality of violence—that females are most likely to be victims of males, not the other way around. Let's briefly review this almost one-way street in gender violence.

Violence against Women

Battering, intimidation, stalking, sexual assault, intimate violence, and physical, emotional, and psychological abuse are among the forms of violence in which the majority of victims are women. Women are more likely than men to experience the most severe forms of spousal assault, as well as

Rent-a-Uterus: Gender and Reproductive Technology

Breakthroughs in reproductive technology have led to a cultural lag. That is, our technology allows forms of reproduction that have outpaced our norms, our standards of right and wrong. Let's look at some real-life examples.

Consider surrogate motherhood:

Mary Beth Whitehead of New Jersey signed a contract for which she was paid to be artificially inseminated with the semen of Bill Stern, whose wife was ill. During pregnancy, Whitehead became emotionally attached to her developing child and decided to keep the baby.

Stern sued Whitehead to enforce the contract. The controversy, known as the "Baby M case," captivated the nation. Should the contract be enforced, or did a "mother's right" supersede the contract? Stern won, not on the basis of the contract, which was ruled illegal, but on the basis of his fathering the baby.

Consider the growth of commercial surrogacy:

In the city of Anand in western India, 15 pregnant women, cared for by a team of maids, cooks, and doctors, live at a clinic at Kaival Hospital, preparing to give birth to children for infertile couples from around the world. Here, surrogate motherhood, or "outsourced pregnancy," has become an enterprise. Couples pro-

vide the egg and sperm and sign a contract, guaranteeing payment of medical expenses and the surrogate's fee. The surrogate mother also signs a contract, promising to hand over the baby after birth. Surrogate motherhood pays the young women well—what would take about 15 years to earn at a regular job. Is this arrangement exploitative of young poor women, who endure the pain and possible complications of pregnancy for relatively low rates of pay? (Wombs for Rent, 2007: p. A6)

Consider artificial insemination for the purpose of abortion:

Rae Leith loved her father, who was suffering the ravages of Alzheimer's disease. She wanted to be inseminated with her father's sperm in order to have an abortion, and then have the brains of the fetus, which would match her father's tissue, transplanted into her father's brain. Her father said no.

Consider postmortem ventilation (PMV), in which a brain-dead body is kept alive by artificial means:

Brain-dead pregnant women have been kept in a ventilated state for several months in order to allow their fetuses to have a better chance to survive. In one case, the man who claimed to be the father of the fetus

requested PMV, but the husband objected. The court ruled that since the woman was dead, the state had the right to make the decision, which it did, ruling in favour of PMV. Seven weeks later, the baby died after a caesarean delivery.

For Your Consideration

What should the relative roles of men and women be in technological conception? In the first case described, should contracts for surrogate motherhood be legally enforceable—and placed higher than a woman's right to motherhood? In the second case, what are the ethics of commercial surrogacy and how are exploitation and globalization together impacting young women's lives and their reproductive health? In the third case, should a woman have an absolute right to do whatever she wishes with her uterus—regardless of whose sperm is used? In the fourth case, should the state be able to determine what happens to a woman's womb and fetus if she is brain-dead? Is this the rightful saving of a child's life, or the state's wrongful control over a woman's womb? Finally, on the basis of this last case, since brain-dead women have no legal rights, could they be used as incubators for the embryos of others—something that is totally within our technological capacity?

Sources: Overvold (1988); Rothman (1989); J. G. Raymond (1993); Wombs for Rent (2007).

---

spousal homicide, sexual assault, and stalking, while men are more likely to be assaulted by a stranger (Statistics Canada, 2006a; Johnson, 2006). There are notable gender differences in rates and patterns of victimization. For example, both in Canada and the United States, convicted rapists are almost exclusively young men, and acts of violence committed by women are likely to occur in their homes, often against their male partners as acts of self-defence or retribution (Johnson, 2006: p. 23).

RAPE Prior to changes in the Canadian Criminal Code in 1983, rape was narrowly defined as a sexual act committed

by a male upon a female who was not his wife and who did not consent to the act. Under this definition, a man could not be charged with raping or sexually abusing his wife, even if they were separated at the time (Duffy & Momirov, 1997; Nelson & Robinson, 1999). Under the reformed code, rape was renamed "sexual assault" and emphasis is now placed on the violence of the act, including the power and intimidation it entails. Women are no longer exempt as perpetrators under this new definition (Duffy & Momirov, 1997).

SEXUAL ASSAULT According to the Canadian Criminal Code, sexual assault is defined as a range of behaviours, from unwanted sexual touching to sexual violence, resulting in injury to the victim (Johnson, 2006: p. 27). Since less than 10 percent of sexual assaults are reported to the police, it is difficult to get an accurate picture of the prevalence of this form of violence. But the incidence of reported cases has been declining since 1993. It is difficult to assess whether the number of cases has actually declined or whether women have resisted making reports. On the positive side, it may be that human rights and awareness campaigns have contributed to the decline.

DATE RAPE Studies have shown that date rape (also known as *acquaintance rape*) is not an isolated event here and there. According to police reports, while incidents of spousal violence have declined since 2000, violent acts perpetrated by boyfriends have increased (Johnson, 2006: p. 12). Date rape most commonly occurs not between relative strangers on first dates, but between couples that have known each other for about a year. Most date rapes go unreported. Those that are reported are difficult to prosecute, for juries tend to believe that if a woman knows the accused, she wasn't "really" raped (Bourque, 1989).

MURDER Although men are more than twice as likely as women to become homicide victims, husbands are about three times more likely to murder their wives than they are to be murdered by their wives (Johnson, 2006: p. 23). One in five homicides in Canada is the murder of an intimate partner (Johnson, 2006: p. 21) Women are far more likely (by about nine times) to be killed by their husbands than by a stranger. Furthermore, the most sensational act of violence

Domestic abuse is one of the most common forms of violence. Until recently, it was treated by the police as a private family matter. Shown here are police pulling a woman from her bathroom window, where she had fled from her armed husband, who was threatening to shoot her.

in the home, familicide, in which a whole family—women, children, and sometimes other family members—are murdered at the same time, is usually committed by men.

MASS MEDIA IN SOCIAL LIFE
Violence as Entertainment

The studio audience at *Super Jockey*, a popular nationally-run comedy show in Japan, waits expectantly. Finally, a young woman, clad in a revealing bikini, walks onto the stage. Cringing with fear, she is lowered into a glass tank of scalding hot water. The audience both at the studio and across the country break into laughter as the girl writhes in pain.

To make sure the young women gets the full treatment, a man ladles hot water over her breasts—just as though he were basting a chicken. The television camera zooms in for a close-up shot of her reddening chest. Most women last only three or four seconds.

The camera follows as the young woman scrambles out of the tub, where she jumps up and down in pain and rubs ice all over her body. The audience howls with glee.

Why do the women do it? For every second they stay in the hot water, they get one second on the program to advertise any product they wish. Most advertise their place of employment, their pain a favour to their boss (Strauss, 1998).

Canadians would suggest that *Super Jockey* wouldn't be tolerated here. Instead of trying to explain why it is seen as amusing in Japan, let's turn the focus to our own culture. Why do we find violence against women a source of entertainment? And entertainment it is, considering the number of television

shows, movies, and sometimes music videos and lyrics centring on violence and woman abuse.

Consider how entertaining our society finds the murder of women. The *Halloween* slasher films are an outstanding example. Audiences, simultaneously titillated and terror-stricken, watch crazed, masked killers hunt down college co-eds with knives, axes, and even chain saws. Audiences seem to find the screams of the victims especially entertaining. And the prettier, shapelier, and more skimpily clad the victim, the higher the entertainment value.

Spouse battering, marital rape, and incest are discussed in Chapter 13.

A Feminist Understanding of Gender Patterns in Violence

Feminist sociologists have been especially effective in bringing violence against women to the public's attention. Some use the perspective of symbolic interactionism, pointing out that to associate strength and virility with violence—as is done in so many areas of Canadian culture—is to produce violence. Others use conflict theory, arguing that as gender relations change, males are losing power, and that some males become violent against females as a way to reassert their power and status.

Focus Question

According to feminist sociologists, how is violence against women explained?

Solutions

There is no magic solution for this problem, but in order to be effective, any solution must break the connection between violence and masculinity. This would require an educational program that incorporates schools, religious institutions, homes, the courts, and the media. Many unions offer well-developed anti-violence and sexual harassment awareness programs. Given the breadth of this problem, the tacit acceptance of the many forms of violence, and current messages in the mass media, it is difficult to be optimistic that a change will come soon.

Our next topics, women in politics and women in sports, however, give us much more reason for optimism.

GENDER AND CHANGE

The Changing Face of Politics

What do these nations have in common?

- Canada
- Argentina, Bolivia, Chile, and Nicaragua in Latin America
- Britain, France, Ireland, and Portugal in Western Europe
- The Philippines in East Asia
- Israel in the Middle East
- Poland in Eastern Europe
- India, Pakistan, and Sri Lanka in South Asia

MASS MEDIA IN SOCIAL LIFE
The Simpsons' Take on Issues of Gender

Spawning a myriad of toys, posters, and other pop culture paraphernalia, *The Simpsons*, one of the longest-running television shows in North America, is familiar to most Canadian households. Woven through the hundreds of episodes are a number of recurring themes, gently poking at traditional values, structures, and institutions and exposing absurdities in American society. Producer Matt Groening's sarcasm, satire, and wit have extended to schools, policing, local politics, the environment, the church, and the values and practices of capitalism. Through feisty Lisa, with her intelligence and strong sense of justice, and Marge, housewife and mother, with her quiet commentary, strong moral convictions, fairness, and willingness to engage in local politics, women's places in family and community are exposed and questioned.

In one notable episode, Lisa's concerns over phrases such as "Let's make cookies for the boys," uttered by the popular talking doll, Malibu Stacy (a doll styled with great similarity to Mattel's Barbie), led her to the executive boardroom.

There Malibu Stacy's creator, who was recently bought out by a giant competitor, listens to Lisa's concerns over the sexist doll and with Lisa recreates the doll with intelligence. Not surprisingly, the new doll is a bomb.

Along with candid commentary on gender socialization and sexism in the marketplace, gender tensions are featured throughout the series: When Marge gets a job as a policewoman, she is assigned the toughest tasks to prove that she should be there; when Marge is employed at the nuclear plant, Mr. Burns tries to fire her because she is married; Bart's daring antics are chalked up to the notion that "boys will be boys"; Marge's unpaid household work is unnoticed by Homer and other family members until she is hospitalized with a broken leg. Often the message is that change is difficult and many give up trying. Lisa's enthusiasm for achievement is met with lukewarm welcome, and Marge's ventures into the paid labour force or into local politics are dismal failures.

Underlying many episodes are serious questions about gender relations, opportunities, and roles. Within our society, poking fun at women, trivializing their concerns and contributions to family and society is highly entertaining. While we are also entertained by Homer's stupidity and obsession with food and Bart's boyish pranks, the humour is bounded by different sets of expectations based on gender and position in the family.

How are the issues of gender relations and roles infused in our sense of humour and in entertainment in Canadian culture?

SUMMARY AND REVIEW

Issues of Sex and Gender

WHAT IS GENDER STRATIFICATION?

The term **gender inequality** refers to unequal access to power, prestige, and property on the basis of sex. Every society establishes a structure that, on the basis of sex and gender, opens and closes access to the group's privileges. p. 147.

HOW DO SEX AND GENDER DIFFER?

Sex refers to biological distinctions between males and females. It consists of both primary and secondary sex characteristics. **Gender**, in contrast, is what a society considers proper behaviours and attitudes for its male and female members. Sex physically distinguishes males from females; gender defines what is "masculine" and "feminine." p. 147.

WHY DO THE BEHAVIOURS OF MALES AND FEMALES DIFFER?

In the "nature versus nurture" debate—whether differences between the behaviours of males and females are caused by inherited (biological) or learned (cultural) characteristics—almost all sociologists take the side of nurture. In recent years, however, the door to biology has opened somewhat. pp. 147–150.

Gender Inequality in Global Perspective

IS GENDER INEQUALITY UNIVERSAL?

George Murdock surveyed information on premodern societies and found not only that all of them have sex-linked activities, but also that all of them give greater prestige to male activities. **Patriarchy**, or male dominance, appears to be universal. Besides work, other areas of discrimination include education, politics, and violence. pp. 150–152.

Gender Inequality in Theoretical Perspective

HOW DID FEMALES BECOME A MINORITY GROUP?

The main theory that attempts to explain how females became a **minority group** in their own societies focuses on the physical limitations imposed by childbirth. The origins of this discrimination, however, are lost in history, and no one knows for sure how this discrimination began. pp. 152–155.

Gender Inequality in Canada

IS THE FEMINIST MOVEMENT NEW?

In what is called the "first wave," feminists made political demands for change in the early 1900s—and were met with much hostility, even violence. The "second wave" of feminism began in the 1960s and continues today. pp. 155–156.

WHAT FORMS DOES GENDER INEQUALITY IN EDUCATION TAKE?

Although more women than men now attend university, each tends to select "feminine" or "masculine" fields. In addition, men outnumber women in most scientific disciplines. Change is indicated by the growing numbers of women in such fields as law and medicine. pp. 156–159.

IS THERE GENDER INEQUALITY IN EVERYDAY LIFE?

Two indications of gender inequality in everyday life are the general devaluation of femininity and the male dominance of conversation. p. 159.

Gender Relations in the Workplace

WHAT GENDER INEQUALITY IS THERE IN THE WORKPLACE?

Over the past century, women have comprised an increasing proportion of the workforce. Nonetheless, a gender gap in pay characterizes all occupations. For university graduates, the lifetime pay gap runs about $800 000 in favour of men. **Sexual harassment** also continues to be a reality in the workplace. pp. 159–165.

Gender and Violence

WHAT FORMS DOES VIOLENCE AGAINST WOMEN TAKE?

The victims of battering, sexual assault, incest, and murder overwhelmingly are females. Conflict theorists point out that men use violence to maintain their power. pp. 165–168.

Gender and Change

WHAT IS THE TREND IN GENDER INEQUALITY IN POLITICS?

A strict division of gender roles—women as child-care providers and housekeepers, men as workers outside the home—has traditionally kept women out of politics. Although women continue to be underrepresented in Canadian politics, the trend toward greater political equality is firmly in place. pp. 168–170.

Glimpsing the Future—with Hope

WHAT PROGRESS HAS BEEN MADE IN REDUCING GENDER INEQUALITY?

In Canada, women are playing a fuller role in the decision-making processes of our social institutions. Men, too, are re-examining their traditional roles. The ultimate possibility of gender equality is a new conception of the human personality, one that allows both males and females to pursue their individual interests unfettered by gender. p. 170.

TALKING ABOUT THEORY

Theoretical Paradigms

	CLASSICAL PARADIGMS		RECENT PARADIGMS	
	Structural-Functional Paradigm	Social-Conflict Paradigm	Feminist Paradigm	Postmodernist Paradigm
What is the level of analysis?	Macro level	Macro level	Micro and macro levels	Micro levels
How is gender inequality explained?	Biological, or inborn differences, explain different behaviours, emotions, temperaments.	Factors of socialization, social structure and social control—not biological factors—explain different behaviours and expectations.	Drawing on conflict theory, feminism argues that patriarchy—men's power and control over property—explains gender inequality.	Gender differences are socially constructed and gender identities should be analyzed from an individual point of view because not all women share similar identities and experiences.

KEY TERMS

agency 169	gender inequality 147	patriarchies 149	sex-typed 150
feminism 154	matriarchies 149	sex 147	sexual harassment 164
gender 147	minority group 150		

WEBLINKS

All URLs listed are current as of the printing of this book.

York University Centre for Feminist Research
www.yorku.ca/cfr
The Centre for Feminist Research at York University engages in research and education in feminist studies. It links with the Women's Studies program at York and with women's research networks in Canada and internationally.

Backlash and Battered Husbands
www.dadsrights.org/articles/
backlash_and_battered_husbands.shtml
"One way to trivialize and dismiss a point of view is to claim it is part of a backlash. That is the contemptuous and deroga-tory characterization often applied when the topic of men's issues arises. Domestic violence is a case in point."

Deceptions of a "Gender-Equal Society"
www.fathermag.com/9607/Leacock
Eleanor Leacock, an anthropologist, published claims of soci-eties that were supposedly egalitarian in regard to both wealth and sex. In her essay "Women In Egalitarian Societies," one of her principal examples was the Montagnais-Naskapi of the Labrador peninsula. The authors argue that it is now clear that the gender equality of that soci-ety has no basis in fact.

CRITICAL THINKING QUESTIONS

1. As some forms of work become increasingly "faceless" due to advances in technology (internet businesses, for example), will gender inequalities among workers be minimized?

2. What evidence is there that the women's world is beginning to mirror the men's world? What factors most significantly contribute to gender inequality?

3. The pay gap is one indicator of gender inequalities in the workplace. Access the Research Navigator through MySocLab, and use it to find five recent articles on gen-der inequality at work. Based on these articles, would you conclude that women's position in the workplace has improved over the past few decades?

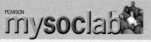

Explore the topics covered in this chapter on MySocLab using the access information provided with this text. Interactive resources for studying include multimedia tutorials, video clips, practice tests, quizzes, and animated maps and figures.

8 Inequalities of Race and Ethnicity

Between 800 000 and 1 million Rwandans died in the slaughter. Although the killings were low-tech—most were done with machetes—it took just 100 days in the summer of 1994 to complete the state-sanctioned massacres (Gourevitch, 1995).

Rwanda has two major ethnic groups. Hutus are stocky and round-faced, dark-skinned, flat-nosed, and thick-lipped. The Tutsis are lankier and longer-faced, lighter-skinned, narrow-nosed, and thin-lipped. The Hutus outnumber the Tutsis six to one. But the two groups, who speak the same language, have intermarried for many years and have difficulty telling each other apart. National identity cards, originally issued by the Belgians when Rwanda was its colony, are a sure way of telling who is who.

During the genocide, a Tutsi card was a passport to death.

The Hutus, who controlled the government, called for the killing of all Tutsis. It was a national duty, said the Hutu leaders. Obediently, neighbours hacked neighbours to death in their homes. Colleagues hacked colleagues to death at work. Even teachers killed their students.

Nkongoli, a Tutsi who is now the vice-president of the Rwandan National Assembly, says, "One expected to die. Not by machete, one hoped, but with a bullet. If you were willing to pay for it, you could ask for a bullet. Death was more or less normal, a resignation. You lose the will to fight" (Gourevitch, 1995).

At the end of World War II, the world was aghast at the Nazis' slaughter of Jews, Slavs, gypsies, and homosexuals. Dark images of gas ovens and emaciated bodies stacked like cordwood haunted the nations of the world. At Nuremberg, the Allies, flush with victory, put the top Nazis on trial, exposing their heinous deeds to a shocked public. Their public executions, everyone assumed, marked the end of genocide, a shameful aberration of history.

Never again would such atrocities be allowed happen—that was the general consensus. Yet mass slaughters did occur. By far, the worst was the Khmer Rouge's killing spree in the 1970s, leaving 2 or 3 million Cambodians dead (Markusen, 1995). This was purely political killing, a ruthless regime against victims of the same race and ethnicity.

Genocide—the attempt to annihilate a people simply because of their presumed race or ethnicity—continues today, as evidenced in the description above. It grows out of the same impulse of hatred displayed by the Nazis. Although the Rwandan killings lacked swastikas and goose-stepping, and machetes replaced poison gas and ovens, the end goal was the same.

There were, of course, other reasons for the slaughter. There always are. The Hutus felt threatened by a Tutsi rebel group, and 20 years earlier the Tutsis had killed 100 000 Hutus. What is significant for our purposes is that it happened, even after the world's vow of "never again" in 1945.

LAYING THE SOCIOLOGICAL FOUNDATION

Race and ethnic relations seldom drop to such a brutal low as they did in Nazi Germany and Rwanda, but in our own society, newspaper headlines and evening newscasts keep race and ethnic relations constantly before us. Sociological findings on the topic, then, can contribute greatly to a better understanding of this aspect of social life. To begin, we will consider to what extent the concept of race is a myth.

Race: Myth and Reality

With 6.5 billion people (United Nations, 2005), the world is home to a diverse range of human shapes and colours. Eyes come in various shades of blue, brown, and green. Lips are thick and thin. Hair can be straight, curly, kinky, black, white, or red—and, of course, all hues of brown.

As humans spread throughout the world, their adaptations to diverse climates and other living conditions resulted in a profusion of complexions, colours, and shapes. In this sense, the concept of **race**, a group with inherited physical characteristics that distinguish it from another group, is a reality. Humans do, indeed, come in a variety of colours and shapes.

COMMON SENSE VERSUS SOCIOLOGY According to common sense, our racial classifications represent biological differences between people. Sociologists, however, stress that what we call "races" are *social* classifications, not biological categories.

Humans show such a remarkable diversity that, as the text explains, there are no pure races. Shown here are Verne Troyer, who weighs about 45 pounds and is 2 feet 8 inches short, and Yao Ming, who weighs 296 pounds and is 7 feet 5 inches tall.

The racial categories common in Canada, for example, constitute merely one of numerous ways that people around the world classify physical appearances. Although different groups use different categories, each group assumes that its categories are natural—merely a response to visible biology.

But what about that biology? Biological differences are real, regardless of how we categorize them, aren't they? It is true that humans have numerous physical differences. But if biology is the main element, then biologists, of all people, should agree on the numbers and characteristics of human races.

But modern geneticists conclude that there is only ONE racial category (genotype) of humans: *Homo sapiens!*

RACIAL SUPERIORITY People are inclined to think that their own "race" is superior to others, regardless of the logical arguments just recounted. The idea of racial superiority haunts humanity.

That race is an arbitrary classification makes little difference to common thinking. "I know what I see, and you can't tell me any different" seems to be a frequent response. "I know what *they* are like. *They* are (fill in the cultural stereotype)." For the race in question, the description becomes reality.

Sociologist W.I. Thomas observed, "If people define situations as real, they are real in their consequences" (Thomas & Thomas, 1928: p. 572). What people *believe* affects social life, for *people act on beliefs, not facts.* As a result, the ideas of race that are firmly embedded in our culture—rather than scientific fact—influence attitudes and behaviour. As you read this chapter, you will examine some of the racial ideas you learned as you were socialized in your culture.

IN SUM

Race, then, is in the eye of the beholder. Humans show such diversity in physical characteristics—skin colour, hair texture, nose shape, head shape, eye colour, and so on—that there is no inevitable, much less universal, way to classify our many biological differences. Because racial classifications are arbitrary, the categories we use change over time.

Ethnic Groups

Whereas people use the term *race* to refer to the supposed biological characteristics that distinguish one group from another, **ethnicity** and **ethnic** apply to cultural characteristics. Derived from the Greek *ethnos*, meaning "people" or "nation," these terms refer to people who identify with one another on the basis of common ancestry and cultural heritage. Their sense of belonging often centres on nation of origin, distinctive foods, dress, family names and relationships, language, music, religion, and other customs.

People often confuse the terms *race* and *ethnic group.* For example, many people, including many Jews, consider the

These photos were selected to illustrate how seriously we must take all preaching of hatred and racial supremacy, even though it may seem to come from harmless or even humorous sources. The result in this instance was the Holocaust, the systematic slaughter of Jews and others deemed racially inferior in Nazi Germany. In the photo on the left, Adolf Hitler is wearing lederhosen, traditional clothing of Bavaria, Germany. He caused the horrific scene depicted in the image on the right, which reflects conditions in the concentration camp in Buchenwald, Germany, where thousands of people died of starvation and diseases amid piles of rotting bodies awaiting burial.

Jews a race. Jews, however, are more properly considered an ethnic group; it is their cultural characteristics, especially religion, that bind them together.

Some of us have a greater sense of ethnicity than others. We can use the term **ethnic work** to refer to the way people construct their ethnicity. For people who have a strong ethnic identity, *ethnic work* refers to how they enhance and maintain their group's distinctions—from clothing, food, and language to religious practices and holidays. For people whose ethnic identity is not as firm, the term refers to attempts to recover their ethnic heritage, such as trying to trace family lines or visiting the country or region of their family's origins.

Focus Question

What is the difference between a race and an ethnic group?

Minority Groups and Dominant Groups

Sociologist Louis Wirth (1945) defined a **minority group** as people who are singled out for unequal treatment *and* who regard themselves as objects of collective discrimination. Physical (racial) or cultural (ethnic) differences can serve as the basis of the unequal treatment.

Surprisingly, the term *minority group* does not necessarily refer to a *numerical* minority. For example, before India's independence in 1947, a handful of British colonial rulers discriminated against millions of Indians. Similarly, when South Africa practised apartheid, a small group of Dutch discriminated against the black majority. All over the world, women are a minority group. Accordingly, sociologists refer to those who do the discriminating not as the *majority*, but, rather, as the **dominant group**, since they have greater power, privileges, and social status.

The dominant group almost always attributes its privileged position to its own innate superiority. Possessing political power and unified by shared physical and cultural traits, a dominant group uses its position to discriminate against those with different—and supposedly inferior—characteristics.

EMERGENCE OF MINORITY GROUPS A group becomes a minority in one of two ways. The first is through the expansion of political boundaries. This often occurs as the result of a decisive military victory. When a group expands its political boundaries, it produces minority groups if it incorporates people with different customs, languages, values, and physical characteristics into one political entity. For example, after defeating the French on the Plains of Abraham, the British seized control of New France. Consequently, the French who remained, who had previously been the dominant group, then became a minority group, a status that significantly influenced their lives (see the section "The Two Charter Groups" on page 182).

The second way a group becomes a minority is through migration. Migration can be voluntary, as with the millions of people who chose to move to Canada, or involuntary, as with Native Canadians, many of whom were forcibly transported to remote regions of the North (see the Down-to-Earth Sociology box called "The Inuit Expulsion" on page 183). Japanese Canadians were labelled "enemy aliens" during World War II, then stripped of their businesses and livelihoods, forcibly relocated from the West Coast, and put to work in concentration camps throughout Canada. Interestingly, the same fate did not befall the many German and Italian Canadians. Instead, cities and towns with identifiable German names were simply renamed.

Because ideas of race and ethnicity are such a significant part of society, all of us are classified according to those ideas. This photo illustrates the difficulty of assumptions in Israel. A group of Jewish Ethiopians, shown here arriving in Israel, although claiming to be Jews, looked so different from other Jews that it took several years for Israeli authorities to acknowledge the group's "true Jewishness."

SHARED CHARACTERISTICS Anthropologists Charles Wagley and Marvin Harris (1958) identified five characteristics shared by minorities worldwide:

1. Membership in a minority group is an ascribed status; that is, it is not voluntary, but comes through birth.

2. The physical or cultural traits that distinguish minorities are held in low esteem by the dominant group.

3. Minorities are unequally treated by the dominant group.

4. Minorities tend to marry within their own group.

5. Minorities tend to feel strong group solidarity (a sense of "we-ness" and of belonging somewhere).

These conditions—especially when combined with collective discrimination—often create a shared sense of identity among minorities, and, in many instances, even a sense of common destiny (Chandra, 1993b).

Prejudice and Discrimination

Prejudice and discrimination are common throughout the world. In Mexico, Hispanic Mexicans discriminate against Native-American Mexicans; in Israel, Ashkenazic Jews, primarily of European descent, discriminate against Sephardic Jews from the Muslim world; and in Japan, the Japanese discriminate against just about anyone who is not Japanese, especially immigrant Koreans and the descendants of the Eta caste. A stigma is still attached to the Eta, now called the Burakumin, who used to perform Japan's dirty work—working with dead animals (stripping hides and tanning leather) and serving as the country's executioners and prison guards (Mander, 1992). All around the world, women are discriminated against by men.

Discrimination is an *action*—unfair treatment directed against someone. When the basis of discrimination is race, it is known as **racism**, but discrimination can be based on many other characteristics—including age, sex, sexual orientation, weight, disease (e.g., AIDS), and disability. Discrimination is often the result of an *attitude* called **prejudice**—prejudgment, usually in a negative sense. Positive prejudice exaggerates the virtues of a group, such as thinking that one group (usually one's own) is more capable than others. Most prejudice, however, is negative, prejudging a group as inferior.

LEARNING FROM ASSOCIATION As with other learned attitudes, we are not born with prejudice; we glean it from the people around us. Kathleen Blee (2005) interviewed women who were members of the KKK and Aryan Nations. Some members were recruited by someone who already belonged to the group, while others learned to be racists after they joined. They were attracted to the community not because it matched their racist beliefs, but because someone they liked already belonged. Blee observed that racism was often not the cause of their joining, but rather the result of their membership.

Focus Question

What is the difference between prejudice and discrimination?

Individual and Institutional Discrimination

Sociologists stress that we need to move beyond thinking in terms of **individual discrimination**, the negative treatment of one person by another. With a focus on the broader picture, sociologists encourage us to examine **institutional discrimination**—that is, how discrimination is woven into the fabric of society to such an extent that it becomes routine, sometimes even a matter of social policy. The system once known as apartheid in South Africa, the forced resettlement and expropriation of property of Japanese Canadians as "enemy aliens" during World War II, or the present-day system of reserves for Native Canadians are all examples of institutional discrimination.

THEORIES OF PREJUDICE

Why are people prejudiced? The common-sense explanation is that they or someone they know has been harmed by some member of a particular group, and they apply their negative perception to all members of that group. Eugene Hartley (1946) showed that much more is involved when he asked people how they felt about various racial and ethnic groups. Besides blacks and Jews, his list included the Wallonians, Pireneans, and Danireans—names he had made up. Most people who expressed dislike for Jews and blacks also expressed dislike for the three fictitious groups. The significance of Hartley's study is twofold. First, people who are prejudiced against one racial or ethnic group tend to also be prejudiced against others. Second, prejudice does not depend on negative experiences with others. People can be—and are—prejudiced against people they have never met—and even against groups that do not exist!

Social scientists have developed several theories to explain prejudice. We will begin by examining psychological theories, then explore sociological views.

Psychological Perspectives

FRUSTRATION AND SCAPEGOATS Psychologist John Dollard suggested that prejudice is the result of frustration. People who are unable to strike out at the real source of their frustration (such as low wages) find someone else to blame.

This **scapegoat**, generally a racial, ethnic, or religious minority they unfairly blame for their troubles, becomes a convenient—and safe—target on which to vent their frustrations. Gender and age also provide common bases for scapegoating.

THE AUTHORITARIAN PERSONALITY With the horrors he had observed under the Nazis fresh in his mind, Theodor Adorno wondered whether there is a certain type of individual who is more likely to fall for the racist utterances and policies of people like Hitler or Mussolini, or groups like the Ku Klux Klan.

To test the idea, Adorno (1950) developed three scales: a series of statements that measured ethnocentrism, anti-Semitism, and support for strong authoritarian leaders. Testing nearly 2000 people, ranging from university professors to prison inmates, Adorno found that people who scored high on one scale also scored high on the other two. For example, people who agreed with anti-Semitic statements also agreed that it was good for a government to be highly authoritarian and that foreign ways of life posed a threat to the nation.

Adorno concluded that highly prejudiced people have several things in common. They are insecure, are highly conformist, have deep respect for authority, and are highly submissive to superiors. He termed this the **authoritarian personality**. Individuals who possess an authoritarian personality believe that things are *either* right *or* wrong. When they confront norms and values that differ from their own, especially in matters of religion or sexual orientation, they become anxious and aggressive.

Sociological Theories

Sociologists find psychological explanations inadequate. They stress that the key to understanding prejudice is not the *internal* state of individuals, but factors *outside* the individual. Thus, sociological theories focus on how some environments foster prejudice, while others reduce it. Let's compare functionalist, conflict, symbolic interactionist, feminist, postmodern, postcolonial, and critical race theories of racism, discrimination, and prejudice.

FUNCTIONALISM In a telling scene from a television documentary, journalist Bill Moyers interviewed Fritz Hippler, a Nazi intellectual who at age 29 was put in charge of the entire German film industry. Hippler said that when Hitler came to power, the Germans were no more anti-Semitic than the French—probably less so. He was told to create anti-Semitism, which he did by producing movies that contained vivid scenes comparing Jews to rats—their breeding threatening to infest the population.

Why was Hippler told to create hatred? The Jews provided a convenient target because they had businesses, bank accounts, and other property to confiscate. They held key positions (university professors, reporters, judges, and so on), which the Nazis could replace with their own flunkies. Hatred also showed its dysfunctional side, as the Nazi officials who were sentenced to death at Nuremberg discovered.

Harnessing the state machinery—schools, police, courts, mass media, and almost all aspects of the government—to promote hatred as the Nazis did is not as uncommon as we would hope. Recall the case of the Rwandan genocide outlined at the start of this chapter.

That prejudice is functional and shaped by social environment was dramatically demonstrated by Muzafer and Carolyn Sherif (1953) in a simple but ingenious experiment. At a boys' summer camp, they assigned friends to different cabins and made cabins the basic units of competition. Each cabin competed against the others in sports and for status.

In only a few days, strong in-groups had formed, and even former lifelong friends were calling one another "crybaby" and "sissy" and showing intense dislike for one another.

The Sherifs' study illustrates four major points. First, the social environment can be deliberately arranged to generate either positive or negative feelings about people. Second, prejudice can be a product of pitting group against group in an "I win, you lose" situation. Third, prejudice is functional in that it creates in-group solidarity. Fourth, prejudice is dysfunctional in that it destroys wider community social relationships.

CONFLICT THEORY Conflict theorists stress that the capitalist class systematically pits group against group. If workers are united, they will demand higher wages and better working conditions. To reduce workers' solidarity, then, is to weaken their bargaining power, drive down costs, and increase profits. Thus the capitalist class exploits racial and ethnic strife to produce a **dual labour market** (also called a *split labour market*)—workers divided along racial, ethnic, and gender lines (Du Bois, 1935/1992; M. Reich, 1972; Lind, 1995). Usually, one ethnic group holds down the good jobs while other identifiable ethnic or racial groups work in low-paying, ordinarily non-unionized jobs.

Unemployment is a useful weapon to help maintain a split labour market. Keeping some people unemployed, however, provides a **reserve labour force** from which owners can draw when they need to expand production. Minority workers, including women, are especially useful as members of the reserve army of labour because their presence poses a potential threat to the dominant group of workers—usually, but not always, white males (see "Feminism: Multiracial Feminism and Inequality" below).

The consequences are devastating, say conflict theorists. Just like the boys in the Sherif experiments, black Canadians, Native Canadians, Quebecois, anglophones, and others see themselves as able to make gains only at one another's expense. Thus, their frustration, anger, and hostility are deflected away from capitalists and directed toward others whom they see as standing in their way. Pitted against one another, racial and ethnic groups learn to fear and distrust each another instead of recognizing their common class interests and working for their mutual welfare (Blackwelder, 1993).

SYMBOLIC INTERACTIONISM Symbolic interactionists stress that no one is born prejudiced. Instead, at birth, each of us becomes a member of some particular family and racial or ethnic group, where we learn our beliefs and values. There we learn to like—or dislike—members of other groups and to perceive them positively or negatively. If discrimination is common practice, we learn to observe it routinely. Just as we learn other attitudes and customs, we learn prejudice and discrimination.

Words are not simply meaningless labels. Rather, *the labels we learn colour the way we see the world*. Symbolic interactionists stress that labels are an essential ingredient of prejudice. Labels cause **selective perception**; that is, they lead people to see certain things and blind them to others. Through labels, people look at the members of racial and ethnic groups as though they are all alike. The terms *honky*, *spic*, *mick*, *kike*, *limey*, *kraut*, *dago*, or any of the other scornful words people use to belittle ethnic groups are not simply nicknames, they are emotionally laden stereotypes. Such words overpower us with emotions, blocking out rational thought about the people they refer to (Allport, 1954).

STEREOTYPES AND DISCRIMINATION: THE SELF-FULFILLING PROPHECY The stereotypes we learn can even produce the behaviour they depict. Let's consider Group X. Negative stereotypes, which characterize Group X as lazy, seem to justify withholding opportunities from this group (because they are lazy and undependable) and placing its members in inferior economic positions. The result is a *self-fulfilling prophecy*. Denied jobs that require high dedication and energy, Group X members are confined to "dirty work," seen as more fitting for "that kind" of people. Since much dirty work is irregular, members of Group X are also liable to be readily visible—standing around on street corners. The sight of their idleness then reinforces the original stereotype of laziness, while the discrimination that created the "laziness" in the first place passes unnoticed.

FEMINISM: MULTIRACIAL FEMINISM AND INEQUALITY Multiracial feminism (otherwise known as multicultural or multiethnic feminism) has emerged from the challenges put forward by women of colour. Simply put, they argue that white men *and women* oppress lower-class women and men of disadvantaged races and ethnicities. However, the inclusion of race and ethnicity in social class inequality complicates the picture. While sex is a dichotomy (generally speaking, you are either a man or a woman), race, ethnicity, and social class are continuums of privileges and disadvantages. Multiracial feminists contend that it is not enough to simply dissect inequality from a woman's point of view. Analysis must include the experiences of women and men of different racial and ethnic groups and their class differences. Therefore, multiracial feminism discusses the outlooks and behaviours of men and women of different ethnic and racial backgrounds, such as black working-class men and women, wealthy white men and women, poor Chinese men and women, and so on.

Eating disorders provide a useful example. Among young white middle-class women who desire a thin, sexually attractive body, anorexia nervosa and bulimia can be the negative consequences of a culture of thinness in Western society. Much has been written about this social problem and a great deal of television time has been devoted to it. Eating disorders are now defined as a significant social problem for this group. Among many African-American and Hispanic women, binge eating and purging are ways of coping with the traumas of their social lives, such as poverty, racism, and sexual abuse. Their eating disorders have not received the same level of attention because of their lower social-class position, or in other words, lack of access to the levers of power make their social problems "invisible."

The important point made by multiracial feminists is that a member of a disadvantaged ethnic or racial group (man or woman) is not oppressed because of her or his gender, race, ethnicity, or social class position alone; it is a multiple system of domination that requires a multifaceted remedy. In contrast to liberal feminists, who have focused their energies on the oppression of women by men and on raising the status of women through legal changes, and to Marxist and other radical feminists, who have argued that women's oppression is linked to working-class political struggles, multiracial feminists point to complexities in the struggle for equality. "Men" are not the enemy, nor is the "ruling class"; the system of oppression experienced by men and women of colour demonstrates the complexity of inequality and how difficult it is to resolve (Lorber, 1998, pp. 134–147).

POSTMODERNISM AND THE ETHNIC/RACIAL EXPERIENCE

The postmodernist position on understanding racism and discrimination is reasonably clear-cut: only those who directly experience racism and discrimination can understand what it means to be "black," "brown," and so on. It is only through their "voices" that we all can come to understand what it means to be a member of a disaffected minority group. According to postmodernists, no middle-class white female or male academic could possibly put her- or himself in the place of a visible minority, let alone write about the social and cultural fabric of these communities.

POSTCOLONIALISM, ETHNICITY, AND CULTURAL IDENTITY

Postcolonialism, also known as postcolonial theory or post-oriental theory, refers to regions of the world that have regained political independence from European domination and are therefore technically no longer colonial. Examples include postcolonial India and postcolonial Algeria. However, long periods of imperialism and forced dependency have profoundly affected the cultural fabric of these societies. As a result, postcolonial theory seeks to understand how the colonial legacy of racism persists in so-called postcolonial societies and interacts with their refusal to accept white European notions of race, ethnicity, and cultural identity (individual and collective). Therefore, most postcolonial theorists are concerned with understanding the cultural products (print and visual media, literature, the arts, and language) of these societies. To what degree are they influenced (even dominated) by their one-time colonial masters?

Franz Fanon, in his 1962 book *The Wretched of the Earth*, laid the theoretical foundation for much postcolonial writing today. A French-speaking native of Martinique, Fanon knew that language played a vital role in shaping the consciousness of colonized people. As we discussed in Chapter 3, a vibrant culture nurtures and is nurtured by an evolving language. The flip side of this equation is that a colonizer's language must denigrate the local indigenous culture if it is to successfully replace it. After decades, even centuries, of English or French as the master language, for example,

indigenous languages and cultures fade into the background. Some locals learn the dominant language and are rewarded. Others may keep their language and culture but pay the price of poverty. Such differences in the response of colonized peoples to the institutions of the colonizer make understanding and theorizing the postcolonial experience a complex and ongoing undertaking.

In the zeal to overthrow cultural imperialism, however, many advocates of postcolonial theory seem willing to toss the baby out with the bath water. A case in point is the issue of homosexuality. For many postcolonials and postcolonial theorists in Africa (Fanon was among the earliest homophobes), the Middle East, and Asia, homosexuality is considered a white European "disease," and any cultural contributions and all experiences of gays and lesbians in the former colonies are prohibited, censored, or ignored. This ignorant and judgmental position is a waste of energy and has become a self-defeating invective in the face of the global AIDS epidemic. In an otherwise progressive movement to affirm the diversity of racial, ethnic, and cultural identities worldwide, throwbacks such as misogyny and homophobia must be rigorously challenged and eradicated.

CRITICAL RACE THEORY

Critical race theory accepts that racism is an "endemic facet of life in our society and that neutrality, objectivity, colorblindness, and meritocracy are all questionable constructs" (Pizarro, 1998, p. 62). This perspective sees racial inequalities in housing, the legal system, employment, and the educational system persisting over time. Research by critical race theorists acknowledges an interactive relationship between researchers and participants (Guba & Lincoln, 1994) and between participants and their stories. Within this world view, people's stories of their experiences are counted as empirical evidence, as fact. This paradigm negates the assumption that narratives from the disenfranchised are biased and subjective. Stories, experiences, and voices are the mediums through which critical race theorists uncover the "hidden past" of racial minorities (Pizarro, 1998, p. 62).

Focus Question

How do sociologists differ from psychologists in their explanations of prejudice?

GLOBAL PATTERNS OF INTERGROUP RELATIONS

In any society, basic patterns develop between the dominant group and minorities. Let's look at each of the patterns shown in Figure 8.1.

Genocide

The twentieth century's most notorious examples of genocide are Hitler's attempt to destroy all Jews and, as depicted in our opening vignette, the Hutus' attempt to destroy all

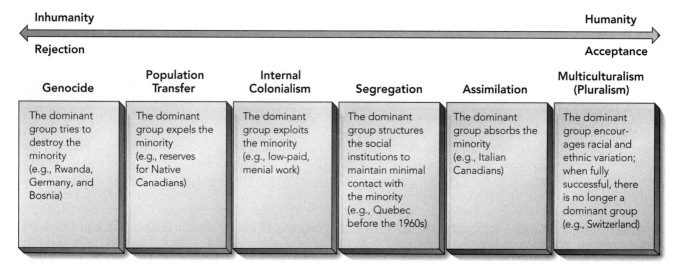

Inhumanity —————————————————————→ Humanity

Rejection   Acceptance

Genocide	Population Transfer	Internal Colonialism	Segregation	Assimilation	Multiculturalism (Pluralism)
The dominant group tries to destroy the minority (e.g., Rwanda, Germany, and Bosnia)	The dominant group expels the minority (e.g., reserves for Native Canadians)	The dominant group exploits the minority (e.g., low-paid, menial work)	The dominant group structures the social institutions to maintain minimal contact with the minority (e.g., Quebec before the 1960s)	The dominant group absorbs the minority (e.g., Italian Canadians)	The dominant group encourages racial and ethnic variation; when fully successful, there is no longer a dominant group (e.g., Switzerland)

FIGURE 8.1   Patterns of Intergroup Relations: A Continuum

Tutsis in Rwanda. One of the most horrifying aspects of these slaughters is that those who participated were ordinary citizens—whose participation was facilitated by labels that singled out the victims as enemies worthy of death.

Labels are powerful forces in human life. Labels that dehumanize others help people to **compartmentalize**—to separate their acts from feelings that would threaten their self-concept and make it difficult for them to participate in killing (Bernard, Ottenberg, & Redl, 1971; Markusen, 1995). Thus, *genocide is facilitated by labelling the targeted group as less than fully human.*

Population Transfer

Population transfer can be indirect and direct. *Indirect* population transfer is achieved by making life so unbearable for members of a minority group that they leave "voluntarily." Under bitter conditions in czarist Russia, for example, millions of Jews made this "choice." *Direct* transfer takes place when a minority is expelled. Examples include the relocation of Native Canadians to reserves and the transfer of Canadians of Japanese descent to relocation camps during World War II.

Internal Colonialism

The term *colonialism* refers to the exploitation of the world's least-industrialized nations by the most-industrialized nations. Conflict theorists use the term **internal colonialism** to refer to a dominant group's exploitation of minority groups. The "routine" form is to use existing social institutions to deny minorities access to the full benefits of a society. The system of reserves for Canada's Native peoples is an example of internal colonialism.

Segregation

Segregation—the formal separation of racial or ethnic groups—accompanies internal colonialism. Segregation

allows a dominant group to exploit the labour of the minority (butlers, chauffeurs, housekeepers, nannies, street cleaners) while maintaining social distance (P.H. Collins, 1986). In the southern United States until the 1960s, by law African-Americans and whites had to use separate public facilities such as hotels, schools, swimming pools, bathrooms, and even drinking fountains. In 38 states, laws prohibited interracial marriage. Violators could be sentenced to one to five years in prison (Mahoney & Kooistra, 1995). The legal structure also upheld residential segregation (Massey & Denton, 1993).

Assimilation

Assimilation is the process by which a minority is absorbed into the mainstream culture. There are two types. In *forced assimilation,* the dominant group refuses to allow the minority to practise its religion, speak its language, or follow its customs. In Armenia prior to the fall of the Soviet Union, for example, the dominant group, the Russians, required that Armenian schoolchildren be taught in Russian and that Armenians honour Russian rather than Armenian holidays. *Permissible assimilation,* in contrast, permits the minority to adopt the dominant group's patterns in its own way and at its own speed. In Brazil, for example, an ideology favouring the eventual blending of diverse racial types into a "Brazilian stock" encourages its racial and ethnic groups to intermarry.

Multiculturalism (Pluralism)

A policy of **multiculturalism**, also called **pluralism**, permits and even encourages racial and ethnic variation. Switzerland provides an outstanding example of multiculturalism. The Swiss are made up of four separate groups—French, Italian, German, and Romansh—who have kept their own languages and live peacefully in political and economic unity. Multiculturalism has been so successful that none of

Amid fears that Japanese Canadians were "enemy aliens" who would sabotage industrial and military installations along the Canadian and American west coast, the property of Japanese Canadians in British Columbia in the early days of World War II was confiscated and the people were transferred to "relocation camps" in other provinces, including small towns in Quebec such as Farnham.

these groups can properly be called a minority. Table 8.4 (page 188) details Canada's initiatives to promote muliticulturalism.

Focus Question
What is the difference between multiculturalism and assimilation?

THE MAJOR CLASSIFICATIONS IN CANADA

Canadians can be classified into three categories: Native peoples, including status Indians, non-status Indians, Métis, and Inuit; the two "charter groups," the French and English white settlers whose historical relations span over 400 years; and other immigrants from all over the world who entered and settled in Canada over the course of the past 100 years or so.

Native Peoples

Native peoples comprise a small but extremely disparate constituency. Roughly 4 percent of Canada's population, or 1 319 980 people, reported in the 2001 census that they had Aboriginal ancestry. Native Canadians encompass a rich diversity of customs, languages, and cultural differences that stretch back to pre-European contact (Frideres & Gadacz, 2001). However, not many of them share or have shared in Canada's development. There are wide differences in access to social, health, and education programs and in levels of development for Native Canadians both on and off the reserve system.

For this and other reasons, Native Canadians did not consent to the patriation of the Canadian constitution (the *British North America Act*) and even sent a delegation to London, England, to lobby British parliament not to pass the *Canada Act*.

The federal government has made efforts to gain Native Canadians' support for the *Charter of Rights and Freedoms* by making provision for their self-government. On April 1,

1999, the territory of Nunavut was created. It is the largest land claim settlement in Canadian history. Nunavut means "Our Land" in the Inuktitut language, and the territory is nearly one-fifth the size of Canada.

Status or registered Indians have the highest profile in Canada. According to the 2001 census, there are 558 180 registered Indians. To be considered a member of this category, a person must (1) be admitted to a general registry in Ottawa; (2) be affiliated with one of the 622 bands; (3) be granted the entitlement to reside on band reserve lands; and (4) come under the legal jurisdiction of the *Indian Act* passed in 1876 (see Chapter 3, Table 3.3, p. 58).

Approximately half of status or registered Indians (49 percent in 2001) live on reserves created by one of the 61 treaties signed with the British Crown. The federal government allocates approximately $5 billion a year to this group. However, only a small percentage of this sum, roughly 5 percent, is directed to the economic development of Native reserves. The bulk of the money is monopolized by administrative costs to run Indian and Northern Affairs Canada (or INAC for short) and social spending.

The interests of status Indians are today represented by 633 chiefs, who make up the Assembly of First Nations; however, not all bands are members, nor are the Métis.

Part 2 of the *Constitution Act, 1982* recognizes Native Indians, Inuit, and Métis. Inuit are Native people whose ancestral home is the Arctic, while Métis are the children of Native and non-Native parents. The Charter entrenches "existing aboriginal and treaty rights" (see Ponting, 1986, p. 302). Nevertheless, the use of the term "existing" remains unsatisfactory to Native groups, because many of their land claims are not recognized by provincial governments. For example, only recently (since 2001) did the government of British Columbia enter into agreements with its First Nations peoples through an initiative called New Era.

Despite much-publicized conflicts with Natives, such as those related to the James Bay project and the "Oka Crisis" (1990), Quebec has a better record, in some respects, than the rest of Canada when it comes to its dealings with Native

Multiculturalism (or pluralism) permits, and even encourages, racial and ethnic variation—in Canada, this allows minority groups to maintain their separate identities but also participate in the country's social institutions.

peoples. Evidence can be found in the favourable rate of Native language retention, the levels of prosperity of Native peoples resident in Quebec compared to other provinces, and lower rates of imprisonment.

The Two Charter Groups

In John Porter's *The Vertical Mosaic* (1965), the term *charter groups* was used to characterize the two linguistic and culturally distinct white settler groups in Canada, the French and the British. This term gained ready use among academics and policymakers. The history of the two charter groups began with the French colonization of North America in 1534, when Jacques Cartier led the first of three voyages of exploration into the St. Lawrence River region. By the beginning of the eighteenth century, the French colony stretched from Hudson Bay to New Orleans. The 13 British Atlantic colonies, later to become the United States of America, were encircled by the French. However, the nucleus of the French Empire in North America was centred along the St. Lawrence and stretched from Montreal to Quebec City, with Louisburg as the military beachhead on Cape Breton.

The population of "New France" never exceeded 65 000. The colony depended on trade in fur, a luxury item used in the making of fashionable clothing for the aristocracy of Europe. Neither agriculture nor industry of any significant kind was developed in New France. Therefore, resources—both material and human—were stretched extremely thin to maintain the presence of the French Empire in North America. War with the British Atlantic colonies was inevitable given the need to expand westward to support a growing and prospering colony. The British succeeded

militarily in expelling the French colonial government from North America in 1763 with the Peace of Paris.

North America was now under British control. American colonists had been known to grumble for more autonomy from their British overlords before 1763, but they had to worry about the French knocking at their door. Now that the French colonial government was gone, renewed interest in political sovereignty quickly gained momentum. The British government, realizing they might lose everything if they lost a war with their American colonists, passed the *Quebec Act of 1774*. This Act extended extraordinary rights to the newly conquered French Catholic colonists to keep them on side in any conflict with their American counterparts. Among these non-assimilationist rights were the right to keep the French civil law and practise Catholicism. The strategy worked; the Americans tried but were unsuccessful in gaining support from the French colonists along the St. Lawrence. The Americans won their war of independence from the British however. Unlike the French government, the British were able to keep the northern tier in their hands.

The nineteenth century was a period of rapid growth in British immigration to its North American colony and the natural expansion of Catholic Quebec. The hundred years leading up to Confederation and beyond witnessed the development of the two charter groups. Each controlled its own institutional elites—the British presided over commerce and the French Catholics controlled the professions (lawyers, doctors, and clergy) and farming. This unequal distribution of economic power between the two charter groups was meant to be balanced by political accommodation, especially at the federal level.

The harm that befalls some communities does not necessarily stem from sinister conspiracies. Even the best intentions can lead to suffering and death. The coerced relocation of Native Canadians from one community to another provides an example of how "helping" can sometimes dissolve into "hurting." It also gives us the opportunity to reconsider who is the guilty party in the so-called "Indian problem."

Native Canadians have been afflicted by about 100 forced removals since Confederation. Consider the case of the Inuit. In 1953, southern Canadian bureaucrats dispatched 10 ill-equipped Inuit families, mostly from Quebec, to a life of northern hardship in a bleak and inhospitable environment. The 85 Inuit were identified by dog tags, kept in cargo holds like livestock throughout the 2000-kilometre trip, separated from their families, abandoned to confront harsh Arctic conditions, left in near-starvation conditions for many years, and discouraged from returning home. The fact that these Inuit had little say in what was happening reflected a callous and arrogant indifference at odds with Canada's increasingly vaunted reputation on the global stage.

The rationale given by the federal government included political expediency, cost-cutting, and human compassion—all justified within the framework of "national interests." Within the federal bureaucracy, the resettlement was viewed as an "experiment" to determine whether the Inuit had gone "soft" or could survive when reunited with a wilderness environment. The government saw Inuit settlements as a bulwark in defence of a de facto sovereignty over the northernmost limits of Canada—not an inconsequential challenge given U.S. strategic interests in the northern Arctic when only 140 permanently settled Canadians provided evidence of Canada's sovereignty in the region.

The relocation was also viewed as a way of paring government costs. The solution lay in providing an environment where the Inuit could once again become self-sufficient through resumption of traditional living patterns. However, relief costs were largely underwritten by the Inuit families themselves. Tragically, these Inuit were forced to subsidize their own victimization; they were charged exorbitant prices for necessities but offered reduced payments for the fur pelts they brought to government supply stores. Old colonial practices of exploitation are hard to break.

The injustice of the relocation is rarely disputed. The Inuit were little more than pawns in a Canadian society-building experiment. The lack of cultural sensitivity to a people who were deeply attached to their homeland contributed to the sorry outcome. They were powerless to resist—a powerlessness that continues to plague many Native communities. While Prime Minister Stephen Harper apologized to Canada's Native peoples in June 2008 for residential schools, the government's refusal to issue an apology or a measure of redress commensurate with the gravity of the 'white collar' crime of relocation is unjust.

Source: Adapted from Fleras & Elliott (1996, pp. 218–219).

As Hubert Guindon (1964, 1968, 1978, 2001) observed, this accommodation "worked" as long as there was room for the French Catholics of Quebec to grow. The late nineteenth and early twentieth century was a time of exploding population in rural Quebec. The province had the highest birth rate in the country. When arable land became scarce in Quebec by the late nineteenth century, and when the vacant Prairie provinces were closed off to emigration, discontent incubated (see the Down-to-Earth Sociology box "The Legacy of Louis Riel"). The solution to the social and political problem of "too many people and not enough arable land" was the industrialization of rural Quebec (see also Hughes, 1943).

Industrialization was welcomed by the people and clergy of Quebec. Most residents were employed and Quebec's Catholic clergy had parishioners. However, all was not well, especially after World War II. Quebec's government had not kept up with the changing times, and a small group of rogue intellectuals—Pierre Elliott Trudeau, Jean Marchand, and Gerald Pelletier—took on the Quebec government of Maurice Duplessis in a journal called *Cité Libre* ("free city"). Duplessis was accused of corruption and anti-democratic politics. The Catholic Church was also singled out for its authoritarian character and support of the Nazis. Quebec, it was argued, had been shackled by the old elites; it was time to modernize her and bring her into the twentieth century as a free, democratic, and secular province.

The death of Maurice Duplessis and his replacement by Paul Sauvé (not Jean Lesage, as Guindon rightly notes) began what became known as the Quiet Revolution in Quebec. It was not and has not been quiet, nor was it much of a revolution. Its goal was the secularization of Quebec society. Where the Catholic Church had once controlled and staffed social welfare, education, and hospitals, the provincial government took over. The provincial government had access to the resources to affect massive changes in these three areas, and did so by creating jobs in the public sector of the economy. Taking over the hydroelectric power plants in the province by the mid-1960s was tantamount to catching up to Ontario, which had nationalized its hydroelectric power facilities half a century earlier.

Focus Question
Can you describe Canada's two charter groups?

At the beginning of the twentieth century, industrialization in rural Quebec had eased the demographic pressure brought on large family farms by keeping sons and daughters in the province. The post-Duplessis era set the agenda for the secularization of Quebec (the Quiet Revolution) by providing good jobs in the public sector. What was the fate of the private sector? That preserve was to be left largely to the English-speaking population of the province, who had enjoyed its privileges for over a hundred years. Some Quebecois thought otherwise, and the not-so-quiet politics of language in Quebec has been the result.

DOWN-TO-EARTH SOCIOLOGY
The Legacy of Louis Riel

The French Canadians who supported Confederation expected to establish many new communities on the Prairies. This was a realistic vision: the first European explorers on the great plains had been French, and their numbers increased with the fur trade. French Canadians and Cree natives intermarried, and their offspring were called Métis, who formed a distinctive community with their own language, Michef. French-Canadian missionaries converted the region's Native population to Catholicism.

French Canadians and Métis comprised the majority of the population when the Prairies entered Confederation through the purchase of the territory from the Hudson's Bay Company.

The first major crisis after Confederation came when the French-Canadian Catholics of the plains protested that they had not been properly consulted regarding the Hudson's Bay Company purchase. The resulting conflict was the Red River Rebellion, the insistence by the residents Red River on negotiating their entry into Confederation. They were successful. A new province was created by the Manitoba Act (1870), and the French-Canadian majority was guaranteed the right to their own school system.

There was a major difference, however, between the liberal spirit of the Manitoba Act and the administration of the new province during its first years. Canadian militia in the province terrorized the French-Canadian leaders, prompting many of them to leave before their land claims could be resolved. However, between 1876 and 1881, over 40 000 immigrants, mainly Ontario British, moved to Manitoba, lured by the prospect of profitable wheat farming. Some leaders, notably Louis Riel, moved to the United States. Most Métis left for present-day Saskatchewan. There, the Second Red River Rebellion, or "Riel Rebellion," broke out in 1885 over a concern about the lack of legal protection for French lands and schools. The rebellion was crushed by 5000 militia. Though Riel was a hero in French Canada, he was vilified in Ontario and executed, despite an appeal for clemency by Queen Victoria. Because the French Canadians were clearly upset about their treatment in the West, their migration to the Prairies slowed to a trickle. Instead, they moved north, to "New Quebec," a region inhabited largely by Native peoples.

When Keewatin, part of the Northwest Territories, was transferred to Manitoba in the latter part of the nineteenth century, no protections were

extended for its French Canadians residents. Public opinion about the matter in Quebec was outrage. By way of appeasement, Ungava, a large territory that today comprises the northern section of the province—and the site of the massive James Bay Hydro-Electric Project—was transferred to Quebec.

Métis leader Louis Riel, who led the Second Red River Rebellion in 1885 over a concern about the protection of French lands and schools on the Prairies.

Source: Adapted from Metta Spencer (1996, p. 379).

The position of Canada's ethnic or multicultural minorities is based on their standing as immigrants or descendants of immigrants. Their interests, therefore, centre more on equality than on political demands.

The chosen few from the English charter group, according to John Porter (1965), kept their status as the pre-eminent economic leaders of the country for several generations. Just as often, though, other members from the English charter group could be found in the country's political and media elites, the upper echelons of the Protestant clergy, and even in the trade union elites. Canada was, in Porter's phrase, a "vertical mosaic"—a pyramid in which the apex was composed of one dominant charter group: the English. A select few from the French charter group constituted a subordinate political elite located mostly, but not exclusively, in the province of Quebec. Even as late as the mid-1960s, immigrant minorities had barely touched any significant levers of power or authority in Canada.

However, Porter believed that once Canada expanded and opened its postsecondary educational institutions to all who qualified, more opportunities would become available to a greater number of Canadians. Moreover, he felt that education would help break down the secrecy and exclusivity of Canada's elites and bring about a more democratic society. The economic benefits of modernization and development could be shared among all Canadians: Natives, both charter group members, and new immigrants.

Unfortunately, according to Wallace Clement (1975, 1977), a student of Porter who updated his mentor's work, the economic elite has grown more insular and exclusive. While the Canadian economy has expanded since Porter's day, Clement, and now others, see a greater integration of Canada's economic elite with powerful economic interests south of the border. And while many Canadians have benefited from the expanding economy and many others have access to postsecondary education, not all Canadians share in these benefits (an exception is our publicly funded health care system, in which we all share equally).

The Other Ethnic Groups in Canada

Canada's ethnic or multicultural minorities occupy a uniquely different status than either the Native peoples or the two charter groups. Their situation in Canada is based on their standing as immigrants or descendants of immigrants. Their interests, therefore, centre on equality instead of the more political demands made by the other groups.

That said, Canada embraces a rich diversity of immigrants and refugees from different parts of the world. At Confederation, barely 8 percent of Canada's population was not British or French. Today, the majority of Canadians have neither British nor French ancestry.

Table 8.1 is based on the 2001 census and provides a breakdown of selected characteristics of eight principal ethnic groups in Canada. All groups are compared with the Canadian average. With the exception of Canada's Native peoples and Jamaicans, all groups reported higher levels of university qualifications than the national average, with Jews reporting the highest at almost 40 percent compared with the national average of 12 percent. Americans and Jews stand out as having the highest average full-time incomes, while Native Canadians and Jamaicans report the lowest incomes. Interestingly, of those respondents who had less than a high school education, Jamaicans reported lower incomes than the national average, but of those with trade certificates, Jamaicans reported higher incomes than the national average. This discrepancy between educational qualifications and income could be due to the more recent immigration of

TABLE 8.1 Ethnic Composition of Canada with Selected Ethnic Groups and Characteristics, 2001

Ethnic Category/Selected Characteristics	Canadian	English	French	Italian	East Indian	Jewish	American	Jamaican	Native/ Aboriginal
Average Full-Time Income	$44 286	$47 698	$42 220	$46 314	$40 622	$73 928	$72 243	$35 505	$30 527
Less than High School Diploma	33.4%*	27.3%	29.7%	35.2%	28.4%	18.1%	22.3%	28.8%	55.2%
University Degree	11.9%*	16.7%	14.9%	14.6%	26%	39.4%	23.9%	9.9%	3.1%
Trades Certificate	11.2%*	10.9%	11.1%	9.8%	6.6%	5.1%	9.6%	11.4%	11.3%
$60 000 and over	8.8%	12.4%	9.5%	11.3%	8.5%	22%	13.4%	6.5%	4.6%
Unemployment Rate	7.7%	6.5%	7.8%	5.4%	8.6%	6%	6.4%	8.6%	24.6%

* Percentages derived from Canadians 15 years and older.

Source: Data derived from Statistics Canada, 2001, *2001 Census*, Catalogue no. 97F0010XCB2001041.

Jamaicans to Canada. Notwithstanding the incredible statistics for Americans and Jews (both groups are small in number compared to the English), the English remain a privileged category in Canada with higher-than-average incomes (over $60 000 on average per year), university degrees, and lower-than-average unemployment rates.

Table 8.2 draws data from the 2001 and 2006 censuses. Canada's population grew by over 1.6 million people to a total of 31 241 030. Of this number, over two-thirds are visible minorities, with Ontario, British Columbia, Quebec, and Alberta reporting the lion's share of the increase. The only province that reported a negative increase for any of the three major visible minorities was Nova Scotia, which reported a decrease in the number of Blacks.

Table 8.3 shows data from the 2006 census of reported ethnic origins for the three major metropolitan areas in Canada: Montreal, Toronto, and Vancouver. Not surprising, Montreal reported the largest number of respondents stating "Canadian" and "Quebecois," evidence that language and politics remain salient. Vancouver and Toronto are important cities for those reporting Chinese and East Indian origins, while Montreal and Vancouver report relatively large Native populations. All three major cities report significant numbers who state English, Scottish, and Irish origins, while Montreal is the only city with a large French origin population. While there is evidence for the increasing ethnic diversity of Canada's three major cities, the two "charter groups" remain numerically significant.

According to Metta Spencer (1996), the actual economic experience of moving to and living in Canada has fallen far short of the expectations of many immigrants. The hope of a better life took longer than expected for most or failed to materialize at all. Faced with unemployment and discrimination, up to 20 percent of some groups, says Spencer, have returned to their native countries. She goes on to say that while British and American immigrants do well in Canada, others are apt to be less successful.

Canada needs immigration to continue benefiting from our renewed prosperity. It is no secret that our population is aging and our fertility rate is too low to keep the population at its present level. Any remaining barriers to jobs based on racial or ethnic discrimination must be eradicated. The past is littered with examples of discrimination against immigrants. At first, the Irish or French were likely taking jobs away from "Canadians," then it was the Italians or Jews, and now it is Asians or Africans or Caribbeans—all myths with terrible consequences for those who have to bear the brunt of such prejudices. Far from taking employment away from Canadians, immigrants create more jobs than they fill (Dirks, 1995). While it is no easy task, it is time that we recognize that we are all "immigrants" in one way or another, and the sooner we get over our hang-ups about our fellow Canadian residents, the better our society and ourselves will be for it.

LOOKING TOWARD THE FUTURE

Canadians will face two major issues as we progress through the twenty-first century. The first is a persistent demand for the increased political autonomy, if not outright independence, of Quebec from Canada. Second, we will encounter

TABLE 8.2 The Changing Ethnic Composition of Canada, Provinces and Territories, Visible Minorities 2001–2006

Province, Territory, Canada	Total Population 2006	Total Population 2001	Total Population Change, Visible Minority	Total Population Change, Chinese	Total Population Change, Black	Total Population Change, South Asian*
Newfoundland & Labrador	500 605	506 075	1870 +49%	404 +44%	60 +7%	585 +58%
PEI	134 205	133 385	650 +55%	45 +22%	270 +73%	nil
Nova Scotia	903 090	897 565	3155 +9%	1010 +31%	-440 -2%	915 +31%
New Brunswick	719 650	719 710	3920 +42%	920 +60%	610 +16%	545 +38%
Quebec	7 435 905	7 125 580	156 380 +31%	23 000 +41%	35 875 +24%	13 340 +22%
Ontario	12 028 895	11 285 550	592 160 +28%	95 475 +20%	62 675 +15%	239 300 +43%
Manitoba	1 113 519	1 103 700	21 980 +25%	1775 +15%	2840 +22%	3680 +28%
Saskatchewan	953 845	963 150	6320 +23%	1420 +18%	925 +22%	1040 +25%
Alberta	3 256 355	2 941 150	124 275 +38%	21 175 +21%	15 685 +50%	34 300 +49%
British Columbia	4 074 385	3 868 875	174 410 +21%	41 735 +11%	2850 +11%	52 000 +25%
Yukon	30 195	28 520	200 +20%	100 +44%	nil	nil
Northwest Territories	41 060	37 100	725 +47%	65 +25%	nil	nil
Nunavut	29 325	26 665	210 +100%	40 +100%	nil	nil
Canada	31 241 030	29 639 030	1 084 245 +27%	187 175 +18%	121 580 +18%	345 795 +38%

* Pakistani, East Indian, or Sri Lankan, for example.

Source: Statistics Canada, 2007, Visible minority groups, 2006 counts for Canada, provinces and territories—20% sample data. Ethnocultural portrait of Canada Highlight 2006 Census, cat no. 97-562-XWE2006002, Ottawa, released April 2, 2008.

new challenges of racial and ethnic diversity due to the immigration of people, including refugees, from less-developed nations. Clearly, there will be increased racial and ethnic diversity and tension, especially in the three major cities of Toronto, Montreal, and Vancouver. And for all intents and purposes, it is already here. Neither issue will be easy to resolve.

What we do about these issues depends on our vision of and for Canadian society. If we seek a tolerant, progressive, and pluralistic society, we can achieve one where Native peoples, the two charter groups, and a racially and ethnically diverse population coexist in harmony. We will be the envy of the world and a model for others to follow.

TABLE 8.3 Top Ethnic Origins Reported for Montreal, Toronto, and Vancouver

Ethnic Origin	Montreal	Toronto	Vancouver
Canadian	1 670 655	651 635	278 360
English	148 095	804 100	464 340
French	936 990	241 395	137 270
Irish	216 410	531 865	251 695
Scottish	119 365	561 050	337 225
Chinese	82 665	537 060	402 000
Italian	85 785	466 155	76 345
Quebecois*	72 445	———	———
German	———**	259 015	203 720
Jewish	68 485	141 685	———**
East Indian	39 305	484 655	181 895
North American Indian	74 565	———**	43 190
TOTAL	3 588 520	5 072 075	2 097 965

* Reported for Montreal only.
** Not among the top 25 reported.

Source: Statistics Canada, 2007, Ethnic origins. 2006 counts for census metropolitan areas and census agglomerations—20% sample data. Ethnocultural portrait of Canada Highlight 2006 Census, cat no. 97-562-XWE2006002, Ottawa, accessed April 28, 2008.

TABLE 8.4 Language and Culture in Canada: Some Important Dates

Federal Initiatives on Language and Culture	Date
Canadian Bill of Rights	1960
Royal Commission on Bilingualism and Biculturalism	1963
Official Languages Act	1969
Promotion of multiculturalism as a national policy (Canada becomes the first country in the world to promote multiculturalism)	1971
Canadian *Human Rights Act*	1977
Canadian Charter of Rights and Freedoms	1982
Multiculturalism Act	1988
Department of Canadian Heritage includes a Secretary of State for Multiculturalism and the Status of Women portfolio	1993
Establishment of the Canadian Race Relations Foundation	1996

Most Canadians do not realize that our citizenship is a relatively new achievement. As late as 1946, Canadians were considered British subjects residing in Canada, not Canadian citizens.

It was not until 1947, with the passage of the first *Citizenship Act*, that the idea of a distinctly Canadian citizenship was introduced. The year 1997 saw the fiftieth anniversary of this step toward true nationhood for Canada.

The *Citizenship Act* came into being largely due to the efforts of Paul Martin, Sr., father of the former prime minister of Canada. It has been said that while visiting a military cemetery in France just after World War II, Paul Martin, Sr. was visibly shaken by the rows and rows of wooden crosses marking the graves of Canadians who had given their lives in the service of their country and for the peace and freedom that everyone now enjoys.

Martin was impressed by the various ethnic and religious backgrounds of the names on the graves. Despite their differences, these soldiers had come together in a struggle against the Nazi dictatorship and fascism and had died for what they believed in. When Martin returned to Canada, he set wheels in motion that led to the establishment of the *Citizenship Act* as a tribute to their memory. On January 1, 1947, Canada took a bold step toward independence when the *Citizenship Act* came into being, and in so doing established a separate Canadian identity, new rights for Canadian women, and our own Canadian passport.

Source: Adapted from Citizenship and Immigration Canada website.

SUMMARY AND REVIEW

Laying the Sociological Foundation

HOW IS RACE BOTH A REALITY AND A MYTH?
In the sense that different groups inherit distinctive physical characteristics, race is a reality. In the sense of one race being superior to another and the idea that there are "pure races," however, race is a myth. The *idea* of race is powerful, shaping basic relationships among people. p. 174.

HOW DO RACE AND ETHNICITY DIFFER?
Race refers to supposed biological characteristics; **ethnicity**, to cultural ones. Ethnic groups identify with one another on the basis of common ancestry and cultural heritage. pp. 174–175.

WHAT ARE MINORITY AND DOMINANT GROUPS?
Minority groups are people singled out for unequal treatment by members of the **dominant group** in society, the group with more power, privilege, and social status. Minorities originate with the expansion of political boundaries or migration. pp. 175–176.

WHY ARE WOMEN A MINORITY?
Women are a minority because they have been singled out for unequal treatment and many regard themselves as objects of collective discrimination. p. 175.

ARE PREJUDICE AND DISCRIMINATION THE SAME THING?
Prejudice is an attitude; **discrimination** is an act. Some people who are prejudiced do not discriminate, while others who are not prejudiced do. p. 176.

HOW DO INDIVIDUAL AND INSTITUTIONAL DISCRIMINATION DIFFER?
Individual discrimination is the negative treatment of one person by another, while **institutional discrimination** is discrimination built into a society's social institutions. Institutional discrimination often occurs without the awareness of either the perpetrator or the object of the discrimination. p. 177.

Theories of Prejudice

HOW DO PSYCHOLOGISTS EXPLAIN PREJUDICE?
Psychological theories of prejudice stress frustration displayed toward **scapegoats** and **authoritarian personalities**. p. 177.

HOW DO SOCIOLOGISTS EXPLAIN PREJUDICE?
Sociological theories focus on how different social environments increase or decrease prejudice. Functionalists stress the benefits and costs that come from discrimination. Conflict theorists look at how groups in power exploit racial and ethnic divisions to hold down wages and otherwise maintain power. Symbolic interactionists stress that labels create **selective perception** and self-fulfilling prophecies. Multiracial feminists argue that white men *and women* oppress lower-class women and men of disadvantaged races and ethnicities. Postmodernists argue that only those who directly experience racism and discrimination can understand it. Postcolonial theorists seek to understand the ways in which the colonial legacy of racism persists in

so-called postcolonial societies. Critical race theorists hold that racial inequalities in housing, the legal system, employment, and the educational system in developed nations persist over time. pp. 177–179.

Global Patterns of Intergroup Relations

WHAT ARE THE MAJOR PATTERNS OF MINORITY AND DOMINANT GROUP RELATIONS?
Beginning with the least humane, they are: **genocide**, **population transfer**, **internal colonialism**, **segregation**, **assimilation**, and **multiculturalism (pluralism)**. pp. 179–181.

The Major Classifications In Canada

WHAT ARE THE MAJOR ETHNIC GROUPS IN CANADA?
The major classifications of ethnic groups in Canada are Native peoples, the two charter groups, and other ethnic groups in Canada. p. 181.

WHY DON'T ALL NATIVE PEOPLES IN CANADA SUPPORT THE *CHARTER OF RIGHTS AND FREEDOMS*?
The use of the term "existing aboriginal and treaty rights" remains unsatisfactory to many Natives because many land claims are not recognized by some provincial governments. pp. 181–182.

WHAT WAS THE "QUIET REVOLUTION" IN QUEBEC?
Rural industrialization and secularization of religious institutions around health, education, and welfare. pp. 182–185.

ARE ALL IMMIGRANTS IN CANADA HAPPY THEY CAME TO THIS COUNTRY?
According to Metta Spencer, the answer is no. She reports that up to 20 percent of some ethnic groups return to their native countries. pp. 185–186.

Looking toward the Future

WHAT ARE THE MAIN ETHNIC ISSUES FACING CANADA?
More political autonomy for Quebec and the challenge of creating a racially and ethnically diverse country. pp. 186–189.

TALKING ABOUT THEORY

Theoretical Paradigms

	CLASSICAL PARADIGMS			RECENT PARADIGMS			
	Structural-Functional Paradigm	Social-Conflict Paradigm	Symbolic-Interaction Paradigm	Feminist Paradigm	Postmodernist Paradigm	Postcolonial Paradigm	Critical Race Paradigm
What is the level of analysis?	Macro level	Macro level	Micro level	Macro level	Micro level	Macro level	Micro level
What is the social significance of the inequalities of race & ethnicity?	Prejudice creates in-group solidarity (inclusive = functional); it also destroys wider community social relationships (exclusive = dysfunctional)	Reduces worker solidarity by exploiting racial and ethnic rivalry; for example, the dual or split labour market.	Labels create selective perception; for example, the self-fulfilling prophecy.	White men and women oppress lower-class women and men of disadvantaged races and ethnicities.	Hear only the "voices" of those who have experienced racism and discrimination.	The persistence of the colonial legacy of racism in postcolonial societies; homosexuality viewed as a white European "disease;" patriarchy and misogyny are indigenous characteristics.	Racism is a fact of life; meritocracy, colour-blindness, objectivity, and neutrality are questionable.
Have the inequalities of race and ethnicity changed over time? How?	No/Yes. Without changing social environments, it is difficult to affect prejudice toward minority groups.	No. Capitalist societies need a reserve army of labour.	Yes. Education and changing social environments.	No/Yes. The complexities of understanding the nature of the oppression of men and women of colour.	N/A	Yes. Confronting the nature of the colonizer's culture, especially language and rules of property and governance.	No/Yes. Racism exists but there is a struggle to make legal changes to discrimination in housing, employment, and so on.

KEY TERMS

assimilation   180
authoritarian
    personality   177
compartmentalize   180
discrimination   176
dominant group   175
dual labour market   178

ethnic (and ethnicity)   174
ethnic work   175
genocide   173
individual
    discrimination   177
institutional
    discrimination   177

internal colonialism   180
minority group   175
multiculturalism (also
    called pluralism)   180
population transfer   180
postcolonialism   179
prejudice   176

race   174
racism   176
reserve labour force   178
scapegoat   177
segregation   180
selective perception   178

WEBLINKS

All URLs listed are current as of the printing of this book.

University of Toronto: Ethnic, Immigration, and Pluralism Studies
www.utoronto.ca/ethnicstudies

The University of Toronto's Robert F. Harney Professorship program in Ethnic, Immigration, and Pluralism Studies is a seat of research, training, and the dissemination of knowledge in the area of ethnic studies. The links page provides access to useful Canadian and non-Canadian web references.

Centre for Refugee Studies
www.yorku.ca/crs/

The Centre for Refugee Studies is engaged in research on refugee issues. It informs public discussion; participates in policy development and practical innovation by international, governmental, advocacy, and service organizations; and supports teaching in refugee and migration studies.

Hate on the Net
www.sociology.org/content/vol003.002/kallen.html

This 1998 paper by Evelyn Kallen of York University shows that messages promoted on the internet by organized political and religious groups incite hatred and promote harmful action against racial, ethnocultural, religious, and same-sex-oriented minorities. High-tech hate-mongering violates minority members' fundamental right to freedom from group defamation and harassment.

CRITICAL THINKING QUESTIONS

1. Is ethnic or cultural assimilation of immigrants to the dominant culture the only workable public policy for a national society such as in the United States, France, or Canada?

2. Many sociologists assume that a society is held together by the common values and beliefs of its members. What beliefs and values hold Canadian society together today?

3. After you have given some thought to what holds Canada together as a society, consider the ethnic or national forces pulling Canada apart. What solutions might you offer to help minimize cultural and national divisions?

4. Does Aboriginal self-government contribute to nation-building in Canada, or do race-based politics serve to undermine the Canadian state?

Access Research Navigator through MySocLab and use keywords such as "assimilation," "emigration and immigration," "ethnic," "multiculturalism," and "public policy" to locate relevant and recent scholarly and popular press publications to help you answer these questions.

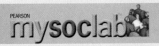

PEARSON mysoclab

Explore the topics covered in this chapter on MySocLab using the access information provided with this text. Interactive resources for studying include multimedia tutorials, video clips, practice tests, quizzes, and animated maps and figures.

Inequalities of Age

9

LEARNING OUTCOMES

After you have studied this chapter, you will be able to answer the following questions:

1. Is aging a global crisis?

2. What does the term "greying of Canada" mean?

3. What factors influence perceptions of aging?

4. How does aging affect men and women differently?

5. Is there conflict among different age groups?

6. What are some of the problems faced by the elderly today?

"I am at the same age my mother was when she was dying of cancer . . . it makes me want to go twice as hard. Because, who knows, I might find myself with cancer a couple of years from now. The paradox being that if I push myself, there is a greater likelihood that I could get cancer. So the challenge to me is how to move forward or create a balance. And, the huge issue for me right now is balance. How do I begin to achieve a balance? How do I begin to care for myself and still continue to do the work I do? How do I begin to have mercy on myself in order that I can continue over these next 10 to 20 years? I also feel I will have more control as I go into the future. More control will manifest itself as not caring as much. Like, I don't care if I go into debt a little bit now. Like, I cared vehemently about it and held myself back for the last 25 years and now all of a sudden, I don't care about that . . . Now I'm letting go of things that I controlled, in order to engage more in my choices, to engage choice, to look at what I am doing here . . . do I want to do that? . . . which direction do I want to go in?"

These comments from a 53-year-old woman speak to the complexity and contradictions of aging. Loss, fear, and fatalism interweave with feelings of freedom, possibility, and accomplishment. For the first time in history, millions of people are living well into their 70s, and sometimes even their 80s. Their experience with the process of aging and struggles with its contradictions are likely to have a dramatic impact on Canadian society in the coming decades.

Source: Edited interview excerpt from Mandell, N., Wilson, S., & Duffy, A. *Connection, Compromise and Control: CanadianWomen Discuss Midlife.* Toronto: Oxford University Press, 2008.

THE "AGE-QUAKE"

Until the 1970s, aging and the elderly received relatively little attention from Canadian social researchers. Other forms of social inequality—racism, sexism, and classism—were all seen as much more consequential. However, as the post-war baby boomers (Canadians born between 1946 and 1965) surge toward the final chapters of their lives, efforts to examine the social construction of aging in Canada have gained increasing prominence. By 1999, the International Year of Older Persons, the federal government had instituted the National Advisory Council on Aging to advise the federal minister of health; scholars had established the Canadian Association on Gerontology; and almost every university in Canada had created a gerontology or aging studies program. These and various other efforts are providing increased insight into the personal and societal dimensions of aging.

For most of us, aging and old age will become an issue in the course of our personal lives. We will experience important shifts in our fundamental sense of self. Not only will this be necessitated by biological changes—declining physical fitness and increasing disabilities—but also by profound alterations in our social roles. Important elements that were carefully socialized into our identities when we were children and young adults will eventually be pruned away. Our grandparents and parents will die, and we will no longer be grandchildren or sons and daughters. With divorce or widowhood, the maturation of children, and changes or losses in employment identities because of retirement, we will learn to think of ourselves in terms of a dramatically different constellation of relationships and abilities.

For young people reading this text, the intellectual understanding of these changes may seem perfectly clear, but it is difficult to actually enter into the lived experiences of the elderly. In his classic study of racism, *Black Like Me* (1961), John Griffin, a white social researcher, dyed his skin brown and travelled throughout the southern United States in the late 1950s. He sought to truly know the experience of being black and living in a racist society. It would be wonderfully instructive if, for a few hours, young people could similarly immerse themselves in the lives of seniors.

Walking down a street, the senior is often socially invisible. Unlike "attractive" young men and women, the senior fades into the social setting and often passes unnoticed. As reinforced in popular culture, and particularly in the mass media, our culture is not about the elderly, and their images are rarely reflected in movies, television, or magazines. If they do appear, they are often caricatures—the snoopy old woman, the cranky old man. There are, of course, a few notable exceptions—particularly older white men, such as Christopher Plummer, Gordon Pinsent, and Farley Mowat, who remain important cultural figures well past age 65. However, in most instances, cultural images are about the relatively young. Indeed, celebrity women are typically only able to hang on to their status if they maintain a youthful appearance. In the films nominated for Academy Awards in 2005, 2006, and 2007, for example, seniors were almost completely absent from the storylines. An alien visitor might legitimately assume that the elderly are extremely uncommon (and unimportant) in the social landscape or that they have little of significance to communicate about the human condition. In a recent study of animated Disney films, researchers found that although the majority of older characters were portrayed positively, a significant number were depicted in such a way that children might develop negative feelings toward them (Robinson, Callister, Magoffin & Moore, 2007). Older characters, for example, might appear as toothless, feeble, and hunched over, with cracking voices. Older men might be depicted as sinister, conniving villains, while older women often play witches (or witch-like characters) with sagging breasts, unshapely bodies, and unattractive features. A similar portrayal is presented on television, where seniors are either absent as characters, contestants on games shows, or are presented in a negative light (Katz, 2005).

A variety of popular ageist values underlie this tendency to ignore or gloss over seniors. Often, the unstated assumption when interacting with seniors is that they are not intellectually sharp, not up to date, incapable of learning new skills, unambitious and unfocused, and simply not worthy of attention. In a society in which attention is dispensed based on social power and position, the lack of attention shown to seniors speaks volumes.

Examining the way we, as a society, socially construct aging is not only important for one's own future life course and for a full understanding of social inequalities in Canada, it is key to any formulations about our future evolution. Throughout the world's industrialized nations, the population bubble that appeared after World War II has matured into senior citizenry. The result is a historically unparalleled transformation in the age structure of industrialized society. The possible outcomes are raising concerns among many analysts.

With industrialization, urbanization, and modernization came a dramatic increase in lifespan and a remarkable swell in the numbers of seniors in the population. The combination of improved sanitation, nutrition, and medical care ensures that Canadians—and the citizens of industrialized countries around the world—have an excellent likelihood of living into their 70s, 80s, or 90s (see Figures 9.1 and 9.2). The demographic effects of industrialization were magnified by World War II. From 1939 to 1945, birthrates dropped as military conflict and the large deployment of soldiers overseas interrupted family patterns. At the end of the war, men and women made up for lost time by marrying and forming families. A period of economic prosperity encouraged couples to have relatively large numbers of children. The net result was the "baby boom"—a dramatic increase in the population generated between 1946 and 1965. Today, the baby boomers range in age from 41 to 60 and, according to the 2006 census, represent nearly a third of the total Canadian population (Statistics Canada, 2007). Today, one in seven Canadians—a record 13.7 percent of the population—is age 65 or over (Statistics

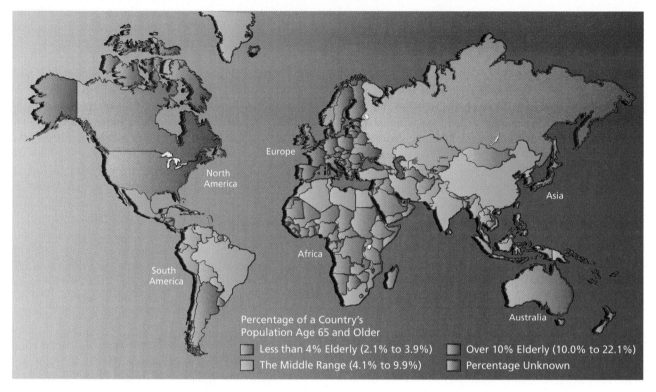

FIGURE 9.1   The Greying of the Globe

Source: By the author. Based on *Statistical Abstract, 2007:* Table 1309.

Canada, 2007a). Figure 9.3 illustrates the steady increase in the number of seniors in Canada over the 50-year period from 1956 to 2006. The post–World War II shift in the age profile of developed countries was so momentous that it is sometimes referred to as an "age-quake."

Since 1965, there has been a decline in the number of children born into a typical family. Improved access to reliable birth control, the advent of the women's movement, the decline in family income, and an increased need for mothers to enter paid employment all contributed to a "baby bust" from 1966 to 1979. There was a brief relief from the yearly decline in births when the baby boomers reached the age of marriage and began to have children between 1980 and 1995. The growth spurt was short-lived, however, and in the years following 1996 there has been a decline in the number of births per year in Canada. Between 2001 and 2006, the population of Canadians under the age of 15 declined by 2.5 percent, while the number of seniors (65 and over) increased by 11.5 percent (Statistics Canada, 2007a). Without the influx of immigrants (approximately 225 000 per year), our total population would be in decline (Statistics Canada, 2007a).

The net result is that the age pyramid that characterizes most traditional societies—many children, fewer adults, and very few elders—has been turned on its head in Canada and most other industrialized nations, and older Canadians increasingly predominate the population. This is reflected in the median age of Canadians—that is, the point at which exactly half of the population is older and the other half is younger. In 1901, the median age in Canada was 22.7; in 1966, it was marginally higher at 25.4 years. According to the census results, the median age in 2006 was 39.5, a number that is expected to increase to 44 by 2031 (Statistics Canada, 2007a).

The shift in Canada toward an older society poses significant issues. Will older citizens who continue to occupy positions in the labour force block the entry and advancement of younger Canadians? With the elimination of mandatory retirement, will today's university and college students find it increasingly difficult to gain a foothold in the economy? Or will older workers increasingly become the victims of ageist discrimination in the workplace—denied the opportunity for training and retraining on the assumption that they are too old to learn (McDaniel, 2002b)? Will older workers continue to be pushed out of the productive arena, expected to take up "volunteer" unpaid work, while pension provisions become increasingly insecure and insufficient?

Will seniors who are disabled or ill become an overwhelming burden for young citizens who are directly or indirectly (through taxation) involved in the provision of care for the elderly? As a nation's elderly population increases, so too does the bill footed by its younger citizens to provide for

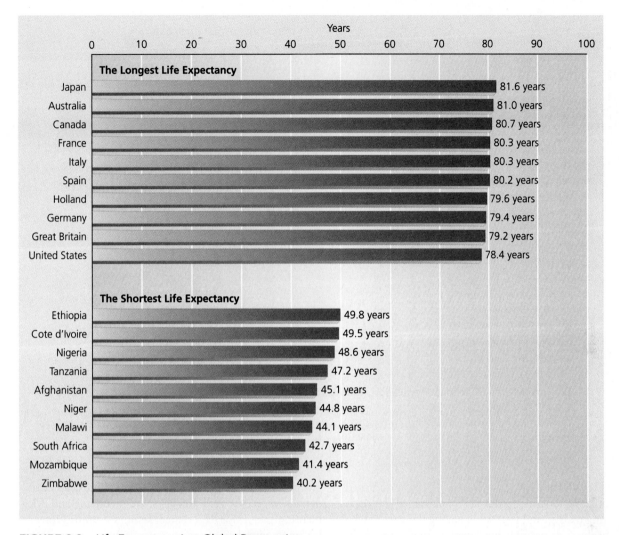

FIGURE 9.2 Life Expectancy in a Global Perspective

Source: By the author. Based on *Statistical Abstract, 2007*: Table 1310.

their needs. In the world's most industrialized countries, this bill has become a major social issue. As shown in Table 9.1, despite Canadians' complaints about taxes, the Canadian rate of taxation to support the elderly is relatively moderate compared to that of some Western European nations. In the least industrialized countries, as occurred in Canada in the past, there are few or no social security taxes, and families are expected to care for their own elderly.

As the senior population continues to grow, and particularly the number of aged seniors (80 years and older), it is likely that debates over other public expenditures, such as health care, will greatly intensify. Over the past five years, the proportion of seniors aged 65 and over increased in every province and territory in Canada, whereas the number of youth aged 15 and under declined (Statistics Canada, 2007a). There are now 1.2 million octogenarians in Canada and the number of centenarians (4635) has

increased by 22 percent since 2001 (Ibid.). These changes raise the question of how scarce resources will be allocated when the interests of seniors conflict with those of the young. For example, should limited research funding be directed toward the diseases of the elderly, such as arthritis and heart disease, or health concerns of the young, such as reproductive technologies? Is a 65-year-old man a less worthy candidate for surgery than a baby born prematurely? Will we be able to provide for the consumption needs of increasing numbers of elderly, many of whom will presumably join the ranks of the retired (Bosworth & Keys, 2004)? Should provisions for euthanasia be established so that seniors suffering from dementia or experiencing negligible quality of life can be afforded the choice to opt for death?

These complex societal issues swirl around the shifting age profile in Canada. Certainly, some commentators predict

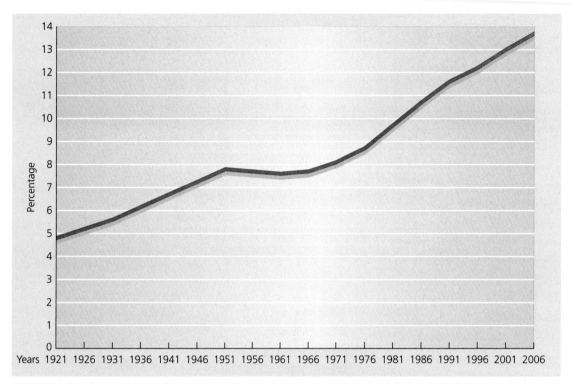

FIGURE 9.3 Proportion of the Canadian Population Aged 65 Years and Over, 1956–2006

Sources: Statistics Canada, 2007a. 2006 Census: Portrait of the Canadian Population, By Age and Sex: National Portrait. July 16, 2007. www12.statcan.ca/english/census06/analysis/agesex/charts/chart2.htm, from Statistics Canada, Censuses of Population, 1956 to 2006. Derived from Statistics Canada, 2002. *Profile of the Canadian Population by Age and Sex: Canada Ages.* Catalogue No. 96F0030XIE2001002.

increased tension and conflict between the young and aged if appropriate action is not taken, and others argue that there is a growing malaise and frustration among the young, who see themselves increasingly burdened by their aging societies. There have been a variety of important developments on age-related matters. As explored later in the chapter, academics, especially gerontologists, are theorizing and documenting the senior experience; seniors' organizations are lobbying governments against age discrimination and for changes in retirement practices and options; individuals are

TABLE 9.1 Payroll Taxes and the Elderly (2003)

Country	Total Population	Percentage Over 65	Percentage of Payroll Paid in Taxes to Support Elderly
France	60 181 000	16.3	39
Germany	82 398 000	17.8	34
Italy	58 103 000	18.8	32
Canada	32 207 000	12.9	24
Japan	126 600 000	18.6	22
United States	290 343 000	12.4	14
Mexico	106 203 000	5.3	13

Source: Derived from *Statistical Abstract of the United States*, 2004–2005 Edition. Tables 1347, 1322, and 1321. Available at www.census.gov/prod/www/statistical-abstract-04.html.

taking claims of age discrimination to court (see Selvin & Goldman, 2007: p. D16); and governments in many industrialized countries are actively exploring ways to maintain old age social security benefits as the first wave of baby boomers reaches retirement age. In a number of societies, seniors and their caregivers are mobilizing in support of a re-examination of the relationship between the state and assisted suicide and demanding the legalization of euthanasia. Most promising, as discussed below, a number of analysts are investigating the possibility of using the broad issue of ageism to rethink the structure and meaning of our lives. Pursued from this perspective, the study of ageism may join racism, sexism, and heterosexism as a core element in social justice campaigns and as a source of fundamental positive social change.

The Greying of Canada

Figure 9.3 documents the dramatic increase in the numbers of seniors (65+) in the Canadian population over the past 50 years. In large measure, this is the result of marked improvements in Canadian **life expectancy**. A hundred years ago, the majority of Canadians would not live to see age 65; by 2041, wholly a quarter of all Canadians will be over that age, according to some projections (Ferguson 2004, p. A4). In fact, analysts project that the population of centenarians may triple by 2031 to over 14 000 (Statistics Canada, 2007a). Indeed, the average Canadian woman born in 1901 could expect to live to age 50, and the average man to age 47. Of course, these figures reflected high mortality rates among infants and children in the early twentieth century. As shown in Table 9.2, a Canadian woman today can expect to live to age 83 and a man to78. Despite illness, accidents, and other factors that may cut life short, the overwhelming majority of Canadians live at least to retirement age. More than 80 percent of men and almost 90 percent of women can expect to live to at least age 65 (Gorrie, 2001; Martel & Belanger, 2000). Further, life expectancy continues to increase, so that every five years Canadians can add about another year to their life expectancy. It is clear that more and more Canadians are living longer lives. What is not clear and has momentous implications is whether the growing population of seniors will be able to participate as productive members of society or whether many—aged seniors, in particular—will continue to experience high rates of disability, frailty, and dependency (Aaron & Harris, 2003).

The term **greying of Canada** has been coined to refer to this increasing proportion of older people in the Canadian population. According to the 2006 census, there are over 4.3 million Canadian seniors, including more than 1.1 million octogenarians, comprising 13.7 percent of the population (Statistics Canada, 2007a). Canadian society has become so "grey" that by 2016 there will be more seniors than

TABLE 9.2 Life Expectancy in a Global Context

High and Low Life Expectancies at Birth by Region, 2005–2010	Women	Men
Africa		
High: Reunion	81	72
Low: Swaziland	39	40
North/Central America		
High: Canada	83	78
Low: Haiti	63	59
South America		
High: Chile	82	75
Low: Guyana	70	64
Asia		
High: China, Hong Kong	85	79
Low: Afghanistan	44	44
Europe		
High: Iceland	83	80
Low: Ukraine	74	62
Oceania		
High: Australia	84	79
Low: Papua New Guinea	60	55

Source: Derived from United Nations, 2007, *Statistics and Indicators on Women and Men*, Table 3a. Life Expectancy. http://unstats.un.org/unsd/demographic/products/indwm/tab3a.htm

children aged 14 and younger (Lu, 2001). And the greying is far from complete: the number of Canadians aged 55 to 64 and nearing retirement has reached a new peak, totalling 3.7 million in 2006 (Statistics Canada, 2007a). Although Canada's life expectancy ranks among the highest in the world (see Table 9.2), other countries, such as Japan and Italy, have surpassed us in terms of the proportion of seniors in their populations (St. Arnaud, Beaudet, & Tully, 2005: p.44). As Canada follows suit in the coming years, seniors will take an increasingly prominent place in our society.

The impact of this aging population has not been felt uniformly across the country. As with so much of Canadian social life, important regional differences exist. Saskatchewan reported the highest proportion of seniors over 65 in 2006 (15.4 percent), while Nunavut reported the lowest (2.7 percent) (Statistics Canada, 2007a). In general, an east-west split exists, with the Atlantic provinces and Quebec having older populations than the Canadian average. As a result of low fertility and outmigration, Atlantic Canada and Quebec are expected to continue to age more rapidly than the rest of the country over the next decade. Higher-than-average fertility rates in the Prairie provinces means those provinces have relatively younger populations. Further, populations of urban areas are generally younger than those of rural areas, since most young rural adults leave their communities for school or work. However, the downtown areas of Canada's largest cities tend to have older populations, while the suburbs are generally younger, as families with young children migrate from downtown cores in search of more affordable and more spacious housing in the suburbs. We can therefore reasonably anticipate that the impact of the aging population—such as increased pressure on the health care system—will be experienced disproportionately throughout the country.

Seniors Organize

As seniors have become a more prominent demographic and economic element in Canadian society, they have predictably established their own support groups and organizations. Some of these efforts are intended to provide assistance and support to seniors in terms of specific issues and concerns, while others provide a more general sense of community and solidarity and advance their interests and perspectives. While interest in current events varies by level of education, overall the majority of seniors (89 percent) report keeping up with news and current affairs on a daily basis, outnumbering their younger counterparts at all educational levels (Turcotte & Schellenberg, 2007: pp. 171–172). A recent study suggests that seniors carry their interest in current events to the ballot box, as they are more likely than younger Canadians to vote regularly. A 2003 survey found that 77 percent of seniors aged 65 to 74—compared to 34 percent of those aged 25 to 34—voted in the last federal, provincial, and municipal elections (Ibid.: p. 180). However, seniors, and particularly those over 75, are less likely than younger Canadians to engage in political activities such as signing petitions, boycotting products for ethical reasons, or taking part in marches or demonstrations (Ibid.). Differences in active political participation between seniors and younger groups, as well as between "older" and "younger" seniors, may simply relate in large part to mobility issues rather than lack of interest.

The first significant step in advancing the interests of seniors was taken in the 1960s when Margaret Kuhn helped establish the Gray Panthers in the United States. This organization played a foundational role in advocating seniors' issues and providing a focus for mobilizing older people around a variety of social concerns. Since that time, a growing number of organizations have flourished in Canada and the United States. In 1973, the Fédération de

l'Âge d'Or du Québec was created, which lobbies the government on seniors' issues, publishes a newspaper, and writes briefs regarding senior concerns. Similarly, Albertans established the Alberta Council of Aging in the 1970s to identify seniors' needs and mobilize senior leaders to act (Novak, 1993).

In the ensuing years, a variety of groups emerged. Grandparents Raising Grandchildren provides support and advocacy for grandparents who become primary caregivers for their grandchildren. Across the country, there are organizations that target elder abuse—the Ontario Network for the Prevention of Elder Abuse, for example—and seek to educate the public and provide support for victims (Community Information Centre of Metropolitan Toronto, 1997).

The ability of Canadian seniors to mobilize quickly and effectively around a social issue was demonstrated in their response to 1985 government efforts to de-index government pensions. Under pressure from the business community to cut government spending and reduce the national debt, Finance Minister Michael Wilson proposed that Old Age Security (OAS) and Guaranteed Income Supplement (GIS) pensions no longer be automatically increased in

CARP (Canada's Association for the Fifty-Plus), in collaboration with the Ontario Human Rights Commission, developed a campaign to combat age discrimination.

response to increases in the cost of living (the Consumer Price Index). Rather, he suggested that pension payments should only be increased when the cost of living rose by more than 3 percent. If the cost of living increased by 5 percent, for example, then pensions would be increased by 2 percent. If it rose by 3 percent, there would be no increase in pension payments. The government predicted that this policy—scheduled to be implemented on January 1, 1986—would save the government $1.6 billion in 1990–91. However, it would effectively reduce the income of all seniors—rich and poor—since they would have to make up any 3 percent increases in living costs.

The response from seniors across the country was immediate and overwhelming. Drawing on traditional methods of protest, seniors and their supporters made pension de-indexation a front-page issue. Petitions were circulated, news conferences held, and politicians confronted. The nation-wide efforts were capped in the summer of 1985 with a massive protest on Parliament Hill. A variety of other social advocacy groups also rallied their support and urged the government not to fight the deficit on the backs of seniors, especially poor seniors. Anti-poverty advocates pointed out that the proposed changes would consign hundreds of thousands of low-income seniors to poverty. In the face of five weeks of protests, the federal government backed down and abandoned the legislation (Novak, 1993).

Subsequent governments have been careful to avoid twisting the lion's tail. Clearly, seniors are able to mobilize effectively and rapidly across the country in response to important issues. Since this time, seniors have become not only more numerous but better organized. The Canadian Association of Retired Persons (CARP, now known as Canada's Association for the Fifty-Plus), with local chapters across Canada, launched a vigorous nationwide campaign against age discrimination. Working with the Ontario Human Rights Commission, the group helped create a province-wide campaign to increase public awareness of ageism and its impact. Its publications communicate that discrimination against older workers is detrimental to business, since older workers are highly productive, have on-the-job experience, and have lower absenteeism and turnover rates than younger workers (Pasternak, 2002). Other initiatives, such as demanding improvements in the health care system and challenging efforts to increase long-term institutional care costs, reflect the dynamism of this and other seniors' organizations. In short, it is clear that Canadian seniors have in place a number of organizations through which they can ensure that their voices are heard and their interests protected.

Not all seniors' organizations are formal or mainstream. The Raging Grannies, founded in 1987 in Victoria, British Columbia, is made up of groups of older women in communities across Canada, the United States, Australia, and the United Kingdom who have lent support to a variety of social justice movements. Dressed as stereotypical "old ladies"—with big hats and frilly dresses—the Raging Grannies sing songs poking fun at governments, prime ministers, and presidents. They have been a visible presence at protests against the U.S. military's invasion of Iraq and the World Trade Organization (Acker & Brightwell, 2004).

Aging: Differences by Gender, Social Class, and Ethnicity

Not everyone in society has an equal chance of becoming old. Prior to 1951, men were more likely than women to reach old age since many women died in childbirth. Once medical care for mothers improved, the average Canadian woman could reasonably expect to live longer than the average male. However, since the late 1970s, men have been catching up in terms of life expectancy as differences in gender mortality narrow. Accordingly, in 1991 there were 72 senior men for every 100 senior women, while in 2001 there were 75 senior men for every 100 senior women. The gender gap has not been

Israeli Arab Mariam Amash recently applied for a new Israeli identity card and claims she was born 120 years ago—a claim that, if confirmed, would make her the oldest person in the world. The Guinness Book of Records currently lists 114-year-old Edna Parker of Shelbyville, Indiana, as holding that title.

eliminated and is certainly evident among the growing numbers of Canadian octogenarians: of the over 1.1 million Canadians aged 80 or over in 2006, about two-thirds were women (Statistics Canada, 2007a). Women's life expectancy is nearly five years longer than men's. Not surprisingly, as a result, women tend to predominate in the ranks of older Canadians. Currently, women comprise 75 percent of Canadians 90 years of age and older and about 52 percent of seniors aged 65 to 69 (Turcotte & Schellenberg, 2007: p. 14). This greater percentage of women, especially among aged seniors, is one of the reasons aging often draws the attention of feminist researchers (discussed in more detail below).

In old age, as in other stages of life, having money improves your prospects for health and longevity. Not surprisingly, research indicates that socioeconomic factors such as income and education are directly related to health. Healthy Canadians over the age of 50 with higher incomes and levels of education are less likely to see their health deteriorate over a two-year period than are those with lower education and income levels (Statistics Canada, 2004a). However, the relationship to social class is complicated. For men (but not women) aged 65 or older, higher levels of education and economic affluence were found to be significantly associated with a decreased likelihood of dying in the period between 1994–95 and 2000–01 (Statistics Canada, 2003d). Clearly, social class—in complex association with gender—deeply colours the aging experience.

Twenty-five years ago, Canada's population of poor seniors was a social embarrassment. More than a third (33.9 percent) of Canadian seniors were living below the Statistics Canada low-income cut-offs in 1980 and many were deeply impoverished. By the end of the twentieth century (thanks in large measure to improved government income support for seniors through Old Age Security, the Guaranteed Income Supplement, and the Canada/Quebec pension plans), those figures have been dramatically reduced. Although improvements have levelled off in recent years, only about one in six Canadians over age 65 was poor and living below the low-income cut-offs in 2006 (Turcotte & Schellenberg, 2007: p. 68).

However, many older people continue to live in poverty or near the poverty line, and the economic well-being of certain groups of seniors is particularly precarious. Currently, almost one in five women over 65 (17.8 percent), in contrast to fewer than one in ten (7.3 percent) men in the same age group, are poor (National Council of Welfare, 2007). Senior women who are divorced or separated figure significantly among the poorest of the poor (Statistics Canada, 2004a). The 45 percent of all women over age 65 who are widowed also fair poorly in economic terms and are likely to slip into long-term low-income status (Statistics Canada, 2004b). In short, gender, social class, and age intersect to put women at an increased risk of impoverishment as they age. Not surprisingly, additional factors such as advanced age, visible minority status, and recent immigration intensify the likelihood that older women will be poor.

Finally, research suggests that ethnic and cultural differences intersect with social class and gender to affect the structure and experience of aging. People living in remote and northern areas of Canada, the majority of whom are Aboriginal, have markedly lower life expectancies than the average Canadian. For example, residents of Region de Nunavik in Quebec have the lowest life expectancy in Canada, at 66.7 years for both males and females. This means that their life course is more in line with individuals living in the Dominican Republic or Egypt than with Canadians living in large urban centres. Of course, the argument here is not that some groups are inherently less healthy. Rather, some ethnic populations (Aboriginals in Canada and African-Americans in the United States) are more likely to be affected by socioeconomic circumstances (high rates of impoverishment and social marginalization)

The socially accepted definition of old age, along with social expectations of seniors' activities, varies around the world. This photo by James Henslin of a 65-year-old bonded labourer in Chennai, India, reveals how culturally relative our views may be. This "senior" woman makes her living carrying heavy rocks all day in the burning, tropical sun. She works alongside her 18-year-old son, who breaks the rocks into a size his mother can carry.

that ultimately lead to dramatically reduced life expectancy (Statistics Canada, 2005b; National Council of Welfare, 2006).

Focus Question
Why did industrialization have such an impact on the greying of Canada?

The number of years you will spend as a senior and your quality of life appear to be affected by ethnicity. An examination of two French-speaking communities in Moncton and Montreal indicate that social integration and strong networks of family and friends were positively associated with self-reports of good health among men and women over age 65 (Zunzunegui et al., 2004). General research also confirms that among senior men, social integration, as reflected in being married and participating in social organizations, improved longevity (Statistics Canada, 2003d). Since degree of social integration is likely to vary among ethnic groups and between immigrant and non-immigrant populations in Canada, it is probable that the experience of aging varies considerably by ethnicity. For example, research indicates that immigrants, especially those living in Toronto, Montreal, and Vancouver—cities with large immigrant communities— are less likely than native-born Canadians to commit suicide. Analysts suggest that the social and emotional support provided by ethnic communities, especially in large urban centres, may account for a portion of these differences (Statistics Canada, 2004h).

IN SUM

As a result of industrialization and its accompanying improvements in sanitation, disease prevention, nutrition, and so on, more humans around the globe are growing old. The shift in the age pyramid of industrialized countries poses a variety of important issues, such as the distribution of national resources and the role of citizens in and out of the paid labour force. As with other social categories such as gender and ethnicity, we should refrain from "essentializing" seniors; that is, viewing them as an undifferentiated group. Seniors comprise a diverse population and the experience of aging is importantly distinguished along gender, social class, and ethnic lines.

SYMBOLIC INTERACTIONIST PERSPECTIVES ON AGING

To study how aging is socially constructed, symbolic interactionists examine how the symbols associated with age affect our perceptions. Let's look, then, at how culture underlies our ideas of when a person becomes "old" and how negative stereotypes and the mass media may affect the self-perceptions of older Canadians.

Labelling and the Onset of Old Age

You can probably remember when you thought a 12-year-old was "old"—and anyone older than that was beyond reckoning, just "up there" someplace. You were probably five or six at the time. Similarly, to a 12-year-old, someone of 21 seems "old." At 21, 30 may mark that line, and 40 may seem "very old." And so our patterns of perception persist, with "old" gradually receding from the self. To people who turn 40, 50 seems old; at 50, the late 60s look old (not the early 60s). The passing of years seems to accelerate as we age, and at 50, the 60s don't seem far from the horizon (Thorpe, 2002).

At some point, an individual must apply the label "old" to him- or herself. Often, cultural definitions of age force this label on people sooner than they are ready to accept it. In the typical case, the individual has become used to what he or she sees in the mirror. Changes have taken place very gradually, and each change, if not exactly taken in stride, has been accommodated. Consequently, it comes as a shock when meeting a friend one has not seen in years to see how much that person has changed. At class reunions, no one can believe how much older *the others* appear!

If there is no single point at which people automatically cross a magical line and become "old," what, then, puts someone in this category? We can point to several factors that spur people to apply the label to themselves.

The first factor is *biology*, which seems to establish very broad parameters for aging. Within these biological boundaries, one person may experience "signs" of aging—wrinkles, balding, aches, difficulty in doing some things he or she used to take for granted—much earlier than another. Consequently, one person might feel "old" at an earlier or later age than others, and only at that time *adopt the role of an "old person"*—that is, begin to act in ways that old people in their society are thought to act. In short, our experience with and perception of biological changes affect our sense of "self." Laura Hurd Clarke (2001) looked at how women's aging bodies—including the deterioration of health and functional abilities—affected women's sense of identity. Interestingly, many of her female research participants indicated they came to experience their bodies as a mask and a prison for their "real" self.

Personal history or biography is a second factor that influences the point at which people consider themselves old. The death of close friends is likely to mark an important signpost in the process of aging. Indeed, the loss of close relationships may come to be seen as a normative indicator. In the words of one woman, "I just noticed that I'm at the stage in my life where in one page of obituaries, among the decedents, one half are below my age and one half are above. Up to now they were always older than me" (quoted in de Vries & Johnson, 2002, p. 315).

Consider a woman who gave birth to a daughter at 16, who in turn had a child at 18. In this scenario, the first woman became a biological grandmother at 34. Most likely,

As evident in this cover photograph from the October 2003 edition of *50Plus* magazine, media images of seniors can play an important role in creating a more positive public perception of the "old." Given the growing numbers of Canadian seniors and their high degree of organization, media campaigns are likely to continue to promote a more vital and healthy view of aging Canadians.

"old" or "not old." One cultural group may choose a particular birthday, such as the sixtieth or sixty-fifth, or a particular physical event, such as menopause, to signal the onset of old age. Our biology is also influenced by social forces (as evidenced by increasing longevity in industrialized societies), so it is not surprising that our social timetables are regularly amended. Today, many analysts refer to a "third age" (a period of good health, free of many work and family obligations) followed by a "fourth age" (a period when health deteriorates and activity is limited). Further, as discussed in "The Dependency Crisis" section of this chapter (see p. 210), it appears that the dependence-free "third age" is expanding as more Canadians adopt healthy lifestyles (Martel & Belanger, 2000).

Canadian Society: Changing Social Constructions of Aging

Physician Robert Butler coined the term **ageism** in 1969 to refer to prejudice, discrimination, and hostility directed against people because of their age (Blytheway & Johnson, 2005). Research into ageism in Canada suggests that the elderly were neither uniformly venerated nor detested in the past (Markson, 2003, p. 93). In traditional Canadian Inuit culture, for example, elders were valued members of the group as long as they contributed to its survival. At the point that they became a drain on resources, they were expected to "remove" themselves (by allowing themselves to die from exposure). Today, Inuit seniors continue to understand their value through the transmission of accumulated wisdom and knowledge to younger generations, but also express frustration at the physical limitations that reduce their ability to contribute directly to their households. For contemporary Inuit, old age is not perceived as a positive life stage. It is a difficult period that is managed more or less successfully only as long as men are able to participate in hunting and travelling and women are able to continue their involvement in domestic activities in the home and community (Collings, 2001).

It seems likely that there was never a "golden era" in human history when a society's elderly were uniformly respected and valued. An elderly individual's experience of well-being and social status has always been rooted in his or her health and physical abilities and relative social ranking as determined by the interplay between age and other personal characteristics such as gender, social rank, and ethnicity.

Recognizing that the history of aging is complex and contradictory, it can be argued that the Industrial Revolution corresponded not only with an increase in the numbers of seniors but also with a significant downturn in the social position of the great majority of seniors—those who were working-class, female, immigrants, and/or disabled. The new industrial order experienced by workers was decidedly a young man's—and, to a lesser degree, a young woman's—world. Any respect that older individuals might have accrued from their skills in domestic work or crafts or through the apprenticeship system was rapidly eroded as skilled

the woman will not play any stereotypical role—spending her days in a rocking chair, for example—but *knowing* she is a grandmother has an impact on her self-concept. At a minimum, she must *deny* that she is old.

A third factor in determining when people label themselves as "old" is societal **timetables**, the signals societies use to inform their members of their aged status. As noted throughout this text, societal forces play a crucial role in establishing our self-definition and expectations about aging. Further, our expectations are interwoven with gender, sexual orientation, ethnicity, (dis)ability, and social class. With this complex array of factors at work, there is no predefined age at which people become "old." The definition varies around the world and throughout history and is communicated through a variety of means (Gilleard, 2002). Government and workplace regulations around retirement and pension eligibility, media images of "seniors," advertising campaigns for cosmetics, and day-to-day comments from friends and family combine in complex ways with our biology and personal history to create our sense of ourselves as

craftsmen and household workers were displaced by machinery and mass-marketed products. At the centre of the new order was the industrial factory, which made unrelenting demands on even the most fit men and women. As economic opportunities for many seniors were undermined, so too were social institutions—notably the patriarchal family and traditional religious structures—that tended to support an age-based system of respect and deference.

Modern Canadian society has inherited long-held contradictory perspectives on aging and the elderly along with the economic marginalization of many seniors, as reflected in the popular acceptance of a range of stereotypes about the elderly. Certainly, old age is not seen as necessarily synonymous with disability, frailty, incompetence, or dependence—and positive notions of older citizens do exist. However, research suggests that since seniors are often denied important productive social roles, they tend to be stereotyped in negative terms: as having lower status than young individuals and as physically and cognitively inept and passive. These stereotypes are tempered by slightly more positive notions that seniors are warm and socially sensitive and are to be pitied (Cuddy & Fiske, 2002).

The popular media tend to reflect this ambivalent perception of older Canadians. Consider, for example, the traditionally negative mother-in-law stereotype at the centre of Jane Fonda's recent film *Monster-in-Law* (2005). Admittedly, the media—for example, advertisers—employ scenarios in which healthy seniors plan cruises, are sexually active, and learn new skills. However, such positive representations exist alongside persistent negative stereotypes. In particular, the aged senior (who "looks" his or her age) and the senior with physical infirmity tend to be pitied, marginalized, or obliterated from media imagery or represented in stereotypically negative terms—that is, as dependent, incompetent, and needy.

Negative representations of aging are not restricted to any particular category of seniors. In pursuit of a mother lode of profits, the consumer market economy—which relies on the creation of need and personal dissatisfaction—taps into our societal and personal discomfort with aging. Today, the media intensively cultivate a powerful fear and loathing of the aging process. The net result has been a billion-dollar market in goods and services designed to delay, counteract, or camouflage aging. From Viagra and Botox to teeth whiteners and hair dyes, an enormous amount of economic activity is directed toward the message that age is a personal problem and a stigma that must be constantly battled if self-worth is to be maintained.

MASS MEDIA IN SOCIAL LIFE
The Social Construction of Age as a Contemporary Social Problem

In his book *Forever Young* (2003), University of Toronto social analyst Marcel Danesi argues that contemporary Western culture has embraced the view that age is bad and youth is good. Consider, for example, the images of adults in 1950s sitcoms such as *Father Knows Best* and *The Adventures of Ozzie and Harriet*. Whatever their foibles, the parents were mature and in charge and were capable of skillfully guiding their children. In contrast, in the late 1960s and early 1970s, the father on the popular television program *All in the Family* was portrayed as an uneducated, uninformed bigot and the mother as a simpleton. By the 1990s, the dumbing down of adults was complete with the rise in popularity of *The Simpsons* (1987) and *Family Guy* (1999), programs that imply that many adults are rude and stupid. Danesi suggests that the message here and elsewhere in popular culture is

clear: only the young are "cool," and aging is a deterioration to be fought on every front.

These are not free-floating ideas. The consumer economy has a tremendous vested interest in perpetuating these notions, since not only can numerous symbols of "cool" be sold to the young, but masses of products—from makeup to hair colour and soft drinks—can be marketed to post-adolescents who want to retain the public impression of youthfulness. The net result is a culture in which adults vainly attempt to mimic the young while failing to cultivate the skills, experience, and wisdom that should be the companions of age. In his provocative book, Danesi suggests that Western cultures would dramatically benefit from a rethinking of their current social constructions of aging and adolescence.

These conclusions are echoed by feminist author Margaret Morganroth

Gullette, who argues in her book *Aged by Culture* (2004) that cultural messages encourage an obsession with trying to stay young. Like Danesi, she sees these messages embedded in negative media portrayals of "greedy boomers" and in the workplace experiences of many middle-aged workers, who find themselves "downsized" into unemployment or working for younger and less experienced supervisors. Who would want to grow older when it translates into not only a decline in our physical abilities but also social and economic marginalization? Like Danesi, Gullette calls for a fight against the cultivation of middle-ageism and gerontophobia with respect to both interpersonal and global economic manifestations. Ultimately, these authors' voices join others not only in challenging ageism but also in demanding a more positive social construction of what it means to grow old (Chapman, 2005).

As discussed earlier, a basic principle of symbolic interactionism is that people perceive both themselves and others according to the symbols of their culture. In terms of aging, we are being assailed by mixed messages not only about seniors' wisdom and experience, but also the undesirability of being viewed as old. Predictably, young and old Canadians are struggling to sort out the personal and societal meanings attached to aging.

In a recent provocative study, Canadian researchers Julie Ann McMullin and John Cairney (2004) explored the relationships between self-esteem, age, class, and gender. Using data (from Statistics Canada's National Population Health Survey) on 19 600 Canadian households, they found that self-reported self-esteem levels tended to decline as men and women aged, that women of all ages reported lower levels than men, and that higher social class characteristics are related to higher self-esteem results. Examining the interrelationships between these characteristics, they reported that after about age 62, men and women in the high social class enjoy higher self-esteem than their lower-class counterparts. Men, more than women, were particularly advantaged by social class as they aged.

These results lend credence to the view that aging is socially constructed as a negative experience in contemporary Canada and that certain groups, notably women and the less well-off, are particularly vulnerable to the negative conceptions of age in our culture. However, the stigma attached to aging and the elderly reflects an ongoing struggle over the symbolic meanings of these constructs in Canada.

Today, the burgeoning senior population is able to support seniors' organizations and groups, as reflected in Canadian magazines such as *Today's Seniors*, *The Seniors' Review*, and *50Plus*, which actively campaign for positive

images of seniors and stress the active, healthy lifestyles enjoyed by many older Canadians. In these media, older individuals are likely to be portrayed as important and involved members of society who are healthy, capable, and active (Roberts & Zhou, 1997). However, it should be noted that such campaigns may be faulted for creating new sets of stereotypes that are equally constraining while continuing to exclude a wide range of alternative images of aging (for example, political protestors or gay seniors) (Blytheway & Johnson, 2005).

Stereotypes, which play a profound role in social life, are a basic area of sociological investigation. In contemporary society, the mass media are a major creator of stereotypes.

MASS MEDIA IN SOCIAL LIFE
Sexy Seniors: Media Blackout

A particularly important source of societal notions of aging and the elderly are the images promoted in the mass media. As noted above, the caricaturizing—and the invisibility—of seniors conveys a powerful message about our prevailing beliefs and values. Representation of seniors as either sexless or inappropriately sexual ("dirty old men and women") is especially significant in a culture where sexuality and sexual attractiveness are related to social powerfulness in complex ways.

As pointed out by researcher Thomas Walz (2002), the popular media, notably television and movies, are averse to representing seniors as sexual beings. While there are exceptions to this rule, the sexuality of older persons is frequently presented in terms of negative stereotypes. From dirty old men to frigid old women, the message concerning senior sexuality is both contradictory and unflattering. Frequently, seniors are presented as simply sexless—either uninterested in or incapable of sex. In the

film *Grumpy Old Men*, for example, the protagonists talk about sex but actually spend their time golfing and fishing. When older men or women are depicted as sexually driven, they generally are involved with younger partners, a pattern that presents a stereotype of senior sexual predators (e.g., Humbert in *Lolita* or Mrs. Robinson in *The Graduate*).

Media representation of senior sexuality is particularly interesting since it flies in the face of what we know from sexual research. Over and over, researchers have documented that the majority of older people remain sexually interested and able, and their activity levels would be even greater if not for losses of partners due to age and infirmity (Walz, 2002, p. 109; Fraser, Maticka-Tyndate & Smylie, 2004).

In the 2003 film *Something's Gotta Give*, the character played by Jack Nicholson gives up the much younger woman he is romancing (played by Amanda Peet) because of his attraction to her mother, played by Diane Keaton. Meanwhile, the mother rejects the prospect of romance with a much younger man, played by Keanu Reeves. Perhaps this film suggests a softening of ageist attitudes, but it is worth noting that Diane Keaton, as with so many "older" actresses, is celebrated in part because she does not "look her age."

It will be fascinating to discover whether the wave of aging baby boomers forces a reconsideration of media stereotypes, a more realistic portrayal of senior sexuality, and a popularization of the sexy senior. CARP's *50Plus* magazine recently ran a cover story titled "Looking Hot After 50" (Righton, 2002). It doesn't appear likely that the boomers will easily accept traditional negative stereotypes of aging.

IN SUM

Symbolic interactionists have drawn our attention to a number of important aspects of aging. First, whether someone is labelled old or labels him- or herself as such depends on a variety of factors, not simply biological age. Physical signs of aging, such as wrinkles, may contribute to the labelling process, but personal history (having grandchildren at a young age) and gender (men "mature" while women "age") may also have an impact on how we see ourselves getting older. Finally, societies set certain timetables, such as retirement at age 65, that tend to be seen as key signals of aging. Given that aging responds to a variety of social factors, it is not surprising that attitudes toward the elderly vary considerably from one society to another. Further, these attitudes may shift over time. For example, industrialization and related changes in Canadian society served to diminish the social position of many seniors as traditional age-structured institutions, such as the patriarchal family and the craft guild, were replaced. In recent times, the consumer market economy has played a central role in promoting negative societal perceptions of aging and the elderly. At the same time, improved health and nutrition allow increasing numbers of older Canadians to lead healthy, longer lives and prolong their positions as powerful members of society. The media play a particularly important role in promoting both negative and positive images of the aging process. On one hand, seniors are often ignored, pitied, or trivialized in media images. On the other, media may be mobilized by seniors' interest groups to increasingly promote a more positive and inclusive perspective on aging and the elderly.

Focus Question

How do popular television programs, such as *Survivor*, reflect our attitudes toward aging and the elderly?

FEMINIST PERSPECTIVES

As women who were active in the modern women's movement moved into "middle age" in the 1980s and 1990s, aging was increasingly viewed as a feminist issue (Macdonald & Rich, 1991). Many of the most well-known spokeswomen of the movement—including Betty Friedan (1993), Germaine Greer (1991), and Gloria Steinem (1992)—examined their own personal experiences of growing older and exposed the inequities faced by older women. In more recent years, as feminists sought to embrace the diversities and complexities of women's experiences, they incorporated various intersecting patterns of privilege, domination, and oppression (such as sexual orientation, ethnicity, and disability) into the feminist paradigm (Reinharz, 1997; Shaw & Lee, 2001; Abu-Laban & McDaniel, 2005). Today, although ageism is still not as central a concern in society as it is within feminist scholarship (Colasanti, Slevin, & King, 2006), an increasing number of feminists are playing key roles in challenging mainstream gerontology and articulating a critical approach to the study of aging.

Feminist analysts have pointed out that aging exacerbates the problems of power and inequality for women (Copper, 2001). As women age, they are likely to find themselves increasingly marginalized and dismissed. This is apparent in patterns of marriage, for example. Around the globe, compared to women, most men are able to marry much younger spouses. Indeed, the popular media often poke fun at older men with much younger "trophy" wives. In part, this pattern reflects the belief that men retain their attractiveness and sexuality longer than women. On men, greying hair and even a few wrinkles may be seen as signs of "maturing," while on women those same features are likely to be interpreted as signs of being "old." As Canadian sociologists Sharon McIrvin Abu-Laban and Susan McDaniel (2005) state, "Women are said to be older sooner than men. While aging is seen as empowering for many men, it is not seen to be so for women. *His* facial lines are seen as signs of character; *her* lines are signs of decrepitude and decreasing sexual attractiveness" (p. 101). This difference in the social evaluation of "old women" and "mature men" is also revealed when older male news anchors are likely to be retained, while female anchors of the same age are likely to be transferred to less visible positions. Hillary Clinton faced the critical eye of the media as she ran unsuccessfully for the Democratic presidential nomination in the United States. Similarly, in movies, older men are much more likely than older women to play leads—often opposite much younger female stars (such as Richard Gere and Winona Ryder in *Autumn in New York*). Canadian actress Kim Cattrall (Samantha Jones in *Sex and the City*), who is over 50, said of the ageist-sexist Hollywood ideal, "'You can't ever talk about the big 5-0 . . . You turn 35 in Hollywood and your auditions get cut in half. They're just not interested'" (Goodman, 2008: p. Go19).

The relative "attractiveness" or "beauty" of women is related in a complex way to their social and economic positions in society. Access to the best cosmetics, health clubs and spas, and cosmetic surgeons requires considerable time and economic resources. Only elite women (Oprah Winfrey is a high-profile example) can afford the personal chefs, personal trainers, and other assistants who make the beauty ideal attainable. The overwhelming majority of women must accept that as they age they will fall further and further short of this artificial, socially prescribed goal (Abu-Laban & McDaniel, 2005).

Women's lack of economic resources is, in turn, related to their traditional role in the economy. Numerous women who are now approaching senior status have devoted themselves to home and family, and while they may have had paid employment, they often interrupted their careers or worked part-time. As a result, as discussed in Chapter 7, the overwhelming majority of corporate chiefs, leaders in professions such as medicine and law, and social-political power elite are male (Carroll, 2004). Indeed, many women, particularly if they never marry, divorce, or become widowed, will find that contributions to the family do not result in economic security in old age. It is likely that such patterns of economic marginalization and insecurity contribute to images of older women as "unattractive."

Needless to say, older women struggling with additional societal prejudices are likely to have even more difficulties. As Abu-Laban and McDaniel (2005) observe, "The prospects for women of colour, Aboriginal women, women with disabilities, or lesbian women are even worse. Aged women with out-of-date eyewear, bad teeth, unfashionably sized bodies, limited education, and whose only (or main) work experience is raising children on social assistance" are even more likely to end up economically and socially peripheralized in old age (p. 109).

There are exceptions to these general patterns. Some women marry much younger men, and we have seen increasing numbers of female celebrities (Goldie Hawn, Susan Sarandon, and Jane Fonda, for example) employed in their 50s and 60s. However, such exceptions, simply because they are noteworthy, are evidence of the powerful social norms surrounding women and aging. For example, the "mature" women celebrities are outstanding in large measure because of their youthful appearance rather than their age. In an interesting comparison of the media's portrayal of Jane Fonda (born 1937) and Barbara Bush (born 1925), Myra Dinnerstein and Rose Weitz (2002) observed that Bush, despite her social position as the wife of a former president and mother of a serving president, is often depicted as someone in need of a "make-over," given her matronly figure, white hair, and wrinkled face. Bush herself employs self-deprecating humour to deflect anticipated criticisms of her appearance and often appears defensive when discussing the "naturalness" of her appearance. In contrast, Fonda, who attributes her appearance to health and fitness while acknowledging a years-long battle with bulimia, is presented in magazines as an enviable (if unattainable) role model for aging women. In short, even powerful, respected women find themselves constrained by corrosive cultural standards of femininity.

The Mass Media: Invisible Older Women

Much contemporary postmodern feminism has explored cultural representations of gender and age in mediums such as art, literature, and the mass media. Contemporary efforts to deconstruct embedded messages have exposed the complex and nuanced meanings that society attaches to gender and age. However, no deconstruction is needed to reveal the messages about gender and aging that are incorporated into contemporary media.

Undertaking your own examination of mass media images of older women can be very revealing. This is what U.S. feminist Betty Friedan did when she began researching her book on aging, *The Fountain of Age*. Not surprisingly, of 290 identifiable faces in *Vogue*, Friedan found that only one belonged to a woman who might be over 60. Of 116 identifiable faces in *Vanity Fair*, there were two women over 60—the Queen Mother and Imelda Marcos—and 10 older men, all powerful or famous (Friedan, 1993, p. 37). The implication is that most seniors, except the rich, famous, and powerful, do not count, a message especially true of senior women.

Media images of older women are not *entirely* negative or absent. Carol Matthews (1996) contends that older women have, on occasion, been portrayed positively in a variety of Canadian literature. Prominent Canadian authors, including Margaret Laurence, Margaret Atwood, Sylvia Fraser, and Sheila Watson, have depicted older women as a powerful presence and significant forces in their novels.

CONFLICT PERSPECTIVES: THE POLITICAL ECONOMY OF AGING

Various conflict perspectives suggest that the guiding principles of social life are competition, disequilibrium, and change. Conflict analysts draw attention to the potential for discord among society's age groups. Recent comments from Canada's Association for the Fifty-Plus (CARP) speak to this concern: "Predictions that seniors will break the health care and pension banks are myths. But, if we don't prepare for the aging population now, these myths could become realities" (Gleberzon & Cutler, 2005 p. 5). As the baby boomer generation retires, analysts project that in 2031 there will be two workers for every retired person in Canada, which represents a dramatic fall from five workers per retiree in the 1980s (CBC News, 2008). The ongoing tensions over retirement issues provide a revealing example of the complexities and contradictions in age-based struggles.

Mandatory Retirement and Generational Conflict

Until recently, almost all Canadians were required by law to retire at age 65. This tradition reflects a standard established in 1889 by Count Otto von Bismarck, Germany's first chancellor. At this point in history, most citizens in industrialized economies were in physical decline by age 65 and increasingly incapable of work. Further, few survived many years postretirement. Clearly, we now live in a very different world. Improvements in medical care, nutrition, physical fitness, and technology have meant that many workers are capable of continuing their paid employment well beyond the traditional age of retirement. At the same time, dramatic increases in the numbers of retiring seniors have raised concerns about the long-term viability of publicly funded pension schemes. Some analysts predict that younger workers contributing to government pension payments will find that when they reach retirement age themselves, the pension funds will be depleted (Girard, 2002).

In particular, analysts are concerned about the dwindling numbers of active workers and the swelling population of retirees. The fear is that the number of people who collect government pensions will grow, while the proportion of working people—those who pay for these benefits out of their wages—will shrink. Currently, there are four working taxpayers for every non-working pensioner. But when this ratio drops to two to one, as analysts predict, will the public pension plans be sustainable?

Some see this shift in the **dependency ratio**—the number of workers compared with the number of QPP/CPP recipients—as especially troubling not only in terms of monies available to fund pensions, but also in relation to adequate support for the health care system. According to the Association of Canadian Pension Management (ACPM), "The combined forces of the retirement of the Boomer Generation, rising life expectancies, and falling birth rates will seriously strain, and could possibly rupture our retirement and health care systems in the next 30 years" (ACPM, 2000, p. 2). Given that poor Canadian seniors (65 and older) currently derive between 91 and 95 percent of their total incomes from government transfer payments (Old Age Security pensions, Guaranteed Income Supplement for seniors, the Canada/Quebec pension plans), any failure in these systems could have potentially disastrous results (National Council of Welfare, 2004, p. 82).

As a result of these and other social pressures, a movement has emerged powered in part by seniors' groups, professional organizations, and employers intent on ending the policy of mandatory retirement at age 65. The argument can be made that mandatory retirement should be seen as a form of age discrimination and consequently banned under the provisions of the *Charter of Rights and Freedoms* (1982). In 1990, the Canadian Supreme Court upheld mandatory retirement on the grounds that such discrimination was justified in a free and democratic society. The social benefits for society include the opening up of job and promotion opportunities for younger workers. However, in the past 15 years, the issue has been repeatedly brought before the courts, and subsequent judicial rulings suggest that mandatory retirement is not *always* justified. On July 1, 2009, when new legislation was enacted in Nova Scotia, mandatory retirement was eliminated in all provinces and territories (CBC News, 2008). Table 9.3 highlights the regional differences in retirement rules across Canada.

Many jurisdictions have continued to allow mandatory retirement on two grounds: age discrimination legislation does not apply to individuals over age 65, and retirement and pension plans are exempted from age discrimination legislation. Currently, only Manitoba bans mandatory retirement through its human rights legislation. The federal government has voluntarily eliminated mandatory retirement for civil servants, and Quebec (since 1982) has banned the practice through its *Employment Standards Act*. In short, the issues of mandatory retirement and retirement age are far from clear (in contrast to the United States, where mandatory retirement is banned) and are likely to continue to be hotly debated.

The position of many older workers is that, if required to retire, they may be effectively blocked from finding other forms of employment since they could be considered over-experienced or overqualified and are likely to confront ageist assumptions that they will be unable to manage new technologies (Thomas, 2005). Older women workers may be particularly affected by mandatory retirement provisions, since they have not typically been able to spend as much time in the paid labour force as their male counterparts and, as a result, have built up fewer retirement resources. This pattern becomes of particular concern when older women are divorced or widowed. In addition, older employees argue that they do not want to be required to retire from work they enjoy, feel they are entirely capable of carrying on with their work and have much to contribute as workers, and/or are concerned about a decline in lifestyle if required to retire (Pupo & Duffy, 2005). Groups and individuals opposed to mandatory retirement would like to see older workers offered a variety of alternate possibilities, such as continuing to work as long as they are able, phased-in retirement, or part-time employment (Ferguson, 2004, p. A4).

Younger workers tend not to have been represented by particular lobby groups, but their views—in particular, the concern that the elimination of mandatory retirement will result in fewer opportunities for entrance or advancement in the labour market—have been presented by college and university student organizations and in media coverage of the debate. It is suggested that many young Canadians face high rates of unemployment and are forced to settle for "McJobs"

TABLE 9.3 Regional Differences in Retirement Rules across Canada

Province or Territory	Retirement Rules
Nunavut	No mandatory retirement age
Northwest Territories	No mandatory retirement age
Yukon	No mandatory retirement age
British Columbia	Law to eliminate mandatory retirement took effect January 1, 2008
Alberta	No mandatory retirement age
Saskatchewan	Law to eliminate mandatory retirement took effect in November 2007
Manitoba	No mandatory retirement age
Ontario	Law to eliminate mandatory retirement took effect December 12, 2006
Quebec	No mandatory retirement age
New Brunswick	No mandatory retirement, but companies are allowed to enforce it under the terms and conditions of any retirement or pension plan
Nova Scotia	Mandatory retirement at age 65, if required by the employer. Law to eliminate this took effect July 1, 2009
Prince Edward Island	No mandatory retirement age
Newfoundland and Labrador	Law to eliminate mandatory retirement took effect May 26, 2007

Source: CBC News, February 21, 2008. Available at: www.cbc.ca/news/background/retirement/mandatory_retirement.html.

with low pay and little challenge in the retail or service industries and feel they are being denied the opportunities enjoyed by their parents and grandparents. Some youth believe that the "good" jobs and the opportunities for a prosperous life are being obstructed by a "boomer bottleneck" in which older Canadians continue to hang on to their positions for privilege, power, and wealth. The resulting resentment may be compounded by concerns that the younger generation will face the no-win choice of either higher taxes or reduced services in order to provide pensions and health care for the boomer generation.

What does the end of mandatory retirement mean for older workers? Are many hanging on to their jobs well past the age of 65? Today, only 6 percent of workers continue to work full time after they turn 65, and the average age of retirement in Canada is 62 (CBC News, 2008). Patterns vary, with some workers phasing into retirement by reducing their hours and others finding part-time work in another capacity. Some seniors prefer to draw upon their past work experiences and skills to start small businesses (Pupo and Duffy, 2005). Between 2001 and 2005, the number of small businesses started by entrepreneurs over the age of 55 grew by 35 percent. Today, one in four self-employed Canadians is 55 or older, and the majority of these so-called "seniorpreneurs" (two-thirds) work alone without paid staff (Ebden, 2006: p. E6).

Not surprisingly, some groups, including younger workers in certain occupations, argue that youthfulness may be a bona fide occupational qualification. In other words, if you are "old," you simply cannot handle certain jobs (for example, an airline pilot, police officer, firefighter, or bus driver). However, given the variability with which people age and the diversity in our beliefs and expectations about seniors, it is difficult to establish a particular age at which all seniors should be banned from specific kinds of work. Perhaps a reasonable accommodation may mean accepting that specific seniors can indeed continue to perform well in physically demanding occupations.

Employers tend not to assume one clear position on the issue. On one hand, some employers would benefit from being able to retain older skilled workers; on the other, some may resist the costs of maintaining a senior workforce that, because of its seniority, is being paid at the highest levels. To some degree, a standard retirement date facilitates economic planning for employers and also allows for downsizing. While retaining experienced workers may reduce training costs, it may also hinder the hiring of workers with new ideas and perspectives.

Segments of the labour movement are vigorously opposed to efforts to do away with retirement legislation. The right to retire and draw upon pension funds was a hard-won victory for workers who, during the early industrial period, were expected to work until they died. From the perspective of some unionists, eliminating retirement provisions is a step backward in the struggle to reduce the number of hours and years we must spend in paid employment (MacQueen, 2005).

Given the preceding discussion, it is clear that the issue of mandatory retirement is wrought with controversy and cannot be understood simply in terms of generational conflict. There are a variety of competing interests and concerns that do not necessarily divide along age lines. Young people will, after all, be faced with the issue of retirement age at some point in their lives. As a result, their long-term interests may be at odds with their short-term concerns.

Related concerns about the depletion of old age social security plans and mushrooming medical costs are by no means established facts. Analysts argue that as long as there is continued economic growth, the dependency ratio will not pose a problem. Currently in Canada and the United States, many seniors and retirees function as productive members of the paid labour force rather than drawing on public monies (Bowlby, 2002; Duchesne, 2002). Further, as the population ages, there will be cost savings in terms of day care and education, which can then be transferred to other areas of the economy, such as health care (Gorrie, 2002). Perhaps most important, research suggests that other social cleavages—gender, race, social class, and political affiliation—are likely to mitigate any clear-cut divisions by age (Hamil-Luker, 2001).

We have only to look at other industrialized countries, many of which are already experiencing the senior boom that looms in Canada's future, to see that talk of crisis and generational conflict may be hyperbole. Italy, Greece, Sweden, Japan, Spain, Belgium, Germany, France, and the United Kingdom already have many more citizens aged 65 and older than Canada. In many of these countries, almost a fifth of the population is 65 or older, and yet generational conflict has not become rampant. It appears that by encouraging people to work past age 65 (by reducing pension benefits, discouraging early retirement, and increasing mandatory retirement ages), providing a reduced workweek, providing incentives for direct pension contributions from employees, and facilitating home-based eldercare rather than institutional care, these countries are managing to avoid the pitfalls of bankrupt social security and health care systems. They may serve as useful models of how to avert future conflict between the interests of the young and old (Ross, 2002).

Critical Social Gerontology

Not surprisingly, the advancing age of the baby boomer generation has helped to stimulate an upsurge of academic interest in aging and the elderly. In recent years, analysts have increasingly challenged traditional gerontological approaches to the study of seniors. In particular, the tendency to approach age in biomedical terms, almost as an ailment that can be "cured" by medical intervention, has been extensively criticized as homogenizing seniors rather than acknowledging the important differences among them (Auger & Tedford-Litle, 2002). Today, pressure continues to mount for more societal and psychological investigation into the aging process and an improved awareness of the diversity (ethnicity, immigrant/non-immigrant status, gender, rural/urban residence, etc.) of the aging population (Chappell et al.,

2003). This has resulted in many more studies of the actual experiences of seniors, as well as increasing interest in global research and cross-cultural comparisons (Bosworth & Keys, 2004; de Jong, Gierveld, & Havens, 2004; van Dijk, 2004).

Other analysts are mounting a strong argument against the separation of elderly studies as a separate and distinct discipline. They contend that aging must be located in terms of the overall life course and that seniors should be considered within a complex web of relationships. Canadian sociologist Susan McDaniel (2002a) made a particularly important contribution to these developments with her concept of *intergenerational interlinkages (IGILs)*. In contrast to earlier formulations that tend to locate seniors in terms of relationships (care-giving relationships between adult children and their parents, for example) and transfer from one generation to another (such as provision of public health care), she suggests an approach that moves beyond one-dimensionality and narrowness to explore intergenerational linkages in a variety of directions, contexts, and forms. In a three-generation typology—parents, children, and grandchildren—each generation is both receiving and giving, and transfers between generations are monetary, public, and global (including intangibles such as attention and joy). In short, McDaniel's approach challenges our assumptions about seniors and family life and opens a wide array of research possibilities, in particular regarding "whether or how generation works with or against other dimensions of societal cleavage such as class, gender, ethnicity, and/or immigration recency" (p. 59).

A useful example of this new approach is its perspective on the popular notion of the "sandwich generation." For decades, this term has been employed to refer to the burden experienced by mid-life women and men who must satisfy the simultaneous demand of their teenage children and elderly parents. According to a 2004 Statistics Canada study, 30 percent of Canadians aged 45 to 64 with unmarried children living at home were also caring for an aging relative (Johne, 2008: p. E5). Women in this group spent on average 29 hours a month caring for seniors while their male counterparts spent 13 hours. Eighty percent of these individuals also had paid employment (Stobert & Cranswick, 2004). Not surprisingly, a significant number of family caregivers (40 percent) faced financial costs as a result of their "labours of love," including the costs of renting medical equipment, reducing work hours, and forfeiting extra income (Johne, 2008: p. E5).

Over the past 30 years, the rate of institutionalization of seniors declined and the vast majority (93 percent) currently live in private households (Turcotte & Schellenberg, 2006: p. 138). About one in three seniors aged 75 and over lives alone, and nearly one in six lives with children or grandchildren (Ibid.: p. 191). Whether seniors are living alone or with family members, care and social support arrangements are complexly interwoven into the schedules of adult children, who may share the responsibilities with their siblings. Analysts question what the future will hold for the baby boomers, who, on average, have had fewer children than their parents and may therefore have a smaller circle of family members involved in their support in their later years.

Caught between these two "slices" of responsibility, the "sandwich" generation today presumably feels pressured and conflicted. Drawing on McDaniel's notion of intergenerational interlinkages, Joseph Tindale et al. (2002) suggest that we need an approach that is not premised on generational conflict between seniors and their caregivers and that recognizes the possibility of intergenerational support between parents in their 70s and their children in their 40s and 50s. Senior parents may provide a very useful sounding board in dealing with the trials of parenting a teenager, for example. When viewed from this nuanced perspective, a more apt metaphor might be lasagna, in which the layers intermingle (p. 224).

The push toward increasingly complex theoretical approaches reflects a wider understanding of the global context of changes in family relations, community, state, and social support. Although aging is experienced at the individual and local levels, it is influenced not only by societal but also global social and economic changes. Adopting this perspective means appealing to dominant global institutions—the World Trade Organization, the International Monetary Fund, the International Labour Organization, the World Bank, and the United Nations—with regard to their impact on the social construction of aging around the world. The World Bank, for example, has been influential in promoting a minimal role for the state in basic pension provision and in advocating a system of individual defined-contribution retirement accounts. Debates about the future of old age social security need to be considered in terms of these global pressures. Critical social gerontologists press for older people to be viewed as participants in these new global realities, which are more fluid, mobile, and uncertain than prior social arrangements (Phillipson, 2003).

IN SUM

Conflict theorists contend that all members of a society do not share common interests, and the interests of the young may be in direct opposition to those of seniors. For example, as a society we must decide on the allocation of resources. Seniors might prioritize health care issues such as Alzheimer's disease and other dementia research; younger generations may want to focus on fertility and childhood illnesses. With finite resources, difficult decisions must be made. One source of potential conflict is the role of seniors in the paid labour force. At present there is much discussion in the media about the prospects for generational conflict as seniors and younger workers contest the question of age of retirement. However, closer examination suggests that the issue is much more nuanced than a generational dispute, and experiences in other, "greyer" nations suggest that it is possible to employ innovative social policies to avert such clashes. Critical social gerontologists suggest that such policies depend on a rethinking of our approach to aging and the elderly.

What difference, if any, has the elimination of mandatory retirement in Canada made in your life?

THE DEPENDENCY CRISIS

As seniors age, there is no question that most will become increasingly vulnerable to physical and mental disability. It is not surprising, therefore, that most Canadian seniors (81 percent) living at home have at least one chronic health problem—heart disease, diabetes, rheumatism, or arthritis—and that one in four are living with chronic pain (Lindsay, 1999; Crompton, 2000). In 2003, 44 percent of seniors aged 65 to 74 and 51 percent of those over age 75 reported having arthritis or rheumatism, the most common chronic conditions among seniors (Turcotte & Schellenberg, 2006: p. 47). In addition, one in three reported cognitive difficulties—forgetfulness or difficulty thinking (Lindsay, 1999). Currently, about 450 000 Canadian seniors suffer from Alzheimer's or a related disease, and it is estimated that by 2031 this number will mushroom to 750 000 (Alzheimer's Society, 2008). These figures prompt the question of who will care for dependent seniors.

The eldercare scene in Canada is characterized by an uneven mix of home care, hospital care, and institutional care. About 5 percent of seniors over age 65 and 18 percent of those 80 and over are cared for in an institution. Seniors living at home are typically cared for by elderly spouses (usually wives), adult daughters, and to a lesser degree adult sons. In addition, there is an evolving network of community care centres intended to provide support for ailing seniors who do not need hospitalization but are unable to access outpatient care. For example, in Ontario, the Ontario Association of Community Care Access Centres (CCACs) coordinates various services—food delivery, in-home assistance, nursing, and nutritional counselling—allowing many Canadians to live independently in their homes (OACCAC, 2005). In 2003, about one in seven seniors living at home required home care, including nursing and personal care, and help with housework, meal preparation, and shopping (*The Daily*, February 7, 2006).

Analysts question whether this patchwork of solutions will adequately address the masses of seniors flooding the systems. As the baby boom generation ages, and as disease and disability take their toll, the pressure on caregivers, both paid and unpaid, will dramatically intensify. Already, concern is being raised about the emotional and physical pressures on adult daughters and sons, most with their own family and paid-work responsibilities, who provide informal care for a seriously disabled senior family member (Ho et al., 2003). Research with family caregivers suggests a litany of problems, including "difficulty balancing work and family, lack of free time, wishing that someone else would take over and anger with the person they were looking after" (Frederick & Fast, 1999; Keating et al., 1999). Further, the expectation that wives and daughters will shoulder the lion's share of this burden is seen by many to perpetuate traditional patterns of gender inequity, in which women are expected to provide family care and service—to the likely detriment of their careers and economic well-being—only to end up living by themselves in old age.

However, paid community providers and institutional caregivers are not necessarily the solution. Analysts complain that many such public facilities and services are underfunded, resulting in long waiting lists, poorly trained workers, and inadequate supervision of patient treatment (Martin-Matthews, 2005). Recent media coverage of the abuse and neglect of seniors in seniors' residences underscores these concerns. In addition, private facilities and services may be so prohibitively expensive that they are only available to the wealthiest seniors.

Some commentators argue that the composite of isolation, disability, illness, and dependency accounts for many of the social problems with which aged seniors are identified. For example, this constellation is seen as the root cause of the high rates of suicide among men over age 75 (24.5 suicides per 100 000 population) when compared to men aged 60 to 74 (5 suicides per 100 000 population) (Langlois & Morrison, 2002). It is also seen as an important factor in the increasing numbers of murder-suicides in the United States in which older males kill their wives and then themselves. At present, older American adults (55 years and older) are twice as likely as younger adults (under age 55) to commit such acts. Predictably, causes are seen as linked to undiagnosed depression, failing health, caregiver stress, and loss of independence (Vann, 2002).

For some aged seniors, suicide may be a valued escape from chronic suffering and disease. The dramatic growth in the number of aged seniors has triggered discussion of the "right to die," especially euthanasia (mercy killing) and assisted suicide. Currently, a number of right-to-die advocates are urging that the Canadian government create social policies that recognize that the terminally ill and those who suffer from debilitating, irreversible, and slow-moving diseases have the right to a "timely death." Again, given the numbers of seniors appearing on the demographic horizon and the current problems associated with the care of frail, disabled, and ill aged seniors, this debate is likely to intensify in coming years.

At present, there are only four jurisdictions in the world that legally and openly allow assisted dying for patients: the state of Oregon (physician-assisted suicide since 1997); the Netherlands (voluntary euthanasia and physician-assisted suicide since 2002); Switzerland (physician and nonphysician assisted suicide since 1941); and Belgium (euthanasia, without a specific method, since 2002) (www.assistedsuicide.org, 2005). Dutch law permits doctors to inject a sedative and a lethal dose of muscle relaxant at the request of adult patients suffering great pain and with no hope of relief. Very recently, the Dutch doctors' association began to consider guidelines for the euthanizing of ill people with no "free will," including ill babies, children, the severely mentally retarded, and people left in irreversible coma after an accident (Sterling, 2004, p. A12). Given the mushrooming elderly population, dramatic increases in health care costs, and improvements in medicine's ability to prolong biological life, along with polls that indicate that three-quarters of Canadians support doctor-assisted suicide for the terminally ill, control over one's own death will likely become a hotly contested issue in the near future (Pollard, 2001). The very existence of this debate in Canadian society speaks strongly to the fact that death and dying, like aging,

DOWN-TO-EARTH SOCIOLOGY
Connecting Isolation, Dependency, Dementia, and Abuse

It is important to realize that the issues of dependency, disability, and isolation may intersect with other social concerns, such as elder neglect and abuse. The recent New Brunswick case of 82-year-old Kenneth Leadlay, who pleaded guilty to killing his 81-year-old wife, speaks to these interconnections.

Alice Leadlay suffered from severe dementia and, as a result, often roamed the house and sometimes screamed for hours on end. In September 2004, Kenneth, desperate after days without sleep, tied his wife up and gagged her. She apparently suffocated as a result.

The judge ruled that the husband had been negligent and was clearly responsible for his wife's death. He was sentenced to two years to be served in the community.

In his defence, Kenneth affirmed his love for his wife, whom he had met when she was 12 years old, and who had been not only his sweetheart but also his best friend. Other witnesses testified to the happy, loving relationship between the couple, and the judge noted that there were no prior indications of abuse.

Although Kenneth Leadlay was punished for his "bad judgment," it seems likely that other societal factors entered into the tragic end to their relationship. While the husband may be at fault for refusing to admit that his wife was "too big a burden to him," the local community and society at large should consider its failure to be aware of the situation and to provide adequate support and alternatives.

Source: CBC News. (2005, April 7). Elderly man sentenced in wife's gagging death. Available at: www.cbc.ca/story/canada/ national/2005/ 04/06/nb-elder-050406.html.

are as much socially constructed as they are biological events.

As critical social gerontologists would be quick to emphasize, the interplay between dependency, care giving, illness, and state funding are not restricted to the plight of Canadian seniors. All individuals, regardless of age, who are so ill or disabled that they are incapable of participating productively in the economic order risk societal marginalization. While numbers of affected seniors are higher, the social attitudes toward their plight, the underfunding of support services, and the downloading of responsibilities onto family members are by no means peculiar to this group. The mentally and physically disabled, regardless of age or cause, have typically been invisible in modern society. Seriously addressing their plight and that of their caregivers necessarily raises fundamental questions about the social value placed on life, the meaning of "quality of life," and the responsibility of the state and community in maintaining minimal standards. The sheer numbers of seniors will likely require that Canadian society face these issues in the near future.

Dependency and Elder Abuse

By the 1980s, activists working on family violence issues—child abuse, wife abuse, and so on—increasingly recognized that seniors were also subject to violence, both within families and outside. The first national survey of elder abuse was undertaken in 1992, and today we have an extensive body of research on the topic. Canadians now generally understand that seniors are vulnerable to a variety of forms of victimization, including physical, sexual, financial, mental, and emotional abuse. The abuse may be perpetrated by a spouse, son or daughter or other relative, neighbour, paid caregiver or caregiver in an institutional setting, or by the senior him- or herself. The physical and mental deterioration that accompanies aging renders them both dependent upon others and vulnerable to victimization. The precise form of abuse varies considerably—from a physically abusive spouse or family member to financial con artists to attendants in seniors' residences who neglect their patients. Within these broad parameters, it is estimated that approximately 10 percent of Canadian seniors are subject to some form of physical, psychological, and/or financial abuse (Brennan, 2002). Predictably, very few of these incidents are included in police reports, and those that are tend to involve non-family members. Of the family abuse that was reported in 2002, males were the overwhelming majority (80 percent) of the perpetrators, and most of the victims were female. In many instances, the abuse involved husbands and sons of the victims (AuCoin, 2005). Alarmingly, there were significant increases in family violence against older females and males between 1998 and 2002. Older Canadians are also vulnerable to victimization outside the home. Although we know very little about abuse

in institutional settings, surveys of nurses and nursing assistants suggest that many have witnessed rough handling (hitting, shoving patients, inappropriate use of restraints) and emotional abuse (yelling, swearing, and humiliation of patients) (Brzozowski, 2004b).

Why do children, spouses, and other relatives abuse their own elderly? Apparently, one precipitating cause may be situational: stress from caring for a person who is highly dependent, demanding and, in some cases, violent (Pillemer & Suitor, 1992). A history of family violence may lay the foundation for abuse against seniors. Recently, researchers have emphasized the relevance of feminist analysis to elder abuse. Canadian researchers, for example, suggest that a feminist perspective (focusing on gender inequalities and the subordination of women), along with a situational model, are helpful in identifying elderly individuals that are more likely to be victims of physical abuse (Smith & Hightower, 2004). Gender is an important factor in senior victimization. The feminist perspective on the issue does not discount that other factors—such as ethnicity, recent immigrant status, and rural residence—may compound the vulnerability of older women. For example, South Asian women in Toronto report that speaking out is doubly difficult in their community since older women fear not only shaming their families but also being shunned by their society (Dinshaw, 2004).

IN SUM

Aging, especially for older seniors, almost always involves becoming frail and dependent. Although both men and women confront the issue, women in particular are likely to end up on their own and potentially isolated from the larger society. Isolation may become a serious issue when coupled with disability, particularly dementia. Chronic illness requires intense support from families and/or health care institutions. As the number of seniors grows, senior disability is likely to become an increasingly important social issue. The health care system is already experiencing severe pressures, and the burden of family support often falls disproportionately on adult women. In this context, it is troubling to note that elder abuse and neglect may be taking place. Isolated and/or disabled seniors may be particularly vulnerable to abuse from both professional and family caregivers. These concerns could be compounded by the economic vulnerability of seniors. Although government policies have improved the financial situation of many Canadian seniors, many still live in or near poverty.

Focus Question

Is it reasonable to rely on family members to provide care and support for aging seniors, or should other social support mechanisms be put in place?

The "Age-Quake"

IS AGING A GLOBAL CRISIS?
No. The so-called developed countries are experiencing a dramatic increase in the proportion of seniors in their populations. Differences between developed and developing countries are reflected in differing life expectancy rates, dependency ratios, and age profiles. Globally, the trend is for more people to live longer, but this a concern primarily of developed countries. pp. 193–197.

WHAT DOES THE TERM "GREYING OF CANADA" MEAN?
The phrase **greying of Canada** refers to the growing proportion of Canadians reaching old age. The cost of health care for the elderly has become a social issue, and sentiment about the elderly may be shifting. pp. 197–198.

Symbolic Interactionist Perspectives on Aging

WHAT FACTORS INFLUENCE PERCEPTIONS OF AGING?
Symbolic interactionists stress that, by itself, reaching a particular age has no meaning. They identify three factors that influence when people label themselves as "old": biological changes, biographical events, and cultural timetables. Cross-cultural comparisons demonstrate the role of culture in determining how individuals experience aging. **Ageism**, or negative reaction to the elderly, is based on stereotypes, which are influenced by the mass media. pp. 201–205.

Feminist Perspectives

HOW DOES AGING AFFECT MEN AND WOMEN DIFFERENTLY?
Extensive feminist analysis has shown that the aging process affects men and women differently. Aging women are more likely to be socially marginalized and dismissed, as evidenced by the popular belief that men are more attractive and sexual at an older age than women. Women are also likely to find themselves economically disadvantaged, particularly if they have taken "time out" to devote themselves to their home and family. Finally, older women who are also members of minority groups—Aboriginal women, lesbians, disabled women—are likely to experience additional societal prejudices. pp. 205–206.

Conflict Perspectives: The Political Economy of Aging

IS THERE CONFLICT AMONG DIFFERENT AGE GROUPS?
Government legislation is an example of one generation disputing the demands made by another generation for limited resources. As the **dependency ratio**—the number of workers who support one retired person—decreases, workers may become resentful. pp. 206–210.

The Dependency Crisis

WHAT ARE SOME OF THE PROBLEMS FACED BY THE ELDERLY TODAY?
Due to differences in mortality and work histories, older women are more likely to live alone and to be poor. pp. 210–212.

Theoretical Paradigms

	CLASSICAL PARADIGMS			RECENT PARADIGMS	
	Structural-Functional Paradigm	Social-Conflict Paradigm	Symbolic-Interaction Paradigm	Feminist Paradigm	Postmodernist Paradigm
What is the level of analysis?	Macro level	Macro level	Micro level	Micro and macro levels	Micro and macro levels
How is age discrimination explained?	Older people are not discriminated against, but are regarded as being in a separate and distinct stage of life. They contribute to the maintenance of tradition within families and communities.	Older people generally stand outside of productive activity, as they are no longer in the labour force, and they have fewer resources within society.	Older people are labelled in such ways that they appear to be less capable and require more help with everyday tasks than younger people.	Aging exacerbates problems of power and inequality for women. Older women are even more marginalized than their younger counterparts.	Older people—particularly older women—are invisible in cultural representations such as art, literature and mass media. Images are often negative or absent—giving the impression that the elderly do not count.

KEY TERMS

ageism   202

dependency ratio   207

greying of Canada   197

life expectancy   197

timetables   202

WEBLINKS

All URLs listed are current as of the printing of this book.

Elderweb
www.elderweb.org
An online community of older adult computer users.

Division of Aging and Seniors
www.phac-aspc.gc.ca/seniors-aines/index_pages/
whatsnew_e.htm
Health Canada's Division of Aging and Seniors provides federal leadership in areas pertaining to aging and seniors, and serves as a focal point for information and a centre of expertise.

Canadian Association on Gerontology
www.cagacg.ca
The Canadian Association on Gerontology (CAG-ACG) is a national, multidisciplinary association established to provide leadership in matters relating to the aging population in Canada. CAG fosters research, education, and policy aimed at improving the quality of life of the elderly in Canada.

Canadian Network for the Prevention of Elder Abuse
www.cnpea.ca
The CNPEA website provides information and raises awareness about abuse and neglect in later life. This information includes Canadian laws on abuse and neglect and strategies for preventing abuse.

Alzheimer Society
www.alzheimers.ca
The Alzheimer Society of Canada is dedicated to preventing and treating the cognitive decline of Alzheimer's disease and to providing practical, up-to-the-minute information that empowers caregivers to manage the disease more confidently, effectively, and economically.

Canada's Association for the Fifty-Plus (CARP)
www.carp.ca
CARP provides information of interest to Canadian seniors 50 and over and seeks to lobby on their behalf with federal, provincial, and local governments.

CRITICAL THINKING QUESTIONS

1. When you envision your own life course, how do you imagine your mid-life and old age, and how does that vision relate to your attitudes toward the elderly in Canada today?

2. In what ways are gender differences in aging intensified or reduced by other factors such as being a recent immigrant, belonging to a specific ethnic group, or being well-off?

3. What kinds of research projects on aging would critical social gerontologists want to pursue?

4. Thinking about the last half-dozen movies you watched, do you think that media images of older men or women are becoming more positive?

5. If the social construction of adolescence and old age are going to be revised in the next generation, what kinds of changes in our values and social institutions would have to take place?

6. Do you think it is likely that seniors and young Canadians will face conflict over access to resources such as health care and employment? Access the Research Navigator through MySocLab and use keywords such as "ageism," "seniors," and "retirement" to locate relevant and recent scholarly and popular press publications to help you answer this question.

 **PEARSON mysoclab** Explore the topics covered in this chapter on MySocLab using the access information provided with this text. Interactive resources for studying include multimedia tutorials, video clips, practice tests, quizzes, and animated maps and figures.

10 Bureaucracy and the Corporation

LEARNING OUTCOMES

After you have studied this chapter, you will be able to answer the following questions:

1. **How did the rationalization of society come about?**

2. **What are formal organizations?**

3. **What dysfunctions are often associated with bureaucracies?**

4. **What are the functions of voluntary associations?**

5. **What is the "iron law of oligarchy"?**

6. **How does the corporate culture affect workers?**

7. **What does "humanizing a work setting" mean?**

8. **What is lean production?**

This was an exciting day for Jennifer. She would be starting university in a week's time and today was the day her electronic window would open, allowing her to enroll in first-year courses. She had circled this date in her calendar on the last day of high school, and was ready to begin her online registration promptly at 9:00 a.m. Jennifer had been advised that a number of the courses she wished to take would fill quickly and that she should enroll without delay on the day her registration window opened. She sat down at her computer, prepared with a list of courses and course codes, her student number, and tuition payment information.

The summer had gone by quickly. High school had ended with such pleasant memories: the prom, graduation—how proud she had felt at that moment. But best of all had been her final term's marks and university admission scholarship. Everyone, especially Jennifer, had been pleasantly surprised as she read aloud her letter of admission to the program in health sciences, her top choice.

Her guidance and career advisors had assured Jennifer that there would be an endless number of opportunities now open to her. As she sat at her computer to begin the registration process, she thought about the final farewell party she had been planning with friends, whom she most likely wouldn't see until Thanksgiving or later. She suddenly snapped out of her reverie, however. Registering online was not as simple as she thought it would be. After an hour at the computer spent repeatedly typing in her nine-digit student number, she had still not gained access and, like hundreds of other students, felt increasingly frustrated with her first university experience. When she finally accessed her registration, she excitedly typed in all the codes of the courses she had carefully selected and pressed the tab to confirm her enrollment. But the message that popped up caught Jennifer by surprise: REGISTRATION DENIED.

In tears, she called the university and after several attempts to get through, was told by a clerk in the registrar's office that students are required to pay tuition or submit proof of scholarship *before* registering in courses and that, unfortunately, this information was accidentally left out of the early admissions letters that had been sent to students in March. Despite the error, no exceptions would be made. Jennifer would have to clear the matter with financial services, then hope that the classes she had been planning to take were not full.

Jennifer felt thoroughly confused. Dejected, she logged on to the university's website again, located financial services, typed in her nine-digit student number, and waited for access. Paying tuition and enrolling in courses—tasks Jennifer thought would take less than an hour, took the better part of a day during her last week of summer vacation.

THE RATIONALIZATION OF SOCIETY

We can all understand Jennifer's dismay. Things could have been clearer—a lot clearer. The problem is that many universities must register thousands of students, most of whom will start classes on the same day. To do so, they have broken up the admissions and registration process into tiny bits, with each piece making a small contribution to the task as a whole. As Jennifer discovered, however, things don't always go as planned.

In this chapter, we will examine how society is organized to "get jobs done." As you read, you may be able to trace the source of some of your frustrations to this form of social organization, as well as see how your welfare depends on it.

Over the course of history, societies have undergone transformations so extensive that whole new types of societies emerged. In addition to these transformations, a major development has been **rationality**—the idea that rules, efficiency, and practical results should guide human affairs. An emphasis on rationality underlies even the relatively recent shift to a globalized information society. Let's examine how this approach to life—which we often take for granted today—came about.

The Contribution of Max Weber

Max Weber (1864–1920), a sociologist whose studies incorporated an amazingly broad sweep of world history, concluded that until recently, the world's groups and nations were immersed in a **traditional orientation** to life—that is, the idea that the past is the best guide for the present. In this view, deep, lifelong obligations and responsibilities and personal relationships characterize society. What exists is good because it has passed the test of time. Customs—and relationships based on them—have served people well and should not be lightly abandoned. A central orientation of traditional society is to protect the status quo. Change is viewed with suspicion and comes slowly, if at all.

The traditional orientation stands in the way of industrialization, which requires willingness—even eagerness—to change. If a society is to industrialize, a deep-seated shift must occur in people's thinking—from wanting to keep things as they are to seeking the most efficient means of accomplishing tasks. Under capitalism, the "bottom line" (results) becomes the primary concern and rule-of-thumb methods are replaced by explicit rules and procedures for measuring results. This change requires an entirely different way of looking at life and is in opposition to the basic orientation of all human societies prior to industrialization. Weber referred to this change as the **rationalization of society**. This new *rationality* meant that things were to be judged according to the bottom line instead of by personal relationships and considerations. Rationality has become so deeply embedded in our ways of life that it is difficult to grasp how fundamentally different society and human relationships were prior to industrialization. How, then, did the rationalization of society come about? How did people break through their profound resistance to change?

To Weber, this problem was like an unsolved murder is to a detective. Weber's primary clue was that capitalism thrived only in certain parts of Europe. If he could determine why this was so, he was convinced he could discover the root of this fundamental change in human society. As Weber pursued the matter, he concluded that religion held the key, given that capitalism flourished in Protestant countries while Roman Catholics held on to tradition and were relatively untouched by the ideology.

Why did Roman Catholics resist change while Protestants embraced the new emphasis on practical results? Weber's answer to this puzzle has been the source of controversy since it was first proposed in his highly influential book, *The Protestant Ethic and the Spirit of Capitalism* (1904–05/1958). He concluded that essential differences between the two religions held the answer. Roman Catholic doctrine emphasized the acceptance of present arrangements, not change: "God wants you where you are. You owe primary allegiance to the Church, to your family, to your community and country. Accept your lot in life and remain rooted." But Protestant theology, especially Calvinism, was quite different, Weber argued. Calvinists (followers of the teachings of John Calvin, 1509–1564) believed that before birth, people are destined to go either to heaven or to hell—and they would not know their destiny until after death. Weber believed that this idea filled Calvinists with an anxiety that pervaded their entire lives. Salvation became their chief concern in life—they wanted to know now where they were going after death.

To resolve their spiritual dilemma, Calvinists came up with an ingenious solution: God did not want those chosen for heaven to be ignorant of their destiny. Consequently, he would bestow signs of approval on them. But what signs? The answer, they claimed, was to be found not in mystical, spiritual experiences, but in tangible achievements that people could see and measure. The sign of God's approval became success: those whom God had predestined for heaven would be blessed with visible success in life.

This idea transformed Calvinists' lives, serving as an extraordinary motivation. Because Calvinists also believed that thrift is a virtue, their dedication to work led to an accumulation of money. Calvinists could not spend the excess on themselves, however, for to purchase items beyond the basic necessities was considered sinful. **Capitalism**, the investment of capital in the hope of producing profits, became an outlet for excess money, while the success of such investments became a further sign of God's approval. As such, worldly success was transformed into a spiritual virtue, and other branches of Protestantism, although less extreme, adopted the creed of thrift and hard work.

When society began to rationalize, production of goods was broken up into its various components, with individuals assigned only specific tasks. This painting of a pottery shop in England in the late nineteenth century is by Alfred Morgan (1862–1904).

Consequently, said Weber, Protestant countries embraced capitalism.

What does this have to do with rationalization? Simply put, capitalism demands *rationalization*, the careful calculation of practical results. If profits are your goal, you must compute income and expenses. You must calculate inventories and wages, the cost of producing goods, and how much they bring in. You must find ways to lower your costs, which often means decreasing labour costs. For example, you might require that workers produce more units per hour or that work be intensified in such a way that fewer workers are needed to do the job. You must determine "the bottom line." Under this arrangement, efficiency, not tradition, becomes the drum to which you march. Traditional ways of doing things, if inefficient, must be replaced, for what counts are the results.

Marx on Rationalization

Another sociologist, Karl Marx (1818–1883), the originator of conflict theory, also observed that tradition had given way to rationality. When he analyzed the problem, however, Marx came up with an entirely different explanation. Marx dismissed Weber's notion that commitment to particular religious beliefs accounted for the rise of capitalism. He did not think religion had anything to do with breaking the bondage of tradition. Rather, Marx concluded that the switch to rationality was the result of capitalism itself. When people saw that capitalism was more efficient, that it produced things they wanted in much greater abundance, and that it amassed profit and wealth, they embraced rationality, giving up their traditional thinking. Thus, Marx reversed the equation: the transition to capitalism, he said, changed the way people thought about life, not the other way around.

Marx criticized capitalism's rationality and emphasis on efficiency. He argued that capitalism produces inequalities within societies, separating people on the basis of wealth, social class, ideologies, and power. He argued that the values and practices of capitalism contributed to feelings of **alienation**. The needs of workers became secondary to the interests of capital and the capitalists' persistent pursuit of profit—often at any cost.

Who is correct? Weber, with his conclusion that Protestantism produced rationality, which then paved the way for capitalism? Or Marx, who concluded that capitalism produced rationality? No analyst has yet reconciled the two opposing answers to the satisfaction of sociologists.

Focus Question

How did Marx and Weber differ in their views on rationality and how it came to permeate society?

FEMINIST AND CRITICAL APPROACHES TO THE STUDY OF ORGANIZATIONS

For many years, textbooks and studies of organizations have presented facts about organizational structures, but have overlooked the characteristics and roles of the people who make up organizations. Feminists and other critical thinkers contend that this omission presents a problem for women and minorities, whose voices and perspectives are not taken into account in "generic" descriptions of the organization. These critics argue that the "generic" presentations are not "faceless," but rather are representations of a dominant (male) perspective (Mills, Simmons, & Mills, 2005).

Feminist analyses of organizations take into account the ways in which women are affected by organizational arrangements. They question the distribution of power and authority and seek to understand why and how women are discriminated against within organizational structures. They ask, for example, why women are rarely found in corporate boardrooms as decision-makers, despite their high numbers in the lower levels of organizational hierarchies and in clerical or other female-dominated fields. Radical feminists take such questions further, seeking change to organizational structures that allow men to dominate.

Following this critical tradition of questioning the ways in which organizations are gendered are more recent approaches that include the experiences of diverse groups and how their concerns and rights as workers, consumers, and clients may be excluded, ignored, or cast aside within organizations. Along with concerns raised by feminists, the new critical approaches to organizations are inclusive, accounting for the experiences of racialized minorities, Aboriginal peoples, people with visible and invisible disabilities, and sexually diverse groups—gay, lesbian, bisexual, and transgendered people.

FORMAL ORGANIZATIONS AND BUREAUCRACY

Regardless of whether Marx or Weber was right about its cause, rationality was a totally different way of thinking that came to permeate society. This new orientation transformed the way society is organized. As a result, **formal organizations**—secondary groups designed to achieve explicit objectives—have become a central feature of contemporary society. We engage in multiple and complex sets of interactions with formal organizations—in schools, workplaces, hospitals and other care-providing institutions, governments, religious organizations, businesses, and so on. In our daily routines—attending classes, shopping, visiting a nursing home resident, paying a parking ticket, playing organized sports, or picking up dinner from a fast-food chain—we interact with dozens of formal organizations, most of which share similar central characteristics.

Formal Organizations

Prior to industrialization, only a few formal organizations existed. The guilds of Western Europe during the twelfth century are an example. People who performed similar work organized to control their craft in a local area. They set prices and standards of workmanship (Bridgwater, 1953; Guilds, 2005). Much like modern unions, guilds also prevented outsiders (those who were not members) from working at a particular craft. Another example of an early formal organization is the army, with its structure of senior officers, junior officers, and ranks. Formal armies date back to early history.

With industrialization, secondary groups became common. Today we take their existence for granted and, beginning with grade school, spend a good deal of time participating in them. Formal organizations tend to develop into bureaucracies and, in general, the larger the formal organization, the more likely it is to be bureaucratic.

The Essential Characteristics of Bureaucracies

Although a police department, post office, university, and General Motors may not seem to have much in common,

they are all bureaucracies. As Weber (1913/1947) analyzed them, the essential characteristics of a **bureaucracy** are as follows:

1. *A hierarchy with assignments flowing downward and accountability flowing upward.* The organization is divided into clear-cut levels. Each level assigns responsibilities to the level beneath it, while each lower level is accountable to the level above for fulfilling those assignments. The bureaucratic structure of a typical university is shown in Figure 10.1.

2. *A division of labour.* Every member of a bureaucracy has a specific task to fulfill, and all tasks are then coordinated to accomplish the purpose of the organization. In a university, for example, a professor does not run the heating system, the president does not teach, and a secretary does not evaluate textbooks. These tasks are distributed among people who have been trained to do them.

3. *Written rules.* In their attempt to become efficient, bureaucracies stress written procedures. In general, the longer a bureaucracy exists and the larger it grows, the more written rules it has. The rules of bureaucracies may cover just about every imaginable situation. Often an organization's rules are bound in handbooks, with separate sections for each department and specific guidelines for submitting annual or regular reports to superiors.

4. *Written communications and records.* Records, now often in digital formats, are kept of much of what occurs in a bureaucracy. Consequently, workers in bureaucracies spend a fair amount of time sending memos, emailing messages back and forth, and keeping detailed records—sometimes referred to as "paper trails"—of all their interactions and correspondence. Universities, for example, require that each faculty member keep his or her curriculum vitae up to date and that departments write an annual report listing what was accomplished in teaching, research, and service. These materials go to committees whose task it is to evaluate the relative performance of the university's departments and the courses offered.

5. *Impersonality and replaceability.* It is the office that is important in a bureaucracy, rather than the individual who holds the office. Ultimately, you work for the organization. Your supervisor or boss simply heads a post in the organization, is responsible for one or more employees, and, like you, is replaceable. Consequently, members of a bureaucracy owe allegiance to the office, not to particular people. If you work in a bureaucracy, you become a small cog in a large machine. Each worker is a replaceable unit, and many others are available to fulfill each particular function.

These five characteristics not only help bureaucracies reach their goals, but also allow for their growth and

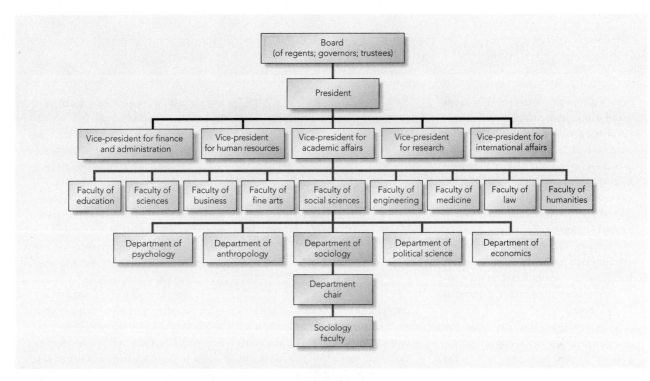

FIGURE 10.1 Typical Bureaucratic Structure of a Medium-Sized University

This is a scaled-down version of a university's bureaucratic structure. The actual lines of authority in a university are likely to be much more complicated than those depicted here. A university may have a chancellor and several vice-presidents, each responsible for a certain campus or major function. Although extensions of authority are given only for the vice-president of academic affairs and the faculty of social sciences in this figure, each of the other vice-presidents and faculties has similar positions. If the figure were to be extended, departmental administrators and student advisors would be shown and eventually, somewhere, even students.

endurance. If the head of a bureaucracy dies, retires, or resigns, the organization continues, hardly skipping a beat. Unlike in a "mom and pop" operation, the functioning of a bureaucratic unit does not depend on the individual who heads it. The expansion (or domination, according to some) of bureaucracies in contemporary society is illustrated by the McDonaldization example in the Down-to-Earth Sociology box on the next page.

Today's armies, no matter what their country of allegiance, are bureaucracies. They have a strict hierarchy of rank, division of labour, and impersonality (emphasis on the office rather than the individual) and stress written records, rules, and communications—essential characteristics as identified by Max Weber. This army in India, though its outward appearance differs from Western standards, is no exception to the principle.

Sociologist George Ritzer (1993) believes that the thousands of McDonald's restaurants that dot the North American landscape—and increasingly, the world—have much greater significance than the convenience of fast food. He coined the term "the **McDonaldization** of society" to refer to the increasing rationalization of the routine tasks of everyday life. Ritzer argues that the modern fast-food restaurant presents a better paradigm for rationalization than Weber's conceptualization of bureaucracy (Ritzer, 1998).

He points out that Ray Kroc, the founder of McDonald's, applied principles developed by Henry Ford to the preparation and serving of food. A 1958 operations manual spelled out exact procedures:

> It told operators exactly how to draw milk shakes, grill hamburgers, and fry potatoes. It specified precise cooking times for all products and temperature settings for all equipment. It fixed standard portions on every food item, down to the quarter ounce of onions placed on each hamburger patty and the thirty-two slices per pound of cheese. It specified that french fries be cut at nine thirty-seconds of an inch thick... Those working the grill were instructed to put hamburgers down on the grill moving from left to right,

McDonald's in Beijing, China.

creating six rows of six patties each. And because the first two rows were farthest from the heating element, they were instructed (and still are) to flip the third row first, then the fourth, fifth, and sixth before flipping the first two.

Ritzer stresses that "McDonaldization" refers to more than the robot-like assembly of food. Rather, this process, occurring throughout society, is transforming our lives. Shopping malls are controlled environments of approved design, logos, colours, and opening and closing hours. Travel agencies transport middle-class tourists to 10 European capitals in 14 days, with each visitor experiencing exactly the same hotels, restaurants, and other predictable settings. Varied television stations produce the same bland, instant news—in short, non-analytic pieces that can be

consumed between gulps of the McShake or the McBurger.

Efficiency may bring reduced prices and dependability, but at a cost—the loss of something difficult to define, a quality of life washed away by rationalization—as predictability replaces spontaneity. If you travel and take packaged tours, for example, you may never have enjoyable, eye-opening experiences that could add to your appreciation of human diversity.

In any event, the future has arrived, with a strong trend toward the McDonaldization of human experience. For good or bad, our social destiny seems to be to live in prepackaged settings. When education becomes rationalized—which is now in process—our children will no longer have to put up with the idiosyncrasies of real professors, people who think ideas must be discussed endlessly and who never come to decisive answers anyway. We seem to want instant, preformed solutions to social issues, like those we find in mathematics and engineering. Fortunately, our children will be instructed in computerized courses, in which everyone learns the same answers—approved, "politically correct," precise, and proper ways to think about social issues. This will certainly be efficient—and proof that the "iron cage" of bureaucracy has entrapped us, as Weber predicted.

In an attempt to demonstrate the impact of the fast-food industry on our health and well-being, culture, and environment (i.e., McDonaldization), filmmaker Morgan Spurlock produced the award-winning documentary *Super Size Me*, in which he chronicled his own "journey" as he lived on nothing but McDonald's fast food for an entire month. The film is a critical look at the billion-dollar fast-food industry, its impact on our health and way of life, its addictiveness, and its influence on a global level (www.supersizeme.com).

While McDonaldization refers to the organization of work and aspects of culture and everyday life, the term

Walmartization refers to profound transformations in regional and global economies brought about by the sheer size, influence, and power of the big-box department store Wal-Mart. Worldwide, Wal-Mart now tops the Global 500, *Fortune*'s annual list of the top 500 corporations in the world, with over $351 billion in sales, 1.9 million workers (Demos & Tkaczyk, 2007), and more than 176 million customers worldwide every week in 2006 (Pier, 2007: p. 24). The largest employer in the United States, Wal-Mart's policy of low prices is maintained by paying workers substandard wages and providing them with few, if any, benefits. When Wal-Mart moves into a community, many

Technology has changed our lives fundamentally. As shown in this 1904 photo, telephone operators used to make connections by hand. Labour was so intensive and problems so numerous that it required about one supervisor for every four workers. Long distance calls, with their numerous hand-made connections, were not only slower, but also more expensive—perhaps 100 times higher than what they now cost.

smaller businesses, unable to compete, go bankrupt and invariably close their doors. Without competition, Wal-Mart is free to raise its prices. According to Wal-Mart Watch, an organization of citizens affected by Wal-Mart's policies, three jobs are lost for every two that are created when Wal-Mart moves into a community (Ribeiro, 2005; Fishman, 2003).

Wal-Mart is aggressively anti-union, has intimidated unionists (Pier, 2007; Marotte, 2005), and has closed stores (as in Jonquière, Quebec) or threatened closure (as in Saint-Hyacinthe, Quebec) at the mention of unionization (Peritz, 2005). Moreover, it uses sophisticated technologies and tracking devices to monitor consumer choices and customers' buying patterns in different geographical areas, not only through cash register and bar coding systems, but through the implantation of microchips that allow information to be relayed through wireless technologies long after products have left manufacturers and warehouses in China. For many, Wal-Mart is synonymous with power and control.

"Ideal" versus "Real" Bureaucracy

Just as people's actions often stray from the norm, so do those of bureaucracies. The characteristics of bureaucracies identified by Weber are ideal types; that is, they are a composite of characteristics based on many specific examples. Think of a judge at a dog show. He or she has a mental image of what a certain breed of dog should look like and judges each dog according to that mental image. No one dog will have all the characteristics, but all dogs of that breed put together have them. Thus, a particular organization may be ranked high or low on some characteristic and still qualify as a bureaucracy. Instead of labelling a particular organization as a "bureaucracy" or "not a bureaucracy," it might make more sense to think in terms of the *extent* to which an organization is bureaucratized (Udy, 1959; R.H. Hall, 1963).

As such, a bureaucracy often differs from its ideal image. The actual lines of authority in an organization ("going through channels"), for example, may be quite different from those portrayed on organizational charts such as that shown in Figure 10.1. Suppose that before being promoted, a university president taught in the history department. As a result, friends from that department may have direct access to him or her. In giving their "input" (ranging from opinions about how to solve problems to personal grievances or even gossip), these individuals may skip their chairperson or even the dean of their faculty altogether.

Dysfunctions of Bureaucracies

Although Weber recognized that no other form of social organization has been found to be more efficient in the long run, his model accounts for only some of the characteristics of bureaucracies. They do not always operate smoothly and efficiently. We will now discuss some of bureaucracy's dysfunctions—red tape, lack of communication, alienation, goal displacement, and incompetence. The Thinking Critically about Social Controversy box on p. 223 presents a teenager's dilemma as she is caught between bureaucracies and their policies.

RED TAPE: A RULE IS A RULE As Jennifer from the opening vignette discovered, bureaucracies can be filled with so much red tape that they impede the purpose of the organization.

For a single parent trying to escape poverty and make life a little more comfortable for her children, for example, rules regarding eligibility for benefits are too inflexible. After working only a few extra hours at her part-time job as a bank teller, provincial social services declared a single mother ineligible for a daycare subsidy because she earned a few dollars

This is the way that some people view bureaucracies; stilted, slow-moving, and destructive to the individual. Bureaucracies can be like this, but not all bureaucracies are alike. Some are innovative and unleash creative energy.

more than the maximum allowed (Daly, 2006). Her choices were to quit her job and apply for welfare or keep the job and pay the full cost of day care. Neither option is very appealing. Unable to afford day care without a subsidy and unable to live on the income from her part-time job, this mother found herself between the proverbial "rock and a hard place."

LACK OF COMMUNICATION BETWEEN UNITS Each unit within a bureaucracy performs specialized tasks, which are designed to contribute to the organization's overall goals. At times, units fail to communicate with one another and end up working at cross-purposes. In Granada, Spain, for example, the local government was concerned about the rundown appearance of buildings along one of its main roads. Consequently, one unit of the government fixed the fronts of these buildings, painting and repairing concrete, iron, and stonework. The results were impressive, and the unit was proud of what it had accomplished. The only problem was that another unit of the government had slated these same buildings for demolition (Arías, 1993). With neither unit of the bureaucracy knowing what the other was doing, a huge expense and effort ended in a heap of rubble.

BUREAUCRATIC ALIENATION Many workers find it disturbing to deal with others in terms of roles, rules, and functions rather than as individuals. Similarly, they may dislike writing memos and sending messages instead of talking to people face to face. It is not surprising, then, that workers in large organizations sometimes feel more like objects than people, or, as Weber (1922/1978) described, ". . . only a small cog in a ceaselessly moving mechanism which prescribes to [them] an endlessly fixed routine. . ." Because workers must deal with one another formally, and because they constantly perform routine tasks, some come to feel that no one cares about them and that they are misfits in their surroundings.

Marx termed these reactions *alienation* and attributed them to the fact that workers are cut off from the finished product of their labour. Although assigning workers to repetitive tasks makes for efficient production, Marx argued that it also reduces their satisfaction by limiting their creativity and sense of contribution to the finished product. Underlying alienation is the workers' loss of control over their work, because they no longer own their own tools or make decisions. Before industrialization, individual workers used their own tools to produce an entire product, such as a chair or table. Now, capitalists own the machinery and tools and assign each worker only a single step or two in the entire production process. Relegated to repetitive tasks that seem remote from the finished product, workers lose a sense of identity with what they produce. Ultimately, they come to feel estranged not only from their products but from the work environment as a whole.

RESISTING ALIENATION Alienation is not a pleasant experience. Because workers want to feel valued and have a sense of control over their work, they resist alienation. Forming primary groups is a major form of such resistance. Workers band together in informal settings—at lunch, around desks, for a drink after work—to give one another approval for jobs well done and express sympathy for the shared need to put up with cantankerous bosses, meaningless routines, and endless rules. They relate to one another not just as workers, but as people of value. They laugh and tell jokes, talk about their families, problems, goals, and often, their love lives.

Consider the common sight of work areas in an office decorated with family and vacation photos. The sociological implication is that of workers striving to overcome alienation. By staking a claim to individuality, they are rejecting an identity of mere machines performing functions. Adding multidimensionality to work relationships restores workers' sense of being individuals rather than mere cogs in an endlessly moving machine.

One bureaucracy's rules may clash with another's, creating a situation in which it is impossible for people to have their needs met fairly. Bureaucratic dysfunction may inadvertently result in tremendous disadvantage to people who question or challenge rules, policies, or procedures, or even jeopardize their opportunities or threaten their well-being.

Consider the case of Jackie B., a high school student and athlete. After graduating with honours from her local public middle school, Jackie left her friends behind to attend a separate secondary school in her area. Her reason was simple, or so she thought: Jackie was a highly competitive soccer player and wanted to take up the sport of rowing. The separate school supported not only a rowing team, but also the most highly successful and well-regarded girls' soccer program in the province.

Jackie's Grade 9 school year began with the usual awkwardness experienced by most students beginning high school. But soon after the year began, Jackie found herself a victim of bullying and harassment. At first she ignored it and fully expected that it would end as she continued to prove herself on the field and as an outstanding newcomer to the rowing crew. As the year went on, she became increasingly despondent. She found herself alone and depressed and her marks began to drop. She feared reporting the bullies. The situation was brought to the attention of the school's senior administration, and when pressed, Jackie divulged the name of one of the leading bullies. However, the situation was poorly handled, and Jackie's sense of security both within the school and in public places, such as movie theatres, was threatened. For many, the solution would be simple: transfer to the public high school. For an athlete, however, this simple solution can be very costly.

To prevent coaches from "shopping" for star athletes and luring students from one school to another, either inside or outside home boundaries, all provincial athletic associations have a rule regarding transfers. If a student transfers schools, she or he will not be allowed to participate in any sport (falling under the association's umbrella) in which she or he was involved during the previous school year. Jackie was devastated by her situation. Transferring schools would possibly mean sitting out of sports for a year, and staying put would be increasingly difficult to deal with. However, exceptions are sometimes made to this rule, and Jackie had an opportunity to appeal her case. Her chances of winning were slim but would be considerably improved if she could obtain a statement by an official from the separate school confirming that she had been a victim of bullying and harassment and transferred as a result.

Jackie's coaches and teachers at the new school were highly accommodating and helped her and her parents with the appeal. Nevertheless, they ran into a major roadblock: no one from Jackie's previous school would help. Her parents' phone calls were not returned and the situation was swept under the carpet. Even several teachers who had been well aware of the problems Jackie had experienced refused to help her. It seems that they were under strict orders from the principal not to get involved. Worried that perhaps their careers might suffer, they turned a blind eye to Jackie's plight, despite their knowledge of the situation and their willingness to agree that bullying and harassment are serious problems in schools and that steps should be taken to eliminate them.

Without supporting documents from the separate school, Jackie lost her appeal. She paid the price for being on the receiving end of the bullies' actions. It would have cost her, whether or not she had chosen to transfer. If she had remained at the separate school, she would have continued to be victimized at the expense of her marks and well-being. Her decision to transfer to the public high school was supported by family and friends as the only reasonable choice, but the price she paid for this decision was clearly outrageous.

For Your Consideration

How was Jackie limited by bureaucratic decision-making? What does her situation tell us about bureaucratic alienation, careerism, communication within or between bureaucracies, and lines of authority? What message would this incident have given to the bullies?

When they decide to take collective action about workplace struggles, workers form a union. A union provides strength in numbers, a source of action and support, and a legal avenue through which workers' rights are sanctioned and their concerns addressed.

THE ALIENATED BUREAUCRAT Not all workers succeed in resisting alienation, however, and some become extremely alienated. They remain in an organization because they see no viable alternative or because they have "only so many years until retirement." They hate every minute of it, and it shows—in their attitudes toward clients, fellow workers, and especially toward authority in the organization. The alienated bureaucrat does not take initiative, will not do anything for the organization beyond what he or she is absolutely required to do, and uses rules to justify doing as little as possible. If

Jennifer in the chapter's opening vignette had come across an alienated bureaucrat behind the registration window, she might have been told: "What's the matter with you—can't you read? Everyone else manages to pay their fees before going online to register for courses, why can't you? I don't know what kind of students they are sending us nowadays." If the worker had been even more alienated, he or she might even have denied knowledge of how to resolve the problem.

Recently, there has been an increase in the incidence of "work rage," in which workers who are stressed and facing growing workloads or are disrespected by co-workers or managers vent their frustrations at work by hurling things across a room, yelling at or threatening others, or swearing. A British survey of over 1200 workers found that almost four out of five admitted losing their tempers and lashing out at the office (Immen, 2008). With the growth in technology and new expectations that workers be available to respond instantaneously to clients' and managers' requests, levels of stress and anxiety are hitting the roof. Such circumstances are detrimental to all workers. Managers might find ways to ease workers' frustrations by involving them in decisions regarding their jobs and re-assessing workloads and unreasonable demands on their time.

Some managers deal with such situations poorly by shunting off alienated workers into small bureaucratic corners, where they are assigned trivial tasks and have little chance of coming into contact with the public or even other workers. This treatment only alienates them further.

GOAL DISPLACEMENT Bureaucracies sometimes take on a life of their own, adopting new goals in place of old ones. In this process, called **goal displacement**, even when the goal of an organization has been achieved and there is no longer any reason for it to carry on, it does anyway. A good example is The War Amps, founded as a fraternal organization in 1918 to provide counselling, self-help, and assistance to servicemen who lost one or more limbs or complete eyesight on the front lines during World War I. The organization grew quickly and became well known around the world for its innovative programs for amputees. However, as the population of war amputees declined and as amputees drew upon other existing services and programs in their communities, The War Amps turned its attention to child amputees and in 1975 started the Child Amputee Program (CHAMP), providing prosthetics, education, and counselling to children with amputations (www.waramps.ca/about/history.html).

In insidious attempts to sell more and maximize profits, corporations sometimes misrepresent, confuse, or extend the potential uses of their products. The executives of Taser International, for example, describe the company as primarily concerned with public safety. Yet the company has been engaging in aggressive marketing practices to push its C2 model as a "personal protector"—available in pink, leopard print, or flaming red (for Valentine's Day), complete with a holster and built-in MP3 player (Klein, 2008). The marketing message for this product, directed mainly at men, is that if you love her, you'll protect her. This campaign is not only sexist, it's completely off the mark with regard to safety.

Thousands of Canadians were horrified by the video of Robert Dziekanski's death by taser at the Vancouver Airport late in 2007. Mr. Dziekanski, a Polish visitor to Canada, became agitated after he was unable to locate his relatives, and rather than attempting to calm him down, the RCMP zapped him with a taser gun. According to Amnesty International, 310 people in North America died in 2001 after being shocked with a taser (Klein, 2008). Given this figure, the outcry following Mr. Dziekanski's death, and the discovery that in 2006 in Toronto, of the 156 incidents involving tasers, the vast majority (147) of those targeted were in some type of crisis or appeared to have a "mental disorder" (Klein, 2008), the public should be asking whether the millions of dollars spent on electroshock weapons would be better spent on housing, or social and mental health services.

BUREAUCRATIC INCOMPETENCE In a tongue-in-cheek analysis of bureaucracies, Laurence Peter proposed what has become known as the **Peter principle**: each employee of a bureaucracy should be promoted to his or her *level of incompetence* (Peter & Hull, 1969). People who perform well in a bureaucracy would come to the attention of those higher up the chain of command and be promoted. If they again perform well, they will again be promoted. This process would continue until, finally, they would be promoted to a level at which they could no longer handle the responsibilities well— their level of incompetence. There they would hide behind the work of others, taking credit for what those under their direction might accomplish. Although the Peter principle contains a grain of truth, if it were generally true, bureaucracies would be staffed entirely by incompetents, and none could succeed. In reality, bureaucracies are remarkably efficient.

Focus Question

What are some of the ways bureaucracies become inefficient and dysfunctional?

The Sociological Significance of Bureaucracies

Perhaps the main sociological significance of bureaucracies is that they represent a fundamental change in how people relate to one another. When work is rooted in social relationships, much more is at stake than efficiency in performing tasks and keeping an eye on the bottom line. Seeing that all family members are employed, or that everyone in a community has a chance to make a living, for example, may be determining factors in making decisions. Bureaucracies, or the rationalization of society, changes this view (Volti, 1995).

VOLUNTARISM AND VOLUNTARY ORGANIZATIONS

Although bureaucracies have become the dominant form of organization for large, task-oriented groups and most often are structures of employment, **voluntary associations**—groups made up of volunteers who organize on the basis of some mutual interest—are also commonly found in our communities. A vast array of voluntary associations exist within every community, which may be local, regional, national, or international in scope. These organizations run on a not-for-profit basis and are distinguished from profit-making corporations. They are located within the broad public sector and may be governmental or non-governmental organizations, often referred to as NGOs. In some, members are exclusively involved in voluntary (unpaid) activities. For example, local historical societies, little league sports teams, and Kiwanis, Lions, and Rotary are linked to provincial or national bodies but are run at the local level solely on a voluntary basis. Sometimes, voluntary associations such as local hospitals or other institutions involved in care-related work or nationally recognized organizations such as the Canadian Cancer Society operate with a mix of paid staff and management who work in a centralized headquarters with an army of volunteers in local communities.

In the 1830s, a Frenchman travelled across the United States, observing the customs of this new nation. Alexis de Tocqueville wrote a widely read book about his observations, *Democracy in America* (1835/1966), which is still quoted for its insights into character. As an outsider, de Tocqueville was able to see patterns that people immersed in them could not. One such observation was that Americans joined a lot of voluntary associations.

Like their American neighbours, Canadians are proud of their commitment to voluntary associations. Visitors entering small towns across the country are often greeted by signs proclaiming which volunteer associations a particular town is involved with: Girl Scouts, Boy Scouts, Kiwanis, Lions, Knights of Columbus, Chamber of Commerce, Canadian Legion, or a host of others. One form of voluntary association is so prevalent that a separate sign usually indicates which denominations are present in the town: Roman Catholic, Jewish, Muslim, Buddhist, Lutheran, Anglican, and so on. Many other voluntary associations are not listed, such as political parties, unions, health clubs, social planning councils, minor hockey associations, the National Anti-Poverty Organization, Alcoholics Anonymous, the Canadian Cancer Society, and Citizens United For or Against This and That.

With the exception of people between the ages of 25 and 34, the percentage of Canadians who volunteer decreases as age increases. Over half of all youths aged 15 to 24 volunteered in 2004, whereas about a third of seniors 65 and older volunteered. However, the average number of hours volunteered rises with age, from an annual average of 139 hours for youth to 245 hours for seniors (Hall et al., 2006: p. 37).

Volunteers might work in a variety of settings: organizing community events, fundraising, campaigning, canvassing, and sitting on boards. With cutbacks in funding to hospitals and social service agencies, volunteer work has become essential in meeting many public organizations' service goals. Major organizations, like hospitals, sometimes hire full-time volunteer coordinators who provide training and support to this army of unpaid workers. Although most volunteers describe their work as personally rewarding, from a critical perspective it is sometimes argued that these workers are not valued highly enough for their contributions and are exploited by administrators and governments whose primary concern is cost-saving.

Through voluntary associations, Canadians express a wide range of interests, goals, opinions, and even dissatisfactions. Some groups are local, consisting of only a few volunteers; others are national, with paid professional staffs. Some are temporary, organized to accomplish a specific task, such as arranging a town's next Labour Day parade; others, such as the Scouts and political parties, are permanent, large, secondary organizations with clear lines of command—and they are also bureaucracies. Many voluntary organizations are complexly interconnected with formal organizations and corporations. For example, we often see McDonald's cold drink coolers at events for children; Tim Horton's sponsors "Timbits" hockey programs for young kids, and a variety of companies buy strategically placed ads in and around minor league sporting events, support local teams, and supply equipment. Such arrangements are often made by volunteers.

Most people who spend their time volunteering do so freely. However, young people in particular face the paradox of coercive volunteerism, as examined in the Thinking Critically about Social Controversy box on the next page.

Shared Interests

Voluntary associations represent no single interest or purpose. They can be reactionary, dragged screaming into the present as their nails claw the walls of the past, or they can lead the vanguard for social change, announcing their vision of a better world. The anti-globalization movement, for example, extends across the globe, bringing together scientists and activists who question policies such as NAFTA and raise awareness of human rights, labour, and environmental issues while examining the decisions of organizations such as the World Bank and International Monetary Fund.

In spite of their amazing diversity, however, a common thread runs through all voluntary associations: mutual interest. Although the particular interest varies from group to group, shared interest in some view or activity provides the tie that binds each group's members together.

Although members are united by shared interests, their motivations for joining a volunteer group differ widely. Some join because they have strong convictions concerning the stated purpose of the organization; others simply because

During my graduate class last fall, someone referred to the requirement in Ontario that high school students complete a minimum of 40 hours of volunteer work before graduation. Most of my graduate students were unfamiliar with this policy, having come to York University from outside Ontario or Canada or having been simply too far removed from the Ontario high school scene. They were outraged that graduation is now contingent upon completion of these hours and that the requirement is strict enough that if a student fails to complete the work, his or her high school graduation will be delayed. The government warns schools not to bend the rules on this requirement. In my community, the local paper has printed a number of articles about the problems faced by students who delay volunteering until the end of their last term and then have to scramble to find a job to fulfill the requirement. It's a "tough love" experience for those who are unsuccessful.

While most of us would support the notion of youth contributing to communal welfare, this policy is severely flawed and is based on the false notion that volunteer work is truly advantageous for students' future well-being. Sending students to seek out "opportunities" in their communities and the process of matching students to jobs reflects divisions of class, opportunity, privilege, and access that are intrinsic to most educational and work experiences and are replicated in a variety of ways, including annual "bring-your-kids-to-work" days. Who benefits from this program of community service? Is voluntarism confused with coercion? And in this confusion, what messages are relayed?

In reflecting on my graduate students' reaction to the mandatory volunteering requirement, I began to think about the hidden curriculum in schools and the ways in which students are made to embrace particular status quo ideologies and political positions appropriate for the ongoing social order. What does the mandatory volunteer program teach about work and who gets it?

Consider some of the lessons hidden in the process of coercive volunteerism. A number of concerns about access to work are immediately apparent. Middle-class students—those whose parents are in white-collar or professional jobs—often have the best access to meaningful work, thereby widening the gap between students, schools, and communities. Some people, only a minority, get good jobs that they enjoy, that are fulfilling, and that draw upon their skills. Young athletes, for example, often coach younger children in sports such as basketball and swimming. They are able to draw on their own skills and are rewarded with respect and admiration from youngsters. This experience also enhances their own array of skills in that they learn to teach others their techniques and to develop patience in doing so.

If the purpose of the program is simply to provide students with work experience, it is clearly unnecessary. By the end of their senior high school year, most students have more work experience than they need. In fact, the overlap between school and paid work characterizes teenagers' lifestyles, and for many, there is no longer a distinction between years spent in school and years spent in the labour force, as there was for earlier generations. Recent surveys indicate that by Grade 11, the majority of students hold part-time jobs. These senior students are joined by over a third of Grade 10 students who also work for pay. And while many experts agree that working part-time hours may keep young people focused and teach them to organize their time, others caution that undertaking too much work robs them of time they could spend engaging in other activities—sports, for example—and distracts them from school and the joys of being young. While many students may be working a minimum number of hours, a sizable number work as many hours as possible, most often out of necessity. Their time is spent in a confusing and stressful pattern of school and work, often with little time to enjoy intellectual, political, and social life or to set a reasonable pace for learning and developing skills. There is a fine line between the benefits and drawbacks of part-time work for students. There are no clear and easy answers to the questions of how much they should do, what they should do, and when they should do it.

Forty hours of volunteer work is not enough to have a meaningful work experience or develop skills. This volunteer work comes with real costs. There are huge numbers of students who need to spend their time at their paid jobs and can ill afford to undertake volunteer work at this point in their lives. Considering the decline in real wages among families in Canada, the pressure on students to work as much as possible has increased remarkably. Summer jobs are not as lucrative as they once were, and as a result, more students have greater difficulties in making ends meet. Moreover, employers are often reluctant to change work schedules to allow for the flexibility required to host a concurrent voluntary position.

Despite the picture we can present of the stresses of young people and of their prodigious work experience, some will continue to promote the benefits of students' voluntary work as developing a sense of responsibility unmatched by in-class experience. However, for most young people, what is really acquired is yet another lesson about contingent work and the vulnerability of workers in the labour market. Young volunteers in public services in care-giving work—such as hospitals or nursing homes, for example—catch glimpses of restructured workplaces where staff are stretched to the limit and run off their feet. The few highly paid workers have little time to engage with other paid workers—let alone with teenaged student volunteers—about the rewards of their jobs, nor to mentor such temporary helpers. Yet some workers in public services may now be in a position where they have to rely on this help to get the work done. In nursing homes, for example, the need for volunteers exposes the working conditions faced by full-time workers who no longer have time in their schedules to talk to the residents and approach care work as they once did. Clearly we should be concerned about whether volunteers are taking on tasks that were once paid jobs.

Among the leading service positions for students in my community is the job of collecting and sorting groceries for the local food bank. Here, the lesson for student volunteers is that for many Canadians, frequent trips to the food bank have become a way of life—that a growing number of Canadians are working poor. They are reminded that even hard work does not provide adequate wages, even for the necessities, and that social assistance is inadequate. As a result, they learn to hang on to their after-school McJobs, hoping to avoid such insecurity, despite the inadequate wages and poor working conditions most experience.

Many critics argue that this type of labour market experience—contingent, underpaid, unorganized—is what corporatized schooling (the presence and influence of corporations on campuses and in schools) may be preparing youth for. In his critical analysis of schooling as edu-tainment, Randle Nelsen (2002), a professor at Lakehead University, argues that the corporatization of schools prepares students for the cultural context of work in a globalized economy. The mandatory 40-hour community service program fits this profile, with student workers "filling in"—taking up some of the tasks in what has become a compartmentalized and fragmented public service. The program is exploitative, providing neither real opportunities for valuable labour market experience nor fair access to the most coveted positions. While the program may offer students a gloomy yet realistic glimpse of their future work lives, most teenagers could simply use the time off.

Source: Pupo (2004). Adapted and reprinted by permission.

membership gives them a chance to make contacts that will help them politically or professionally. Some even join for social reasons. Others, like seniors, derive satisfaction and a sense of pride from using their skills and experience in a meaningful way.

With varied motivations for joining and diverse levels of commitment to goals, volunteer organizations often have a high turnover. Within every organization, however, is an inner core of individuals who stand firmly behind the group's goals, or at least are firmly committed to maintaining the organization itself. If this inner core loses commitment, the group is likely to fold.

The Problem of Oligarchy

Most organizations are run by a small number of members (Cnaan, 1991). Building on the term *oligarchy*, a system in which many are ruled by a few, sociologist Robert Michels (1876–1936) coined the term the **iron law of oligarchy** to refer to the way formal organizations come to be dominated by a small, self-perpetuating elite. The majority of members become passive, and an elite inner group maintains power by passing the leading positions from one clique member to another.

What many find depressing about the iron law of oligarchy is that it applies even to organizations strongly committed to democratic principles. Even Canadian political parties, for example, supposedly the backbone of the nation's representative government, have fallen prey to it. Run by an inner group that may or may not represent the community, political parties often pass their leadership positions from one elite member to another.

The iron law of oligarchy is not without limitations. Do members of an organization simply adopt a passive stance, thereby allowing a small group to continue to lead, or are the voices of the majority silenced or not heard by an elite that insulates itself? To maintain democracy, members of the inner group must remain attuned to the opinions of the others, regardless of their personal feelings. If the oligarchy gets too far out of line, the majority may rebel and throw the elite group out of office. Good leadership remains responsive to the needs and interests of the group.

Focus Question
How is the power structure within most formal organizations described?

WORKING WITHIN BUREAUCRACIES

Most of you will spend the majority of your working years working within a bureaucracy. Even if you are self-employed, you will spend a great amount of time interfacing with corporations of various sizes as well as with governments and agencies within the public sector. Although entrepreneurs often talk about setting up their own businesses in order to escape the drudgery of the inflexible hours and rules associated with working in a bureaucratic organization, it is almost impossible to avoid

Volunteer work has become an intricate part of the social fabric of Canadian communities. With cutbacks in funding to hospitals, social service agencies, long-term care facilities, and other public sector organizations, Canadians relying on these agencies have come to depend on this army of unpaid workers.

conducting business or settling one's affairs without interaction with bureaucrats.

The Corporate Culture: Consequences of Hidden Values

Who gets ahead in a large corporation? Although we might like to think that success is the consequence of intelligence and hard work, many factors other than merit underlie salary increases and promotions. Historically in Canada, family ties have secured many individuals to the power structure, or what author Peter C. Newman refers to as the "Canadian Establishment." Although a number of historically dominant family dynasties, such as the Eatons, have recently tumbled, others, such as the Irvings, Sobeys, Ganongs, Molsons, and McCains, maintain control over their corporate empires (Newman, 1999). A few among the group of Canada's most wealthy and powerful may trace their roots back to more humble origins. Paul Desmarais, CEO of Power Corporation, launched his career by revitalizing a small one-route bus line in Sudbury, Ontario; Jean Coutu and Murray Koffler, retail pharmacy magnates, each started with one corner drugstore; and diving for salvage was the first job of Newfoundland's premier businessman, Craig Dobbin, a lumberjack's son (Newman, 1999).

While hard work and a cunning business sense certainly helped a number of Canada's most prominent corporate executives, the largest group succeeded with the help of familial and social interrelations. Some have even enjoyed continued prosperity despite incompetence. Senior executives with companies such as Bell Canada, Dofasco Inc., Montreal Trust, Confederation Life, and others have, at one time or another, misjudged business prospects, and for their poor decision-making were actually promoted and given raises with bonuses (Newman, 1999). As sociologist Rosabeth Moss Kanter (1977, 1983) stresses, the **corporate culture**—the orientation that characterizes a corporate work setting—is crucial in determining people's corporate fate. She explains how a corporation's "hidden values"—those not officially part of the organization, but that nevertheless powerfully influence its members—operate as self-fulfilling stereotypes. The elite hold ideas about who are the best workers and colleagues, and those who fit this mould get better access to information and networking and are put in "fast-track" positions. Not surprisingly, these people perform better and become more committed to the organization, thus confirming initial expectations. In contrast, those judged to be outsiders find opportunities few and far between. They tend to work at a level beneath their capacity, come to think poorly of themselves, and become less committed to the organization.

Some members of the "Canadian Establishment," such as Paul Desmarais, CEO of Power Corporation, trace their roots to humble origins and owe their powerful positions to their own entrepreneurial efforts. Others secured their positions within the Canadian power structure through family ties.

and rewarded according to gendered and racialized assumptions and stereotypes (Jackson, 2005).

While a number of sociologists have discussed the ways in which women are overlooked in their pursuit of upward social mobility and how organizations may become more open to promoting women, Kathy Ferguson, in her 1984 book *The Feminist Case Against Bureaucracy,* identifies the power structures within bureaucratic capitalist society as a primary source of oppression for both women and men. She advocates elimination, rather than amelioration, of these structures (Ferguson, 1984). Moreover, it is important to develop a critical approach to organizations that focuses on inequalities of power and opportunity within hierarchical structures and to examine how women, minorities, Aboriginal people, and the working class are disadvantaged within organizations (Mills & Simmons, 1999; 2005).

Kanter found that the level people reach in an organization shapes their behaviour and even their attitudes toward themselves and others. In general, the higher people go, the higher their morale. "This is a good company," they say to themselves; "they recognize my abilities." With their greater satisfaction, people in higher office also tend to be more helpful to subordinates and flexible in their style of leadership. In contrast, people who don't get very far in an organization become frustrated and tend to have lower morale. A less-apparent result of their blocked opportunity, however, is that they are likely to be rigid supervisors and strong defenders of whatever privileges they have. Because the workers in a corporation tend to see only the level that is readily visible, they usually ascribe differences in behaviours and attitudes to people's personalities. Sociologists probe beneath this level to examine how corporate culture shapes people's attitudes and, by extension, the quality of their work.

The hidden values that create the self-fulfilling prophecy remain invisible to most. What are visible are the promotions of people with superior performances and greater commitment to the company.

The Down-to-Earth Sociology box on the next page explores how ideas are often judged in corporations not by their merit, but according to *who* expresses them. You can see how hidden values contribute to the iron law of oligarchy, for the corporate elite—the tight inner group that heads a corporation—sets in motion a self-fulfilling prophecy that tends to reproduce itself with people who "look" like its members, generally white males. Although women and minorities who don't match the stereotype are often "showcased"—placed in highly visible positions with little power—in order to demonstrate to the public that the company engages in diversity practices, looking beyond these few reveals that workers are often placed, promoted,

MANAGEMENT STRATEGIES AND THE CORPORATE CULTURE

Bureaucracies have transformed society by harnessing people's energies to specific goals and monitoring progress toward those goals. Weber (1946a) predicted that because bureaucracies are so efficient and have the capacity to replace themselves indefinitely, they would come to dominate social life. More than any prediction in sociology, this one has stood the test of time (Rothschild & Whitt, 1986; Perrow, 1991).

The recent film *The Corporation* explores the power and dominance of corporations over everyday life. Based on a book by Joel Bakan, *The Corporation: The Pathological Pursuit of Profit and Power,* the award-winning film explores the nature and development of this dominant institution and examines the major corporation's hold on our decisions and our lives. In assessing the "personality" of the corporation, deemed in the mid-1880s to have the legal status of a person,

Manoeuvring the Hidden Culture: Women Surviving the Male-Dominated Business World

I work for a large insurance company. Of its 2500 employees, about 75 percent are women. Only 5 percent of the upper management positions, however, are held by women.

I am one of the more fortunate women—I hold a position in middle management. I am also a member of the 12-member junior board of directors, of whom nine are men and three are women.

Recently, one of the female members of the board suggested that the company become involved in Horizons for Tomorrow, a program designed to provide internships for disadvantaged youth. Two other women and I spent many days developing a proposal for the company's participation.

We needed to determine the best way to sell the proposal to the company president. From past experience, we knew that if he saw it as a "woman's project," it would be shelved in the second tier of "maybes." He hates what he calls "aggressive bitches."

We decided, reluctantly, that the proposal only had a chance if it were presented by a man. We decided that Bill was the logical choice. We also knew we had to "stroke" Bill if we were going to get his co-operation.

We asked Bill if he would "show us how to present our proposal." (It is ridiculous to have to play the role of the "less capable female" today, but, unfortunately, corporate culture sometimes dictates this strategy.) To clinch matters, we puffed up Bill even more by saying, "You're the logical choice as the next chair of the board."

Bill, of course, came to our next planning session, where we "prepped" him on what to say.

At our meeting with the president, Bill gave the basic presentation. We backed him up, providing the background and rationale for why the president should endorse the project. As we answered the president's questions, we carefully deferred to Bill.

The president's response? "An excellent proposal," he concluded. "An appropriate project for our company."

To be successful, we had to manoeuvre through the treacherous waters of the "hidden culture" (actually not so "hidden" to women who have been in the company for a while). The proposal was not sufficient on its own merit, for the "who" behind it was at least as significant as the proposal itself.

"We shouldn't have to play these games," Laura said, summarizing our feelings.

We all know that we have no choice, however. To become labelled "pushy" is to commit "corporate suicide"—and we're no fools.

Source: Written by an insurance executive in Henslin's introductory sociology class who, out of fear of retaliation at work, has chosen to remain anonymous.

---

the film demonstrates that it has "a highly anti-social 'personality': it is self-interested, inherently amoral, callous, and deceitful; it breaches social and legal standards to get its way; it does not suffer from guilt, yet it can mimic the human qualities of empathy, caring, and altruism" (www.thecorporation.com). The various practices within corporations shape their character and affect working conditions and services or products provided.

Keeping Corporate Images Untarnished

Among the major concerns of large corporations is maintaining a clean and ethical image. Many companies have faced controversy and public outcry over unfair labour practices, unethical behaviour, and sweatshop working conditions. Talk-show host Kathie Lee Gifford was challenged on U.S. national television in 1996 when news came forward that the clothing line bearing her name and sold by Wal-Mart was made by girls between the ages of 12 and 15 working 75 hours a week for 31 cents an hour in a Honduran sweatshop under horrendous conditions. With this pronouncement, Gifford initially broke down, but rallied to establish a monitoring program in all factories that produced her label. She also pushed Wal-Mart to revisit working practices at the Honduran plant.

It is difficult for consumers to obtain inside information on corporate practices, including where the goods they sell or buy are made and whether or not the codes of conduct at their suppliers meet at least minimum standards (Marr, 2006). You have to be a sleuth, digging deep into corporate practices, to find answers. Corporations loathe to be identified with distasteful images. Name brands such as Nike, Liz Claiborne, Gap, and countless others, at one time or another guilty of engaging in shoddy manufacturing and workplace practices, have spoken publicly about taking steps such as adopting a code of labour standards for their subcontractors in order to re-establish themselves as fair-minded companies in the minds of consumers.

For example, in late 2007, Gap moved quickly to withdraw tens of thousands of items from its Christmas orders because it was revealed that items bearing the Gap label had been made in New Delhi and other backstreet workshops by children under slave-like conditions (McDougall, 2007). Since 2000, when an investigation by the BBC exposed the company's working conditions in Cambodia, Gap has declared its abhorrence of the use of child labour and its commitment to embrace fair standards for workers in factories manufacturing under its label. This step was taken to restore the shine on the company's image, and in light of stiff competition in the garment industry, Gap moved quickly to distance itself from the allegations. This move made good business sense.

Companies work hard to build their images through branding, expensive advertising, and other gimmicks. Large corporations dedicate entire departments to the construction and maintenance of their images. But for the consumer, what lies beneath the shiny surface is difficult to access.

Diversity Training

The successes of the women's movement and of civil rights activism have encouraged pride in heritage and other diversities and have made many Canadians comfortable with being different from the dominant group. Consequently, people are now less amenable to **assimilation**, the process by which minorities are absorbed into the dominant culture. Assimilation involves relinquishing distinctive cultural patterns of behaviour in favour of those of the dominant culture. Recognizing that assimilation is likely not the way of the future, most major companies, unions, and public service commissions sponsor "diversity training," sending employees to lectures and workshops to learn to work with colleagues of diverse cultures and racial/ethnic backgrounds, and sometimes even to incorporate new ways of thinking and doing to replace traditional models.

A general argument in favour of diversity training is that it helps participants develop an appreciation of differences that facilitates understanding and people's ability to work together to meet common goals.

Critical approaches to the study of organizations suggest that diversity training programs alone will not eliminate the problems confronting racialized groups within organizations today. In fact, critics argue that diversity training and multiculturalism may gloss over underlying sentiments of racism. It is not enough to respect or to know about various cultures; it is necessary to ensure that each has equal access to positions, rewards, and statuses within an organization (Mills & Simmons, 1999; 2005).

Scientific Management

During the late 1880s, Frederick Winslow Taylor, an American industrial engineer, developed the **principles of scientific management** (often referred to as Taylorism), which sought to reduce waste and inefficiency in production. When management draws upon the principles of scientific management as a means of organizing work, the workplace may be described as being *Taylorized*. Using these principles, management was able to regulate work precisely by controlling the pace of work, the level of production, and all decisions pertaining to the labour process. In order for management to maintain or re-establish control over work, Taylor recommended dividing complex tasks into a number of sub-tasks and separating knowledge or conceptual work from the execution of tasks. He used a series of time and motion studies to detail the exact movements required by workers to carry out each task and the length of time needed to complete them. The data were then used by management to specify exactly how work was to be done, and it was the worker's responsibility to carry out his or her assigned task to management's precise specifications. By adopting the principles of scientific management, employers were able to hire less-skilled, lower-paid workers (Braverman, 1974). While Taylor's principles were originally applied in factories, eventually the rules were used in offices, call centres, fast-food restaurants, reservation services, and Canada Post and Air Canada (Ritzer, 1998; Schlosser, 2002; Shalla, 1997).

Humanizing Work

Bureaucracies appear likely to remain our dominant form of social organization, and most of us, like it or not, are

Humanizing the work setting means making the work site a more pleasant place in order to better meet the needs of workers. In this photo, workers are taking a yoga class. As sociologist Arlie Hochschild discovered, work places have become so rewarding that employees sometimes prefer work to the tensions of family life.

destined to spend our working lives in bureaucracies. Many people have become concerned about the negative side of bureaucracies, however, and would like to make them more humane. **Humanizing a work setting** means organizing work in such a way that it develops rather than impedes human potential. Such work settings offer access to opportunities on the basis of ability and contributions rather than personal characteristics, distribute power more equally, and have less rigid rules and more open decision-making. In short, more people are involved in making decisions, their contributions are more readily recognized, and individuals feel freer to participate.

Can bureaucracies adapt to such a model? Contrary to some popular images, not all bureaucracies are unyielding, unwieldy monoliths. There is nothing in the nature of bureaucracies that makes them *inherently* insensitive to people's needs or that prevents them from humanizing corporate culture. However, the pursuit of efficiency and profit relegates social relationships and people's needs or interests to the "back court."

Moreover, to humanize corporate culture does not necessarily require huge expense; nor does it mean loss rather than profit. Kanter (1983) compared 47 companies that were rigidly bureaucratic with more flexible competitors of the same size. The more flexible companies were also more profitable—probably because their greater flexibility encouraged greater company loyalty, creativity, and productivity. Claims of efficiency and profits are a matter of degrees. The garment industry, for example, is noted for its "sweatshop" conditions. Historically, the term **sweating** has been used in reference to working conditions in the garment industry, with its detailed division of labour separating the craft process (design, cutting, and marketing) from the labour-intensive tasks of sewing and finishing. Under this form of organization, even today, garment workers—who are primarily women—are among the most exploited workers worldwide, receiving very low rates of pay despite their extraordinary sewing skills. Sweatshops are located around the world, and giant retailers import their stock or have their own private labels made in countries where there are no, or very few, policies protecting workers (Ross, 1999). Small clothing manufacturing operations with "no sweat" and "fair trade" practices may be profitable and efficiently run, but they present little competition to corporate giants in the industry.

Quality Circles

In light of such findings, many corporations have taken steps to humanize their work settings, motivated not by any altruistic urge to make life better for their workers but by self-interest—the desire to make their organization more competitive. Companies, both large and small, have begun to reform their work organizations. Some have developed **quality circles**, which consist of perhaps a dozen workers and a manager or two who meet regularly to try to improve the quality of both the work setting and the company's products.

However, many companies report that quality circles yield few benefits. Disappointed with the results, companies such as Whirlpool and GE have abandoned the idea. (Part of the reason may be that they set up quality circles for reasons of publicity, not intending to take employee suggestions seriously.) Regardless of whether they formally implement such measures, companies often solicit ideas from their employees, who have a wealth of knowledge about how things might work best. In some cases, workers are not credited for their ideas, but in others, companies might use town hall–type meetings to allow employees to air their ideas publicly and/or may reward workers with cash and stock options.

Employee Stock Ownership

Many companies offer an opportunity for their employees to purchase stock at a discount or as part of their salary, and numerous Canadian companies, including Canadian Tire Corporation, are now partially owned by employees. Because each employee typically owns only a tiny amount of stock, such "ownership" is practically meaningless. In a small percentage of companies, however, employees own the majority of the stock. On average, companies with at least 10 percent of stock owned by employees are more profitable than other firms, probably because the workers are more committed and managers take a longer-term view (White, 1991).

One might think that employee ownership of a company's stock would eliminate problems between workers and management. Profitability, however, not ownership, appears to be the key to reducing these problems. Unprofitable firms put more pressure on their employee-owners, creating tension between workers and managers, while profitable companies resolve problems more quickly.

Work Teams

Pioneered in the computer industry to increase productivity and cut down on absenteeism, small work groups, or self-managed teams, have become increasingly common. Work teams stimulate creative ideas and imaginative solutions to problems, and employees who work in them feel a greater sense of loyalty to the company, work harder, and reduce their absenteeism. Workers in these groups also react more quickly to threats posed by technological change and competitors' advances. Even IBM has found that people work more effectively in a small group than in a distant, centralized command structure (Drucker, 1992).

The small work group establishes primary relationships among its members, and workers' identities become tied up with their group. This reduces alienation; rather than being lost in a bureaucratic maze, workers' individuality is appreciated and their contributions more readily recognized. The group's successes become the individual's successes—as do its failures—reflecting positively or negatively on the individual. As a consequence of their expanded personal ties, workers make more of an effort. The results have been so good that, in what is known as "worker empowerment," some self-managed teams even replace bosses in controlling everything from schedules to hiring and firing (Lublin, 1991).

Workplace Day Care

Another way to humanize the work setting is to set up daycare facilities at workplaces. This eases the strain on parents, especially new mothers, who are able to go to work and still keep an eye on a baby or young child. Parents are also able to spend time with their children during breaks and lunch hours. Mothers can even nurse a child at these times.

With fewer families with a stay-at-home parent, there may be increasing pressure on firms to offer childcare services as part of a benefits package to attract and hold capable workers.

Say Hello to the New Taste in Town

There is a rich vein of gold in Northern Ontario. That liquid gold is St. Joseph Island maple syrup and it is as much a part of life today as it was when it was first tapped generations ago. The sterling reputation of St. Joe Island as a source of world-class maple syrup is well deserved. The region boasts plentiful sugar maples, rooted in limestone-rich soil, growing in just the right climate.

Red Maple Premium Lager is made using amber maple syrup from St. Joe Island producers. Its characteristic maple flavour gently balances the natural bitterness created by the blend of imported hops. When combined with premium black roasted barley malt, and pure Pre-Cambrian Shield waters of Lake Superior, the result is an uncommonly smooth beer with a uniquely Northern character. In essence, Red Maple Premium Lager is a gift of nature, from the North.

503 Bay Street, Sault Ste. Marie

OPEN Mon.-Sat. 9 a.m. to 11 p.m.
Sunday 11 a.m. to 6 p.m.

Debit card, Visa, MasterCard, American Express accepted.

Co-operatives provide workers with an alternative work arrangement. As owners, organization members collectively make decisions, determine goals and policies, and set salaries and work tasks. Decision-making, even on routine matters, is often very time-consuming, since all members participate. Co-operatives strive to provide members with a high level of satisfaction for work performed.

Developing an Alternative: The Co-operative

While measures such as those described above generally make the workplace more hospitable to workers, these management strategies are ultimately aimed at increasing profit and productivity. In the 1970s, many workers across North America, especially those opposed to capitalism and what they considered to be the deadening effects of bureaucracy, began to seek an alternative organizational form. They began to establish co-operatives—organizations owned by members who collectively make decisions, determine goals, evaluate resources, set salaries, and assign work tasks. Tasks are carried out without a hierarchy of authority, and all members can participate in the decisions of the organization. In Canada there are approximately 286 worker-managed companies, most of which are located in Quebec. All together, these companies have over 17 000 members and employ over 11 400 workers (Cooperatives Secretariat, 2003: p. 5). As sociologists Joyce Rothschild and Allen Whitt (1986) state, co-operatives are not new. Farmers' co-operatives, once popular in western Canada, have a long and rich history. Co-operatives attempt to achieve some specific social good (such as lowering food prices and improving food quality) and provide a high level of personal satisfaction for their members as they work toward that goal. Most self-managed enterprises are small companies in which workers are ultimately concerned with controlling their own labour. Some companies were bought out by workers in order to save their jobs. One such company is Northern Breweries in Sault Ste. Marie, Ontario, the first employee-owned brewing company in North America (Rinehart, 1996; www.northernbreweries.com). Because all members can participate in decision-making, co-operatives spend huge amounts of time deciding even routine matters.

The economic results of co-operatives are mixed. Many are less profitable than private organizations, others more so. A few have been so successful that they have been bought by major corporations.

The Conflict Perspective

Conflict theorists suggest that the basic relationship between workers and owners is confrontational regardless of how a work organization is structured (R. Edwards, 1979; Rinehart, 2006). Each walks a different path, with one exploiting workers to extract a greater profit, and the other trying to resist that exploitation. Since their basic interests are fundamentally opposed, conflict theorists argue, employers' attempts to humanize the work setting (or to manage diversity) are mere window dressing—efforts to conceal their fundamental goal of exploiting workers. If these efforts are not camouflage, they are worse—attempts to manipulate workers into active co-operation in their own exploitation. This analysis does not apply to co-operatives, however, since they are owned by the workers.

Technology and the Control of Workers

The microchip has rapidly changed our lives. Many people continue to rejoice over the computer's capacity to improve their quality of life. They are pleased with the control of manufactured goods and the reduction of drudgery. Records are much easier to keep, and we can type just one letter and let the computer print and address it to 10 people—or 10 000.

Computers also hold the potential for severe abuse. They may allow governments to operate a police state, monitoring our every move. The Big Brother in George Orwell's classic novel, *1984*, may turn out to be a computer. Technology has, in many ways, transformed work into Aldous Huxley's vision of a "Brave New World," according to writer and activist Heather Menzies. In the new workplace, individuals play a secondary role to advanced technologies that are not only capable of levels of production and efficiency beyond human capability, but also simultaneously connect to and manage facilities and labour forces across the globe (Menzies, 1996). The technologically advanced workplace has the capacity to eliminate and de-skill workers, resulting in high levels of unemployment and a deep sense of insecurity experienced by workers in various settings (Noble, 1995; Huws, 2003).

Whether this happens or not, the computer gives managers much greater control over workers. Social psychologist Shoshana Zuboff (1991) and many others contend that computers allow managers to increase surveillance without face-to-face supervision (Silverman, 2008). They let managers know the number of strokes a word processor makes every minute or hour, or inform supervisors how long each teleworker takes per call. Call centre workers who are "underperforming" are singled out for discipline. It does not matter that the slower operators may be more polite or more helpful, only that the computer reports slower performance.

As sociologist Gary Marx (1985, 1986, 1995) says, with computers able to measure motion, air currents, vibrations, odours, pressure changes, and voice stress, and video cameras that need only a pinhole for their spying eye, we may be moving to a "maximum-security" workplace. When workers at a leading hotel punch in, a device scans their eyes, comparing their retinas with computerized data on file. This prevents employees from punching in one another's time cards.

Although companies employ monitoring techniques to increase productivity, researchers have found that excessive surveillance may have the opposite effect on workers. In a British study, researchers discovered that workers whose activities, including keyboard strokes and emails, were highly monitored reported feeling exhausted and anxious compared to workers who were not monitored (Silverman, 2008). A truck driver at Safeway used to enjoy his job. He says, "No one was looking over your shoulder, and you felt like a human being." Now, the driver says he feels "pushed around." A small computer in the dashboard of his truck (called, appropriately, a Tripmaster) keeps track of his speed, shifting, excessive idling, and even reports when and how long he stops for lunch or a coffee break. The driver says he will retire early.

"Maximum-security workplace" seems an apt term for what is coming. And, as many fear, with the computer's awesome capacities this kind of workplace may be just one part of a "maximum-security society" (Marx, 1995).

Focus Question
From the worker's perspective, what are some of the advantages and disadvantages of the various techniques or strategies employed by management to "humanize" the corporate culture?

Virtual Organizations

Virtual organizations are companies "without walls," often transcending time, space, and culture. The image of the virtual organization is that of an edgeless, permeable entity, capable of rapid results and characterized by temporary, depersonalized relationships. Some companies engage in what has come to be known as **hotelling**, whereby they provide employees with laptops, but only assign desks on a temporary basis to whoever needs them, much like one rents a room in a hotel—only when needed. With its highly mobile labour force, in order to save money, IBM is adopting the hotelling model for its 19 000 Canadian employees (Shimo, 2008). While this arrangement has its drawbacks and certainly dissuades the development of a work "community" or identification with a work *place,* with workers out on business calls or at off-site meetings, proponents of hotelling see underused office space as dollars lost in profits. Such dollar amounts are especially significant in major cities like Toronto, Montreal, and Vancouver, where land costs are at a premium.

A twist on the idea of hotelling is the newer craze of co-working, with sites popping up around the globe from "Argentina to Australia and many places in between" (Fost, 2008). In co-working, a company or lone entrepreneur sets up an office and rents out the desks to people who have different jobs but who desire a community of others with whom they might share ideas. For some people, this arrangement combines the idea of a "traditional" office with the contemporary notion that workers' physical location is of minor importance in a networked world.

Most of us have had experiences interacting through tele-mediated business processes—perhaps having had an evening meal interrupted by a telemarketer attempting to sell us insurance, vacation packages, financial services, or any other number of goods or services. The telemarketer may be calling from a location thousands of miles away from your Canadian home—even from as far away as India! He or she will have been trained to develop a Canadian "accent" and will rely on a script to deliver his or her sales pitch. Similarly, when you call for hotel reservations, the reservations clerk may be half a world away from the hotel of your choosing

To meet the goal of production efficiency, under lean production most workers are replaced by machinery. Even in very large production facilities, there are few workers on the shop floor.

and therefore may not be able to answer your questions about the weather at the hotel location or the distance from the hotel to a particular landmark.

Professor Ursula Huws has studied the revolution in microtechnology and the ways in which it has transformed work. Huws (2003) notes that in industrialized countries, information technology (IT) has affected skills and the division of labour, and has also sometimes removed work from a central location to remote areas, including workers' homes—a process known as telework. Huws has studied off-shoring or outsourcing and argues that IT has enabled information processing work to be relocated across the globe, thereby creating an "internationalization of the division of labour in white collar work." Even fast-food restaurants may engage in outsourcing. In an effort to reduce waiting times at their drive-throughs, McDonald's is now testing the use of remote call centres in the United States to process orders. Your order from a drive-through off the Interstate in Missouri may be taken by a call centre worker in Colorado Springs, more than 900 miles from your car. With lightning speed,

your order will be sent by high-efficiency data lines to the McDonald's outlet where you are making your purchase (Fitzgerald, 2004). Centralizing order taking in this manner is expected to keep the individual outlet's workers focused on the already Taylorized, subdivided, and scripted work process within the restaurant. Moreover, this is another step toward complete standardization of the service and product, allowing for minimal variation from one location to the next.

LEAN PRODUCTION AND CORPORATE EFFICIENCY

How were the Japanese able to arise from the defeat of World War II, including the nuclear destruction of two of their main cities, to become a giant in today's global economy? Some analysts trace part of the answer to the way their major corporations are organized. One of the Japanese production techniques contributing to organizational efficiency is **lean production**. Unlike Fordist production, which relies on enormous inventories of parts and massive warehouse spaces, lean production employs a **just-in-time (JIT) strategy**. Under this system, parts inventories are limited to the amount needed at the time, reducing the demand for huge parts warehouses and large work stations. Work is flexible. Workers easily rotate through various jobs and share job classifications. Overall, there are fewer problems with faulty assemblies and poor-quality production (Rinehart, 2006).

Central to the process of lean production is work standardization. The Japanese model incorporates the practice of **kaizen**, which means continuous improvement. Under kaizen, production techniques are constantly evaluated in search of more efficient and improved methods. While workers are involved in discussions around these improvements, ultimately the goal of kaizen and lean production is to reduce the labour force, minimizing inefficiency. Lean production is particularly pertinent in the auto industry, and the success of Toyota has attracted the attention of the North American auto makers. In Canada, the CAMI plant in Ingersoll, Ontario, a joint venture of General Motors and Suzuki, is organized according to lean production techniques. Despite the reputation of lean production strategies for minimizing labour disputes, workers at the CAMI plant have engaged in strikes and protests after realizing that work rotation and continuous improvement in practice eliminated jobs and intensified their work (Rinehart, 2006).

Although there are many facets to the Japanese organizational model in addition to lean production and kaizen, another interesting aspect is the commitment to lifetime security. Once hired, employees can expect to work for the same firm for the rest of their lives. Similarly, the firm expects them to be loyal to the company, to stick with it through good times and bad. On one hand, employees will not be laid off or fired; on the other, they do not go job shopping, and their careers—and many aspects of their lives—are wrapped up in one firm.

In North America, lifetime security is unusual, limited primarily to some university professors (who receive what is called *tenure*). Companies lay off workers in slow times, and if they restructure, it often means that whole divisions are eliminated altogether or moved overseas. Given this context, workers "look out for number one," which includes job shopping and job hopping and constantly seeking better pay and opportunities elsewhere.

Patterns of shorter job tenure and the phenomenon of moving from job to job are relatively recent in Canada. Past generations of workers (typically males) prided themselves on long-term employment with one company and were commonly rewarded with a gold watch for 25 years or more of service. Retirees became members of their workplaces' "Quarter Century Clubs," an honour bestowed for their loyalty. Today's seniors—among them dads who spent 35 years at General Motors, in the steel plant, or in the local fire department—worry that their sons and grandsons are disloyal as they continually seek out newer and better places of employment.

With lifetime security comes greater degrees of involvement in the workplace. In Japan, work is like marriage. The employee and the company are committed to each other. The employee supports the company with loyalty and long hours of dedicated work, and the company, in turn, supports the worker with lifetime security, health services, recreation, sports and social events, and even a home mortgage. Involvement with the company does not stop when workers leave the building. They are likely to spend evenings with co-workers in places of entertainment, and are perhaps part of a company study or exercise group.

In North America, work relationships are assumed to be highly specific. An employee is hired to do a specific job, and employees who have done their jobs have thereby fulfilled their obligation to the company. The rest of their hours are their own. They go home to their private lives, which are usually highly separated from their work.

In Japan, workers are trained more broadly within the firm so that they gain a more comprehensive picture of the corporation and how the specific jobs they are assigned fit into the bigger picture. Within this context, workers are also involved to a greater degree in decision-making and thereby made to feel that they are an essential part of the organization, not simply cogs in a giant wheel.

SUMMARY AND REVIEW

The Rationalization of Society

HOW DID THE RATIONALIZATION OF SOCIETY COME ABOUT?
Weber used the phrase **rationalization of society** to refer to a transformation in people's thinking and behaviours—the change from protecting time-honoured ways to a concern with efficiency and practical results. Weber traced the rationalization of society to Protestant theology, which he said brought about capitalism, while Marx attributed rationalization to capitalism itself. pp. 216–217.

Formal Organizations and Bureaucracy

WHAT ARE FORMAL ORGANIZATIONS?
Formal organizations are secondary groups designed to achieve specific objectives. Their dominant form is the **bureaucracy**, which Weber characterized as consisting of a hierarchy, a division of labour, written rules, written communications, and impersonality of positions—characteristics that allow bureaucracies to be efficient and enduring. pp. 218–221.

WHAT DYSFUNCTIONS ARE OFTEN ASSOCIATED WITH BUREAUCRACIES?
The dysfunctions of bureaucracies include alienation, red tape, lack of communication between units, **goal displacement**, and incompetence (as seen in the **Peter principle**). In Weber's view, the impersonality of bureaucracies tends to produce **alienation** among workers—the feeling that no one cares about them and that they don't really fit in. Marx's view of alienation is somewhat different—workers are separated from the product of their labour because they participate in only a small part of the production process. pp. 221–224.

Voluntarism and Voluntary Organizations

WHAT ARE THE FUNCTIONS OF VOLUNTARY ASSOCIATIONS?
Voluntary associations are groups made up of volunteers who organize on the basis of common interests. These associations further mutual interests, provide a sense of identity and purpose, help to govern and maintain order, mediate between the government and the individual, give training in organizational skills, help provide access to political power, and pave the way for social change. pp. 225–227.

WHAT IS THE "IRON LAW OF OLIGARCHY"?
Sociologist Robert Michels noted that formal organizations have a tendency to become controlled by a small group that limits leadership to its own inner circle. The dominance of a formal organization by an elite inner circle that keeps itself in power is called the **iron law of oligarchy**. p. 227.

Working within Bureaucracies

HOW DOES THE CORPORATE CULTURE AFFECT WORKERS?
The term **corporate culture** refers to an organization's traditions, values, and unwritten norms. Much of corporate

culture, such as its hidden values, is not readily visible. Often, a self-fulfilling prophecy is at work: people who match a corporation's hidden values are put on tracks that enhance their chance of success, while those who do not match these values are set on a course that minimizes their performance. pp. 227–230.

Management Strategies and the Corporate Culture

WHAT DOES "HUMANIZING A WORK SETTING" MEAN?

Humanizing a work setting means organizing it in a way that develops rather than impedes human potential. Among the characteristics of more humane bureaucracies are expanded opportunities on the basis of ability and contributions rather than personal characteristics, a more even distribution of power, less rigid rules, and more open decision-making. Attempts to modify bureaucracies include quality circles, small work groups, and self-managed teams.

Employee ownership plans give workers a greater stake in the outcomes of their work organizations. These humanizing techniques are management strategies designed to increase productivity and profit and are not real alternatives. Co-operatives are an alternative to bureaucracies. Conflict theorists see attempts to humanize work as a way of manipulating workers. pp. 230–235.

Lean Production and Corporate Efficiency

WHAT IS LEAN PRODUCTION?

Central to the process of **lean production**, originally a Japanese production model, is work standardization and continuous improvement. Production techniques are constantly evaluated in search of more efficient and improved methods. Lean production is particularly pertinent in the auto industry, and the success of Toyota has attracted the attention of the North American auto makers, which have begun to employ similar strategies. pp. 235–236.

TALKING ABOUT THEORY

Theoretical Paradigms

	CLASICAL PARADIGMS			RECENT PARADIGMS
	Structural-Functional Paradigm	Social-Conflict Paradigm	Symbolic-Interaction Paradigm	Feminist Paradigm
What is the level of analysis?	Macro level	Macro level	Micro level	Micro and macro levels
Why are bureaucratic organizations a central feature of contemporary society? Are they efficient?	In complex societies, bureaucracies are an efficient way to organize societal functions, tasks, and the division of labour.	Bureaucratic organizations are hierarchical systems of power and mirror the structure of power within the broader society. Conflict theorists ask: efficient for whom?	Symbolic interactionists seek to understand relationships within organizations and ask whether relations among participants within a bureaucracy may improve.	The distribution of power and authority within organizations discriminates against women and other minorities, rendering them invisible and relegating them to the lowest rungs of the hierarchy.

KEY TERMS

WEBLINKS

All URLs listed are current as of the printing of this book.

Formal Organization
www.spc.uchicago.edu/ssr1/PRELIMS/orgs.html
Summaries of classic studies in formal organization from the University of Chicago.

Organizational Learning Resources
http://choo.fis.utoronto.ca/fis/OrgCog/
A selection of web-based resources on organizational learning, organizational cognition, information management, knowledge management, environment scanning, and scenario planning.

Organizational Leadership and Supervision
www.tech.purdue.edu/ols/
The Organizational Leadership and Supervision Center, based at Purdue University, stimulates education and research in all areas of collaborative work systems.

Innovisions Canada: Canadian Telework Association (CTA)
www.ivc.ca/cta/index.htm
The website of an association dedicated to promoting telework in Canada.

CRITICAL THINKING QUESTIONS

1. To what extent has Canadian society become over-rationalized?

2. What are some of the difficulties co-operative organizations might encounter in their interactions with hierarchically structured organizations?

3. Why is it difficult for many Canadians to adjust to the expectations and culture of co-operative or alternative organizational structures?

4. Access the Research Navigator through MySocLab and use it to find articles in which authors consider the advantages and disadvantages of telework for managers and workers.

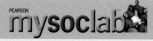

PEARSON mysoclab Explore the topics covered in this chapter on MySocLab using the access information provided with this text. Interactive resources for studying include multimedia tutorials, video clips, practice tests, quizzes, and animated maps and figures.

The Economy: Money and Work

The alarm pounded in Kim's ears. "Not Monday already," she groaned. "There must be a better way of starting the week." She pressed the snooze button on the clock (from Germany) to sneak another 10 minutes' sleep. After what seemed like only 30 seconds, the alarm shrilly insisted she get up and face the week.

Still bleary-eyed after her shower, Kim peered into her closet and picked out a silk blouse (from China), a plaid wool skirt (from Scotland), and leather shoes (from India). She nodded, satisfied, and added a pair of simulated pearls (from Taiwan). Running late, she hurriedly ran a brush (from Mexico) through her hair. As Kim wolfed down a bowl of cereal (from Canada) topped with milk (from Canada), bananas (from Costa Rica), and sugar (from the Dominican Republic), she turned on her kitchen television (from Korea) to see the weather forecast.

Gulping the last of her coffee (from Brazil), Kim grabbed her briefcase (from Wales), purse (from Spain), and jacket (from Malaysia) and quickly climbed into her car (from Japan). As she glanced at her watch (from Switzerland), she hoped the traffic would be in her favour. She muttered to herself as she glimpsed the gas gauge at a street light (from Great Britain). She muttered again when she paid for gas (from Saudi Arabia) at the gas station, for the price had risen once more. "My paycheque never keeps up with prices," she moaned to herself as she finished her drive to work.

The office was abuzz. Six months earlier, Vancouver headquarters had put the company up for sale, but there had been no takers. The big news today was that both a Japanese and an American corporation had put in bids over the weekend. No one got much work done that day, as the whole office speculated about how things might change.

LEARNING OUTCOMES

After you have studied this chapter, you will be able to answer the following questions:

1. How are economic systems linked to types of societies?

2. How do the major economic systems differ?

3. What are the differences between neoliberalism and social conservatism?

4. How do four of the major sociological perspectives apply to work?

5. What are the three economic sectors of the labour force?

6. How has the ratio of women in the workforce changed?

7. What is the underground economy?

8. How have patterns of work and leisure changed?

THE TRANSFORMATION OF ECONOMIC SYSTEMS

Today's **economy**—our system of producing, distributing, and exchanging goods and services—differs radically from the economies of all but our most recent past. The products used by Kim in the opening vignette make it apparent that today's economy knows no national boundaries. Moreover, the economy is essential to our welfare, for it affects our chances of buying a new home, working a dead-end job, or entering the fast track of an up-and-coming company.

The term *market* refers to much more than the personal touch you get when you buy fruits, vegetables, and meats from local farmers or when you shop at a flea market or buy something at a yard or garage sale. It maintains its original definition of buying and selling, but now refers to much more impersonal exchanges. Today's **market**, the mechanism by which we establish values in order to exchange goods and services, means the Toronto, Montreal, or Vancouver stock exchanges, the Dow Jones Industrial Average in New York City, and the Nikkei Index in Tokyo. "Market" also means the movement of vast amounts of goods across international borders, and even across oceans and continents. The definition also encompasses brokers taking orders for IBM and speculators trading international currencies.

To better understand how global forces affect the Canadian economy—and your own life—we will begin with an overview of sweeping historical changes.

Preindustrial Societies: The Birth of Inequality

The earliest human groups, hunting and gathering societies, had a simple **subsistence economy**. Groups of 25 to 40 people lived off the land, gathering what they could and moving from place to place as their food supply ran low. With no excess to accumulate, everybody possessed about the same as everyone else.

People soon discovered how to breed animals and cultivate plants, which allowed the production of a surplus. The primary sociological significance of surplus and trade was that it fostered *social inequality*, with some people accumulating more possessions than others and passing them on to their children. The effects of surplus and trade remain with us today.

The invention of the plow made land much more productive. As *agricultural societies* developed, trade expanded and gave rise to trading centres, which blossomed into cities. The result was even greater social, political, and economic inequality.

Industrial Societies: The Birth of the Machine

The steam engine, invented in 1765, ushered in industrial societies. Based on fuel-powered machines, these societies created surpluses unlike anything seen before. Trade among nations was stimulated, bringing even greater social inequality. A handful of individuals opened factories and exploited the labour of many. Later on, bloody battles occurred as workers unionized to improve their working conditions.

More efficient machines created ever larger surpluses. The emphasis in the economy changed from the production of goods to their consumption. Sociologist Thorstein Veblen (1912) used the term **conspicuous consumption** to describe this fundamental change in people's orientations. Veblen meant that the Protestant ethic identified by Weber—an emphasis on hard work, savings, and a concern for

The common-sense meaning of *market* is a place where people exchange or buy and sell goods. Old-fashioned markets are still common in less industrialized nations, such as this one in Guatemala. Here people find social interaction every bit as rewarding as the goods and services they exchange.

Nine-year-old Alone Banda works in an abandoned quarry in Zambia. Using a bolt, he breaks rocks into powder. In a week, he makes enough powder to fill half a cement bag. Alone gets $3 for the half bag.

Three dollars doesn't sound like much, but without it he and his grandmother would starve to death.

Alone faces a slow death. Robbed of his childhood and breathing rock dust continuously, he is likely to contract what his fellow quarry workers call a "heavy chest," an early sign of silicosis.

As the mothers of children—some as young as seven—who work at the quarry say, "If I feel pity for them, what are they going to eat?" (Wines, 2006a).

In Ghana, six-year-old Mark Kwadwo, who only weighs about 30 pounds,

works for a fisherman. For up to 14 hours a day, seven days a week, he paddles a boat and takes fish out of nets. Exhausted, he falls asleep at night in a little mud hut that he shares with five other boys.

Mark is still too little to dive, but he knows what is coming when he is older. His fear is that he will dive to free a tangled net—and never resurface.

If Mark doesn't paddle hard enough, or pull in the fish from a net fast enough, Takyi, the fisherman, will hit him on the head with a paddle.

"I prefer to have older boys work for me," says Takyi, "but I can't afford them. That's why I go for these."

Around the world, children are forced to work. Like Mark, some work in the fishing industry, and some work

in quarries like Alone. Others are employed in construction, and still other children work as miners, pesticide sprayers, street vendors, and household servants. Children weave carpets in India, race camels in the Middle East, and, all over the world, work as prostitutes.

The underlying cause of children working is poverty so severe that the few dollars the children bring in can make the difference between life and death. In Ghana, where Mark works on the fishing boat, two out of three people live on less than $1 a day (LaFraniere, 2006).

There is a cultural dynamic. Many cultures do share the Western views that children have the right to be educated and to be spared from adult burdens.

With prosperity comes this perspective, however. In the meantime, people do what they must to survive, even if it requires desperate measures.

For Your Consideration

How do you think the industrialized nations can help alleviate the suffering of child workers? Prior to industrialization, and for a period afterward, employing children in hard jobs was also common in the West. Just because our economic system has changed, bringing with it different ideas of childhood and of the rights of children, what right do we have to impose our changed ideas on other nations?

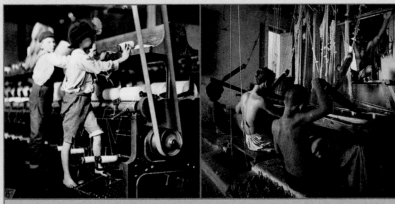

One of the negative consequences of early industrialization in the West was the use of child labour. In the photo of the U.S. textile industry in the 1800s, spindle boys are at work in a Georgia cotton mill. Today's least developed nations are experiencing the same negative consequence as they industrialize. The photo shows boys at work in a contemporary textile factory in Varanas, India.

---

salvation (discussed in Chapter 10)—had been replaced with an eagerness to show off wealth by the "elaborate consumption of goods."

Postindustrial Societies: The Birth of the Information Age

In 1973, sociologist Daniel Bell noted that an entirely new type of society was emerging, which he called a *postindustrial society*. He identified six characteristics of such a society:

(1) a service sector so large that it employs the majority of workers; (2) a huge surplus of goods; (3) extensive trade among nations; (4) a wide variety and quantity of goods available to the average person; (5) an "information explosion"; and (6) a "global village"—that is, the linking of people around the world by instantaneous communications, transportation, and trade.

The rise of the postindustrial society witnessed the replacement of paper money with credit cards and the **debit card**, a device by which a purchase is charged against the

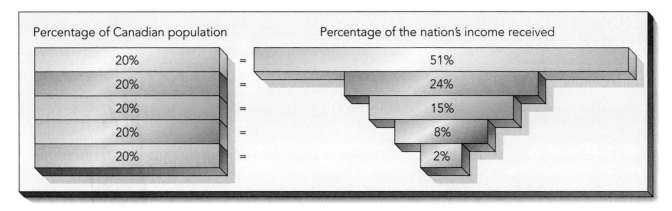

FIGURE 11.1 The Inverted Income Pyramid: The Proportion of Income Received by Each Fifth of the Canadian Population

Source: Based on Statistics Canada, 2003a, Income in Canada, Catalogue no. 96F0030XIE2001014, p. 107.

purchaser's bank account. Like credit cards, debit cards are a guarantee that their user has enough currency on deposit to cover a purchase. Postindustrial monetary exchange also includes e-cash—the electronic transfer of money over the internet. Many of us now do our banking on the web and/or buy goods from online retailers such as eBay.

Increasingly, spending in a postindustrial society means not an exchange of physical money—paper or coins—but rather the electronic transfer of numbers residing in computer memory banks. In effect, this new form of exchange is itself part of the information explosion.

The consequences of this explosion are unevenly distributed. Most of us will become as comfortable with the new society as our predecessors were with theirs, but not everyone will find a comfortable niche in the global village.

Focus Question
What are the differences between preindustrial, industrial, and postindustrial societies?

Bioeconomic Societies: Merging Biology and Economics

We may be on the verge of yet another new type of society that is being ushered in by advances in biology—in particular, the deciphering of the human genome system. While the specifics have yet to emerge, a bioeconomic society centres around the application of genetics—human genetics for medicine and plant and animal genetics for the production of food. The marriage of biology and economics has given us, for example, irradiated foods, which supposedly last longer and are free of harmful bacteria.

Social Inequality in Canada

In preceding chapters, we examined inequalities—from global stratification to inequalities of social class, gender, race, and age in Canada. There is little to add to that extensive presentation, but an overall snapshot of how income is distributed in Canada may be useful.

Consider the inverted pyramid shown in Figure 11.1. The proportion of the nation's income going to the wealthiest fifth of the Canadian population is at the top; the proportion going to the poorest fifth, at the bottom. Note that *51 percent* of the country's income is directed toward just one-fifth of Canadians, while only *2 percent* goes to the poorest fifth. What is more significant is that between 1996 and 2003, the gap between the richest and poorest quintile increased by 23 percent (Statistics Canada, 2003a, p. 86). Recent data (presented in Table 11.1) convey an even more dramatic story. Between 1980 and 2005, controlling for

TABLE 11.1 Changes in Top, Middle, and Bottom 20 Percent of Canadian Income Earners

Group	1980 Median Income*	2005 Median Income	Change
Top 20%	$74 084	$86 253	+16.4%
Middle 20%	$41 348	$41 401	+0.1%
Bottom 20%	$19 367	$15 375	-20.6%
*All figures in 2005 dollars			

Source: Statistics Canada, Income and Earnings, 2006 Census, Catalogue no.: 97-563-XWE2006001

TABLE 11.2 Young Canadians Are Poorer

Year	Men	Women
1980	$43 767	$32 813
2005	$37 680	$32 104
*All figures in 2005 dollars		

Source: Statistics Canada, Income and Earnings, 2006 Census, Catalogue no.: 97-563-XWE2006001

inflation and other factors, the top 20 percent of Canada's income earners reported an increase of more than 16 percent while the bottom 20 percent fell by over 20 percent. Rather than ushering in equality, the postindustrial society perpetuates the income inequalities of the industrial society. Will the new bioeconomic society bring even greater disparities?

While the percentage of income going to each segment of the population in Canada resembles the skewed distribution in the United States, the inequalities between the richest and poorest Canadians are still less extreme than they are in the United States, largely due to federal government transfer payments to individuals.

As presented in Table 11.2, the recent Statistics Canada (2008) census figures show that younger workers, especially young men, earned less in 2005 than their parents did a generation earlier.

For the 25- to 29-year-old group, Statistics Canada paints a picture of falling fortunes. The median earnings of young men tumbled from $43 767 in 1980 to $37 680 in 2005. For women of the same age, the median income fell by a much smaller $709 in the same period to $32 104.

WORLD ECONOMIC SYSTEMS

Now that we have outlined the main economic changes in history, let's compare capitalism and socialism.

Capitalism

If we distill the businesses of Canada into their basic components, we can see that **capitalism** has three essential features: (1) **private ownership of the means of production** (individuals own the capital, land, machines, and factories and decide what shall be produced); (2) the pursuit of profit (selling something for more than it costs); and (3) **market competition** (an exchange of items between willing buyers and sellers).

WELFARE (OR STATE) CAPITALISM VERSUS LAISSEZ-FAIRE CAPITALISM Pure capitalism, known as **laissez-faire capitalism** (loosely, "leave alone"), means that **market forces** operate without interference from the government. Such is not the case in Canada or the United States, where many restraints to the laissez-faire model are in force. The current form of Canadian capitalism is **welfare or state capitalism**, in which private citizens acting as individuals or in groups, such as credit unions, co-operatives, or the *caisses populaires* ("people's banks") of Quebec and Ontario, together with the provincial and federal governments, own the means of production and pursue profits in a system of laws designed to protect the welfare of the population.

Consider a few Canadian examples. Crown corporations are companies owned by the provincial or federal government but managed at "arm's length" (see Table 11.3). The largest federal Crown corporation is Canada Post, which reported a profit every year for the past 13 years and in 2006 earned $119 million with over 72 000 full- and part-time employees.

Before the provincial government passed legislation that split it into separate entities, the largest provincial Crown corporation in Canada was Ontario Hydro, with 1998 profits of almost $2 billion and 26 000 persons on the payroll. The largest provincial Crown corporation today is Hydro-Québec, with a 2006 profit of more than $2.8 billion and a full-time workforce numbering over 19 500.

Why does the development of capitalism require continuous government intervention? Suppose you have discovered what you think is a miracle tonic: it will grow hair,

TABLE 11.3 Five Largest Federal Crown Corporations Ranked by Assets, July 2007

Federal Crown Corporation	Total Assets ($ Billions)	Employment
Canada Mortgage and Housing Corporation	$124.2	1877
Export Development Canada	$22.8	1056
Farm Credit Canada	$13.8	1194
Business Development Bank of Canada	$10.8	1733
Canada Post Corporation	$4.9	61 000

Source: Treasury Board of Canada Secretariat, Crown Corporations and Other Corporate Interests of Canada, 2007, http://www.tbs-sct.gc.ca/reports-rapports/cc-se/2007/cc-se03-eng.asp.

Canada's state capitalism at work: pictured here is one of the newer "convenience store" postal outlets of Canada Post. Canada Post is the largest Canadian federal Crown corporation, with reported earnings of $119 million in 2006 and a staff of over 72 000 full- and part-time employees.

erase wrinkles, and dissolve excess fat. If your product works, you will become an overnight sensation—not only a millionaire, but also the toast of television talk shows.

Before you count your money, you must reckon with **market restraints**, the laws and regulations of welfare capitalism that limit your capacity to sell what you produce. First, you must comply with municipal, provincial, and federal rules. You are required to register your company's name with a provincial registry—or, better yet, obtain a charter of incorporation from the province, a business license from your municipality if you are operating a retail store or outlet, and a GST number from the federal government that allows you to make untaxed purchases.

Second, you cannot simply take your item to local stores and ask them to sell it; you must first seek approval from federal agencies that monitor compliance with the *Food and Drug Act* (FDA). In addition, the *Hazardous Products Act* forbids the advertising, sale, or import of unsafe products that might be an ingredient in your "miracle" cure or the cure itself. This means you must prove that your product will not cause harm to the public. Moreover, you must be able to substantiate your claims—or face being shut down by provincial and federal agencies that monitor the market for fraud.

Suppose you succeed in overcoming these obstacles, your business starts to prosper, and you begin hiring. Other provincial and federal agencies will monitor your compliance with regulations concerning employment. For example, if your employees are not unionized, you must comply with the provincial *Employment Standards Act*. If they become unionized, relations with your employees will fall under the *Labour Relations Act* of your province. Provincial and federal

human rights statutes cover discrimination in the workplace on the basis of sex, race, ethnicity, and—at the federal level and in almost every province—sexual orientation. Income tax, employment insurance, and CPP contributions are handled by the federal government, and on occasion the Supreme Court of Canada has adjudicated issues dealing with unionized workplaces (see Glenday, 1997).

Focus Question
What makes Canada a welfare capitalist society?

IN SUM

As currently practised, capitalism is far from the classical laissez-faire model. Canada's economic system encourages the first two components of capitalism: private ownership of the means of production and the pursuit of profit. A vast system of government regulations both protects and restricts the third, market competition.

Socialism/Communism

Socialism also has three essential components: (1) public ownership of the means of production; (2) central planning; and (3) the distribution of goods without a profit motive.

In the few socialist/communist economies that remain in the world (China, North Korea, and Cuba), the governments own the means of production—not only factories, but also land, railroads, oil wells, and gold mines. In a socialist economy, *everyone* in the economic chain works for the

This advertisement from 1885 represents an earlier stage of capitalism. Today, the production and marketing of goods take place under detailed, complicated government regulations.

government. By narrowing the huge pay gaps that characterize capitalist nations, socialist nations are able to establish considerably greater equality of income.

DEMOCRATIC SOCIALISM Dissatisfied with the greed and exploitation of capitalism and the lack of freedom and individuality of socialism, most European Union nations developed **democratic socialism**, or welfare socialism. In this form of socialism, both the state and individuals engage in production and distribution for profit (see the discussion of Canada's Crown corporations on pages 243–244).

Criticisms of Capitalism and Socialism

The primary criticism levelled against capitalism is that it leads to social inequality. Capitalism, according to critics, produces a tiny top layer comprised of wealthy, powerful people who exploit a vast bottom layer of poorly paid workers, many of whom are underemployed (**underemployment** is having to work at a job beneath one's training and abilities or being able to find only part-time work). Another major criticism is that the tiny top layer wields vast political power. To further their own wealth, the few who own the means of production and reap huge profits are able to get legislation passed that goes against the public good.

The primary criticism levelled against socialism is that it does not respect individual rights (Berger, 1991). In the case

of China, the government even controls how many children families may have (Mosher, 1983). Critics also argue that central planning is grossly inefficient (Kennedy, 1993) and that socialism is not capable of producing sufficient quantities of consumer goods.

Changes in Capitalism and Socialism

CHANGES IN CAPITALISM Over the years, Canada has adopted several public policy practices, such as universal health care and accessible, free education, into which the federal and provincial governments redistribute tax dollars to pay for benefits given to all Canadians, no matter where they live in the country. Besides health care and education, Canadians have access to Employment Insurance (formerly Unemployment Insurance, established in 1940), welfare, the Canada Pension Plan (1966), and Old Age Security (1952).

CHANGES IN SOCIALISM In 1989, the Soviet Union, which headed a bloc of Eastern European nations (East Germany, Czechoslovakia, and Hungary, among others), concluded that its system of central planning had failed. Suffering from shoddy goods and plagued by shortages, the former Soviet Union began to reinstate market forces.

China, the second major socialist power, watched in dismay as its one-time mentor abandoned the basic principles of socialism (Szelenyi, 1987). In 1989, at the cost of many lives and despite world opposition, Chinese authorities put down a hunger strike by students and workers in Tiananmen Square who were demanding greater freedom and economic reforms. Despite its repressive measure, however, China began to endorse capitalism. Its leaders solicited Western investment and encouraged farmers to cultivate their own plots on communal farms. They allowed the use of credit cards, approved a stock market, and even permitted pieces of the Great Wall to be sold as souvenirs for profit (McGregor, 1992). While still officially proclaiming Marxist-Leninist-Maoist principles, the Communist Party, under the slogan "One China, two systems," hopes to make Shanghai the financial centre of East Asia (McGregor, 1993; Schlesinger, 1994).

Neoliberalism and Social Conservatism

As a capitalist business and political ideology, neoliberalism is not the same as classical market liberalism, even though they share a belief in the centrality of private property, inheritance, and the pursuit of profit. Market liberalism or classical liberalism has origins in the Enlightenment ideas of human rights or individual rights to life, liberty, and the pursuit of property. According to classical liberalism, the state should protect these rights. The opposite of market liberalism is communism.

Neoliberalism refers to expansion of the free market in time and space: nothing less than a 24-hour global economy

Socialism has the virtue of making people more equal. Socialism's equality, however, tends to mean that poverty is distributed throughout a society. Under socialism, almost everyone becomes equally poor.

Capitalism, in contrast, has the virtue of producing wealth. A lot of people remain poor under this system, however, leaving a sharp contrast in wealth and poverty that produces envy and sometimes creates social unrest.

Since the adoption of capitalism in China, wealth is being produced. The poor aren't happy with their lot, especially when their land is taken away to help make others wealthy. Anger and resentment have kept the Communist Party busy, for its army has been forced to squelch numerous riots.

In Beijing, the capital of China, stands a mansion recently built by Zhang Yuchen that is a twin of the Château Maisons-Laffitte, an architectural landmark on the Seine River outside Paris.

At a cost of $50 million, the Beijing replica matches the original edifice detail for detail. Built using the original blueprints of the French château, it even features the same Chantilly stone.

The replica château built by Zhang Yuchen.

The Chinese version of the château—and its accompanying acreage set aside for a proposed development of luxury homes, also to be developed by Yuchen—made 800 farmers landless.

But not to worry. The spiked fence, moat, and armed guards—looking sharp in their French-style uniforms complete with capes and kepis—keep the peasants off the grounds.

In most places, you need connections to become wealthy. In China, this means connections with the Communist Party, the group that holds the power. Yuchen has those connections. As a member of the party, his job involves directing Beijing's construction projects. Yuchen was able to have the wheat fields that had been farmed by peasants re-designated as a "conservation area." He was also able to divert a river to construct the moat, one of the finishing touches on his architectural wonder.

The peasants haven't been left with nothing: as part of Yuchen's deal, he gives $45 a month to each of the elderly. Younger peasants can work in the vineyards that Yuchen is planting. French wine will top off the project.

Source: based on Kahn, 2004, 2007b.

---

will satisfy neoliberals. This type of economy is made possible by the rapid growth of global information and telecommunications technologies. In contrast to classical liberalism, neoliberalism emphasizes the contract over property, and especially the labour contract. More important, neoliberalism sees the time period of contracts reduced and, by extension, the number of contracts greatly increased. For example, a service contract to clean offices might be reduced from one year to three months, and then to one month. Labour or service contracts multiply rapidly under neoliberalism, increasing the control and flexibility enjoyed by companies and the employment instability and exploitation suffered by employees and service providers. Long-term labour contracts, which became the norm after industrialization, are today an anomaly.

SOCIAL CONSERVATISM In the developed world, including Canada and the United States, social conservatism, a set of beliefs often linked to the economic changes associated with neoliberalism, has been on the rise for the past ten years or so. **Social conservatism** is a value system characterized by the belief in conventional morality and social mores and a desire to preserve them, often aggressively, through civil law and regulation. For Protestants or Roman Catholics, for example, social conservativism means politically supporting the legal definition of marriage as a union only between a man and woman. Another example is abortion, as social conservatives believe it is their right to use the government to enact laws that make abortion illegal. This point of view is unlike that held by classical conservatives in the United States and elsewhere, who embrace similar beliefs about family, church, and public morality, but are suspicious, even intolerant, of government intervention in the private lives of a nation's citizens.

In addition to their political support for morally conservative agendas, social conservatives defend patriotism and strongly identify with the existing government and its defenders: the police, the military, and national cultural icons and musicians. In the United States, a subgroup of social conservatives supports a more self-confident foreign policy. This doctrine reverses the traditional conservative position of American isolationism.

Thus, in many ways, social conservatives in the United States are nothing like their conservative grandparents. It is curious that in our current period of history, noted for rapid social and economic change brought on by the information explosion, a significant segment of the U.S. population seeks refuge behind outdated, even unkind, beliefs and values.

IN SUM

At this point in history, we must note that there is no pure capitalism (and likely never was). Today, capitalism speaks in a variety of accents, some softer than others, with versions in China, the former Soviet Union, Great Britain, Japan, Germany, Sweden, Canada, and the United States each differing from the others.

APPLYING SOCIOLOGICAL THEORIES
The Symbolic Interactionist Perspective

PROFESSION OR JOB? WORK AS A STATUS SYMBOL We know that selling hamburgers from a drive-through window is not a profession, but why isn't selling shoes? Sociologists who adopt a symbolic interactionist perspective on work identify five characteristics of **professions** (Parsons, 1954; W. J. Goode, 1960; Greenwood, 1962; Etzioni, 1969).

1. *Rigorous education.* Today, the professions require not only a university degree but also completion of graduate school, followed by an examination that determines whether you will be allowed to practise in the field.

2. *Theory.* Education is theoretical, not just "hands-on." For example, in medicine, microbes, viruses, and genetics are used to explain disease, while in sociology, social structure and social interaction are used to explain human behaviour.

3. *Self-regulation.* Members of a profession claim that only they possess sufficient knowledge to determine the profession's standards and to certify those qualified to be admitted. A group's members also determine who shall be decertified as a result of incompetence or moral problems.

4. *Authority over clients.* Members of a profession claim authority over clients on the basis of their specialized education and theoretical understanding. Unlike carpentry, in which any of us can see that a nail is bent, members of a profession claim that related matters are complex and therefore entreat the client to follow their exclusive instructions.

5. *Professional culture.* Public good, or service to society, not self-interest, lies at the heart of a professional culture. The professions claim that they exist "to provide service to whomever requests it, irrespective of the requesting client's age, income, kinship, politics, race, religion, sex, [sexual orientation,] and social status" (Greenwood, 1962; Hall, 1994).

TABLE 11.4 The Education–Job Market Connection

Change in Number of People Employed, 1990–2001	Level of Education (25–65 Years Old)
Grade 8 or less	–285 000
Some high school	–560 000
High school graduate	–198 000
Some postsecondary	–32 800
Postsecondary certificate	+834 000
University degree (bachelor's)	+1 110 300
Above bachelor's degree	+172 600
Total	+1 041 100

Source: Statistics Canada, March 2002, *Labour Force Historical Review 2001* (revised edition). Catalogue no. 71F0004XCB.

Today, we expect the basic motivation of a physician to be not unlike that of a businessperson or automobile mechanic—that is, making money. However, educational credentials, membership in professional associations, and the professional culture of physicians distinguish their work from that of automobile mechanics and businessmen.

As shown in Table 11.4, there has been a significant gain in employment among the better educated, and a net loss of jobs among the less educated in Canada in the past decade. This trend is indicative of the increase in status of the many new professional careers created as a result of the information explosion, something we have discussed and that will continue to be a point of interest later in this chapter and in subsequent chapters.

The Functionalist Perspective

Work is functional for society. It is because people work that we have electricity, hospitals, schools, automobiles, and homes. Beyond this obvious point, however, lies a basic sociological principle: *work binds us together.* Let's review Durkheim's principles of mechanical and organic solidarity.

MECHANICAL SOLIDARITY In preindustrial societies, people do similar work, directly share most aspects of life, and look at the world in similar ways. Durkheim used the term **mechanical solidarity** to refer to the sense of unity that arises from performing similar activities.

ORGANIC SOLIDARITY As societies industrialize, a division of labour develops, and people work in different occupations. Functioning as an organism, each is part of the same economic system, and the welfare of each depends on the others. Durkheim called this economic interdependence **organic solidarity**.

The Conflict Perspective

Central to conflict theory is an emphasis on the benefit of the wealthy at the expense of workers. Conflict theorists also focus on the impact of technology and the economic and political power of capitalism's inner circle.

TECHNOLOGY: WHO BENEFITS? Conflict theorists suggest that the jobs destroyed by new technologies are not located at the top levels of the multinationals, nor are they held by the wealthy individuals who own large blocks of stock. For the power elite, by lowering production costs, new technologies increase profits and fatten their dividend cheques. The people who bear the brunt of the change are low-level workers, who suffer the ravages of uncertainty, the devastation of job loss, and, often, the wrenching adjustments that come with being forced into lower-paying jobs.

THE INNER CIRCLE OF POWER Multinational corporations are headed by a group that Michael Useem (1984) calls the *inner circle*. Members of the inner circle consult with high-level politicians, promote legislation favourable to big business, and serve as trustees for foundations and universities. They also endorse political candidates who stand firmly for the private ownership of property. On a global level, they fiercely promote the ideology of capitalism and move capital from one nation—or region—to another in their relentless search for greater and more immediate profits.

As stressed in previous chapters, conflict theorists focus on power. Although multinational corporations enshroud much of their activities in secrecy, on occasion their subterranean abuse of power comes to light. One of the most notable examples occurred in 1973, when a U.S. multinational, the International Telephone & Telegraph Company (ITT), joined the CIA in a plot to unseat Chile's elected government. They first attempted to bring about the economic collapse of Chile. When this failed, they plotted a coup d'état, which resulted in the assassination of the Chilean president, Salvador Allende (Coleman, 1995).

Feminist Perspectives

As discussed in Chapter 1, there are a range of feminist theories that tackle the various issues facing women in the world today. In some respects, these theories correspond to the distinctive stages or "waves" of feminism. "First-wave" feminists were primarily concerned with the political right to vote and were known as "suffragists." In Canada and the United States, women were granted the vote after World War I. In France, Charles de Gaulle enfranchised women after World War II for their courage and determination in the underground fight against the Nazis and the collaborationist Vichy government. In some Muslim countries, women still cannot vote, leave the house without their husband's permission, drive cars, or appear in public unveiled.

Rights concerned with property ownership, earning a living, and achieving higher education—many of which were

In their march toward globalization, multinational companies locate their corporate headquarters in one country, manufacture components in another, assemble them in still another, and sell the finished product throughout the world. This factory in Guangzhou, China, fills orders from North American corporations.

THE GLOBAL DIVISION OF WORK Organic solidarity has expanded far beyond anything Durkheim envisioned. People who live in Vancouver or Calgary—or even St. John's, Newfoundland—depend on workers in Tokyo to produce cars. Tokyo workers, in turn, depend on Saudi Arabian workers for oil, South American workers to operate ships, and South African workers for palladium for their catalytic converters. Although we do not feel unity with one another—in fact, we sometimes feel threatened and hostile—interdependence links us all in the same economic web.

Driving this interdependence is the dominance of capitalism. As capitalism globalizes, the world's nations are being divided into three primary trading blocs: North and South America, dominated by the United States; Europe, dominated by Germany; and Asia, dominated by Japan. Multinational corporate giants, benefiting from the new world structure, promote free trade. If free trade is put into practice worldwide, its functions will include greater competition over scarce resources on a global scale. Another dysfunctional consequence—already felt by millions of U.S., U.K., French, and German workers—is the vast loss of production jobs in the most industrialized nations.

granted at the end of the nineteenth century—contributed to increasing women's economic independence in twentieth-century Canada and the United States.

Second-wave feminism is believed to have begun with the publication of Simone de Beauvoir's *The Second Sex* in France in 1949. She argued that men were the first sex because they dominated the economic realm and set the standards and values women were to follow. De Beauvoir insisted that this inequality was not the result of biological differences but was a *social creation*. It wasn't until the 1960s, however, that second-wave feminism took hold and the struggle for equality in the workplace gained momentum. Equal pay for equal work and employment equity (in Canada) or Affirmative Action (in the United States) became the rallying cry of women for several decades. While many have made advances in the world of work and entrepreneurship, job ghettoes and glass ceilings remain in force. **Job ghettoes** (also called **pink ghettoes**) are those employment areas where women dominate, such as nursing, elementary school teaching, child care, and so on. **Glass ceiling** refers to the barriers to social advancement that many women face in the work world.

Third-wave feminism concentrates on sex, sexuality, and gender and offers very little to our understanding of inequality in the workplace. Today, the feminist view of what makes women and men unequal is less unified than it was with first-wave feminism, in large part because of a new focus on the complexity of gender inequality.

Focus Question

What are the differences between the symbolic interactionist, functionalist, conflict, and feminist perspectives on work?

WORK IN CANADIAN SOCIETY

We will now turn our focus to work in Canadian society. To understand the present situation, we must review the large-scale changes that have taken place in what are called *economic sectors*.

Three Economic Sectors

Sociologists divide economic life into three sectors: primary, secondary, and tertiary. In the **primary sector**, workers extract natural resources from the environment. Canadians who fish for a living or mine copper and gold in northern Ontario and Quebec work in the primary sector. So do hunters, cattle raisers, farmers, and lumberjacks. In the **secondary sector**, workers turn raw materials into manufactured goods. They package fish, process copper into electrical wire, and turn trees into lumber and paper. The secondary sector dominates industrial economies.

The main focus of the **tertiary sector** is providing services. Some workers, such as computer technicians and automobile mechanics, install or service products. Others, such as private detectives and cab drivers, provide personal services. Although most of the labour force in postindustrial societies works in the tertiary sector, all three sectors exist side by side. Consider the common lead pencil. People who extract lead and cut timber work in the primary sector; those who turn wood and lead into pencils are employed in the secondary sector; and those who advertise and sell pencils work in the tertiary sector.

Farming provides a remarkable example of the change in sector employment in Canada (Drucker, 1987, 1994). Table 11.5 shows the dramatic decline in employment in farming (the primary sector) since World War II in Canada, from a high of almost 20 percent in 1951 to its present low of 0.8 percent. There has been a similar trend in the other primary sectors (forestry, mining, oil, and natural gas) of the Canadian economy. Manufacturing (the secondary sector) also shows a decline in employment from two in seven workers in 1951 to only one in seven today. In both cases, the declines arose because technological changes in the way food is grown and goods are produced dramatically increased crop yields and manufacturing output. For example, while the production of steel in Canada increased threefold to almost 14.5 million tonnes a year since 1960, the number of people employed fell from 36 500 to 27 200 in 2002 (*Maclean's*, January 23, 2003, p. 32).

Although a postindustrial society requires fewer people to produce food or basic materials and fewer people to process them, the information explosion demands that large numbers of people work in the tertiary sector. Consequently, we have experienced a surge in "knowledge and information work"—managing information and designing, servicing, and marketing products—that requires higher levels of education, as illustrated in Table 11.5.

Table 11.5 shows that between 1961 and 1971, a major transition occurred in Canada. Employment in community, business, and personal services grew rapidly and remains the major engine of job growth in the Canadian economy today.

On the other hand, the reported average weekly earnings of people employed in mining and petroleum businesses and utilities are considerably higher than the average weekly earnings of those in booming tourist and food services enterprises. This difference is due in large part to two major factors: the increased productivity of technological changes and the highly unionized nature of the workforce.

Focus Question

What are the three highest-paying jobs in Canada (by average full-time weekly earnings)?

Women and Work

One of the chief characteristics of the Canadian workforce has been the steady increase in the number of women in paid employment outside the home. In the early 1900s, only one

TABLE 11.5 Employment by Industry, 1951–2004 (percentage of total employed), and Average Weekly Full-Time Earnings, April 2004

Industry	1951	1961	1971	1981	1991	1997	2004	Average Weekly Full-Time** Earnings, April 2004
Agriculture	18.4%	11.2%	6.3%	4.3%	3.4%	1.9%	0.8%	$461.79
Other primary (mining, oil, natural gas, and forestry)	4.4%	3.0%	2.8%	3.0%	2.4%	1.8%	1.7%	$1042.74
Manufacturing	26.5%	24.0%	22.0%	19.5%	15.4%	15.0%	16.3%	$787.63
Construction	6.8%	6.2%	6.1%	6.3%	6.5%	5.6%	4.7%	$824.05
Transportation								$811.12
Utilities								$1080.37
Trade	14.1%	16.9%	16.5%	17.0%	17.5%	16.5%	16.3%	$638.17
Finance, insurance, and real estate	3.0%	3.9%	4.8%	5.3%	5.9%	6.0%	N/A	$831.09
Community, business, and personal service	18%	19.5%	26.2%	29.6%	35.0%	36.6%	N/A	N/A
Educational services								$939.94
Health care and social assistance								$757.36
Accommodation and food/ beverage services								$448.57
Information, culture, and recreation								$791.74
Public administration		5.9%	6.4%	6.8%	6.5%	5.4%	6.1%	$953.76
Professional, scientific, and technical services								$951.85
Total	100%*	100%*	100%*	100%*	100%*	100%*		
Total number employed in Canada	5097	6055	8078	12 131	14 083	15 534		$777.73

* Where totals do not add up to 100%, unclassified workers make up the remainder.
** Part-time employment earnings in all categories are substantially lower than full-time earnings.

Source: By Dan Glenday. Data from Labour Division, Statistics Canada, *Labour Force Annual Averages*, Catalogues 71-529, 71-201; *Employment Earnings and Hours*, Catalogue 72-002.

in six women worked in the paid labour force, while today the proportion has narrowed to one in two. As Figure 11.2 illustrates, this ratio is one of the highest in the industrialized world.

The likelihood of a woman working in the paid labour force depends on several factors. One is marital status. In a recent study by Statistics Canada, families in which the wife reported employment income had higher household incomes than in other family structures. In 1995, less than 5 percent of two-income families had a total income of less than $20 000 while 14 percent had an income of over $100 000. These findings stand in contrast to one-income families, where 21 percent had incomes of less than $20 000 and

less than 5 percent reported incomes of at least $100 000 (Statistics Canada, 1998a, pp. 12–17).

Researchers have found some major distinctions between women and men in the world of work. For one, women tend to be more concerned than men with maintaining a balance between their work and family lives (Statham, Miller, & Mauksch, 1988). For another, men and women generally follow different models for success: Men tend to emphasize individualism, power, and competition, while women are much more likely to stress collaboration, persuasion, and helping (Miller-Loessi, 1992). A primary concern of many women is the extent to which they must adopt the male model of leadership in order to be successful in their careers.

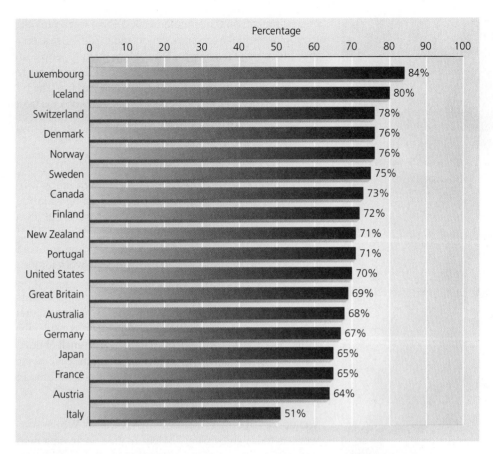

FIGURE 11.2 What Percentage of Women Is in the Labour Force?

Source: By the author. Based on *Statistical Abstract* 2007: Table 1339.

Note that these findings reflect tendencies only and many people can and do diverge from them.

"THE QUIET REVOLUTION" Because the changes it has brought about have been both gradual and profound, sociologists in the United States use the term **quiet revolution** to refer to the growing proportion of women in the labour force. This trend has transformed consumer patterns, relations at work, self-concepts for both men and women, and relationships with husbands and children. One of the most significant aspects of the quiet revolution is the increased proportion of women with preschool children working for wages. In 1981, 47 percent of married women in Canada were employed; by 1997 that proportion had increased to 57 percent. As previously discussed, dual-income families tend to be better off than single-income families, and are increasingly becoming the norm in the Canadian labour force. The implications of these and other related changes to Canada's families are discussed in Chapter 13.

The Underground Economy

It has a sinister ring—suggestive of dope deals struck in alleys and wads of dollar bills hastily exchanged. The underground economy is this, but is also a lot more. If you pay the plumber with "cash," if you purchase a pair of sunglasses from a street vendor or a kitchen gadget at a yard sale, if you so much as hand a neighbour's kid a $20 bill (or accept one) to mow the lawn or baby sit, you are participating in the underground economy (Pennar & Farrell, 1993).

The **underground economy**, also known as the *informal economy* and the *off-the-books economy*, consists of economic activities—legal or illegal—that aren't reported to the government. As a 20-year-old childcare worker who also works as a prostitute two or three nights a week said, "Why do I do this? For the money! Where else can I make this kind of money in a few hours? And it's all tax-free" (Jim Henslin's files).

Because of its subaltern nature, no one knows the exact size of Canada's underground economy, but it likely comprises 15 to 20 percent of the regular economy. Since the 2002 gross domestic product (GDP) of Canada was $940 billion, the current underground economy probably runs over $140 billion. It is so huge that it distorts the country's official GDP statistics, and the Canada Revenue Agency loses millions of dollars in taxes each year.

Shrinking Paycheques

The record profits reported by Canada's banks and other corporations give weight to the assumption that the pay of Canadian employees is increasing. On the contrary,

The term *underground economy* has a sinister ring to it. Part of the underground economy consists of drug deals furtively transacted in back alleys, but the term refers to any unreported, untaxed commercial transaction. Most are as innocuous and common as that depicted in this photo.

According to a recent study, household income growth has declined dramatically over the past 20 years (*Financial Post*, November 13, 1998, p. C7). As shown in Table 11.5, the average weekly earnings of workers in 2004 appeared high in some sectors of the Canadian economy such as utilities, mining, oil, and natural gas. However, even with the sharp rise in the number of working mothers, the study concludes that the standard of living of average Canadians is falling relative to much of the rest of the industrial world. GDP per capita fell below the OECD average in 1993, and the decline continues. Canadian consumers have responded by going increasingly into debt. This is not a recipe for a financially secure future.

Some workers, however, aren't able to bring home even shrinking paycheques. Could you imagine making payments on rent, a car, food, and, if you had anything left over,

entertainment, on the approximately $450 a week provided to employees in the accommodation and food/beverage services industries (see Table 11.5)? Many young people are forced to work two or more jobs and "bunk up" with others their age, or return home to live with their parents. The following Perspectives box looks at some of the problems faced by Canadians in today's job market.

Patterns of Work and Leisure

TRENDS IN LEISURE **Leisure** is time not taken up by work or required activities such as eating and sleeping. Consider driving a car. If you do it for pleasure, it is leisure, but if you are an on-duty police officer or commuting to the office, it is work. If done for enjoyment, horseback riding and reading a book are leisure—but these activities are work for jockeys and students.

Patterns of leisure change with the life course, as illustrated by the U-curve shown in Figure 11.3. Young children enjoy the most leisure, but teenagers still have considerably more leisure than their parents. Parents with small children have the least leisure, but after their children leave home, leisure picks up again. After the age of 60 or so, the amount of leisure enjoyed by adults peaks.

WORK IN THE POSTINDUSTRIAL SOCIETY While some workers today enjoy plenty of leisure time, increasing numbers of Canadian workers are feeling the stress of working more but enjoying life less. Over the past several decades, unionization helped many Canadians increase the amount of time they could spend in leisure activities. Today, the assault on trade unions by businesses and governments makes increasing vacation time for their members a luxury when faced with more pressing issues such as job security.

Shortening the workweek is one way to increase leisure time. In Germany, for example, the workweek is currently 35 hours, with Friday afternoons off. Volkswagen was the world's

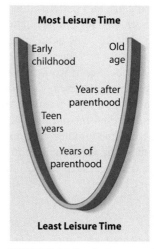

FIGURE 11.3 Leisure and the Life Course: The "U" Curve of Leisure

What is it like for some Canadians to find work? Below are two typical stories that shed light on the personal problems faced by increasing numbers of Canadians, both young and old.

On March 2, 1990, Garrie Manser punched out at the north-end picture-frame plant for the last time. K-D Manufacturing was moving across the river to Watertown, New York. Manser, a painter at K-D for 21 years, remembers the exact date three years later. He can also remember his first day working for the organization: November 13, 1968. He was 22 at the time.

After K-D shut down, Manser managed to find work with Dustbusters (a contract cleaning outfit) and the Ministry of Transport. He liked the government job; it involved painting highway guardrails, and he could use his experience. But both jobs ended soon after they began. Manser then found six weeks of work at a door and window maker, but left because chemicals in the wood preservatives used gave him an unbearable rash.

"There's so darn many people out of work, they don't know who to pick," says Manser. His 21 years working in one place didn't appear to carry any weight. "They want a Grade 12 education. The jobs you see in the paper are for bartenders, cooks, and like that. They want experience."

Russ Jackson is typical of his generation. His father commuted every day to work in Ford's Windsor foundry. Born in nearby Chatham in 1959, Jackson married Brenda Ritchie, the girl next door, after teaching her how to drive the family car. At age 18, he followed his father and started work at the Ford foundry, then watched as his parents and their friends retired and began spending half the year in winter homes purchased in Florida. Before he was to be laid off in 1979, Jackson took a job at Brant Casting, a newly opened foundry that supplied forged engine parts to the Big Three auto makers. Ten years after he signed on at Brant Casting, Jackson and his mates punched out for the last time when the plant closed permanently, one of the first of many factories to feel the first bite of the recession that began in 1990. For 10 years, Jackson had been living from paycheque to paycheque, saving little. By this time, his wife was working as a moulder in a plastic factory run by the Complax company, now that their youngest daughter was ready to be left with a caregiver. Less than a half a year later, the Complax plant, though new, also closed down. "There is no other plant in Canada or in the U.S. with the high technology we have," company president Ralph Zarboni had bragged when the plant opened in the 1980s. "It's state of the art," Brenda Jackson says. She is still proud of her former workplace.

"The days of getting hired somewhere and spending 30 years there are done," says Russ Jackson. "Now you'll be jumping from job to job. You can feel it in the town, the insecure feeling that most people have. It's affected our kids." He relates that his daughter wanted to go ice skating but couldn't because her skates didn't fit. "She didn't want to ask for the 10 bucks for another pair." In 10 years at Brant Castings, Russ Jackson managed to put $600 into an RRSP, and now he can't rely on getting a pension. "People who jump from job to job don't have that. That's the scary part. We're all going to get older. How will we live then?" The very notion of retirement—to say nothing of the "early" retirement now aimed at saving the jobs of young employees—was only being invented when Russ Jackson's dad entered the work world 50 years earlier.

Source: Glenday, Duffy, & Pupo (1997).

first global corporation to adopt a 30-hour workweek (Rifkin, 1995). In addition, German workers are guaranteed six weeks of paid vacation each year. Unlike Western Europe, however, the trend in Canada and the United States is the opposite: Canadian workers now average 2036 hours of work a year, with U.S. workers averaging 1948 hours. For Japanese workers, the norm is 2120 hours (DeGraff, 2003).

THE FUTURE: FACING THE CONSEQUENCES OF GLOBAL CAPITALISM

A little over a decade and a half ago, a small number of sociologists in Great Britain and France were celebrating the coming "Leisure Revolution" (Sherman, 1985; Jenkins & Sherman, 1981; Gorz, 1982, 1985). We were told then that within our lifetime, the application of new microelectronics-based technology by businesses and governments would steer us into a future where the nature of work and the work ethic would be defined by what we did in our leisure time, be it simple relaxation or starting our own business. True, we would still have to work at something that was not of our own choosing; however, there would be limitations on the length of time we would be exposed to this kind of work.

As one of the "Paths to [this] Paradise," André Gorz (1985) spoke of a lifetime work schedule of 20 000 hours. Can you imagine working for only 20 years at a rate of only 6 hours a day, 4 days a week, for 42 weeks a year? Imagine starting employment after university with a four-day workweek, two-and-a-half months' paid vacation, and retirement before your forty-fifth birthday!

As capitalism globalizes, it is not just the products but also the cultures of the dominant capitalist nations that are exported around the world. Shown here is an outdoor ad in Tokyo. What aspects of Western culture can you identify in the ad?

Clearly, this is not our present-day reality, nor is it likely to become reality in the immediate future. What happened to the transformation of work? Is the idea of a shortened workweek and meaningful jobs an impossible utopia?

The new realities of work deal with the nature of jobs and skills-based change. The transformation of work has witnessed the rise of a knowledge/information/service economy based on the universal application of microelectronics technology that has created new occupational categories—a rush of change that has left in its wake thousands of lost jobs, leaving most of the remaining positions "retooled."

What does this mean for the future of occupational choice for young Canadians? When governments are divesting themselves of people and assets and large companies are shedding "excess" human resources, what are the prospects for the future? Will there be enough good service jobs created by the private sector in this country? What would it take to rescue the dream of the "Leisure Revolution"?

The Thinking Critically about Social Controversy box that follows focuses on the far-reaching implications of the global transformation of our economy.

THINKING CRITICALLY ABOUT SOCIAL CONTROVERSY
New Technology and the Restructuring of Work: What Type of New Society?

What are we to base prospective discussions on when debating the new realities of work? Economic nationalism is no longer on the political agenda in Canada. As a modest beginning, let us explore two possible scenarios.

The first reflects the changes taking place in Canadian society today, where large, lean, or agile corporations such as General Motors are continuing their strategy of cost-cutting, otherwise known as "downsizing" or "reengineering," with layoffs, redundancies, and early retirement of unionized or non-unionized employees and large segments of lower and middle management. Between 2002

and 2005, employment in the manufacturing industry in Canada fell by nearly 149 000 full-time jobs, or about 6.4 percent, to a little over 2 173 000. About two-thirds of the decline happened in 2005 alone.

Only three weeks after recent negotiations with General Motors, the Canadian Auto Workers Union (CAW) and the public were told on June 3, 2008, that General Motors planned to cease production of its half-tonne trucks at its plant in Oshawa, Ontario, in 2009 instead of the previously negotiated date of 2011, effectively eliminating 2600 jobs. For two weeks, CAW work-

ers blocked the entrance to GM's headquarters in Oshawa. On Thursday, June 12, between 2000 and 3000 unionized workers led a solidarity march in Oshawa in support of the CAW workers.

It is not only the private sector that is open to pressures from globalization. The public sector relies on tax revenues to sustain and expand its services. What happens when governments promise to cut taxes, such as income taxes and the GST? Where will the money come from? Therefore, included in this "economic necessity" are governments, at all levels, who are slashing good paying jobs and eliminating, privatizing, or contracting out public service careers.

Nowadays, it is not uncommon for television personalities, business consultants, government bureaucrats, and many others to point out that today's redundant blue- and white-collar employees will need time to adjust to the new realities of work in an information age. Often this means acquiring new skills through retraining programs, upgrading existing skills, or even getting a basic education. Just as often, new entrants into the labour market are told that to be competitive, computer skills, the ability to work in teams, and networking are prerequisites for increasingly elusive good jobs. Even armed with these skills, competition from other job seekers is often so great that landing a job remains a challenge for many. Insecurity about the future breeds suspicion, anxiety, and frustration for increasing numbers of young Canadians. The sign of these times is flatter, leaner, and meaner corporations and governments, where all levels of the work force are multi-skilled and government employees and corporate citizens are "working more for less."

The ruling orthodoxy maintains the promise of new and better jobs for the casualties of corporate restructuring and government re-engineering. We are told that information technology is responsible for eliminating all the good jobs in traditional industries, especially manufacturing, but that new jobs in the service sector are being created rapidly, and that the private sector, if unfettered by government regulations, will create more and better jobs than those lost in manufacturing and the public sector. University graduates are led to believe that they will be sought after by those companies Edward Luttwak calls the "New Titans" of the information age—Microsoft and Intel. Yet, as Luttwak (1996) rightly points out, Microsoft and Intel, whose value on Wall Street is much greater than that

of General Motors, had a combined total of only 48 100 employees worldwide by the mid 1990s, while Ford alone payrolled 325 000 employees! Clearly, the good jobs from the "New Titans" have not materialized. Not only have they not materialized, Luttwak argues in his latest book, *Turbo Capitalism* (1999), the result of globalization is an "Upstairs-Downstairs" society in which the privileged few are served by the rest of us.

What's more, what comes after school/university for most Canadians are not good jobs and plenty of leisure time. There is little prospect for new graduates of a secure future with better-compensated leisure time. On the contrary, we are told that we can't afford our lifestyle, that governments have to cut and corporations must become global and more competitive. While retail stores carry a wider variety of products available for consumption than at any previous time in recorded history—from Benetton clothes to IKEA furniture, Macintosh computers, and Toyota Camrys—these products are made in various parts of the globe with a shrinking proportion of well-paid factory and office workers.

If this scenario holds, Canada's occupational structure could take on the appearance of a bottom-heavy hourglass, replacing the traditional pyramid—otherwise known as the "shrinking middle." This new society would restrict access to the limited numbers of good jobs or careers defined by a high degree of employment security, high pay, and relatively decent working conditions, while promoting a burgeoning secondary sector comprised of openly competitive, insecure, and nonstandard "work arrangements." It would see entrenched bipolar occupational estates offering less and less opportunity for advancement into good jobs and could give rise to a new set of dangerous populist politics.

The second scenario involves the promise of a better, prosperous life as

a result of the revolution in new information technologies—a promise kept alive by characters like *The Jetsons* or the vision of Gene Roddenberry's *Star Trek*, where poverty has been eliminated and ethnic violence is a forgotten memory.

The basis for this second and more optimistic scenario, too, is the dramatic increase in the productive capacity of the world economy generated by microelectronics-based information technology. The capability to produce increasing amounts for less money could mean that more people would be freed from wage slavery. The drudgery, danger, and pain associated with factory, longshore, mining, and forestry jobs would be dramatically reduced. Instead of men, women, and children destroying themselves at work, the microelectronics-based information revolution could give almost everyone a chance for self-fulfillment and meaning.

This dream of a liberated future has been superseded by an uncertain present. For most Canadians, holding a steady, full-time job is probably more important now than it was 30 years ago. Nevertheless, some analysts argue that the disruptions brought about by the sustained advance to an information-based, service economy are much like the dramatic changes in the world's economic livelihood brought about by the Industrial Revolution. Time was needed for those displaced from their agricultural way of life to adapt to the discipline of the factory regime. Our society is in a period of transition, they contend; eventually, the good jobs will appear.

Can the more positive scenario be realized by simply waiting and leaving well enough alone? Or will it require Canadians, Americans, the British, the French, and citizens in other developed and less developed countries to pressure their governments to step in and challenge the path chosen by those who wield economic and political power?

This poorly paid worker carrying sulphur from the Ijen crater in Java is an expendable part of the profit system that drives the economic machine called capitalism.

SUMMARY AND REVIEW

The Transformation of Economic Systems

HOW ARE ECONOMIC SYSTEMS LINKED TO TYPES OF SOCIETIES?

The earliest societies, hunting and gathering societies, were **subsistence economies**: small groups lived off the land and produced little or no surplus. Economic systems grew more complex as people discovered how to domesticate and cultivate, farm (agricultural societies), and manufacture (industrial societies). Each of these methods allowed people to produce a *surplus*, which fostered trade. Trade, in turn, brought social inequality as some people began to accumulate more than others. pp. 240–243.

World Economic Systems

HOW DO THE MAJOR ECONOMIC SYSTEMS DIFFER?

The world's two major economic systems are capitalism and socialism. In **capitalism**, private citizens own the means of production and pursue profits. In **socialism**, the state owns the means of production and determines production with no goal of profit. pp. 243–245

WHAT ARE THE DIFFERENCES BETWEEN NEOLIBERALISM AND SOCIAL CONSERVATISM?

Neoliberalism is a version of the capitalist economic system based on the realization of a 24-hour global economy.

This type of economy is made possible by the rapid expansion of global information and telecommunications technologies. **Social conservatism** is a value system characterized by a belief in conventional morality and social mores and a desire to preserve them, often aggressively, through civil law and regulation. For example, a social conservative politically supports the legal definition of marriage as a union only between a man and a woman and is against abortion. pp. 245–247.

Applying Sociological Theories

HOW DO FOUR OF THE MAJOR SOCIOLOGICAL PERSPECTIVES APPLY TO WORK?

Symbolic interactionists analyze meanings and self-perceptions, asking why work is a job or a profession, what gives work status, and what makes work satisfying. From the *functionalist perspective*, work is a basis of social solidarity. Preindustrial societies foster **mechanical solidarity**, identifying with others who perform similar tasks. With industrialization comes **organic solidarity**, economic interdependence brought about by the division of labour. *Conflict theorists*, who focus on worker exploitation and alienation, note how the new technology and global capitalism affect workers and owners. Workers lose jobs to automation, while the inner circle maintains its political power and profits from these changes. *Feminist theories* concentrate on gender inequality and how men dominate the more important good jobs while women can be found in **pink ghettoes**. Those that do enter the mostly male occupations tend to experience **glass ceilings**. pp. 247–249.

Work in Canadian Society

WHAT ARE THE THREE ECONOMIC SECTORS OF THE LABOUR FORCE?

In the **primary sector**, workers extract raw materials from the environment. In the **secondary sector**, workers turn raw products into manufactured goods. In the **tertiary sector**, workers produce services. Most Canadians now work in the tertiary, or service, sector. p. 249.

HOW HAS THE RATIO OF WOMEN IN THE WORKFORCE CHANGED?

In 1921, one in five Canadian women participated in paid employment. Today, this figure is almost one in two, one of the highest ratios in the industrialized world. pp. 249–251.

WHAT IS THE UNDERGROUND ECONOMY?

The **underground economy** consists of any economic activity not reported to the government, from babysitting to prostitution. The size of the underground economy is likely 15 to 20 percent of the regular economy. p. 251.

HOW HAVE PATTERNS OF WORK AND LEISURE CHANGED?

Industrialization initially brought a dramatic decrease in **leisure**, but workers have gained some back. Among the industrialized nations, currently only the Japanese work more hours per year than Canadian workers. pp. 252–253.

The Future: Facing the Consequences of Global Capitalism

Expanding global trade, new technologies, and downsizing will continue to force a restructuring of work. Choices made now can lead to either a better society or a fortress mentality. pp. 253–256.

TALKING ABOUT THEORY

Theoretical Paradigms

	CLASSICAL PARADIGMS			RECENT PARADIGMS
	Structural-Functional Paradigm	Social-Conflict Paradigm	Symbolic-Interaction Paradigm	Feminist Paradigm
What is the level of analysis?	Macro level	Macro level	Micro level	Micro and macro levels
What is the social significance of the economy?	Work binds us together as a society and increasingly as members of a global economy (inclusive = functional). Globalization divides the world into three trading blocks (exclusive = dysfunctional).	The economic system maintains the status quo. New technology benefits the few at the expense of the many.	The distinction between working at a job and having a career as a professional.	"Pink ghettoes" and the "glass ceiling" point to the social mechanisms of discrimination in the workplace.
Has the economy changed over time? How?	Yes. Globalization divides the world into three trading blocks.	No. As changing technology provides new opportunities for capital and profit, the wealthy benefit economically.	Yes. New information and communications technologies have created new professions.	Yes/No. Changes in legal prohibitions against sexual harassment and workplace discrimination are significant positive changes. Patriarchy remains.

KEY TERMS

WEBLINKS

All URLs listed are current as of the printing of this book.

Centre for Research on Work and Society (CRWS)
www.yorku.ca/crws

The Centre for Research on Work and Society at York University brings together academic researchers with labour movement partners to engage in research and education on work and labour matters. One of the centre's most recent projects is an electronic journal entitled *Just Labour*. You can reach the *Just Labour* website through the CRWS home page.

Canadian Business
www.canadianbusiness.com

The homepage for Canada's premier business periodical. Each year, it carries the most complete and authoritative list of that year's most successful Canadian companies and business personalities.

World Economic Forum
www.weforum.org

The World Economic Forum is an independent, non-partisan international organization committed to improving the state of the world by engaging leaders in partnerships to shape global, regional, and industry agendas. The World Economic Forum was incorporated as a foundation in 1971 and is based in Geneva, Switzerland.

The Canadian Economy Online
http://canadianeconomy.gc.ca/english/economy/

A Government of Canada website offering a wealth of information on the Canadian economy, including links to key Canadian economic indicators for the past 10 years.

CRITICAL THINKING QUESTIONS

1. Some sociologists and most public officials believe that microelectronics-based computer technologies hold the promise of a better future for most Canadians. Do you believe this is an accurate assessment?

2. Most students today work while going to university. Describe the ways you would make your workplace a better place to work. Why can't you implement your ideas? Do you think having a trade union in your workplace would matter?

3. Some sociologists believe work is important because it provides all of us with status and meaning. It is not uncommon to hear someone say, "I am a sociologist" or "I am a university student" or "I am a teacher." If work is important for our well-being, why do so many people hate their jobs and look forward to retirement?

   Access the Research Navigator through MySocLab and use keywords such as "new technology," "work," and "future" to locate relevant and recent scholarly and popular press publications to help you answer these questions.

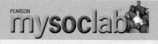 **PEARSON** mysoclab

Explore the topics covered in this chapter on MySocLab using the access information provided with this text. Interactive resources for studying include multimedia tutorials, video clips, practice tests, quizzes, and animated maps and figures.

12 Politics: Power and Authority

LEARNING OUTCOMES

After you have studied this chapter, you will be able to answer the following questions:

1. What is the difference between micropolitics and macropolitics?
2. How are authority and coercion related to power?
3. What kinds of authority are there?
4. How are the types of government related to power?
5. What are the main characteristics of the Canadian political system?
6. What political parties are there at present in the House of Commons?
7. What is at the root of the political strife in Quebec politics?
8. Is Canada controlled by a ruling class?
9. How successful has employment equity been as a federal public policy?
10. How are war and terrorism related to politics, and what are their costs?
11. Is humanity headed toward a one-world political order?

In the 1940s, George Orwell wrote *1984*, a novel about a future in which the government, known as "Big Brother," dominates society, dictating almost every aspect of everyone's life. To love someone is considered a sinister activity, a betrayal of the unquestioning allegiance all citizens owe Big Brother.

Two characters, Winston and Julia, fall in love. Because of Big Brother, they meet furtively, always with the threat of discovery and punishment hanging over their heads. When informers turn them in, expert interrogators separate the pair. They swiftly proceed to break their affection—to restore their loyalty to Big Brother.

Then follows a remarkable account of Winston and his tormentor, O'Brien. Winston is strapped so tightly into a chair that he can't even move his head. O'Brien explains that everyone has a breaking point, some worst thing that will push them over the edge.

O'Brien tells Winston that he has discovered his worst fear. He sets on the table a cage with two giant, starving sewer rats, then picks up a mask connected to the door of the cage and places it over Winston's head. In a quiet voice, O'Brien explains that when he presses the lever, the door of the cage will slide up and the rats will shoot out like bullets and bore straight into Winston's face. Still speaking so quietly that Winston has to strain to hear him, O'Brien adds that the rats sometimes attack the eyes first, but sometimes burrow through the cheeks and devour the tongue. When O'Brien places his hand on the lever, Winston realizes that the only way out is for someone to take his place. But who? Then he hears his own voice screaming, "Do it to Julia! . . . Tear her face off, strip her to the bones. Not me! Julia! Not me!"

Orwell does not describe Julia's interrogation, but when Julia and Winston see each other later they realize that each has betrayed the other. Their love is gone. Big Brother has won. Although Orwell pictures an extreme form of totalitarianism, politics is always about power and authority, the focus of this chapter.

MICROPOLITICS AND MACROPOLITICS

Although the images that come to mind when we think of politics are those of government—kings, queens, coups, dictatorships, running for office, voting—politics, in the sense of power relations, is also an inevitable part of everyday life (M. Schwartz, 1990). As Weber (1922/1968) said, **power** is the ability to carry out your will in spite of resistance, and in every group, large or small, some individuals have power over others. Symbolic interactionists and feminists use the term **micropolitics** to refer to the exercise of power in everyday life. Routine situations in which people jockey for power include several employees trying to impress a new boss, who will decide which one of them will be promoted to manager, efforts by parents to enforce their curfew on a reluctant daughter or son, and the struggle over a remote control to a television. *Every group is political, for in every group there is a power struggle of some sort.*

In contrast, **macropolitics**—the focus of this chapter—refers to the exercise of large-scale power over a large group. Governments, whether the dictatorship faced by Winston in the opening vignette or the elected forms in the United States and Canada, are examples of macropolitics.

POWER, AUTHORITY, AND VIOLENCE

Power is linked to leadership; that is, we perceive power as either legitimate or illegitimate. Weber used the term **authority** to refer to legitimate power—power that we accept as right and just. In contrast, illegitimate power, or **coercion**, is power that we do not accept as morally correct.

Imagine you are driving to university to take a sociology exam, and on the way you stop to buy a high-end DVD player on sale for $250. As you approach the store, a man jumps out of an alley and shoves a gun in your face. He demands your money. Frightened for your life, you hand it over. After filing a police report, you are running late. Afraid you might miss the test, you step on the gas. As the needle hits 130, you see flashing blue and red lights in your rearview mirror. Your explanation about the robbery doesn't faze the officer—or the judge who hears your case a few weeks later. She lectures you on safety and orders you to pay $50 in court costs plus $200 for travelling 30 kilometres per hour over the speed limit. You pay the $250.

What's the difference? The mugger, the police officer, and the judge each has power, and in both cases you part with $250. The difference is that the mugger has no authority. His power is illegitimate—he has no *right* to do what he did because he personally assaulted you. In contrast, you may grudgingly acknowledge that the officer has the right to stop you and that the judge has the right to fine you. Theirs is *authority,* or legitimate power.

Focus Question
What is the difference between power and authority?

Authority and Legitimate Violence

The **state**, a term synonymous with government, claims the exclusive right to use violence and the right to punish anyone else who does (Max Weber, 1946a, 1922/1968). This point is critical to our understanding of macropolitics. If someone owes you a debt, you cannot imprison that person or even forcibly take the money. The state can. As Berger (1963) summarized, *"Violence is the ultimate foundation of any political order."*

Before we explore the origins of the modern state, let's look at what happens when the state loses legitimacy.

THE COLLAPSE OF AUTHORITY Sometimes a state oppresses its people, who resist their government as they would a mugger. **Revolution**, armed resistance with the intention to overthrow a government, is not only a people's rejection of a government's claim to rule over them but also a rejection of its monopoly on violence. The American Revolution of 1776, the Cuban and Chinese Communist revolutions, and the Russian Revolution of 1917, which resulted in the establishment of the Soviet Communist regime and lasted until 1989, are examples of the use of violence to achieve a fundamental change in government.

What some see as coercion, however, others see as authority. Consequently, some people might remain loyal to a government, willingly defend it, and perhaps even die for it, while others are ready to take up arms against it. *The more its power is seen as legitimate, the more stable a government is.* The Canadian system of democracy is seen by most Canadians as legitimate, and therefore Canadian people do not seek a radical transformation in how it is run.

Why do people accept power as legitimate? Max Weber (1922/1968) identified three sources of authority: traditional, rational-legal, and charismatic.

Traditional Authority

Throughout history, the most common form of authority has been tradition. **Traditional authority** is based on custom. Simply because of their bloodline, for example, specific individuals become chief, king, or queen. Queen Elizabeth II is Canada's titular head of government. She wasn't elected queen, she was crowned because of her royal lineage or kinship.

Gender relations in most human groups are a good example of traditional authority, since they are based on custom. In the villages of Spain and Portugal, for example, widows are expected to wear only black until they remarry—which generally means they wear black for the rest of their lives, or risk being ostracized by the community.

Traditional authority is undermined by industrialization, because people are exposed to new experiences. This opens up new perspectives on life and traditional authority no longer goes unchallenged. Thus, in Spain and Portugal, you can still see old women dressed in black from head to toe—and you immediately know their marital status. Younger widows, however, are likely to be indistinguishable from other women.

For centuries, widows in the Mediterranean were expected to dress in black. Their long dresses were matched by black stockings, black shoes, and black head coverings. Widows conformed to this socially defined expression of ongoing sorrow not because of law, but because of custom. Today, however, as industrialization erodes traditional authority, few widows follow this practice.

One of the best examples of charismatic authority is Joan of Arc, shown here at the coronation of Charles VII, whom she was instrumental in making king. Uncomfortable at portraying Joan of Arc wearing only a man's coat of armor, the artist depicted her with plenty of makeup, and a ludicrous skirt.

Even in postindustrial societies, parental authority provides an excellent example of traditional authority (M. Schwartz, 1990). From generations past, we inherit the idea that parents are responsible for providing their children with food and shelter and also have the right to discipline them, choose their doctors and schools, and teach them religion and morality.

Rational-Legal Authority

Rational-legal authority, the second type of authority identified by Weber, is based on written rules. "Rational" means reasonable, and "legal" means part of law. Matters agreed to may be as broad as a constitution that specifies the rights of all members of a nation or as narrow as a contract between two individuals. Because bureaucracies are based on written rules, rational-legal authority is also called *bureaucratic authority*.

Rational-legal authority comes from the position an individual holds, not from the person who holds the position. In a democracy, for example, the prime minister's authority comes from the office, as specified in a written constitution, not from custom or the individual's personal characteristics. Her/his pronouncements are subject to the law, rather than the law being subject to her/his personal fads and foibles.

Charismatic Authority

A charismatic individual is someone to whom people are drawn because they believe that person has been touched by God or has been endowed by nature with exceptional qualities (Lipset, 1993). Joan of Arc is an example of someone with **charismatic authority**, the third type of authority identified by Weber. (*Charisma* is a Greek word that describes a gift freely and graciously given [Arndt & Gingrich, 1957].) People followed her because they were drawn to her outstanding traits. They saw her as a messenger of God, fighting on the side of justice, and accepted her leadership as a result of these appealing qualities.

THE THREAT POSED BY CHARISMATIC LEADERS Queen Elizabeth II owes allegiance to tradition, while Prime Minister Harper is bound to written laws. To what do charismatic leaders owe allegiance? Their authority resides in their ability to attract followers, which is often based on their sense of special mission or calling. Not tied to tradition or the rule of law, charismatic leaders pose a threat to the established political system. Accordingly, they can inspire followers to disregard—or even overthrow—traditional and rational-legal authorities.

Focus Question
What are Max Weber's three bases for authority?

Pierre Elliott Trudeau at the 1968 Liberal leadership convention. Trudeau is a good example of someone who combined rational-legal and charismatic authority.

Authority as Ideal Type

Weber's classifications—traditional, rational-legal, and charismatic—represent ideal types of authority. Any given leader may show a combination of characteristics.

Consider Pierre Elliott Trudeau, who combined rational-legal and charismatic authority. As the elected head of the Canadian government, Trudeau represented rational-legal authority. Yet his mass appeal, especially in English-speaking Canada, was so great that his public speeches could arouse feelings of patriotism and national identity.

On the other hand, for nationalists in Quebec, Trudeau's authority was far from legitimate. Trudeau's policy of bilingualism and biculturalism (later changed to multiculturalism) was portrayed as an exercise in the assimilation of the French majority in Quebec because it did not challenge the entrenched privileges of the anglophone minority in the province. In addition, Quebec francophones' hostility toward Trudeau's actions during both the October Crisis (see page 270) and the air traffic controllers' and airline pilots' strike of 1976 had a significant role in the subsequent election of the nationalistic Parti Québécois (PQ) to power in 1976 (Guindon, 1988, 2001). Trudeau may have had mass appeal in English Canada, but he was far from a hero in his home province of Quebec. Such are the "dangers" of a charismatic leader. Not everyone supports his or her cause, and there are many who will openly oppose it.

Charismatic and traditional authority can also overlap. The Ayatollah Khomeini of Iran, for example, was a religious leader, holding the traditional position of ayatollah. His embodiment of the Iranian people's dreams, however, along with his austere life and devotion to the principles of the Koran, gave him such mass appeal that he was also a charismatic leader. Khomeini's followers were convinced he had been chosen by God, and his speeches could arouse tens of thousands of followers into action.

The Transfer of Authority

The orderly transfer of authority from one leader to another is critical for social stability. Under traditional authority, people generally know who is next in line. Under rational-legal authority, people may not know who the next leader will be, but they do know how that person will be selected. South Africa provides a remarkable example of the orderly transfer of authority under a rational-legal organization. In spite of being ripped apart by decades of racial strife accompanied by deep suspicions, hatreds, and many murders, South Africa was able to peacefully transfer power from the white minority group led by President de Klerk to the black majority group led by Nelson Mandela by maintaining its rational-legal authority.

Charismatic authority has no such rules of succession, which makes it inherently less stable than either traditional or rational-legal authority. Because charismatic authority is built around an individual, the death or incapacitation of such a leader can mean a bitter struggle for succession. Consequently, some charismatic leaders make arrangements for an orderly transition of power by appointing a successor. This does not guarantee orderly succession, of course, for followers may not perceive the designated heir in the same way as they did the earlier leader. A second strategy is for a charismatic leader to build an organization, which then develops a system of rules or regulations, thus transforming itself into a rational-legal leadership. Weber used the term **routinization of charisma** to refer to the transition of authority from a charismatic leader to rational-legal authority.

TYPES OF GOVERNMENT

How do the various types of government—monarchies, democracies, dictatorships, and oligarchies—differ?

Monarchies: The Rise of the State

City-states were the first type of government. Each had its own **monarchy**, with a king or queen whose right to rule was considered hereditary. If you drive through the countrysides of Spain, France, or Germany, you can still see evidence of former city-states.

Prime Minister Stephen Harper being sworn in. The Governor General of Canada, Michaëlle Jean (sitting in the background), presides over the ceremony. As the Queen's representative in Canada, Jean is Canada's head of state. Harper, whose Conservative Party was democratically elected, is the head of government.

Although a city controlled the immediate area around it under this system, the areas between cities remained in dispute. City-states often quarrelled, and wars were common. The victors extended their rule, and eventually a single city-state was able to wield power over an entire region. As the size of these regions grew, the people slowly developed an identity with the larger region. That is, they began to see distinct inhabitants as a "we" instead of a "they." What we define as a state—a political entity that claims a monopoly on the use of violence within a territory—came into being.

Democracies: Citizenship as a Revolutionary Idea

Both Canada and the United States have governments that are called **democracies**. (The word *democracy* is derived from two Greek words—*kratos* [power] and *demos* [common people]—literally, "power to the people.")

The democracies of the two countries differ in that the government of the United States grew out of a revolutionary past with Great Britain, while Canada's grew out of accepting our colonial heritage with Great Britain and pre-Revolutionary France.

Because of their size, some small legal-rational organizations, such as tribes and cities, practised **direct democracy**. They were small enough for eligible voters to meet, express opinions, and vote publicly—much like a town hall meeting today. Direct democracy is not possible with the large populations of Canada and the United States. Therefore, **representative democracy** was invented.

Today, we take the idea of citizenship for granted. There is nothing natural about citizenship, however—it is simply one way that people choose to define themselves. Throughout most of human history, people were thought to *belong* to a clan, tribe, or even a ruler. The idea of **citizenship**—that by virtue of birth and residence, people have basic rights—is relatively new to the human scene (B. Turner, 1990).

The concept of representative democracy based on citizenship was revolutionary. Its implementation meant *the reversal of traditional ideas, since the government was to be responsive to the people's wishes, not the people to the wishes of the government.*

The idea of **universal citizenship**—of everyone having the same basic rights by virtue of being born in a country (or by immigrating and becoming a naturalized citizen)—flowered very slowly, and came into practice only through fierce struggle. Initially, only certain citizens (male land owners) in Canada voted for men to represent them—first in Montreal, which was the first city of representative government in British North America, and later in Ottawa.

It seems inconceivable today that anyone should be denied the right to vote, hold office, make a contract, testify in court, or own property on the basis of their gender or race/ethnicity. For earlier generations of Canadians, however, it seemed just as inconceivable that women, the poor, Native Canadians, or Asian Canadians should have such rights. Table 12.1 details the evolution of the right to vote in Canada.

Over the years, rights have been extended, and citizenship and its privileges now apply to all Canadians. Property, sex, and ethnicity no longer determine the civil rights of citizens.

TABLE 12.1 Women, Equity, and the Right to Vote

Year	Event
1867	British North America Act excludes women's right to vote.
1873	Women property owners in British Columbia become the first women to gain the right to vote in a municipal election.
1885	Sir John A. Macdonald introduces, then withdraws, an elections act amendment giving women the vote.
1894	House of Commons votes down the Women's Christian Temperance Union petition for women's suffrage.
1914	Flora Denison publishes the first suffrage journal, entitled *War and Women*.
1916	Women in Manitoba become the first in Canada to win the vote in provincial elections. In March and April, Saskatchewan and Alberta follow Manitoba's lead.
1918	On May 24, women vote in federal elections but must be 21 years or older, not be alien-born, and meet the property requirements in the province where they reside.
1919	Electoral law amended so that women can stand for federal office.
1920	Federal law amended to include universal female and male suffrage regardless of provincial law.
1921	The first federal election in which women vote under universal franchise.
1940	Women gain the provincial franchise in Quebec.
1948	Disqualifications based on race eliminated from federal election law.
1955	Final restrictions based on religion removed from Federal Elections Act.
1960	Diefenbaker's government extends the franchise to "Registered Indians."
1970	Voting age lowered to 18. Eighteen-year-olds vote for the first time in the 1972 federal election.
1982	Charter of Rights and Freedoms entrenches the right to vote.
1993	Special ballot for Canadians living or travelling abroad who are unable to vote on election day.
1996	The times for opening and closing polls on election day is increased from 11 to 12 hours.
1997	National Register of Electors created; eliminates door-to-door enumeration. By eliminating enumeration, the election period is reduced from a minimum of 47 days to 36.
2000	Bill C-2 guarantees people with physical or other disabilities the right to vote in their own home in the presence of an election officer and a witness chosen by the elector. The Chief Electoral Officer is empowered to devise and test electronic voting techniques for future use.

Source: Elections Canada, 2000, Catalogue no. CA1 TB #52, ISSN 12022454. Adapted with the permission of the Minister of Public Works and Government Services Canada. Also, Elections Canada website, www.elections.ca.

Focus Question

Why is the parliamentary system in Canada a form of democracy?

Dictatorships and Oligarchies: The Seizure of Power

A government run by a single person who has seized power is known as a **dictatorship**. If a small group seizes power, the government is called an **oligarchy**. Although one individual may be named president, often a group of high-ranking military officers, working behind the scenes, makes the decisions. If their designated president becomes uncooperative, they remove him from office and designate another.

Monarchies, dictatorships, and oligarchies vary in the amount of control they exert over their people. **Totalitarianism** is almost *total* control of a people by a government. As illustrated in our opening vignette, totalitarian regimes tolerate no opposing opinion. In Nazi Germany, for example, Hitler kept the populace in tight control through the Gestapo, a ruthless secret police force that looked for any sign of dissent. Control was so thorough that spies even watched moviegoers' reactions to newsreels, reporting those who did not respond "appropriately" (Hippler, 1987). A more recent example is the armed squads in Taliban-ruled Afghanistan that patrolled the streets looking for anyone who transgressed the religious rules of the regime. Women were often the prime targets of these vigilante-style operations. Another incidence of totalitarianism is the deterioration of women's rights in Ayatollah Khomeini's Iran, as described in Azar Nafisi's *Reading Lolita in Tehran* (2004).

The ideas of citizenship and representative democracy are appealing to people around the world. Those who have no say in their government's decisions or who face prison for expressing dissent find hope for a brighter future in these ideas. With today's electronic communications, people no longer remain ignorant of whether they are more or less privileged politically than others. This knowledge produces pressure for greater citizen participation in government. With

continued development in communications, this pressure will continue to mount.

THE CANADIAN POLITICAL SYSTEM

The Canadian system of government can be described as a parliamentary democracy. Parliament is, constitutionally, the supreme national lawmaking authority for all matters that fall within its jurisdiction. Canada has a federal system of government. This means that some areas of legal jurisdiction or real powers of enforcement are reserved for the federal parliament and other residual powers are distributed among provincial and municipal governments. Examples of Parliament's powers include interprovincial and international trade, communications, banking and finance, and some criminal matters. However, in Canada, the provinces have evolved a number of separate and significant powers of their own, such as control over natural resources, most labour legislation (approximately 90 percent of trade union members come under provincial jurisdiction), and most criminal matters.

Canada is a democracy, as the people elect their politicians in periodic elections. Since World War II, between 70 and 80 percent of Canadians have participated in the electoral process (see Table 12.2). This contrasts with only 50 to

TABLE 12.2 Voter Turnout at Federal Elections

Date of Election	Population	Number of Electors	Total Ballots Cast	Voter Turnout (%)
March 31, 1958	16 073 970	9 131 200	7 357 139	79.4
June 18, 1962	18 238 247	9 700 325	7 772 656	79.0
April 8, 1963	18 238 247	9 910 757	7 958 636	79.2
November 8, 1965	18 238 247	10 274 904	7 796 728	74.8
June 25, 1968	20 014 880	10 860 888	8 217 916	75.7
October 30, 1972	21 568 311	13 000 778	9 974 661	76.7
July 8, 1974	21 568 311	13 620 353	9 671 002	71.0
May 22, 1979	22 992 604	15 233 653	11 541 000	75.7
February 18, 1980	22 992 604	15 890 416	11 015 514	69.3
September 4, 1984	24 343 181	16 774 941	12 638 424	75.3
November 21, 1988	25 309 331	17 639 001	13 281 191	75.3
October 25, 1993	27 296 859	19 906 796	13 863 135	70.9
June 2, 1997	28 846 761	19 662 522	13 171 628	67.0
November 27, 2000	30 769 669	21 243 473	12 997 185	64.1
June 28, 2004	30 007 094	22 466 621	13 564 702	60.5
January 26, 2006	31 612 897	23 054 615	14 908 703	64.7
October 14, 2008	32 976 026	23 401 064	13 832 972	59.1

Source: Adapted from *A History of the Vote in Canada*, Elections Canada, 1997, and Elections Canada website: www.elections.ca/scripts/OVR2004/default.html and http://enr.elections.ca/National_e.aspx. Reproduced with permission of the Minister of Public Works and Government Services, 2002, and courtesy of Elections Canada.

55 percent of Americans who voted for their president and less than a majority of eligible voters who casted ballots for their representatives to Congress. Since the 1990s, however, a downward trend in voter turnout in Canada may be evidence of a growing cynicism toward our political system among the electorate in Canada. Interestingly, we are approaching the U.S. average voter turnout for presidential elections. Can you think of ways to get more Canadians excited about their political system? Some Canadians believe proportional representation is a solution. This option will be discussed later in the chapter.

Canada's form of federal government is unlike a **unitary state**, in which all power resides with the central government. Neither does Canada's parliamentary democracy resemble a **confederal union**, in which provinces have most of the powers and the central government has little authority to enforce national decisions on the "sovereign" provinces.

Canada has evolved a system of government that is somewhere in between the two extremes. Nevertheless, to most Canadians, the year 1867 is commonly known as that of "Confederation." As Garth Stevenson notes, the use of that term to denote our system of government is inaccurate. The Fathers of Confederation desired a unity state. Many citizens in Quebec, New Brunswick, Nova Scotia, and Prince Edward Island, however, were interested in preserving their distinctive cultural and social qualities and meeting the particular economic needs of their provinces. This could only be accomplished if they could retain control over matters that would allow them to preserve their local character and institutions. Therefore, a unitary national state of any kind was out of the question, and a confederal union was appealing to Quebec and the Maritime provinces. Stevenson goes so far as to say that the use of the word "Confederation" to denote our federal system of government was purposely encouraged to "confuse those [such as the people of the Maritimes and Quebec] who might find such a project [a unitary state] alarming" (1987, p. 9).

What Is the Parliamentary System in Canada?

Constitutionally, there are three major levels of national government in Canada: the Queen, the Senate, and Parliament. However, the Queen has no powers to make laws in Canada, and the Senate, an appointed body, is a minor player in the lawmaking process. Therefore, only Parliament has the ultimate power to make law in Canada.

While Parliament makes the laws, there are limits to what it can do. It cannot make laws in areas reserved exclusively for the provinces. And, since 1982, Parliament's formal powers have been limited by the Charter of Rights and Freedoms.

Most Canadians, however, realize that the lion's share of the federal government's policymaking authority comes from the prime minister's office and the Cabinet. The power to spend money and introduce tax legislation is limited to the Cabinet, while the prime minister has the exclusive power to open, postpone, and dissolve Parliament. Ultimately, the prime minister wields the real power in Canada's federal government. He or she appoints the Cabinet, whose members become the heads of various federal government departments such as Finance, Human Resources, Transportation, and so on.

The role of the opposition parties is basically adversarial. During Question Period, they debate the government's policies and other related matters. However, there are rules to follow, and all Members of Parliament must conduct themselves in an appropriate manner. The Speaker of the House presides over, but is not permitted to participate in, the debates in the House of Commons. For the first time in our nation's political history, Canadians elected back-to-back minority governments at the federal level in 2006 (and again in 2008). We elected a Liberal minority government in 2004 under Paul Martin, then two short years later, Canadians voted for a Conservative minority government under Stephen Harper. Table 12.3 provides details of the final election results.

TABLE 12.3   Back-to-Back Minority Governments in Canada, 2004, 2006, 2008

Political Party	2004 Federal General Election		2006 Federal General Election		2008 Federal General Election	
	Number of Seats	Percentage Vote	Number of Seats	Percentage Vote	Number of Seats	Percentage Vote
Liberal	135	36.7%	103	30.2%	76	26.2%
Conservative	99	29.6%	124	36.2%	143	37.6%
Bloc Québécois	54	12.4%	51	10.5%	50	10%
New Democratic Party	19	15.7%	29	17.5%	37	18.2%
Independent	1	1.4%	1	0.5%	2	0.7%
Other (including the Green Party)	0	4.3%	0	5%	0	7.9%
Voter Turnout		60.5%		64.7%		59.1%

Source: www.cbc.ca/canadavotes/2004,2006 and http://www.cbc.ca/news/canadavotes/

The previous minority government in Canada was elected in May 1979, when Joe Clark, leader of the Progressive Conservative Party, became Canada's youngest prime minister.

Table 12.4 provides a chronology of the prime ministers in Canada since Confederation, their political party affiliations, the dates they held office, and the lengths of their tenures as prime minister. (The only woman prime minister in Canada's history has been Kim Campbell, whose short-lived status as the head of government came after Brian Mulroney left the post late in his second term of office.)

The Evolution of the Political Party System in Canada: From the Two-Party to the Multiple-Party System

John A. Macdonald was Canada's first prime minister (1867–1873). He headed a coalition Conservative government comprised of Ontario Tories and Quebec Liberals, or *Bleus*, as they were called. His first term in office as head of the coalition ended in scandal (the "Pacific Scandal") when it was revealed that he and a number of his colleagues had accepted large sums of money as kickbacks from the

TABLE 12.4 Prime Ministers of Canada from Confederation to the Present

Prime Minister	Political Party	Dates in Office	Tenure
John A. Macdonald	Liberal-Conservative	1867–1873	
John A. Macdonald	Conservative	1878–1891	19 years
Alexander Mackenzie	Liberal	1873–1878	5 years
John Abbott	Conservative	1891–1892	1 year
John Thompson	Conservative	1892–1894	2 years
Mackenzie Bowell	Conservative	1894–1896	1 year
Charles Tupper	Conservative	1896	2 months
Wilfrid Laurier	Liberal	1896–1911	15 years
Robert Borden	Conservative	1911–1920	9 years
Arthur Meighen	Conservative	1920–1921	2 years
William Lyon Mackenzie King	Liberal	1921–1930	
William Lyon Mackenzie King	Liberal	1935–1948	22 years
R. B. Bennett	Conservative	1930–1935	5 years
Louis St. Laurent	Liberal	1948–1957	9 years
John Diefenbaker	P.C.	1957–1963	6 years
Lester Pearson	Liberal	1963–1968	5 years
Pierre Elliott Trudeau	Liberal	1968–1979	
Joe Clark	P.C.	1979–1980	9 months
Pierre Elliott Trudeau	Liberal	1980–1984	15 years
John Turner	Liberal	1984	2 months
Brian Mulroney	P.C.	1984–1993	9 years
Kim Campbell*	P.C.	1993	2 months
Jean Chrétien	Liberal	1993–2003	10 years
Paul Martin	Liberal	2003–2006	18 months
Stephen Harper	Conservative	2006–present	

*Canada's first woman prime minister.

promoters of the Canadian Pacific Railway. By 1878, there were two political parties in Canada—the Conservatives and the Liberals.

Canada, in 1867, counted only five provinces. Manitoba was added in 1870, and British Columbia in 1871. Alberta and Saskatchewan did not enter Confederation until 1905. As Canada was still in the process of nation-state building, the two-party system of the Liberals and the Conservatives dominated Canadian politics until well into the twentieth century.

The end of World War I (1914–1918) saw the emergence of a coalition of farmers' organizations based in Alberta and extending to Ontario that became known as the Progressive Movement. It was populist in ideology (i.e., grassroots democracy with regional agricultural-based policies) and had a short life nationally. However, the party continued to dominate western provincial governments until World War II. The end of the Progressive era in Canadian politics came when Manitoba premier John Bracken moved to the federal Conservative party in 1942 on the condition that its name be changed to the Progressive Conservative Party.

The demise of the Progressive movement in the West led to the dramatic election in the 1935 Alberta legislature of another grassroots, populist protest party known as Social Credit. Unlike the Progressive Movement, the Social Credit Party was able to achieve a beachhead in Quebec with its sister party, known as the Ralliement des Créditistes, under the leadership of Réal Caouette, a Rouyn-Noranda, Quebec, radio commentator. Except for the one-time electoral success of the Ralliement des Créditistes in the 1962 federal election (26 seats from rural Quebec), Social Credit remained a provincial party contender in Manitoba, Alberta, and British Columbia until the early 1970s, when it disappeared for good from Canada's political landscape.

The CCF (Cooperative Commonwealth Federation), later the NDP (New Democratic Party), was founded by representatives from the cooperative movement, labour leaders, and academics in Regina, Saskatchewan, in 1933. The founding principles of the party are contained in the Regina Manifesto. The party remains Canada's national social democratic party. Its provincial strongholds are Saskatchewan, Manitoba, and British Columbia. While never achieving a majority in the House of Commons, the NDP formed a coalition government with the Liberals for two years from 1972–1974.

The Conservative Party of Canada is the latest addition to the federal political landscape. On December 8, 2003, the Canadian Alliance Party (formerly the Reform Party) merged with the Progressive Conservative Party to become the Conservative Party. Before the merger, the Progressive Conservatives held 15 seats in the House of Commons and the Canadian Alliance held 63 seats. Stephen Harper and Peter MacKay acted as principal spokespersons for the Canadian Alliance and Progressive Conservative caucuses respectively. Once the two parties merged, Harper ran for the leadership of the newly formed party in January 2004, along

with Belinda Stronach and Tony Clement. Harper won the leadership contest in March 2004, and MacKay become deputy leader.

Like its predecessor, the Canadian Alliance Party, the Conservative Party does not have provincial parties as the Liberals and the NDP do. Instead, the Conservative Party maintains relationships with provincial Progressive Conservative parties at the provincial level.

The Conservative Party occupies the "right" of the political spectrum in Canada. The party endorses the major tenets of social conservatism, such as upholding and valuing traditional, intolerant views about the nation (e.g., anti-multiculturalism, anti–Aboriginal rights, anti-immigration, and pro-military), family, and religion, as well as promoting a strong work ethic and stricter law enforcement. These values came to the party via the western Canada–based Canadian Alliance Party. Unlike their right-wing Republican counterparts in the United States, the party tends to endorse greater decentralization of power. That is, there is support for more provincial rights and, by extension, more power to Quebec.

The lack of a coherent political right in Canada is in fact probably due to at least two factors not shared with the United States. First, although there are pockets of right-wing Christian fundamentalism in Canada, especially in western Canada and parts of Ontario, this votership is dramatically less than south of the border. Indeed, as will be discussed in Chapter 14, one of the largest growing segments of the population is those who profess to have no religion. Second, unlike the United States, Canada is not a superpower with a large military to support. Therefore, while there will be continued support for the Conservative Party of Canada, its association with social conservatism will keep many Canadians (and certainly most Quebecois) from voting for the party.

First elected in 1990, the Bloc Québécois is the newest social democratic political party on the national scene in Canada. Its roots are exclusively in the province of Quebec. Unlike the NDP, the Bloc Québécois was formed from a coalition of dissident Quebec MPs who had left the Liberal and Progressive Conservative parties. It upholds a social democratic platform of policies and is committed to increased sovereignty for Quebec. The party was initially led by Lucien Bouchard, the one-time minister of the environment in Brian Mulroney's Cabinet. Bouchard left the Bloc (now led by Gilles Duceppe) to become the leader of the Parti Québécois and the premier of Quebec from 1996 until his resignation on January 10, 2001, over the Yves Michaud affair. Michaud's views about the anti-sovereignist sentiments of the Jewish minority in Quebec sparked a controversy within the PQ. Michaud's beliefs and his right to express them were covered extensively in the Quebec media. As the discussions heated, both Michaud and Bouchard resigned from provincial politics and the controversy dissipated. Today, Quebec is governed by the Quebec Liberal Party led by Jean Charest.

The Structure of the Canadian Bureaucracy

Today, employees of the federal government who work for one of the ministries are called *public servants*. Under the 1967 *Public Service Employment Act*, public servants were allowed the right to bargain collectively with their employer. However, *public sector employees* in Canada are a much larger group, which includes both federal and provincial public servants and employees of Crown corporations, the military, and other nondepartmental agencies of the government. Taken together, all categories of public sector employees at all levels of government make up over 40 percent of the total labour force.

The *federal bureaucracy* is comprised of employees in the armed forces, the RCMP, various government agencies, and the public service. At the federal level, the main categories of the bureaucracy are government departments, departmental corporations, Crown corporations, the Canadian Armed Forces (115 000 employees), and the RCMP (22 500 employees).

Quebec: The Social Basis for the Quiet Revolution and the Rise of the Sovereignty Movement

Politically, the Quiet Revolution in Quebec began in 1959 with the death of Maurice Duplessis and his replacement by Paul Sauvé, his right-hand man in the Union Nationale Party. Premier Sauvé died after only a hundred days in office but had begun the process of modernization in Quebec. The election of the provincial Liberal Party under the leadership of Jean Lesage in 1960 carried forward the initiatives begun by Sauvé: the creation of professionally qualified jobs in the modernizing sectors of the health, education, and welfare bureaucracies of the provincial government and the eventual nationalization of the hydroelectric power companies under Hydro-Québec.

The social basis for the rapid expansion of the public sector in Quebec during the 1960s began with the industrialization of rural Quebec in the first half of the twentieth century. During this time, rural Quebec came under the pressure of a "demographic contradiction"; that is, there were too many people and not enough arable lands to settle. Where was the surplus population to go? Some went to northern Quebec and northern Ontario to work in the mines; others went in search of work to Montreal and towns springing up in the Eastern Townships, such as Drummondville; still others went to the New England states of Vermont, New York, and New Hampshire. The only employment open to the children of rural farmers was labouring jobs in the factories owned by foreign or English Canadian capital.

Everett Hughes, in his classic study of the industrialization of rural Quebec entitled *French Canada in Transition* (1943), paints a graphic picture of what he calls an "ethnic division of labour," in which the bosses in the factories were all English-speaking and Protestant while the workers were all French-speaking and Catholic. Contrary to what one might expect, Hughes argued that it was not the rural working-class Quebecois that had difficulty adapting to their new situation, it was members of the traditional Quebec middle class of lawyers and doctors. According to Hughes, so long as Quebec remained rural and agricultural, members of the small middle class could survive by passing on to their sons (and some daughters) their education and class privileges. Industrialization changed this system, however, because the workers' sons and daughters would soon acquire better educations and would be able to compete for the small number of middle-class jobs once held by their class "betters." The only remedy for the situation was to expand the number of middle-class jobs available. Modernizing and

A French-only sign in Quebec. The language debate has been escalating in that province since the Report of the Royal Commission on Bilingualism and Biculturalism in 1968.

professionalizing the Quebec government bureaucracy was a viable solution. Moreover, and equally important, jobs in the public sector would ensure the continuation of the French language and culture (but not religion) in the decades subsequent to the Quiet Revolution. This was not an easy task, however, and it had to wait until the death of Maurice Duplessis and the election of Jean Lesage and the provincial Liberal Party in order to be successful.

The Quiet Revolution gave hope to many Quebecois seeking to modernize their province through the expansion of the health, education, and welfare bureaucracies while taking on other more daring projects such as nationalizing the province's hydroelectric power companies. It unleashed a tidal wave of energy in the province that included the rise of the terrorist group known as the FLQ (Front de Libération du Québec) and the creation of the Parti Québécois.

In 1970, the bubble burst with the October Crisis: the FLQ kidnappings of James Cross, the British trade commissioner, on October 5, and Pierre Laporte, the Quebec minister of labour in the ruling provincial Liberal Party, on October 10. Prime Minister Trudeau invoked the *War Measures Act* on October 16, 1970, marking the first time these extraordinary powers were used in peacetime. On October 17, Pierre Laporte was found dead in the trunk of a parked car at the airport in St. Hubert, Quebec.

This was an unsettling period for many Canadians both inside and outside Quebec. The fact that the kidnappers had been found by conventional police methods strongly indicated to many that the invocation of the *War Measures Act* was at best an overreaction on the part of Pierre Trudeau and the federal Liberals, and at worst a disguised attempt to undermine the credibility of the Parti Québécois and the sovereignty movement in the province. In any event, the tide shifted back toward the sovereignty movement when, in 1976, the Parti Québécois was elected for the first time. One of the first pieces of legislation passed by the newly formed PQ government was Bill 101—"the language law."

Language in the workplace had become a major political issue in Quebec before 1976. Starting with the Report of the Royal Commission on Bilingualism and Biculturalism in 1968, the stage was set for a lingering feud over language in the province that continues to this day. The passage of Bill 22, the *Official Languages Act*, by the Liberal Party of Quebec in 1972 and Bill 101 by the dissatisfied Parti Québécois in response should have been wake-up calls to the rest of Canada—reminders that language and culture are significant social issues that go beyond petty party politics.

What is the social basis for the politics of language in Quebec? For those of us in the rest of Canada to begin to understand, we need to set aside the complex political wrangling over the repatriation of the Constitution in 1982 and the "failures" of the Meech Lake Accord (1987) and the Charlottetown Accord (1992). Instead, we must see the preservation of language and culture in Quebec as tied to

"jobs." A language does not flourish by being taught at school. Languages are nurtured or languish in the workplace. Speaking a language at work is the primary vehicle for sustaining its survival and culture. We constantly exercise our language at work, a place where cultural experiences are shared and nurtured. Therefore, making French the language of work for everyone in Quebec makes sense to the majority of French speakers in the province. The English-speaking minority recognizes the significance of work for language preservation and the struggles against the majority's language bills.

This is the essence of the political strife in Quebec. The struggles over language in that province are just as much struggles over who gets which jobs. In other words, the social basis of language and culture is a necessary starting point for all of us if we hope to achieve an understanding of the growing complexity of politics of Quebec, either in or out of Canada. To bury our heads in the sand or to fall back on old and tired clichés will not resolve our difficulties as a maturing nation. As Canadians, we must begin an intelligent and reasonable discussion of the issues if we are to participate in their resolution.

Focus Question
Why are language and culture so important for many Quebecois?

Democratic Systems in Europe

We tend to take our political system for granted and assume that any other democracy looks like ours. This is not the case. To achieve a comparative understanding, let's look at the European system.

Most European countries base their elections on a system of **proportional representation**; that is, the seats in the national legislature are divided according to the proportion of votes received by each political party. If one party wins 51 percent of the vote, for example, that party is awarded 51 percent of the seats; a party with 49 percent of the votes receives 49 percent of the seats, and so on.

Proportional representation encourages minority parties. The proportional representation followed in most European countries means that if a party gets 10 percent of the voters to support its candidate, it will get 10 percent of the seats. This system encourages the formation of **noncentrist parties**, those that propose less popular ideas.

Three main results follow from being able to win even a few seats in the national legislature. First, if a minority party has officeholders, it gains access to the media throughout the year, receiving publicity that helps keep its issues alive. Second, because many parties compete in elections, no single party is likely to gain a majority of the seats in the national legislature. To muster the required votes to make national decisions, the party with the most seats must align itself with one or more of the smaller parties and form a

coalition government. A party with only 10 or 15 percent of the seats, then, may be able to trade its vote on some issues for the larger party's support on others. Third, because coalitions break down, the governments tend to be less stable. Italy, for example, has had more than 50 different governments since World War II, in contrast to the 13 prime ministers of Canada (see Table 12.3).

In April 2001, Fair Vote Canada (FVC) was launched in Ottawa. Its goal is to bring some form of proportional representation to Canada's political system by a national referendum. Voters during the recent Ontario election rejected the mixed member proportional (MMP) system advocated by the FVC. The group remains active and is committed to electoral reform in Canada (see www.fairvotecanada.org).

WHO RULES CANADA?
The Functionalist Perspective: Pluralism

Functionalists view the state as having arisen out of the basic needs of a social group.

Functionalists say that **pluralism**, a diffusion of power among many interest groups, prevents any one group from gaining control of a government and using it to oppress the people. In other words, the Canadian government functions like a healthy human body (Polsby, 1959; Huber & Form, 1973; Dahl, 1961, 1982).

From the functionalist perspective, ethnic groups, women, men, farmers, the unemployed, and the retired are all parts of our pluralist society. As special-interest groups such as women or the disabled negotiate with one another

and reach compromises, conflict is minimized, and the resulting policies gain wide support.

The Conflict Perspective: Power Elite/Ruling Class

Conflict theorists propose a different answer. The important question is who holds the power that determines the overarching policies for Canada. For example, who determines how many Canadians will be out of work by raising or lowering interest rates? Who sets policies that transfer jobs from Canada to the United States or countries with low-cost labour? And the ultimate question of power: Who is behind decisions to go or not to go to war?

C. Wright Mills (1956) took the position that the decisions that have the greatest impact on the lives of Americans—and of Canadians and people across the globe—are made by a coalition of individuals whose interests coincide and who have access to the centre of political power in the United States. Mills called them the **power elite**. As depicted in Figure 12.1, the power elite consists of the top leaders of the largest corporations, the most powerful generals and admirals of the armed forces, and certain elite politicians. They wield the most power and make the decisions that direct the country—and shake the world (Hellinger & Judd, 1991; Ferguson, 1995).

Conflict theorists contend that we should not think that the behaviour of the ruling class stems from some grand conspiracy to control the country. Rather, it is grounded in mutual interests in solving problems faced by large businesses (Useem, 1984). The ruling class consists of people

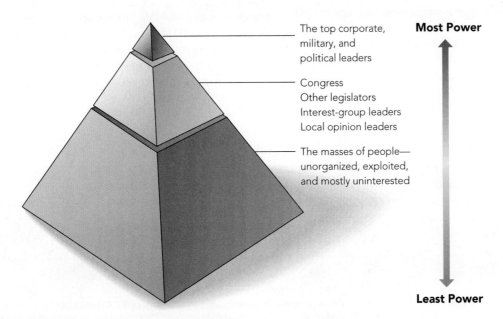

The top corporate, military, and political leaders

Congress
Other legislators
Interest-group leaders
Local opinion leaders

The masses of people—unorganized, exploited, and mostly uninterested

Most Power

Least Power

FIGURE 12.1 Power in the United States: The Model Proposed by C. Wright Mills

Source: Based on Mills (1956).

whose backgrounds and orientations to life are so similar—they attend prestigious private schools, belong to exclusive private clubs, and are millionaires many times over—that they automatically share the same values and goals.

As mentioned in other chapters, in *The Vertical Mosaic* (1965), John Porter identified several elites in Canadian society, not just the industrial-military complex identified by C. Wright Mills for the United States. In addition to the economic elite, he identified elites in the media, religion, organized labour, and the political sector of Canadian society.

The common characteristics of an elite presented by Porter were similar to those put forth by C. Wright Mills. The Canadian economic elite, for example, attended similar if not the same private schools as members of the U.S. elite and completed their education at the "right" universities. British Protestants (primarily Anglican) still dominate the Canadian group, with very few French-Canadians, Jews, or Catholics. The members of the economic elite attend the same social (private) clubs and recruit one another to serve on various boards of directors.

Wallace Clement's (1975, 1977, 1983) studies classified three components of Canada's corporate elite: a Canadian component based mainly in banking, insurance, and other related financial institutions; a foreign (mainly U.S.) component that dominates the manufacturing and natural resource sectors of the economy; and a component Clement calls a *comprador* elite—native-born directors and senior managers of foreign-controlled corporations operating in Canada.

Dennis Olsen (1980), a graduate student of John Porter, studied the Canadian state elite. While Olsen discovered that members of the federal bureaucratic elite (judges, politicians, and senior federal and provincial bureaucrats such as deputy ministers) were more open to recruitment and were a much larger group than the economic elite, most came from middle-class backgrounds and were channelled to executive positions through "acceptable" bureaucratic means. They were able to stay in regular contact through what Olsen calls "executive federalism."

Unfortunately, very little recent research has been carried out to investigate the changing social characteristics of Canada's political elites.

Feminist Perspectives: Gender Reform, Resistance, and Rebellion

Current feminist theorizing about the nature of gender inequality is linked to whether theorists seek to reform the present system or struggle to achieve some fundamental change. That is, the main reasons given for women having a lesser social status and fewer advantages than men of similar education, class background, race/ethnicity, and religion lead to proposed solutions or remedies, including political ones. Proponents of liberal feminism, for example, hold the current system of democratic government as legitimate. They have been instrumental in making visible the pervasiveness of overt discrimination. The solutions they have proposed, such as pay and employment equity in Canada and Affirmative Action in the United States, have sparked debate and discussion.

EMPLOYMENT EQUITY Since the 1970s, the Canadian government has attempted to change the manner by which employees are recruited into the federal bureaucracy. The major policy initiative has been employment equity, or recruitment targeting the designated groups of women, Aboriginal people, visible minorities, and the physically disabled. Table 12.5 provides a portrait of the "success" of this policy at the "executive category" level.

Clearly, women have made important strides since the early 1990s, though they remain underrepresented at the "executive level." Aboriginal numbers remain low, at just under 3 percent, and visible minorities have made only minor advances, holding just 4.2 percent of executive-level positions in 2003.

In addition, the number of jobs at this level over the six-year period from 1993 until 1999 decreased from a high of 4155 in 1993 to a low of 3421 in 1999, a drop of nearly

TABLE 12.5 Employment Equity at the "Executive Category" Level in the Federal Civil Service

Executive Employment Category	1993		1999		2001		2003		2006	
	Number	%	Number	%	Number	%	Number	%	Number	%
Women	731	17.6	919	26.9	1057	30.0	1424	33.8	1749	38.8
Aboriginal people	44	1.1	64	1.9	70	2.0	114	2.7	153	3.4
People with disabilities	81	1.9	101	3.0	125	3.5	193	4.6	248	5.5
Visible minority	N/A		103	3.0	118	3.4	177	4.2	247	5.5
Total executive category	4155		3421		3522		4213		4505	

Source: Adapted from Treasury Board of Canada, *Employment Equity in the Federal Public Service—Annual Report*, Ottawa, Communications and Coordination Directorate, 1994–present.

20 percent. The number rose somewhat between 1999 and 2001, although it was still 15 percent lower than in 1993. By 2003, however, the numbers advanced to 4213—a marginal increase of 1 percent over the 1993 figure. It has taken 10 years to reach levels comparable to those in 1993.

Gender resistance feminisms, such as radical and lesbian feminisms, claim that the gender order cannot be made gender-neutral by seeking legislative changes. Instead, these feminists propose a woman-centred society and seek to create a women-oriented culture, ethics, and even religion. Gender rebellion feminisms, such as multiracial, postmodern, and queer theories, attack the gender order directly by undermining the boundaries that separate men from women, male from female, and homosexual from heterosexual. Using the language of postmodernism, these feminists deconstruct the categories of sex, sexuality, and gender and thereby undermine the legitimacy of favouring one group over another.

WAR AND TERRORISM: A MEANS TO IMPLEMENT POLITICAL OBJECTIVES

As previously noted, an essential characteristic of the state is that it claims a monopoly on violence. **War**—armed conflict between nations or politically distinct groups—is often part of national policy.

Is War Universal?

War is one option that groups may choose for dealing with disagreements, but not all societies choose this option. The Mission Indians of North America, the Arunta of Australia, the Andaman Islanders of the South Pacific, and the Inuit of the Arctic, for example, follow procedures to handle aggression and quarrels, but do not have organized battles that pit one tribe or group against another. These groups do not even have a word for war (Lesser, 1968).

Why Nations Go to War

Sociologist Nicholas Timasheff (1965) found that war is likely if a country's leaders see the antagonistic situation as an opportunity to achieve one of the following objectives:

1. To exact revenge or settle "old scores" from previous conflicts.

2. To dictate their will to a weaker nation.

3. To enhance the nation's prestige or save its "honour."

4. To unite rival groups within their country.

5. To protect or exalt their own position.

6. To satisfy the national aspirations of ethnic groups, bringing under their rule "our people" who are living in another country.

7. To forcibly convert others to religious and ideological beliefs.

Focus Question

What are some examples of recent wars that would fit one or more of Timasheff's objectives?

Sowing the Seeds of Future Wars

With incredible hypocrisy, the most industrialized nations of the world lament regional conflicts that can escalate into larger wars while zealously pursuing profits by selling advanced war technology to the least industrialized nations. When one least industrialized nation buys high-tech weapons, its neighbours get nervous, sparking an arms race among them (Cole & Lubman, 1994; Ricks, 1994).

Table 12.6 illustrates that the United States is the chief merchant of death, even though the Cold War is over and it can no longer claim the "communist threat" as a reason for arming the free world. The seeds of future wars are also sown by nuclear proliferation, and several least industrialized

TABLE 12.6 The Business of Death

The Top Arms Sellers, 2001–2004	The Top Arms Buyers, 2001–2004
1. $28 billion, United States	1. $19 billion, Saudi Arabia
2. $16 billion, Russia	2. $9 billion, China
3. $12 billion, Great Britain	3. $7 billion, United Arab Emirates
4. $9 billion, France	4. $6 billion, Egypt
5. $3 billion, China	5. $6 billion, India
6. $2 billion, Israel	6. $4 billion, Israel
7. $1 billion, Germany	7. $4 billion, Taiwan
8. $1 billion, Ukraine	8. $3 billion, South Korea

Source: By the author. Based on Gimmett 2005: Tables 2F, 2I

nations, such as India, Pakistan, and China, now have nuclear weapons. Always a threat to the world's safety, in the hands of a dictator these weapons can mean blackmail or an attack to settle personal or nationalistic grudges.

Terrorism

With hatred fanned across generations, terrorism directed against a civilian population is a continuing threat. Groups nurture bitterness by endlessly chronicling the atrocities committed by their arch-enemy. One of the few options open to a weaker group looking to retaliate against a powerful country for its suppression is "suicide terrorism"—which usually involves bombs capable of blowing up only a few people at a time. However, as we witnessed on September 11, 2001, suicide terrorism can also strike on a grander scale, killing thousands.

War and Dehumanization

> Proud of his techniques, the U.S. trainer was demonstrating to the South American soldiers how to torture a prisoner. As the victim screamed in anguish, the trainer was interrupted by a phone call from his wife. His students could hear him say, "A dinner and a movie sound nice. I'll see you right after work." Hanging up the phone, he then continued the lesson. (Stockwell, 1989)

Exposure to brutality and killing often causes **dehumanization**, the process of reducing people to objects that do not deserve to be treated as humans.

As we review findings on dehumanization and see how it breeds callousness and cruelty, perhaps we can better understand how O'Brien from the opening vignette could have unleashed rats onto someone's face. Consider the four characterizations of dehumanization (Bernard, Ottenberg, & Redl, 1971):

1. *Increased emotional distance from others.* People are seen as subhuman—as "the enemy."

2. *An emphasis on following procedures.* People are likely to say, "We all have to die some day. What difference does it make if these people die now?"

3. *Inability to resist pressures.* Fears of losing one's job, losing the respect of one's peers, or having one's integrity and loyalty questioned take precedence over individual moral decisions.

4. *A diminished sense of personal responsibility.* People do not see themselves as responsible for what they do because they are simply following orders.

A Vietnam vet who read this section remarked, "You missed the major one we used. We killed kids. Our dehumanizing technique was a saying, 'The little ones are the soldiers of tomorrow.'"

Dehumanization does not always insulate the self from guilt, however, and its failure to do so can bring severe personal consequences. During a war, soldiers are surrounded by army buddies who agree that the enemy is less than human and deserves inhuman treatment. After a solider returns home, the concept of dehumanizing is more likely to break down. Many soldiers find themselves seriously disturbed by what they did during a war.

POST-TRAUMATIC STRESS DISORDER (PTSD) While trauma-stress reactions date back to descriptions in Classical Greek literature, it was not until 1980 that the American Psychiatric Association Diagnostic and Statistical Manual recognized post-traumatic stress disorder. The surge of scientific and clinical interest in the condition over the past two decades has been largely the result of an awareness of problems associated with returning Vietnam combat veterans in the United States and advocacy by the feminist movement on behalf of rape victims. PTSD is a severe psychological disorder. To date, the rate of post-traumatic stress among Canada's soldiers is as high as 20 percent, according to the military ombudsman's office in Canada (CBC News *In Depth*, July 2006, www.cbc.ca/news/background/health/posttraumaticstress.html).

A NEW WORLD ORDER?

The globalization of capitalism, accompanied by the world-wide flow of information, capital, and goods discussed in Chapter 11, is little affected by national boundaries. The United States, Canada, and Mexico formed the North American Free Trade Association, to which all of South America will eventually belong. European countries have formed an economic and political unit known as the European Union, which supersedes their national boundaries. The Euro is now the single cross-national currency, with only one exception—the United Kingdom. Similarly, the United Nations, transcending national borders and moderating disputes between countries, can authorize the use of international force against individual nations—as it did against North Korea in 1950, Iraq in 1990, and on a smaller scale Somalia in 1993 and Bosnia in 1994 and 1997.

Will this process continue until a single state or empire envelops the earth? This is a possibility. Set against it is the demand for self-determination and self-government from nations within the bosom of states in the developed part of the world. Examples include Scottish and Quebec independence, the Palestinians, Aboriginals, and so on. As borders shift, as occurred with the breakup of the Soviet Union, previously unincorporated nations such as Lithuania and Azerbaijan demand their independence and the right to full statehood. The Perspectives box explores the tension between capitalist globalization and the rise of nationalism.

If global political and economic unity does come about, it is fascinating to speculate on what type of government will result. If Hitler had had his way, his conquests would have resulted in world domination—by a world dictator and a world totalitarian regime based on racial identification. If a progressive world order emerges from current trends—that's a big "if"—the potential for human welfare is tremendous.

PERSPECTIVES

Cultural Diversity around the World: The Rise of Nationalism versus the Globalization of Capitalism—Implications for a New World Order

Shown here are Russian troops in what remains of downtown Grozny, the capital of Chechnya. Russia bombed the city in order to stop the former colony from gaining independence.

The world has about 5000 nations. What makes each a *nation* is that its people share a language, culture, territory, and political organization. A *state*, in contrast, claims a monopoly on violence over a territory. A state may contain many nations. The Kayapo Indians are one nation within the state of Brazil. The Chippewa and Sioux are two nations within the state of the United States and, to some, Quebec is a nation within Canada. To nation peoples, group identity transcends political affiliation. The world's nations have existed for hundreds, even thousands, of years. In contrast, most of the world's 194 states have been around only since World War II.

Most modern states are empires, and they are increasingly seen as such by the nations that have been incorporated into them—usually by conquest. Some states have far better records than others, but overall, no ideology, left or right, religious or sectarian, has protected nations or promoted pluralism much better or worse than any other. In fact, the twentieth century has probably seen more genocide and ethnocide (the destruction of an ethnic group) than any other.

Palestinians who live within Israel's borders will not soon identify themselves as Israelis. Twenty-two million Kurds don't consider themselves first and foremost Turks, Iranians, Iraqis, or Syrians. There are about 130 nations in the former Soviet Union, 180 in Brazil, 90 in Ethiopia, 450 in Nigeria, and 350 in India. That so many nations are squeezed into so few states is the crux of the problem.

In most states, power lies in the hands of a few elites, who operate by a simple credo: winner take all. They control foreign investment and aid, and use both to reinforce their power. They set local commodity prices, control exports, levy taxes, and buy weapons. They confiscate the resources of nations, whether Indian land in North and South America or oil from the Kurds in Iraq. When nations resist, the result is open conflict.

About half of the debt of the least industrialized states and nearly all debt in Africa comes from the purchase of weapons by states to fight their own citizens. Most of the world's 12 million refugees are the offspring of such conflicts, as are most of the 100 million internally displaced people who have been uprooted from their homelands.

A vicious cycle forms. The appropriation of a nation's resources leads to conflict, conflict leads to weapons purchases, weapons purchases lead to debt, and debt leads to the appropriation of more resources. This self-feeding cycle helps ensure the co-operation of the elites of the least industrialized states as the most industrialized states divide the globe's resources among themselves.

The fly in the ointment in the march to the "new world order" is the existence of fierce **nationalism**—identity with and loyalty to a nation. Nationalism threatens to undermine the developing new order. Based on nationalism, the shooting wars increase—fought over issues, grudges, and animosities rooted in long history, only faintly understood by those who are not a party to the events but vividly alive in the folklore and collective memory of these nations. These wars threaten the fragile coalitions of the powerful states that are dividing up the world's resources.

Currently, we are witness to an oppositional struggle: nationalism versus the formation of global coalitions. We are likely to see many more seemingly contradictory fruits of these two forces: the globe divided into huge regional trading blocs controlled by the most industrialized states, matched by the simultaneous outbreak of small-scale shooting wars as nations struggle for independence.

Sources: Clay (1990); Kanter (1995); Ohmae (1995); Jáuregui (1996); Marcus (1996).

Micropolitics and Macropolitics

WHAT IS THE DIFFERENCE BETWEEN MICROPOLITICS AND MACROPOLITICS?

The essential nature of politics is **power**, and every group is political. The term **micropolitics** refers to the exercise of power in everyday life; **macropolitics** refers to large-scale power, such as governing a nation. p. 260.

Power, Authority, and Violence

HOW ARE AUTHORITY AND COERCION RELATED TO POWER?

Authority is power that people view as legitimately exercised over them, while **coercion** is power they consider unjust. The **state** is a political entity that claims a monopoly on violence over a particular territory. If enough people consider a state's power illegitimate, **revolution** is possible. p. 260.

WHAT KINDS OF AUTHORITY ARE THERE?

Max Weber identified three types of authority. Power in **traditional authority** stems from custom—patterns set down in the past serve as rules for the present. Power in **rational-legal authority** (also called *bureaucratic authority*) is based on law and written procedures. In **charismatic authority**, power is based on loyalty to an individual to whom people are attracted. Charismatic authority, which undermines traditional and rational-legal authority, has built-in problems in its transference to a new leader. pp. 260–262.

Types of Government

HOW ARE THE TYPES OF GOVERNMENT RELATED TO POWER?

In a **monarchy**, power is based on hereditary rule; in a **democracy**, power is given to a ruler by citizens; and in a **dictatorship**, power is seized by an individual or small group. pp. 262–265.

The Canadian Political System

WHAT ARE THE MAIN CHARACTERISTICS OF THE CANADIAN POLITICAL SYSTEM?

Canada is a federal state with a parliamentary democracy. Sometimes, though rarely, Canada's parliamentary system can have a **coalition government** unlike the "winner take all" system of the United States. Most European democracies have **proportional representation**, with legislative seats divided among political parties according to the percentage of votes each receives. If no single party wins a majority of votes, proportional representation creates the need for a coalition government. pp. 265–267.

WHAT POLITICAL PARTIES ARE THERE AT PRESENT IN THE HOUSE OF COMMONS?

The Liberal Party, the Conservative Party, the Bloc Québécois, and the New Democratic Party. pp. 267–268.

WHAT IS AT THE ROOT OF THE POLITICAL STRIFE IN QUEBEC POLITICS?

The preservation of language and culture in Quebec is tied to jobs. Speaking at work is the primary vehicle for sustaining a language and culture. We constantly exercise our language at work, a place where cultural experiences are shared and nurtured. This is the essence of the political strife in Quebec. pp. 269–270.

Who Rules Canada?

IS CANADA CONTROLLED BY A RULING CLASS?

In a view known as **pluralism**, functionalists contend that no single group holds power, that a country's many competing interest groups balance one another. Conflict theorists, who focus on the top level of power, believe that Canada is governed by a **power elite**, a ruling class made up of the top corporate, military, and political leaders. In Canada, John Porter, Wallace Clement, and Dennis Olsen describe Canada's power elites. Feminist perspectives include liberal feminism, which seeks to fight overt discrimination from within the system by winning legislative advances, and radical forms of feminism, which believe change must be much more fundamental. pp. 271–272.

HOW SUCCESSFUL HAS EMPLOYMENT EQUITY BEEN AS A FEDERAL PUBLIC POLICY?

Women have made important strides since the early 1990s, although they still remain underrepresented at the executive level. Visible minorities, on the other hand, have made even smaller advances. pp. 272–273.

War and Terrorism: A Means to Implement Political Objectives

HOW ARE WAR AND TERRORISM RELATED TO POLITICS, AND WHAT ARE THEIR COSTS?

War, common in human history, is a means of attempting to reach political objectives. The least industrialized nations, which can least afford it, spend huge amounts of money on technologically advanced weapons. Another cost is **dehumanization**, whereby people no longer see others as worthy of human treatment. pp. 273–274.

A New World Order?

IS HUMANITY HEADED TOWARD A ONE-WORLD POLITICAL ORDER?

The global expansion of communications, transportation, and trade; the widespread adoption of capitalism and the retreat of socialism; and the trend toward larger political unions may indicate that a world political system is developing. The oppositional trend is fierce **nationalism**. If a new world order develops, the possible consequences for human welfare range from excellent to calamitous. pp. 274–275.

Theoretical Paradigms

	CLASSICAL PARADIGMS		RECENT PARADIGMS
	Structural-Functional Paradigm	Social-Conflict Paradigm	Feminist Paradigm
What is the level of analysis?	Macro level	Macro level	Micro and macro levels
What is the social significance of politics?	Various interest groups compete (inclusive = functional)	A power elite or ruling class dominates politics. The members usually come from upper class backgrounds.	Male domination at the societal level (patriarchy) explains the continued inequality of women in politics.
Have politics changed over time? How?	Yes. Different interest groups, such as women, ethnic groups and gays/lesbians, can effect changes in legislation.	No.	Yes/No. Changes in the legal prohibitions against women voting and pay and employment equity are significant positive changes. Patriarchy remains.

KEY TERMS

WEBLINKS

All URLs listed are current as of the printing of this book.

Mother Jones Online
www.mojones.com
Mother Jones is a magazine of investigation and ideas for independent thinkers. Provocative and unexpected articles inform readers and inspire action toward positive social change.

Canadian Political Parties
www.synapse.net/radio/can-pol.htm
A comprehensive array of links to parties and to other indexes. Highly recommended.

Fair Vote Canada
www.fairvotecanada.org
Fair Vote Canada is committed to electoral reform and has the goal of bringing some form of proportional representation to Canada's political system.

CRITICAL THINKING QUESTIONS

1. According to Max Weber, the state is an organization with a monopoly on the legitimate use of violence. In a democracy, what other forms of power are there for citizens to express their point of view?

2. Some sociologists contend that democracy as a form of government and capitalism as an economic system are two sides of the same coin. Is it true that democracy and capitalism are directly related?

3. The democratic institutions we have inherited in Canada are apparently unable to resolve some of the political demands being made by Quebec nationalists. Is Quebec sovereignty inevitable? Can you think of any public policy alternatives to the present dilemma, or do we need to completely change the way we practise politics in Canada?

4. Access the Research Navigator through MySocLab and use keywords such as "Quebec," "independence," and "sovereignty" to locate relevant and recent scholarly and popular press publications to help you answer the previous question.

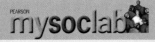

PEARSON mysoclab Explore the topics covered in this chapter on MySocLab using the access information provided with this text. Interactive resources for studying include multimedia tutorials, video clips, practice tests, quizzes, and animated maps and figures.

13

The Family: Initiation into Society

Mayra collapsed in exhaustion on the living-room couch. Her mind raced but her 60-year-old body was completely out of energy.

In an hour, her husband, Jean-Paul, would be back from his business trip and she would have to tell him that their son Colin and his husband, Rick, would be living temporarily in the home office space.

Mayra had left work early so that she could spend the afternoon moving filing cabinets around and squeezing the office desk into a corner, but all her efforts didn't solve the problem. With the sofa bed set up and suitcases piled around, the room looked like a crowded maze.

A few months earlier, Colin had been laid off from his position with an accounting firm and Rick had learned that his graduate studies scholarship would not be renewed. While Colin had finally landed work last week, he was only on a six-month contract and Rick still needed to finish writing his thesis. Until they got back on their feet, they needed a cheap place to live . . . so it was back to Mom and Dad.

Mayra sighed deeply as she pondered the new living arrangements. Yes, Colin and Rick would be out during the day, so Jean-Paul could work uninterrupted in his home office, but she knew he wouldn't like the intrusion into "his" space. Too bad five years earlier they had downsized to a condo.

Her thoughts were suddenly interrupted by a phone ringing. As Mayra lifted the receiver, she didn't know that her daughter Satie was phoning to tell her that her 90-year-old mother had just suffered a stroke. Nor did she know that in the coming months, her concerns about Colin and Rick living in her home would be dwarfed by her own forced retirement and her frantic efforts to locate and manage chronic care for her aged mother. In fact, having Colin and Rick around would actually provide her with invaluable moral support as she came to terms with her mother's declining health and impending death.

Adult children returning home, women juggling the combined pressures of paid work and family responsibilities, gay marriages, middle-aged couples juggling their "sandwich generation" roles as parents and as sons and daughters, the transformation of the home into a site for paid work—all reflect important changes in family lives in Canada today.

Despite the fact that the media often refer to some abstract notion of "the family," it's not clear what it means to *live* in a family. Everyone has heard the phrase "nothing is more important than family," but what does this signify and whom does it include? As we will see, family lives are complex, nuanced, and sometimes conflicted experiences and many Canadian families are in the midst of dramatic transformations. To navigate through these changes and come to terms with the new realities of many families, we need to appreciate the established patterns, significant diversities, and emerging trends that characterize contemporary family living.

MARRIAGES AND FAMILIES IN A GLOBAL PERSPECTIVE

To better understand Canadian patterns of marriage and family, let's first sketch a cross-cultural portrait of family lives.

Defining Families

When asked what the "ideal" family arrangement is, 58 percent of Canadians, especially older adults, describe the traditional family: a married man and woman with at least one biological child. A sizable minority (40 percent), especially younger adults, opt for a more diverse view of the family, stating that there is "no one family ideal." (Bibby 2004–5, pp. 3, 4). It appears that this youthful view captures the emerging realities of Canadian family life.

According to the 2006 census, most Canadians (84 percent) live in some kind of census family (married, common-law, or lone parent) rather than alone or with non-relatives. However, the numbers of non-traditional forms of families—common-law couples and lone parent families—are growing most rapidly. Only 34.6 percent of all census families in 2006 were comprised of married couples with children aged 24 and under. This figure is down dramatically from the 49.4 percent of families that were "traditional" according to the 1986 census. Meanwhile, the percentage of common-law couples (with and without children), lone parent families (with and without children), and married couples without children grew between 1986 and 2006 (Milan, Vezina, & Wells, 2007). Clearly, we live in a time of transition in terms of both our beliefs about family life and our lived experiences (Meadow & Stacey, 2006: 55).

This growing diversity in family experiences is consistent with what social scientists, especially anthropologists, have been documenting for generations. Around the globe, there is no single clear standard for *the* family. In some cultures, men are expected to have more than one wife (**polygyny**) and in others women have more than one husband (**polyandry**). Consider, for example, the Banaro of New Guinea. Among this group a young woman must give birth before she can marry, and she cannot marry the father of her child (Murdock, 1949).

And so it goes. For just about every element you might consider essential to marriage or family, some group has a different custom. Even the sex of a bride and groom may not be what you expect. Although in almost every instance a bride and groom are female and male, there are exceptions. In some Native American tribes, for example, a man or woman who want to be a member of the opposite sex go through a ceremony (*berdache*) and are *declared* to be of that sex. From then on, the "new" man or woman not only perform the tasks associated with that sex, but are also allowed to marry—in which case, the husband and wife are of the same biological sex (Whittington & Gordon, 2005). Even to say that the family is the unit in which children are disciplined and their parents are responsible for their material needs is not universally true. Among the Trobriand Islanders, the wife's eldest brother is responsible for making certain that his sister's children are fed and are properly disciplined when they misbehave (Malinowski, 1927).

Even sexual relationships don't universally characterize a husband and wife. The Nayar of Malabar never allow a bride and groom to have sex. After a three-day celebration of a marriage, they send the groom packing—and never *allow* him to see his bride again (La Barre, 1954). (In case you are wondering, the groom comes from another tribe, and Nayar women are allowed to have sex, but only with approved lovers—who can never be their husband. This system keeps family property intact along matrilineal lines.)

Focus Question

What might the following families have in common: a refugee family recently arrived from Pakistan living in downtown Toronto; a single-parent Native family living in northern Alberta; and a childless gay couple living in a Victoria retirement community?

DOWN-TO-EARTH SOCIOLOGY
Polygamous Canada

We do not need to look to other countries or ancient history to realize that conceptions of family life vary considerably. In Bountiful, British Columbia, a polygamist commune has existed for more than 50 years. A breakaway sect of the Mormon Church, the 1000-strong community believes that polygamy is ordained by God as a key to redemption; therefore, husbands have multiple wives and teenage girls are "assigned" marriages to older men in the community. From their point of view, they are "just a normal bunch of people" doing what they think is right. Needless to say, since polygamy is illegal in Canada, the practices have been challenged as immoral and abusive. However, despite ongoing RCMP investigations, the provincial government has not intervened, apparently fearing the charge of violating religious freedoms (Bramham, 2008; Girard, 2005, p. A15).

Common Cultural Themes

In spite of this diversity, several common themes run through many marriages and families. Table 13.1 illustrates the ways in which traditional and industrial/postindustrial societies typically pattern mate selection, descent, inheritance, and family authority.

These patterns, however, are situated in history, which means they are also changing. Fifty years ago, for example, child birth routinely occurred in hospitals and was attended only by medical staff. Family and friends were exiled to the waiting room. Today, many Canadian women opt for home birth or birthing centres and increasing varieties of family relations and friends. Not only the baby's father, but also the couple's children, their mothers and fathers, and various friends are sometimes invited to be present for a birth (Sokoloff, 2008: p. L1).

NORMS OF MATE SELECTION Every human group establishes formal or informal norms to govern who marries whom. Norms of **endogamy** specify that people should marry within their own group. Groups may prohibit interracial marriages, for example. In contrast, norms of **exogamy** specify that people must marry outside their group. The best example is the *incest taboo*, which prohibits sex and marriage between designated relatives. Even when informal, these norms are powerful. For example, in North America most people marry within their own "racial" and social class groups. A recent study of marriage patterns in Greater Toronto found that 75 percent of the 710 000 unions in 2001 involved couples of the same cultural background (ethnic endogamy) (Keung, 2008: p. ID1).

RECKONING PATTERNS OF DESCENT How are you related to your father's father or your mother's mother? The explanation is found in your society's **system of descent**, the way people trace kinship over generations. To us, a **bilateral** system seems logical—and natural—for we think of ourselves as related to both our mother's and our father's side of the family. "Doesn't everyone?" you might ask. Interestingly, this is only one logical way to reckon descent. In a **patrilineal** system, descent is traced only on the father's side, and children are not considered to be related to their mother's relatives. In a **matrilineal** system, descent is figured only on the mother's side, and children are not considered to be related to their father's relatives.

RIGHTS OF INHERITANCE Marriage and family—in whatever forms are customary in a society—are also used to compute rights of inheritance. In the bilateral system, property is passed to both males and females, in the patrilineal system only to males, and in the matrilineal system (the rarest form) only to females. Each system matches a people's ideas of justice and logic.

TABLE 13.1 Common Cultural Themes: Marriage in Traditional and Industrial Societies

Perspective	Traditional Societies	Industrial (and Postindustrial) Societies
What is the structure of marriage?	Extended (marriage embeds spouses in a large kinship network of explicit obligations)	Nuclear (marriage brings fewer obligations toward the spouse's kin)
What are the functions of marriage?	Economic production, socialization, care of the sick and aged, recreation, sexual control, and reproduction	More limited (many traditional social functions are fulfilled by other institutions)
Who holds authority?	Highly patriarchal (authority is held by males)	Although some patriarchal features remain, authority is more evenly divided
How many spouses at one time?	Most have one spouse (monogamy), while some have several (polygamy)	One spouse
Who selects the spouse?	The parents, usually the father	Individuals choose their own spouse
Where does the couple live?	Most commonly with the groom's family (patrilocal residence), less commonly with the bride's family (matrilocal residence)	In a new home (neolocal residence)
How is descent figured?	Most commonly from male ancestors (patrilineal kinship); less commonly from female ancestors (matrilineal kinship)	From male and female ancestors equally (bilateral kinship)
How is inheritance figured?	Rigid system of rules; usually patrilineal, but may be matrilineal	Highly individualistic; usually bilateral

Non-traditional families take many forms. Families from across Canada have moved to Alberta to take advantage of the high paying jobs provided by the oil industry. In many instances, husbands are away at remote work locations for weeks or months at a time. Meanwhile, their wives—termed "oil patch widows"—must take on all the responsibilities of parenting, household maintenance, and, in many instances, paid employment (Agrell, 2008).

PATTERNS OF AUTHORITY Historically, some form of - **patriarchy**, a social system in which men dominate women, has formed a thread running through most societies. Our marriage and family customs developed within a framework of patriarchy. Today, in Canada, Europe, and elsewhere around the globe, many individuals, especially younger women, are embracing more **egalitarian** attitudes toward, for example, household work and child care (Blau, Brinton, & Grusky, 2006). However, many customs persist that are rooted in our patriarchal past. Naming patterns, for example, reflect patriarchy.

In spite of recent trends, the typical bride (outside the province of Quebec) still takes the groom's last name; children, too, are usually given the father's last name. Even in progressive Norway, there appears to be a recent trend away from keeping the bride's birth-given name (Noack & Wiik, 2008; Arichi, 1999).

What are some of the fundamental differences in family life as it is lived around the globe?

Definitions of "the Family": The Problem of Monolithic Bias

Until relatively recently, North American sociologists have tended to downplay the amazing diversity in family life and focused on common cultural themes and functions. As a result, they broadly define the **family** as two or more people who consider themselves related by blood, marriage, or adoption. A **household** may or may not be a family since it is defined as consisting of all people who occupy the same housing unit—a house, apartment, or other living quarters. Within these broad categories, some sociologists then classify families as **nuclear** (husband, wife, and children) and **extended** (including people such as grandparents, aunts, uncles, and cousins in addition to the nuclear unit). Sociologists also refer to the **family of orientation** (the family in which an individual grows up) and the **family of procreation** (the family formed when a couple have their first child). Regardless of its form, **marriage** can be viewed as a group's approved mating arrangements—usually marked out by a ritual of some sort (a wedding) to indicate a couple's new public status.

While it is important to recognize these terms that appear frequently in sociological literature, it is also crucial to realize that many Canadian sociologists have explicitly rejected any approach to "the family" as a **monolithic structure**, along with any discussions of *the family*. In particular, noted Canadian sociologist Margrit Eichler developed an extensive critique of this approach to family studies (1988a, 1997). As she suggests, the popular definition of the nuclear family appears to support a very limited view of family life. If we assume that all or most families include a mother and father who are married to one another, who live together, and who have biological children who reside with them, we are ignoring the hundreds of thousands of Canadians who live in single-parent families, or who do not live together, or who do not have children, or do not have children living at home, or have stepchildren, or have adopted children, or are working so that their children can join them as immigrants to Canada (Milan, Vezina, & Wells, 2007; Mandell & Duffy, 2005). We would also tend to overlook in our research gay and lesbian families, families in which the couple are joined by common-law marriage, families in which the partners live apart for significant periods of time (immigrating families, commuting couples, truck drivers, military personnel), and adults and children who are residing not with family but in institutional settings (prisons, group homes, hospitals, and so on). Indeed, the list of exceptions seems to become longer and longer as we examine the complex realities of family life.

The **monolithic bias** not only lends itself to a very incomplete approach, but also tends to support a conservative bias. The monolithic approach implies that the "normal" and "natural" family is the one composed of two heterosexual adults who reside with and raise their biological (or adopted) children. This perspective may tend to ignore the numerous difficulties and shortcomings attached to many so-called "normal" nuclear families—for example, child abuse, woman abuse, senior abuse, and incest. It may also tend to devalue as "'deviant' or even dismiss families that exist outside the traditional boundaries—for example, gay and lesbian families, common-law or single-parent families, families of culturally or ethnically nondominant groups in Canada, families created through adoption, surrogacy, or donor insemination. As we discuss below, this conservative bias is particularly evident in the structural-functionalist theoretical perspective on family life.

Focus Question

Why does Canadian sociologist Margrit Eichler reject the monolithic approach to the family?

IN SUM

The question of what is a family is much more complex than we might think. Not only is there tremendous variation in family life around the globe, there are great diversities within the North American family. Further, certain definitions of the family may carry an unspoken agenda. If the "real" family is restricted to heterosexual couples with male primary breadwinners, female secondary breadwinners, biological children living at home, and so on, then the majority of Canadians are, according to this narrow definition, not living in a family and, significantly, fewer and fewer Canadians each year are living in "real" families (Milan, Vezina, & Wells, 2007). If such narrow definitions are then used to determine which families do or do not qualify to receive taxation benefits or social welfare support, for example, then the political implications are very apparent.

MARRIAGE AND FAMILY IN THEORETICAL PERSPECTIVE

The Functionalist Perspective: Functions and Dysfunctions

As noted in Chapter 1, functionalists stress that to survive, a society must meet certain basic needs, or functions. When functionalists look at families, they examine how families are related to other parts of society, especially how they contribute to the well-being of society.

IS THE FAMILY UNIVERSAL? Functionalists argue that although the form of families may vary from one human group to another, families are universal because they fulfill six needs basic to every society's well-being. As described in Table 13.1, these needs, or functions, are economic production, socialization of children, care of the sick and aged, recreation, sexual control, and reproduction.

As Eichler and other sociologists would be quick to point out, many groups that consider themselves "families" do not in fact fulfill all or even most of these "basic needs" (1997). Childless couples and couples whose children are grown up do not actively socialize children, yet will likely consider themselves members of a family. In some families, the socialization of children is entirely the responsibility of others—consider, for example, children placed in homes for young offenders or sent to boot camps, or those attending private residential schools or who are raised by nannies. Similarly, families do not necessarily provide a medium for legitimate sexual activity. Some families engage in illegal and/or socially stigmatized sexual behavior, such as marital rape, child sexual abuse, or "swinging." In some families, the "couple" has no sexual relations or only has sexual relations with partners outside the family relationship. The examples are endless. The bottom line is that any enumeration of "universal needs or functions" fulfilled by families should be understood only as a useful analytic tool, not as an accurate or complete description of familial realities and not as a foundation for social policies.

MASS MEDIA IN SOCIAL LIFE
Media Messages about Parenting

Various media are an important source of our images of family life.

Even children's picture books have a role to play in constructing societal images of family life. In their examination of gender stereotypes in children's picture books, David Anderson and Mykol Hamilton found that a very traditional (and inaccurate) image of father-ing was often presented. In 200 prominent children's picture books, fathers were largely underrepresented and, when they were visible, were presented as withdrawn and ineffectual parents (2005).

Recent Canadian research suggests that contrary to these stereotypes, there are men "who mother" and who fully assume primary care-giving roles with their children (Doucet 2006). Further, there are various indications that men are assuming a growing presence as primary parents. For example, lone-parent families headed by men are growing faster than such families headed by women (Milan, Vezina & Wells, 2007).

Recent U.S. research on the beliefs of college women also suggests there may be a shift toward parenting beliefs premised on the equal ability of fathers and mothers to provide primary nurturing care (Deutsch, Kokot, & Binder, 2007: p. 925). In this context, media stereotypes of invisible and inadequate fathers are both troubling (*Canadian Social Trends*, Winter 2007: pp. 39-40) and outdated (Troilo & Coleman, 2008).

Media socialization of familial roles also occurs among adults. For example, in recent decades, the media has sought to play an explicit role in explaining to parents what their roles should be. As Linda Quirke explains in her fascinating examination of parenting magazines, in Canada, the United States, the United Kingdom, and Australia between 1959 and 2003, there was a dramatic expansion in the numbers of magazines that explicitly detailed child-rearing practices. Where parents might once have turned to their own parents or other older relatives or neighbours for advice, today, the latest issue of *Parents Magazine* or *Mon Bebe* provides answers to questions even before they are asked.

While this may seem to be a benign development—one in which parents are informed by experts rather than folk lore—it is not clear that the outcome is uniformly positive. In her detailed examination of the content of Canadian parenting magazines, Quirke found that in the mid 1970s and early 1980s, magazine articles focused on children's health and safety or on fun activities to keep kids occupied. Beginning in the 1990s, the emphasis shifted, so that now articles in parenting magazines directly or indirectly encourage parents to provide intellectual stimulation and academic support for their children. For example, articles explain how to make sure your child doesn't "fall behind" during the summer holidays. In this new media reality, the good parent is implicitly one who intensely engages in activities to ensure that his or her child succeeds in school (Quirke 2006).

CONNECTION TO OTHER PARTS OF SOCIETY Functionalists make the important point that the family is not an isolated unit, but is vitally connected to other parts of society. They note, for example, that industrialization and urbanization made the family more fragile. It ushered in formal organizations, some of which began to replace the family's traditional functions. Medical treatment began to be provided by hospitals, recreation by businesses, and sex education by schools. To weaken family functions is to weaken the "ties that bind," to reduce the motivation to struggle together against hardships. One consequence is more divorce. From the functionalist perspective, increased divorce does not represent "incompatible personalities" or personal conflicts. Rather, changes in other parts of society impact our most intimate relationships.

ISOLATION AND EMOTIONAL OVERLOAD Functionalists also analyze the dysfunctions that arise from the relative isolation of today's nuclear family (another consequence of industrialization and urbanization). Unlike extended families in traditional societies, which are enmeshed in kinship networks, members of nuclear families can count on fewer people for material and emotional support. This makes nuclear families vulnerable to "emotional overload." That is, the stress that comes with crises such as the loss of a job—or even the routine stress of a harried life—is spread around among fewer people. This puts a greater strain on each family member. In addition, the relative isolation of the nuclear family makes it vulnerable to a "dark side"—which we will examine later in the chapter.

The Conflict Perspective: Gender, Conflict, and Power

As we have discussed, central to conflict theory is the struggle over scarce resources. The recurring struggle over who

In Hindu marriages, the roles of husband and wife are firmly established. Neither this woman nor her husband questions whether she should carry the family wash to the village pump. As India rapidly industrializes, as happened in the West, who does the wash will be questioned—and may become a source of strain between married couples.

does housework is actually an example of such a struggle over time, energy, and the leisure to pursue interesting activities. Feminist sociologists in particular continue to draw attention to the social issues surrounding housework.

THE POWER STRUGGLE OVER HOUSEWORK When the second wave of feminism swept through North America and Western Europe in the 1960s, social researchers began to realize that the person who washed the dishes and who diapered the baby reflected significant social issues. In particular, American feminist Betty Friedan developed a stinging indictment of a society that produced extremely well-educated women and then sequestered them as unpaid housewives for the majority of their adult lives (Friedan, 1963). Canadian sociologists working from a conflict perspective quickly picked up on the issue and developed a wealth of material on the experience of Canadian women. Among the most notable work was that of Meg Luxton, an anthropologist who lived for several years in Flin Flon, Manitoba, and chronicled the day-to-day lives of women in that community (1980). From this and other research, it became clear that in Canada, as elsewhere, women were doing the lion's share of housework and child care. The implicit agreement in many Canadian families, especially in the 1950s and 1960s, was that the husband would "bring home the bacon" and the wife would "cook it" while also taking care of the home and children.

Unfortunately, as the research record increasingly documented, this unspoken arrangement contained significant drawbacks for women and seemed to be rooted in women's relative lack of power in the family. Like many forms of low-paid, semiskilled work, housework was often tedious, time-consuming, repetitious, boring and socially marginalized. Women with young children reported shouldering onerous amounts of work while receiving little support within their families or communities (Mandell, Wilson, & Duffy, 2008;

Duffy, Mandell, & Pupo, 1989). Indeed, for many women, housework and child care was an isolating experience in which some felt completely cut off from adult stimulation. These problems were, of course, intensified for women who were poor or were recent immigrants or disabled. Most important, unlike other work, housework and child care was unpaid, and, in a variety of ways, this reality could have devastating implications in women's lives. Women whose marriages failed or who became widows (as most eventually would) often found that years of cooking, cleaning, and care translated into impoverishment when they were on their own.

The booming 1950s, when many families could afford to have a mother working at home as a full-time homemaker, were short-lived. Growing financial pressure on family resources has meant that few families can afford a full-time parent in the home. Instead, family members are working longer hours—the total workday (paid and unpaid work) of parents has increased by almost one hour over the past decade as both parents have to cut back on personal care and leisure activities (Fast, Frederick, Zukewich, & Franke, 2001, p. 21). Not surprisingly, increased time devoted to paid employment during the typical workday has directly contributed to fewer hours spent with the family (Turcotte, 2007: p. 5). Additionally, as part of this general shift toward more work time, increasing numbers of wives and mothers have moved into the paid labour force (see Figure 13.1).

Interestingly, despite the movement of most mothers into paid employment, equality in the division of domestic labour has not been achieved. Although most Canadians agree that both parents should take equal responsibility for raising children and carrying out household duties (Bibby, 2004–5, p. 9), survey research continues to document that women, even when employed full-time, are still undertaking the lion's share of unpaid household work, including child care, eldercare, and domestic work.

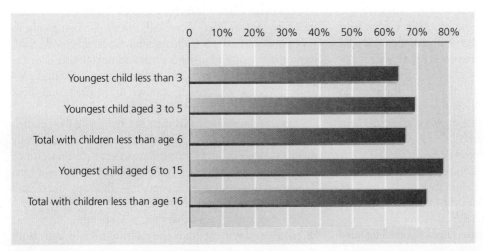

FIGURE 13.1 Percentage of Employed Mothers Working Full-Time, by Age of Youngest Child, 2004

Yes, there have been changes. Overall, Canadian couples are spending less time on household work (presumably thanks to labour-saving appliances and products) and men have increased their contributions to household work, including child care. However, equality in the home remains out of reach for many couples. In 2005, women aged 25 to 54 averaged 2.8 hours per day in housework while comparable men averaged only 1.8 hours. If we narrow the focus to men and women with children at home, women were doing 1.3 hours more housework per day than their male counterparts (Marshall, 2006). This means that over the course of a week, many Canadian women are working a full workday (approximately 8 to 9 hours) and putting more time toward unpaid household work than their male counterparts.

This patterned inequality is not restricted to Canada. Australia and other "developed" countries retain very similar patterns of inequality in domestic labour, although some—Sweden, East Germany—have been able to introduce social policies that improve gender equity in the home (Baxter, Hewitt, & Haynes, 2008; Cooke 2007).

Predictably, as a result of this inequity, many women are experiencing considerable stress (MacDonald, Phipps, & Lethbridge, 2005). A recent U.S. examination of time distributions in families reported that mothers reported feeling more time-stressed than fathers and that they felt they didn't spend "enough" time with their children (Bianchi, Robinson, & Milkie, 2006). Canadian research echoes these patterns. Among Canadian couples with the longest workday (combined housework and paid work) and with children at home, two thirds of women reported being time-stressed compared to only half of men (Marshall, 2006: p. 15). Further, analysts argue that the continuing inequity is rooted, at least in part, in continuing patterns of gender inequality in Canadian society (Gazso-Windle & McMullin, 2003). It seems that, despite social changes, many women are returning from a day of paid employment to find that groceries still have to be bought, meals prepared, children looked after, dishes washed, laundry done, and so on and so on.

According to American sociologist Arlie Hochschild (1989), women's "second shift" at home is, at least in part, the result of continued male resistance to household equality. For example, according to her series of in-depth interviews with nearly 50 American families, many men never volunteer to do chores around the house or they passively resist the work by responding glumly or with irritation when asked to "help out." A number of men "play dumb"; that is, they burn the dinner or lose the grocery list or forget to stop off at the dry cleaners. Some men use a "needs reduction" strategy in which they tell their wives not to bother to iron their clothes because they don't mind walking around in a wrinkled shirt, or that they don't need to tidy up because they don't mind the mess, or, when on their own, that they have a bowl of cereal for supper because that's all they want. When this strategy works,

women feel guilty and self-conscious—they want their husband and their home to appear neat and tidy. They then provide the tidying, the ironed shirts, or the cooked dinner. In some cases, men offer appreciation and rewards—expressing admiration for their wife's ability to manage the double day and providing her with a dishwasher to help out with the dishes—rather than actually increasing their own labour contribution to the home.

Recent research in Western Europe suggests that these patterns of resistance are very much still with us. Despite much public discussion of the "new fathers," in fact, there has been relatively little change. In France, for example, nearly one father in three with a young child is not involved in parental tasks. They may "help out" when a baby arrives by shopping or doing some laundry or they may "baby sit" while their wife goes out on errands, but the improvement is very small relative to the dramatic increase in domestic work requirements made by having an infant in the family. Other evidence suggests that men are selective about the kind of domestic work they do and often opt for particular tasks—cooking and washing up, for example—while leaving mothers with the overwhelming majority of parental work. The researchers conclude that "sharing" family and home responsibilities is more a popular fuzzy and warm ideology than a practical reality (Devreux, 2007).

However, despite their apparent reluctance and resistance, men in many countries of the world, including Canada, are slowly increasing their household and familial contributions. Over the past several decades, while wives and mothers have been directing more of their time to paid work, Canadian fathers have been reorienting some of their paid "work" time to child care, household maintenance, and meal preparation. In 1986, when 56 percent of couples with dependent children were dual earner families, only 54 percent of men participated daily in housework; by 2005, when 69 percent of families were dual earner, 71 percent of men were doing daily housework. Similarly, men's participation rate in primary child care (reading to children, helping with homework, driving them to activities, and so on) in dual earner families increased from 57 percent in 1986 to 73 percent in 2005 (Marshall, 2006). Unfortunately, as we have discussed, these changes have not produced equality in the division of unpaid work and negotiating the time crunch remains a significant concern for many families—especially those with young children in the home and those caring for both children and aging parents.

The combined facts that men are increasing their contributions to household work and child care and that family members, especially mothers, still experience the time crunch suggest that the problem is not due simply to resistant husbands. Many professional careers—held by men and women—allow little time for attending to family responsibilities, and average Canadians are now spending more time in paid employment than they did a decade ago. Both husbands and wives, particularly at certain points of their family lives, are simply "running as fast as they can" (Turcotte, 2007). Noted Canadian researchers Roderic Beaujot and Robert Andersen conclude from their research that solving the time crunch in Canadian families requires a reduction in hours of paid work for both men and women (2007: p. 311). We are simply spending too many hours at work.

These problems, as well as how wives and husbands cope with them, are discussed in the next Thinking Critically about Social Controversy box.

Focus Question
Why would feminist conflict theorists reject a strictly functional explanation of mothers' increased participation in paid employment?

Focus Question
Why do employed mothers still assume most of the responsibility for household work?

The Symbolic Interactionist Perspective: Gender and its Meanings in Marriage

As noted in Chapter 1, symbolic interactionists focus on the meanings people give to the roles they play in society. Let's apply this perspective to some surprising findings about marriage.

HOUSEWORK, PAYCHEQUES, AND MASCULINITY The first pattern of findings is probably what you'd expect—the more a woman earns from her paid employment, the more

THINKING CRITICALLY ABOUT SOCIAL CONTROVERSY
Is it Greed or Need? Why Canadian Mothers Work for Pay

From the 1970s to the end of the 1990s, the Canadian family mobilized increasing numbers of income earners. Wives, mothers, and teenage family members moved into the paid labour force. Not only are more family members employed, but they are working more continuously. The overwhelming majority of mothers (87 percent) who gave birth in 1999 returned to work in the first year after childbirth. Further, they stay employed. Eighty-four percent of mothers who gave birth in 2001 were employed in 2004 and fewer than 6 percent of women who gave birth in the early 2000s quit the labour market in the first three years after childbirth (The Daily, December 19, 2007). At one time, new mothers might take a few years off while their children were young. In Canada as well as the Netherlands and the United Kingdom, the trend has been for mothers to return more and more quickly to paid work (Smeaton, 2006; Vlasblom & Schippers, 2006).

Much has been made of the reasons why family members, particularly mothers, have become so deeply involved with paid work, particularly when it often results in considerable time stress for not only mothers but all family members. Why do mothers spend so much time in

paid work? There has been an ongoing debate in the media between those who are advocates for mothers who "opt out" of high-pressure professional careers and those who urge stay-at-home moms to get to work in order to find financial and personal freedom in paid employment (Stone, 2007; Hirshman, 2006). Both positions tend to involve a fair amount of hyperbole. Most women do not have the luxury of leaving a prestigious professional career and most stay-at-home mothers will find the path to economic freedom bumpy. Rather than "choosing" whether or not to have a paid job, most women and their families face harsh economic pressures that typically demand several incomes.

Controlling for inflation, incomes in Canada have grown only minimally for almost two decades. Average hourly wages are actually lower now than they were 15 years ago and overall (salary and hourly wages) wages are up only $0.25 since 1991. Average income (after taxes and government transfers) for Canadian households increased marginally from $52 300 in 1980 to $55 800 in 2006. If not for major income tax reductions in 2001 and 2002, family incomes in recent years would have been flat or declining. Given that real income gains per house-

hold grew by a mere 5 percent from 1990 to 2006 while household spending increased by over 18 percent, it is not surprising that the average household saving rate dropped to less than 1 percent in 2004—the same as the average rate during the Great Depression of the 1930s.

In order to make ends meet amid dramatic increases in the costs of education, energy, medical care, health services, and so on, families are cashing in their RRSPs (the rate of withdrawals from RRSPs doubled from 1993 to 2001) and going deeper into debt. Average total consumer debt (including mortgages) increased from $30 000 in the early 1980s to $76 000 in 2004 (Sauve, 2005, 2007; The Daily, May 1 2008; May 5, 2008). It seems that the dearth of secure, well-paying, full-time jobs along with dramatic increases in costs, especially for housing and education, are taking a toll on the average Canadian family. In this economic context, it is not surprising to see many families, middle-income and poor, mobilizing every available wage-earner.

Women have played a particularly important income-earning role as they have increased the average number of hours they work. Between 1980 and 2004, a woman aged 25 to 34 with a university degree increased her working hours by 20 percent while her male counterpart saw his working hours reduced by 1 percent. Further, especially among women without a university degree, weekly earnings dramatically improved for women but not for comparable men in the same time period. Men aged 25 to 34 with a non-university diploma or certificate saw their earnings drop by 7 percent while their female counterparts increased their wages by 1 percent (Sauve, 2005). For all these reasons, women play an increasingly crucial role in family economics. Currently, employed wives are contributing on average about 30 percent of family income, and couples with only one income earner have a poverty rate five times larger than dual-earner families (Sauve, 2007). Consider what it would mean to your family to lose almost a third of its income. While many Canadian families could "survive" without women's income, and some women work for reasons other than economic survival, it is important to realize the pivotal role played by economic pressures.

The issue of economic pressures is addressed in Meg Luxton and June Corman's award-winning book, *Getting By in Hard Times* (2001). Based on a case study conducted from 1980 to 1996 among families where at least one person was employed at Stelco's steel manufacturing plant in Hamilton, Ontario, their work reveals a great deal about the impact of economic globalization on the day-to-day realities of family life. Economic restructuring, including the movement of many industrial jobs to other countries with lower labour costs, the loss of industrial jobs to technological innovation, and the growth of poorly paid service jobs shook traditional families to their core. Where a job at the steel plant had once promised lifelong economic security, families are now faced with layoffs and insecurity.

Not surprisingly, Luxton and Corman found that many of the working-class families in their study moved away from a pattern in which women were full-time housewives and men were income earners to one where women were also income earners. For many, standards of living needed to be lowered, and family members, especially mothers, needed to intensify their unpaid work at home to help make ends meet.

The resultant upheaval reverberated through family and personal life. Tensions over the division of household work and child care intensified. These pressures on individual families and their members, in turn, affected the larger community. There was little in the way of time or energy to direct toward strong friendship networks and community organizations or to organize protest movements. The day-to-day demands of the family took precedence, and opportunities for collective actions—from the union movement to local community initiatives—were undermined.

Further, frustration with increasing economic insecurity led to increased racial, ethnic, and gender conflict. Immigrants in general, along with specific ethnic groups and women's organizations, were blamed for putting obstacles in the employment paths of white, able-bodied men. Affirmative action policies were seen as evidence of increasing patterns of unfairness in which "others" were always the first to get jobs.

By locating family life in the midst of these crucial larger social issues, Luxton and Corman dramatically exposed the complex ways in which economic pressures, exacerbated by cutbacks in government services, can force families to turn inward, away from possibilities of progressive social change. Given recent declines in manufacturing-based employment, particularly in the auto industry, it is likely such changes will continue to reverberate through Canadian families.

For Your Consideration

Identify the sources of economic pressure for the contemporary Canadian family. Consider strategies that family members might employ to lessen these pressures.

Researchers June Corman and Meg Luxton, pictured here, continue to chronicle the impact of large social trends, such as economic restructuring, on ordinary Canadian families.

housework men tend to take on (Marshall, 2006: p. 11). (However, when women are the primary wage earners, husbands do not typically equal or surpass their wives' household work time.) Today, more than a quarter of wives (29 percent) in dual earner couples earn more than their husbands. This is a remarkable increase from 11 percent in 1967 (Marshall, 2006: p. 10). Rather than the husbands in these families taking over household responsibilities while the wives occupy the traditional breadwinner role, these couples are more likely to purchase home services such as cleaning or child care. And, further, when women earn much more than their husbands, couples may engage in complicated "systems of shifting money" to maintain the appearance that the man is the major provider (Marshall, 2006: p. 11). You might think husbands who earn less than their wives would want to balance things out—to do more around the house. Researchers suggest that the key is gender role. Not only are boys socialized to perform certain tasks in the home, but they also associate their self-esteem with a particular notion of masculinity. If a wife earns more than her husband, it is likely to threaten his masculinity if he endorses traditional gender roles. He may take it as a sign that he has failed in the manly role of family provider. To do housework—"women's work," in his eyes—threatens it even further. By avoiding housework, he "reclaims" his masculinity (Pitt & Borland, 2008; Hochschild, 1989; Brines, 1994).

TWO MARRIAGES IN ONE Another interesting finding of symbolic interactionists is how husbands and wives perceive their marriages. When asked how much housework each does, they give different answers. They even disagree about whether they fight over doing housework (Sanchez, 1994). Groundbreaking sociologist Jessie Bernard studied this marital gulf and noted in a classic work (1972) that when researchers

> ask husbands and wives identical questions about the union they often get quite different replies. There is usually agreement on the number of children they have and a few other such verifiable items, although not, for example, on length of premarital acquaintance and of engagement, on age at marriage and interval between marriage and birth of first child.

Why don't husbands and wives agree on such a basic matter as how frequently they have sex? The answer lies in differing *perceptions* of lovemaking. It appears that in a typical marriage, the wife desires greater emotional involvement from her husband, while the husband desires more sex (Komter, 1989; Barbeau, 1992). When questioned about sex, then, the husband, feeling deprived, tends to underestimate it, while the wife, more reluctant to participate in sex because of unsatisfied intimacy needs, overestimates it (Bernard, 1972).

Symbolic interactionists conclude that because husbands and wives hold such different viewpoints, they perceive marriage differently. Their experiences contrast so sharply that *every marriage contains two separate marriages—his and hers.*

IN SUM

Working from very different and sometimes opposing theoretical orientations, sociologists of the family have focused on a number of important features of family life. Functionalists tend to emphasize the interconnections between families and other social institutions such as the education system and the economy. The conflict perspective, and feminist sociologists in particular, emphasize conflicts, including those over scarce resources (such as time) that often emerge in family life. Nowhere is this strain more apparent than in the struggle over who should be responsible for housework, particularly in a dual-earner family. Symbolic interactionists explore the meaning family members attach to family life and roles within the family. Not surprisingly, given differences in gender socialization, men and women approach the meaning of family activities in very different ways. This is so much the case that it is reasonable to refer to "his" marriage and "her" marriage.

Focus Question
In what way do male and female perceptions of lovemaking and housework reveal the differences between "his" and "her" marriage? What are the implications?

THE FAMILY LIFE CYCLE

We have seen that forms of marriage and family vary widely, and have examined marriage and family from different sociological perspectives. Now let's discuss love, courtship, and the family life cycle.

Love and Courtship in Global Perspective

Until recently, social scientists thought romantic love originated in Western Europe during the medieval period (Mount, 1992). When anthropologists William Jankowiak and Edward Fischer (1992) surveyed the data available on 166 societies around the world, they found that this was not so. **Romantic love**—people being sexually attracted to and idealizing one another—showed up in 88 percent (147) of these groups. The role of love, however, differs sharply from one society to another. For example, people in India don't expect love to occur until *after* marriage—if at all.

Romantic love usually begins with sexual attraction. We find ourselves sexually attracted to someone and spend time with that person. If we discover mutual interests, we may eventually label our feelings as "love." As such, romantic love has two components. The first is emotional, a feeling of sexual attraction. The second is cognitive, a label we attach to our feelings. If we attach this label, we describe ourselves as being "in love."

Focus Question
Using a functional perspective, explain why notions of romantic love vary from one culture to another.

Finding a "Significant e-Other": Looking for Romance in All the New Places

Canadians are increasingly turning to the internet to find friends, dates, and potential mates. Numerous sites advertise that they offer thousands of potential companions, lovers, or spouses. For a low monthly fee, you, too, can meet the person of your dreams—a person scientifically matched to your specific profile!

On some websites, there is a fascinating array of photographs of people searching for a relationship. Some seem to be lovely, attractive, and vivacious, and one wonders why they are posting their photos and personal information online. Internet dating sites appear to be frequented by people of every description—the needy, the pitiful, the desperate, and, of course, regular, ordinary people. In an increasingly time-stressed culture, it is not surprising that many people embrace these efficient, cost-effective mechanisms for meeting suitable potential mates. Predictably, internet postings and online services are losing their stigma and more singles are finding mates via electronic matchmaking.

Facebook and MySpace also offer alternatives for finding potential dates and mates (Gray, 2007). This is part of Facebook's allure. To find people with similar interests, simply type that interest in the search field. If you enjoy clubbing, making out, or Japanese films, you can find people who share these interests with a mouse-click. If you see a cute girl or guy in class, you can learn not only their e-mail address but also the other classes they are taking and their interests.

A huge advantage for cash-strapped college and university students is that Facebook is free. Just answer a few questions, post your picture, and start making a social network. A photo appears on your computer screen whenever someone asks to be listed as part of your group. If you click yes, you have just "friended" him or her. You have control. You can set your own privacy settings to determine who can view which parts of your profile: contact information, personal information, courses you are taking, or your list of friends.

The "wall" is a favourite feature of Facebook. On your virtual "wall," friends can scrawl messages, either fanciful ("Meathead is here") or private ("My love

for you grows with each passing minute. I can't wait until I'm in your arms again."). In the "'old days," lovers etched their initials on trees; today they can proclaim their love through cyberspace. Needless to say, these new technologies for forming relationships are fraught with difficulties. When online interest from a prospective "friend" is too intense or unwelcome, it may transform into cyberstalking or cyberharassment.

Often, profiles and photos are not an accurate representation and resultant face-to-face meetings can be, at the least, disappointing. The possibility of endless dating prospects may make "commitment" all the more difficult. It's important to keep in mind that online postings are available to a great many people. Employers have used Facebook to check out some well-dressed, serious job applicants, and discovered that their prospective employees were bragging about getting drunk, getting laid, and smoking substances other than tobacco (Henslin, 2008).

Marriage

The overwhelming majority (80 percent) of Canadians view marriage as very or somewhat important, and 95 percent agree or strongly agree that ideally, marriage should last a lifetime (Bibby, 2004–5, p. 6). Clearly, marriage remains a central social value. It is envisioned as a path to commitment, children, and a sense of family.

THE SOCIAL CHANNELS OF LOVE AND MARRIAGE In the typical Canadian case, marriage is expected to be preceded by "love." However, when viewed from a societal perspective, love and marriage are not random events. Rather, through this process we often cement social bonds and perpetuate societal traditions.

When we marry, we generally think we have freely chosen our spouse. With few exceptions, however, our choices follow highly predictable social channels, especially age, education, social class, race, and religion (Tucker & Mitchell-Kerman, 1990; Kalmijn, 1991). A young woman with a university degree whose parents are both physicians is likely to fall in love with and marry a young man slightly older than her who has graduated from university. Similarly, a female high-school dropout whose parents are on welfare is likely to fall in love with and marry a male who comes from a background similar to hers.

Sociologists use the term **homogamy** to refer to the tendency of people with similar characteristics to marry one another. Homogamy occurs largely as a result of *propinquity*, or spatial nearness. That is, we tend to fall in love with and marry people who live near us or whom we meet at school, church, or work. The people with whom we associate are far from a random sample of the population, for social filters produce neighbourhoods, schools, and churches that follow racial-ethnic and social class lines.

Not all marriages are between people of similar backgrounds. In a multicultural country such as Canada, many persons enter into "mixed unions"; that is, they form unions across cultural lines or across visible minority lines. In 2006, 3.9 percent of Canadians (247 600 couples) were living in mixed unions comprised of one visible minority member and one non–visible minority member, an increase of 33.1 percent since 2001 (Statistics Canada, 2008: p. 16). By forming unions across cultural and minority status lines, such individuals may be seen as an important "engine of social change" (Milan & Hamm, 2004). "Mixed" unions may not only challenge "racial" categories but also provide a mechanism for social integration and, as discussed below, social mobility.

In a very contentious survey involving mixed marriages in Toronto, Spanish social scientist Rodriguez-Garcia found that visible minorities were more likely to marry whites even if whites were less educated and earned a lower income. The author suggested that members of minority groups tend to compensate for their relative status by bringing more educational or economic resources to the marriage market when they marry someone from an ethnic group with higher social standing. Needless to say, these suggestions were considered offensive by some readers, but the logic of Rodriguez-Garcia's analysis underscores the point that mate selection follows patterns other than simply romance and love (Keung, 2008).

Childbirth

In 1947, at the beginning of the baby boom years, Canada's fertility rate was 3.6 children per woman, and the rate did not peak until 1959, when nearly 500 000 babies were born. Since that time, the birth rate has followed a fairly steady decline (see Figure 13.2). In 2005, despite a much larger general population, only 342 276 babies were born, or 1.54 children per woman (*The Daily,* September 21, 2007). However, despite this decline, almost 70 percent of Canadian adults have children (down from 77 percent in 1975), and 90 percent of Canadian adults indicate that having children was or is important "for them to do in their lifetimes" (Bibby, 2004–5, p. 9).

MARITAL SATISFACTION A sociological finding that surprises many is that marital satisfaction usually *decreases* with the birth of a child (Whyte, 1992; Bird, 1997). Recent Canadian research, for example, tracked 577 Canadian university graduates for seven years and found that the transition to parenthood was associated with increased anger, especially among mothers (Galambos & Krahn, 2008). Think about the implications of coping with a newborn—less free time (feeding, soothing, and diapering), less sleep, and heavier expenses. If

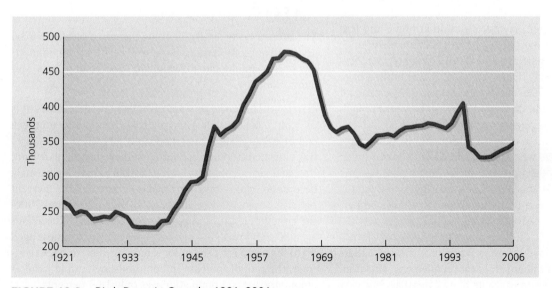

FIGURE 13.2 Birth Rates in Canada, 1921–2006

we consider the intensification of work time alone, it is clear that parenthood may be a stressful time. New mothers average four extra hours of unpaid work a day and new fathers two extra hours (Baxter, Hewitt, & Haynes, 2008). Mothers cut back on their paid work time and, along with fathers, decrease their leisure time. Further, the division of labour in the home tends to become more gendered, with mothers taking on more of the household responsibilities (Zukewich, 2003).

To add to the pressures, many women experience a drop in income (the motherhood wage penalty) as a result of motherhood—a particularly troubling prospect when the average expenditures on a child from birth to age 17 among middle-income, husband-wife families is about $190 000 (Glauber, 2007; Carr, 2007: p. 62). These difficulties are often not anticipated or planned for since prevailing cultural beliefs (reinforced through the media and targeting women) suggest that babies more or less "guarantee a happy, healthy, rewarding life" (Simon, 2008). Given all this, it is not surprising that parenthood may be a time of difficult adjustments and reduced relationship satisfaction.

Focus Question

Why would marital satisfaction decline with the birth of a child, and why might social class affect this decline?

Child-Rearing: New Realities

As discussed with respect to socialization, childhood has changed dramatically over the past several generations. For example, there are fewer children in the average family. According to the latest census data (2006), for the first time in Canadian history there were more couple families that did not have children (42.7 percent) than those that did (41.4 percent). In sharp contrast, from 1986 to 2006, the proportion of married couples with children (the traditional "family") declined from 49.4 percent of census families to 34.6 percent.

The number of children in a family also continued to drop, with more than a third (37.3 percent) of census (2006) families with children having one child at home and less than a fifth (18.9 percent) having three or more children.

Further, since marriage and childrearing are more frequently delayed today than in the past, more children have older parents. In 2006, almost one in ten (9.4 percent) of children aged four and under had a mother between the ages of 40 and 49 (Milan, Vezina, & Wells, 2007).

As discussed earlier, increasing numbers of families have mothers and fathers who are both in the paid labour force. As a result, the modern process of childrearing has become more complex and varied and, not surprisingly, new parents often find the first year in the transition to parenthood particularly onerous (Claxton & Perry-Jenkins, 2008).

Of particularly troubling concern is the provision of child care for employed parents. Many mothers and fathers find initial decisions about child care challenging. However, despite parental concerns, research indicates that child care

does not necessarily undermine the parenting experience. The children of employed parents feel loved and valued, provided they know they are their parents' priority (Galinsky, 1999). Indeed, the Canadian National Longitudinal Survey of Children and Youth suggests that although child care has drawbacks, such as fewer positive mother-child interactions and less reading with parents at ages two and four, children in non-parental care exhibit lower hyperactivity, more pro-social behavior, and less anxiety at age four. In short, depending on the type and quality of child care and the mothers' parenting, child care may benefit children (Nomaguchi, 2006). Further, recent research indicates that employed mothers are spending as many hours a week with their children as stay-at-home moms did in 1981, and fathers are spending more time with their children, up from 19 hours a week in 1981 to 24 in 1997 ("Kids Spending More Time with Parents," 2001, p. M10; Zukewich, 2003). So, while non-familial child care is more common, parental child-rearing still remains an important aspect of family life.

We should also point out that many children are being parented in the context of family separation and divorce. This means they are living in lone-parent families or, if their parent(s) remarry, in new blended families. Results from the Canadian National Longitudinal Survey on Children and Youth indicate that marital dissolution has a particularly negative impact on the role of the father in childrearing. Of children living with their mothers in 1994/1995, almost half saw their fathers frequently (27 percent saw them at least once a week, 22 percent saw them every two weeks). One in three saw their father irregularly—every month or on holidays. One in five (19 percent) had, at most, phone or mail contact with their father. These patterns appeared to persist over time, with many fathers maintaining regular or irregular contact and a significant minority becoming essentially absent from their children's lives (*The Daily*, October 29, 2007)

The Family in Later Life

The later stages of family life bring their own pleasures to be savoured and problems to be solved. Let's look at common-law unions among older Canadians, "boomerang" kids, and living alone.

COMMON-LAW UNIONS AMONGST OLDER CANADIANS It is difficult to believe that in the not-too-distant past, entering a common-law relationship (at one time termed "shacking up") was considered somewhat daring and even socially deviant. In recent years, common-law relationships have increasingly become accepted, something that is reflected in the emergent patterns among older Canadians. Between 2001 and 2006, the growth rate in common-law relationships for Canadians aged 50 to 54 was 43.5 percent; 63.9 percent for those aged 55 to 59, and 77.1 percent for seniors aged 60 to 64. In contrast, the rate of increase in common-law-couple families among the general population was only 18.9 percent.

This dramatic increase among older Canadians likely reflects a variety of factors. The size of the boomer generation means that as they age, boomers will impact on all marriage forms, but it is also likely that adults who have been living their lives in common-law families for a long time are now entering the ranks of older Canadians—the Woodstock generation is growing old.

It seems that new normative patterns have emerged. After the dissolution of an earlier marriage, many individuals choose a common-law form for their subsequent relationships. Reflecting general trends, older Canadians are increasingly likely to find themselves divorced (Milan, Vezina, & Wells, 2007: pp. 21–22). The proportion of divorced persons among seniors tripled from 1981 to 2001, and by 2001, 11 percent of women aged 55 to 64 had been divorced (Turcotte & Schellenberg, 2006: p. 139). In addition, it seems that after age 50, people who have been widowed also often opt for common-law arrangements. Together, these factors underscore the fact that throughout the life cycle, marriage is becoming less frequently defined as a legal contract or religious ceremony.

Focus Question
Considering the changes that are currently impacting the Canadian family, what kinds of issues might be faced by a man and woman living in a common-law relationship as they mature from 50 to 70 years of age?

BOOMERANG KIDS A generation ago, analysts were discussing the impact of "empty nest" syndrome on older parents. Having devoted much of their adult lives to the care and well-being of their children, fathers and, in particular, mothers, it was suggested, were troubled by their abrupt lack of purpose in life. While the empty nest theory has always been questioned, it has become outdated as a result of recent trends. Today, many mothers have long been employed full-time in the paid labour force, so the exit of adult children and the transition to reduced familial responsibilities may create more of a sense of relief than a personal vacuum.

More significantly, adult children are not moving out. As a result of various factors, including extended patterns of education, increased education costs, an uncertain employment market, and dramatic rises in the costs of housing in metropolitan centres, many mothers and fathers are finding that their adult children are not leaving home or are returning.

In the past, reflecting patterns of earlier marriage and child-bearing, young adults tended to leave the parental home to form their own households. In 1986, slightly less than a third of young adults (20 to 29) were still living with their parents. In contrast, in 2006, almost half (43.5 percent) had either stayed in their parental homes or had moved back. While the figures are particularly high for those in the first half of their twenties (60.3 percent), even among young adults aged 25 to 29, more than one in four (26.0 percent) were living "'at home' (Milan, Vezina, & Wells, 2007).

Not surprisingly, certain types of families are more likely to have adult children in the home. Lone-parents, parents living in a large metropolitan area (where housing may be particularly costly), parents who were born in Europe and Asia, and parents who own a single detached home (with adequate space for additional adults) are more likely to have their adult children living with them. Clearly, practical considerations—the availability of space in the home and the costs of housing in the area—along with cultural considerations—traditions that encourage young adults to live with their parents until marriage—may be involved in this new pattern of family life (Turcotte, 2006).

Whether this trend will be long-lived depends on a variety of social factors. However, there is no doubt that at present there is a new reality in many families and not all families have been able to settle comfortably into these new social arrangements. As reflected in recent movies—notably, *Failure to Launch* (2007)—and popular humour on the topic ("for my kids, when they're 24, it's out the door!"), the presence or even possibility of "boomerang" kids may be unsettling. The daily presence of adult children may result in frustrations for parents who must continue to share their living space. However, Canadian research suggests that typically, this inconvenience is balanced by a personal satisfaction from their roles as parents. The quality of the parents' marriages may also be subject to pressures as parents argue over adult children's contributions to chores or the drain on family resources, and opportunities for couple intimacy are reduced. However, again, the evidence does not suggest that significant family turmoil is common (Turcotte, 2006, 2007).

In fact, research suggests that once adult children marry, intergenerational ties with parents tend to diminish and married adult children have less time (than divorced or single adult children) to stay in touch or give or receive emotional, financial, or practical help (Sarkisian & Gerstel, 2008). As a result, boomerang children in the home may provide an important opportunity for the two generations to bond. At present, families are working out these new dynamics and there are few norms about what to expect and how to act.

LIVING ALONE As they enter their senior years, men and women may find that they are "on their own." However, it has long been the case that women, more than men, find themselves living alone. The cultural pattern of women marrying older men and higher longevity rates for women increase the likelihood that even when marriages endure for decades, a woman is more likely than her male partner to be widowed. Cultural patterns surrounding ageism, beauty, and economic wealth also mean that in the event of divorce, women are less likely to remarry than their male counterparts (Cruikshank, 2003). The net effect of these patterns is that although seniors in general are likely to end up alone, it is particularly the case for senior women.

According to census data (2001), more than a fifth (22 percent) of Canadians aged 65 to 74 and more than a third (34 percent) of seniors aged 85 and over were living on their own. Although men's life expectancy has improved in recent decades, women are still more likely than men to face widowhood. In 2001, 28 percent of women aged 65 to 74 were widowed. Meanwhile, increases in divorce have also impacted senior women. Between 1981 and 2001, the percentage of women aged 55 to 64 who were divorced increased threefold to 11 percent. As a result, many more senior women (aged 75 to 84) are living on their own (43 percent) than senior men (18 percent). Even among aged seniors, 38 percent of men aged 85 and older live with a spouse, compared to only 7 percent of women in the same age group (Turcotte & Schellenberg, 2007).

Only recently, social researchers have begun to examine the quality of life and experiences of post-family older women. The picture is far from bleak, particularly for women with sufficient economic resources and good health. Many maintain extensive social networks with friends and family and live busy, fulfilled lives. However, older women on their own tend to be subject to economic problems and ageist stereotypes. As the rapidly aging boomer generation of women matures, it is highly likely the economic and societal marginalization of older women will be increasingly challenged (Mandell, Wilson, & Duffy, 2008).

IN SUM

Following the family through the life course—from romance and courtship to widowhood and death—provides us with an appreciation for the complexities of family life. Certainly, not every family follows the same path, and an examination of other cultures and other historical periods reveals profoundly different experiences of love, childbirth, and childrearing. However, within this diversity, interesting patterns emerge.

DIVERSITY IN CANADIAN FAMILIES

It is important to emphasize that there is no such thing as *the* Canadian family. Rather, family life varies widely throughout Canada.

Ethnic Diversities

For generations, population growth in Canada has been primarily the result of immigration. As the birth rate decreased, our reliance on immigration intensified and, according to the 2006 census, the proportion of foreign-born people in Canada has reached its highest level in 75 years. For a number of years, Canadian fertility has been below the "replacement level"; that is, the numbers of children born to Canadians are not sufficient to maintain the country's population size. Coupled with the "aging" of the Canadian population and the increased number of retirees, the continuing need for immigrant labour is clear. Between 1945 and 1966,

125 000 immigrants arrived yearly in the country. Throughout the 1970s and 1980s, the pattern remained much the same. During the 1990s, 2.2 million immigrants came to Canada, and current government policy maintains a goal of between 250 000 and 300 000 immigrants (including refugees) annually. In this context, it is not surprising to learn that there are members of more than 200 different ethnic groups in Canada and that immigrants make up almost 20 percent of our population (Statistics Canada, 2008; *The Daily*, December 4, 2007; Momirov & Kilbride, 2005, p. 88).

Given the increasing diversity of immigrants, it is also not surprising to find that more than 16.2 percent of Canadians are visible minorities (usually Chinese, South Asian, or black)—a 27.2 percent increase between 2001 and 2006—and in certain areas, the numbers are much higher. For example, 42.9 percent of Torontonians are members of a visible minority group (Statistics Canada, 2008).

These statistics underscore the continuing importance of recognizing the diversity of cultures that influence Canadian families. Some differences, as in national costume or dates of religious events, may seem trivial, but many, such as differences in mother tongue or cultural beliefs and values, may have a profound impact on almost every aspect of family life. Depending on their cultural background, families embrace varying views on the rights and responsibilities of family members. Issues as crucial and diverse as whether marriages should be arranged or whether wives should have paid employment will be approached differently depending upon ethnic origins. This ethnic diversity is apparent, for example, in patterns of home-leaving among young adult Canadians. In contrast to Canadians with a British ethnic background, Indian, Chinese, and Southern European young adults are likely to delay their first home-leaving. It appears that, in complex interaction with other factors such as religiosity, "normative expectations about appropriate timing and pathways out of the home, such as when to marry or whether to pursue advanced education" are embedded in ethno-cultural backgrounds and directly impact the decision to leave the parental home (Mitchell, Wister, & Gee, 2004).

Ethnic diversity similarly affects the nature and significance of families in Canada's First Nations. In the 2006 census, 1 678 200 people (5.4 percent of the Canadian population) reported Aboriginal ancestry. There is considerable diversity within this population, since these individuals are divided among 48 First Nations, ranging from the 120 000-member Cree to the 85-member Potawatomi, and some are living in large metropolitan areas while others are on remote reserves. However, family life for members of the First Nations is still conditioned by long-standing patterns that have tended to marginalize Native Canadians economically and socially (Castellano, 2002). While individual lives vary, simply by reason of being a Native Canadian you are more likely to be in a low-income category, more likely to commit suicide, more likely to have a variety of serious illnesses, and less likely to have high levels of formal education (Federal,

Provincial, and Territorial Advisory Committee, 1999, p. 47). Aboriginal analysts are pointing to the importance of families—extended family networks in rural communities and reserves; nuclear families and two-generation families in urban and rural communities; and "intentional families" of the heart (voluntary communities)—in supporting efforts to create a vibrant, new Aboriginal presence in Canada (Castellano, 2002).

This significance of family relationships is also apparent among Chinese immigrants to Canada. As of 2001, 93 percent of Chinese Canadians were living in a family household, in comparison to 87 percent of the general population. Strength of family is particularly evident among senior family members. Of Chinese people aged 65 or older, 16 percent were living with a family member, four times the rate in the general population, and only 1 in 10 senior Chinese Canadians lived alone, compared to 3 in 10 in the general population (Chui, Tran, & Flanders, 2005). Clearly, the family is an important resource for both Chinese individuals and the larger Chinese community.

It is important to keep in mind that the family lives of members of various racial and ethnic groups are also affected by the explicit responses of the dominant culture. Members of visible minorities, including immigrants and Native peoples, have frequently been subjected to direct and indirect manifestations of discrimination and cultural domination that have affected the quality, and even the possibility, of family life among minority communities. Historically, immigration policies have intentionally blocked family formation among working-class Chinese, South Asian, and Japanese men and women, and more recently black Caribbean women. Missionary-led residential schools and, later, non-Native child-welfare agencies similarly jeopardized family life among Canadian Native peoples by removing children from their Native communities, undermining familial relationships—especially between children and parents—and terminating Native cultures, languages, religions, education, and economies (Das Gupta, 2000).

One-Parent Families

From television talk shows to government officials, the growing numbers of one-parent families have long been a matter of concern. The increase is no myth, although it is often overstated. After all, in the early 1930s, more than 1 family in 10 was a single-parent family. However, the overwhelming majority of those families were created by the death of a parent. As the adult death rate lessened, so did the proportion of single-parent families. By 1961, there were only 347 400 single-parent families in Canada. The country then began to witness an enormous increase. As of the 2006 census, there were 1 414 060 such families in Canada and 15.9 percent (a staggering one in six) of all census families were lone-parent families—the highest recorded census figure in the last 75 years. The majority (80.1 percent) of single-parent families are headed by women; however, the numbers of father-headed lone-parent families grew by 14.6 percent between 2001 and 2006, while mother-headed lone-parent families grew by only 6.3 percent (Statistics Canada, 2008).

Not surprisingly, this shift in family configuration has triggered a heated debate on the implications of divorce and single-parent families for children.

To understand many one-parent families, we need to view them through the lens of poverty, for that is often the primary source of strain. When a household becomes essentially reliant on the income of one income-earner or when a household's income must be divided to support two separate units, there are frequently not enough financial resources to go around. As a result, the median total annual income for couple families in Canada was $70 400, and for lone-parent families it was $33 000. A third of children living with single mothers were in low income households (*The Daily*, May 5 & June 11, 2008).

The results are serious, not just for these parents and their children but for society as a whole. Children from poor families are penalized with respect to physical, mental, and social health. Level of income is clearly related to a sense of identity and purpose, social contacts, and opportunities for personal growth. For example, children from low-income families are likely to achieve lower levels of education, which, in turn, is likely to translate into higher levels of unemployment (National Council of Welfare, 2004). Although poverty does not inevitably repeat generation after generation, children of poor families are certainly not set up to succeed.

Childless or Childfree Families?

Why do some couples not have children? Sociologist Kathleen Gerson (1985) found that some women see their marriage as too fragile to withstand the strains a child would bring. Other women believe they would be stuck at home—bored and lonely with diminishing career opportunities. Many couples see a child as too expensive or feel that having a child would limit their options in life. With trends firmly in place—more education and careers for women; technological advances in contraception, abortion, and sterilization; and the high cost of rearing children—the proportion of women who never bear children is likely to increase.

According to 2006 census data, 42.7 percent of census families (married and common-law couples) have no children living in the home (Milan, Vezina, & Wells, 2007) (see Table 13.2). This was the first time that there were more census families "without" than "with" children. Many of these families are not child-free by choice. Reflecting the dramatic impact of the baby boom generation, many are empty-nesters whose children have gone off to establish families of their own (Berry et al., 1999, p. 72) and many others are young couples who have not yet had children. However, in the past 20 years, the proportion of married couples with children has declined from almost half (49.4 percent) to slightly more than a third (34.6 percent) (Milan, Vezina, & Wells, 2007).

TABLE 13.2 Percentage of Canadian Families by Living Arrangement, 2006

Married couples with children	34.6
Married couples with no children	34.0
Common-law couples with children	6.8
Common-law couples with no children	8.7
Lone-parent mother-headed families	12.7
Lone-parent father-headed families	3.2

Source: Derived from Milan, Vezina, & Wells, 2007.

Some analysts suggest that one factor at work here is a shift toward the acceptance of childlessness as an acceptable family form. Currently, research suggests that about 10 percent of Canadian women never give birth (Nelson & Robinson, 2002). In part, this reflects the intentions of some men and women not to have children—7 percent of Canadian women and 8 percent of Canadian men aged 20 to 34 indicate that they do not intend to have children (Stobert & Kemeny, 2003). Recent U.S. surveys suggest that there has been a shift toward more positive attitudes among students about childlessness as a life choice and an acceptance that parenthood will be delayed (Koropeckyj-Cox, Romano, & Moras, 2007). In particular, it seems that women are increasingly accepting childlessness as "one possible life path" (Koropeckyj-Cox & Pendell, 2007).

On occasion, the popular media has paid positive attention to voluntary childlessness as a life option (as embodied, for example, in Oprah Winfrey or Condoleza Rice) and challenged the pro-natalist view that all women want to become mothers. Several social groups have also emerged that are devoted to extolling the virtues of adults-only communities, vacation spots, and so forth. For example, the nonprofit social club "No Kidding" provides support for couples who don't have or never want children. Created in 1984, the organization now has 70 chapters throughout North America, with 7000 members and a very active website (McNeely, 2002).

Focus Question

In what ways have major changes in Canadian society increased the likelihood of both single-parent and childless-by-choice families?

Blended Families

An increasingly significant type of family formation found in Canada is the **blended family**, resulting from the remarriage of adults who are parenting one or more children from prior relationships and possibly one or more children they have had together. In 2006, 5.3 percent of all census families were stepfamilies; that is, families in which at least one of the children was from a previous relationship of one of the parents, and 2.4 percent of Canadian families were blended stepfamilies where children of both spouses from one or more unions along with one or more children from the current union were members (Bechard, 2007). With divorce common, many children spend some of their childhood in stepfamilies or blended families. In addition, even if they grow up in a single-parent home, they may have biological parents living elsewhere with new partners and new half-siblings.

SOCIOLOGY AND THE NEW TECHNOLOGY
High-Tech Reproduction and the Formation of Families

One of the unintended consequences of delayed marriage and child-bearing has been an upsurge in infertility among married couples. In response, a variety of technological solutions—such as in vitro fertilization (IVF), the use of donor insemination and donor eggs—have gained public attention. The first successful IVF took place in 1978, when a woman in England gave birth to Louise, the world's first "test-tube" baby. Well over 250 000 children worldwide have been born as a result of the procedure since then (T. Harper, 2000, pp. L1, L3).

The vast majority of IVF children are the biological offspring of the parents who rear them. In some instances, however, single women, both lesbian and heterosexual, have purchased sperm from sperm banks. The resulting child typically does not know the identity of the biological father.

Needless to say, ongoing technological advances in the field have generated heated public debate over the ethical implications. Should 65-year-old women be allowed to use this technology to become mothers? Who should "own" the frozen embryos of deceased couples? Should donors and surrogates be allowed to "sell" their services? Which fertility services—IVF costs about $7000 (including required medication)—should be covered by the government-funded health insurance program? Since the treatment is often unsuccessful, how many attempts should be allowed? And so on. Since each year, an estimated 330 000 Canadian couples seek fertility assistance, this is an important social issue that is likely to stay with us.

Research suggests that only half of children born today will live in a household with their original parents; indeed, one in five Canadian children are not born into a "traditional" family of mother, father, and joint children (Carey, 2001b, p. D3; Mclanahan, 2002). Although still relatively uncommon, the trend toward step- or blended families is important, since research suggests that growing up in either family form may be particularly difficult (Kerr & Michalski, 2007).

Focus Question

What kinds of societal issues are raised by the use of high-tech reproduction assistance by infertile couples?

Gay Families

In 1989, Denmark became the first country to legalize marriage between people of the same sex. Since then, the Netherlands (2001), Belgium (2003), Spain (2005), South Africa (2006), Norway, and Sweden have made same-sex

These septuplets, born to Bobbi McCaughey (an Alberta-born seamstress currently living in Iowa), reflect not only the diversity amongst our families, but also the impact of modern reproductive technologies on our family lives.

marriage legal. In 2001, the Netherlands provided same-sex couples with the right to marriage, adoption, and divorce, placing them at the vanguard of gay rights internationally (Deutsch, 2000). In recent years, Canadian federal and provincial governments have moved increasingly toward legally recognizing gay families. In 1996, the government amended the Canadian Human Rights Code, adding sexual orientation as a prohibited ground of discrimination. Health care benefits were extended to same-sex partners, and the term "common-law spouse" in collective agreements was interpreted to include same-sex couples. In 1998, British Columbia became the first jurisdiction in North America to give same-sex couples the same privileges and obligations as opposite-sex couples (including custody, access, and child support) (O'Brien & Goldberg, 2000). On July 12, 2002, the Ontario Superior Court ruled that the current legal definition of marriage is discriminatory and ordered it changed to include recognition of same-sex marriages. And in June 2005, the Canadian federal government fully recognized and legalized same-sex unions (Larocque, 2006).

These changes reflect greater social acceptance of the 45 300 same-sex couples enumerated in the 2006 census. This census also recorded for the first time the number of married same-sex couples: 7500, or 16.5 percent. In Canada, as in other countries such as New Zealand, Australia, Ireland, and the United States, it appears that slightly less than 1 percent of all households indicate they are same-sex households. In most of these countries, including Canada but excluding New Zealand, male same-sex couples tend to predominate.

Over half of same-sex married couples (53.7 percent) in Canada were male in 2006 and 46.3 percent were female. Children were present in slightly less than one in ten (9 percent) of same-sex-couple homes. Women in same-sex couples were more likely (16.3 percent) than comparable men (2.9 percent) to have children in the home, and same-sex married couples were more likely to have children in the home. As a result of these combined factors, almost a quarter (24.5 percent) of women in same-sex married couples have children. Possibly reflecting the recent changes in social attitudes, men and women in same-sex couples tend to be younger than opposite-sex couples. A quarter of same-sex couples were aged 34 or younger in 2006, and only 3.8 percent were aged 65 or older; less than one-fifth (18.1 percent) of opposite-sex couples were 34 and under (Milan, Vezina, & Wells, 2007).

These new national statistics suggest that there is greater social acceptance of gay and lesbian families. A recent survey reported that almost half of Canadians approve of same-sex marriages and of adoption by homosexual men and women, and the majority (61 percent) of respondents indicated that they feel same-sex couples "can do a good job of raising children." Among young Canadians (under aged 35 years), 74 percent saw same-sex couples as good potential parents (Bibby, 2004–5, p. 9). However, it's important to recognize that many gay and lesbian relationships in Canada and elsewhere continue to be directly affected by a sometimes hostile, even violent, social context (Faulkner, 2001). There has been a long tradition of legal discrimination against gays and lesbians, and growing up gay, lesbian, transgendered, or two-spirited continues to be a difficult and stressful process as negative stereotypes and discriminatory practices continue to abound. In this context, families and communities may take on even greater significance.

Intentional Families

The segmented relationships of contemporary society may make many of us feel emotionally aloof or disconnected from others. Many would like to find a solution to this problem—to enjoy long-term relationships and feel closer to others. To overcome problems of loneliness, some people have started **intentional families**. The members, though not related by blood or marriage, declare themselves a family. They often live separately, but near one another. They meet regularly and share experiences, which adds satisfaction to their lives. The first intentional family, formed in Providence, Rhode Island, has been together for 25 years (Graham, 1996). Analysts suggest that a similar phenomenon exists among contemporary "urban tribes." With growing numbers of 30-something singles living in urban centres (consider the close-knit groups featured on television shows such as *Friends* and *Sex and the City*), young adults may be creating their own family-like support structures to provide a sense of community and belonging (Watters, 2003).

Focus Question

Why would be it be very important for a Grade 1 school teacher to be aware of the possible diversity of family forms?

IN SUM

It is important to keep in mind not only the patterning of family life, but also the diversity of experiences within these patterns. We have considered racial and ethnic diversities, one-parent families, families without children, families formed through reproductive technology, blended families, gay families, and intentional families. Many families combine these diversities, and there are other diversities not included here.

TRENDS IN CANADIAN FAMILIES

Marriage and family life patterns in Canada are in the midst of profound change. The number of "traditional" Canadian family households, comprised of a married heterosexual couple with children, continues to decline. By 2006, only about 39 percent of Canadian census families were heterosexual married couples with children (Milan, Vezina, & Wells, 2007). The remainder of families consisted of married couples (same-sex and opposite sex) without children, same-sex married couples with children, common-law couples with and without children at home, single-mother headed families, and single-father headed families.

Alongside the decline in "traditional" families, there has been a dramatic increase in non-traditional arrangements. The incidence of common-law-couple families continues to increase and is growing faster than married-couple families. Between 2001 and 2006, the number of common-law-couple families grew by 18.9 percent, while married-couple families increased by only 3.5 percent. The 2006 census recorded for the first time that unmarried Canadians (aged 15 and older) outnumbered married Canadians. Over half of the population aged 15 and older had never been married, divorced, separated, or widowed, and only 48.5 percent were legally married in 2006. Twenty years ago, only 38.6 percent of this population was unmarried.

In large part as a result of increased rates of divorce, lone-parent families also grew faster than married-couple families. Reflecting a trend toward more joint-custody arrangements, lone-father families grew by 14.6 percent between 2001 and 2006 and lone-mother families also increased, but by only 6.3 percent. Due to our aging population and reduced numbers of children in families, for the first time the census reported more couples without children than with children. The number of households made up of individuals living alone continued to increase—from 9 percent of households in 1961 to 26.8 percent in 2006 (Milan, Vezina, & Wells 2007: p. 16).

When linked with other changes in the experiences of family life—the dramatically aging population, the shift toward employed mothers, the dramatic growth in the immigrant population, the general urbanization of Canadians, delays in relationship formation and child-bearing, and so on—it is not far-fetched to suggest that many Canadian families are in the midst of foundation-shaking turmoil.

Postponing Marriage and Parenting

After declining since the 1920s, the average age of first-time brides and grooms began an upward trend in the 1980s. In 1925, the average bride was 25 and her groom was almost 30. By 1975, the brides averaged 22 years of age and grooms only 24. Today, the average bride and groom are older than at any other time in the twentieth century (see Table 13.3).

This increased age reflects the fact that both marriage and child-bearing are increasingly being postponed. Growing pressures to spend longer periods in education and employment prior to getting married and having children mean that many women and men are waiting longer before starting families. In 1979, 40.7 percent of women giving birth were aged 24 and under; in 2004 these young women made up only 20.6 percent of all mothers. Conversely, in 2004, births to women aged 35 and older increased almost four times over the pattern 25 years earlier (*The Daily,* July 31, 2006).

TABLE 13.3 Changes in the Average Age of Marriage, Canada, 1925–2003

| Year | Average Age of Marriage | |
	Brides	Grooms
1925	25.3	29.8
1930	25.0	29.2
1935	25.0	29.0
1940	24.4	27.7
1945	25.5	29.0
1950	25.3	28.5
1955	25.1	28.0
1960	24.7	27.7
1965	24.5	27.2
1970	24.9	27.3
1975	22.0	24.4
1980	22.8	25.0
1985	24.1	26.2
1990	25.5	27.4
1995	27.1	29.0
1998	27.6	29.0
2003	28.5	30.6

Source: Statistics Canada e-Book, 2005h, "Marriage," *The People*. Available at http://142.206.72.67/02/02d/02d_001a_e.htm; *The Daily*, January 17, 2007.

Delays in child-bearing have reverberated in terms of reductions in the numbers of children in families. In 1961, about one in six Canadian families was made up of six or more persons, and the average family size was 3.9 people. Today, large families are an oddity, making up a scant 2.6 percent of families, and the average family size has been reduced to 3.0 persons (Statistics Canada e-Book, 2005e). It is now estimated the average woman will have 1.53 children in her lifetime, up only slightly from the record-low fertility rate for Canada set in 2000 (*The Daily*, July 31, 2006). Interestingly, the number stands in sharp contrast to the U.S. fertility rate, which is 2.1.

Focus Question

Does the postponement of marriage and childrearing, along with increases in divorce, signal disillusionment with family life?

Common-Law Marriage

At one time, most Canadians would have been scandalized by the notion of two people living together without a formal married union. Since the 1981 census—the first time the number of common-law families was counted—the numbers have increased by 200 percent (Statistics Canada e-Book, 2005d). Today, over 40 percent of Canadians report that they have lived in a common-law relationship (see Figure 13.3) (Bibby, 2004–5, p. 9), and 18.4 percent of all current couples are common-law. In Quebec, where common-law relationships are particularly popular, 34.6 percent of all couples are common-law unions. This sharply contrasts not only with the rest of Canada, but with other countries, such as Sweden (25.4 percent), Finland (23.9 percent), New Zealand (23.7 percent), and Denmark (22.2 percent) (Milan, Vezina, & Wells, 2007).

For some common-law couples, the relationship is a trial run. They live together as long as the relationship works, and if it sours, they can move out. In line with this pattern, first common-law relationships are twice as likely as first marriages to end in separation. Not surprisingly, children of separated parents are more likely to opt for this kind of trial run, and almost half of common-law relationships end within five years. Further, those common-law couples that do marry are more likely to divorce than those that did not cohabit first (Statistics Canada, 2002c; *The Daily* June 13, 2007).

PERSPECTIVES
Delays in Marriage and Child-Bearing in East Asia

Tendencies toward later marriages, later child-bearing, and reduced fertility are not restricted to the most industrialized countries. In the growing middle class in Vietnam, Thailand, and the Philippines, more and more young women are postponing marriage as they pursue education and careers. As with Canadians, these delays may ultimately result in late or foregone marriage and fewer or no children. Echoing complaints heard in North America during the first wave of the women's movement in the 1920s, there is much talk in the popular press of a "flight" from marriage and the family. Not surprisingly, educated women are being criticized for "imperiling the country's future (i.e., the next generation)" by putting personal interests and careers ahead of traditional responsibilities as wives and mothers (Williams & Guest, 2005).

Although it is important to be aware of the enormous changes occurring in family life, it is also important to locate this change in the context of continuity and tradition. Much has been made, for example, about the new role of many grandparents, who, due to emotional, financial, or other difficulties, end up raising their children's children. In 2006 in Canada, 62 500 grandparents were living with their grandchildren without either of the child's parents being present. Sometimes referred to as "skip-generation households," these arrangements clearly imply a very different relationship between grandchildren and

grandparents (Milan, Vezina, & Wells, 2007). There has also been considerable public discussion of whether grandparents' rights of access to grandchildren in the event of divorce should be enshrined in law (Chau, 2005, p. 22).

It would seem that even grandparenting is in the midst of upheaval. However, changes in grandparenting roles must also be seen as complexly interwoven with tradition. Adult grandchildren, for example, are not abandoning their relationships with their grandparents but are instead seeking a new balance. According to recent research, they juggle competing pres-

sures to "spend time with and respect senior family members" and to satisfy work and educational obligations along with a desire for personal independence. Similarly, most grandparents also negotiate conflicting influences and expectations, not wanting to subject grandchildren to interference yet wanting to be involved and respected (Kemp, 2004). In short, we need to remain attuned to the diversity and complexity of family life and focus on the ways in which new roles and expectations are negotiated in the midst of traditional norms and expectations.

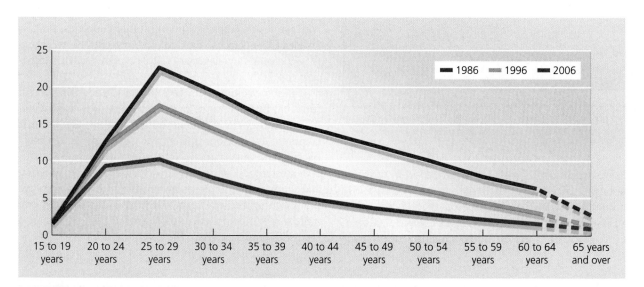

FIGURE 13.3 Persons in Common-Law Couples Increasing for All Age Groups

Divorce and Remarriage

A discussion of the family would not be complete without considering marriage breakup. Many analysts have pointed to increases in divorce as evidence not only that the family is in decline but that our society and its basic social values are in jeopardy. Divorce may be a catastrophic event for a family, with long-term negative consequences for all family members. Sixty-eight percent of Canadians who were children in divorced/separated families indicate that "life was

harder for us" because of their parents' divorce/separation (Bibby, 2004–5, p. 10). Similarly, the Canadian National Longitudinal Survey of Children and Youth, which tracked children over time, found that children whose parents later divorced exhibited higher levels of anxiety, depression, and antisocial behaviour than children whose parents remained married (Strohschein, 2005). However, it is important to be aware that although many marriages end in divorce, most divorces (except in Quebec) end in remarriages (Nelson & Robinson, 2002, p. 347). When marriages fail, Canadian men and women frequently try again, and the overwhelming majority (80 percent) of people with new partners expect their new relationships to last the remainder of their lives (Bibby, 2004–5, p. 10).

In the past, divorce was a distinctly uncommon phenomenon. Until 1968, adultery was the only legal grounds for divorce in most of Canada. Predictably, formal divorces were uncommon, but informal separations and family desertions provided a way out for many unhappy husbands and wives.

In 1968, in response to social pressure, the *Divorce Act* was changed, the grounds for divorce were expanded, and a number of "no-fault, no-blame grounds" were added. In particular, if a couple could demonstrate that they had lived separately for three or more years, they could petition for divorce.

This change in the law opened the floodgates to a backlog of divorce actions. Couples that had been informally divorced made their status official and legitimate. In 1985, the *Divorce Act* was amended again: A couple living separately for a period of not less than one year, as well as adultery or mental or physical cruelty, were viewed as indicative of marriage breakdown and legitimate grounds for divorce (Nelson & Robinson, 2002, pp. 343–344).

The new changes in the law were again reflected in dramatic increases in the number of Canadians obtaining divorces. Table 13.4 reveals increases from 1921 to the mid 1980s and a more recent levelling-off. Today, about 38 percent of Canadians will divorce by their thirtieth wedding anniversary. The rate varies across the country and is much lower for Newfoundlanders and higher for Quebecers. By 2003, the average length of a marriage ending in divorce had increased to 14.2 years and the average age at divorce had risen to 43 for men and 40.5 for women. Only 31 percent of divorces involve custody orders, with 48 percent of primary

TABLE 13.4 Rates of Divorce* in Canada, 1921–2003

1921	6.4
1941	21.4
1968**	54.8
1969	124.2
1981	271.8
1985†	253.6
1987††	362.3
1997	224.8
2003	224.0

*Rate of divorce indicates the number of divorces per 100 000 population.
**Reform of divorce laws
†Divorce Act (no fault)
††Peak Year

Source: Ambert, 2005a, p. 5.

custody arrangements being awarded to mothers (down from 78.2 percent in 1980), 10 percent to fathers, and 42 percent joint custody (Ambert, 2005a, pp. 1, 7, 8, 9; Milan, Vezina, & Wells, 2007).

Focus Question

What sociological factors would be particularly important in explaining the negative impact of divorce and remarriage on children?

THINKING CRITICALLY ABOUT SOCIAL CONTROVERSY
Social Policy and Changes in the Family

Divorce rates provide an excellent example of the interplay between social policy and social patterns. Once divorce laws changed, we witnessed a shift in divorce rates, which then fed further changes in attitudes toward divorce, which were in turn reflected in further liberalization of divorce laws. This underscores the importance of the role of social policy in changing the possibilities in family life. For example, changes in the provision of maternity and parental leave in Canada in 1971, 1990, and 2000 have improved the nature and amount of government support that new mothers and fathers can expect. These changes have resulted in more mothers staying home on parental leave for longer periods of time and more fathers availing themselves of parental leave. In this way, paid employment is experienced as less of an obstacle to caring for very young children (Marshall, 2003; *The Daily*, June 13, 2007).

Divorce is a global phenomenon. Our neighbour to the south has the highest divorce rate in the industrialized world, with about 40 percent of men and women in their 50s indicating they have been divorced at some point in their lives and more than a million children a year learning that their parents are divorcing (Henslin, 2008: p. 486). Further, there are likely to be continued changes in the global patterns of divorce (see Table 13.5). Despite the prevailing impression that Islamic cultures are conservative and opposed to women's rights within marriage, significant shifts are occurring in the Muslim world. Tunisia and, more recently, Egypt (March 2000) have enacted laws that allow women to seek a unilateral, no-questions-asked divorce; in short, women in these countries have gained divorce rights similar to those of men (United Nations Population Fund, 2000, p. 55). As occurred in Canada, changes in divorce laws often precede dramatic changes in the rates of divorce.

In the wake of divorce, men are more likely to remarry and to remarry more quickly than women. This may reflect not only the smaller pool of potential partners for women, but also men's greater motivation to remarry. Research has consistently indicated that men derive greater benefit from marriage—in terms of increased life expectancy, for example—than women. Presumably, men derive considerable benefit from the familial gender

roles in which women are expected to bring to the marriage: companionship skills as well as housekeeping abilities. In line with this, women who possess very high levels of education and income are less likely to remarry than their less-educated, less well-to-do counterparts (Nelson & Robinson, 2002, pp. 347–348). Evidently, women who are more educated and more independent (no children) can afford to be more selective.

TABLE 13.5 Rates of Divorce: International Perspective, 2000 (per 1000 population aged 15 to 64)

Canada	3.4
Denmark	4.0
France (1999)	3.1
Ireland	1.0
Italy	1.0
Japan	3.1
Spain	1.4
Sweden	3.8
United Kingdom	4.0
United States	6.2

Source: U.S. Census Bureau, 2005, *Statistical Abstract of the United States, 2004–2005.* Table 1327, p. 847.

IN SUM

Not only is it vital to appreciate the variety of family forms in Canada, but we must recognize that families are in the midst of important changes. Increasing numbers of Canadians are postponing marriage and parenting. They are also much more likely to enter into common-law relationships. As more Canadians become seniors, middle-aged Canadians are finding that family responsibilities involve providing care for aging parents. Although divorce statistics appear to have hit a plateau, divorce is becoming an increasingly common ingredient of family life for Canadians.

Focus Question

What social factors would be useful in explaining the different rates of divorce around the world?

TWO SIDES OF FAMILY LIFE

Family life may bring with it enormous personal benefits and satisfactions; conversely, it may incorporate the worst aspects of human existence. First, let's discuss the troubled family and then consider the prospects for happier familial relations.

The Dark Side of Family Life: Child Abuse, Battering, and Incest

CHILD ABUSE Most of us are appalled by child abuse—helpless children victimized by their own parents, the adults who are supposed to love, protect, and nurture them. The most gruesome of these cases make the evening news—a four-year-old girl beaten and raped by her mother's boyfriend or six-to-ten-year-old children videotaped in sex acts by their stepfather. But few of the less-sensational child abuse cases come to our attention: children who live in filth, those who are neglected, those who are left alone for hours or days at a time, and those who are "disciplined" with extension cords.

The latest available crime statistics indicate that in 2005, 163 out of every 100 000 children and youth were the victims of physical or sexual assault by a parent. Of all family members, including siblings and extended family members, parents were much more likely to commit assaults on their children. Most of the violence is physical, with physical assault rates three times higher than sexual assault rates by parents. Reflecting gendered patterns of violence, male family members were identified as the "accused" in 97 percent of all family-related sexual assaults and 71 percent of physical assaults against children and youth. Specifically, fathers comprised 38 percent of accused family members, with extended male family members (31 percent) and brothers (28 percent) filling out the ranks. Female family members were rarely identified as perpetrators of violence against children and youth. However, in instances of female-perpetrated physical assaults on children, mothers were accused in 82 percent of the cases.

Not surprisingly, girls are much more likely (three times) to be victims of sexual assault by family members than boys.

Reflecting the intersecting patterns of sexuality, gender, and age, boys are more likely to be sexually assaulted when they are between the ages of 3 and 5, while girls' rates are highest between 12 and 15 years of age.

Suggesting that physical violence may be rooted in power struggles among family members, overall rates of family-related physical assaults tended to increase with the age of the victim. Physical assaults peaked at age 17 for girls and at age 12 for boys.

Family violence against children and youth is not insignificant. A third (36 percent) suffered a minor physical injury and 1 percent a major injury in 2005 (according to police reports) (Brzozowksi, 2007). Indeed, of the 60 children or youth murdered in 2005, a third were killed by family members, most often parents. Between 1996 and 2005, 56 percent of children and youth killed by a family member were killed by their fathers, 33 percent by their mothers, and 11 percent by other family members. The majority of victims of family violence were infants (28 percent), with family homicide rates declining as children grew older (McGechie, 2007).

While physical and sexual abuse and murder capture the headlines, numerous Canadian children are abused by being neglected or exposed to growing up in a violent home. Recent research suggests that when children witness physical fights between adults or teenagers in their home, they are more likely to be physically aggressive, to commit property offences, and to display emotional disorders ("The harm that family violence does to children," 2001, p. 19).

Globally, we know that in many countries, accepted social practices result in the routine abuse of children, especially female children. The routine acceptance of physical punishment (including spanking) of children continues to contribute to child maltreatment and child deaths (Gracia & Herrero, 2008). In some countries, it has been socially accepted to deliberately allow certain children to die of exposure or to deliberately smother or drown unwanted children. Age-old patterns of infanticide and neglect (along with sex-selective abortion) are reported to have resulted in the elimination of 60 million girls from Asian populations. Honour killings (or rapes) of young girls suspected of dishonouring their families by losing their virginity or acting in an "unchaste" manner are a socially sanctioned form of child murder. Female genital mutilation, which has been performed on at least 130 million girls and often results in persistent gynecological problems, may be viewed as a socially accepted expression of child sexual abuse. Child labour, particularly in the form of child prostitution, is a culturally embedded practice that destroys childhoods around the world. It is estimated that 2 million girls between the ages of 5 and 15 are introduced, often by family members, to the commercial sex market each year, some ending up on the streets of Toronto and Vancouver (United Nations Population Fund, 2000; Seager, 2003). Child abuse, when viewed from this perspective, is a complex, growing, and global reality.

BATTERING Thanks in large measure to Statistics Canada's landmark 1993 *Canadian Violence Against Women Survey* and the now yearly family violence statistical profiles, we have excellent national statistics concerning wife battering. In the 1993 survey, almost one woman in three (29 percent) who had ever married or lived in a common-law relationship revealed at least one episode of violence by a husband or live-in partner (H. Johnson, 1996). Although spousal violence reported to police has declined in recent years, it remains an important social issue, with 55 350 incidents in 2002 and 74 homicides in 2005. Eighty-five percent of the victims of spousal violence are women and spousal homicide rates against females were three to five times higher than those against males from 1975 to 2005 (Brzozowski, 2004c, p. 5; Ogrodnik, 2007).

The global picture is alarmingly similar. A quick review of the literature indicates that violence against women in intimate relationships remains commonplace. In South Africa, 13 to 29 percent of women say they have experienced physical abuse by a male intimate; in India, 26 to 40 percent, and in Norway, 18 percent (Seager, 2003, pp. 26–27; Amnesty International, 2004). In the United States between 2000 and 2006, more than 8000 women were killed by the intimate males in their lives (Vallee, 2008). In some countries, abuse is amplified by a cultural tolerance for violence against women—a view shared by both men and women. In rural Egypt, for example, 80 percent of women surveyed said that beatings were common and justified, especially if the woman refused her partner sex. In some countries (such as the case of dowry murder in India), prevailing laws and practices mean that male attackers will seldom be punished and women have little access to alternative shelter (United Nations Population Fund, 2000; Rudd, 2001).

Focus Question

How is violence in the family connected to gender inequalities in society?

OTHER FORMS OF FAMILY VIOLENCE This brief discussion leaves aside other significant aspects of family violence. A quick survey of your friends will reveal that sibling violence is very common and not always innocuous, for example. In addition, although assumed to be relatively uncommon, analysts are paying increasing attention to violence against men in intimate relationships (Lupri & Grandin, 2004). Growing research is also documenting the extent to which parents may be the victims of violence at the hands of their children (Beauchamp, 2007; Cottrell, 2003).

The Brighter Side of Family Life

After examining divorce and family abuse, one could easily conclude that marriages and families seldom work. That would be far from the truth. Ninety-seven percent of Canadians in a recent survey indicated they would agree or strongly agree that they would describe their marriages as

While contemporary families are under tremendous pressures from society, they remain for their members an important source of joy, fulfillment, and social connection.

"very happy" or "pretty happy." Further, 95 percent of those who were married or widowed indicated that they would marry again if they had it to do over (Bibby, 2004–5, p. 6). Although they recognize a negative side to marriage—in terms of tensions around money, children, household duties, and communication—they also point out the benefits marriage offers, such as security, a sense of belonging, and a unique relationship (Bibby, 2004–5, p. 6).

There are some general social factors that help predict "lasting" marriages. Being wealthy, religious, college-educated, not living common-law before marriage, and postponing marriage to at least age 20 are all factors associated with low rates of divorce ("U.S. study tries to unravel mysteries of lasting marriages," 2002, p. A12). Further, research suggests that those who devote energy to maintaining their marriages will reap benefits in terms of the marital bond. Older people generally rate the quality of their relationships highly and, with increasing age, feel increasingly positive about their relationships (Chalmers & Milan, 2005).

IN SUM

Social researchers are increasingly aware that numerous families are often troubled and even violent. Abuse is particularly troublesome when the victims are children or seniors, since they are often trapped by the power of their "caregivers." Women are also common victims of family violence. Given that family life may go tragically wrong, it is important to be aware of the ingredients for a good marriage. As a society, we are increasingly aware of family dynamics, and we can reasonably anticipate that in the immediate future, many families will continue to evolve as they struggle to keep up with larger societal changes.

The Future of Marriage and Family

What can we expect of marriage and family in the future?

Certain trends are firmly in place. Family events—home-leaving, first marriage, first child—will continue to be delayed. There will be increasing individualization in terms of both the timing of family changes and the nature of family forms. For example, cohabitation, mother-headed families, and blended families will continue to signify a diversity of family types. More married women will join the workforce, and they will continue to gain marital power. There is likely to be a continued shift toward greater equality in family life as men spend more of their youth living independently (in college dorms, for example) and learning the skills needed to share the housework (Pitt & Borland 2008). The number of elderly will continue to increase, and more couples will find themselves "sandwiched" between caring for their parents and their own children.

Our culture will continue to be haunted by distorted images of marriage and family: the bleak ones portrayed in the mass media and the rosy ones painted by cultural myths. Sociological research can help correct these distortions and allow us to see how our own family experiences fit into the patterns of our culture. Sociological research also can help to answer the big question of how to formulate social policy that will support and enhance family life as we move ever more into "uncharted territory" (Bianchi, Robinson, & Milkie, 2006).

Focus Question
What will the Canadian family look like in 20 years?

SUMMARY AND REVIEW

Marriage and Families in a Global Perspective

WHY DO CONTEMPORARY SOCIOLOGISTS REFER TO "FAMILIES" RATHER THAN "THE FAMILY"?

The notion of "the family" implies that there is one standard type of family. Certainly for a short period of time in the past, the expected family form was a mother and father, legally joined in marriage, living with their biological children in a common residence. Today, a minority of families share these characteristics. One-parent, blended, same-sex, and other forms of families have proliferated. As a result, using the term "the family" harkens back to this "traditional" model of families and is not only inaccurate but may hide a conservative agenda; that is, that families ought to have these characteristics. pp. 280–283.

Marriage and Families in a Theoretical Perspective

WHAT ARE THE DIFFERENCES BETWEEN THE FUNCTIONCTIONALIST, CONFLICT/FEMINIST, AND SYMBOLIC INTERACTIONIST THEORETICAL APPROACHES TO FAMILY LIFE?

Functionalists tend to examine families in terms of the services they provide for the larger society and for other institutions in that society. They are inclined to argue, for example, that all societies have families because they must have a mechanism of socializing children, caring for the sick and aged, and providing for the production of the next generation. Conflict theorists tend to focus on the power struggles and inequalities within and between families. For example, feminists have focused on the struggle over the division of household work and the pressures on women to contribute to household incomes as important elements in family satisfaction and changes in familial roles. Symbolic interactionists are particularly interested in the construction and perpetuation of meanings in family lives. Being a father is complexly interwoven with the meanings attached to masculinity in a particular society. Men may avoid certain aspects of the fathering role because they believe some acts (changing diapers) may mean (to themselves or to others) that they are less manly. pp. 283–289.

The Family Life Cycle

WHAT ARE THE MAJOR PATTERNS THAT EXIST WITHIN THE RICH DIVERSITY OF FAMILY LIFE EXPERIENCES?

From a life cycle perspective, families typically go through a series of stages. First, there is some form of mate selection and relationship formation. In many western societies, couples date, fall in love, and become engaged (often reflected in a decision to live common-law). Whether or not they formalize their relationship with a legal and/or religious ceremony, most couples will confront childrearing. The majority of couples will adopt or bear children and will spend several decades raising these children. In later life, contemporary couples may find that their adult children remain in the home. As a result of divorce or widowhood, most parents (especially mothers) will find themselves on their own in their later years. pp. 289–294.

Diversity in Canadian Families

WHAT ARE THE OUTSTANDING FAMILY FORMS IN CANADA?

Contemporary Canadian families include married couples with and without children, common-law couples with and without children, and lone-parent families headed by either mothers or fathers. These families include same-sex families, step-, and blended families. pp. 294–298.

Trends in Canadian Families

WHAT KINDS OF CHANGES IN CANADIAN FAMILY LIVES ARE CURRENTLY OCCURRING?

There are trends toward decreased numbers of traditional families and increased numbers of common-law families, blended/stepfamilies, and father-headed lone-parent families. There are increased numbers of households made up of individuals living alone. Marriage and child-bearing are being delayed longer. Mothers continue to move into the paid labour force. More fathers are taking time off work to partake of parental leave when their children are born. There are more Canadians families without children. pp. 298–302.

Two Sides of Family Life

WHAT ARE SOME OF THE SOCIAL CAUSES OF FAMILY VIOLENCE AND ABUSE?

Long-standing patterns of gender inequality contribute to abuse of children and wives. The patriarchal tradition in many societies has tended to legitimate violence against girls and women. This tradition continues to echo in some familial relationships; for example, husbands may feel they own their children or wives and may treat them as property. The long-standing acceptance of punishment of children (and, previously, wives) also serves to provide a rationale for contemporary "disciplining" of children. Many other forms of child abuse—notably, neglect—are the direct results of poverty and patterned economic inequality. pp. 302–304.

Theoretical Paradigms

	CLASSICAL PARADIGMS		RECENT PARADIGMS
	Structural-Functional Paradigm	Symbolic-Interaction Paradigm	Feminist Paradigm
What is the level of analysis?	Macro level	Micro level	Macro level
What is the importance of families for society?	Society depends on families for reproduction, socialization of children, support for educational processes, and economic activities.	Family roles are crucial to our sense of meaning and identity. Being a father or a mother, for example, is a key ingredient in the social construction of masculinity or femininity.	Struggles over division of household labour within the home reflect larger social patterns of inequality surrounding gender. The expectation that women will do the "lion's share" in the home reflects and reinforces the generalized subordination of women in society.
Have families changed over time? How?	Yes, many of the traditional functions of the family have been taken over by other agents—including the school system, daycare centres, and even Molly Maid.	Yes, the meanings people attach to family roles have shifted. Being a mother, for example, is now generally accepted as compatible with paid employment.	Yes and no. The division of domestic labour has moved toward greater equality, but there still remains a tendency for women to take the majority of responsibilities for children and chores.

KEY TERMS

WEBLINKS

All URLs listed are current as of the printing of this book.

National Clearinghouse on Family Violence
www.phac-aspc.gc.ca/nc-cn/
The National Clearinghouse on Family Violence is a national resource centre for all Canadians seeking information about violence inside the family and looking for new resources being used to address it. The Clearinghouse seeks to help Canadian communities work toward the eventual elimination of all forms of family violence.

Vanier Institute of the Family
www.vifamily.ca
The Vanier Institute of the Family was established in 1965 under the patronage of their Excellencies Governor General Georges P. Vanier and Madame Pauline Vanier. It is a national voluntary organization dedicated to promoting the well-being of Canada's families through research, publications, public education, and advocacy. The website is a very useful resource for examining trends in Canadian families.

Children's Defense Fund
www.childrensdefense.org
The mission of the Children's Defense Fund is to "ensure every child a Healthy Start, a Head Start, a Fair Start, a Safe Start, and a Moral Start in life and successful passage to adulthood with the help of caring families and communities."

CRITICAL THINKING QUESTIONS

1. How would the participants in "successful" marriages address the issue of the division of household work?

2. How are the interconnections between the family and other societal institutions—the economic system, the education system—likely to change in the near future?

3. Given that the Canadian family is going through a number of important changes, what particular family issues confront children and adolescents today?

4. Have the dramatic changes in family life in Western countries benefited women or not? Access the Research Navigator through MySocLab and use keywords such as "divorce," "single-parents," and "housework" to locate relevant and recent scholarly and popular press publications to help you answer this question.

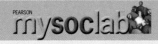 PEARSON mysoclab

Explore the topics covered in this chapter on MySocLab using the access information provided with this text. Interactive resources for studying include multimedia tutorials, video clips, practice tests, quizzes, and animated maps and figures.

14 Education and Religion

Neha still feels resentment when she recalls the memo that greeted her that Monday morning:

> With growing concern about international competition for our products, the management is upgrading several positions. The attached listing of jobs states the new qualifications that must be met.

Neha quickly scanned the list. The rumours had been right, after all. The new position the company was opening up—the job she had been slated to get—was listed.

After regaining her composure somewhat, but still angry, Neha marched into her supervisor's office. "I've been doing my job for three years," she said. "You always gave me good evaluations, and you said I'd get that new position."

"I know, Neha. You'd be good at it. Believe me, I gave you a high recommendation. But what can I do? You know what the higher-ups are like. If they decide they want someone with a university degree, that's just what they'll get."

"But I can't go back to university now, not with all my responsibilities. It's been five years since I was in university, and I still have a year to go."

The supervisor was sympathetic, but she insisted that her hands were tied. Neha would have to continue working at the lower job classification—and stay at the lower pay.

It was Neha's responsibility to break in Melissa, the newcomer with the freshly minted university degree. Those were the toughest two weeks Neha ever spent at work—especially since she knew that Melissa was already being paid more than she was.

TODAY'S CREDENTIAL SOCIETY

Sociologist Randall Collins (1979) observed that industrialized nations have become **credential societies**, that employers use diplomas and degrees to determine who is eligible for a job. In many cases, the diploma or degree is irrelevant for the work that must be performed. The new job that Neha wanted, for example, did not suddenly change into a task requiring a university degree. Her immediate supervisor knew Neha's abilities well and was sure she could handle the responsibility just fine—but the new company policy required a credential that Neha didn't have. Similarly, a high school diploma is not necessary to pump gas or to sell shoes, yet employers routinely require such credentials.

In fact, it is often on the job, not at school, that employees learn the specific knowledge or skills a job requires. A high school diploma teaches no one how to sell tacos or be polite to customers. Neha had to teach Melissa the ropes. Why do employers insist on diplomas and degrees? Why don't they simply use on-the-job training?

A major reason credentials are required is the large size, urbanization, and consequent anonymity of industrial societies. Diplomas and degrees serve as automatic sorting devices. Because employers don't know potential workers personally or even by reputation, they depend on schools to weed out the capable from the incapable. By hiring graduates, the employer assumes that they are hiring responsible people; for evidently they have shown up on time for numerous classes, have turned in scores of assignments, have obeyed—or at least have not detoured too far from—the many rules of universities, and have demonstrated basic writing and thinking skills. The specific job skills that a position requires can then be grafted onto this base certified by the academic institution.

In other cases, specific job skills must be mastered before an individual is allowed to perform certain work. As a result of changes in technology and knowledge, simple on-the-job training will not suffice for physicians, engineers, and airline pilots, which is precisely why doctors prominently display their credentials. Their framed degrees declare that they have been certified by an institution of higher learning, that they are qualified to work on our bodies.

A high school diploma is regarded as the minimum qualification for young Canadians entering the labour market. Analysts suggest that two thirds of new jobs created between 2004 and 2008 require postsecondary education or management training (Shaienks, Eisl-Culkin, & Bussiere, 2006: p. 6).

In general, unemployment rates are lower among the more highly educated. In Canada in 2006, the unemployment rate among university graduates aged 25 to 54 was 4.2 percent. In contrast, within the same age group, 9.4 percent of those who did not finish high school were unemployed (Statistics Canada, March 2008: p. 15).

Without the right credentials, you won't get hired. It doesn't matter that you can do the job better than someone else. You will never have the opportunity to prove what you can do, if, like Neha, you lack the credentials to even be considered for the job.

THE DEVELOPMENT OF MODERN EDUCATION

Credentials are only one indicator of how central the educational institution is in our lives. Before exploring the role of education in contemporary society, let us first look at education in earlier societies, and trace the development of universal education.

Education in Earlier Societies

In earlier societies, there was no separate social institution called education. There were no special buildings called schools, and no people who earned their livings as teachers. Rather, as an integral part of growing up, children learned what was necessary to get along in life. If hunting or cooking were essential skills, then people who already possessed those skills taught them. *Education was synonymous with* **acculturation**, the transmission of culture from one generation to the next—as it still is in today's tribal groups.

Education can be a dangerous thing. Socrates, who taught in Greece about 400 years before the birth of Christ, was forced to take poison because his views challenged those of the establishment. Usually, however, educators reinforce the perspectives of the elite, teaching students to take their place within the social structure. This fresco is from Rome, circa 50 B.C.

In some societies, when a sufficient surplus accumulated—as in China, North Africa, and classical Greece—a separate institution developed. Some people then devoted themselves to teaching, while those who had leisure time—the children of the wealthy—became their students. In ancient China, for example, Confucius taught a few select pupils, while in Greece, Aristotle, Plato, and Socrates taught science and philosophy to upper-class boys. **Education** came to be something quite distinct from informal acculturation; education is a group's *formal* system of teaching knowledge, values, and skills. Such instruction stood in marked contrast to the learning of traditional skills such as farming or hunting, for it was clearly intended to develop the mind.

Education flourished during the period roughly marked by the birth of Christ, then slowly died out. During the Dark Ages in Europe (the thirteenth and fourteenth centuries), the candle of enlightenment was kept burning by monks, who, except for a handful of the wealthy and nobility, were the only people who could read and write. Although they delved into philosophy, the intellectual activities of the monks centred on learning Greek, Latin, and Hebrew so that they could read early texts of the Bible and writings of the church fathers. Similarly, Jews kept formal learning alive as they studied the Torah.

Formal education, however, remained limited to those who had the leisure to pursue it. (In fact, school comes from a Greek word meaning "leisure.") Industrialization transformed this approach to learning, as new machinery and new types of jobs brought a general need to be able to read, write, and work accurately with figures—the classic "three Rs" of the nineteenth century ("Reading, 'Riting, and 'Rithmetic").

Industrialization and Universal Education

The development of universal education is linked to industrialization. Let's see how free universal education developed in Canada.

Prior to Confederation, mainly religious groups were most involved in education. The primary goal, particularly among Christian groups, was to "civilize" First Nations Canadians, along with other children, by teaching them a curriculum based on the "three Rs." The church's influence on education, however, was significant, and lessons usually included guidance in morality and obedience. Both Catholic and Protestant (or public) school systems were created even before Confederation. The *School Act* of 1851 provided Roman Catholics with public funds for their schools, a topic of ongoing controversy even today. The development of higher education was also linked to religious bodies. North America's oldest institution of higher learning, Laval University in Quebec City, was founded by Jesuit priests in 1636. The founders of both the University of Toronto and McGill University were linked to the Church of England.

By the time of Confederation, the makings of a free and universal education system had been firmly entrenched. A number of school acts were passed throughout Upper and Lower Canada providing for schools within bounded areas, and school attendance gradually began to increase as the value of education was recognized across communities. Commitment to education was regarded not only as a personal benefit, but also as a civic responsibility, since schooling the masses was considered to be the means to social improvement. Education was a matter of **political socialization**, the way young people would be inculcated with beliefs, ideas, and values and would embrace the civil order, all of which was necessary for the developing capitalist and industrial order. A universal system of schooling based on standardized texts instilled patriotism and taught the principles of democratic government.

In Ontario, Reverend Egerton Ryerson, who was the province's superintendent of schools from 1844 to 1876, was instrumental in establishing the system of free, publicly supported schools. His work in Ontario was eventually followed by educational activists throughout Canada. Prior to Ryerson's work, formal education was optional for working-class children. Most children learned from their parents in and around the home or in small workshops that dotted the Canadian landscape. Upper-class children attended costly private schools or were taught in their homes by tutors. In 1871, schooling was made compulsory and the relationship between the school and the state tightened. The common school became "a public institution in the modern sense of the term, an institution not only paid for out of public funds, but with publicly defined goals" (Prentice, 1977, p. 17). It is no coincidence that universal education and industrialization occurred simultaneously. Seeing that the economy was undergoing fundamental change, political and civic leaders recognized the need for an educated workforce. They also feared the influx of foreign values and looked on public education as a way to socialize immigrants into the Canadian way of life.

Over time, the amount of education considered necessary continued to expand. By 1920, most provinces had compulsory education laws requiring children to attend school, usually until they had completed Grade 8 or turned 16, whichever came first. In the early 1900s, graduation from Grade 8 was considered to be a full education for most people. "Dropouts" were students who did not complete grade school. High school, as its name implies, was viewed as a form of "higher" education.

As industrialization progressed and as fewer people made their living from agriculture, formal education came to be thought of as essential to the well-being of society. Industrialized nations then developed some form of the credential society described earlier. Graduation with a post-secondary certificate or university degree is increasingly common in Canada. Between 1980 and 2005, the income gap between less educated young workers and those who were well-educated widened significantly. There are a number of reasons why this difference in income levels exists.

Some argue that technological change requiring a more highly skilled labour force accounts for the difference, while others point to losses in manufacturing and other highly unionized jobs together with growth in economic sectors, such as retail, where wages are typically low (Chung, 2006: p. 5). With the loss of many assembly jobs as industries move to China, India, or other lower-wage countries, there have been fewer opportunities available to Canadian workers who do not graduate from high school (Ibid.). Predominant among those who have not completed high school are older workers over the age of 55. Between 1980 and 2005, the percentage of Canadians in the labour force without a high school diploma decreased from 29 percent of those aged 25 to 34 in 1980 to 9 percent in 2005. Among Canadians aged 35 to 54, 47 percent had some high school or less in 1980 but only 13 percent had less than a high school diploma in 2005 (Chung, 2006: p. 5). Today, the majority of university graduates (60 percent) are women (Frenette & Zeman, 2007). Women with college diplomas outnumber college-educated men, while the majority of those holding trade certificates or licenses are men. Overall, 44 percent of working-age Canadians—evenly split between university and college or vocational programs—have attained a postsecondary degree or diploma (Brown, 2006: p. A4).

Canadians who don't make it through high school, however, are condemned to a difficult economic life. Analysts have estimated that university graduates may earn up to $1 million more over their lifetimes than high school graduates (Brown, 2006: p. A4). On average, the unemployment rate among high school leavers is higher, their wages are lower, and they are less likely to work full-time, full-year compared to high school graduates (Morisette, Ostrovsky, & Picot, 2004; Chung, 2006). Moreover, the International Adult Literacy Survey concluded that, as compared to their counterparts in other countries, poorly educated Canadians with less than a high school education tend to perform poorly in simple daily literacy tasks (Statistics Canada, 2004d). The rates of high school graduation are not evenly distributed across the provinces. Relatively higher numbers in Newfoundland, the Northwest Territories, Prince Edward Island, and Saskatchewan leave school before completing high school. To some degree, the rates of school leaving correlate with the distribution of poverty within the provinces, with the relatively poorer provinces having a higher number of school leavers and the relatively well-off having greater numbers of university graduates.

Canada ranks fourth among developed countries for the percentage of its labour force holding a university degree (20 percent). Canada is behind Norway (26 percent) and the Netherlands (21 percent), and ahead of the United Kingdom (18 percent), Sweden (17 percent), Korea (17 percent), and Australia (19 percent). However, Canada ranks second (21 percent), trailing only Iceland (22 percent), in the percentage of the labour force holding college diplomas (Organization for Economic Cooperation and Development (OECD), 2002). If we consider only younger adults aged 25 to 34, Canadians have shown considerable improvements in postsecondary attainment as compared to other OECD countries. In 2007, Canada and Korea stood well ahead of other OECD countries, with over 50 percent of those aged 25 to 34 having obtained higher educational credentials (Ischinger, 2007). However, Canada's commitment to education may be questioned. Canada ranked fifteenth among 39 OECD countries in 2005 on the proportion of the GDP it spent on research and development, a number that had not changed since 2001. And on another measure, Canada ranked tenth out of 11 OECD countries in the number of science and engineering degrees as a percentage of all new degrees granted in 2005 (Canadian Council on Learning, 2007: p. 13).

Focus Question

How are education and industrialization linked?

Focus Question

What is political socialization and how does it take place through education?

THE FUNCTIONALIST PERSPECTIVE: PROVIDING SOCIAL BENEFITS

As stressed in previous chapters, a central position of functionalism is that when the parts of society are working properly, each contributes to the well-being or stability of the society as a whole. The intended consequences of people's actions are known as **manifest functions**, while those that are not intended are called **latent functions**. As we examine the functions of education, its manifest and latent functions will become evident.

Teaching Knowledge and Skills

Education's most obvious manifest function is to teach knowledge and skills, whether they are the traditional three Rs or more contemporary competencies such as computer literacy and internet skills. Every society must train the next generation to fulfill its significant positions. From a functionalist perspective, this is the reason that schools are founded, supported by parents, and financed by taxes.

Cultural Transmission of Values

At least as significant as teaching knowledge and skills is a function of education called **cultural transmission**, a process by which schools pass on a society's core values from one generation to the next. In addition to responding to the demands of the economy, the need to produce an informed electorate, and the desire to "Canadianize" immigrants, in what other ways does the educational system reflect—and transmit—cultural values?

Schools are such an essential part of Canadian culture that it is difficult to know where to begin. Outside Quebec, instruction takes place primarily in English, reflecting the dominant British influence on Canadian institutions and culture. The perspective conveyed in the classroom is predominantly Western. The Western perspective, essentially the point of view of the dominant group, neglects to tell the stories of minority groups, often those who have suffered at the hands of these dominant groups. Aboriginal or First Nations groups are sometimes portrayed in negative ways or might be absent from school texts and discussions. Slavery and other acts of discrimination, such as the treatment of Japanese-Canadians during World War II, are introduced as unfortunate, inexcusable, and isolated events that should not have happened, but are now in the past. There is little in the curriculum on working-class or union history, politics, arts, and culture. Similarly, the architecture of school buildings themselves reflects Western culture, and their often distinctive appearance—typically low rise boxy buildings with adjacent playing fields or running tracks—identify them as schools on sight.

If we think of political teaching and cultural training within schools as running on a continuum from a very conservative approach to one incorporating more liberal viewpoints, then situated on the extreme right would be fundamentalist groups from the Christian right. The recent Oscar-nominated and award winning documentary *Jesus Camp* (2006) follows the lives of a group of young children as they are trained to assume leadership roles within a particular sect of evangelical Christianity. This training includes homeschooling, thereby isolating the children from a wider range of viewpoints and ideas. Many question the extreme training practices in which the children are repeatedly reduced to tears to atone for their sins. Coupled with homeschooling, where the children are taught that creationism has all the answers and that science is evil, these practices are considered by many to be intense forms of indoctrination.

With just under 5.3 million students attending elementary and high schools in 2004/05 (Statistics Canada, August 30, 2007), and over 1 million enrolled in universities in 2005/06 (Statistics Canada, February 8, 2008), Canadian education is big business. In 2004/05, the total expenditure on public education was $44.5 billion, or, in other words, the cost to Canadian taxpayers was $9040 per student (Statistics Canada, August 30, 2007). Education institutions at all levels have become major employers, providing relatively well-paid work for thousands of professionals. In addition to classroom teachers and university professors, thousands more work providing classroom support as aides, administrators, bus drivers, janitors, and secretaries. Others earn their living in industries that service schools—from building schools to manufacturing pencils, paper, computers, and desks to providing insurance, cleaning supplies, and food. In 2002, 44 percent of Canadian households each spent an average of $2119 on educational expenses for books, supplies, and tuition (Statistics Canada, 2005b). Overall, Canada spends billions on education, recording the second highest level of total expenditure in relation to the GDP among the G-7 countries (Canadian Education Statistics Council, 2006, p. 21).

To better understand the connection between education and values, let's look at how the educational system transmits individualism, competition, and patriotism.

INDIVIDUALISM Individualism forms a thread integrally woven into the Canadian educational system. Unlike their Japanese counterparts, Canadian teachers and students

Corporations can sometimes play a significant role in the education system. Over the years, some schools have negotiated agreements with specific corporations in return for funding. However, while students may benefit from the extra money their school has managed to acquire in this way, the students' ideas, values, and overall school experiences are often influenced by that company's corporate agenda.

seldom focus on teamwork. Where Japanese schools stress that the individual is only one part of a larger, integrated whole, Canadian students learn that the individual exists on his or her own. Pervasive but often subtle, such instruction begins in the early grades, when teachers point out the success of a particular student. They might say, for example, "Everyone should be like Joey," or "Why can't you be like María, who got all the answers right?" In such seemingly innocuous statements, the teacher thrusts one child ahead of the rest, holding the individual up for praise. Schools continue to select class valedictorians, reward high achievers, sponsor athlete-of-the-year banquets, and participate in science fairs, math competitions, and spelling bees. In each of these events, in the end, usually only one student takes home the coveted prize.

COMPETITION Competitive games in the classroom and the schoolyard provide an apt illustration of how schools transmit this core value. In the classroom, a teacher may divide the class into competitive groups for a spelling bee, while on the playground children are encouraged to play hard-driving competitive games and sports. A school's formal sports programs—baseball, football, basketball, soccer, hockey, volleyball, and so on—pit students against one another as they try out for spots on the teams and then pit team against team in head-to-head confrontations, driving home the lesson that the competitive spirit is highly valued. Although organized sports stress teamwork, the individual is held up for praise. The custom of nominating an "outstanding player" (emphasizing which of these persons is the best) reinforces the related lesson of individualism.

PATRIOTISM As in schools around the world, schools in North America teach patriotism. Canadian students are taught that Canada is the best country in the world; Americans learn that no country is better than the United States; and French, German, British, Spanish, Japanese, Chinese, Afghani, and Egyptian students all learn the same about their respective countries. To instill patriotism, elementary school teachers in every country extol the virtues of their society's founders, their struggle for freedom from oppression, and the goodness of the country's basic social institutions.

Sociologist Randle Nelsen (2002) argues that, in today's schools, education has become infused with popular culture in such a way that education has evolved into "edu-tainment" and the corporate presence at schools and on college and university campuses represents the encroachment of the corporate agenda into curriculums and therefore into the heart of education. In the U.S., the amount of company sponsorship at the elementary and high schools levels has rapidly increased, with global and local companies footing bills for sports programs and football stadiums. It is becoming commonplace to see advertisements around schoolyards, on uniforms, on walls, and even sculpted into the landscape (Pennington, 2004).

In step with practices in the U.S., highbrow fundraisers are becoming commonplace in Canada. A recent national study by the Canadian Teachers' Federation found that public schools on average raised almost $16 000 per year, with some schools netting close to $50 000. At the far end, one Ontario high school raised $250 000 (Alphonso, 2005: p. A6). Corporate sponsorships buy basics, including textbooks, library materials, and classroom technology, and pay for special events, such as school trips and athletic programs and clubs. Many parents and educators worry about the long-term outcomes of what might seem like innocuous activities. In particular, concerns have been raised that fundraising and corporate sponsorships recreate inequality. Schools in wealthier neighbourhoods are generally more successful in raising adequate and even surplus amounts of money for the basics and beyond. This leaves many communities questioning the responsibility of the state in providing equal opportunities to children and youth through education.

As elaborated in the Thinking Critically about Social Controversy box on page 314, not only have schools, and particularly university and college campuses, taken on a "shopping mall" appearance, but the transformation in the appearance of the "ivy walls" represents long-term contracts and agreements that institutions have struck with big business—and such relationships that have affected dominant values, ideas, and experiences of the school system.

Focus Question
How does the educational system transmit values of individualism and competition?

Schools socialize students politically by incorporating, however subtly, dominant values, ideas, and experiences. Most school lessons are taught primarily from a white, middle-class, male, non-Native perspective.

For decades, critics have exposed the intricate ways that the corporate agenda has directed and shaped the structural forms and intellectual pathways of educational institutions, starting with the seemingly linear links realized through individuals who play pivotal roles in connecting the two. The encroachment of the corporate agenda into the sphere of education is no longer debated as it was throughout the last century, when those defending the form and structure of educational institutions argued that non-partisan educational decision-makers should be drawn from among those men (and sometimes women) who held esteemed positions within the economy and broader society. With insights drawn from their professional experience largely within the corporate world and as members of academic governing boards, these prominent players were expected to protect the academy's autonomy and ensure that its researchers and educators maintained their course in the pursuit of knowledge while drawing interest, respect, and material support from corporate and political networks.

In the past, corporate connections to education were less obvious, and were traced by critics primarily through members of boards of governors, the majority of whom had résumés that included an impressive list of directorships in both top-ranking and local business concerns. Schools maintained their autonomy, at least in appearance. Today, corporate presence is striking, and academic administrators covet long-term contracts and reciprocal agreements with big business. Ontario university campuses, for example, have become the site of Pepsi–Coke cola wars. A number of schools have signed deals with either company, stipulating that the competitor's products will not be sold anywhere on campus.

The agreements give Pepsi or Coke full rights at the exclusion of the other (as well as the less popular brands), thereby guaranteeing a market of primarily young consumers whose preferences (for Pepsi or Coke) may be formulated or confirmed during their years at school. Similar binding agreements are signed with fast-food chains, many of which are located within the same corporate empire, such as the well-known Pepsi–Pizza Hut relation. And these agreements are not only signed at colleges and universities, where it is generally easier for students and staff to access alternative businesses within their local communities, but an increasing number of high schools have committed to such arrangements in exchange for sponsorship of events (basketball tournaments, band exchanges, ski trips) and the provision of resources and equipment (sports scoreboards, computers).

For the institutions, a successful corporate campaign has been key to economic survival. Those spearheading corporate fund-raising campaigns argue that such initiatives are necessary to support an increasingly expensive academic infrastructure, particularly in light of the state's dismantling of the welfare state, including its former commitments to higher education and its adoption of a monetarist economic program. Within the context of globalization, one of the primary goals for the state is to reduce the costs of production and reproduction. This is accomplished in part through cutbacks in health care, social programs, and education. For some, the invitation to establish corporate agreements is a reasonable course in heading off the inevitable tide of privatization. However, as Nelsen (2002) poignantly observes, "education becomes edu-tainment" and a student culture, marked by political dissent, is replaced by popular culture. The campus, once a site of protest and resistance, becomes even more firmly ensconced within the throes of corporatism.

As schooling is transformed into edu-tainment, the educator steps into the role of performer. Those professors who have taught large undergraduate classes with any degree of success will readily describe the experience as physically exhausting, largely because of demands for a flawless performance that is somewhat entertaining and well-paced to maintain interest and allow for salient points to be noted. Within mass culture, scholarship and intellect may be confused with Trivial Pursuit. Game shows like *Who Wants to Be a Millionaire?* to some degree condition our understanding of intellect and provide rewards for straight-forward facts. As schools become further corporatized, it is within similarly narrow parameters that their curricula and institutional form will be shaped as corporatization demands compartmentalization. We may not wish to reconstruct the traditional academy of past decades and we certainly do not want to reproduce the exclusivity of the past. However, we might struggle to revive the intellectual culture that is today lost within the edu-business framework.

Source: Adapted from Pupo (2002).

Social Integration

Schools also perform the function of social integration, helping to mould students into a more or less cohesive unit. Indeed, as just discussed, forging a national identity by integrating immigrants into a common cultural heritage was one of the manifest functions of establishing a publicly funded system of education in Canada. When children enter school, they come from many different backgrounds. Their particular family and social class may have taught them speech patterns, dress, and other behaviours or attitudes that differ from those generally recognized as desirable or acceptable. In the classroom and on the playground, those backgrounds take new shape. The end result is that schools help socialize students into the mainstream culture.

Peer culture is especially significant, since most students are eager to fit in. From their peers, they learn ideas and norms that go beyond their family and their little corner of the world. Guided by the powerful world of mass media, many succumb to peer pressure, particularly during early and middle adolescence (Ambert, 2001; 2006). While peer pressure may result in students in all parts of the country sporting the same brands and styles of jeans, shirts, shoes, and jackets and using similar speech patterns, sharing ideas, and interacting with the opposite sex in similar ways, there are aggressive, nasty, harmful, and even violent sides to peer pressure (Corsaro, 2004).

Peer culture may also turn awry, with those not seen as fitting in becoming targets for insults, pranks, or more serious and violent words and actions, as evident in the increased incidence of bullying in Canadian schools. Bullying, often a topic for community forums, professional development days, and public discussion, is considered a serious and growing problem among adolescents. It has also been the theme of a number of recent films, including the highly acclaimed *Welcome to the Dollhouse* (1996). The popular film *Napoleon Dynamite* (2004) exposes the ways in which "life at high school is a daily misery for Napoleon," the title character, who is "tall, ungainly, depressed and happy to be left alone" (Ebert, 2004). As well-publicized cases in British Columbia, in Taber, Alberta, and at Columbine High School in the United States, among others, indicate, bullying in its extreme form has pushed many to suicide and others to violent actions, including murder. The case of Reena Virk, who was swarmed, beaten, and drowned by seven girls and a boy, aged 14 to 17, under a bridge in Saanich on Vancouver Island in 1997 stands as testimony to strong pressures teens face to fit in and the price they may pay in doing so.

The classroom itself helps to produce social integration. As students learn about Confederation and the Canadian Charter of Rights and Freedoms, take Civics class in high school, or sing "O Canada," they become aware of the "greater government," and their sense of national identity grows. One indicator of how education promotes political integration is the millions of immigrants who have attended Canadian schools, learned mainstream ideas, and given up their earlier national and cultural identities as they became Canadians. Schools also socialize students politically by incorporating and emphasizing, however subtly, dominant values, ideas, and experiences. Teaching is primarily from a white, middle-class, male, non-Native perspective. Many critics have exposed the ways structural barriers, such as racism, classism, and sexism, operate within the Canadian school system to limit the level of participation and success of minority students (C. James, 2003).

How significant is this integrative function of education? It goes far beyond similarities of appearance or speech. To forge a national identity is to stabilize the political system. If people identify with a society's social institutions and perceive them as the basis of their welfare, they have no reason to question or rebel. This function is especially significant when it comes to the working classes, in which the greatest desire for and the strongest pursuit of social and political change ordinarily develops. The wealthy already have a vested interest in maintaining the status quo, but to get the working classes to identify with the Canadian social system as it is goes a long way toward its preservation.

Gatekeeping

Gatekeeping, or determining which people will enter what occupations, is another major function of education. Credentialling, the subject of the opening vignette, is an example of gatekeeping. Because Neha did not have the required credentials, but Melissa did, education closed the door to one person and opened it to the other. Yet, as sociologist David Livingstone (1999) argues, many workers are vastly underemployed, and this may be so because we usually focus on the question of how schools should prepare students for work, rather than how work might make use of people's education, continuing learning capacities, and knowledge. As feminists argue, knowledge and skills acquired through cultural teachings and practices, or through experience in managing households or engaging in caring and other family and community-related work, for example, are disregarded. Exclusively emphasizing school learning as preparation for jobs disadvantages those who are unable to acquire the specified credentials.

Essential to the gatekeeping function is **tracking**, or sorting students into different educational programs on the basis of real or perceived abilities. Tests are used to determine which students should be directed into "university-bound" programs, while others are put on a vocational track. The impact is life-long. As we saw with Neha and Melissa, throughout adulthood, opportunities for jobs, raises, and promotions open or close on the basis of education.

Tracking begins in elementary school, where, on the basis of test results, most students take regular courses, but some are placed in programs for the "gifted" or in advanced sections of English and mathematics. In high school, tracking becomes more elaborate. In many schools, students are funnelled into university-bound, non-university-bound, or vocational programs. Others are placed in classes for students with "special needs." All students who complete their sequence of courses receive high school diplomas, but not all graduates are eligible to go on to higher education. Those in vocational or non-academic streams are most likely to enter the workforce after high school or perhaps will take a vocational or trade course; those in the academic streams enter university; and those in between may attend a community college to obtain a diploma or certificate in one of a number of semiprofessional, technological, or vocational fields.

Recent studies have confirmed results consistent with a number of previous studies that indicate that in general, the likelihood of attending university increases as family incomes increase (Drolet, 2005; Canadian Council on Learning, 2007). The university attendance rate of children from families whose incomes are $100 000 or more is twice the rate of those from families with incomes below $25 000 (Drolet, 2005). In Ontario, for example, over 82 percent of families whose annual earnings were $120 000 or more in 2001, compared to 53 percent of those earning between $30 000 and $50 000 that year, had saved for their children to attend college or university (Canadian Council on Learning, 2007: p. 75). Along with income, parents' education is also strongly related to participation in higher education. In 2001, only 17 percent of youth whose parents had a high school education or less attended university, compared to 28 percent of youth whose parents were college-educated and 50 percent whose parents were university-educated (Drolet, 2005). Tables 14.1 and 14.2 provide data on postsecondary participation by household income and by parental education.

In an earlier study of Ontario schools, researchers concluded that children whose parents are in unskilled jobs are 10 times more likely than children whose parents are professionals to be directed toward non-college-or-university-bound high school programs. Also, working-class children are far less likely than others from higher social class backgrounds to go to university, a result of the way the school system sorts students. Not only is this a shameful waste of human potential, but it discriminates against working-class and poor children (Curtis, Livingstone, & Smaller, 1992).

Besides academic achievement, which many suggest is related to social class, students are provided with opportunities on the basis of other characteristics, such as gender. Today, the educational attainment of females in Canada is surpassing that of males. In 2006, 58 percent of students in bachelor degree programs in Canadian universities were women. This represents an enormous increase in female participation rates since the 1970s, when only one in three students in full-time programs was female. In addition, today women account for about half of Master's students and 45 percent of Ph.D. students (Canadian Council on Learning, 2007: p. 77). Not only are women outnumbering males in classrooms and lecture halls, but the graduation rates for women have been consistently increasing since the 1970s, whereas the rates for males have been declining (Ibid.). The most recent figures, from the 2006 census, indicate that 60 percent of university graduates aged 25 to 29 are women (Statistics Canada, April 29, 2008).

However, some fields, such as engineering, are still male-dominated. Males earn over 75 percent of engineering degrees, and at the undergraduate level, women are underrepresented in mathematics and the physical sciences. At the same time, men are underrepresented in nursing, rehabilitation medicine, social work, languages, education, and a number of the social sciences, including psychology and sociology (Statistics Canada, 2004e). Considering these patterns, we might conclude that males and females are sent down separate gender-specific career paths and that these paths are to some degree mapped out by their school-related experiences, including advice from guidance counsellors, encouragement from teachers and parents, and reception from other students.

TABLE 14.1 Postsecondary Participation by Household Income in Canada, 2001

Before Tax Parental Income Range	University Participation Rate	College Participation Rate	Total Participation Rate
Less than $25 000	20%	29%	49%
$25 001–$50 000	23%	37%	60%
$50 001–$75 000	25%	38%	63%
$75 001–$100 000	38%	38%	76%
More than $100 000	46%	32%	77%

Source: Berger, J., Motte, A., & Parkin, A. *The Price of Knowledge 2006–07*. Canada Millennium Scholarship Foundation, 2007, cited in Canadian Council on Learning, 2007, p. 76.

TABLE 14.2 Postsecondary Participation by Parental Education in Canada, 2001

Highest Level of Parental Education	University Participation Rate	College Participation Rate	Total Participation Rate
University	50%	32%	81%
Postsecondary certificate/diploma	28%	40%	68%
High school or less	17%	36%	53%

Source: Berger, J., Motte, A., & Parkin, A. *The Price of Knowledge 2006–07*. Canada Millennium Scholarship Foundation, 2007, cited in Canadian Council on Learning, 2007, p. 76.

Gatekeeping sorts people on the basis of merit, according to functionalists. Sociologists Talcott Parsons (1940), Kingsley Davis, and Wilbert Moore (1945), who pioneered this view, also known as **social placement**, argue that a major task of society is to fill its positions with capable people. Some positions, such as that of a physician, require a high intellect and many years of arduous education. Consequently, to motivate capable people to postpone immediate gratification and submit to many years of rigorous education, high income and prestige are held out as rewards. Other jobs require far fewer skills and can be performed by people of lesser intelligence. Thus, functionalists look on education as a system that, to the benefit of society, sorts people according to their abilities. Clearly education plays a role in promoting personal change, broadening people's outlooks, networks, and perspectives, and often contributes to social change

Mainstreaming

A new function of education is **mainstreaming**, incorporating people with disabilities into regular social activities. As a matter of routine policy, students with disabilities used to be placed in special schools. Educators concluded that in these settings, such students learned to adjust only to a world of the disabled, leaving them ill-prepared to cope with the dominant world. The educational philosophy then changed to having students with disabilities attend regular schools.

Mainstreaming is easiest for students whose disabilities are minor, since they fit more easily into regular schools. For people who cannot walk, schools (and other public facilities) have been required to build wheelchair ramps; for those who cannot hear, "signers" (interpreters who use their hands) may attend classes with them. Most blind students still attend special schools, as do people with severe learning disabilities.

Replacing Family Functions

Canadian schools have begun to rival some family functions. Child care is an example. Elementary schools do double duty as babysitting services for working parents. Child care always has been a *latent* function of formal education, as it was an unintended consequence of schooling. Now, however, since most families have two wage earners, child care has become a manifest function. Some schools even offer child care both before and after formal classes. Another example is providing sex education and birth control advice, which has stirred controversy. Some families resent this function being taken from them. Many parents object to schools usurping their role, and to their children being taught values that violate their own. Many would condemn a graphic presentation of how to put on a condom.

THE CONFLICT PERSPECTIVE: REPRODUCING THE SOCIAL CLASS STRUCTURE

Unlike functionalists, who see education as a social institution that performs functions for the benefit of society, conflict theorists see the educational system as a tool used by those in the controlling sector of society to maintain their dominance and keep people in line.

The Hidden Curriculum

The term **hidden curriculum** refers to the unwritten rules of behaviour and attitudes, such as obedience to authority and conformity to cultural norms, that are taught in schools in addition to the formal curriculum (Gillborn, 1992). Conflict theorists contend that this hidden curriculum perpetuates social inequalities.

According to conflict theorists, the primary functions of bureaucratically organized schools are to teach acceptance of hierarchical control, obedience to authority, and acceptance of rules regardless of their logic or purpose.

To better understand this central point, consider the values and work habits that students are taught in school: obedience to the teacher, punctuality, and turning in neat work on time. These traits are highly desired by employers, who want dependable, docile, subordinate workers. Or just consider the emphasis on "proper" English. Members of the elite need people to run their business empires, and they are more comfortable if their managers possess the "refined" language and manners that they themselves are used to. Consequently, middle-class schools, whose teachers know where their pupils are headed, stress "proper" English and "good" manners. In contrast, because fewer children from working-class or minority backgrounds will occupy managerial positions, their teachers will be more lenient in allowing street language in the classroom and are less concerned with students' grammatical skills.

Each type of school helps reproduce the social class structure, then, by preparing students to work in positions similar to those of their parents. They are "taught" to internalize negative perceptions of the working class that reproduce their status and, therefore, reinforce such perceptions, creating and perpetuating the cycle (Willis, 1981). Some children, socially destined for higher positions, learn "refined" speech and manners. Others are simply taught to obey rules so they can take their place in the closely supervised, low-status positions for which they are socially destined (Bowles & Gintis, 1976; Olneck & Bills, 1980). From the conflict perspective, even kindergarten has a hidden curriculum, as illustrated in the Down-to-Earth Sociology box.

Tilting the Tests: Discrimination by IQ

Even intelligence tests play a part in keeping the social class system intact. For example, how would you answer the following question?

A symphony is to a composer as a book is to a(n)

paper _____

sculptor _____

musician _____

author _____

man _____

You probably had no difficulty coming up with "author" as your choice. Wouldn't any intelligent person have done the same?

In point of fact, this question raises a central issue regarding biases in intelligence and standardized testing. Not all intelligent, capable, or skilled people would know the answer, because the question contains *cultural biases*. In other words, children from some backgrounds are more familiar with the concepts of symphonies, composers, sculptors, and musicians than other children. Consequently, the test is tilted in their favour (Turner, 1972; Ashe, 1992).

Perhaps asking a different question will make the bias clearer. How would you answer the following question?

If you throw dice and "seven" is showing on top, what is facing down?

seven _____

snake eyes _____

box cars _____

little Joes _____

eleven _____

This question, suggested by Adrian Dove (n.d.), a social worker in Watts, is slanted toward a working-class experience. It surely is obvious that this *particular* cultural bias tilts the test so that children from some social backgrounds will perform better than others.

Speaking a language students understand is key to reaching them. Working with youth in detention centers, Ras Mo Moses, an anti-violence educator, draws on rap to get through to young offenders. Recognizing that youth listened to and identified with rap, he turned to dub poetry, a Jamaican art form popularized in the 1970s. By writing new lyrics and maintaining the rhythm of rap, Moses captured students' attention because his approach was, in his words, "culturally appropriate, something they could relate to" (Borcea, 2007: p. A3).

It is no different with IQ (intelligence quotient) tests that use such words as *composer* and *symphony*. A working-class child may have heard about rap, rock, hip hop, or jazz, but not about symphonies. In other words, IQ tests measure not only intelligence but also culturally acquired knowledge. Everything else aside, the cultural bias built into the IQ tests used in schools is clearly not tilted in favour of the working classes.

A second inadequacy of IQ tests is that they focus on mathematical, spatial, symbolic, and linguistic abilities. Intelligence, however, consists of more than these components. The ability to compose music, to be empathetic to the feelings of others, or to be humorous or persuasive are also components of intelligence. Questions regarding who composes test questions, what the tests are trying to achieve, and who they are geared toward should be raised. In addition, many parents and educators are aware that standardized testing neglects learning disabilities and different ways of learning and expression.

The significance of these factors, according to conflict theorists, is that culturally biased IQ tests favour the middle classes and discriminate against students from lower-class backgrounds. An important consequence is that children from poor families or who are recent immigrants whose first language may not be English may score lower on average on standardized tests, and on this basis may be assigned to less demanding courses or streams thought to appropriately match their test scores. This affects their education, and ultimately, their work futures. Conflict theorists view standardized tests as maintaining the social class structure across generations.

Kindergarten as Boot Camp

After conducting participant observation in a kindergarten, sociologist Harry Gracey (2007) concluded that kindergarten is a sort of boot camp for the entire educational system. Here, tender students from diverse backgrounds are drilled in the behaviours and attitudes deemed appropriate for the "student role" and made to follow classroom routines. The goal of kindergarten is to mould many individuals from diverse backgrounds into a compliant group that will, on command, unthinkingly follow classroom routines.

Kindergarten's famous "show and tell," for example, is not merely a tool for encouraging children to be expressive. It also teaches them to talk only when they are asked to speak ("It's your turn, Jarmay"). The practice also instructs children to request permission to talk ("Who knows what Letitia has?") by raising a hand and being acknowledged. Show and tell also teaches children to acknowledge the teacher's ideas as superior. She is the one who has the capacity to evaluate students' activities and ideas.

Gracey found a similar *hidden curriculum* in the other activities he observed. Whether drawing pictures, listening to records, or participating in snack time or rest time, teachers would quiet talkative students, even scolding them at times, while giving approval for conforming behaviours. In short, the message is that the teacher—and, by inference, the entire school system—is the authority.

Gracey concluded that this is not merely a side issue—it is *the* purpose of kindergarten. The kindergarten teacher's job is to teach children to "follow orders with unquestioning obedience." To accomplish this, kindergarten teachers "create and enforce a rigid social structure in the classroom through which they effectively control the behaviour of most of the children for most of the school day." This produces three kinds of students: (1) "good" students, those who submit to school-imposed discipline and come to identify with it; (2) "adequate" students, those who submit to the school's discipline but do not identify with it; and (3) "bad" students, those who refuse to submit to school routines.

Children in the third category are called "problem children." To bring them into line, tougher drill sergeants, such as the principal and the school psychologist or social worker, are called in. If that doesn't work, "problem children" are drugged into docility with Ritalin.

These early lessons extend well beyond the classroom. As Gracey notes, school serves as a boot camp, preparing students for the routines of the work world, whether on the assembly line or at the office. Mastering the student role prepares them to become docile workers and to follow unquestioningly the routines imposed by "the company."

Stacking the Deck: Unequal Funding

Conflict theorists stress the central role that funding for education plays in perpetuating social inequalities. Funding is a scarce resource unequally distributed among rich and poor students. The vast regional inequality in Canada affects access to education and the unequal distribution of resources pushes education out of the reach of students in poorer areas. A greater percentage of the population over age 25 in the relatively richer provinces have university degrees, while at the other end, the relatively poorer provinces have the highest proportion of adults with less than a Grade 9 education (Davies & Guppy, 2006). Moreover, a greater percentage of Aboriginal students compared to non-Aboriginal students drop out of school, although there are fewer dropping out today as compared to the number of dropouts in earlier decades (Canadian Education Statistics Council, 2000; Canadian Council on Learning, 2007). Although there has been a significant increase in the participation of Native groups in higher education, particularly over the past 20 years, attendance and participation rates of Aboriginal people lag far behind the rates for all Canadians. First Nations peoples living on reserves have identified a number of barriers preventing them from attending university or college. These barriers include inadequate funding, poor academic preparation, having to support their families, and feeling unwelcome on campuses (Canadian Council on Learning, 2007: p. 76).

The low rate of school completion in the Northwest Territories in part reflects the abysmal way schooling has been provided for Aboriginal Canadians. Under the residential school system, formally operated by the Canadian government through the *Indian Act* of 1876, between 1892 and 1969, Native children were separated from their families, often by force, and taken to boarding schools, where they were stripped of their Indianness. They were not allowed to speak in their Native languages, nor were they provided with opportunities to learn from within and about their own cultures. Many students suffered sexual, physical, and emotional abuse in these schools, which were eventually abolished (MacKinnon, 1999). Overall, about 130 000 Native children were taken into the country's 130 residential schools. After 1969, some of the schools remained in operation, but were run by churches and eventually by band councils. Akaitcho Hall in Yellowknife, the last residential school to remain open, was finally closed in 1994 (Mironowicz, 2002).

Since then, overall education levels on reserves have increased, but there are still wide gaps between levels of school completion for Native populations and those for Canada as a whole. In 2001, about 48 percent of Aboriginals aged 20 to 24 living off reserves had not completed secondary school. While this represented a drop from previous years, it compares poorly with the general rate for all Canadians in that age group. By 2001, only 26 percent of the general population aged 20 to 24 had not completed secondary school (Turcotte & Zhou, 2004). The dropout rate among Canadian youth is relatively low. Calculations indicate that it steadily declined from 21 percent to 14 percent for males and from 16 percent to 9 percent for females between 1990/91 and 2005/06 (Raymond, 2008: p. 9). In general, school leavers face a number of labour market challenges. Not only are they less likely to find work, but the jobs they do find typically have lower wages, higher rates of unemployment, and less security than those of high school or postsecondary graduates (Raymond, 2008; Canadian Council on Learning, 2007). Across Canada, the rate of dropping out varies, and currently the highest rate is in Quebec (Zeman, 2007). School leavers tend to be from lower socioeconomic backgrounds, often from single- and no-parent families, and usually experience pressures to enter the labour market.

On the plus side, an increasing number of dropouts return to school. Three out of ten re-entered in 2005/06, and this upward trend may be the result of increasing labour market pressures and rising job requirements, as well as new programs designed to give those who dropped out a second chance. Men and women drop out of school for different reasons. For girls, it is most often for personal reasons—29 percent of female dropouts in 2006 were mothers with one or more children (Faulkner, 2008: p. A4). Boys' reasons tend to relate to jobs—labour market conditions and wages—or to their performance—grades and disinterest (Ibid.). Among those who dropped out of high school, 21 percent of girls, compared to 14 percent of boys, went on to post secondary education in 2004 (Shaienks, Eisl-Culkin, & Brussiere, 2006: p. 32).

The disparities across Canada in educational attainment may be explained by a variety of additional factors, including distance from a postsecondary institution (Statistics Canada, 2004f) and parents' educational attainment. Education is a provincial matter and there are vast economic differences between provinces in the tax bases from which funding is drawn. Decisions made by local school boards may also account for variations between and within provinces. Some provinces have larger urban areas, and generally rural areas are relatively poorer. In urban areas, the demand for higher educational credentials is higher and relates to the types of industries and work available. Provinces such as Ontario, for example, house high-profile law and medical schools that attract students from across Canada. The existence of a degree-granting institution within a community is a drawing card for a highly educated workforce. The Northwest Territories does not have a university. Many young residents who leave never return, eventually settling in the community where they graduated (Humphreys, 1998).

Conflict theorists go beyond these observations, however. They stress that in each province and community, the deck is stacked against the poor. Because public schools are largely supported by local property taxes, the richer communities (where property values are higher) have more to spend on their children, while the poorer communities end up with much less. Consequently, the richer communities are able to offer higher salaries (and take their pick of the most highly qualified and motivated teachers); afford the latest textbooks and computers, teach additional courses in languages, music, and arts; and provide better opportunities for young athletes interested in sports programs. Because schools so closely reflect the Canadian social class system, the children of the privileged emerge from elementary and middle schools best equipped for success in high school. Wealthier families are often more able to afford opportunities such as private schooling or tutoring in addition to being more likely to afford university or a prestigious postsecondary institution. In turn, they come out of high school best equipped for success in university. Their greater likelihood of success in university, and in high-status professional programs such as medicine and law, in turn, serves to maintain their dominance.

The Correspondence Principle

Conflict sociologists Samuel Bowles and Herbert Gintis (1976) used the term **correspondence principle** to refer to the ways schools reflect the social structure of society. This term means that what is taught in a nation's schools corresponds to the characteristics of that society. Thus education helps to perpetuate a society's social inequalities. The following list provides some examples.

CHARACTERISTICS OF SOCIETY

1. Capitalism

2. Social inequality

3. Racial-ethnic prejudice

4. Bureaucratic structure of the corporation

5. Need for submissive workers

6. Need for dependable workers

7. Need to maintain armed forces and agents of control

CHARACTERISTICS OF SCHOOLS

1. Promote competition

2. Unequal funding of schools, track the poor to job training

3. Make minorities feel inferior, track minorities to job training

4. Provide a model of authority in the classroom

5. Make students submissive, as in the kindergarten boot camp

6. Enforce punctuality in attendance and homework

7. Promote nationalism (to fight for capitalism)

Thus, conclude conflict theorists, the Canadian educational system is designed to produce dependable workers that will not question their bosses, and produce some individuals who will go on to be innovators in thought and action but can still be counted on to be loyal to the social system as it exists (Olneck & Bills, 1980).

The Bottom Line: Family Background and the Educational System

The end result of unequal funding, standardized tests, and so on is that family background proves more important than test scores in predicting who attends university. In 1977, sociologist Samuel Bowles compared the college attendance of the brightest 25 percent of high school students in the United States with the intellectually weakest 25 percent. Of the brightest 25 percent, 90 percent of those from affluent homes went to college, while only half of those from low-income homes did. Of the weakest students, 26 percent from affluent homes went to college, while only 6 percent from poorer homes did.

Canadian sociologists also found that in Canada, students from a higher class background were far more likely to go to university than poorer students within the same cohort (Porter, Porter, & Blishen, 1979; Davies & Guppy, 2006). And today? The same general relationship still holds. If you rank families from the poorest to the richest, as the income increases, the likelihood that the children will attend institutions of higher learning also increases (Manski, 1992–1993; Curtis, Livingstone & Smaller, 1992; Davies & Guppy, 2006).

Conflict theorists point out that the educational system reproduces the wealth-poverty divide within the Canadian social class structure. Like Neha in the opening vignette, those without degrees have less access to jobs with better pay and potential for advancement. Then, too, there is the program and the type of institution attended. Wealthy

Canadians are more likely than others to attend private schools and prestigious and internationally renowned universities.

The purpose of the educational system, according to conflict theorists, is to reproduce inequality, to help keep the social class structure intact from one generation to the next. Consequently, most children from less privileged families are funnelled into job training programs, while children of the middle classes attend universities and community colleges. The offspring of the elite, in contrast, attend exclusive private schools, such as Upper Canada College, where their learning environment includes small classes and well-paid teachers (Persell et al., 1992). Here they inherit a cozy social network between the school's advisors and the admissions officers of the nation's and the world's most elite institutions. Some of these networks are so efficient that a majority of these private schools' graduating classes are admitted to McGill, University of Toronto Law School, or University of Western Ontario's Business School, or to Harvard, Yale, or Princeton in the United States.

Focus Question
What are some of the ways the education system reproduces inequality?

THE FEMINIST PERSPECTIVE

Feminist approaches to the sociology of education raise questions regarding women's place in schools at all levels, in knowledge production and distribution, and in the construction of research questions and programs about education. A primary concern of feminism is to promote social justice, and in developing their analysis of education and schools, feminist approaches are interconnected with analyses of inequalities, including race, class, disabilities, sexual orientation, and ageism.

Liberal feminists are most concerned with basic equality issues within schools and educational institutions. They want to see women have equal opportunities, and catch up to men with regard to educational attainment, access to educational programs, and respect and consideration in academic circles. Radical feminists are more interested in giving women a "voice" within classrooms, within the sphere of knowledge production, and within all levels of education. Their concern is less in accessing the avenues that will allow them to achieve equity with men, but more in developing a woman-centred approach to education that denies men systematic power and dominance over women. In this scenario, women's experiences and understandings of social processes are foremost. Socialist feminists are concerned with the intersections of race, class and gender, and argue that patriarchal relations, including those intertwined in the fabric of schools and educational programs and processes, must be dismantled in order to establish a truly just society.

THE SYMBOLIC INTERACTIONIST PERSPECTIVE: TEACHER EXPECTATIONS AND THE SELF-FULFILLING PROPHECY

Whereas functionalists look at how education functions to benefit society and conflict theorists examine how education perpetuates social inequality, symbolic interactionists study face-to-face interactions in the classroom. They have found that the expectations of teachers have profound consequences for their students.

The Rist Research

Symbolic interactionists have uncovered some of the dynamics of educational tracking. In what has become a classic study, sociologist Ray Rist conducted participant observation in an African-American grade school with an African-American faculty. Rist (1970) found that after only eight days in the classroom, the kindergarten teacher felt that she knew the children's abilities well enough to assign them to three separate worktables. To Table 1, Mrs. Caplow assigned those she considered to be "fast learners." They sat at the front of the room, closest to her. Those whom she saw as "slow learners," she assigned to Table 3, located at the back of the classroom. She placed "average" students at Table 2, in between the other tables.

This pattern seemed strange to Rist. He knew that the children had not been tested for ability, yet the teacher was certain that she could differentiate between bright and slow children. Investigating further, Rist found that social class was the underlying basis for assigning the children to the different tables. Middle-class students were separated out for Table 1, children from poorer homes to Tables 2 and 3. The teacher paid the most attention to the children at Table 1, who were closest to her, less to Table 2, and the least to Table 3. As the year went on, children from Table 1 perceived that they were treated better and came to see themselves as smarter. They became the leaders in class activities and even ridiculed children at the other worktables, calling them "dumb." Eventually, the children at Table 3 disengaged themselves from many classroom activities. Not surprisingly, at the end of the year only the children at Table 1 had completed the lessons that prepared them for reading.

This early tracking stuck. When these students entered Grade 1, their new teacher looked at the work they had accomplished and placed students from Table 1 at her Table 1. She treated her tables much as the kindergarten teacher had, and the children at Table 1 again led the class.

The children's reputations continued to follow them. The Grade 2 teacher reviewed their scores and also divided her class into three groups. The first she named the "Tigers," and, befitting their name, gave them challenging readers. Not surprisingly, the Tigers came from the original Table 1 in kindergarten. The second group she called the "Cardinals." They came from the original Tables 2 and 3. Her third group consisted of children she had failed the previous year, whom she called the "Clowns." The Cardinals and Clowns were given less advanced readers.

Rist concluded that the child's journey through school was determined at the eighth day of kindergarten! What had occurred was a **self-fulfilling prophecy**, a term coined by sociologist Robert Merton (1949/1968) to refer to an originally false assumption of what is going to happen that comes true simply because it was predicted. Labels are powerful. They can set people on courses of action that affect the rest of their lives. That, of course, is the significance of Rist's observations of these grade school children.

How Do Teacher Expectations Work?

How do teacher expectations work? Observations of classroom interaction give us some idea (Leacock, 1969; Rist, 1970; Buckley, 1991; Farkas, 1996; Farkas, Sheehan, & Grobe, 1990b; Farkas, Grobe, Sheehan, & Shuan, 1990a). A teacher's own middle-class background comes into play, for teachers are pleased when middle-class students ask probing questions. They take these as a sign of intelligence. When working-class students ask similar questions, however, teachers are more likely to interpret their questions as "smart aleck." In addition, working-class children are more likely to reflect a subculture that "puts down" intellectual achievements, an attitude that causes teachers to react negatively. As with social class, there are also questions regarding the intersection of race and education. While most educators do not see racism as present in the school system, many teachers and students have preconceived notions pertaining to members of racial minorities. In his studies, James Ryan (1998) found that both teachers and students perceived and treated Asian students as intellectually gifted compared to other students, and students from African backgrounds as less able academically than others. As a result, unfair expectations or unrealistic demands are placed on some students based on their backgrounds and minority group status.

We do not yet have enough information on how teachers form their expectations, how they communicate them to students, or exactly how these expectations influence teacher–student interaction. Nor do we know very much about how students "signal" messages to teachers. (As discussed in the Sociology and the New Technology box, technology is producing new forms of student–teacher interaction and "signalling.")

RETHINKING SCHOOLS: PROBLEMS AND SOLUTIONS

To conclude this section on education, let's list some of the major problems facing Canadian education today—and consider potential solutions.

The Rising Tide of Mediocrity

While more and more Canadians are staying in school longer, a significant number of Canadians experience illiteracy. At the same time, dropout rates have declined significantly across the country. Teachers' groups may claim that teachers are doing a better job. They are getting more students to stay in high school and to go on to university. Is it possible that higher retention rates today mean that fewer students are failing due to poorer standards and a deflation in expectations?

In the United States, sociologist Robert Benford (2007) obtained a copy of a 20-question final examination given to basketball players taking a credit course on coaching at the University of Georgia. Some of the questions were:

1. How many goals are on a basketball court? a. 1 b. 2 c. 3 d. 4

2. How many players are allowed to play at one time on any one team in a regular game? a. 2 b. 3 c.4 d. 5

3. How many halves are in a college basketball game? a. 1 b. 2 c. 3 d. 4

4. How many points does a three-point field goal count for in a basketball game? a. 1 b. 2 c. 3 d. 4

Some point their fingers at low standards: "frill" courses, less homework, fewer term papers, grade inflation, and burned-out teachers who often find themselves working under dismal classroom conditions due to recent cutbacks and restructuring in many areas of the school system. Professors in Canadian universities often find students in their classes who experience great difficulties in summarizing researchers' findings in social science courses, who read too slowly or without adequate comprehensive skills to keep up with weekly reading assignments, or who are unable to write well.

Cheating and Essay-Writing Mills

Almost every year, stories of essay-writing services are uncovered in major centres. These services offer recycled or hastily prepared essays for sale. With enough cash, students may purchase a made-to-order term paper that conforms closely to the particular requirements of their course. These illegal operations boom at peak periods during the academic year, and the arrogance of their proprietors is demonstrated by their bold advertisements littering Canadian campuses.

In addition to buying these services, some students engage in other forms of academic dishonesty, including plagiarism, cheating, and misrepresentation at examinations. The extent of such problems is unknown, possibly due to difficulties in detection.

Grade Inflation, Social Promotion, and Functional Illiteracy

At the same time that learning may be declining, grades are going up. In the 1960s, high school teachers gave out about twice as many Cs as As, but now the As exceed the Cs. Grade inflation in the face of declining standards has been accom-panied by social promotion, the practice of passing students from one grade to the next even though they have not mastered basic materials. One unfortunate result is functional illiteracy, difficulty with reading and writing even though one has graduated from high school. Some high school graduates cannot fill out job applications; others can't figure out if they are being given the right change at the grocery store.

Peer Groups

A team of two psychologists and a sociologist studied 20 000 high school students in California and Wisconsin (Steinberg, Dornbusch, & Brown, 1996). They found that of all the influences affecting these teenagers, peer group is the most important. Simply put, those who hang out with good students tend to do well; those who hang out with poor students tend to do poorly. The subcultures students develop include informal norms about educational achievement: some groups set up norms of classroom excellence, others sneer at getting good grades. What's cool or not cool according to the group is the guiding code of conduct. The question that arises from this research is how to build educational achievement into student culture.

Violence in Schools

The shooting spree at Columbine High School in the spring of 1999, a jolting incident and the subject of Michael Moore's documentary film *Bowling for Columbine,* and what has been called the worst mass shooting in U.S. history on the Virginia Tech campus in April 2007 in many ways represent the intensity of the violence many young people live with on a daily basis. Many U.S. schools have deteriorated to the point that basic safety is an issue, putting students' lives at risk, a condition that decades earlier would have been unimaginable. In some schools, uniformed guards have become a fixture, while in others students can gain entrance only after passing through metal detectors. While Canadian schools are much safer, the growing number of incidents of violence, including the possession and use of weapons, beatings, drug trafficking, and other serious offences, have prompted school boards to adopt "zero tolerance" policies, which expel or suspend students at their first offence for even minor infractions. Without programs in place to prevent students from committing "offensive" behaviour in the first place, critics say that such policies are too punitive and may backfire, turning students away from school altogether (Canadian Press, 2002, p. A3). However, a recent report on the Toronto District School Board, the country's largest school system, found it to be rife with violence, including robberies and sexual assaults, and most of which was not reported by school officials or staff, who felt that exposing the violence would be akin to criticizing the Board, something they thought would have career implications for them (Alphonso & El Akkad, 2008: pp. A1, A10). It was not until the unfortunate

Distance learning, courses taught to students who are not physically present with their instructor, is not new. For decades, we have had correspondence courses.

Today, however, telecommunications—satellites, computers, television, iPods, and video cameras—are changing the face of education by making cybercolleges part of mainstream learning. With computer linkups, students may watch the professor on their laptop. Clicking an icon, they can "raise their hands" to ask a question. Programs let the instructor know who is e-mailing others and who is not participating. Such software is also capable of scrutinizing the instructor by storing information that may be retrieved by department chairs or deans on how long it takes him or her to answer students' questions by e-mail.

Until recently, most distance learning has been either slow (a correspondence course) or one-way (students passively receiving instruction, usually providing feedback only through tests). New technologies, such as teleconferencing, however, permit students and teachers to see one another, talk with one another, and share documents worldwide.

The potential is staggering. Why should our learning be limited to walled classrooms? When studying human culture, for example, wouldn't it be intriguing to be able to compare notes on eating, dating, or burial customs with fellow students in Thailand, Iceland, South Africa, Germany, Egypt, China, and Australia?

Some educators suggest that new technologies—such as digital podcasts—allow students to self-direct and "attend" lectures at their own convenience. As a bonus, this flexible learning system provides a solution to the "space crunch" in university lecture halls and to the "time crunch" experienced by most students (Faulkner, 2006: p. A7).

While the virtual classroom has been part of the educational system for many years, new technologies are reshaping administrative structures within academic circles. With the development of telephone and internet registration options, long line-ups of students waiting to enroll in classes, pay tuition, or access administrative services within universities and colleges have disappeared. The application and recruitment processes have also been recently reorganized. Using the very latest technology for iPods,

This student is taking a credit course in economic crime investigation from home.

recruiters for the engineering program at McMaster University have created "podcasts" to lure potential students to campus by advertising the program, the university, and the local culture through this relatively cheap and highly portable device (Faulkner, 2005).

Will we eventually go from kindergarten to graduate school, proceeding at our own pace, with classmates from around the world? While it may sound intriguing, no walls also means no flirting after class, no joking in the hallway or dorm, and no keg parties.

---

shooting death of Jordon Manners, a 15-year-old victim of violence on school property, that the depth of the problem began to come to light.

Solutions: Retention, Safety, Standards, and Other Reforms

It is one thing to identify problems, quite another to find solutions for them.

A SECURE LEARNING ENVIRONMENT The first criterion for a good education is security, a guarantee of students' physical safety and freedom from fear. Fortunately, most Canadian schools are relatively trouble-free, and those that are not can be changed. School administrators and teachers can reclaim the schools by expelling all students who threaten the welfare of others and by refusing to tolerate threats, violence, drugs, and weapons. However, the extent of problems such as bullying and harassment—problems that may be even less obvious and that are difficult to address—are beginning to surface. Unfortunately, many school administrators seem to "bury their heads in the sand" when it comes to confronting these problems head on.

HIGHER STANDARDS Within a secure learning environment, steps can be taken to improve the quality of education.

Students perform better when they are expected to achieve. Somehow, this basic principle seems to be lost on many teachers, who end up teaching at a low level—and on school administrators, who accept low student performance. The reason is probably not their lack of awareness of such basics, but rather the organizational constraints in which

A secure learning environment is basic to a good education. The growing number of violent incidents in Canadian schools has prompted school boards to confront the problem with strict, no-nonsense policies such as "zero tolerance."

they find themselves, the bureaucracies in which ritual often replaces performance. This notion has been the theme of a number of popular films, including *Dead Poets Society* (1989) and *Dangerous Minds* (1995). (To understand this point better, you may wish to review Chapter 10.) Ultimately, we must not only expect more from students, but also from teachers and administrators.

Reform in anything needs a guiding principle. The problem lies not with the ability of students, but rather with the educational system itself. That this is true becomes apparent when we consider the results reported in the Thinking Critically about Social Controversy box on page 326.

RELIGION: ESTABLISHING MEANING

With a call from his mother, Tom's world began to crumble. Amid sobs, she had told him that she had left his father. After 22 years, their marriage was over. Why? It just didn't make sense. Tom knew that his mother and father had problems, that they argued quite a bit. But they always had. And didn't every married couple? Where was he going to go for the summer? His parents had put the house up for sale, and each had moved to a small apartment. There was no home anymore.

Life seemed a little brighter when Tom met Amy in English class. She was the only one he could talk to about his feelings—Amy's parents had divorced three years before, and she understood. When Amy was invited to a meeting of the Unification Church (the church of the "Moonies," followers of Reverend Sun Myung Moon), Tom agreed to go with her.

The meeting was a surprise. Everyone was friendly, and everything was low-key. And everyone seemed so sure. They all believed that Judgment Day was just around the corner.

Amy and Tom found the teachings rather strange, but, since the people had been so friendly, they came back. After Tom and Amy attended meetings for about a month, they became good friends with Marcia and Ryan. Later they moved into an apartment house where Marcia, Ryan, and other Moonies lived. After a while, they dropped out of university and immersed themselves in a new life as Moonies.

What Is Religion?

Sociologists who research religion analyze the relationship between society and religion and study the role religion plays in people's lives. They do not seek to make value judgments about religious beliefs. Nor is their goal to verify or to disprove anyone's faith. Religion is a matter of faith; sociologists deal with empirical matters, things they can observe or measure. Thus sociologists can measure the extent to which people are religious and can study the effects of religious beliefs and practices on people's lives. They can analyze how religion is organized and how systems of belief are related to culture, stratification systems, and other social institutions.

In 1912, Emile Durkheim published an influential book, *The Elementary Forms of the Religious Life*, in which he tried to identify the elements common to all religions. He found that all religions, regardless of their name or teaching, separate the sacred from the profane. By **profane**, he meant

Called "the best teacher in America," Jaime Escalante taught in an East Los Angeles inner-city school plagued with poverty, crime, drugs, gangs, and miserably low student scores. In this self-defeating environment, he taught calculus. His students scored so highly on national tests that test officials, suspecting cheating, asked his students to retake the tests. They did. Again they passed—this time with even higher scores.

How did Escalante overcome such odds? His success was *not* due to a recruitment of the brightest students. Students' poor academic performance did not stand in the way of being admitted to the math program. The *only* requirement was an interest in math. What did Escalante do right, and what can we learn from his approach?

"Success starts with attitude" could be Escalante's motto. Few Latino students were taking math. Most were tracked into craft classes and made jewelry and birdhouses. "Our kids are just as talented as anyone else. They just

need the opportunity to show it. And for that, they must be motivated," he said. "They just don't think about becoming scientists or engineers."

Here are the keys to what Escalante accomplished. First, teaching and learning can't take place unless there is discipline. For that, the teachers, not gangs, must control the classroom. Second, students must believe in themselves. The teacher must inspire students with the idea that they *can* learn (remember teacher expectations). Third, students must be motivated to perform, in this case to see learning as a way out of the *barrio*, as a path to good jobs.

Escalante uses a team approach. He has his students think of themselves as a team, of him as the coach, and the national exams as a sort of Olympics for which they are preparing. To stimulate team identity, the students wear team jackets, caps, and T-shirts with logos that identify them as part of the team. Before class, his students do "warmups" (hand-clapping and foot-stomping to a rock song).

His team has practice schedules as rigorous as a championship football team. Students must sign a contract that binds them to participate in the summer program he has developed, to complete the daily homework, and to attend Saturday morning and after-school study sessions. To get into his class, even the students' parents have to sign the contract. To show his students that the principle that self-discipline pays off, Escalante covers his room with posters of sports figures in action—Michael Jordan, Jerry West, Babe Ruth, and Tiger Woods.

The sociological point is that the problem was not the ability of the students. Their failure to do well in school was not the result of something within them. The problem was the system, the way classroom instruction was arranged. When Escalante changed the system of instruction, both attitudes and performance changed. Escalante makes this very point—that student performance does not depend on the charismatic personality of a single person, but on how we

To say that today's schoolchildren can't learn as well as previous schoolchildren would be to blame the victim. Jaime Escalante, shown here, demonstrated that teachers can motivate even highly deprived students to study hard and excel in learning. His experience challenges us to rethink our approach to education.

aspects of life that are not concerned with religion or religious purposes but, instead, are part of everyday life. By **sacred**, Durkheim referred to aspects of life having to do with the supernatural that inspire awe, reverence, deep respect, and even fear. Durkheim also found that all religions develop a community around their practices and beliefs. He summarized his findings as follows: a religion is a unified system of beliefs and practices relative to sacred things, that is to say, things set apart and forbidden—beliefs and practices that unite into one single moral community.

Thus, he argued, a **religion** is defined by three elements:

1. Beliefs that some things are sacred (forbidden, set off from the profane);

2. Practices (rituals) centring around the things considered sacred;

3. A moral community resulting from a group's beliefs and practices. (1912/1965)

From his review of world religions, Durkheim concluded that all religions have beliefs, practices, and a moral community. Shown here are the colourful and expressive statutes on the roof of a Hindu temple in Chattisgargh, India. The figures represent some of the numerous gods worshipped by Hindus.

Durkheim used the term *moral community* not to imply morality in the sense familiar to most of us. A **moral community** is simply a group of people united by their religious practices—which includes Aztec priests or Jehovah's Witnesses.

To better understand the sociological approach to religion, let's see what pictures emerge when we apply the major theoretical perspectives.

THE FUNCTIONALIST PERSPECTIVE

Functions of Religion

Around the world, religions provide answers to perplexing questions—such as the purpose of life, why people suffer, and the existence of an afterlife.

Similarly, religious rituals that enshroud critical events such as illness and death provide emotional comfort at times of crisis. The individual knows others care and can find consolation in following familiar rituals.

Religious teachings and practices unite believers into a community that shares values and perspectives ("we Jews," "we Christians," "we Muslims"). The religious rituals that surround marriage, for example, link a bride and groom with a broader community. So do other religious rituals, such as those that celebrate birth and mourn death.

Religion not only provides guidelines for everyday life, but also controls people's behaviours. An example is religious teachings that are incorporated into criminal law. In Ontario, for example, laws once prohibited the sale of alcohol before noon on Sunday. Thankfully, that law no longer exists!

Religion can help people adapt to new environments. By keeping their native languages alive and preserving familiar rituals and teachings, religion provides continuity with immigrants' cultural pasts.

Most religions provide support for the government. An obvious example is the Canadian flag prominently displayed in many Anglican and other churches. Another example is the Queen (or King) of England's coronation as head of state

One of the many functions of religion is social solidarity. Can you see instances of this function in this photo of a Hindu service?

Tommy Douglas, pictured here, combined his personal experiences with the compelling message of the Social Gospel teachings he received while studying theology at Brandon University, which emphasized the church's responsibility to reform society. He is credited with helping to establish two important institutions in Canada: Medicare and Crown corporations.

(for Great Britain and Canada), which means she (or he) is also the head of the Church of England. The reading of the Lord's Prayer remains a hallmark of the Ontario legislature, although MPPs voted in June 2008 to add a moment of silence and a rotation of prayers from other beliefs as well.

Although religion is often so bound up with the prevailing order that it resists social change, occasionally it spearheads progressive social and political change. In Canada, a notable example is J. S. Woodsworth's religious movement that began in Saskatchewan and eventually led to the founding of the Cooperative Commonwealth Federation (the CCF), now known as the New Democratic Party (NDP).

Dysfunctions of Religion

Functionalists also examine ways in which religion can be dysfunctional; that is, how it can bring about harm. Two main dysfunctions are war and religious persecution. However, a recent study by Gregory Paul (2005) found that highly secular democracies, such as in France, Japan and Scandinavia, consistently enjoy low rates of societal dysfunction, while pro-religious and anti-evolution America performs poorly. Among the measures of dysfunction he used were homicide, teen pregnancy, STD infection rates, and abortion.

WAR AND TERRORISM History is filled with wars based on religion. Between the eleventh and fourteenth centuries, Christian monarchs conducted nine bloody Crusades in an attempt to wrest control of the Holy Land from the Muslims. Unfortunately, such wars are not a relic of the past. Even in recent years, we have seen Protestants and Catholics kill one another in Northern Ireland, and Jews and Muslims in Israel and Christians and Muslims in Bosnia follow suit. Terrorist acts also are sometimes committed in the name of a god. In the United States, Paul Hill, a minister, was executed in Florida for killing a doctor who had carried out abortions. Another example is Dr. Baruch Goldstein, who was convinced that God (Yahweh) wanted him to go to the Tomb of the Patriarchs and shoot into a crowd of praying Palestinian men and boys (Juergensmeyer: 2000). The all-too-familiar 9/11 acts of terror in New York and Washington were done in the name of religious jihad. It should be noted, however, that religious terrorism often carries a political agenda.

PERSECUTION Beginning in the 1200s and continuing into the 1800s, in what has become known as the Inquisition, special commissions of the Roman Catholic Church tortured women to elicit confessions that they were witches and burned them at the stake. In 1692, Protestant leaders in Salem, Massachusetts, drowned women who were accused of being witches. (The last execution for witchcraft was in Scotland in 1722 [Bridgwater, 1953]). In short, religion has been used to justify oppression and a number of brutal acts.

THE SYMBOLIC INTERACTIONIST PERSPECTIVE

Symbolic interactionists focus on the meanings people give their experiences, especially how they use symbols. Let's apply this perspective to religious symbols, rituals, and beliefs to see how they help to forge a community of like-minded people.

Religious Symbols

All religions use symbols to provide identity and social solidarity for their members. A symbol is a condensed way of communicating. In other words, for Muslims, the primary symbol is the crescent moon and star, for Jews the Star of David, and for Christians the cross. For members, these are not ordinary symbols, but sacred symbols that evoke feelings of awe and reverence.

Rituals

Rituals—ceremonies or repetitive practices—are also symbols that help unite people in a moral community. Some rituals, such as the bar mitzvah for Jewish boys and Holy Communion for Christians, are designed to create in the devout a feeling of closeness and unity with one another. Rituals include kneeling and praying at set times, bowing, crossing oneself, singing, lighting candles and incense, a liturgy, scripture readings, processions, baptisms, weddings, and funerals. Boys and, later, men are normally accorded special status/privileges when compared to girls and women. Later, you will read how women in some of the major religions such as Christianity, Judaism, and Islam are struggling for equality.

Beliefs

Symbols, including rituals, develop from beliefs. A belief may be vague ("God is") or highly specific ("God wants us to prostrate ourselves and face Mecca five times each day"). Religious beliefs include not only **values** (what is considered good and desirable in life—how we ought to live) but also a **cosmology**, a unified picture of the world. For example, the Jewish, Christian, and Muslim belief that there is only one God, who created the universe, is concerned about the actions of humans, and will hold us accountable for what we do, is a cosmology. It presents a unifying picture of the universe.

One of the functions of religion is to create community—a sense of being connected with one another and, in this case, a sense of being connected with God. To help accomplish this, religions often use rituals. Shown here are Javanese Muslim women in Aramaribo as they celebrate Eid al Fatr at the end of Rammadan.

Community

Finally, the shared meanings that come through symbols, rituals, and beliefs unite people into a moral community. People in a moral community feel a bond with one another: their beliefs and rituals bind them together while separating them from those that do not share their unique symbolic world. Mormons, for example, feel a "kindred spirit" (as it is often known) with other Mormons. So do Baptists, Jews, Jehovah's Witnesses, and Muslims with members of their respective faiths.

Removal from a community is a serious matter for people whose identity is bound up in their religious community. Sociologists John Hostetler (1980), William Kephart, and William Zellner (1994) describe the Amish practice of shunning—ignoring an offender in all situations. Persons who are shunned are treated as though they do not exist. Shunning is so thorough that even family members, who themselves remain in good standing in the congregation, are not allowed to talk to the person being shunned.

"We're thinking maybe it's time you started getting some religious instruction. There's Catholic, Protestant, and Jewish—any of those sound good to you?"

Religion can be a serious matter for those who find slight differences of faith to be significant or an opportunity to explore the teachings of several religions.

THE CONFLICT PERSPECTIVE

The conflict perspective provides an entirely different focus. Conflict theorists examine how religion supports the status quo and helps to maintain social inequalities.

Opium of the People

In general, conflict theorists are highly critical of religion. Karl Marx set the tone for conflict theorists with his most famous statement on this subject: "Religion is the sigh of the oppressed creature, the sentiment of a heartless world. . . . It is the opium of the people" (Marx, 1844/1964). By this statement, Marx meant that oppressed workers, sighing for release from their suffering, escape into religion. For them, religion is like a drug that helps them forget their misery. By diverting their eyes to future happiness in a coming world, religion takes them from their suffering in this one, thereby greatly reducing the possibility that they will rebel against their oppressors.

A Reflection of Social Inequalities

Conflict theorists stress that religious teachings and practices are a mirror of a society's inequalities. Gender inequality illustrates this point. In the mid-nineteenth century, when Canada was evolving into a nation, the Church (like Parliament and other institutions of society that were dominated by men) ordained only men, limiting women to such activities as teaching children's Sunday school or preparing meals for congregational get-togethers, which were considered appropriate "feminine" activities. As women's roles in the broader society changed, however, religion reflected those changes. First, many religious groups allowed women to vote. Then, as women attained prominent positions in the business world and professions, some Protestant and Jewish groups allowed women to be ordained. Similarly, just as women still face barriers in secular society, some congregations still refuse to ordain women. In some religious communities the barriers remain so high that women are still not allowed to vote.

A Legitimation of Social Inequalities

Conflict theorists say that religion legitimates the social inequalities of the larger society. By this, they mean that religion teaches that the existing social arrangements of a society represent what God desires.

In what is perhaps the supreme technique of legitimating the social order, the religion of ancient Egypt held that the Pharaoh was a god. The Emperor of Japan was similarly declared divine. Today, in matters of faith and morals, all Catholics must believe in the infallibility of the Pope.

Conflict theorists point to many other examples of how religion legitimates the social order. One of the more remarkable took place in the decades before the U.S. Civil War. Southern ministers used scripture to defend slavery, saying it was God's will—while northern ministers legitimated their region's social structure and used scripture to denounce slavery as evil (Ernst, 1988; Nauta, 1993; White, 1995). In India, Hinduism supports the caste system by teaching that an individual who tries to change caste will come back in the next life as a member of a lower caste—or even as an animal.

THE FEMINIST PERSPECTIVE
Female Spirituality

According to Johanna Stuckey (1998), there are a number of reasons to study female spirituality from a feminist perspective. First, the feminist commitment to diversity leads to an acceptance of exploring the positive spiritual experiences of women. Second, feminist endorsement of the personal should recognize that the spiritual is deeply personal. Third, spirituality and its manifestations in religion help to reveal how the male-dominated system controls both women and men. Fourth, the separation of mind and body or rationality and spirituality is a fabrication of Western male epistemologies (i.e., theories of knowledge), which feminists must avoid. And fifth, half the human population—that is, women—have been neglected in religious studies. It is time to include women's religious roles, women's understanding of spirituality, and women-centred religious symbols.

Stuckey (1998) outlines four main categories of the feminist study of spirituality. **Revisionists** are those who believe that the basic message of the major religions is liberating. The major changes to the teachings revisionists would defend include replacing sexist prose with sex-neutral language. **Reformists** advocate revealing the "liberating core" of religious teachings with female imagery and exposing and refusing to accept rituals that are clearly sexist. **Revolutionaries** seek to change the established orthodoxy by importing language, images, and rituals from other traditions. **Rejectionists** are feminists who judge the traditional teachings to be hopelessly sexist and have abandoned them in order to establish a new spiritual tradition. Most practise "Feminist Goddess Worship," which is understood to be completely different from any other religious expression of spirituality.

Themes in Christian Feminism

Several themes have been expressed by feminists interested in female spirituality within the Christian tradition. First is overcoming sexism by taking account of women's experiences in the church. Second, and a very productive area of Christian feminism, is the recovery of Christian women's histories. Rescued names and lives of women from the past include the twelfth-century prophet Hildegard of Bingen, Shaker Ann Lee, and Roman Catholic social activist Dorothy Day. Third is exploring the meaning of Jesus, a debate that has produced heated encounters. One telling example is the statue "Crucified Woman" that stands outside Emmanuel College at the University of Toronto (Dyke, 1991). Fourth, the issue of Christian feminist ethics has produced a burgeoning literature tackling issues such as abortion, homophobia, power and sexuality, and suffering and evil.

Themes in Judaism and Feminism

Jewish feminists, like their Christian counterparts, have been questioning the male dominance of their religion and the masculinity of God. For the most part, Jewish feminists are revisionists in that they believe in the core meanings of Judaism and seek to change Judaism from the inside by challenging blatantly sexist rituals and teachings. They have fought to take part in public rituals and to fill leadership roles. Within non-Orthodox Judaism, for example, there are a number of female rabbis. In Conservative, Reform, and Reconstructionist Judaism, women read the Torah in public and can take part in the *minyan*, the formerly "10 males" prayer ceremony (Elwell, 1996).

Themes in Feminism and Islam

The theoretical core of Islamic feminism is grounded in an interpretation of the teachings of the Qur'an. The central focus remains the clarification of gender equality in Islam. The first international conference on Islamic feminism, held in Barcelona in 2005, drew participants from old and new Muslim societies. One important Canadian Muslim woman is Irshad Manji, a Canadian journalist and author of *The Trouble with Islam Today: A Muslim's Call for Reform in Her Faith* (2005) who has been published in almost 30 countries. Another example of bringing Islamic issues including feminist themes to a wider Canadian audience is the CBC television program *Little Mosque on the Prairie*.

Feminist spirituality is a recent development within second-wave feminism. However, the thrust of feminist spirituality resides in the Christian and Jewish traditions and is only now beginning to have an impact on Islam and other world religions. For the most part, feminists interested in spirituality have not given up on their religious upbringing. Very few profess rejectionist sentiments. Most are working for change from within an established religious tradition.

POSTMODERNISM AND RELIGION

Unlike modernism, which celebrated the virtues of individualism, science, reason, and progress, postmodernism extols the intrinsic worth of socially contextualized individual experience, spirituality, and cultural diversity. According to postmodernism, all of our thinking is contextual. There is no place for objective truth derived from science or organized religion. Instead, we find "local narratives" or stories that work for particular communities but are not considered valid outside these communities. Indeed, there is no room for any absolute, universal truths within postmodernism. All religions that profess to know the truth are classed as "meta-narratives" (comprehensive world views) and abandoned. However, there is space for individuals to seek out their spirituality. In some ways, postmodernism is the spiritual "'re-enchantment' of the world that modernity tried so hard to disenchant" (Bauman, 1994). However, there are a great many forms this "re-enchantment" can take, which is probably why postmodernism has contributed to the rise of New Age religions and all things "spiritual."

Focus Question

What explanations are provided by the functionalist, symbolic interactionist, conflict, feminist, and postmodernist perspectives for the existence of religion in society?

RELIGION AND THE SPIRIT OF CAPITALISM

Weber was intrigued with the question of why some societies embraced capitalism while others clung to their traditional ways. As he explored the problem, he concluded that religion held the key to **modernization**—the transformation of traditional societies to industrial societies.

To explain his conclusions, Weber wrote *The Protestant Ethic and the Spirit of Capitalism* (1904–1905/1958). His explanation is briefly summarized here.

1. Capitalism represents a fundamentally different way of thinking about work and money. To accumulate money (capital) as an end in itself, and to consider it a duty to invest money in order to make profits Weber called the **spirit of capitalism**.

2. Why did the spirit of capitalism develop in Europe, and not, for example, in China or India, where the people had similar intelligence, material resources, education, and so on? According to Weber, religion was the key.

3. What was different about Protestantism, especially Calvinism? Calvinists concluded that church members had a duty to prove that they were one of God's elect and to live as though they were predestined to heaven. This conclusion motivated Calvinists to lead highly moral lives and to work hard, to not waste time, and to be frugal—for idleness and needless spending were signs of worldliness. Weber called this hard-working, self-denying approach to life 'inner-worldly asceticism" or the **Protestant ethic**.

4. As people worked hard and spent money only on necessities, they accumulated wealth, because spending made people pompous and greedy. Therefore, a Calvinist could never be certain, but believed that a frugal way of life, or inner worldly asceticism, was close to what God wanted from "His" followers on earth. Accumulated capital, since it couldn't be spent, was invested—which led to a surge in production.

5. Thus, a change in religion to Protestantism, especially Calvinism, led to a fundamental change in thought and behaviour (the Protestant ethic). The result was the spirit of capitalism. Hence capitalism originated in Europe, and not in places where religion did not encourage capitalism's essential elements: the accumulation of capital through frugality and hard work, and its investment and reinvestment.

Today, the Protestant ethic and the spirit of capitalism are not confined to any specific religion or part of the world. Rather, they have become cultural traits that have spread to societies around the globe (Greeley, 1964; Yinger, 1970). Canadian Catholics have about the same approach to life as Canadian Protestants. In addition, Hong Kong, Japan, Malaysia, Singapore, South Korea, Taiwan, and, today, China—not exactly Protestant countries—have embraced capitalism (M. J. Levy, 1992).

THE WORLD'S MAJOR RELIGIONS

Of the thousands of religions in the world, most people practise Judaism, Christianity, Islam, Hinduism, Buddhism, or Confucianism (see Figure 14.1). Let us briefly review each.

Judaism

Judaism is one of the first recorded religions based on **monotheism**, the belief that there is only one God.

Contemporary Judaism comprises three main branches: Orthodox, Reform, and Conservative. Orthodox Jews adhere to the laws espoused by Moses. They eat only foods prepared in a designated manner (kosher), observe the Sabbath in a traditional way, and segregate males and females in their religious services. During the 1800s, a group that wanted to make its practices more compatible with the secular (nonreligious) culture broke from this tradition. This liberal group, known as Reform Judaism, mostly uses the vernacular (a country's language) in its religious ceremonies and has reduced much of the ritual. The third branch, Conservative Judaism, falls somewhere between the other two.

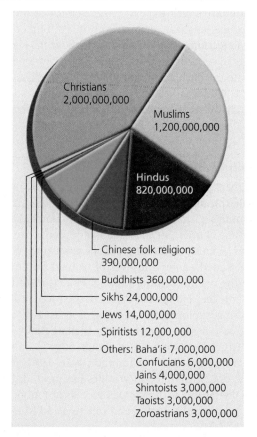

FIGURE 14.1 The World's Largest Religions

Note: The classification of religions is often confusing. Animists, for example, although numerous, are not listed as a separate group in the source. It is sometimes difficult to tell what groups are included in what categories.

Source: Adherents of All Religions, by Six Continental Areas, (2003). *World Almanac and Book of Facts.*

The history of Judaism is marked by conflict and persecution. For most of Jewish history, they faced prejudice, discrimination, and persecution (called **anti-Semitism**) by many peoples and rulers. The most horrendous example is Hitler's attempt to eliminate the Jews as a people in the Nazi Holocaust of World War II. Under the Nazi occupation of Europe and North Africa, about 6 million Jews were slaughtered, perhaps half dying in gas ovens constructed specifically for this purpose.

Christianity

Christianity, which developed out of Judaism, is also monotheistic. Christians believe that Jesus Christ is the Messiah. At about the age of 30, he began a preaching and healing ministry and was as a result punished by the ruling Romans with death.

The 12 main followers of Jesus, called *the apostles*, believed that Jesus rose from the dead. The new religion spread rapidly, and in A.D. 317, Christianity became the Roman empire's official religion.

During the first 1000 years of Christianity, there was only one church organization: the Roman Catholic Church. In the eleventh century, after disagreement over doctrine and politics, Greek Orthodoxy was established. It was headquartered in Constantinople (now Istanbul, Turkey).

Although Martin Luther's (1483–1546) original goal of advancing what has become known as the 96 Resolutions was to reform the Roman Catholic Church, the Protestant Reformation of the sixteenth century began a splintering of Christianity. The schism coincided with the breakup of feudalism and the beginning of capitalism.

Today, Christians are divided into hundreds of groups, some with doctrinal differences so slight that only members can appreciate the extremely fine distinctions that significantly separate them from others.

Islam

Islam, whose followers are known as Muslims and number 1 billion people, began in the same part of the world as Judaism and Christianity. Islam is the world's third monotheistic religion. It was founded by Muhammad, who was born in Mecca (now in Saudi Arabia) about A.D. 570. His teachings were written in a book called the Koran. When he found out that there was a plot to murder him, Muhammad fled to Medina, where he found a more receptive audience. There he established a *theocracy* (a government based on the principle that God is the ruler, his laws the statutes of the land, and priests his earthly administrators), and founded the Muslim empire. In A.D. 630 he returned to Mecca, this time as a conqueror (Bridgwater, 1953).

After Muhammad's death, a struggle for control over the empire split Islam into two branches that remain today, the Sunni and the Shi'ite. Shi'ites are generally more conservative and inclined to **fundamentalism**, the belief that modernism threatens religion and that the faith as it was originally practised should be restored. Sunni, who do not share this belief, are generally more liberal.

Like Jews, Muslims trace their ancestry to Abraham. For Muslims, also, Jerusalem is a holy city. It is the duty of each Muslim to make a pilgrimage to Mecca during his or her lifetime.

Hinduism

Unlike the other religions described, Hinduism has no specific founder. For about 4000 years, Hinduism has been the chief religion of India. The term *Hinduism*, however, is Western, and in India the closest word is *dharma* (law). Unlike Judaism, Christianity, and Islam, Hinduism has no texts thought to be inspired by a God. Instead, several books, including the *Brahmanas*, *Bhagavad-Gita*, and *Upanishads*, expound on moral qualities that people should strive after.

Hindus are *polytheists*; that is, they believe there are many gods. They believe one of these gods, Brahma, created the universe. Brahma, along with Shiva (the Destroyer) and Vishnu (the Preserver), form a triad at the centre of modern Hinduism. A central belief is *karma*, or spiritual progress.

Depictions of Buddha are found throughout the world. Many Buddhists keep small statues in their homes and businesses, to which they make daily offerings of food. This golden Buddha statue is in Bangkok, Thailand.

There is no final judgment, but, instead, **reincarnation**, a cycle of life, death, and rebirth. Death involves only the body, and every person's soul comes back in a form that matches the individual's moral progress in the previous life (which centres on proper conduct in following the rules of one's caste). If an individual reaches spiritual perfection, he or she has attained *nirvana*. This marks the end of the cycle of death and rebirth, when the soul is reunited with the universal soul. When this occurs, *maya*, the illusion of time and space, has been conquered.

Buddhism

About 600 B.C., Siddhartha Gautama founded Buddhism. (Buddha means "enlightened one," a term Gautama was given by his disciples.) Gautama was the son of an upper-caste Hindu ruler in an area north of Benares, India. At the age of 29, he renounced his life of luxury and became an ascetic.

Through meditation, he discovered the following "four noble truths," all of which emphasize self-denial and compassion:

1. Existence is suffering.
2. The origin of suffering is desire.
3. Suffering ceases when desire ceases.
4. The way to end desire is to follow the "noble eightfold path."

The noble eightfold path consists of

1. right belief
2. right resolve (to renounce carnal pleasure and to harm no living creature)
3. right speech
4. right conduct
5. right occupation or living
6. right effort
7. right-mindedness (or contemplation)
8. right ecstasy

The central symbol of Buddhism is the eight-spoked wheel. Each spoke represents one aspect of the path. Buddhists teach that all things are temporary, even the self. Because all things are destined to pass away, there is no soul. By the fifth century A.D., Buddhism reached the height of its popularity in India, after which it died out. However, Buddhism had been adopted in Sri Lanka, Myanmar, Tibet, Laos, Cambodia, Thailand, China, Korea, and Japan, where it flourishes today.

Confucianism

About the time that Gautama lived, K'ung Fu-tsu (551–479 B.C.) was born in China. Confucius (his name strung together in English), a public official, was distressed by the corruption that he saw in government. He urged social reform and developed a system of morality based on peace, justice, and universal order. His teachings were incorporated into writings called the Analects.

Confucianism was originally atheistic, simply a set of moral teachings without reference to the supernatural. As the centuries passed, however, local gods were added to the teachings and Confucius himself was declared a god. Confucius's teachings became the basis for the government of China.

The basic moral principle of Confucianism is to maintain *jen*, sympathy or concern for other humans. The key to *jen* is maintaining right relationships—being loyal and placing morality above self-interest. In what is called the "Confucian Golden Rule," Confucius stated a basic principle for *jen*: to treat those who are subordinate to you as you would like to be treated by people superior to yourself. Confucius taught that right relationships within the family (loyalty, respect) should be the model for society. He also taught the "middle way," an avoidance of extremes.

TYPES OF RELIGIOUS GROUPS

Sociologists have identified four types of religious groups: cults, sects, churches, and ecclesias. Why are some of these groups met with hostility, while others are accepted? For an explanation, consider Figure 14.2.

Cult

Cults sometimes make instant headlines around the world, as did the ones described in the next Down-to-Earth Sociology box (on page 336). Cults, however, are not necessarily weird, and few practise "brainwashing" or bizarre rituals. In fact, all religions began as cults (R. Stark, 1989).

Cults often begin with the appearance of a **charismatic leader**, an individual who inspires people because he or she seems to have extraordinary qualities. Finding something highly appealing about the individual, people feel drawn to both the person and his or her message.

A **cult**, then, is simply a new or different religion, with few followers, whose teaching and practices put it at odds with the dominant culture and religion.

Every cult meets with rejection from society. Its message is considered bizarre, its approach to life, strange. Its members antagonize the majority, who are convinced that they have a monopoly on the truth. The new message may claim revelation, visions, visits from God and angels, some form of enlightenment, or seeing the true way to God. The cult demands intense commitment, and its followers, confronting a hostile world, pull into a tight circle, separating themselves from nonbelievers.

Most cults fail. Not many people believe the new message, and the cult fades into obscurity. Some, however, succeed and make history. Over time, large numbers of people may come to accept the message and become followers

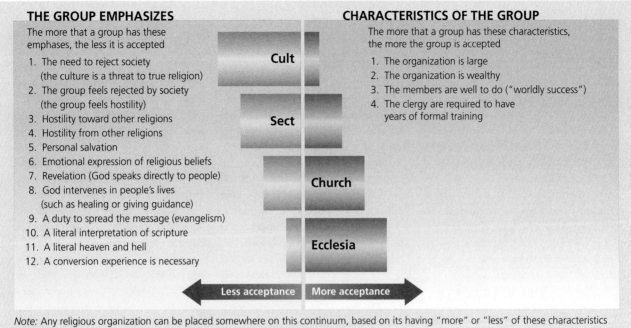

THE GROUP EMPHASIZES

The more that a group has these emphases, the less it is accepted

1. The need to reject society (the culture is a threat to true religion)
2. The group feels rejected by society (the group feels hostility)
3. Hostility toward other religions
4. Hostility from other religions
5. Personal salvation
6. Emotional expression of religious beliefs
7. Revelation (God speaks directly to people)
8. God intervenes in people's lives (such as healing or giving guidance)
9. A duty to spread the message (evangelism)
10. A literal interpretation of scripture
11. A literal heaven and hell
12. A conversion experience is necessary

CHARACTERISTICS OF THE GROUP

The more that a group has these characteristics, the more the group is accepted

1. The organization is large
2. The organization is wealthy
3. The members are well to do ("worldly success")
4. The clergy are required to have years of formal training

Cult

Sect

Church

Ecclesia

Less acceptance ← → More acceptance

Note: Any religious organization can be placed somewhere on this continuum, based on its having "more" or "less" of these characteristics and emphases. The varying proportions of the rectangles are intended to represent the group's relative characteristics and emphases.

FIGURE 14.2 Religious Groups: From Hostility to Acceptance

Source: By the author. Troeltsch (1931); Pope (1942); Johnson (1963).

of the religion. If this happens, the new religion changes from a cult to a *sect*.

Sect

A **sect** is a group larger than a cult. Its members still feel a fair amount of tension with the prevailing beliefs and values of the broader society. The sect may even be hostile to the society that surrounds it.

Ordinarily, sects are loosely organized and fairly small. They emphasize personal salvation, and extemporaneous prayers are hallmarks of sects. Like cults, sects also stress **evangelism**, the active recruitment of new members. One example would be Jehovah's Witnesses.

If a sect grows, its members gradually tend to make peace with the rest of society. They become more respectable in the eyes of the majority and feel much less hostility and little, if any, isolation. To appeal to the new, broader base, the sect shifts some of its doctrines, redefining matters to remove some of the rough edges that created tension between it and the rest of society. If a sect follows this course and becomes larger and more integrated into society, it changes into an *institutionalized religion,* such as the Roman Catholic Church or Confucianism.

Institutionalized Religion

When a sect becomes an **institutionalized religion**, it becomes highly bureaucratized—probably with national and international headquarters that give directions to local congregations, enforce rules about who can be ordained, and control finances. Rather than being recruited from the outside by fervent, personal evangelism, most new members come from within, from children born to existing members. At some designated age, children may be asked to affirm the group's beliefs in a confirmation or bar mitzvah ceremony.

Ecclesia

Some groups become so well integrated into a culture and so strongly allied with their government that it is difficult to tell where one leaves off and the other takes over. In these state religions, also called **ecclesias**, the government and religion work together to try to shape society. How extensively religion and government intertwine in an ecclesia is illustrated by Sweden, where in the 1800s all citizens had to memorize Luther's Small Catechism and be tested on it yearly (P. Anderson, 1995). Today, Lutheranism is still the state religion, but most Swedes come to church only for baptisms, marriages, and funerals.

Variations in Patterns

Not all religious groups go through all of these stages—from cult to sect to institutionalized religion to ecclesia. Some die out because they fail to attract enough members. Others, such as the Amish, remain sects. And very few religions ever become ecclesias, with notable exceptions such as Iran.

Although all religions began as cults, not all varieties of a given religion may have done so. For example, some

The news made instant headlines around the world in late March 1997: 39 bodies had been found in an exclusive San Diego neighbourhood draped in purple, diamond-shaped shrouds. Some of the men had been castrated. There was no sign of a struggle.

Reports followed on the beliefs of those who had died—members of the Heaven's Gate cult. A spaceship was hiding behind the Hale-Bopp comet ready to transport them to a new life. To be beamed aboard, they had to leave their "containers" behind. That meant suicide. For their space travels, each cult member put on new Nike sneakers. Each also packed a bag with clothing, $5 bills, and quarters—and a passport.

Then there is the garbage-eating Brotherhood led by an ex-Marine who claims he is Jesus. His long-haired followers rummage through dumpsters, carefully removing any mould before dining on rotting scraps of the material world they so disdain. They blame their stomachaches on Satan (O'Neill, 1997).

Other Messiahs have been just as influential. In the 1970s, hundreds followed Jim Jones to Guyana. More than 900 committed suicide—or were murdered. In the 1990s, 74 members of the Solar Temple in Switzerland, France, and Canada arranged themselves in the shape of a cross and set themselves afire. They believed they would be transported to the star Sirius (Lacayo, 1997).

Why would anyone fall for such "obvious" deception? Finding *meaning* in life lies at the centre of religion. Always, people seek to satisfy their spiritual longings. And with today's rapid social change, our traditional meanings are constantly challenged and sometimes uprooted. Newcomers are isolated, cut off from family and friends who would provide a balancing perspective on reality. As a group's views are regularly confirmed by people one has come to like and respect, the bizarreness of these beliefs gradually wears off. Instead, cult members come to be viewed as "insiders" privy to secret messages beyond the grasp of ordinary people.

Heaven's Gate, and its many counterparts throughout the world, matches the public's image of cults—bizarre people with strange teachings whose followers act in repugnant ways. As has been stressed, however, the *sociological* meaning of "cult" is different. All new religions begin as cults. Some grow and become sects. Others even develop into churches and ecclesias.

denominations—"brand names" within a major religion, such as Methodism or Reform Judaism—may begin as splinter groups. A large group within an institutionalized religion may disagree with some aspects of the religion's teachings (not its major message) and break away to form its own organization.

When Religion and Culture Conflict

Cults and sects represent a break with the past. Consequently, they challenge the social order. Three major patterns of adaptation occur when religion and the culture in which it is embedded find themselves in conflict.

First, the members of a religion may reject the dominant culture and have as little as possible to do with nonmembers of their religion. The practice of polygamy by a breakaway Mormon sect in Bountiful, British Columbia, is a recent example. Withdrawn into a closed community, it is unlikely that the BC government can or will prosecute, even though polygamy is illegal in Canada.

In the second pattern, a cult or sect rejects only specific elements of the prevailing culture. Most elements of the main culture, however, are accepted. Although specific activities are forbidden, members of the religion are able to participate in most aspects of the broader society. They resolve this mild tension either by adhering to the religion or by "sneaking," conducting the forbidden acts on the sly. An example might be Jehovah's Witnesses.

In the third pattern, the society rejects the religious group and may even try to destroy it. The early Christians are an example. The Roman emperor declared them enemies

While attendance at religious services in Canada has declined over the past five decades, the vast majority of Canadians still retain a belief in God.

of Rome and ordered all Christians hunted down and destroyed.

CHARACTERISTICS OF RELIGION IN CANADA

How can we generalize about religion in Canada, with its hundreds of denominations and sects? What do these many religious groups have in common? It certainly isn't doctrine, but doctrine is not the focus of sociology. Sociologists are interested in the relationship between society and religion, and the role religion plays in people's lives. To better understand religion in Canadian society, we shall focus first on characteristics of members of religious groups, then on the groups themselves.

The picture of religion in Canada is a changing one—but one that recognizes diversity and a degree of continuity with the past.

Historically, Canada has been predominantly Christian. Most of the population is divided between Protestants, living mostly outside the province of Quebec, and Roman Catholics, of whom the majority continue to live in Quebec. Between 1986 and 2001, Roman Catholics numbered approximately 40 percent of the adult population in Canada, while the proportion of established Protestants, such as Anglican, United, and so on, dropped from 28 percent to 20 percent of the adult population in the country. However, the more right-wing, conservative Protestants continue to number approximately 6 percent of the population.

The only religious groups in Canada that grew to any significant degree over this time period were the Eastern, non-Christian religions of Islam, Hinduism, and Buddhism. While the proportion is small—5 percent of the adult Canadian population—the numbers increased from approximately 300 000 in 1986 to over 1.5 million in 2001, or a percentage increase of 400 percent in 15 years (see Table 14.3).

What is changing in Canada in terms of religion and religious identity? Since the 1961 census, the incidence of those reporting "no religion" increased dramatically from a low of less than 1 percent in 1961 to over 18 percent at the beginning of the millennium. Compared to the United States, proportionally more Canadians profess not to be part of any religious tradition, a trend that does not appear to be slowing down.

Another significant change has been the proportion of Canadians who regularly attend religious services. Since the post–World War II period, Canadians have been attending religious services on a less frequent basis. Over two-thirds of Canadians in 1951 stated they had attended religious services during the previous week. The General Social Survey in 1996 reported that fewer than 20 percent of adult Canadians attend religious services every week.

While this is true for all age groups in Canada, over a third of seniors aged 65 and over attended religious services weekly in 1996. This percentage is twice that reported for 15- to 24-year-olds.

TABLE 14.3 Religion in Canada, 1986–2001 (in millions)

Religion	1986	1991	1996	2001
Roman Catholic	9.0	9.3	10.4	12.8
Eastern Orthodox	0.3	0.2	0.2	0.25
Established Protestants	5.6	5.0	4.8	
Right-wing Protestants	1.2	1.1	1.4	
Other Protestants	0.7	0.7	1.2	
Total Protestants				8.65*
Jewish	0.2	0.2	0.2	0.33
Eastern non-Christian	0.3	0.5	0.7	1.5
No religion	2.0	3.5	3.4	4.9
Not stated	0.4	0.5	1.2	nil

* 2001 census did not distinguish among different categorizations of Protestantism.

Source: Statistics Canada, *General Social Survey*, 1996; Statistics Canada, 2001, *Census 2001*. Catalogue nos. 97F0022XCB2001041, 97F0022XCB2001001, and 97F0022XCB2001006.

While attendance at religious services may be down and there is a growing trend toward Canadians expressing no religious affiliation, Reginald Bibby, in his 1995 Project Canada survey, found that the vast majority of Canadians—81 percent—still believe in God.

When compared to Americans, Canadians show a dramatic difference when it comes to non-religious residents. In 1971, less than 1 percent of Canadians reported having no religion. In 2001, the data showed a dramatic increase to 16 percent, or just fewer than 4.8 million. Table 14.4 illustrates that younger Canadians, or those under 25, are more likely to say they have no religion. In 1996, Queen's University

TABLE 14.4 Canadians Reporting "No Religion" by Age Group, 2001.

Age Group	No Religion (%)	Total Population (%)
0–14 years	23.1	19.4
15–24 years	16.2	13.5
25–44	45	30.5
45–54	13.2	14.9
55–64	6.3	9.6
65 years and over	6.2	12.2

Source: Statistics Canada, Cat. # 96F0030XIE2001015—Religions in Canada

TABLE 14.5 Expressions of Religious Tradition for Canada and the United States, 1996

Religious Tradition	Canada		United States	
Christian	69.0%	(2070)	76.5	(2313)
Jewish	1.0%	(29)	2.1%	(63)
Muslim	0.4%	(13)	0.3%	(9)
Other non-Christian	0.8%	(23)	1.2%	(36)
Agnostic	3.1%	(92)	2.1%	(64)
Atheist	3.2%	(97)	0.9%	(26)
Nothing	16.0%	(481)	10.1%	(304)
Something	5.4%	(162)	6.0%	(180)
Don't know	1.1%	(33)	0.9%	(28)

Source: Adapted from *God and Society in North America Survey*, Queen's University, 1996, with the permission of the American Religious Data Archive.

conducted the only recent North American survey, titled "God and Society in North America" (see Table 14.5). In the survey, those expressing no religious affiliation were separated into the following categories: "Agnostic," "Atheist," "Nothing," and "Don't Know." In each category, Canadians scored higher (in percentage terms) than Americans. In total, almost a quarter (23.4 percent) of Canadians fell into these categories, while only one in seven (14 percent) of Americans expressed these sentiments (see Table 14.5).

While established and non-established Christian religions continue to dominate the Canadian religious landscape, questions about spirituality or the human spirit are increasing.

Focus Question

What are the religious differences between Canada and the United States?

THE FUTURE OF RELIGION

Marx was convinced that religion would crumble when the workers threw off their chains of oppression. In a new society based on justice, he argued, there will no longer be a need for religion, for religion is the refuge of the miserable, and people will no longer be miserable. Religion will wither away when people see that thoughts about an afterlife are misdirected (De George, 1968).

After communist countries were established, however, people continued to be religious. At first, the leaders thought this was simply a remnant of the past that would eventually dwindle. Old people might cling to the past, but the young would give it up, and with the coming generation religion would cease to exist.

The new Marxist states, avowing atheism, were not content to let this withering occur on its own, and they tried to eradicate religion from their midst. (Keep in mind that Marx

In its common usage, to "evangelize" means to make converts. As *Peanuts* so humorously picks up, evangelization is sometimes accomplished through means other than pronouncements.

said he was not a Marxist. He did not advocate the persecution of religion, for he felt that religion would crumble on its own.) The Communist government in the Soviet Union confiscated church buildings and turned them into museums or government offices. The school curriculum was designed to ridicule religion, and a civil marriage ceremony was substituted for the religious ceremony (complete with an altar and a bust of Lenin), while a ceremony dedicating newborns to the state was substituted for baptism.

In spite of severe, extended persecution, religion remained strong, even among many youth. Table 14.6 shows the results of the first scientific sampling of the Russian population after the collapse of the Soviet Union. Three out of four Russians believe there is a God, and one out of three believes there is a heaven.

Science can simply never replace religion. Nor can political systems, as demonstrated by the experience of socialist and communist countries. Science can describe death and

TABLE 14.6   Religious Beliefs in Russia

Percentage of Russians Who Believe in the Following:	
God	74%
Life after death	40%
Miracles	33%
Heaven	33%
Hell	30%

Source: Greeley (1994).

compute consequences, but it cannot dictate the moral superiority of any action.

There is little doubt that religion could last as long as humanity lasts—or until humans develop adequate functional alternatives.

SUMMARY AND REVIEW

Education: Transferring Knowledge and Skills

Today's Credential Society

WHAT IS A CREDENTIAL SOCIETY, AND HOW DOES IT DEVELOP?

A **credential society** is one in which employers use diplomas and degrees to determine who is eligible for a job. One reason that credentialling developed is that large, anonymous societies lack the personal knowledge common to smaller groups; educational certification provides evidence of a person's ability. p. 309.

The Development of Modern Education

HOW DID MODERN EDUCATION DEVELOP?

In most of human history, education consisted of informal learning, equivalent to **acculturation**. In some earlier societies, centres of formal education developed, such as among the Arabians, Chinese, Greeks, and Egyptians. Because modern education came about in response to industrialization, formal education is much less common in the least industrialized nations. pp. 309–311.

The Functionalist Perspective: Providing Social Benefits

WHAT IS THE FUNCTIONALIST PERSPECTIVE ON EDUCATION?

Among the functions of education are the teaching of knowledge and skills, **cultural transmission** of values, social integration, **gatekeeping**, promoting personal and social change, and **mainstreaming**. Functionalists also note

that education has replaced some traditional family functions. pp. 311–317.

The Conflict Perspective: Reproducing the Social Class Structure

WHAT IS THE CONFLICT PERSPECTIVE ON EDUCATION?

The basic view of conflict theorists is that education reproduces the social class structure; that is, through such mechanisms as unequal funding and operating different schools for the elite and for the masses, education reinforces a society's basic social inequalities. pp. 317–321.

The Symbolic Interactionist Perspective: Teacher Expectations and the Self-Fulfilling Prophecy

WHAT IS THE SYMBOLIC INTERACTIONIST PERSPECTIVE ON EDUCATION?

Symbolic interactionists focus on face-to-face interaction. In examining what occurs in the classroom, they have found a **self-fulfilling prophecy**: that student performance tends to conform to teacher expectations, whether they are high or low. p. 322.

Rethinking Schools: Problems and Solutions

WHAT ARE THE CHIEF PROBLEMS THAT FACE CANADIAN EDUCATION?

The major problems are low achievement, grade inflation, social promotion, functional illiteracy, and violence. pp. 322–324.

WHAT ARE THE PRIMARY SOLUTIONS TO THESE PROBLEMS?

The primary solution is to restore high educational standards, which can be done only after providing basic security for students. Any solution for improving quality must be based on raising standards and expecting more of both students and teachers. pp. 324–325.

Religion: Establishing Meaning

What Is Religion?

WHAT IS RELIGION?

Durkheim identified three essential characteristics of **religion**: beliefs that set the **sacred** apart from the **profane**, **rituals**, and a **moral community**. pp. 325–327.

The Functionalist Perspective

WHAT ARE THE FUNCTIONS AND DYSFUNCTIONS OF RELIGION?

Among the functions of religion are answering questions about ultimate meaning, providing emotional comfort, social solidarity, guidelines for everyday life, social control, adaptation, support for the government, and fostering social change. Groups or activities that provide these same functions are called functional equivalents of religion. Among the dysfunctions of religion are war and religious persecution. pp. 327–329.

The Symbolic Interactionist Perspective

WHAT ASPECTS OF RELIGION DO SYMBOLIC INTERACTIONISTS STUDY?

Symbolic interactionists focus on the meanings of religion for its followers. They examine religious symbols, rituals, beliefs, experiences, and the sense of community provided by religion. pp. 329–330.

The Conflict Perspective

WHAT ASPECTS OF RELIGION DO CONFLICT THEORISTS STUDY?

Conflict theorists examine the relationship of religion to social inequalities, especially how religion is a conservative force that reinforces a society's social stratification. p. 330.

The Feminist Perspective

WHAT ASPECTS OF RELIGION DO FEMINISTS STUDY?

Feminists focus on female spirituality. There are four main categories of the feminist study of spirituality: **revisionists**, **reformists**, **revolutionaries**, and **rejectionists**. All attempt to eliminate sexist ritual and teachings. pp. 330–331.

Postmodernism and Religion

WHAT IS THE POSTMODERN PERSPECTIVE ON RELIGION?

Postmodernism extols the intrinsic worth of socially contextualized individual experience, spirituality, and cultural diversity. According to postmodernism, all of our thinking is contextual. There is no place for objective truth derived from science or organized religion. Instead, we find "local narratives" or stories that work for particular communities but are not considered valid outside these communities. There is no room for any absolute, universal truths within postmodernism. All religions that profess to know the truth are classed as "metanarratives" (comprehensive world views) and abandoned. However, there is space for individuals to seek out spirituality. p. 331.

Religion and the Spirit of Capitalism

WHAT DOES THE SPIRIT OF CAPITALISM HAVE TO DO WITH RELIGION?

Max Weber disagreed with Marx's conclusion that religion impedes social change. In contrast, Weber saw religion as a primary source of social change. He analyzed how Protestantism gave rise to the **Protestant ethic**, which stimulated what he called the **spirit of capitalism**. The result was capitalism, which transformed society. p. 332.

The World's Major Religions

WHAT ARE THE WORLD'S MAJOR RELIGIONS?

Judaism, Christianity, and Islam, all **monotheistic** religions, can be traced to the same Old Testament roots. Hinduism, the chief religion of India, has no specific founder, unlike Judaism (Abraham), Christianity (Jesus), Islam (Muhammad), Buddhism (Gautama), and Confucianism (K'ung Fu-tsu). Specific teachings and history of these six religions are given in the text. pp. 332–334.

Types of Religious Groups

WHAT TYPES OF RELIGIOUS GROUPS ARE THERE?

Sociologists divide religious groups into cults, sects, churches, and ecclesias. All religions began as **cults**. Those that survive tend to develop into **sects** and eventually into **institutionalized religions**. Sects, often led by **charismatic leaders**, are unstable. Some are perceived as a threat and persecuted by the state. **Ecclesias**, or state religions, are rare. pp. 334–337.

Characteristics of Religion in Canada

WHAT ARE THE MAIN TRENDS IN RELIGION IN CANADA?

Most Canadians are either Protestant or Roman Catholic. The only religious groups that have grown by any significant degree in the past decade and a half are the Eastern non-Christian religions of Islam, Hinduism, and Buddhism. Since 1961, the incidence of those reporting "no religion" has increased dramatically from a low of less than 1 percent to an approximate high today of over 18 percent. p. 337.

WHAT IS ONE OF THE PRINCIPAL DIFFERENCES BETWEEN CANADA AND THE UNITED STATES WITH REGARD TO RELIGION?

When compared to Americans, Canadians show a dramatic difference when it comes to the non-religious affiliation category. Almost a quarter (23.4 percent) of Canadians reported no religious affiliation, while only one in seven (14 percent) of Americans expressed the same sentiment. pp. 337–338.

The Future of Religion

Because science and political systems cannot answer questions about ultimate meaning, the need for religion will remain. In any foreseeable future, religion—or its functional equivalents—will prosper. pp. 338–339.

TALKING ABOUT THEORY

Theoretical Paradigms

	CLASSICAL PARADIGMS			RECENT PARADIGMS	
	Structural-Functional Paradigm	Social-Conflict Paradigm	Symbolic-Interaction Paradigm	Feminist Paradigm	Postmodernist Paradigm
What is the level of analysis?	Macro level	Macro level	Micro level	Macro level	Micro and macro levels
What is the social significance of religion?	Religion provides answers to troubling questions about human purpose, choice, and emotional comfort (inclusive = functional). Religion divides us into believers and non-believers, resulting in conflict between different religious groups (exclusive = dysfunctional).	Religion reinforces social inequality by acting much like a drug, facilitating escape from personal misery.	Religion creates a feeling of belonging to a larger community through symbols, rituals, and cosmology.	Concentrates on how the world's religions have avoided or, more often, suppressed female spirituality.	Emphasizes local narratives as expressions of human spirituality. For example, the rise of New Age religions.
Has religion changed over time? How?	Yes/No. When linked to outstanding political objectives, religious messages change. For example, Christian fundamentalism and social conservatism.	No. All religions, regardless of cosmetic changes, remain false consciousness.	Yes/No. Changing social environments can lead to changes in rituals but not fundamental symbols and cosmology. For example, Catholic mass no longer in Latin.	Yes. Recovering the role of women and female spirituality from the three major world religions.	N/A

KEY TERMS

WEBLINKS

All URLs listed are current as of the printing of this book.

Canadian Montessori Academy
www.montessori-academy.com/about_montessori.htm
This page explains the philosophy of the Montessori Method of early education, in which the teacher creates a prepared environment supported by specialized materials that help children teach themselves.

Infidel Guy
www.infidelguy.com
Website of a free thought organization that rejects all doctrine.

Becoming a Pagan
www.spiralgoddess.com/Pagan101.html
This website provides information and links about paganism.

CRITICAL THINKING QUESTIONS

1. With technology providing greater out-of-classroom educational opportunities (courses through the internet, for example), will education's role in reproducing inequality be diminished?

2. How might education become a liberator for the poor and other minority groups?

3. What are some of the pressures high school students experience in today's economy and how might these pressures contribute to growing violence within the schools?

4. What are some of the ways the education system reproduces inequality? Access the Research Navigator through MySocLab and use keywords such as "hidden curriculum," "political socialization," "gender inequalities" and "racial inequalities" to locate relevant and recent scholarly and popular press publications to help you answer this question.

5. Compared to Americans, a much larger percentage of Canadians report that they have no religious affiliation. What do you think accounts for this difference? Do Weber's ideas of secularization have any merit?

6. Generally speaking, why do you think people from different classes in Canada also differ in their religious preferences? Compare the religious affiliation of small businessmen with the rich and the more underprivileged members of Canadian society.

 **Explore the topics covered in this chapter on MySocLab using the access information provided with this text. Interactive resources for studying include multimedia tutorials, video clips, practice tests, quizzes, and animated maps and figures.**

15

Medicine: Health and Illness in Canada

Rudy Johnson had a problem—how to transport a long extension ladder on a short pickup truck. Against her better judgment, his wife, Norma, consented to sit on the ladder while Rudy moved it. That worked out just fine—until Rudy took a curve too fast and Norma and the ladder spilled out.

This was not Norma's lucky day. She landed on her head.

An emergency medical team answered the 911 call. Determining that the unconscious woman was near death, the team ordered a helicopter to fly Norma to a trauma centre, where emergency specialists sprang into action. The trauma surgeon ordered X-rays, which revealed haziness in her lungs, probably from aspirated vomit. A CAT scan revealed a brain hemorrhage and a skull fracture. When a blood test showed that the oxygen level in her blood had fallen to a dangerously low level, an anesthesiologist inserted a breathing tube into Norma's trachea and administered 100 percent oxygen.

Norma's condition worsened. The trauma surgeon inserted a tube into her chest to expand a collapsed lung. The cardiologist pushed an ultrasound probe down her throat to take pictures of her beating heart and evaluate its pumping efficiency. The neurosurgeon drilled a hole in Norma's skull and inserted a pressure gauge to monitor her swollen brain.

To improve the blood flow to her lungs, a special bed rocked Norma from side to side that night. Her condition stabilized, and she lived. Norma vowed never again to ride in the back of a pickup—at least not on top of an extension ladder.

Source: Based on J.J. Miller (1995).

SOCIOLOGY AND THE STUDY OF MEDICINE

The technology that saved Norma Johnson's life, available in only a few places in the world, opens up fascinating possibilities in health care. It also contributes to skyrocketing medical costs and creates such dilemmas as whether or not such expensive technology should be rationed, topics we will explore in this chapter.

As we look at such issues, the role of sociology in the study of **medicine**—society's standard ways of dealing with illness and injury—will become apparent. Medicine is a profession, a bureaucracy, and a publicly funded institution in Canada. In the midst of our publicly funded, universally accessible medicare system in Canada stands what is called the Health-Industrial Complex. The Health-Industrial Complex comprises the pharmaceutical industries, private health insurance companies such as Blue Cross and Green Shield that provide extra medical coverage for Canadians, privately operated home-care industries, and many other for-profit industries that extend across the health and medicine sector of our economy.

Sociologists study how this important and extensive sector is influenced by ideas of self-regulation, the bureaucratic structure, and public policy in Canada. Sociologists also study how illness and health are much more than biological matters—how they are intimately related to cultural beliefs, lifestyle, and social class. Because of such emphases, the sociology of medicine is one of the applied fields of sociology.

THE SYMBOLIC INTERACTIONIST PERSPECTIVE

The Role of Culture in Defining Health and Illness

There are biological components of health—a nutritious diet, exercise, the use of antibiotics, and so on. However, there is also an important cultural dimension to physical well-being that is the focus of health and medical sociology.

Consider mental "illness" and mental "health." If a Canadian talks aloud to spirits that no one else can see, and takes direction from them, he or she is likely to be defined as mentally ill. In some tribal societies, someone who talks to invisible spirits might be honoured for being in close contact with the spiritual world—and, for everyone's good, declared a **shaman** (or healer) who will diagnose and treat medical problems.

Around the world, every culture provides guidelines its people use to determine whether they are "healthy" or "sick."

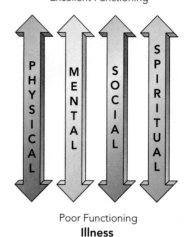

FIGURE 15.1   A Continuum of Health and Illness

This is another example of the vital role the social construction of reality plays in our lives.

What Is Health?

In 1941, international health experts identified three components of **health**: physical, mental, and social (World Health Organization, 1946). (See Figure 15.1. In light of recent feminist and postmodern interest in the "spiritual" side of well-being, we have added a spiritual component to the diagram.)

As symbolic interactionists stress, an important concern of sociologists is not to define what "true" health or "true" illness is. Instead, it is to analyze the effects of people's ideas of health and illness on their lives.

THE FUNCTIONALIST PERSPECTIVE

If society is to function well, its people need to be healthy enough to perform their normal roles. One way to control sickness is through a system of medical care societies. Another is to make rules that keep too many people from "being sick."

The Sick Role

Do you remember when you were young and your throat began to hurt and mom or dad took your temperature? The thermometer may have registered 39°C (37C is normal), and your parents perhaps took you to the doctor. Despite your protests that the next day was (your birthday or the first day of vacation), you had to spend the next three days in bed taking medicines. You were forced to play what sociologists call the **sick role**. What is meant by this term?

ELEMENTS OF THE SICK ROLE   Talcott Parsons (1953), who first analyzed the sick role, pointed out that it has

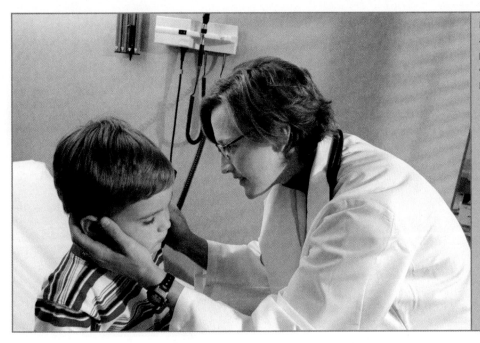

How do you think this doctor's assumptions of the cause and proper treatment of illness might contrast with those of the immigrant parents of her patient?

four elements—that you are not held responsible for being sick, that you are exempt from normal responsibilities, that you don't like the role, and that you will get competent help so you can return to your routines. People who don't seek competent help can be denied the right to claim sympathy from others and to be excused from their normal routines.

AMBIGUITY IN THE SICK ROLE Instead of a fever of 39°C, suppose the thermometer registers 37.4°C. Do you then "become" sick, or not? That is, do you decide to claim the sick role? Decisions to claim the sick role often are based more on social considerations than physical conditions. Let's also suppose you are facing a midterm for which you are drastically underprepared, and you are allowed to make it up. The more you think about the test, the worse you are likely to feel—legitimating to yourself the need to claim the sick role. Now assume that you have no test, but your friends are coming over to take you out to celebrate your nineteenth birthday. You are much less likely to play the sick role. Note that in the two cases your physical condition is the same.

GATEKEEPERS TO THE SICK ROLE Parents and physicians are the primary gatekeepers to the sick role. That is, they mediate between our feelings of illness and our claim to being sick. Before parents call the school to excuse a child's absence, they decide whether the child is faking or has genuine symptoms serious enough to allow him or her to remain home. For adults, physicians are the main gatekeepers of the sick role. A "doctor's excuse"—actually official permission to play the sick role—removes the need for employers and teachers to pass judgment on an individual's claim.

THE CONFLICT PERSPECTIVE

As stressed in earlier chapters, the primary focus of conflict theorists is how people struggle over scarce resources. Since medical treatment is one of those resources, let's examine this competition in a global perspective.

Effects of Global Stratification on Health Care

Our review in Chapter 5 of how globalization stratified the world economy stressed that the nations that industrialized obtained the economic and military power that allowed them to become rich and dominate the globe. One consequence is the globalization of medical care.

Consider the opening vignette as an example. The least industrialized nations cannot even begin to afford the technology that saved Norma Johnson's life. Life expectancy also illustrates globalization. Whereas most people in the industrialized world can expect to live to about 75, *most* people in Afghanistan, Angola, Cambodia, Haiti, and Rwanda die before they reach 50. The infant mortality rates shown in Figure 15.2 also tell the story. This figure lists the world's countries where fewer than 7 out of every 1000 babies die before they are a year old. *All* of them are industrialized nations. The contrast is stark—close to 150 of every 1000 babies born in Afghanistan and Angola never reach their first birthdays (*Statistical Abstract*, 1997, Table 1336).

Globalization, then, is a matter of life and death. Suppose you were born in a least industrialized nation located in the tropics. During your much shorter life, you would face illness and death from four major sources: malaria (from mosquitoes), internal parasites (from contaminated water), diarrhea

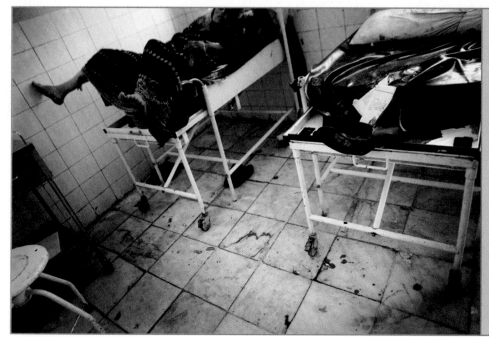

This woman has just given birth in a hospital in Badakshan, Afghanistan, a province that has the highest mortality rate recorded in human history: 64 percent of women of reproductive age die. If you examine this photo carefully, you probably can pinpoint part of the reason for these deaths.

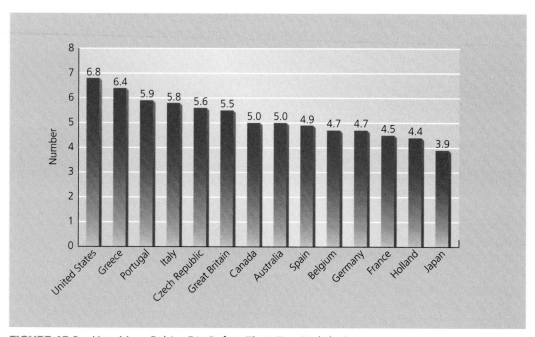

FIGURE 15.2   How Many Babies Die Before Their First Birthday?

Note: All countries listed in the source with an infant mortality rate below that of the United States. That this is not a complete list is evident from Austria, Switzerland, Hong Kong, and Sweden being dropped from the source, all of which had lower rates in the 1997 *Statistical Abstract*. Infant mortality is defined as the number of babies that die before their first birthday, per 1000 live births.

Source: By the author. Based on *Statistical Abstract* 2002, Table 1312.

(from food and soil contaminated with human feces), and malnutrition. A longer life expectancy in the developed industrial nations depends on diseases you are not likely to contract that could kill you early in life. Or, if you do contract malaria or diarrhea, there are "cures" available to you.

Focus Question

What are the differences between the functionalist and the conflict perspectives on health?

THE FEMINIST PERSPECTIVE

As discussed throughout the text, the primary focus of feminist theorists is how sexism pervades our social institutions and social life. Since medical treatment is an important institution in our society, let's examine how sexism works in medicine and health.

Sexism in Medicine

Although usually quite subtle, often even below people's awareness, sexism in medicine can carry serious consequences. As we saw in the Down-to-Earth Sociology box entitled "Making the Invisible Visible: The Deadly Effects of Sexism" in Chapter 7 (page 156), physicians don't take women's health complaints as seriously as men's. As a result, women with heart disease are operated on at a later stage, making it more likely they will die from their surgery.

Bias *against* women's reproductive organs has also been reported. Sue Fisher (1986) conducted participant observation in a hospital. When she heard doctors recommend a total hysterectomy (removal of both the uterus and the ovaries) although no cancer was present, she asked why. The doctors explained that the uterus and ovaries are "potentially disease-producing" organs. Also, they added, they are unnecessary after the child-bearing years, so why not remove them?

To "convince" the woman to have this surgery, the doctor tells her that, unfortunately, the examination uncovered fibroids in her uterus—and that they *might* turn into cancer. This statement is often sufficient, since it frightens women, who visualize themselves ready to be buried. What the surgeon does *not* say is that the fibroids will probably not turn into cancer and that many nonsurgical alternatives are available.

Underlying this sexism is the male dominance of medicine in Canada. This is not a worldwide phenomenon. In the former Soviet Union, for example, three out of four physicians are women (Knaus, 1981). Following changes in gender relations, the percentage of Canadian medical degrees earned by women has risen from only 24.3 percent in 1975 to 40.5 percent today (Altman, 1993). Today, 52 percent of doctors under the age of 35 are women. This changing sex ratio should help to reduce sexism in medical practice.

The Gendered Experience of Health and Illness: Some Explanations

There are gender differences in causes of death (discussed in the next section) and, although the gap is narrowing, in life expectancy (see Chapter 9). Moreover, we know that men and women experience health and illness differently. For example, having social support is a more important predictor of good health for women than for men.

What could account for these and other gendered differences? Leaving aside any biological answers, there are five sociological explanations for gender differences in the experience of health and illness.

1. First, there is *role accumulation*. This theory suggests that the more roles a person has, the better their health. However, this simple explanation fails to take into account the kinds of roles a woman performs. For example, the benefits of being married and having a job, such as increased income and social support, may be offset by the added burdens of the parental role. Therefore, modifications to this explanation have centred on the kinds of roles women and men perform.

2. A second explanation put forward for the gendered differences in health and illness concentrates on the negative effects of women's roles on their health and well-being. The demands of the *double day* (i.e., family and employment responsibilities) lead to increased stress and excessive demands on women's time and energy.

3. *Social acceptability*, the third explanation, suggests that due to the socialization of women into traditional roles, women are more willing than men to admit to being sick and accept help in dealing with their health problems. On the other hand, men are socialized to control their experiences of pain or illness and so are reluctant to adopt the sick role, and as a result, talk about their health. Therefore, women are more likely to share information about the types of symptoms they are experiencing. While men rely on their spouses for social support, women tend to turn to their friends and their children for help.

4. The fact that women experience more illness than men is explained by the *nurturing* tendencies of women. In their role as primary caregiver for their spouses, children, and aging parents, women experience considerable stress with little, if any, time left for themselves. As a result, they may neglect their own health.

5. Finally, there is the suggestion that men are socialized to take more risks than women while women are socialized to be cautious. This *competitive* view of gender role differences sees men engaging in more risky behaviours, such as smoking, alcohol, and accidents, while women take on more preventive and protective behaviours, such as seeking help early.

All these theories have been advanced in order to make sense of the complex differences between the social characteristics of men and women and their impact on the gendered experience of health and illness.

Focus Question

Is there a gendered experience of health and illness?

HISTORICAL PATTERNS OF HEALTH

How have patterns of health and illness in Canada changed? The answer to this question takes us into the field of **epidemiology**, the study of how medical disorders are distributed throughout a population.

The Doctor–Nurse Game

Leonard Stein (1988), a physician who observed nurses and doctors for many years, analyzed their interactions in terms of a game. Because physicians have higher status, nurses must try to give the impression that the doctor is always "in control." Although nurses spend more time with patients and, therefore, are often more familiar with their needs, nurses can never be perceived as giving recommendations to a doctor. Consequently, nurses disguise their recommendations. Consider the following dialogue between a nurse and a resident physician whom the nurse has called at 1 a.m. The rotating resident does not know the patient.

"This is Dr. Jones." (*An open and direct communication.*)

"Dr. Jones, this is Nurse Smith on 2W. Mrs. Brown learned today that her father died, and she is unable to fall asleep." (*This apparently direct, open communication of factual information— that the patient is unable to sleep and has learned of a death in the family— contains a hidden recommendation. The nurse has diagnosed the cause of the sleeplessness and is suggesting that a sedative be prescribed.*)

The conversation continues: "What sleeping medication has been helpful to Mrs. Brown in the past?" (*This communication, supposedly a mere request for facts, is actually a request for a recommendation of what to prescribe.*)

"Pentobarbital, 100 milligrams, was quite effective the night before last." (*This is actually a specific recommendation from the nurse to the physician, but it comes disguised in the form of factual information.*)

"Pentobarbital, 100 milligrams before bedtime, as needed for sleep. Got it?" (*This communication is spoken with audible authority—a little louder, a little firmer.*)

"Yes, I have, and thank you very much, Doctor."

The two successfully played the doctor–nurse game. The lower-status person made a recommendation to the higher-status person in a covert manner that required neither of them to acknowledge what really occurred and did not threaten their relative statuses.

According to Stein, incidences of the doctor–nurse game are decreasing because of the larger number of men in nursing, the feminist movement's challenging of male authority, and the larger number of women physicians. As a consequence, nurses are less subservient and physicians are less able to exert unquestioned authority.

Some version of the game will continue to be played, however, as long as status differences remain. The rules will simply be modified to meet changing circumstances.

Physical Health

Table 15.1 provides recent data for the leading causes of death among Canadians. The top three causes of death—cancer, heart disease, and cerebrovascular diseases such as strokes—affected 70 percent of men and women in Canada who died in 2002. Gender differences do exist when it comes to cancer and respiratory diseases, however, as women are slightly less likely than men to die of these causes. Women are more likely than men to die from nutritional and metabolic diseases such as diabetes, and from mental and behavioural disorders such as eating disorders. Also among the top 10 causes of death are infectious diseases such as HIV/AIDS and viral hepatitis, from which both men and women have a similar chance of dying. HIV/AIDS remains an important social and medical issue in Canada.

Between the provinces, Quebec reported the highest mortality rates for lung and colon cancer, while Alberta reported the lowest rates of lung cancer and British Columbia the lowest rates of colon cancers. Deaths due to suicide have declined in all provinces except Saskatchewan, Alberta, and Quebec. Quebec's rate not only remained the highest but exceeded the margin set the year before for all the provinces and territories in Canada. The reason or reasons for this cause of death is a matter of serious research and public policy remedies in Quebec. Having said this, the highest rates of suicide in Canada are among our Aboriginal populations, especially those located in the Yukon and the Northwest Territories. This must become a high priority for Indian and Northern Affairs Canada (INAC).

WERE CANADIANS HEALTHIER IN THE PAST? Mortality rates can help us answer this question. Because most people today live longer than their ancestors, we can conclude that contemporary Canadians are healthier.

Mental Health

When it comes to mental health, we have no rational basis for making comparisons. All groups have had their share of mental problems—and common-sense beliefs that mental illness is worse today represent perceptions, not measured reality. Since we don't know how extensive mental illness is now (M. W. Miller, 1993), we certainly can't judge how much there was in the past.

TABLE 15.1 Selected Leading Causes of Death, by Sex, 2007

	Deaths Both Sexes Total Number	Deaths Both Sexes Total %	Deaths Both Sexes Rate	Males Rate	Females Rate
All causes	215 669	100.0	658.7	844.0	521.6
Cancers	58 703	27.2	181.5	229.7	148.5
Diseases of the heart	57 417	26.6	173.0	230.8	129.7
Cerebrovascular diseases	16 051	7.4	47.8	52.8	43.9
Chronic obstructive pulmonary diseases and allied conditions	9618	4.5	29.0	44.5	20.1
Unintentional injuries	8626	4.0	27.6	37.8	17.9
Pneumonia and influenza	8032	3.7	23.7	31.5	19.2
Diabetes mellitus	5699	2.6	17.4	20.6	14.8
Hereditary and degenerative diseases of the central nervous system	5049	2.3	15.0	16.7	13.9
Diseases of the arteries, arterioles, and capillaries	4767	2.2	14.3	19.5	10.6
Psychoses	4645	2.2	13.6	13.3	13.4
Suicide	3681	1.7	12.0	19.5	4.9
Nephritis, nephrotic syndrome, and nephrosis	2654	1.2	8.0	11.0	6.1
Chronic liver diseases and cirrhosis	2030	0.9	6.4	8.9	4.2
Neurotic disorders, personality disorders, and other nonpsychotic mental disorders	1163	0.5	3.5	4.8	2.5
HIV infection	626	0.3	2.0	3.6	0.5

1. Age-standardized mortality rate per 100 00 population.

Source: Statistics Canada, Health Statistics Division. www40.statcan.ca/l01/cst01/health36.htm?sdi=leadingcausesdeath. Last modified: 2008-05-08.

ISSUES IN HEALTH CARE

Health Care in Canada

While the provision of health care in Canada is a provincial responsibility, the federal government has played a major role in the past in financing the health care services available to all Canadians.

The primary purpose of national health insurance in Canada is the elimination of financial barriers to health care. Universal, government-funded medical, hospital, and other related health insurance has been available only since 1971, even though there was a federal hospital insurance program in the 1950s and a federal medical insurance program covering physicians and related services in the mid 1960s.

Under Canada's medicare system, hospitals are financed on the basis of annually negotiated planned-for budgets. Physicians are reimbursed on a fee-for-service basis (as is the case in the United States). However, these fees are determined by province-wide, negotiated, uniform fee schedules.

Private insurance companies offer coverage only for various forms of additional services, such as private-room accommodation in hospitals, eyeglasses (up to a certain dollar limit), and pharmaceutical drugs. (Note that as of 2004, Ontario no longer covers eye examinations under medicare.)

In 1984, the *Canada Health Act* came into force to ensure that necessary health services would be available to all Canadians regardless of their financial circumstances. The Act sets out a national standard for the provision of Canada's health care with which the provinces are obligated to comply under penalty of withholding transfer payments.

Table 15.2 outlines the five basic criteria: comprehensive scope, universal coverage, public administration, portability, and accessibility.

Federal funding for health care took a severe slashing during Paul Martin's later years as finance minister (1997 and following), when he was tackling the federal deficit and, as a result, slashed health care contributions to the provinces

TABLE 15.2 *Canada Health Act, 1984*

Criterion	Description
Comprehensive	A province must cover all services provided by physicians (general practitioners and specialists)
Universal	A province must provide insured services to all insured residents and must not impose a residential or waiting period longer than three months
Public administration	A provincial plan must be administered and operated on a nonprofit basis by a public authority
Portability	The benefits must be available to insured persons temporarily absent from the province (e.g., on vacation) and to those who move to another province until such time as they qualify for medicare benefits in that province
Accessibility	A province's health care services must be reasonably accessible to all insured persons

(see Table 15.3). Beginning in 1996–1997, the older Established Programs Financing (EPF) was replaced by the Canada Health and Social Transfer program (CHST). Unlike the EPF, which was divided into separate categories of health insurance, extended health care, and postsecondary education, the CHST is a block transfer payment to the provinces. This makes determining the federal share of health costs extremely difficult. However, we know that the federal government's share of health care funding has been dramatically cut. Even recently, the federal contribution has barely

TABLE 15.3 Federal and Provincial Expenditures on Health, 1989–2007

Year	Federal Expenditures Millions of $	% of Total	Provincial Expenditures Millions of $	% of Total
1989	7723	18.7	33 449	81.3
1990	7818	17.4	37 026	82.6
1991	7397	15.6	39 859	84.4
1992	8081	15.4	44 397	84.6
1993	9803	17.6	45 859	82.4
1994	9803	17.5	46 041	82.5
1995	9392	16.8	46 416	83.2
1996	9024	15.9	47 641	84.1
1997	1177	2.4	47 951	97.6
1998	1327	2.6	49 553	97.4
1999	1509	2.7	54 354	97.3
2000	1730	2.9	57 821	97.1
2001	3630	5.4	63 584	94.6
2002	3286	4.7	66 594	95.3
2003	3498	4.7	70 893	95.3
2004	6044	7.3	76 758	92.7
2005	23 774	22.6	81 615	77.4
2006	21 823	20.2	86 233	79.8
2007	22 901	19.7	93 289	80.3
2008	25 805	20.4	100 454	79.6

Source: Dan Glenday and Kevin Manual, Brock University Library Consultant. Data from Statistics Canada, 2005, CANSIM II database, Table 358-0002.

reached pre-1997 funding levels although expenditures have skyrocketed. Despite several years of record budget surpluses, there is little evidence that the federal government has reversed its course voluntarily. Even after Roy Romanow's report (from the Commission on the Future of Health Care in Canada), *Building on Values: The Future of Health Care in Canada*, was tabled in Parliament in November 2002, there was little sustained momentum for advancing the benefits of publicly funded health care. The recent (2003–2005) transfer of health care monies to the provinces may begin the process of re-establishing the federal government's commitments to publicly funded health care in Canada. However, a June 2005 ruling in Quebec protecting a patient's right to access private services may become more important for the future health of medicare.

Data for the 2000–2001 fiscal year reveal a total transfer to the provinces and territories under the CHST of almost $33 billion. What amounts go directly to medical health care and what goes to social spending is determined mainly by individual provinces and territories.

One issue that occasionally surfaces is the use of *extra billing*, or charging patients "a little extra" as a means of cutting down on "unnecessary" visits by patients to general practitioners. As early as 1968–1972, Saskatchewan instituted a regime of modest extra billing. This measure was devastating to the poor and the elderly, and little evidence could be found to support the contention that extra billing cut down on unnecessary visits to doctors. On the contrary, R. G. Evans, a health care economist, concluded from his study of the province's "experiment" in extra billing that it involved "perverse wealth transfers from the ill to the healthy and from low-to-high income classes" (Barer, Evans, & Stoddart, 1979, p. 111).

More recently, British Columbia, Alberta, Newfoundland, Manitoba, and Nova Scotia have experimented with extra billing. However, under the *Canada Health Act*, the federal government penalized each province. Alberta, for example, lost almost $4 million, and Newfoundland was penalized $270 000, Nova Scotia $157 000, and Manitoba $1.3 million before banning user fees.

Focus Question

Describe the publicly funded health care system in Canada.

SARS (Severe Acute Respiratory Syndrome)

SARS (Severe Acute Respiratory Syndrome) recently became a health issue in Canada. According to the World Health Organization (WHO), a total of 8098 people worldwide became sick with SARS during the 2003 outbreak. With only sporadic cases reported since the original outbreak, SARS has receded from the public's attention.

It is widely recognized that SARS had a dramatic impact on the tourism industry in Canada. Not until 2005 was there any sign of relief that the industry may be on the rebound. Table 15.4 provides a brief annotated history of the outbreak of the disease.

The Development of the Sociology of Health in Canada

The sociology of health in Canada has passed through at least two major stages. During the 1970s, or stage one, it focused on matters related to the complexity of the health care system, such as the changing relationships between health care professionals, the challenges posed by nurses and chiropractors to the dominance of the traditional model of medicine, and the dynamics of the sick role and patient illness behaviour. During the 1980s, the second stage brought the inclusion of other themes, such as the impact of population aging on health and health care delivery.

The principal focus of research in the field of health care has been the use of large surveys to gauge the health status of Canadians. The most recent is the ongoing longitudinal *National Population Health Survey (NPHS)*, conducted by Health Canada and Statistics Canada. This large survey, begun in 1994 and continuing every second year thereafter, is an important source of information about the health and health behaviours of Canadians. The NPHS, which relies on respondents' self-reported health information, surveys the same group of respondents every two years for up to 20 years. In the studies that have been conducted recently, the most significant finding centres on the *causal* links between social status and health status. That is, social factors such as socioeconomic status (e.g., income and education) and gender, age, and ethnicity play a vital part in determining how healthy Canadians are. The recent Health Behaviour in School-Aged Children study (2008) examined the health, well-being, and health behaviours of young people (aged 11 to 15 years) and their social settings and conditions, especially the school environment. The survey is a continuing, cross-national research project conducted in collaboration with the WHO Regional Office for Europe. The findings are numerous, but a few pertinent results include: obesity is on the rise among this age group for both boys and girls, almost two fifths of students reported being victims of bullying, daily smoking is down from 2002, and condom use during respondents' last sexual intercourse is reported by four-fifths of sexually active boys in Grades 9 and 10. A 2005 study by Morris et al. provides data on an opposite phenomenon— the "drift hypothesis," or how a deterioration in a person's health can lead to a reduction in her or his income. In addition to these studies, others have confirmed that the organization of work and family life are important predictors of the health status of Canadians.

Focus Question

What is the sociology of health in Canada?

Depersonalization

One of the main criticisms levelled against the medical profession is its **depersonalization**, the practice of dealing

CHAPTER 15 Medicine: Health and Illness in Canada 351

TABLE 15.4 A Brief Chronology of SARS (Severe Acute Respiratory Syndrome)

Date	Event
Feb. 15, 2003	China reports 305 cases of atypical pneumonia (later classified as SARS).
March 5, 2003	Sui-chu Kwan, a 78-year-old woman who had travelled to Hong Kong in February, dies of SARS in Toronto.
March 12, 2003	The World Health Organization (WHO) issues a global SARS alert.
March 17, 2003	Health Canada announces 11 suspected cases of SARS in Canada: 9 in Ontario, 1 in B.C., and 1 in Alberta.
March 21, 2003	Canadian scientists say they have isolated the virus that causes SARS. The virus comes from the same family that gives people mumps or measles.
March 26, 2003	Ontario declares a public health emergency and orders thousands of people to quarantine themselves in their homes. There are 27 probable cases of SARS in the province. Toronto hospitals begin barring visitors.
April 1, 2003	WHO advises travellers to stay away from Hong Kong and China.
April 23, 2003	WHO warns against all unnecessary travel to Toronto, Beijing, and China's Shanxi province because of the SARS outbreak. The three locations join Hong Kong and China's Guangdong province on the WHO list.
April 24, 2003	Health Canada sends a formal letter of protest to the WHO, demanding that the UN health agency take back its Toronto travel advisory. Health Canada says the WHO based its warning on outdated information.
	The U.S. Centers for Disease Control and Prevention says it doesn't believe a travel advisory is warranted for Toronto since public health officials understand the patterns of transmission in the city. British medical officers, meanwhile, support the advisory.
April 29, 2003	The WHO announces it will lift its travel advisory against Toronto, effective April 30, 2003.
May 30, 2003	Thirty SARS-related deaths in Canada are reported—all of them in the Toronto area.
July 2, 2003	WHO removes Toronto from its list of SARS-affected cities.
September 29, 2003	Ontario's SARS inquiry opens the first of three days of public hearings in Toronto.

Source: Dan Glenday. Data from CBC News *Timeline*, December 15, 2003, www.cbc.ca/news/background/sars/timeline.html.

with people as though they are cases and diseases, not individuals. Many patients get the impression they are being treated by a physician who, while talking to them, is impatiently counting minutes.

Participant observation of medical students at McMaster University by sociologists Jack Haas and William Shaffir (1978/1993) provides insight into how physicians learn to depersonalize patients. Haas and Shaffir found that students begin medical school wanting to "treat the whole person." As vast amounts of material are thrown at them, their feelings for patients are overpowered by the need to be efficient. These students' statements pick up on the change:

> Somebody will say, "Listen to Mrs. Jones' heart." It's just a little thing flubbing on the table. And *you forget about the rest of her* . . . The advantage is that *you can go in a short time and see a patient, get the important things out of the patient, and leave* [italics added].

> . . . Someone comes in who has croaked (died) [and you say], "Well, come on. Here is a chance to practise your intubation" [inserting a tube in the throat].

Medicalization of Society

As we have seen, women's reproductive organs have become defined as medical matters. Sociologists use the term **medicalization** to refer to the process of turning something that was not previously considered medical into a medical matter. Examples include balding, weight, wrinkles, acne, anxiety, depression, a sagging chin or buttocks, small breasts, and even the inability to achieve orgasm. There is nothing inherently medical in such human conditions, yet we have become so used to medicalization that we tend to consider them somehow naturally medical concerns. As Susan Sontag (1994) says, even many criminal behaviours have become matters to be medically understood and treated.

BIOETHICS

Medicine and ethics are by no means strangers—on the contrary, medicine started out as an aspect of early philosophy. Bioethics began with the Oath of Hippocrates, some of whose tenets included: treat the sick to the best of one's ability, preserve patient privacy, and teach the secrets of medicine to the next generation. Today, the advent of new reproductive and genetic technologies has opened the door to a number of new ethical concerns never contemplated by Hippocrates. Human cloning, stem cell research, abortion, euthanasia, and the selling of organs are a few of the issues we are confronted with today. Let's look at euthanasia.

Medically Assisted Suicide

Should doctors be able to write lethal prescriptions for terminally ill patients? Jack Kevorkian, a retired pathologist, has helped over 100 people commit suicide (Denzin, 1992). Some defend Kevorkian as a courageous trailblazer, while others decry his acts as perverted. A how-to book on suicide, *Final Exit*, has sold over half a million copies. The Hemlock Society is a group advocating voluntary **euthanasia**—mercy killing—for terminally ill people. The case of "Nancy B." (a pseudonym), a terminally ill patient at Hôtel Dieu hospital in Quebec City, although considered by some to be an instance of euthanasia, is more properly an example of the right to refuse medical treatment. For 2 1/2 years, Nancy suffered from a neurological disease called Guillain-Barré syndrome, from which there was no cure. She was totally helpless and physically dependent on the health care staff at the hospital. Nancy wanted to have her life-sustaining equipment disconnected, and when she went to court in 1992 to plead for this right, Justice Jacques Dufour ruled in favour of the patient's right to self-determination. Some argue that the Nancy B. case is an example of "passive euthanasia," a situation in which the person is rational (according to legal definitions) but requires assistance to stop artificial treatment of an incurable illness.

At the opposite end of the euthanasia spectrum is the situation depicted in the Oscar-winning film *Les Invasions Barbares* (*The Barbarian Invasions*) by acclaimed Quebec director Denys Arcand. The film tells the moving story of Rémy, a history professor in his 50s who is dying of cancer. Rémy opts to die while he is still in control of his faculties. Assisted by his son, Sébastien, his family, and close friends, Rémy is administered an overdose of morphine and dies quietly in the countryside, surrounded by those who love him.

With new technology that can keep the body alive even after the heart, lungs, and other vital organs no longer function on their own, a burning question, yet undecided, is "Who has the right to pull the plug?" Should someone's body be kept alive for years even though their mind can no longer work? To resolve this issue, some people sign a **living will**—a declaration they make while in good health of what they want medical personnel to do in case they become dependent on artificial life support systems.

Our technology and the acts of Dr. Kevorkian have brought us face to face with matters of death that are both disturbing and unresolved. Should "medically assisted suicide" be legal? Few find this medical-ethical issue easy to resolve. The following Thinking Critically about Social Controversy box explores these issues.

THINKING CRITICALLY ABOUT SOCIAL CONTROVERSY
Euthanasia in the Netherlands

Proponents of euthanasia base their claim on "people's right to die." "If someone wants to be disconnected from feeding tubes," they say, "he or she should be able to die in peace. And if someone wants to commit suicide, that person should have the right to do so. What right does the rest of society have to interfere?"

If the issue is framed this way, many Canadians would agree that euthanasia should be permitted. The problem, say its opponents, is that most euthanasia involves other types of dying.

The best example, critics point out, is the Netherlands, which has allowed euthanasia for over 20 years. According to Dutch law, a physician can assist a patient in dying if the patient makes "a free, informed, and persistent request."

Euthanasia must be a "last resort," and physicians are accountable to the courts for following the letter of the law.

The most recent Dutch study commissioned by the government indicates that since 1996, the number of cases of euthanasia that were reported increased from 41 percent to 54 percent. Researchers estimated that overall, 3500 cases occurred in 2001, or 2.5 percent of all deaths, as compared to 3200 (or 2.4 percent) in 1995. The number of assisted suicides decreased from 400 in 1995 to 300 in 2001. The total number of requests for euthanasia remained the same, at about 9700. Of these, 39 percent were accepted by a doctor in 2001, a similar percentage to that in 1995 (BMJ, 2003: www.bmj.com/cgi/content/full/326/7400/1164?etoc).

Leading Dutch physicians who practise euthanasia oppose its legalization in the United States, which has a private, for-profit health care system (unlike Canada and the Netherlands, where health care is publicly funded). Said one, "If euthanasia were allowed in the United States, I would not want to be a patient there. In view of the financial costs that the care of patients can impose on relatives and society under the United States health care system, the legalization of euthanasia in America would be an open door to get rid of patients."

For Your Consideration
What do you think?

Sources: Gomez (1991); Markson (1992); Angell (1996).

THREATS TO HEALTH

In this section we will examine the following threats to health: AIDS, the globalization of disease, drugs, and disabling environments.

AIDS

Perhaps one of the most pressing health issues today in Canada—and globally—is AIDS (Acquired Immune Deficiency Syndrome). Let's look at some of its major characteristics.

ORIGIN The origin of AIDS is unknown. The most prevalent theory is that the virus was first present in monkeys in Africa and then transmitted to humans. If so, how the transmission to humans took place remains a matter of conjecture. It may have occurred during the 1920s and 1950s, when, in a peculiar experiment for malaria, people were inoculated with blood from monkeys and chimpanzees. The blood may have been infected with viral ancestors of HIV (Rathus & Nevid, 1993). Since monkeys are considered food in several parts of Africa, another possibility is that the virus was transmitted through inadequately cooked meat. Some suggest an opposite theory, that the disease originated in Europe or the United States and was somehow transmitted to Africa (Rushing, 1995).

THE TRANSMISSION OF AIDS AIDS is known to be transmitted through the exchange of blood and semen, and, in rare cases, through mother's milk to newborns. Since the virus can be present in all bodily fluids, including sweat, tears, spittle, and urine, some people think AIDS can also be transmitted

in these forms. The U.S. Centers for Disease Control and Prevention, however, says that AIDS cannot be transmitted by casual contact in which traces of these fluids would be exchanged. The correct use of condoms is the best preventative measure against AIDS and other STDs (see Figure 15.3.)

THE STIGMA OF AIDS One of the most significant sociological aspects of AIDS is its stigma, another example of how social factors are essential to health and illness. From the outset, the notion of AIDS as a "gay disease" was spread rapidly by television evangelists and other Christian conservatives in Canada and the United States. Even today, in many parts of the world including our own, some remain convinced that AIDS is a "divine" message from God. Some people even refuse to be tested because they fear the stigma they would have to bear if they tested positive. One unfortunate consequence is the further spread of AIDS by people who "don't want to know." The stigma is so great in Africa and some Asian countries that government officials refuse to acknowledge how widespread the disease is. Burying their heads in the sand, however, makes them unable to sponsor preventive measures, so the epidemic grows (Shenon, 1995). If this disease is to be brought under control, its stigma must be overcome: AIDS must be thought of as being, like other lethal diseases, simply the work of a destructive biological organism.

THE GLOBALIZATION OF AIDS Today's global travel has facilitated the globalization of this disease. Africa has been hit hardest (Haub, 1997). In some countries ravaged by AIDS, life expectancy may be cut in half (Olshansky, Carnes, Rogers, & Smith, 1997). Botswana, Uganda, and Zimbabwe

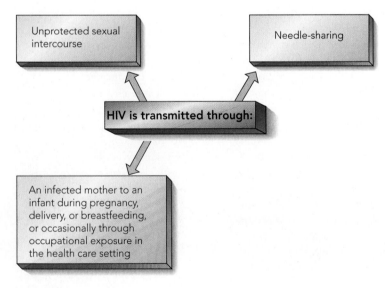

Unprotected sexual intercourse

Needle-sharing

HIV is transmitted through:

An infected mother to an infant during pregnancy, delivery, or breastfeeding, or occasionally through occupational exposure in the health care setting

FIGURE 15.3 How Do I Get HIV/AIDS?

AIDS is devastating huge areas of Africa. In some countries, a third or more of the population has AIDS. Millions of children have been orphaned. Governments that first ignored the problem are now trying to battle the disease. This anti-AIDS billboard is posted in Nairobi, Kenya.

are likely to lose a quarter of their populations (Stout, 1992). In Kampala and Kigali, a third of all pregnant women have AIDS (Scommegna, 1996). The bubonic plague is considered to have killed about 30 million people in medieval Europe. The U.S. Census Bureau projects that by 2010, as a result of AIDS deaths and the loss of future population from the deaths of women of child-bearing age, sub-Saharan Africa will have 71 million fewer people than it would otherwise (Christensen, 2000). In the former Soviet Union, AIDS is multiplying, primarily due to the rise in prostitution and drug use since the fall of communism (Kaminski & Palchikoff, 1997). AIDS is also flourishing in Asia, partly because of its huge sex industry.

IS THERE A CURE FOR AIDS? The number of deaths due to AIDS in Canada began to decline in 1996. Does this mean we have found a cure? With thousands of scientists searching, the media have heralded every new breakthrough in research as a possible cure, but this has yet to appear.

The most promising treatment to date, the one that lies behind the reduction in deaths, was spearheaded by David Ho, a virologist (virus researcher). If patients in the very early stages of the disease take a "cocktail" of drugs (a combination of protease inhibitors, AZT, and 3TC), the "visible" signs of the virus can be erased from their bodies. Their immune systems then rebound (C. Gorman, 1997b). No one is yet calling this a cure, however; apparently the virus lingers undetected, ready to flourish if the drugs are withdrawn.

While most praise this new treatment, some researchers have issued a warning (Rotello, 1996). They suggest that the cocktail may become this decade's penicillin. When penicillin

was introduced, everyone was ecstatic with its results. But over the years, the microbes it targets mutated, producing "super bugs" against which we have no protection. If this is the case with AIDS, then a new, "super AIDS" virus may hit the world with even more fury than the first devastating wave.

The Globalization of Disease

In the movie *Outbreak*, when a new disease threatened the world, government epidemiologists were transformed into Indiana Jones–style heroes in order to save it. But despite its overdramatization, the movie's depiction of the rapid spread of disease is not far from reality. Modern travel has wiped out the frontiers that used to contain diseases.

New diseases keep appearing on the world scene, and antibiotics are ineffective against many of them. The only way Ebola, with its particularly hideous death, could be contained was to isolate an entire region in Zaire. When SARS appeared in 2003 (discussed earlier in the chapter), the fear was that it would encircle the globe, killing millions of people in a short time. Each person with SARS was isolated and cities and regions were declared off limits to visitors. The same thing happened with outbreaks of Asian bird flu (avian influenza) and the Marburg virus in Angola, which causes death from fever, diarrhea, vomiting, and bleeding (LaFraniere, 2005).

When such deadly diseases for which there are no cures break out, world health officials send out emergency medical teams to seal off affected areas. They have been successful in containing diseases so far, but fear that they won't always be so fortunate. (Olshansky et al., 1997).

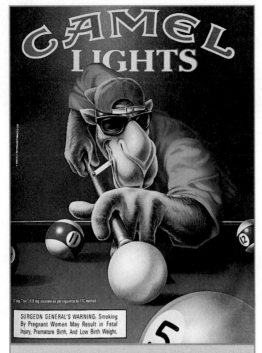

Do you think that this magazine ad is designed to make cigarettes appealing to male youths? Although tobacco industry officials denied they were trying to entice youth to smoke, evidence such as this ad is overwhelmingly against them. After pressure from the U.S. Congress, in 1997 Camel agreed to terminate its Joe Camel ads.

Drugs: Alcohol and Nicotine

Let's examine some of the health consequences of alcohol and nicotine, the most frequently used drugs in Canada.

ALCOHOL Alcohol is the standard recreational drug of Canadians. Is it bad for your health? This beverage cuts both ways. About two drinks a day for men and one drink for women reduce the risk of heart attacks and blood vessel diseases. (Women weigh less on average and produce fewer enzymes that metabolize alcohol.) Beyond these amounts, however, alcohol increases the risk of a variety of diseases, from cancer to stroke. It also increases the likelihood of birth defects.

NICOTINE Of all drugs, nicotine is the most harmful to human health. Smokers in their 30s are six times more likely to have heart attacks than nonsmokers of the same age (Winslow, 1995). Smoking doubles the risk of blindness in old age (Lagnado, 1996). It also causes progressive emphysema and several types of cancer that kill an increasing number of Canadians every year. Between 1991 and 2001, deaths due to smoking increased from over 41 000 to almost 47 000, or over 20 percent of *all* deaths in Canada. By far, nicotine is the most lethal of all recreational drugs.

Stressing the health hazards of smoking and of secondhand smoke, an anti-tobacco campaign is being waged successfully in Europe and North America. It helped end smoking on Canadian airlines and led to nonsmoking regulations in bars, restaurants, and offices across the country.

Why do people still smoke? There are two main reasons. First, nicotine is addictive, maybe even as addictive as heroin (Tolchin, 1998). The second reason is advertising. Although the tobacco companies deny it, they target youth, often by associating cigarette smoking with success, high fashion, and independence. The tobacco industry is relentless in its pursuit of adolescent smokers, and in 2004 introduced cigarettes spiked with candy flavours in the U.S. (O'Connell: 2004).

Disabling Environments

A **disabling environment** is one harmful to health. The health risk of some occupations is evident: mining and the construction industry are obvious examples. In many occupations, however, people become aware of the risk only years after they worked at jobs they thought were safe. For example, several million people worked with asbestos during and after World War II. Now the government estimates that a quarter of them will die of cancer from having breathed asbestos dust. It is likely that many other substances we have

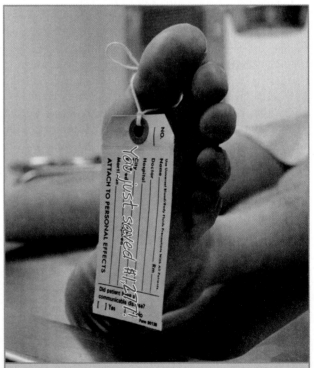

In a mind-boggling attempt to justify cigarette smoking, Philip Morris reported that the Czech government saves $1227 in pensions and health care every time a smoker dies. Following this reasoning, to reduce government deficits we might want to require smoking classes in kindergarten—for the sooner people begin to smoke, the sooner they get sick and die, and the more the government saves.

not yet identified also cause slowly developing cancers (Meier, 1987).

Although industrialization has increased the world's standard of living, it also threatens to disable the basic environment of the human race, posing what may be the greatest health hazard of all time. The burning of vast amounts of carbon fuels is leading to the *greenhouse effect*, a warming of the earth that may change the globe's climate, melt its polar icecaps, and flood the earth's coastal shores. Use of fluorocarbon gases in such items as aerosol cans, refrigerators, and air conditioners is threatening the *ozone shield*, the protective layer of the earth's upper stratosphere that screens out a high proportion of the sun's ultraviolet rays. High-intensity ultraviolet radiation is harmful to most forms of life. In humans, it causes skin cancer. The pollution of land, air, and water, especially by nuclear waste, pesticides, herbicides, and other chemicals, poses additional risks to life on our planet.

To identify environmental threats to world health is only the first step. The next is to introduce short- and long-term policies to reduce such problems. The sociology of the environment is discussed in Chapter 17.

THE SEARCH FOR ALTERNATIVES

What alternatives are there to the way medicine is usually practised? The suggestion we explore here is to shift the emphasis away from the *treatment* of disease to the *prevention* of it.

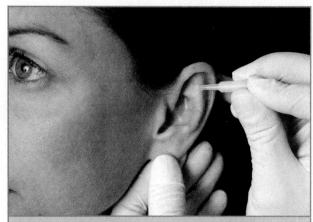

In auriculotherapy, reflex points of the ear are stimulated to relieve chronic pain and alleviate substance abuse.

Treatment or Prevention?

EFFECTS OF VALUES AND LIFESTYLES Prevention implies both an individual and a group responsibility. At the individual level, exercising regularly, eating nutritious food, having protected sex, and avoiding smoking and alcohol abuse go a long way to preventing disease. Following these guidelines can add years to our lives.

At the group level, one alternative is preventive medicine. Instead of the treatment of disease, medicine could have "wellness" as its goal. What would it require to implement

---

SOCIOLOGY AND THE NEW TECHNOLOGY

Who Should Live and Who Should Die? Technology and the Dilemma of Medical Rationing

Visiting a doctor or a hospital today is not without risk, but the risk is small compared to the time in history when physicians bled and purged their patients. Today's physicians are well trained, and medical care is supported by scientific studies. Our new technology even allows us to cure medical conditions that just a short time ago doomed people to premature death. In other instances, the medical condition remains, but the patient is able to live a long life.

And there's the rub. Some technology is limited, and there isn't enough to go around to everyone who needs it.

Other technology is so costly that it would bankrupt society if it were made available to everyone who has a particular condition. Who, then, should receive the benefits of new medical technology?

At the heart of the issue of how to spend limited resources are questions not only of cost, but also of fairness, of how to distribute equitably the benefits of advanced medical technology.

For Your Consideration

The dilemma is harsh: if we choose medical rationing, many sick people will be

allowed to die. If we don't, we may go bankrupt. In more specific terms, should a federal Cabinet minister who is an alcoholic be given a liver transplant when he is already dying of cancer? Use ideas, concepts, and principles presented in this and other chapters to develop a reasonable answer to this pressing issue. Also note how this dilemma changes shape if you view it from the contrasting perspectives of conflict, functionalism, and symbolic interactionism.

a national policy of "prevention, not intervention" This would necessitate a program of education in schools and the media showing how some practices of nutrition, exercise, sex, and judicious prescription drug use pay off with healthier lives. For example, diet is a significant factor in many types of cancer, and an educational program to replace fatty, low-fibre foods with a diet rich in fruits, vegetables, and green tea would go a long way in saving lives. Unfortunately, rather than making such basic changes, most Canadians still seem to prefer that their doctors prescribe drugs.

On yet a broader scale is comprehensive prevention—eliminating disabling environments and the use of harmful drugs. Some businesses continue to spew industrial wastes into the air and use rivers and oceans as industrial sewers, while others use advertising to seduce youths to use harmful drugs. These acts are unconscionable. Since we now live in a global village, the creation and maintenance of a health-producing environment requires international controls and co-operation.

SUMMARY AND REVIEW

Sociology and the Study of Medicine

WHAT IS THE ROLE OF SOCIOLOGY IN THE STUDY OF MEDICINE?
Sociologists study **medicine** as a social institution. As practised in Canada, three of its primary characteristics are professionalization, bureaucracy, and public policy. p. 344.

The Symbolic Interactionist Perspective

WHAT IS THE SYMBOLIC INTERACTIONIST PERSPECTIVE ON HEALTH AND ILLNESS?
Health is not only a biological matter but is also intimately related to society. Illness is not only an objective matter; it can be viewed from within the framework of culture, and such definitions vary from one group to another. p. 344.

The Functionalist Perspective

WHAT IS THE FUNCTIONALIST PERSPECTIVE ON HEALTH AND ILLNESS?
The **sick role** is society's permission to not perform one's usual activities. In return for this permission, the individual assumes responsibility to seek competent help and to co-operate in getting well so he or she can quickly resume normal activities. pp. 344–345.

The Conflict Perspective

WHAT IS THE CONFLICT PERSPECTIVE ON HEALTH AND ILLNESS?
Health care is one of the scarce resources over which groups compete. On a global level, health care follows the international stratification we studied in Chapter 6, with the best health care available in the industrialized nations and the worst in the least industrialized nations. pp. 345–346.

The Feminist Perspective

WHAT IS THE FEMINIST PERSPECTIVE ON HEALTH AND ILLNESS?
Sexism is one source of gender inequality in medicine. More recently, five explanations have been advanced to account for the gendered experience of health and illness: role accumulation, double day, social acceptability, nurturing tendencies of women, and competition. p. 347.

Historical Patterns of Health

WHAT ARE THE GENDER DIFFERENCES IN CAUSES OF DEATH?
The three leading causes of death—cancer, heart disease, and cerebrovascular diseases such as strokes—are the same for both men and women in Canada. Women are more likely than men to die from nutritional and metabolic diseases such as diabetes, and from mental and behavioural disorders such as eating disorders. Among the top 10 causes of death are infectious diseases such as HIV/AIDS and viral hepatitis, of which both men and women have a similar chance of dying. HIV/AIDS remains an important social and medical issue in Canada. pp. 347–349.

Issues in Health Care

WHICH LEVEL OF GOVERNMENT IN CANADA IS RESPONSIBLE FOR HEALTH CARE?
While the provision of health care in Canada is a provincial responsibility, the federal government has played a major role in financing the health care services available to all Canadians. p. 349.

WHAT ARE THE FIVE PROVISIONS OF THE *CANADA HEALTH ACT* (1984)?
The five provisions of the *Canada Health Act* (1984) are comprehensive scope, universal coverage, public administration, portability, and accessibility. pp. 349–350.

IS EXTRA BILLING A GOOD IDEA FOR CUTTING COSTS TO THE HEALTH CARE SYSTEM IN CANADA?
Research has shown that although extra billing has meant that the poor and the elderly were dissuaded from going to their general practitioner, there was no support for the contention that extra billing cut down on unnecessary visits to doctors. p. 351.

WHAT IS ONE OF THE MAJOR FINDINGS OF THE SOCIOLOGY OF HEALTH RESEARCH IN CANADA?

The most significant finding centres on the *causal* links between social status and health status of Canadians. p. 351.

Bioethics

WHY IS MEDICALLY ASSISTED SUICIDE AN ISSUE NOW?

As a result of advanced technology, people can be kept technically alive even when they have no brain waves. Physicians who openly assist in suicides have come under severe criticism. Research findings on **euthanasia** in the Netherlands have fuelled this controversy. pp. 352–353.

Threats to Health

WHAT ARE SOME THREATS TO THE HEALTH OF CANADIANS?

AIDS, alcohol and nicotine—the most lethal drugs used by Canadians—and **disabling environments**—environments harmful to human health that lead to work-related diseases or pollution of air and water. pp. 353–357.

The Search for Alternatives

ARE THERE ALTERNATIVES TO OUR CURRENT HEALTH CARE SYSTEM?

The primary alternative discussed in this chapter is a change from treatment to the prevention of disease. pp. 357–358.

TALKING ABOUT THEORY

Theoretical Paradigms

	CLASSICAL PARADIGMS			RECENT PARADIGMS
	Structural-Functional Paradigm	Social-Conflict Paradigm	Symbolic-Interaction Paradigm	Feminist Paradigm
What is the level of analysis?	Macro level	Macro level	Micro level	Micro and macro levels
What is the social significance of medicine?	The sick role and sick role behaviours allow individuals to be exempt from normal responsibilities. The sick role is a temporary, medically sanctioned form of deviant behaviour.	The globalization of health care increases the risks of illness and death in less developed nations.	Different cultures provide guidelines for who is "healthy" and who isn't.	Gendered differences in the diagnosis and treatment of illness.
Has the sociological study of medicine changed over time?	No.	Yes/No. As changing technology provides new opportunities for curing illness, those with the fewest resources in either rich or less developed countries will be denied access.	Yes. As social attitudes change toward what constitutes health and the role of medicine.	Yes/No. Changes in legal prohibitions against women in medicine are significantly positive. Patriarchy remains.

KEY TERMS

WEBLINKS

All URLs listed are current as of the printing of this book.

World Health Organization (WHO)
www.who.int
The WHO's objective is the attainment by all peoples of the highest possible level of health—defined in the WHO constitution as a state of complete physical, mental, and social well-being and not merely the absence of disease or infirmity.

Centers for Disease Control and Prevention
www.cdc.gov
An agency of the U.S. Department of Health and Human Services, located in Atlanta, Georgia. Its mission is to "promote health and quality of life by preventing and controlling disease, injury, and disability."

AIDS Treatment News Archive Online
www.aids.org/atn/
Complete archive, including the current issue, of *AIDS Treatment News,* an internationally recognized newsletter for persons living with HIV/AIDS and looking for information on new therapies. *AIDS Treatment News* has been published twice a month since 1986.

Canadian Alliance on Mental Illness and Mental Health
www.camimh.ca/
Established in 1998, the Canadian Alliance on Mental Illness and Mental Health (CAMIMH) is an alliance of mental health organizations comprised of health care providers and the mentally ill and their families.

Canadian Bioethics Society
www.bioethics.ca
The Canadian Bioethics Society has over 600 current members, both individuals and organizations, from a wide variety of fields, including medicine, law, theology, philosophy, and public health. The organization's site is intended as a resource for anyone interested in bioethical issues.

CRITICAL THINKING QUESTIONS

1. Canadians are not all equally likely to become sick or to suffer an injury. Some are more likely to develop particular diseases or disabilities. Why do you think there are differences in the health and illness of Canadians based on sex and class?

2. Virtually everyone recognizes the life-saving value of medicine and the advances being made in medical research on such diseases as cancer and AIDS. However, are there any social factors that negatively contribute to our physical, mental, and spiritual well-being?

3. Is the medicalization of society a good thing? Apply the functionalist and conflict perspectives to help answer this question.

4. How do lifestyles and values affect our health? What does this have to do with sociology? Access the Research Navigator through MySocLab and use keywords such as "lifestyles," "health," and "values" to locate relevant and recent scholarly and popular press publications to help you answer this question.

 **Explore the topics covered in this chapter on MySocLab using the access information provided with this text. Interactive resources for studying include multimedia tutorials, video clips, practice tests, quizzes, and animated maps and figures.**

Crime and Social Deviance

Chicago Blackhawk defenceman Steve Smith's bloodied and pulpy face and the pile of writhing bodies on the ice were, of course, nothing new for the National Hockey League. But the sight of Blackhawk Stu Grimson, a thug on skates if ever there was one, running amok—with the home crowd roaring approval—was unforgettable. As the fight subsided on the ice, Grimson, glassy-eyed and stripped down to his sweat-soaked undershirt, simply came unglued. Suddenly, his own coach, Mike Keenan, couldn't hold him back at the bench. Breaking from Keenan's grasp, Grimson first tracked down, then grabbed one of the linesmen by the head as if hoping to dash his brains out against the glass. When Grimson finally went to the showers, there was a telling moment when teammate Ed Balfour gave him a congratulatory send-off tap on the rear with his goal stick. It was disgusting.

Starting with this episode of goonery, the NHL must clamp down on the violence that gives hockey a bad name. Sitting in the comfort of their living rooms, Don Cherry–types may covet this kind of rock-em, sock-em stuff on skates. But if it ever happened in a bar or a back alley somewhere, there'd be criminal charges—and maybe even a trip to the cooler [jail].

Violence on the ice also filters to the junior and minor hockey league teams across Canada. The recent (2008) incident involving Patrick Roy's son who repeatedly pounded an opponent in a Quebec Remparts and Chicoutimi Sagueneens game caught national attention when it was repeatedly broadcast across the country. The incident led the minister responsible for sport in Quebec to request a report from the president of the Quebec Major Junior Hockey League (QMJHL) containing anti-fighting proposals to be in her hands by the end of June 2008. It is doubtful that the recommendations from this report or other similar measures to curb violence in hockey, whether it be on the ice or in the stands by parents of children playing hockey, will be successful in the wake of the lure of high salaries, the heightened expectation of sport bravado, and the need for quick headline grabbers in the print and electronic media.

Source: *Toronto Star* editorial (1992), Cnews, March 28, 2008.

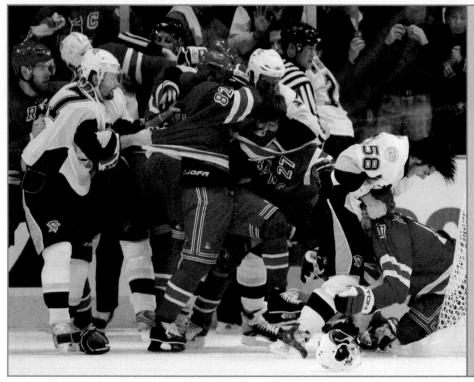

Violence has always been part of NHL hockey. In recent years, however, the level and intensity of violence has dramatically increased. Instead of throwing down the gloves, the hockey stick has become the weapon of choice for some players. A culture of violence has emerged—encouraged, in part, by the demand for bigger and stronger players, the competition for huge salaries, and by some in the media.

GAINING A SOCIOLOGICAL PERSPECTIVE ON CRIME AND SOCIAL DEVIANCE

In Canadian society, violence has become culturally acceptable in sports, particularly in hockey. We frequently hear that a game was good because of a "good brawl" (or brawls). But when does "acceptable" violence in a sport step over the line and become criminal? One example of this line-crossing occurred in a 1988 hockey game, when Minnesota North Star Dino Ciccarelli pleaded guilty to assault charges in Toronto for slashing Maple Leaf Luke Richardson in the head. He was jailed for only one day. Another more recent example is Vancouver Canuck Todd Bertuzzi's attack on Colorado Avalanche player Steve Moore, an incident in which the courts interceded because the severity of the injuries to Moore required more than the standard fines and suspended games.

Whether the NHL should police its own players or whether the responsibility should fall to the state is a complex issue. The nature of, and reaction to, violence in sports depends on a society's culture. Whether the subject is violence in the bull-fight or violence in soccer, much can be learned about a society as a whole by studying its sports.

Examples such as the Dino Ciccarelli/Luke Richardson and Todd Bertuzzi/Steve Moore cases demonstrate that cultural norms, values, and mores shape the social acceptance or non-acceptance of certain behaviours. However, these norms, values, and mores are not perceived or acted upon in a monolithic manner. Rather, Canadians continually debate what is acceptable and unacceptable behaviour, whether related to sports, morality, or the criminal justice system. What Canadians view as criminal behaviour or social deviance, then, depends on whose behaviour it is, who is affected by it, and in what context it occurs.

How Norms Make Social Life Possible

Norms make social life possible by making behaviour predictable. Only because we can count on most people most of the time meeting the expectations of others can social life as we know it exist.

You can depend on grocery clerks to sell you milk. You also can depend on paying the same price as everyone else and not being forced to attend a party in the store. Why is this so? Because we are socialized to follow norms, to play the basic roles society assigns to us.

Norms lay out the basic guidelines for how we play our roles and how we interact with others. In short, norms allow for **social order**, a group's usual and customary social arrangements. Our lives are based on these arrangements, which is why social deviance and criminal behaviour in particular are often seen as threatening, for they undermine predictability, the foundation of social life. Consequently, human groups develop a system of **social control**, formal (legal) and informal means of enforcing norms.

Comparing Psychological, Biological, and Sociological Explanations

Since norms are essential for society, why do people violate them? To better understand the reasons, it is useful to know how sociological explanations differ from biological and psychological ones, and to examine how the five sociological perspectives explain crime, social deviance, and social control.

Psychologists and *sociobiologists* explain crime and social deviance by looking for answers *within* individuals. They assume that something in the makeup of people leads them to become criminal or socially deviant.

Some *psychologists* focus on abnormalities *within* the individual, or what are called **personality disorders**. Their supposition is that deviating individuals have deviating personalities (Barnes, 2001; Mayer, 2007). That is, various unconscious urges drive people to criminal activity or social deviance.

Biological explanations, like their psychological counterparts, focus on **genetic predispositions** to such social deviance as juvenile delinquency and crime (Lombroso, 1911; Goozen et al., 2007). When it comes to explaining criminal behaviours, biological explanations include (but are not restricted to) the following three theories: (1) intelligence—low intelligence leads to crime; (2) the "XYY" theory—an extra Y chromosome in males leads to crime; and (3) body type—people with "squarish, muscular" bodies are more likely to commit **street crimes**, acts such as mugging, rape, and burglary.

How do these theories hold up? Some criminals are very intelligent, and most people of low intelligence do not commit crimes. Most criminals have the normal "XY" chromosome combination, and most men with the "XYY" combination do not become criminals; in addition, no women have this combination of genes, so the theory is lacking in explanation for female criminals. Criminals also run the range of the body types exhibited by humanity, and most people with "squarish, muscular" bodies do not become street criminals. No specific childhood experience is invariably linked with social deviance or criminality. For example, children who had "bad toilet training," "suffocating mothers," or "emotionally aloof fathers" may become good accountants—or embezzling bookkeepers. Just as university students, professors, and police officers represent a variety of good—and bad—childhood experiences, so do social deviants and criminals. Similarly, people with "suppressed anger" can become military heroes or freeway snipers—or anything else. In short, these supposed "causes" of criminal behaviours are even more common among the general population of people who do not commit crimes. There is no inevitable outcome of any childhood experience. Therefore, the causes of criminal behaviours and social deviance cannot be answered by biological or psychological explanations that focus solely on personality or genetic "disorders." One sociological explanation, for example, is that some of the expectations of the masculine role in Canadian society—to be braver, tougher, more independent, and less tolerant of insult—increase the likelihood that males will become involved in violence.

In contrast to the biological and psychological perspectives, *sociologists* search for factors *outside* the individual. Since crime and social deviance are relative, why, they ask, should we expect to find anything constant within people to account for a behaviour that is conforming in one society and socially deviant in another? Sociologists also look for social influences that "recruit" some people rather than others to break norms. To account for why people commit crimes, for example, sociologists examine such external influences as socialization, subcultural membership, and social class. *Social class*, a concept discussed in depth in Chapter 6 and the next two chapters, refers to people's relative standing in terms of education, occupation, and especially income and wealth.

The Relativity of Social Deviance

> In just a few moments I was to meet my first Yanomamo. What would it be like? I looked up (from my canoe) and gasped when I saw a dozen burly, naked, men staring at us down the shafts of their drawn arrows. Immense wads of green tobacco were stuck between their lower teeth and lips, and strands of dark-green slime dripped or hung from their noses. We arrived at the village while the men were blowing a hallucinogenic drug up their noses.

> I wondered why I ever decided to switch from civil engineering to anthropology in the first place . . . [Soon] I was covered with red pigment, the result of a dozen or so complete examinations. . . The Indians would blow their noses into their hands, flick as much of the mucus off that would separate in a snap of the wrist, wipe the residue into their hair, and then carefully examine my face, arms, legs, hair, and the contents of my pockets. I said (in their language), "Your hands are dirty"; my comments were met in the following way: they would "clean" their hands by spitting a quantity of slimy tobacco juice into them, rub them together, and then proceed with the examination (Chagnon, 1977).

Sociologists use the term **social deviance** to refer to any violation of norms—whether the infraction is as minor as jaywalking, as serious as murder, or as humorous as Chagnon's encounter with the Yanomamo. This deceptively simple definition takes us to the heart of the sociological perspective of social deviance, which sociologist Howard S. Becker (1966) identified this way: *It is not the act* itself, but the reactions to the act, that make something socially deviant. In other words, people's behaviours must be viewed from the framework of the culture in which they take place. What was socially deviant to Chagnon was *conforming* to the Yanomamo. From their viewpoint, you *should* check out strangers, as they did—and nakedness is natural, as are hallucinogenic drugs.

Chagnon's abrupt introduction to the Yanomamo allows us to see the *relativity of social deviance*. Thus, acts perfectly acceptable in one culture—or in one group within a

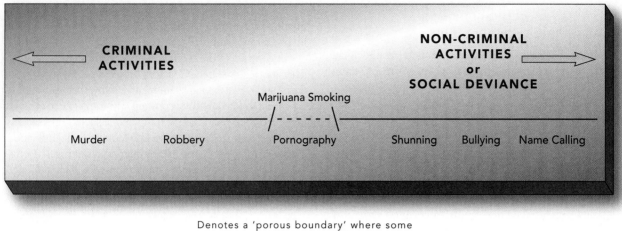

Denotes a 'porous boundary' where some
- - - - - - activities straddle both social deviance
and criminal activities/behaviours

FIGURE 16.1   Crime and Social Deviance—A Continuum

society—may be considered socially deviant in another culture, or in another group within the same society.

Unlike the general public, sociologists use the term *social deviance* nonjudgmentally, to refer to any act to which people respond negatively. To sociologists, then, *all of us* are social deviants of one sort or another, for we all violate norms from time to time. Figure 16.1 depicts the violation of norms along a continuum, from non-criminal to criminal activities.

To be considered socially deviant, a person may not even have to *do* anything. Sociologist Erving Goffman (1963) used the term **stigma** to refer to attributes that discredit people. These attributes include violations of norms of ability (blindness, deafness, mental handicaps) and norms of appearance (a facial birthmark, obesity). They also include involuntary membership in groups, such as being the victim of AIDS or a close friend of Paul Bernardo or Karla Homolka. The stigma becomes a person's *master status*, defining him or her as socially deviant. Recall from Chapter 5 that a master status cuts across all other statuses that a person occupies.

Knowing how relative social deviance is, sociologists wonder why anyone would expect to find factors within people to explain social deviance. For example, because **crime** is the violation of norms that have been written into law, what a crime is varies from one human group to another. Why, then, should we expect to find anything constant within people to account for crime—or any other behaviour that is conforming in one group but socially deviant in another? Even the media often insist on "explaining" criminal behaviours as the result of "abnormal" or nonconforming personality traits.

Who Defines Social Deviance?

If social deviance does not lie in the act, but in definitions of the act, where do those definitions come from? To see how sociologists explain social deviance, especially criminal behaviour, let's contrast the five main sociological perspectives—

symbolic interactionism, functionalism, conflict theory, feminism, and postmodernism.

Focus Question
What is social deviance? What is crime?

IN SUM

In sociology, the term *social deviance* refers to all violations of social rules, regardless of their seriousness. In other words, social deviance can be viewed as a continuum, with minor rule- or norm-breaking at one end and serious criminal violations at the other. The term is not a judgment about the behaviour. Social deviance is relative; what is socially deviant in one group may be conforming in another. Consequently, we must consider social deviance from within a group's own framework, for it is the *group's* meanings that motivate its members' behaviour.

THE SYMBOLIC INTERACTIONIST PERSPECTIVE

As we examine symbolic interactionism, it will become more evident why sociologists are not satisfied with explanations of social deviance that are rooted in biology or personality. A basic principle of symbolic interactionism is that each of us acts according to our interpretations of situations, not according to blind predispositions. Let's consider how our membership in social groups influences our views of life, which affect our individual behaviours.

Differential Association Theory of Criminal Behaviours

THE THEORY Contrary to theories of biology and personality, sociologist Edwin Sutherland stressed that people *learn* criminal behaviours. He coined the term **differential association** to indicate that learning to deviate or to conform to society's norms is influenced most by the people with whom we associate (Sutherland, 1924, 1947; Sutherland & Cressey, 1974; Sutherland, Cressey, & Luckenbill, 1992). On the most obvious level, boys and girls who join street gangs learn a way of looking at the world that is more likely to get them into trouble with the law than boys and girls who join the Boy Scouts or Girl Guides.

Sutherland's theory is actually more complicated, but his basic assertion was that social deviance is learned rather than the result of biology or personality.

FRIENDS AND NEIGHBOURHOODS The longer someone has friends who commit criminal acts, the more likely he or she will follow in the friends' footsteps (Warr, 1993). This comes as no surprise to parents, who generally are eager to keep their kids away from "bad" friends or neighbours.

SUBCULTURES All subcultures contain particular attitudes about social deviance and conformity learned by their members. According to sociologist Ruth Horowitz (1983, 1987), who conducted participant observation in a Chicago Chicano neighbourhood, a man in that society must have honour. An insult is a threat to one's honour; therefore, to not stand up to someone is to be less than a real man. Suppose you were a young man growing up in this neighbourhood. You would likely do a fair amount of fighting, for you would see many statements and acts as infringing on your honour. You might make certain that you carried a knife or had access to a gun—words and fists won't always do. Along with members of your group, you would define fighting, knifing, and shooting quite differently than the way most people do.

For members of the Mafia, ideas of manliness are also intertwined with criminal behaviour. In that society, *killing is a primary measure of their manhood.* Not all killings are accorded the same respect, however: "the more awesome and potent the victim, the more worthy and meritorious the killer" (Arlacchi, 1980). Some killings are very practical matters. A member of the Mafia who gives information to the police, for example, has violated the *omerta* (a vow of secrecy taken by all members). Such an offence can never be tolerated, for it threatens the very existence of the group. This example further illustrates how relative even criminal behaviour is. Although the act of killing breaks a legal norm of mainstream society, for the Mafia, *not* killing after certain rules are broken, such as "squealing" to the cops, is the criminal act.

PRISON OR FREEDOM? Symbolic interactionists stress that we are not mere pawns in the hands of others. We are not destined by our group membership to think and behave as our groups dictate. Rather, *we help produce our own orientations to life.* Our choice of membership (differential association), for example, helps to shape the self. One university student may join a feminist group that is trying to change the treatment of women in university; another may associate with a group of women who smoke cigarettes. Their choice of groups points them in two different directions. The one who associates with cigarette smokers may or may not find herself becoming a smoker, while the one who joins the feminist group may develop an even greater interest in producing social change.

Focus Question
According to symbolic interactionists, are we mere pawns in the hands of others when we socialize with either "bad people" or "good people"?

Labelling Theory

Labelling theory focuses on the significance of labels (names, reputations) given to people. Labels tend to become a part of our self-concept. Depending on the kind of pressure coming from others, labels such as whore, slob, genius, or entrepreneur help set people on paths that propel them into or divert them from social deviance and crime.

REJECTING LABELS: HOW PEOPLE NEUTRALIZE SOCIAL DEVIANCE Most people resist the negative labels others try to pin on them. Some are so successful that even though they persist in criminal behaviour, they still consider themselves conformists. For example, some bullies consider themselves to be conforming members of society, even though they beat up people. How do they do it?

Sociologists Gresham Sykes and David Matza (1988) studied boys in this exact situation. They found that they used these five **techniques of neutralization** to help deflect society's norms:

1. *Denial of responsibility.* The youths frequently said, "I'm not responsible for what happened because . . ." The act may have been an "accident," or they may see themselves as "victims" of society, with no control over what happened—like billiard balls shot around the pool table of life.

2. *Denial of injury.* Another favourite explanation of the boys was "What I did wasn't wrong because no one got hurt." Vandalism becomes "mischief," gang fighting is seen as a "private quarrel," and stealing cars is simply "borrowing." The boys might acknowledge that they have done something illegal, but claim it was "just having a little fun."

3. *Denial of a victim.* Sometimes the boys thought of themselves as avengers. Vandalizing a teacher's car would be getting revenge for an unfair grade, while shoplifting might even the score with "crooked" store owners. In short, they protected their self-concept by claiming that people "deserved what they got."

4. *Condemnation of the condemners.* Another technique the boys used was to accuse people who pointed their fingers at them of being "a bunch of hypocrites": the police are

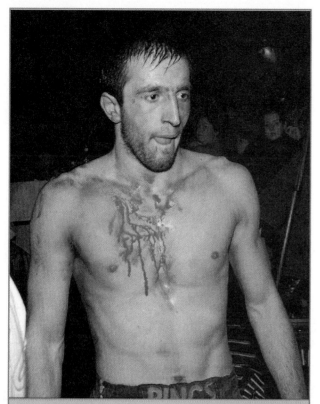

UFC (Ultimate Fighting Championship, sometimes called cage fighting) has a large following in Canada and the United States among both men and women. Many Canadians label those who watch this form of violence social deviants. What do you think?

"on the take," teachers have "pets," and parents cheat on their taxes. In short, they say, "Who are *they* to accuse *me* of something?"

5. *Appeal to higher loyalties.* A final technique to justify antisocial activities was to consider loyalty to the gang more important than following the norms of society. They might say, "I had to help my friends. That's why I got in the fight."

IN SUM

The five techniques of neutralization have implications far beyond these boys. It is not only delinquents who try to neutralize the norms of mainstream society. Consider them again: (1) "I couldn't help myself." (2) "Who really got hurt?" (3) "Don't you think she deserved that, after what *she* did?" (4) "Who are *you* to talk?" (5) "I had to help my friends—wouldn't you have done the same thing?" Do these statements have a familiar ring? All of us attempt to neutralize some of the labels we are given.

REJECTING LABELS: BECOMING A PROSTITUTE Sociologist Nanette Davis (1978) interviewed young prostitutes to find out how they had entered the profession and discovered that most had made a gradual transition from sexual promiscu-

ity to prostitution. Their first acts of selling sex were casual. As one girl said, "I never thought about it one way or another." At this point, the girls were in a stage of social deviance that sociologist Edwin Lemert (1972) termed **primary social deviance**—fleeting acts that do not become part of the self-concept. The young women did not yet think of themselves as prostitutes.

Girls who are engaged in the "business" for a longer time, however, do come to think of themselves as prostitutes. When this occurs, they have entered **secondary social deviance**.

The movement from primary to secondary social deviance may be gradual. Through *self-labelling*, bit by bit, the social deviance becomes part of the self-concept. Self-jarring labels such as "pervert" and "whore" tend to lock people out of conforming groups and push them into contact with others like themselves.

In **tertiary social deviance**, socially deviant behaviour is normalized by *relabelling* it as nondeviant (Kitsuse, 1980; de Young, 1989). Most people in this stage simply reject the judgment that the behaviour is wrong. For example, prostitutes in Canada have formed an organization called CORP (Canadian Organization for the Rights of Prostitutes). This group takes the position that prostitutes perform a service to society, and it is therefore a reasonable occupational choice and legislation should allow prostitutes to operate without interference from the government. Similar organizations exist in the United States (COYOTE—Call Off Your Old Tired Ethics), Europe (ICPR—International Committee for Prostitutes' Rights), and Australia (PROS—Prostitutes Rights Organization for Sex Workers).

INVITING LABELS: THE EMBRACE OF SOCIAL DEVIANCE Although most of us resist being labelled socially deviant, others revel in a socially deviant identity. Some teenagers, for example, make certain by their choice of clothing, music, and hairstyles that no one misses their intentional rejection of adult norms. Their status among fellow members of a subculture—goths, for example—within which they are almost obsessive conformists, is vastly more important than any status outside it.

One of the best examples of a group that embraces criminal activities is motorcycle gangs. Sociologist Mark Watson (1988/2006) conducted participant observation with outlaw bikers. He rebuilt Harleys with them, hung around their bars and homes, and went on "runs" (trips). He concluded that outlaw bikers see the world as "hostile, weak, and effeminate," while they pride themselves on looking "dirty, mean, and generally undesirable"—and take great pleasure in provoking shocked reactions to their appearance. Holding the conventional world in contempt, they also pride themselves on getting into trouble, laughing at death, and treating women as lesser beings whose primary value is to provide them with services—especially sex. Ironically, outlaw bikers also regard themselves as losers, a factor that becomes woven into their unusual embrace of social deviance.

The display of deviants on the *Jerry Springer* show offers viewers a sense of being involved with socially deviant behaviour. As Springer and others like him continue to parade deviants before the public, the shock and surprise wear off, making the deviance seem "more" normal. What is occurring is the *mainstreaming of deviance*—disapproved behaviours moving into the mainstream, or becoming more socially acceptable.

THE POWER OF LABELS: THE SAINTS AND THE ROUGHNECKS We can see how powerful labelling is by referring to Chambliss's study (1973/2007) of two groups of high school boys known as the "Saints" and the "Roughnecks." Both groups of high school boys were "constantly occupied with drinking, wild parties, petty theft, and vandalism," yet their teachers looked on the Saints as "headed for success" and the Roughnecks as "headed for trouble." By the time they finished high school, not one Saint had been arrested, while the Roughnecks had been in constant trouble with the police.

Why did the community perceive these groups differently? Chambliss concluded that the double vision was the result of family background, especially *social class*. The Saints came from respectable, middle-class families, while the Roughnecks came from less respectable, working-class families. Because of their respective backgrounds, teachers and other authorities expected good, law-abiding behaviour from the Saints and trouble from the Roughnecks. And, like the rest of us, both the teachers and police saw what they expected to.

Social class allowed the Saints' lawbreaking to be *less visible*. They had automobiles, and they made their drinking and vandalism inconspicuous by spreading it around neighbouring towns. Without cars, the Roughnecks couldn't even make it to the edge of town. Day after day, they hung around the same street corners, where their boisterous behaviour made them conspicuous, confirming the negative ideas that the community held about them.

The boys' social class backgrounds had equipped them with distinct *styles of interaction*. When questioned by police or teachers, the Saints put on apologetic and penitent faces. Their "respect for authority" elicited positive reactions from teachers and the police, allowing them to avoid serious legal problems. People in authority believed them. In contrast, the Roughnecks' attitudes often expressed open hostility to the authorities, and even when they showed respect, their teachers and the police did not believe they were sincere. Consequently, while the police let the Saints off with warnings, they came down hard on the Roughnecks, interrogating and arresting them when they had the chance.

While a lifetime career is not determined by a label alone, the Saints and the Roughnecks lived up to the labels the community had given them. All but one of the Saints went on to university, after which one earned a doctorate, one became a lawyer, one a doctor, and the others business managers. In contrast, only two Roughnecks went to university, both on athletic scholarships, after which they became coaches. The other Roughnecks did not fare as well. Two of them dropped out of high school, later became involved in separate killings, and received long prison sentences. One became a local bookie, and no one knows the whereabouts of the other.

How do labels work? While the matter is extremely complex, involving self-concept and individual reactions, we can observe that labels open and close the doors of opportunity. In many respects, how others in authority react to what is expected from members of the lower social classes affects how we are labelled. It is not *what* they do so much as *who* they do it to.

IN SUM

Symbolic interactionists examine how people's definitions of a situation underlie their rejection of or conformity to social norms. They focus on group membership (differential association) and the significance of labels placed on people (labelling theory).

THE FUNCTIONALIST PERSPECTIVE

When we think of crime and social deviance, its dysfunctions are likely to come to mind. Functionalists, in contrast, are as likely to stress the functions of social deviance rather than dysfunction itself.

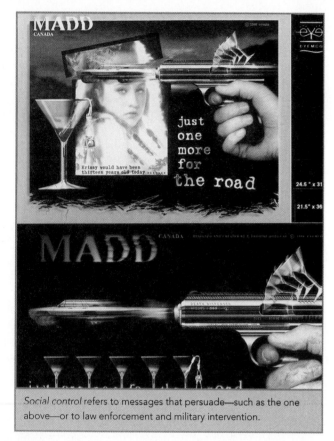

Social control refers to messages that persuade—such as the one above—or to law enforcement and military intervention.

How Crime and Social Deviance Are Functional for Society

According to Emile Durkheim (1893/1933, 1895/1964), social deviance, including crime, is functional for society. Its three main functions are as follows:

1. *Crime and social deviance clarify moral boundaries and affirm norms.* A group's ideas about how people should act and think mark its *moral boundaries*. Social deviance, and especially more serious crimes, challenge those boundaries. To say, in effect, "You broke an important rule, and we cannot tolerate that," affirms a group's norms and clarifies the distinction between conforming and deviating behaviour.

2. *Crime and social deviance promote social unity.* To affirm a group's moral boundaries fosters a "we" feeling among the group's members. In saying, "You can't get away with that," the group collectively affirms the rightness of its own ways.

3. *Crime and social deviance promote social change.* Groups do not always agree on what to do with people who push beyond their acceptable ways of doing things. Boundary violations that gain enough support become new, acceptable behaviours. Thus, social deviance may force a group to rethink and redefine its moral boundaries, helping groups, and whole societies, change their customary ways. Same-sex marriage in Canada is a case in point.

FUNCTIONALISM AND SOCIAL CONTROL If some group threatens to upset the equilibrium, efforts are made to restore balance. For example, in a pluralistic society, the central government often plays a mediating role between groups. In Canada, the federal and provincial governments and the Supreme Court mediate the demands of the various groups that make up our society, accommodating diverse communities whose basic ideas deviate from those held by most members of Canadian society (Porter, 1965). This view of mediation and balance among competing groups is broadly representative of what may be called the Canadian Mosaic or the **pluralistic theory of social control**.

Focus Question
Are crime and social deviance always bad for society?

Strain Theory: How Social Values Produce Crime

Functionalists argue that crime is a *natural* part of society, not an aberration or some alien element in our midst. To understand how the acceptance of mainstream values can generate crime, they say, we must consider what sociologists Richard Cloward and Lloyd Ohlin (1960) identified as the crucial problem of the industrialized world: the need to locate and train the most talented people of every generation—whether born in wealth or in poverty—to enable them to take over the key technical jobs of modern society. To get the most talented people to compete with one another, society tries to motivate everyone to strive for success. It does this by arousing discontent—making people feel dissatisfied with what they have so that they will try to "better" themselves.

Most people, then, end up with strong desires to achieve **cultural goals**, such as wealth, high status, or "the good life." Not everyone, however, has equal access to society's **institutionalized means**, the legitimate ways of achieving success. Some people, for example, find their path to higher education and good jobs blocked. The more entrepreneurial among these people experience *strain* or frustrations and find it difficult to identify with these norms. They may even feel wronged by the system, and its rules may seem illegitimate.

This perspective, known as **strain theory**, was developed by sociologist Robert Merton (1956, 1968). Merton's classic outline of how people react to cultural goals and institutionalized means is depicted in Table 16.1. The first reaction, which Merton said is the most common, is *conformity*, using socially acceptable means to strive to reach cultural goals. In industrialized societies, most people try to get good jobs, a good education, and so on. If well-paid jobs are unavailable, they take less desirable jobs. Others take night classes and attend vocational schools. In short, most people take the socially acceptable road.

FOUR SOCIALLY DEVIANT PATHS The remaining four responses represent reactions to strain. *Innovators* are people who accept the goals of society but use illegitimate means to try

TABLE 16.1 How People Match Their Goals to Their Means

Do They Feel the Strain That Leads to Anomie?	Mode of Adaptation	Cultural Goals	Institutionalized Means
No	Conformity	Accept	Accept
Yes	**Deviant Paths:**		
	1. Innovation	Accept	Reject
	2. Ritualism	Reject	Accept
	3. Retreatism	Reject	Reject
	4. Rebellion	Reject/Replace	Reject/Replace

Source: Based on Merton 1968.

to reach them. Drug dealers, for instance, accept the goal of achieving wealth but reject legitimate avenues for doing so. Other examples are embezzlers, robbers, and con artists.

The second socially deviant path is taken by people who become discouraged and give up on achieving cultural goals, but who still cling to conventional rules of conduct. Merton called this response *ritualism*. Although ritualists have given up on excelling and advancing in position, they survive by following the rules. Teachers who suffer from "burnout" but continue to go through the motions of classroom performance after their idealism is shattered are examples of ritualists.

People who choose the third path, *retreatism*, reject both cultural goals and the institutionalized means of achieving them. Those who drop out of the pursuit of success by way of membership in mystical religious sects are retreatists. So are long-term welfare recipients. Such people do not even try to appear as though they share the goals of their society.

The final type of response is *rebellion*. Rebels, like retreatists, reject both society's goals and its institutionalized means. Unlike retreatists, however, they seek to replace existing goals with new ones. Revolutionaries are the most committed type of rebels. More important are those who seek change in the name of social justice, such as environmentalists, gay and lesbian activists, or feminists.

Strain theory underscores the main sociological point about social deviance—namely, that social deviants are not pathogenic individuals. Simply put, if a society emphasizes the goal of material success, groups deprived of access to this goal will be more involved in property crime. During periods of economic recession, we can expect to find an increase in property crimes simply because there aren't enough good jobs to go around to all who want or need them, especially hard-hit young males (see the following Down-to-Earth Sociology box).

Illegitimate Opportunity Theory: Explaining Social Class and Crime

Social class position is an important predictor of economic success in our society. Just as different classes carry different cultures of dress, speech, and mannerisms, social classes have distinct styles of crime.

DOWN-TO-EARTH SOCIOLOGY
Mean Streets and Hard Time: Youth Unemployment and Crime in Canada

Newspaper headlines from western Canada in 1993 announced that "Tough Times Drive Kids out of Class, into Crime" (*Winnipeg Free Press*, September 5, 1993). A few months earlier, the same newspaper reported that "Young Canadians have the highest unemployment rate, account for a large share of criminal activity and are especially vulnerable to economic downturns" (March 16, 1993, p. A3). According to the same article, students who work more than 15 hours a week are more likely to drop out of school. Even those who stay in school see grim prospects for good jobs. Corey, a 15-year-old, said, "There are more offers from gangs than offers of jobs."

Among Canadian criminologists, the link between unemployment and property crimes has been ignored in favour of more "sophisticated" theories. "Dysfunctional" family background is often used by more conservative theorists who point out single-parent households or a parent's alcoholism as negatively affecting the children's actions. Others are more prone to differential association theory—that is, a person's prior exposure to socially deviant beliefs—and/or labelling theory—that is, a person's passage through successive stages of negative stigmatization.

Clearly, youth unemployment affects different young people differently. In Great Britain, the increase in suicide rates among young people has been linked

THE POOR AND CRIME Functionalists point out that industrialized societies have no trouble socializing the poor into wanting to possess things. Like others, they, too, are bombarded with messages urging them to buy everything from the latest iPod to Xboxes and cellphones. The vivid images in movies and on television of the middle class enjoying luxurious lives reinforce the myth that all Canadians can afford society's many goods and services. The bombardment of messages also unintentionally produces the idea that all Canadians have a *right* to these items.

The school system, however, which constitutes the most common route to success, fails the poor. It is run by the middle class, and when poor children enter it, they are already at an educational disadvantage, confronting a bewildering world for which their background ill prepares them. Their grammar and nonstandard language—liberally punctuated by what the middle class considers obscene and foul words and phrases—their ideas of punctuality and neatness, and their lack of preparation in computer skills are a mismatch with their new environment. Facing these barriers, the poor drop out of school in larger numbers than their more privileged counterparts. Educational failure, in turn, closes the door on many legitimate avenues to financial success (recall from Chapter 14 our discussion of the "hidden curriculum").

Not infrequently, however, a different door opens to them, one that sociologists Richard Cloward and Lloyd Ohlin (1960) called **illegitimate opportunity structures**. Woven into the texture of life in poor urban neighbourhoods are gambling and other remunerative crimes, commonly called "hustles" (Liebow, 1967/1999; E. Anderson, 1978, 1990, 2006; Bourgois, 1994). For many of the poor, the "hustler" is a role model—glamorous, in control, the image of "easy money," and one of the few people in the area who comes close to the cultural goal of success. Those who tell their urban "buds" that they have made lots of money from internet casino gambling point out it is an "easy way" to make it for the less educated but talented poor. For some, then, such illegal income-producing activities are functional—they provide income—and they attract disproportionate numbers of the poor.

WHITE-COLLAR AND STREET CRIME The more privileged social classes are not crime free, but they find a different illegitimate opportunity structure beckoning. More privileged people encounter "opportunities" for income tax evasion, bribery of public officials, stock manipulation, embezzlement, false advertising, and so on. Sociologist Edwin Sutherland (1949) used the term **white-collar crime** to refer to crimes that people of respectable and high social status commit in the course of their occupations.

Although the general public seems to think that the lower classes are more crime prone, numerous studies show the devastating impact of corporate crime (Weisburd, Wheeler, & Waring, 1991; Zey, 1993). This difference in perception is based largely on visibility. While crimes committed by the poor are given much publicity, the crimes of

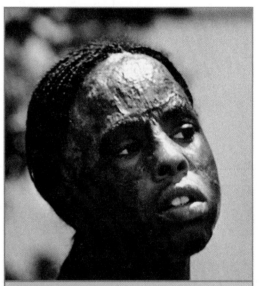

Most white-collar crime is a harmless nuisance, but some result in horrible consequences. Shown here is Alisha Parker, who, with three siblings, was burned when the gas tank of her 1979 Chevrolet Malibu exploded after a rear-end collision. Although General Motors executives knew about the problem with the Malibu gas tanks, they had ignored it. Outraged at the callousness of GM's conduct, the jury awarded these victims the staggering sum of $4.9 billion.

It is ironic that the one-time media mogul Conrad Moffat Black found himself on the opposite side of the media cameras facing criminal charges in the United States. He was found guilty of three counts of mail fraud and one count of obstruction of justice, but acquitted of the other nine charges, including wire fraud and racketeering. In December 2007, he was sentenced to 6 1/2 years in prison.

the more privileged classes seldom make the evening news and go largely unnoticed. Yet the dollar cost of "crime in the suites" is considerably higher than "crime in the streets," totalling in the billions of dollars a year. This estimate refers only to dollar costs, however. No one has yet figured out a way to compare, for example, the suffering of a rape victim with the pain experienced by an elderly couple who have lost their life savings to white-collar fraud.

Although white-collar crime is not as dramatic as a street killing or an abduction and rape—and therefore usually considered less newsworthy—it, too, can involve physical harm, and sometimes even death. Unsafe working conditions, for example, many resulting from executive decisions to put profits ahead of workers' safety, killed 2 million workers worldwide in 2002, according to the International Labour Organization (ILO) (ILO, 2002).

In Canada, work-related fatalities kill 1000 Canadians each year. Of five countries surveyed for the ILO, Canada's record for occupational injuries at work was the worst in all three economic sectors surveyed—manufacturing, mining, and construction (Glenday, 1996). Nevertheless, Canadians are becoming more and more worried about street crime, since the media is diligent about reporting any and almost all encounters with violence on the street.

IN SUM

Functionalists conclude that much street crime is the consequence of socializing the lower social classes into equating success with material possessions, while denying them the means to attain that success. People from higher social classes are exposed to opportunities to commit fraud or embezzlement or to do nothing even when they know that intervention could save lives and property.

THE CONFLICT PERSPECTIVE
Class, Crime, and the Criminal Justice System

Conflict theorists stress that the state's machinery of social control, which includes the **criminal justice system**—the police, courts, and prisons that deal with people who are accused of having committed crimes—represents the interests of the wealthy and powerful.

The Law as an Instrument of Oppression

According to conflict theorists, the idea that the law is a social institution that operates impartially and administers a code shared by all is a cultural myth promoted by the capitalist class. In contrast, they see the law as an instrument of oppression, a tool designed to maintain the powerful in their privileged position (Spitzer, 1975; Reiman, 2004; Chambliss, 2000, 2007). Because the working class holds the potential to rebel and overthrow the current social order, when its members get out of line they are arrested, tried, and imprisoned. Wealthy property holders, on the other hand, are punished much less severely.

CONFLICT THEORY AND SOCIAL CONTROL Conflict theorists stress that every society is dominated by a group of elite, powerful people, and that the basic purpose of social control is to maintain the current power arrangements. For this reason, the criminal justice system does not focus on the owners of corporations and the harm they do through manufacturing unsafe products, creating pollution, and manipulating prices. Instead, it directs its energies against violations by the working and middle classes. The violations of the capitalist class cannot be ignored totally, however, for if they become too outrageous or oppressive, the working class may rise up and revolt. To prevent this, a flagrant violation by a member of the capitalist class is occasionally prosecuted. The publicity given to the case helps to stabilize the social system by providing evidence of the "fairness" of the criminal justice system.

Although political power is not as naked in Canada as it is in dictatorships, conflict theorists note that an elite group of wealthy, largely white, males maintains power, working behind the scenes to control the federal government by making certain that the group's interests are represented in Cabinet (Porter, 1965; Clement & Myles, 1994; Olsen, 1980; McQuaig, 1995). Thus, it is this group's views of capital and property—the basis of its power—that are represented in the laws of society.

The Trouble with Official Statistics

Both the findings of symbolic interactionists concerning authorities' reactions to such groups as the Saints and the Roughnecks and the conclusions of conflict theorists that the criminal justice system exists to serve the ruling elite demonstrate the need for caution in interpreting official crime statistics. Statistics are not objective, tangible objects, like apples in a supermarket, waiting to be picked up. They are a human creation, produced within a specific social and political context for some particular purpose.

According to official statistics, working-class boys clearly emerge as much more delinquent than middle-class boys. Yet, as we have seen, who actually gets arrested for what is directly affected by social class, a point that has far-reaching implications. As symbolic interactionists point out, the police use a symbolic system as they enforce the law. Their ideas of "typical criminals" and "typical good citizens," for example, permeate their work. The more a suspect matches their ideas of the "criminal profile," the more likely that person is to be arrested. *Police discretion,* or the decision whether or not to arrest someone or even to ignore a matter, is a routine part of police work. Consequently, official crime statistics always reflect these and many other biases.

Usually, the powerful bypass the courts altogether, appearing instead before some agency with no power to imprison. Most cases of illegal sales of stocks and bonds, price-fixing, restraint of trade, collusion, and so on are handled by "gentlemen overseeing gentlemen." Such agencies are directed by people from wealthy backgrounds who sympathize with the intricacies of the corporate world. It is not surprising, then, that the typical sanction is a token fine. In contrast, the property crimes of young offenders from the lower classes are handled by courts that do have the power to imprison. Burglary, armed robbery, and theft by the poor and their children not only threaten the sanctity of private property but, ultimately, the positions of the powerful.

IN SUM

From the perspective of conflict theory, the small penalties imposed for crimes committed by the powerful are typical of a legal system designed to mask injustice, play down workplace health and safety interests of the majority of the country's workers and, ultimately, stabilize the social order. From this perspective, law enforcement is a cultural device through which the capitalist class carries out self-protective and oppressive policies (Silver, 1977).

THE FEMINIST PERSPECTIVE

Feminist theories stress the importance of gender inequality in society. Patriarchy implies male power over women, and social deviance from a feminist perspective evokes male violence against women. Let's examine this aspect of social deviance.

Feminist Theories and Male Violence against Women

As has been mentioned in previous chapters, there are several feminist theories—Marxist feminist theories, liberal feminist theories, non-Marxist radical feminist theories, and postmodern feminist theories. However, when it comes to feminist theories of social deviance—more specifically, male violence against women—a number of common principles are shared by all feminist theories, of which the most important is patriarchy.

First and foremost, **patriarchy** is characterized as a "sexual system of power in which the male possesses superior power and economic privilege" (Eisenstein, 1980, p. 16). Michael Smith (1990) identified two related forms of patriarchy, the "social" and the "familial." The first refers to male domination at the societal level, whereas the latter pertains to male control in domestic arrangements, including dating and nonmarriage or common-law relationships.

When it comes to male violence against women, virtually all feminist theorists agree that men assault their female partners to maintain control over them and, if they happen to live in a relationship, over their "domestic" situation. Control over women has been measured as (1) sexual fidelity, (2) obedience, (3) respect, (4) loyalty, (5) dependency, and (6) sexual access.

Several studies have been conducted that confirm the relationship of a patriarchal ideology of control and male violence against women (D.E. Smith, 1987, 1990). Feminist contributions to our understanding of male violence against women are pioneering. However, this approach is not without its detractors and progressive critics. Conservative critics, for example, are quick to regard theories of patriarchy as political philosophies rather than social scientific theories (Gelles & Cornell, 1985; Levinson, 1989). The empirical work of Smith and others challenges this notion.

More serious criticisms come from those who point out that feminist theories ignore the effects of class and ethnicity/race on violence against women. It is too simple to point to some empirical studies that have shown that violence against women is more prevalent among lower-class males. And, as we have seen in this chapter, official statistics tend to hide as much as they may reveal about criminal activity. These critics entreat feminists to explain how certain class-based cultural characteristics interact with gender relations and how these circumstances put some women more at risk than others.

Ethnicity/race is another significant factor in assessing male violence against marginalized women. For example, Statistics Canada data show that Aboriginal women are murdered at rates between 5 and 10 times higher than those for non-Aboriginal women (Gartner et al., 1998). Recently, Amnesty International (2004) took issue with the Canadian government's failure to protect Aboriginal women from violence. The report noted that Aboriginal women aged 25 to 44 were five times more likely than other Canadian women of the same age to die of violence. Further, despite controversy about its composition (due to alleged under-representation of marginalized women), the Canadian Panel on Violence Against Women (1993) reported that lesbians, teenagers, and seniors are also especially vulnerable. In fact, a 1993 Statistics Canada Survey found that just over half (51 percent) of all sexual assaults were on young women between the ages of 16 and 27. Feminist theories and researchers are only now becoming sensitive to the issue of violence in same-sex relationships, whether gay or lesbian. The fact that there is little research on violence in these relationships does not signify its absence. Same-sex relationships may be an accepted social fact among many urban-based gays and lesbians in Canada, but violence in such relationships is probably still in the closet (Kinsman, 2001). A recent National Film Board film entitled *Prisoners of Violence: Same Sex Partner Abuse* (2003) spoke to this growing issue. The video stressed the importance of education and awareness to break down barriers. Domestic violence is violence, regardless of sexual orientation.

Feminist Theories and Issues of Public Policy in Canada

Four strategies for coping with male violence against women are discussed in this section: policing, job creation, social services, and anti-sexist male collectives. The first involves raising the sensitivity of police to the reality of male violence against women. Where once police officers, most of whom are males, would not want to arrest or lay charges against a man, today there has been a change in attitude and training across Canada. This change has been largely the result of feminist research findings and effective lobbying. This is not to say all is well—far from it. For example, while arrests for violence against women have increased, some feminists charge that simply enforcing arrest policies can make a bad situation even worse. They contend that many women do not want to report their husbands, companions, or boyfriends simply because they believe their partner's arrest will destroy the relationship. They suggest that only imple-

menting aggressive charging policies fails to address wider issues of patriarchy, including many women's economic dependence on men.

The second strategy includes all levels of government participating in good job-creation programs. DeKeseredy and Hinch (1991), for example, argue that economic policy reforms such as paid work leaves, flexible hours (flextime), pay equity, and improving the quality of work available to disadvantaged people, to name just a few, can lower the rate of male violence against women.

The need for expanded social services such as short-term emergency shelters and housing assistance is the third strategy for coping with male violence against women. Since 1979, the number of Canadian women's shelters has tripled. Nevertheless, most emergency shelters in this country are usually overcrowded and understaffed. All levels of government, in their cost-cutting frenzy, were quick to cut these essential social services. Instead of returning to their violent partners, women who find themselves with little money and who are unable to buy a house or rent an apartment should be assured of some measure of safety and autonomy by living in state-subsidized housing or co-ops.

Anti-sexist self-help groups for violent men are beneficial so long as the men are attending for the right reasons. If men are attending because they were told to change before returning home, or were caught by the police and ordered by a judge to take counselling, the success of these programs may be jeopardized. Only if there is a genuine willingness to change can the issues have any hope of being resolved. Examples of anti-sexist male self-help groups include AMEND, EMERGE, New Directions, and Vivre sans Violence.

The costs for these initiatives should not come from the limited amount of money available for the victims of violence. Shelters for women and other social services are beneficial and necessary to cope with male violence against women. Instead, governments must adequately fund both initiatives.

POSTMODERN THEORIES OF CRIME AND SOCIAL DEVIANCE

The postmodern approach emphasizes the need to "deconstruct" or decode the meaning of concepts such as "law and order" and the "criminal justice system." Postmodern feminist analyses of "the law," for example, have uncovered the ingrained bias of the legal system against women because certain aspects of this system are premised on conceptions of the "reasonable man" (Naffine, 1990). Many postmodern analysts try to uncover the "hidden text" of oppression. More often than not, the media are singled out as the major culprit in the creation of a false public perception of "reality." When television or newspapers "expose the truth" about crime in a city by using particular images, text, or film that focus on particular groups, postmodernists seek out the hidden agendas—the biased subtexts—of these stories.

Postmodern theorists also argue that we are living in a "**risk society**." That is, whether sitting at home, driving, or walking on the streets, we are bombarded by information in the media about the risks that we take—from air pollution and environmental hazards on and off the job to everyday choices about what we eat and drink. The postmodern conception of society is characterized by risk and how it should be managed at both the institutional and personal levels. Canadians and Americans are increasingly feeling at risk of being victimized by crime, based on what they read and see in the media. This is what postmodernists call the media-created "risk society" (see, for example, the now classic work by Ulrich Beck, 1992).

Let's look at the representations of youth crime in Canada as one example of a risk society.

YOUTH CRIME AND THE RISK SOCIETY Canadian society, like American society, is focused on the notion that the criminal element has taken over almost all aspects of everyday living. This widespread belief in crime as a pervasive and global phenomenon helps to create a risk society. In the media's discussion of youth crime, for example, today's youth are presented as the source of the perceived risk we all face. In response to this media-created "reality" of the high incidence of youth crime, social policymakers and criminal law legislators impose rules and regulations in an attempt to effectively manage the perceived dangers of the risk society.

In an attempt to uncover the facts about youth crime, sociologists and criminologists study (1) the external forces that create the social conditions leading to youth crime, (2) the incidence of youth crime, and (3) the nature of the crimes themselves, in order to "decode" the messages generated by the media. Public perceptions of the increase in youth crime have, in fact, been disproved by a study conducted by the John Howard Society of Alberta (1999). Researchers used official statistics to demonstrate that youth crime is actually decreasing. Furthermore, while the statistics in Table 16.2 show a slight increase in the number of youth crimes committed related to drug possession, drug trafficking, and uttering threats, they also show significant evidence that other major youth crimes, including robbery, have decreased.

Popular opinion would tell us that young offenders commit crimes, get a slap on the wrist, and are then released without receiving effective rehabilitation, which results in most young offenders re-offending. This public perception is overwhelmingly generated by media reports (John Howard Society of Alberta, 1999). Public concerns regarding the "deficiencies" of the current criminal justice system and the treatment of young offenders, as presented by the media, led to the replacement of the *Young Offenders Act* by the more stringent (yet still ineffective) *Youth Criminal Justice Act* in April 2003 (Gardner, 2004). Negative public sentiment hinders the implementation of more effective alternative programs such as vocational instruction, alternate custodial arrangements, and so forth. The example in the Perspectives box on page 376 is indicative of how the current treatment of young offenders by the criminal justice system in the United States and Canada is ineffective in preventing further crime.

The Need for Multiple Theories

Feminist theories, differential association, labelling, blocked opportunities, illegitimate opportunities, and the privileged position of the elite all help explain the range of social deviance in society, including crime.

THE CANADIAN CRIMINAL JUSTICE SYSTEM

The Canadian criminal justice system comprises three principal components: the police, the courts, and the corrections system. Each division is made up of its own subsystems that include both public and private sectors. Some provinces, such as Ontario and Quebec, have their own provincial police forces, while others, such as New Brunswick and Saskatchewan, rely on the Royal Canadian Mounted Police (RCMP). (The Canadian court system is discussed in detail below.) The corrections system includes such facilities as federal penitentiaries, provincial correctional centres, halfway houses, treatment programs, youth programs, boot camps, and parole.

The Organization of the Court System in Canada

The court system in Canada is composed of four basic levels. At the lowest, most local level, are the provincial courts, which handle the great majority of cases that come into the system: most criminal offences, family law matters (except divorce, which is dealt with at the federal level), young offenders (from the ages of 12 to 17), and traffic violations. At the second level are the provincial and territorial superior courts, which deal with more serious crimes and also take appeals from provincial court judgments. There is also the Federal Court Trial Division. At the third level are the provincial courts of appeal and the Federal Court of Appeal. The Supreme Court of Canada comprises the fourth and highest level (see Figure 16.2).

Federal Authority over Criminal Courts

Unlike the United States, where states' rights prevail in criminal matters, in Canada the federal government has exclusive authority over the procedures in the criminal court. While criminal cases are tried in provincial courts, any appeals go to a superior court, the highest level of court in the provinces. The federal government appoints and pays provincial superior court judges. The highest-level court of appeal in Canada is the Supreme Court, which has nine judges, three of whom must be from Quebec. The Supreme Court also has a second function: to decide important questions concerning the Constitution and controversial areas of public law.

TABLE 16.2 Cases in Youth Criminal Court, 1998–2002

	1998	2000	2002
	Total All Decisions (number)		
Total Cases	92 867	87 617	84 592
Criminal Code total (not including traffic offences)	76 297	69 791	66 592
Crimes against persons	23 204	22 674	22 462
Homicide	37	38	44
Attempted murder	64	46	43
Robbery	3327	2714	2932
Sexual assault	1236	1146	1115
Other sexual offences	565	615	566
Major assaults	4910	4791	4935
Common assaults	9671	9229	8968
Uttering threats	2770	3360	3244
Criminal harassment	151	240	208
Other crimes against persons	473	495	407
Crimes against property	40 148	34 694	32 465
Theft	15 234	13 611	12 913
Breaking and entering	11 021	8223	7415
Fraud	1784	1653	1411
Mischief	4393	4213	4247
Possession of stolen property	7215	6452	6039
Other property crimes	501	542	440
Administration of justice	8154	7917	7790
Other *Criminal Code* offences	4791	4506	4267
Criminal Code traffic offences	1240	1166	1225
Impaired driving	793	697	658
Other *Criminal Code* traffic offences	447	469	567
Other federal statutes	15 330	16 660	16 383
Drug possession	2725	3773	4137
Drug trafficking	1575	1994	1770
Young Offenders Act	10 916	10 766	10 325
Residual federal statutes	114	127	151

Source: Adapted from Statistics Canada, 2005, "Court, Youth Cases by Decision." CANSIM Table 252-0030: Available at www.statcan.ca/english/Pgdb/legal25a.htm

The criminal justice system in Canada is a complex web of institutions, organizations, professional and voluntary associations (e.g., police associations), and groups with particular vested interests in matters such as abortion or youth justice. It is a system of criminal and law enforcement behaviours and organizations that all the major theories discussed in this chapter—functionalist, conflict, symbolic interactionist, postmodern, and feminist—have something to say about.

In Florida, prosecutors decide whether a teenager will be tried as a juvenile or an adult. Practice varies greatly from county to county. Researchers compared teens who had committed similar crimes but had been sent to different court systems in their respective counties and found that 30 percent of teens sent to adult court had re-offended within two years, compared with 19 percent of those sent to juvenile court. Teens put in adult court also re-offended sooner and at a higher rate than those who had stayed in the juvenile system. They were also more likely to have been rearrested for serious offences. These studies, and many others like them, were reviewed by the U.S. Surgeon General's office in its 2001 report on youth violence. The report's conclusion was blunt: treating young offenders as adult criminals is a terrible mistake. "Evaluations of these programs suggest that they increase future criminal behaviour rather than deter it, as advocates of this approach had hoped."

When a teenager is caught and sent to a youth justice system that emphasizes help over vengeance, he is told, in effect, that he's got problems that he must straighten out. But if he's convicted and imprisoned as an adult, the message is that he's simply a no-good criminal who must be isolated and punished. Sociologists call this practice "labelling," and it is particularly harmful for teenagers who are already alienated from school, family, and community—precisely the sort of teenager who often gets into trouble. That experience breeds more and more anti-social behaviour, and a true criminal is created.

Source: Gardner (2004).

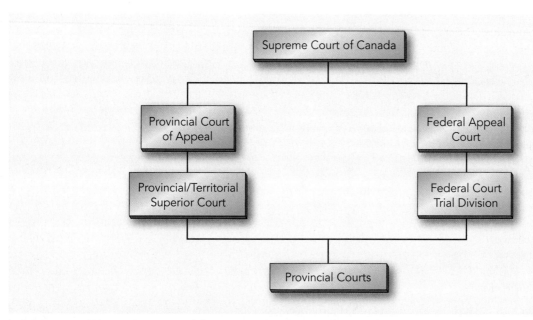

FIGURE 16.2   The Organization of the Court System in Canada

REACTIONS TO SOCIAL DEVIANCE

Whether cheating on a sociology quiz or drinking under the legal age, any violation of norms invites reaction.

Sanctions

Responding to social deviance is vital to the welfare of groups, since groups must maintain their boundaries if they are to continue to claim a unique identity. Disapproval of social deviance, called **negative sanctions**, ranges from frowns and gossip for breaking folkways to imprisonment and capital punishment for breaking mores. **Positive sanctions**, in contrast—from smiles to formal awards—are used to reward people for conforming to norms. Getting a raise is a positive sanction; being fired for misconduct is a negative sanction. Getting an A in basic sociology is a positive sanction; getting an F is a negative one.

Degradation ceremonies are intended to humiliate norm violators and mark them as "not members" of a group. This photo was taken by the U.S. army in 1945 after U.S. troops liberated Cherbourg, France. Members of the French resistance shaved the heads of these women, who had "collaborated" (had sexual contact) with the occupying Nazis. They then marched the shamed women down the streets of the city, while the public shouted insults and spat on them.

Degradation Ceremonies

Sociologist Harold Garfinkel (1956) referred to formal attempts to mark an individual with the status of an outsider as **degradation ceremonies**. The individual is called to account before a group, witnesses denounce him or her, the offender is pronounced guilty and, most importantly in sociological terms, steps are taken to *strip the individual of his or her identity as a group member*. Following a court martial, for example, officers found guilty stand at attention before their peers while the insignia of rank are ripped from their uniforms. A priest may be defrocked before a congregation; a citizen forced to wear a prison uniform. These procedures indicate that the individual is no longer a member of the group—no longer able to command soldiers, to preach or offer sacraments, or to move about freely.

Focus Question
What is the more important strategy for reducing crime—punishment or rehabilitation?

Imprisonment

Today, the prison experience follows a degradation ceremony involving a public trial and the public pronouncement that the person is "unfit to live among decent, law-abiding people" for some specified period of time.

IN SUM

Reactions to the spectrum of criminals and social deviants vary from such mild sanctions as frowns and stares to such severe responses as imprisonment and death. Some sanctions are formal—court hearings, for example—although most are informal, as when friends refuse to talk to each other. One sanction is to label someone a social deviant, which can have powerful consequences for the person's life, especially if the label closes off conforming activities and opens up socially deviant ones. The degradation ceremony, in which someone is publicly labelled "not one of us," is a powerful sanction. So is imprisonment. Official statistics must be viewed with caution, for they reflect a strong social class bias.

The Medicalization of Social Deviance: Mental Illness

Another way society deals with social deviance is to *medicalize* it. To medicalize something is to make it a form of illness that properly belongs in the care of physicians.

NEITHER MENTAL NOR ILLNESS? For the past 100 years or so, especially since the time of Sigmund Freud (1856–1939), the Viennese physician who founded psychoanalysis, there has been a growing tendency toward the **medicalization of social deviance**. In this view, social deviance, including crime, is a sign of mental sickness. Rape, murder, theft, cheating, and so on are external symptoms of internal disorders, consequences of a confused or tortured mind.

Thomas Szasz (1986, 1998), a renegade in his profession of psychiatry, argues that *mental illnesses are neither mental nor illnesses. They are simply problem behaviours*. Some forms of so-called mental illnesses have organic causes; that is, they are physical illnesses that result in unusual perceptions and behaviour. Some depression, for example, is caused by a chemical imbalance in the brain, which can be treated with drugs. Depression, however, manifests as crying, long-term sadness, and the inability to become interested in anything. When a person becomes socially deviant in ways that disturb others, who cannot find a satisfying explanation for why

There are substantial differences between the United States and Canada in terms of rates of violent crime and other forms of social deviance. According to James Henslin, between 1970 and 1995, the population of the United States grew by 28 percent, while the prison population grew 20 times as fast, increasing by 560 percent. If the number of prisoners had increased at the same rate as the general population, there would be about 250 000 people in prison, or a fifth of the actual number. By contrast, the increase in the prison population in Canada between 1980 and 1990 was 12 percent, or 81.1 to 92.1 per 100 000.

These differences in incarceration or imprisonment have been explained in a number of ways. A widely recognized theory was offered by Seymour Martin Lipset (1990), who pointed to our counter-revolutionary history and its traditions of respect for institutional authority. The revolutionary history of the United States, by contrast, boasts of traditions respecting "rugged individualism" and irreverence for authority. What is more, the U.S. constitution guarantees every individual the right to life, liberty, the pursuit of happiness, and to bear arms. This makes for a lethal cultural cocktail. In Canada, the *British North America Act* promises peace, order, and good government while the *Charter of Rights and Freedoms* contains provisions for both individual and collective rights.

Canadian economic history has also been used to explain the cultural differences between the two countries. Canada has relied much more on large commercial enterprises, such as the Canadian Pacific Railroad, for nation-building, while major U.S. industries were frequently begun by individuals, often "robber barons" known to bend the rules on their way to fame and fortune. Because of the size of Canadian enterprises, our economic development relied more heavily on government subsidies than that of our U.S. capitalist counterparts. Therefore, the government and the police were active in the settlement of western Canada, in contrast to the "frontier spirit" of conquest over nature and people that symbolized U.S. westward expansion.

the person is "like that," they conclude that a "sickness in the head" causes the inappropriate, unacceptable behaviour.

All of us have troubles. Some of us face a constant barrage of problems as we go through life. Most of us continue the struggle, encouraged by relatives and friends, motivated by jobs, family responsibilities, and life goals. Even when the odds seem hopeless, we carry on, not perfectly, but as best we can.

Some people, however, fail to cope well with the challenges of daily life. Overwhelmed, they become depressed, uncooperative, or hostile. Some strike out at others, while some, in Merton's terms, become retreatists and withdraw into their apartments or homes and refuse to come out. These are *behaviours, not mental illnesses*, stresses Szasz. They may be inappropriate coping devices, but they are coping devices, nevertheless, not mental illnesses. Thus, Szasz concludes that "mental illness" is a myth foisted on a naive public by a medical profession that uses pseudoscientific jargon to expand its area of control and force nonconforming people to accept society's definitions of "normal."

Szasz's extreme claim forces us to look anew at the forms of social deviance called mental illness. To explain behaviour that people find bizarre, he directs our attention not to "things hidden deep within the subconscious," but instead to how people learn such behaviours. To ask, "What is the origin of inappropriate or bizarre behaviour?" then becomes similar to asking, "Why do some women steal?" "Why do some men rape?" "Why do some teenagers cuss their parents and stalk out of the room slamming doors?" *The answers depend on people's particular experiences in life, not some illness*

in their mind. In short, some sociologists find Szasz's renegade analysis refreshing because it indicates that *social experiences*, not illness of the mind, underlie bizarre behaviours—as well as social deviance in general.

THE HOMELESS MENTALLY ILL

Jamie was sitting on the low wall surrounding the landscaped area of an exclusive restaurant. She appeared unaware of the stares elicited by her many layers of mismatched clothing, her dirty face, and the ever-present shopping cart overflowing with her meagre possessions.

Every once in a while Jamie would pause, concentrate, and point to the street. I asked her what she was doing.

"I'm directing traffic," she replied. "I control where the cars go. Look, that one turned right there," she said, now withdrawing her finger.

"Really?" I said.

After a while she confided that her cart talked to her.

"Really?" I said again.

"Yes," she replied. "You can hear it, too." At that, she pushed the shopping cart a bit.

"Did you hear that?" she asked.

When I shook my head, she demonstrated again. Then it hit me. She was referring to the squeaking wheels!

I nodded.

When I left Jamie, she was looking toward the sky, her finger upraised, for, as she told me, she also controlled the flight of airplanes.

The homeless are located at the bottom of the social class ladder. Why do you think a society as wealthy as Canada has homeless people?

No one will talk to you, and you withdraw further into yourself. You begin to build a fantasy life. You talk openly to yourself. People stare, but so what? They stare anyway. Besides, they are no longer important to you.

How long would it take us to engage in bizarre behaviours if we were homeless? What if we were homeless and hopeless for years? The point is that *just being on the streets can cause mental illness*—or whatever we want to label socially inappropriate behaviours that we find difficult to classify (McCarthy, 1983; Belcher, 1988; R.K. Nelson, 1989). *Homelessness and mental illness are reciprocal*: Just as "mental illness" can cause homelessness, so the trials of being homeless, of living on cold, hostile streets, can lead to unusual and unacceptable thinking and behaviours.

THE NEED FOR A MORE HUMANE APPROACH

As Durkheim (1895/1938, pp. 68–69) pointed out, social deviance is inevitable—even in a group of saints:

> Imagine a society of saints... Crimes, properly so called, will there be unknown; but faults which appear [invisible] to the layman will create there the same scandal that the ordinary offense does in ordinary [society].

With social deviants being inevitable, one measure of a society is how it treats them. Social class position remains an important predictor. White-collar criminals continue to get by with a slap on the wrist, while street criminals are severely punished. Taking refuge in shelters and cardboard boxes in city streets is not a humane answer to homelessness. Neither is enforcing arrest policies the answer for violence against women. Although no one has *the* answer, it does not take much reflection to see that there are more humane approaches than these.

The larger issues of social deviance involve protecting people from socially deviant behaviours that are harmful to themselves or others, tolerating those that are not, and developing systems of fairer treatment for social deviants. In the absence of the fundamental changes that would bring about a truly equitable social system, most efforts are, unfortunately, Band-Aid work. What is needed is a more humane social system, one that would prevent the social inequalities that were the focus of Chapters 6 through 9.

To most of us, Jamie's behaviour and thinking are bizarre. They simply do not match any reality we know. Jamie might be mentally ill. Some organic problem, such as a chemical imbalance in her brain, might underlie her behaviour. But perhaps not. Could you or I become Jamie?

Suppose for a bitter moment that you are homeless and have to live on the streets. You have no money, no place to sleep, no bathroom, do not know *if* you are going to eat, much less where, have no friends or anyone you can trust, and live with the constant threat of rape and violence. Do you think this might be enough to drive you "over the edge"?

Consider the problems involved in not having a place to bathe. (Shelters are often so dangerous that the homeless prefer to take their chances sleeping in public settings.) At first, you might try to wash in the toilets of gas stations, bars, the bus station, or a shopping centre. But you are dirty, and people stare when you enter and call the management when they see you wash your feet in the sink. You are thrown out and told in no uncertain terms never to come back. So you get dirtier and dirtier. Eventually you come to think of being dirty as a fact of life. Soon, maybe, you don't even care. No longer do the stares bother you—at least not as much.

HOW DO PSYCHOLOGICAL, BIOLOGICAL, AND SOCIOLOGICAL EXPLANATIONS OF SOCIAL DEVIANCE DIFFER?

To explain why people deviate, psychologists and biologists look for reasons *within* the individual, such as **genetic predispositions** or **personality disorders**. Sociologists, in contrast, look for explanations *outside* the individual, in social relations. pp. 363–364.

The Symbolic Interactionist Perspective

HOW DO SYMBOLIC INTERACTIONISTS EXPLAIN SOCIAL DEVIANCE?

Symbolic interactionists have developed several theories to explain social deviance such as **crime** (the violation of norms written into law). According to **differential association** theory, people learn to deviate from associating with others. **Labelling theory** focuses on how labels (names, reputations) help to propel people into or divert people away from social deviance. Many people commit socially deviant acts and still think of themselves as conformists. They apparently use five **techniques of neutralization**. Studies of prostitutes show three ways in which the self-concept is involved in socially deviant acts. In **primary social deviance**, the acts are fleeting and have little effect on the self-concept. In **secondary social deviance**, people incorporate their socially deviant acts into their self-concept. In **tertiary social deviance**, acts commonly considered socially deviant are relabelled as normal. Although most people resist being labelled socially deviant, some embrace social deviance. pp. 364–367.

The Functionalist Perspective

HOW DO FUNCTIONALISTS EXPLAIN SOCIAL DEVIANCE?

Functionalists point out that social deviance, including criminal acts, is functional for society. Functions include affirming norms and promoting social unity and social change. According to **strain theory**, societies socialize their members into desiring **cultural goals**, but many people are unable to achieve these goals in socially acceptable ways—by **institutionalized means**. Social deviants, then, are people who either give up on the goals or use socially deviant means to attain them. Merton identified five types of responses to cultural goals and institutionalized means: conformity, innovation, ritualism, retreatism, and rebellion. Illegitimate opportunity theory stresses that some people have easier access to illegal means of achieving goals. pp. 367–371.

The Conflict Perspective

HOW DO CONFLICT THEORISTS EXPLAIN SOCIAL DEVIANCE?

Conflict theorists see power and social inequality as the primary characteristics of society. They stress that the state's machinery of social control, which includes the **criminal justice system**—the police, courts, and prisons that deal with the accused—represents the interests of the wealthy and powerful, a group that determines the basic laws essential to preserving its own power. pp. 371–372.

ARE OFFICIAL STATISTICS ON CRIME RELIABLE?

The conclusions of both symbolic interactionists (that the police operate with a large measure of discretion) and conflict theorists (that the legal system is controlled by the capitalist class) cast doubt on the accuracy of official crime statistics. p. 372.

The Feminist Perspective

WHY DO MEN COMMIT ACTS OF VIOLENCE AGAINST WOMEN?

When it comes to male violence against women, virtually all feminist theorists agree that men assault their female partners to maintain control over them and, if they happen to live in a relationship, their "domestic" situation. Control over women has been measured as (1) sexual fidelity, (2) obedience, (3) respect, (4) loyalty, (5) dependency, and (6) sexual access. pp. 372–373.

WHAT CAN BE DONE ABOUT MALE VIOLENCE AGAINST WOMEN?

Four strategies for coping with male violence against women are: (1) training the police to identify and charge offenders; (2) good job-creation strategies; (3) social services such as shelters and co-op housing; and (4) anti-sexist male collectives. DeKeseredy and Hinch, for example, argue that economic policy reforms such as paid work leaves, flexible hours (flextime), pay equity, and improving the quality of work available to disadvantaged people, to name just a few, can lower the rate of male violence against women. p. 373.

Postmodern Theories of Crime and Social Deviance

WHAT IS THE POSTMODERN PERSPECTIVE ON CRIME AND SOCIAL DEVIANCE?

The postmodern approach emphasizes the need to "deconstruct" or decode the meaning of concepts such as "law and order" and the "criminal justice system." Postmodern theorists also argue that whether we are sitting at home, driving, or walking on the streets, we are bombarded by information in the media about the risks we take—from air pollution and environmental hazards on and off the job to everyday choices about what we eat and drink. pp. 373–374.

The Canadian Criminal Justice System

WHAT ARE THE MAIN COMPONENTS OF THE CANADIAN CRIMINAL JUSTICE SYSTEM?

The Canadian criminal justice system comprises three principal components: the police, the courts, and the corrections system. The court system in Canada is composed of four basic levels. The first level is the provincial courts, which handle most criminal offences, family law matters (except divorce, which is dealt with at the federal level), and traffic violations. At the second level are the provincial and territorial superior courts, which deal with more serious crimes and also take appeals from provincial court judgments. There is also the Federal Court Trial Division. At the third level are the provincial courts of appeal and the Federal Court of

Appeal. The Supreme Court of Canada comprises the fourth and highest level. pp. 374–376.

Reactions to Social Deviance

HOW DO SOCIETIES REACT TO SOCIAL DEVIANCE?
Deviance results in **negative sanctions**, acts of disapproval ranging from frowns to capital punishment. Some groups use **degradation ceremonies** to impress on their members that certain violations will not be tolerated. pp. 376–377.

WHAT IS THE MEDICALIZATION OF SOCIAL DEVIANCE?
The medical profession has attempted to **medicalize** many forms of social deviance, claiming that they represent men-tal illnesses. Thomas Szasz disagrees, claiming that they are just problem behaviours, not mental illnesses. Research on homeless people illustrates how problems in living can lead to bizarre behaviour and thinking. pp. 377–379.

The Need for a More Humane Approach

Social deviance is inevitable, so the larger issues are protecting people from social deviance that harms themselves and others, tolerating social deviance that is not harmful, and developing systems of fairer treatment for social deviants. p. 379.

TALKING ABOUT THEORY

Theoretical Paradigms

	CLASSICAL PARADIGMS			RECENT PARADIGMS	
	Structural-Functional Paradigm	Social-Conflict Paradigm	Symbolic-Interaction Paradigm	Feminist Paradigm	Postmodernist Paradigm
What is the level of analysis?	Macro level	Macro level	Micro level	Micro and macro levels	Micro and macro levels
What is the social significance of crime and social deviance?	Social deviance and crime clarify and affirm normative boundaries for the majority (positive, or functional). The capitalist ethic that says that happiness and the good life come as a result of affluence influences some individuals in minority groups to resort to crime as the quickest means to achieve the good life (negative, or dysfunctional).	The criminal justice system maintains the status quo.	The groups that individuals associate with directly influences their attitudes and behaviours.	Male domination at the societal and familial level (patriarchy) explains violence toward women as a means of control.	The media-created "risk society" generates anxieties over the perpetrators of crime, such as visible minorities and youth.
Have crime and social deviance changed over time? How?	No. Social deviance and crime continue to have the same root causes and explanations. (For example, Merton's four paths of social deviance and "illegitimate opportunity structures" to explain social class and crime.)	Yes/No. As changing technology provides new opportunities for capital and profit, the laws must change to maintain class privilege and power.	Yes. As social attitudes change toward social deviance, old labels carry less weight.	Yes/No. Changes in legal prohibitions against women's right to vote and discrimination at work are significant positive changes. Patriarchy remains.	N/A

KEY TERMS

WEBLINKS

All URLs listed are current as of the printing of this book.

Journal of Prisoners on Prisons
www.jpp.org
A prisoner-written, academically oriented journal with the purpose of bringing "the knowledge and experience of the incarcerated to bear upon more academic arguments and concerns and to inform public discourse about the current state of our carceral institutions."

SocioSite
www.sociosite.net
A site designed to provide access to information and resources relevant to sociologists and other social scientists. Subjects include crime and deviance.

Internet Crime Archives
www.mayhem.net/Crime/archives.html
Information on all manners of illegal deviant behaviour.

American Society of Criminology
www.asc41.com
An international organization concerned with criminology that embraces scholarly, scientific, and professional knowledge concerning the etiology, prevention, control, and treatment of crime and delinquency.

Art Crimes: The Writing on the Wall
www.graffiti.org
A gallery of graffiti art from cities around the world, providing cultural information and resources that aim to preserve and document constantly disappearing graffiti paintings. "We do not advocate breaking the law, but we think art belongs in public spaces and that more legal walls should be made available for this fascinating art form."

CRITICAL THINKING QUESTIONS

1. According to Robert K. Merton, when people lack the opportunities to legitimately pursue culturally approved goals, they may turn to crime. Two ways of circumventing this are to (1) teach people to be satisfied with less and (2) provide more legitimate opportunities. If you alone had the means to decrease crime in Canadian society, which strategy would you pursue and why?

2. According to one of the authors of this book (Dan Glenday), Canadian criminologists have largely ignored the link between unemployment and property crimes in Canada. Instead, they have focused on more "sophisticated" theories that suggest "dysfunctional family backgrounds" as the cause for property crimes or differential association and labelling theories. Why do you think Canadian criminologists have ignored the link between unemployment and property crimes?

3. Probation officers and social workers usually want to identify "young offenders" as early as possible so that they may be "treated" before their "socially deviant" character is firmly established. Is this the right or wrong approach to take with young offenders?

4. What do you think should be done about the Canadian crime problem? What sociological theories either support or oppose your view? Access the Research Navigator through MySocLab and use keywords such as "crime," "solution," and "Canada" to locate relevant and recent scholarly and popular press publications to help you answer this question.

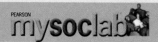
PEARSON mysoclab Explore the topics covered in this chapter on MySocLab using the access information provided with this text. Interactive resources for studying include multimedia tutorials, video clips, practice tests, quizzes, and animated maps and figures.

Population, Urbanization, and the Environment

The image still haunts me. There stood Celia, age 30, her distended stomach obvious proof that her thirteenth child was on its way. Her oldest was only 14 years old! A mere boy by our standards, he had already gone as far in school as he ever would. Every morning, he joined the men to work in the fields. Every evening around twilight, we saw him return home, exhausted from hard labour in the sun.

My wife and I, who were living in Colima, Mexico, had eaten dinner at Celia and Angel's home, which clearly proclaimed the family's poverty. A thatched hut consisting of only a single room served as home for all 14 members of the family. At night, the parents and younger children crowded into a double bed, while the eldest boy slept in a hammock. As in many other homes in the village, the others slept on mats spread on the dirt floor.

The home was meagerly furnished. It had only a gas stove, a cabinet where Celia stored her cooking utensils and dishes, and a table. With no closets, clothes were hung on pegs in the walls. There were no chairs, not even one. This really startled us. The family was so poor that they could not afford even a single chair.

Celia beamed as she told us how much she looked forward to the birth of her next child. Could she really mean it? It was hard to imagine that any woman would want to be in her situation.

Yet Celia meant every word. She was as full of delightful anticipation as she had been with her first child—and with all the others in between.

Source: Based on the personal experience of James Henslin.

How could Celia have wanted so many children—especially when she lived in such poverty? Celia's story takes us into the heart of **demography**, the study of the size, composition, growth, and distribution of human populations. It brings us face to face with questions of whether our planet will be able to support its growing population. Will chronic famine and mass starvation be the sorry fate that awaits most of us in this millennium? Let's look at how these concerns began, and then at what today's demographers have to say.

A PLANET WITH NO SPACE TO ENJOY LIFE?

Sometimes, the cultural diffusion of a simple item can have far-reaching consequences on nations. An example is the potato, which the Spanish Conquistadors found among the natives of the Andes. When the Spanish brought this food back to Europe, the people there came to gradually accept it. Eventually, the potato became the principal food of the lower classes. With more abundant food, fertility increased and the death rate dropped. As a result, Europe's population soared, almost doubling during the 1700s (McKeown, 1977).

This rapid growth alarmed Thomas Malthus (1766–1834), an English Protestant theologian. He saw it as a sign of coming doom. In 1798, he wrote *An Essay on the Principle of Population,* a book that became world famous. In it, Malthus proposed what became known as the **Malthus theorem**. He argued that while population grows geometrically (from 2 to 4 to 8 to 16, and so forth), the food supply increases only arithmetically (from 1 to 2 to 3 to 4, and so on). This meant, he claimed, that if births go unchecked, the population of a country, or even of the world, will outstrip its food supply. War and famine would be the inevitable result.

The New Malthusians

Was Malthus right? One group, which can be called the "New Malthusians," is convinced that today's situation is at least as grim as if not grimmer than what Malthus ever imagined. Figure 17.1 shows how fast the world's population is growing. *In just the time it takes you to read this chapter, another 15 000 to 20 000 babies will be born!*

The New Malthusians point out that the world's population is following an **exponential growth curve**. To illustrate, sociologist William Faunce (1981) told a parable about a man who saved a rich man's life. The rich man was grateful and said that he wanted to reward the man for his heroic deed:

> The man replied that he would like his reward to be spread out over a four-week period, with each day's amount being twice what he received on the preceding day. He also said he would be happy to receive only one penny on the first day. At the end of the first week, the rich man owed only $1.27. . . On the twenty-first day, however the total had grown to $20 971.51. When the twenty-eighth day arrived the rich man was shocked to discover that he owed $1 342 177.28 for that day alone and that the total reward had jumped to $2 684 354.56!

This kind of situation is precisely what alarms the New Malthusians. They contend that it took all of human history for the world's population to reach its first billion around 1800. It then took about 130 years (1930) to add the second billion. Just 30 years later (1960), the world population hit three billion. The time needed to reach the fourth billion was cut in half, to only 15 years (1975). Today, the world population has surpassed six billion (Haub & Yinger, 1994; Cohen, 1996).

The Anti-Malthusians

It seems obvious that no one wants to live in a shoulder-to-shoulder world and fight for scraps. How, then, can anyone argue with the New Malthusians?

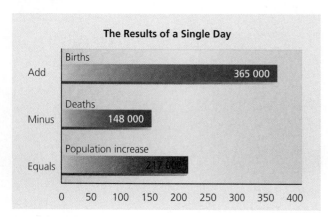

The Results of a Single Day

Add	Births	365 000
Minus	Deaths	148 000
Equals	Population increase	217 000

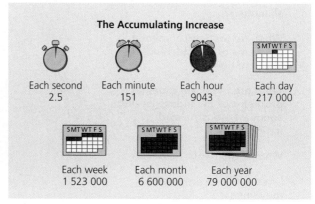

The Accumulating Increase

Each second 2.5	Each minute 151	Each hour 9043	Each day 217 000
Each week 1 523 000	Each month 6 600 000	Each year 79 000 000	

FIGURE 17.1   How Fast is the World's Population Growing?

Source: Based on Haub 2002c.

In earlier generations, large farm families were common. Having many children was functional—there were many hands to help with crops, food production, and food preparation. As the country industrialized and urbanized, this changed—children became expensive and nonproducing. Consequently, the size of families shrank as we entered Stage 3 of the *demographic transition* (see below), and today Canadian families with 10 children are practically non-existent.

A much more optimistic group of demographers, whom we can call the "Anti-Malthusians," claim that such an image of the future is ridiculous. Anti-Malthusians argue that people simply do not blindly reproduce until they run out of room (Simon, 1992, 1996; Mosher, 1994, 1997).

The Anti-Malthusians believe that Europe's **demographic transition** provides a more accurate picture of the future. This transition is diagrammed in Figure 17.2. During most of its history, Europe was in Stage 1. High birth rates offset by high death rates led to a fairly stable population. Stage 2, the "population explosion," was what upset Malthus. Europe's population surged because birth rates remained high, while death rates went down. Finally, Europe made the transition to Stage 3—the population stabilized as people brought their birth rates into line with the lower death rates.

This, contend the Anti-Malthusians, is what will happen in the least industrialized nations. Their current surge in growth simply indicates that they have reached the second stage of the demographic transition. Hybrid seed and modern medicine imported from the most industrialized nations have cut their death rates, but their birth rates remain high. When they move into the third stage, we will wonder what all the fuss was about.

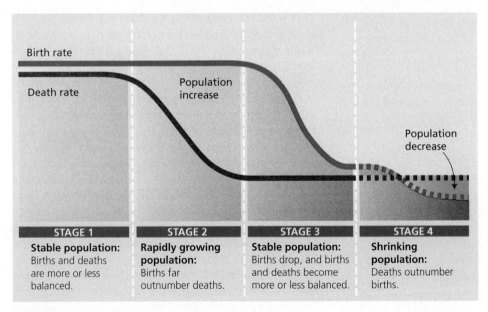

FIGURE 17.2 The Demographic Transition

Note: The standard demographic transition is depicted by Stages 1–3. Stage 4 has recently been suggested by some Anti-Malthusians.

Some Anti-Malthusians go even further (Mosher, 1997). As shown at the far right of Figure 17.2, they foresee a "demographic free fall." They predict that the world's population will peak at about 7 billion around the year 2030, and then begin a long descent. As countries industrialize, women will become more educated, postpone marriage, and reduce the number of children they bear. The result will be **population shrinkage**.

The shrinking population of Europe—Germany and Italy already fill more coffins than cradles—has begun to alarm policymakers. Closer to home, the demographic picture of Quebec society over the past 50 years illustrates the Anti-Malthusian claim. Quebec went from having the highest birth rate in the country to one of the lowest in just two generations. In recent years, the birth rate has inched upward, but still remains at a dismal 1.54 children per woman. The number of births dropped to a 55-year low in 2000. Since then, the number of births has gone up every year except 2002. In 2005, 342 418 babies were born in Canada, a jump of 1.5 percent from the previous year. The two main concerns for Anti-Malthusians are not enough young workers to support a rapidly growing elderly population, and race–ethnic problems that develop as workers from other parts of the world migrate to depopulating countries. Surprising almost everyone, the fourth stage of the demographic transition has also begun to hit Asia: Japan and South Korea do not produce enough children to maintain their populations (Chesnais, 1997). In short, stress the Anti-Malthusians, the world's problem will not be a population explosion, but *population shrinkage*—too few children in the world rather than too many.

Who Is Correct?

Who is right? Like the proverbial pessimists who see the glass of water half empty, the New Malthusians interpret population growth negatively. And like the optimists who see the same glass half full, the Anti-Malthusians view the figures positively.

However, in addition to the Mathusian debate, we should consider another perspective: feminism and population control.

Feminism and the Population Debate

Feminists reject the "solutions" favoured by the New Malthusians to limit population growth in the industrializing and least industrialized countries. The New Malthusians proposed, for example, forced sterilization of women in the industrializing and least industrialized nations. This idea and others like it were rightly analyzed as patriarchal policies. That is, such heavy-handed decisions, thought up by governments, are mainly rules created by older men to be imposed on younger men, women, and children. Feminists object to these policies because they deprive women of the freedom to make decisions for themselves—decisions about their own bodies.

The feminist perspective on the topic of population control begins with the emancipation of women from patriarchal decision-making. Feminists argue that women's rights, especially the right to decide about one's reproductive future, must be recognized as basic human rights. Unlike their Victorian predecessors, who rejected contraception, the contemporary feminist perspective recognizes the importance of birth control.

How should population control be achieved? By providing women with economic opportunities, education about birth control, and rights. Women who work, especially in cities, generally want to limit the number of children they will bear. This is a "policy" that does not have to be imposed; it simply involves making available opportunities for employment. There is strong evidence to support the argument that educating women is another important step. Women who can read are better able to care for their children, leading to lower infant mortality rates and lower fertility rates.

For most feminists, the course of action is clear: Empower women by giving them opportunities to find and keep meaningful employment, provide free public education, and enshrine women's rights in national and international legislation, and they will voluntarily lower their fertility.

Focus Question
What is the feminist viewpoint on the population debate?

Why Are People Starving?

Pictures of starving children haunt us. Why don't children around the world have enough food?

The basic question is this: Does the world produce enough food to feed everyone? On this issue, the Anti-Malthusians make a point that seems irrefutable. As Figure 17.3 shows, *the amount of food produced for each person in the world is now much more than it was in 1950.* Although the world's population has more than doubled during this time, improved seeds and fertilization have made more food available for every person on earth.

Then why do people die of hunger? From Figure 17.3, we can conclude that some countries produce more food than their people can consume; others make less than they need for survival. In short, the cause of starvation is an imbalance between supply and demand. It is important to understand the underlying basis of such human misery, some of which could certainly be alleviated by transferring food from nations that have a surplus.

One of the most notable examples is that at the same time as widespread famine is ravishing West Africa, Canadian farmers are having trouble selling their grain on the global market. The result: the lack of adequate incomes from cash crops has forced many western Canadian family farmers to give up and move to the cities.

Photos of starving people, such as this mother and child, haunt Canadians and other citizens of the most industrialized nations. Many of us wonder why, when some people are starving, we should live in the midst of such abundance, often overeating and even casually scrapping excess food. We even have eating contests to see who can eat the most food in the least time. The text discusses reasons for such unconscionable disparities.

Africa has been the site of recent pockets of starvation. Many images presented in the media leave the impression that Africa is overpopulated. Why else would all those people be starving? The truth, however, is far different. Africa has 22 percent of the earth's land surface, but only 10.5 percent of the world's population (Nsamenang, 1992). In fact, Africa contains some of the world's largest untapped land suitable for agriculture. The reason for famines in Africa, then, is not too many people living on too little land (Bender & Smith, 1997). Rather, famine is the result of two primary causes: outmoded farming techniques and political instability—revolutions and other warfare—that disrupt harvests and food distribution.

POPULATION GROWTH
Why the Least Industrialized Nations Have So Many Children

To understand why populations increase so much more rapidly in the least industrialized nations, let's figure out why

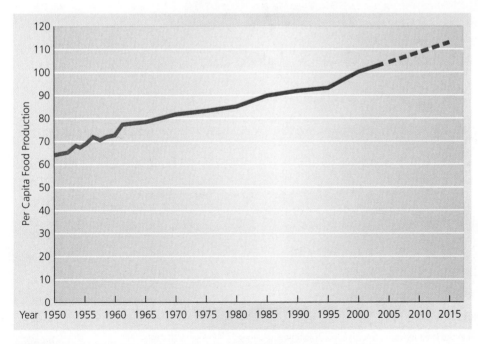

FIGURE 17.3 How Much Food Does the World Produce Per Person?

Source: By the author. Based on Simon 1981; Food and Agriculture Organization of the United Nations 2006.

Celia is so happy about having her thirteenth child. Consider three scenarios.

First, in the least industrialized nations, the more children a woman bears, the more she is thought to have achieved the purpose for which she was born—motherhood. Similarly, a man proves his manhood by fathering children. The more children he fathers, especially sons, the better—for through them his name lives on.

Second, the community views children as a blessing and encourages a couple to have many children. The barren woman, not the woman with a dozen children, is to be pitied.

Third, poor people in the least industrialized nations consider children economic assets. They have no social insurance or medical and employment insurance. As a result, when parents become sick or too old to work—or when no work is to be found—the more children they have, the broader their base of support. Moreover, like the eldest son of Celia and Angel, children begin contributing to the family income at a young age. Figure 17.4 illustrates how children can be net income earners for a least industrialized nation family. For example, consider the following incident, reported by a government worker in India:

Thaman Singh [a very poor man, a water carrier] . . . I have six sons and two daughters and I sit at home in leisure. They are grown up and they bring me money. *Now, you see, because of my large family I am a rich man.*" (Mamdani, 1973, italics added)

The Chinese government uses billboards to remind people of its "one couple, one child" policy. The fat on the child's face on this billboard in Shanghai carries an additional message—that curtailing childbirth brings prosperity and abundant food for all.

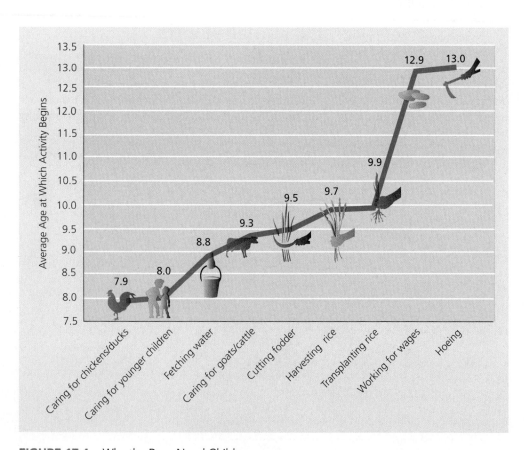

FIGURE 17.4 Why the Poor Need Children

Surviving children are an economic asset in the least industrialized nations. This figure, based on a survey in Indonesia, shows that boys and girls can be net income earners for their families by the age of nine or ten.

Source: U.N. Fund for Population Activities.

Feminists offer a different view of why women in poor nations bear so many children. They stress that in these cultures, men dominate women in all spheres of life, including reproduction. Feminists argue that Celia has internalized values that support male dominance. For example, in Latin America, *machismo* is common. This emphasis on male virility and dominance includes fathering many children as a means of achieving status in the community. From a feminist perspective, then, another reason poor people have so many children is that men control women's reproductive choices.

Estimating Population Growth: The Three Demographic Variables

How many people will live in Canada 50 years from now? What will the world's population be then? These are important questions. Educators want to know how many schools to build. Manufacturers want to anticipate changes in demand for their products. The government needs to know how many doctors, engineers, and executives to train, as well as how many people will be paying taxes and how many young people will be available to fight a war.

To project population trends, demographers use three **demographic variables**: fertility, mortality, and net migration.

FERTILITY The **fertility rate** is the number of children the average woman bears. A term sometimes confused with fertility is **fecundity**, the number of children that women are *capable* of bearing. The fecundity of women around the world is around 20 children each. Their fertility rate, however (the actual number of children they bear), is much lower. The world's overall fertility rate is 3.0, which means that the average woman in the world bears three children during her lifetime. As we saw earlier in the chapter, at 1.54 (2005), the fertility rate of Canadian women is considerably less than the world average.

To compute the fertility rate of a country, demographers figure the country's **crude birth rate**, the annual number of live births per 1000 population.

MORTALITY The second demographic variable, **crude death rate**, is the number of deaths per 1000 population.

MIGRATION The third major demographic variable is the **net migration rate**, the difference between the number of *immigrants* (people moving in) and *emigrants* (people moving out) per 1000 population. To understand migration, we need to look at both *push* and *pull* factors. Push factors are the things people want to escape—poverty, a lack of religious and political freedoms, even political persecution. Pull factors are the magnets that draw people to a new land, such as a chance for higher wages and better jobs.

Around the world, the flow of migration is from the least industrialized nations to the more industrialized countries (Kalish, 1994). After "migrant paths" are established, immigration often accelerates as networks of kin and friends become further magnets that attract more people from the same nation—and even from the same villages.

Table 17.1 shows the demographic profile of Canada from the first census taken in 1851 up to 2006. Note the rapid increase in births just after World War II, signalling the beginning of the "baby boom" generation. Also take note of the periods on the table from 1986–1991, 1991–1996, and 1996–2001. The number of deaths increased due to an aging population, while the number of births remained stagnant over the 1986–1996 period and *declined significantly* over the last period (1996–2001). Immigration to Canada is the key to supporting population growth and with it sustaining our standard of living.

The Basic Demographic Equation and Problems in Forecasting Population Growth

The total of the three demographic variables—fertility, mortality, and net migration—gives us a country's **growth rate**, the net change after people have been added to and subtracted from a population. What demographers call the **basic demographic equation** is quite simple:

Growth rate = Births − Deaths + Net migration

With such a simple equation, it might seem that it would be a simple matter to project a country's future population. But social factors—economic booms and busts, wars, plagues, and famines—push rates up or down.

The primary factor that influences a country's growth rate is its rate of industrialization. *In every country that industrializes, the growth rate declines.* Not only does industrialization open up economic opportunities, it also makes children more expensive. Significantly, the basis for conferring status also changes—from having children to attaining education and displaying material wealth. People like Celia and Angel then begin to see life differently, and their motivation to have many children drops sharply. Not knowing how rapidly industrialization will progress or how quickly changes in values and reproductive behaviour will follow adds to the difficulty of making accurate projections.

Because of such complications, demographers play it safe by making several projections of population growth (Haub, 1997). For example, what will the population of Canada be in the year 2010? Perhaps we will be at **zero population growth**, with every 1000 women giving birth to 2100 children. (The extra 100 children make up for those who do not survive.) Will a larger proportion of women go to university? (The more education women have, the fewer children they bear.) How will immigration change during the coming years? Will AIDS be brought under control? Will some other horrible disease appear? What will happen to the global economy?

THE CHALLENGE OF THE TWENTY-FIRST CENTURY

Let's look at a different aspect of population: where people live. Since the world is rapidly becoming urban, we will concentrate on urban trends and urban life.

TABLE 17.1   Demographic Profile of Canada from the First Census in 1851–2007 (thousands)[1]

Period	Total Population Growth[2]	Births	Deaths	Immigration	Emigration	Population of Canada at the End of the Period
1851–1861	793	1281	670	352	170	3230
1861–1871	460	1370	760	260	410	3689
1871–1881	636	1480	790	350	404	4325
1881–1891	508	1524	870	680	826	4833
1891–1901	538	1548	880	826	380	5371
1901–1911	1835	1925	900	1550	740	7207
1911–1921	1581	2340	1070	1400	1089	8788
1921–1931	1589	2420	1060	1200	970	10 377
1931–1941	1130	2294	1072	149	241	11 507
1941–1951	2141	3186	1214	548	379	13 648
1951–1956	2071	2106	633	783	185	16 081
1956–1961	2157	2362	687	760	278	18 238
1961–1966	1777	2249	731	539	280	20 015
1966–1971	1553	1856	766	890	427	21 568
1971–1976	1488	1755	824	1053	496	23 550
1976–1981	1371	1820	843	771	377	24 820
1981–1986	1280	1872	885	677	384	26 101
1986–1991	1930	1933	946	1189	256	28 031
1991–1996	1641	1936	1027	1170	480	29 672
1996–2001	1409	1660	1114	1137	321	31 081
2006–2007	N/A	353	238	260	41	31 240

[1] Includes Newfoundland since 1951.
[2] Figures are approximate.

Source: Statistics Canada, *Annual Demographic Statistics*, 2001 (corrected), Catalogue no. 91-213-XPB; CANSIM table 051-0004.

URBANIZATION

The Development of Cities

Perhaps as early as 7000 to 10 000 years ago, people built small cities with massive defensive walls, such as the biblically famous Jericho (Homblin, 1973).

The key to the origin of cities is the development of efficient agriculture (Lenski & Lenski, 1987). Only when farming produces a surplus can some people stop being food producers and gather in cities to spend time in other pursuits. The invention of the plow between 5000 and 6000 years ago created widespread agricultural surpluses, stimulating the development of towns and cities (Curwin & Hart, 1961). A **city** can be defined as a place in which a large number of people are permanently based and do not produce their own food.

Most early cities were tiny in comparison to those of today, merely a collection of a few thousand people in agricultural centres or on major trade routes. The most notable exceptions are two cities that reached populations of 1 million for a brief period before they declined—Changan in China around A.D. 800 and Baghdad in Persia around

A.D. 900 (Chandler & Fox, 1974). By 1900, the number of such cities jumped to 16 as a result of the Industrial Revolution, which drew people to cities by providing work. The Industrial Revolution also stimulated rapid transportation and communication, and allowed people, resources, and products to be moved efficiently—all essential factors (called infrastructure) upon which large cities depend. Figure 17.5 illustrates the global growth in the number of cities that are home to a million or more people (Brockerhoff, 2000).

The Process of Urbanization

Although cities are not new to the world scene, urbanization is. **Urbanization** refers to masses of people moving to cities, giving cities a growing influence on society. Urbanization is worldwide. Just 200 years ago, in 1800, only 3 percent of the world's population lived in cities (Hauser & Schnore, 1965). In 2007, for the first time in history, more people lived in cities than in rural areas. Today, about 77 percent of people in the industrialized world and 41 percent in the least industrialized nations live in cities (Haub, 2006; Robb, 2007).

To understand the city's attraction, we need to consider the "pull" of urban life. Due to its exquisite division of labour, the city offers incredible variety—music ranging from rock and rap to country and classic, diets for vegetarians and diabetics and imported delicacies from around the world.

PERSPECTIVES
Cultural Diversity around the World: Killing Little Girls—An Ancient and Thriving Practice

The Mysterious Case of the Missing Girls could have been the title of this box. For every 100 girls born around the world, about 105 boys are born. In China, however, for every 100 baby girls, there are 120 baby boys. Given China's huge population, this means that China has several million fewer baby girls than it should. Why?

The answer is *female infanticide*, the killing of baby girls. When a Chinese woman goes into labour, the village midwife sometimes grabs a bucket of water. If the newborn is a girl, she is plunged into the water before she can draw her first breath.

Economics lie at the root of China's sexist infanticide. The people are poor and have no pensions. When parents can no longer work, sons support them. In contrast, a daughter must be married off, at great expense, at which point her obligations transfer to her husband and his family.

In the past few years, the percentage of boy babies has grown. The reason, again, is economics, but this time it has a new twist. As China opened the door to capitalism, travel and trade opened up—but primarily to men, for it

is not thought appropriate for women to travel alone. With men finding themselves in a better position to bring profits home to the family, parents have one more reason to want male children.

The gender ratio is so lopsided that for people in their twenties, there are six bachelors for every five potential brides. Concerned about this gender imbalance, officials have begun a campaign to stop the drowning of girl babies. They are also trying to crack down on the abortions of female fetuses.

Female infanticide is also common in India. Many Indian women use ultrasounds to learn the sex of their child and then abort the fetus if it is a girl. Doctors take portable ultrasound machines from village to village, charging $8 for the test

and $44 for the abortion. Although the use of ultrasounds for this purpose is illegal, the practice accounts for the abortion of about 3 million girls a year.

It is likely that the preference for boys, and the resulting female infanticide, will not disappear until the social structures that perpetuate sexism are dismantled. This is unlikely to take place until women hold as much power as men, a development that, should it ever occur, apparently lies far in the future.

In the meantime, politicians have become concerned about a primary sociological implication of female infanticide—that large numbers of young men who cannot marry pose a political threat. These "bare branches," as they are referred to in China, disgruntled and lacking the stabilizing influences of marriage and children, could become a breeding ground for political dissent. This threat could motivate the national elites to take steps against female infanticide.

Sources: Jordan, 2000; Dugger, 2001; Eckholm, 2002; Raghunathan, 2003; French, 2004; Hudson & den Boer, 2004; Riley, 2004; Wonacott, 2007; Yardley, 2007.

Early cities were small economic centres surrounded by walls to keep out enemies. These cities had to be fortresses, for they were constantly threatened by armed, roving tribesmen and by leaders of nearby city-states who raised armies to enlarge their domain and enrich their coffers by sacking neighbouring cities. Pictured here is Cologne, Germany, as depicted in a 1545 manuscript.

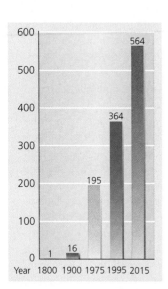

FIGURE 17.5   The Global Growth of Cities with over 1 Million Residents

Sources: By the author. Based on Chandler and Fox, 1974; Brockerhoff, 2000.

Cities also offer anonymity, which many people find highly refreshing in light of the much tighter social controls of village and small-town life. And the city offers work—of all kinds.

The term **metropolis** refers to a central city surrounded by smaller cities and their suburbs. They are connected economically, sometimes politically through county boards and regional governing bodies, and physically by ties of transportation and communication.

Some metropolises have grown so large and influential that the term **megalopolis** is used to describe them. This term refers to an overlapping area consisting of at least two metropolises and their many suburbs. When a city's population hits 10 million, it is called a *megacity*. In 1950, New York City was the only megacity in the world. Today, there are 19, including Tokyo, Shanghai, Buenos Aires, and Mexico City. There are no Canadian megacities.

Urban Patterns in Canada

In 1871, only 18 percent of the Canadian population lived in what could be called small cities. Industrialization had not taken off in Canada, so these early cities were geographically small with limited transportation routes connecting the various districts. By 1921, however, in a period of rapid industrialization that saw the influx of thousands of European immigrants, the percentage of Canadians living in cities had jumped to almost half the population. Today, if we rely on Statistics Canada's definition of "urban," over four-fifths of Canadians live in cities. The Statistics Canada definition of urban as 1000 people or more has recently been criticized as overstating the urban character of Canada (MacGregor, 2007).

Not all cities are the same size, however, nor do they grow at the same rate or carry the same commercial or financial weight. There is a hierarchy of urban centres in Canada.

One measure of the importance of cities in Canada is based on population size and its rate of growth over a period of time. In some instances, several towns expand until they run together and form a continuous urban area even though their municipal governments are still separate. Federal statisticians classify a continuous, built-up region of this kind with a population of 100 000 or more as a census metropolitan area (CMA).

Between 1996 and 2001, 6 of the 10 fastest-growing census metropolitan areas were located in Ontario: Oshawa, Toronto, Kitchener, Windsor, Ottawa-Hull, and Hamilton, in that order. The remaining CMAs were Edmonton (third place), Vancouver (fourth place), Abbotsford (Quebec), and Ottawa-Hull (Quebec part). For 2006, the three CMAs with the largest populations were Toronto (5 406 300), Montreal (3 666 300), and Vancouver (2 236 100). Calgary (36.1 percent) and Edmonton (26.2 percent) had the largest increases.

MODELS OF URBAN GROWTH

The Concentric Zone Model

To explain how cities expand, using Chicago as his model city, sociologist Ernest Burgess (1925) proposed a *concentric-zone model*. As shown in segment A of Figure 17.6, Burgess noted that a city expands outward from its centre.

Burgess observed, however, that no "city fits perfectly this ideal scheme." Some cities have physical obstacles, such as lakes, rivers, or railroads, which cause their expansion to depart from the model (Palen, 1987; Milbank, 1995a).

The Sector Model

Sociologist Homer Hoyt (1939, 1971) noted that a city's concentric zones do not form a complete circle, and modified Burgess's model of urban growth. As shown in segment B of Figure 17.6, a concentric zone might contain several sectors—one of working-class housing, another of expensive homes, a third of businesses, and so on—all competing for the same land.

What sociologists call an **invasion-succession cycle** is an example of the dynamic competition of urban life. When poor immigrants or migrants enter a city, they settle in the lowest-rent areas. As their numbers swell, they spill over into adjacent areas. Upset at their presence, the middle class moves out, thus expanding the sector of low-cost housing. The invasion-succession cycle is never complete, because

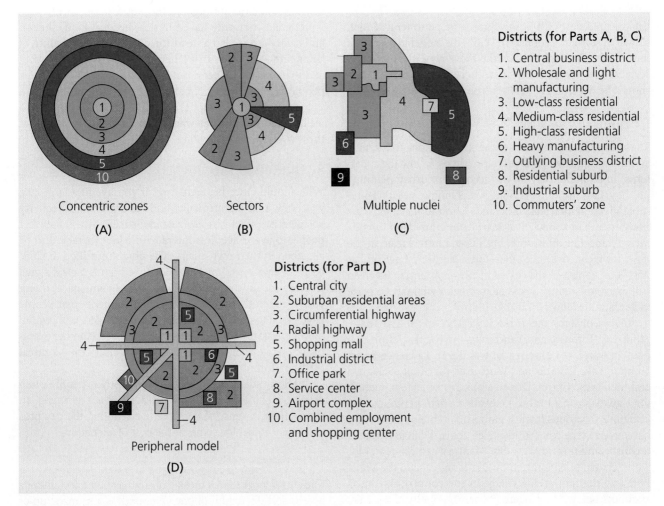

Concentric zones
(A)

Sectors
(B)

Multiple nuclei
(C)

Peripheral model
(D)

Districts (for Parts A, B, C)
1. Central business district
2. Wholesale and light manufacturing
3. Low-class residential
4. Medium-class residential
5. High-class residential
6. Heavy manufacturing
7. Outlying business district
8. Residential suburb
9. Industrial suburb
10. Commuters' zone

Districts (for Part D)
1. Central city
2. Suburban residential areas
3. Circumferential highway
4. Radial highway
5. Shopping mall
6. Industrial district
7. Office park
8. Service center
9. Airport complex
10. Combined employment and shopping center

FIGURE 17.6 How Cities Develop: Models of Urban Growth

Sources: Cousins and Nagpaul, 1970; Harris, 1997.

later, another group will replace this earlier one, or it may be gentrified by other migrants. **Gentrification** is the movement of middle-class people into rundown areas of a city. They are attracted by low prices for quality housing that can be restored. Montreal's famous St. Urban/St. Lawrence Boulevard corridor has been the home of Jewish, Italian, Portuguese, Spanish, and other ethnic groups for the past 100 years. Toronto's Cabbagetown and Spadina Avenue corridors are other examples.

The Multiple-Nuclei Model

Geographers Chauncey Harris and Edward Ullman observed that some cities have several centres or nuclei (Harris & Ullman, 1945; Ullman & Harris, 1970). As shown in segment C of Figure 17.6, each nucleus is the focus of some specialized activity. A familiar example is the clustering of malls and fast-food restaurants in one area and automobile dealerships in another. Thus, push-pull factors separate areas by activities, and services are not evenly spread throughout an urban area.

The Peripheral Model

Chauncey Harris (1997) developed the peripheral model, shown in segment D of Figure 17.6. This model portrays the impact of radial highways on the movement of people and services away from a city's periphery or outskirts. It also shows the development of industrial and office parks.

Critique of the Models

These models tell only part of the story. For one thing, they are time-bound, for medieval cities didn't follow these patterns. In addition, they do not account for urban planning policies. England, for example, has planning laws that preserve green belts (trees, farmlands) around its cities. This prevents urban sprawl: Wal-Mart cannot buy land outside the city and put up a store, but instead must locate in the downtown core, with the other stores. Norwich, England has 250 000 people, yet the city suddenly ends, and in its green belt, pheasants skitter across plowed fields while sheep graze in verdant meadows (Milbank, 1995b).

Like Chicago, the three largest cities of Canada—Montreal, Toronto, and Vancouver—grew in relation to a body of water. For Montreal, it was the St. Lawrence River; Toronto, Lake Ontario; and Vancouver, the Strait of Georgia and the Pacific Ocean. Due to a number of factors, including Canada's constitution, innovative urban planning, and coalitions of various interest groups in each city, these cities have reversed the patterns identified above. With its dynamic linguistic and territorial duality, Montreal can claim an old-world character epitomized by Old Montreal and the Vieux Port and the largest gay village in the country. Toronto's Harbourfront, a 28.3 hectare (70 acre) property along Lake Ontario, mixes recreational, cultural, residential, and commercial elements (Church, Greenberg, & McPhedran, 1997).

Vancouver boasts the 1000-acre Stanley Park as part of its topographical diversity and is home to the third-largest Chinatown in North America after San Francisco and New York City.

The models also fall short when it comes to cities in the least industrialized nations. Here, the wealthy often claim the inner city, where fine restaurants and other services are readily accessible. Tucked behind tall walls and protected from public scrutiny, they enjoy luxurious homes and gardens. In contrast, the poor, especially rural migrants, settle unclaimed fringe areas outside the city (see the Perspectives box on the next page).

Focus Question

What are the three models of urban growth? What are their limitations?

CITY LIFE

Cities are intended to be solutions to problems. They hold hope of gainful employment, education, and other advantages. The perception of such opportunities underlies mass migration to cities throughout the world.

Humans not only have physical needs—food, shelter, and safety—but also a need for **community**, a feeling of belonging—the sense that others care what happens to you, and that you can depend on the people around you. Some people find this sense of community in cities; others find only its opposite, *alienation*, a sense of not belonging, and a feeling that no one cares what happens to you. Let's look at these two aspects of city life.

Alienation in the City

Why should cities be alienating? If you live in a large city, you know that impersonality and self-interest are ordinary characteristics. As you navigate city streets, you can expect people to avoid needless interaction with others and to be absorbed in their own affairs. The ubiquitous iPod or similar MP3 device strapped around a head sends a clear signal to everyone on the street—"I am in my own space, thank you. Don't bother me." These are adjustments that people have made to deal with the crowds of strangers with whom they temporarily share the same urban space. Another example of people avoidance is travelling on either the Montreal Metro or Toronto's subway system.

Lacking identification with one another, people often develop an attitude of "It's simply none of *my* business." In short, the very sense of personal freedom that the city provides may come, for some, at the cost of alienation.

Community

The city is more than a mosaic of strangers who feel disconnected and distrustful of one another. It is also made up of a series of smaller worlds, within which people find *community*, a sense of belonging. Here they live, work, shop, and

Thoughts of the least industrialized nations often conjure images of people tending animals or harvesting crops, enjoying a peaceful life in the lush, green countryside or along babbling brooks. Such images no longer represent the reality faced by most people in the least industrial nations—if they ever did. The rural poor of these countries are flocking to the cities at such a rate that the least industrialized nations now contain most of the world's largest cities. In the most industrialized nations, industrialization generally preceded urbanization, but in the least industrialized nations *urbanization is preceding industrialization*. These cities cannot support their swelling populations.

Settlement patterns are also different in these cities. When rural migrants and immigrants move to U.S. cities, they usually settle in deteriorating housing near a city's centre. The wealthy reside in suburbs and luxurious city enclaves. Migrants to cities of the least industrialized nations, in contrast, establish illegal squatter settlements outside cities. They build shacks from scrap boards, cardboard, and bits of corrugated metal. Even flattened tin cans are scavenged for building material. Squatters enjoy no city facilities—roads, public transportation, water, sewers, or garbage pickup. After thousands of squatters have settled an area, the city reluctantly acknowledges their right to live there and adds bus services and minimal water lines. Hundreds

This photo, taken outside Buenos Aires, Argentina, illustrates the settlement pattern common in the least industrialized and industrializing nations.

of people use a single spigot. About *5 million* of Mexico City's residents live in such squalid conditions, with hundreds of thousands more pouring in each year.

Why is there a rush to live in cities under such miserable conditions? At its core are the "push" factors that arise from a breakdown of traditional rural life. With a safer water supply and the importation of modern medicine, the death rate in rural areas dropped. As a result, rural populations multiplied, and there is no longer enough land for parents to divide up among their children. Without land or jobs, there is hunger. People are deeply dissatisfied with the resulting hardscrabble character of rural life. There are also "pull" factors that draw people to cities—jobs, schools, housing, and even a more stimulating life.

At the bottom of a ravine near Mexico City is a dismal bunch of shacks. Some of the parents in the small community have up to 14 children. "We used to live up there," Señora Gonzalez gestured toward the mountain, "in those caves. Our only hope was one day to have a place to live. And now we do." She smiled with pride at the jerry-built shacks. Each one had a collection of flowers planted in tin cans. "One day, we hope to extend the water pipes and drainage—perhaps even pave . . ."

What was the name of this community? Señora Gonzalez beamed. "Esperanza!" (McDowell, 1984: p. 172). *Esperanza* is the Spanish word for hope. This is what lies behind the rush to cities—the hope of a better life. This is also why the rush won't slow down. In 1930, only one Latin American city had over a million people—now 50 do! The world's cities are growing by a million people each week (Brockerhoff, 2000).

Will the least industrialized nations adjust to this vast migration? They have no choice. Authorities in Brazil, Guatemala, Venezuela, and other countries have sent in the police and even the army to evict settlers. It doesn't work. It just leads to violence, and settlers keep streaming in. The adjustments will be painful. Infrastructure (roads, water, sewers, electricity, and so on) must be built, but poor countries don't have the resources to build them. As the desperate rural poor flock to the cities, the problems will only worsen.

play. Slums, which to outsiders seem threatening, provide a sense of belonging. In a classic study, sociologist Herbert Gans noted:

> After a few weeks of living in the West End [of Boston], my observations—and my perceptions of the area—changed drastically. Since much of the area's life took place on the street, faces became familiar very quickly. I met my neighbours on the

stairs and in front of my building. And, once a shopping pattern developed, I saw the same storekeepers frequently, as well as the area's "characters" who wandered through the streets on a fairly regular route and schedule.

Living in Boston's West End, Gans gained an insider's perspective. He had located a community, discovering that its residents visited back and forth with relatives and were involved

The type of dweller Gans identified as *ethnic villagers* find community in cities. Living in tightly knit neighbourhoods, they know many other residents. Some first-generation immigrants have even come from the same village in the "old country."

in extensive networks of friendships and acquaintances. Gans therefore titled his book *The Urban Villagers* (1962).

Types of Urban Dwellers

Whether you find alienation or community in city life largely depends on who you are, for the city offers both. People from different backgrounds experience the city differently. Gans (1962, 1968, 1991a) identified the types of people who live in the city. The first three types live in cities by choice, and have found a sense of community.

THE COSMOPOLITANS The cosmopolitans are a city's students, intellectuals, professionals, musicians, artists, and entertainers. They value its conveniences and cultural benefits.

THE SINGLES Young, unmarried people, who may team up to rent apartments, come to a city seeking jobs and entertainment. Businesses and services such as singles bars, singles apartment complexes, and computer dating services cater to their needs. Their stay in the city often reflects a temporary stage in their life course. After they marry, many move to the suburbs, where housing is usually cheaper than in the city core.

THE ETHNIC VILLAGERS These people live in tightly knit neighbourhoods that resemble villages and small towns. United by race/ethnicity and social class, their neighbourhoods place an emphasis on family and friends. By doing so, they try to isolate themselves from the dangers and problems of urban life.

THE TRAPPED This group of people have little choice about where they live. Outcasts of industrial society, they are alienated and always skirting the edge of disaster. They consist of

four subtypes: those who could not afford to move when their neighbourhood was "invaded" by another ethnic group; elderly people who are not wanted elsewhere; alcoholics and other drug addicts; and the "downwardly mobile," people who have fallen from a higher social class. The trapped suffer high rates of assault, mugging, robbery, and rape. The homeless are made up of all four types of urban dwellers.

Gans's typology provides insight into the variety of ways urban dwellers experience city life. Some find the streets a stimulating source of cultural contrasts. For others, however, the same events pose a constant threat as they try to survive in what for them amounts to an urban jungle.

Focus Question
Why has the world's population tended to move into urban settlements?

Urban Sentiment: Finding a Familiar World

Sociologists note that *the city is divided into little worlds* that people come to know, down to their smallest details. Gregory Stone (1954) and Herbert Gans (1970) observed how city people create a sense of intimacy for themselves by *personalizing* their shopping. By frequenting the same stores, they become recognized as "regulars," and after a period of time customers and clerks greet each other by name. Particular taverns, restaurants, laundromats, and shops are more than just buildings in which to purchase items and services. They become meeting places where neighbourhood residents build social relationships with one another and share informal news about the community.

Spectator sports also help urban dwellers find a familiar world (Hudson, 1991). When the Hamilton Tiger Cats won the Grey Cup in 1999, the city of Hamilton celebrated the victory of "their" team with a downtown parade and week-long festivities. And when the underdog Toronto Argonauts won in 2004, the victory parade went from Union Station north up Bay Street and ended in Nathan Phillips Square. The 2007 Grey Cup, the Battle of the Underdogs, ended with the Saskatchewan Roughriders as the victors. Sociologists David Karp and William Yoels (1990) note that such identification is so intense that long after moving to other parts of the country, many people maintain an emotional allegiance to the sports teams of the city in which they grew up.

As sociologists Richard Wohl and Anselm Strauss (1958) observed, city dwellers even develop strong feelings for particular objects and locations in the city, such as buildings, rivers, lakes, parks, and even trees and street corners. In some cases, objects become a type of logo that represents the city—for example, Kensington Market in Toronto, the Latin Quarter in Montreal, or Granville Island in Vancouver.

> For those who live in these respective cities, such objects and places do not merely identify the city; they are also sources for personal identification with the city. (Karp, Stone, & Yoels, 1991)

Urban dwellers find their community, then, not in buildings and space, but in their social relationships. Regardless of where they live in the city, people who are not integrated into social networks find alienation, while those who are integrated find community.

Suburbanization

Suburbanization, which refers to people moving from cities to **suburbs**—the communities located just outside a city—is not new. The dream of a place of one's own with green grass, a few trees, and kids playing in the yard was not discovered by this generation (Riesman, 1970). For the past 100 years or so, as transportation became more efficient, especially with the development of automobiles, people have moved to towns next to the cities in which they work.

Deindustrialization and Globalization

The development of a global market has left a heavy imprint on Canadian cities. As sociologist Victor Rodríguez (1994) points out, to compete in the global market, many industries have abandoned local communities and moved their factories to places where labour costs are lower. This process has eliminated millions of manufacturing jobs, locking many poor people out of the postindustrial economy engulfing some cities in Canada. They are forced to move, usually taking lower-paying jobs in call centres and large box stores such as Wal-Mart and Canadian Tire. Many live in despair as a distant economy charges into the uncharted waters of a brave new world without them (see the Perspectives: Finding Work box in Chapter 11, page 253).

> ## THE ENVIRONMENT

THE NATURAL ENVIRONMENT
Environmental Problems of Past Civilizations

Contrary to common assumptions, environmental problems are not new to human existence. Several civilizations destroyed themselves by destroying the environments on which their very existence depended.

The most famous is the fall of Mesopotamia, a civilization that was located in the lush river basin of the Tigris and Euphrates in what is now Iraq. About 3000 years before Christ, this civilization flourished as a result of an extensive irrigation system that provided abundant food. The irrigation system had no drainage, however. The water constantly evaporated, gradually growing saltier. Over centuries, the underground water table rose, and the land became too salty to support crops. The Mesopotamians had unwittingly destroyed the agricultural base on which their civilization depended (Jacobsen & Adams, 1958). What once was beautiful, lush, green land that produced fruits, vegetables, and grains in abundance, is now desert.

Environmental Problems in the Most Industrialized Nations

Although environmental degradation is not new, the frontal assault on the natural environment did not begin in earnest until nations industrialized. The more extensive the industrialization, the better it was considered for a nation's welfare, and the slogan for the most industrialized nations has been "Growth at any cost."

Industrial growth progressed, but at a high cost to the natural environment. Today, many formerly pristine streams are polluted sewers. Most major Canadian cities have daily air pollution indexes. Montreal's McGill subway station, for example, posts the changing daily pollution count on an overhead electronic bulletin board for commuters to easily see. During the summer months, nearly all Canadian radio and television news programs report on the sun's ultraviolet radiation by telling listeners/viewers how long it is safe to stay outside without sunscreen protection.

Of all the consequences of pollution we could discuss, we will consider—due to space limitations—only the implications of fossil fuels.

FOSSIL FUELS AND ENVIRONMENTAL DEGRADATION The burning of fossil fuels for factories, motorized vehicles, and power plants has been especially harmful to the environment. Fish can no longer survive in some lakes in Canada and the northeastern United States because of **acid rain**. As illustrated in Figure 17.7, acid rain is created when the burning of fossil fuels releases sulphur dioxide and nitrogen oxide, which react with moisture in the air to become sulphuric and nitric acids (Sawyer, 2001).

An invisible but more serious consequence is the **greenhouse effect**. Like the glass of a greenhouse, the gases emitted from burning fossil fuels allow sunlight to enter the earth's atmosphere freely, but inhibit the release of heat. It is as though the gases have closed the atmospheric

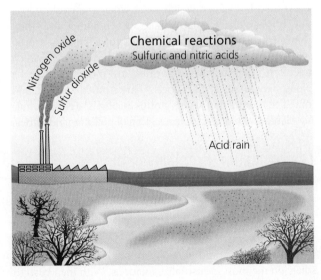

FIGURE 17.7 Acid Rain

window through which our planet breathes. The world's scientists have concluded that the resulting **global warming** will melt the polar icecaps and inundate the world's shorelines, causing the climate boundaries to move several hundred kilometres north and making many animal and plant species extinct (Kanter & Revkin, 2007; Smith & Tirpak, 1988; P. Thomas, 1988; Weisskopf, 1992).

THE ENERGY SHORTAGE AND MULTINATIONAL CORPORATIONS If you have ever read about an energy shortage, you can be sure the report was false. There is no energy shortage, nor can there ever be. The earth holds the potential of producing unlimited low-cost power, which can help raise the living standards of humans across the globe. The sun, for example, produces more energy than humanity could ever use. Boundless energy is also available from the tides and the winds. In some cases, we need better technology to harness these sources of energy; in others, we need only apply technology we already have.

Since burning fossil fuels in internal combustion engines is the main source of pollution in the most industrialized nations, and vast sources of alternative energy are available, why don't we develop the technology to use these alternative sources? From a conflict perspective, alternative sources of energy threaten multinational corporations' oil monopoly. To maintain their profits, these corporations make certain that internal combustion engines remain dominant. The practical development and widespread use of alternative sources of power will wait until the multinationals have cornered the market on the technology that will harness them—so they can continue reaping huge profits.

Environmental Injustice

Unequal power has led to **environmental injustice**, with minority groups and the poor suffering the most from the effects of pollution (Mohal & Saha, 2007). Industries locate where land is cheaper, which is not where the wealthy live. Nor will the rich allow factories to spew pollution near their homes (a phenomenon often referred to as NIMBY—not in my backyard). As a result, low-income communities, which are often inhabited by minorities, are more likely to be exposed to pollution. Sociologists have studied, formed, and joined environmental justice groups that fight to close polluting plants and block the construction of polluting industries.

Environmental Problems in the Industrializing and Least Industrialized Nations

INDUSTRIALIZING NATIONS Negative environmental consequences of industrialization, such as ozone depletion, the greenhouse effect, and global warming, cannot be blamed solely on the most industrialized nations. With their rush to be contenders in global competition, the lack of funds to purchase pollution controls, and few anti-pollution laws, the industrializing nations make their own enormous contributions to this problem. Breathing the polluted air of Mexico City, for example, is the equivalent of smoking two packs of cigarettes a day (Durbin, 1995).

The former Soviet Union is a special case. Until this empire broke up, pollution had been treated as a state secret. Scientists and journalists were forbidden to mention pollution in public. Even peaceful demonstrations to call attention to the problem could net participants two years in prison (Feshbach, 1992). With protest stifled and no environmental protection laws, environmental pollution was everywhere: Almost half of Russia's arable land has been made unsuitable for farming, about a third of Russians live in cities where air pollution is over 10 times greater than levels permitted in Canada, and half of Russia's tap water is unfit to drink. Pollution is so severe that it is likely a contributor to the drop in life expectancy that has occurred in Russia. If so, it is a lesson that should not be lost on the rest of us as we make decisions on how to treat our environment.

LEAST INDUSTRIALIZED NATIONS The great poverty and swelling populations of the least industrialized nations, combined with almost non-existent environmental regulations, destine these countries to become major sources of pollution.

Their lack of environmental protection laws has not gone unnoticed by opportunists in the most industrialized nations, who have seized the opportunity to use these countries as garbage dumps for hazardous wastes and for producing chemicals that their own nations will no longer tolerate (LaDou, 1991; C.S. Smith, 1995). Alarmed at the growing environmental destruction, the World Bank, a monetary arm of the most industrialized nations, has put pressure on the least industrialized nations to reduce pollution and soil erosion (Lachica, 1992). The basic concern of these nations is to produce food and housing first, and to worry about the environment later.

RAIN FORESTS AND EXTINCTION Holding unknown consequences for the future of humanity is the extinction of numerous plant and animal species as tropical rain forests are relentlessly cleared for lumber, farms, and pastures. Although rain forests cover just 7 percent of the earth's land area, they are home to half of its plant species. With these forests disappearing at a rate of nearly *2500 acres (1012 hectares) every hour* (McCuen, 1993), it is estimated that 10 000 species become extinct every year—about one per hour (Durning, 1990). As rain forests are destroyed, so are the native communities that live in them.

Canada and the Kyoto Protocol

The Kyoto Protocol is an agreement entered into by a number of countries that is intended to reduce greenhouse gases (global warming) and thereby contribute to sustainable global development. However, not all national leaders support the goals of the protocol and some don't believe global warming is a problem, even though the world's top 2000 climate experts are all on side.

The Kyoto Protocol came into effect on February 16, 2005, prior to which signing nations were required to "ratify" the protocol—commit to achieving the goals set out in it. The Canadian Parliament ratified on December 17, 2002. One hundred and forty-one countries ratified Kyoto, with the most glaring exception being the largest single polluter in the world: the United States. (Australia and Monaco are the other two industrialized countries that did not sign on.) The United States is responsible for about a quarter of the greenhouse gas emissions believed to be causing global warming.

Ironically, two of the worst—and steadily worsening—polluters, India and China, have not and are not required to sign on to Kyoto because they are industrializing nations. Will the Kyoto Protocol be successful in slowing global warming? Without the United States on board, is it doomed to fail? These are important questions. However, we will have to wait until 2012, when the first phase of the agreement is over, to determine how successful it has been and how much stricter its requirements may need to be.

The Environmental Movement

Concern about environmental problems has produced a worldwide social movement. In some countries, political parties built around environmental concerns, called *green parties*, campaign in local and national elections. In Europe, especially Germany, green parties have become a political force and have won seats in the national legislatures.

Activists in the environmental movement generally seek solutions in politics, legislation, and education. Seeing that pollution continues, the rain forests are still being cleared, and species are becoming extinct, some activists are convinced that the planet is doomed unless immediate steps are taken. Choosing a more radical course, they use extreme tactics to try to arouse indignation among the public and thus force governments to act. Convinced that they stand for morality, many are willing to break the law and go to jail for their actions. Such activists are featured in the Thinking Critically about Social Controversy box below.

THINKING CRITICALLY ABOUT SOCIAL CONTROVERSY
Ecosabotage

Chaining oneself to a giant Douglas fir slated for cutting; pouring sand down the gas tank of a bulldozer; tearing down power lines and ripping up survey stakes; driving spikes into redwood trees; and sinking whaling vessels—are these the acts of dangerous punks, intent on vandalism and with little understanding of the needs of modern society? Or are they the acts of brave men and women willing to put their freedom, and even their lives, on the line on behalf of the planet?

How many 3000-year-old trees remain on Earth? Do fences and picnic tables for backyard barbecues justify cutting them down? Questions like these, as well as the slaughter of seals, the destruction of rain forests, and the drowning of dolphins in mile-long drift nets spawned Earth First! and other organizations devoted to preserving the environment, such as Greenpeace, Sea Shepherds, and the Ruckus Society.

"We feel like there are insane people who are consciously destroying our environment, and we are compelled to

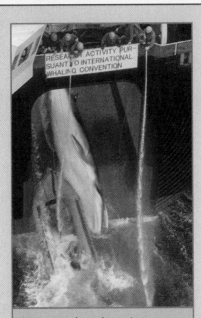

As concern about the environment grows, a social movement to try to change the course of events has developed. Protest groups have rallied around numerous issues, including the seal hunt, whaling, and the destruction of old growth forests on Canada's west coast.

fight back," explains a member of one of the militant groups. "No compromise in defence of Mother Earth!" says another. "With famine and death approaching, we're in the early stages of World War III," adds another.

The dedication of some of these activists has brought them close to martyrdom. When Paul Watson, founder of the Sea Shepherds, sprayed seals with green dye, which destroys the value of their pelts but doesn't hurt the animals, hunters hog-tied him, dragged him across the ice, and threatened to toss him into the sea. "It's no big deal," says Watson, "when you consider that 100 million people in this century have died in wars over real estate."

Radical environmentalists represent a broad range of activities and purposes. They are united on neither tactics nor goals. Some want to stop a specific action, such as the killing of whales, or to destroy all nuclear weapons and dismantle nuclear power plants. Others want everyone to become vegetarians. Still others want the earth's population

Environmental Sociology

Environmental sociology, which examines the relationship between human societies and the environment, emerged as a subdiscipline of sociology around 1970 (Dunlap & Catton 1979, 1983; Buttel, 1987; Freudenburg & Gramling, 1989; Laska, 1993). Its main assumptions are:

1. The physical environment is a significant variable of sociological investigation.

2. Human beings are one species among many that are dependent on the natural environment.

3. Because of intricate feedbacks to nature, human actions have many unintended consequences.

4. The world is finite, so there are potential physical limits to economic growth.

5. Economic expansion requires increased extraction of resources from the environment.

6. Increased extraction of resources leads to ecological problems.

7. These ecological problems place restrictions on economic expansion.

8. Governments create environmental problems by trying to establish conditions for the accumulation of capital.

The goal of environmental sociology is not to stop pollution or nuclear power, but rather to study how humans (their cultures, values, and behaviours) affect the physical environment and how the physical environment affects human activities. Environmental sociologists, however, are generally also environmental activists.

Kathleen Riel is an environmental sociologist in Canada who has written extensively on matters affecting our environment. In Table 17.2, she provides contrasting views of society as seen from environmental and traditional sociological perspectives.

Focus Question
What is the relationship between our physical environment and sociological theory?

ECOFEMINISM AND THE ENVIRONMENT

Ecofeminists believe human beings are connected to one another and to the nonhuman world—animal, vegetable, or mineral. They point out that we do violence to each other and to nature, congratulating ourselves on providing material abundance for some while militarily protecting our self-interests in the exploitation of the earth's natural resources, such as fossil fuels and other valuable minerals and ores.

They explain the harm done to humanity and the environment by pointing to patriarchy's hierarchical, dualistic, and oppressive ways of thinking. For example, women are "naturalized" when they are described in animal terms such as "foxes, cows, chicks, bird-brains" and so on, while nature is "feminized" when "she" is "raped, conquered, mastered, penetrated, subdued" or "worshipped" as the grandest "mother" of them all. In biblical terms, man is lord over nature and over nature's analogue, woman. These dualistic, hierarchical, and oppressive ways of thinking have brought humanity to the brink of disaster by disrespecting nature and women.

Ecofeminists disagree on the proper "solutions" to this social problem, but most agree that a fundamental and radical change in our thinking must be a necessary start. We can begin individually by respecting ourselves and nature and conserving resources through, for example, recycling and refusing to eat animals that have been grown under cruel conditions, and collectively by supporting environmental causes.

Technology and the Environment: The Goal of Harmony

It is inevitable that humans will continue to develop new technologies. The abuse of our environment by those technologies is not inevitable, however.

TABLE 17.2 Comparison of Competing Paradigms, Selected Items

New Environmental Paradigm	Dominant Sociological Paradigm
I. High valuation of nature	*I. Lower valuation of nature*
Environmental protection over economic growth	Human domination over nature
II. Generalized compassion	*II. Compassion only for those near and dear*
Concern for other species, peoples, and generations	Concern for present generation only
III. Careful planning and acting to avoid risk	*III. Acceptance of risk to maximize wealth*
Regulation to protect nature and humans is the government's responsibility	Deregulation by governments—individual responsibility
IV. Limits to growth	*IV. No limits to growth*
Conservation	Production and consumption
V. Completely new society	*V. Present society fine (maintain the status quo)*
Openness and participation	Competition and emphasis on the market
VI. New Politics	*Old Politics*
Emphasis on foresight and planning	Emphasis on market control

Source: *Canadian Society: Meeting the Challenges of the Twenty-First Century,* 2001, Dan Glenday and Ann Duffy, eds. Toronto: Oxford University Press, copyright © 2001.

If we are to have a world that is worth passing on to coming generations, we must seek harmony between technology and the natural environment. This will not be easy. At one extreme are people who claim that to protect the environment we must eliminate industrialization and return to some sort of preindustrial way of life. At the other extreme are people unable to see the harm being done to the natural environment, and who want the entire world to continue industrializing at full speed. Somewhere, there must be a middle ground, one that recognizes that industrialization is here to stay but that we can control it, for it is our creation.

Controlled industrialization can enhance our quality of life. As a parallel to the development of technologies, then, we must develop systems to reduce or eliminate their harm to the environment. This includes mechanisms to globally monitor the production, use, and disposal of technology. The question is whether we have the resolve to take the steps that will preserve the environment for future generations. The stakes—no less than the welfare of the entire planet—are surely high enough to motivate us to make the correct choices.

SUMMARY AND REVIEW

Population in Global Perspective

A Planet with No Space to Enjoy Life?
WHAT DEBATE DID THOMAS MALTHUS INITIATE?
In 1798, Thomas Malthus analyzed the surge in Europe's population. His conclusion, called the **Malthus theorem**, was that because the population grows geometrically but food only arithmetically, the world population will outstrip its food supply. The debate between today's New Malthusians and those who disagree, the Anti-Malthusians, continues, while feminists offer their own analysis and solutions. pp. 384–386.

WHY ARE PEOPLE STARVING?
Starvation is not due to a lack of food in the world, for there is now more food for every person on the planet than there was 50 years ago. Starvation is due, rather, to a maldistribution of food. pp. 386–387.

Population Growth

WHY DO THE POOR NATIONS HAVE SO MANY CHILDREN?
In the least industrialized nations, children are generally viewed as gifts from God, cost little to rear, and represent parents' social security. Consequently, people are motivated to have large families. pp. 387–389.

WHAT ARE THE THREE DEMOGRAPHIC VARIABLES?
To compute population growth, demographers use *fertility*, *mortality*, and *migration*. The **basic demographic equation** is Births – Deaths + Net migration = Growth Rate. p. 389.

WHY IS FORECASTING POPULATION DIFFICULT?
A nation's growth rate is affected by unanticipated variables—from economic conditions, wars, plagues, and famines to government policies and industrialization. p. 389.

Urbanization

WHAT IS THE RELATIONSHIP OF CITIES TO FARMING?
Cities can develop only if there is a large agricultural surplus, which frees people from having to participate in food production. The primary impetus to the development of cities was the invention of the plow about 5000 or 6000 years ago. pp. 390–392.

WHAT ARE METROPOLISES AND MEGALOPOLISES?
Urbanization is so extensive that some cities have become **metropolises**, dominating the areas adjacent to them. The areas of influence of some metropolises have merged, forming **megalopolises**. p. 392.

Models of Urban Growth

WHAT MODELS OF URBAN GROWTH HAVE BEEN PROPOSED?
The primary models are a concentric zone model, a sector model, and a multiple-nuclei model. These models fail to account for medieval cities, as well as many European cities and those in the least industrialized nations. pp. 393–394.

City Life

IS THE CITY INHERENTLY ALIENATING?
Some people experience alienation in the city; others find **community**. What people find depends largely on their background and urban networks. The types of people who live in cities are cosmopolitans, singles, ethnic villagers, and the trapped. pp. 394–397.

The Environment

The Natural Environment

WHAT ARE THE ENVIRONMENTAL PROBLEMS OF THE MOST INDUSTRIALIZED NATIONS?
The environmental problems of the most industrialized nations are severe, ranging from city smog and **acid rain** to the **greenhouse effect**. Scientists debate whether the greenhouse effect is real; if it is, it may cause **global warming** that will fundamentally affect social life. The burning of fossil fuels in internal combustion engines lies at the root of many environmental problems, but alternative sources of energy are unlikely to be developed until the multinational corporations can turn them to profitable ventures. pp. 397–398.

WHAT ARE THE ENVIRONMENTAL PROBLEMS OF THE INDUSTRIALIZING AND LEAST INDUSTRIALIZED NATIONS?
Some of the worst environmental problems are found in the former Soviet Union, a legacy of the unrestrained exploitation of resources by the Communist Party. The rush of the least industrialized nations to industrialize is adding to our environmental decay. p. 398.

WHAT IS THE KYOTO PROTOCOL?
The Kyoto Protocol is an agreement, entered into by a number of countries, intended to reduce greenhouse gases (global warming) and thereby contribute to sustainable global development. However, not all national leaders support the goals of the protocol and some don't believe global warming is a problem at all, even though the world's top 2000 climate experts are all on side. pp. 398–399.

WHAT IS THE ENVIRONMENTAL MOVEMENT?
The environmental movement is an attempt to restore a healthy environment for the world's people. This global movement takes many forms, from peacefully influencing the political process to *ecosabotage*, sabotaging the efforts of people thought to be harming the environment. p. 399.

WHAT IS ENVIRONMENTAL SOCIOLOGY?
Environmental sociology is not an attempt to change the environment, but a study of the relationship between humans and the environment. Environmental sociologists are generally also environmental activists. p. 400.

Ecofeminism and the Environment

WHAT IS ECOFEMINISM?
While there are several variants of ecofeminism, they all agree that the human and nonhuman worlds are interconnected. According to ecofeminists, patriarchy's hierarchical, dualistic, and oppressive ways of thinking explain the environmental predicament facing our planet today. pp. 400–401.

KEY TERMS

WEBLINKS

All URLs listed are current as of the printing of this book.

Environment Canada
www.ec.gc.ca/envhome.html
Environment Canada's internet resource for weather and environmental information.

WWICS Comparative Urban Studies Project
www.wilsoncenter.org/index.cfm?fuseaction=topics.home&topic_id=1410
This project of the Woodrow Wilson International Center for Scholars brings together scholars and policymakers to discuss problems of urban management from a multidisciplinary, multiregional perspective. Participants organize international conferences and disseminate findings through policy briefs, occasional papers, books, and other publications.

The Office of Population Research, Princeton University
http://opr.princeton.edu
The oldest population research centre in the United States. Many of its graduates occupy important professional positions in developing countries; others are on university faculties worldwide.

EnviroLink: The Online Environmental Community
www.envirolink.org
EnviroLink is a non-profit organization that has been providing access to thousands of online environmental resources since 1991.

CRITICAL THINKING QUESTIONS

1. Should governments try to limit population growth by using such traditional techniques as family planning?

2. All major municipalities in Canada have urban planners. However, their advice for more urban green space, for example, is often ignored because it conflicts with powerful economic interests that benefit from the increases in the price of land that result from building huge skyscrapers, stadiums, or other concrete structures in our cities. How would you try to resolve these conflicts of interest if you were an urban planner promoting the public use of a segment of waterfront or riverfront property in your city?

3. Why is there such a shortage of affordable housing in booming cities like Vancouver, Calgary, and Toronto?

4. Is it true that famine, overpopulation, and disease are destroying the social fabric of our planet? Access the Research Navigator through MySocLab and use keywords such as "famine" and "overpopulation" to locate relevant and recent scholarly and popular press publications to help you answer this question.

PEARSON
mysoclab

Explore the topics covered in this chapter on MySocLab using the access information provided with this text. Interactive resources for studying include multimedia tutorials, video clips, practice tests, quizzes, and animated maps and figures.

Social Movements and Social Change

18

The news spread like wildfire. A police officer had been killed. In just 20 minutes, the white population was armed and heading for the cabin. Men and mere boys, some not more than 12 years old, carried rifles, shotguns, and pistols.

The mob, now about 400, surrounded the log cabin of a local black man. Tying a rope around the man's neck, they dragged him to the centre of town. While the men argued about the best way to kill him, the women and children shouted their advice—some to hang him, others to burn him alive.

Someone pulled a large wooden box out of a store and placed it in the centre of the street. Others filled it with straw. Then they lifted the man, the rope still around his neck, and shoved him head first into the box. One of the men poured oil over him. Another lit a match.

As the flames shot upward, the man managed to lift himself out of the box, his body a mass of flames. Trying to shield his face and eyes from the fire, he ran the length of the rope, about 20 feet, when someone yelled, "Shoot!" In an instant, dozens of shots rang out. Men and boys walked to the lifeless body and emptied their guns into it.

They dragged the man's body back to the burning box, then piled on more boxes from the stores, and poured oil over them. Each time someone threw more oil onto the flames, the crowd roared shouts of approval.

Standing about 75 feet away, I could smell the poor man's burning flesh. No one tried to hide their identity. I could clearly see town officials help in the burning. The inquest, dutifully held by the coroner, concluded that the man met death "at the hands of an enraged mob unknown to the jury." What else could he conclude? Any jury from this town would include men who had participated in the man's death.

They dug a little hole at the edge of the street, and dumped in it the man's ashes and what was left of his body.

The man's name was Sam Pettie, known by everybody to be quiet and unoffensive. I can't mention my name. If I did, I would be committing suicide.

Source: A May 1914 letter to *The Crisis*.

Why did the people in this little town "go mad"? These men—and the women who watched in agreement—were ordinary, law-abiding citizens. Even some of the "pillars of the community" joined in the vicious killing of Sam Pettie, who may have been innocent.

Lynching is a form of **collective behaviour**, a group of people bypassing the usual norms that guide their behaviour and doing something unusual (Turner & Killian, 1987; Lofland, 1993). Collective behaviour is a very broad term, for it includes not only such violent acts as lynchings and riots, but also panics, rumours, fads, and fashions. Before examining its specific forms, we will discuss theories that seek to explain collective behaviour.

EARLY EXPLANATIONS: THE TRANSFORMATION OF THE INDIVIDUAL

When people can't figure something out, they are apt to say, "He must have 'gone nuts,' or he wouldn't have shot into the crowd." Early explanations of collective behaviour were not far from such assumptions. Let's look at how these ideas developed.

How the Crowd Transforms the Individual

The study of collective behaviour began when British journalist Charles Mackay (1814–1889) observed that "country folks," who ordinarily are reasonable sorts of people, sometimes "went mad" and did "disgraceful and violent things" in crowd situations. The best explanation Mackay (1852) could come up with was that people had a "herd mentality"—they were like a herd of cows that could suddenly stampede.

About 50 years later, Gustave LeBon (1841–1931) noted that people feel anonymous in crowds, less accountable for what they do. Some even develop feelings of invincibility and come to think that they can do virtually anything. A **collective mind** develops, he said, and people are swept up by almost any suggestion. Contagion, something like mass hypnosis, then takes over, releasing the destructive instincts that society so carefully represses.

The Acting Crowd

Herbert Blumer (1900–1987) synthesized LeBon's ideas with those of another sociologist, Robert Park. As shown in Figure 18.1, Blumer (1939) identified five stages that precede what he called an **acting crowd**, an excited group that moves toward a goal. This model still dominates today's police manuals on crowd behaviour (McPhail, 1989).

1. *Tension or unrest*. At the root of collective behaviour is a background condition of tension or unrest. An example of such a background condition occurred when the PC government of Mike Harris decided in 1997 to place control of Ontario's $14 billion public education system firmly in the hands of the provincial government, and by so doing, eliminate between 7500 and 10 000 jobs and

Until the 1960s, the public facilities in the South were segregated. Some were reserved for whites only, others for blacks only. This *apartheid* was broken by blacks and whites who worked together and risked their lives to bring about a fairer society. Shown here is a 1963 sit-in at a Woolworth's lunch counter in Jackson, Mississippi. Sugar, ketchup, and mustard are being poured over the heads of demonstrators.

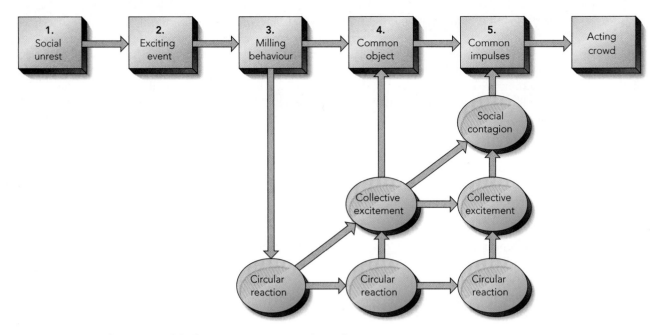

FIGURE 18.1 Blumer's Model of How an Acting Crowd Develops

Source: Based on McPhail (1991, p. 11).

cut billions of dollars from the education budget. As a result, five unions, representing 126 000 teachers, pulled their members out of the classroom and onto the streets of Ontario's cities and towns. This was the first Ontario-wide teachers' strike in more than two decades and the largest strike in Ontario history. It lasted two weeks, from November 3 to 16, 1997, with the leaders of the unions ultimately deciding that little more could be done to effect changes in government policy (Jenish, 1997, p. 18).

2. *Exciting event.* An exciting event occurs, one so startling that people become preoccupied with it. In the instance described at the beginning of this chapter, that event was the killing of a police officer.

3. *Milling.* Next comes **milling**, people standing or walking around, talking about the exciting event. A circular reaction then sets in. That is, as people pick up cues as to the "right" way of thinking and feeling and reinforce them in one another.

4. *A common object of attention.* In this stage, people's attention becomes riveted on some aspect of the event. They get caught up in the collective excitement.

5. *Common impulses.* People get the feeling that they are in agreement about what should be done. These common impulses are stimulated by social contagion, a sense of excitement that is passed from one person to another. In the opening vignette, people concluded that the killer had to be punished, and that only an immediate, public death would be adequate vengeance—as well as a powerful warning for other African-Americans who might think about getting "out of line."

Acting crowds aren't always negative or destructive, for they also include spontaneous demonstrations or sit-ins directed against oppression, such as Amnesty International's efforts to free political prisoners in many parts of the globe or the Ontario-wide teachers strike. Nor are they all serious—even "food fights" are acting crowds!

THE CONTEMPORARY VIEW: THE RATIONALITY OF THE CROWD

If we were to witness a lynching—or a screaming mob or prison riot—most of us probably would agree with LeBon that some sort of "madness" had swept over the crowd. Sociologists today, however, point out that crowds are actually quite rational. By this, they mean that crowds take deliberate steps to reach some desired goal.

The Minimax Strategy

A general principle of capitalist behaviour is that we try to minimize our costs and maximize our rewards. Sociologist Richard Berk (1974) calls this a **minimax strategy**. The fewer costs and the more rewards we anticipate from something, the more likely we are to do it. For example, if we believe that others will approve an act, the likelihood that we will do it increases. Whether in yelling for a referee's blood at a bad call in football, or shouting for the release of a political prisoner, this principle applies.

Emergent Norms

Sociologists Ralph Turner and Lewis Killian (1987) use the term **emergent norms** to express the idea that something

Most of the demonstrators at the 1997 APEC conference in Vancouver came from middle-class backgrounds. One of their goals was to increase public awareness of the corporate agenda of this transnational organization.

new has happened. They suggest that life typically proceeds pretty much as we expect it to, making our usual norms adequate for dealing with everyday events. If something disrupts our customary ways of doing things, our ordinary norms may not cover the new situation. To deal with this situation, new norms may emerge. People may even develop novel definitions of right and wrong, feeling that the new circumstances justify actions that they otherwise would consider wrong.

To understand how new norms emerge, we need to keep in mind that not everyone in a crowd has the same point of view (Snow, Zurcher, & Peters, 1993; Rodríguez, 1994). Turner and Killian (1987) contend that there are five kinds of crowd participants:

1. The *ego-involved* feel a personal stake in the extraordinary event.

2. The *concerned* have a personal interest in the event, but less so than the ego-involved.

3. The *insecure* care little about the particular issue, but they join the crowd because it gives them a sense of power and security.

4. The *curious spectators* also care little about the issue, but they are inquisitive about what is going on.

5. The *exploiters* do not care about the event, but are entrepreneurial and use it for their own purposes, such as hawking food or T-shirts.

Most important for setting a crowd on a particular course of action are the *ego-involved*. Some make suggestions about what should be done; others simply start doing something. As the *concerned* join in, they, too, influence the crowd. If things heat up, the *insecure* and the *curious spectators* may also participate. Although the *exploiters* are unlikely to get involved, they do lend passive support to the crowd. Once a common mood develops, emergent norms are likely to replace the usual norms of accepted behaviour. Activities "not OK" in everyday life may now seem "OK"—whether throwing bottles at police officers or protesting a provincial government's cuts to public education or health care.

Focus Question

Why don't all sociologists describe collective behaviour in terms of emotions?

FORMS OF COLLECTIVE BEHAVIOUR

Sociologists treat collective behaviour the same as other forms of behaviour (Turner & Killian, 1987; Lofland, 1993; Turner, 1993). They view it as ordinary people responding to extraordinary situations (Rodríguez, 1994). They ask their usual questions about interaction, such as: How do people influence one another? What is the significance of the members' age, gender, and social class? What role do pre-existing attitudes play? How are people's perceptions translated into action?

Collective behaviour takes many forms, including riots, panics, moral panics, rumours, fads, fashions, and urban legends. Let's look at each.

Riots or Demonstrations

White Los Angeles police officers were caught on videotape beating an African-American traffic violator with their nightsticks on April 29, 1992. Television stations around the United States—and the world—broadcast the pictures to stunned audiences.

When the officers went on trial 14 months later for beating the man identified as Rodney King, how could the verdict be anything but guilty? Yet a jury of eleven whites and one Asian-American found the officers innocent of using excessive force. The result was a **riot**—violent crowd behaviour aimed against people and property. Within minutes of the verdict, angry crowds began to gather in Los Angeles. That night, mobs set fire to businesses in south-central Los Angeles, and looting and arson began in earnest. The rioting spread to other cities, including Atlanta, Georgia; Tampa, Florida; and even Madison, Wisconsin and Las Vegas,

Nevada. Whites and Koreans were favourite targets of violence.

On the third night, after 4000 fires had been set and more than 30 people killed, President George Bush announced on national television that the U.S. Justice Department had appointed prosecutors to investigate possible federal charges against the police officers for violating the civil rights of Rodney King. He then stated that he had ordered the Seventh Infantry, SWAT teams, and the FBI into Los Angeles. He also placed the California National Guard under the command of General Colin Powell, the African-American chairman of the Joint Chiefs of Staff. Even Rodney King went on television and tearfully pleaded for peace.

The Los Angeles riot was the bloodiest in recent U.S. history. Before it was over, 54 people had lost their lives, 2328 people had been treated in hospital emergency rooms, thousands of small businesses had been burned, and about $1 billion of property had been destroyed. Two of the police officers were later sentenced to two and a half years in prison on federal charges, and King was awarded several million dollars in damages (Rose, 1992; Stevens & Lubman, 1992; Holden & Rose, 1993; Cannon, 1998).

Urban riots are usually caused by frustration and anger at deprivation. Frustration at being kept out of mainstream society —limited to a meagre education, denied jobs and justice, and kept out of good neighbourhoods—builds to such a boiling point that it takes only a precipitating event to erupt in collective violence. In the Los Angeles riot, all these conditions existed, with the jury's verdict the precipitating event.

Sociologists have found that it is not only the deprived, however, who participate in riots or **demonstrations**. During the November 1997 demonstration against the APEC (Asia Pacific Economic Cooperation) summit in Vancouver, over four dozen people were arrested while many others were hosed with pepper spray by the RCMP. APEC is a group of 18 member nations that comprise half the world's economic strength and whose aims include "free trade" among member states by the year 2020. The APEC demonstrators were part of the 700 delegates from around the world attending the People's Summit on APEC. Most of the demonstrators were university students, environmentalists, trade unionists, educators, and others from stable middle-class backgrounds. Why would middle-class people participate in demonstrations? The answer, says sociologist Victor Rodríguez (1994), is the same: frustration and anger. Even though most of the demonstrators had good jobs and were living middle-class lives, they faced a situation in which they were treated as second-class citizens. They, too, can have simmering resentments that a precipitating event brings to the surface.

Panics

On the night before Halloween, a radio program of dance music was interrupted with a report that explosions had been observed on the surface of Mars. The announcer breathlessly added that a cylinder of unknown origin had been discovered embedded in the ground on a farm in New Jersey. The radio station then switched to the farm, where an alarmed reporter gave details of horrible-looking Martians coming out of the cylinder. Their weapons had destructive powers unknown to humans. An interview with an astronomer confirmed that Martians had invaded the Earth.

Nearly six million North Americans heard this broadcast by Orson Wells in 1938. In adapting his book *The War of the Worlds* for a radio play, H.G. Wells made an important change: under his direction, the play was written and performed to sound like a news broadcast about an invasion from Mars, a technique that was intended to heighten the dramatic effect. And it did! About a million listeners were frightened, and thousands panicked. Unknown numbers burst into tears, while thousands more grabbed weapons and hid in their basements or ran into the streets.

Of course, there was no invasion. Although the panic reactions to this radio program may appear humorous to us today, to anyone who is in a panic the situation is anything but humorous. **Panic** occurs when people become so fearful that they cannot function normally, and may even flee.

Why did people panic? Psychologist Hadley Cantril (1941) attributed the result to widespread anxiety about world conditions. The Nazis were marching in Europe. War jitters, he said, created fertile ground for the broadcast to ignite a panic.

Contemporary analysts, however, question whether there even was a panic. Sociologist William Bainbridge (1989) acknowledges that some people were frightened, but says most of this famous panic was an invention of the news media. Reporters found a good story and milked it, exaggerating as they went along.

Bainbridge points to a 1973 event in Sweden. To dramatize the dangers of atomic power, Swedish Radio broadcast a play about an accident at a nuclear power plant. Knowing about the 1938 broadcast in the United States, Swedish sociologists were waiting to see what would happen. Might some people fail to realize that it was a dramatization and panic at the threat of ruptured reactors spewing out radioactivity? The sociologists found no panic. A few people became frightened, and some telephoned family members and the police—reasonable responses, considering what they thought had occurred.

The Swedish media, however, reported a panic. Apparently, a reporter telephoned two police departments and learned that each had received calls from concerned citizens. With a deadline hanging over his head, the reporter decided to gamble. He reported that police and fire stations were jammed with citizens, that people were flocking to shelters, and that others were fleeing south (Bainbridge, 1989).

Panics do occur—which is why nobody has the right to shout "Fire!" in a public building when no such danger exists (if people fear immediate death, they will lunge toward the nearest exit in a frantic effort to escape). Such a panic occurred on January 7, 1995, at a 30-storey apartment building in suburban North York, Ontario. In the early morning hours, around 5 o'clock, residents were awoken by a fire alarm. Most on the lower floors were able to race out of the building while others screamed from balconies as acrid smoke from a fire that had started on the fifth floor slowly gripped the whole building. In the end, six bodies—two men and four women, one of whom had been six months pregnant, were found dead in the smoke-filled stairwell. One eyewitness, who lived on the eighteenth floor, decided to leave her apartment and descend the stairwell to the ground floor. By the time she reached the eleventh floor, she said,

> The stairwell was full of panicking, half-asleep people carrying their pets, and then the smoke became so thick we couldn't go any further—everybody was choking—I knew we had to turn back, but we had to get everybody turned around because the stairwells were lined. It became even harder to breathe because you're puffing from climbing the stairs (Canadian Press Newswire, January 5, 1995).

Sociologists have found what other researchers have discovered in analyzing disasters. *Not everybody panics.* In disturbances, many people continue to act responsibly. Sociologists use the term **role extension** to describe these actions. Especially important are primary group bonds. Parents help their children, for example (Morrow, 1995). Gender roles also persist, and more men help women than women help men (N.R. Johnson, 1993). Even work roles continue to guide some behaviour.

Moral Panics

Moral panics occur when large numbers of people become intensely concerned, even fearful, about some behaviour thought to threaten morality, and the fear is out of proportion to any supposed danger (Cauthen & Jasper, 1994; Goode & Ben-Yehuda, 1994). The threat is seen as enormous, and hostility builds toward those thought responsible. The most infamous of moral panics is the fear of witches in Europe between 1400 and 1650, resulting in the Inquisition—investigations, torture, and burning at the stake of people accused of witchcraft.

Another example is Joan of Arc. Luc Besson's film *The Messenger* (1999) captured the moral panic this young woman caused among France's religious and political leaders after her successful military campaigns against the English.

Today, moral panics are fuelled by the media. Like other panics, moral panics centre around a sense of danger. Moral panics are further fuelled by **rumour**, information for which there is no discernible source and which is usually unfounded. For example, a rumour, still continuing, is that missing children are sold to Satanists who abuse them sexually and then ritually murder them. This rumour is intensely believed by some, and has been supported by testimony from people who claim to have been involved in such sacrifices. Investigations by the police, however, have uncovered no evidence to substantiate it.

Moral panics thrive on uncertainty and anxiety. Today's changing family serves up a rich source of anxiety. Concerns that children are receiving inadequate care because many mothers have left home to join the workforce become linked with thoughts of dangers to children from sinister sources lurking almost everywhere.

Focus Question
Why aren't all crowds destructive mobs?

Rumours

> In *Aladdin*, the handsome young title character murmurs, "All good children, take off your clothes." In *The Lion King*, Simba, the cuddly lion star, stirs up a cloud of dust that, floating off the screen, spells S-E-X. Then there is the bishop in *The Little Mermaid*, who, presiding over a wedding, becomes noticeably aroused.

Thriving in conditions of ambiguity, rumours function to fill in missing information (Turner, 1964; Shibutani, 1966). In response to this rumour, Disney reports that Aladdin really says "Scat, good tiger, take off and go." The line is hard to hear clearly, however, leaving enough ambiguity for others to continue to hear what they want, even to insist that it is an invitation to a teenage orgy. Similar ambiguity remains around Simba's dust and the aroused bishop.

Rumours have swirled around the Magic Kingdom's supposed plots to undermine the morality of youth. Could Mickey Mouse be a dark force, and children his victims? As humorous as this may seem, some have taken these rumours seriously.

Most rumours are short-lived. They arise in a situation of ambiguity, only to dissipate when they are replaced by factual information—or by another rumour. For example, despite a publication ban about the brutal killing of Leslie Mahaffy and Kristin French during the 1993 trial of Karla Homolka and Paul Bernardo, rumours about the details of the crimes were said to be available on the internet for those curious enough to find them.

Why do people believe rumours? Three main factors have been identified. First, rumours deal with a subject that is important to an individual. Second, they replace ambiguity with some form of certainty. Third, they are attributed to a creditable source. An office rumour may be preceded by "Jane has it on good authority that . . ." or "Bill overheard the boss say that. . . ." Ambiguity or uncertainty is especially important in giving life to rumours.

Fads and Fashions

A **fad** is a novel form of behaviour that briefly catches people's attention. The new behaviour appears suddenly and spreads by suggestion, imitation, and identification with people already involved in the fad. Publicity by the mass media also helps spread fads (Aguirre, Quarantelli, & Mendoza, 1993).

Sociologist John Lofland (1985) identified four types of fads. First are object fads, such as the Hula Hoop in the 1950s, pet rocks in the 1970s, the Rubik's Cube and Cabbage Patch Dolls in the 1980s, and the pogs, beanie babies, and Pokémon in the 1990s. Second are activity fads, such as eating goldfish in the 1920s, bungee jumping in the 1990s, and tattooing and body piercing in the 1990s–2000s. Third are idea fads, such as astrology. Fourth are personality fads, such as Elvis Presley, Princess Diana, and Wayne Gretzky. Some fads are extremely short-lived, such as "streaking" (running naked in a public place) or "Tickle Me Elmo" dolls. When a fad lasts, it is called a **fashion**. Some fashions, as with clothing, are the result of a coordinated international marketing system that includes designers, manufacturers, advertisers, and retailers. Billions of dollars worth of clothing are sold by manipulating the tastes of the public. Fashion, however, also refers to hairstyles, home decorating, and even the design and colours of buildings. Sociologist John Lofland (1985) pointed out that fashion even applies to language, as demonstrated by these roughly comparable terms: "Neat!" in the 1950s, "Right on!" in the 1960s, "Really!" in the 1970s, "Awesome!" in the 1980s, and "Bad!" and the resurrection of "cool" and "buddy" in the 1990s–2000s.

Urban Legends

> Jerry [or whoever] went to a nightclub last weekend. He met a good-looking woman, and they hit it off. They spent the night in a motel, and when he awoke the next morning, the woman was gone. When he went into the bathroom, he saw a message scrawled on the mirror in lipstick: "Welcome to the wonderful world of AIDS."

Urban legends are stories with an ironic twist that sound realistic but are false. Although untrue, they are usually told by people who believe that they happened.

Another rumour as urban legend making the rounds via email is that Listerine can be used as a mosquito killer.

> The best way of getting rid of mosquitoes is Listerine, the original medicinal type. The dollar-store type works, too. I was at a deck party a while back, and the bugs were having a ball biting everyone. A man at the party sprayed the lawn and deck floor with Listerine, and the little demons disappeared. The next year I filled a four-ounce spray bottle and used it around my seat whenever I saw mosquitoes. And voilà! That worked as well. It worked at a picnic where we sprayed the area around the food table, the children's swing area, and the standing water nearby. During the summer, I don't leave home without it . . . Pass it on.

Folklorist Jan Brunvand (1981, 1984, 1986) reported that urban legends are passed on by people who think that the event happened just one or two people down the line of transmission, often to a "friend of a friend." Brunvand views urban legends as "modern morality stories," each teaching a moral lesson about life.

If we apply Brunvand's analysis to these two urban legends, three major points emerge. First, their moral serves as a warning. "The wonderful world of AIDS" warns young people that they should be careful about where they go, with whom they go, and what they do. The world is an unsafe place, and "messing around" is risky. "Listerine as mosquito repellant" contains a different moral: Do you *really* know what chemicals you are rubbing on your skin to protect it from insects?

Second, each story is related to social change: "The wonderful world of AIDS" to changing sexual morality; "Listerine as mosquito repellant" to our changing relationship with the physical environment. Third, each is calculated to instill guilt and fear: guilt—failing to protect your family—and fear, the dangerous unknown, whether unprotected sex or West Nile virus. The ultimate moral of these stories is that we should not abandon traditional roles or the safety of the home.

Social Movements

Social movements consist of large numbers of people who organize to promote or resist social change. They have strong ideas about what is wrong with the world—or some part of it—and how to make things right. Examples include the temperance movement, the women's movement, the animal rights crusade, the Quebec sovereignty movement, and the environmental movement.

At the heart of social movements lie grievances and dissatisfactions. For some people, a current condition of society is intolerable, and their goal is to *promote* social change. Theirs is called a **proactive social movement**. In contrast, others feel threatened because some condition of society is changing, and they organize to *resist* that change. Theirs is a **reactive social movement**.

To further their goals, people develop **social movement organizations**. Those whose goal is to promote social change develop such organizations as the National Action Committee on the Status of Women (with over 700 member groups), the Council of Canadians, and the National Indian Brotherhood. In contrast, for those who are trying to resist these changes, the National Citizens Coalition, the Western Guard, and REAL Women of Canada serve this purpose. To recruit followers and sympathizers, leaders of social movements use various attention-getting devices, from marches and protest rallies to sit-ins and boycotts. To publicize their grievances, they also may try to stage "media events."

The Quiet Revolution in Quebec, which began in the early 1960s, was a response to the two-decades-long failure of Maurice Duplessis's Union Nationale government to modernize the state institutions of health, education, and welfare in that province. But the Quiet Revolution also unleashed many other social movements, including the *indépendence* movement and the Front de Libération du Québec (FLQ).

TYPES AND TACTICS OF SOCIAL MOVEMENTS

Let's see what types of social movements there are and then examine their tactics.

Types of Social Movements

Since social change is always their goal, we can classify social movements according to their *target* and the *amount of change* they seek. Figure 18.2 summarizes the classification developed by sociologist David Aberle (1966). If you read across, you will see that the target of the first two types of social movements is *individuals*. **Alterative social movements** seek only to alter some particular behaviour of people. An example of a powerful social movement today is Mothers Against Drunk Driving (MADD), whose goal is to get people to stop driving if they have been drinking any alcohol. Its members are convinced that if they could stop drunk drivers, there would be many fewer deaths on our highways. **Redemptive social movements** also target individuals, but here the aim is for *total* change. An example is a religious social movement that stresses conversion. In fundamentalist Christianity, for example, when someone converts to a particular view of Jesus Christ, the entire person is supposed to change, not just some specific behaviour. The individual becomes a "true believer" of that religious sect or cult.

The target of the next two types of social movements is *society*. **Reformative social movements** seek to *reform* some specific aspect of society. The environmental movement, for example, seeks to reform the ways society treats the environment, from its disposal of garbage and nuclear wastes to

Trade unions in Canada are important social movements with a clearly defined organization and goals. However, the role trade unions should play in Canadian society has never been clear. Often, they are portrayed in the media as adversarial organizations hell-bent on pitting management against employees and sometimes worker against worker. Advocates, on the other hand, argue that unions provide employees with an effective voice to express their views and achieve positive resolutions to their grievances against the many arbitrary decisions made by management.

The views of the two sides could not be more incompatible. Those who favour trade unions' contributions to Canadian society look at the over 3 million trade union members as examples of men and women exercising their basic human right to organize for a better life and national community. Those who gather around the anti-union banner see unions as harmful to society because union leaders fight for their own members' interests at the expense of everyone else.

For those on either side of the barricade, there is little likelihood of reconciling such contrary attitudes. Each sees the other as unreasonable and extremist. Each uses propaganda by focusing on either worst- or best-case scenarios: anti-unionists point out examples of corruption and undemocratic factions within specific unions; pro-unionists point out that trade unions have been in the forefront of the struggle for maintaining, even strengthening, universal social programs such as health care and government pensions.

As each side fights in the political arena for what it considers basic rights, each encounter reinvigorates the other camp. When the *Charter of Rights and Freedoms* came into effect in 1982, trade unions across Canada faced formidable challenges from their adversaries. The Canadian Labour Congress (CLC) did not participate in the original discussions, due largely to the determination of senior Quebec Federation of Labour officials. As a result, the "rights" of trade unionists were never seriously discussed for possible inclusion in the Charter. Several Supreme Court of Canada cases later, each side has won and lost some battles. The contest continues.

Because the two sides see reality in very different ways, advocates and detractors of the trade union movement in Canada are not likely to give up their struggle in the foreseeable future. Nothing to such committed activists is ever complete. Rather, each action is only a step in a prolonged struggle.

Nellie McClung and Emmeline Pankhurst in 1916. What kind of tactics did the suffragettes use in their social movement?

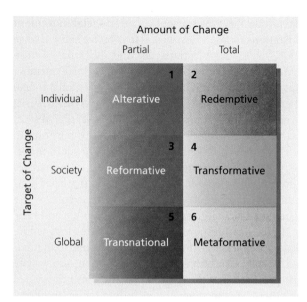

FIGURE 18.2   Types of Social Movements

Source: The first four types are from Aberle (1966); the last two are by the author.

communist and fascist movements of the first half of the twentieth century are examples. Today, examples include religious fundamentalism, whether Christian, Islamic, or some other variety. In most cases, metaformative social

its use of forests and water. **Transformative social movements**, in contrast, seek to *transform* the social order itself and to replace it with a new version of the good society. Revolutions such as those in the American colonies, France, Russia, and Cuba are examples.

A new twist in social movements is global orientation. Rather than focusing on changing a condition within a specific country, the goal of a global social movement is to change this condition throughout the world. As with many aspects of life in our new global economy, numerous issues that concern people transcend national boundaries. Participants in transnational social movements want to change some condition that exists not just in their society but also throughout the world (see Cell 5 of Figure 18.2). These social movements often centre on improving quality of life (Melucci, 1989) The women's, environmental, and animal rights movements are examples. Because of this new focus, some sociologists refer to them as **new social movements** (McAdam, McCarthy, & Zald, 1988).

Cell 6 of Figure 18.2 represents a rare type of social movement. The goal of *metaformative* social movements is to change the social order itself—not just of a specific country, but of an entire civilization, or even the whole world. The objective of metaformative social movements is to change concepts and practices of race/ethnicity, class, gender, family, religion, government, and the globalization of nations. The

Women participating in a Take Back the Night march, which takes place annually in communities across Canada and throughout the world.

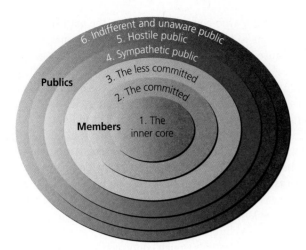

FIGURE 18.3 The Membership and Publics of Social Movements

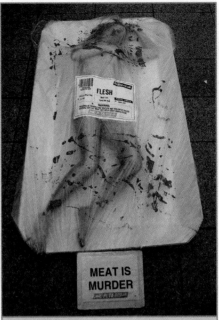

The use of propaganda is popular among those committed to the goals of a social movement. They usually see only one side of the social issue about which they are upset. What attention-getting devices is this demonstrator using? Are they effective? Why is this an example of propaganda?

movements are socially and morally regressive; that is, they seek to replace capitalist modernization with their own specific brand of social and moral order.

Tactics of Social Movements

The leaders of a social movement can choose from a variety of tactics. Should they peacefully boycott, march, or hold an all-night candlelight vigil? Or should they bomb a building, blow up an airplane, or assassinate a key figure? To understand why the leaders of social movements choose particular tactics, we need to examine a group's membership, the publics it addresses (or its audience), and its relationship to authorities.

MEMBERSHIP Figure 18.3 shows the composition of social movements. At the centre is the inner core, those people most committed to the movement. The inner core sets the group's goals, timetables, and strategies, and inspires the other members. Those at the second level are also committed to the movement. People at this level, however, can be counted on to show up for demonstrations and to do grunt work—mailings, passing out petitions and leaflets, making telephone calls. At the third level is a wider circle of people who are less committed and less dependable. Their participation is primarily a matter of convenience. If an activity does not interfere with something else they want to do, they will participate.

The predispositions and backgrounds of the inner core are essential in the choice of tactics. Because of their background, the inner core of some groups is predisposed to use peaceful means while others prefer confrontational means and still others prefer violence. Tactics also depend on the number of committed members. Different tactics are called for if the inner core can count on 700 committed members to show up—as opposed to, say, seven.

THE PUBLICS Outside the membership of a group is the **public**, a dispersed group of people who usually have an interest in the issue. Just outside the third circle of members, and blending into it, is the sympathetic public. Sympathy with the movement's goals makes this public fertile ground for recruiting new members. The second public is hostile; it is keenly aware of the group's goals and dislikes them. This public wants to stop the social movement, for the movement's values go against its own. The third public consists of disinterested people. They are either unaware of the social movement, or if aware, indifferent to it.

RELATIONSHIP TO AUTHORITIES A movement's relationship to authorities is also significant in determining tactics—especially in choosing peaceful or violent tactics. If a social movement is *institutionalized*—accepted by authorities—violence will not be directed against the authorities, as they are on the same side. This, however, does not rule out violence directed against the opposition. If authorities are hostile to a social movement, aggressive or even violent tactics are more likely.

OTHER FACTORS Sociologist Ellen Scott (1993), who studied the movement to stop rape, discovered that close friendships, race, and even size of town are important in determining tactics.

Social Movements and the Media

In selecting tactics, the leaders of social movements are keenly aware of their effects on the mass media (Zald, 1992). Their goal is to influence **public opinion**, how people think about some issue. Pictures of bloodied, dead baby seals, for example, go a long way toward getting one group's message across.

A key to understanding social movements, then, is **propaganda**. Although this word often evokes negative images, it is actually neutral. Propaganda is simply the presentation of information in an attempt to influence people. Its original meaning was positive: *propaganda* referred to a committee of cardinals of the Roman Catholic Church whose assignment was the care of foreign missions. (They were to *propagate* the faith.)

Propaganda, then, in the sense of organized attempts to manipulate public opinion, is a regular part of modern life. Advertisements, for example, are a form of propaganda, presenting a one-sided version of reality.

The mass media play a crucial role in social movements. They can become, in effect, the gatekeepers to social move-

Live 8 was a series of concerts that took place on July 5, 2005, in the G8 nations and South Africa. More than 1000 musicians performed at the concerts, which were broadcast on 182 television networks and 2000 radio networks. The shows were planned to pressure world leaders to drop the debt of the world's poorest nations, increase and improve aid, and negotiate fairer trade rules in the interest of poorer countries. Pictured here is the crowd outside Park Place in Barrie, Ontario.

ments. If those who control and work in the mass media—from owners to reporters—are sympathetic to some particular "cause," it will receive sympathetic treatment in the media. A case in point is the widely televised "LIVE 8—The Long Walk To Justice" concerts in 2005, staged in the major cities of the G8 countries and Johannesburg, South Africa, on the eve of the G8 summit in Gleneagles (near Edinburgh), Scotland. This was a showcase of musical talent from around the world, brought together by Sir Bob Geldof. It is estimated that between 2 and 3 billion people worldwide watched the concerts. The aim of these shows was to pressure the leaders of the G8 nations (Canada, France, Germany, Italy, Japan, Russia, the United Kingdom, and the United States) to do three things to eliminate poverty in Africa: cancel the debt owed by African nations to rich countries, make trade fairer by changing the rules to allow poor countries to develop and build their own industries, and provide more financial aid in areas such as basic health care and education. If it did nothing else, Live 8—and the media's coverage of it—brought an important social issue to the forefront of young people's consciousness.

If you ever get the impression that the media are trying to manipulate your opinions and attitudes on some particular social movement—or some social issue—you are probably right. Far from conducting unbiased reporting, the media are under the control and influence of people who have an agenda to get across. This doesn't mean, however, that we need to be cynical about the role of the media in our lives. It does mean that we need to be critical at times about what is and isn't reported about particular issues and social movements. We need to be aware of the biases of the media establishment—television, radio, newspapers, magazines, and so on—and of the fact that they select which issues they give publicity to, as well as which ones they ignore, and they decide whether they will present favourable or unfavourable treatment of issues and movements.

WHY PEOPLE JOIN SOCIAL MOVEMENTS

As discussed, social movements arise from the conviction that some condition of society is no longer tolerable. Not everyone who feels strongly dissatisfied about an issue joins a social movement, however. Let's look at three explanations for why some people join social movements.

Mass Society Theory

To explain why people are attracted to social movements, sociologist William Kornhauser (1959) proposed **mass society theory**. Kornhauser argued that **mass society**—an impersonal, industrialized, highly bureaucratized society—makes many people feel isolated. Social movements fill a void by offering people a sense of belonging. In geographical areas where social ties are supposedly weaker, such as western Canada, one would expect to find more social movements than in areas where traditional ties are supposedly stronger, such as in Atlantic Canada.

This theory seems to match common-sense observations. Social movements seem to proliferate on the Prairies and the West Coast. But sociologist Doug McAdam (McAdam et al., 1988), who interviewed people who had risked their lives in the civil rights movement, found that these people were firmly rooted in families and communities. It was their strong desire to right wrongs and overcome injustices, not their isolation, that motivated their participation. Ironically, the homeless, among the most isolated, generally do not join anything—except food lines.

Deprivation Theory

A second explanation to account for why people join social movements is *deprivation theory*. According to this theory, people who are deprived of things deemed valuable in society—money, justice, status, or privilege—join social movements in the hope of redressing their grievances. This theory may seem so obvious as to need no evidence. Aren't the Mohawk warriors who occupied their land for 78 days in what became known across Canada as the "Oka Crisis" ample evidence that the theory is true?

Deprivation theory does provide a starting point, but there is more to the matter. We must also pay attention to what Alexis de Tocqueville (1856/1955) noted almost 150 years ago. The peasants of Germany were worse off than the peasants of France, and from deprivation theory we would expect the Germans to have rebelled and overthrown their king. Revolution occurred in France, not Germany, however. The reason, said de Tocqueville, is *relative* deprivation. French peasants had experienced improving living conditions and could imagine even better conditions, while German peasants, having never experienced anything but depressed conditions, had no comparative basis for feeling deprived.

According to **relative deprivation theory**, then, it is not people's actual deprivation that matters. The key to participation is *relative* deprivation—that is, what people *think* they should have relative to what others have or relative to their own recent past or even their perceived future. Relative deprivation theory, which has provided insight into revolutions, holds a surprise. Because improving conditions fuel human desires for even better conditions, *improving* conditions can spark revolutions. As illustrated in Figure 18.4, this occurs when people's expectations outstrip the actual change they experience. It is likely that we can also apply this theory to riots.

Moral Issues and Ideological Commitment

Some people join social movements because of *moral shock*— a sense of outrage at finding out what is "really" going on (Jasper & Poulsen, 1995). They feel they must choose sides

The "Oka Crisis," during which Mohawk warriors occupied their land for 78 days in Quebec, can be viewed as an example of deprivation theory.

and do what they can to make a difference. As sociologists put it, they join because of *ideological commitment* to the movement.

Many members on both sides of the Quebec sovereignty issue see their involvement in such terms. Similarly, most activists in the animal rights movement are convinced that there can be no justification for animals to suffer in order to make safer products for humans. For others, matters of the environment are moral issues, and not to act would be an inexcusable betrayal of future generations. The *moral* component of a social movement, then, is a primary reason for some people's involvement.

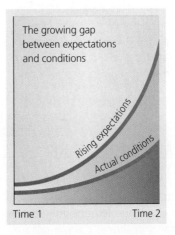

The growing gap between expectations and conditions

Rising expectations

Actual conditions

Time 1   Time 2

FIGURE 18.4   Relative Deprivation and Revolution

A Special Case: The Agent Provocateur

A unique type of social movement participant is the **agent provocateur**, an agent of the government or even of a rival social movement whose job is to spy on the leadership and perhaps sabotage the group's activities. Some are recruited from the membership itself and betray their movement's goals for money, while others are members of the police or a rival group who go underground and join the movement.

Since the social change represented by some social movements is radical, threatening the power elite, the use of agent provocateurs is not surprising. What may be surprising, however, is that some agents get converted to the social movement on which they are spying. Sociologist Gary Marx (1993) explains that, to be credible, agents must share at least some of the class, age, gender, ethnic, racial, or religious characteristics of the group. This makes them more likely to sympathize with the movement's goals and become disenchanted with trying to harm the group. What also may be surprising is how far some agents go. During the 1960s, when a wave of militant social movements rolled across Quebec, the RCMP and other police were busy recruiting agent provocateurs. To sabotage groups, these agents provoked illegal activities that otherwise would not have occurred, setting the leadership up for arrest (Sawatsky, 1980).

Focus Question
Who joins social movements and why?

IN SUM

Perhaps most commonly, people join a social movement because they have friends and acquaintances already in the movement (McCarthy & Wolfson, 1992; Snow, Zurcher, & Ekland-Olson, 1993). Some join because of moral convictions, others to further their own careers, because it is fun, or because they achieve recognition or find a valued identity. As discussed, police officials may join social movements in order to spy on them and sabotage their activities. In no social movement, then, is there a single cause motivating people to join.

ON THE SUCCESS AND FAILURE OF SOCIAL MOVEMENTS

Social movements have brought about extensive social change. The women's movement has led not only to new laws but also to a different way of thinking about relations between women and men. Let's look at the reasons for the success or failure of social movements.

The Life Course of Social Movements

Sociologists have identified five stages in the growth and maturity of social movements (Lang & Lang, 1961; Mauss, 1975; Spector & Kitsuse, 1977; Tilly, 1978; Jasper, 1991).

1. *Initial unrest and agitation.* During this first stage, people are upset about some condition in society and want to change it. Leaders emerge who verbalize people's feelings and crystallize issues. Most social movements fail at this stage. Unable to gain enough support, after a brief flurry of activity they quietly die.

2. *Resource mobilization.* The crucial factor that enables social movements to make it past the first stage is **resource mobilization**. By this term, sociologists mean the mobilization of resources such as time, money, people's skills, technologies such as direct mailing and fax machines, attention by the mass media, and even legitimacy among the public and authorities (Oliver & Marwell, 1992; Buechler, 1993).

3. *Organization.* A division of labour is set up. The leadership makes policy decisions, and the rank and file members carry out the daily tasks necessary to keep the movement going.

4. *Institutionalization.* At this stage, a movement has developed a *bureaucracy*, the type of formal hierarchy described in Chapter 10. The collective excitement is gone, and control lies in the hands of career officers, who may care more about their own position in the organization than the movement for which the organization's initial leaders made sacrifices. They may move the group's headquarters to a "good" location, for example, furnish it with expensive furniture and art work, and take pains to be seen with the "right" people in the "right" places.

5. *Organizational decline and possible resurgence.* During this phase, managing the day-to-day affairs of the organization dominates the leadership. Change in public sentiment may even have occurred and there may no longer be a group of committed people who share a common cause. Decline is not inevitable, however, as we shall see.

If most participants desert and those most committed flounder with little support, it does not necessarily mean the end of a movement. After suffragists won the right to vote in Canada in 1919, their movement declined until nothing but a shell remained. During a period researchers call *abeyance*, only a handful of committed organizers were left, and the best they could do was desperately keep the flame burning. Yet the women's movement was re-energized, and again thrust into national prominence (Taylor, 1997).

The Thinking Critically about Social Controversy box provides an example of the building of a social movement.

Focus Question
Do all social movements have a sociological life (i.e., birth, maturation, and eventual death)?

AN OVERVIEW OF SOCIAL CHANGE

Social change is brought about by people organized into social movements. Before we can interpret these changes, decide whether they are progressive, or even whether there is such a thing as progress, it is necessary to make a few introductory comments about the importance of technology in any theory of social change.

HOW TECHNOLOGY CHANGES SOCIETY

As you may recall from Chapter 3, **technology** carries a double meaning. It refers to both *tools*, items used to accomplish tasks, and the *skills or procedures* to make and use those tools. This broad concept includes in its first meaning tools as simple as a comb and as complicated as computers. Its second meaning refers in this case not only to the skills or procedures used to manufacture combs and computers but also to those required to "produce" an acceptable hairdo or to gain access to the internet. Apart from its particulars, technology always refers to *artificial means of extending human abilities*.

All human groups make and use technology, but the chief characteristic of postindustrial societies (also called **postmodern societies**) is technology that greatly extends our ability to analyze information, communicate, and travel.

These *new information technologies* (ICTs), as they are called, allow us to do what had never been done in history: probe space and other planets, communicate almost instantaneously anywhere on the globe, travel greater distances faster, and store, retrieve, and analyze vast amounts of information.

This level of accomplishment, though impressive, is really very superficial. As we look at how technology spreads, we will stress this sociological aspect of technology—how it affects people's lives.

THINKING CRITICALLY ABOUT SOCIAL CONTROVERSY
Opposing the MAI: What It Takes to Build a Community-Based Social Movement

On September 25, 1997, Saskatchewan's Broadway Theatre in Saskatoon was the site of the first large-scale rally in Canada against the Multilateral Agreement on Investment (MAI). How is it possible for an apparently invisible issue to become so visible?

This can be attributed to organizing that had occurred previously in the community. Two months earlier, a small group got together to talk about the way the MAI was being secretly negotiated, how to break the code of secrecy, and how to build resistance to it. Organizers decided to concentrate on the negative impacts of the MAI, such as potential job losses, increased regional disparities, and the loss of national sovereignty.

The second stage of organizing grew out of an agreement to work toward a major public event in September. Another organizing meeting was held in August. People from different social justice, antinuclear, development, church, labour, farm, health, and other organi-zations in Saskatoon attended. Various people and organizations took on tasks such as distributing posters, developing leaflets, issuing press releases, and getting more groups to support the coming rally. Two Saskatoon organizers wrote articles on the MAI for the local *Saskatoon Star Phoenix*.

Another event helped to spur things forward. A conference of the Asia Pacific Economic Cooperation Forum (APEC) was held in Saskatoon in early September 1997. Because of short notice, only about 30 protestors gathered at the hotel where the conference was being held. As small as it was, the demonstration received positive press coverage; however, as a result of the experience, organizers decided that it was very important to have an active phoning tree.

To keep the momentum growing, the organizing group agreed to meet on a weekly basis leading up to the Broadway Theatre event. Finally, an afternoon workshop on dismantling the corporate agenda was held just prior to the event at the Broadway.

After the rally, participants met at the theatre, where they endorsed a people's charter in opposition to the MAI. Two hundred people signed letters calling for a full and open public debate in the House of Commons and the provincial legislatures. The letters were sent to Prime Minister Jean Chrétien and Premier Roy Romanow.

The key organizing question is how to keep a social movement alive. Participants at the September rally were invited to attend an organizing meeting to be held the next month.

For Your Consideration
Typically, the last stage of a social movement is decline. Does the last stage apply to this social movement? Under what conditions might this movement decline?

Source: Cram & Kossick (1997).

TABLE 18.1   Comparing Traditional and Modern Societies

Characteristics	Traditional Societies	Modern Societies
General Characteristics		
Social change	Slow	Rapid
Size of group	Small	Large
Religious orientation	More	Less
Formal education	No	Yes
Place of residence	Rural	Urban
Family size	Larger	Smaller
Infant mortality	High	Low
Life expectancy	Short	Long
Health care	Home	Hospital
Temporal orientation	Part	Future
Demographic transition	First stage	Third stage (or fourth)
Material Relations		
Industrialized	No	Yes
Technology	Simple	Complex
Division of labour	Simple	Complex
Income	Low	High
Material possessions	Few	Many
Social Relationships		
Basic organization	*Gemeinschaft*	*Gesellschaft*
Families	Extended	Nuclear
Respect for elders	More	Less
Social stratification	Rigid	More open
Statuses	More ascribed	More achieved
Gender equality	Less	More
Norms		
View of life and morals	Absolute	Relativistic
Social control	Informal	Formal
Tolerance of differences	Less	More

Modernization

The term given to the sweeping changes ushered in by the Industrial Revolution is **modernization**. Table 18.1 reviews these changes, presenting an *ideal type* in Weber's sense of the term, for no society exemplifies to the maximum degree all the traits listed here. For example, although most Canadians now work in the service sector of the economy, over 2 million are still employed in the natural resource and manufacturing sectors. Thus, all characteristics shown in Table 18.1 should be interpreted as "more" or "less" rather than "either–or."

As technology from the industrialized world is introduced into traditional societies, we are able to witness how far-reaching the changes are. Consider modern medicine. Its introduction into the least industrialized nations helped reduce death rates while birth rates remained high. As a result, the population exploded, bringing hunger and starvation, mass migration to cities, and mass migration to the industrialized nations.

Ogburn's Theory of Social Change

Sociologist William Ogburn (1922, 1961, 1964) proposed a theory of social change that is based largely on technology. As illustrated in Table 18.2, technology changes society by three processes: invention, discovery, and diffusion. Let's consider each.

INVENTION   Ogburn defined **invention** as the combining of existing elements and materials to form new ones. Although we think of inventions as being only material, such as computers, there also are *social* inventions, such as capitalism and the corporation.

DISCOVERY   Ogburn identified **discovery**, a new way of seeing reality, as the second process of change. However, a

TABLE 18.2 Ogburn's Processes of Social Change

Process of Change	What It Is	Example	Social Changes
Invention	Combination of existing elements to form new ones	1. Cars 2. Computers 3. Plastics	1. Urban sprawl and long commutes to work 2. Telework an Global Positioning System 3. New types of furniture and construction
Discovery	New way of seeing some aspect of the world	1. Columbus—N. America 2. Gold in California 3. DNA	1. Realignment of global power 2. Westward expansion of the United States 3. Positive identification of criminals
Diffusion	Spread of an invention of discovery	1. Airplanes 2. Money 3. Condom	1. Global tourism 2. Global trade 3. Smaller families

Note: For each example, there are many changes. For changes ushered in by the automobile and computer, see pages 420–423. You can also see that any particular change, such as global trade, depends not just on one item, but on several preceding changes.

Source: By the author.

discovery brings extensive change only when it comes at the right time.

DIFFUSION The spread of an invention or discovery from one area to another, called **diffusion**, can have far-reaching effects on human relationships. For example, when missionaries introduced steel axes to the Aborigines of Australia, it upset their whole society. Before this, men controlled the making of axes, using a special stone available only in a remote region and passing axe-making skills from one man to another. Women had to request permission to use a stone axe. When steel axes became common, women also possessed them, and men lost both status and power (L. Sharp, 1995).

Diffusion also involves the spread of ideas. The idea of citizenship, for example, changed political structure, for no longer was the monarch an unquestioned source of authority. Today, the concept of gender equality is circling the globe, with the basic idea that it is wrong to withhold rights on the basis of someone's sex. This idea, though now taken for granted in a few parts of the world, is revolutionary. Like citizenship, it is destined to transform basic human relationships and entire societies.

As noted in Chapter 3, Ogburn coined the term **cultural lag** to describe a situation in which some elements of a culture adapt to an invention or discovery more rapidly than others.

Evaluation of Ogburn's Theory

Some find Ogburn's analysis too one-directional, saying it makes technology the cause of almost all social change. They point out that adapting to changing technology is only one part of the story. The other part consists of people taking control over technology—developing the technology they need.

Technology and social change, then, actually form a two-way street. Just as technology leads to social change, social change leads to new technology. For example, as the numbers of elderly in our society have grown, their needs have stimulated the development of medical technologies to treat Alzheimer's disease. Changing ideas about the disabled have stimulated the development of new types of wheelchairs that allow people who cannot move their legs to play basketball, participate in the Special Olympics, and enter races.

Transforming Society

As discussed in the Sociology and the New Technology box (page 420), it is easy to inaccurately guess the consequences of a new technology. Let's look at five ways technology can change society.

TRANSFORMATION OF EXISTING TECHNOLOGIES The first impact is felt by the technology that is being displaced. For example, IBM electric typewriters, "state of the art" equipment a few decades ago, have been rendered practically useless by desktop and laptop computers.

CHANGES IN SOCIAL ORGANIZATION Technology also changes social organization. For example, machine technology gave birth to the factory. Then it was discovered that workers could produce more items if each did a specialized task. Henry Ford built on this innovation by developing the assembly line: instead of workers moving to the parts, a machine moved the parts to the workers. In addition, the parts were made interchangeable and easy to attach (Womack, Jones, & Roos, 1991).

CHANGES IN IDEOLOGY Technology also spurs new ideologies. For example, Karl Marx saw the change to the factory system as a source of **alienation**. He noted that workers who did repetitive tasks on a small part of a product no

Almost everybody wants to know the future—from the work we'll be doing in five years to how much money we'll have in ten years.

The same applies to technology. Futurists guesstimate the social ramifications of new technologies, predicting far-reaching—and sometimes dire—consequences. Consider the following *totally wrong* predictions:

A new century is at hand. Our new technology will practically annihilate time and space. It will let people live and work wherever they please, creating dynamic new communities linked by electronics. Because of this new technology, many people will move out of cities, doing their work from their homes.

Some social class barriers will crumble, for people will have the power to summon almost anyone. It may even save the family farm by linking farmers with others.

In this amazing future, people will be able to dial up symphonies, presidential speeches, and even three-dimensional Shakespeare plays.

The new technology is not without risk, however. Novels and movie theatres may vanish, people may lose their privacy, and its illicit use can spark a crackdown by the government.

How can we say with certainty that these predictions are *totally wrong*? After all, we are only in the initial stages of the communications revolution, and they all may prove true. The problem is that these predictions were made 100 years ago—and not about the computer, but about the telephone!

A reasonable response to the guesstimates of futurists might be, "Let's wait and see." Plenty of predictions in the past didn't see the light of day. We know that our way of life depends on technology and that new technology can transform society. There will be changes—we can count on it; what we don't know are the exact directions and implications of those changes. For that, we must let the future unfold, taking us with it—sometimes willingly, sometimes reluctantly.

Sources: Marvin, 1988; Fischer, 1995; Pearl, 1995a.

---

longer felt connected to the finished product. They became alienated from the product of their labour, which bred dissatisfaction and unrest.

TRANSFORMATION OF VALUES Today Canadians and Americans brag about cars, hot tubs, and Jacuzzis—and make certain their jeans have the right labels prominently displayed. In short, the particular emphasis on the social value of materialism often depends on the state of technology.

TRANSFORMATION OF SOCIAL RELATIONSHIPS Technology can also change social relationships. New technological changes flourish in our largest cities. And these cities are growing ever larger. Thriving, vibrant cities provide sufficient social space for individuals living in diverse communities to flourish. Ironically, the bigger the city, the "freer" the individual is to be him- or herself and to pursue his or her interests, often with minimal social pressure. In the age of globalization, new social relationships sparked by living in big cities with people from all walks of life and from all parts of the globe lead to the explosion of new ideas and new inventions.

The Automobile

If we try to pick a single item that has had the greatest impact on social life during the past century, among the many candidates would be the automobile. Consider some of the major effects of this innovation.

DISPLACEMENT OF EXISTING TECHNOLOGY In the beginning, people considered the automobile to be cleaner, safer, more reliable, and more economical than horses. Cars also offered the appealing prospect of lower taxes, for no longer would the public have to pay to clean up the tonnes of horse manure that accumulated on city streets each day.

The automobile also replaced a second technology. Canada had developed a vast system of urban transit, with electric streetcar lines radiating outward from the centre of our cities. As the automobile became affordable and more dependable, Canadians demonstrated a clear preference for the greater convenience of private transportation. Instead of walking to a streetcar and then having to wait for one to arrive, people were able to travel directly from home on their own schedules.

EFFECTS ON CITIES The decline in the use of streetcars actually changed the shape of most North American cities, as it stimulated mass suburbanization.

CHANGES IN ARCHITECTURE The automobile's effects on commercial architecture are clear—from the huge parking lots that decorate malls to the drive-up windows of banks and restaurants. But the automobile also fundamentally altered the architecture of North American homes (Flink, 1990). First, new homes were built with a detached garage, located, like the stable, at the back of the home. As the automobile became a more essential part of the North American family, the garage was incorporated into the home by moving

In the photo on the left, Henry Ford proudly displays his 1905 car, the latest in automobile technology. New technology builds on existing technology. At the time this photo was taken, who could have imagined that this vehicle would transform society? Mazda's Nagare is a precursor of future Mazda designs. This concept car is said to embody the word "flow."

it from the backyard to the side of the house and connecting it by a breezeway. The breezeway was eventually removed and the garage integrated into the home so that people could enter their automobiles without even going outside.

CHANGED COURTSHIP CUSTOMS AND SEXUAL NORMS By the 1920s, the automobile was used extensively in dating. In 1925, Jewett introduced cars with a foldout bed, as did Nash in 1937. The Nash version became known as "the young man's model" (Flink, 1990). Since the 1970s, mobile love-making has declined, partly because urban sprawl (itself due

to the automobile) left fewer safe trysting spots, and partly because changed sexual norms made beds more accessible.

EFFECTS ON WOMEN'S ROLES The automobile may also lie at the heart of the changed role of women in Canadian society. Because automobiles required skill rather than strength, women were able to drive as well as men. This new mobility freed women physically from the narrow confines of the home. As Flink (1990) observed, the automobile changed women "from producers of food and clothing into consumers of national-brand canned goods, prepared foods, and ready-made clothes. The automobile permitted shopping at

Most of us take computers for granted, but they are new on the world scene—as are their effects on our lives. This photo captures a significant change in the evolution of computers. The laptop held by the superimposed model has more power than the room-sized ENIAC of 1946.

self-serve supermarkets outside the neighbourhood and in combination with the electric refrigerator made buying food a weekly rather than a daily activity." When women began to do the shopping, they gained greater control over the family budget, and as their horizons extended beyond the confines of the home, they also gained different views of life.

In short, the automobile helped change women's roles at home, including their relationships with their husbands, and facilitated their participation in areas of social life not connected with the home.

IN SUM

With changes this extensive, it would not be inaccurate to say that the automobile shifted basic values and changed the way we look at life. No longer isolated, women and teenagers began to see the world differently. So did husbands and wives, whose marital relationship had also been altered. The automobile even transformed views of courtship, sexuality, and gender relations. No one attributes such fundamental changes solely to the automobile, of course, for many historical events, as well as other technological changes, occurred during this same period, each making its own contribution to social change.

The Computer

The second candidate for bringing about the greatest social change is the computer.

None of us is untouched by the computer. Although it has intruded into our daily lives, most of us never think about it. Our grades are computerized, and probably our paycheques, as well. When we buy groceries, a computer scans our purchases and presents a printout of the name, price, and quantity of each item. The computer's novelty has given way to everyday routine; it is simply another tool.

Let's consider how the computer is changing medicine, education, and the workplace, then examine its likely effects on social inequality.

MEDICINE

The patient's symptoms were mystifying. After exercise, one side of his face and part of his body turned deep red, the other chalky white. He looked as though someone had taken a ruler and drawn a line down the middle of his body.

Stumped, the patient's physician consulted a medical librarian who punched a few words into a personal computer to search for clues in the world's medical literature. Soon, the likely answer flashed on the screen: Harlequin's disease. (Winslow, 1994)

The computer was right, and a neurosurgeon was able to correct the patient's nervous system. With computers, physicians can peer within the body's hidden recesses to determine how its parts are functioning or to see if surgery is necessary. Today, a million tiny fragments of genetic DNA can be crammed onto a disposable microchip. Read by a laser scanner, in just a few minutes the chip can reveal such things as whether a patient carries the cystic fibrosis gene or has grown resistant to AIDS drugs (King, 1994).

As the future is ushered in, the microchip is bringing even more technological wonders. In what is called *telemedicine*, patients have their hearts and lungs checked with a stethoscope—by doctors in another province or country. The data are transmitted by fibre-optic cable (Richards, 1996). Soon a surgeon in Halifax or Vancouver, using a remote-controlled

Technology, which drives much social change, is at the forefront of our information revolution. This revolution, based on the computer chip, allows reality to cross with fantasy, a merging that sometimes makes it difficult to tell where one ends and the other begins. A computer projects an image onto the front of a coat in this image, making its wearer "invisible."

robot and images relayed via satellite to computers, will be able to operate in almost any place or circumstance in the world.

EDUCATION Almost every grade school in Canada introduces its students to the computer. Successful educational programs use a game-like, challenging format that makes students forget they are "studying." Most classrooms are wired to the internet ("Cyberschool Makes Its Debut," 1996).

The question of social inequality becomes significant in this context. Those schools most able to afford the latest in computer technology are able to better prepare their students for the future, thus helping to perpetuate social inequalities that arise from the chance of birth.

The computer has already transformed the experience of university. Students at Mount Allison University in Sackville, New Brunswick, are provided with laptop computers free of charge (if required for their studies) upon their acceptance at the university. And in every university in Canada, students have direct access to the internet and are provided with free email accounts. Overall, "surfing the net" for research and fun is a mainstay of student life at Canadian universities. If you wish, you can go to MySocLab to give yourself a test— at your chosen level of difficulty—to immediately check your mastery of the material.

THE WORKPLACE The computer has also transformed the workplace. In some cases it has returned the work location to the home—an arrangement called *telework*. Already, millions of people perform their jobs at home. As discussed earlier, industrialization caused work to shift from home to factory and office. Since workers can now be "networked" (linked by computers), for many public and private sector workers this historic change is being reversed.

On the negative side are increased surveillance of workers and depersonalization. As a telephone information operator said:

> The computer knows everything. It records the minute I punch in, it knows how long I take for each call . . . I am supposed to average under eighteen seconds per call. . . . Everything I do is reported to my supervisor on his computer, and if I've missed my numbers I get a written warning. I rarely see the guy. . . . It's intense. It's me and the computer all day. I'm telling you, at the end of the day I'm wiped out. Working with computers is the coal mining of the nineties. (Mander, 1992, p. 57)

Cyberspace and Social Inequalities in the Twenty-First Century

The term *information superhighway*, which evokes the idea of information travelling at high speed between homes and businesses, is most apt to describe what is occurring at present around the world. Just as a highway allows physical travel from one place to another, so homes and businesses are being connected by the rapid flow of information. Already about 300 million people around the world are able to communicate by internet, which allows electronic access to libraries of information. Some programs sift, sort, and transmit scanned images, sound, even video. Email allows people to fire off messages without regard to national boundaries. This is the shape of the future: a world linked by almost instantaneous communication, with information readily accessible around the globe, and with few places being considered remote.

The implications of the information superhighway for national and global stratification are severe. At the national level, we may end up with "information have-nots," thereby perpetuating present inequalities. At the global level, the question is: Who will control the information superhighway? The answer is obvious—the most industrialized nations that are developing the system. This leads to one of the more profound issues of the twenty-first century: Will such control destine the least industrialized nations to endless pauper status?

If the answer is yes, how can we reduce the social inequalities created on a global scale? There are no easy answers.

CONTEMPORARY THEORIES OF SOCIAL CHANGE

Table 18.3 categorizes the principal contemporary theories about the causes of social change.

1. *Evolutionary theories* presuppose that societies are moving from the same starting point to some similar ending point. Unilinear theories, which assume the same path for every society, have been replaced with multilinear theories, which assume that different paths can lead to the same stage of development.

2. *Marxist conflict theories* are similar to evolutionary theories of progress except that the final stage, communism— otherwise known as "the end of history"—is the ultimate stage of development.

3. *Cyclical theories*, in contrast, view civilizations as going through a process of birth, youth, maturity, decline, and death.

4. *Feminist theories* assume that all societies, with the possible exception of the earliest hunting-and-gathering tribes, are dominated by patriarchy; and only by women achieving equality of condition and taking action on global human rights can the privileges and liabilities of patriarchy be overcome.

5. *Postmodern theories* assume the present, so that there is no progress or continuity in values, beliefs, and disbeliefs; belief in scientific progress has been replaced with a belief in appearance or form. To postmodernists, any possibility of social change begins with the acceptance of uncertainty, the acknowledgement of diversity, and the refusal to see concepts such as "justice" or "society" as fixed or as governed by unassailable "truths."

TABLE 18.3 Contemporary Theories of Social Change

Theories of Social Change	Assumptions	Path(s) of Social Change
Evolutionary Theories of Social Change	All societies progress from simple to more complicated forms of material organization.	From elementary beginnings to more complex stages of development.
1. Unilinear evolution	All societies follow the same path of development.	One road out of a small village that leads to a town, then a city and beyond.
2. Multilinear evolution	Different routes can lead to a similar stage of development.	Multiple roads out of a small village that lead to a town, then a city and beyond.
Marxist Conflict Theories of Social Change	Similar to evolutionary theories of progress, except communism is the last stage of development, otherwise known as "the end of history."	Multiple roads out of a small village that lead to a town, next a city, and end in paradise.
Cyclical Theories of Change	Civilizations, such as those of Greece, Egypt, or the West, not one particular society, are like organisms: they are born, experience decline, and die.	Airborne fireworks display that begins with a trail upward, then a sudden burst, followed by beautiful colours, ends an exuberant youth, matures, and finally begins the long trail downward to the earth.
Feminist Theories of Social Change	Except for possibly the earliest hunting-and-gathering communities, all societies have been dominated by patriarchy.	A "tug of war" in which more and more women are added to one side of the rope until there is an eventual stalemate.
Postmodern Theories of Social Change	There is no progress or purpose or continuity of values, beliefs, and disbeliefs. Identities and localized situations are basis for change.	A rushing river with multiple currents and fast-moving water, with light sparkling off the top of the water and the surface glimmer being all one sees or wants to see.

Focus Question

Do all sociologists hold the view that humankind is making progress and will keep getting better?

THE DIFFICULT ROAD TO SUCCESS

In spite of their significance in contemporary society, social movements as agents of social change seldom solve all of society's social problems. Resource mobilization helps to explain why. To mobilize resources, a movement must appeal to a broad constituency. For example, the fact that workers at one particular plant are upset about their low wages is not adequate to recruit the broad support necessary for a social movement. At best, it will result in local agitation. The low wages and unsafe working conditions of millions of Canadian workers, however, have a chance of becoming the focal point of a social movement.

Many social movements vitally affect society. The Quebec sovereignty movement comes quickly to mind. Some movements, such as trade unions in Canada, become powerful forces for social change. They highlight problems and turn society onto a path that solves those problems. Others become powerful forces in resisting the social change that its members—and the public it is able to mobilize—consider undesirable.

By their very nature, broad social problems are entrenched in society and are not easy to solve. They require more than merely tinkering with some small part. Just as the problem touches many interrelated components of society, so the solutions require changes in those many parts. Social movements and new technology are among the forces that change society.

SUMMARY AND REVIEW

Early Explanations: The Transformation of the Individual

HOW DID EARLY THEORISTS EXPLAIN THE EFFECTS OF CROWDS ON INDIVIDUALS?
Early theorists argued that individuals are transformed by crowds. Charles Mackay used the term *herd mentality* to explain why people do wild things in crowd settings. Gustave LeBon said that a **collective mind** develops, and people are swept away by suggestions. p. 405.

WHAT STAGES OF CROWD BEHAVIOUR ARE THERE?
Herbert Blumer identified five stages that crowds go through before they become an **acting crowd**: social unrest, an exciting event, **milling**, a common object of attention, and common impulses. pp. 405–406.

The Contemporary View: The Rationality of the Crowd

WHAT IS THE CURRENT VIEW OF CROWD BEHAVIOUR?
Current theorists view crowds as rational. Richard Berk stresses a **minimax strategy**; that is, people try to minimize their costs and maximize their rewards, whether or not they are in crowds. Ralph Turner and Lewis Killian analyze how new norms emerge that allow people to do things in crowds that they otherwise would not do. pp. 406–407.

Forms of Collective Behaviour

WHAT FORMS OF COLLECTIVE BEHAVIOUR ARE THERE?
Some of the major forms of collective behaviour are **demonstrations**, **riots**, **panics**, **moral panics**, **rumours**, **fads**, **fashions**, and **urban legends**. Conditions of discontent or uncertainty provide fertile ground for collective behaviour, and each form provides a way of dealing with these conditions. pp. 407–410.

Social Movements

Types and Tactics of Social Movements

WHAT TYPES OF SOCIAL MOVEMENTS ARE THERE?
Social movements consist of large numbers of people that organize to promote or resist social change. Depending on their target (individuals or society) and the amount of social change desired (partial or complete), social movements can be classified as **alterative**, **redemptive**, **reformative**, or **transformative**. pp. 411–413.

HOW DO SOCIAL MOVEMENTS SELECT THEIR TACTICS?
Tactics are chosen on the basis of a group's membership, its publics (audience), and its relationship to authorities. The three levels of membership are *the inner core*, *the committed*,

and *the less committed*. The predispositions of the inner core are crucial in choosing tactics, but so is the public they wish to address. If relationships with authorities are bad, the chances of aggressive or violent tactics increase. Friendship, size of city, and race of movement participants and their targets may also be significant. p. 413.

HOW ARE THE MASS MEDIA RELATED TO SOCIAL MOVEMENTS?
Because the mass media are gatekeepers for social movements, and their favourable or unfavourable coverage greatly affects a social movement, tactics are chosen with the media in mind. Social movements also make use of **propaganda** to further their cause. p. 414.

Why People Join Social Movements

WHY DO PEOPLE JOIN SOCIAL MOVEMENTS?
There is no single, overriding reason why people join social movements. According to **mass society theory**, social movements relieve feelings of isolation created by an impersonal, bureaucratized society. According to **relative deprivation theory**, people join movements in order to address grievances. Morality, values, and ideological commitment also motivate people to join social movements. The **agent provocateur** illustrates that even people who hate a cause can end up participating in it. pp. 414–416.

On the Success and Failure of Social Movements

WHY DO SOCIAL MOVEMENTS SUCCEED OR FAIL?
Social movements go through several stages—initial unrest and agitation, mobilization, organization, institutionalization, and finally organizational decline with possible resurgence. Groups that appeal to few people cannot succeed. To appeal broadly in order to accomplish **resource mobilization**, a movement must focus on very broad concerns—problems deeply embedded in society—which makes success extremely difficult. p. 416.

How Technology Changes Society

WHAT TYPES OF TECHNOLOGY ARE THERE, AND WHAT EFFECTS CAN A CHANGED TECHNOLOGY HAVE ON SOCIETY?
Because technology is an organizing force in social life, when technology changes its effects can be profound. The automobile and the computer were used as extended examples. The automobile changed the development of cities, buying patterns, architecture, and even courtship and women's roles. We looked at how the computer is changing the way we practise medicine, learn, and work. The information superhighway is likely to perpetuate social inequalities at both a national and a global level. pp. 417–423.

WHAT IS OGBURN'S THEORY OF SOCIAL CHANGE?
Ogburn identified technology as the basic cause of social change, which comes through three processes: invention, discovery, and diffusion. The term **cultural lag** refers to symbolic culture lagging behind changes in technology. pp. 418–419.

Contemporary Theories of Social Change

WHAT ARE THE CONTEMPORARY THEORIES OF SOCIAL CHANGE?
Evolutionary theories presuppose that societies are moving from the same starting point to some similar ending point.

Marxist conflict theories are similar except that communism is the ultimate stage of development. *Cyclical theories* view civilizations as going through a process of birth, youth, maturity, decline, and death. *Feminist theories* assume that societies are mostly dominated by patriarchy, to be overcome by achieving equality of opportunity for women and securing global human rights. In *postmodern theories*, belief in scientific progress has been replaced with a belief in appearance or form; all change is ephemeral. pp. 423–424.

KEY TERMS

acting crowd   405
agent provocateur   416
alienation   419
alterative social
   movements   411
collective behaviour   405
collective mind   405
cultural lag   419
demonstrations   408
diffusion   419
discovery   418
emergent norms   406
fad   410

fashion   410
invention   418
mass society   414
mass society theory   414
milling   406
minimax strategy   406
modernization   418
moral panic   409
new social
   movements   412
panic   408
postmodern
   societies   417

proactive social
   movement   410
propaganda   414
public   413
public opinion   414
reactive social
   movement   410
redemptive social
   movements   411
reformative social
   movements   411
relative deprivation
   theory   415

resource
   mobilization   416
riot   407
role extension   409
rumour   409
social change   417
social movement   410
social movement
   organizations   411
technology   417
transformative social
   movements   412
urban legends   410

WEBLINKS

All URLs listed are current as of the printing of this book.

Collective Behaviour and Social Movements
www.abacon.com/sociology/soclinks/collect.html
A list of useful links on this topic; part of the Allyn and Bacon Sociology Links site.

Social Movements
www.wsu.edu/~amerstu/smc/smcframe.html
This site provides a space for the study of social movements, including those linked to transnational and global movements.

CRITICAL THINKING QUESTIONS

1. To understand the pressures of a social group or social movement, imagine yourself at a hockey game. When the Canadian national anthem is sung, instead of standing up with the other members of the audience, you stay seated. How do you feel when you don't join in? Who is behaving rationally in this situation? You or everyone else?

2. How do the media influence the creation or development of social movements?

3. All too often, sociologists describe social movements as examples of social problems and not as solutions to social problems. Do social movements such as trade unions serve any useful functions in Canadian society?

4. While it is true that technology influences the broad nature of social change, human beings also contribute to the direction of a society's transformation. After having read this book, you should know what sociology is and whether it has anything further to offer you. Do you think sociologists should use their skills and knowledge to directly influence Canadian public policy?

5. In what ways does technology change society? Access the Research Navigator through MySocLab and use keywords such as "teenage" and "authority" to locate relevant and recent scholarly and popular press publications to help you answer this question.

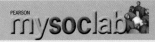

Explore the topics covered in this chapter on MySocLab using the access information provided with this text. Interactive resources for studying include multimedia tutorials, video clips, practice tests, quizzes, and animated maps and figures.

GLOSSARY

acculturation: the transmission of culture from one generation to the next

acid rain: rain containing sulphuric and nitric acids

acting crowd: Herbert Blumer's term for an excited group that collectively moves toward a goal

ageism: prejudice, discrimination, and hostility directed against people because of their age; can be directed against any age group, including youth

agency: individual or collective actions upon social structures and circumstances

agent provocateur: someone who joins a group in order to spy on it and to sabotage it by provoking its members to commit illegal acts

agents of socialization: people or groups that affect our self-concept, attitudes, or other orientations toward life

alienation: Marx's term for workers' lack of connection to the product of their labour; caused by their being assigned repetitive tasks on a small part of a product

alterative social movement: a social movement that seeks to alter only particular aspects of people

animal culture: learned, shared behaviour among animals

anomie: Durkheim's term for a condition of society in which people become detached or cut loose from the norms that usually guide their behaviour

anticipatory socialization: learning part of a future role because one anticipates it

anti-Semitism: prejudice, discrimination, and persecution directed against Jews

applied sociology: the use of sociology to solve problems—from the micro-level of family relationships to the macro-level of crime and pollution

assimilation: the process whereby a minority group is absorbed into the mainstream culture

authoritarian personality: Theodor Adorno's term for people who are prejudiced and rank high on scales of conformity, intolerance, insecurity, respect for authority, and submissiveness to superiors

authority: power that people accept as rightly exercised over them; also called legitimate power

backstage: where people rest from their performances, discuss their presentations, and plan future performances

basic demographic equation: growth rate = births – deaths + net migration

basic sociology: see *pure or basic sociology*

bilateral (system of descent): a system of reckoning descent that counts both the mother's and the father's sides

biological determinism: the belief that the way we act reflects built-in biological traits such as the need to reproduce, the need to survive, and so on

blended family: a family whose members were once part of other families

boomerang kids: young adults who move out of their parents' homes and then move back in as they go through periods of schooling, employment, and family-building

bourgeoisie: Karl Marx's term for capitalists, those who own the means to produce wealth

bureaucracy: a formal organization with a hierarchy of authority; a clear division of labour; emphasis on written rules, communications, and records; and impersonality of positions

capitalism: an economic system characterized by the private ownership of the means of production, the pursuit of profit, and market competition; the investment of capital with the goal of producing profits

caste system: a form of social stratification in which one's status is determined by birth and is life-long

charismatic authority: authority based on an individual's outstanding traits, which attract followers

charismatic leader: an individual who inspires people because he or she seems to have extraordinary qualities

citizenship: the concept that birth (and residence) in a country imparts basic rights

city: a place in which a large number of people are permanently based and do not produce their own food

city-state: an independent city whose power radiates outward, bringing the adjacent area under its rule

clan: an extended network of relatives

clan system: a form of social stratification in which individuals receive their social standing through belonging to an extended network of relatives

class conflict: Marx's term for the struggle between the proletariat and the bourgeoisie

class consciousness: Marx's term for awareness of a common identity based on one's position in the means of production

class system: a form of social stratification based primarily on the possession of money or material possessions

clique: a cluster of people within a larger group who choose to interact with one another; an internal faction

closed-ended questions: questions followed by a list of possible answers to be selected by the respondent

coalition government: a government in which a country's largest party aligns itself with one or more smaller parties

coercion: power that people do not accept as rightly exercised over them; also called illegitimate power

collective behaviour: extraordinary activities carried out by groups of people; includes lynchings, rumours, panics, urban legends, and fads and fashions

collective mind: Gustave LeBon's term for the tendency of people in a crowd to feel, think, and act in extraordinary ways

community: a place people identify with, where they sense that they belong and that others care what happens to them

compartmentalize: to separate acts from feelings or attitudes

confederal union: a system of government in which the provinces have most of the power and the central government has little authority

conflict theory: a theoretical framework in which society is viewed as composed of groups competing for scarce resources

conservative bias: the tendency of analysts to downplay evidence of historical change and to reject evidence of challenges to traditional social patterns

consumer societies: societies in which there has been an explosion in the numbers of goods and services being marketed to meet every possible human need and a dramatic expansion in the time devoted to consumer activities

contradictory class location: Erik Wright's term for a position in the class structure that generates contradictory interests

corporate culture: the orientation that characterizes a corporate work setting

correspondence principle: the sociological principle that schools correspond to (or reflect) the social structure of society

cosmology: teachings or ideas that provide a unified picture of the world

counterculture: a group whose values, beliefs, and related behaviours place its members in opposition to the broader culture

credential society: the use of diplomas and degrees to determine who is eligible for jobs, even though the diploma or degree may be irrelevant to the actual work

crime: the violation of norms that are written into law

criminal justice system: the system of police, courts, and prisons set up to deal with people accused of having committed a crime

critical race theory: linked to the development of African–American legal thought in the post–civil rights era; an interdisciplinary approach that argues that the notions of the social construction of race and race identity, and the reality of discrimination, are ever-present in the writings of known contemporary critical race theorists

crude birth rate: the annual number of births per 1000 population

crude death rate: the annual number of deaths per 1000 population

cult: a new or different religion, with few followers, whose teachings and practices put it at odds with the dominant culture and religion

cultural diffusion: the spread of cultural characteristics from one group to another

cultural goals: the legitimate objectives held out to the members of a society

cultural lag: William Ogburn's term for human behaviour lagging behind technological innovations

cultural levelling: the process by which cultures become similar to one another, and especially by which Western industrial culture is imported and diffused into developing nations

cultural relativism: understanding a people from the framework of its own culture

cultural transmission: in reference to education, the ways schools transmit a society's culture, especially its core values

cultural universal: a value, norm, or other cultural trait that is found in every group

culture: the language, beliefs, values, norms, behaviours, and even material objects passed from one generation to the next

culture of poverty: the assumption that the values and behaviours of the poor make them fundamentally different from other people, that these factors are largely responsible for their poverty, and that parents perpetuate poverty across generations by passing these characteristics on to their children

debit card: a device that allows its owner to charge purchases against his or her bank account

deferred gratification: forgoing something in the present in the hope of achieving greater gains in the future

degradation ceremony: a term coined by Harold Garfinkel to describe an attempt to remake the self by stripping away an individual's

self-identity and stamping a new one in its place; a ritual designed to strip an individual of his or her identity as a group member—for example, a court martial or the defrocking of a priest

dehumanization: the act or process of reducing people to objects that do not deserve the treatment accorded to humans

democracy: a system of government in which authority derives from the people; derived from two Greek words that translate literally as "power to the people"

democratic socialism: a hybrid economic system in which capitalism is mixed with state ownership

demographic transition: a three-stage historical process of population growth: first, high birth rates and high death rates; second, high birth rates and low death rates; and third, low birth rates and low death rates

demographic variables: the three factors that influence population growth: fertility, mortality, and net migration

demography: the study of the size, composition, growth, and distribution of human populations

demonstration: a public meeting, march, etc. for a political or moral purpose

denomination: a "brand name" within a major religion, for example, Methodist or Baptist

dependency ratio: the number of paid workers required so that dependent individuals, usually seniors and children, can be adequately supported

dependency theory: a sociological theory that stresses how the least industrialized nations became dependent on the most industrialized nations

depersonalization: dealing with people as though they are objects—in the case of medical care, as though patients are merely cases and diseases, not persons

dictatorship: a form of government in which power is seized by an individual

differential association: Edwin Sutherland's term to indicate that associating with some groups results in learning an "excess of definitions" of social deviance and, by extension, a greater likelihood that one will become socially deviant

diffusion: the spread of invention or discovery from one area to another; identified by William Ogburn as the final of three processes of social change

direct democracy: a form of democracy in which eligible voters meet together to discuss issues and make their decisions

disabling environment: an environment harmful to health

discovery: a new way of seeing reality; identified by William Ogburn as the second of three processes of social change

discrimination: an act of unfair treatment directed against an individual or a group

divine right of kings: the idea that the king's authority comes directly from God

documents: in its narrow sense, written sources that provide data; in its extended sense, archival material of any sort, including photographs, movies, etc.

dominant group: the group with the most power, greatest privileges, and highest social status

downward social mobility: movement down the social-class ladder

dramaturgical analysis: an approach, pioneered by Erving Goffman, analyzing social life in terms of drama or the stage

dual labour market: workers split along racial, ethnic, gender, age, or any other lines; this split is exploited by owners to weaken the bargaining power of workers

ecclesia (plural ecclesias): a religious group so integrated into the dominant culture that it is difficult to tell where one begins and the other leaves off; also referred to as state religion

economy: a system of distribution of goods and services

education: a formal system of teaching knowledge, values, and skills

egalitarian: authority more or less equally divided between people or groups; for example, between husband and wife in a family

ego: Freud's term for a balancing force between the id and the demands of society

emergent norms: Ralph Turner's and Lewis Killian's term for the development of new norms to cope with a new situation, especially among crowds

endogamy: the practice of marrying within one's own group

environmental injustice: the result of unequal power relations, where minority groups and the poor suffer the most from the effects of pollution

environmental sociology: a subdiscipline of sociology that examines how human activities affect the physical environment and how the physical environment affects human activities

epidemiology: the study of disease and disability patterns in a population

ethnic (and ethnicity): having distinctive cultural characteristics

ethnic work: the way people construct their ethnicity, either through enhancing and maintaining a group's distinctions or recovering ethnic heritage

ethnocentrism: the use of one's own culture as a yardstick for judging the ways of other individuals or societies, generally leading to a negative evaluation of their values, norms, and behaviours

euthanasia: mercy killing

evangelism: an attempt to win converts

exchange mobility: about the same numbers of people moving up and down the social class ladder, such that, on balance, the social class system shows little change

exogamy: the practice of marrying outside one's group

exponential growth curve: a pattern of growth in which numbers double during approximately equal intervals, thus accelerating in the latter stages

export processing zones: tax-free "factory cities" where young Asian women are often lured by the promise of good jobs manufacturing products for export

extended family: a nuclear family plus other relatives, such as grandparents, uncles, and aunts, who live together

fad: a temporary pattern of behaviour that catches people's attention

false consciousness: Karl Marx's term to refer to workers identifying with the interests of capitalists

family: two or more people who consider themselves related by blood, marriage, or adoption

family of orientation: the family in which a person grows up

family of procreation: the family formed when a couple's first child is born

fashion: a pattern of behaviour that catches people's attention and lasts longer than a fad

fecundity: the number of children women are theoretically *capable* of bearing

feminism: the philosophy that men and women should be politically, economically, and socially equal

feminist theories: all three types of feminist theories—Marxist, liberal, and radical—hold that women are oppressed by gender roles that are products of social, historical, and cultural factors

feminization of poverty: the global tendency for adult women to outnumber men among the impoverished population; this tendency is embedded in women's traditional roles in the family and the economy

fertility rate: the number of children the average woman bears

field interview: see qualitative interview

fieldwork: see participant observation

folkways: norms that are not strictly enforced

formal organization: a secondary group designed to achieve explicit objectives

frontstage: where performances are given

functional analysis: a theoretical framework in which society is viewed as composed of various parts, each with a function that, when fulfilled, contributes to society's equilibrium; also known as functionalism and structural functionalism

fundamentalism: the belief that true religion is threatened by modernism and that the faith as it was originally practised should be restored

gatekeeping: the process by which education opens and closes doors of opportunity; another term for the social placement function of education

gender: the social characteristics that a society considers proper for its males and females; masculinity or femininity

gender inequality: males' and females' unequal access to resources, power, prestige, status, and property on the basis of their sex

gender role: the behaviours and attitudes considered appropriate because one is a female or a male

generalizability: the extent to which the findings from one group (or sample) can be generalized or applied to other groups (or populations)

generalized other: the norms, values, attitudes, and expectations of "people in general"; a child's ability to take the role of the generalized other is a significant step in the development of a self

genetic predispositions: inborn tendencies, in this context, to commit socially deviant acts

genocide: the systematic annihilation or attempted annihilation of a people based on their presumed race or ethnicity

gentrification: the displacement of the poor by the relatively affluent, who renovate the former's homes

gestures: the ways in which people use their bodies to communicate with one another

glass ceiling: barriers to social advancement that many women face in some organizations

global warming: an increase in the earth's temperature due to the greenhouse effect

globalization: the extensive movement of capital and ideas between nations due to the expansion of capitalism

goal displacement: replacement of one goal by another; in this context, the adoption of new goals by an organization; also known as goal replacement

greenhouse effect: the buildup of carbon dioxide in the earth's atmosphere that allows light to enter but inhibits the release of heat; believed to cause global warming

greying of Canada: a term that refers to the rising proportion of older people as a percentage of the Canadian population

growth rate: the net change in a population after adding births, subtracting deaths, and either adding or subtracting net migration

habitus: embracing a set of skills and way of looking at the world that reflects (rather than questions or challenges) hierarchical social structures

health: a human condition measured by four components: physical, mental, social, and spiritual

hidden curriculum: the unwritten goals of schools, such as obedience to authority and conformity to cultural norms

homogamy: the tendency of people with similar characteristics to marry one another

hotelling: when companies provide employees with laptops and assign desks only on a temporary basis to whomever needs them, much like one rents a room in a hotel

household: all people who occupy the same housing unit

human agency: the ability to individually or collectively resist social pressures and provide for social change

humanizing a work setting: organizing a workplace in such a way that it develops rather than impedes human potential

hypothesis: a statement of the expected relationship between variables according to predictions from a theory

id: Freud's term for our inborn basic drives

ideology: beliefs about the way things ought to be that justify social arrangements

illegitimate opportunity structures: opportunities for crime that are woven into the texture of life

imperialism: when countries take over other countries so they can expand their markets and gain access to cheap raw materials

indentured service: a fuzzy area between contract and slavery; people whose passage to another country was paid for in exchange for labour; they paid back their transportation costs by serving their master for a specified period of time

individual discrimination: the negative treatment of one person by another on the basis of that person's perceived characteristics

individuation: a growing diversity of individual paths through the life course

in-groups: groups toward which one feels loyalty

institutional discrimination: negative treatment of a minority group that is built into a society's institutions; also called systemic discrimination

institutionalized means: approved ways of reaching cultural goals

institutionalized religion: the formal, highly structured organization, creeds, practices, and rules of conduct intended to assure doctrinal purity and aid believers in their efforts to live by a particular faith

intentional family: people who declare themselves a family and treat one another as members of the same family; originated in the late twentieth century in response to the need for intimacy not met because of distance, divorce, and death

intergenerational mobility: the change that family members make in social class from one generation to the next

internal colonialism: the policy of economically exploiting minority groups

intersectionality: the interrelationships among various inequalities

interview: direct questioning of respondents

invasion-succession cycle: the process of one group of people displacing a group whose racial-ethnic or social class characteristics differ from their own

invention: the combination of existing elements and materials to form new ones; identified by William Ogburn as the first of three processes of social change

iron law of oligarchy: Robert Michels's phrase for the tendency of formal organizations to be dominated by a small, self-perpetuating elite

job ghettoes: also known as pink ghettoes, employment areas dominated by women (and usually lower paid than areas dominated by men)

just-in-time (JIT) strategy: a way of organizing production that minimizes inventory and storage at the production site—components are produced and moved between plants on a just-in-time basis

kaizen: continuous improvement—production techniques are continuously evaluated in search of more efficient and improved methods

labelling theory: the view, developed by symbolic interactionists, that the labels people are given affect their own and others' perceptions of them, thus channelling their behaviour into either social deviance or conformity

laissez-faire capitalism: unrestrained manufacture and trade (loosely, "leave alone" capitalism)

language: a system of symbols that can be combined in an infinite number of ways and can represent not only objects but also abstract thought

latent functions: the unintended consequences of people's actions that help keep a social system in equilibrium

lean production: employs a just-in-time strategy under which parts inventories are reduced to the amount needed at the time, reducing the demand for huge parts warehouses and large work stations

leisure: time not taken up by work or required activities such as eating, sleeping, commuting, childcare, and housework

life expectancy: the number of years an average newborn can expect to live

living will: a statement signed by people in good health that clearly expresses their feelings about being kept alive on artificial life support systems

looking-glass self: a term coined by Charles Horton Cooley to refer to the process by which our self develops through internalizing others' reactions to us

macro-level analysis: an examination of large-scale patterns of society

macropolitics: the exercise of large-scale power, the government being the most common example

macrosociology: analysis of social life focusing on broad features of social structure, such as social class and the relationships of groups to one another; an approach usually used by functionalist and conflict theorists

mainstreaming: helping people become part of the mainstream of society

Malthus theorem: an observation by Thomas Malthus that although the food supply increases only arithmetically (from 1 to 2 to 3 to 4 and so on), population grows geometrically (from 2 to 4 to 8 to 16 and so forth)

manifest function: the intended consequences of people's actions designed to help some part of a social system

market: any process of buying and selling; on a more formal level, the mechanism that establishes values for the exchange of goods and services

market competition: the exchange of items between willing buyers and sellers

market force: the law of supply and demand

market restraints: laws and regulations that limit the capacity to manufacture and sell products

marriage: a group's approved mating arrangements, usually marked by a ritual of some sort

mass media: forms of communication, such as radio, newspapers, and television, directed to mass audiences

mass society: industrialized, highly bureaucratized, impersonal society

mass society theory: an explanation for participation in social movements based on the assumption that such movements offer a sense of belonging to people who have weak social ties

material culture: the material objects that distinguish a group of people, such as their art, buildings, weapons, utensils, machines, hairstyles, clothing, and jewelry

matriarchy: authority vested in females; female control of a society or group; a society in which women dominate men

matrilineal (system of descent): a system of reckoning descent that counts only the mother's side

McDonaldization: a term denoting the increasing rationalization of the routine tasks of everyday life

means of production: the tools, factories, land, and investment capital used to produce wealth

mechanical solidarity: Durkheim's term for the unity that comes from being involved in similar occupations or activities

medicalization: the transformation of something into a matter to be treated by physicians

medicalization of social deviance: to make social deviance a medical matter, a symptom of some underlying illness that needs to be treated by physicians

medicine: one of the major social institutions that sociologists study; a society's organized ways of dealing with sickness and injury

megalopolis: an urban area consisting of at least two metropolises and their many suburbs

meritocracy: a form of social stratification in which all positions are awarded on the basis of merit

metropolis: a central city surrounded by smaller cities and their suburbs

micro-level analysis: an examination of small-scale patterns of society

micropolitics: refers to the exercise of power in everyday life

microsociology: analysis of social life focusing on social interaction; an approach usually used by symbolic interactionists

middle-range theories: explanations of human behaviour that go beyond a particular observation or research but avoid sweeping generalizations that attempt to account for everything

milling: a crowd standing or walking around as they talk excitedly about some event

minimax strategy: Richard Berk's term for the effort people make to minimize their costs and maximize their rewards

minority group: a group discriminated against on the basis of its members' physical or cultural characteristics

modernization: the process by which a *Gemeinschaft* society is transformed into a *Gesellschaft* society; the transformation of traditional societies into industrial societies

monarchy: a form of government headed by a king or queen

monolithic bias: the tendency to ignore the diversity contained within a phenomenon and to focus instead on the most general exterior features; when applied to the family, the bias results in a failure to recognize that traditional notions of the family—male breadwinner, housewife, and biological children—have been supplanted by an amazing diversity of family forms and experiences

monolithic structure: the representation of structure as homogeneous and undiversified; for example, if the family is represented as a monolithic structure, the representation ignores the complex diversity of types and forms incorporated into contemporary experiences of the family

monotheism: the belief that there is only one god

moral community: people united by their religious practices

moral panic: a fear that grips large numbers of people that some evil group or behaviour threatens the well-being of society, followed by intense hostility, sometimes violence, toward those thought responsible

mores: norms that are strictly enforced because they are thought to be essential to core values

multiculturalism (also called pluralism): a philosophy or political policy that permits or encourages ethnic variation

nationalism: a strong identity with a nation, accompanied by the desire for that nation to be dominant

natural sciences: the intellectual and academic disciplines designed to comprehend, explain, and predict events in our natural environment

neocolonialism: coined by Michael Harrington, the shift after World War II where the most industrialized nations turned to international markets as a way of controlling the least industrialized nations

neoliberalism: a version of the capitalist economic system based on the realization of a 24-hour global economy, made possible by the rapid expansion of global information and telecommunications technologies

negative sanction: an expression of disapproval for breaking a norm, ranging from a mild, informal reaction such as a frown to a formal prison sentence or execution

net migration rate: the difference between the number of immigrants and emigrants per 1000 population

new social movements: social movements with a new emphasis on the world, instead of on a condition in a specific country

new technology: the emerging technologies of an era that have a significant impact on social life

noncentrist party: a political party that represents less popular ideas

nonmaterial culture: a group's ways of thinking (including its beliefs, values, and other assumptions about the world) and doing (its common patterns of behaviour, including language and other forms of interaction)

nonverbal interaction: communication without words through gestures, space, silence, and so on

norms: the expectations or rules of behaviour that develop out of values

nuclear family: a family consisting of a husband, wife, and child(ren)

objective method (of measuring social class): a system in which people are ranked according to objective criteria such as their wealth, power, and prestige

objectivity: total neutrality

oligarchy: a form of government in which power is held by a small group of individuals; the rule of the many by the few

operational definitions: the way in which a variable in a hypothesis is measured

organic solidarity: Durkheim's term for the interdependence that results from people needing others to fulfill their jobs; solidarity based on the interdependence brought about by the division of labour

out-groups: groups toward which one feels antagonism

panic: the condition of being so fearful that one cannot function normally, and may even flee

participant observation (or fieldwork): research in which the researcher participates in a research setting while observing what is happening in that setting

patriarchy: authority vested in males; male control of a society or group; a society in which men dominate women

patrilineal (system of descent): a system of reckoning descent that counts only the father's side

peer group: a group of individuals roughly the same age linked by common interests

personal identity kit: items people use to decorate their bodies

personality disorders: the view that a personality disturbance of some sort causes an individual to violate social norms

Peter principle: a bureaucratic "law" according to which the members of an organization are promoted for good work until they reach their level of incompetence, the level at which they can no longer do good work

pink ghettoes: also knows as job ghettoes, employment areas dominated by women (and usually lower paid than areas dominated by men)

pluralism: the diffusion of power among many interest groups, preventing any single group from gaining control of the government

pluralistic society: a society made up of many different groups

pluralistic theory of social control: the view that society is made up of many competing groups, whose interests manage to become balanced

political socialization: the way in which young people are inculcated with beliefs, ideas, and values that embrace the civil order through the education system

polyandry: a marriage in which a woman has more than one husband

polygyny: a marriage in which a man has more than one wife

population: a target group to be studied

population shrinkage: the process by which a country's population becomes smaller because its birth rate and immigration are too low to replace citizens who die and emigrate

population transfer: involuntary movement of a minority group

positive sanction: a reward or positive reaction for approved behaviour, for conformity

positivism: the application of the scientific approach to the social world

postcolonialism: theory concerned with how to understand the cultural products (print and visual media, literature, the arts, and language) coming from societies that were once colonies of Europe

postmodern society: another term for postindustrial society; its chief characteristic is the use of tools that extend the human abilities to gather and analyze information, communicate, and travel

postmodernism: analysis of contemporary social life where the use of images to convey meaning replaces social reality

power: the ability to carry out one's will, even over the resistance of others

power elite: C. Wright Mills's term for those who rule a country: the top people in the leading corporations, the most powerful generals and admirals of the armed forces, and certain elite politicians, who make the nation's major decisions

prejudice: an attitude of prejudging, usually in a negative way

prestige: respect or regard

primary group: a group characterized by intimate, long-term, face-to-face association and co-operation

primary sector: that part of the economy that extracts raw materials from the environment

primary social deviance: Edwin Lemert's term for acts of social deviance that have little effect on the self-concept

principles of scientific management: also referred to as Taylorism, scientific management sought to reduce waste and inefficiency in production by measuring every movement and regulating every step of the work process

private ownership of the means of production: the ownership of machines and factories by individuals who decide what shall be produced

proactive social movement: a social movement that promotes some social change

profane: Durkheim's term for common elements of everyday life

profession: (as opposed to a job) an occupation characterized by rigorous education, a theoretical perspective, self-regulation, authority over clients, and a professional culture that stresses service to society

proletariat: Marx's term for the exploited class, the mass of workers who do not own the means of production

propaganda: in its broad sense, the presentation of information in an attempt to influence people; in its narrow sense, one-sided information used to try to influence people

proportional representation: an electoral system in which seats in a legislature are divided according to the proportion of votes each political party receives

Protestant Ethic: Weber's term to describe the ideal of a self-denying, highly moral life, accompanied by hard work and frugality

public: a dispersed group of people who usually have an interest in the issue on which a social movement focuses; the sympathetic and hostile publics have such an interest, but a third public is either unaware of the issue or indifferent to it

public opinion: how people think about some issue

pure or basic sociology: sociological research whose only purpose is to make discoveries about life in human groups, not to make changes in those groups

qualitative or field interview: an interview in which the researcher is a participant in a conversation with the subject being interviewed

qualitative research methods: research in which emphasis is placed on observing, describing, and interpreting people's behaviour

quality circles: refer to the involvement of rank-and-file workers in detecting and correcting defects and inefficiencies in products and services

quantitative research methods: research in which emphasis is placed on precise measurement, numbers, and statistics

queer theory: an emergent theory that deliberately challenges all notions of a fixed identity; therefore, instead of viewing sex, gender, and desire as a continuum, queer theory smashes these links; gender and desire/pleasure become more "free-floating" and based on individual attraction—regardless of the sex of the other person

questionnaire: a list of questions to be asked

quiet revolution: the fundamental changes in society that occur as a result of vast numbers of women entering the work force

race: inherited physical characteristics that distinguish one group from another

racism: prejudice and discrimination on the basis of race

random sample: a sample in which everyone in the target population has the same chance of being included in the study

rapport: a feeling of trust between researchers and subjects

rationality: the acceptance of rules, efficiency, and practical results as the right way to approach human affairs

rationalization of society: a widespread acceptance of rationality and a social organization largely built around this idea

rational-legal authority: authority based on law or written rules and regulations; also called bureaucratic authority

reactive social movement: a social movement that resists some social change

redemptive social movement: a social movement that seeks to change people totally

reference groups: the groups we use as standards to evaluate ourselves

reformative social movement: a social movement that seeks to change only particular aspects of society

reformists: a category of study of feminist spirituality represented by those who advocate revealing the "liberating core" of religious teachings with female imagery and exposing and refusing to accept rituals that are clearly sexist

reincarnation: in Hinduism and Buddhism, the return of the soul after death in a different form

rejectionists: a category of study of feminist spirituality represented by those who judge the traditional teachings to be hopelessly sexist and have left it to establish a new spiritual tradition

relative deprivation theory: in this context, the belief that people join social movements on the basis of their evaluations of what they think they should have compared with what others have

reliability: the extent to which data produce consistent results

religion: according to Durkheim, beliefs and practices that separate the profane from the sacred and unite its adherents into a moral community

replication: repeating a study to test its findings

representative democracy: a form of democracy in which voters elect representatives to govern and make decisions on their behalf

reputational method (of measuring social class): a system in which people who are familiar with the reputations of others are asked to identify their social class

research method (or research design): one of seven procedures sociologists use to collect data: surveys, participant observation, qualitative interviews, secondary analysis, documents, unobtrusive measures, and experiments

reserve labour force: the unemployed; unemployed workers are thought of as being "in reserve"—capitalists take them "out of reserve" (put them back to work) during times of high production and then lay them off (put them back in reserve) when they are no longer needed

resocialization: the process of learning new norms, values, attitudes, and behaviours

resource mobilization: a theory that social movements succeed or fail on the basis of their ability to mobilize resources such as time, money, and people's skills

respondents: people who respond to a survey, either in interviews or by self-administered questionnaires

revisionists: a category of study of feminist spirituality represented by those who believe that the basic message of the major religions is liberating

revolution: armed resistance designed to overthrow a government

revolutionaries: a category of study of feminist spirituality represented by those who seek to change the established orthodoxy by importing language, images, and rituals from other traditions

riot: violent crowd behaviour aimed against people and property

risk society: in postmodern theory, a term referring to a media-created perception of society that causes Americans and Canadians to feel increasingly at risk of being victimized by crime

rituals: ceremonies or repetitive practices; in this context, religious observances or rites, often intended to evoke awe for the sacred

role extension: the incorporation of additional activities into a role

romantic love: feelings of erotic attraction accompanied by an idealization of the other

routinization of charisma: the transfer of authority from a charismatic figure to either a traditional or a rational-legal form of authority

rumour: unfounded information spread among people

sacred: Durkheim's term for things set apart or forbidden that inspire fear, awe, reverence, or deep respect

sample: the individuals intended to represent the population to be studied

sanctions: expressions of approval or disapproval given to people for upholding or violating norms

sandwich generation: people in the later middle years who find themselves caring not only for their own children but also for their aging parents

Sapir-Whorf hypothesis: Edward Sapir and Benjamin Whorf's hypothesis that language creates ways of thinking and perceiving

scapegoat: an individual or group unfairly blamed for someone else's troubles

science: the application of systematic methods to obtain knowledge and the knowledge obtained by those methods

scientific method: the use of objective, systematic observations to test theories

secondary analysis: the analysis of data already collected by other researchers

secondary group: compared with a primary group, a larger, relatively temporary, more anonymous, formal, and impersonal group based on some interest or activity, whose members are likely to interact on the basis of specific roles

secondary sector: that part of the economy that turns raw materials into manufactured goods

secondary social deviance: Edwin Lemert's term for acts of social deviance incorporated into the self-concept, around which an individual orients his or her behaviour

sect: a group larger than a cult that still feels substantial hostility from and toward society

segregation: the policy of keeping racial or ethnic groups apart

selective perception: seeing certain features of an object or situation, but remaining blind to others

self: the unique human capacity of being able to see ourselves "from the outside"; the picture we gain of how others see us

self-administered questionnaires: questionnaires filled out by respondents

self-fulfilling prophecy: Robert Merton's term for an originally false assertion that becomes true simply because it was predicted

semiperiphery: countries whose economies stagnated as a result of their dependence on trade with the core nations

sex: the biological characteristics that distinguish males and females

sex typing: the association of behaviours with one sex or the other

sexual harassment: the abuse of one's position of authority to force unwanted sexual demands on someone

shaman: the healing specialist of a preliterate tribe who attempts to control the spirits thought to cause a disease or injury; commonly called a witch doctor

sick role: a social role that excuses people from normal obligations because they are sick or injured, while at the same time expecting them to seek competent help and co-operate in getting well

significant other: an individual who significantly influences someone else's life

slavery: a system of social stratification whose essential characteristic is ownership of some people by others

social change: the alteration of culture and societies over time

social class: a large number of people with similar amounts of income and education who work at jobs roughly comparable in prestige; according to Weber, a large group of people who rank closely to one another in wealth, power, and prestige; according to Marx, one of two groups: capitalists who own the means of production or workers who sell their labour

social conservatism: a value system characterized by a belief in conventional morality and social mores and a desire to preserve them, often aggressively, through civil law and regulation; social conservatism is often linked to the economic changes associated with neoliberalism

social control: a group's formal and informal means of enforcing its norms

social deviance: the violation of rules or norms

social facts: Durkheim's term for the patterns of behaviour that characterize a social group

social groups: people who regularly and consciously interact with one another over extended periods of time

social interaction: what people do when they are in one another's presence

social location: the group memberships that people have because of their location in history and society

social mobility: movement up or down the social-class ladder

social movement: a large group of people who are organized to promote or resist social change

social movement organization: an organization developed to further the goals of a social movement

social order: a group's usual and customary social arrangements, upon which its members depend and upon which they base their lives

social placement: a function of education that funnels people into a society's various positions

social sciences: the intellectual and academic disciplines designed to understand the social world objectively by means of controlled and repeated observations

social stratification: the division of large numbers of people into layers according to their relative power, property, and prestige; applies both to nations and to people within a nation, society, or other group

socialism: an economic system characterized by the public ownership of the means of production, central planning, and the distribution of goods without a profit motive

socialization: the process by which people learn the characteristics of their group: the attitudes, values, and actions thought appropriate for them

society: a term used by sociologists to refer to a group of people who share a culture and a territory

sociological imagination: C. Wright Mills's term for a sociological vision— a way of looking at the world that allows links between the apparently private problems of the individual and important social issues

sociological perspective: an approach to understanding human behaviour that entails placing it within its broader social context

sociology: the scientific study of society and human behaviour

spirit of capitalism: Weber's term for the desire to accumulate capital as a duty—not to spend it, but as an end in itself—and to constantly reinvest it

state: a political entity that claims monopoly on the use of violence in some particular territory; commonly known as a country

status: social ranking; the position someone occupies in society or a social group

status consistency: ranking high or low on all three dimensions of social class

status inconsistency (or discrepancy): ranking high on some dimensions of social class and low on others; a contradiction or mismatch between statuses

stigma: "blemishes" that discredit a person's claim to a "normal" identity

strain theory: Robert Merton's term for the strain engendered when a society socializes large numbers of people to desire a cultural goal (such as success) but withholds from many the approved means to reach that goal; one adaptation to the strain is crime, the choice of an innovative means (one outside the approved system) to attain the cultural goal

street crime: crimes such as mugging, rape, and burglary

structural mobility: movement up or down the social-class ladder that is attributable to changes in the structure of society, not to individual efforts

structured conversation: see qualitative or field interview

structured interviews: interviews that use closed-ended questions

subculture: the values and related behaviours of a group that distinguish its members from the larger culture; a world within a world

subjective meanings: the meanings that people give their own behaviour

subjective method (of measuring social class): a system in which people are asked to state the social class to which they belong

subsistence economy: a type of economy in which human groups live off the land with little or no surplus

suburbanization: the movement from the city to the suburbs

suburbs: the communities adjacent to the political boundaries of a city

superego: Freud's term for the conscience, the internalized norms and values of our social groups

survey: the collection of data by having people answer a series of questions

sweating: historically, the term used in reference to exploitative working conditions in the garment industry, with its detailed division of labour separating the craft process (design, cutting, and marketing) from the labour-intensive tasks of sewing and finishing

symbol: something to which people attach meanings and then use to communicate with others

symbolic culture: another term for nonmaterial culture

symbolic interactionism: a theoretical perspective in which society is viewed as composed of symbols that people use to establish meaning, develop their views of the world, and communicate with one another

system of descent: how kinship is traced over generations

taboo: a norm so strong that it brings revulsion if violated

taking the role of the other: putting oneself in someone else's shoes; understanding how someone else feels and thinks and thus anticipating how that person will act

techniques of neutralization: ways of thinking or rationalizing that help people deflect society's norms

technological determinism: the view that technology determines culture, that technology takes on a life of its own and forces human behaviour to follow

technology: often defined as the applications of science, but can be conceptualized as tools (items used to accomplish tasks) and the skills or procedures necessary to make and use those tools

tertiary sector: that part of the economy that consists of service-oriented occupations

tertiary social deviance: the normalizing of behaviour considered socially deviant by mainstream society; relabelling the behaviour as non-deviant

theory: a general statement about how some parts of the world fit together and how they work; an explanation of how two or more facts are related to one another

timetables: the signals societies use to inform their members that they are old; these timetables vary around the world

tool: an object created or modified for a specific purpose

total institution: a place in which people are cut off from the rest of society and are almost totally controlled by the officials who run the place

totalitarianism: a form of government that exerts almost total control over the people

tracking: the sorting of students into different educational programs on the basis of real or perceived abilities

traditional authority: authority based on custom

traditional orientation: the idea—characteristic of tribal, peasant, and feudal societies—that the past is the best guide for the present

transformative social movement: a social movement that seeks to change society totally

triangulation: a research strategy that includes not only the comparison of different data sources, but also the use of different data-gathering techniques and methods to investigate a single phenomenon

underclass: a small group of people for whom poverty persists year after year and across generations

underemployment: the condition of having to work at a job beneath one's level of training and abilities, or of being able to find only part-time work

underground economy: exchanges of goods and services that are not reported to the government and thereby escape taxation

unitary state: a form of government in which all power resides with the central government

universal citizenship: the idea that everyone has the same basic rights by virtue of being born in a country (or by immigrating and becoming a naturalized citizen)

unobtrusive measures: various ways of observing people who do not know they are being studied

upward social mobility: movement up the social-class ladder

urban legend: a story with an ironic twist that sounds realistic but is false

urbanization: the process by which an increasing proportion of a population lives in cities

validity: the extent to which an operational definition measures what was intended

value cluster: a series of interrelated values that together form a larger whole

value contradictions: values that contradict one another; to follow the one means to come into conflict with the other

value-free: an ideal condition in which a sociologist's personal values or biases do not influence social research

values: the standards by which people define what is desirable or undesirable, good or bad, beautiful or ugly; attitudes about the way the world ought to be

variable: a factor or concept thought to be significant for human behaviour, which varies from one case to another

Verstehen: a German word used by Weber that is perhaps best understood as "to have insight into someone's situation"

virtual organizations: companies "without walls," often transcending time, space, and culture

voluntary association: a group made up of volunteers who have organized on the basis of some mutual interest

Walmartization: a term referring to profound transformations in regional and global economies through the sheer size, influence, and power of the big-box department store Wal-Mart

war: armed conflict between nations or politically distinct groups

wealth: property and income

welfare (state) capitalism: an economic system in which individuals own the means of production, but the state regulates many economic activities for the welfare of the population

white-collar crime: Edwin Sutherland's term for crimes committed by people of respectable and high social status in the course of their occupations; for example, bribery of public officials, securities violations, embezzlement, false advertising, and price-fixing

working class: those who sell their labour to the capitalist class

xenophobia: a fear of strangers

zero population growth: a demographic condition in which women bear only enough children to reproduce the population

REFERENCES

100 million children toil full time, forum told. (1997, October 28). *Toronto Star*, p. A5.

Aaron, H. J., & Harris, B. (2003). Our uncertain demographic future. In H. J. Aaron and W. G. Schwartz (Eds.), *Coping with Methuselah: The impact of molecular biology on medicine and society* (pp. 66–93). Washington, D.C.: Brookings Institution Press.

Aberle, D. (1966). *The Peyote religion among the Navaho*. Chicago: Aldine.

Abu-Laban, S. M., & McDaniel, S. A. (2005). Beauty, status, and aging. In N. Mandell (Ed.), *Feminist issues: Race, class and sexuality* (4th ed.). Scarborough, ON: Prentice Hall Allyn and Bacon Canada.

Acker, A., & Brightwell, B. (2004). *Off our rockers and into trouble: The Raging Grannies*. Victoria, B.C.: TouchWood Editions Ltd.

ACPM (Association of Canadian Pension Management). (2000, January). *Dependence or self-reliance: Which way for Canada's retirement income system?* Retrieved October 12, 2000 from, www.acpm.com/ACPMenglish/documents/dep_selfreliance.htm.

Adams, Richard. (2002, December 27). "Fat is a financial issue." *The Guardian.*

Addams, J. (1981). *Twenty years at Hull-House*. (First published 1910). New York: Signet.

Addis, M. E., & Mahalik, J. R. (2003). Men, masculinity and the contexts of help seeking. *American Psychologist, 58*(1), 5–14.

Adherents of All Religions, by Six Continental Areas. (2003). *World Almanac and Book of Facts.*

Adorno, T. W., Frenkel-Brunswick, E., Levinson, D. J., & Sanford, R. N. (1950). *The authoritarian personality*. New York: Harper & Row.

Agrell, S. (2008, January 28). "Oil Industry Takes Its Toll on Domestic Life." *Globe and Mail*, pp. L1, L2.

Aguirre, B. E., Quarantelli, E. L., & Mendoza, J. L. (1993). The collective behavior of fads: The characteristics, effects, and career of streaking. In R. L. Curtis, Jr., & B. E. Aguirre (Eds.), *Collective behavior and social movements* (168–182). Boston: Allyn and Bacon.

Albanese, P. (2006) Small Town, Big Benefits: The Ripple Effect of $7/day Child Care. *Canadian Review of Sociology and Anthropology 43*(2): 125–140.

Albert, E. M. (1963). Women of Burundi: A study of social values. In D. Paulme (Ed.), *Women of tropical Africa* (179–215). Berkeley: University of California Press.

Aldrich, N. W., Jr. (1989). *Old money: The mythology of America's upper class*. New York: Vintage Books.

Allahar, A. L., & Coté, J. E. (1998). *Richer and poorer: The structure of inequality in Canada*. Toronto: James Lorimer & Co.

Allard, Yvon E., Wilkins, Russell, & Berthelot, Jean-Marie. (2004, January). *Premature Mortality in Health Regions with High Aboriginal Populations*. Statistics Canada, Health Reports, Volume 15, Number 1, Catalogue No. 82-003.

Alliance to End Homelessness (Ottawa). (2005). *Experiencing homelessness: The first report card on homelessness in Ottawa*. Available at www.unitedwayottawa.ca.

Allport, F. (1954). *Social Psychology*. Boston: Houghton Mifflin.

Alphonso, Caroline. (2005, July 15). "Schools Rely on 4th 'R': Raising Cash for Basics." *The Globe and Mail*, A6.

Alphonso, Caroline & El Akkad, Omar. "Fears of Career Suicide Stopped Educators from Reporting Violence." *The Globe and Mail*, January 11, 2008: A1, A10.

Alzheimer's Society of Toronto. Statistics. Accessed June 13, 2008. www.alzheimertoronto.org/ad_Statistics.htm.

Ambert, Anne-Marie. (2001) *The Effect of Children on Parents*. Second Edition. New York: The Haworth Press.

Ambert, A. M. (2005). *Same-Sex Couples and Same-Sex-Parent Families: Relationships, Parenting and Issues of Marriage*. The Vanier Institute of the Family, www.vifamily.ca/library/publications/samesexd.html.

Amnesty International. (2004). *Making violence against women count: Facts and figures*. http://web.amnesty.org/libraryindex/ENGACT770362004.

Andersen, M. L. (1988). *Thinking about women: Sociological perspectives on sex and gender*. New York: Macmillan.

Anderson, D. A., and Hamilton, M. (2005). Gender role stereotyping of parents in children's picture books: The invisible father. *Sex Roles, 52*(4/5), 145–151.

Anderson, E. (1978). *A place on the corner*. Chicago: University of Chicago Press.

Anderson, E. (1990). *Streetwise*. Chicago: University of Chicago Press.

Anderson, E. (1997). Streetwise. In J. M. Henslin (Ed.), *Down to earth sociology: Introductory readings* (9th ed., pp. 170–179). New York: Free Press.

Anderson, Elijah. (2006). Streetwise. In J. M. Henslin (Ed.), *Exploring Social Life: Readings to Accompany Essentials of Sociology* (6th ed., pp. 147–156). Boston: Allyn and Bacon.

Anderson, P. (1995, Autumn). God and the Swedish immigrants. *Sweden and America*, 17–20.

Andersson, Hilary. (2005, February 11). "Born to Be a Slave in Niger." BBC, World Edition.

Angell, R. C. (1965). The sociology of human conflict. In E. B. McNeil (Ed.), *The Nature of Human Conflict*. Englewood Cliffs, NJ: Prentice Hall.

Arías, J. (1993, January 2). La Junta rehabilita en Grenada casas que deberá tirar por ruina. *El Pais*, p.1.

Arichi, M. (1999). Is it radical? Women's right to keep their own surnames after marriage. *Women's Studies International Forum, 22*(4), pp. 411–415.

Ariès, P. (1962). *Centuries of childhood: A social history of family life* (R. Baldick, Trans.). New York: Vintage.

Arlacchi, P. (1980). *Peasants and great estates: Society in traditional Calabria*. Cambridge, England: Cambridge University Press.

Arndt, W. F., & Gingrich, F. W. (1957). *A Greek-English lexicon of the New Testament and other early Christian literature*. Chicago: University of Chicago Press.

Arnup, K. (2005) Lesbian and Gay Parents. In N. Mandell, A. Duffy (Eds.), *Canadian Families: Diversity, Conflict and Change* (pp. 176–209). Toronto: Thompson Nelson.

Asch, S. (1952). Effects of group pressure upon the modification and distortion of judgments. In G. Swanson, T. M. Newcomb, & E. L. Hartley (Eds.), *Readings in social psychology*. New York: Holt, Rinehart and Winston.

Ashe, A. (1992, February 27). A zero-sum game that hurts Blacks. *Wall Street Journal*, p. A10.

Ashford, L. S. (2001, March). New population policies: Advancing women's health and rights. *Population Bulletin, 56*(1).

Ashford, L. & Clifton, D. (2005, February). *Women of our world 2005.* Washington, D.C.: Population Reference Bureau.

Assisted Suicide. (2005, June 13). Assisted Suicide Laws Around the World. Accessed June 13, 2008. www.assistedsuicide.org/suicide_laws.html.

AT&T News. (2004, October 8). Glass Ceiling to Boardroom Firmly in Place for Women at Global 200 Companies. www.att.com/gen/press-room?pid=4800&cdvn=news&newsarticleid=21422&phase=check.

Aubin, B. (2001–2002, December 31–January 7). Where the solitudes meet. *Maclean's* (Toronto Edition), *114*(53), p. 32.

AuCoin, Kathy, ed. (2005, July). Family Violence Against Older Adults. *Family Violence in Canada: A Statistical Profile.* Statistics Canada, Catalogue Number 85-224-XIE.www.statcan.ca/english/freepub/85-224-XIE/85-224-XIE2005000.pdf.

Auerbach, J. D. (1990, December). Employer-supported child care as a women-responsive policy. *Journal of Family Issues, 11*(4), 384–400.

Auger, J., & Tedford-Litle, D. (2002). *The inside looking out: Competing ideas about growing old.* Halifax: Fernwood Publishing.

Ayittey, G. B. N. (1998, September 4). Black Africans are enraged at Arabs. *Wall Street Journal*, interactive edition.

Bainbridge, W. S. (1989). Collective behavior and social movements. In R. Stark, *Sociology* (pp. 608–640). Belmont, CA: Wadsworth.

Baker, C. N. (2005). Images of women's sexuality in advertisements: A content analysis of black- and white-oriented women's and men's magazines. *Sex Roles, 52*(1/2), 13–27.

Bales, K. (2002). The social psychology of modern slavery. *Scientific American, 286*, p. 4.

Baltzell, E. D. (1979). *Puritan Boston and Quaker Philadelphia.* New York: Free Press.

Baltzell, E. D., & Schneiderman, H. G. (1988, September/October). Social class in the Oval Office. *Society, 25*, 42–49.

Barbeau, C. (1992). The man–woman crisis. In J. M. Henslin (Ed.), *Marriage and Family in a Changing Society* (4th ed, pp. 193–199). New York: Free Press.

Barnes, F. (1995, June 14). How to rig a poll. *Wall Street Journal*, p. A14.

Barnes, Helen. (2001, June). "A Comment on Stroud and Pritchard: Child Homicide, Psychiatric Disorder and Dangerousness." *British Journal of Social Work*, 31(3).

Baron, R., & Greenberg, G. (1990). *Behavior in organizations.* Boston: Allyn and Bacon.

Bashevkin, S. (2002, May 27). Warning: Duty state under construction. *Toronto Star*, p. A21.

Baudrillard, J. (1983). *Simulations* (P. Foss, P. Patton, & P. Beitchman, Trans.). New York: Semiotext.

Baudrillard, J. (1993). *The transparency of evil: Essays on extreme phenomena* (J. Benedict, Trans.). London; New York: Verso.

Baudrillard, J. (1995). *The Gulf War did not take place* (P. Patton, Trans. and intro.). Bloomington: Indiana University Press.

Bauman, Z. (1994). *Intimations of postmodernity.* London: 1992.

Bauman, Z. (2007) *Consuming Life.*Cambridge: Polity.

Baxter, D. J. (2003). Raising sons. *Transition Magazine* (Vanier Institute of the Family), *33*(1). Available at www.vifamily.ca.

Baxter, J., Hewitt, B., & Haynes, M. (2008) "Life Course Transitions and Housework: Marriage, Parenthood, and Time on Housework." *Journal of Marriage and the Family.* 70 (May), 259–272.

Beagan, B. L. (2007). "'Even If I Don't Know What I'm Doing I Can Make It Look Like I Know What I Am Doing': Becoming a Doctor in the 1990s." In L. Tepperman & H. Dickinson (Eds.), *Reading Sociology: Canadian Perspectives* (pp. 43–47). Don Mills: Oxford University Press.

Beals, R. L., & Hoijer, H. (1965). *An introduction to anthropology* (3rd ed.). New York: Macmillan.

Beauchamp. D. (2007). Parents victimized by their children. P. 24 in L. Ogrodnik (ed.) *Family Violence in Canada: A Statistical Profile 2007.*Statistics Canada catalogue no. 85-224-XIE. Ottawa: Minister of Industry.

Beaujot, R. & Andersen, R. (2007). Time-Crunch: Impact of Time Spent in Paid and Unpaid Work, and its Division in Families. *Canadian Journal of Sociology.* 32(3), 295–315.

Beaupre, P., Turcotte, P., & Milan, A. (2006, August). When is junior moving out? Transitions from the parental home to independence. *Canadian Social Trends.* Summer, 8–14.

Bechard, M. (2007). Family Structure by Region. Statistics Canada catalogue no. 89-625-XIE. Ottawa: Minister of Industry.

Beck, U. (1992). *Risk society: Towards a new modernity.* London: Sage.

Becker, H. S., Geer, B., Strauss, A. L., and Hughes, E. C. (1961). *Boys in white: Student culture in medical school.* Chicago: University of Chicago Press.

Becker, H. S. (1966). *Outsiders: Studies in the sociology of deviance.* New York: Free Press.

Beckett, P. (1996, September 11). Even piñatas sold in Mexico seem to originate in Hollywood now. *Wall Street Journal*, p. B1.

Beeghley, L. (1996). *The structure of social stratification in the United States* (2nd ed.). Boston: Allyn and Bacon.

Belcher, J. R. (1988, Fall). Are jails replacing the mental health system for the homeless mentally ill? *Community Mental Health Journal, 24*(3), 185–195.

Belkin, Lisa. (2008, May 17). The Dinosaurs of Science: More Women are Engineers, Lab and Tech Workers, But They Leave Due to Sexism. *The Hamilton Spectator*, p. A13.

Bell, D. A. (1993). Remembrance of Racism Past: The Civil Rights Decline. In Hill & J. E. Jones (Eds.), *Race in America: The Struggle for Equality* (pp. 73–82). Madison: University of Wisconsin Press.

Benales, C. (1973, January 1). 70 days battling starvation and freezing in the Andes: A chronicle of man's unwillingness to die. *New York Times*, p. 3.

Bender, W., & Smith, M. (1997, February). Population, food, and nutrition. *Population Bulletin, 51*(4), 1–47.

Benford, Robert D. (2007). The College Sports Reform Movement: Reframing the 'Educational' Industry. *The Sociological Quarterly*, 48: 1–28.

Berger, P. L. (1963). *Invitation to sociology: A humanistic perspective.* New York: Doubleday.

Berger, P. L. (1991). *The capitalist revolution: Fifty propositions about prosperity, equality, and liberty.* New York: Basic Books.

Berk, R. A. (1974). *Collective behavior.* Dubuque, Iowa: Brown.

Bernard, J. (1972). *The Future of Marriage.* New York: Bantam.

Bernard, V. W., Ottenberg, P., & Redl, F. (1971). Dehumanization: A composite psychological defense in relation to modern war. In R. Perucci & M. Pilisuk (Eds.), *The triple revolution emerging: Social problems in depth* (pp. 17–34). Boston: Little, Brown.

Berry, L., et al. (1999). *Canadian global almanac 2000.* Toronto: Macmillan Canada.

Bessenoff, G. R. & Del Priore, R. E. (2007). Women, Weight, and Age: Social Comparison to Magazine Images Across the Lifespan. *Sex Roles.* 56, 215–222.

Bianci, S., Robinson, J., & M. Milkie. (2006). *Changing Rhythms of American Family Life.*New York: Russell Sage Foundation.

Bibby, R. W. (1995). *The Bibby report: Social trends Canadian style.* Toronto: Stoddart.

Bibby, R. W. (2004–5). Future families: Surveying our hopes, dreams and realities. *Transition Magazine, 34*(4), 3–16.

Bid to cut mortality rate among children slows. (2005, April 18). *Toronto Star*, p. A16.

Bird, C. E. (1997, August). Gender differences in the social and economic burdens of parenting and psychological distress. *Journal of Marriage and the Family, 59*, 1–16.

Blackwelder, S. P. (1993). Duality of structure in the reproduction of race, class, and gender inequality [Paper presented at the 1993 meetings of the American Sociological Association].

Blakemore, J. E. W., Hill, C. A. (2008). The Child Gender Socialization Scale: A Measure to Compare Traditional and Feminist Parents. *Sex Roles 58*, 192–207.

Blau, F., Brinton, M., & Grusky, D. (Eds.) (2006). *The Declining Significance of Gender?* New York: Russell Sage Foundation.

Blau, P. M. & Duncan, O. D. (1967). *The American Occupational Structure.* New York: John Wiley.

Blee, Kathleen. (2005). "Inside Organized Racism," on Life in Society: Readings to Accompany *Sociology: A Down to Earth Approach, Seventh Edition*, pp. 46–57.

Block, J. (2005). The Politics of Modern Childhood: American Socialisation and the Crisis of Individualism. In J. Goddard, S. McNamee, A. James, A. James (Eds.), *The Politics of Childhood: International Perspectives, Contemporary Developments* (32–49). London: Palgrave Macmillan.

Blumer, H. G. (1939). Collective behavior. In R. E. Park (Ed.), *Principles of Sociology* (pp. 219–288). New York: Barnes and Noble.

Blumer, H. (1966). Sociological implications of the thought of George Herbert Mead. *American Journal of Sociology, 71*, 535–544.

Blytheway, B., & Johnson, J. (2005). Cataloguing old age. In G. J. Andrews & D. R. Phillips (Eds.), *Ageing and place: Perspectives, policy and practice* (pp. 176–187). London: Routledge.

Borcea, Dana. (2007, November 9). Time to Rhyme: Dub Poetry Festival. *The Hamilton Spectator*, p. A3.

Borrelli, P. (1988, Spring). The ecophilosophers. *Amicus Journal, 30*–39.

Bosworth, B. P., & Keys, B. (2004). Increased life expectancy: A global perspective. In H. J. Aaron & W. B. Schwartz (Eds.), *Coping with Methuselah: The impact of molecular biology on medicine and society* (pp. 247–283). Washington, DC: Brookings Institution Press.

Bourdieu, P. & Passeron, J.-C. (1979). *The Inheritors: French Students and their Relations to Culture.* University of Chicago Press, Chicago.

Bourgois, P. (1994). Crack in Spanish Harlem. In J. Curtis & L. Tepperman (Eds.), *Haves and have-nots: An international reader on social inequality* (pp. 131–136). Englewood Cliffs, NJ: Prentice Hall.

Bourque, L. B. (1989). *Defining rape.* Durham, NC: Duke University Press.

Bowlby, G. (2002, Spring). The labour-market: Year-end review 2001. *Perspectives on Labour and Income, 14*, pp. 7–14.

Bowles, S., & Gintis, H. (1976). *Schooling in capitalist America.* New York: Basic Books.

Boyd, N. (2000). *The Beast Within: Why Men Are Violent.* Vancouver: Greystone Books.

Bradshaw, J. (2002). Child poverty and child outcomes. *Children and Society, 16*, 131–140.

Brajuha, M., & Hallowell, L. (1986, January). Legal intrusion and the politics of fieldwork: The impact of the Brajuha case. *Urban Life, 14*(4), 454–478.

Bramham, D. (2008). *The Secret Lives of Saints: Child Brides and Lost Boys in Canada's Polygamous Mormon Sect.* Toronto: Random House Canada.

Brauchli, M. W. (1993, May 10). A satellite TV system is quickly moving Asia into the global village. *Wall Street Journal*, pp. A1, A8.

Braverman, H. (1974). *Labor and monopoly capital: The degradation of work in the twentieth century.* New York: Monthly Review Press.

Brean, Joseph. (2008, February 16). Lottery Winnings Can Sometimes be Fool's Gold. *National Post.* www.nationalpost.com/story-printer.html?id=314008.

Brecher, J., & Costello, T. (1998). *Global Village or Global Pillage: Economic Reconstruction From the Bottom Up.* Cambridge, MA: South End Press.

Brennae, Mark. (2008, March 19). Gender Pay Gap is Widening in Canada: Study. *Montreal Gazette.*

Brennan, R. (2002, March 29). $4.3 million campaign targets elder abuse. *Toronto Star*, p. A3.

Brenner, J. (2000). *Women and the Politics of Class.* New York: Monthly Review Press.

Bridgman, A. (1994, April 6). Report from the Russian front. *Education Week*, pp. 22–29.

Bridgwater, W. (Ed.). (1953). *The Columbia Viking desk encyclopedia.* New York: Viking Press.

Brines, J. (1994, November). Economic dependency, gender, and the division of labor at home. *American Journal of Sociology, 100*(3), 652–688.

Brockerhoff, Martin P. (2000). An Urbanizing World. *Population Bulletin*, 55(3): 1–44.

Bronstein, P., Fox, B. J. Kamon, J. L., & Knolls, M. L. (2007). Parenting and Gender as Predictors of Moral Courage in Late Adolescence: A Longitudinal Study. *Sex Roles.* 56, 661–674.

Brooks, D. (2006, September 20). Mars and Venus Hardwired. *National Post.* p. A19.

Brooks, V. R. (1982). Sex differences in student dominance behavior in female and male professors' classrooms. *Sex Roles, 8*(7), 683–690.

Brown, D. R., & Gary, L. E. (1988). Unemployment and psychological distress among Black American women. *Sociological Focus, 21*, 209–221.

Brown, Louise. (2005, November 24). Native, Minority Kids Twice as Likely to be Poor. *The Hamilton Spectator*, p. A11.

Brown, Louise. (2006, December 8). Boom Lowered on Higher Eduation: Canada Lacks Vision, Training to Compete Globally, Federal Report Warns. *The Toronto Star*, p. A4.

Brunvand, J. H. (1981). *The vanishing hitchhiker: American urban legends and their meanings.* New York: Norton.

Brunvand, J. H. (1984). *The choking Doberman and other "new" urban legends.* New York: Norton.

Brunvand, J. H. (1986). *The study of American folklore.* New York: Norton.

Bryant, C. D. (1993). Cockfighting: America's invisible sport. In J. M. Henslin (Ed.), *Down-to-earth sociology: Introductory readings* (7th ed.). New York: Free Press.

Brym, Robert & St. Pierre, Céline. (1997). Canadian Sociology. *Contemporary Sociology*, Vol. 26(5): 543–546.

Brzozowski, Jodi-Anne. (2004a). Family violence against older adults. In J. Brzozowski (Ed.), *Family violence in Canada: A statistical profile 2004* (pp. 26–34). Ottawa: Statistics Canada. Catalogue no. 85-224-XIE.

Brzozowski, J.-A. (2004b). Spousal violence. In J. Brzozowski (Ed.), *Family violence in Canada: A statistical profile 2004* (pp. 5–15). Ottawa: Statistics Canada. Catalogue no. 85-224-XIE.

Brzozowski, J.-A. (2007). Family violence against children and youth. In L. Ogrodnik (ed.) *Family Violence in Canada: A Statistical Profile 2007*. Statistics Canada catalogue no. 85-224-XIE. Ottawa: Minister of Industry, pp. 22–24.

Buckley, S. (1991, June 17). Shrugging off the burden of a brainy image. *Washington Post,* p. D1.

Buechler, S. M. (1993). Beyond resource mobilization: Emerging trends in social movement theory. *Sociological Quarterly, 34*(2), 217–235.

Bueckert, D. (2003). Truck traffic sickens kids: NAFTA study points to increased air pollution at Mexican border crossing. *Hamilton Spectator,* November 11, p. A16.

Buncombe, Andrew. (2008, March 6). India Paying Cash to Stem Abortions. *The Hamilton Spectator,* p. A12.

Burgess, E. W. (1925). The growth of the city: An introduction to a research project. In R. E. Park, E. W. Burgess, & R. D. McKenzie (Eds.), *The City* (pp. 47–62). Chicago: University of Chicago Press.

Burgess, M. C. R., Stermer, S. P., & Burgess, S. R. (2007). Sex, Lies and Video Games: The Portrayal of Male and Female Characters on Video Game Covers. *Sex Roles.* 57, pp. 419–433.

Burman, P. (1996). *Poverty's bonds: Power and agency in the social relations of welfare.* Toronto: Thompson Educational Publishing.

Bushnik, T. (2006). Child Care in Canada. Statistics Canada Catalogue no. 89-599-MIE2006003. Ottawa: Ministry of Industry.

Butler, Judith. (1993). *Bodies That Matter: On the Discursive Limits of "Sex"* New York: Routledge.

Buttel, F. H. (1987). New directions in environmental sociology. In W. R. Scott & J. F. Short, Jr., (Eds.), *Annual Review of Sociology, 13,* 465–488. Palo Alto, CA: Annual Reviews.

Calamai, P. (2002, September 28). 10 biotech breakthroughs lifesavers for poor. *Toronto Star,* p. A19.

Calvo-Salguero, A., Garcia-Martinex, J. M. A., & Monteoliva, A. (2008). Differences Between and Within Genders in Gender Role Orientation According to Age and Level of Education. *Sex Roles.* 58, pp. 535–548.

Campaign 2000. (2003). Day care "cornerstone" of poverty fight. *Toronto Star.* November 25, p. A26.

Campbell, M. (2001, May 4). Study links racism, wage gap. *Toronto Star,* p. A19.

Canadian Association of Food Banks. (2007). "Hunger Facts 2007" Fact Sheet.

Canadian Council on Learning. (2006, May 31). Why is High-Quality Child Care Essential? The Link Between Quality Child Care and Early Learning. www.ccl-cca.ca/CCL/Reports?LessonsInLearning?20060530LinL.htm?Style=Print.

Canadian Council on Learning. (2007, December). *Post-Secondary Education in Canada: Strategies for Success.* Ottawa.

CCSD (Canadian Council on Social Development). (2008). Stats and Facts: Before/After Tax Poverty Lines, 2006. Ottawa: CCSD .www.ccsd.ca/factsheets/economic_security/poverty/lico_06.htm.

CCSD (Canadian Council on Social Development). (2000). *The Canadian Fact Book on Poverty.* Ottawa: CCSD.

Canadian Education Statistics Council. (2000, February). *Education Indicators in Canada: Report of the Pan-Canadian Education Indicators Program 1999.* Ottawa: Canadian Education Statistics Council.

Canadian Education Statistics Council and Statistics Canada. (2006, April). *Education Indicators in Canada: Report of the Pan-Canadian Education Indicators Program, 2005.* Catalogue No. 81-582-XPE, Ottawa.

Canadian Labour Congress. (2008). *Women in the Work Force: Still a Long Way from Equality.* March 2008. 38pp. http://canadianlabour.ca/updir/womensequalityreportEn.pdf

Canadian Labour Congress. (2008a). "Working Women: Still a Long Way from Equality." Fact Sheet, April 2008. http://canadianlabour.ca/updir/EN-wage-gap-in-general.pdf.

Canadian Labour Congress. (2008b). "Manufacturing Jobs Matter to Women." Fact Sheet, April 2008. http://canadianlabour.ca/updir/EN-manufacturing.pdf.

Canadian Paediatric Society (Adolescent Health Committee). (2004). Dieting in adolescence. *Paediatrics & Child Health.* 9(7), pp. 487–491.

Canadian Panel on Violence Against Women. (1993). *Changing the landscape: Ending violence—achieving equality.* Ottawa: Minister of Supply and Services.

Canadian Press. (2002, July 22). Suspensions soar in schools: Critics are alarmed at trend of punishing young for minor offences. *Toronto Star,* p. A3.

Canadian Press. (2008, April 11). Childcare Spaces Scarce Under Tories, Report Finds. *The Hamilton Spectator,* p. A9.

Canadian Social Trends (2007). Census snapshot of Canada—Families. Winter: pp. 39–40.

Canadian Sociology and Anthropology Association. (1995). *Code of ethics.* Montreal.

Cantril, H. (1941). *The psychology of social movements.* New York: Wiley.

Caplow, T. (1991). The American way of celebrating Christmas. In J. M. Henslin (Ed.), *Down to earth sociology: Introductory readings* (6th ed., pp. 88–97). New York: Free Press.

Capponi, P. (1997). *Dispatches from the poverty line.* Toronto: Penguin Books.

Cardoso, F. H. (1972, July–August). Dependent capitalist development in Latin America. *New Left Review, 74,* 83–95.

Carey, E. (2001, March 16). Rich, poor are even wider apart. *Toronto Star,* pp. A1, A10.

Carey, E. (2001a, April 3). Stress, instability mark of "blended" families. *Toronto Star,* p. D3.

Carpenter, B. (1990, September 17). Redwood radicals. *U.S. News & World Report, 109*(11), 50–51.

Carr, D., Ryff, C. D., Singer, B., & Magee, W. J. (1995). Bringing the "life" back into life course research: A "person-centered" approach to studying the life course. [Paper presented at the 1995 meetings of the American Sociological Association].

Carr, D. (2007). The cost of kids. *Contexts.*6,4,62.

Carrington, T. (1993, September 20). Developed nations want poor countries to succeed on trade, but not too much. *Wall Street Journal,* p. A10.

Carroll, Bill. (2004). *Corporate Power in a Globalizing World.* Toronto: Oxford University Press.

Carroll, Bill & Hackett, Robert A. (2006). *Remaking Media: The Struggle to Democratize Public Communication.* London: Routledge.

Carroll, P. N., & Noble, D. W. (1977). *The free and the unfree: A new history of the United States.* New York: Penguin.

Carroll, W. K. (2004). *Corporate power in a globalizing world: A study in elite social organization.* Toronto: Oxford University Press.

Castellano, M. B. (2002). *Aboriginal family trends: Extended families, nuclear families and families of the heart.* Vanier Institute of the Family, www.vifamily.ca/library/cft/aboriginal.html.

Cauthen, N. K., & Jasper, J. M. (1994, September). Culture, politics, and moral panics. *Sociological Forum, 9*(3), 495–503.

CBC News. (2007, January 2) Diet articles trigger unhealthy behaviour in girls: study. Available at www.cbc.ca/news/story/2007/01/02teens-magazines.html.

CBC News. (2007, November 19) Teenage girls, and increasingly boys, dieting to stay thin: study. Available at www.cbc.ca/health/story/2007/11/29/weightloss-teenagers.html.

CBC News. (2008, February 21). "Retiring Mandatory Retirement." www.cbc.ca/news/background/retirement/mandatory_retirement .html.

CBC News. (2008, March 6). "Canada's Super-rich." www.cbc.ca/news/ background/wealth/.

CBC News. (2008). "Women in Canadian Politics." www.cbc.ca/news/ interactives/map-cda-womenpolitics/.

Centre for Social Justice. (2001). New UN report shows Canada low-down in poverty ranking. Toronto: Centre for Social Justice.

Chafetz, J. S., & Dworkin, A. G. (1986). *Female revolt: Women's movements in world and historical perspective.* Totowa, NJ: Rowman & Allanheld.

Chafetz, J. S. (1990). *Gender equity: An integrated theory of stability and change.* Newbury Park, CA: Sage.

Chagnon, N. A. (1977). *Yanomamo: The fierce people* (2nd ed.). New York: Holt, Rinehart and Winston.

Chalmers, L., & Milan, A. (2005). Marital satisfaction during the retirement years. *Canadian Social Trends* (Spring), 14–17. Catalogue no. 11-008.

Chambliss, William J. (2007). "The Saints and the Roughnecks." In J. M. Henslin, Ed., *Down to Earth Sociology: Introductory Readings,* 14th ed. New York: The Free Press. First published in 1973.

Chambliss, William J. (2000). *Power, Politics, and Crime.* Boulder, CO: Westview Press.

Chandler, D. (1995). Technological or Media Determinism. www.aber.ac .uk/media/Documents/tecdet.

Chandler, T., & Fox, G. (1974). *3000 years of urban growth.* New York: Academic Press.

Chandra, V. P. (1993a). Fragmented identities: The social construction of ethnicity, 1885–1947 [Unpublished paper].

Chandra, V. P. (1993b). The present moment of the past: The metamorphosis [Unpublished paper].

Chapman, S. A. (2005). Theorizing about aging well: Constructing a narrative. *Canadian Journal of Aging, 24*(1), 9–18.

Chappell, N., Gee, E., McDonald, L., & Stones, M. (2003). *Aging in contemporary Canada.* Toronto: Prentice Hall.

Chau, E. (2005, April 15). MPP fights for grandparents. *Niagara This Week,* p. 22.

Cheadle, B. (2000, October 17). Food bank users double in 10 years. *Toronto Star,* p. A1.

Cheng, T. O. (1999). Teenage smoking in China. *Journal of Adolescence, 22,* 607–620.

Chesnais, J.-C. (1997, January). The demographic sunset of the west? *Population Today, 25*(1), 4–5.

Christensen, J. (2000). Africa: Dying by the numbers. Available at www.cnn.com/SPECIALS/2000/aids/stories/overview/AIDS.

Chui, T., Tran, K., & Flanders, J. (2005, Spring). Chinese Canadians: Enriching the cultural mosaic. *Canadian Social Trends,* 24–32. Catalogue no. 11-008.

Chung, Lucy. (2006, June). "Education and Earnings." *Perspectives on Labour and Income.* Statistics Canada, Catalogue No. 75-001-XIE: pp. 5–12.

Church, Gardner, Greenberg, Kenneth, & McPhedran, Marilou. (1997). "Toronto: An Urban Alternative," in Robert Geddes, ed., *Cities in Our Future: Growth and Form, Environmental Health and Social Equity.* Island Press: pp. 93–113.

Clark, S. D. (1942). *The social development of Canada: An introductory study with select documents.* Toronto: University of Toronto Press.

Clark, W. (2007). Delayed Transitions of Young Adults. *Canadian Social Trends* (Fall), pp. 14–22.

Clark, W., Schellenberg, G. (2006). Who's Religious? *Canadian Social Trends 81* (Summer), pp. 2–9.

Clarke, L. H. (2001). Older women's bodies and the self: The construction of identity in later life. *Canadian Review of Sociology and Anthropology, 38,* 441–464.

Claxton, A. & Perry-Jenkins, M. (2008). "No Fun Anymore: Leisure and Marital Quality Across the Transition to Parenthood." *Journal of Marriage and the Family.* 70, February, 28–43.

Clement, W. (1975). *The Canadian corporate elite: An analysis of economic power.* Toronto: McClelland and Stewart.

Clement, W. (1977). *Continental corporate power: Economic elite linkages between Canada and the United States.* Toronto: McClelland and Stewart.

Clement, W. (1983). *Class, power and property: Essays on Canadian society.* Toronto: McClelland and Stewart.

Clement, W., & Myles, J. (1994). *Relations of ruling: Class and gender in postindustrial societies.* Montreal: McGill-Queen's University Press.

Cloward, R. A., & Ohlin, L. E. (1960). *Delinquency and opportunity: A theory of delinquent gangs.* New York: Free Press.

Cnaan, R. A. (1991, December). Neighborhood-representing organizations: How democratic are they? *Social Science Review,* 614–634.

CNN World News. (2002, December 12). "Honor killings" rise in Pakistan. Available at www.cnn.com.

Cohen, A. (1997, April 21). The great American welfare lab. *Time,* 74–76, 78.

Cohen, J. E. (1996, January). How many people can the earth support? *Population Today,* 4–5.

Colapinto, John. (2001). *As Nature Made Him: The Boy Who Was Raised as a Girl.* New York: Harper Collins.

Colasanti, Toni, Slevin, Kathleen F., & King, Neal. (2006, Spring). "Ageism and Feminism: From 'et Cetera' to Center." *National Women's Studies Association Journal,* 18(1): pp. 13–30.

Cole, J., & Lubman, S. (1994, January 28). Weapons merchants are going great guns in post-Cold War era. *Wall Street Journal,* pp. A1, A4.

Coleman, J. W. (1995). Politics and the abuse of power. In J. M. Henslin (Ed.), *Down to earth sociology: Introductory readings* (8th ed., pp. 442–450). New York: Free Press.

Collings, P. (2001). "If you got everything, it's good enough": Perspectives on successful aging in a Canadian Inuit community. *Journal of Cross-Cultural Gerontology, 16,* 127–155.

Collins, P. H. (1996, December). Learning from the outsider within: The sociological significance of Black feminist thought. *Social Problems, 33*(6), 514–532.

Collins, R. (1974). *Conflict sociology: Toward an explanatory science.* New York: Academic Press.

Collins, R. (1979). *The credential society: An historical sociology of education.* New York: Academic Press.

Collins, R. (1988). *Theoretical sociology.* San Diego: Harcourt, Brace Jovanovich.

Collins, R., Chafetz, J. S., Blumberg, R. L., Coltrane, S., & Turner, J. H. (1993). Toward an integrated theory of gender stratification. *Sociological Perspectives, 36*(3), 185–216.

Community Information Centre of Metropolitan Toronto. (1997). *55 plus Ontario: A handbook on services for older adults.* Toronto: The Community Information Centre.

Connell, R. W. (2000). Masculinities and globalization. In M. Zinn, P. Hondagneu-Sotelo, & M. Messner (Eds.), *Gender through the prism of difference* (2nd ed., pp. 49–62). Boston: Allyn and Bacon.

Connell, R. W. (2000). *The men and the boys*. Berkeley: University of California Press.

Conseur, A., Hathcote, J. M., & Kim, S. (2008). Consumer Masculinity Behaviour Among College Students and Its Relationship to Self Esteem and Media Significance. *Sex Roles* 58, 549–555.

Cooke, L. (2007). "Persistent Policy Effects on the Division of Domestic Tasks in Reunified Germany." *Journal of Marriage and the Family*. 69, November, 930–950.

Cooley, C. H. (1902). *Human nature and the social order*. New York: Scribner's.

Cooperatives Secretariat. (2003). *Cooperatives in Canada*. Ottawa: Cooperatives Secretariat, Government of Canada.

Copper, B. (2001). Voices: On becoming old women. In S. Shaw and J. Lee (Eds.), *Women's Voices, Feminist Visions: Classic and Contemporary Readings* (pp. 94–97). Mountain View, California: Mayfield Publishing Company.

Corsaro, William A. (2004). *The Sociology of Childhood*. Second Edition. Thousand Oaks, California: Pine Forge Press.

Coser, L. A. (1977). *Masters of sociological thought: Ideas in historical and social context* (2nd ed.). New York: Harcourt Brace Jovanovich.

Cottrell, B. (2003). Parent abuse. National Clearinghouse on Family Violence, www.phac-aspc.gc.ca/ncfv-cnivf/familyviolence/pdfs/Abuse%20E.pdf.

Courtney, K. (1995). Two sides of the environmental movement: Radical Earth First! and the Sierra Club. [Paper presented at the 1995 meetings of the American Sociological Association].

Cousins, A., & Nagpaul, H. (1970). *Urban man and society*. New York: McGraw-Hill.

Cowley, G. (1996, November 16). Attention: Aging men. *Newsweek*, 66–75.

Cowley, J. (1969). *Pioneers of Women's Liberation*. New York: Merit.

Crane, D. (2000, September 17). Poverty guarantees a nastier world. *Toronto Star*, p. B6.

Cribb, R. & Brazao. (2007 October 20) "Big-box daycare coming to Canada". *Toronto Star*. www.thestar.com/News/Canada/article/268752.

Crompton, S. (2000, Winter). 100 years of . . . health. *Canadian Social Trends*, pp. 12–17.

Crossen, C. (1991, November 14). *Wall Street Journal*, pp. A1, A7.

Cruikshank, M. (2003). *Learning to be Old: Gender, Culture, and Aging*. Lanham: Rowman & Littlefield Publishers, Inc.

Cuddy, A. J. C., & Fiske, S. T. (2002). Doddering but dear: Process, content, and function in stereotyping of older persons. In T. D. Nelson (Ed.), *Ageism: Stereotyping and prejudice against older persons* (pp. 3–26). Cambridge, MA: A Bradford Book/The MIT Press.

Cunningham, G. B. (2008). Creating and Sustaining Gender Diversity in Sport Organizations. *Sex Roles*. 58, pp. 136–145.

Currie, E. (2004). *The Road to Whatever: Middle-Class Culture and The Crisis of Adolescence*.New York: Metropolitan Books.

Curtis, B., Livingstone, D. W., & Smaller, H. (1992). *Stacking the Deck: The Streaming of Working-Class Kids in Ontario Schools*. Montreal: Our Schools/Our Selves Education Foundation.

Curtis, J., Grabb, E., & Guppy, N. (Eds.). (1999). *Social Inequality in Canada: Patterns, Problems, and Policies* (3rd ed.). Toronto: Prentice-Hall.

Curwin, E. C., & Hart, G. (1961). *Plough and pasture*. New York: Collier Books.

Cyberschool makes its debut. (1996, January). *The American Schoolboard*, 183, 1, A11.

Dagg, A. I. (2004). *Love of Shopping Is Not a Gene: Problems with Darwinian Psychology*. Montreal: Black Rose Books.

Dahl, R. A. (1961). *Who governs?* New Haven, CT: Yale University Press.

Dahl, R. A. (1982). *Dilemmas of pluralist democracy: Autonomy vs. control*. New Haven, CT: Yale University Press.

Dahrendorf, R. (1959). *Class and class conflict in industrial society*. Palo Alto, CA: Stanford University Press.

The Daily. (2006, July 31). Births 2004. www.statcan.ca/Daily/English.

The Daily. (2007, June 13). General Social Survey: Navigating family transitions. www.statcan.ca/Daily/English.

The Daily. (2007, October 29). Study: Frequency of contact between separated fathers and their children. www.statcan.ca/Daily/English.

The Daily. (2007, December 4). 2006 Census: Immigration, citizenship, language, mobility and migration. www.statcan.ca/Daily/English/.

The Daily. (2007, December 19). Study: Returning to work after childbirth. www.statcan.ca/Daily/English/.

The Daily. (2008, February 7). Study: Participation in Sports. www.statcan.ca/Daily/English.

The Daily. (2008, May 1). 2006 Census: earnings, income and shelter costs. www.statcan.ca/Daily/English.

The Daily. (2008, May 5) Income of Canadians. www.statcan.ca/Daily/English.

The Daily. (2008, June 11). Family income and related variables: Sub-provincial data. www.statcan.ca/Daily/English.

Daly, Rita. (2006, December 8). "Woman's Extra Pay Costs Her Daycare." *Toronto Star*, p. A4.

Danesi, M. (2003). *Forever young: The "teen-aging" of modern culture*. Toronto: University of Toronto Press.

Darnell, V. (1971, May). Qualitative-quantitative content analysis of graffiti in the public restrooms of St. Louis, Missouri, and Edwardsville, Illinois [Master's thesis]. Edwardsville, IL: Southern Illinois University.

Das Gupta, T. (2000). Families of Native people, immigrants and people of colour. In N. Mandell & A. Duffy, *Canadian families: Diversity, conflict and change* (pp. 146–187). Toronto: Harcourt Brace & Company, Canada.

Davies, Scott. (1999). Stubborn disparities: Explaining class inequalities in schooling. In J. Curtis, E. Grubb, and N. Guppy, (Eds.), *Social Inequality in Canada: Patterns, Problems, Policies*. Toronto: Prentice-Hall.

Davies, Scott & Guppy, Neil. (2006). *The Schooled Society: An Introduction to the Sociology of Education*. Toronto: Oxford University Press.

Davis, A., Gardner, B. B., & Gardner, M. R. (1941). *Deep south: A social-anthropological study of caste and class*. Chicago: University of Chicago Press.

Davis, F. (1959, September). The cabdriver and his fare: Facets of a fleeting relationship. *American Journal of Sociology*, 65, 158–165.

Davis, K., & Moore, W. E. (1945). Some principles of stratification. *American Sociological Review*, 10, 242–249.

Davis, K., & Moore, W. E. (1953). Reply to Tumin. *American Sociological Review*, 18, 394–396.

Davis, N. J., & Robinson, R. V. (1988, February). Class identification of men and women in the 1970s and 1980s. *American Sociological Review*, 53, 103–112.

Davis, N. J. (1978). Prostitution: Identity, career, and legal-economic enterprise. In J. M. Henslin & E. Sagarin (Eds.), *The sociology of sex: An introductory reader* (rev. ed., pp. 195–222). New York: Schocken Books.

De George, R. T. (1968). *The new Marxism: Society and East European Marxism since 1956*. New York: Pegasus.

Deegan, M. J. (1988, Winter). W. E. B. du Bois and the women of Hull-House, 1895–1899. *American Sociologist*, 301–311.

DeGraff, J. (2003, April 12). Workweek woes. *New York Times*, p. 19.

de Jong Gierveld, J., & Havens, B. (2004). Cross-national comparisons of social isolation and loneliness: Introduction and overview. *Canadian Journal on Aging, 23*(2), 109–113.

DeKeseredy, W., & Hinch, R. (1991). *Woman Abuse: Sociological Perspectives*. Toronto: Thompson Educational Publishers.

Del Castillo, D. (2002). A sociology professor in Mauritania fights its slave system. *Chronicle of Higher Education*, May 31, A39–A40.

DeMartini, J. R. (1982). Basic and applied sociological work: Divergence, convergence, or peaceful co-existence? *The Journal of Applied Behavioral Science, 18*(2), 203–215.

DeMause, L. (1975, April). Our forebears made childhood a nightmare. *Psychology Today 8*(11), 85–88.

Demos, Telis & Tkaczyk, Christopher. (2007). "Global 500: The Top 25." Fortune, CNNMoney.com, http://money.cnn.com/galleries/2007/fortune/0707/gallery.global500_top25.fortune/index:html. Accessed: March 10, 2008).

Dentzler, S. (1991, April 22). The vanishing dream. *U.S. News and World Report,* 39–43.

Denzin, N. K. (1992, July–August). The suicide machine. *Society,* 7–10.

Department of Indian Affairs and Northern Development (DIAND). (2001). Basic departmental data. Accessed March 2002 at www.ainc-inac.gc.ca/pr/sts/bdd01/bdd01_e.pdf.

Desroches, Frederick. (1990). 'Tearoom Trade': A research update. *Qualitative Sociology*, Volume 31, Number 1, pp. 39–61.

Deutsch, A. (2000, September 13). Dutch bill gives gays right to marry. *Toronto Star*, p. A13.

Deutsch, F., Kokot, A. & Binder, K. (2007). "College Women's Plans for Different Types of Egalitarian Marriages." *Journal of Marriage and the Family.* 69 (November), 916–929.

Devreux, A. (2007). 'New Fatherhood' in Practice: Domestic and Parental Work Performed by Men in France and in the Netherlands. *Journal of Comparative Family Studies.* 38, 1, 87–103.

De Vries, B., & Johnson, C. (2002). The death of friends in later life. In R. A. Settersten, Jr. & T. J. Owens (Eds.), *New frontiers in socialization* (pp. 299–324). Amsterdam: JAI.

De Waal, F. (2005). *Our Inner Ape.* New York: Riverhead Books.

de Young, M. (1989, March). The world according to NAMBLA: Accounting for deviance. *Journal of Sociology and Social Welfare, 16*(1), 111–126.

Diamond, M. (1982). Sexual identity: Monozygotic twins reared in discordant sex roles and a BBC follow-up. *Archives of Sexual Behavior, 11*(2), 181–186.

Dickson, T., & McLachlan, H. V. (1989). In search of "the spirit of capitalism": Weber's misinterpretation of Franklin. *Sociology, 23*(1), 81–89.

Dill, K. E., & Thill, K. P. (2007). Video Game Characters and the Socialization of Gender Roles: Young People's Perceptions Mirror Sexist Media Depictions. *Sex Roles 58,* 851–864.

Dinnerstein, M., & Weitz, R. (2002). Jane Fonda, Barbara Bush and other aging bodies: Femininity and the limits of resistance. In K. S. Ratcliff (Ed.), *Women and Health: Power, Technology, Inequality, and Conflict in a Gendered World* (pp. 180–190). Boston: Allyn and Bacon.

Dinshaw, F. M. (2004). Elder abuse: South Asian women speak up. *Education Wife Assault Newsletter on Older Woman Abuse, 13*(1).

Dirks, G. E. (1995). *Controversy and Complexity: Canadian Immigration Policy During the 1980s.* Montreal: McGill-Queen's University Press.

Dobriner, W. M. (1969). *Social Structures and Systems.* Pacific Palisades, CA: Goodyear.

Domhoff, G. W. (1978). *Who really rules? New Haven and community power reexamined.* New Brunswick, NJ: Transaction.

Domhoff, G. W. (1983). *Who rules America now? A view of the '80s.* Englewood Cliffs, NJ: Prentice Hall.

Domhoff, G. W. (1990). *The power elite and the state: How policy is made in America.* Hawthorne, NY: Aldine de Gruyter.

Domhoff, G. William. (1996). *State Autonomy or Class Dominance? Case Studies on Policy Making in America.* Hawthorne, N.Y.: Aldine de Gruyter.

Domhoff, G. W. (1997). The Bohemian grove and other retreats. In J. M. Henslin (Ed.), *Down to earth sociology: Introductory readings* (9th ed., pp. 340–352). New York: Free Press.

Domhoff, G. William. (2006). *Who Rules America? Power, Politics, and Social Change. 5th Edition.* New York: McGraw-Hill.

Doren, K., & Jones, C. (2000). *You Go Girl! Winning the Woman's Way.* Kansas City: Andrews McMeel Publishing.

Doucet, A. (2006). *Do Men Mother: Fathering, Care and Domestic Responsibility.* Toronto: University of Toronto Press.

Dowd, M. (2002, December 5). The knife under the tree. *New York Times,* p. 24.

Downe, P. J. (2006) Aboriginal Girls in Canada: Living Histories of Dislocation, Exploitation and Strength. In Y. Jiwani, C. Steenbergen, C. Mitchell (Eds.), *Girlhood: Redefining the Limits.* (pp. 1–14). Montreal: Black Rose.

Doyle, J. A. (1995). *The male experience* (3rd ed.). Madison, WI: WCB Brown & Benchmark Publishers.

Doyle, A. (2002, March 8). Equality coming to boardroom: Norway to require at least 40% of directors be women. *Toronto Star*, p. A12.

Drolet, M. (2002). *The "who, what, when and where" of gender pay differentials.* Ottawa: Statistics Canada, Catalogue 71-584-MIE No. 4.

Drolet, M. (2005). *Participation in postsecondary education in Canada: Has the role of parental income and education changed over the 1990s?* Ottawa: Statistics Canada, Catalogue 11F0019MIE No. 243.

Drucker, P. F. (1987, April 22). The rise and fall of the blue-collar worker. *Wall Street Journal*, p. 36.

Drucker, P. F. (1992, February 11). There's more than one kind of team. *Wall Street Journal*, p. A16.

Drucker, P. F. (1994, November). The age of social transformation. *Atlantic Monthly,* 274(5), 53+.

Du Bois, W. E. B. (1992). *Black reconstruction in America, 1860–1889.* New York: Atheneum. (First published 1935).

Duchesne, D. (2002, Summer). Seniors at work. *Perspectives on Labour and Income, 14,* pp. 33–44.

Duffy, A. (1996). Bad girls in hard times: Canadian female juvenile offenders. In G. M. O'Bireck (Ed.), *Not A Kid Anymore: Canadian Youth, Crime and Subcultures* (pp. 203–220). Toronto: Nelson Canada.

Duffy, A., & Momirov, J. (1997). *Family violence: A Canadian introduction.* Toronto: Lorimer.

Duffy, A. & Pupo, N. (1992). *The part-time paradox: Connecting gender, work and family.* Toronto: McClelland and Stewart.

Duffy, A. & Pupo, N. (1996). Family-friendly organizations and beyond: proposals for policy directions with women in mind. National Forum on Family Security. Ottawa: Canada Council on Social Development.

Duffy, A., Glenday, D., & Pupo, N. (Eds.). (1997). *Good Jobs, Bad Jobs, No Jobs: The Transformation of Work in the 21st Century.* Toronto: Harcourt Brace.

Duffy, A., Mandell, N. & Pupo, N. (1989). *Few choices: Women, work and family.* Toronto: Garamond Press.

Dugger, Celia W. (2001, April 22). "Abortion in India Is Tipping Scales Sharply Against Girls." *New York Times*.

Dunlap, R. E., & Catton, W. R., Jr. (1979). Environmental sociology. *Annual Review of Sociology, 5,* 243–273.

Dunlap, R. E., & Catton, W. R., Jr. (1983). What environmental sociologists have in common whether concerned with "built" or "natural" environments. *Sociological Inquiry, 53*(2/3), 113–135.

Dunphy, Bill. (2006, December 14). "Rich and Poor Gap Widens." *The Hamilton Spectator*, p. A14.

Durbin, S. (1995, July–August). Mexico. *Population Today, 7.*

Durkheim, E. (1933). *The division of labor in society* (G. Simpson, Trans.). New York: Free Press. (First published 1893).

Durkheim, E. (1938, 1958, 1964). *The rules of sociological method* (S. A. Solovay & J. H. Mueller, Trans.). New York: Free Press. (First published 1895).

Durkheim, E. (1965). *The elementary forms of the religious life.* New York: Free Press. (First published 1912).

Durkheim, E. (1966). *Suicide: A study in sociology* (J. A. Spaulding & G. Simpson, Trans.). New York: Free Press. (First published 1897).

Durning, A. (1990). Cradles of life. In L. W. Barnes (Ed.), *Social Problems 90/91* (pp. 231–241). Guilford, CT: Dushkin.

Dyke, D. J. (1991). *Crucified women.* Toronto: United Church.

Ebden, Theresa. (2006, October 30). "Retiring, but Not Quitting." *The Globe and Mail*, pp. E1, E6.

Ebert, R. (2004, June 18). *Napoleon Dynamite* (Review).

Eckholm, Erik. (2002, June 21). "Desire for Sons Drives Use of Prenatal Scans in China." *New York Times*.

Ecklund, E. H. (2008). Religion and Spirituality Among Scientists. *Contexts* 7(1): pp. 12–15.

Eder, K. (1990). The rise of counter-culture movements against modernity: Nature as a new field of class struggle. *Theory, Culture & Society, 7,* 21–47.

Edgerton, R. B. (1992). *Sick societies: Challenging the myth of primitive harmony.* New York: Free Press.

Edwards, R. (1979). *Contested terrain: The transformation of the workplace in the twentieth century.* New York: Basic Books.

Ehrenreich, B., & English, D. (1973). *Witches, midwives, and nurses: A history of women healers.* Old Westbury, NY: Feminist Press.

Eibl-Eibesfeldt, I. (1970). *Ethology: The biology of behavior.* New York: Holt, Rinehart, and Winston.

Eichler, M. (1988a). *Families in Canada today: Recent changes and their policy consequences* (2nd ed.). Toronto: Gage Educational Publishing.

Eichler, M. (1988b). *Nonsexist research methods: A practical guide.* New York: Routledge.

Eichler, M. (1997). *Family shifts: Families, policies and gender equality.* Toronto: Oxford University Press.

Eisenhart, R. W. (1975, Fall). You can't hack it, little girl: A discussion of the covert psychological agenda of modern combat training. *Journal of Social Issues, 31,* 13–23.

Ekman, P., Friesen, W. V., & Bear, J. (1984, May). The international language of gestures. *Psychology Today, 64.*

Elkins, S. M. (1968). *Slavery: A problem in American institutional and intellectual life* (2nd ed.). Chicago: University of Chicago Press.

Elliott, Patricia & Mandell, Nancy. (2001). "Feminist Theories." In N. Mandell, editor. *Feminist Issues: Race, Class and Sexuality.* Toronto: Prentice Hall, pp. 23–48.

Elwell, S. (1996). Women's voices: The challenges of feminism to Judaism. In C. Wessenger (Ed.), *Religious institutions and women's leadership: New roles inside the mainstream* (pp. 331–43). Columbia, SC: University of South Carolina.

Engels, F. (1942). *The origin of the family, private property, and the state.* New York: International Publishing. (First published in 1884).

Epstein, C. F. (1988). *Deceptive distinctions: Sex, gender, and the social order.* New Haven, CT: Yale University Press.

Epstein, C. F. (1989, January 26). Letter to the author.

Epstein, Cynthia Fuchs. (2007, February). Great Divides: The Cultural, Cognitive and Social Bases of the Global Subordination of Women. *American Sociological Review, 72:* pp. 1–22.

Ernst, E. G. (1988). The Baptists. In C. H. Lippy & P. W. Williams (Eds.), *Encyclopedia of the American religious experience: Studies of traditions and movements* (Vol. 1, pp. 555–577). New York: Scribners.

Erturk, Y. (1994). The status of Moslem women in Turkey and Saudi Arabia. In J. Curtis & L. Tepperman (Eds.), *Haves and have-nots: An international reader on social inequality* (pp. 288–293). Englewood Cliffs, NJ: Prentice Hall.

Ethos Strategy Group. (2007). *Homelessness: A Teacher's Guide.* Vancouver: Greater Vancouver Regional Steering Committee on Homelessness.

Etzioni, A. (Ed.). (1969). *The semi-professions and their organization.* New York: Free Press.

Faludi, S. (1999). *Stiffed: The betrayal of the American man.* New York: Willian Morrow & Company.

Fanon, F. (1962). *Wretched of the earth.* New York: Grove Press.

Faris, R. E. L., & Dunham, W. (1939). *Mental disorders in urban areas.* Chicago: University of Chicago Press.

Farkas, G. (1996). *Human capital or cultural capital?: Ethnicity and poverty groups in an urban school district.* New York: Walter DeGruyter.

Farkas, G., Sheehan, D., & Grobe, R. P. (1990, Winter). Coursework mastery and school success: Gender, ethnicity, and poverty groups within an urban school district. *American Educational Research Journal, 27*(4), 807–827.

Farkas, G., Grobe, R. P., Sheehan, D., & Shuan, Y. (1990, February). Cultural resources and school success: Gender, ethnicity, and poverty groups within an urban school district. *American Sociological Review, 55,* 127–142.

Fast, J., Frederick, J., Zukewich, N., & Franke, S. (2001, Winter). The time of our lives. *Canadian Social Trends, 63,* pp. 20–23.

Faulkner, E. M. (2001). Empowering Victim Advocates: Organizing Anti-Gay/Lesbian Violence in Canada. *Critical Criminology. 1,* pp. 1–16.

Faulkner, Rob. (2008, April 11). Getting a Second Chance: More Women Than Men Go Back To Finish High School. *The Hamilton Spectator*, p. A4.

Faunce, W. A. (1981). *Problems of an industrial society* (2nd ed.). New York: McGraw-Hill.

Featherman, D.L. (1979). Opportunities are expanding. *Society, 13,* 4–11.

Featherman, D. L., & Hauser, R. M. (1978). *Opportunity and change.* New York: Academic Press.

Federal, Provincial, and Territorial Advisory Committee on Population Health. (1999). *Statistical report on the health of Canadians.* Ottawa: Health Canada.

Federal, Provincial, and Territorial Advisory Committee on Population Health for the Meeting of Ministers of Health. (1999). *Toward a healthy future: Second report on the health of Canadians.* Ottawa: Minister of Public Works.

Ferguson, K. E. (1984). *The Feminist Case Against Bureaucracy.* Philadelphia: Temple University Press.

Ferguson, R. (2004, August 21). Is 65 just a number? *Toronto Star*, p. A4.

Ferguson, T. (1995). *Golden Rule*. Chicago: University of Chicago.

Feshbach, M., & Friendly, A., Jr. (1992). *Ecocide in the USSR: Health and nature under siege*. New York: Basic Books.

Fidelman, C. (2008, May 6). Abuse alters genetics, McGill study shows. *Montreal Gazette*. Available at www.canada.com.

Finnie, R. (2000, September). The dynamics of poverty in Canada. C.D. Howe Institute Commentary, 145.

Firestone, Shulamith. (1970). *The Dialectic of Sex*. New York: Morrow.

Fisher, S. (1986). *In the patient's best interest: Women and the politics of medical decisions*. New Brunswick, NJ: Rutgers University Press.

Fishman, C. (2003). The Wal-Mart you don't know. *Fast Company*, 77 (December). Accessed at: http://pf.fastcompany.com/magazine/77/walmart.html.

Fitzgerald, M. (2004, July 18). A drive-through lane to the next time zone. *New York Times*, p. BU3.

Flavelle, Dana. (2006, March 2). Gender Gap at the Big Table. *The Hamilton Spectator*, p. A16.

Fleras, A., & Elliott, J. L. (1996). *Unequal Relations: An Introduction to Race, Ethnic, and Aboriginal Dynamics in Canada* (2nd ed.). Scarborough, ON: Prentice Hall.

Flink, J. J. (1990). *The automobile age*. Cambridge, MA: MIT Press.

Foley, D. E. (1997). The great American football ritual. In J. M. Henslin (Ed.), *Down to earth sociology: Introductory readings* (9th ed., pp. 412–475). New York: Free Press.

Foley, L. A., Evancic, C., Karnik, K., King, J., & Parks, A. (1995, February). Date rape: Effects of race of assailant and victim and gender of subjects on perceptions. *Journal of Black Psychology, 21*(1), 6–18.

Food and Agriculture Organization of the United Nations. (2006). "World and Regional Review: Facts and Figures."

Foote, J. (1990, February 5). Trying to take back the planet. *Newsweek, 115*(6), 24–25.

Forbes, G. B., & Frederick, D. A. (2008). "The UCLA Body Project II: Breast and Body Dissatisfaction among African, Asian, European and Hispanic American College Women." *Sex Roles*. 58: 449–457.

Forcese, D. (1997). *The Canadian class structure* (4th ed.). Toronto: McGraw-Hill Ryerson.

Fost, Dan. (2008). "They're Working on Their Own, Just Side by Side." nytimes.com, accessed February 20, 2008 at www.nytimes.com/2008/02/20/business/businessspecial2/20cowork.html?pagewanted=1&_r=1&ref=businessspecial2.

Fouts, G., & Vaughan, K. (2002). Television situation comedies: Male weight, negative references, and audience reactions. *Sex Roles, 46*(11/12), 439–442.

Francis, D. (1986). *Controlling interest: Who owns Canada?* Toronto: Macmillan.

Fraser, J., Maticka-Tyndale, E., & Smylie, L. (2004). Sexuality of Canadian women at midlife. *The Canadian Journal of Human Sexuality, 13*(3–4), 171–187.

Frederick, D. A., Forbes, G. B., Grigorian, K. E., & Jarcho, J. M. (2007). The UCLA Body Project 1: Gender and Ethnic Differences in Self-Objectification and Body Satisfaction Among 2,206 Undergraduates. *Sex Roles*. 57: pp. 317–327.

Frederick, J. A., & Fast, J. E. (1999, Autumn). Eldercare in Canada: Who does how much? *Canadian Social Trends, 54*, 26–30.

French, Howard W. (2004, April 14). As Girls 'Vanish,' Chinese City Battles Tide of Abortions. *New York Times*.

Frenette, M. & Zeman, K. (2007). *Why Are Most University Students Women? Evidence Based on Academic Performance, Study Habits and Parental Influences*. Statistics Canada catalogue no. 11F0019MIF. Ottawa: Minister of Industry.

Frenette, Marc, Hou, Feng, Morissette, Rene, Wannell, Ted, & Webber, Maryanne. (2008, May). *Earnings and Incomes of Canadians Over the Past Quarter Century, 2006 Census*. Statistics Canada, Catalogue 97-563-X.

Freud, S. (1930). *Civilization and its discontents*. Translated and edited by J. Strachey. New York: W.W. Norton.

Freudenburg, W. R., & Gramling, R. (1989, November). The emergence of environmental sociology: Contributions of E. Dunlap and William R. Catton, Jr. *Sociological Inquiry, 59*(4), 439–452.

Frideres, J., & Gadacz, R. (2001). *Aboriginal Peoples in Canada: Contemporary Conflicts* (6th ed.). Toronto: Prentice Hall.

Friedan, B. (1963). *The feminine mystique*. New York: Dell Publishing Co., Inc.

Friedan, B. (1993). *The Fountain of Age*. New York: Simon and Shuster.

Friedl, E. (1990). Society and sex roles. In J. P. Spradley & McCurdy, D. W. (Eds.), *Conformity and conflict: Readings in cultural anthropology* (pp. 229–238). Glenview, IL: Scott, Foresman.

Fulcher, M., Sutfin, E.L., & Patterson, C.J. (2008) Individual Differences in Gender Development: Associations with Parental Sexual Orientation, Attitudes, and Division of Labor. *Sex Roles* 58, 330–341.

Furtado, C. (1984). *The economic growth of Brazil: A survey of colonial to modern times*. Westport, CT: Greenwood Press.

Gabler, J. & Kaufman, J. (2006). Chess, Cheerleading, Chopin: What Gets You Into College? *Contexts*, 5(2): 45–49.

Gagne, L. G. (2003). *Parental work, child-care use and young children's cognitive outcomes*. Research Paper. Statistics Canada Catalogue no. 89-594-XIE. Ottawa: Minister of Industry.

Galabuzi, Grace-Edward. (2006). *Canada's Economic Apartheid: The Social Exclusion of Racialized Groups in the New Century*. Toronto: Canadian Scholars' Press.

Galambos, N. & Krahn, H. (2008). "Depression and Anger Trajectories During the Transition to Adulthood." *Journal of Marriage and the Family*. 70 (February), 15–27.

Galarneau, D. & Morissette, R. (2004, June). Immigrants: Settling for less? *Perspectives on labour and income*, pp. 5–16. Catalogue no. 75-001-XIE.

Galbraith, J. K. (1979). *The nature of mass poverty*. Cambridge, MA: Harvard University Press.

Galinsky, E. (1999). *Ask the children: What America's children really think about working parents*. New York: William Morrow and Company.

Galinsky, E., & Stein, P. J. (1990, December). The impact of human resource policies on employees: Balancing work/family life. *Journal of Family Issues, 11*(4), 368–383.

Galliher, J. F. (1991). *Deviant behavior and human rights*. Englewood Cliffs, NJ: Prentice Hall.

Gallmeier, C. P. (1988). Methodological issues in qualitative sport research: Participant observation among hockey players. *Sociological Spectrum, 8*, 213–235.

Gans, H. J. (1962). *The urban villagers*. New York: Free Press.

Gans, H. J. (1968). *People and plans: Essays on urban problems and solutions*. New York: Basic Books.

Gans, H. J. (1970). Urbanism and suburbanism. In A. N. Cousins & H. Nagpaul (Eds.), *Urban man and society: A reader in urban ecology* (pp. 157–164). New York: Knopf.

Gans, H. J. (1991). *People, plans, and policies: Essays on poverty, racism, and other national urban problems*. New York: Columbia University Press.

Gardner, D. (2004). Getting tough with young offenders. Responding to youth crime: Do get-tough policies work? In J. V. Roberts & M. G. Grossman (Eds.), *Criminal Justice in Canada—A reader* (2nd ed.). Scarborough: Nelson/Thomson.

Garfinkel, H. (1956, March). Conditions of successful degradation ceremonies. *American Journal of Sociology, 61*(2), 420–424.

Garrison, Jessica. (2007, February 3). "This Teacher is No Ordinary Joe." *The Hamilton Spectator*, p. A8.

Gazso-Windle, A., & McMullin, J. A. (2003). Doing domestic labour: Strategizing in a gendered domain. *Canadian Journal of Sociology, 28*(3), 341–366.

Gelles, R. J., & Cornell, C. P. (1985). *Intimate violence in families*. Beverly Hills, CA: Sage Publications.

Gerson, K. (1985). *Hard choices: How women decide about work, career, and motherhood*. Berkeley: University of California Press.

Gerth, H. H., & Mills, C. W. (1958). *From Max Weber: Essays in sociology*. New York: Galaxy.

Giddens, A. (1978). *Emile Durkheim*. New York: Penguin Books.

Giele, J. Z., & Elder, G. H., Jr. (1998). Life course research: Development of a field. In J. Z. Giele & G. H. Elder, Jr. (Eds.), *Methods of life course research: Qualitative and quantitative Approaches* (pp. 5–27). Thousand Oaks: Sage Publications.

Gilbert, D., & Kahl, J. A. (1982). *The American class structure: A new synthesis*. Homewood, IL: Dorsey Press.

Gilbert, D., & Kahl, J. A. (1993). *The American class structure: A new synthesis* (4th ed.). Homewood, IL: Dorsey Press.

Giles, J. (2008 February 2). Born That Way. *New Scientist*. Issue 2641.

Gillborn, D. (1992). Citizenship, "race" and the hidden curriculum. *International Studies in the Sociology of Education, 2*(1), 57–73.

Gilleard, C. (2002, March). Aging and old age in Medieval society and the transition of modernity. *Journal of Aging and Identity, 7*, 25–41.

Gilman, C. P. (1971). *The man-made world or, our androcentric culture*. New York. (First published 1911).

Girard, D. (2002, July 20). The picture if we don't do anything is quite depressing. *Toronto Star*, pp. E1, E3.

Girard, D. (2005, April 20). "We're a normal bunch," B.C. polygamists insist. *Toronto Star*, p. A15.

Gitlin, T. (1997). *The twilight of common dreams: Why America is wracked by culture wars*. New York: Metropolitan Books.

Glauber, R. (2007). Marriage and the Motherhood Wage Penalty Among African Americans, Hispanics and Whites. *Journal of Marriage and the Family*. 69 (November), pp. 951–961.

Gleberzon, B., & Cutler, J. (2005). Age waves: Managing the transition to an older society. *CARP Action*, June, p. 4.

Glenday, D. (1996). Mean streets and hard time: Youth unemployment and crime in Canada. In G. O'Bireck (Ed.), *Not a kid anymore: Canadian youth, crime and subcultures* (pp. 147–174). Toronto: Nelson.

Glenday, D. (1997). Lost horizons, leisure shock: Good jobs, bad jobs, uncertain future. In D. Glenday, *Good jobs, bad jobs, no jobs: The transformation of work in the 21st century* (pp. 8–34). Toronto: Harcourt Brace.

Glenday, D., & McMullan, J. (1970). *An historical examination into the history of the sociology of Québec*. [Paper presented to the Canadian Sociology and Anthropology Association meetings]. Newfoundland.

Goelman, H., Marshall, S. K., & Ross, S., Eds. (2004). *Multiple Lenses, Multiple Images: Perspectives on the Child Across Time, Space and Disciplines*. Toronto: University of Toronto Press.

Goffman, E. (1961). *Asylums: Essays on the social situation of mental patients and other inmates*. Chicago: Aldine.

Goffman, E. (1963). *Stigma: Notes on the management of spoiled identity*. Englewood Cliffs, NJ: Prentice Hall.

Goffman, E. (1977). The arrangement between the sexes. *Theory and Society, 4*, 301–331.

Gold, R. (1952). Janitors versus tenants: A status–income dilemma. *American Journal of Sociology, 58*, 486–493.

Goldberg, S. (1986, September–October). Reaffirming the obvious. *Society*, 4–7.

Goldberg, S. (1993). *Why men rule: A theory of male dominance*. Chicago: Open Court.

Goleman, D. (1993, September 7). Pollsters enlist psychologists in quest for unbiased results. *New York Times*, pp. C1, C11.

Good, G. E., Porter, M. J., & Dillon, M. G. (2002). When men divulge: Portrayals of men's self-disclosure in prime-time situation comedies. *Sex Roles, 46*(11/12), 419–427.

Goode, E., & Ben-Yehuda, N. (1994). Moral panics: Culture, politics, and social construction. *Annual Review of Sociology, 20*, 149–171.

Goode, W. J. (1960, December). Encroachment, charlatanism, and the emerging profession: Psychology, sociology, and medicine. *American Sociological Review, 25*(6), 902–914.

Goodman, Lee-Anne. (2008, June 12). Kim's Basking in Banff. *The Hamilton Spectator*, p. Go19.

Goodwin, G. A., Horowitz, I. L. & Nardi, P. M. (1991, May). Laud Humphreys: A pioneer in the practice of social science. *Sociological Inquiry, 61*, 2, 139–147.

Goozen, Stephanie H. M. van, Graeme Fairchild, Heddeke Snoek, and Gordon T. Harold. (2007). The Evidence for a Neurobiological Model of Childhood Antisocial Behavior. *Psychological Bulletin*, 133(1): 149–182.

Gorman, C. (1997a, January 6). The disease detective. *Time*, 56–65.

Gorman, C. (1997b, March 24). A boy without a penis. *Time*, 83.

Gorrie, P. (2001, June 16). Is Harris right about seniors? *Toronto Star*, p. A17.

Gorrie, P. (2002, July 20). Ultimately an aging society is a victory. *Toronto Star*, pp. E1, E3.

Gorz, A. (1982). *Farewell to the working class. An essay in post-industrial socialism*. London: Pluto Press.

Gorz, A. (1985). *Paths to paradise: On the liberation from work*. London: Pluto Press.

Gourevitch, P. (1995, December 18). After the genocide. *New Yorker*, pp. 78–94.

Gracia, E. & Herrero, J. (2008). Is It Considered Violence? The Acceptability of Physical Punishment of Children in Europe. *Journal of Marriage and the Family*. 70, February, 210–217.

Graham, E. (1996, March 4). Craving closer ties, strangers come together as family. *Wall Street Journal*, pp. B1, B6.

Gray, M. (2007). Face value. *Contexts*. 6, 2, 73–75.

Greeley, A. M. (1964, Spring). The Protestant ethic: Time for a moratorium. *Sociological Analysis, 25*, 20–33.

Greenwood, E. (1962). Attributes of a profession. In S. Nosow & W. H. Form (Eds.), *Man, work, and society: A reader in the sociology of occupations* (pp. 206–218). New York: Basic Books.

Greer, G. (1991). *The Change: Women Aging and the Menopause*. New York: Fawcet Columbine.

Gregory S. Paul. (2005). Cross-National Correlations of Quantifiable Societal Health with Popular Religiosity and Secularism in the Prosperous Democracies A First Look. *Journal of Religion & Society*, Volume 7, pp. 1–17 ISSN 1522-5658.

Griffin, J. H. (1961). *Black like me.* New York: New American Library.

Gross, J. (1998, November 29). In the quest for the perfect look, more girls choose the scalpel. *New York Times.*

Guba, E. G., & Lincoln, Y. S. (1994). Competing paradigms in qualitative research. In N. K. Denzin & Y. S. Lincoln (Eds.), *Handbook of Qualitative Research.* Thousand Oaks, CA: Sage Publications.

Guha, R. (1989, Spring). Radical American environmentalism and wilderness preservation: A third world critique. *Environmental Ethics, 11*(1), 71–83.

"Guilds." (2005). *Columbia Encyclopedia,* 6th Edition. New York: Columbia University Press.

Guindon, H. (1964, Summer). Social unrest, social class, and Québec's bureaucratic revolution. *Queen's Quarterly,* pp. 12–32.

Guindon, H. (1967). Two Cultures: An essay on nationalism, class, and ethnic tension. In R. H. Leach (Ed.), *Contemporary Canada.* Duke, NC: Duke University Press.

Guindon, H. (1978). The modernization of Québec and the legitimacy of the Canadian state. In D. Glenday, H. Guindon, and A. Turowetz (Eds.), *Modernization and the Canadian State* (pp. 212–246). Toronto: Macmillan.

Guindon, H. (1988). *Québec society: Tradition, modernity and nationhood.* Toronto: University of Toronto Press.

Guindon, H. (2001). Québec's social and political evolution since 1945: A view from within. In D. Glenday and A. Duffy, (Eds.), *Canadian Society: Meeting the Challenges of the Twenty-First Century* (pp. 281–320). Toronto: Oxford University Press.

Gullette, M. M. (2004). *Aged by culture.* Chicago: University of Chicago Press.

Haas, J. (1972). Binging: Educational control among high-steel iron workers. *American Behavioral Scientist, 16,* 27–34.

Haas, J., & Shaffir, W. (1987). *Becoming Doctors: The Adoption of a Cloak of Competence.* Greenwich, CT: JAI Press.

Haas, J., & Shaffir, W. (1993). The cloak of competence. In J. M. Henslin (Ed.), *Down to earth sociology: Introductory readings* (7th ed., pp. 432–441). New York: Free Press. (First published 1978).

Hall, Michael, Lasby, David, Gumulka, Glenn, & Tryon, Catherine. (2006). *Caring Canadians, Involved Canadians: Highlights from the 2004 Survey of Giving, Volunteering and Participating.* Catalogue 71-542-XPE. Ottawa: Minister of Industry and Statistics Canada.

Hall, G. S. (1904). *Adolescence: Its psychology and its relations to physiology, anthropology, sociology, sex, crime, religion, and education.* New York: Appleton.

Hall, O. (1994). Work: The sociology of work in Canada. In A. Wipper (Ed.), *Papers in Honour of Oswald Hall.* Ottawa: Carleton University Press.

Hall, R. H. (1963, July). The concept of bureaucracy: An empirical assessment. *American Journal of Sociology, 69,* 32–40.

Hall, S. S. (1999, August 22). The bully in the mirror. *New York Times Magazine,* pp. 30–35, 58, 62, 64–65.

Halle, D. (1984). *America's working man: Work, home, and politics among blue-collar property owners.* Chicago: University of Chicago Press.

Hamermesh, D. S., & Biddle, J. E. (1994, December). Beauty and the Labor Market. *American Economic Review, 84*(5), 1174–1195.

Hamil-Luker, J. (2001). The prospects of age war: Inequality between (and within) age groups. *Social Science Research, 30,* 386–400.

Hamilton, E.A., Mintz, L., & Kashubeck-West, S. (2007). Predictors of Media Effects on Body Dissatisfaction in European American Women. *Sex Roles.* 56, pp. 397–401.

Harper, B., & Tiggemann, M. (2008). The Effect of Thin Ideal Images on Women's Self-Objectification, Mood, and Body Image. *Sex Roles.* 58, 649–657.

Harper, T. (2000, January 15). Law of the seed. *Toronto Star,* pp. L1, L3.

Harrington, M. (1962). *The other America: Poverty in the United States.* New York: Macmillan.

Harrington, M. (1977). *The vast majority: A journey to the world's poor.* New York: Simon & Schuster.

Harris, C., & Ullman, E. (1945). The nature of cities. *Annals of the American Academy of Political and Social Science, 242,* 7–17.

Harris, Chauncey D. (1997). The Nature of Cities and Urban Geography in the Last half Century. *Urban Geography,* Vol. 18.

Harris, M. (1977, November 13). Why men dominate women. *New York Times Magazine,* pp. 46, 115, 117–123.

Harrison, K. (2003). Television viewers' ideal body proportions: The case of the curvaceously thin woman. *Sex Roles, 48*(5/6), 255–264.

Harrison, P. (1993). *Inside the third world: The anatomy of poverty* (3rd ed.). London: Penguin Books.

Hartley, E. (1946). *Problems in prejudice.* New York: King's Crown Press.

Hartmann, Heidi. (1976, Spring). "Capitalism, Patriarchy, and Job Segregation by Sex." *Signs: Journal of Women and Culture in Society.* pp. 137–169.

Harvey, D. (1989). *The condition of postmodernity.* Oxford; New York: Blackwell.

Haub, C. (1997, April). New UN projections depict a variety of demographic futures. *Population Today, 25*(4), 1–3.

Haub, C., & Yinger, N. (1994). The UN long-range population projections: What they tell us. Washington, DC: Population Reference Bureau.

Haub, Carl. (2002, September–August). "Has Global Growth Reached Its Peak?" *Population Today, 30*(6): p. 6.

Haub, Carl. (2006). "World Population Data Sheet." Washington, DC: Population Reference Bureau.

Hauser, P., & Schnore, L. (Eds.). (1965). *The study of urbanization.* New York: Wiley.

Health Canada. (1999). *Statistical Report on the Health of Canadians.* Ottawa: Minister of Public Works and Government Services.

Heath, D. T. (2004). Parents' Socialization of Children in Global Perspective. In J. Macionis, N. Benokraitis, B. Ravelli (Eds.), *Seeing Ourselves: Classic, Contemporary and Cross-cultural Readings in Sociology* (pp. 102–107). Toronto: Pearson Prentice Hall.

Heesterman, W. (2005). Child Labour and Children's Rights: Policy Issues in Three Affluent Societies. In J. Goddard, S. McNamee, A. James, & A. James (Eds.), *The Politics of Childhood: International Perspectives, Contemporary Developments* (pp. 73–89). London: Palgrave Macmillan.

Heisz, A. (2001, Autumn). Low income intensity: Urban and rural families. *Perspectives on Labour and Income, 13,* pp. 14–16.

Hellinger, D., & Judd, D. R. (1991). *The Democratic Facade.* Pacific Grove, CA: Brooks/Cole.

Hendrix, L. (1994, August). What is sexual inequality? On the definition and range of variation. *Gender and Society, 28*(3), 287–307.

Henley, N., Hamilton, M., & Thorne, B. (1985). Womanspeak and manspeak. In A. G. Sargent (Ed.), *Beyond sex roles.* St. Paul, MN: West.

Henslin, J. M. (1967, September). *The cab driver: An interactional analysis of an occupational culture.* Washington University Ph.D. dissertation.

Henslin, J. M. (1990). It's not a lovely place to visit, and I wouldn't want to live there. In R. G. Burgess (Ed.), *Studies in qualitative methodology, a research annual: Reflections on field experiences* (pp. 51–76). Greenwich, CT: JAI Press.

Henslin, J. M. (1993). Trust and cabbies. In J. M. Henslin (Ed.), *Down to earth sociology: Introductory readings* (7th ed., pp. 183–196). New York: Free Press.

Henslin, J. M. (1997a). Sociology and the social sciences. In J. M. Henslin (Ed.), *Down to earth sociology: Introductory readings* (9th ed., pp. 8–18). New York: Free Press.

Henslin, J. M. (1997b). The survivors of the F-227. In J. M. Henslin (Ed.), *Down to earth sociology: Introductory readings* (9th ed., pp. 237–245). New York: Free Press.

Henslin, J. M. (2005). *Sociology: A Down-to-Earth Approach* (7th ed.). Boston: Pearson.

Henslin, J. M., & Biggs, M. A. (1997). Behavior in pubic places: The sociology of the vaginal examination. In J. M. Henslin (Ed.), *Down to earth sociology: Introductory readings* (9th ed., pp. 203–214). New York: Free Press. (Original version published 1971 as Dramaturgical desexualization: The sociology of the vaginal examination in J. M. Henslin (Ed.), *Studies in the sociology of sex* (pp. 243–272). New York: Appleton-Century-Crofts.)

Henslin, J. (2008). *Sociology: A Down-to-Earth Introduction.* 9th Edition. Boston: Pearson Allyn Bacon.

Henslin, James M. (2008). *Social Problems: A Down-to-Earth Approach. 8th Edition.* Boston: Allyn and Bacon.

Hertzler, J. O. (1965). *A sociology of language.* New York: Random House.

Hewa, S. (1993). Sociology and public policy: The debate on value-free social science. *International Journal of Sociology and Social Policy, 13*(1–2), 64–82.

Higley, J., Hoffmann-Lange, U., Kadushin, C., & Moore, G. (1991, May). Elite integration in stable democracies: A reconsideration. *European Sociological Review, 7*(1), 35–53.

Hilbrecht, M., Zuzanek, J., & Mannell, R. C. (2008). "Time Use, Time Pressure and Gendered Behaviour in Early and Late Adolescence." *Sex Roles.* 58: 342–357.

Hippler, F. (1987). Interview in a television documentary with Bill Moyers in *Propaganda,* in the series "Walk Through the 20th Century."

Hirshman, L. (2006). *Get to Work: A Manifesto For Women Of The World.* New York: Viking.

Ho, B., Friedland, J., Rappolt, S., & Noh, S. (2003). Caregiving for relatives with Alzheimer's disease: Feelings of Chinese-Canadian women. *Journal of Aging Studies, 17,* 301–321.

Hochschild, A. (1989). *The second shift: Working parents and the revolution at home.* New York: Viking.

Hoecker-Drysdale, Susan. (1992). *Harriet Martineau: First Woman Sociologist,* New York: Berg.

Hofstede, G. H. (1980). *Culture's consequences: International differences in work-related values.* Beverly Hills, CA: Sage Publications.

Holden, B. A., & Rose, F. (1993, August 5). Two policemen get 2H year jail terms on U.S. charges in Rodney King case. *Wall Street Journal,* p. B2.

Homblin, D. J. (1973). *The first cities.* Boston: Little, Brown, Time-Life Books.

Honeycutt, K. (1995). Disgusting, pathetic, bizarrely beautiful: Representations of weight in popular culture. [Paper presented at the 1995 meetings of the American Sociological Association].

Honore, C. (2008). *Under Pressures: Rescuing Childhood From The Culture of Hyper-parenting.* Toronto: Alfred A. Knopf Canada.

Horowitz, I. L. (1966). *Three worlds of development: The theory and practice of international stratification.* New York: Oxford University Press.

Horowitz, R. (1983). *Honor and the American dream: Culture and identity in a Chicano community.* New Brunswick, NJ: Rutgers University Press.

Horowitz, R. (1987, December). Community tolerance of gang violence. *Social Problems, 34*(5), 437–450.

Hossfeld, Karen J. (2000). 'Their Logic Against Them': Contradictions in Sex, Race, and Class in Silicon Valley. In Maxine Baca Zinn, Pierrette

Hondagneu-Sotelo, and Michael A. Messner (Eds.), *Gender through the Prism of Difference,* 2nd ed. Borson: Allyn and Bacon: 388–400.

Hostetler, J. A. (1980). *Amish society* (3rd ed.). Baltimore: Johns Hopkins University Press.

Hostetler, A. J., Sweet, S., & Moen, P. (2007). Gendered Career Paths: A Life Course Perspective on Returning to School. *Sex Roles* 56, 85–103.

Houtman, D. (1995). What exactly is a "social class"?: On the economic liberalism and cultural conservatism of the "working class." [Paper presented at the 1995 meetings of the American Sociological Association].

Hoyt, H. (1939). *The structure and growth of residential neighborhoods in American cities.* Washington, DC: Federal Housing Administration.

Hoyt, H. (1971). Recent distortions of the classical models of urban structure. In L. S. Bourne (Ed.), *Internal structure of the city: Readings on space and environment* (pp. 84–96). New York: Oxford University Press.

Huber, J. (1990, February). Micro-macro links in gender stratification. *American Sociological Review, 55,* 1–10.

Huber, J., & Form, W. H. (1973). *Income and Ideology.* New York: Free Press.

Hudson, J. R. (1991). Professional sports franchise locations and city, metropolitan and regional identities. [Paper presented at the annual meetings of the American Sociological Association].

Hudson, Valerie M. and Ancrea M. Den Boer. (2004). *Bare Branches: The Security Implications of Asia's Surplus Male Population.* Cambridge, MA: MIT Press.

Huggins, M. K. (1993). Lost childhoods: Assassinations of youth in democratizing Brazil. [Paper presented at the annual meetings of the American Sociological Association].

Hughes, E. C. (1943). *French Canada in transition.* Chicago: University of Chicago Press.

Hughes, J. (2003). *Learning to smoke: Tobacco use in the West.* Chicago: University of Chicago Press.

Human Resources and Social Development Canada. (2007). Family—Overview, Marriage, Age of Mother at Childbirth, Divorce, Young Adults Living with Parent(s). Available at www4.hrsdc.gc.ca. Retrieved May 25, 2008.

Human Rights Watch. www.hrw.org/women/

Hunt, S. (2005). *The life course: A sociological introduction.* New York: Palgrave Macmillan.

Hurtig, M. (1999). *Pay the rent or feed the kids: The tragedy and disgrace of poverty in Canada.* Toronto: McClelland and Stewart.

Hussain, Y. et al. (2006). Violence in the Lives of Girls in Canada: Creating Spaces of Understanding and Change. In Y. Jiwani, C. Steenbergen, C. Mitchell (Eds.), *Girlhood: Redefining the Limits* (pp. 53–69). Montreal: Black Rose.

Huws, U. (2003). *The making of the cybertariat: Virtual work in a real world.* New York: Monthly Review Press.

Hwang, Stephen W. (2001, January 23). "Homelessness and Health." *Canadian Medical Association Journal,* 164:2, pp. 229–233.

Hymowitz, Carol. (2004, November 8). "Through the Glass Ceiling." *Wall Street Journal.*

ILO (International Labour Organization). (2002, May 24). Press Release: *Work-related fatalities reach 2 million annually.* Available at www.ilo.org/public/english/bureau/inf/pr/2002/23.htm.

Immen, Wallace. (2008). "The Latest Rage in the Office is Just That—Workers Lashing Out." *Globeandmail.com,* accessed March 7, 2008. www.theglobeandmail.com/servlet/story/LAC.20080307.CARAGE07/BNPrint//.

International Trade Union Confederation (IUTC). (2008). *The Global Gender Pay Gap.* Brussels: IUTC, 2008).

Ischinger, Barbara. (2007, October). "Can the World be Over-Educated?" *OECD Observer*, No. 263. www.oecdobserver.org/news/printpage.php/aid/2469/.

Iyer, Nitya. (2002, February 28). *Working Through the Wage Gap: Report of the Task Force on Pay Equity*. February 28, 2002. 164pp. www.ag.gov.bc.ca/public/working_through_the_wage_gap.pdf.

Jackson, A., Robinson, D., Baldwin, B., & Wiggins, C. (2000). *Falling Behind: The State of Working Canada 2000*. Ottawa: Canadian Centre for Policy Alternatives.

Jackson, Andrew. (2005). *Work and Labour in Canada: Critical Issues*. Toronto: Canadian Scholars' Press.

Jackson, J. D. (1975). *Community & conflict: A study of French-English relations in Ontario*. Toronto: Holt, Rinehart & Winston of Canada.

Jackson, T., & Chen, H. (2008). Sociocultural Predictors of Physical Appearance Concerns among Adolescent Girls and Young Women in China. *Sex Roles*. 58, pp. 402–411.

Jacobsen, T., & Adams, R. M. (1958, November 21). Salt and silt in ancient Mesopotamian agriculture. *Science*, 1251–1258.

Jaffrelot, Christophe. (2006, April). "The Impact of Affirmative Action in India: More Political Than Socioeconomic." *India Review*, 5(2): 173–189.

Jaggar, A. M. (1990). Sexual difference and sexual equality. In D. L. Rhode (Ed.), *Theoretical perspectives on sexual difference* (pp. 239–254). New Haven, CT: Yale University Press.

James, Carl. (2003). *Seeing Ourselves: Exploring Race, Ethnicity and Culture*. Third Edition. Toronto: Thompson Educational Publishing.

Jankowiak, W. R., & Fischer, E. F. (1992, April). A cross-cultural perspective on romantic love. *Journal of Ethnology*, 31(2), 149–155.

Jansz, J., & Martis, R. G. (2007). The Lara Phenomenon: Powerful Female Characters in Video Games. *Sex Roles*. 56, 141–148.

Jasper, J. M. (1991). Moral dimensions of social movements. [Paper presented at the annual meetings of the American Sociological Association].

Jasper, J. M., & Poulsen, J. D. (1995, November). Recruiting strangers and friends: Moral shocks and social networks in animal rights and anti-nuclear protests. *Social Problems*, 42(4), 493–512.

Jenish, D'Arcy. (1997, November 10). *Maclean's*, 110(45), p. 18.

Jenkins, C., & Sherman, B. (1981). *The Leisure Shock*. London: Eyre Methuen.

Jiwani, Y. (2006). Racialized Violence And Girls and Young Women of Colour. In Y. Jiwani, C. Steenbergen, C. Mitchell (Eds.) *Girlhood: Redefining the Limits*. (pp. 70–88). Montreal: Black Rose.

John Howard Society of Alberta. (1999). Youth crime in Canada: Public perception vs. statistical information, 1997. In J. Winterdyk & D. King, (Eds). *Diversity and justice in Canada*. Toronto: Canadian Scholars' Press.

Johne, Marjo. (2008, January 30). Squeezed in a Generational Sandwich. *The Globe and Mail*, p. E5.

Johnson, H. (1996). *Dangerous domains: Violence against women in Canada*. Toronto: Nelson Canada.

Johnson, Holly. (2006, October). *Measuring Violence Against Women: Statistical Trends 2006*. Statistics Canada, Catalogue No. 85-570-XIE. www.statcan.ca/english/research/85-570-XIE/85-570-XIE2006001.pdf.

Johnson, J. (2002). *Getting By on the Minimum: The Lives of Working-Class Women*. New York: Routledge.

Johnson, N. R. (1993). Panic at "The Who concert stampede": An empirical assessment. In R. L. Curtis, Jr., & B. E. Aguirre (Eds.), *Collective behavior and social movements* (pp. 113–122). Boston: Allyn and Bacon.

Jordan, Miriam. (2000, May 9). "Among Poor Villagers, Female Infanticide Still Flourishes in India." *Wall Street Journal*, pp. A1, A12.

Juergensmeyer, Mark. (2000). *Terror in the Mind of God: The Global Rise of Religious Violence*. Berkeley: University of California Press.

Kalish, S. (1994, March). International migration: New findings on magnitude, importance. *Population Today*, 22(3), 1–2.

Kalmijn, M. (1991, December). Shifting boundaries: Trends in religious and educational homogamy. *American Sociological Review, 56*, 786–800.

Kaminski, M., & Palchikoff, K. (1997, April 14). The crisis to come. *Newsweek*, pp.44–46.

Kantner, James and Andrew C. Revkin. (2007, April 7). Scientists Detail Climate Changes, Poles to Tropics. *New York Times*.

Kanter, R. M. (1977). *Men and women of the corporation*. New York: Basic Books.

Kanter, R. M. (1983). *The change masters: Innovation and entrepreneurship in the American corporation*. New York: Simon & Schuster.

Kanter, R. M. (1997). *World class: Thriving locally in the global economy*. New York: Touchstone Books.

Kanter, R. M., Wiersema, F., & Kao, J. J. (Eds.). (1997). *Innovation: Breakthrough thinking at 3M, DuPont, GE, Pfizer, and Rubbermaid*. New York: HarperBusiness.

Karp, D. A., Stone, G. P., & Yoels, W. C. (1991). *Being urban: A sociology of city life* (2nd ed.). New York: Praeger.

Karp, D. A., & Yoels, W. C. (1990). Sport and urban life. *Journal of Sport and Social Issues, 14*(2), 77–102.

Katz, Abram. (2005, July 16). "Negative Attitudes on TV Toward Aging Affect Elderly." Global Action on Aging. www.globalaging.org/elderrights/us/2005/tv.htm.

Kazanjian, Arminee, Morettin, Demise, & Cho, Robert. (2004). Health Care Utilization by Canadian Women. In Canadian Institute for Health Information. *Women's Health Surveillance Report: Supplementary Chapters*. Ottawa: Health Canada.

Keating, N., Fast, J., Frederick, J., Cranswick, K. & Perrier, C. (1999). *Eldercare in Canada: Context, content and consequences*. Ottawa: Minister of Industry.

Kelley, J., & Evans, M. D. R. (1995, April). Class and class conflict in six Western nations. *American Sociological Review, 60*, 157–178.

Kelso, W. A. (1995). *Poverty and the underclass: Changing perceptions of the poor in America*. New York: New York University Press.

Kemp, C. L. (2004). "Grand" expectations: The experiences of grandparents and adult grandchildren. *Canadian Journal of Sociology*, 29(4), 499–525.

Keniston, K. (1971). *Youth and dissent: The rise of a new opposition*. New York: Harcourt, Brace, Jovanovich.

Kennedy, P. (1993). *Preparing for the twenty-first century*. New York: Random House.

Kenway, J., & Bullen, E. (2001). *Consuming children: Education-entertainment-advertising*. Buckingham, UK: Open University Press.

Kephart, W. M., & Zellner, W. W. (1994). *Extraordinary groups: An examination of unconventional life-styles* (5th ed.). New York: St. Martin's Press.

Kerr, D. & Michalski, J. (2007) Family Structure and Children's Hyperactivity Problems: A Longitudinal Analysis. *Canadian Journal of Sociology* 32, 1, 85–112.

Kerstetter, S. (2001, March 25). Radical change necessary to aid poor. *Toronto Star*, p. A13.

Keung, N. (2008, March 11). A Love Match? That's so last century. *Toronto Star*, pp. ID1, ID2.

Khalif, M. H. (2002, April 30). Bridging the prosperity gap. *Toronto Star*, p. A24.

Kids spending more time with parents. (2001, May 19). *Toronto Star*, p. M10.

Kilbourne, J. (2004). Socialization and the Power of Advertising. In J. Macionis, N. Benokraitis, B. Ravelli (Eds.), *Seeing Ourselves: Class, Contemporary and Cross-cultural Readings in Sociology* (pp. 96–102). Toronto: Pearson Prentice Hall.

King, R. T., Jr. (1994, October 25). Soon a chip will test blood for diseases. *Wall Street Journal*, pp. B1, B11.

Kinsman, G. (2001). Gays and lesbians: Pushing the boundaries. In D. Glenday & A. Duffy (Eds.), *Canadian society: Meeting the challenges of the twenty-first century* (pp. 212–246). Toronto: Oxford University Press.

Kitsuse, J. I. (1980, October). Coming out all over: Deviants and the politics of social problems. *Social Problems, 28*(1), 1–13.

Kivett, D. D., & Warren, C. A. B. (2002). Social control in a group home for delinquent boys. *Journal of Contemporary Ethnography, 31*(1), 3–32.

Klein, Naomi. (2008, February 11). "Push-button Policing: Why Talk When You Can Shock?" *The Globe and Mail*, p. A17.

Kluegel, J. R., & Smith, E. R. (1986). *Beliefs about inequality: America's views of what is and what ought to be.* Hawthorne, NY: Aldine de Gruyter.

Knaus, W. A. (1981). *Inside Russian medicine: An American doctor's first-hand report.* New York: Everest House.

Kobayashi, E. (2007 February 23). Pretty in pink, but it's still a smoke screen. *Toronto Star*, p. E3.

Kohn, M. L. (1977). *Class and conformity: A study in values* (2nd ed.). Homewood, IL: Dorsey Press.

Komter, A. (1989, June). Hidden power in marriage. *Gender and Society, 3*(2), 187–216.

Korda, M. (1973). *Male chauvinism: How it works.* New York: Random House.

Koropeckyj-Cox, T. & Pendell, G. (2007). "The Gender Gap in Attitudes About Childlessness in the United States." *Journal of Marriage and the Family. 69*, November, 899–915.

Koropeckyj-Cox, T., Romano, V., & A. Moras. (2007). "Through the Lenses of Gender, Race, and Class: Students' Perceptions of Childless/Childfree Individuals and Couples." *Sex Roles. 56*, 415–428.

Kornhauser, W. (1959). *The politics of mass society.* New York: Free Press.

Krane, V., Stiles-Shipley, J. A., Waldron, J., & Michalenok, J. (2001). Relationships among body satisfaction, social physique anxiety and eating behaviors in female athletes and exercisers. *Journal of Sport Behavior, 24*(3), 247–264.

Kumar, M.P. (2007). New Sites of Transformation in Aboriginal People's Post-Secondary Education. *Policy Dialogue* 15 (Spring), pp. 18–20.

Kupers, T. A. (1999). *Prison madness: The mental health crisis behind bars and what we must do.* San Francisco: Josey-Bass.

La Barre, W. (1954). *The human animal.* Chicago: University of Chicago Press.

Lacayo, R. (1997, April 7). The lure of the cult. *Time*, pp. 45–46.

Lachica, E. (1992, May 18). Third world told to spend more on environment. *Wall Street Journal*, p. A2.

LaDou, J. (1991, July). Deadly migration: Hazardous industries' flight to the third world. *Technology Review, 94*(5), 46–53.

LaFraniere, Sharon. (2005, April 11). Health Works Race to Block Deadly Virus in Angolan Town. *New York Times.*

LaFraniere, Sharon. (2006, October 29). Africa's World of Forced Labor, in a 6-Year-Old's Eyes. *New York Times.*

Lagnado, L. (1996, October 9). Another peril: Smoking doubles risk of old-age blindness, two studies say. *Wall Street Journal*, p. B8.

Landtman, G. (1968). *The origin of the inequality of the social classes.* New York: Greenwood Press. (First published 1938).

Lang, K., & Lang, G. E. (1961). *Collective Dynamics.* New York: Crowell.

Langlois, S., & Morrison, P. (2002, Autumn). Suicide deaths and attempts. *Canadian Social Trends*, pp. 20–25.

Lannoy, R. (1975). *The speaking tree: A study of Indian culture and society.* New York: Oxford University Press.

Lareau, A., & Weininger, E. B. (2003). Cultural Capital in Educational Research: A Critical Assessment. *Theory and Society*, pp. 567–606.

Larocque, S. (2006). *Gay Marriage: The Story of a Canadian Social Revolution.* Toronto: James Lorimer & Company Ltd.

Laska, S. B. (1993, September). Environmental sociology and the state of the discipline. *Social Forces, 72*(1), 1–17.

Laxer, J. (1998). *The undeclared war: Class conflict in the age of cyber capitalism.* Toronto: Penguin Books.

Lazarsfeld, P. F., & Reitz, J. G. (1989). History of applied sociology. *Sociological Practice, 7*, 43–52.

Leacock, E. (1969). *Teaching and learning in city schools.* New York: Basic Books.

Leacock, E. (1981). *Myths of male dominance.* New York: Monthly Review Press.

Lee, M. (2002, April 18). The Global Divide: Inequality in the World Economy. In Canadian Centre for Policy Alternatives. *Behind the Numbers: Economic Facts, Figures and Analysis, 4*(2).

Lemert, C. (1994). A classic from the other side of the veil: Du Bois's *Souls of Black folk. Sociological Quarterly, 35*(3), 383–396.

Lemert, E. M. (1972). *Human deviance, social problems, and social control* (2nd ed.). Englewood Cliffs, NJ: Prentice Hall.

Lenski, G. (1954). Status crystallization: A nonvertical dimension of social status. *American Sociological Review, 19*, 405–413.

Lenski, G. (1966). *Power and privilege: A theory of social stratification.* New York: McGraw-Hill.

Lenski, G., & Lenski, J. (1987). *Human societies: An introduction to macrosociology* (5th ed.). New York: McGraw-Hill.

Lerner, G. (1986). *The creation of patriarchy.* New York: Oxford.

Lesser, A. (1968). War and the state. In M. Fried, M. Harris, & R. Murphy (Eds.), *War: The anthropology of armed conflict and aggression* (pp. 92–96). Garden City, NY: Natural History.

Levinson, D. J. (1978). *The seasons of a man's life.* New York: Knopf.

Levitt, H. M., Swanger, R. T., & Buttler, J. B. (2008). "Male Perpetrators' Perspectives on Intimate Partner Violence, Religion and Masculinity." *Sex Roles. 58*, 435–448.

Levy, M. J., Jr. (1992, May–June). Confucianism and modernization. *Society, 24*(4), 15–18.

Lewis, Kate. (2007, October 3). Babies Born to Poor Moms At Risk: Study. *The Toronto Star:* p. A10.

Lewis, O. (1966a, October). The culture of poverty. *Scientific American, 115*, pp. 19–25.

Lewis, O. (1966b). *La Vida.* New York: Random House.

Liebow, E. (1967). *Tally's corner: A study of Negro streetcorner men.* Boston: Little, Brown.

Liebow, E. (1997). Tally's corner. In J. M. Henslin (Ed.), *Down to earth sociology: Introductory readings* (9th ed., pp. 330–339). New York: Free Press.

Lind, M. (1995). *The next American nation: The new nationalism and the fourth American Revolution.* New York: Free Press.

Lindsay, C. (1999, Spring). Seniors: A diverse group aging well. *Canadian Social Trends, 52*, pp. 24–26.

Lindsay, C. (1999). *A portrait of seniors in Canada* (3rd ed.). Ottawa: Statistics Canada, Catalogue 89-519-XPE.

Lingard, L., Garwood, K., Schryer, C. F., & Spafford, M. M. (2003). A certain art of uncertainty: Case presentation and the development of professional identity. *Social Science and Medicine, 56*, 603–616.

Linton, R. (1936). *The Study of Man.* New York: Appleton-Century-Crofts.

Lipset, S. M. (1959). Democracy and working-class authoritarianism. *American Sociological Review, 24,* 482–502.

Lipset, S. M. (1990). *Continental divide: The values and institutions of the United States and Canada.* Washington, DC: Canadian-American Committee.

Lipset, S. M. (1993). The social requisites of democracy revisited. Presidential address to the American Sociological Association, Boston, MA.

Lipton, M. (1979). *Why poor people stay poor: Urban bias in world development.* Cambridge, MA: Harvard University Press.

Livingstone, D. W. (1999). *The education-jobs gap: Underemployment or economic democracy.* Toronto: Garamond Press.

Lofland, J. F. (1985). *Protest: Studies of collective behavior and social movements.* New Brunswick, NJ: Transaction Books.

Lofland, J. F. (1993). Collective behavior: The elementary forms. In R. L. Curtis, Jr., & B. E. Aguirre (Eds.), *Collective behavior and social movements* (pp. 70–75). Boston: Allyn and Bacon.

Lombroso, C. (1911). *Crime: Its causes and remedies* (H. P. Horton, Trans.). Boston: Little, Brown.

Lorber, J. (1998). *Gender inequality: Feminist theories and politics.* Los Angeles: Roxbury.

Lowe, G. S. (1987). *Women in the administrative revolution.* Toronto: University of Toronto Press.

Lu, V. (2001, March 14). More seniors than children by 2016. *Toronto Star*, p. A8.

Lu, V. (2002, June 20). Tobacco use will kill 1 billion, group warns. *Toronto Star*, p. A18.

Lublin, J. S. (1991, February 13). Trying to increase worker productivity, more employers alter management style. *Wall Street Journal,* pp. B1, B7.

Lundberg, O. (1991). Causal explanations for class inequality in health— An empirical analysis. *Social Science and Medicine, 32*(4), 385–393.

Lupri, E., & Grandin, E. (2004). *Intimate partner abuse against men.* National Clearinghouse on Family Violence, www.phac-aspc.gc.ca/ncfv-cnivf/familyviolence/html/mlintima_e.html.

Luttwak, E. (1996). Buchanan has it right. *London Review of Books, 18*(9), 6–8.

Luxton, M. (1980). *More than a labour of love.* Toronto: Women's Press.

Luxton, M., & Corman, J. (2001). *Getting By in Hard Times: Gendered Labour at Home and on the Job.* Toronto: University of Toronto Press.

Lyotard, J. F. (1984). *The postmodern condition: A report on knowledge* (G. Bennington & B. Massumi, Trans.; F. Jameson, Foreword). Minneapolis: University of Minnesota Press.

Macdonald, B., with Rich, C. (1991). *Look me in the eye: Old women aging and ageism.* Minneapolis: Spinsters Ink.

MacDonald, M., Phipps, S., & Lethbridge, L. (2005). Taking its toll: The influence of paid and unpaid work on women's well-being. *Feminist Economics 11*(1), 63–95.

MacFadyen, L., Amos, A., Hastings, G., & Parkes, E. (2003). "They look like my kind of people"—perceptions of smoking images in youth magazines. *Social Science and Medicine 56*, 491–499.

MacGregor, Roy. (2007, November 24). Who says we're an urban country? *Globe and Mail,* p. F8.

Mackenzie, Hugh. (2007). *The Great CEO Pay Race: Over Before it Begins.* Ottawa: Canadian Centre for Policy Alternatives.

Mackay, C. (1852). *Memories of extraordinary popular delusions and the madness of crowds.* London: Office of the National Illustrated Library.

Mackie, M. (1987). *Constructing women and men: Gender socialization.* Toronto: Holt, Rinehart and Winston of Canada Limited.

Mackie, M. (1991). *Gender relations in Canada: Further explorations.* Toronto: Butterworths.

MacKinnon, C. A. (1979). *Sexual harassment of working women: A case of sex discrimination.* New Haven, CT: Yale University Press.

MacKinnon, M. (1999, March 1). The lowest incomes in Canada are found on Native reserves. *Globe and Mail.*

MacLennan, H. (1946). *Two solitudes.* London: Cresset Press.

MacQueen, K. (2005, May 13). The new old age: We're living longer and staying healthier. Maybe it's time to rethink mandatory retirement. *Reader's Digest Canada.*

Mahoney, J. S., Jr., & Kooistra, P. G. (1995). Policing the races: Structural factors enforcing racial purity in Virginia (1630–1930). [Paper presented at the 1995 meetings of the American Sociological Association].

Main, J. T. (1965). *The social structure of revolutionary America.* Princeton, NJ: Princeton University Press.

Malinowski, B. (1927). *Sex and repression in savage society.* Cleveland, OH: World.

Malinowski, B. (1945). *The dynamics of culture change.* New Haven, CT: Yale University Press.

Mamdani, M. (1973). The myth of population control: Family, caste, and class in an urban village. New York: Monthly Review Press.

Mandell, N., & Duffy, A. (2005). Explaining family lives. In N. Mandell & A. Duffy (Eds.), *Canadian families: Diversity, conflict and change* (3rd ed., pp. 3–30). Toronto: Thomson Nelson.

Mandell, Nancy, Wilson, Susannah, & Duffy, Ann. (2008). *Connection, Compromise and Control: Canadian Women Discuss Midlife.* Toronto: Oxford University Press.

Mander, J. (1992). *In the absence of the sacred: The failure of technology and the survival of the Indian nations.* San Francisco, CA: Sierra Club Books.

Manski, C. F. (1992–1993, Winter). Income and higher education. *Focus, 14*(3), 14–19.

Markson, E. W. (2003). *Social gerontology today: An introduction.* Los Angeles: Roxbury.

Markusen, E. (1995). Genocide in Cambodia. In J. M. Henslin (Ed.), *Down to earth sociology* (8th ed., pp. 355–364). New York: Free Press.

Marolla, J., & Scully, D. (1986). Attitudes toward women, violence, and rape: A comparison of convicted rapists and other felons. *Deviant Behavior, 7*(4), 337–355.

Marotte, B. (2005, February 26). Wal-Mart intimidated unionists, board rules. *Globe and Mail,* p. A9.

Marr, Lisa Grace. (2006, December 19). The Ethical Consumer. *The Hamilton Spectator,* p. G11.

Marshall, K. (2003). Parental leave: More time off for baby. *Canadian Social Trends* (Winter), pp. 13–18. Ottawa: Statistics Canada, Catalogue no. 11-008.

Marshall, K. (2006). *Converging Gender Roles. Perspectives on Labour and Income.7*(7), pp. 5–17.

Marshall, K. (2007). The Busy Lives of Teens. *Perspectives on Labour and Income* (May): pp. 5–15.

Marshall, S. (1995, November 2). It's so simple: Just lather up, and watch the fat go down the drain. *Wall Street Journal*, p. B1.

Martel, L., & Belanger, A. (2000, Autumn). Dependence-free life expectancy in Canada. *Canadian Social Trends*, pp. 26–29.

Martin, M. (1990, Winter). Ecosabotage and civil disobedience. *Environmental Ethics, 12*(4), 291–310.

Martin, W. G. (1994, Spring). The world-systems perspective in perspective: Assessing the attempt to move beyond nineteenth-century Eurocentric conceptions. *Review, 17*(2), 145–185.

Martindale, Kathleen, with an addendum by Didi Khayatt. (2001). In N. Mandell, editor. *Feminist Issues: Race, Class and Sexuality.* Toronto: Prentice Hall. pp. 49–74.

Martin-Matthews, A. (2005). Aging and families: Ties over time and across generations. In N. Mandell & A. Duffy (Eds.), *Canadian families: Diversity, conflict and change* (3rd ed., pp. 311–345). Toronto: Thomson Nelson.

Marx, G. T. (1985, May–June). The new surveillance. *Technology Review,* 43–48.

Marx, G. T. (1986, November–December). Monitoring on the job: How to protect privacy as well as property. *Technology Review,* 63–72.

Marx, G. T. (1993). Thoughts on a neglected category of social movement participant: The agent provocateur and the informant. In R. L. Curtis, Jr., & B. E. Aguirre (Eds.), *Collective Behavior and Social Movements* (pp. 242–258). Boston: Allyn and Bacon.

Marx, G. T. (1995). The road to the future. In *Triumph of discovery: A chronicle of great adventures in science* (pp. 63–65). New York: Holt.

Marx, K. (1964). Contribution to the critique of Hegel's philosophy of right. In T. B. Bottomore (Ed.), *Karl Marx: Early writings,* (p. 45). New York: McGraw-Hill. (First published 1844).

Marx, K., & Engels, F. (1967). *Communist manifesto.* New York: Pantheon. (First published 1848).

Massey, D. S., & Denton, N. A. (1993). *American apartheid: Segregation and the making of the underclass.* Cambridge, MA: Harvard University Press.

Mathews, F. (2003). The forgotten child: The declining status of boys in Canada. *Transition Magazine* (Vanier Institute of the Family), *33*(1). Available at www.vifamily.ca.

Matthews, C. (1996, Summer). A powerful presence: Images of the grandmother in Canadian literature. *Canadian Journal of Aging, 15*(2), 264–273.

Matthews, B. J. (2005). The body beautiful: Adolescent girls and images of beauty. In B. Ravelli (Ed.), *Exploring Canadian sociology: A reader* (pp. 39–50). Toronto: Pearson/Prentice Hall.

Mauss, A. (1975). *Social problems as social movements.* Philadelphia: Lippincott.

Maxwell, M. P., & Maxwell, J. D. (1971). Boarding school: Social control, space and identity. In D. I. Davies & K. Herman (Eds.), *Social space: Canadian perspectives.* Toronto: New Press.

Mayell, H. (2002, February 12). Thousands of women killed for family "honor." *National Geographic News.* Available at http://news.nationalgeographic.com/news/2002/02/0212_020212_honorkilling.html.

Mayer, John D. (2007). *Personality: A Systems Approach.* Boston: Allyn & Bacon.

Mayo, E. (1966). *Human problems of an industrial civilization.* New York: Viking.

McAdam, D., McCarthy, J. D., & Zald, M. N. (1988). Social movements. In N. J. Smelser (Ed.), *Handbook of sociology* (pp. 695–737). Newbury Park, CA: Sage.

McCabe, J. T., & Ellis, J. E. (1990). Pastoralism: Beating the odds in arid Africa. In J. P. Spradley & D. W. McCurdy (Eds.), *Conformity and conflict: Readings in cultural anthropology* (pp. 150–156). Glenview, IL: Scott, Foresman.

McCall, L. (2001). *Complex Inequality: Gender, Class and Race in the New Economy.* New York: Routledge.

McCall, M. (1980). Who and where are the artists? In W. B. Shaffir, R. A. Stebbins, & A. Turowetz (Eds.), *Fieldwork experience: Qualitative approaches to social research* (pp. 145–158). New York: St. Martin's.

McCarthy, C. (1983, March 5). America's homeless: Three days down and out in Chicago. *Nation, 236*(9), 1, 271.

McCarthy, J. D., & Wolfson, M. (1992). Consensus movements, conflict movements, and the cooperation of civic and state infrastructures. In A. D. Morris & C. M. Mueller (Eds.), *Frontiers in social movement theory* (pp. 273–297). New Haven, CT: Yale University Press.

McCarthy, M. J. (1993, August 25). James Bond hits the supermarket: Stores snoop on shoppers' habits to boost sales. *Wall Street Journal,* pp. B1, B8.

McCloskey, D. (2003). Canadian boys: Growing up male: Introduction. *Transition Magazine* (Vanier Institute of the Family), *33*(1). Available at www.vifamily.ca.

McCormack, Judith. (2007, March 2). Why Myths About Poor Endure. *The Toronto Star*: p. A17

McCuen, G. E. (Ed.). (1993). *Ecocide and genocide in the vanishing forest: The rainforests and native people.* Hudson, WI: GEM Publications.

McDaniel, S. (2002a). Intergenerational interlinkages: Public, family and work. In D. Cheal (Ed.), *Aging and demographic change in Canadian context* (pp. 22–71). Toronto: University of Toronto Press.

McDaniel, S. (2002b). Information and communication technologies: Bugs in the generational ointment. *Canadian Journal of Sociology, 27*(4), 535–546.

McDonnell, K. (2002, March). The hurried child. *The New Internationalist, 343,* pp. 22–23.

McDougall, Dan. (2007). Child Sweatshop Shame Threatens Gap's Ethical Image. *Observer.* Accessed October 28, 2007 at http://observer.guardian.co.uk/print/0,,331090325-119093,00.html.

McDowell, Bart. (1984). Mexico City: An Alarming Giant. *National Geographic,* 166: 139–174.

McGechie, H. (2007). Family-related homicides against children and youth. In L. Ogrodnik (ed.) *Family Violence in Canada: A Statistical Profile 2007.* Statistics Canada catalogue no. 85-224-XIE. Ottawa: Minister of Industry, pp. 24–27.

McGregor, J. (1992, March 20). China's aging leader seems set to carve reformist idea in stone. *Wall Street Journal,* p. A9.

McGregor, J. (1993, September 24). Running bulls. *Wall Street Journal,* p. R16.

McIlroy, A. (2007 December 11). Humans 'evolving away from each other.' *The Globe and Mail,* p. A3.

McKenzie, Michael. (2007, April). *Where are the Scientists and Engineers?* Statistics Canada, Catalogue 88F0006XIE, No. 002.

McKeown, T. (1977). *The modern rise of population.* New York: Academic Press.

McLanahan, S. (2002, Spring). Life without father: What happens to the children? *Contexts, 1*(1), pp. 35–44.

McMullin, J. A., & Cairney, J. (2004). Self-esteem and the intersection of age, class and gender. *Journal of Aging Studies, 18,* 75–90.

McNally, D. (2002). *Another world is possible: Globalization and anti-capitalism.* Winnipeg: Arbeiter Ring Publishers.

McNeely, S. (2002, May 21). Childless—and loving it. *Toronto Star,* pp. C1, C3.

McPhail, C. (1989). Blumer's theory of collective behavior: The development of a non-symbolic interaction explanation. *Sociological Quarterly, 30*(3), 401–423.

McQuaig, L. (1995). *Shooting the hippo: Death by deficit and other Canadian myths.* Toronto: Viking.

McVey, G., Tweed, S., & Blackmore, E. (2004). Dieting among preadolescent and young adolescent females. *CMAJ.170*(10), pp. 1559–1561.

Mead, G. H. (1934). *Mind, self and society.* Chicago: University of Chicago Press.

Meadow, T. & Stacey, J. (2006). Families. *Contexts, 5*(4): pp. 55–57.

Meier, B. (1987, May 12). Health studies suggest asbestos substitutes also pose cancer risk. *Wall Street Journal,* pp. 1, 21.

Melucci, Alberto. (1989). *Nomads of the Present: Social Movements and Individual Needs in Contemporary Society.* Philadelphia: Temple University Press.

Menzies, H. (1996). *Whose brave new world? The information highway and the new economy.* Toronto: Between the Lines.

Merton, R. K. (1949). *Social theory and social structure.* Glencoe, IL: Free Press. (Enlarged ed., 1968).

Merton, R. K. (1956). The social-cultural environment and *anomie.* In H. L. Witmer & R. Kotinsky (Eds.), *New perspectives for research on juvenile delinquency* (pp. 24–50). Washington, DC: U.S. Department of Health, Education, and Welfare.

Merton, R. K., Reader, G. G., & Kendall, P. L. (1957). *The student physician: Introductory studies in the sociology of medical education.* Cambridge, MA: Harvard University Press.

Milan, A., & Hamm, B. (2004, Summer). Mixed unions. *Canadian Social Trends,* 2–6. Ottawa: Statistics Canada, Catalogue no. 11-008.

Milan, A., Vezina, M., & Wells, C. (2007). *Family Portrait: Continuity and Change in Canadian Families and Households in 2006, 2006 Census.* Statistics Canada Catalogue no. 97-553-XIE. Ottawa: Minister of Industry.

Milbank, D. (1995a, May 3). Guarded by greenbelts, Europe's town centers thrive. *Wall Street Journal,* pp. B1, B4.

Milbank, D. (1995b, August 9). Working poor fear welfare cutbacks aimed at the idle will inevitably strike them, too. *Wall Street Journal,* p. A10.

Milgram, S. (1963). Behavioral study of obedience. *Journal of Abnormal and Social Psychology, 67*(4), 371–378.

Milgram, S. (1965, February). Some conditions of obedience and disobedience to authority. *Human Relations, 18,* 57–76.

Miller, J. J. (1995, May 25). Don't close our "golden door." *Wall Street Journal,* p. A14.

Miller, M. K. & Summers, A. (2007). Gender Differences in Video Game Characters' Roles, Appearances, and Attire as Portrayed in Video Game Magazines. *Sex Roles.57,* 733–742.

Miller, M. W. (1993, December 2). Dark days: The staggering cost of depression. *Wall Street Journal,* pp. B1, B6.

Miller, P., Donahue, P., Este, D., & Hofer, M. (2004). Experiences of being homeless or at risk of being homeless among Canadian youth. *Adolescence, 39*(156), 735–755.

Miller-Loessi, K. (1992). Toward gender integration in the workplace: Issues at multiple levels. *Sociological Perspectives, 35*(1), 1–15.

Mills, Albert J., Simmons, Tony, & Helms Mills, Jean C. (2005). *Reading Organization Theory: A Critical Approach to the Study of Organizational Behaviour and Structure.* 3rd Edition. Toronto: Garamond Press.

Mills, A. J., & Simmons, T. (1999). *Reading organization theory: A critical approach to the study of organizational behaviour and structure.* Toronto: Garamond Press.

Mills, A. J., & Simmons, T. (2005). *Reading organization theory: A critical approach to the study of organizational behaviour and structure.* Toronto: Garamond Press.

Mills, C. W. (1956). *The power elite.* New York: Oxford University Press.

Mills, C. W. (1959). *The sociological imagination.* New York: Oxford University Press.

Mironowicz, M. (2002, July 19). Native forum probes legacy of residential schools. *Hamilton Spectator.*

Mitchell, B. A., Wister, A. V., & Gee, E. M. (2004). The ethnic and family nexus of homeleaving and returning among Canadian young adults. *Canadian Journal of Sociology, 24*(4), 543–575.

Mitchell, B. (2007). The Pendulum of Family change: Comparative Life Course Transitions of Young Adults. In. L. Tepperman & H. Dickinson (Eds.) *Reading Sociology: Canadian Perspectives* (pp. 51–55). Don Mills: Oxford University Press.

Mohal, Paul and Robin Saha. (2007). Racial Inequalities in the Distribution of Hazardous Waster: A National-Level Reassessment. *Social Problems,* 54(3): 343–370.

Moir, A., & Moir, B. (1999). *Why Men Don't Iron: The New Reality of Gender Differences.* New York: Harper Collins.

Mokhiber, R., & Weissman, R. (1999, May 4). A moment of silence. *Multinational Monitor—A Web-Based Newsletter.*

Mokhiber, R., & Weissman, R. (2002, May 28). The age of inequality. *Focus on the Corporation.* Accessed October 11, 2002, at www. corporatepredators.org.

Momirov, J., & Kilbride, K. M. (2005). Family lives of Native peoples, immigrants, and visible minorities. In N. Mandell & A. Duffy (Eds.), *Canadian families: Diversity, conflict and change* (3rd ed., pp. 87–113). Toronto: Thomson Nelson.

Money, J., & Ehrhardt, A. A. (1972). *Man and woman, boy and girl.* Baltimore: Johns Hopkins University Press.

Montgomery, S. (2008, June 5). Boys plead guilty to microwave cat killing. *The Toronto Star* www.thestar.com/printArticle/437329.

Morissette, R., Ostrovsky, Y., & Picot, G. (2004). *Relative Wage Patterns Among the Highly Educated in a Knowledge-based Economy.* Ottawa: Statistics Canada, Catalogue 11F0019MIE No. 232.

Morissette, R., & Picot, G. (2005). *Low-paid work and economically vulnerable families over the last two decades.* Research paper. Analytical Studies Branch Research Paper Series. Ottawa: Statistics Canada, Catalogue 11F0010MIE No. 248.

Morissette, R., & Zhang, X. (2001, Summer). Experience low income for several years. *Perspectives on Labour and Income, 13,* pp. 25–36.

Morissette, Rene & Zhang, Xuelin. (2006, December). Revisiting Wealth Inequality. *Perspectives on Labour and Income,* Statistics Canada Catalogue No. 75-001-XIE: pp. 5–16.

Morris, E., et al. (2005). To what extent does poor health precede welfare? *Canadian Journal of Public Health,* May–June, 201–205.

Morris, J. R. (1991, March). Racial attitudes of undergraduates in Greek housing. *College Student Journal, 25*(1), 501–505.

Morrissy, John. (2008, April 26). Lottery Winners Likely to Keep Working: Survey. *The Saskatoon Star Phoenix.* www.canada.com/saskatoonstarphoenix/news/business/story.html?id=a09854e-763d-4672-915a-f90d55304d17.

Morrow, B. H. (1995). Urban families as support after disaster: The case of Hurricane Andrew. [Paper presented at the 1995 meetings of the American Sociological Association].

Moscos, C. C., & Butler, S. (1997). *All that we can be: Black leadership and racial integration the army way.* New York: Basic Books.

Moscovitch, A. (2007). *Good Servant, Bad Master? Electronic Media and the Family.* Ottawa: The Vanier Institute of the Family. Available at www.vifamily.ca.

Mosher, S. W. (1983, July 25). Why are baby girls being killed in China? *Wall Street Journal*, p. 9.

Mosher, S. W. (1994). *A mother's ordeal: One woman's fight against one-child China*. New York: HarperCollins.

Mosher, S. W. (1997, February 10). Too many people? Not by a long shot. *Wall Street Journal*, p. A18.

Mount, F. (1992). *The subversive family: An alternative history of love and marriage*. New York: Free Press.

Murdock, G. P. (1937, May). Comparative data on the division of labor by sex. *Social Forces, 15*(4), 551–553.

Murdock, G. P. (1945). The common denominator of cultures. In R. Linton (Ed.), *The science of man and the world crisis*. New York: Columbia University Press.

Murdock, G. P. (1949). *Social structure*. New York: Macmillan.

Murnen, S. K. & Kohlman, M. H. (2007). Athletic Participation, Fraternity Membership and Sexual Aggression Among College Men: A Meta-analytic Review. *Sex Roles*. 57, pp. 145–157.

Murphy, Brian, Roberts, Paul & Wolfson, Michael. (2007 September). High-income Canadians. *Perspectives on Labour and Income*, Statistics Canada Catalogue No. 75-001-XIE: pp. 5–17.

Murray, G. W. (1935). *Sons of Ishmael*. London: Routledge.

Myrdal, G. (1962). *Challenge to Affluence*. New York: Pantheon Books.

Naffine, N. (1990). *Law and the sexes: Explorations in feminist jurisprudence*. Sydney: Allen & Unwin.

Nafisi, A. (2004). *Reading* Lolita *in Tehran: A memoir in books*. New York: Random House.

National Council of Welfare. (1999). *Poverty profile 1997*. Ottawa: Minister of Public Works and Government Services.

National Council of Welfare. (2000, Spring). *Justice and the poor*. Ottawa: Minister of Public Works and Government Services.

National Council of Welfare. (2001, Summer). *Child poverty profile 1998*. Ottawa: Minister of Public Works and Government Services.

National Council of Welfare. (2001–02, Winter). *The cost of poverty*. Ottawa: Minister of Public Works and Government Services.

National Council of Welfare. (2004, Autumn). *Poverty profile 2001*. Ottawa: Minister of Public Works and Government Services, Catalogue SD25-1/2001E.

National Council of Welfare. (2006, Summer). *Poverty Profile, 2002 and 2003*. National Council of Welfare Reports, Volume 124. Ottawa: Minister of Public Works and Government Services.

National Council of Welfare. (2006, July). Poverty Facts 2003.

National Council of Welfare. (2007, October). Poverty Statistics 2004. www.ncwcnbes.net/en/research/poverty-pauvrete.html.

National Council of Welfare. (2007, March). Poverty Statistics, 2004. Poverty Rates by Age and Sex, 2004. www.ncwcnbes.net/documents/researchpublications/ResearchProjects/PovertyProfile/2004/PovertyRates-ByAgeSexENG.pdf.

Nauta, A. (1993). That they all may be one: Can denominationalism die? [Paper presented at the annual meetings of the American Sociological Association].

Nelsen, R. W. (2002). *Schooling as entertainment: Corporate education meets popular culture*. Kingston: Cedarcreek Publications.

Nelson, A. (2006). *Gender in Canada* (3rd ed.). Toronto: Pearson Education Canada.

Nelson, A., & Robinson, B. W. (2002). *Gender in Canada* (2nd ed.). Toronto: Prentice Hall.

Nelson, E. D., & Robinson, B. W. (1999). *Gender in Canada*. Scarborough: Prentice Hall Allyn and Bacon Canada.

Nelson, R. K. (1989, November 2). Letter to the editor. *Wall Street Journal*, p. A23.

Newman, P. C. (1979). *The Canadian establishment* (Vol. 1). Toronto: McClelland and Stewart.

Newman, P. C. (1999). *Titans: How the new Canadian establishment seized power*. Toronto: Penguin Books Canada Ltd.

Newman, Peter C. (2004). *Here Be Dragons: Telling Tales of People, Passion and Power*. Toronto: McClelland & Stewart.

Ni, Ching-Ching. (2005). Young girls risk death to support poor families. *Hamilton Spectator*, May 24, p. A12.

Noack, T. & Wiik, K. (2008). Women's Choice of Surname Upon Marriage. *Journal of Marriage and the Family*. 70 (May): 507–518.

Noble, D. F. (1995). *Progress without people: New technology, unemployment, and the message of resistance*. Toronto: Between the Lines.

Nolan, S. A., Buckner, J. P., Marzabadi, C. H., & Kuck, V. J. (2008). Training and Mentoring Chemists: A Study of Gender Disparity. *Sex Roles*. 58: 235–250.

Nomaguchi, K. (2006). Maternal Employment, Nonparental Care, Mother-Child Interactions, and Child Outcomes During Preschool Years. *Journal of Marriage and the Family*. 68 (December), pp. 1341–1369.

Novak, M. (1993). *Aging and society: A Canadian perspective* (2nd ed.). Toronto: Nelson Canada.

Nsamenang, A. B. (1992). *Human development in cultural context: A third world perspective*. Newbury Park, CA: Sage.

OACCAC (The Ontario Association of Community Care Access Centres). (2005). *OACCAC Pamphlet*. Ottawa: Author.

O'Bireck, G. M. (1993). *Gettin' tall: Cocaine use within a subculture of Canadian professional musicians: An ethnographic inquiry*. Toronto: Canadian Scholars' Press.

O'Brien, C.-A., & Goldberg, A. (2000). Lesbians and gay men inside and outside families. In N. Mandell & A. Duffy (Eds.), *Canadian families: Diversity, conflict and change* (pp. 115–145). Toronto: Harcourt Brace Canada.

O'Connell, Vanessa. (2004, May 20). Massachusetts Tries to Halt Sale of 'Sweet' Cigarettes. *Wall Street Journal*.

Offen, K. (1990). Feminism and sexual difference in historical perspective. In D. L. Rhode (Ed.), *Theoretical perspectives on sexual difference* (pp. 13–20). New Haven, CT: Yale University Press.

Ogburn, W. F. (1922). *Social change with respect to culture and human nature*. New York: W. B. Huebsch. (Other editions by Viking 1927, 1938, and 1950).

Ogburn, W. F. (1961). The hypothesis of cultural lag. In T. Parsons, E. Shils, K. D. Naegele, & J. R. Pitts (Eds.), *Theories of society: Foundations of modern sociological theory* (Vol. 2, pp. 1270–1273). New York: Free Press.

Ogburn, W. F. (1964). *On culture and social change: Selected papers*, O. D. Duncan (Ed.) Chicago: University of Chicago Press.

Ogletree, S. M., & Drake, R. (2007). College Students' Video Game Participation and Perceptions: Gender Differences and Implications. *Sex Roles* 56: 537–542.

Ogrodnik, L. (2007). Spousal homicide or attempts and prior police contact for spousal abuse. In L. Ogrodnik (ed.) *Family Violence in Canada: A Statistical Profile 2007*. Statistics Canada catalogue no. 85-224-XIE. Ottawa: Minister of Industry, pp. 9–16.

Olive, David. (2007, January 13). A State of Constant Dread: Poverty Today. *The Toronto Star*, p. A1, A21.

Oliver, P. E., & Marwell, G. (1992). Mobilizing technologies for collective action. In A. D. Morris & C. C. Mueller (Eds.), *Frontiers in social movement theory* (pp. 251–272). New Haven, CT: Yale University Press.

Olneck, M. R., & Bills, D. B. (1980). What makes Sammy run? An empirical assessment of the Bowles-Gintis correspondence theory. *American Journal of Education, 89,* 27–61.

Olsen, D. (1980). *The state elite*. Toronto: McClelland and Stewart.

Olshansky, S. J., Carnes, B., Rogers, R. G., & Smith, L. (1997, July). Infectious diseases—New and ancient threats to world health. *Population Bulletin, 52*(2), 1–51.

O'Neill, H. (1997, April 6). Strange, strange worlds. *Alton Telegraph*, p. A10.

Organization for Economic Cooperation and Development (OECD). (2002). *Level of Educational Attainment in the Population Aged 25 to 64, OECD Countries, 2000*.

Palen, J. J. (1987). *The Urban World* (3rd ed.). New York: McGraw-Hill.

Pancevski, B. (2007, February 12). Imprisoned girls 'may never recover.' *The Australian*. Available at: www.theaustralian.news.com.

Parfit, M. (1990, April). Earth First!ers wield a mean monkey wrench. *Smithsonian, 21*(1), pp. 184–204.

Parsons, T. (1940). An analytic approach to the theory of social stratification. *American Journal of Sociology, 45,* 841–862.

Parsons, T. (1953). Illness and the role of the physician: A sociological perspective. In C. Kluckhohn & H. A. Murray (Eds.), *Personality in nature, society, and culture* (2nd ed., pp. 609–617). New York: Knopf.

Parsons, T. (1954). The professions and social structure. In T. Parsons (Ed.), *Essays in Sociological Theory* (Rev. ed., pp. 34–49). New York: Free Press.

Pasternak, J. (2002, October). Definition of ageism. *50 Plus*, pp. 99–100.

Pearce, Tralee. (2008, March 11). Men Twice as Likely to Get Knee Surgery. *The Globe and Mail,* pp. L1, L4.

Pennar, K., & Farrell, C. (1993, February 15). Notes from the underground economy. *Business Week*, pp. 98–101.

Pennington, B. (2004, October 18). Reading, writing and corporate sponsorships. *New York Times*.

Peritz, I. (2000, February 22). Sex-change soldier hails Canada's liberal attitudes. *Globe and Mail*, pp. A1, A17.

Peritz, I. (2005, February 11). Unionized Wal-Mart employees fear second Quebec store to shut. *Globe and Mail*, p. A7.

Perkel, Colin. (2007, January 28). Female Profs Lag in Pay, Promotions. www.thestar.com/printArticle/175746.

Perrow, C. (1991, December). A society of organizations. *Theory and Society, 20*(6), 725–762.

Persell, C. H, Catsambis, S., & Cookson, P. W., Jr. (1992). Family background, school type, and college attendance: A conjoint system of cultural capital transmission. *Journal of Research on Adolescence, 2*(1), 1–23.

Peter, L. J., & Hull, R. (1969). *The Peter Principle: Why things always go wrong*. New York: Morrow.

Peters, D. (2007). Courage under Fire: Rescue Heroes Mike Landry, Andy Hilderman, Mark Barnard. *Readers Digest Canada*. www.readersdigest.ca/mag/2008/01/heroes_of_the_year_5.php.

Peterson, K. A., Paulson, S. E., & Williams, K. K. (2007). Relations of Eating Disorder Symptomology with Perceptions of Pressures from Mothers, Peers, and Media in Adolescent Girls and Boys. *Sex Roles.* 57, pp. 629–639.

Petras, J., & Veltmeyer, H. (2001). *Globalization unmasked: Imperialism in the 21st century*. Halifax: Fernwood Books.

Phillipson, C. (2003). Globalization and the new reconstruction of old age: New challenges for critical gerontology. In S. Biggs, A. Lowenstein, & J. Hendricks (Eds.), *The need for theory: Critical approaches to social gerontology* (pp. 163–179). Amityville, NY: Baywood.

Philp, M. (2000, June 5). Canadians enjoy long and healthy lives: But 12th-place ranking lags behind nations with more aggressive programs. *Globe and Mail*.

Picard, A. (2008, February 14). Smoking Deaths An Epidemic in India. *The Globe and Mail*. p. A15.

Pier, Carol. (2007). *Discounting Rights: Wal-Mart's Violation of US Workers' Right to Freedom of Association*. New York: Human Rights Watch.

Pike, J. J., & Jennings, N. A. (2005). The effects of commercials on children's perceptions of gender appropriate toy use. *Sex Roles, 52*(1/2), 83–91.

Pillemer, K., & Suitor, J. J. (1992). Violence and violent feelings: What causes them among family caregivers? *Journal of Gerontology, 47*(4), 165–172.

Pitt, R. & Borland, E. (2008). "Bachelorhood and Men's Attitudes about Gender Roles." *Journal of Men's Studies*. 16,1, pp. 140–158.

Pitts, G. (2002, March 1). For the billionaire set, it was a very ugly year. *Globe and Mail*, pp. A1, A7.

Pizarro, M. (1998). Chicana/o power! Epistemology and methodology for social justice and empowerment in chicana/o communities. *Qualitative Studies in Education, 11*(1), 57–80.

Pollard, J. (2001, Fall). The impact of religious affiliation and religious practices on attitudes toward euthanasia. *York University Institute for Social Research Newsletter, 16*, pp. 1–4.

Polsby, N. W. (1959, December). Three problems in the analysis of community power. *American Sociological Review, 24*(6), 796–803.

Pomerantz, S. (2006). "Did You See What She Was Wearing?" The Power and Politics of Schoolgirl Style. In Y. Jiwani, C. Steenbergen, C. Mitchell (Eds.) *Girlhood: Redefining the Limits* (pp. 173–190). Montreal: Black Rose.

Ponting, J. R. (Ed.). (1986). *Arduous Journey: Canadian Indians and Decolonization*. Toronto: McClelland and Stewart.

Porter, J. (1965). *The vertical mosaic: An analysis of social class and power in Canada.* Toronto: University of Toronto Press.

Porter, J., Porter, M., & Blishen, B. (1979). *Does money matter?* (Rev. ed.). Toronto: Macmillan.

Prentice, A. (1977). *The school promoters: Education and social class in mid-nineteenth century Upper Canada*. Toronto: McClelland and Stewart.

Prus, R. (2007). Activities and Interdependencies in the Educational Process: An Interactionist Approach to Student Ventures in Learning. In L. Tepperman & H. Dickinson (Eds.) *Reading Sociology: Canadian Perspectives* (pp. 113–115). Don Mills: Oxford University Press.

Pupo, N. (2004, Spring). Community service: Coercion or volunteerism? *CRWS News, 29*.

Pupo, N., & Duffy, A. (2005). Locating "mandatory retirement" in the midst of economic and social transformations. In C. T. Gillin,

Putney, N. M., & Bengston, V. L. (2002). Socialization and the family revisited. In R. A. Settersen, Jr., & T. J. Owens (Eds.), *New Frontiers in Socialization* (pp. 165–194). Amsterdam: JAI Press.

Pyper, W. (2002, Autumn). Falling behind. *Perspectives on Labour and Income, 14*, pp. 21–27.

Quart, A. (2003). *Branded: The buying and selling of teenagers*. New York: Basic.

Quinn, J. (2002, March 31). Food bank clients often well-educated immigrants. *Toronto Star*, p. A12.

Quirke, L. (2006). 'Keeping Young Minds Sharp': Children's Cognitive Stimulation and the Rise of Parenting Magazines, 1959–2003. *Canadian Review of Sociology and Anthropology.* 43, 4: pp. 387–406.

Raby, R. (2007). "Polite, Well-dressed, and On Time: Secondary School Conduct Codes and the Production of Docile Citizens." In. L. Tepperman & H. Dickinson (Eds.) *Reading Sociology: Canadian Perspectives* (pp. 116–119). Don Mills: Oxford University Press.

Raghunathan, V. K. (2003, February 8). Millions of Baby Girls Killed in India. *The Straits Times*.

Raphael, D. (2001, August 20). Poverty is at root of heart disease. *Toronto Star*, p. A17.

Rathus, S., & Nevid, J. (1993). *Human Sexuality in a World of Diversity*. Boston: Allyn and Bacon.

Raymond, Melanie. (2008, April). *High School Dropouts Returning to School*. Statistics Canada, Catalogue No. 81-595-MIE, www.statcan.ca/english/research/81-595-MIE/81-595-MIE2008055.pdf.

Read, P. P. (1974). *Alive. The story of the Andes survivors*. Philadelphia: Lippincott.

Reed, S., & Benet, L. (1990, April 16). Ecowarrior Dave Foreman will do whatever it takes in his fight to save Mother Earth. *People Weekly, 33*(15), 113–116.

Rees, W. E. (2002, April 22). Squeezing the poor. *Toronto Star*, p. A17.

Reich, M. (1972). The economics of racism. In R. C. Edwards, M. Reich, & T. E. Weiskopf (Eds.), *The capitalist system* (pp. 313–321). Englewood Cliffs, NJ: Prentice Hall.

Reiman, J. (2001). *The Rich Get Richer and the Poor Get Prison: Ideology, Class and Criminal Justice*. Boston: Allyn and Bacon.

Reiman, Jeffrey. (2004). *The Rich Get Richer and the Poor Get Prison: Ideology, Class, and Criminal Justice* (7th ed.). Boston: Allyn and Bacon.

Reimer, M. (2008). Academic Women in Pre-Tenure Years: Applying Bourdieu. M.A. Thesis, Brock University.

Reimer, M. & Mueller, A. (2007). University Restructuring and the Female Liberal Arts Undergraduate Student: Does She Get 'Value for the Money' at Corporate U? In. L. Tepperman & H. Dickinson (Eds.) *Reading Sociology: Canadian Perspectives* (pp. 123–128.). Don Mills: Oxford University Press.

Reinharz, S. (1997). Friends or foes: Gerontological and feminist theory. In M. Pearsall (Ed.), *The Other within Us: Feminist Explorations of Women and Aging* (pp. 73–94). Boulder, CO: Westview.

Restoule, J. P. (2005). Aboriginal Identity: The Need for Historical and Contextual Perspectives. In B. Ravelli (Ed.), *Exploring Canadian Sociology* (pp. 159–168). Toronto: Pearson Prentice Hall.

Ribeiro, Silvia. (2005, January 16). The costs of "Walmartization." *Znet*.

Richards, B. (1996, January 17). Doctors can diagnose illnesses long distance, to the dismay of some. *Wall Street Journal*, pp. A1, A8.

Ricks, T. E. (1994, February 14). Pentagon considers selling overseas a large part of high-tech weaponry. *Wall Street Journal*, p. A16.

Ridley, M. (2003). *The Agile Gene: How Nature Turns On Nurture*. New York: Harper Collins.

Riesman, D. (1970). The suburban dislocation. In A. N. Cousins & H. Nagpaul (Eds.), *Urban man and society: A reader in urban ecology* (pp. 172–184). New York: Knopf.

Rifkin, J. (1995). *The end of work: The decline of the global labor force and the dawn of the post-market era*. New York: Putnam.

Righton, B. (2002, October). Well Done. *50 Plus*, pp. 42–46.

Riley, Nancy E. (2004, June). China's Population: New Trends and Challenges. *Population Bulletin, 59*(2): 3–36.

Rinehart, James W. (2006). *The Tyranny of Work: Alienation and the Labour Process. Fifth Edition*. Toronto: Nelson Thomson.

Rist, R. C. (1970, August). Student social class and teacher expectations: The self-fulfilling prophecy in ghetto education. *Harvard Educational Review, 40*(3), 411–451.

Ritzer, G. (1993). *The McDonaldization of society: An investigation into the changing character of contemporary life*. Thousand Oaks, CA: Pine Forge Press.

Ritzer, G. (1998). *The McDonaldization Thesis: Explorations and Extensions*. London: Sage Publications.

Robb, John. (2007, Summer). The Coming Urban Terror. *City Journal*. Online.

Roberts, S. D., & Zhou, N. (1997, June). The 50 and older characters in advertisements of modern maturity: Growing older, getting better. *Journal of Applied Gerontology, 16*(2), 208–220.

Robertson, I. (1987). *Sociology* (3rd ed.). New York: Worth.

Robinson, Tom, Callister, Mark, Magoffin, Dawn, & Moore, Jennifer. (2007, August). "The Portrayal of Older Characters in Disney Animated Films." *Journal of Aging Studies*, Volume 21, Number 3, pp. 203–213.

Rodríguez, V. M. (1994, Spring). Los Angeles, USA 1992: A house divided against itself. *SSSP Newsletter, 5*–12.

Roethlisberger, F. J., & Dickson, W. J. (1939). *Management and the worker*. Cambridge, MA: Harvard University Press.

Roper, E. A. & Halloran. E. (2007). "Attitudes toward Gay Men and Lesbians Among Heterosexual Male and Female Student-Athletes." *Sex Roles* 57, 919–928.

Rosaldo, M. Z. (1974). Women, culture and society: A theoretical overview. In M. Z. Rosaldo & L. Lamphere (Eds.), *Women, culture, and society*. Stanford: Stanford University Press.

Rose, F. (1992, May 5). Los Angeles tallies losses; curfew is lifted. *Wall Street Journal*, pp. A3, A18.

Rosenthal, E. (1999, December 9). China's chic waistline: Convex to concave. *New York Times*.

Ross, A. (Ed.). (1999). *No sweat: Fashion, free trade, and the rights of garment workers*. New York and London: Verso.

Ross, O. (2002, July 20). World shows Canada how to cope with elderly. *Toronto Star*, p. E8.

Ross, S. R. & Shinew, K. J. (2008). Perspectives of Women College Athletes on Sport and Gender. *Sex Roles*. 58, 40–57.

Rossi, A. S. (1977). A biosocial perspective on parenting. *Daedalus, 106*, 1–31.

Rossi, A. S. (1984). Gender and parenthood. *American Sociological Review, 49*, 1–18.

Rotello, G. (1996, July 14). The risk in a "cure" for AIDS. *New York Times*.

Rothschild, J., & Whitt, J. A. (1986). *The cooperative workplace: Potentials and dilemmas of organizational democracy and participation*. Cambridge, England: Cambridge University Press.

Rubin, Gayle S. (1984). Thinking sex: Notes for a radical theory of the politics of sexuality. In Henry Abelove, Michele Aina Barale, & David M. Halperin (Eds.), *The Lesbian and Gay Studies Reader* (pp. 3–44). New York & London: Routledge.

Rubin, L. B. (1976). *Worlds of pain: Life in the working-class family*. New York: Basic Books.

Rudd, J. (2001). Dowry-Murder: An example of violence against women. *Women's Studies International Forum, 24*, pp. 513–522.

Ruggles, P. (1989, June). Short and long term poverty in the United States: Measuring the American "underclass." Washington, DC: Urban Institute.

Rushing, W. A. (1995). *The AIDS epidemic: Social dimensions of an infectious disease*. Boulder, CO: Westview Press.

Rushowy, K. (2000, March 23). Tuition deters poor, study finds. *Toronto Star*, p. A8.

Russell, D. (1987, Fall). The monkeywrenchers. *Amicus Journal*, 28–42.

Ryan, J. (1998, Fall). Understanding racial/ethnic stereotyping in schools: From image to discourse. *Alberta Journal of Educational Research, 44*(3), 30–42.

Sachs, J. D. (2005, March 14). The end of poverty. *Time Magazine* (Canadian Edition), pp. 32ff.

Sainath, P. (1996). *Everybody loves a good drought*. London: Review.

Samuelson, P. A., & Nordhaus, W. D. (1989). *Economics* (13th ed.). New York: McGraw-Hill.

Sanchez, L. (1994, December). Gender, labor allocations, and the psychology of entitlement within the home. *Social Forces, 13*(2), 533–553.

Santos, M. G. (2006). *Inside: Life Behind Bars in America.* New York: St. Martin's Griffin.

Sapir, E. (1949a). The status of linguistics as science. In D. G. Mandelbaum (Ed.), *Culture, language, and personality.* Berkeley, CA: University of California Press.

Sapir, E. (1949b). Selected writings of Edward Sapir. In D. G. Mandelbaum (Ed.), *Culture, language, and personality.* Berkeley, CA: University of California Press.

Sargent, J. D. et al. (2007). Exposure to Smoking Depictions in Movies: Its Association with Established Adolescent Smoking. *Archives of Pediatrics and Adolescent Medicine.* 161(9), 849–856.

Sarkisian, N. & Gerstel, N. (2008). "Till Marriage Do Us Part: Adult Children's Relationships With Their Parents." *Journal of Marriage and the Family.* 70, May, 360–376.

Sarlo, C. (1992). *Poverty in Canada.* Vancouver: The Fraser Institute.

Saturday Special. (2002, March 23). *Toronto Star,* pp. A24, 25.

Sauve, R. (2005). *The current state of Canadian family finances—2004 report.* The Vanier Institute of the Family, www. vifamily.ca/library/publications/state04_pub.html.

Sauve, R. (2007). "Family Finances . . . The Rest of the Story." *Transition Magazine 37,* 1 (Spring). www.vifamily.ca/library/transition/371/371.html.

Sawatsky, J. (1980). *Men in the Shadows: The RCMP Security Service.* Toronto: Doubleday Canada.

Sawyer, R. (2001). Dire new acid rain study. *Conservation Matters, 8*(1), 23–34.

Scarce, R. (1993a, June 12–13). Rik Scarce responds: A clear-cut case of academic freedom at risk. *Daily News* (Moscow-Pullman), p. 1B.

Scarce, R. (1993b, June 15). Turnabout: Jailed for no crime at all. *Morning Tribune* (Lewiston).

Scarce, R. (1994, July). (No) trial (but) tribulations. *Journal of Contemporary Ethnography, 23*(2), 123–149.

Schaefer, R. T. (1989). *Sociology* (3rd ed.). New York: McGraw-Hill.

Scheff, T. J. (2006). *Goffman Unbound: A New Paradigm for Social Science.* Boulder, Colorado: Paradigm Publishers.

Schlesinger, J. M. (1994, January 31). For what ails Japan, some think the cure is a good hot slogan. *Wall Street Journal,* pp. A1, A7.

Schlosser, E. (2002). *Fast food nation: The dark side of the all-American meal.* New York: Perennial Books.

Schor, J. B. (2004). *Born to Buy.* New York: Scribner.

Schur, E. M. (1984). *Labeling women deviant: Gender, stigma, and social control.* New York: Random House.

Schwartz, F. N. (1989, January–February). Management women and the new facts of life. *Harvard Business Review, 89*(1), 65–76.

Schwartz, M. A. (1990). *A sociological perspective on politics.* Englewood Cliffs, NJ: Prentice Hall.

Scommegna, P. (1996, August). Teens' risk of AIDS, unintended pregnancies examined. *Population Today, 24*(8), 1–2.

Scott, E. K. (1993, August). How to stop the rapists: A question of strategy in two rape crisis centers. *Social Problems, 40*(3), 343–361.

Scott-Dixon, K. (2004). *Doing IT: Women working in information technology.* Toronto: Sumach Press.

Scully, D. (1990). *Understanding sexual violence: A study of convicted rapists.* Boston: Unwin Hyman.

Scully, D., & Marolla, J. (1984, June). Convicted rapists' vocabulary of motive: excuses and justifications. *Social Problems, 31*(5), 530–544.

Scully, D., & Marolla, J. (1985, February). Riding the bull at Gilley's: Convicted rapists describe the rewards of rape. *Social Problems, 32*(3), 251–263.

Seager, J. (2003). *The Penguin atlas of women in the world.* New York: Penguin Books.

Selvin, Molly & Goldman, Abigail. (2007, April 10). Boomers Facing Fresh Battle at Work. *The Toronto Star,* p. D16.

Settersten, R. A., & Owens, T. J. (Eds.). (2002). *New frontiers in socialization: Advances in life course research.* Kidlington, Oxford: Elsevier Science Ltd.

Sexual identity is inborn trait, according to study. (1997, March 16). *Alton Telegraph,* p. A6.

Shaienks, Danielle, Eisl-Culkin, Judy, & Brussiere, Patrick. (2006, July). Follow-Up on Education and Labour Market Pathways of Young Canadians Aged 18 to 20—Results from YITS, Cycle 3. Research Paper, Statistics Canada and Human Resources and Social Development Canada, Catalogue No. 81-595-MIE, No. 045.

Shalla, V. (1997). Technology and the deskilling of work: The case of passenger agents at Air Canada. In A. Duffy, D. Glenday, & N. Pupo (Eds.), *Good jobs, bad jobs, no jobs: The transformation of work in the 21st century.* Toronto: Harcourt Brace.

Sharma, S. S. (1994). Untouchables and Brahmins in an Indian village. In J. Curtis & L. Tepperman (Eds.), *Haves and have-nots: An international reader on social inequality* (pp. 299–303). Englewood Cliffs, NJ: Prentice Hall.

Sharp, L. (1995). Steel axes for stone-age Australians. In J. M. Henslin (Ed.), *Down to earth sociology: Introductory readings* (8th ed., pp. 453–462). New York: Free Press.

Shaw, R. (2003). *The epidemic: The rot of American culture, absentee and permissive parenting and the resultant plague of joyless, selfish children.* New York: Regan Books/HarperCollins.

Shaw, S. M., & Lee, J. (2001). *Women's voices, feminist visions: Classic and contemporary readings.* Mountain View, CA: Mayfield Publishing Company.

Shimo, Alexandra. (2008). "Book Your Desk Now—Spaces Are Limited." *globeandmail.com,* accessed January 21, 2008 at www.theglobeandmail.com/servlet/story/RTGAM.20080121. wlhotel21/BNStory/life/Work/#.

Shenon, P. (1995, January 2). AIDS epidemic, late to arrive, now explodes in populous Asia. *New York Times,* pp. A1, A12.

Sherif, M., & Sherif, C. (1953). *Groups in harmony and tension.* New York: Harper & Row.

Sherman, B. (1985). *Working at Leisure.* London: Methuen.

Shibutani, T. (1966). *Improvised news: A sociological study of rumor.* Indianapolis, IN: Bobbs-Merrill.

Shields, M., & Tremblay, S. (2002). *The Health of Canada's Communities.* Ottawa: Statistics Canada, Supplement to Health Reports, 13, Catalogue 82-003.

Shields, N. (2002). Anticipatory socialization, adjustment to university life, perceived stress: Generational and sibling effects. *Social Psychology of Education, 5,* 365–392.

Silver, I. (1977, March–April). Crime and conventional wisdom. *Society, 14*(9), 15–19.

Silverman, Craig. (2008, March 24). Smile, Big Brother's Watching. *The Globe and Mail,* p. L3.

Simkin, John. (n.d.). Harriet Martineau, www.spartacus.schoolnet.co.uk/Wmartineau.htm.

Simon, J. L. (1981). *The ultimate resource.* Princeton, NJ: Princeton University Press.

Simon, J. L. (1992). Population growth is not bad for humanity. In K. Finsterbusch & G. McKenna (Eds.), *Taking sides: Clashing views on controversial social issues* (pp. 347–352). Guilford, CT: Dushkin.

Simon, J. L. (1996). *The ultimate resource 2.* Princeton, NJ: Princeton University Press.

Simon, R. (2008). "The joys of parenthood reconsidered." *Contexts.*7, 2, pp. 40–45.

Simpson, Mark. (1994). *Male Impersonators: Men Performing Masculinity.* Routledge.

Sklair, L. (2001). *Globalization: Capitalism and its alternatives* (3rd ed.). New York: Oxford University Press.

Smeaton, D. (2006). "Work return rates after childbirth in the UK—trends, determinants and implications." *Work, employment and society.* 20, 1, pp. 5–25.

Smith, C. S. (1995, October 9). China becomes industrial nations' most favored dump. *Wall Street Journal,* p. B1.

Smith, D. E. (1987). *The everyday world as problematic: A feminist sociology.* Boston: Northeastern University Press.

Smith, D. E. (1990). *Texts, facts and femininity: Exploring the relations of ruling.* London: Routledge.

Smith, D. E. (1999). *Writing the social: Critique, theory, and investigations.* Toronto: University of Toronto Press.

Smith, G. (2006). *Erving Goffman.* New York: Routledge.

Smith, J. B., & Tirpak, D. A. (1988, October). *The potential effects of global climate change in the United States.* Washington, DC: U.S. Environmental Protection Agency.

Smith, L. (1987, July 20). The war between the generations. *Fortune,* pp. 78–82.

Smith, M. (Ed.). (1990). *Breaking chains: Social movements and collective action.* New Brunswick, NJ: Transaction Publishers.

Smith, M. J., & Hightower, J. (2004). What's age got to do with it? *Education Wife Assault Newsletter on Older Woman Abuse, 13*(1). Available at www.womanabuseprevention.com/html/elder_abuse_newsletter.htm.

Smith-Lovin, L., & Brody, C. (1989). Interruptions in group discussions: The effects of gender and group composition. *American Sociological Review, 54,* 424–435.

Snow, D. A., Zurcher, L. A., & Peters, R. (1993). Victory celebrations as theater: A dramaturgical approach to crowd behavior. In R. L. Curtis, Jr., & B. E. Aguirre (Eds.), *Collective behavior and social movements* (pp. 194–208). Boston: Allyn and Bacon.

Snow, D. A., Zurcher, L. A., & Ekland-Olson, S. (1993). Social networks and social movements: A microstructural approach to differential recruitment. In R. L. Curtis, Jr., & B. E. Aguirre (Eds.), *Collective behavior and social movements* (pp. 323–334). Boston: Allyn and Bacon.

Sokoloff, H. (2002, October 10). Quarter of children at risk: study. *Toronto Star,* pp. A1, A8.

Sokoloff, H. (2008, February 26). Grandpa says: 'Push.' *Globe and Mail,* pp. L1, L3.

Sontag, S. (1994). As quoted in C. K. Riessman, Women and medicalization: A new perspective. In H. D. Schwartz (Ed.), *Dominant issues in medical sociology* (3rd ed., pp. 190–211). New York: McGraw-Hill.

Sorenson, J. (2003). "Everybody is a racist; it's part of human nature." In J. Blackwell, M. Smith, J. Sorenson (Eds.), *Culture of Prejudice: Arguments in Critical Social Science* (pp. 37–45). Toronto: Broadview Press.

Spector, M., & Kitsuse, J. (1977). *Constructing social problems.* Menlo Park, CA: Cummings.

Spencer, M. (1996). *Foundations of modern sociology,* (7th ed.). Toronto: Prentice Hall.

Spitzer, S. (1975, June). Toward a Marxian theory of deviance. *Social Problems, 22,* 608–619.

Srole, L., et al. (1978). *Mental health in the metropolis: The midtown Manhattan study.* New York: New York University Press.

St. Arnaud, Beaudet & Tully, Patricia. (2005, November 16). Life Expectancy. *Health Reports,* Volume 17, Number 1, Statistics Canada.

Stark, E. (1989). Friends through it all. In J. M. Henslin (Ed.), *Marriage and family in a changing society* (3rd ed., pp. 441–449). New York: Free Press.

Stark, R. (1989). *Sociology* (3rd ed.). Belmont, CA: Wadsworth.

Starna, W. A., & Watkins, R. (1991, Winter). Northern Iroquoian slavery. *Ethnohistory, 38*(1), 34–57.

Starrels, M. (1992, September). The evolution of workplace family policy research. *Journal of Family Issues, 13*(3), 259–278.

Statham, A., Miller, E. M., & Mauksch, H. O. (1988). The integration of work: Second-order analysis of qualitative research. In A. Statham, E. M. Miller, & H. O. Mauksch (Eds.), *The worth of women's work: A qualitative synthesis* (pp. 11–35). Albany, NY: State University of New York Press.

Statistical Abstract of the United States. (Published annually). Washington DC: Bureau of the Census.

Statistics Canada. (Selected years). *General Social Survey.*

Statistics Canada. (1998). *Family incomes.* Ottawa: Minister of Supply and Services, Catalogue 13-208.

Statistics Canada. (2002, July). *General social survey—Changing conjugal life in Canada.* Ottawa: Minister of Industry, Catalogue 89-576-XIE.

Statistics Canada. (2003a). *Income of Canadian families.* 2001 Census: Analysis Series. Ottawa: Minister of Industry, Catalogue 96F0030XIE2001014.

Statistics Canada. (2003b). *Earnings of Canadians: Making a living in the new economy.*2001 Census: Analysis Series. Ottawa: Minister of Industry, Catalogue 96F0030XIE2001013.

Statistics Canada. (2003c). *Profile of Canada's labour force. Census of Canada.* Available at www12.statcan.ca/english/census01/products/analytic/companion/paid/canada.cfm.

Statistics Canada. (2003d, May 23). Social support and mortality among seniors. *The Daily.* Ottawa: Minister of Industry.

Statistics Canada. (2004a, December 13). Research data centres: Social and economic aspects of aging. *The Daily.* Ottawa: Minister of Industry.

Statistics Canada. (2004b, July 2). Study: Economic consequences of widowhood. *The Daily.* Ottawa: Minister of Industry.

Statistics Canada (2004c). *Overview: Canadians better educated than ever. 2001 census.* Available at www12.statcan.ca/english/census01/Products/Analytic/companion/educ/canada.cfm.

Statistics Canada. (2004d). *University qualifications granted by field of study, by sex* (Table, 2001 Census). Available at www.statcan.ca/english/Pgdb/educ21.htm.

Statistics Canada. (2004e). *Distance as a postsecondary access issue.* Available at www.statcan.ca/english/freepub/81-004-XIE/200404/dist.htm.

Statistics Canada. (2004f, March 29). Suicide in Canada's immigrant population. *The Daily.* Ottawa: Minister of Industry.

Statistics Canada. (2005, November 4). "Study: Socio-Economic Status and Obesity in Children." *The Daily,* November 4, 2005.

Statistics Canada. (2005a, February 1). Health indicators. *The Daily.* Available at www.statcan.ca.

Statistics Canada. (2005b). *Life expectancy at birth, by sex, by provinces.* Available at www.statcan.ca. Last modified February 17, 2005.

Statistics Canada. (2005c, February 10). Study: Trends in income inequality in Canada from an international perspective. *The Daily.* Available at www.statcan.ca.

Statistics Canada. (2006, February 7). "Health Reports: Seniors' Health Care Use." *The Daily.* www.statcan.ca/Daily/English/060207/d060207a.htm.

Statistics Canada. (2006, April). *Low Wage and Low Income.* Catalogue No.: 75F0002MIE, Volume 6.

Statistics Canada. (2006, April). Income Statistics Division. "Low Wage and Low Income." Catalogue No. 75 F0002MIE.

Statistics Canada. (2006, December 12). "Survey of Household Spending." *The Daily.*

Statistics Canada. (2006). *Women in Canada: A Gender-based Statistical Report.* 5th Ed. Catalogue no. 89-503-XPE. Ottawa: Minister of Industry.

Statistics Canada. (2006a). "Violence Against Women: A Statistical Profile." *The Daily,* October 2, 2006. www.statcan.ca/Daily/English/061002/d061002a.htm.

Statistics Canada. (2007, April). *Women in Canada: Work Chapter Updates.* Catalogue 89F0133XIE7.

Statistics Canada. (2007, May 29). "Family Income," *The Daily.* www.statcan.ca/Daily/English/070529/d070529e.htm.

Statistics Canada. (2007, August 30). "Public School Indicators." *The Daily.* www.statcan.ca/Daily/English/070830/d070830d.htm.

Statistics Canada. (2007). 2006 Census: Portrait of the Canadian Population, By Age and Sex: National Portrait. November 7, 2007. www12.statcan.ca/english/census06/analysis/agesex/NatlPortrait8.cfm.

Statistics Canada. (2007). *Family Portrait: Continuity and Change in Canadian Families and Households in 2006, 2006 Census.* Catalogue no. 97-53-XIE. Ottawa: Minister of Industry.

Statistics Canada, (2007a). 2006 Census: Portrait of the Canadian Population, By Age and Sex: National Portrait. July 16, 2007. www12.statcan.ca/english/census06/analysis/agesex/NatlPortrait2.cfm.

Statistics Canada. (2008, February 8). "Study: Participation in Sports." *The Daily.* Available at www.statcan.ca.

Statistics Canada. (2008, February 8). "University Enrolment." *The Daily.* www.statcan.ca/Daily/English/080207/d080207a.htm.

Statistics Canada. (2008, March). "Canada's Changing Labour Force, 2006 Census." Catalogue No. 97-559-X.

Statistics Canada. (2008, April 29). "Why are the Majority of University Students Women?" *Education Matters,* Catalogue 81-004-XIE, Volume 5, No. 1. www.statcan.ca/english/freepub/81-004-XIE/2008001/article/10561-en.htm.

Statistics Canada. (2008). *Canada's Ethnocultural Mosaic, 2006 Census.* Catalogue no. 97-562-X. Ottawa: Minister of Industry.

Statistics Canada, (2008a). 2006 Census: Analysis Series. *Educational Portrait of Canada, 2006 Census: National Picture.* "Male and Female University Graduates Study in Different Fields." www12.statcan.ca/english/census06/analysis/education/male_female.cfm.

Statistics Canada, (2008b). 2006 Census: Analysis Series. *Educational Portrait of Canada, 2006 Census: National Picture.* "Field of Study: One in Five Postsecondary Graduates Studied in Business, Management, Marketing and Related Support Services." www12.statcan.ca/english/census06/analysis/education/field_study.cfm.

Statistics Canada. (2008c). "Census Snapshot: Canada's Changing Labour Force, 2006 Census." *Canadian Social Trends.* Statistics Catalogue No. 11-008, June 3, 2008, pp. 69–72. http://dsp-psd.pwgsc.gc.ca/collection_2008/statcan/11-008-X/11-008-XIE2008001.pdf.

Statistics Canada e-Book. (2005a). Common law. *The people.* Available at http://142.206.72.67/02/02d/02d_001b_e.htm.

Statistics Canada e-Book. (2005b). Family arrangements. *The people.* Available at http://142.206.72.67/02/02d/02d_001_e.htm.

Statistics Canada and Human Resource Development Canada. (2005). *National longitudinal survey of children and youth: Report.* Catalogue No. 89M0015XCB.

Stein, L. I. (1988). The doctor–nurse game. In J. M. Henslin (Ed.), *Down to earth sociology: Introductory readings* (5th ed., pp. 102–109). New York: Free Press.

Steinberg, L., Dornbusch, S., & Brown, B. (1996). *Beyond the classroom.* New York: Simon & Shuster.

Steinem, G. (1992). *Revolution from within.* Boston: Little, Brown and Company.

Sterling, T. (2004, December 1). Dutch hospital admits to euthanasia of ill babies. *Toronto Star,* p. A12.

Sternheimer, K. (2007). Do Video Games Kill? *Contexts.* 6(1) pp. 13–17.

Stevens, A., & Lubman, S. (1992, May 1). Deciding moment of the trial may have been five months ago. *Wall Street Journal,* p. A6.

Stevenson, G. (1987). *The politics of Canada's airlines from Diefenbaker to Mulroney.* Toronto: University of Toronto Press.

Stinson, K. (2001). *Women and dieting culture: Inside a commercial weight loss group.* New Brunswick, N.J.: Rutgers University Press.

Stobert, S., & Cranswick, K. (2004, Autumn). Looking after seniors: Who does what for whom? *Canadian Social Trends, 74,* pp. 2–6.

Stobert, S., & Kemeny, A. (2003, Summer). Childfree by choice. *Canadian Social Trends,* pp. 7–13. Ottawa: Statistics Canada, Catalogue No. 11-008.

Stockard, J., & Johnson, M. M. (1980). *Sex roles: Sex inequality and sex role development.* Englewood Cliffs, NJ: Prentice Hall.

Stockwell, J. (1989, February). The dark side of U.S. foreign policy. *Zeta Magazine,* pp. 36–48.

Stone, G. P. (1954, November). City shoppers and urban identification: Observations on the social psychology of city life. *American Journal of Sociology, 60,* 276–284.

Stone, P. (2007). *Opting Out? Why Women Really quit Careers and Head Home.* Berkeley: University of California Press.

Stouffer, S. A., Lumsdaine, A. A., Lumsdaine, M. H., Williams, R. M., Jr., Smith, M. B., Janis, I. L., et al. (1949). *The American soldier: Combat and its aftermath* (Vol. 2). New York: Wiley.

Stout, H. (1992, June 4). Harvard team says that AIDS is accelerating. *Wall Street Journal,* p. B10.

Straus, R. A. (1991). The sociologist as a marketing research consultant. *Journal of Applied Sociology, 8,* 65–75.

Strauss, Neil. (1998, July 14). Critic's notebook: A Japanese TV show that pairs beauty and pain. *New York Times.*

Strohschein, L. (2005). Parental Divorce and Child Mental Health Trajectories. *Journal of Marriage and the Family.* 67, December, 1286–1300.

Strough, J. et al. (2007). From Adolescence to Later Adulthood: Femininity, Masculinity, and Androgyny in Six Age Groups. *Sex Roles.* 57, 385–396.

Stryker, S. (1990). Symbolic interactionism: Themes and variations. In M. Rosenberg & R. H. Turner (Eds.), *Social psychology: Sociological perspectives* New Brunswick, NJ: Transaction.

Sumner, W. G. (1906). *Folkways: A study in the sociological importance of usages, manners, customs, mores, and morals*. New York: Ginn.

Sussman, D., & Tabi, M. (2004, Summer). Minimum wage workers. *Perspectives on Labour and Income*, pp. 5–14. Catalogue 75-001-XPE.

Sutfin, E. L., Flulcher, M., Bowles, R. P., & Patterson, C. J. (2008). How Lesbian and Heterosexual Parents Convey Attitudes about Gender to their Children: The Role of Gendered Environments. *Sex Roles*. 58, 501–513.

Sutherland, E. H. (1924). *Criminology*. Philadelphia: Lippincott.

Sutherland, E. H. (1947). *Principles of criminology* (4th ed.). Philadelphia: Lippincott.

Sutherland, E. H. (1949). *White collar crime*. New York: Dryden Press.

Sutherland, E. H., & Cressey, D. (1974). *Criminology* (9th ed.). Philadelphia: Lippincott.

Sutherland, E. H., Cressey, D. R., & Luckenbill, D. F. (1992). *Principles of criminology* (11th ed.). Dix Hills, NY: General Hall.

Swift, J. (1995). *Wheel of fortune: Work and life in the age of falling expectations*. Toronto: Between the Lines.

Sydie, R. A. (1987). *Natural women cultured men: A feminist perspective on sociological theory*. Toronto: Methuen.

Sykes, G. M., & Matza, D. (1988). Techniques of neutralization. In J. M. Henslin (Ed.), *Down to earth sociology: Introductory readings* (5th ed., pp. 225–231). New York: Free Press. (First published 1957).

Szasz, T. S. (1986). *The myth of mental illness* (Rev. ed.). New York: Harper & Row.

Szasz, T. S. (1998). Mental illness is still a myth. In L. M. Salinger (Ed.), *Deviant behavior 96/97* (pp. 200–205). Guilford, CT: Dushkin.

Szelenyi, S. (1987). Social inequality and party membership: Patterns of recruitment in the Hungarian Socialist Workers' Party. *American Sociological Review*, 52, 559–573.

Talaga, T. (1999, September 26). How poor are caught in heart-attack trap. *Toronto Star*, pp. A1, A8.

Tandia, B. (2001). The plight of black Mauritanians. *Black Renaissance*, 3, p. 3.

Tannen, Deborah. (2007). "'But What Do You Mean?' Women and Men in Conversation." In *Down-To-Earth Sociology: Introductory Readings*. 14th edition. James M. Henslin, editor. New York: The Free Press.

Tate, W. F. (1996). Critical race theory. *Review of Research in Education*, 22, 201–247.

Taylor, Norman W. (1964). "The French-Canadian Industrial Entrepreneur and His Social Environment," in Marcel Rioux & Yves Martin (eds), *French-Canadian Society*, Volume #1, Ottawa: McClelland & Stewart, pp. 271–295.

Taylor, V. (1997). Social movement continuity: The women's movement in abeyance. In D. McAdam & D. A. Snow (Eds.), *Social movements: Readings on their emergence, mobilization, and dynamics* (pp. 409–420). Los Angeles: Roxbury Publishing.

Tenenbaum, H. R., & Leaper, C. (2003). Parent–child conversations about science: The socialization of gender inequities. *Developmental Psychology* 39(1), 34–47.

Teotonio, Isabel. (2006, December 11). Equity Key to Child Health: Report. *The Toronto Star*, p. A10.

Thomas, D. (2005, Spring). I am Canadian. *Canadian Social Trends*, pp. 2–7.

Thomas, K. (2005, April 13). IT's old-age conundrum. *National Post*, p. FP9.

Thomas, P. (1988, October 21). EPA predicts global impact from warming. *Wall Street Journal*, p. B5.

Thomas, W. I. & Thomas, Dorothy Swaine. (1928). *The Child in America: Behavior Problems and Programs*. Knopf.

Thorpe, D. (2002). Aging, language and culture. In D. Cheal (Ed.), *Aging and demographic change in Canadian context* (pp. 72–104). Toronto: University of Toronto Press.

Thurer, S. L. (2005). *The End of Gender: A Psychological Autopsy*. New York: Routledge, Taylor & Francis Group.

Tilly, C. (1978). *From mobilization to revolution*. Reading, MA: Addison-Wesley.

Timasheff, N. S. (1965). *War and revolution* (J. F. Scheuer, Ed.). New York: Sheed & Ward.

Timerman, J. (1981). *Prisoner without a name, cell without a number*. New York: Knopf.

Tindale, J., Norris, J. E., & Abbot, K. (2002). Catching up with diversity in intergenerational relations. In D. Cheal (Ed.), *Aging and demographic change in Canadian context* (pp. 245–247). Toronto: University of Toronto Press.

Tinkler, P. (2001). Rebellion, modernity and romance: Smoking as a gendered practice in popular young women's magazines, Britain 1918–1939. *Women's Studies International Forum*, 24(1), pp. 111–122.

Tocqueville, A. de. (1955). *The old regime and the French Revolution* (S. Gilbert, Trans.). Garden City, NY: Doubleday Anchor. (First published 1856).

Tocqueville, A. de. (1966). *Democracy in America* (J. P. Mayer & M. Lerner, Eds.). New York: Harper & Row. (First published 1835).

Tokoro, Masabumi. (2005). The Shift Towards American-style Human Resource Management Systems and the Transformation of Workers' Attitudes at Japanese Firms. *Asian Business and Management*, 4: pp. 23–44.

Tolchin, M. (1988, May 17). Surgeon general asserts smoking is an addiction. *New York Times*, pp. A1, C4.

Tordoff, W. (1992). The impact of ideology on development in the third world. *Journal of International Development*, 4(1), 41–53.

Troilo, S. & Coleman, M. (2008). "College Student Perceptions of the Content of Father Stereotypes." *Journal of Marriage and the Family*. 70 (February), 218–227.

Tucker, B. M., & Mitchell-Kernan, C. (1990). New trends in Black American interracial Marriage: The social structural context. *Journal of Marriage and the Family*, 52, 209–218.

Tumin, M. M. (1953, August). Some principles of social stratification: A critical analysis. *American Sociological Review* 18, 394.

Turcotte, Martin & Zhou, John. (2004, July). *A Portrait of Aboriginal Children Living in Non-Reserve Areas: Results from the 2001 Aboriginal Peoples Survey*. Statistics Canada, Catalogue No. 89-597-XIE. www.statcan.ca/english/freepub/89-597-XIE/2001001/pdf/89-597-XIE2001001.pdf.

Turcotte, M. (2006). Parents with adult children living at home. *Canadian Social Trends*. Spring, 80, 2–9.

Turcotte, M. (2007). Staying at home longer to become homeowners? *Canadian Social Trends*. Winter, 81, 32–36.

Turcotte, M. & Schellenberg. G. (2007). *A Portrait of Seniors in Canada 2006*. Statistics Canada Catalogue no. 89-519-XIE. Ottawa: Minister of Industry.

Turcotte, Martin & Schellenberg, Grant. (2007, February). *A Portrait of Seniors in Canada*. Statistics Canada, Catalogue No. 89-519-XPE. www.statcan.ca/english/freepub/89-519-XIE/89-519-XIE2006001.pdf.

Turk, J. L. (Ed.). (2000). *The corporate campus: Commercialization and the dangers to Canada's colleges and universities*. Toronto: James Lorimer.

Turkle, Sherry. (1984/2005). The Second Self: Computers and the Human Spirit. Simon and Schuster, New York; second revised edition, MIT Press, 2005.

Turkle, Sherry. (1995). *Life on the Screen: Identity in the Age of the Internet.* Simon and Schuster, New York.

Turner, B. S. (1990, May). Outline of a theory of citizenship. *Sociology, 24*(2), 189–217.

Turner, J. H. (1978). *The structure of sociological theory.* Homewood, IL: Dorsey.

Turner, R. H. (1964). Collective behavior. In R. E. L. Faris (Ed.), *Handbook of modern sociology* (pp. 382–425). Chicago: Rand McNally.

Turner, R. H. (1993). Race riots past and present: A cultural-collective behavior approach. [Paper presented at the annual meetings of the American Sociological Association].

Turner, R. H., & Killian, L. M. (1987). *Collective behavior* (2nd ed.). Englewood Cliffs, NJ: Prentice Hall.

U.S. study tries to unravel mysteries of lasting marriages. (2002, July 25). *Toronto Star*, p. A12.

Udy, S. H., Jr. (1959, December). Bureaucracy and rationality in Weber's organizational theory: An empirical study. *American Sociological Review, 24,* 791–795.

Ullman, E., & Harris, C. (1970). The nature of cities. In A. N. Cousins & H. Nagpaul (Eds.), *Urban man and society: A reader in urban ecology* (pp. 91–100). New York: Knopf.

UNESCO. (2006). *Education for All Global Monitoring Report.*

United Nations. (2001). *Human development report 2001.* New York: United Nations.

United Nations. (2003). *Human Development Report 2003.* New York: Oxford University Press.

United Nations. (2005). *Statistics and Indicators on Women and Men.* Table 3a: Life Expectancy. Available at http://unstats.un.org/unsd/demographic/products/indwm/ww2005/tab3a.htm.

United Nations, Interparliamentary Union (IPU). (2005, October). "The Participation of Women and Men in Decision-Making: The Parliamentary Decision." www.un.org/womenwatch/daw/egm/eql-men/docs/BP.2%20Background%20Paper%20IPU.pdf.

United Nations Population Fund. (2000). *Lives together, worlds apart: Men and women in a time of change.* New York: United Nations.

University of Waterloo. (2006, June 21). UW-led research team looks at impact of child-care choices on children's development. http://newsrelease.uwaterloo.ca/news.php?id=4751.

Urquia, Marcelo L., Frank, John W., Glazier, Richard H., & Moineddin, Rahim. (2007, November). Birth Outcomes By Neighbourhood Income and Recent Immigration in Toronto. Statistics Canada, Health Reports, Volume 18, Number 4, Catalogue 82-003.

Useem, M. (1984). *The inner circle: Large corporations and the rise of business political activity in the U.S. and U.K.* New York: Oxford University Press.

Vallee, B. (2008). *The War on Women.* Toronto: Key Porter Books.

Valpy, Michael. (2008, April 26). Wealth Gap Exposes Fresh Labour Challenge. *The Globe and Mail,* p. A14.

van Dijk, J. (2004). The role of ethnicity and religion in the social support system of older Dutch Canadians. *Canadian Journal of Aging, 23*(1), 21–34.

Van Lawick-Goodall, J. (1971). *In the shadow of man.* Boston: Houghton Mifflin.

Vann, K. (2002, March 2). Elderly murder-suicides on rise. *Toronto Star,* p. C9.

Veblen, T. (1912). *The Theory of the Leisure Class.* New York: Macmillan.

Vlasblom, J. & Schippers, J. (2006). Changing dynamics in female employment around childbirth: evidence from Germany, the Netherlands and the UK. *Work, employment and society.* 20, 2, 329–347.

Volti, R. (1995). *Society and technological change* (3rd ed.). New York: St. Martin's Press.

Von Hoffman, N. (1970, May). Sociological snoopers. *Transaction 7*(4), 6.

Wagley, C., & Harris, M. (1958). *Minorities in the new world.* New York: Columbia University Press.

Waldholz, M. (1991, December 2). Computer "brain" outperforms doctors in diagnosing heart attack patients. *Wall Street Journal,* p. 7B.

Waldman, P. (1995, June 12). Riots in Bahrain arouse ire of feared monarchy as the U.S. stands by. *Wall Street Journal,* pp. A1, A8.

Wallerstein, I. (1974). *The modern world system: Capitalist agriculture and the origins of the European world-economy in the sixteenth century.* New York: Academic Press.

Wallerstein, I. (1979). *The capitalist world-economy.* New York: Cambridge University Press.

Wallerstein, I. (1984). *The politics of the world-economy: The states, the movements, and the civilizations.* Cambridge, UK: Cambridge University Press.

Wallerstein, I. (1990). Culture as the ideological battleground of the modern world-system. In M. Featherstone (Ed.), *Global culture: Nationalism, globalization, and modernity* (pp. 31–55). London: Sage.

Walters, J. (1990, May 18–20). Chimps in the mist. *USA Weekend,* p. 24.

Walz, T. (2002, June). Crones, dirty old men, sexy seniors: Representations of the sexuality of older persons. *Journal of Aging and Identity, 4,* 112.

Warner, W. L., & Hunt, P. S. (1941). *The social life of a modern community.* New Haven, CT: Yale University Press.

Warner, W. L., Hunt, P. S., Meeker, M., & Eels, K. (1949). *Social class in America.* New York: Harper.

Warr, M. (1993). Age, peers, and delinquency. *Criminology, 31*(1), 17–40.

Watson, J. M. (1988). Outlaw motorcyclists. In J. M. Henslin (Ed.), *Down to earth sociology: Introductory readings* (5th ed., pp. 203–213). New York: Free Press.

Watters, E. (2003). *Urban tribes: A generation redefines friendship, family and commitment.* New York: Bloomsbury.

Webb, E. J., Campbell, D. T., Schwartz, R. D., & Sechrest, L. (1966). *Unobtrusive measures: Nonreactive research in the social sciences.* Chicago: Rand McNally.

Weber, M. (1946). *From Max Weber: Essays in sociology* (H. Gerth & C. Wright Mills, Trans. and Ed.). New York: Oxford University Press.

Weber, M. (1947). *The theory of social and economic organization* (A. M. Henderson & T. Parsons, Trans., T. Parsons, Ed.). Glencoe, IL: Free Press. (First published 1913).

Weber, M. (1958). *The Protestant ethic and the spirit of capitalism.* New York: Scribner's. (First published 1904–1905).

Weber, M. (1968). *Economy and society* (E. Fischoff, Trans.). New York: Bedminster Press. (First published 1922).

Weber, M. (1978). *Economy and society* (G. Roth & C. Wittich, Eds.). Berkeley: University of California Press. (First published 1922).

Weisburd, D., Wheeler, S., & Waring, E. (1991). *Crimes of the middle classes: White-collar offenders in the federal courts.* New Haven, CT: Yale University Press.

Weisskopf, M. (1992). Scientist says greenhouse effect is setting in. In Washington Post Writers Group (Eds.), *Ourselves and others: The Washington Post sociology companion* (pp. 297–298). Boston: Allyn and Bacon.

Wente, M. (2000, January 29). How David found his manhood. *Globe and Mail.*

Wente, Margaret. (2007, January 27). The Ozzie and Harriet Gap. *Globe and Mail,* p. A25.

Wente, M. (2007, December 8). Why do men still rule the world? *Globe and Mail.* p. A29.

Wente, M. (2008, January 5). Hark! A shriek-inducing wake-up call. *Globe and Mail.* p. A19.

West, C., & Garcia, A. (1988). Conversational shift work: A study of topical transitions between women and men. *Social Problems, 35,* 551–575.

Westell, J. (2008, February 11). Canadian trucker a finalist for Goodyear Highway Hero award. *Truck News.* Available at www.trucknews.com.

White, Emily. (2002). *Fast Girls: Teenage Tribes and The Myth of the Slut.* New York: Scribner.

White, J. A. (1991, February 13). When employees own big stake, it's a buy signal for investors. *Wall Street Journal,* pp. C1, C19.

White, J. E. (1995, July 3). Forgive us our sins. *Time,* p. 29.

Whitehead, S. M., & Barrett, F. J. (Eds). (2001). *The Masculinities Reader.* Cambridge: Polity Press.

Whittington, L., & Gordon, S. (2005, June 21). PM makes push on same-sex legislation. *Toronto Star,* p. A6.

Whorf, B. (1956). *Language, thought, and reality* (J. B. Carroll, Ed.). Cambridge, MA: MIT Press.

Whyte, M. K. (1992, March–April). Choosing mates—The American way. *Society,* 71–77.

Whyte, W. H. (1989). *The city: Rediscovering the center.* New York: Doubleday.

Whyte, W. H. (1997). Street corner society. In J. M. Henslin (Ed.), *Down to earth sociology: Introductory readings* (9th ed., pp. 59–67). New York: Free Press.

Wilkins, Russell, Uppel, Sharanjit, Fines, Philippe, Senecal, Sacha, Guimond, Eric, & Dion, Rene. (2008, January). Life Expectancy in the Inuit-Inhabited Areas of Canada, 1989 to 2003. Statistics Canada, Health Reports, Volume 19, Number 1, Catalogue 82-003.

Williams, C. L. (1995). *Still a man's world: Men who do women's work.* Berkeley: University of California Press.

Williams, Cara. (2006, February). Disability in the Workplace. *Perspectives on Labour and Income,* Statistics Canada Catalogue No, 75-001-XIE: pp. 10–24.

Williams, J. (2004). *50 Facts that should change the world.* Duxford, Cambridge: Icon Books.

Williams, L., & Guest, M. P. (2005). Attitudes toward marriage among the urban middle-class in Vietnam, Thailand, and the Philippines. *Journal of Comparative Family Studies.* (Spring), pp. 163–188.

Willis, P. (1981). *Learning to labour: How working class kids get working class jobs.* New York: Columbia University Press.

Wilson, B., & Jette, S. (2005). Making sense of the cultural activities of Canadian youth. In N. Mandell & A. Duffy (Eds.), *Canadian families: Diversity, conflict and change* (3rd ed., pp. 64–86). Toronto: Thomson Nelson.

Wilson, S. J. (1991). *Women, families, and work.* Toronto: McGraw-Hill Ryerson.

Wilson, W. J. (1996). *When work disappears: The world of the new urban poor.* Chicago: University of Chicago Press.

Wines, Michael. (2006, August 24). Africa Adds to Miserable Ranks of Child Workers. *New York Times.*

Winslow, R. (1994, October 7). More doctors are adding online tools to their kits. *Wall Street Journal,* pp. B1, B4.

Winslow, R. (1995, August 18). Smoking increases heart-attack risk fivefold for people in their 30s and 40s. *Wall Street Journal,* p. B5.

Wirth, L. (1945). The problem of minority groups. In R. Linton (Ed.), *The science of man in the world crisis.* New York: Columbia University Press.

Wohl, R. R., & Strauss, A. (1958, March). Symbolic representation and the urban milieu. *American Journal of Sociology, 63,* 523–532.

Womack, J. P., Jones, D. T., & Roos, D. (1991). *The machine that changed the world: The story of lean production.* New York: Harper Perrenial.

Wombs for Rent: Growth of Commercial Surrogacy. (2007, December 31). *The Hamilton Spectator,* p. A6.

Wonacott, Peter. (2007, April 18). India's Skewed Sex Ratio Puts GE Sales in Spotlight. *Wall Street Journal.*

World Health Organization. (1946). *Constitution of the World Health Organization.* New York: World Health Organization Interim Commission.

Wright, E. O. (1985). *Class.* London: Verso.

Wrigley, J. & Dreby, J. (2006). Violent fatalities in child care. *Contexts.* 5, 4, pp. 35–40.

Yalnizyan, Armine. (2007, March). *The Rich and the Rest of Us: The Changing Face of Canada's Growing Gap.* Ottawa: Canadian Centre for Policy Alternatives.

Yardley, Jim. (2007, May 13). Faces of Abortion in China: A Young Single Woman. *New York Times.*

Yelaja, P. (2002, May 3). Female heart attack victims less likely to be rehabilitated. *Toronto Star,* p. A17.

Yinger, J. M. (1970). *The scientific study of religion.* New York: Macmillan.

Young, L. E. (1995). The overlooked contributions of women to the development of American sociology: An examination of AJS articles from 1895–1926. [Paper presented at the 1995 meetings of the American Sociological Association].

Zachary, G. P. (1995, November 22). Behind stocks' surge is an economy in which big U.S. firms thrive. *Wall Street Journal,* pp. A1, A5.

Zald, M. N. (1992). Looking backward to look forward: Reflections on the past and the future of the resource mobilization research program. In A. D. Morris & C. M. Mueller (Eds.), *Frontiers in social movement theory* (pp. 326–348). New Haven, CT: Yale University Press.

Zeitlin, I. M. (1990). *Ideology and the development of sociological thought* (4th ed.). Englewood Cliffs, NJ: Prentice Hall.

Zeman, Klarka. (2007, June). A First Look at Provincial Differences in Educational Pathways From High School to College and University. *Education Matters.* Statistics Canada, Catalogue 81-004-XIE, www.statcan.ca/english/freepub/81-004-XIE/2007002/provdiff.htm.

Zey, M. (1993). *Banking on fraud: Drexel, junk bonds, and buyouts.* Hawthorne, NY: Aldine de Gruyter.

Zou, H. F. (1994, July). "The spirit of capitalism" and long-run growth. *European Journal of Political Economy, 10*(2), 279–293.

Zuboff, S. (1991). New worlds of computer-mediated work. In J. M. Henslin (Ed.), *Down to earth sociology: Introductory readings* (6th ed., pp. 476–485). New York: Free Press.

Zukewich, N. (2003). *Work, parenthood and the experience of time scarcity.* Ottawa: Minister of Industry. Statistics Canada, Catalogue no. 89-584-MIE No. 1.

Zukin, S. (2005). *Point of Purchase: How Shopping Changed American Culture.* New York: Routledge, Taylor & Francis Group.

Zunzunegui, M. V., Kone, A., Johri, M., Beland, F., Wolfson, C., & Bergman, H. (2004). Social networks and self-rated health in two French-speaking Canadian community dwelling populations over 65. *Social Science and Medicine, 58,* 2069–2081.

NAME INDEX

SUBJECT INDEX

me, 90
means, 30
means of production, 115, 127, 243, 244
mechanical solidarity, 247
media. *See* mass media
media events, 411
median, 30
medicalization, 352
medicalization of social deviance, 377–379
medicare. *See* health care
medicine, 344
   computers and, 422–423
   prevention and, 357–358
   sexism in, 347
Meech Lake Accord, 270
megacities, 392
megalopolis, 392
membership, 412–413, 414–416
men
   changing roles for, 169–170
   masculinity and, 79, 84–87, 169–170,
     288–289, 363, 365, 389
   mass media and, 76
   socialization of, 78–79
men's feminism, 20
mental health, 132, 344, 348
mental illness, 363, 377–379
meritocracy, 124
Mesopotamia, 397
messiahs, 336
metaformative social movements, 412
metanarratives, 331
Métis, 181, 184
metropolis, 392
Mexico, 110, 131, 176, 196, 395, 398
micro-level analysis, 22
micropolitics, 260
microsociology, 2–4, 21
middle class, 115, 128–129, 318
middle-range theories, 16
mid-life crisis, 89
milling, 406
minimax strategy, 406
minority governments, 266
minority groups, 150, 175–176
   aging and, 201
   in Canada, 187
   education and, 312, 315, 321, 326–327
   rationalization of society and, 218
   as reserve labour, 178
minyan, 331
mode, 30
modernity, 20–21
modernization, 418
mommy track, 161, 164
monarchy, 125–126, 260, 262–263, 266
monolithic bias, 282–283
monolithic structure, 282
Montreal, 186–188, 201, 394
moral community, 327, 330
moral issues, 21, 327, 334, 415
moral panics, 409
moral shock, 415
mores, 51, 56
Mormons, 280, 336
mortality, 389

motherhood, 287–288, 296
motherhood wage penalty, 292
multiculturalism, 180–181
multicultural/multiethnic feminism, 178
Multilateral Agreement on
   Investment (MAI), 417
multinational corporations, 248, 398
multiracial feminism, 178
murder-suicide, 211

N

names, 161, 282
Napoleon Dynamite (film), 315
National Advisory Council on Aging, 193
nation, 275
nationalism, 275, 321
   Quebec, 54, 187, 269–270, 274, 415
National Longitudinal Survey of Children
   and Youth, 82
National Population Health
   Survey (NPHS), 33
National Population Health
   Survey (NPHS), 351
Native people, 58–59
   education and, 185, 312, 313, 319–320
   families and, 294–295
   health and, 131, 200
   as minority group, 175, 176
   as population classification, 181–183
   population transfer of, 180
   poverty and, 137, 140
   schooling and, 82
   status or registered, 181
   suicide and, 348
   violence against women and, 373
natural sciences, 5
nature *vs.* nurture, 67, 68, 147–150
Nazism, 173, 183–184, 189, 265, 333,
   377, 408
needs reduction, 286
negative sanction, 51, 376
neocolonialism, 105
neoliberalism, 241–245
Netherlands, 140, 211, 297, 353
net migration rate, 389
neutralization, 365
New Democratic Party, 268, 328
new information technologies (ICTs), 417
New Malthusians, 384, 386
news, 104
new social movements, 412
new technology, 61–62
New Zealand, 297, 299
nicotine, 356
NIMBY, 398
noncentrist parties, 270
non-governmental
   organizations (NGOs), 225
nonmaterial culture, 47
nonverbal interaction, 22
norms, 51, 52
   deviance and, 362, 368
   emergent, 406–407
Norway, 162, 297
nouveau riche, 122, 128
nuclear family, 282, 283, 284, 292

nuclear weapons, 274
Nunavut, 181, 197, 200
nurses, 348

O

Oath of Hippocrates, 352
objective method, of measuring social
   class, 117
objectivity, 11
observation, 30–31
October Crisis, 270
Official Languages Act, 270
off-the-books economy, 251
Ogburn's theory of social change, 418–420
oil industry, 398
oil patch widows, 282
Oka Crisis, 415
Old Age Security (OAS), 198, 207, 214, 245
old money, 122, 128
oligarchy, 227, 229, 264
omerta, 365
Ontario Hydro, 243
Ontario Network for the Prevention of Elder
   Abuse, 198
operational definitions, 38
organic solidarity, 247
organizations
   rational (*See* rationalization)
   virtual, 234–235
   voluntary, 225
Orthodox Church, 337
Outbreak (film), 355
out-groups, 79, 82
outsourcing, 235
ozone shield, 357, 398

P

Pacific Scandal, 267–268
panics, 408–409
parenting, 163–164, 283–284
parliamentary democracy, 265–270
participant observation, 30–31
Parti Québécois, 262, 270
paternity leave, 301
patriarchy, 19–20, 149, 152, 153, 202–203,
   205, 281, 282, 372
patrilineal systems of descent, 281
patriotism, 313, 315
pay gap, 151, 160–161
peer groups, 83, 323
pensions, 207, 210, 245, 391
periphery, 103
permissible assimilation, 180
persecution, 328–329, 333
personal identity kit, 86
personality, 71–73
personality disorders, 363
Peter principle, 224
petty bourgeoisie, 127
pharmaceutical companies, 344
physical fitness, 83
pink ghettoes, 249
plagiarism, 40, 323
play stage, of role development, 70
pluralism, 180–271
pluralistic society, 54

police,   374, 375, 395, 405, 416
police discretion,   372
political parties,   267–268, 399
political science,   5
political socialization,   310
politics
    in Canada,   265–270
    corporations and,   243
    democratic facade and,   122
    gender and,   133–169
    minority groups and,   175
    oligarchy in,   227
    seniors and,   198, 199, 206–209
    social class and,   132
polyandry,   280
polygamy,   280, 281, 336
polygyny,   280
polytheism,   333–334
population,   29
    in feminist theory,   386
    global,   384–386
    growth of,   387–390
    hunger and,   386–387
population shrinkage,   386
population transfer,   180
populism,   268
pornography,   21
positive sanction,   51, 376
positivism,   3–8, 13
postcolonialism,   179
postindustrial societies,   241–242, 249,
    254–255
    authority in,   261
    marriage in,   281
    work in,   252–253
postmodern feminism,   20, 273, 372, 373
postmodernist theory,   20–21, 22
    crime and deviance in,   373–374
    gender in,   154–155, 169
    health in,   344
    prejudice in,   179
    in Quebec,   57
    religion in,   331
    social change in,   423, 424
postmodern societies,   427
postmortem ventilation (PMV),   166
post-oriental theory,   179
post-traumatic stress disorder (PTSD),   274
poverty. *See also* social stratification
    aging and,   200–201, 206, 207
    in Canada,   118–120, 121, 134–135, 136,
        242–243
    capitalism and,   117, 245
    children and,   137, 139–141, 241
    class and,   129, 130
    crime and,   370–371
    culture of,   104, 139–141
    demographics of,   137–141
    education and,   311, 321, 370
    family types and,   295, 387–388
    globalization and,   98–99, 107–108
    health and,   131–132, 345–346
    long-term,   141
    myths about,   136–137
    sports and,   83
    starvation and,   386–387

    urbanization and,   395
    women and,   120, 138, 166, 206,
        207, 285
    work, income, and,   118–121, 129
poverty line,   135–136
power,   260
    aging and,   205
    authority and,   260–262
    in Canada,   271–273
    crime and,   372
    gender and,   205, 250
    globalization and,   274–275
    government as,   262–265
    ideology and,   125–127
    inner circle of,   248
    legitimate,   260
    micro- vs. macro-,   260
    social class and,   115, 116, 121–122
    violence and,   260
power elites,   122, 271
prejudice,   176, 177–179, 320
premature births,   131
prestige,   116
    gender and,   152
    old money and,   128
    social class and,   115, 122
    symbols of,   122
    of work,   151
prevention,   357–358
primary groups,   79
primary sector,   249
primary social deviance,   366
prime ministers,   266, 267
prisons,   86
private ownership of the means of
        production,   243
private property,   245, 248
privilege,   175
proactive social movements,   410
profane,   325–327
professions,   84, 247
Progressive Conservative Party,   268
Progressive Movement,   268
proletariat,   19, 115
propaganda,   411, 414
property
    in capitalism,   245–248
    crimes against,   370
    gender and,   151
    patriarchy and,   153
    social class and,   115–116, 117–118
    women and,   248
proportional representation,   270
prostitution,   21, 146, 151, 241, 303, 355,
        366, 370
Protestant Ethic,   11, 216, 240, 332
Protestantism,   332, 333, 337–338
protests,   406, 407–408, 413
psychoanalysis,   71
psychologists,   363
psychology,   5–6
public opinion,   414
publics,   412, 413
public servants,   269, 272
Public Service Employment Act,   269
pure sociology,   22–23

Q

qualitative analysis,   38
qualitative interviews,   31–32
qualitative research methods,   34–35
quality circles,   232
quantitative analysis,   38
quantitative research methods,   34–35
Quebec,   184, 262, 268, 301, 386, 411, 416
    aging in,   198, 207
    as Charter group,   182–185
    culture in,   56–57
    families in,   299
    health in,   348, 351
    identity in,   55
    marriage in,   57
    as minority group,   175
    nationalism in,   54, 186–187, 269–270,
        274, 415
    Native people in,   181–182
    sexual mores in,   56
    sociology in,   13
    values in,   57
Quebec Act of 1774,   182
queer theory,   21, 30, 154, 273
questionnaires,   30
questions,   30–31
Quiet Revolution,   13, 55, 251,
    269–270, 411

R

race
    education and,   322
    myths about,   174
    poverty and,   137
    women and,   178–179, 373
race theory,   22
racism,   16, 59, 136, 140, 176, 193
    biological determinism and,   67
    in feminist theory,   20, 178–179
    in schools,   315
    slavery and,   113
    social class and,   134
    superiority and,   174–175
radical feminist theory,   20, 273, 321
Raging Grannies,   199
rainforests,   398
Ralliement des Créditistes,   268
random sample,   29
rapport,   30
rationality,   216, 217
rationalization of society,   216
    bureaucracy and,   218–224
    religion and,   216–217
rational-legal authority,   261, 262
reactive social movements,   410
reasonable accommodation debate,   13
rebellion,   369
records,   218
redemptive social movements,   411
Red River Rebellions,   184
red tape,   221
reengineering,   254, 255
reference groups,   79
reformative social movements,   411
reformists,   331
Reform Party,   268

reincarnation, 334
rejectionists, 331
relabelling, 366
relative deprivation theory, 415
reliability, 38
religion, 81, 86, 325–327
  in Canada, 182–185, 269, 337–338
  capitalism and, 11, 216, 332
  in conflict theory, 330
  conservatism and, 246
  control and, 126
  in feminist theory, 330–331
  in functionalist theory, 327–329
  future of, 338–339
  gender and, 330, 331
  institutionalized, 335
  major, 332–334
  marriage, family and, 280
  political power and, 268
  in postmodernist theory, 331
  rationalization and, 216–217
  social class and, 132
  suicide and, 9
  in symbolic interactionist theory, 329–330
  types and groups in, 334–337
remarriage, 300–301
replaceability, 218
replication, 11, 40
representative democracy, 263
reputational method, of measuring social
    class, 117
research
  analysis of, 38
  controversial, 35–36
  ethics in, 40–42
  methods of, 29–40
  model of, 37
  need for, 28–29
  purpose and use of, 11
  quantitative vs. qualitative, 34–35
  theory and, 42–43
  unobtrusive measures, 33–34
  values in, 11–12
research designs, 29
research methods, 38
reserve labour force, 178
resocialization, 73, 86–87
resource mobilization, 416
respondents, 30
retirement, 194, 197, 207–209
retreatism, 369
revisionists, 331
revolutionaries, 331
revolutions, 260, 411–412, 415
riots, 407–408
risk society, 374
ritualism, 369
ritual pollution, 113, 332
rituals, 329
robber barons, 378
role accumulation, 347
role extension, 409
roles, 69–71
  aging and, 201
  gender (See gender roles)
  sick, 344–345

romantic love, 289, 290–291
routinization of charisma, 262
rules, 218, 221, 244
rumours,
Russia, 140, 180, 245, 339, 347, 355, 398,
    409–410
Rwanda, 173, 180, 345

S

sacred, 327
sadomasochism, 21
same-sex families, 282
sample, 29
sanctions, 51, 376
  negative vs. positive, 51, 376
sandwich generation, 89, 209, 210
Sapir -Whorf hypothesis, 49
scapegoats, 177
Scarce research, 41
scarcity, 125
School Act, 310
schools, 82–83, 310–311
  characteristics of, 82–321
  expectations of, 322
  problems in, 322–325
  social integration in, 315
  success in, 326–327
  virtual, 324
science, 4–6
scientific management, 231, 235
scientific method, 8
Scotland, 274
Sea Shepherds, 399
secondary analysis, 32–33
secondary groups, 79
secondary sector, 249
second shift, 286
sects, 335
secularization, 81
segregation, 180–181
selective perception, 178
self, 69
self-administered questionnaires, 30
self-fulfilling prophecies, 178, 322
self-labelling, 366
self-regulation, 247
semiperiphery, 103
seniorpreneurs, 208
seniors. See age; aging
seniors homes, 209–210, 211
seniors organizations, 198–199
Severe Acute Respiratory
    Syndrome (SARS), 351, 352, 355
sex, 147
sexism, 12–13, 59, 140
  in medicine, 347
  in schools, 315
sex offenders, 43
sex roles, 12
sex-selective abortion, 303
sex typing, 150
sexual assault, 43, 165–167
sexual harassment, 164–165
sexuality
  seniors and, 204–205
  teenage, 56

sexual orientation, 373
  aging and, 202
  families and, 75, 297–298
sex workers, 366
shaman, 344
Shiites, 333
Shudras, 113
shunning, 330
sick role, 344–345
signalling, 322
significant others, 69, 74
Simpsons, The, 168
single-parent families, 8, 136, 280, 282,
    283, 292, 293, 295, 298
singles, 396
sit-ins, 405
skip-generation households, 300
slavery, 106–108, 112–113, 231,
    312, 330
social acceptability, 347
social change, 417
  challenges of, 424
  contemporary theories about, 423–424
  Ogburn's theory of, 418–420
  technology and, 417–418, 419–423
  theories of, 424
social class, 116–117
  aging and, 199–201, 202, 204
  components of, 117–123
  consequences of, 130–132
  crime and, 363, 367, 370–371, 372
  education and, 316, 317–321, 322,
    326–327
  impact of, 132
  measuring, 117
  theories about, 127–130
  Weber's three components of, 115–116
social conservatism, 245–247, 268
social control, 362, 368, 371–372, 373
Social Credit Party, 268
social deviance, 363
  continuum of, 364
  primary, secondary, and tertiary, 366
social facts, 12
social groups, 79–85
social integration, 10, 315
social interaction, 2
socialism, 244–245
socialization, 67
  age and, 87–90
  agents of, 80
  anticipatory, 83, 84
  biology and, 67–69
  gender and, 74–79, 147–150
  globalization, 72–73
  groups and, 79–85
  institutionalization and, 86–87
  limitations of, 90
  political, 310
  school and, 132, 315
  self, mind, emotions in, 69–74
  smoking and, 72–73
  work and, 84–85
social location, 2
social mobility, 114, 133–134
social movement organizations, 411

PHOTO CREDITS

Collection, New York; page 246, © Catherine Panchout/Corbis; page 248, Guang Niu/Getty Images; page 252, photo by Michael Setbourn/Getty Images; page 254, © Tatsuyuki Tayama/ Fujifotos/The Image Works; page 256, © Edy Puronomo/The Image Works.

CHAPTER 12

Page 259, courtesy of TF Chen Cultural Center, NY; page 261 (left), Marion Kaplan/Alamy; page 261 (right), Jean-Auguste-Dominique Ingres, Jeanne d'Arc. 1854. Musee du Louvre, Paris. Photo AKG London; page 262, PHC Archives; page 263, CP PHOTO/ Tom Hanson; page 264, Gary Markstein © Milwaukee Journal Sentinal; page 269, Victor Last/Geographic Visuals; page 275, AP Images.

CHAPTER 13

Page 279, *Circle of Love* by Michael Escoffery, 1996. Mixed media. Private Collection. Photo © Michael Escoffery/Art Resource, NY. © 2009 Michael Escoffery/Artists Rights Society (ARS), New York; page 282, © Kevin M. Law/Alamy; page 284, © James M. Henslin; page 288 (left), June Corman; page 288 (right), Meg Luxton; page 290, © Tribune Media Services, Inc. All rights reserved. Reprinted with permission; page 297, © Brooks Kraft/Sygma/Corbis; page 304, David Ellis/Digital Vision/Getty Images.

CHAPTER 14

Page 308, "School Bus, Conception Bay", 1972 serigraph, 6/90 by Reginald Shepherd. The Rooms Provincial Art Gallery, Memorial University of Newfoundland Collection; page 309, © The Art Archive/Corbis; page 312, Tricia Yourkevich; page 313, CP PHOTO/Winnipeg Free Press/Marc Gallant; page 317 © Masterfile; page 319, Myrleen Ferguson Cate/PhotoEdit, Inc.; page 324, © Najlah Feanny/Corbis; page 325, CP PHOTO/Ryan Remiorz; page 326, © David Butow/Corbis SABA; page 327, Will & Deni McIntyre/Photo Researchers, Inc.; page 328 (top), © David H. Wells/Corbis; page 328 (bottom), CP PHOTO Archives/Globe and Mail/ Boris Spremo; page 329, © Stapleton Collection/Corbis; page 330, © The New Yorker Collection, 2000 Robert Mankoff from cartoonbank.com. All rights reserved; page 333, © Redlinks/Corbis; page 336, SuperStock/Liz Strenk; page 338, PEANUTS ® by Charles M. Schulz.

CHAPTER 15

Page 343, *Harlem Hospital* by Jacob Lawrence, 1953. Egg tempera on hardboard, 20 x 24 in. Michael Rosenfeld Gallery. Photo © The Jacob and Gwendolyn Lawrence Foundation/Art Resource, NY. © 2009 The Jacob and Gwendolyn Lawrence Foundation, Seattle/Artists Rights Society (ARS), New York; page 345, Jupiter Unlimited; page 346, Jean Chung/WpN; page 355, © Sven Torfinn/Panos; page 356 (left), David Young-Wolff/PhotoEdit; page 356 (right), © Shuji Kobayashi/Stone/ Getty Images; page 357, © GARO/PHANIE/Photo Researchers, Inc.

CHAPTER 16

Page 361, *Prisoners Exercising (After Gustave Dore's Print)* by Vincent van Gogh, 1890. Oil on canvas, 80 x 64 cm. Pushkin Museum of Fine Arts, Moscow. © Alinari Archives/Corbis; page 362, AP PHOTO/Julie Jacobson; page 366, © Boris Kudriavov/R.P.G./Sygma/Corbis; page 367, Ralf-Finn Hestoft/Corbis; page 368, courtesy of MADD; page 370, Carolyn Cole//Tribune Media Services/TMS Reprints; page 371, photo by Tasos Katopodis/Getty Images; page 377, © UPI/Bettman/Corbis; page 379, Joe Raedle/Getty Images.

CHAPTER 17

Page 383, © Franklin McMahon/Corbis; page 385, © Corbis; page 387 (left), © Reuters/Landov; page 387 (right), © David Paul Morris/Getty Images; page 388, © Wolfgang Kaehler/Corbis; page 391, Raveendran/AFP/Getty Images; page 392, © Roger-Viollet/The Image Works; page 395, Mariana Bazo/Reuters/Corbis; page 396, © Lee Snider/The Image Works; page 399, Cunningham/Greenpeace.

CHAPTER 18

Page 404, *Exhaust Fumes from Cars and Factories Contribute to Global Warming* by Roy Scott. © Roy Scott/Images.com; page 405, Fred Blackwell; page 407, CP PHOTO/Chuck Stoody; page 409, Sebastian D'Souza/AFP/Getty Images; page 412 (left), Glenbow Archives NC-6-1746; page 412 (right), CP PHOTO/Tony Caldwell; page 413, EM-PICS/Landov; page 414, CP PHOTO/Adrian Wyld; page 415, CP PHOTO/Shaney Komulainen; page 421 (top left), Hulton Collection/Liaison/Getty Images; page 421 (top right), © Car Culture/Corbis; page 421 (bottom), courtesy The Computer Museum History Center/Model photo Dennis Bourke; page 422, AP Images.

Saint Simon (1760–1825)

Mary Wollstonecraft (1759–1797)
Vindication of the Rights of Women

Karl Mannheim (1893–1947)
Ideology and Utopia

Harriet Martineau (1802–1876)
Society in America

Karl Marx (1818–1883)
Capital

George Simmel (1858–1918)
Conflict and the Web of Group Affiliations

Talcott Parsons (1902–1979)
The Structure of Social Action

SOCIOLOGY TIMELINE

1800

1900

Auguste Comte (1798-1857)
Positive Philosophy

Herbert Spencer (1820–1903)
The Study of Sociology

Emile Durkheim (1858–1917)
Suicide

Max Weber (1864–1920)
Economy and Society

George H. Mead (1863–1931)
Mind, Self and Society

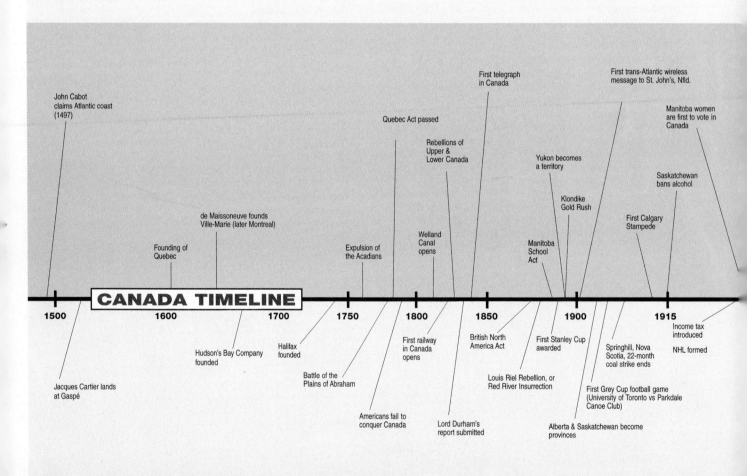

First telegraph
in Canada

First trans-Atlantic wireless
message to St. John's, Nfld.

John Cabot
claims Atlantic coast
(1497)

Manitoba women
are first to vote in
Canada

Quebec Act passed

Rebellions of
Upper &
Lower Canada

Yukon becomes
a territory

Saskatchewan
bans alcohol

Klondike
Gold Rush

de Maissoneuve founds
Ville-Marie (later Montreal)

First Calgary
Stampede

Founding of
Quebec

Expulsion of
the Acadians

Welland
Canal
opens

Manitoba
School
Act

CANADA TIMELINE

1500   **1600**   **1700**   **1750**   **1800**   **1850**   **1900**   **1915**

Income tax
introduced

Hudson's Bay Company
founded

Halifax
founded

First railway
in Canada
opens

British North
America Act

First Stanley Cup
awarded

Springhill, Nova
Scotia, 22-month
coal strike ends

NHL formed

Jacques Cartier lands
at Gaspé

Battle of the
Plains of Abraham

Louis Riel Rebellion, or
Red River Insurrection

First Grey Cup football game
(University of Toronto vs Parkdale
Canoe Club)

Americans fail to
conquer Canada

Lord Durham's
report submitted

Alberta & Saskatchewan become
provinces